THE
COMPLETE WORKS OF
WILLIAM SHAKESPEARE
VOLUME IV

A NOTE TO THE READER

For each work in this set the editors have provided supplementary material that will help the reader better understand the work as both a play to be performed and a literary work.

In his general Foreword, Joseph Papp brings Shakespeare alive as he has for the audiences at his productions. The reader is also acquainted with the theater in which the plays were originally performed.

More detailed information precedes the text of each work: an Introduction places the work in context and discusses its structure and action, and performance notes give a director's view of the problems presented by the characters and themes of each work as interpreted in previous productions.

Each work is followed by a brief record of what is known about the original publication and performance and an attempt to date them; textual departures from the copy text; and an extensive essay on Shakespeare's sources. There are also suggestions for further reading on each work.

THE COMPLETE WORKS OF WILLIAM SHAKESPEARE

VOLUME IV

JULIUS CAESAR

TWELFTH NIGHT

TROILUS AND CRESSIDA

ALL'S WELL THAT ENDS WELL

MEASURE FOR MEASURE

OTHELLO

BANTAM BOOKS
Toronto · New York · London · Sydney · Auckland

THIS EDITION CREATED BY
QUALITY PAPERBACK BOOK CLUB

A Bantam Book / published by arrangement
with Scott, Foresman and Company

PRINTING HISTORY
Scott, Foresman edition published/January 1980
Bantam edition, with newly edited text and substantially
revised, edited, and amplified notes, introductions, and
other materials, published/February 1988
Valuable advice on staging matters has been
provided by Richard Hosley.
Collations checked by Eric Rasmussen.
Additional editorial assistance by Claire McEachern

Cover and display type designed by Charlotte Staub.

Bantam Books are published by Bantam Books,
a division of Bantam Doubleday Dell Publishing Group, Inc.
Its trademark, consisting of the words "Bantam Books"
and the portrayal of a rooster, is Registered in U.S. Patent
and Trademark Office and in other countries. Marca Registrada.
Bantam Books, 666 Fifth Avenue, New York, NY 10103.
Printed in the United States of America.

Foreword

It's hard to imagine, but Shakespeare wrote all of his plays with a quill pen, a goose feather whose hard end had to be sharpened frequently. How many times did he scrape the dull end to a point with his knife, dip it into the inkwell, and bring up, dripping wet, those wonderful words and ideas that are known all over the world?

In the age of word processors, typewriters, and ballpoint pens, we have almost forgotten the meaning of the word "blot." Yet when I went to school, in the 1930s, my classmates and I knew all too well what an inkblot from the metal-tipped pens we used would do to a nice clean page of a test paper, and we groaned whenever a splotch fell across the sheet. Most of us finished the school day with ink-stained fingers; those who were less careful also went home with ink-stained shirts, which were almost impossible to get clean.

When I think about how long it took me to write the simplest composition with a metal-tipped pen and ink, I can only marvel at how many plays Shakespeare scratched out with his goose-feather quill pen, year after year. Imagine him walking down one of the narrow cobblestoned streets of London, or perhaps drinking a pint of beer in his local alehouse. Suddenly his mind catches fire with an idea, or a sentence, or a previously elusive phrase. He is burning with impatience to write it down—but because he doesn't have a ballpoint pen or even a pencil in his pocket, he has to keep the idea in his head until he can get to his quill and parchment.

He rushes back to his lodgings on Silver Street, ignoring the vendors hawking brooms, the coaches clattering by, the piteous wails of beggars and prisoners. Bounding up the stairs, he snatches his quill and starts to write furiously, not even bothering to light a candle against the dusk. "To be, or not to be," he scrawls, "that is the—." But the quill point has gone dull, the letters have fattened out illegibly, and in the middle of writing one of the most famous passages in the history of dramatic literature, Shakespeare has to stop to sharpen his pen.

Taking a deep breath, he lights a candle now that it's dark, sits down, and begins again. By the time the candle has burned out and the noisy apprentices of his French Huguenot landlord have quieted down, Shakespeare has finished Act 3 of *Hamlet* with scarcely a blot.

Early the next morning, he hurries through the fog of a London summer morning to the rooms of his colleague Richard Burbage, the actor for whom the role of Hamlet is being written. He finds Burbage asleep and snoring loudly, sprawled across his straw mattress. Not only had the actor performed in *Henry V* the previous afternoon, but he had then gone out carousing all night with some friends who had come to the performance.

Shakespeare shakes his friend awake, until, bleary-eyed, Burbage sits up in his bed. "Dammit, Will," he grumbles, "can't you let an honest man sleep?" But the playwright, his eyes shining and the words tumbling out of his mouth, says, "Shut up and listen—tell me what you think of *this*!"

He begins to read to the still half-asleep Burbage, pacing around the room as he speaks. ". . . Whether 'tis nobler in the mind to suffer the slings and arrows of outrageous fortune—"

Burbage interrupts, suddenly wide awake, "That's excellent, very good, 'the slings and arrows of outrageous fortune,' yes, I think it will work quite well. . . ." He takes the parchment from Shakespeare and murmurs the lines to himself, slowly at first but with growing excitement.

The sun is just coming up, and the words of one of Shakespeare's most famous soliloquies are being uttered for the first time by the first actor ever to bring Hamlet to life. It must have been an exhilarating moment.

Shakespeare wrote most of his plays to be performed live by the actor Richard Burbage and the rest of the Lord Chamberlain's men (later the King's men). Today, however, our first encounter with the plays is usually in the form of the printed word. And there is no question that reading Shakespeare for the first time isn't easy. His plays aren't comic books or magazines or the dime-store detective novels I read when I was young. A lot of his sentences are complex. Many of his words are no longer used in our everyday speech. His profound thoughts are often condensed into poetry, which is not as straightforward as prose.

Yet when you hear the words spoken aloud, a lot of the language may strike you as unexpectedly modern. For Shakespeare's plays, like any dramatic work, weren't really meant to be read; they were meant to be spoken, seen, and performed. It's amazing how lines that are so troublesome in print can flow so naturally and easily when spoken.

I think it was precisely this music that first fascinated me. When I was growing up, Shakespeare was a stranger to me. I had no particular interest in him, for I was from a different cultural tradition. It never occurred to me that his plays might be more than just something to "get through" in school, like science or math or the physical education requirement we had to fulfill. My passions then were movies, radio, and vaudeville—certainly not Elizabethan drama.

I was, however, fascinated by words and language. Because I grew up in a home where Yiddish was spoken, and English was only a second language, I was acutely sensitive to the musical sounds of different languages and had an ear for lilt and cadence and rhythm in the spoken word. And so I loved reciting poems and speeches even as a very young child. In first grade I learned lots of short nature verses— "Who has seen the wind?," one of them began. My first foray into drama was playing the role of Scrooge in Charles Dickens's *A Christmas Carol* when I was eight years old. I liked summoning all the scorn and coldness I possessed and putting them into the words, "Bah, humbug!"

From there I moved on to longer and more famous poems and other works by writers of the 1930s. Then, in junior high school, I made my first acquaintance with Shakespeare through his play *Julius Caesar*. Our teacher, Miss McKay, assigned the class a passage to memorize from the opening scene of the play, the one that begins "Wherefore rejoice? What conquest brings he home?" The passage seemed so wonderfully theatrical and alive to me, and the experience of memorizing and reciting it was so much fun, that I went on to memorize another speech from the play on my own.

I chose Mark Antony's address to the crowd in Act 3,

scene 2, which struck me then as incredibly high drama. Even today, when I speak the words, I feel the same thrill I did that first time. There is the strong and athletic Antony descending from the raised pulpit where he has been speaking, right into the midst of a crowded Roman square. Holding the torn and bloody cloak of the murdered Julius Caesar in his hand, he begins to speak to the people of Rome:

> If you have tears, prepare to shed them now.
> You all do know this mantle. I remember
> The first time ever Caesar put it on;
> 'Twas on a summer's evening in his tent,
> That day he overcame the Nervii.
> Look, in this place ran Cassius' dagger through.
> See what a rent the envious Casca made.
> Through this the well-belovèd Brutus stabbed,
> And as he plucked his cursèd steel away,
> Mark how the blood of Caesar followed it,
> As rushing out of doors to be resolved
> If Brutus so unkindly knocked or no;
> For Brutus, as you know, was Caesar's angel.
> Judge, O you gods, how dearly Caesar loved him!
> This was the most unkindest cut of all . . .

I'm not sure now that I even knew Shakespeare had written a lot of other plays, or that he was considered "timeless," "universal," or "classic"—but I knew a good speech when I heard one, and I found the splendid rhythms of Antony's rhetoric as exciting as anything I'd ever come across.

Fifty years later, I still feel that way. Hearing good actors speak Shakespeare gracefully and naturally is a wonderful experience, unlike any other I know. There's a satisfying fullness to the spoken word that the printed page just can't convey. This is why seeing the plays of Shakespeare performed live in a theater is the best way to appreciate them. If you can't do that, listening to sound recordings or watching film versions of the plays is the next best thing.

But if you do start with the printed word, use the play as a script. Be an actor yourself and say the lines out loud. Don't worry too much at first about words you don't immediately understand. Look them up in the footnotes or a dictionary, but don't spend too much time on this. It is more profitable (and fun) to get the sense of a passage and sing it out. Speak naturally, almost as if you were talking to a friend, but be sure to enunciate the words properly. You'll be surprised at how much you understand simply by speaking the speech "trippingly on the tongue," as Hamlet advises the Players.

You might start, as I once did, with a speech from *Julius Caesar*, in which the tribune (city official) Marullus scolds the commoners for transferring their loyalties so quickly from the defeated and murdered general Pompey to the newly victorious Julius Caesar:

> Wherefore rejoice? What conquest brings he home?
> What tributaries follow him to Rome
> To grace in captive bonds his chariot wheels?
> You blocks, you stones, you worse than senseless
>   things!
> O you hard hearts, you cruel men of Rome,
> Knew you not Pompey? Many a time and oft
> Have you climbed up to walls and battlements,
> To towers and windows, yea, to chimney tops,
> Your infants in your arms, and there have sat
> The livelong day, with patient expectation,
> To see great Pompey pass the streets of Rome.

With the exception of one or two words like "wherefore" (which means "why," not "where"), "tributaries" (which means "captives"), and "patient expectation" (which means patient waiting), the meaning and emotions of this speech can be easily understood.

From here you can go on to dialogues or other more challenging scenes. Although you may stumble over unaccustomed phrases or unfamiliar words at first, and even fall flat when you're crossing some particularly rocky passages, pick yourself up and stay with it. Remember that it takes time to feel at home with anything new. Soon you'll come to recognize Shakespeare's unique sense of humor and way of saying things as easily as you recognize a friend's laughter.

And then it will just be a matter of choosing which one of Shakespeare's plays you want to tackle next. As a true fan of his, you'll find that you're constantly learning from his plays. It's a journey of discovery that you can continue for the rest of your life. For no matter how many times you read or see a particular play, there will always be something new there that you won't have noticed before.

Why do so many thousands of people get hooked on Shakespeare and develop a habit that lasts a lifetime? What can he really say to us today, in a world filled with inventions and problems he never could have imagined? And how do you get past his special language and difficult sentence structure to understand him?

The best way to answer these questions is to go see a live production. You might not know much about Shakespeare, or much about the theater, but when you watch actors performing one of his plays on the stage, it will soon become clear to you why people get so excited about a playwright who lived hundreds of years ago.

For the story—what's happening in the play—is the most accessible part of Shakespeare. In *A Midsummer Night's Dream*, for example, you can immediately understand the situation: a girl is chasing a guy who's chasing a girl who's chasing another guy. No wonder *A Midsummer Night's Dream* is one of the most popular of Shakespeare's plays: it's about one of the world's most popular pastimes—falling in love.

But the course of true love never did run smooth, as the young suitor Lysander says. Often in Shakespeare's comedies the girl whom the guy loves doesn't love him back, or she loves him but he loves someone else. In *The Two Gentlemen of Verona*, Julia loves Proteus, Proteus loves Sylvia, and Sylvia loves Valentine, who is Proteus's best friend. In the end, of course, true love prevails, but not without lots of complications along the way.

For in all of his plays—comedies, histories, and tragedies—Shakespeare is showing you human nature. His characters act and react in the most extraordinary ways—and sometimes in the most incomprehensible ways. People are always trying to find motivations for what a character does. They ask, "Why does Iago want to destroy Othello?"

The answer, to me, is very simple—because that's the way Iago is. That's just his nature. Shakespeare doesn't explain his characters; he sets them in motion—and away they go. He doesn't worry about whether they're likable or not. He's interested in interesting people, and his most fascinating characters are those who are unpredictable. If you lean back in your chair early on in one of his plays, thinking you've figured out what Iago or Shylock (in *The Merchant of Venice*) is up to, don't be too sure—because that great judge of human nature, Shakespeare, will surprise you every time.

He is just as wily in the way he structures a play. In *Macbeth*, a comic scene is suddenly introduced just after the bloodiest and most treacherous slaughter imaginable, of a guest and king by his host and subject, when in comes a drunk porter who has to go to the bathroom. Shakespeare is tickling your emotions by bringing a stand-up comic on-stage right on the heels of a savage murder.

It has taken me thirty years to understand even some of these things, and so I'm not suggesting that Shakespeare is immediately understandable. I've gotten to know him not through theory but through practice, the practice of the *living* Shakespeare—the playwright of the theater.

Of course the plays are a great achievement of dramatic literature, and they should be studied and analyzed in schools and universities. But you must always remember, when reading all the words *about* the playwright and his plays, that *Shakespeare's* words came first and that in the end there is nothing greater than a single actor on the stage speaking the lines of Shakespeare.

Everything important that I know about Shakespeare comes from the practical business of producing and directing his plays in the theater. The task of classifying, criticizing, and editing Shakespeare's printed works I happily leave to others. For me, his plays really do live on the stage, not on the page. That is what he wrote them for and that is how they are best appreciated.

Although Shakespeare lived and wrote hundreds of years ago, his name rolls off my tongue as if he were my brother. As a producer and director, I feel that there is a professional relationship between us that spans the centuries. As a human being, I feel that Shakespeare has enriched my understanding of life immeasurably. I hope you'll let him do the same for you.   *Joseph Papp*

Joseph Papp gratefully acknowledges the help of Elizabeth Kirkland in preparing this Foreword.

The Playhouse

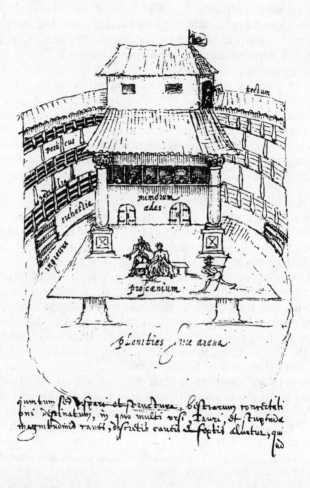

This early copy of a drawing by Johannes de Witt of the Swan Theatre in London (c. 1596), made by his friend Arend van Buchell, is the only surviving contemporary sketch of the interior of a public theater in the 1590s.

From other contemporary evidence, including the stage directions and dialogue of Elizabethan plays, we can surmise
that the various public theaters where Shakespeare's plays
were produced (the Theatre, the Curtain, the Globe) resembled the Swan in many important particulars, though there
must have been some variations as well. The public playhouses were essentially round, or polygonal, and open to
the sky, forming an acting arena approximately 70 feet in
diameter; they did not have a large curtain with which to
open and close a scene, such as we see today in opera and
some traditional theater. A platform measuring approximately 43 feet across and 27 feet deep, referred to in the de
Witt drawing as the *proscaenium*, projected into the yard,
planities sive arena. The roof, *tectum*, above the stage and
supported by two pillars, could contain machinery for as-
cents and descents, as were required in several of Shakespeare's late plays. Above this roof was a hut, shown in the
drawing with a flag flying atop it and a trumpeter at its
door announcing the performance of a play. The underside
of the stage roof, called the heavens, was usually richly dec-
orated with symbolic figures of the sun, the moon, and the
constellations. The platform stage stood at a height of 5½
feet or so above the yard, providing room under the stage
for underworldly effects. A trapdoor, which is not visible in
this drawing, gave access to the space below.

The structure at the back of the platform (labeled *mi-
morum aedes*), known as the tiring-house because it was the
actors' attiring (dressing) space, featured at least two
doors, as shown here. Some theaters seem to have also had
a discovery space, or curtained recessed alcove, perhaps between the two doors—in which Falstaff could have hidden
from the sheriff (*1 Henry IV,* 2.4) or Polonius could have
eavesdropped on Hamlet and his mother (*Hamlet,* 3.4). This
discovery space probably gave the actors a means of access
to and from the tiring-house. Curtains may also have been
hung in front of the stage doors on occasion. The de Witt
drawing shows a gallery above the doors that extends
across the back and evidently contains spectators. On occasions when action "above" demanded the use of this space,
as when Juliet appears at her "window" (*Romeo and Juliet,*
2.2 and 3.5), the gallery seems to have been used by the actors, but large scenes there were impractical.

The three-tiered auditorium is perhaps best described by Thomas Platter, a visitor to London in 1599 who saw on that occasion Shakespeare's *Julius Caesar* performed at the Globe:

The playhouses are so constructed that they play on a raised platform, so that everyone has a good view. There are different galleries and places [*orchestra, sedilia, porticus*], however, where the seating is better and more comfortable and therefore more expensive. For whoever cares to stand below only pays one English penny, but if he wishes to sit, he enters by another door [*ingressus*] and pays another penny, while if he desires to sit in the most comfortable seats, which are cushioned, where he not only sees everything well but can also be seen, then he pays yet another English penny at another door. And during the performance food and drink are carried round the audience, so that for what one cares to pay one may also have refreshment.

Scenery was not used, though the theater building itself was handsome enough to invoke a feeling of order and hierarchy that lent itself to the splendor and pageantry onstage. Portable properties, such as thrones, stools, tables, and beds, could be carried or thrust on as needed. In the scene pictured here by de Witt, a lady on a bench, attended perhaps by her waiting-gentlewoman, receives the address of a male figure. If Shakespeare had written *Twelfth Night* by 1596 for performance at the Swan, we could imagine Malvolio appearing like this as he bows before the Countess Olivia and her gentlewoman, Maria.

From the 1962 New York Shakespeare Festival production of *Julius Caesar*, with Richard Roat as Mark Antony, directed by Joseph Papp at the Heckscher Theater.

JULIUS CAESAR

JULIUS CAESAR

Foreword

Julius Caesar holds a special place in my heart as my first encounter with Shakespeare. I fell in love with the oratory, especially, as I've said before, the great speeches of Antony. "Friends, Romans, countrymen, lend me your ears," is probably the single most famous line in Shakespeare, with the possible exception of "O Romeo, Romeo, wherefore art thou Romeo?" There are many eloquent speeches throughout the play, especially the marvelous rhetoric of Mark Antony over the dead body of Caesar.

My favorite scene is the quarrel between Brutus and Cassius in Act 4, scene 3. Here the emotional nuances—guilt, accusation, defensiveness, anger, hurt—are so skillfully wrought that you can almost touch them. One of the finer moments in this great scene occurs after bitter words have passed between these comrades-in-arms, at the point where Brutus says, "Portia is dead." Cassius, who has been carrying on like a petulant child, painfully recognizes that Brutus had been bearing in his bosom the news of his own wife's death throughout the entire contretemps, and Cassius is filled with deep shame—"How scaped I killing when I crossed you so? / O insupportable and touching loss!"

I like Mark Antony for his passion and his loyalty to Caesar. Cassius I find interesting, but very childish. His petty competition with Caesar, and his hateful determination to bring Caesar down to his own level, makes his role less than honorable.

Frankly, I've never liked Brutus, because his ideals lack an emotional base and therefore become subject to rationalizations that justify the murder of Caesar. Even his remarks to his co-conspirators before they butcher Julius Caesar, though high sounding, lack compassion for the man who had befriended him: "Let's carve him as a dish fit for the gods, / Not hew him as a carcass fit for hounds." But no amount of intellectualization can obscure the fact that Brutus, as Antony tells the crowd, inflicted "the most unkindest cut of all."

Joseph Papp

Joseph Papp gratefully acknowledges the help of Elizabeth Kirkland in preparing this Foreword.

Introduction

Julius Caesar stands midway in Shakespeare's dramatic career, at a critical juncture. In some ways it is an epilogue to his English history plays of the 1590s; in other ways it introduces the period of the great tragedies. The play was evidently first performed at the new Globe Theater in the fall of 1599, shortly after *Henry V* (the last of Shakespeare's history plays about medieval England) and around the time of *As You Like It* (one of the last of Shakespeare's happy romantic comedies). It shortly preceded *Hamlet*. It is placed among the tragedies in the Folio of 1623, where it was first published, and is entitled *The Tragedy of Julius Caesar*, but in the table of contents it is listed as *The Life and Death of Julius Caesar* as though it were a history.

Julius Caesar shares with Shakespeare's history plays an absorption in the problems of civil war and popular unrest. Rome, like England, suffers an internal division that is reflected in the perturbed state of the heavens themselves. The commoners, or plebeians, are easily swayed by demagogues. Opportunists prosper in this atmosphere of crisis, although fittingly even they are sometimes undone by their own scheming. Politics seems to require a morality quite apart from that of personal life, posing a tragic dilemma for Brutus as it did for Richard II or Henry VI. The blending of history and tragedy in *Julius Caesar*, then, is not unlike that found in several English history plays. Rome was a natural subject to which Shakespeare might turn in his continuing depiction of human political behavior. Roman culture had recently been elevated to new importance by the classical orientation of the Renaissance. As a model of political organization it loomed larger in Elizabethan consciousness than it does in ours because so few other models were available, and because Greek culture was less accessible in language and tradition. According to a widely accepted mythology, Elizabethans considered themselves descended from the Romans through another Brutus, the great grandson of Aeneas.

Yet the differences between Roman and English history are as important as the similarities. Rome's choice during her civil wars lay between a senatorial republican form of government and a strong single ruler. Although the monarchical English might be inclined to be suspicious of republicanism, they had no experience to compare with it—certainly not their various peasants' revolts such as Jack Cade's rebellion (in *2 Henry VI*). On the other hand, Roman one-man rule as it flourished under Octavius Caesar lacked the English sanctions of divine right and monarchical primogeniture. Rome was, after all, a pagan culture, and Shakespeare carefully preserves this non-Christian frame of reference. The gods are frequently invoked and appear to respond with prophetic dreams and auguries, but their ultimate intentions are baffling. Humans strive blindly; the will of the gods is inscrutable. The outcome of *Julius Caesar* is far different from the restoration of providentially ordained order at the end of *Richard III*. Calm is restored and political authority reestablished, but we are by no means sure that a divine morality has been served. Roman history for Shakespeare is history divested of its divine imperatives and located in a distant political setting, making dispassionate appraisal less difficult. In Plutarch's *Lives of the Noble Grecians and Romans* as translated by Sir Thomas North, Shakespeare discovered a rich opportunity for pursuing the ironies of political life to which he had been increasingly attracted in the English histories. In fact he was drawn throughout his career to Plutarch: to the portrait of Portia in "The Life of Marcus Brutus" not only for Portia in *Julius Caesar* but for Lucrece in *The Rape of Lucrece*, Kate in *1 Henry IV*, and Portia in *The Merchant of Venice*; to "The Life of Theseus" for the Duke of *A Midsummer Night's Dream*; and to various Lives for *Julius Caesar, Coriolanus, Antony and Cleopatra*, and *Timon of Athens*. Freed from the orthodoxies of the Elizabethan world view, Shakespeare turned in the Roman or classical plays toward irony or outright satire (as in *Troilus and Cressida*) and toward the personal tragedy of political dilemma (as in *Coriolanus* and *Julius Caesar*). These are to be the dominant motifs of the Roman or classical plays, as distinguished from both the English histories and the great tragedies of evil, in which politics plays a lesser part (*Hamlet, Othello, King Lear, Macbeth*).

Julius Caesar is an ambivalent study of civil conflict. As in *Richard II*, the play is structured around two protagonists rather than one. Caesar and Brutus, men of extraordinary abilities and debilitating weaknesses, are more like each other than either would care to admit. This antithetical balance reflects a dual tradition: the medieval view of Dante and Geoffrey Chaucer condemning Brutus and Cassius as conspirators, and the Renaissance view of Sir Philip Sidney and Ben Jonson condemning Caesar as a tyrant.

Caesar is a study in paradox. He is unquestionably a great general, astute in politics, decisive in his judgments, and sharp in his evaluation of men—as, for example, in his distrust of Cassius with his "lean and hungry look" (1.2.194). Yet this mightiest of men, who in Cassius' phrase bestrides the narrow world "Like a Colossus" (l. 136), is also deaf in one ear, prone to fevers and epilepsy, unable to compete with Cassius by swimming the Tiber fully armed, and afflicted with a sterile marriage. Physical limitations of this sort are common enough, but in Caesar they are constantly juxtaposed with his aspirations to be above mortal weakness. He dies boasting that he is like the "northern star," constant, unique, "Unshaked of motion" (3.1.61–71). He professes to fear nothing and yet is notoriously superstitious. He calmly reflects that "death, a necessary end, / Will come when it will come," and then arrogantly boasts in the next moment that "Danger knows full well / That Caesar is more dangerous than he" (2.2.36–45). As his wife puts it, Caesar's "wisdom is consumed in confidence" (l. 49). He willfully betrays his own best instincts and ignores plain warnings through self-deception. He stops a procession to hear a soothsayer and then dismisses the man as "a dreamer" (1.2.24). He commissions his augurers to determine whether he should stay at home on the ides of March and then persuades himself that acting on their advice would be a sign of weakness. Most fatally, he thinks himself above flattery and so is especially vulnerable to it. So wise and powerful a man as this cannot stop the process of his own fate, because his fate and character are interwoven: he is the victim of his own hubris. His insatiable desire for the crown overbalances his judgment; no warnings of the gods can save him. Even his virtues conspire against him, for he regards himself as one who puts public interest ahead of personal affairs and brushes aside the letter of Artemidorus that would have told him of the conspiracy.

Brutus, for all his opposition to Caesar, is also a paradoxical figure. His strengths are quite unlike those of Caesar, but his weaknesses are surprisingly similar. Brutus is a noble Roman from an ancient family whose glory it has been to defend the personal liberties of Rome, the republican tradition. Brutus' virtues are personal virtues. He enjoys an admirable rapport with his courageous and intelligent wife and is genuinely kind to his servants. In friendship he is trustworthy. He deplores oaths in the conspiracy because his word is his bond. He finds Caesar's ambition for power distasteful and vulgar; his opposition to Caesar is both idealistic and patrician. Brutus' hubris is a pride of family, and on this score he is vulnerable to flattery. As Cassius reminds him, alluding to Brutus' ancestor Lucius Junius Brutus, who founded the Roman Republic in 509 B.C.: "There was a Brutus once that would have brooked / Th' eternal devil to keep his state in Rome / As easily as a king" (1.2.159–161). Should not Marcus Brutus be the savior of his country from a return to tyranny? Is not he a more fit leader for Rome than Caesar? " 'Brutus' and 'Caesar.' What should be in that 'Caesar'? / Why should that name be sounded more than yours?" (ll. 142–143). Cassius' strategy is to present to Brutus numerous testimonials "all tending to the great opinion / That Rome holds of his name" (ll. 318–319). Cassius plays the role of tempter here, but the notion he suggests is not new to Brutus.

Cassius works on Brutus' pride much as, in a parallel and adjoining scene, Decius works on Caesar's ambition (2.1 and 2.2). In these two scenes, the protagonists enter alone during the troubled night, call for a servant, receive the conspirators, and dispute the wise caution of their wives. Both men are predisposed to the temptations that are placed before them. Brutus has often thought of himself as the indispensable man for the preservation of Rome's liberties. Despite his good breeding and coolly rational manner, he is as dominating a personality as Caesar, as hard to move once his mind is made up. Indeed, the conspiracy founders on Brutus' repeated insistence on having his way. He allows no oaths among the conspirators and will not kill Antony along with Caesar. He permits Antony to speak after him in Caesar's funeral. He vetoes Cicero as a fellow conspirator. In each instance the other conspirators are unanimously opposed to Brutus' choice but yield to him. Brutus cuts off Cassius' objections before hearing them fully, being accustomed to having his way without dispute. His motives are in part noble and idealistic: Brutus wishes to have the conspirators behave generously and openly, as heroes rather than as henchmen. Yet there is something loftily patrician in his desire to have the fruits of conspiracy without any of the dirty work. His willingness to have Antony speak after him betrays a vain confidence in his own oratory and an unjustified faith in the plebeian mob. Moreover, when Brutus overrides Cassius once more in the decision to fight at Philippi and is proved wrong by the event, no idealistic motive can excuse Brutus' insistence on being obeyed; Cassius is the more experienced soldier. Still, Brutus' fatal limitations as leader of a coup d'état are inseparable from his virtues as a private man. The truth is that such a noble man is, by his very nature, unsuited for the stern exigencies of assassination and civil war. Brutus is strong-minded about his ideals, but he cannot be ruthless. The means and the end of revolution drift further and further apart. He cannot supply his troops at Philippi because he will not forage among the peasants of the countryside and will not countenance among his allies the routine corruptions of an army in time of war—though at the same time that he upbraids Cassius for not sending him gold, he does not stop to ask where the gold would come from. Even suicide is distasteful for Brutus, obliging him to embarrass his friends by asking their help. Brutus is too high-minded and genteel a man for the troubled times in which he lives.

The times indeed seem to demand ruthless action of the sort Antony and Octavius are all too ready to provide. The greatest irony of Brutus' fall is that the coup he undertakes for Roman liberty yields only further diminutions of that liberty. The plebeians are not ready for the commonwealth Brutus envisages. From the first they are portrayed as amiable but "saucy" (even in the opinion of their tribunes, Flavius and Marullus). They adulate Caesar at the expense of their previous idol, Pompey. When Brutus successfully appeals for a moment to their changeable loyalties, they cry "Let him be Caesar," and "Caesar's better parts / Shall be crowned in

Brutus" (3.2.51–52). If Brutus were not swayed by this hero worship, he would have good cause to be disillusioned. To his credit he is not the demagogue the plebeians take him for and so cannot continue to bend them to his will. Cassius, too, for all his villainlike role as tempter to Brutus, his envious motive, and his Epicurean skepticism, reveals a finer nature as the play progresses. Inspired perhaps by Brutus' philosophic idealism, Cassius turns philosopher also and accepts defeat in a noble but ineffectual cause. Yet even his death is futile; Cassius is misinformed about the fate of his friend Titinius and so stabs himself just when the battle is going well for the conspirators.

The ultimate victors are Antony and Octavius. Antony, whatever finer nature he may possess, becomes under the stress of circumstance a cunning bargainer with the conspirators and a masterful rhetorician who characterizes himself to the plebeians as a "plain blunt man" (3.2.219). In sardonic soliloquy at the end of his funeral oration he observes, "Now let it work. Mischief, thou art afoot. / Take thou what course thou wilt" (ll. 261–262). He is, to be sure, stirred by loyalty to Caesar's memory, but to the end of avenging Caesar's death he is prepared to unleash violence at whatever risk to the state. He regards Lepidus contemptuously as a mere creature under his command. Antony is older than Octavius and teaches the younger man about political realities, but an Elizabethan audience would probably savor the irony that Octavius will subsequently beat Antony at his own game. At Philippi, Octavius' refusal to accept Antony's directions in the battle (5.1.16–20) gives us a glimpse of the peremptory manner for which he is to become famous, like his predecessor. Antony and Octavius together are in any case a fearsome pair, matter-of-factly noting down the names of those who must die, including their own kinsmen. They cut off the bequests left to the populace in Caesar's will (4.1), by which Antony had won the hearts of the plebeians. Many innocent persons are sacrificed in the new reign of terror, including Cicero and the poet unluckily named Cinna. In such deaths, art and civilization yield to expediency. Rationality gives way to frenzied rhetoric and to a struggle for power in which Rome's republican tradition is buried forever. Such is the achievement of Brutus' noble revolution.

Appropriately for such a depiction of ambivalent political

strife, *Julius Caesar* is written chiefly in the oratorical mode. It resembles its near contemporary, *Henry V,* in devoting so much attention to speeches of public persuasion. The famous orations following Caesar's assassination, one by Brutus in the so-called Laconic style (that is, concise and sententious) and one by Antony in the Asiatic style (that is, more florid, anecdotal, and literary), are only the most prominent of many public utterances. In the first scene, Marullus rebukes the plebeians for their disloyalty to Pompey, and for the moment dissuades them from idolizing Caesar. Decius Brutus changes Caesar's presumably unalterable mind about staying home on the ides of March (2.2). Caesar lectures the Senate on the virtues of constancy. Before Philippi, the contending armies clash with verbal taunts. Octavius ends the play with a tribute to the dead Brutus. In less public scenes, as well, oratory serves to win Brutus over to the conspirators, to urge unavailingly that Brutus confide in his wife, or to warn the unheeding Caesar of his danger. The decline of the conspirators' cause is reflected in their descent from rational discourse to private bickering (4.3). The play gives us a range of rhetorical styles, from the deliberative (having to do with careful consideration of choices) to the forensic (analogous to pleading at law, maintaining one side or the other of a given question), to the epideictic (for display, as in set orations). The imagery, suitably public and rhetorical in its function, is of a fixed star in the firmament, a Colossus bestriding the petty world of men, a tide of fortune in the affairs of men, a statue spouting fountains of blood. The city of Rome is a vivid presence in the play, conveyed at times through Elizabethan anachronisms such as striking clocks, sweaty nightcaps, "towers and windows, yea, . . . chimney tops" (1.1.39), but in an eclectic fusion of native and classical traditions wherein anachronisms become functionally purposeful. Style affords us one more way of considering *Julius Caesar* as a Janus play looking back to Shakespeare's history plays and forward to his tragedies.

A structural pattern to be found in *Julius Caesar* is the replicating action of rise and fall by which the great men of ancient Rome succeed one another. The process antedates the play itself, for Pompey's faded glory mentioned in Act 1 is a reminder—or should be a reminder—that any person's rise to fortune lasts but a day. We behold Caesar at the point of his greatest triumph and his imminent decline to death. "O mighty Caesar! Dost thou lie so low?" asks Antony when he sees the prostrate body of the once most powerful man alive. "Are all thy conquests, glories, triumphs, spoils, / Shrunk to this little measure?" (3.1.150–152). Brutus and Cassius step forward into prominence only to be supplanted by Antony and Octavius. Antony is unaware, though presumably the audience is aware, that Antony is to fall at the hands of Octavius. The process of incessant change, reinforced by such metaphors as the tide in the affairs of men (already noted), offering its mocking comment on Caesar's self-comparison to the fixed northern star, is not simply a meaningless descent on the grand staircase of history, for Octavius' *Pax Romana* lies at the end of the cycle from republic to empire. Still, that resting place is beyond the conclusion of this open-ended play. What we see here again and again is a human blindness to history through which a succession of protagonists repeat one another's errors without intending to do so. Cassius, like Caesar, goes to his death in the face of unpropitious omens that he now partly believes true. The eagles that accompanied Cassius and his army to Philippi desert him as the moment of battle approaches. These omens suggest a balance between character and fate, for, though the leaders of Rome have one by one fallen through their own acts and choices, they have also, it seems, fulfilled a prearranged destiny. Brutus, confronted by the Ghost of Caesar and assured that he will see this spirit of Caesar at Philippi, answers resolutely, "Why, I will see thee at Philippi, then" (4.3.288). Defeated in battle as he sensed he would be, Brutus unwillingly takes his life in disregard of the stoic creed that has governed the conduct of his entire life. Cassius dies on his birthday. *Sic transit gloria mundi.*

Julius Caesar
in Performance

As a play about political conflict, *Julius Caesar* has lent itself again and again to political interpretation. No reports have survived from Shakespeare's own day to let us know what his contemporaries thought of the play politically (though it seems to have been popular, and some inferences may be drawn from the fact that the play was performed before Charles I in 1637 and again the following year), but to the Restoration and eighteenth century the play clearly was a ringing defense of republicanism and freedom versus the tyranny of Caesar. Thomas Betterton until 1707, Barton Booth until 1728, and James Quin until 1751 played Brutus as the eloquent and noble soul of liberty. The play was predominantly Brutus'; he was, as the actor and dramatist Colley Cibber wrote, a "philosopher and the hero," and the play's "lesson" was a warning against the kind of autocratic rule from which England had struggled to free herself in the seventeenth century.

Performance of the play was intended to stir feelings of national pride and love of liberty. Oratorical skill in delivering impassioned noble sentiments mattered more than nuance of character. Brutus' death became, with some added lines, one last noble sacrifice made for freedom, a protest against "poor slavish Rome" in the grip of Caesarism. Mark Antony, as acted by Edward Kynaston, Robert Wilks, and William Milward, was either cast in Brutus' shadow or made to appear to be, like Brutus, another defender of freedom. Other textual modifications reduced Julius Caesar to the tyrant that audiences expected. Minor figures were cleared away, such as Cinna the Poet (3.3) and the poet of Act 4, scene 3; Artemidorus and the Soothsayer were often merged into one, and Casca's role was usually expanded to include the lines of Marullus in Act 1, scene 1, and Titinius later in the play. The play's supposed improprieties were purified; for example, Portia was reported to have wounded herself in the arm instead of her thigh.

Between 1812 and his retirement in 1817, John Philip

Kemble had great success with the play at the Theatre Royal, Covent Garden, performing it along similar lines, simplifying the plot and intensifying the idealization of Brutus through a Romantic interest in Roman grandeur. Kemble added to the usual excisions still another cut: the disillusioning scene (4.1) in which Antony consents with Octavius to the proscribing of a number of their political enemies, even close relations. Costuming, always at least partly Roman even in Shakespeare's day (though blended at that time with anachronistic touches of contemporary dress), in the nineteenth century became a matter of scrupulous archaeological restoration. Kemble took inordinate trouble with stage picture, grouping large numbers of supernumeraries in front of painted scenery inspired by Joshua Reynolds and the Royal Academy, where pictorial interest in the inspiring antiquities of Rome had wide currency. Kemble's Brutus was more than ever the lofty patriot, while Antony, played by Kemble's brother Charles, avenged the death of Caesar from the best of motives. The cutting of the text aimed at symmetry between opposing forces and simplification of character. Kemble's version gave its spectators what they wanted, and thereafter in the nineteenth century *Julius Caesar* was seldom absent from the repertory.

The play appeared regularly onstage in the United States as well, where it no doubt appealed to the new republic's political sympathies. Lewis Hallam produced the play several times in the late eighteenth century, acting Brutus, most notably at New York's John Street Theatre in 1794. In the early nineteenth century, Thomas Abthorpe Cooper drew record crowds with his productions at the Park Theatre in New York and on tour, including a performance at Charleston, South Carolina, in 1819 attended by President Monroe.

Though critics praised Cooper's acting, they did occasionally complain, as did a Boston critic in 1818, that he had "not introduced into his performance all the stage business which has been recently invented in England." Two developments were increasingly evident on the British stage in the years after Kemble: the use of expensive realistic sets and costuming, and a political shift toward the viewpoint of the people of Rome. Nineteenth-century productions were often so lavish in their zeal for naturalistic stage pictures that the scenery determined what was to remain in the text. William Charles Macready, at Covent Garden in 1838 and five years later at the Theatre Royal, Drury Lane, bestowed on the play a passion for the details of historical setting that had begun with Kemble. Macready used painted shutters with accurate representations of Roman scenes, and employed over a hundred supernumeraries in order to give material substance to the participation of Rome's citizenry. Edwin Booth provided sets of even greater splendor for his production in New York at Booth's Theatre in 1871. The assassination of Caesar took place in a replica of the Roman Senate House based on a painting by Gérôme, with overarching paneled ceilings, rows of statuary, classical columns, banks of seats for the senators, and a seat of state for the ill-fated Caesar. Herbert Beerbohm Tree's production in 1898 at Her Majesty's Theatre was a culmination of the grand style, a spectacular three-act version rearranged to highlight the scenery and Tree himself. The middle act, given over entirely to the Forum scene, focused on Antony (played by Tree) as he spoke to an immense crowd, with handsome facades and details of the ancient Roman Forum in the background. In each act Tree was allowed to have the tableau curtain chiefly to himself, and his role was ennobled by the cutting of those scenes and speeches not to Antony's credit.

A shift in political interest manifested itself in the attention newly paid to characters other than Brutus. Macready sometimes chose to play not Brutus but Cassius, who fascinated Macready with his energy, rancorous ambition, and keen intellect. Even when Macready took the more usual role for the lead actor, that of Brutus, he brought out a more complex figure than had been seen heretofore, abhorring tyranny still, of course, but tender, gentle, self-subdued. Samuel Phelps also played both Cassius and Brutus, the former in Macready's productions of 1838 and 1843 and the latter chiefly at the Sadler's Wells Theatre between 1846 and 1862. (Brutus was in fact his farewell role at Sadler's Wells on November 6, 1862.) Edwin Booth played Brutus in his spectacular production of 1871, but he also later played both Cassius and Antony, gaining thereby an insight into the contending sides in the political struggle for Rome. The Duke

of Saxe-Meiningen's company, playing in German at Drury
Lane in 1881, presented a startling, well-orchestrated crowd
scene in which the spirit of a disturbing political movement appeared much larger than Brutus or Caesar as individuals. The populace of Rome was at last gaining in
importance onstage.

A major trend of twentieth-century interpretation has
been to ironize the play, to see it as a portrait of conflict in
which all politicians are fundamentally alike and in which
the chief causes for which people strive are illusory. At its
best, as in an Old Vic production in 1932 with Ralph Richardson as Brutus and Robert Speaight as Cassius, and
another at Stratford-upon-Avon in 1950 directed by Anthony
Quayle and Michael Langham, this ironic distancing has
led to a balanced view of political struggle, one in which
Brutus and Caesar are indeed often alike; the parallel and
adjoining scenes 1 and 2 in the second act offer directors
ample opportunity to point up similarities as Brutus and
then Caesar receive the conspirators at their houses and
disregard the advice of their wives. Strong acting on the
part of John Gielgud (Cassius) and Andrew Cruickshank
(Caesar) in 1950 provided a healthy counterpart to the usual
dominance of Brutus and Antony (played on this occasion
by Harry Andrews and Anthony Quayle), resulting in an impartial and wryly compassionate wholeness of view. The
set, as in most other twentieth-century productions, eschewed the heavy realistic scenery of the nineteenth century in favor of a sparse symbolism. Joseph Mankiewicz's
film version of *Julius Caesar* (1953), embarrassingly cast
with Marlon Brando as Antony and James Mason as a be-
mused and irritatedly indecisive Brutus, but with Gielgud
once again as Cassius, Louis Calhern as Caesar, and Deb-
orah Kerr as Portia, sought at least a kind of symmetry in
its star casting that allowed the play to speak for itself. Joseph Papp's 1962 swift-paced production at the Heckscher
Theater in New York used Thea Neu's simple, imaginative
set and strong performances from its principal actors to
keep the play's political energies in provocative balance.
Terry Hands's production at Stratford-upon-Avon in 1987
found a more telling equilibrium in subordinating the political opposition between Caesar and Brutus to an emphasis

upon what Hands called the debilitating "effects of power in a male dominated world."

Inevitably, in some productions a darker view of political machination has taken a more ideologically determined shape when the director has deliberately chosen to unbalance the play's symmetries and aim at a partisan effect. Orson Welles, in a production subtitled *Death of a Dictator* (New York, Mercury Theater, 1937), drew an analogy between Caesar and Benito Mussolini. The killing of Cinna the Poet demonstrated the pathetic vulnerability of innocence in the face of the inhuman brutality of an angry mob. Caesar was a caricature of the modern dictator, with thrust-out chin and Fascist uniform; Antony was a rabble-rouser of ominous rhetorical ability. Brutus was a thoughtful man, able to inspire his followers with dedication but ultimately victimized by his own idealism, since he was unable to do more than release the forces of chaos that mocked his dream of freedom from tyranny. Welles added to the contemporary relevance with technical aspects of production: he employed the episodic format of a film script, using lighting and sound effects rather than scenery changes to move rapidly from one scene to another. Dallas Bower, directing the play for BBC television in July of 1938, similarly exploited the play's relevance to the contemporary political situation, prophetically ending his modern-dress version with the sound of bombers overhead. Late in the autumn of 1939, with Europe now at war, Henry Cass, at London's Embassy Theatre, polemically set the play in Fascist Europe, to the point of dressing Antony in an SS uniform and providing field telephones for the commanding officers during the battle in Act 5.

Since World War II, the modern world has not failed to provide new targets for this kind of pointed political comment. Brewster Mason, playing Caesar with haughty demeanor and humorless authority in John Barton's Royal Shakespeare Company production of 1968, reminded audiences of General Charles de Gaulle. In 1969 at the Guthrie Theater in Minneapolis, Edward Payson Call used sets and costumes to evoke the atmosphere of a Latin American dictatorship. The political frame of reference can also be meaningful and contemporary when it is less specific, as at

Stratford-upon-Avon in 1972, when Trevor Nunn, Evan Smith, and Buzz Goodbody generalized the portrait of Caesarism to embrace all political oppression. A colossal statue of Caesar, onstage throughout much of the play subsequent to the assassination, towered impassively above those who still struggled against their destiny, and presided with grim satisfaction over the demise of those who had conspired against him. In 1977 at London's National Theatre, the Caesar of John Gielgud similarly remained wordlessly and ominously onstage in the wake of his murder, and at Philippi four "Caesars" surrounded Brutus to indicate the impossibility of escape from Caesarism in human history.

Even without the explicit context of fascism, then, the play in the twentieth century has retained its political relevance. Modern productions have generally seen Caesar as the embodiment of tyranny but have been unwilling to see Brutus as a viable alternative. A world grown skeptical of politics and politicians has tended to find neither Brutus nor Caesar a compelling hero; if Caesar is arrogant, Brutus is self-deceived. Modern productions have accordingly traced the dispiriting cycle by which revolution generates counterrevolution and tyranny gives way to new tyranny. Such a vision of the play no doubt tells us more about our politics than about Shakespeare's, but it testifies also to the play's remarkable ability to elicit responses as complex as the ceaseless struggle for power the play depicts.

JULIUS
CAESAR

PINDARUS, *Cassius' servant*
LUCIUS,
STRATO, } *Brutus' servants*
Caesar's SERVANT
Antony's SERVANT
Octavius' SERVANT

CARPENTER
COBBLER
Five PLEBEIANS
Three SOLDIERS *in Brutus' army*
Two SOLDIERS *in Antony's army*
MESSENGER

GHOST *of Caesar*

Senators, Plebeians, Officers, Soldiers, and Attendants

SCENE: *Rome; the neighborhood of Sardis; the neighborhood of Philippi*]

1.1

Enter Flavius, Marullus, and certain commoners over the stage.

FLAVIUS

Hence! Home, you idle creatures, get you home!
Is this a holiday? What, know you not,
Being mechanical, you ought not walk   3
Upon a laboring day without the sign   4
Of your profession? Speak, what trade art thou?

CARPENTER   Why, sir, a carpenter.

MARULLUS

Where is thy leather apron and thy rule?
What dost thou with thy best apparel on?
You, sir, what trade are you?

COBBLER   Truly, sir, in respect of a fine workman, I am 10
but, as you would say, a cobbler.   11

MARULLUS

But what trade art thou? Answer me directly.

COBBLER   A trade, sir, that I hope I may use with a safe
conscience, which is indeed, sir, a mender of bad soles. 14

FLAVIUS

What trade, thou knave? Thou naughty knave, what
trade?   15

COBBLER   Nay, I beseech you, sir, be not out with me. 16
Yet if you be out, sir, I can mend you.   17

MARULLUS

What mean'st thou by that? Mend me, thou saucy fellow?

COBBLER   Why, sir, cobble you.   19

FLAVIUS   Thou art a cobbler, art thou?

COBBLER   Truly, sir, all that I live by is with the awl. I
meddle with no tradesman's matters nor women's 22
matters, but withal I am indeed, sir, a surgeon to old 23

1.1. Location: Rome. A street.
3 mechanical of the class of artisans   **4 sign** garb and implements
10 in . . . workman (1) as far as skilled work is concerned (2) compared
with a skilled workman   **11 cobbler** (1) one who works with shoes
(2) bungler   **14 soles** (with pun on *souls*)   **15 naughty** good-for-
nothing   **16–17 out** (1) out of temper (2) having worn-out soles
17 mend (1) reform (2) repair   **19 cobble** (The meaning "to pelt with
stones" suggests itself here, though perhaps not in general use until
later in the seventeenth century.)   **22–23 meddle, women's matters**
(with sexual suggestion)   **23 withal** yet (with pun on *with awl*)

shoes. When they are in great danger, I recover them. ²⁴
As proper men as ever trod upon neat's leather have ²⁵
gone upon my handiwork. ²⁶

FLAVIUS
But wherefore art not in thy shop today?
Why dost thou lead these men about the streets?
COBBLER   Truly, sir, to wear out their shoes, to get my-
self into more work. But indeed, sir, we make holiday
to see Caesar and to rejoice in his triumph. ³¹

MARULLUS
Wherefore rejoice? What conquest brings he home?
What tributaries follow him to Rome ³³
To grace in captive bonds his chariot wheels?
You blocks, you stones, you worse than senseless things! ³⁵
O you hard hearts, you cruel men of Rome,
Knew you not Pompey? Many a time and oft ³⁷
Have you climbed up to walls and battlements, ³⁸
To towers and windows, yea, to chimney tops, ³⁹
Your infants in your arms, and there have sat
The livelong day, with patient expectation,
To see great Pompey pass the streets of Rome. ⁴²
And when you saw his chariot but appear,
Have you not made an universal shout,
That Tiber trembled underneath her banks ⁴⁵
To hear the replication of your sounds ⁴⁶
Made in her concave shores?
And do you now put on your best attire?
And do you now cull out a holiday? ⁴⁹
And do you now strew flowers in his way
That comes in triumph over Pompey's blood? ⁵¹
Begone!

24 recover (1) resole (2) cure   **25 proper** handsome.   **as . . . leather** as
ever wore shoes. (Proverbial.)   **neat's leather** cowhide   **26 gone** walked
31 triumph triumphal procession. (Caesar had overthrown the sons of
Pompey in Spain at the Battle of Munda, March 17, 45 B.C. The triumph
was held that October.)   **33 tributaries** captives who will pay ransom
(tribute)   **35 senseless** insensible like stone (hence, stupid)   **37 Pompey**
(Caesar had overthrown the great soldier and onetime triumvir at the
Battle of Pharsalus in 48 B.C., and Pompey fled to Egypt where he was
murdered.)   **38–39 battlements . . . chimney tops** (The details are
appropriate to an Elizabethan city or town.)   **42 great** (Alludes to
Pompey's epithet, *Magnus*, great.)   **pass** pass through   **45 Tiber** the
Tiber River   **46 replication** echo   **49 cull out** select, pick out
51 Pompey's blood (1) Pompey's offspring (2) the blood of the Pompeys

Run to your houses, fall upon your knees,
Pray to the gods to intermit the plague   54
That needs must light on this ingratitude.   55
FLAVIUS
Go, go, good countrymen, and for this fault
Assemble all the poor men of your sort;   57
Draw them to Tiber banks, and weep your tears
Into the channel, till the lowest stream
Do kiss the most exalted shores of all.   60
                              Exeunt all the commoners.
See whe'er their basest mettle be not moved.   61
They vanish tongue-tied in their guiltiness.
Go you down that way towards the Capitol;
This way will I. Disrobe the images   64
If you do find them decked with ceremonies.   65
MARULLUS   May we do so?
You know it is the Feast of Lupercal.   67
FLAVIUS
It is no matter. Let no images
Be hung with Caesar's trophies. I'll about   69
And drive away the vulgar from the streets;   70
So do you too, where you perceive them thick.
These growing feathers plucked from Caesar's wing
Will make him fly an ordinary pitch,   73
Who else would soar above the view of men   74
And keep us all in servile fearfulness.   *Exeunt.*

54 intermit withhold   **55 needs must** must necessarily   **57 sort** rank
60 kiss i.e., touch.   **most exalted shores** highest banks   **61 See . . . moved**
see how even their ignoble natures can be appealed to.   **whe'er**
whether.   **mettle** (1) temperament (2) substance, *metal*. (*Metal* and *mettle*
are variants of the same word. A *base metal* is one that is easily changed
or *moved*, unlike gold; compare 1.2.309.)   **64 images** statues (of Caesar in
royal regalia, set up by his followers)   **65 ceremonies** ceremonial trappings of state   **67 Feast of Lupercal** a feast of purification (*Februa*,
whence *February*) in honor of Pan, celebrated from ancient times in Rome
on February 15 of each year. (Historically, this celebration came some
months after Caesar's triumph in October of 45 B.C. The celebrants,
called *Luperci*, raced around the Palatine Hill and the Circus carrying
thongs of goatskin with which they struck those who came in their way.
Women so lashed were supposed to be cured of barrenness; hence Caesar's wish that Antony would strike Calpurnia, 1.2.6–8.)   **69 about** go
about   **70 vulgar** commoners, plebeians   **73 pitch** highest point in flight.
(A term from falconry.)   **74 else** otherwise

1.2   *Enter Caesar, Antony for the course, Calpurnia,*
Portia, Decius, Cicero, Brutus, Cassius, Casca, a
Soothsayer; after them, Marullus and Flavius;
[citizens following].

CAESAR
  Calpurnia!
CASCA   Peace, ho! Caesar speaks.
CAESAR   Calpurnia!
CALPURNIA   Here, my lord.
CAESAR
  Stand you directly in Antonius' way
  When he doth run his course. Antonius!
ANTONY   Caesar, my lord?
CAESAR
  Forget not, in your speed, Antonius,
  To touch Calpurnia; for our elders say
  The barren, touchèd in this holy chase,
  Shake off their sterile curse.
ANTONY   I shall remember.   9
  When Caesar says "Do this," it is performed.
CAESAR
  Set on, and leave no ceremony out.   [*Flourish.*] 11
SOOTHSAYER   Caesar!
CAESAR   Ha? Who calls?
CASCA
  Bid every noise be still. Peace yet again!
                              [*The music ceases.*]

CAESAR
  Who is it in the press that calls on me?   15
  I hear a tongue shriller than all the music
  Cry "Caesar!" Speak. Caesar is turned to hear.
SOOTHSAYER
  Beware the ides of March.
CAESAR   What man is that?   18
BRUTUS
  A soothsayer bids you beware the ides of March.

1.2. Location: A public place or street, perhaps as in the previous scene.
s.d. for the course i.e., stripped for the race, carrying a goatskin
thong **9 sterile curse** curse of sterility **11 Set on** proceed **15 press**
throng **18 ides of March** March 15

CAESAR
    Set him before me. Let me see his face.
CASSIUS
    Fellow, come from the throng. [*The Soothsayer comes forward*.] Look upon Caesar.
CAESAR
    What sayst thou to me now? Speak once again.
SOOTHSAYER   Beware the ides of March.
CAESAR
    He is a dreamer. Let us leave him. Pass.   24
        Sennet. Exeunt. Manent Brutus and Cassius.

CASSIUS
    Will you go see the order of the course?   25
BRUTUS   Not I.
CASSIUS   I pray you, do.
BRUTUS
    I am not gamesome. I do lack some part   28
    Of that quick spirit that is in Antony.   29
    Let me not hinder, Cassius, your desires;
    I'll leave you.
CASSIUS
    Brutus, I do observe you now of late.
    I have not from your eyes that gentleness
    And show of love as I was wont to have.   34
    You bear too stubborn and too strange a hand   35
    Over your friend that loves you.
BRUTUS   Cassius,
    Be not deceived. If I have veiled my look,   37
    I turn the trouble of my countenance
    Merely upon myself. Vexèd I am   39
    Of late with passions of some difference,   40
    Conceptions only proper to myself,   41
    Which give some soil, perhaps, to my behaviors.   42
    But let not therefore my good friends be grieved—
    Among which number, Cassius, be you one—

---

24 s.d. Sennet trumpet call signaling the arrival or departure of a dignitary. **Manent** they remain onstage **25 order of the course** ritual of the race **28 gamesome** fond of sports, merry **29 quick spirit** liveliness, responsiveness **34 wont** accustomed **35 stubborn** rough. (The metaphor is from horsemanship.) **strange** unfriendly **37 veiled my look** i.e., been introverted, seemed less friendly **39 Merely** entirely **40 of some difference** conflicting **41 only proper to** relating only to **42 soil** blemish

Nor construe any further my neglect   45
Than that poor Brutus, with himself at war,
Forgets the shows of love to other men.

CASSIUS
Then, Brutus, I have much mistook your passion,
By means whereof this breast of mine hath buried   49
Thoughts of great value, worthy cogitations.   50
Tell me, good Brutus, can you see your face?

BRUTUS
No, Cassius, for the eye sees not itself
But by reflection, by some other things.

CASSIUS   'Tis just.   54
And it is very much lamented, Brutus,
That you have no such mirrors as will turn
Your hidden worthiness into your eye,
That you might see your shadow. I have heard   58
Where many of the best respect in Rome,   59
Except immortal Caesar, speaking of Brutus
And groaning underneath this age's yoke,
Have wished that noble Brutus had his eyes.   62

BRUTUS
Into what dangers would you lead me, Cassius,
That you would have me seek into myself
For that which is not in me?

CASSIUS
Therefore, good Brutus, be prepared to hear;
And since you know you cannot see yourself
So well as by reflection, I, your glass,   68
Will modestly discover to yourself   69
That of yourself which you yet know not of.
And be not jealous on me, gentle Brutus.   71
Were I a common laughter, or did use   72
To stale with ordinary oaths my love   73

45 construe interpret. **further** otherwise   **49–50 By . . . value** i.e.,
because of which misunderstanding (my assuming you were displeased
with me) I have kept to myself important thoughts   **54 just** true
58 shadow image, reflection   **59 best respect** highest repute and station   **62 had his eyes** (1) could see things from the perspective of Caesar's critics, or (2) could see better with his own eyes   **68 glass**
mirror   **69 modestly discover** reveal without exaggeration   **71 jealous
on** suspicious of.   **gentle** noble   **72 laughter** laughingstock.   **did use**
were accustomed   **73 stale** cheapen, make common.   **ordinary**
(1) commonplace (2) customary (3) tavern

To every new protester; if you know   74
That I do fawn on men and hug them hard
And after scandal them, or if you know   76
That I profess myself in banqueting   77
To all the rout, then hold me dangerous.   78

                    Flourish, and shout.

BRUTUS
What means this shouting? I do fear the people
Choose Caesar for their king.
CASSIUS   Ay, do you fear it?
Then must I think you would not have it so.
BRUTUS
I would not, Cassius, yet I love him well.
But wherefore do you hold me here so long?
What is it that you would impart to me?
If it be aught toward the general good,
Set honor in one eye and death i' th' other
And I will look on both indifferently;   87
For let the gods so speed me as I love   88
The name of honor more than I fear death.
CASSIUS
I know that virtue to be in you, Brutus,
As well as I do know your outward favor.   91
Well, honor is the subject of my story.
I cannot tell what you and other men
Think of this life; but, for my single self,
I had as lief not be as live to be   95
In awe of such a thing as I myself.   96
I was born free as Caesar, so were you;
We both have fed as well, and we can both
Endure the winter's cold as well as he.
For once, upon a raw and gusty day,
The troubled Tiber chafing with her shores,   101
Caesar said to me, "Dar'st thou, Cassius, now
Leap in with me into this angry flood
And swim to yonder point?" Upon the word,

---

74 protester i.e., one who protests or declares friendship   **76 scandal**
slander   **77 profess myself** make declarations of friendship   **78 rout**
mob   **87 indifferently** impartially   **88 speed me** make me prosper
91 favor appearance   **95 as lief not be** just as soon not exist   **96 such**
... myself i.e., a fellow mortal   **101 chafing with** raging against

Accoutered as I was, I plungèd in   105
And bade him follow; so indeed he did.
The torrent roared, and we did buffet it
With lusty sinews, throwing it aside
And stemming it with hearts of controversy.   109
But ere we could arrive the point proposed,   110
Caesar cried, "Help me, Cassius, or I sink!"
Ay, as Aeneas, our great ancestor,   112
Did from the flames of Troy upon his shoulder
The old Anchises bear, so from the waves of Tiber
Did I the tirèd Caesar. And this man
Is now become a god, and Cassius is
A wretched creature and must bend his body   117
If Caesar carelessly but nod on him.
He had a fever when he was in Spain,
And when the fit was on him I did mark   120
How he did shake. 'Tis true, this god did shake.
His coward lips did from their color fly,   122
And that same eye whose bend doth awe the world   123
Did lose his luster. I did hear him groan.   124
Ay, and that tongue of his that bade the Romans
Mark him and write his speeches in their books,
Alas, it cried, "Give me some drink, Titinius,"
As a sick girl. Ye gods, it doth amaze me
A man of such a feeble temper should   129
So get the start of the majestic world   130
And bear the palm alone.   *Shout. Flourish.*   131
BRUTUS Another general shout?
I do believe that these applauses are
For some new honors that are heaped on Caesar.
CASSIUS
Why, man, he doth bestride the narrow world   135

---

105 Accoutered fully armed, dressed   **109 stemming** making headway
against.   **hearts of controversy** hearts fired up by rivalry   **110 arrive**
arrive at   **112 Aeneas** hero of Virgil's *Aeneid*, the legendary founder of
Rome (hence *our great ancestor*), who bore his aged father Anchises out
of burning Troy as it was falling to the Greeks   **117 bend his body**
bow   **120 mark** notice   **122 color** (1) i.e., normal healthy hue (2) military colors, flag. (The lips are personified as deserters.)   **123 bend**
glance, gaze   **124 his** its   **129 temper** constitution   **130 get the start of**
outstrip   **131 palm** victor's prize   **135 bestride** straddle

Like a Colossus, and we petty men   136
Walk under his huge legs and peep about
To find ourselves dishonorable graves.   138
Men at some time are masters of their fates.
The fault, dear Brutus, is not in our stars,
But in ourselves, that we are underlings.
"Brutus" and "Caesar." What should be in that
    "Caesar"?
Why should that name be sounded more than yours?
Write them together, yours is as fair a name;
Sound them, it doth become the mouth as well;
Weigh them, it is as heavy; conjure with 'em,
"Brutus" will start a spirit as soon as "Caesar."   147
Now, in the names of all the gods at once,
Upon what meat doth this our Caesar feed   149
That he is grown so great? Age, thou art shamed!
Rome, thou hast lost the breed of noble bloods!
When went there by an age since the great flood   152
But it was famed with more than with one man?   153
When could they say, till now, that talked of Rome,
That her wide walks encompassed but one man?
Now is it Rome indeed, and room enough,   156
When there is in it but one only man.
O, you and I have heard our fathers say
There was a Brutus once that would have brooked   159
Th' eternal devil to keep his state in Rome   160
As easily as a king.   161
BRUTUS
That you do love me, I am nothing jealous.   162
What you would work me to, I have some aim.   163

136 **Colossus** (A 100-foot-high bronze statue of Helios, the sun god, one
of the seven wonders of the ancient world, was commonly supposed to
have stood astride the entrance to the harbor of Rhodes.)
138 **dishonorable graves** the ignoble deaths of slaves   147 **start** raise
149 **meat** food   152 **flood** i.e., the classical analogue of Noah's flood,
one in which all humanity was destroyed except for Deucalion and his
wife Pyrrha   153 **famed with** famous for   156 **Rome, room** (Pronounced alike.)   159 **Brutus** i.e., Lucius Junius Brutus, who expelled
the Tarquins and founded the Roman republic (c. 509 B.C.).   **brooked**
tolerated   160 **keep his state** i.e., set up his throne   161 **As ... king** as
readily as he would tolerate a king   162 **nothing jealous** not at all
doubtful   163 **work** persuade.   **aim** inkling and intention

How I have thought of this and of these times
I shall recount hereafter. For this present,   165
I would not, so with love I might entreat you,   166
Be any further moved. What you have said   167
I will consider; what you have to say
I will with patience hear, and find a time
Both meet to hear and answer such high things.   170
Till then, my noble friend, chew upon this:
Brutus had rather be a villager
Than to repute himself a son of Rome
Under these hard conditions as this time
Is like to lay upon us.
CASSIUS   I am glad that my weak words
Have struck but thus much show of fire from Brutus.

    Enter Caesar and his train.

BRUTUS
The games are done and Caesar is returning.
CASSIUS
As they pass by, pluck Casca by the sleeve,
And he will, after his sour fashion, tell you
What hath proceeded worthy note today.   181
BRUTUS
I will do so. But look you, Cassius,
The angry spot doth glow on Caesar's brow,
And all the rest look like a chidden train.   184
Calpurnia's cheek is pale, and Cicero
Looks with such ferret and such fiery eyes   186
As we have seen him in the Capitol,
Being crossed in conference by some senators.   188
CASSIUS
Casca will tell us what the matter is.
CAESAR   Antonius!
ANTONY   Caesar?
CAESAR
Let me have men about me that are fat,

165 **present** present moment   166 **so . . . you** if I might entreat you in
the name of friendship   167 **moved** urged   170 **meet** fitting
181 **worthy note** worthy of notice   184 **chidden** scolded, rebuked.   **train**
retinue   186 **ferret** ferretlike, i.e., small and red   188 **crossed in conference** opposed in debate

Sleek-headed men, and such as sleep o' nights.
Yond Cassius has a lean and hungry look.
He thinks too much. Such men are dangerous.
ANTONY
Fear him not, Caesar, he's not dangerous.
He is a noble Roman, and well given.   197
CAESAR
Would he were fatter! But I fear him not.
Yet if my name were liable to fear,
I do not know the man I should avoid
So soon as that spare Cassius. He reads much,
He is a great observer, and he looks
Quite through the deeds of men. He loves no plays,   203
As thou dost, Antony; he hears no music.   204
Seldom he smiles, and smiles in such a sort   205
As if he mocked himself and scorned his spirit
That could be moved to smile at anything.
Such men as he be never at heart's ease
Whiles they behold a greater than themselves,
And therefore are they very dangerous.
I rather tell thee what is to be feared
Than what I fear, for always I am Caesar.
Come on my right hand, for this ear is deaf,
And tell me truly what thou think'st of him.
               Sennet. Exeunt Caesar and his train. [Casca
                    remains with Brutus and Cassius.]
CASCA   You pulled me by the cloak. Would you speak 215
with me?
BRUTUS
Ay, Casca. Tell us what hath chanced today,   217
That Caesar looks so sad.   218
CASCA   Why, you were with him, were you not?
BRUTUS
I should not then ask Casca what had chanced.
CASCA   Why, there was a crown offered him; and, being
offered him, he put it by with the back of his hand, 222
thus, and then the people fell a-shouting.

197 given disposed   **203 through** i.e., into the motives of   **204 hears no music** (Regarded as a sign of a morose and treacherous character.)   **205 sort** manner   **215 cloak** (Elizabethan costume; see also *sleeve*, l. 179, and *doublet*, l. 265)   **217 chanced** happened   **218 sad** serious   **222 by** aside

BRUTUS   What was the second noise for?

CASCA   Why, for that too.

CASSIUS

　They shouted thrice. What was the last cry for?

CASCA   Why, for that too.

BRUTUS   Was the crown offered him thrice?

CASCA   Ay, marry, was 't, and he put it by thrice, every   229
　time gentler than other, and at every putting-by mine
　honest neighbors shouted.   231

CASSIUS   Who offered him the crown?

CASCA   Why, Antony.

BRUTUS

　Tell us the manner of it, gentle Casca.   234

CASCA   I can as well be hanged as tell the manner of it.
　It was mere foolery; I did not mark it. I saw Mark An-
　tony offer him a crown—yet 'twas not a crown nei-
　ther, 'twas one of these coronets—and, as I told you,   238
　he put it by once; but for all that, to my thinking, he
　would fain have had it. Then he offered it to him again;   240
　then he put it by again; but to my thinking he was
　very loath to lay his fingers off it. And then he offered
　it the third time. He put it the third time by, and still   243
　as he refused it the rabblement hooted and clapped   244
　their chapped hands, and threw up their sweaty night-   245
　caps, and uttered such a deal of stinking breath be-   246
　cause Caesar refused the crown that it had almost
　choked Caesar, for he swooned and fell down at it.
　And for mine own part I durst not laugh for fear of
　opening my lips and receiving the bad air.

CASSIUS

　But soft, I pray you. What, did Caesar swoon?   251

CASCA   He fell down in the marketplace, and foamed at
　mouth, and was speechless.

BRUTUS

　'Tis very like. He hath the falling sickness.   254

---

229 marry i.e., indeed. (Originally, "by the Virgin Mary.")   **231 honest**
worthy. (Said contemptuously.)   **234 gentle** noble   **238 coronets** chap-
lets, garlands   **240 fain** gladly   **243–244 still as** whenever
245–246 nightcaps (Scornful allusion to the *pilleus*, a felt cap worn by
the plebeians on festival days.)   **251 soft** i.e., wait a minute   **254 like**
likely.   **falling sickness** epilepsy. (But Cassius takes it to mean "falling
into servitude.")

CASSIUS
    No, Caesar hath it not, but you and I,
    And honest Casca, we have the falling sickness.
CASCA   I know not what you mean by that, but I am
    sure Caesar fell down. If the tag-rag people did not   258
    clap him and hiss him, according as he pleased and
    displeased them, as they use to do the players in the   260
    theater, I am no true man.   261
BRUTUS
    What said he when he came unto himself?
CASCA   Marry, before he fell down, when he perceived
    the common herd was glad he refused the crown, he
    plucked me ope his doublet and offered them his throat   265
    to cut. An I had been a man of any occupation, if I   266
    would not have taken him at a word, I would I might
    go to hell among the rogues. And so he fell. When he
    came to himself again, he said if he had done or said
    anything amiss, he desired their worships to think it
    was his infirmity. Three or four wenches where I
    stood cried, "Alas, good soul!" and forgave him with
    all their hearts. But there's no heed to be taken of
    them; if Caesar had stabbed their mothers they would   274
    have done no less.
BRUTUS
    And after that, he came thus sad away?   276
CASCA   Ay.
CASSIUS   Did Cicero say anything?
CASCA   Ay, he spoke Greek.
CASSIUS   To what effect?
CASCA   Nay, an I tell you that, I'll ne'er look you i' the
    face again. But those that understood him smiled at
    one another and shook their heads; but, for mine own
    part, it was Greek to me. I could tell you more news
    too. Marullus and Flavius, for pulling scarves off Cae-   285
    sar's images, are put to silence. Fare you well. There   286
    was more foolery yet, if I could remember it.

258 **tag-rag** ragtag, riffraff   260 **use** are accustomed   261 **true** honest   265 **plucked me ope** pulled open.   **doublet** Elizabethan upper
garment, like a jacket   266 **An** if.   **man . . . occupation** (1) working man
(2) man of action   274 **stabbed** (with bawdy connotation)   276 **sad**
seriously   285 **scarves** decorations, festoons   286 **put to silence** dismissed from office. (So reported in Plutarch.)

CASSIUS   Will you sup with me tonight, Casca?

CASCA   No, I am promised forth.   289

CASSIUS   Will you dine with me tomorrow?

CASCA   Ay, if I be alive, and your mind hold, and your
dinner worth the eating.

CASSIUS   Good. I will expect you.

CASCA   Do so. Farewell both.   *Exit.*

BRUTUS
What a blunt fellow is this grown to be!
He was quick mettle when he went to school.   296

CASSIUS
So is he now in execution
Of any bold or noble enterprise,
However he puts on this tardy form.   299
This rudeness is a sauce to his good wit,   300
Which gives men stomach to digest his words   301
With better appetite.

BRUTUS
And so it is. For this time I will leave you.
Tomorrow, if you please to speak with me,
I will come home to you; or, if you will,
Come home to me, and I will wait for you.

CASSIUS
I will do so. Till then, think of the world.   307

                                        Exit Brutus.

Well, Brutus, thou art noble. Yet I see
Thy honorable mettle may be wrought   309
From that it is disposed. Therefore it is meet   310
That noble minds keep ever with their likes;
For who so firm that cannot be seduced?
Caesar doth bear me hard, but he loves Brutus.   313

---

289 promised forth engaged to dine out   **296 quick mettle** of a lively
temperament   **299 However** however much.   **tardy form** appearance of
sluggishness   **300 rudeness** rough manner.   **wit** intellect   **301 stomach**
appetite, inclination   **307 the world** i.e., the state of the world
309 mettle (As often, the word combines the senses of *mettle*, temperament, and *metal*, substance. The latter meaning continues here in the
chemical metaphor of metal that is *wrought* or transmuted. As *honorable mettle* [or noble metal], gold cannot be transmuted into base
substances, and yet Cassius proposes to do just that with Brutus.
Compare 1.1.61.)   **309–310 wrought . . . disposed** i.e., turned away from
its natural disposition   **310 meet** fitting   **313 bear me hard** bear me a
grudge

If I were Brutus now, and he were Cassius,
He should not humor me. I will this night   315
In several hands in at his windows throw,   316
As if they came from several citizens,
Writings, all tending to the great opinion   318
That Rome holds of his name, wherein obscurely
Caesar's ambition shall be glancèd at.   320
And after this let Caesar seat him sure,   321
For we will shake him, or worse days endure.   *Exit.*

❖

1.3   *Thunder and lightning. Enter, [meeting,] Casca*
            [with his sword drawn] and Cicero.

CICERO
Good even, Casca. Brought you Caesar home?   1
Why are you breathless? And why stare you so?
CASCA
Are not you moved, when all the sway of earth   3
Shakes like a thing unfirm? O Cicero,
I have seen tempests when the scolding winds
Have rived the knotty oaks, and I have seen   6
Th' ambitious ocean swell and rage and foam
To be exalted with the threatening clouds;   8
But never till tonight, never till now,
Did I go through a tempest dropping fire.
Either there is a civil strife in heaven,
Or else the world, too saucy with the gods,   12
Incenses them to send destruction.
CICERO
Why, saw you anything more wonderful?   14

315 **He** i.e., Brutus.   **humor** cajole (Cassius may be saying, if he, Brutus, were in my shoes, he wouldn't be so smug in his behavior toward
me as he is now; or, he wouldn't sway me as I sway him. Or he may
mean, if I were in Brutus' shoes, Caesar wouldn't cajole me so.)
316 **several hands** different handwriting   318 **tending to** concerning;
confirming   320 **glancèd** hinted   321 **seat him sure** seat himself securely in power (i.e., watch out)

1.3. Location: A street.
1 **Brought** escorted   3 **sway** established order   6 **rived** split   8 **exalted**
with raised to the level of   12 **saucy** insolent   14 **more** else.   **wonder-**
ful wondrous

CASCA
> A common slave—you know him well by sight—
> Held up his left hand, which did flame and burn
> Like twenty torches joined, and yet his hand,
> Not sensible of fire, remained unscorched.   18
> Besides—I ha' not since put up my sword—   19
> Against the Capitol I met a lion,   20
> Who glazed upon me and went surly by   21
> Without annoying me. And there were drawn   22
> Upon a heap a hundred ghastly women,   23
> Transformèd with their fear, who swore they saw
> Men all in fire walk up and down the streets.
> And yesterday the bird of night did sit   26
> Even at noonday upon the marketplace,
> Hooting and shrieking. When these prodigies   28
> Do so conjointly meet, let not men say,   29
> "These are their reasons, they are natural,"
> For I believe they are portentous things
> Unto the climate that they point upon.   32

CICERO
> Indeed, it is a strange-disposèd time.
> But men may construe things after their fashion,   34
> Clean from the purpose of the things themselves.   35
> Comes Caesar to the Capitol tomorrow?

CASCA
> He doth; for he did bid Antonius
> Send word to you he would be there tomorrow.

CICERO
> Good night then, Casca. This disturbèd sky
> Is not to walk in.

CASCA   Farewell, Cicero.   *Exit Cicero.*

> *Enter Cassius.*

CASSIUS
> Who's there?

---

18 Not sensible of not feeling   **19 put up** sheathed   **20 Against** opposite or near   **21 glazed** stared glassily   **22 annoying** harming   **22–23 drawn . . . heap** huddled together   **23 ghastly** pallid   **26 bird of night** owl, a bird of evil omen   **28 prodigies** abnormalities, wonders   **29 conjointly meet** coincide   **32 climate** region   **34 construe** interpret.   **after their fashion** in their own way   **35 Clean . . . purpose** contrary to the actual import or meaning

CASCA   A Roman.
CASSIUS   Casca, by your voice.
CASCA
  Your ear is good. Cassius, what night is this!   42
CASSIUS
  A very pleasing night to honest men.
CASCA
  Who ever knew the heavens menace so?
CASSIUS
  Those that have known the earth so full of faults.
  For my part, I have walked about the streets,
  Submitting me unto the perilous night,
  And thus unbracèd, Casca, as you see,   48
  Have bared my bosom to the thunder-stone;   49
  And when the cross blue lightning seemed to open   50
  The breast of heaven, I did present myself
  Even in the aim and very flash of it.   52
CASCA
  But wherefore did you so much tempt the heavens?
  It is the part of men to fear and tremble   54
  When the most mighty gods by tokens send   55
  Such dreadful heralds to astonish us.   56
CASSIUS
  You are dull, Casca, and those sparks of life
  That should be in a Roman you do want,   58
  Or else you use not. You look pale, and gaze,
  And put on fear, and cast yourself in wonder,   60
  To see the strange impatience of the heavens.
  But if you would consider the true cause
  Why all these fires, why all these gliding ghosts,
  Why birds and beasts from quality and kind,   64
  Why old men, fools, and children calculate,   65
  Why all these things change from their ordinance,   66
  Their natures, and preformèd faculties,   67
  To monstrous quality—why, you shall find   68

---

42 what night what a night   **48 unbracèd** with doublet unfastened
49 thunder-stone thunderbolt   **50 cross** forked, jagged   **52 Even in the
aim** at the exact place at which it was aimed   **54 part** appropriate role
55 tokens signs   **56 astonish** stun   **58 want** lack   **60 put on** adopt, show
signs of   **64 from ... kind** (behaving) contrary to their true nature
65 old men dotards.   **calculate** prophesy   **66 ordinance** established nature   **67 preformèd** innate, congenital   **68 monstrous** unnatural

That heaven hath infused them with these spirits
To make them instruments of fear and warning
Unto some monstrous state.   71
Now could I, Casca, name to thee a man
Most like this dreadful night,
That thunders, lightens, opens graves, and roars
As doth the lion in the Capitol—
A man no mightier than thyself or me
In personal action, yet prodigious grown   77
And fearful, as these strange eruptions are.   78

CASCA
'Tis Caesar that you mean, is it not, Cassius?

CASSIUS
Let it be who it is. For Romans now
Have thews and limbs like to their ancestors;   81
But, woe the while, our fathers' minds are dead,   82
And we are governed with our mothers' spirits.
Our yoke and sufferance show us womanish.   84

CASCA
Indeed, they say the senators tomorrow
Mean to establish Caesar as a king,
And he shall wear his crown by sea and land
In every place save here in Italy.

CASSIUS
I know where I will wear this dagger then;
Cassius from bondage will deliver Cassius.
Therein, ye gods, you make the weak most strong;   91
Therein, ye gods, you tyrants do defeat.
Nor stony tower, nor walls of beaten brass,   93
Nor airless dungeon, nor strong links of iron,
Can be retentive to the strength of spirit;   95
But life, being weary of these worldly bars,   96
Never lacks power to dismiss itself.
If I know this, know all the world besides,   98

71 **monstrous state** government or commonwealth in an unnatural
condition   **77 prodigious** ominous   **78 fearful** inspiring fear   **81 thews**
sinews, muscles.   **like** similar   **82 woe the while** alas for the age
84 yoke and sufferance patience under the yoke   **91 Therein** i.e., in the
ability to commit suicide   **93 Nor** neither   **95 be . . . spirit** confine a
resolute spirit   **96 bars** (1) prison bars (2) burdens (such as tyranny)
98 know . . . besides let the rest of the world know

That part of tyranny that I do bear
I can shake off at pleasure.   *Thunder still.*

CASCA   So can I.
So every bondman in his own hand bears
The power to cancel his captivity.

CASSIUS
And why should Caesar be a tyrant, then?
Poor man, I know he would not be a wolf
But that he sees the Romans are but sheep;
He were no lion, were not Romans hinds.   106
Those that with haste will make a mighty fire
Begin it with weak straws. What trash is Rome,
What rubbish and what offal, when it serves   109
For the base matter to illuminate   110
So vile a thing as Caesar! But, O grief,
Where hast thou led me? I perhaps speak this
Before a willing bondman; then I know
My answer must be made. But I am armed,   114
And dangers are to me indifferent.   115

CASCA
You speak to Casca, and to such a man
That is no fleering telltale. Hold. My hand.   117
Be factious for redress of all these griefs,   118
And I will set this foot of mine as far
As who goes farthest.   [*They shake hands.*]

CASSIUS   There's a bargain made.
Now know you, Casca, I have moved already   121
Some certain of the noblest-minded Romans
To undergo with me an enterprise
Of honorable-dangerous consequence;
And I do know by this they stay for me   125
In Pompey's porch. For now, this fearful night,   126

106 hinds (1) female of the red deer (2) servants, menials   **109 offal**
rubbish, wood shavings   **110 matter** i.e., fuel   **114 My answer . . . made**
I will have to answer (to Caesar) for what I have said.   **armed** (1) provided with weapons (2) morally fortified   **115 indifferent** unimportant
117 fleering sneering, scornful.   **Hold. My hand** enough; here is my
hand   **118 factious** active as a partisan.   **griefs** grievances   **121 moved**
urged   **125 by this** by this time.   **stay** wait   **126 Pompey's porch** the
colonnade of Pompey's great open theater, dedicated in 55 B.C. (Caesar
was assassinated there, though Shakespeare has the assassination take
place in the Capitol [i.e., the Senate chamber].)

There is no stir or walking in the streets,
And the complexion of the element   128
In favor's like the work we have in hand,   129
Most bloody, fiery, and most terrible.

  Enter Cinna.

CASCA
Stand close awhile, for here comes one in haste.   131
CASSIUS
'Tis Cinna; I do know him by his gait.
He is a friend.—Cinna, where haste you so?
CINNA
To find out you. Who's that? Metellus Cimber?
CASSIUS
No, it is Casca, one incorporate   135
To our attempts. Am I not stayed for, Cinna?
CINNA
I am glad on 't. What a fearful night is this!   137
There's two or three of us have seen strange sights.
CASSIUS   Am I not stayed for? Tell me.
CINNA
Yes, you are. O Cassius, if you could
But win the noble Brutus to our party—
CASSIUS
Be you content. Good Cinna, take this paper,
       [Giving papers]
And look you lay it in the praetor's chair,   143
Where Brutus may but find it. And throw this   144
In at his window. Set this up with wax
Upon old Brutus' statue. All this done,   146
Repair to Pompey's porch, where you shall find us.   147
Is Decius Brutus and Trebonius there?
CINNA
All but Metellus Cimber, and he's gone
To seek you at your house. Well, I will hie,   150
And so bestow these papers as you bade me.

128 element sky **129 favor's** appearance is **131 close** concealed,
still **135 incorporate** admitted as a member **137 on 't** of it
143 praetor's chair official seat of a praetor, Roman magistrate ranking
next below the consul. (Brutus was praetor, one of sixteen.) **144 Where
. . . it** where Brutus cannot help finding it **146 old Brutus** (Lucius
Junius Brutus; Brutus was reputed to be his descendant.) **147 Repair**
proceed (also in l. 152) **150 hie** go quickly

CASSIUS
    That done, repair to Pompey's theater.   *Exit Cinna.*
    Come, Casca, you and I will yet ere day
    See Brutus at his house. Three parts of him   154
    Is ours already, and the man entire
    Upon the next encounter yields him ours.

CASCA
    O, he sits high in all the people's hearts;
    And that which would appear offense in us,
    His countenance, like richest alchemy,   159
    Will change to virtue and to worthiness.   160

CASSIUS
    Him and his worth, and our great need of him,
    You have right well conceited. Let us go,   162
    For it is after midnight, and ere day
    We will awake him and be sure of him.   *Exeunt.*

❖

154 parts i.e., quarters   **159 countenance** (1) support, approval (2) (honorable) appearance.   **alchemy** pseudoscience the chief object of which was
the transmutation of metals into gold   **160 virtue** (In addition to its literal
meaning, a technical term for what the alchemists hoped to attain.)
162 conceited (1) conceived, grasped (2) expressed in a figure

2.1   *Enter Brutus in his orchard.*

BRUTUS   What, Lucius, ho!—
I cannot by the progress of the stars
Give guess how near to day.—Lucius, I say!—
I would it were my fault to sleep so soundly.—
When, Lucius, when? Awake, I say! What, Lucius!

   Enter Lucius.

LUCIUS   Called you, my lord?
BRUTUS
   Get me a taper in my study, Lucius.   7
   When it is lighted, come and call me here.
LUCIUS   I will, my lord.   *Exit.*
BRUTUS
   It must be by his death. And for my part
   I know no personal cause to spurn at him,   11
   But for the general. He would be crowned.   12
   How that might change his nature, there's the question.
   It is the bright day that brings forth the adder,
   And that craves wary walking. Crown him that,   15
   And then I grant we put a sting in him
   That at his will he may do danger with.
   Th' abuse of greatness is when it disjoins
   Remorse from power. And to speak truth of Caesar,   19
   I have not known when his affections swayed   20
   More than his reason. But 'tis a common proof   21
   That lowliness is young ambition's ladder,   22
   Whereto the climber-upward turns his face;
   But when he once attains the upmost round   24
   He then unto the ladder turns his back,
   Looks in the clouds, scorning the base degrees   26
   By which he did ascend. So Caesar may.
   Then, lest he may, prevent. And since the quarrel

2.1. Location: Rome. Brutus' orchard, or garden.
7 Get me put.   **taper** candle   **11 spurn** kick   **12 general** general cause,
i.e., common good   **15 craves** requires.   **that** i.e., king, emperor
19 Remorse mercy, compassion   **20 affections** passions.   **swayed**
ruled   **21 proof** experience   **22 lowliness** i.e., pretended humbleness
24 round rung   **26 base degrees** (1) lower rungs (2) persons of lower
social station

Will bear no color for the thing he is,   29
Fashion it thus: that what he is, augmented,   30
Would run to these and these extremities.
And therefore think him as a serpent's egg
Which, hatched, would, as his kind, grow mischievous; 33
And kill him in the shell.

    Enter Lucius.

LUCIUS
The taper burneth in your closet, sir.   35
Searching the window for a flint, I found
This paper, thus sealed up, and I am sure
It did not lie there when I went to bed.
                        Gives him the letter.

BRUTUS
Get you to bed again. It is not day.
Is not tomorrow, boy, the ides of March?   40
LUCIUS   I know not, sir.
BRUTUS
Look in the calendar and bring me word.
LUCIUS   I will, sir.   *Exit.*
BRUTUS
The exhalations whizzing in the air   44
Give so much light that I may read by them.
                  Opens the letter and reads.
"Brutus, thou sleep'st. Awake, and see thyself!
Shall Rome, et cetera? Speak, strike, redress!"
"Brutus, thou sleep'st. Awake!"
Such instigations have been often dropped
Where I have took them up.
"Shall Rome, et cetera?" Thus must I piece it out:
Shall Rome stand under one man's awe? What, Rome?
My ancestors did from the streets of Rome
The Tarquin drive, when he was called a king.
"Speak, strike, redress!" Am I entreated
To speak and strike? O Rome, I make thee promise,   56

29 Will . . . is i.e., can carry no appearance of justice so far as his
conduct to date is concerned   **30 Fashion it** put the matter   **33 as his
kind** according to his nature.   **mischievous** harmful   **35 closet** private
chamber, study   **40 ides** fifteenth day   **44 exhalations** meteors   **56 I
make thee promise** I promise thee

If the redress will follow, thou receivest   57
Thy full petition at the hand of Brutus.

    Enter Lucius.

LUCIUS   Sir, March is wasted fifteen days. *Knock within.*
BRUTUS
  'Tis good. Go to the gate; somebody knocks.
                           [*Exit Lucius.*]
  Since Cassius first did whet me against Caesar,   61
  I have not slept.
  Between the acting of a dreadful thing
  And the first motion, all the interim is   64
  Like a phantasma or a hideous dream.   65
  The genius and the mortal instruments   66
  Are then in council; and the state of man,   67
  Like to a little kingdom, suffers then
  The nature of an insurrection.

    Enter Lucius.

LUCIUS
  Sir, 'tis your brother Cassius at the door,   70
  Who doth desire to see you.
BRUTUS   Is he alone?
LUCIUS
  No, sir, there are more with him.
BRUTUS   Do you know them?
LUCIUS
  No, sir. Their hats are plucked about their ears,
  And half their faces buried in their cloaks,
  That by no means I may discover them   75
  By any mark of favor.
BRUTUS   Let 'em enter.   [*Exit Lucius.*] 76
  They are the faction. O conspiracy,
  Sham'st thou to show thy dangerous brow by night,

---

57 If . . . follow i.e., if striking Caesar will lead to the reform of grievances **61 whet** incite **64 motion** proposal **65 phantasma** hallucina-
tion **66–67 The genius . . . council** i.e., the immortal part of man, his
rational soul, deliberates or debates with his lower or mortal faculties,
his physical and passionate side **67 state of man** i.e., man as a microcosm, a tiny kingdom **70 brother** i.e., brother-in-law. (Cassius had
married a sister of Brutus.) **75 discover** identify **76 favor** appearance

When evils are most free? O, then by day   79
Where wilt thou find a cavern dark enough
To mask thy monstrous visage? Seek none, conspiracy!
Hide it in smiles and affability;
For if thou path, thy native semblance on,   83
Not Erebus itself were dim enough   84
To hide thee from prevention.   85

> *Enter the conspirators, Cassius, Casca, Decius,*
> *Cinna, Metellus [Cimber], and Trebonius.*

CASSIUS
I think we are too bold upon your rest.   86
Good morrow, Brutus. Do we trouble you?
BRUTUS
I have been up this hour, awake all night.
Know I these men that come along with you?
CASSIUS
Yes, every man of them, and no man here
But honors you; and every one doth wish
You had but that opinion of yourself
Which every noble Roman bears of you.
This is Trebonius.
BRUTUS   He is welcome hither.
CASSIUS
This, Decius Brutus.
BRUTUS   He is welcome too.
CASSIUS
This, Casca; this, Cinna; and this, Metellus Cimber.
BRUTUS   They are all welcome.
What watchful cares do interpose themselves   98
Betwixt your eyes and night?
CASSIUS   Shall I entreat a word?
> *They [Brutus and Cassius] whisper.*
DECIUS
Here lies the east. Doth not the day break here?
CASCA   No.

79 **free** free to roam at will   83 **path** proceed, walk about.   **thy . . . on**
wearing your true appearance   84 **Erebus** region of darkness between
earth and Hades   85 **prevention** detection and being forestalled
86 **upon** in intruding upon   98 **watchful cares** worries preventing sleep

CINNA

O, pardon, sir, it doth; and yon gray lines
That fret the clouds are messengers of day.   104

CASCA

You shall confess that you are both deceived.   105
Here, as I point my sword, the sun arises,
Which is a great way growing on the south,   107
Weighing the youthful season of the year.   108
Some two months hence, up higher toward the north
He first presents his fire; and the high east   110
Stands, as the Capitol, directly here.

BRUTUS [*Coming forward*]

Give me your hands all over, one by one.   112

CASSIUS

And let us swear our resolution.

BRUTUS

No, not an oath. If not the face of men,   114
The sufferance of our souls, the time's abuse—   115
If these be motives weak, break off betimes,   116
And every man hence to his idle bed;   117
So let high-sighted tyranny range on   118
Till each man drop by lottery. But if these,   119
As I am sure they do, bear fire enough
To kindle cowards and to steel with valor
The melting spirits of women, then, countrymen,
What need we any spur but our own cause
To prick us to redress? What other bond   124
Than secret Romans that have spoke the word
And will not palter? And what other oath   126
Than honesty to honesty engaged   127
That this shall be or we will fall for it?
Swear priests and cowards and men cautelous,   129

104 fret mark with interlacing lines   **105 deceived** mistaken
107 growing on toward   **108 Weighing** considering, in consequence of
110 high due   **112 all over** one and all   **114 face of men** i.e., grave look of
all concerned persons in the state   **115 sufferance** state of suffering.
time's abuse corruptions of the present day   **116 betimes** at once
117 idle unused, empty   **118 high-sighted** upward-gazing (cf. 2.1.26); or
haughty, looking down from an Olympian height   **119 by lottery** i.e., as
the capricious tyrant chances to pick on him.   **these** i.e., these injustices
just cited   **124 prick** spur   **126 palter** use trickery   **127 honesty** personal
honor   **129 Swear** make swear.   **cautelous** deceitful; cautious

Old feeble carrions, and such suffering souls   130
That welcome wrongs; unto bad causes swear
Such creatures as men doubt; but do not stain
The even virtue of our enterprise,   133
Nor th' insuppressive mettle of our spirits,   134
To think that or our cause or our performance   135
Did need an oath, when every drop of blood
That every Roman bears—and nobly bears—
Is guilty of a several bastardy   138
If he do break the smallest particle
Of any promise that hath passed from him.

CASSIUS
But what of Cicero? Shall we sound him?   141
I think he will stand very strong with us.

CASCA
Let us not leave him out.

CINNA   No, by no means.

METELLUS
O, let us have him, for his silver hairs
Will purchase us a good opinion   145
And buy men's voices to commend our deeds.
It shall be said his judgment ruled our hands;
Our youths and wildness shall no whit appear,
But all be buried in his gravity.

BRUTUS
O, name him not. Let us not break with him,   150
For he will never follow anything
That other men begin.

CASSIUS   Then leave him out.

CASCA   Indeed he is not fit.

DECIUS
Shall no man else be touched but only Caesar?

CASSIUS
Decius, well urged. I think it is not meet   156

130 carrions men who resemble corpses.   **suffering** long-suffering
133 even steadfast, consistent   **134 insuppressive** not to be suppressed   **135 or . . . or** either . . . or   **138 several bastardy** i.e., individual dishonorable act. (A noble Roman failing to keep his promise
would be charged with a separate desecration of his birthright for
each drop of blood in his body.)   **141 sound him** find out his feelings   **145 purchase** procure (playing on *silver* in l. 144 as money)
150 break with confide in   **156 meet** fitting

Mark Antony, so well beloved of Caesar,
Should outlive Caesar. We shall find of him   158
A shrewd contriver; and you know his means,
If he improve them, may well stretch so far   160
As to annoy us all. Which to prevent,   161
Let Antony and Caesar fall together.
BRUTUS
Our course will seem too bloody, Caius Cassius,
To cut the head off and then hack the limbs,
Like wrath in death and envy afterwards;   165
For Antony is but a limb of Caesar.
Let's be sacrificers, but not butchers, Caius.
We all stand up against the spirit of Caesar,
And in the spirit of men there is no blood.
O, that we then could come by Caesar's spirit   170
And not dismember Caesar! But, alas,
Caesar must bleed for it. And, gentle friends,   172
Let's kill him boldly but not wrathfully;
Let's carve him as a dish fit for the gods,
Not hew him as a carcass fit for hounds.
And let our hearts, as subtle masters do,
Stir up their servants to an act of rage   177
And after seem to chide 'em. This shall make
Our purpose necessary, and not envious;   179
Which so appearing to the common eyes,
We shall be called purgers, not murderers.
And for Mark Antony, think not of him;
For he can do no more than Caesar's arm
When Caesar's head is off.
CASSIUS   Yet I fear him,
For in the engrafted love he bears to Caesar—   185
BRUTUS
Alas, good Cassius, do not think of him.
If he love Caesar, all that he can do
Is to himself—take thought and die for Caesar.   188
And that were much he should, for he is given   189
To sports, to wildness, and much company.

158 of in   **160 improve** exploit, make good use of   **161 annoy** injure
165 envy malice   **170 come by** get hold of   **172 gentle** noble   **177 their
servants** i.e., our hands   **179 envious** malicious   **185 engrafted** firmly
implanted   **188 take thought** become melancholy   **189 much he should**
more than is to be expected of him, hence unlikely

TREBONIUS
   There is no fear in him. Let him not die,   191
   For he will live, and laugh at this hereafter.   192

                                    Clock strikes.

BRUTUS
   Peace! Count the clock.
CASSIUS   The clock hath stricken three.
TREBONIUS
   'Tis time to part.
CASSIUS   But it is doubtful yet
   Whether Caesar will come forth today or no;
   For he is superstitious grown of late,
   Quite from the main opinion he held once   197
   Of fantasy, of dreams, and ceremonies.
   It may be these apparent prodigies,   199
   The unaccustomed terror of this night,
   And the persuasion of his augurers
   May hold him from the Capitol today.
DECIUS
   Never fear that. If he be so resolved,
   I can o'ersway him; for he loves to hear
   That unicorns may be betrayed with trees,   205
   And bears with glasses, elephants with holes,   206
   Lions with toils, and men with flatterers;   207
   But when I tell him he hates flatterers,
   He says he does, being then most flattered.
   Let me work;
   For I can give his humor the true bent,   211
   And I will bring him to the Capitol.
CASSIUS
   Nay, we will all of us be there to fetch him.
BRUTUS
   By the eighth hour. Is that the uttermost?   214
CINNA
   Be that the uttermost, and fail not then.

191 no fear nothing to fear   **192 s.d. Clock strikes** (A much-commented-upon anachronism; the mechanical clock was not invented until c. 1300.) **197 from the main** contrary to the strong   **199 apparent** obvious **205 unicorns . . . trees** i.e., by having the unicorn imprison itself by driving its horn into a tree as it charges at the hunter   **206 glasses** mirrors (enabling the hunter to approach the bear while it vainly admires itself in the mirror).   **holes** pitfalls   **207 toils** nets, snares   **211 humor** disposition.   **true bent** right direction   **214 uttermost** latest

METELLUS

Caius Ligarius doth bear Caesar hard,   216
Who rated him for speaking well of Pompey.   217
I wonder none of you have thought of him.

BRUTUS

Now, good Metellus, go along by him.   219
He loves me well, and I have given him reasons;   220
Send him but hither, and I'll fashion him.   221

CASSIUS

The morning comes upon 's. We'll leave you, Brutus.
And, friends, disperse yourselves; but all remember
What you have said, and show yourselves true Romans.

BRUTUS

Good gentlemen, look fresh and merrily;
Let not our looks put on our purposes,   226
But bear it as our Roman actors do,
With untired spirits and formal constancy.   228
And so good morrow to you every one.   229

                          Exeunt. Manet Brutus.

Boy! Lucius! Fast asleep? It is no matter.   230
Enjoy the honey-heavy dew of slumber.
Thou hast no figures nor no fantasies   232
Which busy care draws in the brains of men;
Therefore thou sleep'st so sound.

      Enter Portia.

PORTIA   Brutus, my lord!

BRUTUS

Portia, what mean you? Wherefore rise you now?
It is not for your health thus to commit
Your weak condition to the raw cold morning.

PORTIA

Nor for yours neither. You've ungently, Brutus,   238
Stole from my bed. And yesternight, at supper,
You suddenly arose, and walked about

---

216 bear Caesar hard bear a grudge toward Caesar   **217 rated** angrily
rebuked   **219 by him** by way of his house   **220 reasons** i.e., for loving
me   **221 fashion** shape (to our purposes)   **226 put on** display, wear in
open view   **228 formal constancy** steadfast appearance, decorum
229 s.d. Manet he remains onstage   **230 Lucius** (Brutus calls to his
servant, who is evidently within, asleep, after having admitted the conspirators at l. 85; later, at l. 310, he is still within when Brutus calls to him.)
232 figures imaginings   **238 ungently** discourteously, unkindly

Musing and sighing, with your arms across,   241
And when I asked you what the matter was,
You stared upon me with ungentle looks.
I urged you further; then you scratched your head
And too impatiently stamped with your foot.
Yet I insisted, yet you answered not,   246
But with an angry wafture of your hand   247
Gave sign for me to leave you. So I did,
Fearing to strengthen that impatience
Which seemed too much enkindled, and withal   250
Hoping it was but an effect of humor,   251
Which sometimes hath his hour with every man.   252
It will not let you eat, nor talk, nor sleep,
And could it work so much upon your shape
As it hath much prevailed on your condition,   255
I should not know you Brutus. Dear my lord,   256
Make me acquainted with your cause of grief.

BRUTUS
I am not well in health, and that is all.

PORTIA
Brutus is wise and, were he not in health,
He would embrace the means to come by it.

BRUTUS
Why, so I do. Good Portia, go to bed.   261

PORTIA
Is Brutus sick? And is it physical   262
To walk unbracèd and suck up the humors   263
Of the dank morning? What, is Brutus sick,
And will he steal out of his wholesome bed
To dare the vile contagion of the night,
And tempt the rheumy and unpurgèd air   267
To add unto his sickness? No, my Brutus,
You have some sick offense within your mind,   269
Which by the right and virtue of my place

---

241 **across** folded (A sign of melancholy.)   246 **Yet . . . yet** still . . .
still   247 **wafture** waving   250 **withal** indeed   251 **humor** mood
252 **his** its   255 **condition** inner state of mind   256 **know you** recognize you as   261 **so I do** (Said with a double meaning not perceived by
Portia: I seek through Caesar's death the means to better the health of
the state.)   262 **physical** healthful   263 **unbracèd** with loosened
clothing.   **humors** damps, mists   267 **rheumy** damp.   **unpurgèd**
not purified (by the sun)   269 **sick offense** harmful disturbance

I ought to know of. [*She kneels.*] And upon my knees
I charm you, by my once-commended beauty,   272
By all your vows of love, and that great vow
Which did incorporate and make us one,
That you unfold to me, your self, your half,
Why you are heavy, and what men tonight   276
Have had resort to you; for here have been   277
Some six or seven, who did hide their faces
Even from darkness.

BRUTUS   Kneel not, gentle Portia.
                                        [*He raises her.*]

PORTIA
I should not need if you were gentle Brutus.
Within the bond of marriage, tell me, Brutus,
Is it excepted I should know no secrets   282
That appertain to you? Am I your self
But as it were in sort or limitation,   284
To keep with you at meals, comfort your bed,   285
And talk to you sometimes? Dwell I but in the suburbs 286
Of your good pleasure? If it be no more,
Portia is Brutus' harlot, not his wife.

BRUTUS
You are my true and honorable wife,
As dear to me as are the ruddy drops
That visit my sad heart.

PORTIA
If this were true, then should I know this secret.
I grant I am a woman, but withal   293
A woman that Lord Brutus took to wife.
I grant I am a woman, but withal
A woman well-reputed, Cato's daughter.   296
Think you I am no stronger than my sex,
Being so fathered and so husbanded?
Tell me your counsels, I will not disclose 'em.   299

---

272 charm conjure, entreat   **276 heavy** sad   **277 had resort to** visited
282 excepted made an exception that   **284 in . . . limitation** only up to a
point   **285 keep** stay, be   **286 suburbs** periphery. (In Elizabethan
London, prostitutes frequented the suburbs.)   **293 withal** in addition
296 Cato's daughter (Cato of Utica was famous for his integrity; he
sided with Pompey against Caesar in 48 B.C. and later killed himself
rather than submit to Caesar's tyranny. He was Brutus' uncle as well as
his father-in-law.)   **299 counsels** secrets

I have made strong proof of my constancy,
Giving myself a voluntary wound
Here, in the thigh. Can I bear that with patience,
And not my husband's secrets?
BRUTUS   O ye gods,
Render me worthy of this noble wife!
                                        Knock [within].
Hark, hark, one knocks. Portia, go in awhile,
And by and by thy bosom shall partake
The secrets of my heart.
All my engagements I will construe to thee,   308
All the charactery of my sad brows.   309
Leave me with haste.   *Exit Portia.*
          Lucius, who's that knocks?

          *Enter Lucius and [Caius] Ligarius [wearing a
          kerchief].*

LUCIUS
Here is a sick man that would speak with you.   311
BRUTUS
Caius Ligarius, that Metellus spake of.
Boy, stand aside. [*Exit Lucius.*] Caius Ligarius, how?   313
LIGARIUS
Vouchsafe good morrow from a feeble tongue.   314
BRUTUS
O, what a time have you chose out, brave Caius,   315
To wear a kerchief! Would you were not sick!
LIGARIUS
I am not sick, if Brutus have in hand
Any exploit worthy the name of honor.
BRUTUS
Such an exploit have I in hand, Ligarius,
Had you a healthful ear to hear of it.
LIGARIUS
By all the gods that Romans bow before,
I here discard my sickness! Soul of Rome!
                    [*He throws off his kerchief.*]

308 construe explain fully   **309 charactery** handwriting, i.e., what is
figured there   **311 sick man** (In Elizabethan medicine, not Roman, a
poultice was often applied to the forehead of a patient and wrapped in a
handkerchief; hence the kerchief in l. 316.)   **313 how** i.e., how are you
314 Vouchsafe deign (to accept)   **315 brave** noble

Brave son, derived from honorable loins!
Thou like an exorcist hast conjured up   324
My mortifièd spirit. Now bid me run,   325
And I will strive with things impossible,
Yea, get the better of them. What's to do?
BRUTUS
A piece of work that will make sick men whole.   328
LIGARIUS
But are not some whole that we must make sick?
BRUTUS
That must we also. What it is, my Caius,
I shall unfold to thee as we are going
To whom it must be done.
LIGARIUS   Set on your foot,   332
And with a heart new-fired I follow you
To do I know not what; but it sufficeth
That Brutus leads me on.   *Thunder.*
BRUTUS   Follow me, then.   *Exeunt.*

❖

2.2 *Thunder and lightning. Enter Julius Caesar, in
his nightgown.*

CAESAR
Nor heaven nor earth have been at peace tonight.   1
Thrice hath Calpurnia in her sleep cried out,
"Help, ho, they murder Caesar!"—Who's within?

        Enter a Servant.

SERVANT My lord?
CAESAR
Go bid the priests do present sacrifice   5
And bring me their opinions of success.   6
SERVANT I will, my lord.   *Exit.*

---

324 **exorcist** conjurer   325 **mortifièd** deadened   328 **whole** healthy, i.e.,
free of the disease of tyranny   332 **To whom** i.e., to him to whom

2.2. Location: Caesar's house.
s.d. nightgown dressing gown   **1 Nor** neither   **5 present** immediate.
sacrifice examination of the entrails of sacrificed animals for omens
6 success the result, what will follow

Enter Calpurnia.

CALPURNIA
What mean you, Caesar? Think you to walk forth?
You shall not stir out of your house today.

CAESAR
Caesar shall forth. The things that threatened me   10
Ne'er looked but on my back. When they shall see
The face of Caesar, they are vanishèd.

CALPURNIA
Caesar, I never stood on ceremonies,   13
Yet now they fright me. There is one within,
Besides the things that we have heard and seen,
Recounts most horrid sights seen by the watch.   16
A lioness hath whelpèd in the streets,   17
And graves have yawned and yielded up their dead.   18
Fierce fiery warriors fight upon the clouds   19
In ranks and squadrons and right form of war,   20
Which drizzled blood upon the Capitol.
The noise of battle hurtled in the air;   22
Horses did neigh, and dying men did groan,
And ghosts did shriek and squeal about the streets.
O Caesar, these things are beyond all use,   25
And I do fear them.

CAESAR   What can be avoided
Whose end is purposed by the mighty gods?
Yet Caesar shall go forth; for these predictions
Are to the world in general as to Caesar.   29

CALPURNIA
When beggars die there are no comets seen;
The heavens themselves blaze forth the death of princes.   31

CAESAR
Cowards die many times before their deaths;
The valiant never taste of death but once.
Of all the wonders that I yet have heard,
It seems to me most strange that men should fear,

---

10 forth go forth   **13 stood on ceremonies** attached importance to
omens   **16 watch** (An anachronism, since there was no *watch*, or body
of night watchmen, in Caesar's Rome.)   **17 whelpèd** given birth
18 yawned gaped   **19 fight** did fight   **20 right form** regular formation
22 hurtled clashed   **25 use** normal experience   **29 Are to** are as applicable to   **31 blaze forth** proclaim (in a blaze of light)

Seeing that death, a necessary end,
Will come when it will come.

    Enter a Servant.

                          What say the augurers?

SERVANT
They would not have you to stir forth today.
Plucking the entrails of an offering forth,
They could not find a heart within the beast.

CAESAR
The gods do this in shame of cowardice.
Caesar should be a beast without a heart
If he should stay at home today for fear.
No, Caesar shall not. Danger knows full well
That Caesar is more dangerous than he.
We are two lions littered in one day,
And I the elder and more terrible;
And Caesar shall go forth.

CALPURNIA   Alas, my lord,
Your wisdom is consumed in confidence.   49
Do not go forth today! Call it my fear
That keeps you in the house, and not your own.
We'll send Mark Antony to the Senate House,
And he shall say you are not well today.
Let me, upon my knee, prevail in this.   [*She kneels.*]

CAESAR
Mark Antony shall say I am not well,
And for thy humor I will stay at home.   56

                     [*He raises her.*]

    Enter Decius.

Here's Decius Brutus. He shall tell them so.

DECIUS
Caesar, all hail! Good morrow, worthy Caesar.
I come to fetch you to the Senate House.

CAESAR
And you are come in very happy time   60
To bear my greeting to the senators
And tell them that I will not come today.

49 consumed in confidence destroyed by overconfidence   **56 humor**
whim   **60 happy** opportune

Cannot, is false, and that I dare not, falser;
I will not come today. Tell them so, Decius.
CALPURNIA
Say he is sick.
CAESAR   Shall Caesar send a lie?
Have I in conquest stretched mine arm so far
To be afeard to tell graybeards the truth?
Decius, go tell them Caesar will not come.
DECIUS
Most mighty Caesar, let me know some cause,
Lest I be laughed at when I tell them so.
CAESAR
The cause is in my will: I will not come.
That is enough to satisfy the Senate.
But for your private satisfaction,
Because I love you, I will let you know.
Calpurnia here, my wife, stays me at home.   75
She dreamt tonight she saw my statue,   76
Which like a fountain with an hundred spouts
Did run pure blood; and many lusty Romans   78
Came smiling and did bathe their hands in it.
And these does she apply for warnings and portents   80
And evils imminent, and on her knee
Hath begged that I will stay at home today.
DECIUS
This dream is all amiss interpreted;
It was a vision fair and fortunate.
Your statue spouting blood in many pipes,
In which so many smiling Romans bathed,
Signifies that from you great Rome shall suck
Reviving blood, and that great men shall press   88
For tinctures, stains, relics, and cognizance.   89
This by Calpurnia's dream is signified.
CAESAR
And this way have you well expounded it.

75 stays detains   **76 tonight** last night   **78 lusty** lively, merry   **80 apply for** interpret as   **88 press** crowd around   **89 tinctures** handkerchiefs dipped in the blood of martyrs, with healing powers; or colors in a coat of arms. (*Tinctures, stains,* and *relics* are all venerated properties, as though Caesar were a saint.)   **cognizance** heraldic emblems worn by a nobleman's followers

DECIUS
    I have, when you have heard what I can say;
    And know it now. The Senate have concluded
    To give this day a crown to mighty Caesar.
    If you shall send them word you will not come,
    Their minds may change. Besides, it were a mock   96
    Apt to be rendered for someone to say   97
    "Break up the Senate till another time
    When Caesar's wife shall meet with better dreams."
    If Caesar hide himself, shall they not whisper
    "Lo, Caesar is afraid"?
    Pardon me, Caesar, for my dear dear love
    To your proceeding bids me tell you this,   103
    And reason to my love is liable.   104
CAESAR
    How foolish do your fears seem now, Calpurnia!
    I am ashamèd I did yield to them.
    Give me my robe, for I will go.

        Enter Brutus, Ligarius, Metellus, Casca,
        Trebonius, Cinna, and Publius.

    And look where Publius is come to fetch me.
PUBLIUS
    Good morrow, Caesar.
CAESAR   Welcome, Publius.
    What, Brutus, are you stirred so early too?
    Good morrow, Casca. Caius Ligarius,
    Caesar was ne'er so much your enemy
    As that same ague which hath made you lean.   113
    What is 't o'clock?
BRUTUS   Caesar, 'tis strucken eight.
CAESAR
    I thank you for your pains and courtesy.

        Enter Antony.

    See, Antony, that revels long o' nights,
    Is notwithstanding up. Good morrow, Antony.
ANTONY   So to most noble Caesar.

96–97 mock . . . rendered witty remark apt to be made **103 proceeding**
advancement **104 reason . . . liable** my reason or sense of propriety is
overruled by my love **113 ague** fever

CAESAR [*To a Servant*]   Bid them prepare within.   119
                              [*Exit Servant.*]
I am to blame to be thus waited for.
Now, Cinna. Now, Metellus. What, Trebonius,
I have an hour's talk in store for you;
Remember that you call on me today.
Be near me, that I may remember you.

TREBONIUS
Caesar, I will. [*Aside.*] And so near will I be
That your best friends shall wish I had been further.

CAESAR
Good friends, go in and taste some wine with me,
And we, like friends, will straightway go together.

BRUTUS [*Aside*]
That every like is not the same, O Caesar,   129
The heart of Brutus earns to think upon!   *Exeunt.* 130

❖

2.3   *Enter Artemidorus [reading a paper].*

ARTEMIDORUS   "Caesar, beware of Brutus; take heed of
   Cassius; come not near Casca; have an eye to Cinna;
   trust not Trebonius; mark well Metellus Cimber; Decius Brutus loves thee not; thou hast wronged Caius
   Ligarius. There is but one mind in all these men, and
   it is bent against Caesar. If thou beest not immortal, 6
   look about you. Security gives way to conspiracy. The 7
   mighty gods defend thee! Thy lover,   8
                                   Artemidorus."
   Here will I stand till Caesar pass along,
   And as a suitor will I give him this.   11
   My heart laments that virtue cannot live

---

119 prepare within i.e., set out a repast of wine in the other room, or
prepare to leave. (Perhaps addressed to the servant who entered at
l. 37, or to Calpurnia.)   **129 That . . . same** i.e., that everyone who seems
a friend is not actually so. (Proverbial.)   **130 earns** grieves

2.3. Location: A street near the Capitol.
6 bent directed   **7 Security** overconfidence.   **gives way** opens a path
8 lover friend   **11 as a suitor** as if I were a petitioner

Out of the teeth of emulation.   13
If thou read this, O Caesar, thou mayest live;
If not, the Fates with traitors do contrive.   *Exit.* 15

❖

2.4   *Enter Portia and Lucius.*

PORTIA
   I prithee, boy, run to the Senate House.
   Stay not to answer me, but get thee gone.—
   Why dost thou stay?
LUCIUS   To know my errand, madam.
PORTIA
   I would have had thee there and here again
   Ere I can tell thee what thou shouldst do there.
   [*Aside.*] O constancy, be strong upon my side;   6
   Set a huge mountain 'tween my heart and tongue!
   I have a man's mind, but a woman's might.
   How hard it is for women to keep counsel!—   9
   Art thou here yet?
LUCIUS   Madam, what should I do?
   Run to the Capitol, and nothing else?
   And so return to you, and nothing else?
PORTIA
   Yes, bring me word, boy, if thy lord look well,
   For he went sickly forth; and take good note   14
   What Caesar doth, what suitors press to him.
   Hark, boy, what noise is that?
LUCIUS   I hear none, madam.
PORTIA   Prithee, listen well.
   I heard a bustling rumor, like a fray,   19
   And the wind brings it from the Capitol.
LUCIUS   Sooth, madam, I hear nothing.   21

   Enter the Soothsayer.

---

13 Out . . . emulation i.e., beyond the reach of grudging envy
15 contrive conspire

2.4. Location: Before the house of Brutus.
6 constancy resolution   **9 counsel** a secret   **14 take good note** observe
closely   **19 bustling rumor** confused sound   **21 Sooth** truly

PORTIA
  Come hither, fellow. Which way hast thou been?
SOOTHSAYER   At mine own house, good lady.
PORTIA
  What is 't o'clock?
SOOTHSAYER   About the ninth hour, lady.   24
PORTIA
  Is Caesar yet gone to the Capitol?
SOOTHSAYER
  Madam, not yet. I go to take my stand,
  To see him pass on to the Capitol.
PORTIA
  Thou hast some suit to Caesar, hast thou not?
SOOTHSAYER
  That I have, lady, if it will please Caesar
  To be so good to Caesar as to hear me:
  I shall beseech him to befriend himself.
PORTIA
  Why, know'st thou any harms intended towards him?
SOOTHSAYER
  None that I know will be, much that I fear may chance.
  Good morrow to you. Here the street is narrow.
  The throng that follows Caesar at the heels,
  Of senators, of praetors, common suitors,   36
  Will crowd a feeble man almost to death.
  I'll get me to a place more void, and there   38
  Speak to great Caesar as he comes along.   *Exit.*
PORTIA
  I must go in. Ay me, how weak a thing
  The heart of woman is! O Brutus,
  The heavens speed thee in thine enterprise!
  Sure, the boy heard me.—Brutus hath a suit
  That Caesar will not grant.—O, I grow faint.—
  Run, Lucius, and commend me to my lord;
  Say I am merry. Come to me again
  And bring me word what he doth say to thee.
                                   Exeunt [separately].

❖

24 **the ninth hour** i.e., 9 A.M. (In Roman reckoning the ninth hour would
be 3 P.M.) 36 **praetors** judges 38 **void** empty, uncrowded

3.1 *Flourish. Enter Caesar, Brutus, Cassius, Casca,*
Decius, Metellus [Cimber], Trebonius, Cinna,
Antony, Lepidus, Artemidorus, Publius,
[Popilius Lena,] and the Soothsayer; [others
following].

CAESAR [*To the Soothsayer*]   The ides of March are come.
SOOTHSAYER   Ay, Caesar, but not gone.
ARTEMIDORUS   Hail, Caesar! Read this schedule.   3
DECIUS
  Trebonius doth desire you to o'erread,
  At your best leisure, this his humble suit.
ARTEMIDORUS
  O Caesar, read mine first, for mine's a suit
  That touches Caesar nearer. Read it, great Caesar.
CAESAR
  What touches us ourself shall be last served.
ARTEMIDORUS
  Delay not, Caesar, read it instantly.
CAESAR
  What, is the fellow mad?
PUBLIUS   Sirrah, give place.   10
CASSIUS
  What, urge you your petitions in the street?
  Come to the Capitol.

      [*Caesar goes to the Capitol and takes his place,*
      the rest following.]

POPILIUS [*To Cassius*]
  I wish your enterprise today may thrive.
CASSIUS   What enterprise, Popilius?
POPILIUS [*To Cassius*]   Fare you well.
                            [*He advances to Caesar.*]
BRUTUS   What said Popilius Lena?
CASSIUS
  He wished today our enterprise might thrive.
  I fear our purpose is discoverèd.

3.1. Location: **Before the Capitol, and, following l. 12, within the**
Capitol.
s.d. others following (Citizens may be present, though not certainly so;
see ll. 83 and 93–94.)   **3 schedule** document   **10 Sirrah** fellow. (A form
of address to a social inferior.)   **place** way

BRUTUS
• Look how he makes to Caesar. Mark him.   19
                    [*Popilius speaks apart to Caesar.*]
CASSIUS
  Casca, be sudden, for we fear prevention.   20
  Brutus, what shall be done? If this be known,
  Cassius or Caesar never shall turn back,   22
  For I will slay myself.
BRUTUS   Cassius, be constant.   23
  Popilius Lena speaks not of our purposes;
  For look, he smiles, and Caesar doth not change.   25
CASSIUS
  Trebonius knows his time, for look you, Brutus,
  He draws Mark Antony out of the way.
                    [*Exit Trebonius with Antony.*]
DECIUS
  Where is Metellus Cimber? Let him go
  And presently prefer his suit to Caesar.   29
BRUTUS
  He is addressed. Press near and second him.   30
CINNA
  Casca, you are the first that rears your hand.
                    [*They press near Caesar.*]
CAESAR
  Are we all ready? What is now amiss
  That Caesar and his Senate must redress?
METELLUS [*Kneeling*]
  Most high, most mighty, and most puissant Caesar,
  Metellus Cimber throws before thy seat
  An humble heart—
CAESAR   I must prevent thee, Cimber.   36
  These couchings and these lowly courtesies   37
  Might fire the blood of ordinary men,   38
  And turn preordinance and first decree   39
  Into the law of children. Be not fond   40

19 **makes to** advances toward   20 **sudden** swift in action.   **prevention**
being forestalled   22 **turn back** i.e., return alive   23 **constant** resolute   25 **change** change expression   29 **presently prefer** immediately
present   30 **addressed** ready   36 **prevent** forestall   37 **couchings,**
lowly courtesies submissive bows   38 **fire the blood of** incite
39 **preordinance . . . decree** matters already firmly decided   40 **law of**
children i.e., laws to be changed as children change rules in their
games.   **fond** so foolish as

To think that Caesar bears such rebel blood   41
That will be thawed from the true quality   42
With that which melteth fools—I mean, sweet words,
Low-crookèd curtsies, and base spaniel fawning.   44
Thy brother by decree is banishèd.
If thou dost bend and pray and fawn for him,   46
I spurn thee like a cur out of my way.   47
Know, Caesar doth not wrong, nor without cause
Will he be satisfied.
METELLUS
  Is there no voice more worthy than my own
  To sound more sweetly in great Caesar's ear
  For the repealing of my banished brother?   52
BRUTUS [*Kneeling*]
  I kiss thy hand, but not in flattery, Caesar,
  Desiring thee that Publius Cimber may
  Have an immediate freedom of repeal.   55
CAESAR
  What, Brutus?
CASSIUS [*Kneeling*]   Pardon, Caesar! Caesar, pardon!
  As low as to thy foot doth Cassius fall,
  To beg enfranchisement for Publius Cimber.   58
CAESAR
  I could be well moved, if I were as you;
  If I could pray to move, prayers would move me.   60
  But I am constant as the northern star,   61
  Of whose true-fixed and resting quality   62
  There is no fellow in the firmament.   63
  The skies are painted with unnumbered sparks;
  They are all fire and every one doth shine;
  But there's but one in all doth hold his place.
  So in the world: 'tis furnished well with men,
  And men are flesh and blood, and apprehensive;   68
  Yet in the number I do know but one

41 rebel i.e., rebellious against the law and against his own firm nature   **42 true quality** i.e., proper firmness and stability   **44 Low-
crookèd** bent low   **46 bend** bow   **47 spurn** kick   **52 repealing** recall
55 freedom of repeal permission to be recalled   **58 enfranchisement**
liberation (from the decree of banishment)   **60 pray to move** make
petition (as you do)   **61 northern star** polestar   **62 true-fixed** firmly
fixed, unmovable.   **resting** unchanging   **63 fellow** equal
68 apprehensive capable of perception

That unassailable holds on his rank, 70
Unshaked of motion. And that I am he, 71
Let me a little show it even in this—
That I was constant Cimber should be banished,
And constant do remain to keep him so.
CINNA [*Kneeling*]
  O Caesar—
CAESAR   Hence! Wilt thou lift up Olympus? 75
DECIUS [*Kneeling*]
  Great Caesar—
CAESAR   Doth not Brutus bootless kneel? 76
CASCA Speak, hands, for me!
          They stab Caesar, [Casca first, Brutus last].
CAESAR *Et tu, Brutè?* Then fall, Caesar!   *Dies.* 78
CINNA
  Liberty! Freedom! Tyranny is dead!
  Run hence, proclaim, cry it about the streets.
CASSIUS
  Some to the common pulpits, and cry out 81
  "Liberty, freedom, and enfranchisement!"
BRUTUS
  People and senators, be not affrighted.
  Fly not; stand still. Ambition's debt is paid. 84
CASCA
  Go to the pulpit, Brutus.
DECIUS   And Cassius too.
BRUTUS Where's Publius? 86
CINNA
  Here, quite confounded with this mutiny. 87
METELLUS
  Stand fast together, lest some friend of Caesar's
  Should chance—
BRUTUS
  Talk not of standing.—Publius, good cheer. 90

70 rank place in line or file, position **71 Unshaked of motion** (1) un-
swayed by petitions (2) with perfectly steady movement **75 Olympus**
mountain dwelling of the Greek gods **76 bootless** in vain **78 Et tu,
Brutè** and thou, Brutus **81 common pulpits** public platforms or
rostra **84 Ambition's debt** what Caesar's ambition deserved
86 Publius (An old senator, too confused to flee.) **87 mutiny** uprising
90 standing resistance

There is no harm intended to your person,
Nor to no Roman else. So tell them, Publius.

CASSIUS
And leave us, Publius, lest that the people,
Rushing on us, should do your age some mischief.

BRUTUS
Do so, and let no man abide this deed   95
But we the doers.   [*Exeunt all but the conspirators.*]

          Enter Trebonius.

CASSIUS
Where is Antony?

TREBONIUS   Fled to his house amazed.   97
Men, wives, and children stare, cry out, and run
As it were doomsday.

BRUTUS   Fates, we will know your pleasures.   99
That we shall die, we know; 'tis but the time,
And drawing days out, that men stand upon.   101

CASCA
Why, he that cuts off twenty years of life
Cuts off so many years of fearing death.

BRUTUS
Grant that, and then is death a benefit.
So are we Caesar's friends, that have abridged
His time of fearing death. Stoop, Romans, stoop,
And let us bathe our hands in Caesar's blood
Up to the elbows and besmear our swords.
Then walk we forth even to the marketplace,   109
And, waving our red weapons o'er our heads,
Let's all cry "Peace, freedom, and liberty!"

CASSIUS
Stoop, then, and wash. [*They bathe their hands and
    weapons.*] How many ages hence
Shall this our lofty scene be acted over
In states unborn and accents yet unknown!   114

BRUTUS
How many times shall Caesar bleed in sport,   115

95 abide (1) stand the consequences of (2) remain here with   **97 amazed**
stunned   **99 As** as if   **101 drawing . . . upon** prolonging their lives, that
men attach importance to   **109 the marketplace** i.e., the Forum
114 accents languages   **115 in sport** for entertainment

That now on Pompey's basis lies along   116
No worthier than the dust!
CASSIUS   So oft as that shall be,
So often shall the knot of us be called   119
The men that gave their country liberty.
DECIUS
What, shall we forth?
CASSIUS   Ay, every man away.
Brutus shall lead, and we will grace his heels   122
With the most boldest and best hearts of Rome.

    Enter a Servant.

BRUTUS
Soft, who comes here? A friend of Antony's.
SERVANT [*Kneeling*]
Thus, Brutus, did my master bid me kneel;
Thus did Mark Antony bid me fall down,
And being prostrate, thus he bade me say:
"Brutus is noble, wise, valiant, and honest;
Caesar was mighty, bold, royal, and loving.
Say I love Brutus and I honor him;
Say I feared Caesar, honored him, and loved him.
If Brutus will vouchsafe that Antony   132
May safely come to him and be resolved   133
How Caesar hath deserved to lie in death,
Mark Antony shall not love Caesar dead
So well as Brutus living, but will follow
The fortunes and affairs of noble Brutus
Thorough the hazards of this untrod state   138
With all true faith." So says my master Antony.
BRUTUS
Thy master is a wise and valiant Roman;
I never thought him worse.
Tell him, so please him come unto this place,   142
He shall be satisfied and, by my honor,
Depart untouched.

116 Pompey's basis pedestal of Pompey's statue.   **along** prostrate, at full
length   **119 knot** group   **122 grace** do honor to (by following closely)
132 vouchsafe allow   **133 be resolved** receive an explanation
138 Thorough through.   **untrod state** new state of affairs   **142 so** if it
should

SERVANT   I'll fetch him presently.   144

Exit Servant.

BRUTUS
I know that we shall have him well to friend.   145

CASSIUS
I wish we may. But yet have I a mind
That fears him much, and my misgiving still   147
Falls shrewdly to the purpose.   148

Enter Antony.

BRUTUS
But here comes Antony.—Welcome, Mark Antony.

ANTONY
O mighty Caesar! Dost thou lie so low?
Are all thy conquests, glories, triumphs, spoils,
Shrunk to this little measure? Fare thee well.—
I know not, gentlemen, what you intend,
Who else must be let blood, who else is rank;   154
If I myself, there is no hour so fit
As Caesar's death's hour, nor no instrument
Of half that worth as those your swords, made rich
With the most noble blood of all this world.
I do beseech ye, if you bear me hard,   159
Now, whilst your purpled hands do reek and smoke,   160
Fulfill your pleasure. Live a thousand years,   161
I shall not find myself so apt to die;   162
No place will please me so, no means of death,
As here by Caesar, and by you cut off,
The choice and master spirits of this age.

BRUTUS
O Antony! Beg not your death of us.
Though now we must appear bloody and cruel,
As by our hands and this our present act
You see we do, yet see you but our hands

---

144 presently immediately   **145 to friend** for a friend   **147 fears** distrusts.
my misgiving still i.e., such misgiving on my part always or generally
148 Falls . . . purpose falls ominously close to the mark   **154 let blood** bled,
i.e., killed.   **rank** diseased and in need of bleeding (with pun on "overgrown,
too powerful")   **159 bear me hard** bear ill will to me   **160 purpled** bloody.
reek steam   **161 Live** if I should live   **162 apt** ready

And this the bleeding business they have done.
Our hearts you see not. They are pitiful;   171
And pity to the general wrong of Rome—
As fire drives out fire, so pity pity—   173
Hath done this deed on Caesar. For your part,
To you our swords have leaden points, Mark Antony.   175
Our arms in strength of malice, and our hearts   176
Of brothers' temper, do receive you in   177
With all kind love, good thoughts, and reverence.
CASSIUS
Your voice shall be as strong as any man's   179
In the disposing of new dignities.   180
BRUTUS
Only be patient till we have appeased
The multitude, beside themselves with fear,
And then we will deliver you the cause   183
Why I, that did love Caesar when I struck him,
Have thus proceeded.
ANTONY   I doubt not of your wisdom.
Let each man render me his bloody hand.
                 [*He shakes hands with the conspirators.*]
First, Marcus Brutus, will I shake with you;
Next, Caius Cassius, do I take your hand;
Now, Decius Brutus, yours; now yours, Metellus;
Yours, Cinna; and, my valiant Casca, yours;
Though last, not least in love, yours, good Trebonius.
Gentlemen all—alas, what shall I say?
My credit now stands on such slippery ground   193
That one of two bad ways you must conceit me,   194
Either a coward or a flatterer.
That I did love thee, Caesar, O, 'tis true!
If then thy spirit look upon us now,
Shall it not grieve thee dearer than thy death   198
To see thy Antony making his peace,
Shaking the bloody fingers of thy foes—

---

171 pitiful full of pity   **173 pity pity** i.e., pity for the general wrong of
Rome drove out pity for Caesar   **175 leaden** i.e., blunt   **176–177 Our
. . . temper** i.e., both our arms, though seeming strong in enmity, and
our hearts, full of brotherly feeling   **179 voice** vote, authority
180 dignities offices of state   **183 deliver** report to   **193 credit** credibility   **194 conceit** think, judge   **198 dearer** more deeply

Most noble!—in the presence of thy corpse?
Had I as many eyes as thou hast wounds,
Weeping as fast as they stream forth thy blood,
It would become me better than to close   204
In terms of friendship with thine enemies.
Pardon me, Julius! Here wast thou bayed, brave hart,   206
Here didst thou fall, and here thy hunters stand,
Signed in thy spoil and crimsoned in thy lethe.   208
O world, thou wast the forest to this hart,
And this indeed, O world, the heart of thee!
How like a deer, strucken by many princes,
Dost thou here lie!

CASSIUS
  Mark Antony—
ANTONY   Pardon me, Caius Cassius.
  The enemies of Caesar shall say this;   214
  Then in a friend it is cold modesty.   215

CASSIUS
  I blame you not for praising Caesar so,
  But what compact mean you to have with us?   217
  Will you be pricked in number of our friends,   218
  Or shall we on and not depend on you?

ANTONY
  Therefore I took your hands, but was indeed
  Swayed from the point by looking down on Caesar.
  Friends am I with you all, and love you all,
  Upon this hope, that you shall give me reasons
  Why and wherein Caesar was dangerous.

BRUTUS
  Or else were this a savage spectacle.   225
  Our reasons are so full of good regard   226
  That were you, Antony, the son of Caesar,
  You should be satisfied.
ANTONY   That's all I seek,

204 close come to an agreement   **206 bayed** brought to bay.   **hart** stag
(with pun on *heart*)   **208 Signed . . . spoil** marked with the tokens of
your slaughter.   **lethe** river of oblivion in the underworld, here associated with death and blood (perhaps fused with Cocytus, river of blood
in the underworld)   **214 The enemies** even the enemies   **215 cold**
sober.   **modesty** moderation   **217 compact** agreement   **218 pricked in
number** marked off on a list   **225 else were this** otherwise this would
be   **226 regard** account, consideration

And am moreover suitor that I may
Produce his body to the marketplace,   230
And in the pulpit, as becomes a friend,   231
Speak in the order of his funeral.   232
BRUTUS
You shall, Mark Antony.
CASSIUS   Brutus, a word with you.
    [*Aside to Brutus*.] You know not what you do. Do not
        consent
    That Antony speak in his funeral.
    Know you how much the people may be moved
    By that which he will utter?
BRUTUS [*Aside to Cassius*]   By your pardon:
    I will myself into the pulpit first
    And show the reason of our Caesar's death.
    What Antony shall speak, I will protest   240
    He speaks by leave and by permission,
    And that we are contented Caesar shall
    Have all true rites and lawful ceremonies.
    It shall advantage more than do us wrong.
CASSIUS [*Aside to Brutus*]
    I know not what may fall. I like it not.   245
BRUTUS
    Mark Antony, here, take you Caesar's body.
    You shall not in your funeral speech blame us,
    But speak all good you can devise of Caesar,
    And say you do 't by our permission.
    Else shall you not have any hand at all
    About his funeral. And you shall speak
    In the same pulpit whereto I am going,
    After my speech is ended.
ANTONY   Be it so.
    I do desire no more.
BRUTUS
    Prepare the body then, and follow us.   255
                        Exeunt. Manet Antony.
ANTONY
    O, pardon me, thou bleeding piece of earth,

230 **Produce** bring forth   231 **pulpit** public platform   232 **order** ceremony   240 **protest** announce   245 **fall** befall, happen   255 **s.d. Manet**
he remains onstage

That I am meek and gentle with these butchers!
Thou art the ruins of the noblest man
That ever livèd in the tide of times.   259
Woe to the hand that shed this costly blood!   260
Over thy wounds now do I prophesy—
Which, like dumb mouths, do ope their ruby lips
To beg the voice and utterance of my tongue—
A curse shall light upon the limbs of men;
Domestic fury and fierce civil strife
Shall cumber all the parts of Italy;   266
Blood and destruction shall be so in use
And dreadful objects so familiar   268
That mothers shall but smile when they behold
Their infants quartered with the hands of war,   270
All pity choked with custom of fell deeds;   271
And Caesar's spirit, ranging for revenge,   272
With Ate by his side come hot from hell,   273
Shall in these confines with a monarch's voice   274
Cry "Havoc!" and let slip the dogs of war,   275
That this foul deed shall smell above the earth   276
With carrion men, groaning for burial.

    Enter Octavius' Servant.

You serve Octavius Caesar, do you not?
SERVANT   I do, Mark Antony.
ANTONY
Caesar did write for him to come to Rome.
SERVANT
He did receive his letters, and is coming,
And bid me say to you by word of mouth—
O Caesar!   [*Seeing the body.*]
ANTONY
Thy heart is big. Get thee apart and weep.   284
Passion, I see, is catching, for mine eyes,

---

259 tide of times course of all history   **260 costly** (1) valuable (2) fraught
with dire consequences   **266 cumber** entangle   **268 objects** sights
270 quartered cut to pieces   **271 custom ... deeds** the familiarity of
cruel deeds   **272 ranging** roaming up and down in search of prey
273 Ate goddess of discord and moral chaos   **274 confines** regions
275 Havoc (The signal for sack, pillage, and slaughter.)   **let slip**
unleash   **276 That** so that   **284 big** swollen with grief

Seeing those beads of sorrow stand in thine,
Began to water. Is thy master coming?
SERVANT
He lies tonight within seven leagues of Rome.   288
ANTONY
Post back with speed and tell him what hath chanced.
Here is a mourning Rome, a dangerous Rome,
No Rome of safety for Octavius yet;
Hie hence and tell him so. Yet stay awhile;   292
Thou shalt not back till I have borne this corpse
Into the marketplace. There shall I try,   294
In my oration, how the people take
The cruel issue of these bloody men,   296
According to the which thou shalt discourse   297
To young Octavius of the state of things.   298
Lend me your hand.   *Exeunt [with Caesar's body]*.

❖

3.2   *Enter Brutus and [presently] goes into the
pulpit, and Cassius, with the Plebeians.*

PLEBEIANS
We will be satisfied! Let us be satisfied!   1
BRUTUS
Then follow me, and give me audience, friends.
Cassius, go you into the other street
And part the numbers.   4
Those that will hear me speak, let 'em stay here;
Those that will follow Cassius, go with him;
And public reasons shall be renderèd
Of Caesar's death.
FIRST PLEBEIAN   I will hear Brutus speak.
SECOND PLEBEIAN
I will hear Cassius, and compare their reasons
When severally we hear them renderèd.   10
          [Exit Cassius, with some of the Plebeians.]

288 seven leagues about 20 miles   **292 Hie** hasten   **294 try** test
296 issue deed   **297 the which** the outcome of which   **298 young
Octavius** (He was eighteen in March of 44 B.C.)

3.2. Location: The Forum.
1 be satisfied have an explanation   **4 part** divide   **10 severally** individually, separately

THIRD PLEBEIAN
  The noble Brutus is ascended. Silence!
BRUTUS   Be patient till the last.
  Romans, countrymen, and lovers, hear me for my 13
  cause, and be silent that you may hear. Believe me for
  mine honor, and have respect to mine honor, that you
  may believe. Censure me in your wisdom, and awake 16
  your senses, that you may the better judge. If there be 17
  any in this assembly, any dear friend of Caesar's, to
  him I say that Brutus' love to Caesar was no less than
  his. If then that friend demand why Brutus rose
  against Caesar, this is my answer: not that I loved Caesar less, but that I loved Rome more. Had you rather
  Caesar were living and die all slaves, than that Caesar
  were dead, to live all free men? As Caesar loved me, I
  weep for him; as he was fortunate, I rejoice at it; as he
  was valiant, I honor him; but, as he was ambitious, I
  slew him. There is tears for his love; joy for his fortune; honor for his valor; and death for his ambition.
  Who is here so base that would be a bondman? If any,
  speak, for him have I offended. Who is here so rude 30
  that would not be a Roman? If any, speak, for him
  have I offended. Who is here so vile that will not love
  his country? If any, speak, for him have I offended. I
  pause for a reply.
ALL   None, Brutus, none!
BRUTUS   Then none have I offended. I have done no
  more to Caesar than you shall do to Brutus. The ques- 37
  tion of his death is enrolled in the Capitol, his glory 38
  not extenuated wherein he was worthy, nor his 39
  offenses enforced for which he suffered death.   40

    *Enter Mark Antony [and others] with Caesar's
    body.*

13 lovers friends. (This speech by Brutus is in what Plutarch calls the
Lacedemonian or Spartan style, brief and sententious. Its content is
original with Shakespeare.)   **16 Censure** judge   **17 senses** intellectual
powers   **30 rude** barbarous   **37 shall** i.e., should, if I were to do as
Caesar did   **37–38 The question . . . enrolled** the considerations that
necessitated his death are recorded   **39 extenuated** minimized
40 enforced exaggerated, insisted upon

Here comes his body, mourned by Mark Antony, who,
though he had no hand in his death, shall receive the
benefit of his dying, a place in the commonwealth, as
which of you shall not? With this I depart, that, as I
slew my best lover for the good of Rome, I have the　45
same dagger for myself when it shall please my country to need my death.

ALL　Live, Brutus, live, live!

　　　　　　　　　　　　　　　[*Brutus comes down.*]

FIRST PLEBEIAN
　Bring him with triumph home unto his house.

SECOND PLEBEIAN
　Give him a statue with his ancestors.　　　　　　50

THIRD PLEBEIAN
　Let him be Caesar.

FOURTH PLEBEIAN　　　Caesar's better parts
　Shall be crowned in Brutus.

FIRST PLEBEIAN
　We'll bring him to his house with shouts and clamors.

BRUTUS
　My countrymen—

SECOND PLEBEIAN　　　Peace, silence! Brutus speaks.

FIRST PLEBEIAN　　Peace, ho!

BRUTUS
　Good countrymen, let me depart alone,
　And, for my sake, stay here with Antony.
　Do grace to Caesar's corpse, and grace his speech　58
　Tending to Caesar's glories, which Mark Antony,　59
　By our permission, is allowed to make.
　I do entreat you, not a man depart,
　Save I alone, till Antony have spoke.　　　　*Exit.*

FIRST PLEBEIAN
　Stay, ho, and let us hear Mark Antony.

THIRD PLEBEIAN
　Let him go up into the public chair.
　We'll hear him. Noble Antony, go up.

---

45 lover friend　**50 Second Plebeian** (Not the same person who exited at
l. 10; the numbering here refers to those who stay to hear Brutus.)
58 Do grace show respect.　**grace his speech** i.e., listen courteously to
Antony's speech　**59 Tending to** relating to, dealing with

ANTONY

For Brutus' sake I am beholding to you.   66

[*He goes into the pulpit.*]

FOURTH PLEBEIAN   What does he say of Brutus?

THIRD PLEBEIAN   He says, for Brutus' sake

He finds himself beholding to us all.

FOURTH PLEBEIAN

'Twere best he speak no harm of Brutus here.

FIRST PLEBEIAN

This Caesar was a tyrant.

THIRD PLEBEIAN   Nay, that's certain.

We are blest that Rome is rid of him.

SECOND PLEBEIAN

Peace! Let us hear what Antony can say.

ANTONY

You gentle Romans—

ALL   Peace, ho! Let us hear him.

ANTONY

Friends, Romans, countrymen, lend me your ears.   75

I come to bury Caesar, not to praise him.

The evil that men do lives after them;

The good is oft interrèd with their bones.

So let it be with Caesar. The noble Brutus

Hath told you Caesar was ambitious.

If it were so, it was a grievous fault,

And grievously hath Caesar answered it.   82

Here, under leave of Brutus and the rest—   83

For Brutus is an honorable man,

So are they all, all honorable men—

Come I to speak in Caesar's funeral.

He was my friend, faithful and just to me;

But Brutus says he was ambitious,

And Brutus is an honorable man.

He hath brought many captives home to Rome,

Whose ransoms did the general coffers fill.

Did this in Caesar seem ambitious?

When that the poor have cried, Caesar hath wept;

66 beholding beholden   **75 Friends** (This speech by Antony is thought to
illustrate the Asiatic or "florid" style of speaking. In it Shakespeare
gathers various hints from Plutarch, Appian, and Dion, but the speech
is Shakespeare's invention.)   **82 answered** paid the penalty for
83 under leave by permission

Ambition should be made of sterner stuff.
Yet Brutus says he was ambitious,
And Brutus is an honorable man.
You all did see that on the Lupercal   97
I thrice presented him a kingly crown,
Which he did thrice refuse. Was this ambition?
Yet Brutus says he was ambitious,
And sure he is an honorable man.
I speak not to disprove what Brutus spoke,
But here I am to speak what I do know.
You all did love him once, not without cause.
What cause withholds you then to mourn for him?
O judgment! Thou art fled to brutish beasts,
And men have lost their reason. Bear with me;
My heart is in the coffin there with Caesar,
And I must pause till it come back to me.

FIRST PLEBEIAN
Methinks there is much reason in his sayings.

SECOND PLEBEIAN
If thou consider rightly of the matter,
Caesar has had great wrong.

THIRD PLEBEIAN   Has he, masters?
I fear there will a worse come in his place.

FOURTH PLEBEIAN
Marked ye his words? He would not take the crown,
Therefore 'tis certain he was not ambitious.

FIRST PLEBEIAN
If it be found so, some will dear abide it.   116

SECOND PLEBEIAN
Poor soul, his eyes are red as fire with weeping.

THIRD PLEBEIAN
There's not a nobler man in Rome than Antony.

FOURTH PLEBEIAN
Now mark him. He begins again to speak.

ANTONY
But yesterday the word of Caesar might
Have stood against the world. Now lies he there,
And none so poor to do him reverence.   122

97 **Lupercal** (See 1.1.67 and note.)   **116 dear abide it** pay a heavy penalty for it   **122 none . . . reverence** i.e., no one, not even the lowliest
person, is below Caesar in fortune now, making obeisance to him

O masters! If I were disposed to stir
Your hearts and minds to mutiny and rage,   124
I should do Brutus wrong, and Cassius wrong,
Who, you all know, are honorable men.
I will not do them wrong; I rather choose
To wrong the dead, to wrong myself and you,
Than I will wrong such honorable men.
But here's a parchment with the seal of Caesar.
I found it in his closet; 'tis his will.   131
                              [*He shows the will.*]
Let but the commons hear this testament—   132
Which, pardon me, I do not mean to read—
And they would go and kiss dead Caesar's wounds
And dip their napkins in his sacred blood,   135
Yea, beg a hair of him for memory,
And dying, mention it within their wills,
Bequeathing it as a rich legacy
Unto their issue.

FOURTH PLEBEIAN
We'll hear the will! Read it, Mark Antony.

ALL
The will, the will! We will hear Caesar's will.

ANTONY
Have patience, gentle friends; I must not read it.
It is not meet you know how Caesar loved you.   143
You are not wood, you are not stones, but men;
And being men, hearing the will of Caesar,
It will inflame you, it will make you mad.
'Tis good you know not that you are his heirs,
For if you should, O, what would come of it?

FOURTH PLEBEIAN
Read the will! We'll hear it, Antony.
You shall read us the will, Caesar's will.

ANTONY
Will you be patient? Will you stay awhile?
I have o'ershot myself to tell you of it.   152
I fear I wrong the honorable men
Whose daggers have stabbed Caesar; I do fear it.

124 mutiny riot, tumult   **131 closet** private chamber   **132 commons**
common people   **135 napkins** handkerchiefs   **143 meet** fitting that
152 o'ershot myself gone further than I should

FOURTH PLEBEIAN
  They were traitors. "Honorable men"!
ALL The will! The testament!
SECOND PLEBEIAN
  They were villains, murderers. The will! Read the will!
ANTONY
  You will compel me then to read the will?
  Then make a ring about the corpse of Caesar
  And let me show you him that made the will.
  Shall I descend? And will you give me leave?
ALL Come down.
SECOND PLEBEIAN Descend.
THIRD PLEBEIAN You shall have leave.
        [*Antony comes down. They gather around Caesar.*]
FOURTH PLEBEIAN A ring; stand round.
FIRST PLEBEIAN
  Stand from the hearse. Stand from the body.   166
SECOND PLEBEIAN
  Room for Antony, most noble Antony!
ANTONY
  Nay, press not so upon me. Stand far off.   168
ALL Stand back! Room! Bear back!
ANTONY
  If you have tears, prepare to shed them now.
  You all do know this mantle. I remember   171
  The first time ever Caesar put it on;
  'Twas on a summer's evening in his tent,
  That day he overcame the Nervii.   174
  Look, in this place ran Cassius' dagger through.
  See what a rent the envious Casca made.   176
  Through this the well-belovèd Brutus stabbed,
  And as he plucked his cursèd steel away,
  Mark how the blood of Caesar followed it,
  As rushing out of doors to be resolved   180
  If Brutus so unkindly knocked or no;   181
  For Brutus, as you know, was Caesar's angel.   182
  Judge, O you gods, how dearly Caesar loved him!

166 hearse bier **168 far** farther **171 mantle** cloak, toga **174 the
Nervii** the Belgian tribe whose defeat in 57 B.C. is described in Caesar's
Gallic War, 2.15–28 **176 rent** tear, hole. **envious** malicious, spiteful
180 be resolved learn for certain **181 unkindly** cruelly and unnatu-
rally **182 angel** i.e., daimon or genius, second self

This was the most unkindest cut of all;   184
For when the noble Caesar saw him stab,
Ingratitude, more strong than traitors' arms,
Quite vanquished him. Then burst his mighty heart,
And in his mantle muffling up his face,
Even at the base of Pompey's statue,
Which all the while ran blood, great Caesar fell.
O, what a fall was there, my countrymen!
Then I, and you, and all of us fell down,
Whilst bloody treason flourished over us.   193
O, now you weep, and I perceive you feel
The dint of pity. These are gracious drops.   195
Kind souls, what weep you when you but behold   196
Our Caesar's vesture wounded? Look you here,   197
Here is himself, marred as you see with traitors.
                    [*He lifts Caesar's mantle.*]
FIRST PLEBEIAN O piteous spectacle!
SECOND PLEBEIAN O noble Caesar!
THIRD PLEBEIAN O woeful day!
FOURTH PLEBEIAN O traitors, villains!
FIRST PLEBEIAN O most bloody sight!
SECOND PLEBEIAN We will be revenged.
ALL Revenge! About! Seek! Burn! Fire! Kill! Slay! Let 205
not a traitor live!
ANTONY Stay, countrymen.
FIRST PLEBEIAN Peace there! Hear the noble Antony.
SECOND PLEBEIAN We'll hear him, we'll follow him,
we'll die with him!
ANTONY
Good friends, sweet friends, let me not stir you up
To such a sudden flood of mutiny.
They that have done this deed are honorable.
What private griefs they have, alas, I know not,   214
That made them do it. They are wise and honorable,
And will no doubt with reasons answer you.
I come not, friends, to steal away your hearts.

---

184 unkindest (1) most cruel (2) most unnatural. (The double superlative
was grammatically acceptable in Shakespeare's day.) **193 flourished**
triumphed insolently **195 dint** impression **196 what** why
197 vesture garment **205 About** to work **214 griefs** grievances

I am no orator, as Brutus is,
But, as you know me all, a plain blunt man
That love my friend, and that they know full well
That gave me public leave to speak of him.   221
For I have neither wit, nor words, nor worth,   222
Action, nor utterance, nor the power of speech   223
To stir men's blood. I only speak right on.
I tell you that which you yourselves do know,
Show you sweet Caesar's wounds, poor poor dumb
     mouths,
And bid them speak for me. But were I Brutus,
And Brutus Antony, there were an Antony
Would ruffle up your spirits and put a tongue   229
In every wound of Caesar that should move
The stones of Rome to rise and mutiny.
ALL
  We'll mutiny!
FIRST PLEBEIAN We'll burn the house of Brutus!
THIRD PLEBEIAN
  Away, then! Come, seek the conspirators.
ANTONY
  Yet hear me, countrymen. Yet hear me speak.
ALL
  Peace, ho! Hear Antony, most noble Antony!
ANTONY
  Why, friends, you go to do you know not what.
  Wherein hath Caesar thus deserved your loves?
  Alas, you know not. I must tell you then:
  You have forgot the will I told you of.
ALL
  Most true, the will! Let's stay and hear the will.
ANTONY
  Here is the will, and under Caesar's seal.
  To every Roman citizen he gives,
  To every several man, seventy-five drachmas.   243
SECOND PLEBEIAN
  Most noble Caesar! We'll revenge his death.

221 **public leave** permission to speak publicly   222 **wit** understanding,
intelligence.   **worth** stature, authority   223 **Action** gesture.   **utterance**
good delivery   229 **ruffle up** stir to anger   243 **several** individual.
drachmas coins. (This is a substantial bequest.)

THIRD PLEBEIAN   O royal Caesar!

ANTONY   Hear me with patience.

ALL   Peace, ho!

ANTONY

Moreover, he hath left you all his walks,
His private arbors, and new-planted orchards,   249
On this side Tiber; he hath left them you,
And to your heirs forever—common pleasures,   251
To walk abroad and recreate yourselves.
Here was a Caesar! When comes such another?

FIRST PLEBEIAN

Never, never! Come, away, away!
We'll burn his body in the holy place
And with the brands fire the traitors' houses.
Take up the body.

SECOND PLEBEIAN   Go fetch fire!

THIRD PLEBEIAN   Pluck down benches!

FOURTH PLEBEIAN   Pluck down forms, windows, anything!   260

Exeunt Plebeians [with the body].

ANTONY

Now let it work. Mischief, thou art afoot.
Take thou what course thou wilt.

Enter Servant.

How now, fellow?

SERVANT

Sir, Octavius is already come to Rome.

ANTONY   Where is he?

SERVANT

He and Lepidus are at Caesar's house.

ANTONY

And thither will I straight to visit him.   266
He comes upon a wish. Fortune is merry,   267
And in this mood will give us anything.

SERVANT

I heard him say Brutus and Cassius
Are rid like madmen through the gates of Rome.   270

---

249 orchards gardens   **251 common pleasures** public pleasure gardens
(in which)   **260 forms** benches. **windows** i.e., shutters   **266 straight**
straightway, at once   **267 upon a wish** just when wanted.   **merry** i.e.,
favorably disposed   **270 Are rid** have ridden

ANTONY
  Belike they had some notice of the people,   271
  How I had moved them. Bring me to Octavius.
                                        Exeunt.

                        ❖

3.3   *Enter Cinna the poet, and after him the*
        Plebeians.

CINNA
  I dreamt tonight that I did feast with Caesar,   1
  And things unluckily charge my fantasy.   2
  I have no will to wander forth of doors,
  Yet something leads me forth.
FIRST PLEBEIAN   What is your name?
SECOND PLEBEIAN   Whither are you going?
THIRD PLEBEIAN   Where do you dwell?
FOURTH PLEBEIAN   Are you a married man or a bachelor?
SECOND PLEBEIAN   Answer every man directly.
FIRST PLEBEIAN   Ay, and briefly.
FOURTH PLEBEIAN   Ay, and wisely.
THIRD PLEBEIAN   Ay, and truly, you were best.   13
CINNA   What is my name? Whither am I going? Where
  do I dwell? Am I a married man or a bachelor? Then
  to answer every man directly and briefly, wisely and
  truly: wisely I say, I am a bachelor.
SECOND PLEBEIAN   That's as much as to say they are
  fools that marry. You'll bear me a bang for that, I fear. 19
  Proceed directly.
CINNA   Directly, I am going to Caesar's funeral.
FIRST PLEBEIAN   As a friend or an enemy?
CINNA   As a friend.
SECOND PLEBEIAN   That matter is answered directly.
FOURTH PLEBEIAN   For your dwelling—briefly.
CINNA   Briefly, I dwell by the Capitol.
THIRD PLEBEIAN   Your name, sir, truly.

271 Belike likely enough.   **of** about; or from

3.3. Location: A street.
1 tonight last night   **2 unluckily . . . fantasy** oppress my imagination
with foreboding   **13 you were best** it would be best for you   **19 bear
. . . bang** get a beating from me

CINNA Truly, my name is Cinna.

FIRST PLEBEIAN Tear him to pieces! He's a conspirator!

CINNA I am Cinna the poet, I am Cinna the poet!

FOURTH PLEBEIAN Tear him for his bad verses, tear him
for his bad verses!

CINNA I am not Cinna the conspirator.

FOURTH PLEBEIAN It is no matter, his name's Cinna.
Pluck but his name out of his heart, and turn him 35
going.   36

THIRD PLEBEIAN Tear him, tear him! Come, brands, ho,
firebrands! To Brutus', to Cassius'; burn all! Some to
Decius' house, and some to Casca's; some to Ligarius'.
Away, go!

       Exeunt all the Plebeians, [dragging off Cinna].

          ❖

35–36 turn him going send him packing

4.1　*Enter Antony [with a list], Octavius, and*
　　　　Lepidus.

ANTONY
　These many, then, shall die. Their names are pricked.　1
OCTAVIUS
　Your brother too must die. Consent you, Lepidus?
LEPIDUS
　I do consent—
OCTAVIUS　　　　Prick him down, Antony.
LEPIDUS
　Upon condition Publius shall not live,
　Who is your sister's son, Mark Antony.
ANTONY
　He shall not live. Look, with a spot I damn him.　6
　But Lepidus, go you to Caesar's house.
　Fetch the will hither, and we shall determine　8
　How to cut off some charge in legacies.　9
LEPIDUS　What, shall I find you here?
OCTAVIUS　Or here or at the Capitol.　　*Exit Lepidus.*　11
ANTONY
　This is a slight unmeritable man,　12
　Meet to be sent on errands. Is it fit,
　The threefold world divided, he should stand　14
　One of the three to share it?
OCTAVIUS　　　　　　　So you thought him,
　And took his voice who should be pricked to die　16
　In our black sentence and proscription.　17
ANTONY
　Octavius, I have seen more days than you;
　And though we lay these honors on this man

4.1. Location: Rome. A table is perhaps set out.
1 pricked marked down on a list (appropriate to the use of the stylus on
waxen tablets or of a pin on paper)　**6 spot** mark (on the list).　**damn**
condemn　**8–9 determine . . . legacies** i.e., find a way to reduce the
outlay of Caesar's estate, by altering the will　**11 Or** either　**12 slight**
unmeritable insignificant and undeserving　**14 threefold** (i.e., including
Europe, Africa, and Asia; alluding also to the triumvirate of Lepidus,
Antony, Octavius)　**16 took his voice** allowed him to decide (i.e., about
Publius), or, asked his opinion　**17 proscription** (Proscription branded a
man as an outlaw, confiscated his property, offered a reward for his
murder, and forbade his sons and grandsons from holding public office.)

To ease ourselves of divers slanderous loads,   20
He shall but bear them as the ass bears gold,
To groan and sweat under the business,
Either led or driven as we point the way;
And having brought our treasure where we will,
Then take we down his load, and turn him off,
Like to the empty ass, to shake his ears   26
And graze in commons.

OCTAVIUS   You may do your will;   27
But he's a tried and valiant soldier.

ANTONY
So is my horse, Octavius, and for that
I do appoint him store of provender.   30
It is a creature that I teach to fight,
To wind, to stop, to run directly on,   32
His corporal motion governed by my spirit.   33
And in some taste is Lepidus but so.   34
He must be taught, and trained, and bid go forth—
A barren-spirited fellow, one that feeds
On objects, arts, and imitations,   37
Which, out of use and staled by other men,   38
Begin his fashion. Do not talk of him   39
But as a property. And now, Octavius,   40
Listen great things. Brutus and Cassius   41
Are levying powers. We must straight make head.   42
Therefore let our alliance be combined,   43
Our best friends made, our means stretched;   44
And let us presently go sit in council   45
How covert matters may be best disclosed   46
And open perils surest answerèd.   47

20 divers . . . loads i.e., some of the burdensome accusations that will be
leveled against us   **26 empty** unloaded   **27 commons** public pasture
30 appoint assign, provide   **32 wind** turn. (Horse trainer's term.)
33 corporal bodily   **34 taste** degree, sense   **37 On . . . imitations** on
curiosities, artificial things, and the following of fashion (?), i.e., copied
things merely, taken up secondhand   **38 staled** made common or
cheap   **39 Begin his fashion** i.e., these outworn fashions are chosen by
him as his fashion   **40 property** tool   **41 Listen** hear   **42 powers**
armies.   **straight make head** immediately raise an army   **43 combined**
coalesced (i.e., let us work as one)   **44 made** mustered.   **stretched** used
to fullest advantage, extended to the utmost   **45 presently** at once
46 How . . . disclosed (to determine) how hidden dangers may best be
discovered   **47 surest answerèd** most safely met

OCTAVIUS
   Let us do so, for we are at the stake   48
   And bayed about with many enemies;   49
   And some that smile have in their hearts, I fear,
   Millions of mischiefs.   *Exeunt.* 51

❖

4.2   *Drum. Enter Brutus, Lucilius, [Lucius,] and the*
      army. Titinius and Pindarus meet them.

BRUTUS   Stand, ho!   1
LUCILIUS   Give the word, ho, and stand!   2
BRUTUS
   What now, Lucilius, is Cassius near?
LUCILIUS
   He is at hand, and Pindarus is come
   To do you salutation from his master.
BRUTUS
   He greets me well. Your master, Pindarus,   6
   In his own change, or by ill officers,   7
   Hath given me some worthy cause to wish
   Things done, undone; but if he be at hand
   I shall be satisfied.
PINDARUS   I do not doubt   10
   But that my noble master will appear
   Such as he is, full of regard and honor.   12
BRUTUS
   He is not doubted.—A word, Lucilius.
         [Brutus and Lucilius speak apart.]
   How he received you let me be resolved.   14
LUCILIUS
   With courtesy and with respect enough,

---

48 at the stake i.e., like a bear in the sport of bearbaiting   **49 bayed about** surrounded as by baying dogs   **51 mischiefs** harms, evils

4.2. Location: Camp near Sardis, in Asia Minor. Before Brutus' tent.
1–2 Stand . . . stand halt! Pass the word   **6 well** i.e., ceremoniously, through Pindarus (who is only a slave; perhaps Brutus is ironic)   **7 In . . . officers** whether from an alteration in his feelings toward me, or through the acts of unworthy subordinates   **10 be satisfied** have things explained to my satisfaction   **12 regard** i.e., consideration of your joint interests   **14 resolved** informed, put out of doubt

But not with such familiar instances   16
Nor with such free and friendly conference   17
As he hath used of old.
BRUTUS   Thou hast described
A hot friend cooling. Ever note, Lucilius,
When love begins to sicken and decay
It useth an enforcèd ceremony.   21
There are no tricks in plain and simple faith.
But hollow men, like horses hot at hand,   23
Make gallant show and promise of their mettle;
                              Low march within
But when they should endure the bloody spur,
They fall their crests and like deceitful jades   26
Sink in the trial. Comes his army on?   27
LUCILIUS
They mean this night in Sardis to be quartered.   28
The greater part, the horse in general,   29
Are come with Cassius.

        Enter Cassius and his powers.

BRUTUS   Hark, he is arrived.
March gently on to meet him.   31
CASSIUS   Stand, ho!
BRUTUS   Stand, ho! Speak the word along.
FIRST SOLDIER   Stand!
SECOND SOLDIER   Stand!
THIRD SOLDIER   Stand!
CASSIUS
Most noble brother, you have done me wrong.
BRUTUS
Judge me, you gods! Wrong I mine enemies?
And if not so, how should I wrong a brother?
CASSIUS
Brutus, this sober form of yours hides wrongs;   40

---

16 familiar instances proofs of intimate friendship   **17 conference**
conversation   **21 enforcèd** constrained   **23 hollow** insincere.   **hot at
hand** restless and full of spirit when held in, at the start   **26 fall their
crests** lower their necks, hang their heads.   **jades** worthless horses
27 Sink give way, fail   **28 Sardis** (The capital city of Lydia in Asia
Minor.)   **29 the horse in general** all the cavalry   **31 gently** mildly, not
hostilely   **40 sober form** dignified manner

And when you do them—
BRUTUS   Cassius, be content;
  Speak your griefs softly. I do know you well.   42
  Before the eyes of both our armies here,
  Which should perceive nothing but love from us,
  Let us not wrangle. Bid them move away.
  Then in my tent, Cassius, enlarge your griefs,   46
  And I will give you audience.
CASSIUS   Pindarus,
  Bid our commanders lead their charges off   48
  A little from this ground.
BRUTUS
  Lucius, do you the like, and let no man
  Come to our tent till we have done our conference.
  Let Lucilius and Titinius guard our door.   52
       Exeunt. Manent Brutus and Cassius. [Lucilius
         and Titinius stand guard at the door.]

4.3

CASSIUS
  That you have wronged me doth appear in this:
  You have condemned and noted Lucius Pella   2
  For taking bribes here of the Sardians,
  Wherein my letters, praying on his side,   4
  Because I knew the man, was slighted off.   5
BRUTUS
  You wronged yourself to write in such a case.
CASSIUS
  In such a time as this it is not meet   7
  That every nice offense should bear his comment.   8

---

42 griefs grievances   **46 enlarge** speak freely   **48 charges** troops
52 Lucilius (The Folio reads *Lucius* here and *Lucilius* in l. 50, but when
Shakespeare interpolated a passage in the next scene at ll. 124–166 he
evidently intended to have Lucilius guarding the door.)

**4.3. Location: The scene is continuous. Brutus and Cassius remain on-
stage, which now represents the interior of Brutus' tent.**
2 noted publicly disgraced.   **Lucius Pella** a Roman praetor in Sardis
4 letters i.e., letter   **5 slighted off** slightingly dismissed   **7 meet** fitting   **8 nice** trivial.   **bear his comment** be made the object of scrutiny

BRUTUS
Let me tell you, Cassius, you yourself
Are much condemned to have an itching palm,   10
To sell and mart your offices for gold   11
To undeservers.
CASSIUS   I an itching palm?
You know that you are Brutus that speaks this,
Or, by the gods, this speech were else your last.   14
BRUTUS
The name of Cassius honors this corruption,   15
And chastisement doth therefore hide his head.   16
CASSIUS   Chastisement?
BRUTUS
Remember March, the ides of March remember.
Did not great Julius bleed for justice' sake?
What villain touched his body that did stab
And not for justice? What, shall one of us,
That struck the foremost man of all this world
But for supporting robbers, shall we now   23
Contaminate our fingers with base bribes,
And sell the mighty space of our large honors   25
For so much trash as may be graspèd thus?   26
I had rather be a dog and bay the moon   27
Than such a Roman.
CASSIUS   Brutus, bait not me.   28
I'll not endure it. You forget yourself
To hedge me in. I am a soldier, I,   30
Older in practice, abler than yourself
To make conditions.   32
BRUTUS   Go to! You are not, Cassius.
CASSIUS   I am.
BRUTUS   I say you are not.

10 condemned to have accused of having   11 mart traffic in   14 else
otherwise   15 honors lends the appearance of honor to, countenances
16 chastisement . . . head i.e., legal authority is afraid to act (because of
Cassius' influence)   23 But only.   robbers i.e., those who would have
robbed Rome of her liberty (?) (According to Plutarch, Caesar "was a
favorer and suborner of all of them that did rob and spoil by his countenance and authority.")   25 the mighty . . . honors the greatness of our
honorable reputations   26 trash i.e., money (despised in Brutus' stoic
philosophy)   27 bay howl at   28 bait harass   30 hedge me in limit my
authority   32 make conditions i.e., for the behavior of such men as
Lucius Pella and for the appointment of my officers

CASSIUS
Urge me no more; I shall forget myself.   36
Have mind upon your health. Tempt me no farther.   37
BRUTUS   Away, slight man!   38
CASSIUS
Is 't possible?
BRUTUS   Hear me, for I will speak.
Must I give way and room to your rash choler?   40
Shall I be frighted when a madman stares?   41
CASSIUS
O ye gods, ye gods! Must I endure all this?
BRUTUS
All this? Ay, more. Fret till your proud heart break.
Go show your slaves how choleric you are
And make your bondmen tremble. Must I budge?   45
Must I observe you? Must I stand and crouch   46
Under your testy humor? By the gods,
You shall digest the venom of your spleen   48
Though it do split you; for, from this day forth,
I'll use you for my mirth, yea, for my laughter,
When you are waspish.
CASSIUS   Is it come to this?   51
BRUTUS
You say you are a better soldier.
Let it appear so; make your vaunting true,   53
And it shall please me well. For mine own part,
I shall be glad to learn of noble men.   55
CASSIUS
You wrong me every way! You wrong me, Brutus.
I said an elder soldier, not a better.
Did I say "better"?
BRUTUS   If you did, I care not.
CASSIUS
When Caesar lived he durst not thus have moved me.   59
BRUTUS
Peace, peace! You durst not so have tempted him.   60

36 Urge provoke   **37 Tempt** provoke   **38 slight** insignificant   **40 give
way and room to** make allowance for and accept.   **choler** wrathful
temperament   **41 stares** looks wildly at me   **45 budge** flinch
46 observe pay reverence to.   **crouch** bow, cringe   **48 digest** swallow.
spleen i.e., irascibility   **51 waspish** hotheaded   **53 vaunting** boasting
55 learn of learn of the existence of; or, learn from (those who have
proved themselves noble)   **59 moved** angered   **60 tempted** provoked

CASSIUS   I durst not?

BRUTUS   No.

CASSIUS

What, durst not tempt him?

BRUTUS   For your life you durst not.

CASSIUS

Do not presume too much upon my love.

I may do that I shall be sorry for.

BRUTUS

You have done that you should be sorry for.

There is no terror, Cassius, in your threats,

For I am armed so strong in honesty

That they pass by me as the idle wind,

Which I respect not. I did send to you   70

For certain sums of gold, which you denied me;

For I can raise no money by vile means.

By heaven, I had rather coin my heart

And drop my blood for drachmas than to wring

From the hard hands of peasants their vile trash

By any indirection. I did send   76

To you for gold to pay my legions,

Which you denied me. Was that done like Cassius?

Should I have answered Caius Cassius so?

When Marcus Brutus grows so covetous

To lock such rascal counters from his friends,   81

Be ready, gods, with all your thunderbolts;

Dash him to pieces!

CASSIUS   I denied you not.

BRUTUS

You did.

CASSIUS   I did not. He was but a fool

That brought my answer back. Brutus hath rived my

   heart.   85

A friend should bear his friend's infirmities,

But Brutus makes mine greater than they are.

BRUTUS

I do not, till you practice them on me.

---

70 respect not pay no attention to   **76 indirection** devious or unjust
means   **81 rascal counters** i.e., paltry sums. (*Counters* were uncurrent
coins used by shopkeepers as discs in making reckonings.)   **85 rived**
cleft, split

CASSIUS
You love me not.
BRUTUS   I do not like your faults.
CASSIUS
A friendly eye could never see such faults.
BRUTUS
A flatterer's would not, though they do appear
As huge as high Olympus.
CASSIUS
Come, Antony, and young Octavius, come,
Revenge yourselves alone on Cassius,
For Cassius is aweary of the world;
Hated by one he loves, braved by his brother,   96
Checked like a bondman, all his faults observed,   97
Set in a notebook, learned and conned by rote   98
To cast into my teeth. O, I could weep
My spirit from mine eyes! There is my dagger,
                    [*He offers his unsheathed dagger*]
And here my naked breast; within, a heart
Dearer than Pluto's mine, richer than gold.   102
If that thou be'st a Roman, take it forth.
I, that denied thee gold, will give my heart.   104
Strike, as thou didst at Caesar; for I know,
When thou didst hate him worst, thou lovedst him better
Than ever thou lovedst Cassius.
BRUTUS   Sheathe your dagger.
Be angry when you will, it shall have scope;   108
Do what you will, dishonor shall be humor.   109
O Cassius, you are yokèd with a lamb   110
That carries anger as the flint bears fire,
Who, much enforcèd, shows a hasty spark   112
And straight is cold again.
CASSIUS   Hath Cassius lived   113
To be but mirth and laughter to his Brutus
When grief and blood ill-tempered vexeth him?   115

96 braved defied **97 Checked** rebuked **98 conned by rote** memorized
102 Dearer more laden with wealth. **Pluto** god of the underworld (confused with Plutus, god of riches) **104 that denied** i.e., who you insist
denied **108 scope** free rein **109 dishonor . . . humor** i.e., I'll regard your
corruption or your flaring temper as something to be humored **110 yokèd
with** allied with (i.e., Brutus compares himself to the lamb) **112 enforcèd**
provoked, struck upon **113 straight** at once **115 blood ill-tempered** i.e.,
disposition imbalanced by the humors of the body

BRUTUS
   When I spoke that, I was ill-tempered too.
CASSIUS
   Do you confess so much? Give me your hand.
BRUTUS
   And my heart too.   [*They embrace.*]
CASSIUS   O Brutus!
BRUTUS   What's the matter?
CASSIUS
   Have not you love enough to bear with me,
   When that rash humor which my mother gave me   120
   Makes me forgetful?
BRUTUS   Yes, Cassius, and from henceforth,
   When you are overearnest with your Brutus,
   He'll think your mother chides, and leave you so.   123

      Enter a Poet [followed by Lucilius and Titinius,
      who have been standing guard at the door].

POET
   Let me go in to see the generals!
   There is some grudge between 'em; 'tis not meet
   They be alone.
LUCILIUS   You shall not come to them.
POET   Nothing but death shall stay me.
CASSIUS   How now? What's the matter?
POET
   For shame, you generals! What do you mean?
   Love and be friends, as two such men should be;
   For I have seen more years, I'm sure, than ye.
CASSIUS
   Ha, ha, how vilely doth this cynic rhyme!   132
BRUTUS
   Get you hence, sirrah. Saucy fellow, hence!
CASSIUS
   Bear with him, Brutus. 'Tis his fashion.
BRUTUS
   I'll know his humor when he knows his time.   135

---

120 that rash humor i.e., choler, anger   **123 leave you so** let it go at
that   **132 cynic** i.e., rude fellow; also one claiming to be a Cynic philosopher, hence outspoken against luxury   **135 I'll . . . time** I'll indulge his
eccentric behavior when he knows the proper time for it

What should the wars do with these jigging fools?   136
Companion, hence!
CASSIUS   Away, away, begone!   *Exit Poet.* 137
BRUTUS
  Lucilius and Titinius, bid the commanders
  Prepare to lodge their companies tonight.
CASSIUS
  And come yourselves, and bring Messala with you
  Immediately to us.   [*Exeunt Lucilius and Titinius.*]
BRUTUS [*To Lucius within*]   Lucius, a bowl of wine.
CASSIUS
  I did not think you could have been so angry.
BRUTUS
  O Cassius, I am sick of many griefs.
CASSIUS
  Of your philosophy you make no use
  If you give place to accidental evils.   145
BRUTUS
  No man bears sorrow better. Portia is dead.
CASSIUS   Ha? Portia?
BRUTUS   She is dead.
CASSIUS
  How scaped I killing when I crossed you so?   149
  O insupportable and touching loss!   150
  Upon what sickness?
BRUTUS   Impatient of my absence,   151
  And grief that young Octavius with Mark Antony
  Have made themselves so strong—for with her death   153
  That tidings came—with this she fell distract
  And, her attendants absent, swallowed fire.   155
CASSIUS
  And died so?
BRUTUS   Even so.
CASSIUS   O ye immortal gods!

---

136 jigging rhyming in jerky doggerel   **137 Companion** fellow
145 accidental evils misfortunes caused by chance (which should be a
matter of indifference to a philosopher like Brutus)   **149 scaped I**
killing did I escape being killed   **150 touching** grievous   **151 Impatient**
of unable to endure   **153 her death** i.e., news of her death
155 swallowed fire (According to Plutarch, as translated by Thomas
North, Portia "took hot burning coals and cast them in her mouth, and
kept her mouth so close that she choked herself.")

Enter Boy [Lucius] with wine and tapers.

BRUTUS
Speak no more of her.—Give me a bowl of wine.—
In this I bury all unkindness, Cassius.   *Drinks.*
CASSIUS
My heart is thirsty for that noble pledge.
Fill, Lucius, till the wine o'erswell the cup;
I cannot drink too much of Brutus' love.   161
                    [*He drinks. Exit Lucius.*]

Enter Titinius and Messala.

BRUTUS
Come in, Titinius. Welcome, good Messala.
Now sit we close about this taper here
And call in question our necessities.   [*They sit.*] 164
CASSIUS
Portia, art thou gone?
BRUTUS   No more, I pray you.
Messala, I have here receivèd letters
That young Octavius and Mark Antony
Come down upon us with a mighty power,   168
Bending their expedition toward Philippi.   169
                    [*He shows letters.*]

MESSALA
Myself have letters of the selfsame tenor.
BRUTUS   With what addition?
MESSALA
That by proscription and bills of outlawry   172
Octavius, Antony, and Lepidus
Have put to death an hundred senators.
BRUTUS
Therein our letters do not well agree;
Mine speak of seventy senators that died
By their proscriptions, Cicero being one.
CASSIUS
Cicero one?

161 s.d. Titinius (Lucilius does not return with Titinius, as he was
ordered to do at ll. 140–141, probably because he was not in Shakespeare's original version of this scene.)   **164 call in question** examine,
discuss   **168 power** army   **169 Bending** directing.   **expedition** rapid
march; military power   **172 proscription** (See 4.1.17, note.)

MESSALA   Cicero is dead,
  And by that order of proscription.
  Had you your letters from your wife, my lord?   180
BRUTUS   No, Messala.
MESSALA
  Nor nothing in your letters writ of her?   182
BRUTUS
  Nothing, Messala.
MESSALA   That, methinks, is strange.
BRUTUS
  Why ask you? Hear you aught of her in yours?
MESSALA   No, my lord.
BRUTUS
  Now, as you are a Roman, tell me true.
MESSALA
  Then like a Roman bear the truth I tell,
  For certain she is dead, and by strange manner.
BRUTUS
  Why, farewell, Portia. We must die, Messala.
  With meditating that she must die once,   190
  I have the patience to endure it now.
MESSALA
  Even so great men great losses should endure.   192
CASSIUS
  I have as much of this in art as you,   193
  But yet my nature could not bear it so.   194
BRUTUS
  Well, to our work alive. What do you think   195
  Of marching to Philippi presently?
CASSIUS
  I do not think it good.
BRUTUS   Your reason?
CASSIUS   This it is:

180–194 Had . . . so (This passage is sometimes regarded as contradictory to and redundant of ll. 142–165. Perhaps it is the original account
of Portia's death, and ll. 142–165 are part of a later interpolation, but it
is also possible that both are intended, the first being Brutus' intimate
revelation of the news to his friend and the second, Brutus' recovery of
his stoic reserve now on display for Messala and Titinius.)   **182 nothing
. . . her** nothing written about her in the letters you've received
190 once at some time   **192 Even so** in just such a way   **193 art** i.e., the
acquired wisdom of stoical fortitude   **195 alive** concerning us who are
alive and dealing with present realities

'Tis better that the enemy seek us.
So shall he waste his means, weary his soldiers,
Doing himself offense, whilst we, lying still,   200
Are full of rest, defense, and nimbleness.

BRUTUS
Good reasons must of force give place to better.   202
The people twixt Philippi and this ground
Do stand but in a forced affection,
For they have grudged us contribution.
The enemy, marching along by them,
By them shall make a fuller number up,
Come on refreshed, new-added, and encouraged;   208
From which advantage shall we cut him off
If at Philippi we do face him there,
These people at our back.

CASSIUS   Hear me, good brother—

BRUTUS
Under your pardon. You must note besides   212
That we have tried the utmost of our friends;
Our legions are brim full, our cause is ripe.
The enemy increaseth every day;
We, at the height, are ready to decline.
There is a tide in the affairs of men
Which, taken at the flood, leads on to fortune;
Omitted, all the voyage of their life   219
Is bound in shallows and in miseries.   220
On such a full sea are we now afloat,
And we must take the current when it serves
Or lose our ventures.

CASSIUS   Then, with your will, go on.   223
We'll along ourselves and meet them at Philippi.   224

BRUTUS
The deep of night is crept upon our talk,
And nature must obey necessity,
Which we will niggard with a little rest.   227
There is no more to say?

200 **offense** harm   202 **of force** necessarily   208 **new-added** reinforced   212 **Under your pardon** i.e., excuse me, let me continue
219 **Omitted** neglected, missed   220 **bound in** confined to
223 **ventures** investments (of enterprise at sea).   **with your will** as you
wish   224 **along** go along   227 **niggard** stint (by sleeping only briefly)

CASSIUS   No more. Good night.
Early tomorrow will we rise and hence.   229
BRUTUS
Lucius! (*Enter Lucius.*) My gown. [*Exit Lucius.*] Fare-
well, good Messala.   230
Good night, Titinius. Noble, noble Cassius,
Good night and good repose.
CASSIUS   O my dear brother!
This was an ill beginning of the night.
Never come such division 'tween our souls!
Let it not, Brutus.

  Enter Lucius with the gown.

BRUTUS   Everything is well.
CASSIUS   Good night, my lord.
BRUTUS   Good night, good brother.
TITINIUS, MESSALA   Good night, Lord Brutus.
BRUTUS   Farewell, everyone.
    Exeunt [*all but Brutus and Lucius*].
Give me the gown. Where is thy instrument?   241
LUCIUS
Here in the tent.
BRUTUS   What, thou speak'st drowsily?
Poor knave, I blame thee not; thou art o'erwatched.   243
Call Claudius and some other of my men;
I'll have them sleep on cushions in my tent.
LUCIUS   Varro and Claudius!

  Enter Varro and Claudius.

VARRO   Calls my lord?
BRUTUS
I pray you, sirs, lie in my tent and sleep.
It may be I shall raise you by and by   249
On business to my brother Cassius.
VARRO
So please you, we will stand and watch your pleasure.   251
BRUTUS
I will not have it so. Lie down, good sirs.

---

229 hence depart   **230 gown** dressing gown   **241 instrument** i.e., lute or
cithern   **243 knave** boy.   **o'erwatched** tired from lack of sleep   **249 raise**
rouse   **251 watch your pleasure** wakefully await your commands

It may be I shall otherwise bethink me.   253
                    [*Varro and Claudius lie down.*]
Look, Lucius, here's the book I sought for so;
I put it in the pocket of my gown.
LUCIUS
I was sure your lordship did not give it me.
BRUTUS
Bear with me, good boy, I am much forgetful.
Canst thou hold up thy heavy eyes awhile
And touch thy instrument a strain or two?   259
LUCIUS
Ay, my lord, an 't please you.
BRUTUS   It does, my boy.   260
I trouble thee too much, but thou art willing.
LUCIUS   It is my duty, sir.
BRUTUS
I should not urge thy duty past thy might;
I know young bloods look for a time of rest.   264
LUCIUS   I have slept, my lord, already.
BRUTUS
It was well done, and thou shalt sleep again;
I will not hold thee long. If I do live,
I will be good to thee.
                    Music, and a song. [*Lucius falls asleep.*]
This is a sleepy tune. O murderous slumber,   269
Layest thou thy leaden mace upon my boy,   270
That plays thee music? Gentle knave, good night;
I will not do thee so much wrong to wake thee.
If thou dost nod, thou break'st thy instrument;
I'll take it from thee. And, good boy, good night.
                    [*He removes Lucius' instrument,
                    and begins to read.*]
Let me see, let me see; is not the leaf turned down
Where I left reading? Here it is, I think.

        Enter the Ghost of Caesar.

253 **otherwise bethink me** change my mind   259 **touch** i.e., play on.
strain tune, musical phrase   260 **an 't** if it   264 **young bloods** youthful
constitutions   269 **murderous** producing the likeness of death
270 **leaden mace** heavy staff of office (used by a sheriff to touch the
shoulder of one being placed under arrest)

How ill this taper burns! Ha! Who comes here?   277
I think it is the weakness of mine eyes
That shapes this monstrous apparition.
It comes upon me.—Art thou any thing?   280
Art thou some god, some angel, or some devil,
That mak'st my blood cold and my hair to stare?   282
Speak to me what thou art.

GHOST
Thy evil spirit, Brutus.

BRUTUS   Why com'st thou?

GHOST
To tell thee thou shalt see me at Philippi.

BRUTUS   Well; then I shall see thee again?

GHOST   Ay, at Philippi.

BRUTUS
Why, I will see thee at Philippi, then.   [*Exit Ghost.*]
Now I have taken heart, thou vanishest.
Ill spirit, I would hold more talk with thee.—
Boy, Lucius! Varro! Claudius! Sirs, awake!
Claudius!

LUCIUS   The strings, my lord, are false.   292

BRUTUS
He thinks he still is at his instrument.
Lucius, awake!

LUCIUS   My lord?

BRUTUS
Didst thou dream, Lucius, that thou so criedst out?

LUCIUS
My lord, I do not know that I did cry.

BRUTUS
Yes, that thou didst. Didst thou see anything?

LUCIUS   Nothing, my lord.

BRUTUS
Sleep again, Lucius. Sirrah Claudius!
[*To Varro.*] Fellow thou, awake!

VARRO   My lord?

CLAUDIUS   My lord?

---

277 How . . . burns (It is part of the machinery of apparitions that lights
burn low and blue.)   **280 upon** toward   **282 stare** stand on end
292 false out of tune

[*They get up.*]

BRUTUS
  Why did you so cry out, sirs, in your sleep?
VARRO, CLAUDIUS
  Did·we, my lord?
BRUTUS   Ay. Saw you anything?
VARRO
  No, my lord, I saw nothing.
CLAUDIUS   Nor I, my lord.
BRUTUS
  Go and commend me to my brother Cassius.   305
  Bid him set on his powers betimes before,   306
  And we will follow.
VARRO, CLAUDIUS   It shall be done, my lord.
                                        Exeunt.

❖

305 commend me deliver my greetings **306 set . . . before** advance his
troops early in the morning, before me

5.1 *Enter Octavius, Antony, and their army.*

OCTAVIUS
Now, Antony, our hopes are answerèd.
You said the enemy would not come down,
But keep the hills and upper regions.   3
It proves not so. Their battles are at hand;   4
They mean to warn us at Philippi here,   5
Answering before we do demand of them.

ANTONY
Tut, I am in their bosoms, and I know   7
Wherefore they do it. They could be content
To visit other places, and come down   9
With fearful bravery, thinking by this face   10
To fasten in our thoughts that they have courage;   11
But 'tis not so.

          Enter a Messenger.

MESSENGER   Prepare you, generals.   12
The enemy comes on in gallant show.
Their bloody sign of battle is hung out,   14
And something to be done immediately.   15

ANTONY
Octavius, lead your battle softly on   16
Upon the left hand of the even field.

OCTAVIUS
Upon the right hand, I. Keep thou the left.

ANTONY
Why do you cross me in this exigent?   19

OCTAVIUS
I do not cross you, but I will do so.   *March.* 20

          Drum. Enter Brutus, Cassius, and their army;
          [Lucilius, Titinius, Messala, and others].

5.1. Location: The plains of Philippi, in Macedonia.
3 keep remain in   **4 battles** armies   **5 warn** challenge   **7 bosoms** secret
councils   **9 visit other places** i.e., be elsewhere.   **come** they come
10 fearful bravery (1) awesome ostentation (2) a show of bravery to
conceal their fear.   **face** pretense (of courage)   **11 fasten** fix the idea
12 'tis not so (1) their plan cannot deceive us (2) they have no courage
14 bloody sign red flag   **15 to be** is to be   **16 softly** warily, with restraint   **19 cross** contradict.   **exigent** critical moment   **20 do so** i.e., do
as I said

BRUTUS   They stand and would have parley.

CASSIUS
Stand fast, Titinius. We must out and talk.   22

OCTAVIUS
Mark Antony, shall we give sign of battle?

ANTONY
No, Caesar, we will answer on their charge.   24
Make forth. The generals would have some words.   25

OCTAVIUS [*To his officers*]   Stir not until the signal.
    [*The two sides advance toward one another.*]

BRUTUS
Words before blows. Is it so, countrymen?

OCTAVIUS
Not that we love words better, as you do.

BRUTUS
Good words are better than bad strokes, Octavius.

ANTONY
In your bad strokes, Brutus, you give good words.   30
Witness the hole you made in Caesar's heart,
Crying, "Long live! Hail, Caesar!"

CASSIUS   Antony,
The posture of your blows are yet unknown;   33
But for your words, they rob the Hybla bees,   34
And leave them honeyless.

ANTONY   Not stingless too?

BRUTUS   O, yes, and soundless too.
For you have stolen their buzzing, Antony,
And very wisely threat before you sting.   39

ANTONY
Villains! You did not so when your vile daggers   40
Hacked one another in the sides of Caesar.
You showed your teeth like apes, and fawned like
  hounds,   42

22 out go out   **24 answer on their charge** respond when they attack
25 Make forth march forward   **30 In . . . words** i.e., as you deliver cruel
blows, Brutus, you use deceiving flattery. (Antony deliberately changes
Brutus' *Good words* in l. 29, "bravely spoken words," into a negative
meaning.)   **33 posture** quality   **34 for** as for.   **Hybla** a mountain and a
town in ancient Sicily, famous for honey   **39 very wisely** (Said ironically; Brutus suggests that Antony is all bluster and no action.)   **threat**
threaten   **40 so** i.e., give warning   **42 showed your teeth** i.e., in smiles

And bowed like bondmen, kissing Caesar's feet,
Whilst damnèd Casca, like a cur, behind
Struck Caesar on the neck. O you flatterers!

CASSIUS
Flatterers? Now, Brutus, thank yourself!
This tongue had not offended so today
If Cassius might have ruled.   48

OCTAVIUS
Come, come, the cause. If arguing make us sweat,   49
The proof of it will turn to redder drops.   50
Look,   [*He draws*]
I draw a sword against conspirators.
When think you that the sword goes up again?   53
Never, till Caesar's three-and-thirty wounds   54
Be well avenged, or till another Caesar
Have added slaughter to the sword of traitors.   56

BRUTUS
Caesar, thou canst not die by traitors' hands,   57
Unless thou bring'st them with thee.

OCTAVIUS   So I hope.   58
I was not born to die on Brutus' sword.   59

BRUTUS
O, if thou wert the noblest of thy strain,   60
Young man, thou couldst not die more honorable.

CASSIUS
A peevish schoolboy, worthless of such honor,   62
Joined with a masker and a reveler!   63

ANTONY
Old Cassius still.

OCTAVIUS   Come, Antony, away!—
Defiance, traitors, hurl we in your teeth.

48 ruled prevailed (in urging that Antony be killed)   **49 the cause** to our
business   **50 proof** trial   **53 up** in its sheath   **54 three-and-thirty**
(Plutarch has it three-and-twenty.)   **56 Have . . . to** has also been slaugh-
tered by   **57–59 Caesar . . . sword** (Brutus says that if there are any
traitors on the battlefield they will perforce be in Octavius' army;
Octavius twists Brutus' taunt by pretending that Brutus meant Octavius
could not die on Brutus' sword.)   **60 if** even if.   **strain** lineage
62 peevish silly, childish.   **schoolboy** (Octavius was 18 at the time of
Caesar's assassination.)   **worthless** unworthy   **63 masker . . . reveler**
i.e., Antony, noted for his reveling

If you dare fight today, come to the field;
If not, when you have stomachs.   67
    Exeunt Octavius, Antony, and army.

CASSIUS
Why now, blow wind, swell billow, and swim bark!   68
The storm is up, and all is on the hazard.   69

BRUTUS
Lo, Lucilius! Hark, a word with you.

LUCILIUS (*Stands forth*) My lord?
    [*Brutus and Lucilius converse apart.*]

CASSIUS Messala!

MESSALA (*Stands forth*) What says my general?

CASSIUS Messala,
This is my birthday; as this very day   75
Was Cassius born. Give me thy hand, Messala.
Be thou my witness that against my will,
As Pompey was, am I compelled to set   78
Upon one battle all our liberties.
You know that I held Epicurus strong   80
And his opinion. Now I change my mind
And partly credit things that do presage.   82
Coming from Sardis, on our former ensign   83
Two mighty eagles fell, and there they perched,   84
Gorging and feeding from our soldiers' hands,
Who to Philippi here consorted us.   86
This morning are they fled away and gone,
And in their steads do ravens, crows, and kites   88
Fly o'er our heads and downward look on us
As we were sickly prey. Their shadows seem   90
A canopy most fatal, under which   91
Our army lies, ready to give up the ghost.

MESSALA
Believe not so.

67 stomachs (1) appetites (for fighting) (2) courage **68 billow** wave
69 on the hazard at stake **75 as** on **78 Pompey** (The reference is to the
battle of Pharsalus, where Pompey was persuaded to fight Caesar
against his own judgment.) **set** stake **80 Epicurus** Greek philosopher
(341–270 B.C.), whose materialistic philosophy spurned belief in omens
or superstitions **82 presage** foretell events **83 former ensign** foremost
standard, the legion's *aquila*, a tall standard surmounted by the image
of an eagle **84 fell** swooped down **86 consorted** accompanied
88 kites birds of prey, belonging to the hawk family **90 As** as if
91 fatal presaging death

CASSIUS   I but believe it partly,   93
  For I am fresh of spirit and resolved
  To meet all perils very constantly.   95
BRUTUS
  Even so, Lucilius.   [*He rejoins Cassius.*]
CASSIUS   Now, most noble Brutus,   96
  The gods today stand friendly, that we may,   97
  Lovers in peace, lead on our days to age!   98
  But since the affairs of men rest still incertain,   99
  Let's reason with the worst that may befall.   100
  If we do lose this battle, then is this
  The very last time we shall speak together.
  What are you then determinèd to do?
BRUTUS
  Even by the rule of that philosophy
  By which I did blame Cato for the death   105
  Which he did give himself—I know not how,
  But I do find it cowardly and vile,
  For fear of what might fall, so to prevent   108
  The time of life—arming myself with patience   109
  To stay the providence of some high powers   110
  That govern us below.
CASSIUS   Then, if we lose this battle,
  You are contented to be led in triumph
  Thorough the streets of Rome?   113
BRUTUS
  No, Cassius, no. Think not, thou noble Roman,
  That ever Brutus will go bound to Rome;
  He bears too great a mind. But this same day
  Must end that work the ides of March begun.
  And whether we shall meet again I know not;
  Therefore our everlasting farewell take.
  Forever and forever farewell, Cassius!
  If we do meet again, why, we shall smile;
  If not, why then this parting was well made.

93 but only   **95 constantly** resolutely   **96 Even so, Lucilius** (This phrase
marks the end of Brutus' private conversation apart with Lucilius.)
97 The gods may the gods   **98 Lovers** friends   **99 still** always
100 reason reckon   **105 Cato** i.e., Marcus Porcius Cato, Brutus' father-
in-law, who killed himself to avoid submission to Caesar in 46 B.C. (See
2.1.296 and note.)   **108 fall** befall.   **prevent** anticipate the end, cut
short   **109 time** term, end   **110 stay** await   **113 Thorough** through

CASSIUS
    Forever and forever farewell, Brutus!
    If we do meet again, we'll smile indeed;
    If not, 'tis true this parting was well made.
BRUTUS
    Why then, lead on. O, that a man might know
    The end of this day's business ere it come!
    But it sufficeth that the day will end,
    And then the end is known. Come, ho, away!

                                    Exeunt.

5.2   *Alarum. Enter Brutus and Messala.*

BRUTUS
    Ride, ride, Messala, ride, and give these bills   1
    Unto the legions on the other side.   2
                    [*He hands him written orders.*]
                                    Loud alarum.

    Let them set on at once; for I perceive   3
    But cold demeanor in Octavius' wing,   4
    And sudden push gives them the overthrow.
    Ride, ride, Messala! Let them all come down.   6

                                    Exeunt.

5.3   *Alarums. Enter Cassius [carrying a standard],*
            and Titinius.

CASSIUS
    O, look, Titinius, look, the villains fly!   1
    Myself have to mine own turned enemy.   2
    This ensign here of mine was turning back;   3

5.2. Location: The plains of Philippi. The field of battle.
s.d. Alarum (This is seemingly an anticipatory stage direction; the battle
actually begins with the *Loud alarum* at l. 2. An *alarum* is offstage
sounds signifying a battle.) **1 bills** orders **2 side** wing (i.e., Cassius'
wing) **3 set on** attack **4 cold demeanor** faintheartedness **6 come
down** i.e., from the hills where they have been awaiting the battle; see
5.1.2–3.

5.3. Location: The field of battle still.
1 the villains i.e., my own troops **2 mine own** my own men
3 ensign bearer of the standard. (A legion's *aquila* or eagle standard had
great moral significance and needed to be guarded.)

I slew the coward and did take it from him.   4
TITINIUS
  O Cassius, Brutus gave the word too early,
  Who, having some advantage on Octavius,
  Took it too eagerly. His soldiers fell to spoil,   7
  Whilst we by Antony are all enclosed.   8

    Enter Pindarus.

PINDARUS
  Fly further off, my lord, fly further off!
  Mark Antony is in your tents, my lord.
  Fly therefore, noble Cassius, fly far off.
CASSIUS
  This hill is far enough. Look, look, Titinius:
  Are those my tents where I perceive the fire?
TITINIUS
  They are, my lord.
CASSIUS   Titinius, if thou lovest me,
  Mount thou my horse and hide thy spurs in him
  Till he have brought thee up to yonder troops
  And here again, that I may rest assured
  Whether yond troops are friend or enemy.
TITINIUS
  I will be here again even with a thought.   *Exit.* 19
CASSIUS
  Go, Pindarus, get higher on that hill.
  My sight was ever thick. Regard Titinius,   21
  And tell me what thou not'st about the field.   22
                    [Pindarus goes up.]
  This day I breathèd first. Time is come round,   23
  And where I did begin, there shall I end.
  My life is run his compass.—Sirrah, what news?   25
PINDARUS (*Above*) O my lord!
CASSIUS What news?

---

4 it i.e., the ensign's standard **7 spoil** looting **8 enclosed** surrounded
19 even . . . thought as quick as thought **21 thick** imperfect, dim. **Regard** observe **22 s.d. Pindarus goes up** (Pindarus may exit and ascend
behind the scenes to the gallery; at l. 35 he does *enter* in order to return.) **23 breathèd first** i.e., is my birthday **25 his compass** its circuit,
circle (as drawn by a geometer's compass)

PINDARUS [*Above*]
   Titinius is enclosèd round about
   With horsemen that make to him on the spur,   29
   Yet he spurs on. Now they are almost on him.
   Now, Titinius! Now some light. O, he   31
   Lights too. He's ta'en. (*Shout.*) And hark! They shout for
      joy.
CASSIUS   Come down, behold no more.
   O coward that I am, to live so long
   To see my best friend ta'en before my face!

      Enter Pindarus [*from above*].

   Come hither, sirrah.
   In Parthia did I take thee prisoner,   37
   And then I swore thee, saving of thy life,   38
   That whatsoever I did bid thee do
   Thou shouldst attempt it. Come now, keep thine oath;
   Now be a freeman, and with this good sword,
   That ran through Caesar's bowels, search this bosom.   42
   Stand not to answer. Here, take thou the hilts,   43
   And when my face is covered, as 'tis now,
   Guide thou the sword. [*Pindarus does so.*] Caesar, thou
      art revenged,
   Even with the sword that killed thee.   [*He dies.*]
PINDARUS
   So, I am free, yet would not so have been   47
   Durst I have done my will. O Cassius!   48
   Far from this country Pindarus shall run,
   Where never Roman shall take note of him.   [*Exit.*]

      Enter Titinius [*with a garland of laurel*] *and*
      Messala.

MESSALA
   It is but change, Titinius; for Octavius   51
   Is overthrown by noble Brutus' power,

---

29 make . . . spur approach him riding rapidly   **31 light** alight, dismount   **37 Parthia** (What is now northern Iran.)   **38 swore . . . of** made you swear, when I spared   **42 search** penetrate   **43 Stand** delay.   **hilts** i.e., sword hilt   **47 so** in this manner   **48 Durst** dared   **51 change** exchange of advantage, quid pro quo

As Cassius' legions are by Antony.
TITINIUS
These tidings will well comfort Cassius.
MESSALA
Where did you leave him?
TITINIUS   All disconsolate,
With Pindarus his bondman, on this hill.
MESSALA
Is not that he that lies upon the ground?
TITINIUS
He lies not like the living. O my heart!
MESSALA
Is not that he?
TITINIUS   No, this was he, Messala,
But Cassius is no more. O setting sun,
As in thy red rays thou dost sink to night,   61
So in his red blood Cassius' day is set!
The sun of Rome is set. Our day is gone;   63
Clouds, dews, and dangers come; our deeds are done!
Mistrust of my success hath done this deed.   65
MESSALA
Mistrust of good success hath done this deed.
O hateful Error, Melancholy's child,   67
Why dost thou show to the apt thoughts of men   68
The things that are not? O Error, soon conceived,
Thou never com'st unto a happy birth,
But kill'st the mother that engendered thee.   71
TITINIUS
What, Pindarus! Where art thou, Pindarus?
MESSALA
Seek him, Titinius, whilst I go to meet
The noble Brutus, thrusting this report
Into his ears. I may say "thrusting" it;
For piercing steel and darts envenomèd   76
Shall be as welcome to the ears of Brutus
As tidings of this sight.

61 to toward   **63 sun** (with pun on *son*)   **65 Mistrust** i.e., Cassius'
doubt   **67 Melancholy's child** i.e., chimera bred of a melancholic temperament   **68 apt** impressionable   **71 the mother** i.e., the melancholy
person who too readily believed the worst   **76 darts** spears

TITINIUS   Hie you, Messala,   78
And I will seek for Pindarus the while.
                              [*Exit Messala.*]
Why didst thou send me forth, brave Cassius?
Did I not meet thy friends? And did not they
Put on my brows this wreath of victory
And bid me give it thee? Didst thou not hear their
    shouts?
Alas, thou hast misconstrued everything.
But, hold thee, take this garland on thy brow.   85
              [*He places a garland on Cassius' brow.*]
Thy Brutus bid me give it thee, and I
Will do his bidding. Brutus, come apace   87
And see how I regarded Caius Cassius.
By your leave, gods! This is a Roman's part.
Come, Cassius' sword, and find Titinius' heart.
                    [*He stabs himself and*] *dies.*

Alarum. Enter Brutus, Messala, young Cato,
Strato, Volumnius, and Lucilius, [*Labeo, and*
Flavius].

BRUTUS
Where, where, Messala, doth his body lie?
MESSALA
Lo, yonder, and Titinius mourning it.
BRUTUS
Titinius' face is upward.
CATO   He is slain.
BRUTUS
O Julius Caesar, thou art mighty yet!
Thy spirit walks abroad and turns our swords
In our own proper entrails.   *Low alarums.*
CATO   Brave Titinius!   96
Look whe'er he have not crowned dead Cassius.   97
BRUTUS
Are yet two Romans living such as these?
The last of all the Romans, fare thee well!
It is impossible that ever Rome
Should breed thy fellow. Friends, I owe more tears

78 Hie hasten   **85 hold thee** wait   **87 apace** quickly   **96 own proper**
very own   **97 whe'er** whether

To this dead man than you shall see me pay.—
I shall find time, Cassius, I shall find time.—
Come, therefore, and to Thasos send his body.   104
His funerals shall not be in our camp,
Lest it discomfort us. Lucilius, come,   106
And come, young Cato, let us to the field.
Labeo and Flavius, set our battles on.   108
'Tis three o'clock, and, Romans, yet ere night
We shall try fortune in a second fight.   *Exeunt.* 110

5.4   *Alarum. Enter Brutus, Messala, [young] Cato,*
          Lucilius, and Flavius.

BRUTUS
    Yet, countrymen, O, yet hold up your heads!
              [*Exit, followed by Messala and Flavius.*]
CATO
    What bastard doth not? Who will go with me?   2
    I will proclaim my name about the field:
    I am the son of Marcus Cato, ho!
    A foe to tyrants, and my country's friend.
    I am the son of Marcus Cato, ho!

         Enter soldiers, and fight.

LUCILIUS
    And I am Brutus, Marcus Brutus I!
    Brutus, my country's friend! Know me for Brutus!
                 [*Young Cato is slain by Antony's men.*]
    O young and noble Cato, art thou down?
    Why, now thou diest as bravely as Titinius,
    And mayst be honored, being Cato's son.
FIRST SOLDIER [*Capturing Lucilius*]
    Yield, or thou diest.
LUCILIUS [*Offering money*]   Only I yield to die.   12

There is so much that thou wilt kill me straight;   13
Kill Brutus, and be honored in his death.

FIRST SOLDIER
We must not. A noble prisoner!

SECOND SOLDIER
Room, ho! Tell Antony, Brutus is ta'en.

    Enter Antony.

FIRST SOLDIER
I'll tell the news. Here comes the General.—
Brutus is ta'en, Brutus is ta'en, my lord.

ANTONY   Where is he?

LUCILIUS
Safe, Antony, Brutus is safe enough.
I dare assure thee that no enemy
Shall ever take alive the noble Brutus.
The gods defend him from so great a shame!
When you do find him, or alive or dead,   24
He will be found like Brutus, like himself.

ANTONY [*To First Soldier*]
This is not Brutus, friend, but, I assure you,
A prize no less in worth. Keep this man safe;
Give him all kindness. I had rather have
Such men my friends than enemies. Go on,
And see whe'er Brutus be alive or dead;   30
And bring us word unto Octavius' tent
How everything is chanced.   *Exeunt* [*separately*]. 32

5.5   *Enter Brutus, Dardanius, Clitus, Strato, and*
      Volumnius.

BRUTUS
Come, poor remains of friends, rest on this rock.
                           ,   [*He sits.*]

13 There ... straight i.e., here is money (or perhaps the inducement of
honor) if you will kill me at once   **24 or alive** either alive   **30 whe'er**
whether   **32 is chanced** has fallen out   **s.d. Exeunt** (The body of
young Cato may be carried off at this point; it is not seen by Brutus et
al. in scene 5.)

5.5. Location: The field of battle still.

CLITUS
 Statilius showed the torchlight, but, my lord,   2
 He came not back. He is or ta'en or slain.   3
BRUTUS
 Sit thee down, Clitus. Slaying is the word.
 It is a deed in fashion. Hark thee, Clitus.
                                        [*He whispers.*]
CLITUS
 What, I, my lord? No, not for all the world.
BRUTUS
 Peace then. No words.
CLITUS   I'll rather kill myself.
BRUTUS
 Hark thee, Dardanius.   [*He whispers.*]
DARDANIUS   Shall I do such a deed?
      [*Dardanius and Clitus move away from Brutus.*]
CLITUS   O Dardanius!
DARDANIUS   O Clitus!
CLITUS
 What ill request did Brutus make to thee?
DARDANIUS
 To kill him, Clitus. Look, he meditates.
CLITUS
 Now is that noble vessel full of grief,
 That it runs over even at his eyes.
BRUTUS
 Come hither, good Volumnius. List a word.   15
VOLUMNIUS
 What says my lord?
BRUTUS   Why, this, Volumnius:
 The ghost of Caesar hath appeared to me
 Two several times by night—at Sardis once,   18
 And this last night here in Philippi fields.
 I know my hour is come.
VOLUMNIUS   Not so, my lord.
BRUTUS
 Nay, I am sure it is, Volumnius.
 Thou seest the world, Volumnius, how it goes;

2 Statilius . . . torchlight (A scout named Statilius has gone to see if
Cassius' camp is still occupied; he signals back, but is taken or
slain.) **3 or ta'en** either taken **15 List** listen to **18 several** separate

Our enemies have beat us to the pit.   *Low alarums.* 23
It is more worthy to leap in ourselves
Than tarry till they push us. Good Volumnius,
Thou know'st that we two went to school together.
Even for that, our love of old, I prithee,   27
Hold thou my sword hilts whilst I run on it.   28
VOLUMNIUS
That's not an office for a friend, my lord.   29
                           Alarum still.

CLITUS
Fly, fly, my lord! There is no tarrying here.
BRUTUS
Farewell to you, and you, and you, Volumnius.
Strato, thou hast been all this while asleep;
Farewell to thee too, Strato. Countrymen,
My heart doth joy that yet in all my life
I found no man but he was true to me.
I shall have glory by this losing day
More than Octavius and Mark Antony
By this vile conquest shall attain unto.   38
So fare you well at once, for Brutus' tongue   39
Hath almost ended his life's history.
Night hangs upon mine eyes; my bones would rest,
That have but labored to attain this hour.   42
         Alarum. Cry within, "Fly, fly, fly!"
CLITUS
Fly, my lord, fly!
BRUTUS   Hence, I will follow.
     [*Exeunt Clitus, Dardanius, and Volumnius.*]
I prithee, Strato, stay thou by thy lord.
Thou art a fellow of a good respect;   45
Thy life hath had some smatch of honor in it.   46
Hold then my sword, and turn away thy face,
While I do run upon it. Wilt thou, Strato?
STRATO
Give me your hand first. Fare you well, my lord.

23 beat driven. **pit** trap for wild animals; also, a grave   **27 that, our
love** that friendship of ours   **28 hilts** i.e., hilt   **29 office** duty   **38 vile**
paltry   **39 at once** all together   **42 That . . . hour** i.e., all their striving
has been toward this moment of death   **45 respect** reputation   **46 some
smatch** some flavor, a touch

BRUTUS
    Farewell, good Strato. [*He runs on his sword.*] Caesar,
      now be still.
    I killed not thee with half so good a will.   *Dies.* 51

      Alarum. Retreat. Enter Antony, Octavius; Messala,
      Lucilius [as prisoners]; and the army.

OCTAVIUS   What man is that?
MESSALA
    My master's man. Strato, where is thy master?
STRATO
    Free from the bondage you are in, Messala.
    The conquerors can but make a fire of him,
    For Brutus only overcame himself,   56
    And no man else hath honor by his death.
LUCILIUS
    So Brutus should be found. I thank thee, Brutus,
    That thou hast proved Lucilius' saying true.   59
OCTAVIUS
    All that served Brutus, I will entertain them.   60
    Fellow, wilt thou bestow thy time with me?
STRATO
    Ay, if Messala will prefer me to you.   62
OCTAVIUS   Do so, good Messala.
MESSALA   How died my master, Strato?
STRATO
    I held the sword, and he did run on it.
MESSALA
    Octavius, then take him to follow thee,   66
    That did the latest service to my master.   67
ANTONY
    This was the noblest Roman of them all.
    All the conspirators save only he
    Did that they did in envy of great Caesar;   70
    He only in a general honest thought
    And common good to all made one of them.

51 s.d. Retreat signal to retire 56 Brutus . . . himself only Brutus
conquered Brutus 59 saying (See 5.4.21–25.) 60 entertain take into
service 62 prefer recommend 66 follow serve 67 latest last 70 that
what. envy of malice toward

His life was gentle, and the elements   73
So mixed in him that Nature might stand up
And say to all the world, "This was a man!"
OCTAVIUS
According to his virtue let us use him,
With all respect and rites of burial.
Within my tent his bones tonight shall lie,
Most like a soldier, ordered honorably.   79
So call the field to rest, and let's away   80
To part the glories of this happy day.   81

Exeunt omnes [with Brutus' body].

73 gentle noble.   **elements** (Man as a microcosm is made up of earth, air, fire, and water, whose qualities were mingled in Brutus in due proportions.)   **79 ordered** treated, arranged for   **80 field** army in the field   **81 part** share   **s.d. omnes** all

Date and Text

Julius Caesar was first published in the First Folio of 1623. The text is an excellent one, based evidently on a theater promptbook or a transcript of it. In the Folio the play is included among the tragedies and entitled *The Tragedy of Julius Caesar*, although the table of contents lists it as *The Life and death of Julius Caesar*.

First performance must have occurred in 1599 or slightly earlier. On September 21, 1599, a Swiss visitor named Thomas Platter crossed the Thames River after lunch with a company of spectators to see "the tragedy of the first Emperor Julius Caesar" performed in a thatched-roofed building. The description fits the Globe, the Rose, and the Swan theaters, but the last of these was not in regular use. The Admiral's men at the Rose are not known to have had a Caesar play, whereas the Chamberlain's men certainly had Shakespeare's play about this time. They had only recently moved from their Theatre in the northeast suburbs of London to the Globe south of the river, and *Julius Caesar* and *Henry V* were probably new plays for the occasion.

John Weever, in *The Mirror of Martyrs* (1601), is surely referring to Shakespeare's play when he describes "the many-headed multitude" listening first to "Brutus' speech that Caesar was ambitious" and then to "eloquent Mark Antony." (The dedication to Weever's book claims he wrote it "some two years ago," in 1599: but since this book has been shown to be heavily indebted to a work that first appeared in 1600, Weever's allusion is not as helpful in limiting the date as was once thought.) Ben Jonson's *Every Man in His Humor*, acted in 1599, may also contain allusions to Shakespeare's play.

Textual Notes

These textual notes are not a historical collation, either of the early folios or of more recent editions; they are simply a record of departures in this edition from the copy text. The reading adopted in this edition appears in bold face, followed by the rejected reading from the copy text, i.e., the First Folio. Only major alterations in punctuation are noted. Changes in lineation are not indicated, nor are some minor and obvious typographical errors.

Abbreviations used:
F the First Folio
s.d. stage direction
s.p. speech prefix

Copy text: the First Folio.

1.1. s.d. [and elsewhere] Marullus Murellus   **37 Pompey . . . oft** Pompey many a time and oft?

1.2. s.d. [and elsewhere] Calpurnia Calphurnia   **3, 4, 6 Antonius', Antonius** Antonio's, Antonio [also l. 190 and 1.3.37]   **24 s.d. Manent** Manet

1.3. 129 In Is

2.1. 40 ides first   **67 of** of a   **122 women, then,** women. Then   **136 oath, when** Oath. When   **214 eighth** eight   **268 his** hit   **281 the** tho   **310 s.d. Enter Lucius** etc. [after "with haste" in l. 310 in F]   **314 s.p. [and through l. 332] Ligarius** Cai

2.2. 23 did neigh do neigh   **46 are** heare

2.3. 1 s.p. Artemidorus [not in F]

3.1. 40 law lane   **114 states** State   **116 lies** lye   **256 s.p. Antony** [not in F] **277 s.d. Octavius'** Octauio's [also at 5.2.4]   **285 for** from

3.2. 106 art are   **205 s.p. All** [not in F]   **222 wit** writ   **260 s.d. Exeunt** Exit **262 s.d. Enter Servant** [after "fellow" in F]

4.2. 34–36 s.p. First, Second, Third Soldier [not in F]   **50 Lucius** Lucillius **52 Lucilius** Lucius   **s.d. Manent** Manet

4.3. 209 off off   **230 s.d. Enter Lucius** [before l. 230 in F]   **244, 246 [and throughout] Claudius** Claudio   **246 [and throughout] Varro** Varrus   **252 will** will it   **303, 307 s.p. Varro, Claudius** Both

5.1. 42 teeth teethes   **67 s.d. Exeunt** Exit   **70** [F has s.d.: "Lucillius and Messala stand forth"]   **71 s.p. Lucilius (Stands forth)** Luc   **73 s.p. Messala (Stands forth)** Messa

5.3. 104 Thasos Tharsus   **108 Flavius** Flauio

5.4. 7 s.p. Lucilius [not in F]   **9 O** Luc. O   **12, 15 s.p. First Soldier** Sold **16 s.d. Enter Antony** [before l. 16 in F]   **17 the news** thee newes   **30 whe'er** where

5.5. 77 With all Withall

Shakespeare's Sources

Julius Caesar represents Shakespeare's first extensive use of the work of the first-century Greek biographer Plutarch, in Thomas North's translation (based on the French, of Jacques Amyot) of *The Lives of the Noble Grecians and Romans* (1579 and 1595). Plutarch was to become Shakespeare's most often used source in the 1600s; prior to 1599 he had consulted it briefly on a number of other occasions. In *Julius Caesar*, he borrows details from three lives: Caesar, Brutus, and Antonius. He uses particular traits of character, such as Caesar's belief that it is "better to die once than always to be afraid of death," Brutus' determination to "frame his manners of life by the rules of virtue and study of philosophy," Cassius' choleric disposition and his "hating Caesar privately more than he did the tyranny openly," and Antonius' inclination to "rioting and banqueting."

The events of the play are substantially present in Plutarch, especially in "The Life of Julius Caesar" (as can be seen in the selection that follows). Antonius runs the course on the Feast of Lupercal to cure barrenness and offers the diadem to Caesar. Flavius and Marullus despoil the images of Caesar. Caesar observes that he mistrusts pale and lean men such as Brutus and Cassius. Papers are thrown by the conspirators where Brutus can find them, proclaiming "Thou sleepest, Brutus, and art not Brutus indeed." Caesar's death is preceded by prodigies: a slave's hand burns but is unconsumed, a sacrificial beast is found to contain no heart. When Caesar encounters the soothsayer who previously had warned him of his fate and boasts that "the ides of March be come," the soothsayer has the last word: "So be they, but yet are they not past." Brutus' wife Portia complains to him of being treated "like a harlot," not like a partner. Brutus commits what Plutarch calls two serious errors when he forbids his fellow conspirators to kill Antonius and when he permits Antonius to speak at Caesar's funeral. Cinna the Poet is slain by an angry crowd mistaking him for Cinna the conspirator. A ghost appears to Brutus shortly before the last battle saying, "I am thy ill angel, Brutus, and thou shalt see me by the city of Phillippes," to which Brutus replies, "Well, I shall see thee then." Antonius says of the vanquished conspirators that "there was none but Brutus only that was moved to do it, as thinking the act commendable of itself: but that all the other conspirators did conspire his death for some private malice or envy." Shakespeare's debt to Plutarch is greater than these few examples can indicate.

Of course Shakespeare reshapes and selects, as in his history plays. He compresses into one day Caesar's triumphant procession, the disrobing of the images, and the offer of the crown to Caesar on the Lupercal, when in fact these events were chronologically separate. Casca is by and large an invented character, and Octavius' role is considerably enlarged. Brutus' servant Lucius is a minor but effective addition, illustrating Brutus' capacity for warmth and humanity. Shakespeare accentuates the irrationality and vacillation of the mob, for in Plutarch the people are never much swayed by Brutus' rhetoric even though they respectfully allow him to speak. They are aroused to violence, in Plutarch's account, not by Antony's speech but by the revelation of Caesar's will and the sight of his mangled body. In fact, the unforgettable speeches of Brutus and Antony are not set down at all in Plutarch. More compression of time occurs after the assassination: in Plutarch, Octavius does not arrive in Rome until some six weeks afterward and does not agree to the formation of the Triumvirate until more than a year of quarreling has taken place. The inexorable buildup of tension in Shakespeare's play is the result of careful selection from a vast amount of material. Shakespeare's borrowing from "The Life of Marcus Brutus" is no less extensive and is at the same time reshaped and given new emphasis, as can be seen in the selection that follows.

Although Shakespeare depended heavily on Plutarch, he was also aware of later and conflicting traditions about Caesar. On the one hand, Dante's *Divine Comedy* (c. 1310–1321) consigns Brutus and Cassius to the lowest circle of hell along with Judas Iscariot and other betrayers of their masters. Geoffrey Chaucer's "The Monk's Tale," from the *Canterbury Tales*, similarly portrays Caesar as the manly and uncorruptible victim of envious attackers. On the other hand, Montaigne stresses the hubris of Caesar in aspiring to divinity. (Shakespeare could have read Montaigne in the French original, or, if he had access to a manuscript, in John Florio's English translation, published in 1603.) A pro-Brutus view could also be found in the Latin *Julius Caesar* of Marc-Antoine Muret (1553) and the French *César* of Jacques Grévin (1561). That Shakespeare knew these works is unlikely, but they kept alive a tradition with which he was certainly familiar. Possibly he knew such Roman works as Lucan's account of Caesar in the *Pharsalia* and Cicero's letters and orations, which were republican in tenor. Other possible sources include the *Chronicle of the Romans' Wars* by Appian of Alexandria (translated 1578), the anonymous play *Caesar's Revenge* (published 1606–1607, performed in the early 1590s at Oxford), and Thomas Kyd's *Cornelia* (translated from the French Senecan tragedy by Garnier). *Il Cesare* by Orlando Pescetti (1594) is now almost universally rejected as a possible source. The result of Shakespeare's acquaintance with both pro- and anti-Caesar traditions is that he subordinates his own political vision to a balanced presentation of history, showing the significant strengths and disabling weaknesses in both Caesar and the conspirators.

The Lives of the Noble Grecians and Romans Compared Together by . . . Plutarch

Translated by Thomas North

FROM THE LIFE OF JULIUS CAESAR

[Plutarch surveys the whole of Julius Caesar's early career: his first consulship, his conquests in Gaul and England, his crossing the Rubicon, his defeat of Pompey the Great at Pharsalia, his making Cleopatra Queen of Egypt, his *"Veni, vidi, vici,"* "I came, I saw, I conquered," after his victory over King Pharnaces, his being chosen perpetual dictator, and his enemies' resentment toward his growing power and ambition.]

But the chiefest cause that made him mortally hated was the covetous desire he had to be called king, which first gave the people just cause, and next his secret enemies honest color,[1] to bear him ill will. This notwithstanding, they that procured him this honor and dignity gave it out[2] among the people that it was written in the Sybilline prophecies how the Romans might overcome the Parthians if they made war with them and were led by a king, but otherwise that they[3] were unconquerable. And furthermore they[4] were so bold besides that, Caesar returning to Rome from the city of Alba, when they came to salute him, they called him king. But the people being offended, and Caesar also angry, he said he was not called king, but Caesar. Then every man keeping silence, he went his way heavy[5] and sorrowful.

When they had decreed divers honors for him in the Senate, the consuls and praetors, accompanied with[6] the whole assembly of the Senate, went unto him in the marketplace, where he was set by the pulpit for orations,[7] to tell him what honors they had decreed for him in his absence. But he, sitting still in his majesty, disdaining to rise up unto them when they came in, as if they had been private men, answered them that his honors had more need to be cut off

1 **color** excuse   2 **gave it out** let it be known   3 **they** i.e., the Parthians
4 **they** i.e., Caesar's supporters   5 **heavy** sad, pensive   6 **with** by   7 **was
set . . . orations** sat beside the pulpit used for public orations

than enlarged. This did not only offend the Senate but the common people also, to see that he should so lightly esteem of[8] the magistrates of the commonwealth, insomuch as every man that might lawfully go his way departed thence very sorrowfully. Thereupon also Caesar, rising, departed home to his house and, tearing open his doublet collar, making his neck bare, he cried out aloud to his friends that his throat was ready to offer to any man that would come and cut it. Notwithstanding it is reported that afterwards, to excuse this folly, he imputed it to his disease, saying that their wits are not perfect which have his disease of the falling evil[9] when, standing of their feet, they speak to the common people but are soon troubled with a trembling of their body and a sudden dimness and giddiness. But that was not true, for he would have risen up to the Senate, but Cornelius Balbus, one of his friends (but rather a flatterer), would not let him, saying: "What, do you not remember that you are Caesar, and will you not let them reverence you and do their duties?"

Besides these occasions[10] and offenses, there followed also his shame and reproach, abusing the tribunes of the people in this sort. At that time the feast Lupercalia was celebrated, the which in old time men say was the feast of shepherds or herdmen and is much like unto the feast of the Lycaeans in Arcadia. But howsoever it is, that day there are divers noblemen's sons, young men, and some of them magistrates themselves that govern then, which run naked through the city, striking in sport them they meet in their way with leather thongs, hair and all on, to make them give place.[11] And many noblewomen and gentlewomen also go of purpose[12] to stand in their way and do put forth their hands to be stricken, as scholars hold them out to their schoolmaster to be stricken with the ferula,[13] persuading themselves that, being[14] with child, they shall have good delivery, and also, being barren,[15] that it will make them to conceive with child. Caesar sat to behold that sport upon the pulpit for orations in a chair of gold, appareled in triumphing

---

8 esteem of esteem   **9 the falling evil** epilepsy   **10 occasions** grounds
(for disapproval)   **11 give place** move out of the way   **12 of purpose**
with intent   **13 ferula** cane or rod used as an instrument of punishment
14 being if they are   **15 also, being barren** and if they are barren

manner. Antonius, who was consul at that time, was one of them that ran this holy course. So when he came into the marketplace, the people made a lane for him to run at liberty,[16] and he came to Caesar and presented him a diadem wreathed about with laurel. Whereupon there rose a certain cry of rejoicing, not very great, done only by a few appointed[17] for the purpose. But when Caesar refused the diadem, then all the people together made an outcry of joy. Then Antonius offering it him again, there was a second shout of joy, but yet of a few. But when Caesar refused it again the second time, then all the whole people shouted. Caesar having made this proof[18] found that the people did not like of it, and thereupon rose out of his chair and commanded the crown to be carried unto Jupiter in the Capitol.

After that, there were set up images of Caesar in the city with diadems upon their heads, like kings. Those the two tribunes, Flavius and Marullus, went and pulled down, and furthermore, meeting with them that first saluted Caesar as king, they committed them to prison. The people followed them rejoicing at it and called them Brutes, because of Brutus who had in old time driven the kings out of Rome and that brought the kingdom of one person unto the government of the Senate and people. Caesar was so offended withal that he deprived Marullus and Flavius of their tribuneships, and accusing them, he spake also against the people and called them Bruti and Cumani, to wit, beasts and fools.

Hereupon the people went straight unto Marcus Brutus, who from his father came of[19] the first Brutus and by his mother of the house of the Servilians, a noble house as any was in Rome, and was also nephew and son-in-law of Marcus Cato. Notwithstanding, the great honors and favor Caesar showed unto him kept him back that of himself alone[20] he did not conspire nor consent to depose him of his kingdom. For Caesar did not only save[21] his life after the Battle of Pharsalia, when Pompey fled, and did at his request also save many more of his friends besides, but furthermore he put a marvelous confidence in him. For he had already pre-

16 at liberty where he wished   **17 appointed** agreed upon, designated
18 proof test   **19 came of** was descended from   **20 that . . . alone** so
that as far as he himself was concerned   **21 save** spare

ferred him[22] to the praetorship for that year and furthermore was[23] appointed to be consul the fourth year after
that, having through Caesar's friendship obtained it before
Cassius, who likewise made suit for the same; and Caesar
also, as it is reported, said in this contention, "Indeed Cassius hath alleged best reason, but yet shall he not be chosen
before Brutus." Some one day[24] accusing Brutus while he
practiced[25] this conspiracy, Caesar would not hear of it, but,
clapping his hand on his body, told them, "Brutus will look
for this skin"—meaning thereby that Brutus for his virtue
deserved to rule after him, but yet that, for ambition's sake,
he would not[26] show himself unthankful or dishonorable.

Now, they that desired change and wished Brutus only
their prince and governor above all other, they durst not
come to him themselves to tell him what they would have
him to do, but in the night did cast sundry papers into the
praetor's seat, where he gave audience, and the most of
them to this effect: "Thou sleepest, Brutus, and art not Brutus indeed." Cassius, finding Brutus' ambition stirred up
the more by these seditious bills,[27] did prick[28] him forward
and egg him on the more for a private quarrel he had conceived against Caesar, the circumstance whereof we have
set down more at large[29] in Brutus' life. Caesar also had
Cassius in great jealousy[30] and suspected him much, whereupon he said on a time[31] to his friends, "What will Cassius
do, think ye? I like not his pale looks." Another time when
Caesar's friends complained unto him of Antonius and Do-
labella, that they pretended[32] some mischief towards him,
he answered them again, "As for those fat men and smooth-
combed heads," quoth he, "I never reckon of them; but
these pale-visaged and carrion lean people, I fear them
most"—meaning Brutus and Cassius.

Certainly destiny may easier be foreseen than avoided,
considering the strange and wonderful[33] signs that were

---

22 **he had already preferred him** i.e., Caesar had already advanced or
promoted Brutus   23 **was** i.e., he, Brutus, was   24 **Some one day** one
day when some persons were   25 **practiced** plotted   26 **for
ambition's . . . not** he would not simply for ambition's sake   27 **bills**
letters, papers   28 **prick** spur   29 **at large** in detail   30 **had Cassius in
great jealousy** i.e., kept a wary eye on Cassius   31 **on a time** on one
occasion   32 **pretended** intended, plotted   33 **wonderful** wondrous

said to be seen before Caesar's death. For, touching the fires in the element[34] and spirits running up and down in the night, and also these solitary birds[35] to be seen at noondays sitting in the great marketplace, are not all these signs perhaps worth the noting, in such a wonderful chance as happened? But Strabo[36] the philosopher writeth that divers men were seen going up and down in fire, and furthermore that there was a slave of the soldiers that did cast a marvelous burning flame out of his hand, insomuch as they that saw it thought he had been burnt, but when the fire was out it was found he had no hurt. Caesar self[37] also, doing sacrifice unto the gods, found that one of the beasts which was sacrificed had no heart; and that was a strange thing in nature, how a beast could live without a heart.

Furthermore there was a certain soothsayer that had given Caesar warning long time afore to take heed of the day of the ides of March, which is the fifteenth of the month, for on that day he should be in great danger. That day being come, Caesar, going unto the Senate House and speaking merrily to the soothsayer, told him, "The ides of March be come." "So be they," softly answered the soothsayer, "but yet are they not past." And the very day before, Caesar, supping with Marcus Lepidus, sealed certain letters, as he was wont to do, at the board.[38] So, talk falling out amongst them[39] reasoning what death was best, he, preventing their opinions,[40] cried out aloud, "Death unlooked-for."

Then going to bed the same night, as his manner was, and lying with his wife Calpurnia, all the windows and doors of his chamber flying open, the noise awoke him and made him afraid when he saw such light, but more when he heard his wife Calpurnia, being fast asleep, weep and sigh and put forth many fumbling[41] lamentable speeches; for she dreamed that Caesar was slain and that she had him in her arms. Others also do deny that she had any such dream,[42]

---

34 touching . . . element as regards fires in the sky   **35 these solitary birds** i.e., owls   **36 Strabo** Stoic traveler and writer, c. 64 B.C.–A.D. 19   **37 self** himself   **38 board** dinner table   **39 talk . . . them** their talk happening to turn to the topic   **40 preventing their opinions** anticipating what they might say, speaking first   **41 fumbling** incoherent   **42 do deny . . . dream** i.e., deny that the dream took this particular form

as, amongst other, Titus Livius writeth that it was in this sort: the Senate having set upon the top of Caesar's house for an ornament and setting forth[43] of the same a certain pinnacle, Calpurnia dreamed that she saw it broken down and that she thought she lamented and wept for it. Insomuch that, Caesar rising in the morning, she prayed him if it were possible not to go out of the doors that day but to adjourn the session of the Senate until another day. And if that he made no reckoning of her dream, yet that he would search further of the soothsayers by their sacrifices to know what should happen him that day. Thereby it seemed that Caesar likewise did fear or suspect somewhat, because his wife Calpurnia until that time was never given to any fear or superstition and then for that[44] he saw her so troubled in mind with this dream she had. But much more afterwards, when the soothsayers, having sacrificed many beasts one after another, told him that none did like[45] them, then he determined to send Antonius to adjourn the session of the Senate.

But in the meantime came Decius Brutus, surnamed Albinus, in whom Caesar put such confidence that in his last will and testament he had appointed him to be his next heir, and yet was of the conspiracy with Cassius and Brutus. He, fearing that if Caesar did adjourn the session that day the conspiracy would be out, laughed the soothsayers to scorn and reproved Caesar, saying that he gave the Senate occasion to mislike with him[46] and that they might think he mocked them, considering that by his commandment they were assembled, and that they were ready willingly to grant him all things and to proclaim him king of all his provinces of the Empire of Rome out of Italy, and that he should wear his diadem in all other places both by sea and land. And furthermore that if any man should tell them from him they should[47] depart for that present time and return again when Calpurnia should have better dreams, what would his enemies and ill-willers[48] say and how could they like of[49] his friends' words? And who could persuade them otherwise

---

43 **setting forth** decorating   44 **for that** because   45 **like** satisfy, please
46 **mislike with him** disapprove of him   47 **tell . . . should** tell them as coming from Caesar that they, the Senators, were to   48 **ill-willers** evil-wishers   49 **like of** approve, believe, trust

but that they would think his dominion a slavery unto them and tyrannical in himself? "And yet if it be so," said he, "that you utterly mislike of[50] this day, it is better that you go yourself in person and, saluting the Senate, to dismiss them till another time." Therewithal he took Caesar by the hand and brought him out of his house.

Caesar was not gone far from his house but a bondman, a stranger, did what he could to speak with him; and when he saw he was put back by the great press and multitude of people that followed him, he went straight unto his house and put himself into Calpurnia's hands to be kept till Caesar came back again, telling her that he had great matters to impart unto him. And one Artemidorus also, born in the isle of Gnidos, a Doctor of Rhetoric in the Greek tongue, who by means of his profession was very familiar with certain of Brutus' confederates and therefore knew the most part of all their practices[51] against Caesar, came and brought him a little bill[52] written with his own hand of all that he meant to tell him. He, marking how Caesar received all the supplications that were offered him and that he gave them straight[53] to his men that were about him, pressed nearer to him and said: "Caesar, read this memorial[54] to yourself, and that quickly, for they be matters of great weight and touch you nearly." Caesar took it of him, but could never read it, though he many times attempted it, for the number of people that did salute him, but holding it still in his hand, keeping it to himself, went on withal into the Senate House. Howbeit others are of opinion that it was some man else that gave him that memorial and not Artemidorus, who did what he could all the way as he went to give it Caesar, but he was always repulsed by the people.

For these things, they may seem to come by chance;[55] but the place where the murder was prepared and where the Senate were assembled, and where also there stood up an image of Pompey dedicated by himself amongst other ornaments which he gave unto the theater—all these were manifest proofs that it was the ordinance of some god that made

50 mislike of disapprove of, mistrust   **51 practices** conspiracies   **52 bill** memorandum   **53 straight** immediately   **54 memorial** memorandum **55 For these . . . chance** as for these things, they may seem to occur merely by chance

this treason to be executed specially in that very place. It is also reported that Cassius, though otherwise he did favor the doctrine of Epicurus, beholding the image of Pompey before they entered into the action of their traitorous enterprise, he did softly call upon it to aid him; but the instant danger of the present time, taking away his former reason, did suddenly put him into a furious passion and made him like a man half beside himself.

Now Antonius, that was a faithful friend to Caesar and a valiant man besides of his hands,[56] him Decius Brutus Albinus entertained out of[57] the Senate House, having begun a long tale of set purpose.[58] So Caesar coming into the house, all the Senate stood up on their feet to do him honor. Then part of Brutus' company and confederates stood round about Caesar's chair, and part of them also came towards him as though they made suit with Metellus Cimber to call home his brother again from banishment. And thus prosecuting still their suit, they followed Caesar till he was set in his chair. Who, denying their petitions and being offended with them one after another because the more they were denied the more they pressed upon him and were the earnester with him, Metellus at length, taking his gown with both his hands, pulled it over his neck, which was the sign given the confederates to set upon him.

Then Casca, behind him, strake him[59] in the neck with his sword. Howbeit the wound was not great nor mortal, because it seemed the fear of such a devilish attempt did amaze him[60] and take his strength from him, that he killed him not at the first blow. But Caesar, turning straight unto him, caught hold of his sword and held it hard; and they both cried out, Caesar in Latin: "O vile traitor Casca, what dost thou?" and Casca, in Greek, to his brother: "Brother, help me!" At the beginning of this stir, they that were present, not knowing of the conspiracy, were so amazed with the horrible sight they saw that they had no power to fly, neither to help him nor so much as once to make an outcry. They on the other side that had conspired his death com-

56 of his hands i.e., with his weapons, in hand-to-hand combat
57 entertained out of engaged, held in conversation outside of   58 of
set purpose devised for the occasion   59 strake him i.e., struck Caesar
60 amaze him i.e., dazzle Casca

passed him in on every side with their swords drawn in their hands, that Caesar turned him nowhere but he was stricken at by some and still had naked swords in his face, and was hacked and mangled among them as[61] a wild beast taken of[62] hunters. For it was agreed among them that every man should give him a wound, because all their parts should be[63] in this murder. And then Brutus himself gave him one wound about his privities. Men report also that Caesar did still[64] defend himself against the rest, running every way with his body; but when he saw Brutus with his sword drawn in his hand, then he pulled his gown over his head and made no more resistance, and was driven either casually or purposedly[65] by the counsel of the conspirators against the base whereupon Pompey's image stood, which ran all of a gore blood[66] till he was slain. Thus it seemed that the image took just revenge of Pompey's enemy, being thrown down on the ground at his feet and yielding up his ghost there for[67] the number of wounds he had upon him. For it is reported that he had three-and-twenty wounds upon his body; and divers of the conspirators did hurt themselves, striking one body with so many blows.

When Caesar was slain, the Senate (though Brutus stood in the midst amongst them, as though he would have said something touching this fact[68]) presently[69] ran out of the house and, flying, filled all the city with marvelous[70] fear and tumult. Insomuch as some did shut to their doors, others forsook their shops and warehouses, and others ran to the place to see what the matter was; and others also that had seen it ran home to their houses again. But Antonius and Lepidus, which were two of Caesar's chiefest friends, secretly conveying themselves away, fled into other men's houses and forsook their own.

Brutus and his confederates on the other side, being yet hot with this murder they had committed, having their swords drawn in their hands, came all in a troop together out of the Senate and went into the marketplace, not as men

---

61 as like   **62 of** by   **63 all their parts should be** they should all take part   **64 still** continually   **65 purposedly** purposely   **66 of a gore blood** all covered with blood   **67 for** because of   **68 fact** deed   **69 presently** immediately   **70 marvelous** inspired by astonishment and the supernatural

that made countenance to fly, but otherwise[71] boldly holding up their heads like men of courage, and called to the people to defend their liberty, and stayed to speak with every great personage whom they met in their way. Of them, some followed this troop and went amongst them as if they had been of the conspiracy, and falsely challenged[72] part of the honor with them; among them was Caius Octavius and Lentulus Spinther. But both of them were afterwards put to death for their vain covetousness of honor by Antonius and Octavius Caesar the younger, and yet had no part of that honor for the which they were put to death, neither did any man believe that they were any of the confederates or of counsel with them. For they that did put them to death took revenge rather of the will they had to offend[73] than of any fact[74] they had committed.

The next morning Brutus and his confederates came into the marketplace to speak unto the people, who gave them such audience that it seemed they neither greatly reproved nor allowed the fact;[75] for by their great silence they showed that they were sorry for Caesar's death and also that they did reverence Brutus. Now, the Senate granted general pardon for all that was past, and to pacify every man ordained besides that Caesar's funerals should be honored as a god,[76] and established[77] all things that he had done, and gave certain provinces also and convenient honors unto Brutus and his confederates, whereby every man thought all things were brought to good peace and quietness again.

But when they had opened Caesar's testament[78] and found a liberal legacy of money bequeathed unto every citizen of Rome, and that[79] they saw his body (which was brought into the marketplace) all bemangled[80] with gashes of swords, then there was no order to keep the multitude and common people quiet, but they plucked up forms,[81] ta-

71 **made countenance to fly, but otherwise** looked as though they were about to flee, but to the contrary   72 **challenged** claimed   73 **of the will . . . offend** i.e., for their having wanted to be part of the conspiracy   74 **fact** deed   75 **allowed the fact** approved of the deed   76 **as a god** as if he were a god   77 **established** enacted permanently   78 **testament** will   79 **that** i.e., when   80 **bemangled** mangled   81 **forms** benches

bles, and stools and laid them all about the body and, setting them afire, burnt the corpse. Then when the fire was well kindled, they took the firebrands and went unto their houses that had slain Caesar to set them afire.[82] Other[83] also ran up and down the city to see if they could meet with any of them to cut them in pieces; howbeit, they could meet with never a man of them because they had locked themselves up safely in their houses.

There was one of Caesar's friends called Cinna that had a marvelous strange and terrible dream the night before. He dreamed that Caesar bade him to supper and that he refused and would not go; then that Caesar took him by the hand and led him against his will. Now Cinna, hearing at that time that they burnt Caesar's body in the marketplace, notwithstanding that he feared his dream and had an ague on him besides, he went into the marketplace to honor his funerals. When he came thither, one of the mean sort[84] asked what his name was. He was straight called by his name. The first man told it to another and that other unto another, so that it ran straight through them all that he was one of them that murdered Caesar; for indeed one of the traitors to Caesar was also called Cinna as[85] himself. Wherefore taking him for Cinna the murderer they fell upon him with such fury that they presently dispatched him in the marketplace.

This stir and fury made Brutus and Cassius more afraid than of all that was past,[86] and therefore within few days after[87] they departed out of Rome. And touching their doings afterwards, and what calamity they suffered till their deaths, we have written it at large in the life of Brutus. Caesar died at six-and-fifty years of age, and Pompey also lived not passing[88] four years more than he. So he reaped no other fruit of all his reign and dominion, which he had so vehemently desired all his life and pursued with such extreme danger, but a vain name only and a superficial glory that procured him the envy and hatred of his country.

But his great prosperity and good fortune that favored

---

82 went . . . afire went to the houses of those who had slain Caesar and set those houses afire   **83 Other** others   **84 of the mean sort** of lower station   **85 as** like   **86 was past** was happening, had happened   **87 after** afterward   **88 passing** exceeding

him all his lifetime did continue afterwards in the revenge of his death, pursuing the murderers both by sea and land till they had not left a man more to be executed of all them that were actors or counselors in the conspiracy of his death. Furthermore, of all the chances that happen unto men upon the earth, that which came to Cassius above all other is most to be wondered at; for he, being overcome in battle at the journey of Philippes, slew himself with the same sword with the which he strake[89] Caesar. Again, of signs in the element[90] the great comet, which seven nights together was seen very bright after Caesar's death, the eighth night after was never seen more. Also the brightness of the sun was darkened, the which all that year through rose very pale and shined not out, whereby it gave but small heat; therefore the air being very cloudy and dark, by the weakness of the heat that could not come forth, did cause the earth to bring forth but raw and unripe fruit which rotted before it could ripe.

But above all, the ghost that appeared unto Brutus showed plainly that the gods were offended with the murder of Caesar. The vision was thus: Brutus, being ready to pass over his army from the city of Abydos to the other coast lying directly against it,[91] slept every night as his manner was in his tent; and being yet awake, thinking of his affairs (for by report he was as careful a captain[92] and lived with as little sleep as ever man did), he thought he heard a noise at his tent door, and looking towards the light of the lamp that waxed very dim, he saw a horrible vision of a man, of a wonderful[93] greatness and dreadful look, which at the first made him marvelously afraid. But when he saw that it did him no hurt but stood by his bedside and said nothing, at length he asked him what he was. The image answered him: "I am thy ill angel, Brutus, and thou shalt see me by the city of Philippes." Then Brutus replied again and said, "Well, I shall see thee then." Therewithal the spirit presently[94] vanished from him.

After that time Brutus, being in battle near unto the city

---

89 strake struck   **90 element** sky, heavens   **91 against it** opposite it (across the Hellespont)   **92 as careful a captain** as watchful and attentive to duty a commanding officer   **93 wonderful** wondrous   **94 presently** immediately

of Philippes against Antonius and Octavius Caesar, at the first battle he wan[95] the victory, and overthrowing all them that withstood him he drave[96] them into young Caesar's camp, which he took. The second battle being at hand, this spirit appeared again unto him but spake never a word. Thereupon Brutus, knowing he should die, did put himself to all hazard in battle, but yet fighting could not be slain. So seeing his men put to flight and overthrown, he ran unto a little rock not far off and there, setting his sword's point to his breast, fell upon it and slew himself; but yet, as it is reported, with the help of his friend that dispatched him.

Text based on *The Lives of the Noble Grecians and Romans Compared Together by That Grave, Learned Philosopher and Historiographer, Plutarch of Chaeronea. Translated out of Greek into French by James Amyot . . . and out of French into English by Thomas North. . . . Thomas Vautroullier . . . 1579.*

95 wan won   **96 drave** drove

The Lives of the Noble Grecians and Romans Compared Together by . . . Plutarch

Translated by Thomas North

FROM THE LIFE OF MARCUS BRUTUS

Any departures from the original text are noted with an asterisk and appear at the bottom of the page in boldface; original readings are in roman.

[After the assassination of Julius Caesar, the triumvirs, Octavius Caesar, Antonius, and Lepidus, divide the Empire of Rome among themselves. Brutus and Cassius meanwhile take their armies into the Middle East, forming alliances and gathering support for their cause. Friction develops between them over Brutus' concern that Cassius is too ready to conquer for his own glory and profit when their only purpose ought to be to free Italy from the dictatorship of the triumvirs. The nations that yield to Brutus, such as the Patareians, find themselves humanely treated.]

So after they had thus yielded themselves, divers other cities also followed them and did the like, and found Brutus more merciful and courteous than they thought they should have done, but specially far above Cassius. For Cassius, about the selfsame time, after he had compelled the Rhodians every man to deliver all the ready money they had in gold and silver in their houses, the which being brought together amounted to the sum of eight thousand talents, yet he condemned the city besides to pay the sum of five hundred talents more. Where Brutus, in contrary manner, after he had levied of all the country of Lycia but a hundred and fifty talents only, he departed thence into the country of Ionia and did them no more hurt. Now Brutus in all this journey did many notable acts and worthy of memory, both for rewarding as also in punishing those that had deserved it. . . .

About that time, Brutus sent to pray Cassius to come to the city of Sardis, and so he did. Brutus, understanding of his coming, went to meet him with all his friends. There, both their armies being armed, they called them both emperors. Now, as it commonly happeneth in great affairs between two persons, both of them having many friends and so many captains under them, there ran tales and complaints betwixt them. Therefore, before they fell in hand with[1] any other matter, they went into a little chamber together, and bade every man avoid[2] and did shut the doors to them. Then they began to pour out their complaints one to the other and grew hot and loud, earnestly accusing one another, and at length fell both a-weeping. Their friends that were without[3] the chamber, hearing them loud within and angry between themselves, they were both amazed and afraid also lest it would grow to further matter. But yet they were commanded that no man should come to them.

Notwithstanding, one Marcus Phaonius, that had been a friend and follower of Cato[4] while he lived and took upon him to counterfeit a philosopher—not with wisdom and discretion, but with a certain bedlam[5] and frantic motion—he would needs[6] come into the chamber, though the men offered[7] to keep him out. But it was no boot to let[8] Phaonius when a mad mood or toy[9] took him in the head, for he was a hot, hasty man and sudden in all his doings, and cared for never a senator of them all. Now, though he used this bold manner of speech after the profession of the Cynic philosophers[10] (as who would say,[11] dogs)[12] yet this boldness did no hurt many times, because they did but laugh at him to see him so mad. This Phaonius at that time, in despite of the doorkeepers, came into the chamber, and with a certain scoffing and mocking gesture, which he counterfeited of purpose,[13] he rehearsed[14] the verses which old Nestor said in Homer:

> My lords, I pray you, hearken both to me,
> For I have seen more years than such ye three.

Cassius fell a-laughing at him, but Brutus thrust him out of

---

1 fell in hand with took up   2 avoid go out of the room   3 without outside   4 Cato Roman philosopher, 231–149 B.C., who opposed extravagance and luxury, advocating a return to primitive agricultural simplicity   5 bedlam mad   6 would needs felt it necessary that he, took it upon himself to   7 offered attempted   8 no boot to let useless to hinder   9 toy whim   10 profession of the Cynic philosophers practice or custom among those philosophers known as Cynics (among whose chief tenets was the despising of ease, riches, and fleshly indulgence)   11 as who would say as one might say   12 dogs (Cynic is derived from the Greek kunikos, doglike, currish. Diogenes, the famous Cynic of the fourth century B.C., was renowned for his snarling and biting criticism.)   13 of purpose on purpose   14 rehearsed recited

the chamber and called him dog and counterfeit Cynic. Howbeit his coming in brake their strife at that time, and so they left each other.

The selfsame night, Cassius prepared his supper in his chamber, and Brutus brought his friends with him. So when they were set at supper, Phaonius came to sit down after he had washed. Brutus told him aloud no man sent for him, and bade them set him at the upper end—meaning indeed at the lower end of the bed. Phaonius made no ceremony but thrust in amongst the midst of them and made all the company laugh at him. So they were merry all suppertime and full of their philosophy.

The next day after, Brutus, upon complaint of the Sardians, did condemn and noted[15] Lucius Pella for a defamed person—that had been a praetor of the Romans and whom Brutus had given charge[16] unto—for that he was accused and convicted of robbery and pilfery in his office. This judgment much misliked[17] Cassius, because he himself had secretly (not many days before) warned two of his friends attainted[18] and convicted of the like offenses and openly had cleared them; but yet he did not therefore leave[19] to employ them in any manner of service as he did before. And therefore he greatly reproved Brutus for that he would show himself so straight[20] and severe in such a time as was meeter to bear a little[21] than to take things at the worst.

Brutus in contrary manner answered that he should remember the ides of March, at which time they slew Julius Caesar, who neither pilled nor polled[22] the country but only was a favorer and suborner[23] of all them that did rob and spoil by his countenance and authority.[24] And if there were any occasion whereby they might honestly set aside justice and equity, they should have had more reason to have suffered[25] Caesar's friends to have robbed and done what wrong and injury they had would than to bear with[26] their

---

15 noted publicly disgraced. (See *Julius Caesar*, 4.3.2.) **16 charge** authority **17 misliked** displeased **18 attainted** i.e., charged **19 leave** refrain, leave off **20 straight** rigid **21 as was meeter . . . little** i.e., when it was more suitable to be a little indulgent **22 pilled nor polled** plundered nor pillaged. (The words are synonymous.) **23 suborner** encourager, one who aids and commissions **24 countenance and authority** (Synonymous terms.) **25 suffered** allowed **26 they had would . . . bear with** they had intended than to excuse, tolerate the conduct of

own men. "For then," said he, "they[27] could but have said they[28] had been cowards;[29] and now they may accuse us of injustice, besides the pains we take and the danger we put ourselves into." And thus may we see what Brutus' intent and purpose was.

But as they both prepared to pass over again out of Asia into Europe, there went a rumor that there appeared a wonderful[30] sign unto him. Brutus was a careful[31] man and slept very little, both for that his diet was moderate as also because he was continually occupied. He never slept in the daytime, and in the night no longer than the time he was driven[32] to be alone and when everybody else took their rest. But now, whilst he was in war and his head ever busily occupied to think of his affairs and what would happen, after he had slumbered a little after supper he spent all the rest of the night in dispatching of his weightiest causes; and after he had taken order for them, if he had any leisure left him, he would read some book till the third watch of the night, at what time the captains, petty captains, and colonels did use to come unto him.

So, being ready to go into Europe, one night very late (when all the camp took quiet rest) as he was in his tent with a little light, thinking of weighty matters, he thought he heard one come in to him and, casting his eye towards the door of his tent, that[33] he saw a wonderful strange and monstrous shape of a body coming towards him and said never a word. So Brutus boldly asked what he was, a god or a man, and what cause brought him thither. The spirit answered him, "I am thy evil spirit, Brutus, and thou shalt see me by the city of Philippes." Brutus, being no otherwise afraid, replied again unto it: "Well, then I shall see thee again." The spirit presently vanished away, and Brutus called his men unto him, who told him that they heard no noise nor saw anything at all. Thereupon Brutus returned again to think on his matters as he did before.

And when the day brake, he went unto Cassius to tell him what vision had appeared unto him in the night. Cassius,

---

27 they i.e., people   **28 they** i.e., Brutus and Cassius   **29 cowards** i.e., for not standing up bravely to corruption   **30 wonderful** portentous
31 careful full of cares, watchful, attentive to duty   **32 driven** obliged
33 that i.e., he thought that

being in opinion an Epicurean[34] and reasoning thereon with Brutus, spake to him touching the vision thus: "In our sect, Brutus, we have an opinion that we do not always feel or see that which we suppose we do both see and feel, but that our senses, being credulous and therefore easily abused (when they are idle and unoccupied in their own objects), are induced to imagine they see and conjecture that which they in truth do not. For our mind is quick and cunning to work, without either cause or matter, anything in the imagination whatsoever. And therefore the imagination is resembled to clay and the mind to the potter who, without any other cause than his fancy and pleasure, changeth it into what fashion and form he will. And this doth the diversity of our dreams show unto us. For our imagination doth upon a small fancy grow from conceit[35] to conceit, altering both in passions and forms of things imagined. For the mind of man is ever occupied, and that continual moving[36] is nothing but an imagination.

"But yet there is a further cause of this in you. For, you being by nature given to melancholic discoursing and of late continually occupied, your wits and senses, having been overlabored, do easilier yield to such imaginations. For to say that there are spirits or angels and, if there were, that they had the shape of men, or such voices, or any power at all to come unto us, it is a mockery. And for mine own part I would there were such, because that we should not only have soldiers, horses, and ships but also the aid of the gods to guide and further our honest and honorable attempts." With these words Cassius did somewhat comfort and quiet Brutus.

When they raised[37] their camp, there came two eagles that, flying with a marvelous force, lighted upon two of the foremost ensigns[38] and always followed the soldiers, which[39] gave them meat and fed them until they came near to the city of Philippes. And there, one day only before the battle, they both flew away.

---

34 Epicurean one who maintains that there is nothing to fear from God and nothing to feel in death, that a good life of plain living and virtue is attainable, and that good is knowable only by the senses as an absence of pain   **35 conceit** notion, idea   **36 that continual moving** the continual motion of the mind   **37 raised** struck, ended, took down   **38 ensigns** standards   **39 which** who

Now Brutus had conquered the most part of all the people and nations of that country; but if there were[40] any other city or captain to overcome, then they made all clear before them and so drew towards the coasts of Thasos. There Norbanus,[41] lying in camp in a certain place called the straits by[42] another place called Symbolon (which is a port of the sea), Cassius and Brutus compassed him in[43] in such sort that he was driven to forsake the place which was of great strength for him, and he was also in danger besides to have lost all his army. For Octavius Caesar could not follow him[44] because of his[45] sickness and therefore stayed behind, whereupon they had taken his army had not Antonius' aid been,[46] which made such wonderful speed that Brutus could scant believe it. So Caesar came not thither of[47] ten days after; and Antonius camped against Cassius and Brutus on the other side against Caesar.

The Romans called the valley between both camps the Philippian fields; and there were never seen two so great armies of the Romans, one before[48] the other, ready to fight. In truth, Brutus' army was inferior to Octavius Caesar's in number of men, but for bravery[49] and rich furniture[50] Brutus' army far excelled Caesar's. For the most part of their armors were silver and gilt, which Brutus had bountifully given them, although in all other things he taught his captains to live in order without excess. But for the bravery of armor and weapon which soldiers should carry in their hands or otherwise wear upon their backs, he thought that it was an encouragement unto them that by nature are greedy of honor, and that it maketh them also fight like devils that love to get[51] and be afraid to lose, because they fight to keep their armor and weapon as also their goods and lands.

Now when they came to muster their armies, Octavius Caesar took the muster of his army within the trenches of

40 if there were i.e., in case there were   41 Norbanus a Roman general of the triumvirate stationed at *Thasos*, an island in the northern Aegean off the coast of northeast Greece   42 by nearby   43 compassed him in surrounded him   44 follow him i.e., follow with support for Norbanus   45 his i.e., Caesar's   46 had not Antonius' aid been had it not been for Antonius' aid   47 came not thither of did not arrive there until   48 before facing, in front of   49 bravery splendor   50 furniture equipment   51 get acquire

his camp and gave his men only a little corn and five silver drachmas to every man to sacrifice to the gods and to pray for victory. But Brutus, scorning this misery[52] and niggardliness, first of all mustered his army and did purify it in the fields according to the manner of the Romans, and then he gave unto every band a number of wethers[53] to sacrifice and fifty silver drachmas to every soldier. So that Brutus' and Cassius' soldiers were better pleased and more courageously bent to fight at the day of the battle than their enemies' soldiers were.

Notwithstanding, being busily occupied about the ceremonies of this purification, it is reported that there chanced certain unlucky signs unto Cassius. For one of his sergeants that carried the rods[54] before him brought him the garland of flowers turned backwards, the which he should have worn[55] on his head in the time of sacrificing. Moreover, it is reported also that at another time before, in certain sports and triumphs[56]* where they carried an image of Cassius' victory of clean[57] gold, it fell by chance, the man stumbling that carried it. And yet further, there were seen a marvelous number of fowls of prey that feed upon dead carcasses, and beehives also were found where bees were gathered together in a certain place within the trenches of the camp—the which place the soothsayers thought good to shut out of the precinct of the camp for to[58] take away the superstitious fear and mistrust men would have of it. The which began somewhat to alter Cassius' mind from Epicurus' opinions and had put the soldiers also in a marvelous fear.

Thereupon Cassius was of opinion not to try this war at one battle but rather to delay time and to draw it out in length, considering that they were the stronger in money and the weaker in men and armors. But Brutus in contrary manner did alway before, and at that time also, desire nothing more than to put all to the hazard of battle as soon as might be possible, to the end he might either quickly re-

---

*triumphs triumphe
52 misery wretchedness, privation   53 wethers male sheep   54 rods
fasces, bundles of rods with a projecting ax blade, borne ceremoniously
before Roman magistrates and dignitaries as a badge of authority
55 he should have worn i.e., Cassius was to have worn   56 triumphs
victory celebrations   57 clean pure   58 for to in order to

store his country to her former liberty or rid him[59] forthwith of this miserable world, being still troubled in following and maintaining of such great armies together. But perceiving that in the daily skirmishes and bickerings[60] they made his men were alway the stronger and ever had the better, that[61] yet quickened his spirits again and did put him in better heart. And furthermore, because that some of their own men had already yielded themselves to their enemies and that it was suspected moreover divers others would do the like, that[62] made many of Cassius' friends, which were of his mind before, when it came to be debated in council whether the battle should be fought or not, that they were then of Brutus' mind.

But yet was there one of Brutus' friends called Atellius that was against it and was of opinion that they should tarry the next winter. Brutus asked him what he should get by tarrying a year longer? "If I get naught else," quoth Atellius again, "yet have I lived so much longer." Cassius was very angry with this answer, and Atellius was maliced[63] and esteemed the worse for it of all men. Thereupon it was presently determined they should fight battle the next day. So Brutus all suppertime looked with a cheerful countenance, like a man that had good hope, and talked very wisely of philosophy and after supper went to bed.

But touching Cassius, Messala reporteth that he supped by himself in his tent with a few of his friends and that all suppertime he looked very sadly and was full of thoughts, although it was against his nature; and that after supper he took him by the hand and, holding him fast, in token of kindness as his manner was, told him in Greek: "Messala, I protest unto thee and make thee my witness that I am compelled against my mind and will, as Pompey the Great was, to jeopard[64] the liberty of our country to the hazard of a battle. And yet we must be lively and of good courage, considering our good fortune, whom we should wrong too much to mistrust her, although we follow evil counsel."[65]

---

59 rid him rid himself   **60 bickerings** skirmishes   **61 that** that realization   **62 that** that consideration   **63 maliced** scorned   **64 jeopard** jeopardize   **65 although . . . counsel** i.e., even if we are obliged to follow Brutus' bad advice and fight inopportunely

Messala writeth that Cassius, having spoken these last words unto him, he bade him farewell and willed him to come to supper to him the next night following because it was his birthday.

The next morning, by break of day, the signal of battle was set out in Brutus' and Cassius' camp, which was an arming[66] scarlet coat. And both the chieftains spake together in the midst of their armies. There Cassius began to speak first and said: "The gods grant us, O Brutus, that this day we may win the field, and ever after to live all the rest of our life quietly, one with another. But sith[67] the gods have so ordained it that the greatest and chiefest things amongst men are most uncertain, and that if the battle fall out otherwise today than we wish or look for, we shall hardly meet again. What art thou then determined to do, to fly, or die?" Brutus answered him, being yet but a young man and not overgreatly experienced in the world: "I trust (I know not how) a certain rule of philosophy, by the which I did greatly blame and reprove Cato for killing of himself, as being no lawful nor godly act touching the gods nor concerning men valiant, not to give place and yield to divine providence and not constantly and patiently to take whatsoever it pleaseth him[68] to send us but to draw back, and fly.[69] But being now in the midst of the danger, I am of a contrary mind. For if it be not the will of God that this battle fall out fortunate for us, I will look no more for hope, neither seek to make any new supply for war again, but will rid me of this miserable world and content me with my fortune. For I gave up my life for my country in the ides of March, for the which I shall live in another more glorious world." Cassius fell a-laughing to hear what he said and, embracing him, "Come on, then," said he, "let us go and charge our enemies with this mind. For either we shall conquer or we shall not need to fear the conquerors."

---

66 arming providing protective covering for the body   **67 sith** since
68 him i.e., God   **69 fly** flee

[The events of the battle, and of Cassius' and Brutus' suicides, are essentially as in Shakespeare's play.]

Text based on *The Lives of the Noble Grecians and Romans Compared Together by That Grave, Learned Philosopher and Historiographer, Plutarch of Chaeronea. Translated out of Greek into French by James Amyot . . . and out of French into English by Thomas North. . . . Thomas Vautroullier . . . 1579.*

Further Reading

Berry, Ralph. "Communal Identity and the Rituals of *Julius Caesar*." *Shakespeare and the Awareness of the Audience*. New York: St. Martin's Press, 1985. Berry finds the roots of the play's tragic action not in individual character but in a "communal identity" derived from the city itself: Rome is "the social determinant of the action." When characters express individuality they do so in response to pressures generated by the city, forcing them into archaic roles that are played out with a "diminishing expectation of success" and are effective only in "the mastering of defeat."

Bonjour, Adrien. *The Structure of "Julius Caesar."* Liverpool, Eng.: Liverpool Univ. Press, 1958. Bonjour explores the antithetical structure of the play and its careful balance of sympathy, "perfectly divided between the victim of the crime and the victim of the punishment." Imagery and characterization confirm the ambivalence of the plotting, deepening the agnostic political vision.

Burckhardt, Sigurd. "How Not to Murder Caesar." *Shakespearean Meanings*. Princeton, N.J.: Princeton Univ. Press, 1968. Likening the conspiracy to a dramatic plot, Burckhardt discovers in the failure of Brutus' political design a series of aesthetic misjudgments. Brutus would fashion the assassination as a "classical, almost Aristotelian" tragedy to be played before "an audience of noble, sturdy republicans," but his assumptions about the appropriate political style are wrong for the reality of imperial Rome.

Burke, Kenneth. "Antony in Behalf of the Play." *Southern Review* 1 (1935): 308–319. Rpt. in *The Philosophy of Literary Form*. Baton Rouge, La.: Louisiana State Univ. Press, 1941. Burke constructs a speech by a garrulous Antony directed not at the Roman populace but at the audience of *Julius Caesar*, explaining the play's "mechanism and its virtues." Burke's Antony exposes the rhetorical manipulations of Shakespeare's play that make the audience complicit in Caesar's murder and then desirous of Brutus' death to "absolve" them of their guilt.

Charney, Maurice. "The Imagery of *Julius Caesar*." *Shake-

speare's Roman Plays: The Function of Imagery in the Drama. Cambridge: Harvard Univ. Press, 1961. Charney's analysis reveals the centrality and ambivalence of the play's imagery of fire, blood, and storms. The ambiguity serves Shakespeare's interest in exploring, rather than arbitrating, conflicting political claims that would have been "of lively contemporary interest."

Daiches, David. *Shakespeare: "Julius Caesar."* London: Edward Arnold, 1976. In an essay designed to introduce the play to students, Daiches examines the unfolding action, tracing Shakespeare's control of his audience's response. The moral balances of the play are delicately maintained: Brutus appears at once idealistic and naive; Caesar, proud and frail. The play's only absolute resides in the grim efficiency of the new political ruler, Octavius.

Doran, Madeleine. " 'What should be in that "Caesar" ?': Proper Names in *Julius Caesar.*" *Shakespeare's Dramatic Language.* Madison, Wis.: Univ. of Wisconsin Press, 1976. Doran notes Shakespeare's unusual emphasis on names in the play and examines how the sounded names establish the tension between the paired protagonists. Only with Antony's eulogy does the disjunction end "between Brutus and Caesar which Cassius began in setting their names against one another."

Mack, Maynard. *"Julius Caesar."* In *Modern Shakespearean Criticism: Essays on Style, Dramaturgy, and the Major Plays,* ed. Alvin B. Kernan. New York: Harcourt, Brace and World, 1970. Mack finds the play's theme in "the always ambiguous impact between man and history." The first half of the play focuses on the efforts of characters to exert their wills upon history, but the second half shows "the insufficiency of reason and rational expectation." Brutus fails because his idealism prevents him from seeing history's limited responsiveness to human influence: he successfully kills Caesar but the spirit he would destroy "must repeatedly be killed but never dies."

Ornstein, Robert. "Seneca and the Political Drama of *Julius Caesar.*" *Journal of English and Germanic Philology* 57 (1958): 51–56. Ornstein discovers in Seneca's *De Beneficiis* a perspective for understanding Brutus' political role, one that lends support to modern ironic readings of the play. Following Seneca, "Shakespeare realizes that the essential drama of Brutus' role in the conspiracy lay not in a conflict of republican and monarchal theories" (for Brutus lacks a clearly defined political ideology) but in a "tragic disparity between naïve illusions and political realities."

Prior, Moody E. "The Search for a Hero in *Julius Caesar*." *Renaissance Drama* n.s. 2 (1969): 81–101. Prior examines the play's structure and finds that it is neither the tragedy of Julius Caesar nor of Brutus. The play is not organized around a single character but, like the *Henry IV* plays, divides its action among several characters and takes its name from a "central figure" in relation to whom events find meaning. The play's treatment of politics, however, is more like the treatment in the tragedies, with a focus on moral rather than historical implications.

Rabkin, Norman. "Structure, Convention, and Meaning in *Julius Caesar*." *Journal of English and Germanic Philology* 63 (1964): 240–254. Rpt. rev. in *Shakespeare and the Common Understanding*. New York: Free Press, 1967. The clear parallels that Rabkin sees between Caesar and Brutus establish the assassination as a "criminal mistake" rather than an "act of public virtue." Antony's speech in the forum declares the failure of Brutus' "naive idealization" of the murder of Caesar and marks a change of course in the drama that is virtually a shift in dramatic convention: Shakespeare turns "what promised to be a tragical history into a revenge play" that reveals the limits of human will and desire.

Ripley, John. *"Julius Caesar" on Stage in England and America, 1599–1973*. Cambridge and New York: Cambridge Univ. Press, 1980. Ripley provides a history of *Julius Caesar* on the stage, as it has diversely served as a "star-vehicle," a "clothes-horse for pageantry," and as a "political medium." His discussion of distinctive productions includes textual changes, stagecraft, and the interpretation of character.

Schanzer, Ernest. "The Tragedy of Shakespeare's Brutus." *ELH* 22 (1955): 1–15. Rpt. rev. in *The Problem Plays of Shakespeare: A Study of "Julius Caesar," "Measure for Measure," and "Antony and Cleopatra."* New York:

Schocken, 1963. Schanzer discusses "the complex and divided attitude to the Caesar story found in Shakespeare's play" and in his sources, and proposes that Shakespeare is less interested in deciding whether or not the assassination is justifiable than in exploring the moral questions to which it gives rise. The denial to an audience of secure "moral bearings" establishes *Julius Caesar* as one of Shakespeare's "genuine problem plays."

Shaw, George Bernard. *"Julius Caesar." Shaw on Shakespeare*, ed. Edwin Wilson. New York: E. P. Dutton, 1961. Shaw is perhaps the most virulent detractor of Shakespeare's handling of the play's political conflict. Declaring that his "truce with Shakespeare is over," Shaw is contemptuous of Shakespeare's "travestying" of Caesar as "a silly braggart" and of the depiction of the conspirators as "statesmen and patriots" when in truth they are merely a "pitiful gang of mischief-makers."

Stirling, Brents. " 'Or Else This Were a Savage Spectacle.' " *PMLA* 66 (1951): 765–774. Rpt. rev. in *Unity in Shakespearian Tragedy*. New York: Columbia Univ. Press, 1956. Stirling examines the centrality of ritual and ceremony to the structure of the play. Brutus' efforts to legitimize his political actions through rituals that represent his acts as noble and necessary are countered by Antony's counter-rituals in the second half of the play, exposing and condemning the contradictions in Brutus' idealism.

Velz, John W. "Undular Structure in *Julius Caesar*." *Modern Language Review* 66 (1971): 21–30. Exploring the marked parallels between the experience and behavior of the play's "successive protagonists," Velz concludes that the play's theme is "the turbulent process by which the commitment of the Romans moved from Pompey to Augustus." The play's presentation of a succession of political rises and falls establishes the theme and gives "unity to this panoramic play."

From the 1963 New York Shakespeare Festival production of *Twelfth Night*, with Peggy Pope as Maria and Albert Quinton as Sir Toby Belch, directed by Joseph Papp at the Heckscher Theater.

TWELFTH NIGHT
—————— OR ——————
WHAT YOU WILL

TWELFTH NIGHT

Introductory Material
Foreword by Joseph Papp
Introduction
Twelfth Night in
Performance

THE PLAY

Supplementary Material
Date and Text
Textual Notes
Shakespeare's Sources
Further Reading

Foreword

I've always loved the scene in *Twelfth Night* where the steward Malvolio discovers the love letter addressed to him that he imagines was written by the Lady Olivia. In having Malvolio read it out loud, Shakespeare gives us a glimpse of a man whose fantastic ambitions and exaggerated sense of his own worth make him an obvious target for those in the play—Sir Toby Belch, Sir Andrew Aguecheek, Maria, and Fabian—who cannot tolerate his pomposity.

There's no question that Malvolio is the character of greatest interest to Shakespeare, because he subjects him to the cruellest kind of treatment at the hands of Olivia's alcoholic uncle and his cohorts. While the audience is led to enjoy the antics and mischief perpetrated on this puritanical figure, Shakespeare (as usual), is not content with a simplistic attitude toward this important character. Instead, the playwright encourages us to feel sympathetic toward Malvolio for his tribulations in the later scene, tribulations that seem overly severe.

At the end of the play, Feste, the Fool, echoes the very words that Malvolio himself uttered in reading the planted letter: "Some are born great, some achieve greatness, and some have greatness thrust upon them." These words linger in our minds as we apply them to the world outside the play. We think of people who *are* born great and seem to have a natural genius; others who achieve greatness through hard work in the arts, in the sciences, in sports, in politics; and still others who unexpectedly have greatness thrust upon them, such as a vice president who may suddenly become the president of the United States after an assassination or a resignation.

Joseph Papp

Joseph Papp gratefully acknowledges the help of Elizabeth Kirkland in preparing this Foreword.

Introduction

Twelfth Night is possibly the latest of the three festive comedies, including *Much Ado about Nothing* and *As You Like It*, with which Shakespeare climaxed his distinctively philosophical and joyous vein of comic writing. Performed on February 2, 1602, at the Middle Temple (one of the Inns of Court, where young men studied law) and written possibly as early as 1599, *Twelfth Night* is usually dated 1600 or 1601. This play is indeed the most festive of the lot. Its keynote is Saturnalian release and the carnival pursuit of love and mirth. Along with such familiar motifs (found, for example, in *As You Like It* and *The Merchant of Venice*) as the plucky heroine disguised as a man, *Twelfth Night* also returns to the more farcical routines of mistaken identity found in Shakespeare's early comedy. As a witness of the 1602 performance, John Manningham, observed, the play is "much like the *Comedy of Errors,* or *Menaechmi* in Plautus, but most like and near to that in Italian called *Inganni.*" Manningham might have added Shakespeare's *The Two Gentlemen of Verona* as another early instance, since it too employs the device of the heroine, Julia, disguised in the service of her unresponsive lover, Proteus.

The carnival atmosphere is appropriate to the season designated in the play's title: the twelfth night of Christmas, January 6, the Feast of Epiphany. (The prologue to *Gl'Ingannati*, perhaps the Italian play referred to by Manningham, speaks of "La Notte di Beffania," Epiphany night.) Although Epiphany has of course a primary Christian significance as the Feast of the Magi, it was also in Renaissance times the last day of the Christmas revels. Over a twelve-day period, from Christmas until January 6, noble households sponsored numerous performances of plays, masques, banquets, and every kind of festivity. (Leslie Hotson argues, in fact, that *Twelfth Night* was first performed on twelfth night in early 1601, in the presence of Queen Elizabeth.) Students left schools for vacations, celebrating release from study with plays and revels of their own. The stern rigors of a rule-bound society gave way temporarily to playful inversions of authority. The reign of the Boy Bishop and the Feast of Fools, for example, gave choristers and minor church functionaries the cherished opportunity to boss the hierarchy around, mock the liturgy with outrageous lampooning, and generally let off steam. Although such customs occasionally got out of hand, the idea was to channel potentially destructive insubordination into playacting and thereby promote harmony. Behind these Elizabethan midwinter customs lies the Roman Saturnalia, with its pagan spirit of gift-giving, sensual indulgence, and satirical hostility to those who would curb merriment.

Shakespeare's choice of sources for *Twelfth Night* underscores his commitment to mirth. Renaissance literature offered numerous instances of mistaken identity among twins and of the disguised heroine serving as page to her beloved. Among those in English were the anonymous play *Sir Clyomon and Sir Clamydes* (c. 1570–1583), Sidney's *Arcadia* (1590), and the prose romance *Parismus* by Emmanuel Forde (1598), featuring both a shipwreck and two characters with the names of Olivia and Violetta. Of particular significance, but largely for negative reasons, is Barnabe Riche's tale of "Apollonius and Silla" in *Riche His Farewell to Military Profession* (1581), which was based on François de Belleforest's 1571 French version of Matteo Bandello's *Novelle* (1554). Here we find most of the requisite plot elements: the shipwreck; Silla's disguise as a page in Duke Apollonius's court; her office as ambassador of love from Apollonius to the Lady Julina, who thereupon falls in love with Silla; the arrival of Silla's twin brother, Silvio; and his consequent success in winning Julina's affection. To Riche, however, this tale is merely a long warning against the enervating power of infatuation. Silvio gets Julina with child and disappears forthwith, making his belated reappearance almost too late to save the wrongly accused Silla. Riche's moralizing puts the blame on the gross and drunken appetite of carnal love. The total mismatching of affection with which the story begins, and the sudden realignments of desire based on mere outward resemblances, are seen as proofs of love's unreasonableness. Shakespeare of course retains and capitalizes on the irrational quality of love, as in *A Midsummer Night's Dream*, but in doing so he minimizes the harm done (Olivia is not made pregnant) and repudiates any negative moral judgments. The added subplot, with its rebuking of Malvolio's censoriousness, may have been conceived as a further answer to Riche, Fenton, and their sober school.

Shakespeare's festive spirit owes much, as Manningham observed, to Plautus and the neoclassical Italian comic writers. At least three Italian comedies called *Gl'Inganni* ("The Frauds") employ the motif of mistaken identity, and one of them, by Curzio Gonzaga (1592), supplies Viola's assumed name of "Cesare," or Cesario. Another play with the same title appeared in 1562. More useful is *Gl'Ingannati* ("The Deceived"), performed in 1531, translated into French in 1543. Besides a plot line generally similar to that of *Twelfth Night*, and the reference to "La Notte di Beffania" (Epiphany), this play offers the suggestive name *Malevolti*, "evil-faced," and *Fabio* (which resembles "Fabian"). It also contains possible hints for Malvolio, Toby, and company, although the plot of the counterfeit letter is original with Shakespeare. Essentially, Shakespeare superimposes his own subplot on an Italianate novella plot, as he did in *The Taming of the Shrew* and *Much Ado about Nothing*. And it is in the Malvolio story that Shakespeare most pointedly defends merriment. Feste, the professional fool, an original stage type for Shakespeare in *Twelfth Night* and in *As You Like It*, also reinforces the theme of seizing the moment of mirth.

This great lesson, of savoring life's pleasures while one is still young, is something that Orsino and Olivia have not yet learned when the play commences. Although suited to each other in rank, wealth, and attractiveness, they are unable to overcome their own willful posturing in the elaborate charade of courtship. Like Silvius in *As You Like It*, Orsino is the conventional wooer trapped in the courtly artifice of love's rules. He opens the play on a cloying note of self-pity. He is fascinated with his own degradation as a rejected suitor, and bores his listeners with his changeable moods and fondness for poetical "conceits." He sees himself as a hart pursued by his desires "like fell and cruel hounds," reminding us that enervating lovesickness has in fact robbed him of his manly occupation, hunting. He sends ornately contrived messages to Olivia but has not seen her in so long that his passion has become unreal and fantastical, feeding on itself.

Olivia plays the opposite role of chaste, denying woman-hood. She explains her retirement from the world as mourning for a dead brother (whose name we never learn) but this withdrawal from life is another unreal vision. Olivia's practice of mourning, whereby she will "water once a day her chamber round / With eye-offending brine" (1.1.28–29), is a lifeless ritual. As others view the matter, she is senselessly wasting her beauty and affection on the dead. "What a plague means my niece to take the death of her brother thus?" Sir Toby expostulates (1.3.1–2). Viola, though she too has seemingly lost a brother, is an important foil in this regard, for she continues to hope for her brother's safety, trusts his soul is in heaven if he is dead, and refuses to give up her commitment to life in any case. We suspect that Olivia takes a willful pleasure in self-denial not unlike Orsino's self-congratulatory suffering. She appears to derive satisfaction from the power she holds over Orsino, a power of refusal. And she must know that she looks stunning in black.

Olivia's household reflects in part her mood of self-denial. She keeps Malvolio as steward because he too dresses somberly, insists on quiet as befits a house in mourning, and maintains order. Yet Olivia also retains a fool, Feste, who is Malvolio's opposite in every way. Hard-pressed to defend his mirthful function in a household so given over to melancholy, Feste must find some way of persuading his mistress that her very gravity is itself the essence of folly. This is a paradox, because sobriety and order appeal to the conventional wisdom of the world. Malvolio, sensing that his devotion to propriety is being challenged by the fool's prating, chides Olivia for taking "delight in such a barren rascal" (1.5.80–81).

Feste must argue for an inversion of appearance and reality whereby many of the world's ordinary pursuits can be seen to be ridiculous. As he observes, in his habitually elliptical manner of speech, "*cucullus non facit monachum* [the cowl doesn't make the monk]; that's as much to say as I wear not motley in my brain" (1.5.52–54). Feste wins his case by making Olivia laugh at her own illogic in grieving for a brother whose soul she assumes to be in heaven. By extension, Olivia has indeed been a fool for allowing herself to be deprived of happiness in love by her brother's death ("there is no true cuckold but calamity"), and for failing to consider the brevity of youth ("beauty's a flower"). Yet, paradoxically, only one who professes to be a fool can point this out, enabled by his detachment and innocence to perceive simple but profound truths denied to supposedly rational persons. This vision of the fool as naturally wise, and of society as self-indulgently insane, fascinated Renaissance writers, from Erasmus in *In Praise of Folly* and Cervantes in *Don Quixote* to Shakespeare in *King Lear*.

Viola, although not dressed in motley, aligns herself with Feste's rejection of self-denial. Refreshingly, even comically, she challenges the staid artifice of Orsino's and Olivia's lives. She is an ocean traveler, like many of Shakespeare's later heroines (Marina in *Pericles*, Perdita in *The Winter's Tale*), arriving on Illyria's shore plucky and determined. On her first embassy to Olivia from Orsino, she exposes with disarming candor the willfully ritualistic quality of Olivia's existence. Viola discards the flowery set speech she had prepared and memorized at Orsino's behest; despite her charmingly conceited assertion that the speech has been "excellently well penned," she senses that its elegant but empty rhetoric is all too familiar to the disdainful Olivia. Instead, Viola departs from her text to urge seizing the moment of happiness. "You do usurp yourself," she lectures Olivia, "for what is yours to bestow is not yours to reserve" (1.5.183–184). Beauty is a gift of nature, and failure to use it is a sin against nature. Or, again, "Lady, you are the cruel'st she alive / If you will lead these graces [Olivia's beauty] to the grave / And leave the world no copy" (236–238). An essential argument in favor of love, as in Shakespeare's sonnets, is the necessity of marriage and childbearing in order to perpetuate beauty. This approach is new to Olivia, and catches her wholly by surprise. In part she reacts, like Phoebe in *As You Like It*, with perverse logic, rejecting a too-willing wooer for one who is hard to get. Yet Olivia is also attracted by a new note of sincerity, prompting her to reenter life and accept maturely both the risks and rewards of romantic involvement. Her longing for Cesario is of course sexually misdirected, but the appearance of Viola's identical twin, Sebastian, soon puts all to rights.

The motifs of Olivia's attraction for another woman (both

actors would have been boys), and of Orsino's deep fondness for Cesario that matures into sexual love, delicately evoke homosexual suggestions as in *As You Like It*. Once again, however, we must approach the notion circumspectly, remembering that these elements are also found in Shakespeare's sources and reflect a convention wholly different from a modern psychological analysis of sexual aberration. Like Rosalind, Viola uses her male attire to win Orsino's pure affection, in a friendship devoid of sexual interest since both seemingly are men. Viola as Cesario can teach Orsino about the conventions of love in relaxed and frank conversations that would not be possible if she were known to be a woman. She teaches him to avoid the beguiling but misleading myths of Petrarchan love (named after the Italian sonneteer Francis Petrarch, whose poems embody the idealization of courtly love), and so prepares him for the realities of marriage. Comparing men and women in love, she confides, "We men may say more, swear more, but indeed / Our shows are more than will; for still we prove / Much in our vows, but little in our love" (2.4.116–118). Once she and Orsino have achieved an instinctive rapport all the more remarkable for their talking so often at cross-purposes, Viola's unmasking can make possible a physical communion as well. The friendship of Sebastian and Antonio, sorely tested by the mix-ups of the mistaken identity plot, presents further insight into the debate of love and friendship.

The belowstairs characters of the subplot, Sir Toby and the rest, share with Feste and Viola a commitment to joy. As Sir Toby proclaims in his first speech, "care's an enemy to life" (1.3.2–3). Even the simpleton Sir Andrew, although gulled by Sir Toby into spending his money on a hopeless pursuit of Olivia, seems none the worse for his treatment; he loves to drink in Sir Toby's company and can afford to pay for his entertainment. Sir Toby gives us some of the richly inventive humor of Falstaff, another lovable fat roguish knight. In this subplot, however, the confrontations between merriment and sobriety are more harshly drawn than in the main plot. Whereas the gracious Olivia is won away from her folly, the obdurate Malvolio can only be exposed to ridicule. He is chiefly to blame for the polarization of attitudes, for he insists on rebuking the mirth of others. His name (*Mal-volio*, the "ill-wisher") implies a self-satisfied determination to impose his rigid moral code on others. As Sir Toby taunts him, "Dost thou think, because thou art virtuous, there shall be no more cakes and ale?" (2.3.114–115). Malvolio's inflexible hostility provokes a desire for comic vengeance. The method is satiric: the clever manipulators, Maria and Toby, invent a scheme to entrap Malvolio in his own self-deceit. The punishment fits the crime, for he has long dreamed of himself as Count Malvolio, rich, powerful, in a position to demolish Toby and the rest. Without Malvolio's infatuated predisposition to believe that Olivia could actually love him and write such a letter as he finds, Maria's scheme would have no hope of success. He tortures the text to make it yield a suitable meaning, much in the style of Puritan theologizing.

Indeed, Malvolio does in some ways resemble a Puritan, as Maria observes (2.3.139–147), even though she qualifies the assertion by saying that he is not a religious fanatic but a "time-pleaser." She directs her observation not at a religious group but at all who would be killjoys; if the Puritans are like that, she intimates, so much the worse for them. This uncharacteristic lack of charity gives a sharp tone to the vengeance practiced on Malvolio, evoking from Olivia a protestation that "He hath been most notoriously abused" (5.1.379). The belated attempt to make a reconciliation with him seems, however, doomed to failure, in light of his grim resolve to "be revenged on the whole pack of you." At the height of his discomfiture he has been tricked into doing the two things he hates most: smiling affably, and wearing sportive attire. The appearance of merriment is so grossly unsuited to him that he is declared mad and put into safe-keeping. The apostle of sobriety in this play thus comes before us as a declared madman, while the fool Feste offers him sage comment in the guise of a priest. Wisdom and folly have changed places. The upside-down character of the play is epitomized in Malvolio's plaintive remark to Feste (no longer posing as the priest): "I am as well in my wits, Fool, as thou art" (4.2.88). Malvolio's comeuppance is richly deserved, but the severity of vengeance and counter-vengeance suggests that the triumph of festival will not last long. This brevity is, of course, inherent in the nature of such holiday release from responsibility. As Feste sings, "What's to come is still unsure. / In delay there lies no plenty."

Twelfth Night
in Performance

Although *Twelfth Night* has almost always been popular on-stage, many theatrical producers in past years have treated the play as though its stage popularity had to be achieved in defiance of the text rather than through it. Not until recently have they trusted the play to conjure up its own sense of magic and imagination; too often they have relied, counterproductively, on excessively detailed realism instead of theatrical evocation. This literalized and revisionistic approach dominated much of the play's stage history during the Restoration and the eighteenth and nineteenth centuries, despite evidence that *Twelfth Night* (presumably as Shakespeare wrote it) was very popular in his own day and for some time after. Following his death the play was staged at court in 1618 and 1622, and, along with *Much Ado about Nothing*, it was identified by the poet Leonard Digges in 1640 as still among Shakespeare's most popular dramas. Digges suggested one important reason for this popularity when he commented that crowds were filling the theater "To hear *Malvolio*, that cross-gartered gull." Digges's observation also points to a distortion that would occur in subsequent productions of *Twelfth Night:* the play would become a vehicle for lead actors and actresses in a few key roles at the expense of the play as a whole. Revision of this sort was common in the Restoration and eighteenth century, whereas scenic overemphasis came to be a predictable feature of much nineteenth-century production.

The diarist Samuel Pepys saw a version of *Twelfth Night* on three occasions in the 1660s and thought it "a silly play." What Pepys objected to can perhaps be surmised from Charles Burnaby's adaptation in 1703, called *Love Betrayed, or the Agreeable Disappointment,* in which Burnaby undertook to "improve" the play with the kind of symmetry and neoclassical unity that he evidently felt it lacked. In this version, produced at the theater in Lincoln's Inn Fields, London, Malvolio, having been merged with the character of Sir Andrew, is tricked into fighting an abortive comic duel with the disguised Viola, whom he believes to be his rival for the love of Olivia. Maria becomes two characters, one an old servant in love with Sir Toby and the other a confidante of Olivia. Sebastian is provided with a wise-cracking servant. The characters are all renamed, and only some fifty-eight lines of Shakespeare's text (including "If music be the food of love, play on") remain intact. The major effect of Burnaby's revision is to reduce the number of subplots and to bring to the foreground the opposition of Malvolio and Viola. Malvolio is no longer the focus of a separate comic plot but at the center of the play, where, audiences evidently felt, he belonged.

Something more like Shakespeare's original of *Twelfth Night* did return in 1741, to the Theatre Royal, Drury Lane, evidently at the actor Charles Macklin's instigation (and with Macklin as Malvolio), and enjoyed during the next century a number of popular runs. John Henderson and John Philip Kemble, among others, took the part of Malvolio, while Hannah Pritchard, Peg Woffington, Dorothea Jordan (paired with her brother, George Bland, as Sebastian), Sarah Siddons, and Helen Faucit played Viola. Feste's concluding song, customarily absent throughout the eighteenth century, was finally restored in 1799. Nevertheless, adaptation continued to be a major factor in eighteenth- and nineteenth-century productions of the play. Songs were frequently added. Frederic Reynolds produced an operatic version in 1820 at the Theatre Royal, Covent Garden, with an overture compiled from various composers including Thomas Morley, Thomas Ravenscroft, and Mozart. "Full many a glorious morning" was introduced from the sonnets, "Even as the sun" from *Venus and Adonis,* "Orpheus with his lute" from *Henry VIII,* and "Come unto these yellow sands" from *The Tempest,* all set off by elegant scenery in what was supposed to be the style of the architect and set designer Inigo Jones.

Even when Shakespeare's text was treated with more respect, the emphasis on lead actors and actresses remained an unavoidable feature of nineteenth-century production. At the Haymarket Theatre in London in 1846, Charlotte and Susan Cushman, famous for their epicene Romeo and Juliet, starred as Viola and Olivia and made their pairing the center of the theatrical experience. When Samuel Phelps produced the play at the Sadler's Wells Theatre in 1848 and again in 1857, he gave prominence to his own portrayal of Malvolio as a grave and self-important Spanish grandee. In 1849, at the Theatre Royal, Marrylebone, Cora Mowatt and Fanny Vining (who, like the Cushmans, had done an epicene *Romeo and Juliet*) emulated their predecessors by pairing themselves in the roles of Olivia and Viola.

Twelfth Night does not call for the spectacular effects of battle sieges and royal pageantry that gave such impressive scope to the epic productions of the history plays by Charles Kean and others (as, for example, in Kean's *King John*), but theater managers who were insistent on visual opulence soon found a way to dress *Twelfth Night* in the splendor they wished to emphasize. Kean opened at the Princess's Theatre in 1850 with *Twelfth Night* and performed it some forty times, bestowing upon the play every realistic scenic device known to nineteenth-century theater. Henry Irving chose for his 1884 production, at the Lyceum Theatre, London, a Venetian setting in the age of Queen Elizabeth. Orsino's palace and Olivia's scarcely less palatial villa were sumptuously Palladian in decor, while the art of landscape gardening, as a contemporary observer marveled, appeared "to have reached a very high pitch of excellence." Olivia's house featured an adjoining cloister. No less impressive were the depictions of the seacoast, the courtyard and terrace of Olivia's house, the road near Olivia's house, and the dungeon for Malvolio. Ellen Terry played a spritely Viola opposite Irving's sentimental Malvolio, and although the performance was not a success, it was not for lack of handsome scene design.

In 1894, not to be outdone, producer Augustin Daly, at his Daly's Theatre in London, began with an exciting storm scene worthy of *The Tempest*. Unexpectedly, Daly showed his audiences the landing of Sebastian and Antonio rather than that of Viola and the Captain, which allowed the production's star, Ada Rehan (Viola), to enter more impressively in the next scene. The rearrangement also made possible the employment of an elaborate set for the Duke's palace. So elaborate was this set that, in order to keep it in use for a continuous stretch of dramatic action, Daly ran together Act 1, scene 1 (showing Orsino's love melancholy), with Act 1, scene 4 (in which Viola as Cesario is dispatched to Olivia), before making the cumbersome shift to Olivia's house. Once there, Daly devised another long composite scene, in which Toby and Andrew carouse (1.3), Olivia receives Viola-Cesario (1.5), and Malvolio returns the ring to Viola-Cesario (2.2). Music was prominent throughout the production. During its first scene, for instance, on the seacoast after the storm happy villagers sang "Come unto these yellow sands" from *The Tempest;* other songs were introduced into the scenes at Olivia's house. Moonlight beamed onto the set as Orsino's minstrels sang "Who is Olivia?" (taken from "Who is Sylvia?" in *The Two Gentlemen of Verona*) set to music by Franz Schubert. Rehan, the scenery, and the music made the play a great success; it ran for 119 performances.

Herbert Beerbohm Tree's *Twelfth Night,* at Her Majesty's Theatre in 1901, achieved a kind of pinnacle in the verisimilar staging of *Twelfth Night.* His set for Olivia's house featured a terrace that extended to the extreme back of the stage and a garden complete with real grass, fountains, pathways, and descending steps. It was, according to an eyewitness report, literally an Italian garden, going beyond anything hitherto seen in beauty and realistic illusion. As in Daly's production, the set was so nearly immovable that scenes had to be rearranged extensively, even to the point of staging in Olivia's garden some dramatic material that properly belonged at Orsino's court or elsewhere. Tree also focused, in traditional nineteenth-century fashion, on the leading characters, playing Malvolio himself to the Viola of Lily Brayton.

Nonetheless, a major new direction was at hand. Already, in 1895, *Twelfth Night* had become the first of the revivals by actor-manager William Poel and the Elizabethan Stage Society, who staged it once at Burlington Hall, Savile Row, and again at St. George's Hall. Featuring Elizabethan costumes, a stage bare of scenery, and a single ten-minute intermission, the production tried to approximate the conditions of Shakespeare's own theater. Two years later, in a production in the Hall of the Middle Temple (one of the Inns of Court, where young men studied law in London), Poel sought to produce the play as it might have been done at Shakespeare's Blackfriars Theatre. A table and chair were the only props on the raised platform stage, which was surrounded by halberdiers (guards); costumes were based on the dress of the Elizabethan court, and the songs were, wherever possible, given their original settings and played on sixteenth-century instruments.

In the spirit of Poel's reforms, the twentieth century has generally turned against the excesses of nineteenth-century verisimilar staging. The anti-illusionism implicit in Poel's attempts to restore Elizabethan staging practices was successfully translated into a more modern idiom in a swift-moving ensemble production directed by Harley Granville-Barker at London's Savoy Theatre in 1912, and then in a performance on an apron stage (i.e., a stage thrust out in front of the proscenium) directed by Barry Jackson at the Birmingham Repertory Theatre in 1913, which was revived in 1916 with an uncut text. Since then the play has had its share of new settings and adaptations, including a rock musical version called *Your Own Thing* (1968), but on the whole, of all Shakespeare's comedies *Twelfth Night* seems the least in need of being made "relevant." Allowed to speak for itself, the play has had memorable theatrical triumphs. Tyrone Guthrie's London production at the Old Vic in 1937 successfully doubled Jessica Tandy as Viola and Sebastian and had Laurence Olivier as Toby and Alec Guinness as Andrew Aguecheek. In 1954 the play again graced the Old Vic, directed by Denis Carey, with Claire Bloom as an energetic, almost ferocious Viola and Richard Burton as Toby. A year later, John Gielgud directed Vivien Leigh as Viola and Olivier as Malvolio at Stratford-upon-Avon. John Barton's 1969 Stratford-upon-Avon production was movingly autumnal, dominated by Emrys James's melancholy Feste.

Elizabethan costuming, which was used in Barton's production, seems admirably suited to the play's winsome blend of satire and foolery about love; onstage the play seems quintessentially of Shakespeare's age and yet timeless. It can fully employ the talents of repertory companies expert in ensemble work and willing to distribute the acting honors beyond the roles of Viola, Toby, and Feste. It is a favorite of amateurs, and acts well out-of-doors. It has become a staple of summer festivals at Stratford, in Canada, at Ashland, in Oregon, and many others, where a sturdy and rollicking performance can be counted on to pack the house. New interpretation is usually a matter not of a wholly new or of an anachronistic setting but of nuance, as in the 1969 Barton production when Malvolio, played by Donald Sinden, coming onstage in Act 3, scene 4, stopped to correct the sundial by consulting his pocket watch; the gratuitous officiousness of the gesture was comically eloquent.

Apron, or thrust, stages and quick-paced productions of recent years enable actors to stage *Twelfth Night* much as it must have been performed in Shakespeare's Globe Theatre. The scene of eavesdropping on Malvolio (2.5), for instance, requires only that the actors playing Sir Toby and his belowstairs companions hide themselves where their antics can be visible to spectators during the reading of the letter; on Shakespeare's stage, the pillars would have been especially convenient for such a purpose. When they performed the play at Middle Temple Hall, in February of 1602, as John Manningham's diary tells us, the actors would have had the magnificent screen with its two arched doorways and other architectural features in which to hide from Malvolio or, later, for use as a makeshift prison in which to incarcerate him. The comic duel of Sir Andrew and Viola-Cesario requires only that the contenders approach one another from opposite entrances, with Sir Toby and Fabian moving back and forth between the two unwilling contenders to frighten them or propose terms.

When, in Act 2, scene 2, Malvolio hastens after Viola-Cesario and encounters him in a street, no stage business is required other than that they enter *at several* (i.e., separate) *doors*. They need not (and indeed are instructed that they should not) enter one after the other by the same door to signify that they are coming from Olivia's house, for doors are not used in this illusionistic way on the Shakespearean stage. The previous scene, in any case, has been located in an entirely different part of Illyria, so that Shakespeare makes no attempt to provide a visual continuity between the end of Act 1, scene 5, when Cesario-Viola leaves Olivia's house with Malvolio in pursuit, and their meeting in Act 2, scene 2. Instead, Elizabethan theatrical convention asks the audience to understand that actors entering by separate doors are encountering one another. Realistically identified doorways, or, in the scene of eavesdropping, real shrubbery, not only slow down changes of scene but miss the point by literalizing Illyria. The world in which *Twelfth Night* is located is, or should be, one of theatrical imagination. Illyria is above all a place of the artist's creation, his play world, his theater. *Twelfth Night* frequently calls attention to its self-reflexive quality, as when Fabian says of Malvolio's comic discomfiture, "If this were played upon a stage now, I could condemn it as an improbable fiction" (3.4.129–130). Shakespeare's play revels in this paradox of illusion, making improbable fiction wholly convincing and defying the more ordinary conventions by which dramatic art is made to appear "real."

TWELFTH NIGHT
OR
WHAT YOU WILL

[*Dramatis Personae*

ORSINO, *Duke (or Count) of Illyria*
VALENTINE, *gentleman attending on Orsino*
CURIO, *gentleman attending on Orsino*

VIOLA, *a shipwrecked lady, later disguised as Cesario*
SEBASTIAN, *twin brother of Viola*
ANTONIO, *a sea captain, friend to Sebastian*
CAPTAIN *of the shipwrecked vessel*

OLIVIA, *a rich countess of Illyria*
MARIA, *gentlewoman in Olivia's household*
SIR TOBY BELCH, *Olivia's uncle*
SIR ANDREW AGUECHEEK, *a companion of Sir Toby*
MALVOLIO, *steward of Olivia's household*
FABIAN, *a member of Olivia's household*
FESTE, *a clown, also called* FOOL, *Olivia's jester*

A PRIEST
FIRST OFFICER
SECOND OFFICER

Lords, Sailors, Musicians, and other Attendants

SCENE: *A city in Illyria, and the seacoast near it*]

1.1 *Enter Orsino Duke of Illyria, Curio, and other lords [with musicians].*

ORSINO
If music be the food of love, play on;
Give me excess of it, that surfeiting,
The appetite may sicken and so die.
That strain again! It had a dying fall;   4
O, it came o'er my ear like the sweet sound
That breathes upon a bank of violets,
Stealing and giving odor. Enough, no more.
'Tis not so sweet now as it was before.
O spirit of love, how quick and fresh art thou,   9
That, notwithstanding thy capacity
Receiveth as the sea, naught enters there,
Of what validity and pitch soe'er,   12
But falls into abatement and low price   13
Even in a minute. So full of shapes is fancy   14
That it alone is high fantastical.   15
CURIO
Will you go hunt, my lord?
ORSINO   What, Curio?
CURIO   The hart.
ORSINO
Why, so I do, the noblest that I have.   17
O, when mine eyes did see Olivia first,
Methought she purged the air of pestilence.
That instant was I turned into a hart,
And my desires, like fell and cruel hounds,   21
E'er since pursue me.

        Enter Valentine.

                            How now, what news from her?   22

1.1. Location: Orsino's court.
s.d. **Illyria** country on the east coast of the Adriatic Sea **4 fall** cadence **9 quick and fresh** keen and hungry **12 validity** value. **pitch** superiority. (Literally, the highest point of a falcon's flight.) **13 abatement** depreciation **14 shapes** imagined forms. **fancy** love **15 it . . . fantastical** it surpasses everything else in imaginative power **17 the noblest . . . have** i.e., my noblest part, my heart (punning on *hart*) **21 fell** fierce **22 pursue me** (Alludes to the story in Ovid of Actaeon, who, having seen Diana bathing, was transformed into a stag and killed by his own hounds.)

VALENTINE
So please my lord, I might not be admitted,
But from her handmaid do return this answer:
The element itself, till seven years' heat,   25
Shall not behold her face at ample view;
But like a cloistress she will veilèd walk,   27
And water once a day her chamber round
With eye-offending brine—all this to season   29
A brother's dead love, which she would keep fresh   30
And lasting in her sad remembrance.

ORSINO
O, she that hath a heart of that fine frame   32
To pay this debt of love but to a brother,
How will she love, when the rich golden shaft   34
Hath killed the flock of all affections else   35
That live in her; when liver, brain, and heart,   36
These sovereign thrones, are all supplied, and filled   37
Her sweet perfections, with one self king!   38
Away before me to sweet beds of flowers.
Love thoughts lie rich when canopied with bowers.

                                        Exeunt.

❖

1.2   *Enter Viola, a Captain, and sailors.*

VIOLA   What country, friends, is this?
CAPTAIN   This is Illyria, lady.
VIOLA
And what should I do in Illyria?
My brother he is in Elysium.   4

25 element sky.   **seven years' heat** seven summers   **27 cloistress** nun
secluded in a religious community   **29 season** keep fresh (playing on
the idea of the salt in her tears)   **30 brother's dead** dead brother's
32 frame construction   **34 golden shaft** i.e., of Cupid   **35 affections else**
other feelings   **36 liver, brain, and heart** (In medieval and Elizabethan
psychology these organs were the seats of the passions, of thought, and
of feeling.)   **37 supplied** filled   **37–38 and . . . perfections** and her sweet
perfections filled   **38 self king** single lord (the object of her entire
affection)

1.2. Location: The seacoast.
4 Elysium classical abode of the blessed dead

Perchance he is not drowned. What think you, sailors? 5
CAPTAIN
It is perchance that you yourself were saved.   6
VIOLA
O, my poor brother! And so perchance may he be.
CAPTAIN
True, madam, and to comfort you with chance,   8
Assure yourself, after our ship did split,
When you and those poor number saved with you
Hung on our driving boat, I saw your brother,   11
Most provident in peril, bind himself,
Courage and hope both teaching him the practice,
To a strong mast that lived upon the sea;   14
Where, like Arion on the dolphin's back,   15
I saw him hold acquaintance with the waves
So long as I could see.
VIOLA   For saying so, there's gold. [*She gives money.*]
Mine own escape unfoldeth to my hope,   19
Whereto thy speech serves for authority,   20
The like of him. Know'st thou this country?   21
CAPTAIN
Ay, madam, well, for I was bred and born
Not three hours' travel from this very place.
VIOLA   Who governs here?
CAPTAIN
A noble duke, in nature as in name.
VIOLA   What is his name?
CAPTAIN   Orsino.
VIOLA
Orsino! I have heard my father name him.
He was a bachelor then.
CAPTAIN
And so is now, or was so very late;
For but a month ago I went from hence,

5–6 Perchance . . . perchance perhaps . . . by mere chance   **8 chance**
i.e., what one may hope that chance will bring about   **11 driving** drift-
ing, driven by the seas   **14 lived** i.e., kept afloat   **15 Arion** a Greek poet
who so charmed the dolphins with his lyre that they saved him when he
leaped into the sea to escape murderous sailors   **19–21 unfoldeth . . .
him** i.e., offers a hopeful example that he may have escaped similarly, to
which hope your speech provides support

And then 'twas fresh in murmur—as, you know,   32
What great ones do the less will prattle of—   33
That he did seek the love of fair Olivia.
VIOLA   What's she?
CAPTAIN
A virtuous maid, the daughter of a count
That died some twelvemonth since, then leaving her
In the protection of his son, her brother,
Who shortly also died; for whose dear love,
They say, she hath abjured the sight
And company of men.
VIOLA   O, that I served that lady,
And might not be delivered to the world   42
Till I had made mine own occasion mellow,   43
What my estate is!
CAPTAIN   That were hard to compass,   44
Because she will admit no kind of suit,
No, not the Duke's.
VIOLA
There is a fair behavior in thee, Captain,
And though that nature with a beauteous wall
Doth oft close in pollution, yet of thee
I will believe thou hast a mind that suits
With this thy fair and outward character.   51
I prithee, and I'll pay thee bounteously,
Conceal me what I am, and be my aid
For such disguise as haply shall become   54
The form of my intent. I'll serve this duke.   55
Thou shalt present me as an eunuch to him.   56
It may be worth thy pains, for I can sing
And speak to him in many sorts of music
That will allow me very worth his service.   59
What else may hap, to time I will commit;
Only shape thou thy silence to my wit.   61

32 **murmur** rumor   33 **less** i.e., social inferiors   42 **delivered** revealed,
made known   43 **mellow** ready or convenient (to be made known)
44 **estate** position in society.   **compass** bring about, encompass
51 **character** face or features as indicating moral qualities   54 **become** suit   55 **form of my intent** nature of my purpose (with suggestion
of outward appearance in *form*)   56 **eunuch** castrato, high-voiced
singer   59 **allow me** cause me to be acknowledged   61 **wit** plan,
invention

CAPTAIN
  Be you his eunuch, and your mute I'll be;
  When my tongue blabs, then let mine eyes not see.
VIOLA   I thank thee. Lead me on.   *Exeunt.*

❖

1.3   *Enter Sir Toby [Belch] and Maria.*

SIR TOBY   What a plague means my niece to take the
  death of her brother thus? I am sure care's an enemy
  to life.
MARIA   By my troth, Sir Toby, you must come in earlier
  o' nights. Your cousin, my lady, takes great exceptions 5
  to your ill hours.
SIR TOBY   Why, let her except before excepted.   7
MARIA   Ay, but you must confine yourself within the
  modest limits of order.   9
SIR TOBY   Confine? I'll confine myself no finer than I am. 10
  These clothes are good enough to drink in, and so be
  these boots too. An they be not, let them hang them- 12
  selves in their own straps.
MARIA   That quaffing and drinking will undo you. I
  heard my lady talk of it yesterday, and of a foolish
  knight that you brought in one night here to be her
  wooer.
SIR TOBY   Who, Sir Andrew Aguecheek?
MARIA   Ay, he.
SIR TOBY   He's as tall a man as any's in Illyria.   20
MARIA   What's that to the purpose?
SIR TOBY   Why, he has three thousand ducats a year.
MARIA   Ay, but he'll have but a year in all these ducats. 23
  He's a very fool and a prodigal.
SIR TOBY   Fie, that you'll say so! He plays o' the viol-de- 25
  gamboys, and speaks three or four languages word for 26

1.3. Location: Olivia's house.
5 cousin i.e., kinswoman   **7 except before excepted** (Plays on the legal
phrase *exceptis excipiendis*, "with the exceptions before named." Sir
Toby means that enough exceptions to his behavior have already been
taken.)   **9 modest** moderate   **10 confine myself** dress myself (playing
on Maria's use of *confine*, limit).   **finer** (1) better (2) tighter   **12 An** if
20 tall brave   **23 he'll ... ducats** i.e., he'll spend all his money within a
year   **25–26 viol-de-gamboys** viola da gamba, leg-viol, bass viol

word without book, and hath all the good gifts of 27
nature.

MARIA He hath indeed, almost natural, for, besides that 29
he's a fool, he's a great quarreler, and but that he hath
the gift of a coward to allay the gust he hath in quar- 31
reling, 'tis thought among the prudent he would
quickly have the gift of a grave.

SIR TOBY By this hand, they are scoundrels and sub- 34
stractors that say so of him. Who are they? 35

MARIA They that add, moreover, he's drunk nightly in
your company.

SIR TOBY With drinking healths to my niece. I'll drink
to her as long as there is a passage in my throat and
drink in Illyria. He's a coward and a coistrel that will 40
not drink to my niece till his brains turn o' the toe like
a parish top. What, wench? *Castiliano vulgo!* For here 42
comes Sir Andrew Agueface. 43

Enter Sir Andrew [Aguecheek].

SIR ANDREW Sir Toby Belch! How now, Sir Toby Belch?
SIR TOBY Sweet Sir Andrew!
SIR ANDREW Bless you, fair shrew.
MARIA And you too, sir.
SIR TOBY Accost, Sir Andrew, accost. 48
SIR ANDREW What's that?
SIR TOBY My niece's chambermaid. 50
SIR ANDREW Good Mistress Accost, I desire better ac-
quaintance.
MARIA My name is Mary, sir.
SIR ANDREW Good Mistress Mary Accost—

---

27 without book by heart   **29 natural** (with a play on the sense "born
idiot")   **31 allay the gust** moderate the taste   **34–35 substractors** i.e.,
detractors   **40 coistrel** horse-groom, base fellow   **42 parish top** a large
top provided by the parish to be spun by whipping, apparently for
exercise in cold weather.   **Castiliano vulgo** (Of uncertain meaning.
Castilians were noted for their decorum, and possibly Sir Toby is urging
Maria to behave politely to Sir Andrew.)   **43 Agueface** (Like *Aguecheek,*
this name betokens the thin, pale countenance of one suffering from an
ague.)   **48 Accost** go alongside (a nautical term), i.e., greet her, address
her   **50 chambermaid** lady in waiting (a gentlewoman, not one who
would do menial tasks)

SIR TOBY You mistake, knight. "Accost" is front her, board her, woo her, assail her.   56

SIR ANDREW By my troth, I would not undertake her in this company. Is that the meaning of "accost"?

MARIA Fare you well, gentlemen.   [*Going.*]

SIR TOBY An thou let part so, Sir Andrew, would thou 60 mightst never draw sword again.

SIR ANDREW An you part so, mistress, I would I might never draw sword again. Fair lady, do you think you have fools in hand?   64

MARIA Sir, I have not you by the hand.

SIR ANDREW Marry, but you shall have, and here's my 66 hand.

MARIA Now, sir, thought is free. I pray you, bring your 68 hand to the buttery-bar, and let it drink.   69

SIR ANDREW Wherefore, sweetheart? What's your metaphor?

MARIA It's dry, sir.   72

SIR ANDREW Why, I think so. I am not such an ass but I can keep my hand dry. But what's your jest?

MARIA A dry jest, sir.   75

SIR ANDREW Are you full of them?

MARIA Ay, sir, I have them at my fingers' ends. Marry, now I let go your hand, I am barren.   *Exit Maria.* 78

SIR TOBY O knight, thou lack'st a cup of canary! When 79 did I see thee so put down?

SIR ANDREW Never in your life, I think, unless you see canary put me down. Methinks sometimes I have no more wit than a Christian or an ordinary man has. But I am a great eater of beef, and I believe that does harm to my wit.

SIR TOBY No question.

---

56 board greet, approach (as though preparing to board in a naval encounter)   **60 An . . . part** if you let her leave   **64 have . . . hand** i.e., have to deal with fools. (But Maria puns on the literal sense.)   **66 Marry** i.e., indeed. (Originally, "By the Virgin Mary.")   **68 thought is free** i.e., I may think what I like. (Proverbial; replying to *do you think . . . in hand*, above.)   **69 buttery-bar** ledge on top of the half-door to the buttery or wine cellar   **72 dry** thirsty; also dried up, a sign of age and debility   **75 dry** (1) ironic (2) dull, barren (referring to Sir Andrew)   **78 barren** i.e., barren of jests and of Andrew's hand   **79 canary** a sweet wine from the Canary Islands

SIR ANDREW   An I thought that, I'd forswear it. I'll ride
home tomorrow, Sir Toby.

SIR TOBY   *Pourquoi*, my dear knight?   89

SIR ANDREW   What is *"pourquoi"*? Do or not do? I
would I had bestowed that time in the tongues that I   91
have in fencing, dancing, and bearbaiting. O, had I
but followed the arts!   93

SIR TOBY   Then hadst thou had an excellent head of hair.

SIR ANDREW   Why, would that have mended my hair?   95

SIR TOBY   Past question, for thou seest it will not curl by
nature.

SIR ANDREW   But it becomes me well enough, does 't
not?

SIR TOBY   Excellent. It hangs like flax on a distaff, and I   100
hope to see a huswife take thee between her legs and
spin it off.   102

SIR ANDREW   Faith, I'll home tomorrow, Sir Toby. Your
niece will not be seen, or if she be, it's four to one
she'll none of me. The Count himself here hard by   105
woos her.

SIR TOBY   She'll none o' the Count. She'll not match
above her degree, neither in estate, years, nor wit; I   108
have heard her swear 't. Tut, there's life in 't, man.   109

SIR ANDREW   I'll stay a month longer. I am a fellow o' the
strangest mind i' the world; I delight in masques and
revels sometimes altogether.

SIR TOBY   Art thou good at these kickshawses, knight?   113

SIR ANDREW   As any man in Illyria, whatsoever he be,
under the degree of my betters, and yet I will not com-   115
pare with an old man.   116

SIR TOBY   What is thy excellence in a galliard, knight?   117

---

89 Pourquoi why   **91 tongues** languages. (Perhaps also suggests *tongs*,
curling irons.)   **93 the arts** the liberal arts, learning. (But Sir Toby plays
on the phrase as meaning "artifice," the antithesis of *nature*.)   **95 mended**
improved   **100 distaff** a staff for holding the flax, tow, or wool in
spinning   **102 spin it off** i.e., cause you to lose hair as a result of venereal disease, gotten from the *huswife* (suggesting *hussy*, "whore")
105 Count i.e., Duke Orsino, sometimes referred to as Count.   **hard**
near   **108 degree** social position.   **estate** fortune, social position
109 there's life in 't i.e., while there's life there's hope   **113 kick-**
shawses delicacies, fancy trifles. (From the French, *quelque chose*.)
115 under . . . betters excepting those who are above me   **116 old**
man experienced person (?)   **117 galliard** lively dance in triple time

SIR ANDREW   Faith, I can cut a caper.   118
SIR TOBY   And I can cut the mutton to 't.
SIR ANDREW   And I think I have the back-trick simply as   120
strong as any man in Illyria.
SIR TOBY   Wherefore are these things hid? Wherefore have
these gifts a curtain before 'em? Are they like to   123
take dust, like Mistress Mall's picture? Why dost thou   124
not go to church in a galliard and come home in a
coranto? My very walk should be a jig; I would not so   126
much as make water but in a sink-a-pace. What dost   127
thou mean? Is it a world to hide virtues in? I did think,   128
by the excellent constitution of thy leg, it was formed
under the star of a galliard.   130
SIR ANDREW   Ay, 'tis strong, and it does indifferent well   131
in a dun-colored stock. Shall we set about some re-   132
vels?
SIR TOBY   What shall we do else? Were we not born under Taurus?   135
SIR ANDREW   Taurus? That's sides and heart.
SIR TOBY   No, sir, it is legs and thighs. Let me see thee
caper. Ha, higher! Ha, ha, excellent!
                              [*Sir Andrew capers.*] *Exeunt.*

❖

1.4   *Enter Valentine, and Viola in man's attire.*

VALENTINE   If the Duke continue these favors towards
you, Cesario, you are like to be much advanced. He
hath known you but three days, and already you are
no stranger.

---

118 cut a caper make a lively leap. (But Sir Toby puns on the *caper* used
to make a sauce served with mutton. *Mutton* in turn suggests "whore.")
120 back-trick backward step in the galliard   **123–124 like to take**
likely to collect   **124 Mistress Mall's picture** i.e., perhaps the portrait
of some woman protected from light and dust, as many pictures were,
by curtains   **126 coranto** lively running dance   **127 sink-a-pace** dance
like the galliard. (French *cinquepace*.)   **128 virtues** talents   **130 under
. . . galliard** i.e., under a star favorable to dancing   **131 indifferent**
moderately   **132 stock** stocking   **135 Taurus** zodiacal sign. (Sir Andrew
is mistaken, since Leo governed sides and hearts in medical astrology.
Taurus governed legs and thighs, or, more commonly, neck and throat.)
1.4. Location: Orsino's court.

VIOLA You either fear his humor or my negligence, that 5
you call in question the continuance of his love. Is he
inconstant, sir, in his favors?
VALENTINE No, believe me.

Enter Duke [Orsino], Curio, and attendants.

VIOLA I thank you. Here comes the Count.
ORSINO Who saw Cesario, ho?
VIOLA On your attendance, my lord, here.
ORSINO
Stand you awhile aloof. [*The others stand aside.*]
 Cesario,
Thou know'st no less but all. I have unclasped
To thee the book even of my secret soul.
Therefore, good youth, address thy gait unto her; 15
Be not denied access, stand at her doors,
And tell them, there thy fixèd foot shall grow 17
Till thou have audience.
VIOLA   Sure, my noble lord,
If she be so abandoned to her sorrow
As it is spoke, she never will admit me.
ORSINO
Be clamorous and leap all civil bounds 21
Rather than make unprofited return.
VIOLA
Say I do speak with her, my lord, what then?
ORSINO
O, then unfold the passion of my love;
Surprise her with discourse of my dear faith. 25
It shall become thee well to act my woes; 26
She will attend it better in thy youth
Than in a nuncio's of more grave aspect. 28
VIOLA
I think not so, my lord.
ORSINO   Dear lad, believe it;
For they shall yet belie thy happy years
That say thou art a man. Diana's lip

---

5 humor changeableness **15 address thy gait** go **17 them** i.e., Olivia's
servants **21 civil bounds** bounds of civility **25 Surprise** take by storm.
(A military term.) **26 become** suit **28 nuncio's** messenger's

Is not more smooth and rubious; thy small pipe 32
Is as the maiden's organ, shrill and sound, 33
And all is semblative a woman's part. 34
I know thy constellation is right apt 35
For this affair.—Some four or five attend him;
All, if you will, for I myself am best
When least in company.—Prosper well in this,
And thou shalt live as freely as thy lord,
To call his fortunes thine.
VIOLA   I'll do my best
To woo your lady. [*Aside.*] Yet a barful strife! 41
Whoe'er I woo, myself would be his wife.   *Exeunt.*

❖

1.5   *Enter Maria and Clown [Feste].*

MARIA   Nay, either tell me where thou hast been, or I
will not open my lips so wide as a bristle may enter in
way of thy excuse. My lady will hang thee for thy absence.
FESTE   Let her hang me. He that is well hanged in this
world needs to fear no colors. 6
MARIA   Make that good. 7
FESTE   He shall see none to fear.
MARIA   A good lenten answer. I can tell thee where that 9
saying was born, of "I fear no colors."
FESTE   Where, good Mistress Mary?
MARIA   In the wars, and that may you be bold to say in 12
your foolery.
FESTE   Well, God give them wisdom that have it; and
those that are fools, let them use their talents. 15

32 rubious ruby red.   **pipe** voice, throat   **33 shrill and sound** high and
clear, uncracked   **34 semblative** resembling, like   **35 constellation** i.e.,
nature as determined by your horoscope   **41 barful strife** endeavor full
of impediments

1.5. Location: Olivia's house.
6 fear no colors i.e., fear no foe, fear nothing (with pun on *colors*,
worldly deceptions, and *collars*, halters or nooses)   **7 Make that good**
explain that   **9 lenten** meager, scanty (like lenten fare)   **12 In the wars**
(where *colors* would mean "military standards")   **15 talents** abilities
(also alluding to the parable of the talents, Matthew 25:14–29)

MARIA   Yet you will be hanged for being so long absent;
or to be turned away, is not that as good as a hanging   17
to you?

FESTE   Many a good hanging prevents a bad marriage;
and for turning away, let summer bear it out.   20

MARIA   You are resolute, then?

FESTE   Not so, neither, but I am resolved on two
points.   23

MARIA   That if one break, the other will hold; or if both
break, your gaskins fall.   25

FESTE   Apt, in good faith, very apt. Well, go thy way;
if Sir Toby would leave drinking, thou wert as witty a   27
piece of Eve's flesh as any in Illyria.   28

MARIA   Peace, you rogue, no more o' that. Here comes
my lady. Make your excuse wisely, you were best.   30

                                    [*Exit.*]

              Enter Lady Olivia with Malvolio [and attendants].

FESTE   Wit, an 't be thy will, put me into good fooling!   31
Those wits that think they have thee do very oft prove
fools, and I that am sure I lack thee may pass for a wise
man. For what says Quinapalus? "Better a witty fool   34
than a foolish wit."—God bless thee, lady!

OLIVIA   Take the fool away.

FESTE   Do you not hear, fellows? Take away the lady.

OLIVIA   Go to, you're a dry fool. I'll no more of you. Be-   38
sides, you grow dishonest.   39

FESTE   Two faults, madonna, that drink and good   40
counsel will amend. For give the dry fool drink, then
is the fool not dry. Bid the dishonest man mend himself; if he mend, he is no longer dishonest; if he cannot, let the botcher mend him. Anything that's   44

17 **turned away** dismissed (possibly also meaning "turned off,"
"hanged")   20 **for** as for.   **let . . . out** i.e., let mild weather make dismissal endurable   23 **points** (Maria plays on the meaning "laces used to
hold up hose or breeches.")   25 **gaskins** wide breeches   27–28 **thou . . .
Illyria** (Feste may be observing ironically that Maria is as likely to prove
witty as Sir Toby is to give up drinking; or he may hint at a match
between the two.)   30 **you were best** it would be best for you   31 **an 't**
if it   34 **Quinapalus** (Feste's invented authority.)   38 **dry** dull   39 **dishonest** unreliable; wicked   40 **madonna** my lady   44 **botcher** mender of
old clothes and shoes

mended is but patched; virtue that transgresses is but patched with sin, and sin that amends is but patched with virtue. If that this simple syllogism will serve, so; if it will not, what remedy? As there is no true cuckold 48 but calamity, so beauty's a flower. The lady bade take 49 away the fool; therefore I say again, take her away.

OLIVIA Sir, I bade them take away you.

FESTE Misprision in the highest degree! Lady, *cucul-* 52 *lus non facit monachum;* that's as much to say as I 53 wear not motley in my brain. Good madonna, give me 54 leave to prove you a fool.

OLIVIA Can you do it?

FESTE Dexterously, good madonna.

OLIVIA Make your proof.

FESTE I must catechize you for it, madonna. Good my 59 mouse of virtue, answer me.   60

OLIVIA Well, sir, for want of other idleness, I'll bide 61 your proof.

FESTE Good madonna, why mourn'st thou?

OLIVIA Good Fool, for my brother's death.

FESTE I think his soul is in hell, madonna.

OLIVIA I know his soul is in heaven, Fool.

FESTE The more fool, madonna, to mourn for your brother's soul, being in heaven. Take away the fool, gentlemen.

OLIVIA What think you of this fool, Malvolio? Doth he not mend?   71

MALVOLIO Yes, and shall do till the pangs of death shake him. Infirmity, that decays the wise, doth ever make the better fool.

FESTE God send you, sir, a speedy infirmity, for the better increasing your folly! Sir Toby will be sworn that I am no fox, but he will not pass his word for two-pence that you are no fool.

48–49 As ... flower i.e., Olivia has wedded calamity but will not be faithful to it, for the natural course is to seize the moment of youth and beauty before we lose it **52 Misprision** mistake, misunderstanding (a legal term meaning a wrongful action or misdemeanor) **52–53 cucullus ... monachum** the cowl does not make the monk **54 motley** the many-colored garment of jesters **59–60 Good ... virtue** my good virtuous mouse. (A term of endearment.) **61 idleness** pastime. **bide** endure **71 mend** i.e., improve, grow more amusing. (But Malvolio uses the word to mean "grow more like a fool.")

OLIVIA How say you to that, Malvolio?

MALVOLIO I marvel your ladyship takes delight in such
a barren rascal. I saw him put down the other day with 81
an ordinary fool that has no more brain than a stone.
Look you now, he's out of his guard already. Unless 83
you laugh and minister occasion to him, he is gagged. 84
I protest I take these wise men that crow so at these set 85
kind of fools no better than the fools' zanies.   86

OLIVIA O, you are sick of self-love, Malvolio, and taste
with a distempered appetite. To be generous, guiltless,
and of free disposition is to take those things for bird- 89
bolts that you deem cannon bullets. There is no slan- 90
der in an allowed fool, though he do nothing but rail; 91
nor no railing in a known discreet man, though he do
nothing but reprove.

FESTE Now Mercury endue thee with leasing, for 94
thou speak'st well of fools!

Enter Maria.

MARIA Madam, there is at the gate a young gentleman
much desires to speak with you.

OLIVIA From the Count Orsino, is it?

MARIA I know not, madam. 'Tis a fair young man, and
well attended.

OLIVIA Who of my people hold him in delay?

MARIA Sir Toby, madam, your kinsman.

OLIVIA Fetch him off, I pray you. He speaks nothing
but madman. Fie on him! [*Exit Maria.*] Go you, Mal- 104
volio. If it be a suit from the Count, I am sick, or not at
home; what you will, to dismiss it. (*Exit Malvolio.*)
Now you see, sir, how your fooling grows old, and 107
people dislike it.

FESTE Thou hast spoke for us, madonna, as if thy eldest son should be a fool; whose skull Jove cram with
brains, for—here he comes—

81 with by   **83 out of his guard** defenseless, unprovided with a witty
answer   **84 minister occasion** provide opportunity (for his fooling)
85 protest avow, declare.   **crow** laugh stridently.   **set** artificial, stereotyped   **86 zanies** assistants, aping attendants   **89 free** magnanimous
89–90 bird-bolts blunt arrows for shooting small birds   **91 allowed**
licensed (to speak freely)   **94 Now . . . leasing** i.e., may Mercury, the god
of deception, make you a skillful liar   **104 madman** i.e., the words of
madness   **107 old** stale

Enter Sir Toby.

one of thy kin has a most weak *pia mater*.   112

OLIVIA   By mine honor, half drunk. What is he at the
gate, cousin?

SIR TOBY   A gentleman.

OLIVIA   A gentleman? What gentleman?

SIR TOBY   'Tis a gentleman here—[*He belches.*] A plague o'
these pickle-herring! How now, sot?   118

FESTE   Good Sir Toby.

OLIVIA   Cousin, cousin, how have you come so early by
this lethargy?

SIR TOBY   Lechery? I defy lechery. There's one at the
gate.

OLIVIA   Ay, marry, what is he?

SIR TOBY   Let him be the devil, an he will, I care not.
Give me faith, say I. Well, it's all one.   *Exit.* 126

OLIVIA   What's a drunken man like, Fool?

FESTE   Like a drowned man, a fool, and a madman.
One draft above heat makes him a fool, the second 129
mads him, and a third drowns him.

OLIVIA   Go thou and seek the crowner, and let him sit 131
o' my coz; for he's in the third degree of drink, he's 132
drowned. Go, look after him.

FESTE   He is but mad yet, madonna; and the fool shall
look to the madman.   [*Exit.*]

Enter Malvolio.

MALVOLIO   Madam, yond young fellow swears he will
speak with you. I told him you were sick; he takes on
him to understand so much, and therefore comes to
speak with you. I told him you were asleep; he seems
to have a foreknowledge of that too, and therefore
comes to speak with you. What is to be said to him,
lady? He's fortified against any denial.

OLIVIA   Tell him he shall not speak with me.

MALVOLIO   He's been told so; and he says he'll stand at

---

112 **pia mater** i.e., brain (actually the soft membrane enclosing the
brain)   118 **sot** (1) fool (2) drunkard   126 **Give me faith** i.e., to resist the
devil.   **it's all one** it doesn't matter   129 **draft** drinking portion.   **above
heat** above the point needed to make him normally warm   131 **crowner**
coroner   131–132 **sit o' my coz** hold an inquest on my kinsman (Sir Toby)

your door like a sheriff's post, and be the supporter to 145
a bench, but he'll speak with you.

OLIVIA What kind o' man is he?

MALVOLIO Why, of mankind.

OLIVIA What manner of man?

MALVOLIO Of very ill manner. He'll speak with you,
will you or no.

OLIVIA Of what personage and years is he?

MALVOLIO Not yet old enough for a man, nor young
enough for a boy; as a squash is before 'tis a peascod, 154
or a codling when 'tis almost an apple. 'Tis with him 155
in standing water, between boy and man. He is very 156
well-favored and he speaks very shrewishly. One 157
would think his mother's milk were scarce out
of him.

OLIVIA Let him approach. Call in my gentlewoman.

MALVOLIO Gentlewoman, my lady calls.   *Exit.*

    Enter Maria.

OLIVIA

Give me my veil. Come, throw it o'er my face.
We'll once more hear Orsino's embassy.

                             [Olivia veils.]

    Enter Viola.

VIOLA The honorable lady of the house, which is she?

OLIVIA Speak to me; I shall answer for her. Your will?

VIOLA Most radiant, exquisite, and unmatchable
beauty—I pray you, tell me if this be the lady of the
house, for I never saw her. I would be loath to cast
away my speech; for besides that it is excellently well
penned, I have taken great pains to con it. Good beau- 170
ties, let me sustain no scorn; I am very comptible, even 171
to the least sinister usage.   172

OLIVIA Whence came you, sir?

VIOLA I can say little more than I have studied, and that

---

145 sheriff's post post before the sheriff's door on which proclamations
and notices were fixed   **154 squash** unripe pea pod.   **peascod** pea pod
155 codling unripe apple   **156 in standing water** at the turn of the
tide   **157 well-favored** good-looking.   **shrewishly** sharply   **170 con**
learn by heart   **171 comptible** susceptible, sensitive   **172 least sinister**
slightest discourteous

question's out of my part. Good gentle one, give me modest assurance if you be the lady of the house, that I may proceed in my speech. 176

OLIVIA Are you a comedian? 178

VIOLA No, my profound heart; and yet, by the very fangs of malice, I swear I am not that I play. Are you the lady of the house? 179

OLIVIA If I do not usurp myself, I am. 182

VIOLA Most certain, if you are she, you do usurp yourself; for what is yours to bestow is not yours to reserve. But this is from my commission. I will on with my speech in your praise, and then show you the heart of my message. 183 184 185

OLIVIA Come to what is important in 't. I forgive you the praise. 188

VIOLA Alas, I took great pains to study it, and 'tis poetical.

OLIVIA It is the more like to be feigned. I pray you, keep it in. I heard you were saucy at my gates, and allowed your approach rather to wonder at you than to hear you. If you be not mad, begone; if you have reason, be brief. 'Tis not that time of moon with me to make one in so skipping a dialogue. 195 196 197

MARIA Will you hoist sail, sir? Here lies your way.

VIOLA No, good swabber, I am to hull here a little longer.—Some mollification for your giant, sweet lady. Tell me your mind; I am a messenger. 199 200

OLIVIA Sure you have some hideous matter to deliver, when the courtesy of it is so fearful. Speak your office. 203

VIOLA It alone concerns your ear. I bring no overture of

---

176 modest reasonable   **178 comedian** actor   **179 profound** very wise, figuratively deep   **182 do . . . myself** am not an impostor   **183–184 usurp yourself** i.e., betray yourself, by withholding yourself from Orsino
185 from outside of   **188 forgive you** excuse you from repeating   **195 If . . . mad** i.e., if you don't have madness to excuse your saucy behavior (?) Possibly an error for *If . . . but mad* (?)   **reason** sanity   **196 moon** (The moon was thought to affect lunatics according to its changing phases.)
196–197 make one take part   **199 swabber** one in charge of washing the decks. (A nautical retort to *hoist sail*.)   **hull** lie with sails furled
200 Some . . . for i.e., please mollify, pacify.   **giant** i.e., the diminutive Maria who, like many giants in medieval romances, is guarding the lady   **203 courtesy** i.e., introduction.   **office** commission

war, no taxation of homage. I hold the olive in my 205
hand; my words are as full of peace as matter.

OLIVIA Yet you began rudely. What are you? What
would you?

VIOLA The rudeness that hath appeared in me have I
learned from my entertainment. What I am, and what 210
I would, are as secret as maidenhead—to your ears,
divinity; to any other's, profanation.

OLIVIA Give us the place alone; we will hear this divinity. [*Exeunt Maria and attendants.*] Now, sir, what is
your text?

VIOLA Most sweet lady—

OLIVIA A comfortable doctrine, and much may be said 217
of it. Where lies your text?

VIOLA In Orsino's bosom.

OLIVIA In his bosom? In what chapter of his bosom?

VIOLA To answer by the method, in the first of his 221
heart.

OLIVIA O, I have read it; it is heresy. Have you no more
to say?

VIOLA Good madam, let me see your face.

OLIVIA Have you any commission from your lord to ne-
gotiate with my face? You are now out of your text.
But we will draw the curtain and show you the picture. [*Unveiling.*] Look you, sir, such a one I was this 229
present. Is 't not well done?   230

VIOLA Excellently done, if God did all.

OLIVIA 'Tis in grain, sir; 'twill endure wind and 232
weather.

VIOLA

'Tis beauty truly blent, whose red and white   234
Nature's own sweet and cunning hand laid on.   235
Lady, you are the cruel'st she alive
If you will lead these graces to the grave
And leave the world no copy.   238

205 **taxation** demand for the payment   210 **entertainment** reception
217 **comfortable** comforting   221 **To . . . method** i.e., to continue the
metaphor (of delivering a sermon, begun with *divinity* and *what is your
text* and continued in *doctrine, heresy,* etc.)   229–230 **this present** at this
present time. (Since it was customary to hang curtains in front of pictures,
Olivia in unveiling speaks as if she were displaying a picture of herself.)
232 **in grain** fast dyed   234 **blent** blended   235 **cunning** skillful   238 **copy**
i.e., a child. (But Olivia uses the word to mean "transcript.")

OLIVIA   O, sir, I will not be so hardhearted. I will give
  out divers schedules of my beauty. It shall be inven- 240
  toried, and every particle and utensil labeled to my will: 241
  as, item, two lips, indifferent red; item, two gray eyes, 242
  with lids to them; item, one neck, one chin, and so
  forth. Were you sent hither to praise me?   244

VIOLA
  I see you what you are, you are too proud;
  But, if you were the devil, you are fair.   246
  My lord and master loves you. O, such love
  Could be but recompensed, though you were crowned 248
  The nonpareil of beauty!

OLIVIA   How does he love me?

VIOLA
  With adorations, fertile tears,   250
  With groans that thunder love, with sighs of fire.

OLIVIA
  Your lord does know my mind; I cannot love him.
  Yet I suppose him virtuous, know him noble,
  Of great estate, of fresh and stainless youth;
  In voices well divulged, free, learned, and valiant,   255
  And in dimension and the shape of nature
  A gracious person. But yet I cannot love him.   257
  He might have took his answer long ago.

VIOLA
  If I did love you in my master's flame,   259
  With such a suffering, such a deadly life,   260
  In your denial I would find no sense;
  I would not understand it.

OLIVIA   Why, what would you?

VIOLA
  Make me a willow cabin at your gate,   263
  And call upon my soul within the house;   264
  Write loyal cantons of contemnèd love,   265

---

240 schedules inventories   **241 utensil** article, item.   **labeled** added as
a codicil   **242 indifferent** somewhat   **244 praise** appraise   **246 if** even
if   **248 but . . . though** no more than evenly repaid even though
250 fertile copious   **255 In . . . divulged** well reported in public opinion.   **free** generous   **257 gracious** graceful, attractive   **259 flame**
passion   **260 deadly** deathlike   **263 willow cabin** shelter, hut. (Willow
was a symbol of unrequited love.)   **264 my soul** i.e., Olivia   **265 cantons**
songs.   **contemnèd** rejected

And sing them loud even in the dead of night;
Hallow your name to the reverberate hills,   267
And make the babbling gossip of the air   268
Cry out "Olivia!" O, you should not rest
Between the elements of air and earth
But you should pity me!

OLIVIA   You might do much.
What is your parentage?

VIOLA
Above my fortunes, yet my state is well: 273
I am a gentleman.

OLIVIA   Get you to your lord.
I cannot love him. Let him send no more—
Unless, perchance, you come to me again
To tell me how he takes it. Fare you well.
I thank you for your pains. Spend this for me.

                              [*She offers a purse.*]

VIOLA
I am no fee'd post, lady; keep your purse.   279
My master, not myself, lacks recompense.
Love make his heart of flint that you shall love,   281
And let your fervor, like my master's, be
Placed in contempt! Farewell, fair cruelty.   *Exit.*

OLIVIA   "What is your parentage?"
"Above my fortunes, yet my state is well:
I am a gentleman." I'll be sworn thou art!
Thy tongue, thy face, thy limbs, actions, and spirit
Do give thee fivefold blazon. Not too fast! Soft, soft!   288
Unless the master were the man. How now?
Even so quickly may one catch the plague?
Methinks I feel this youth's perfections
With an invisible and subtle stealth
To creep in at mine eyes. Well, let it be.
What ho, Malvolio!

        Enter Malvolio.

MALVOLIO   Here, madam, at your service.

267 **Hallow** (1) halloo (2) bless   268 **babbling . . . air** echo   273 **state**
social standing   279 **fee'd post** messenger to be tipped   281 **Love . . .**
love may Love make the heart of the man you love as hard as flint
288 **blazon** heraldic description

OLIVIA
Run after that same peevish messenger,
The County's man. He left this ring behind him,   296
                    [*Giving a ring*]
Would I or not. Tell him I'll none of it.   297
Desire him not to flatter with his lord,   298
Nor hold him up with hopes; I am not for him.
If that the youth will come this way tomorrow,
I'll give him reasons for 't. Hie thee, Malvolio.
MALVOLIO   Madam, I will.   *Exit.*
OLIVIA
I do I know not what, and fear to find
Mine eye too great a flatterer for my mind.   304
Fate, show thy force. Ourselves we do not owe;   305
What is decreed must be, and be this so.   [*Exit.*]

❖

296 **County's** Count's, i.e., Duke's   297 **Would I or not** whether I
wanted it or not   298 **flatter with** encourage   304 **Mine . . . mind** i.e.,
that my eyes (through which love enters the soul) have betrayed my
reason   305 **owe** own, control

2.1 *Enter Antonio and Sebastian.*

ANTONIO   Will you stay no longer? Nor will you not that ₁
I go with you?

SEBASTIAN   By your patience, no. My stars shine darkly ₃
over me. The malignancy of my fate might perhaps ₄
distemper yours; therefore I shall crave of you your ₅
leave, that I may bear my evils alone. It were a bad
recompense for your love to lay any of them on you.

ANTONIO   Let me yet know of you whither you are
bound.

SEBASTIAN   No, sooth, sir; my determinate voyage is ₁₀
mere extravagancy. But I perceive in you so excellent ₁₁
a touch of modesty that you will not extort from me
what I am willing to keep in; therefore it charges me ₁₃
in manners the rather to express myself. You must ₁₄
know of me then, Antonio, my name is Sebastian,
which I called Roderigo. My father was that Sebastian
of Messaline whom I know you have heard of. He left ₁₇
behind him myself and a sister, both born in an hour. ₁₈
If the heavens had been pleased, would we had so
ended! But you, sir, altered that, for some hour before ₂₀
you took me from the breach of the sea was my sister ₂₁
drowned.

ANTONIO   Alas the day!

SEBASTIAN   A lady, sir, though it was said she much resembled me, was yet of many accounted beautiful. But
though I could not with such estimable wonder over- ₂₆
far believe that, yet thus far I will boldly publish her: ₂₇
she bore a mind that envy could not but call fair. She
is drowned already, sir, with salt water, though I seem
to drown her remembrance again with more.

2.1. Location: Somewhere in Illyria.
1 Nor will you not do you not wish   **3 patience** leave   **4 malignancy**
malevolence (of the stars; also in a medical sense)   **5 distemper** disorder, disturb   **10 sooth** truly.   **determinate** intended, determined upon
11 extravagancy aimless wandering   **13 am willing ... in** wish to keep
secret   **13–14 it ... manners** it is incumbent upon me in all courtesy
14 express reveal   **17 Messaline** probably Messina, or, more likely,
Massila (the modern Marseilles). In Plautus' *Menaechmi*, Massilians and
Illyrians are mentioned together.   **18 in an hour** in the same hour
20 some hour about an hour   **21 breach of the sea** surf   **26 estimable**
wonder admiring judgment   **27 publish** proclaim

ANTONIO Pardon me, sir, your bad entertainment. 31
SEBASTIAN O good Antonio, forgive me your trouble. 32
ANTONIO If you will not murder me for my love, let me 33
be your servant.
SEBASTIAN If you will not undo what you have done,
that is, kill him whom you have recovered, desire it 36
not. Fare ye well at once. My bosom is full of kindness, 37
and I am yet so near the manners of my mother that 38
upon the least occasion more mine eyes will tell tales
of me. I am bound to the Count Orsino's court. Fare-
well.   *Exit.*
ANTONIO
The gentleness of all the gods go with thee!
I have many enemies in Orsino's court,
Else would I very shortly see thee there.
But come what may, I do adore thee so
That danger shall seem sport, and I will go.   *Exit.*

❖

2.2 *Enter Viola and Malvolio, at several doors.*

MALVOLIO Were not you even now with the Countess
Olivia?
VIOLA Even now, sir. On a moderate pace I have since
arrived but hither.
MALVOLIO She returns this ring to you, sir. You might
have saved me my pains, to have taken it away yourself. She adds, moreover, that you should put your
lord into a desperate assurance she will none of him. 8
And one thing more, that you be never so hardy to 9
come again in his affairs, unless it be to report your
lord's taking of this. Receive it so.
VIOLA She took the ring of me. I'll none of it.   12

---

31 **entertainment** reception, hospitality 32 **your trouble** the trouble
I put you to 33 **murder me for** i.e., be the cause of my death in
return for 36 **recovered** rescued, restored 37 **kindness** tenderness,
natural emotion (of grief) 38 **manners of my mother** womanish
qualities

2.2. Location: Outside Olivia's house.
s.d. several different **8 desperate** without hope **9 hardy** bold **12 She
. . . it** (Viola tells a quick and friendly lie to shield Olivia.)

MALVOLIO   Come, sir, you peevishly threw it to her, and
her will is it should be so returned. [*He throws down
the ring.*] If it be worth stooping for, there it lies, in   15
your eye; if not, be it his that finds it.   *Exit.*   16
VIOLA [*Picking up the ring*]
   I left no ring with her. What means this lady?
   Fortune forbid my outside have not charmed her!
   She made good view of me, indeed so much   19
   That sure methought her eyes had lost her tongue,   20
   For she did speak in starts distractedly.
   She loves me, sure! The cunning of her passion
   Invites me in this churlish messenger.   23
   None of my lord's ring? Why, he sent her none.
   I am the man. If it be so—as 'tis—
   Poor lady, she were better love a dream.
   Disguise, I see, thou art a wickedness
   Wherein the pregnant enemy does much.   28
   How easy is it for the proper false   29
   In women's waxen hearts to set their forms!   30
   Alas, our frailty is the cause, not we,
   For such as we are made of, such we be.   32
   How will this fadge? My master loves her dearly,   33
   And I, poor monster, fond as much on him;   34
   And she, mistaken, seems to dote on me.
   What will become of this? As I am man,
   My state is desperate for my master's love;
   As I am woman—now, alas the day!—
   What thriftless sighs shall poor Olivia breathe!   39
   O Time, thou must untangle this, not I;
   It is too hard a knot for me t' untie.   [*Exit.*]

❖

15–16 **in your eye** in plain sight   19 **made good view of** took a careful
look at   20 **lost** caused her to lose; or, ruined   23 **Invites** tries to
attract   28 **pregnant** quick, resourceful.   **enemy** i.e., Satan   29 **proper
false** men who are handsome and deceitful   30 **waxen** i.e., malleable,
impressionable.   **set their forms** stamp their images (as of a seal)
32 **such as . . . of** i.e., feminine frailty   33 **fadge** turn out   34 **monster**
i.e., being both man and woman.   **fond** dote   39 **thriftless** unprofitable

2.3   *Enter Sir Toby and Sir Andrew.*

SIR TOBY   Approach, Sir Andrew. Not to be abed after
midnight is to be up betimes; and *diluculo surgere,* 2
thou know'st—

SIR ANDREW   Nay, by my troth, I know not, but I know
to be up late is to be up late.

SIR TOBY   A false conclusion. I hate it as an unfilled can. 6
To be up after midnight and to go to bed then, is early;
so that to go to bed after midnight is to go to bed
betimes. Does not our lives consist of the four ele- 9
ments?   10

SIR ANDREW   Faith, so they say, but I think it rather con-
sists of eating and drinking.

SIR TOBY   Thou'rt a scholar; let us therefore eat and
drink. Marian, I say, a stoup of wine!   14

   Enter Clown [Feste].

SIR ANDREW   Here comes the Fool, i' faith.

FESTE   How now, my hearts! Did you never see the
picture of "we three"?   17

SIR TOBY   Welcome, ass. Now let's have a catch.   18

SIR ANDREW   By my troth, the Fool has an excellent
breast. I had rather than forty shillings I had such a 20
leg, and so sweet a breath to sing, as the Fool has. In
sooth, thou wast in very gracious fooling last night,
when thou spok'st of Pigrogromitus, of the Vapians 23
passing the equinoctial of Queubus. 'Twas very good, 24
i' faith. I sent thee sixpence for thy leman. Hadst it? 25

FESTE   I did impeticos thy gratillity; for Malvolio's 26
nose is no whipstock. My lady has a white hand, and 27

2.3. Location: Olivia's house.
2 betimes early.   **diluculo surgere [saluberrimum est]** to rise early is most
healthful. (A sentence from Lilly's *Latin Grammar.*)   **6 can** tankard
9–10 four elements i.e., fire, air, water, and earth, the elements that were
thought to make up all matter   **14 stoup** drinking vessel   **17 picture of**
"we three" picture of two fools or asses inscribed "we three," the specta-
tor being the third   **18 catch** round   **20 breast** voice   **23–24 Pigrogromitus**
. . . Queubus (Feste's mock erudition.)   **25 leman** sweetheart   **26 impeticos**
thy gratillity (Suggests "impetticoat, or pocket up, thy gratuity.")
27 whipstock whip handle. (Possibly suggests that Malvolio is not very
formidable as overseer in Olivia's household; or, just nonsense.)   **has a**
white hand i.e., is ladylike. (But Feste's speech may be mere nonsense.)

the Myrmidons are no bottle-ale houses.   28

SIR ANDREW Excellent! Why, this is the best fooling,
when all is done. Now, a song.

SIR TOBY Come on, there is sixpence for you. [*He gives
money.*] Let's have a song.

SIR ANDREW There's a testril of me too. [*He gives money.*] 33
If one knight give a—

FESTE Would you have a love song, or a song of good 35
life?   36

SIR TOBY A love song, a love song.

SIR ANDREW Ay, ay, I care not for good life.

FESTE (*Sings*)
        O mistress mine, where are you roaming?
        O, stay and hear, your true love's coming,
            That can sing both high and low.
        Trip no further, pretty sweeting;
        Journeys end in lovers meeting,
            Every wise man's son doth know.

SIR ANDREW Excellent good, i' faith.

SIR TOBY Good, good.

FESTE [*Sings*]
        What is love? 'tis not hereafter;
        Present mirth hath present laughter;
            What's to come is still unsure.
        In delay there lies no plenty,
        Then come kiss me, sweet and twenty;   51
            Youth's a stuff will not endure.

SIR ANDREW A mellifluous voice, as I am true knight.

SIR TOBY A contagious breath.

SIR ANDREW Very sweet and contagious, i' faith.

SIR TOBY To hear by the nose, it is dulcet in contagion. 56
But shall we make the welkin dance indeed? Shall we 57

---

28 Myrmidons followers of Achilles.   **bottle-ale houses** (Used contemptuously of taverns because they sold low-class drink.)   **33 testril** i.e.,
tester, a coin worth sixpense   **35–36 good life** virtuous living. (Or perhaps Feste means simply "life's pleasures," but is misunderstood by
Sir Andrew to mean "virtuous living.")   **51 sweet and twenty** i.e., sweet
and twenty times sweet   **56 To . . . nose** i.e., to describe hearing in
olfactory terms.   **dulcet in contagion** (Sir Toby may be mocking Sir
Andrew's unfortunate choice of words.)   **57 make . . . dance** i.e., drink
till the sky seems to turn around

rouse the night owl in a catch that will draw three 58
souls out of one weaver? Shall we do that?   59
SIR ANDREW   An you love me, let's do 't. I am dog at a 60
catch.   61
FESTE   By 'r Lady, sir, and some dogs will catch well.
SIR ANDREW   Most certain. Let our catch be "Thou
knave."
FESTE   "Hold thy peace, thou knave," knight? I shall
be constrained in 't to call thee knave, knight.
SIR ANDREW   'Tis not the first time I have constrained
one to call me knave. Begin, Fool. It begins, "Hold thy
peace."
FESTE   I shall never begin if I hold my peace.
SIR ANDREW   Good, i' faith. Come, begin.   *Catch sung.*

Enter Maria.

MARIA   What a caterwauling do you keep here! If my
lady have not called up her steward Malvolio and bid
him turn you out of doors, never trust me.
SIR TOBY   My lady's a Cataian, we are politicians, Mal- 75
volio's a Peg-a-Ramsey, and [*Sings*] "Three merry 76
men be we." Am not I consanguineous? Am I not of 77
her blood? Tillyvally! Lady! [*Sings*.] "There dwelt a 78
man in Babylon, lady, lady."   79
FESTE   Beshrew me, the knight's in admirable fooling.
SIR ANDREW   Ay, he does well enough if he be disposed,
and so do I too. He does it with a better grace, but I
do it more natural.   83
SIR TOBY   [*Sings*]   "O' the twelfth day of December"— 84

58–59 draw three souls (Refers to the threefold nature of the soul,
vegetal, sensible, and intellectual; or to the three singers of the three-
part catch; or, just a comic exaggeration.)   **59 weaver** (Weavers were
often associated with psalm-singing.)   **60 dog at** very clever at. (But
Feste uses the word literally.)   **61 catch** round. (But Feste uses it to
mean "seize.")   **75 Cataian** Cathayan, i.e., Chinese, a trickster; or, just
nonsense.   **politicians** schemers, intriguers   **76 Peg-a-Ramsey** character
in a popular song. (Used here contemptuously.)   **76–77 Three . . . we** (A
snatch of an old song.)   **77 consanguineous** i.e., a blood relative of
Olivia   **78 Tillyvally** i.e., nonsense, fiddle-faddle   **78–79 There . . . lady**
(The first line of a ballad, "The Constancy of Susanna," together with
the refrain, "Lady, lady.")   **83 natural** naturally (but unconsciously
suggesting idiocy)   **84 O'. . . December** (Possibly part of a ballad about
the Battle of Musselburgh Field, or Toby's error for the "twelfth day of
Christmas," i.e., Twelfth Night.)

MARIA   For the love o' God, peace!

Enter Malvolio.

MALVOLIO   My masters, are you mad? Or what are you?
Have you no wit, manners, nor honesty but to gabble
like tinkers at this time of night? Do ye make an alehouse of my lady's house that ye squeak out your coz- 89
iers' catches without any mitigation or remorse of 90
voice? Is there no respect of place, persons, nor time in
you?

SIR TOBY   We did keep time, sir, in our catches. Sneck 93
up!   94

MALVOLIO   Sir Toby, I must be round with you. My 95
lady bade me tell you that though she harbors you as
her kinsman, she's nothing allied to your disorders. If
you can separate yourself and your misdemeanors,
you are welcome to the house; if not, an it would
please you to take leave of her, she is very willing to
bid you farewell.

SIR TOBY [*Sings*]
   "Farewell, dear heart, since I must needs be gone." 102

MARIA   Nay, good Sir Toby.

FESTE [*Sings*]
   "His eyes do show his days are almost done."

MALVOLIO   Is 't even so?

SIR TOBY [*Sings*]
   "But I will never die."

FESTE
   Sir Toby, there you lie.

MALVOLIO   This is much credit to you.

SIR TOBY [*Sings*]
   "Shall I bid him go?"

FESTE [*Sings*]
   "What an if you do?"

SIR TOBY [*Sings*]
   "Shall I bid him go, and spare not?"

FESTE [*Sings*]
   "O, no, no, no, no, you dare not."

89–90 coziers' cobblers'   **90 mitigation or remorse** i.e., considerate
lowering   **93–94 Sneck up** go hang   **95 round** blunt   **102 Farewell . . . gone** (From the ballad "Corydon's Farewell to Phyllis.")

SIR TOBY   Out o' tune, sir? Ye lie. Art any more than a
steward? Dost thou think, because thou art virtuous,
there shall be no more cakes and ale?

FESTE   Yes, by Saint Anne, and ginger shall be hot i'   116
the mouth too.

SIR TOBY   Thou'rt i' the right. Go, sir, rub your chain   118
with crumbs. A stoup of wine, Maria!   119

MALVOLIO   Mistress Mary, if you prized my lady's favor
at anything more than contempt, you would not give   121
means for this uncivil rule. She shall know of it, by   122
this hand.   *Exit.*

MARIA   Go shake your ears.   124

SIR ANDREW   'Twere as good a deed as to drink when a
man's a-hungry, to challenge him the field, and then   126
to break promise with him and make a fool of him.

SIR TOBY   Do 't, knight. I'll write thee a challenge, or I'll
deliver thy indignation to him by word of mouth.

MARIA   Sweet Sir Toby, be patient for tonight. Since the
youth of the Count's was today with my lady, she is
much out of quiet. For Monsieur Malvolio, let me
alone with him. If I do not gull him into a nayword   133
and make him a common recreation, do not think I   134
have wit enough to lie straight in my bed. I know I
can do it.

SIR TOBY   Possess us, possess us, tell us something of   137
him.

MARIA   Marry, sir, sometimes he is a kind of puritan.   139

SIR ANDREW   O, if I thought that, I'd beat him like a
dog.

SIR TOBY   What, for being a puritan? Thy exquisite reason, dear knight?

---

116 Saint Anne mother of the Virgin Mary. (Her cult was derided in the
Reformation.)   **ginger** (Commonly used to spice ale.)   **118–119 Go . . .
crumbs** i.e., scour or polish your steward's chain; attend to your own
business and remember your station   **121–122 give means** i.e., supply
drink   **122 rule** conduct   **124 your ears** i.e., your ass's ears   **126 the
field** i.e., to a duel   **133 gull** trick.   **nayword** byword   **134 recreation**
sport   **137 Possess** inform   **139 puritan** (Maria's point is that Malvolio
is sometimes a *kind* of puritan, insofar as he is precise about moral
conduct and censorious of others for immoral conduct, but that he is
nothing consistently except a time-server. He is not then simply a
satirical type of the Puritan sect. The extent of the resemblance is left
unstated.)

SIR ANDREW I have no exquisite reason for 't, but I have
reason good enough.

MARIA The devil a puritan that he is, or anything constantly, but a time-pleaser; an affectioned ass, that cons 147
state without book and utters it by great swaths; the 148
best persuaded of himself, so crammed, as he thinks, 149
with excellencies, that it is his grounds of faith that all 150
that look on him love him; and on that vice in him
will my revenge find notable cause to work.

SIR TOBY What wilt thou do?

MARIA I will drop in his way some obscure epistles of
love; wherein, by the color of his beard, the shape of
his leg, the manner of his gait, the expressure of his 156
eye, forehead, and complexion, he shall find himself 157
most feelingly personated. I can write very like my 158
lady your niece; on a forgotten matter we can hardly
make distinction of our hands.

SIR TOBY Excellent! I smell a device.

SIR ANDREW I have 't in my nose too.

SIR TOBY He shall think, by the letters that thou wilt
drop, that they come from my niece, and that she's in
love with him.

MARIA My purpose is indeed a horse of that color.

SIR ANDREW And your horse now would make him an
ass.

MARIA Ass, I doubt not.   169

SIR ANDREW O, 'twill be admirable!

MARIA Sport royal, I warrant you. I know my physic 171
will work with him. I will plant you two, and let the
Fool make a third, where he shall find the letter. Observe
his construction of it. For this night, to bed, and
dream on the event. Farewell.   *Exit.* 175

SIR TOBY Good night, Penthesilea.   176

---

147 time-pleaser time-server, sycophant. **afffectioned** affected
147–148 cons . . . book learns by heart the phrases and mannerisms of
the great **149 best persuaded** having the best opinion **150 grounds of
faith** creed, belief **156 expressure** expression **157 complexion** countenance **158 personated** represented **169 Ass, I** (with a pun on
"as I") **171 physic** medicine **175 event** outcome **176 Penthesilea**
Queen of the Amazons. (Another ironical allusion to Maria's diminutive
stature.)

SIR ANDREW   Before me, she's a good wench.   177
SIR TOBY   She's a beagle true-bred and one that adores
  me. What o' that?
SIR ANDREW   I was adored once too.
SIR TOBY   Let's to bed, knight. Thou hadst need send for
  more money.
SIR ANDREW   If I cannot recover your niece, I am a foul   183
  way out.   184
SIR TOBY   Send for money, knight. If thou hast her not
  i' the end, call me cut.   186
SIR ANDREW   If I do not, never trust me, take it how you
  will.
SIR TOBY   Come, come, I'll go burn some sack. 'Tis too   189
  late to go to bed now. Come, knight; come, knight.

                                                              Exeunt.

                                    ❖

2.4   *Enter Duke [Orsino], Viola, Curio,*
         and others.

ORSINO
  Give me some music. Now, good morrow, friends.
  Now, good Cesario, but that piece of song,   2
  That old and antique song we heard last night;   3
  Methought it did relieve my passion much,
  More than light airs and recollected terms   5
  Of these most brisk and giddy-pacèd times.
  Come, but one verse.
CURIO   He is not here, so please your lordship, that
  should sing it.
ORSINO   Who was it?
CURIO   Feste the jester, my lord, a fool that the Lady
  Olivia's father took much delight in. He is about the
  house.

177 Before me i.e., on my soul   **183 recover** win   **183–184 foul way out**
i.e., miserably out of pocket. (Literally, out of my way and in the mire.)
186 cut a horse with a docked tail; also, a gelding, or the female genital
organ   **189 burn some sack** warm some Spanish wine

2.4. Location: Orsino's court.
2 but i.e., I ask only   **3 antique** old, quaint, fantastic   **5 recollected
terms** studied and artificial expressions (?)

ORSINO
  Seek him out, and play the tune the while.
                       [Exit Curio.] Music plays.
  Come hither, boy. If ever thou shalt love,
  In the sweet pangs of it remember me;
  For such as I am, all true lovers are,
  Unstaid and skittish in all motions else   18
  Save in the constant image of the creature
  That is beloved. How dost thou like this tune?

VIOLA
  It gives a very echo to the seat   21
  Where Love is throned.

ORSINO   Thou dost speak masterly.
  My life upon 't, young though thou art, thine eye
  Hath stayed upon some favor that it loves.   24
  Hath it not, boy?

VIOLA   A little, by your favor.   25

ORSINO
  What kind of woman is 't?

VIOLA   Of your complexion.

ORSINO
  She is not worth thee, then. What years, i' faith?

VIOLA About your years, my lord.

ORSINO
  Too old, by heaven. Let still the woman take   29
  An elder than herself; so wears she to him,   30
  So sways she level in her husband's heart.   31
  For, boy, however we do praise ourselves,
  Our fancies are more giddy and unfirm,
  More longing, wavering, sooner lost and worn,
  Than women's are.

VIOLA   I think it well, my lord.

ORSINO
  Then let thy love be younger than thyself,
  Or thy affection cannot hold the bent;   37
  For women are as roses, whose fair flower
  Being once displayed, doth fall that very hour.

---

18 motions else other thoughts and emotions **21 the seat** i.e., the heart
24 stayed . . . favor rested upon some face **25 by your favor** (1) if you
please (2) like you in feature **29 still** always **30 wears she** she adapts
herself **31 sways she level** she keeps steady, constant **37 hold the bent**
hold steady (like the tension of a bow)

VIOLA
And so they are. Alas, that they are so,
To die, even when they to perfection grow!   41

    Enter Curio and Clown [Feste].

ORSINO
O fellow, come, the song we had last night.
Mark it, Cesario, it is old and plain;
The spinsters and the knitters in the sun,   44
And the free maids that weave their thread with bones, 45
Do use to chant it. It is silly sooth,   46
And dallies with the innocence of love,
Like the old age.   48
FESTE   Are you ready, sir?
ORSINO   Ay, prithee, sing.   *Music.*

       The Song.

FESTE
Come away, come away, death,
   And in sad cypress let me be laid.   52
Fly away, fly away, breath;
   I am slain by a fair cruel maid.
My shroud of white, stuck all with yew,   55
    O, prepare it!
My part of death, no one so true   57
    Did share it.   58

Not a flower, not a flower sweet
   On my black coffin let there be strown;   60
Not a friend, not a friend greet
   My poor corpse, where my bones shall be thrown.
A thousand thousand sighs to save,
    Lay me, O, where
Sad true lover never find my grave,
    To weep there!

---

41 even when just as   **44 spinsters** spinners   **45 free** carefree, innocent.
bones bobbins on which bone-lace was made   **46 Do use** are accustomed.
silly sooth simple truth   **48 Like . . . age** as in the good old times   **52 cy-**
press i.e., a coffin of cypress wood, or bier strewn with sprigs of cypress
55 yew i.e., yew sprigs. (Emblematic of mourning, like cypress.)   **57–58 My**
. . . it i.e., no one died for love so true to love as I   **60 strown** strewn

ORSINO   There's for thy pains.   [*Offering money.*]

FESTE   No pains, sir. I take pleasure in singing, sir.

ORSINO   I'll pay thy pleasure then.

FESTE   Truly, sir, and pleasure will be paid, one time 70
or another. 71

ORSINO   Give me now leave to leave thee. 72

FESTE   Now, the melancholy god protect thee, and the 73
tailor make thy doublet of changeable taffeta, for thy 74
mind is a very opal. I would have men of such constancy put to sea, that their business might be every- 76
thing and their intent everywhere, for that's it that 77
always makes a good voyage of nothing. Farewell. 78
                                          Exit.

ORSINO
Let all the rest give place.
                    [*Curio and attendants withdraw.*]
                    Once more, Cesario, 79
Get thee to yond same sovereign cruelty.
Tell her my love, more noble than the world,
Prizes not quantity of dirty lands;
The parts that fortune hath bestowed upon her, 83
Tell her, I hold as giddily as fortune; 84
But 'tis that miracle and queen of gems 85
That nature pranks her in attracts my soul. 86

VIOLA   But if she cannot love you, sir?

ORSINO
I cannot be so answered.

VIOLA   Sooth, but you must.
Say that some lady, as perhaps there is,

70–71 pleasure . . . another i.e., sooner or later one must pay for
indulgence   **72 leave to leave** permission to take leave of, dismiss
73 the melancholy god i.e., Saturn, whose planet was thought to control the melancholy temperament   **74 doublet** close-fitting jacket.
changeable taffeta a silk so woven of various-colored threads
that its color shifts with changing perspective   **76–77 that . . .
everywhere** i.e., so that in the changeableness of the sea their inconstancy could always be exercised   **77–78 for . . . nothing** i.e., because such inconstant men would (1) make a good voyage come to
nothing but (2) think a voyage that led anywhere a good one   **79 give
place** withdraw   **83 parts** attributes such as wealth or rank   **84 I . . .
fortune** i.e., I esteem as carelessly as does fortune, that fickle goddess
85 miracle . . . gems i.e. her beauty   **86 pranks** adorns.   **attracts** i.e.,
that attracts

Hath for your love as great a pang of heart
As you have for Olivia. You cannot love her;
You tell her so. Must she not then be answered?
ORSINO   There is no woman's sides
Can bide the beating of so strong a passion   94
As love doth give my heart; no woman's heart
So big, to hold so much; they lack retention.   96
Alas, their love may be called appetite,
No motion of the liver, but the palate,   98
That suffer surfeit, cloyment, and revolt;   99
But mine is all as hungry as the sea,
And can digest as much. Make no compare
Between that love a woman can bear me
And that I owe Olivia.
VIOLA   Ay, but I know—   103
ORSINO   What dost thou know?
VIOLA
Too well what love women to men may owe.
In faith, they are as true of heart as we.
My father had a daughter loved a man
As it might be perhaps, were I a woman,
I should your lordship.
ORSINO   And what's her history?
VIOLA
A blank, my lord. She never told her love,
But let concealment, like a worm i' the bud,
Feed on her damask cheek. She pined in thought,   112
And with a green and yellow melancholy
She sat like Patience on a monument,   114
Smiling at grief. Was not this love indeed?
We men may say more, swear more, but indeed
Our shows are more than will; for still we prove   117
Much in our vows, but little in our love.
ORSINO
But died thy sister of her love, my boy?

94 bide withstand   **96 retention** constancy, power of retaining
98 motion impulse.   **liver . . . palate** (Real love is a passion of the liver,
whereas fancy, light love, is born in the eye and nourished in the palate.)   **99 cloyment** satiety.   **revolt** sickness, revulsion   **103 owe** have
for   **112 damask** pink and white like the damask rose   **114 on a monument** carved in statuary on a tomb   **117 more than will** greater than
our feelings.   **still** always

VIOLA
    I am all the daughters of my father's house,
    And all the brothers too—and yet I know not.
    Sir, shall I to this lady?
ORSINO   Ay, that's the theme.
    To her in haste; give her this jewel. [*He gives a jewel.*] Say
    My love can give no place, bide no denay.   *Exeunt.* 124

❖

2.5   *Enter Sir Toby, Sir Andrew, and Fabian.*

SIR TOBY   Come thy ways, Signor Fabian.
FABIAN   Nay, I'll come. If I lose a scruple of this sport, 2
    let me be boiled to death with melancholy.   3
SIR TOBY   Wouldst thou not be glad to have the nig-
    gardly rascally sheep-biter come by some notable 5
    shame?
FABIAN   I would exult, man. You know he brought me
    out o' favor with my lady about a bearbaiting here.
SIR TOBY   To anger him we'll have the bear again, and
    we will fool him black and blue. Shall we not, Sir 10
    Andrew?
SIR ANDREW   An we do not, it is pity of our lives.   12

    Enter Maria.

SIR TOBY   Here comes the little villain.—How now, my 13
    metal of India?   14
MARIA   Get ye all three into the boxtree. Malvolio's
    coming down this walk. He has been yonder i' the sun
    practicing behavior to his own shadow this half hour.
    Observe him, for the love of mockery, for I know this
    letter will make a contemplative idiot of him. Close, in 19
    the name of jesting! [*The others hide.*] Lie thou there

___

124 can . . . denay cannot yield or endure denial

2.5. Location: Olivia's garden.
2 scruple bit   **3 boiled** (with a pun on *biled;* black bile was the "humor"
of melancholy)   **5 sheep-biter** a dog that bites sheep, i.e., a nuisance
10 fool . . . blue mock him until he is figuratively black and blue
12 pity of our lives a pity we should live   **13 villain** (Here a term of
endearment.)   **14 metal** gold, i.e., priceless one   **19 contemplative** i.e.,
from his musings.   **Close** i.e., keep close, stay hidden

[*Throwing down a letter*]; for here comes the trout that
must be caught with tickling.   *Exit.* 22

  Enter Malvolio.

MALVOLIO 'Tis but fortune, all is fortune. Maria once
told me she did affect me; and I have heard herself 24
come thus near, that should she fancy, it should be 25
one of my complexion. Besides, she uses me with a
more exalted respect than anyone else that follows 27
her. What should I think on 't?
SIR TOBY Here's an overweening rogue!
FABIAN O, peace! Contemplation makes a rare turkey-
cock of him. How he jets under his advanced plumes! 31
SIR ANDREW 'Slight, I could so beat the rogue!   32
SIR TOBY Peace, I say.
MALVOLIO To be Count Malvolio.
SIR TOBY Ah, rogue!
SIR ANDREW Pistol him, pistol him.
SIR TOBY Peace, peace!
MALVOLIO There is example for 't. The lady of the Stra- 38
chy married the yeoman of the wardrobe.   39
SIR ANDREW Fie on him, Jezebel!   40
FABIAN O, peace! Now he's deeply in. Look how imag-
ination blows him.   42
MALVOLIO Having been three months married to her,
sitting in my state—   44
SIR TOBY O, for a stone-bow, to hit him in the eye!   45
MALVOLIO Calling my officers about me, in my
branched velvet gown; having come from a daybed, 47
where I have left Olivia sleeping—
SIR TOBY Fire and brimstone!
FABIAN O, peace, peace!
MALVOLIO And then to have the humor of state; and 51

22 tickling (1) stroking gently about the gills—an actual method of
fishing (2) flattery   **24 she** i.e., Olivia.   **affect** have fondness for
25 fancy fall in love   **27 follows** serves   **31 jets** struts.   **advanced**
raised   **32 'Slight** by His (God's) light   **38 example** precedent
38–39 lady of the Strachy (Apparently a lady who had married below
her station; no certain identification.)   **40 Jezebel** the proud queen of
Ahab, King of Israel   **42 blows** puffs up   **44 state** chair of state
45 stone-bow crossbow that shoots stones   **47 branched** adorned with a
figured pattern suggesting branched leaves or flowers.   **daybed** sofa,
couch   **51 have . . . state** adopt the imperious manner of authority

after a demure travel of regard, telling them I know my 52
place as I would they should do theirs, to ask for my
kinsman Toby—   54

SIR TOBY Bolts and shackles!

FABIAN O, peace, peace, peace! Now, now.

MALVOLIO Seven of my people, with an obedient start,
make out for him. I frown the while, and perchance
wind up my watch, or play with my—some rich 59
jewel. Toby approaches; curtsies there to me—

SIR TOBY Shall this fellow live?

FABIAN Though our silence be drawn from us with 62
cars, yet peace.   63

MALVOLIO I extend my hand to him thus, quenching
my familiar smile with an austere regard of control— 65

SIR TOBY And does not Toby take you a blow o' the lips 66
then?

MALVOLIO Saying, "Cousin Toby, my fortunes having
cast me on your niece give me this prerogative of
speech—"

SIR TOBY What, what?

MALVOLIO "You must amend your drunkenness."

SIR TOBY Out, scab!   73

FABIAN Nay, patience, or we break the sinews of our
plot.

MALVOLIO "Besides, you waste the treasure of your
time with a foolish knight—"

SIR ANDREW That's me, I warrant you.

MALVOLIO "One Sir Andrew—"

SIR ANDREW I knew 'twas I, for many do call me fool.

MALVOLIO What employment have we here?   81

[*Taking up the letter.*]

FABIAN Now is the woodcock near the gin.   82

SIR TOBY O, peace, and the spirit of humors intimate 83
reading aloud to him!

---

52 demure . . . regard grave survey of the company. **telling** indicating
to **54 Toby** (Malvolio omits the title *Sir*.) **59 play with my** (Malvolio
perhaps means his steward's chain, but checks himself in time; as
"Count Malvolio" he would not be wearing it. A bawdy meaning is also
suggested.) **62–63 with cars** with chariots, i.e., by force **65 familiar**
friendly. **regard of control** look of authority **66 take** deliver **73 scab**
scurvy fellow **81 employment** business **82 woodcock** (A bird proverbial for its stupidity.) **gin** snare **83 humors** whim, caprice

MALVOLIO By my life, this is my lady's hand. These be
her very c's, her u's, and her t's; and thus makes she 86
her great P's. It is in contempt of question her hand. 87
SIR ANDREW Her c's, her u's, and her t's. Why that?
MALVOLIO [*Reads*] "To the unknown beloved, this, and
my good wishes."—Her very phrases! By your leave, 90
wax. Soft! And the impressure her Lucrece, with 91
which she uses to seal. 'Tis my lady. To whom should 92
this be?   [*He opens the letter.*]
FABIAN This wins him, liver and all.   94
MALVOLIO [*Reads*]
        "Jove knows I love,
            But who?
        Lips, do not move;
            No man must know."
"No man must know." What follows? The numbers 99
altered! "No man must know." If this should be thee,
Malvolio?
SIR TOBY Marry, hang thee, brock!   102
MALVOLIO [*Reads*]
        "I may command where I adore,
            But silence, like a Lucrece knife,
        With bloodless stroke my heart doth gore;
            M.O.A.I. doth sway my life."
FABIAN A fustian riddle!   107
SIR TOBY Excellent wench, say I.
MALVOLIO "M.O.A.I. doth sway my life." Nay, but
first, let me see, let me see, let me see.
FABIAN What dish o' poison has she dressed him!   111
SIR TOBY And with what wing the staniel checks 112
at it!   113
MALVOLIO "I may command where I adore." Why, she
may command me; I serve her, she is my lady. Why,

86 c's . . . t's i.e., *cut*, slang for the female pudenda **87 great** (1) upper-
case (2) copious. **in contempt of** beyond **90–91 By . . . wax** (Addressed
to the seal on the letter.) **91 Soft** softly, not so fast. **impressure** device
imprinted on the seal. **Lucrece** Lucretia, chaste matron who, ravished
by Tarquin, committed suicide **92 uses** is accustomed **94 liver** i.e., the
seat of passion **99 numbers** meter **102 brock** badger. (Used contemptuously.) **107 fustian** bombastic, ridiculously pompous **111 dressed**
prepared for **112 staniel** kestrel, a sparrow hawk. (The word is used
contemptuously because of the uselessness of the staniel for falconry.) **112–113 checks at it** turns to fly at it

this is evident to any formal capacity. There is no ob- 116
struction in this. And the end—what should that al-
phabetical position portend? If I could make that resemble something in me! Softly! M.O.A.I.—

SIR TOBY   O, ay, make up that. He is now at a cold scent. 120

FABIAN   Sowter will cry upon 't for all this, though it be 121
as rank as a fox. 122

MALVOLIO   M—Malvolio! M! Why, that begins my
name!

FABIAN   Did not I say he would work it out? The cur is
excellent at faults. 126

MALVOLIO   M—But then there is no consonancy in the 127
sequel that suffers under probation: A should follow, 128
but O does.

FABIAN   And O shall end, I hope. 130

SIR TOBY   Ay, or I'll cudgel him, and make him cry O!

MALVOLIO   And then I comes behind.

FABIAN   Ay, an you had any eye behind you, you might
see more detraction at your heels than fortunes before 134
you.

MALVOLIO   M.O.A.I. This simulation is not as the for- 136
mer. And yet, to crush this a little, it would bow to
me, for every one of these letters are in my name. Soft!
Here follows prose.
[*Reads.*] "If this fall into thy hand, revolve. In my stars 140
I am above thee, but be not afraid of greatness. Some
are born great, some achieve greatness, and some have
greatness thrust upon 'em. Thy Fates open their
hands; let thy blood and spirit embrace them; and, to
inure thyself to what thou art like to be, cast thy hum- 145

116 formal capacity normal mind   **120 O, ay** (playing on *O.I.* of
M.O.A.I.)   **make up** work out   **121 Sowter** cobbler. (Here, the name for
a hound.)   **cry upon 't** bay aloud (as though picking up the scent)
122 rank as a fox (i.e., Malvolio is so crude a hunter that he will leave
the trail of a hare and follow the rank scent of a fox.)   **126 at faults** i.e.,
at maneuvering his way past breaks in the line of scent   **127–128 consonancy in the sequel** pattern in the following letters. (In fact, the
letters M.O.A.I. represent the first, last, second, and next to last letters
of Malvolio's name.)   **128 suffers under probation** stands up under
examination   **130 O shall end** (1) O ends Malvolio's name (2) a noose
shall end his life (3) omega ends the Greek alphabet (4) his cry of pain
will end the joke   **134 detraction** defamation   **136 simulation** disguised
meaning   **140 revolve** consider.   **stars** fortune   **145 inure** accustom.
cast cast off

ble slough and appear fresh. Be opposite with a kins- 146
man, surly with servants. Let thy tongue tang argu- 147
ments of state; put thyself into the trick of singularity. 148
She thus advises thee that sighs for thee. Remember
who commended thy yellow stockings, and wished to
see thee ever cross-gartered. I say, remember. Go to, 151
thou art made, if thou desir'st to be so. If not, let me
see thee a steward still, the fellow of servants, and not
worthy to touch Fortune's fingers. Farewell. She that
would alter services with thee,   155
                       The Fortunate-Unhappy."
Daylight and champaign discovers not more! This is 157
open. I will be proud, I will read politic authors, I will 158
baffle Sir Toby, I will wash off gross acquaintance, I 159
will be point-devise the very man. I do not now fool 160
myself, to let imagination jade me; for every reason 161
excites to this, that my lady loves me. She did commend my yellow stockings of late, she did praise my
leg being cross-gartered; and in this she manifests herself to my love, and with a kind of injunction drives
me to these habits of her liking. I thank my stars, I am 166
happy. I will be strange, stout, in yellow stockings, 167
and cross-gartered, even with the swiftness of putting
on. Jove and my stars be praised! Here is yet a post-
script. [*Reads.*] "Thou canst not choose but know who I
am. If thou entertain'st my love, let it appear in thy
smiling; thy smiles become thee well. Therefore in my
presence still smile, dear my sweet, I prithee." Jove, I
thank thee. I will smile; I will do everything that
thou wilt have me.   *Exit.*
FABIAN   I will not give my part of this sport for a pension of thousands to be paid from the Sophy.   177
SIR TOBY   I could marry this wench for this device.

---

146 slough skin of a snake; hence, former demeanor of humbleness.
opposite contradictory   **147 tang** sound loud with   **148 state** politics,
statecraft.   **trick of singularity** eccentricity of manner   **151 cross-gartered**
wearing garters above and below the knee so as to cross behind it
155 alter services i.e., exchange place of mistress and servant   **157 champaign** open country   **158 politic** dealing with state affairs   **159 baffle**
deride, degrade (a technical chivalric term used to describe the disgrace
of a perjured knight).   **gross** base   **160 point-devise** correct to the letter
161 jade trick   **166 these habits** this attire   **167 happy** fortunate.   **strange**
aloof.   **stout** haughty   **177 Sophy** Shah of Persia

SIR ANDREW   So could I too.

SIR TOBY   And ask no other dowry with her but such another jest.

Enter Maria.

SIR ANDREW   Nor I neither.

FABIAN   Here comes my noble gull-catcher.

SIR TOBY   Wilt thou set thy foot o' my neck?

SIR ANDREW   Or o' mine either?

SIR TOBY   Shall I play my freedom at tray-trip, and be-   186
come thy bondslave?

SIR ANDREW   I' faith, or I either?

SIR TOBY   Why, thou hast put him in such a dream that
when the image of it leaves him he must run mad.

MARIA   Nay, but say true, does it work upon him?

SIR TOBY   Like aqua vitae with a midwife.   192

MARIA   If you will then see the fruits of the sport, mark
his first approach before my lady. He will come to her
in yellow stockings, and 'tis a color she abhors, and
cross-gartered, a fashion she detests; and he will smile
upon her, which will now be so unsuitable to her disposition, being addicted to a melancholy as she is, that
it cannot but turn him into a notable contempt. If you   199
will see it, follow me.

SIR TOBY   To the gates of Tartar, thou most excellent   201
devil of wit!

SIR ANDREW   I'll make one too.   *Exeunt.*

❖

186 play gamble.   **tray-trip** a game of dice, success in which depended
on throwing a three *(tray)*   **192 aqua vitae** brandy or other distilled
liquors   **199 notable contempt** notorious object of contempt
201 Tartar Tartarus, the infernal regions

3.1 *Enter Viola, and Clown [Feste, playing his pipe and tabor].*

VIOLA Save thee, friend, and thy music. Dost thou live 1
by thy tabor? 2
FESTE No, sir, I live by the church.
VIOLA Art thou a churchman?
FESTE No such matter, sir. I do live by the church; for
I do live at my house, and my house doth stand by the
church.
VIOLA So thou mayst say the king lies by a beggar, if 8
a beggar dwell near him; or, the church stands by thy 9
tabor, if thy tabor stand by the church. 10
FESTE You have said, sir. To see this age! A sentence 11
is but a cheveril glove to a good wit. How quickly the 12
wrong side may be turned outward!
VIOLA Nay, that's certain. They that dally nicely with 14
words may quickly make them wanton. 15
FESTE I would therefore my sister had had no name,
sir.
VIOLA Why, man?
FESTE Why, sir, her name's a word, and to dally with
that word might make my sister wanton. But indeed, 20
words are very rascals since bonds disgraced them. 21
VIOLA Thy reason, man?
FESTE Troth, sir, I can yield you none without words,
and words are grown so false I am loath to prove reason with them.
VIOLA I warrant thou art a merry fellow and car'st for
nothing.
FESTE Not so, sir, I do care for something; but in my
conscience, sir, I do not care for you. If that be to care
for nothing, sir, I would it would make you invisible. 30
VIOLA Art not thou the Lady Olivia's fool?

3.1. Location: Olivia's garden.
1 Save God save **1–2 live by** earn your living with. (But Feste uses the
phrase to mean "dwell near.") **2 tabor** small drum **8 lies by** dwells
near **9–10 stands by . . . stand by** (1) is maintained by (2) is placed
near **11 sentence** maxim, judgment, opinion **12 cheveril** kidskin
14 dally nicely play subtly **15 wanton** i.e., unmanageable **20 wanton**
unchaste **21 since . . . them** i.e., since sworn statements have been
needed to make them good **30 invisible** i.e., nothing; absent

FESTE   No indeed, sir, the Lady Olivia has no folly.
She will keep no fool, sir, till she be married, and fools
are as like husbands as pilchers are to herrings; the 34
husband's the bigger. I am indeed not her fool, but
her corrupter of words.

VIOLA   I saw thee late at the Count Orsino's.   37

FESTE   Foolery, sir, does walk about the orb like the 38
sun; it shines everywhere. I would be sorry, sir, but 39
the fool should be as oft with your master as with my
mistress. I think I saw your wisdom there.   41

VIOLA   Nay, an thou pass upon me, I'll no more with thee. 42
Hold, there's expenses for thee.   [*She gives a coin.*]

FESTE   Now Jove, in his next commodity of hair, send 44
thee a beard!

VIOLA   By my troth, I'll tell thee, I am almost sick for
one—[*Aside*] though I would not have it grow on my
chin.—Is thy lady within?

FESTE   Would not a pair of these have bred, sir?

VIOLA   Yes, being kept together and put to use.   50

FESTE   I would play Lord Pandarus of Phrygia, sir, to 51
bring a Cressida to this Troilus.

VIOLA   I understand you, sir. 'Tis well begged.
                        [*She gives another coin.*]

FESTE   The matter, I hope, is not great, sir, begging 54
but a beggar; Cressida was a beggar. My lady is 55
within, sir. I will conster to them whence you come. 56
Who you are and what you would are out of my
welkin—I might say "element," but the word is 58
overworn.   *Exit.*

VIOLA
This fellow is wise enough to play the fool,
And to do that well craves a kind of wit.

34 **pilchers** pilchards, fish resembling herring   37 **late** recently   38 **orb**
earth   39 **but** unless   41 **your wisdom** i.e., you   42 **pass upon me** fence
(verbally) with me, joke at my expense   44 **commodity** supply   50 **put
to use** put out at interest   51 **Pandarus** the go-between in the love story
of Troilus and Cressida; uncle to Cressida   54–55 **begging . . . Cressida**
(A reference to Henryson's *Testament of Cresseid* in which Cressida
became a leper and a beggar. Feste desires another coin to be the mate
of the one he has, as Cressida, the beggar, was mate to Troilus.)
56 **conster** construe, explain   58 **welkin** sky.   **element** (The word can be
synonymous with *welkin*, but the common phrase *out of my element*
means "beyond my scope.")

He must observe their mood on whom he jests,
The quality of persons, and the time,   63
And, like the haggard, check at every feather   64
That comes before his eye. This is a practice   65
As full of labor as a wise man's art;
For folly that he wisely shows is fit,   67
But wise men, folly-fall'n, quite taint their wit.   68

    Enter Sir Toby and [Sir] Andrew.

SIR TOBY Save you, gentleman.
VIOLA And you, sir.
SIR ANDREW *Dieu vous garde, monsieur.*   71
VIOLA *Et vous aussi; votre serviteur.*   72
SIR ANDREW I hope, sir, you are, and I am yours.
SIR TOBY Will you encounter the house? My niece is   74
  desirous you should enter, if your trade be to her.   75
VIOLA I am bound to your niece, sir; I mean she is the   76
  list of my voyage.   77
SIR TOBY Taste your legs, sir, put them to motion.   78
VIOLA My legs do better understand me, sir, than I un-   79
  derstand what you mean by bidding me taste my legs.
SIR TOBY I mean, to go, sir, to enter.
VIOLA I will answer you with gait and entrance.—But   82
  we are prevented.   83

    Enter Olivia and Gentlewoman [Maria].

Most excellent accomplished lady, the heavens rain
odors on you!
SIR ANDREW That youth's a rare courtier. "Rain odors,"
well.

---

63 quality character **64 haggard** untrained adult hawk, hence unmanageable **64–65 check . . . eye** strike at every bird it sees, i.e., dart
adroitly from subject to subject **65 practice** exercise of skill **67 folly
. . . fit** the folly he displays is a proper skill **68 folly-fall'n** having fallen
into folly. **taint** impair **71 Dieu . . . monsieur** God keep you, sir
72 Et . . . serviteur and you, too; (I am) your servant. (Sir Andrew is
not quite up to a reply in French.) **74 encounter** (High-sounding word
to express "enter.") **75 trade** course, path. (Viola picks up the commer-
cial meaning of the word in her reply.) **76 I am bound** I am on a
journey. (Continues Sir Toby's metaphor in *trade*.) **77 list** limit, destination **78 Taste** try **79 understand** stand under, support **82 gait and
entrance** going and entering **83 prevented** anticipated

VIOLA   My matter hath no voice, lady, but to your own 88
most pregnant and vouchsafed ear.   89
SIR ANDREW   "Odors," "pregnant," and "vouchsafed."
I'll get 'em all three all ready.   91
OLIVIA   Let the garden door be shut, and leave me to
my hearing. [*Exeunt Sir Toby, Sir Andrew, and Maria.*]
Give me your hand, sir.
VIOLA
My duty, madam, and most humble service.
OLIVIA   What is your name?
VIOLA
Cesario is your servant's name, fair princess.
OLIVIA
My servant, sir? 'Twas never merry world
Since lowly feigning was called compliment.   99
You're servant to the Count Orsino, youth.
VIOLA
And he is yours, and his must needs be yours;
Your servant's servant is your servant, madam.
OLIVIA
For him, I think not on him. For his thoughts,   103
Would they were blanks, rather than filled with me!   104
VIOLA
Madam, I come to whet your gentle thoughts
On his behalf.
OLIVIA   O, by your leave, I pray you.
I bade you never speak again of him.
But, would you undertake another suit,
I had rather hear you to solicit that
Than music from the spheres.
VIOLA   Dear lady—   110
OLIVIA
Give me leave, beseech you. I did send,
After the last enchantment you did here,

---

88 hath no voice cannot be uttered   **89 pregnant** receptive.   **vouchsafed**
proffered, i.e., attentive   **91 all ready** i.e., for future use   **99 lowly
feigning** affected humility.   **was called** began to be called   **103 For** as
for   **104 blanks** blank spaces or empty sheets of paper   **110 music
from the spheres** (The heavenly bodies were thought to be fixed in
hollow concentric spheres that revolved one about the other, producing
a harmony too exquisite to be heard by human ears.)

A ring in chase of you; so did I abuse
Myself, my servant, and, I fear me, you.
Under your hard construction must I sit,   115
To force that on you in a shameful cunning   116
Which you knew none of yours. What might you think?
Have you not set mine honor at the stake   118
And baited it with all th' unmuzzled thoughts   119
That tyrannous heart can think? To one of your
  receiving   120
Enough is shown; a cypress, not a bosom,   121
Hides my heart. So, let me hear you speak.

VIOLA
I pity you.

OLIVIA   That's a degree to love.

VIOLA
No, not a grece; for 'tis a vulgar proof   124
That very oft we pity enemies.

OLIVIA
Why then methinks 'tis time to smile again.   126
O world, how apt the poor are to be proud!   127
If one should be a prey, how much the better
To fall before the lion than the wolf!   *Clock strikes.* 129
The clock upbraids me with the waste of time.
Be not afraid, good youth, I will not have you;
And yet, when wit and youth is come to harvest,
Your wife is like to reap a proper man.   133
There lies your way, due west.

VIOLA   Then westward ho!   134
Grace and good disposition attend your ladyship.
You'll nothing, madam, to my lord by me?

OLIVIA Stay.
I prithee, tell me what thou think'st of me.

115 **hard construction** harsh interpretation   **116 To force** for forcing
118 **stake** (The figure is from bearbaiting.)   **119 baited** harassed (as
dogs *bait* a bear)   **120 tyrannous** cruel.   **receiving** capacity, intelligence   **121 cypress** a thin, gauzelike, black material   **124 grece** step.
(Synonymous with *degree* in the preceding line.)   **vulgar proof** common
experience   **126 smile** i.e., cast off love's melancholy   **127 the poor** i.e.,
the unfortunate and rejected (like Olivia).   **proud** i.e., of their distress
129 To fall . . . wolf i.e., to fall before a noble adversary   **133 proper**
handsome, worthy   **134 westward ho** (The cry of Thames watermen to
attract westward-bound passengers from London to Westminster.)

VIOLA
That you do think you are not what you are.   139

OLIVIA
If I think so, I think the same of you.   140

VIOLA
Then think you right. I am not what I am.

OLIVIA
I would you were as I would have you be!

VIOLA
Would it be better, madam, than I am?
I wish it might, for now I am your fool.   144

OLIVIA
O, what a deal of scorn looks beautiful
In the contempt and anger of his lip!
A murderous guilt shows not itself more soon
Than love that would seem hid; love's night is noon.   148
Cesario, by the roses of the spring,
By maidhood, honor, truth, and everything,
I love thee so that, maugre all thy pride,   151
Nor wit nor reason can my passion hide.   152
Do not extort thy reasons from this clause,   153
For that I woo, thou therefore hast no cause;   154
But rather reason thus with reason fetter,   155
Love sought is good, but given unsought is better.

VIOLA
By innocence I swear, and by my youth,
I have one heart, one bosom, and one truth,
And that no woman has, nor never none
Shall mistress be of it save I alone.
And so adieu, good madam. Nevermore
Will I my master's tears to you deplore.   162

---

139 That . . . are i.e., that you think you are in love with a man, and you
are mistaken   **140 If . . . you** (Olivia may interpret Viola's cryptic
statement as suggesting that Olivia "does not know herself," i.e., is
distracted with passion; she may also hint at her suspicion that "Cesario" is higher born than he admits.)   **144 fool** butt   **148 love's . . . noon**
i.e., love, despite its attempt to be secret, reveals itself as plain as day
151 maugre in spite of   **152 Nor** neither   **153–154 Do . . . cause** i.e., do
not rationalize your indifference along these lines, that because I am the
wooer you have no cause to reciprocate   **155 But . . . fetter** but instead
take possession of your reasoning with the following reason   **162 deplore**
beweep

OLIVIA

  Yet come again; for thou perhaps mayst move
  That heart, which now abhors, to like his love.

                              Exeunt [separately].

❖

3.2   *Enter Sir Toby, Sir Andrew, and Fabian.*

SIR ANDREW   No, faith, I'll not stay a jot longer.

SIR TOBY   Thy reason, dear venom, give thy reason.   2

FABIAN   You must needs yield your reason, Sir Andrew.

SIR ANDREW   Marry, I saw your niece do more favors to
  the Count's servingman than ever she bestowed upon
  me. I saw 't i' the orchard.   6

SIR TOBY   Did she see thee the while, old boy? Tell me
  that.

SIR ANDREW   As plain as I see you now.

FABIAN   This was a great argument of love in her toward   10
  you.

SIR ANDREW   'Slight, will you make an ass o' me?   12

FABIAN   I will prove it legitimate, sir, upon the oaths of 13
  judgment and reason.

SIR TOBY   And they have been grand-jurymen since before Noah was a sailor.

FABIAN   She did show favor to the youth in your sight
  only to exasperate you, to awake your dormouse valor,   18
  to put fire in your heart and brimstone in your liver.
  You should then have accosted her, and with some
  excellent jests, fire-new from the mint, you should
  have banged the youth into dumbness. This was   22
  looked for at your hand, and this was balked. The dou- 23
  ble gilt of this opportunity you let time wash off, and 24
  you are now sailed into the north of my lady's opinion, 25

3.2. Location: Olivia's house.
2 venom i.e., person filled with venom   **6 orchard** garden   **10 argu-**
ment proof   **12 'Slight** by his (God's) light   **13 oaths** i.e., testimony
under oath   **18 dormouse** i.e., sleepy   **22 banged** struck   **23 balked**
missed, neglected   **23–24 double gilt** thick layer of gold, i.e., rare
worth   **25 north** i.e., out of the warmth and sunshine of her favor

where you will hang like an icicle on a Dutchman's 26
beard, unless you do redeem it by some laudable at- 27
tempt either of valor or policy. 28

SIR ANDREW An 't be any way, it must be with valor,
for policy I hate. I had as lief be a Brownist as a poli- 30
tician. 31

SIR TOBY Why, then, build me thy fortunes upon the 32
basis of valor. Challenge me the Count's youth to fight
with him; hurt him in eleven places. My niece shall
take note of it; and assure thyself, there is no love-bro- 35
ker in the world can more prevail in man's commen- 36
dation with woman than report of valor.

FABIAN There is no way but this, Sir Andrew.

SIR ANDREW Will either of you bear me a challenge to
him?

SIR TOBY Go, write it in a martial hand. Be curst and 41
brief; it is no matter how witty, so it be eloquent and
full of invention. Taunt him with the license of ink. If 43
thou "thou"-est him some thrice, it shall not be amiss; 44
and as many lies as will lie in thy sheet of paper, al- 45
though the sheet were big enough for the bed of Ware 46
in England, set 'em down. Go, about it. Let there be
gall enough in thy ink, though thou write with a 48
goose pen, no matter. About it. 49

SIR ANDREW Where shall I find you?

SIR TOBY We'll call thee at the cubiculo. Go. 51

Exit Sir Andrew.

FABIAN This is a dear manikin to you, Sir Toby. 52

SIR TOBY I have been dear to him, lad, some two thou- 53
sand strong, or so.

26–27 icicle . . . beard (Alludes to the arctic voyage of William Barentz
in 1596–1597.) **28 policy** stratagem **30 Brownist** (Early name of the
Congregationalists, from the name of the founder, Robert Browne.)
30–31 politician intriguer **32 build me** i.e., build **35–36 love-broker**
agent between lovers **41 curst** fierce **43 with . . . ink** i.e., with the
freedom that may be risked in writing but not in conversation
44 "thou"-est ("Thou" was used only between friends or to inferiors.)
45 lies charges of lying **46 bed of Ware** (A famous bedstead capable of
holding twelve persons, about eleven feet square, said to have been at
the Stag Inn in Ware, Hertfordshire.) **48 gall** (1) bitterness, rancor (2) a
growth found on certain oaks, used as an ingredient of ink **49 goose
pen** (1) goose quill (2) foolish style **51 call thee** call for you. **cubiculo**
little chamber **52 manikin** puppet **53 dear** expensive (playing on *dear,*
fond, in the previous speech)

FABIAN We shall have a rare letter from him; but you'll not deliver 't?

SIR TOBY Never trust me, then; and by all means stir on the youth to an answer. I think oxen and wainropes 58 cannot hale them together. For Andrew, if he were 59 opened and you find so much blood in his liver as will 60 clog the foot of a flea, I'll eat the rest of th' anatomy. 61

FABIAN And his opposite, the youth, bears in his vis- 62 age no great presage of cruelty.

Enter Maria.

SIR TOBY Look where the youngest wren of nine 64 comes.

MARIA If you desire the spleen, and will laugh your- 66 selves into stitches, follow me. Yond gull Malvolio is turned heathen, a very renegado; for there is no Chris- 68 tian that means to be saved by believing rightly can ever believe such impossible passages of grossness. 70 He's in yellow stockings.

SIR TOBY And cross-gartered?

MARIA Most villainously; like a pedant that keeps a 73 school i' the church. I have dogged him like his mur- derer. He does obey every point of the letter that I dropped to betray him. He does smile his face into more lines than is in the new map with the augmen- 77 tation of the Indies. You have not seen such a thing as 'tis. I can hardly forbear hurling things at him. I know my lady will strike him. If she do, he'll smile and take 't for a great favor.

SIR TOBY Come, bring us, bring us where he is.

Exeunt omnes.

58 **wainropes** wagon ropes 59 **hale** haul 60 **liver** (Seat of the pas-sions.) 61 **anatomy** cadaver 62 **opposite** adversary 64 **youngest . . . nine** i.e., the last hatched and smallest of a nest of wrens 66 **the spleen** a laughing fit. (The spleen was thought to be the seat of immoderate laughter.) 68 **renegado** renegade, deserter of his religion 70 **passages of grossness** improbable statements (i.e., in the letter) 73 **villainously** i.e., abominably. **pedant** schoolmaster 77 **new map** (Probably a reference to a map made by Emmeric Mollineux in 1599 for the pur-chasers of Hakluyt's *Voyages*, showing more of the East Indies, includ-ing Japan, than had ever been mapped before.)

3.3   *Enter Sebastian and Antonio.*

SEBASTIAN
   I would not by my will have troubled you,
   But since you make your pleasure of your pains,
   I will no further chide you.

ANTONIO
   I could not stay behind you. My desire,
   More sharp than filèd steel, did spur me forth;
   And not all love to see you, though so much   6
   As might have drawn one to a longer voyage,
   But jealousy what might befall your travel,   8
   Being skilless in these parts, which to a stranger,   9
   Unguided and unfriended, often prove
   Rough and unhospitable. My willing love,
   The rather by these arguments of fear,   12
   Set forth in your pursuit.

SEBASTIAN   My kind Antonio,
   I can no other answer make but thanks,
   And thanks; and ever oft good turns   15
   Are shuffled off with such uncurrent pay.   16
   But were my worth, as is my conscience, firm,   17
   You should find better dealing. What's to do?   18
   Shall we go see the relics of this town?   19

ANTONIO
   Tomorrow, sir. Best first go see your lodging.

SEBASTIAN
   I am not weary, and 'tis long to night.
   I pray you, let us satisfy our eyes
   With the memorials and the things of fame
   That do renown this city.

ANTONIO   Would you'd pardon me.   24
   I do not without danger walk these streets.
   Once in a sea fight 'gainst the Count his galleys   26

3.3. Location: A street.
6 not all not only, not altogether   **8 jealousy** anxiety   **9 skilless in**
unacquainted with   **12 The rather** the more quickly   **15 And . . . turns**
(This probably corrupt line is usually made to read, "And thanks and
ever thanks; and oft good turns.")   **16 uncurrent** worthless (such as
mere thanks)   **17 worth** wealth.   **conscience** i.e., moral inclination to
assist   **18 dealing** treatment   **19 relics** antiquities   **24 renown** make
famous   **26 Count his** Count's, i.e., Duke's

I did some service, of such note indeed
That were I ta'en here it would scarce be answered.   28
SEBASTIAN
Belike you slew great number of his people?   29
ANTONIO
Th' offense is not of such a bloody nature,
Albeit the quality of the time and quarrel
Might well have given us bloody argument.   32
It might have since been answered in repaying   33
What we took from them, which for traffic's sake   34
Most of our city did. Only myself stood out,
For which, if I be lapsèd in this place,   36
I shall pay dear.
SEBASTIAN   Do not then walk too open.
ANTONIO
It doth not fit me. Hold, sir, here's my purse.
                              [*He gives his purse.*]
In the south suburbs, at the Elephant,   39
Is best to lodge. I will bespeak our diet,   40
Whiles you beguile the time and feed your knowledge
With viewing of the town. There shall you have me.
SEBASTIAN   Why I your purse?
ANTONIO
Haply your eye shall light upon some toy   44
You have desire to purchase; and your store   45
I think is not for idle markets, sir.   46
SEBASTIAN
I'll be your purse-bearer and leave you
For an hour.
ANTONIO   To th' Elephant.
SEBASTIAN   I do remember.
                              Exeunt [*separately*].

❖

28 it . . . answered i.e., I'd be hard put to offer a defense   **29 Belike**
probably, perhaps   **32 bloody argument** cause for bloodshed   **33 an-**
swered compensated   **34 traffic's** trade's   **36 lapsèd** i.e., caught
39 Elephant (The name of an inn.)   **40 bespeak our diet** order our
food   **44 toy** trifle   **45 store** store of money   **46 idle markets** unnecessary purchases, luxuries

3.4   *Enter Olivia and Maria.*

OLIVIA [*Aside*]
  I have sent after him; he says he'll come.   1
  How shall I feast him? What bestow of him?   2
  For youth is bought more oft than begged or borrowed.
  I speak too loud.—
  Where's Malvolio? He is sad and civil,   5
  And suits well for a servant with my fortunes.
  Where is Malvolio?
MARIA He's coming, madam, but in very strange man-
  ner. He is, sure, possessed, madam.   9
OLIVIA Why, what's the matter? Does he rave?
MARIA No, madam, he does nothing but smile. Your
  ladyship were best to have some guard about you if
  he come, for sure the man is tainted in 's wits.
OLIVIA
  Go call him hither. [*Maria summons Malvolio.*] I am as
  mad as he,
  If sad and merry madness equal be.

    Enter Malvolio.

  How now, Malvolio?
MALVOLIO Sweet lady, ho, ho!
OLIVIA Smil'st thou? I sent for thee upon a sad occasion.
MALVOLIO Sad, lady? I could be sad. This does make
  some obstruction in the blood, this cross-gartering,
  but what of that? If it please the eye of one, it is with
  me as the very true sonnet is, "Please one and please   23
  all."   24
OLIVIA Why, how dost thou, man? What is the matter
  with thee?
MALVOLIO Not black in my mind, though yellow in my   27
  legs. It did come to his hands, and commands shall be   28
  executed. I think we do know the sweet Roman hand.   29

3.4. Location: Olivia's garden.
1 he . . . come i.e., suppose he says he'll come   **2 of** on   **5 sad and civil**
sober and decorous   **9 possessed** i.e., possessed with an evil spirit
23 sonnet song, ballad   **23–24 Please . . . all** (The refrain of a ballad.)
27 black i.e., melancholic   **28 It** i.e., the letter   **29 Roman hand** fashionable Italian style of handwriting

OLIVIA   Wilt thou go to bed, Malvolio?

MALVOLIO   To bed? Ay, sweetheart, and I'll come to   31
thee.   32

OLIVIA   God comfort thee! Why dost thou smile so and
kiss thy hand so oft?

MARIA   How do you, Malvolio?

MALVOLIO   At your request? Yes, nightingales answer   36
daws.   37

MARIA   Why appear you with this ridiculous boldness
before my lady?

MALVOLIO   "Be not afraid of greatness." 'Twas well writ.

OLIVIA   What mean'st thou by that, Malvolio?

MALVOLIO   "Some are born great—"

OLIVIA   Ha?

MALVOLIO   "Some achieve greatness—"

OLIVIA   What sayst thou?

MALVOLIO   "And some have greatness thrust upon
them."

OLIVIA   Heaven restore thee!

MALVOLIO   "Remember who commended thy yellow
stockings—"

OLIVIA   Thy yellow stockings?

MALVOLIO   "And wished to see thee cross-gartered."

OLIVIA   Cross-gartered?

MALVOLIO   "Go to, thou art made, if thou desir'st to
be so—"

OLIVIA   Am I made?

MALVOLIO   "If not, let me see thee a servant still."

OLIVIA   Why, this is very midsummer madness.   58

Enter Servant.

SERVANT   Madam, the young gentleman of the Count
Orsino's is returned. I could hardly entreat him back.
He attends your ladyship's pleasure.

OLIVIA   I'll come to him. [*Exit Servant.*] Good Maria, let
this fellow be looked to. Where's my cousin Toby? Let
some of my people have a special care of him. I would

31–32 Ay . . . thee (Malvolio quotes from a popular song of the day.)
36–37 nightingales answer daws i.e., (to Maria), do you suppose a fine
fellow like me would answer a lowly creature (a *daw*, a crow) like you
58 midsummer madness (A proverbial phrase; the midsummer moon
was supposed to cause madness.)

not have him miscarry for the half of my dowry.   65
         Exeunt [Olivia and Maria, different ways.]

MALVOLIO O ho, do you come near me now? No worse 66
man than Sir Toby to look to me! This concurs directly
with the letter. She sends him on purpose that I may
appear stubborn to him, for she incites me to that in
the letter. "Cast thy humble slough," says she; "be opposite with a kinsman, surly with servants; let thy
tongue tang with arguments of state; put thyself into
the trick of singularity." And consequently sets down 73
the manner how: as, a sad face, a reverend carriage, a 74
slow tongue, in the habit of some sir of note, and so 75
forth. I have limed her, but it is Jove's doing, and Jove 76
make me thankful! And when she went away now,
"Let this fellow be looked to." "Fellow!" Not "Malvo- 78
lio," nor after my degree, but "fellow." Why, every- 79
thing adheres together, that no dram of a scruple, no 80
scruple of a scruple, no obstacle, no incredulous or un- 81
safe circumstance—What can be said? Nothing that 82
can be can come between me and the full prospect of
my hopes. Well, Jove, not I, is the doer of this, and he
is to be thanked.

      Enter [Sir] Toby, Fabian, and Maria.

SIR TOBY Which way is he, in the name of sanctity? If
all the devils of hell be drawn in little, and Legion him- 87
self possessed him, yet I'll speak to him.

FABIAN Here he is, here he is.—How is 't with you, sir?
How is 't with you, man?

MALVOLIO Go off. I discard you. Let me enjoy my pri- 91
vate. Go off.   92

MARIA Lo, how hollow the fiend speaks within him!

---

65 miscarry come to harm **66 come near** understand **73 consequently**
thereafter **74 sad** serious **75 habit . . . note** attire suited to a gentleman of distinction **76 limed** caught like a bird with birdlime (a sticky
substance spread on branches) **78 Fellow** (Malvolio takes the original
meaning, "companion.") **79 after my degree** according to my position **80 dram** (Literally, one-eighth of a fluid ounce.) **scruple** (Literally, one-third of a dram.) **81 incredulous** incredible **81–82 unsafe**
uncertain, unreliable **87 drawn in little** gathered into a small space,
i.e., in Malvolio's heart. **Legion** (Cf. "My name is Legion, for we are
many," Mark 5:9.) **91–92 private** privacy

Did not I tell you? Sir Toby, my lady prays you to have
a care of him.

MALVOLIO Aha, does she so?

SIR TOBY Go to, go to! Peace, peace, we must deal
gently with him. Let me alone.—How do you, Mal-   98
volio? How is 't with you? What, man, defy the devil!
Consider, he's an enemy to mankind.

MALVOLIO Do you know what you say?

MARIA La you, an you speak ill of the devil, how he 102
takes it at heart! Pray God he be not bewitched!

FABIAN Carry his water to the wisewoman.   104

MARIA Marry, and it shall be done tomorrow morning,
if I live. My lady would not lose him for more than
I'll say.

MALVOLIO How now, mistress?

MARIA O Lord!

SIR TOBY Prithee, hold thy peace; this is not the way.
Do you not see you move him? Let me alone with
him.

FABIAN No way but gentleness, gently, gently. The
fiend is rough, and will not be roughly used.

SIR TOBY Why, how now, my bawcock? How dost 115
thou, chuck?   116

MALVOLIO Sir!

SIR TOBY Ay, biddy, come with me. What, man, 'tis not 118
for gravity to play at cherry-pit with Satan. Hang him, 119
foul collier!   120

MARIA Get him to say his prayers, good Sir Toby, get
him to pray.

MALVOLIO My prayers, minx?

MARIA No, I warrant you, he will not hear of godliness.

MALVOLIO Go hang yourselves all! You are idle shallow things; I am not of your element. You shall know 126
more hereafter.   *Exit.* 127

SIR TOBY Is 't possible?

---

98 Let me alone leave him to me **102 La you** look you **104 water**
urine (for medical analysis) **115 bawcock** fine fellow. (From French
beau-coq.) **116 chuck** (A form of "chick," term of endearment.)
118 biddy chicken **119 for gravity** suitable for a man of your dignity.
cherry-pit a children's game consisting of throwing cherry stones into a
hole **120 collier** i.e., Satan. (Literally, a coal vendor.) **126–127 know
more** i.e., hear about this

FABIAN   If this were played upon a stage now, I could condemn it as an improbable fiction.

SIR TOBY   His very genius hath taken the infection of the 131 device, man.

MARIA   Nay, pursue him now, lest the device take air 133 and taint. 134

FABIAN   Why, we shall make him mad indeed.

MARIA   The house will be the quieter.

SIR TOBY   Come, we'll have him in a dark room and bound. My niece is already in the belief that he's mad. We may carry it thus, for our pleasure and his penance, till our very pastime, tired out of breath, prompt us to have mercy on him; at which time we will bring the device to the bar and crown thee for a finder of 142 madmen. But see, but see!

Enter Sir Andrew [with a letter].

FABIAN   More matter for a May morning. 144

SIR ANDREW   Here's the challenge. Read it. I warrant there's vinegar and pepper in 't.

FABIAN   Is 't so saucy? 147

SIR ANDREW   Ay, is 't, I warrant him. Do but read.

SIR TOBY   Give me. [*Reads.*] "Youth, whatsoever thou art, thou art but a scurvy fellow."

FABIAN   Good, and valiant.

SIR TOBY [*Reads*]   "Wonder not, nor admire not in thy 152 mind, why I do call thee so, for I will show thee no reason for 't."

FABIAN   A good note, that keeps you from the blow of 155 the law.

SIR TOBY [*Reads*]   "Thou com'st to the Lady Olivia, and in my sight she uses thee kindly. But thou liest in thy throat; that is not the matter I challenge thee for."

FABIAN   Very brief, and to exceeding good sense—less.

SIR TOBY [*Reads*]   "I will waylay thee going home, where if it be thy chance to kill me—"

FABIAN   Good.

---

131 genius i.e., soul, spirit   **133–134 take ... taint** become exposed to air (i.e., become known) and thus spoil   **142 bar** i.e., bar of judgment
144 matter ... morning sport for Mayday   **147 saucy** (1) spicy
(2) insolent   **152 admire** marvel   **155 note** observation, remark

SIR TOBY [*Reads*]   "Thou kill'st me like a rogue and a villain."

FABIAN   Still you keep o' the windy side of the law. 166 Good.

SIR TOBY [*Reads*]   "Fare thee well, and God have mercy upon one of our souls! He may have mercy upon mine, but my hope is better, and so look to thyself. Thy friend, as thou usest him, and thy sworn enemy,
                              Andrew Aguecheek."
If this letter move him not, his legs cannot. I'll give 't him.

MARIA   You may have very fit occasion for 't. He is now in some commerce with my lady, and will by and by 176 depart.

SIR TOBY   Go, Sir Andrew. Scout me for him at the cor- 178 ner of the orchard like a bum-baily. So soon as ever 179 thou seest him, draw, and as thou draw'st, swear hor- rible; for it comes to pass oft that a terrible oath, with a swaggering accent sharply twanged off, gives man- hood more approbation than ever proof itself would 183 have earned him. Away!

SIR ANDREW   Nay, let me alone for swearing.   *Exit.* 185

SIR TOBY   Now will not I deliver his letter; for the behav- ior of the young gentleman gives him out to be of good capacity and breeding; his employment between his lord and my niece confirms no less. Therefore this letter, being so excellently ignorant, will breed no ter- ror in the youth. He will find it comes from a clodpoll. 191 But, sir, I will deliver his challenge by word of mouth, set upon Aguecheek a notable report of valor, and drive the gentleman, as I know his youth will aptly receive it, into a most hideous opinion of his rage, skill, fury, and impetuosity. This will so fright them both that they will kill one another by the look, like cockatrices.   198

---

166 windy windward, i.e., safe, where the law may get no scent of you
176 commerce conference   **178 Scout me** keep watch   **179 bum-baily** minor sheriff's officer employed in making arrests   **183 approbation** reputation (for courage).   **proof** performance   **185 let . . . swearing** don't worry about my ability in swearing   **191 clodpoll** blockhead   **198 cockatrices** basilisks, fabulous serpents reputed to be able to kill by a mere look

Enter Olivia and Viola.

FABIAN   Here he comes with your niece. Give them way   199
till he take leave, and presently after him.   200
SIR TOBY   I will meditate the while upon some horrid   201
message for a challenge.
[Exeunt Sir Toby, Fabian, and Maria.]
OLIVIA
I have said too much unto a heart of stone
And laid mine honor too unchary on 't.   204
There's something in me that reproves my fault,
But such a headstrong potent fault it is
That it but mocks reproof.
VIOLA
With the same havior that your passion bears
Goes on my master's griefs.
OLIVIA *[Giving a locket]*
Here, wear this jewel for me. 'Tis my picture.   210
Refuse it not; it hath no tongue to vex you.
And I beseech you come again tomorrow.
What shall you ask of me that I'll deny,
That honor, saved, may upon asking give?   214
VIOLA
Nothing but this: your true love for my master.
OLIVIA
How with mine honor may I give him that
Which I have given to you?
VIOLA   I will acquit you.   217
OLIVIA
Well, come again tomorrow. Fare thee well.
A fiend like thee might bear my soul to hell.   *[Exit.]*   219
Enter [Sir] Toby and Fabian.

SIR TOBY   Gentleman, God save thee.
VIOLA   And you, sir.
SIR TOBY   That defense thou hast, betake thee to 't. Of
what nature the wrongs are thou hast done him, I

199 **Give them way** stay out of their way   200 **presently** immediately
201 **horrid** terrifying (literally, "bristling")   204 **laid** hazarded.   **unchary on 't** recklessly on it   210 **jewel** (Any piece of jewelry; here,
seemingly, a locket.)   214 **That . . . give** i.e., that can be granted without
compromising any honor   217 **acquit you** release you of your promise
219 **like** resembling

know not; but thy intercepter, full of despite, bloody 224
as the hunter, attends thee at the orchard end. Dis- 225
mount thy tuck, be yare in thy preparation, for thy 226
assailant is quick, skillful, and deadly.

VIOLA   You mistake sir. I am sure no man hath any
quarrel to me. My remembrance is very free and clear
from any image of offense done to any man.

SIR TOBY   You'll find it otherwise, I assure you. Therefore, if you hold your life at any price, betake you to
your guard; for your opposite hath in him what youth,
strength, skill, and wrath can furnish man withal.

VIOLA   I pray you, sir, what is he?

SIR TOBY   He is knight, dubbed with unhatched rapier 236
and on carpet consideration, but he is a devil in 237
private brawl. Souls and bodies hath he divorced
three, and his incensement at this moment is so im-
placable that satisfaction can be none but by pangs of
death and sepulcher. Hob, nob, is his word; give 't or 241
take 't.

VIOLA   I will return again into the house and desire
some conduct of the lady. I am no fighter. I have heard 244
of some kind of men that put quarrels purposely on
others, to taste their valor. Belike this is a man of that 246
quirk. 247

SIR TOBY   Sir, no. His indignation derives itself out of a
very competent injury; therefore, get you on and give 249
him his desire. Back you shall not to the house, unless
you undertake that with me which with as much 251
safety you might answer him. Therefore, on, or strip
your sword stark naked; for meddle you must, that's 253
certain, or forswear to wear iron about you. 254

VIOLA   This is as uncivil as strange. I beseech you, do
me this courteous office, as to know of the knight what

---

224 intercepter i.e., he who lies in wait.   **despite** defiance   **224–225 bloody as the hunter** bloodthirsty as a hunting dog   **225–226 Dismount thy tuck** draw your rapier   **226 yare** ready, nimble   **236 unhatched** un-hacked, unused in battle   **237 carpet consideration** (A carpet knight was one whose title was obtained not in battle but through connections at court.)   **241 Hob, nob** have or have not, i.e., give it or take it.   **word** motto   **244 conduct** escort   **246 taste** test   **247 quirk** peculiar humor   **249 competent** sufficient   **251 that** i.e., to give satisfaction in a duel   **253 meddle** engage (in conflict)   **254 forswear . . . iron** give up your right to wear a sword

my offense to him is. It is something of my negligence,
nothing of my purpose.
SIR TOBY   I will do so. Signor Fabian, stay you by this
gentleman till my return.   *Exit Toby.*
VIOLA   Pray you, sir, do you know of this matter?
FABIAN   I know the knight is incensed against you, even
to a mortal arbitrament, but nothing of the circum- 263
stance more.
VIOLA   I beseech you, what manner of man is he?
FABIAN   Nothing of that wonderful promise, to read 266
him by his form, as you are like to find him in the 267
proof of his valor. He is, indeed, sir, the most skillful,
bloody, and fatal opposite that you could possibly
have found in any part of Illyria. Will you walk towards him? I will make your peace with him if I can.
VIOLA   I shall be much bound to you for 't. I am one that
had rather go with Sir Priest than Sir Knight. I care not 273
who knows so much of my mettle.   *Exeunt.*

   Enter [Sir] Toby and [Sir] Andrew.

SIR TOBY   Why, man, he's a very devil; I have not seen
such a firago. I had a pass with him, rapier, scabbard, 276
and all, and he gives me the stuck in with such a mor- 277
tal motion that it is inevitable; and on the answer, he 278
pays you as surely as your feet hits the ground they
step on. They say he has been fencer to the Sophy.
SIR ANDREW   Pox on 't, I'll not meddle with him.
SIR TOBY   Ay, but he will not now be pacified. Fabian
can scarce hold him yonder.
SIR ANDREW   Plague on 't, an I thought he had been valiant and so cunning in fence, I'd have seen him
damned ere I'd have challenged him. Let him let the
matter slip, and I'll give him my horse, gray Capilet. 287
SIR TOBY   I'll make the motion. Stand here, make a good 288
show on 't. This shall end without the perdition of 289
souls. [*Aside, as he crosses to meet Fabian.*] Marry, I'll 290
ride your horse as well as I ride you.

---

263 **mortal arbitrament** trial to the death   266–267 **read . . . form** judge
him by his appearance   273 **Sir Priest** (*Sir* was a courtesy title for priests.)
276 **firago** virago.   **pass** bout   277 **stuck in** stoccado, a thrust in fencing   278 **answer** return hit   287 **Capilet** i.e., "little horse." (From "ca-
pel," a nag.)   288 **motion** offer   289–290 **perdition of souls** loss of lives

Enter Fabian and Viola.

[*To Fabian.*] I have his horse to take up the quarrel. I   292
have persuaded him the youth's a devil.

FABIAN   He is as horribly conceited of him, and pants   294
and looks pale as if a bear were at his heels.

SIR TOBY [*To Viola*]   There's no remedy, sir, he will fight
with you for 's oath's sake. Marry, he hath better bethought him of his quarrel, and he finds that now
scarce to be worth talking of. Therefore draw, for the
supportance of his vow; he protests he will not hurt   300
you.

VIOLA [*Aside*]   Pray God defend me! A little thing
would make me tell them how much I lack of a man.

FABIAN   Give ground, if you see him furious.

SIR TOBY [*Crossing to Sir Andrew*]   Come, Sir Andrew,
there's no remedy. The gentleman will, for his
honor's sake, have one bout with you. He cannot by
the *duello* avoid it. But he has promised me, as he is   308
a gentleman and a soldier, he will not hurt you. Come
on, to 't.

SIR ANDREW   Pray God he keep his oath!

VIOLA   I do assure you, 'tis against my will.

[They draw.]

Enter Antonio.

ANTONIO
Put up your sword. If this young gentleman
Have done offense, I take the fault on me;
If you offend him, I for him defy you.

SIR TOBY   You, sir? Why, what are you?

ANTONIO
One, sir, that for his love dares yet do more
Than you have heard him brag to you he will.

SIR TOBY
Nay, if you be an undertaker, I am for you.   319

[They draw.]

Enter Officers.

292 take up settle, make up   294 He . . . him i.e., Cesario has as
horrible a conception of Sir Andrew   300 supportance upholding
308 duello duelling code   319 undertaker one who takes upon himself a
task or business; here, a challenger.   for you i.e.; ready for you

FABIAN   O good Sir Toby, hold! Here come the officers.

SIR TOBY [*To Antonio*]   I'll be with you anon.

VIOLA [*To Sir Andrew*]   Pray, sir, put your sword up, if
you please.

SIR ANDREW   Marry, will I, sir; and for that I promised
you, I'll be as good as my word. He will bear you eas- 325
ily, and reins well.

FIRST OFFICER   This is the man; do thy office.

SECOND OFFICER
Antonio, I arrest thee at the suit
Of Count Orsino.

ANTONIO   You do mistake me, sir.

FIRST OFFICER
No, sir, no jot. I know your favor well,   330
Though now you have no sea-cap on your head.—
Take him away. He knows I know him well.

ANTONIO
I must obey. [*To Viola.*] This comes with seeking you.
But there's no remedy, I shall answer it.   334
What will you do, now my necessity
Makes me to ask you for my purse? It grieves me
Much more for what I cannot do for you
Than what befalls myself. You stand amazed,
But be of comfort.

SECOND OFFICER   Come, sir, away.

ANTONIO
I must entreat of you some of that money.

VIOLA   What money, sir?
For the fair kindness you have showed me here,
And part being prompted by your present trouble,   343
Out of my lean and low ability
I'll lend you something. My having is not much;   345
I'll make division of my present with you.   346
Hold, there's half my coffer.   [*She offers money.*] 347

ANTONIO   Will you deny me now?
Is 't possible that my deserts to you   349
Can lack persuasion? Do not tempt my misery,   350
Lest that it make me so unsound a man   351

325 **He** i.e., the horse   330 **favor** face   334 **answer it** suffer for it   343 **part**
partly   345 **having** wealth   346 **present** present store   347 **coffer** purse.
(Literally, strong box.)   349–350 **deserts . . . persuasion** claims on you
can fail to persuade you to help me   351 **unsound** weak

As to upbraid you with those kindnesses
That I have done for you.
VIOLA   I know of none,
Nor know I you by voice or any feature.
I hate ingratitude more in a man
Than lying, vainness, babbling drunkenness,
Or any taint of vice whose strong corruption
Inhabits our frail blood.
ANTONIO   O heavens themselves!
SECOND OFFICER   Come, sir, I pray you, go.
ANTONIO
Let me speak a little. This youth that you see here
I snatched one half out of the jaws of death,
Relieved him with such sanctity of love,
And to his image, which methought did promise   364
Most venerable worth, did I devotion.   365
FIRST OFFICER
What's that to us? The time goes by. Away!
ANTONIO
But, O, how vile an idol proves this god!
Thou hast, Sebastian, done good feature shame.   368
In nature there's no blemish but the mind;
None can be called deformed but the unkind.   370
Virtue is beauty, but the beauteous evil   371
Are empty trunks o'erflourished by the devil.   372
FIRST OFFICER
The man grows mad. Away with him! Come, come, sir.
ANTONIO   Lead me on.   *Exit [with Officers]*.
VIOLA [*To herself*]
Methinks his words do from such passion fly
That he believes himself; so do not I.   376
Prove true, imagination, O, prove true,
That I, dear brother, be now ta'en for you!
SIR TOBY   Come hither, knight; come hither, Fabian.

364 image what he appeared to be (playing on the idea of a religious
icon to be venerated)   **365 venerable worth** worthiness of being venerated   **368 Thou . . . shame** i.e., you have shamed physical beauty by
showing that it does not always reflect inner beauty   **370 unkind**
unnatural   **371 beauteous evil** those who are outwardly beautiful but
evil within   **372 trunks** (1) chests (2) bodies.   **o'erflourished** (1) covered with ornamental carvings (2) made outwardly beautiful   **376 so
. . . I** i.e., I do not believe myself (in the hope that has arisen in me)

We'll whisper o'er a couplet or two of most sage saws. 380
                              [*They gather apart from Viola.*]

VIOLA
He named Sebastian. I my brother know   381
Yet living in my glass; even such and so   382
In favor was my brother, and he went
Still in this fashion, color, ornament,
For him I imitate. O, if it prove,   385
Tempests are kind, and salt waves fresh in love!
                                        [*Exit.*]

SIR TOBY   A very dishonest, paltry boy, and more a cow- 387
ard than a hare. His dishonesty appears in leaving his 388
friend here in necessity and denying him; and for his 389
cowardship, ask Fabian.

FABIAN   A coward, a most devout coward, religious in it.

SIR ANDREW   'Slid, I'll after him again and beat him.   392

SIR TOBY   Do, cuff him soundly, but never draw thy
sword.

SIR ANDREW   An I do not—   [*Exit.*]

FABIAN   Come, let's see the event.   396

SIR TOBY   I dare lay any money 'twill be nothing yet.   397
                                        Exeunt.

❖

380 **saws** sayings   381–382 **I . . . glass** i.e., I know my brother is virtually alive every time I look in a mirror, because we looked so much
alike   385 **prove** prove true   387 **dishonest** dishonorable   388 **dishonesty** dishonor   389 **denying** refusing to acknowledge   392 **'Slid** i.e., by
his (God's) eyelid   396 **event** outcome   397 **yet** nevertheless, after all

4.1   *Enter Sebastian and Clown [Feste].*

FESTE   Will you make me believe that I am not sent for
you?

SEBASTIAN   Go to, go to, thou art a foolish fellow. Let
me be clear of thee.

FESTE   Well held out, i' faith! No, I do not know you, 5
nor I am not sent to you by my lady to bid you come
speak with her, nor your name is not Master Cesario,
nor this is not my nose neither. Nothing that is so is so.

SEBASTIAN   I prithee, vent thy folly somewhere else. 9
Thou know'st not me.

FESTE   Vent my folly! He has heard that word of some
great man, and now applies it to a fool. Vent my folly!
I am afraid this great lubber, the world, will prove a 13
cockney. I prithee now, ungird thy strangeness and 14
tell me what I shall vent to my lady. Shall I vent to her
that thou art coming?

SEBASTIAN   I prithee, foolish Greek, depart from me. 17
There's money for thee. [*He gives money.*] If you tarry
longer, I shall give worse payment.

FESTE   By my troth, thou hast an open hand. These 20
wise men that give fools money get themselves a good
report—after fourteen years' purchase.   22

Enter [Sir] Andrew, [Sir] Toby, and Fabian.

SIR ANDREW   Now, sir, have I met you again? There's
for you!   [*He strikes Sebastian.*]

SEBASTIAN   Why, there's for thee, and there, and there!
[*He beats Sir Andrew with the hilt of his dagger.*]
Are all the people mad?

SIR TOBY   Hold, sir, or I'll throw your dagger o'er the
house.

FESTE   This will I tell my lady straight. I would not be 29
in some of your coats for twopence.   [*Exit.*]

4.1. Location: Before Olivia's house.
5 held out kept up   **9 vent** give vent to   **13 lubber** lout   **14 cockney**
effeminate or foppish fellow.   **ungird thy strangeness** put off your
affectation of being a stranger   **17 Greek** i.e., buffoon. (From "merry
Greek.")   **20 open** generous   **22 after . . . purchase** i.e., at great cost.
(Land was ordinarily valued at the price of twelve years' rental; the Fool
adds two years to this figure.)   **29 straight** at once

SIR TOBY   Come on, sir, hold!   [*He grips Sebastian.*]

SIR ANDREW   Nay, let him alone. I'll go another way to
work with him; I'll have an action of battery against   33
him, if there be any law in Illyria. Though I struck him
first, yet it's no matter for that.

SEBASTIAN   Let go thy hand!

SIR TOBY   Come, sir, I will not let you go. Come, my
young soldier, put up your iron. You are well fleshed;   38
come on.

SEBASTIAN
I will be free from thee. [*He breaks free and draws his
sword.*] What wouldst thou now?
If thou dar'st tempt me further, draw thy sword.

SIR TOBY   What, what? Nay, then I must have an ounce
or two of this malapert blood from you.   [*He draws.*]   43

          Enter Olivia.

OLIVIA
Hold, Toby! On thy life I charge thee, hold!

SIR TOBY   Madam—

OLIVIA
Will it be ever thus? Ungracious wretch,
Fit for the mountains and the barbarous caves,
Where manners ne'er were preached! Out of my sight!
Be not offended, dear Cesario.
Rudesby, begone!
          [*Exeunt Sir Toby, Sir Andrew, and Fabian.*]
                    I prithee, gentle friend,   50
Let thy fair wisdom, not thy passion, sway
In this uncivil and unjust extent   52
Against thy peace. Go with me to my house,
And hear thou there how many fruitless pranks
This ruffian hath botched up, that thou thereby   55
Mayst smile at this. Thou shalt not choose but go.
Do not deny. Beshrew his soul for me!   57
He started one poor heart of mine, in thee.   58

---

33 action of battery lawsuit for beating (me)   **38 fleshed** initiated into
battle   **43 malapert** saucy, impudent   **50 Rudesby** ruffian   **52 extent**
attack   **55 botched up** clumsily contrived   **57 Beshrew** curse   **58 He**
. . . thee i.e., he alarmed half of my heart, which lies in your bosom.
(The word *started* also suggests a play on *heart, hart*.)

SEBASTIAN [*Aside*]
  What relish is in this? How runs the stream?
  Or I am mad, or else this is a dream.   60
  Let fancy still my sense in Lethe steep;   61
  If it be thus to dream, still let me sleep!
OLIVIA
  Nay, come, I prithee. Would thou'dst be ruled by me!
SEBASTIAN
  Madam, I will.
OLIVIA   O, say so, and so be!   *Exeunt.*

❖

4.2   *Enter Maria [with garments] and Clown
         [Feste].*

MARIA   Nay, I prithee, put on this gown and this beard;
  make him believe thou art Sir Topas the curate. Do it 2
  quickly. I'll call Sir Toby the whilst.   [*Exit.*] 3
FESTE   Well, I'll put it on, and I will dissemble myself 4
  in 't, and I would I were the first that ever dissembled
  in such a gown. [*He disguises himself in gown and
  beard.*] I am not tall enough to become the function 7
  well, nor lean enough to be thought a good student; 8
  but to be said an honest man and a good housekeeper 9
  goes as fairly as to say a careful man and a great
  scholar. The competitors enter.   11

      Enter [Sir] Toby [and Maria].

SIR TOBY   Jove bless thee, Master Parson.

60 Or either   **61 fancy** imagination.   **still** ever.   **Lethe** the river of
forgetfulness in the underworld; i.e., forgetfulness

4.2. Location: Olivia's house.
2 Sir (Honorific title for priests.)   **Topas** (A name perhaps derived from
Chaucer's comic knight in the "Rime of Sir Thopas" or from a similar
character in Lyly's *Endymion*. Topaz, a semiprecious stone, was believed to be a cure for lunacy.)   **3 the whilst** in the meantime   **4 dissemble** disguise (with a play on "feign")   **7 become** grace, adorn.
function profession   **8 student** scholar (in divinity)   **9 said** called,
known as.   **housekeeper** household manager, hospitable person
11 competitors associates, partners

FESTE *Bonos dies*, Sir Toby. For, as the old hermit of 13
Prague, that never saw pen and ink, very wittily said 14
to a niece of King Gorboduc, "That that is, is"; so I, 15
being Master Parson, am Master Parson; for what is
"that" but "that," and "is" but "is"?

SIR TOBY To him, Sir Topas.

FESTE What, ho, I say! Peace in this prison!

[*He approaches the door*
behind which Malvolio is confined.]

SIR TOBY The knave counterfeits well; a good knave.

MALVOLIO (*Within*) Who calls there?

FESTE Sir Topas the curate, who comes to visit Malvolio the lunatic.

MALVOLIO Sir Topas, Sir Topas, good Sir Topas, go to
my lady—

FESTE Out, hyperbolical fiend! How vexest thou this 26
man! Talkest thou nothing but of ladies?

SIR TOBY Well said, Master Parson.

MALVOLIO Sir Topas, never was man thus wronged.
Good Sir Topas, do not think I am mad. They have
laid me here in hideous darkness.

FESTE Fie, thou dishonest Satan! I call thee by the
most modest terms, for I am one of those gentle ones
that will use the devil himself with courtesy. Sayst
thou that house is dark?   35

MALVOLIO As hell, Sir Topas.

FESTE Why, it hath bay windows transparent as bar- 37
ricadoes, and the clerestories toward the south north 38
are as lustrous as ebony; and yet complainest thou of
obstruction?

MALVOLIO I am not mad, Sir Topas. I say to you this
house is dark.

FESTE Madman, thou errest. I say there is no darkness but ignorance, in which thou art more puzzled
than the Egyptians in their fog.   45

---

13 Bonos dies good day   **13–14 hermit of Prague** (Probably another invented authority.)   **15 King Gorboduc** a legendary king of ancient Britain,
protagonist in the English tragedy *Gorbobuc* (1562)   **26 hyperbolical**
vehement, boisterous.   **fiend** i.e., the devil supposedly possessing Malvolio   **35 house** i.e., room   **37–38 barricadoes** barricades   **38 clerestories**
windows in an upper wall   **45 Egyptians . . . fog** (Alluding to the darkness
brought upon Egypt by Moses; see Exodus 10:21–23.)

MALVOLIO I say this house is as dark as ignorance,
though ignorance were as dark as hell; and I say there
. was never man thus abused. I am no more mad than
you are. Make the trial of it in any constant question. 49
FESTE What is the opinion of Pythagoras concerning 50
wildfowl?   51
MALVOLIO That the soul of our grandam might haply 52
inhabit a bird.
FESTE What think'st thou of his opinion?
MALVOLIO I think nobly of the soul, and no way ap-
prove his opinion.
FESTE Fare thee well. Remain thou still in darkness.
Thou shalt hold th' opinion of Pythagoras ere I will
allow of thy wits, and fear to kill a woodcock lest thou 59
dispossess the soul of thy grandam. Fare thee well.
         [*He moves away from Malvolio's prison.*]
MALVOLIO Sir Topas, Sir Topas!
SIR TOBY My most exquisite Sir Topas!
FESTE Nay, I am for all waters.   63
MARIA Thou mightst have done this without thy beard
and gown. He sees thee not.
SIR TOBY To him in thine own voice, and bring me
word how thou find'st him. I would we were well rid
of this knavery. If he may be conveniently delivered, I 68
would he were, for I am now so far in offense with
my niece that I cannot pursue with any safety this
sport to the upshot.—Come by and by to my chamber. 71
                         Exit [*with Maria*].
FESTE [*Singing as he approaches Malvolio's prison*]
     "Hey, Robin, jolly Robin,   72
     Tell me how thy lady does."   73
MALVOLIO Fool!
FESTE "My lady is unkind, pardie."   75
MALVOLIO Fool!

---

49 constant question set problem   **50–51 Pythagoras . . . wildfowl** (An
opening for the discussion of transmigration of souls, a doctrine held by
Pythagoras.)   **52 haply** perhaps   **59 allow of thy wits** i.e., certify your
sanity.   **woodcock** (A proverbially stupid bird, easily caught.)   **63 for all
waters** i.e., ready for anything   **68 delivered** i.e., delivered from prison
71 upshot conclusion   **72–73 Hey, Robin . . . does** (Another fragment of
an old song, a version of which is attributed to Sir Thomas Wyatt.)
75 pardie i.e., by God, certainly

FESTE   "Alas, why is she so?"

MALVOLIO   Fool, I say!

FESTE   "She loves another—" Who calls, ha?

MALVOLIO   Good Fool, as ever thou wilt deserve well at my hand, help me to a candle, and pen, ink, and paper. As I am a gentleman, I will live to be thankful to thee for 't.

FESTE   Master Malvolio?

MALVOLIO   Ay, good Fool.

FESTE   Alas, sir, how fell you beside your five wits?   86

MALVOLIO   Fool, there was never man so notoriously abused. I am as well in my wits, Fool, as thou art.

FESTE   But as well? Then you are mad indeed, if you be no better in your wits than a fool.

MALVOLIO   They have here propertied me, keep me in   91 darkness, send ministers to me—asses!—and do all they can to face me out of my wits.   93

FESTE   Advise you what you say. The minister is here.   94 [*He speaks as Sir Topas.*] Malvolio, Malvolio, thy wits the heavens restore! Endeavor thyself to sleep, and leave thy vain bibble-babble.

MALVOLIO   Sir Topas!

FESTE [*In Sir Topas's voice*]   Maintain no words with him, good fellow. [*In his own voice.*] Who, I, sir? Not I, sir. God b' wi' you, good Sir Topas. [*In Sir Topas's voice.*]   101 Marry, amen. [*In his own voice.*] I will, sir, I will.

MALVOLIO   Fool! Fool! Fool, I say!

FESTE   Alas, sir, be patient. What say you, sir? I am shent for speaking to you.   105

MALVOLIO   Good Fool, help me to some light and some paper. I tell thee I am as well in my wits as any man in Illyria.

FESTE   Welladay that you were, sir!   109

MALVOLIO   By this hand, I am. Good Fool, some ink,

---

86 beside out of.   **five wits** (The intellectual faculties, usually listed as common wit, imagination, fantasy, judgment, and memory.)   **91 propertied me** i.e., treated me as property and thrown me into the lumber-room   **93 face . . . wits** brazenly represent me as having lost my wits   **94 Advise you** take care   **101 God b' wi' you** God be with you. (Feste uses two voices in this passage to carry on a dialogue between himself and "Sir Topas.")   **105 shent** scolded, rebuked   **109 Welladay** alas, would that

paper, and light; and convey what I will set down to
my lady. It shall advantage thee more than ever the
bearing of letter did.

FESTE   I will help you to 't. But tell me true, are you
not mad indeed, or do you but counterfeit?

MALVOLIO   Believe me, I am not. I tell thee true.

FESTE   Nay, I'll ne'er believe a madman till I see his
brains. I will fetch you light and paper and ink.

MALVOLIO   Fool, I'll requite it in the highest degree. I
prithee, begone.

FESTE [*Sings*]

    I am gone, sir,
    And anon, sir,
  I'll be with you again,
    In a trice,
    Like to the old Vice,   125
  Your need to sustain;

    Who, with dagger of lath,   127
    In his rage and his wrath,
  Cries "Aha!" to the devil;
    Like a mad lad,
    "Pare thy nails, dad?
  Adieu, goodman devil!"   *Exit.* 132

❖

4.3   *Enter Sebastian [with a pearl].*

SEBASTIAN
  This is the air; that is the glorious sun;
  This pearl she gave me, I do feel 't and see 't;
  And though 'tis wonder that enwraps me thus,
  Yet 'tis not madness. Where's Antonio, then?
  I could not find him at the Elephant;
  Yet there he was, and there I found this credit,   6
  That he did range the town to seek me out.

125 Vice comic tempter of the morality plays   **127 dagger of lath** comic
weapon of the Vice   **132 goodman** title for a person of substance but
not of gentle birth

4.3. Location: Olivia's garden.
6 was was previously.   **credit** report

His counsel now might do me golden service;
For though my soul disputes well with my sense   9
That this may be some error, but no madness,
Yet doth this accident and flood of fortune
So far exceed all instance, all discourse,   12
That I am ready to distrust mine eyes
And wrangle with my reason that persuades me
To any other trust but that I am mad,   15
Or else the lady's mad. Yet if 'twere so,
She could not sway her house, command her followers, 17
Take and give back affairs and their dispatch,   18
With such a smooth, discreet, and stable bearing
As I perceive she does. There's something in 't
That is deceivable. But here the lady comes.   21

    Enter Olivia and Priest.

OLIVIA
Blame not this haste of mine. If you mean well,
Now go with me and with this holy man
Into the chantry by. There, before him,   24
And underneath that consecrated roof,
Plight me the full assurance of your faith,
That my most jealous and too doubtful soul   27
May live at peace. He shall conceal it
Whiles you are willing it shall come to note,   29
What time we will our celebration keep   30
According to my birth. What do you say?   31

SEBASTIAN
I'll follow this good man, and go with you,
And having sworn truth, ever will be true.

OLIVIA
Then lead the way, good Father, and heavens so shine
That they may fairly note this act of mine!   *Exeunt.* 35

9 my soul . . . sense i.e., both my rational faculties and my physical
senses come to the conclusion   **12 instance** precedent.   **discourse**
reasoning   **15 trust** belief   **17 sway** rule   **18 Take . . . dispatch** undertake matters of business and see to their execution   **21 deceivable**
deceptive   **24 chantry by** privately endowed chapel nearby   **27 jealous**
anxious, mistrustful.   **doubtful** full of doubts   **29 Whiles** until.   **come
to note** become known   **30 What time** at which time.   **our celebration**
i.e., the actual marriage; what they are about to perform is a binding
betrothal   **31 birth** social position   **35 fairly note** look upon with favor

5.1   *Enter Clown [Feste] and Fabian.*

FABIAN   Now, as thou lov'st me, let me see his letter.

FESTE   Good Master Fabian, grant me another request.

FABIAN   Anything.

FESTE   Do not desire to see this letter.

FABIAN   This is to give a dog and in recompense desire   5
my dog again.   6

Enter Duke [Orsino], Viola, Curio, and lords.

ORSINO   Belong you to the Lady Olivia, friends?

FESTE   Ay, sir, we are some of her trappings.   8

ORSINO   I know thee well. How dost thou, my good fellow?

FESTE   Truly, sir, the better for my foes and the worse   10
for my friends.

ORSINO   Just the contrary; the better for thy friends.

FESTE   No, sir, the worse.

ORSINO   How can that be?

FESTE   Marry, sir, they praise me, and make an ass of
me. Now my foes tell me plainly I am an ass; so that
by my foes, sir, I profit in the knowledge of myself,
and by my friends I am abused; so that, conclusions to   18
be as kisses, if your four negatives make your two af-   19
firmatives, why then the worse for my friends and the   20
better for my foes.

ORSINO   Why, this is excellent.

FESTE   By my troth, sir, no; though it please you to be
one of my friends.   24

ORSINO   Thou shalt not be the worse for me. There's gold.
[He gives a coin.]

FESTE   But that it would be double-dealing, sir, I   26
would you could make it another.

5.1. Location: Before Olivia's house.
5–6 This . . . again (Apparently a reference to a well-known reply of Dr.
Bulleyn when Queen Elizabeth asked for his dog and promised a gift of
his choosing in return.)   8 trappings ornaments, decorations   10 for
because of   18 abused flatteringly deceived   18–20 conclusions . . .
affirmatives i.e., as when a young lady, asked for a kiss, says "no, no"
really meaning "yes, yes"; or, as the four lips of two contrary lovers
come together to make one passionate kiss   24 friends i.e., those who,
according to Feste's syllogism, flatter him   26 But except for the fact.
double-dealing (1) giving twice (2) deceit, duplicity

ORSINO   O, you give me ill counsel.

FESTE   Put your grace in your pocket, sir, for this once, 29
and let your flesh and blood obey it.

ORSINO   Well, I will be so much a sinner to be a double-
dealer. There's another.   [*He gives another coin.*]

FESTE   *Primo, secundo, tertio* is a good play, and the 33
old saying is, the third pays for all. The triplex, sir, is 34
a good tripping measure; or the bells of Saint Bennet, 35
sir, may put you in mind—one, two, three.

ORSINO   You can fool no more money out of me at this
throw. If you will let your lady know I am here to 38
speak with her, and bring her along with you, it may
awake my bounty further.

FESTE   Marry, sir, lullaby to your bounty till I come
again. I go, sir, but I would not have you to think that
my desire of having is the sin of covetousness; but as
you say, sir, let your bounty take a nap, I will awake
it anon.   *Exit.*

Enter Antonio and Officers.

VIOLA
Here comes the man, sir, that did rescue me.

ORSINO
That face of his I do remember well,
Yet when I saw it last it was besmeared
As black as Vulcan in the smoke of war.   49
A baubling vessel was he captain of,   50
For shallow draft and bulk unprizable,   51
With which such scatheful grapple did he make   52
With the most noble bottom of our fleet   53
That very envy and the tongue of loss   54

---

29 Put . ∴. pocket (1) pocket up your virtue, your grace before God
(2) reach in your pocket or purse and show your customary grace or
munificence   **33 play** (Perhaps a children's game or game of dice.)
34 triplex triple time in music   **35 Saint Bennet** church of St. Bene-
dict   **38 throw** (1) time (2) throw of the dice   **49 Vulcan** Roman god of
fire and smith to the other gods; his face was blackened by the fire
50 baubling insignificant, trifling   **51 For** because of.   **draft** depth of
water a ship draws.   **unprizable** of value too slight to be estimated, not
worth taking as a "prize"   **52 scatheful** destructive   **53 bottom** ship
54 very envy i.e., even those who had most reason to hate him, his
enemies.   **loss** i.e., the losers

Cried fame and honor on him. What's the matter?
FIRST OFFICER
Orsino, this is that Antonio
That took the Phoenix and her freight from Candy,   57
And this is he that did the *Tiger* board
When your young nephew Titus lost his leg.
Here in the streets, desperate of shame and state,   60
In private brabble did we apprehend him.   61
VIOLA
He did me kindness, sir, drew on my side,
But in conclusion put strange speech upon me.   63
I know not what 'twas but distraction.   64
ORSINO
Notable pirate, thou saltwater thief,
What foolish boldness brought thee to their mercies
Whom thou in terms so bloody and so dear   67
Hast made thine enemies?
ANTONIO   Orsino, noble sir,
Be pleased that I shake off these names you give me.   69
Antonio never yet was thief or pirate,
Though I confess, on base and ground enough,   71
Orsino's enemy. A witchcraft drew me hither.
That most ingrateful boy there by your side
From the rude sea's enraged and foamy mouth
Did I redeem; a wrack past hope he was.   75
His life I gave him, and did thereto add
My love, without retention or restraint,   77
All his in dedication. For his sake
Did I expose myself—pure for his love—   79
Into the danger of this adverse town,   80
Drew to defend him when he was beset;
Where being apprehended, his false cunning,
Not meaning to partake with me in danger,
Taught him to face me out of his acquaintance   84

---

57 from Candy on her return from Candia, or Crete   **60 desperate . . . state** recklessly disregarding disgrace and his status as a wanted man **61 brabble** brawl   **63 put . . . me** spoke to me strangely   **64 but distraction** unless (it was) madness   **67 dear** costly, grievous   **69 Be pleased that** allow me to   **71 base and ground** solid grounds   **75 wrack** goods from a wrecked vessel   **77 retention** reservation   **79 pure** entirely, purely   **80 Into** unto. **adverse** hostile   **84 face . . . acquaintance** brazenly deny he knew me

And grew a twenty years' removèd thing   85
While one would wink; denied me mine own purse,   86
Which I had recommended to his use   87
Not half an hour before.

VIOLA   How can this be?

ORSINO   When came he to this town?

ANTONIO
Today, my lord; and for three months before,
No interim, not a minute's vacancy,
Both day and night did we keep company.

Enter Olivia and attendants.

ORSINO
Here comes the Countess; now heaven walks on earth.
But for thee, fellow—fellow, thy words are madness.
Three months this youth hath tended upon me;
But more of that anon. Take him aside.

OLIVIA
What would my lord—but that he may not have—   98
Wherein Olivia may seem serviceable?
Cesario, you do not keep promise with me.

VIOLA   Madam?

ORSINO   Gracious Olivia—

OLIVIA
What do you say, Cesario? Good my lord—

VIOLA
My lord would speak; my duty hushes me.

OLIVIA
If it be aught to the old tune, my lord,
It is as fat and fulsome to mine ear   106
As howling after music.

ORSINO   Still so cruel?

OLIVIA   Still so constant, lord.

ORSINO
What, to perverseness? You uncivil lady,
To whose ingrate and unauspicious altars

85–86 grew . . . wink in the twinkling of an eye acted as though we had
been estranged for twenty years   **87 recommended** consigned   **98 but
that** except that which.   **he . . . have** i.e., my love   **106 fat and fulsome**
gross and offensive

My soul the faithfull'st offerings have breathed out
That e'er devotion tendered! What shall I do?
OLIVIA
Even what it please my lord that shall become him.
ORSINO
Why should I not, had I the heart to do it,
Like to th' Egyptian thief at point of death,   116
Kill what I love?—a savage jealousy
That sometimes savors nobly. But hear me this: 118
Since you to nonregardance cast my faith,   119
And that I partly know the instrument
That screws me from my true place in your favor,   121
Live you the marble-breasted tyrant still.
But this your minion, whom I know you love,   123
And whom, by heaven I swear, I tender dearly,   124
Him will I tear out of that cruel eye
Where he sits crownèd in his master's spite.—   126
Come, boy, with me. My thoughts are ripe in mischief.
I'll sacrifice the lamb that I do love,
To spite a raven's heart within a dove.   [*Going.*]
VIOLA
And I, most jocund, apt, and willingly,
To do you rest, a thousand deaths would die.   131
                                                 [*Going.*]
OLIVIA
Where goes Cesario?
VIOLA   After him I love
More than I love these eyes, more than my life,
More by all mores than e'er I shall love wife.   134
If I do feign, you witnesses above
Punish my life for tainting of my love!
OLIVIA
Ay me, detested! How am I beguiled!

---

116 Egyptian thief (An allusion to the story of Theagenes and Chariclea
in the *Ethiopica*, a Greek romance by Heliodorus. The robber chief,
Thyamis of Memphis, having captured Chariclea and fallen in love with
her, is attacked by a larger band of robbers; threatened with death, he
attempts to slay her first.)   **118 savors nobly** is not without nobility
119 nonregardance neglect   **121 screws** pries, forces   **123 minion**
darling, favorite   **124 tender** regard   **126 in . . . spite** in defiance of his
master   **131 do you rest** give you ease   **134 by all mores** by all such
comparisons

VIOLA
Who does beguile you? Who does do you wrong?

OLIVIA
Hast thou forgot thyself? Is it so long?
Call forth the holy father.   [*Exit an Attendant.*]

ORSINO [*To Viola*]   Come, away!

OLIVIA
Whither, my lord? Cesario, husband, stay.

ORSINO
Husband?

OLIVIA   Ay, husband. Can he that deny?

ORSINO
Her husband, sirrah?

VIOLA   No, my lord, not I.

OLIVIA
Alas, it is the baseness of thy fear
That makes thee strangle thy propriety.   145
Fear not, Cesario, take thy fortunes up;
Be that thou know'st thou art, and then thou art   147
As great as that thou fear'st.

          Enter Priest.

                    O, welcome, Father!   148
Father, I charge thee by thy reverence
Here to unfold, though lately we intended
To keep in darkness what occasion now
Reveals before 'tis ripe, what thou dost know
Hath newly passed between this youth and me.

PRIEST
A contract of eternal bond of love,
Confirmed by mutual joinder of your hands,   155
Attested by the holy close of lips,   156
Strengthened by interchangement of your rings,
And all the ceremony of this compact
Sealed in my function, by my testimony;   159
Since when, my watch hath told me, toward my grave
I have traveled but two hours.

ORSINO
O thou dissembling cub! What wilt thou be

145 **strangle thy propriety** deny what you are   147 **that** that which
148 **that thou fear'st** him you fear, i.e., Orsino   155 **joinder** joining
156 **close** meeting   159 **Sealed** ratified

When time hath sowed a grizzle on thy case?   163
Or will not else thy craft so quickly grow
That thine own trip shall be thine overthrow?   165
Farewell, and take her, but direct thy feet
Where thou and I henceforth may never meet.

VIOLA
My lord, I do protest—
OLIVIA   O, do not swear!
Hold little faith, though thou hast too much fear.   169

Enter Sir Andrew.

SIR ANDREW   For the love of God, a surgeon! Send one
presently to Sir Toby.
OLIVIA   What's the matter?
SIR ANDREW   He's broke my head across and has given   173
Sir Toby a bloody coxcomb too. For the love of God,   174
your help! I had rather than forty pound I were at
home.
OLIVIA   Who has done this, Sir Andrew?
SIR ANDREW   The Count's gentleman, one Cesario. We
took him for a coward, but he's the very devil incar-   179
dinate.   180
ORSINO   My gentleman, Cesario?
SIR ANDREW   'Od's lifelings, here he is!—You broke my   182
head for nothing, and that that I did, I was set on to
do 't by Sir Toby.
VIOLA
Why do you speak to me? I never hurt you.
You drew your sword upon me without cause,
But I bespake you fair, and hurt you not.   187
SIR ANDREW   If a bloody coxcomb be a hurt, you have
hurt me. I think you set nothing by a bloody cox-   189
comb.

Enter [Sir] Toby and Clown [Feste].

Here comes Sir Toby halting; you shall hear more. But   191

---

163 a grizzle gray hair.   **case** sheath, skin   **165 trip** wrestling trick (i.e.,
you'll get overclever, and trip yourself up)   **169 little** i.e., a little
173 broke broken the skin, cut   **174 coxcomb** fool's cap resembling the
crest of a cock; here, head   **179–180 incardinate** (for *incarnate*)
182 'Od's lifelings by God's little lives   **187 fair** courteously   **189 set
nothing by** regard as insignificant   **191 halting** limping

if he had not been in drink, he would have tickled you
othergates than he did.   193
ORSINO   How now, gentleman? How is 't with you?
SIR TOBY   That's all one. He's hurt me, and there's th'
end on 't.—Sot, didst see Dick surgeon, sot?   196
FESTE   O, he's drunk, Sir Toby, an hour agone; his
eyes were set at eight i' the morning.   198
SIR TOBY   Then he's a rogue, and a passy measures   199
pavane. I hate a drunken rogue.   200
OLIVIA   Away with him! Who hath made this havoc
with them?
SIR ANDREW   I'll help you, Sir Toby, because we'll be   203
dressed together.   204
SIR TOBY   Will you help? An ass-head and a coxcomb
and a knave, a thin-faced knave, a gull!
OLIVIA
Get him to bed, and let his hurt be looked to.
            [*Exeunt Feste, Fabian, Sir Toby, and Sir
                                                            Andrew.*]

      Enter Sebastian.

SEBASTIAN
I am sorry, madam, I have hurt your kinsman;
But, had it been the brother of my blood,
I must have done no less with wit and safety.—   210
You throw a strange regard upon me, and by that   211
I do perceive it hath offended you.
Pardon me, sweet one, even for the vows
We made each other but so late ago.
ORSINO
One face, one voice, one habit, and two persons,   215
A natural perspective, that is and is not!   216
SEBASTIAN
Antonio, O my dear Antonio!

193 othergates otherwise   **196 Sot** (1) fool (2) drunkard   **198 set** fixed
or extinguished, closed   **199–200 passy measures pavane** a slow-moving
eight-bar grave and stately dance (suggesting Sir Toby's impatience to
have his wounds dressed)   **203–204 be dressed** i.e., have our wounds
surgically dressed   **210 with wit and safety** with intelligent concern for
my own safety   **211 strange regard** look such as one directs at a stranger
215 habit dress   **216 natural perspective** an optical device or illusion
created by nature

How have the hours racked and tortured me
Since I have lost thee!

ANTONIO   Sebastian are you?

SEBASTIAN   Fear'st thou that, Antonio?   221

ANTONIO
How have you made division of yourself?
An apple cleft in two is not more twin
Than these two creatures. Which is Sebastian?

OLIVIA   Most wonderful!

SEBASTIAN [*Seeing Viola*]
Do I stand there? I never had a brother;
Nor can there be that deity in my nature
Of here and everywhere. I had a sister,   228
Whom the blind waves and surges have devoured.   229
Of charity, what kin are you to me?   230
What countryman? What name? What parentage?

VIOLA
Of Messaline; Sebastian was my father.
Such a Sebastian was my brother too;
So went he suited to his watery tomb.   234
If spirits can assume both form and suit,
You come to fright us.

SEBASTIAN   A spirit I am indeed,
But am in that dimension grossly clad   237
Which from the womb I did participate.   238
Were you a woman, as the rest goes even,   239
I should my tears let fall upon your cheek,
And say "Thrice welcome, drownèd Viola!"

VIOLA
My father had a mole upon his brow.

SEBASTIAN   And so had mine.

VIOLA
And died that day when Viola from her birth
Had numbered thirteen years.

SEBASTIAN
O, that record is lively in my soul!   246

---

221 Fear'st thou that do you doubt that   **228 here and everywhere**
omnipresence   **229 blind** heedless, indiscriminating   **230 Of charity**
(tell me) in kindness   **234 suited** dressed; clad in human form
237 in . . . clad clothed in that fleshly shape   **238 participate** possess
239 as . . . even since everything else agrees   **246 record** recollection

He finishèd indeed his mortal act
That day that made my sister thirteen years.

VIOLA
If nothing lets to make us happy both   249
But this my masculine usurped attire,
Do not embrace me till each circumstance
Of place, time, fortune, do cohere and jump   252
That I am Viola—which to confirm,
I'll bring you to a captain in this town,
Where lie my maiden weeds; by whose gentle help   255
I was preserved to serve this noble count.
All the occurrence of my fortune since
Hath been between this lady and this lord.

SEBASTIAN [*To Olivia*]
So comes it, lady, you have been mistook.
But nature to her bias drew in that.   260
You would have been contracted to a maid;
Nor are you therein, by my life, deceived.
You are betrothed both to a maid and man.   263

ORSINO
Be not amazed; right noble is his blood.
If this be so, as yet the glass seems true,   265
I shall have share in this most happy wrack.   266
[*To Viola.*] Boy, thou hast said to me a thousand times
Thou never shouldst love woman like to me.

VIOLA
And all those sayings will I over swear,   269
And all those swearings keep as true in soul
As doth that orbèd continent the fire   271
That severs day from night.

ORSINO   Give me thy hand,
And let me see thee in thy woman's weeds.

VIOLA
The captain that did bring me first on shore
Hath my maid's garments. He upon some action   275

249 lets hinders   **252 jump** coincide, fit exactly   **255 weeds** clothes
260 nature . . . that nature followed her bent in that   **263 a maid** i.e., a
virgin man   **265 glass** i.e., the *natural perspective* of l. 216   **266 wrack**
goods from a wrecked vessel   **269 over swear** swear again   **271 As . . .**
fire i.e., as the sphere of the sun keeps the fire   **275 action** legal charge

Is now in durance, at Malvolio's suit,   276
A gentleman and follower of my lady's.
OLIVIA
He shall enlarge him. Fetch Malvolio hither.   278
And yet, alas, now I remember me,
They say, poor gentleman, he's much distract.

Enter Clown [Feste] with a letter, and Fabian.

A most extracting frenzy of mine own   281
From my remembrance clearly banished his.
How does he, sirrah?
FESTE Truly, madam, he holds Belzebub at the stave's   284
end as well as a man in his case may do. He's here   285
writ a letter to you; I should have given 't you today
morning. But as a madman's epistles are no gospels,   287
so it skills not much when they are delivered.   288
OLIVIA Open 't, and read it.
FESTE Look then to be well edified, when the fool de-   290
livers the madman. [*Reads loudly.*] "By the Lord,   291
madam—"
OLIVIA How now, art thou mad?
FESTE No, madam, I do but read madness. An your
ladyship will have it as it ought to be, you must allow
vox.   296
OLIVIA Prithee, read i' thy right wits.
FESTE So I do, madonna; but to read his right wits is
to read thus. Therefore perpend, my princess, and   299
give ear.
OLIVIA [*To Fabian*] Read it you, sirrah.
FABIAN [*Reads*] "By the Lord, madam, you wrong me,
and the world shall know it. Though you have put me
into darkness and given your drunken cousin rule
over me, yet have I the benefit of my senses as well as

---

276 durance captivity   **278 enlarge** release   **281 extracting** i.e., that
obsessed me and drew all thoughts except of Cesario from my mind
284–285 holds . . . end i.e., keeps the devil at a safe distance   **287 a
madman's . . . gospels** i.e., there is no truth in a madman's letters. (An
allusion to readings in the church service of selected passages from the
epistles and the gospels.)   **288 skills** matters   **290–291 delivers** speaks
the words of   **296 vox** voice, i.e., an appropriately loud voice   **299 perpend** consider, attend

your ladyship. I have your own letter that induced me
to the semblance I put on, with the which I doubt not   307
but to do myself much right or you much shame.
Think of me as you please. I leave my duty a little
unthought of and speak out of my injury.

                              The madly used Malvolio."
OLIVIA   Did he write this?
FESTE   Ay, madam.
ORSINO   This savors not much of distraction.
OLIVIA
See him delivered, Fabian; bring him hither.   315
                              [*Exit Fabian.*]
My lord, so please you, these things further thought on,   316
To think me as well a sister as a wife,   317
One day shall crown th' alliance on 't, so please you,   318
Here at my house and at my proper cost.   319
ORSINO
Madam, I am most apt t' embrace your offer.
[*To Viola.*] Your master quits you; and for your service
   done him,   321
So much against the mettle of your sex,   322
So far beneath your soft and tender breeding,
And since you called me master for so long,
Here is my hand. You shall from this time be
Your master's mistress.
OLIVIA   A sister! You are she.

   Enter [Fabian, with] Malvolio.

ORSINO
Is this the madman?
OLIVIA   Ay, my lord, this same.
How now, Malvolio?
MALVOLIO   Madam, you have done me wrong,
Notorious wrong.
OLIVIA   Have I, Malvolio? No.

307 the which i.e., the letter   **315 delivered** released   **316 so . . . on** if
you are pleased on further consideration   **317 To . . . wife** to regard
me as favorably as a sister-in-law as you had hoped to regard me as a
wife   **318 crown . . . on 't** i.e., serve as occasion for two marriages
confirming our new relationship   **319 proper** own   **321 quits** releases
322 mettle natural disposition

MALVOLIO

Lady, you have. Pray you, peruse that letter.

[*He gives letter.*]

You must not now deny it is your hand.
Write from it, if you can, in hand or phrase,   332
Or say 'tis not your seal, not your invention.   333
You can say none of this. Well, grant it then,
And tell me, in the modesty of honor,   335
Why you have given me such clear lights of favor,
Bade me come smiling and cross-gartered to you,
To put on yellow stockings, and to frown
Upon Sir Toby and the lighter people?   339
And, acting this in an obedient hope,
Why have you suffered me to be imprisoned,
Kept in a dark house, visited by the priest,
And made the most notorious geck and gull   343
That e'er invention played on? Tell me why?   344

OLIVIA

Alas, Malvolio, this is not my writing,
Though, I confess, much like the character;   346
But out of question 'tis Maria's hand.   347
And now I do bethink me, it was she
First told me thou wast mad; then cam'st in smiling,   349
And in such forms which here were presupposed   350
Upon thee in the letter. Prithee, be content.
This practice hath most shrewdly passed upon thee;   352
But when we know the grounds and authors of it,
Thou shalt be both the plaintiff and the judge
Of thine own cause.

FABIAN   Good madam, hear me speak,
And let no quarrel nor no brawl to come
Taint the condition of this present hour,
Which I have wondered at. In hope it shall not,
Most freely I confess, myself and Toby
Set this device against Malvolio here,

---

332 from it differently   **333 invention** composition   **335 modesty of
honor** sense of propriety belonging to honorable persons   **339 lighter**
lesser   **343 geck** dupe   **344 invention** contrivance   **346 character**
handwriting   **347 out of** beyond   **349 cam'st** you came   **350 presupposed** specified beforehand   **352 shrewdly** cruelly, grievously.   **passed
upon** imposed on

Upon some stubborn and uncourteous parts 361
We had conceived against him. Maria writ 362
The letter at Sir Toby's great importance, 363
In recompense whereof he hath married her.
How with a sportful malice it was followed 365
May rather pluck on laughter than revenge, 366
If that the injuries be justly weighed
That have on both sides passed.

OLIVIA
Alas, poor fool, how have they baffled thee! 369

FESTE Why, "some are born great, some achieve greatness, and some have greatness thrown upon them." I was one, sir, in this interlude, one Sir Topas, 372 sir, but that's all one. "By the Lord, Fool, I am not mad." But do you remember? "Madam, why laugh you at such a barren rascal? An you smile not, he's gagged." And thus the whirligig of time brings in his 376 revenges.

MALVOLIO   I'll be revenged on the whole pack of you!
[*Exit.*]

OLIVIA
He hath been most notoriously abused.

ORSINO
Pursue him, and entreat him to a peace.
He hath not told us of the captain yet.
When that is known, and golden time convents, 382
A solemn combination shall be made
Of our dear souls. Meantime, sweet sister,
We will not part from hence. Cesario, come—
For so you shall be, while you are a man;
But when in other habits you are seen,
Orsino's mistress and his fancy's queen.
Exeunt [*all, except Feste*].

FESTE (*Sings*)
When that I was and a little tiny boy,
With hey, ho, the wind and the rain,

361 **Upon** on account of. **parts** qualities, deeds **362 conceived against him** seen and resented in him **363 importance** importunity **365 followed** carried out **366 pluck on** induce **369 baffled** disgraced, quelled **372 interlude** little play **376 whirligig** spinning top **382 convents** (1) summons, calls together (2) suits

A foolish thing was but a toy,
  For the rain it raineth every day.

But when I came to man's estate,
  With hey, ho, the wind and the rain,
'Gainst knaves and thieves men shut their gate,
  For the rain it raineth every day.

But when I came, alas, to wive,
  With hey, ho, the wind and the rain,
By swaggering could I never thrive,
  For the rain it raineth every day.

But when I came unto my beds,
  With hey, ho, the wind and the rain,
With tosspots still had drunken heads,   403
  For the rain it raineth every day.

A great while ago the world begun,
  With hey, ho, the wind and the rain,
But that's all one, our play is done,
  And we'll strive to please you every day.

                                    [*Exit.*]

403 tosspots drunkards

Date and Text

Twelfth Night was registered with the London Company of Stationers (booksellers and printers) in 1623 and first published in the First Folio that year in a good text set up from what may have been a scribal transcript of Shakespeare's foul papers, or draft manuscript. There was a brief delay in printing *Twelfth Night* in the First Folio, possibly because a transcript was being prepared. The play was first mentioned, however, on Candlemas Day, February 2, 1602, in the following entry from the *Diary* of a Middle Temple (one of the Inns of Court, where law was studied) law student or barrister named John Manningham:

> At our feast wee had a play called "Twelue Night, or What you Will," much like the Commedy of Errores, or Menechmi in Plautus, but most like and neere to that in Italian called *Inganni*. A good practise in it to make the Steward beleeve his Lady widdowe was in love with him, by counterfeyting a letter as from his Lady in generall termes, telling him what shee liked best in him, and prescribing his gesture in smiling, his apparaile, & c., and then when he came to practise making him beleeue they tooke him to be mad.

This entry was once suspected to be a forgery perpetrated by John Payne Collier, who published the *Diary* in 1831, but its authenticity is now generally accepted. The date accords with several possible allusions in the play itself. When Fabian jokes about "a pension of thousands to be paid from the Sophy" (2.5.176–177), he seems to be recalling Sir Anthony Shirley's reception by the Shah of Persia (the Sophy) in 1599–1600. An account of this visit was entered in the Stationers' Register in November of 1601. Viola's description of Feste as "wise enough to play the fool" (3.1.60) may recall a poem beginning "True it is, he plays the fool indeed" published in 1600–1601 by Robert Armin (who had played the role of Feste). Maria's comparison of Malvolio's smiling face to "the new map with the augmentation of the Indies" (3.2.77–78) refers to new maps of about 1600 in which America (the Indies) was increased in size. Leslie Hotson (*The First Night of Twelfth Night*, 1954) has argued for a first performance at court on Twelfth Night in January of 1601, when Queen Elizabeth entertained Don Virginio Orsino, Duke of Bracciano, but this hypothesis has not gained general acceptance partly because the role of Orsino in the play would scarcely flatter such a noble visitor and partly because there is no proof that any of Shakespeare's plays were originally commissioned for private performance. Nevertheless, a date between 1600 and early 1602 seems most likely. Francis Meres does not mention the play in 1598 in his *Palladis Tamia: Wit's Treasury* (a slender volume on contemporary literature and art; valuable because it lists most of Shakespeare's plays that existed at that time).

Textual Notes

These textual notes are not a historical collation, either of the early folios or of more recent editions; they are simply a record of departures in this edition from the copy text. The reading adopted in this edition appears in boldface, followed by the rejected reading from the copy text, i.e., the First Folio. Only a few major alterations in punctuation are noted. Changes in lineation are not indicated, nor are some minor and obvious typographical errors.

Abbreviations used:
F the First Folio
s.d. stage direction
s.p. speech prefix

Copy Text: the First Folio.

1.1. 1 s.p. [and throughout] Orsino Duke **11 sea, naught** sea. Nought

1.2. 15 Arion Orion

1.3. 51 s.p. Sir Andrew Ma **54 Mary Accost** Mary, accost **96 curl by** coole my **98 me** we **132 dun** dam'd. **set** sit **136 That's** That

1.5. 5 s.p. [and throughout] Feste Clown **163 s.d. Viola** Uiolenta **296 County's** Countes **306 s.d.** [F adds "Finis, Actus primus"]

2.2. 31 our O **32 of** if

2.3. 25 leman Lemon

2.4. 51 s.p. Feste [not in F] **53 Fly . . . fly** Fye . . . fie **55 yew** Ew **88 I** It

2.5. 112 staniel stallion **118 portend?** portend, **142 born** become. **achieve** atcheeues **173 dear** deero **203 s.d.** [F adds "Finis Actus secundus"]

3.1. 8 king Kings **68 wise men** wisemens **91 all ready** already

3.2. 7 thee the the **64 nine** mine

3.4. 15 s.d. [at l. 14 in F] **25 s.p. Olivia** Mal **65 s.d. Exeunt** Exit **72 tang** langer **175 You** Yon **222 thee** the **249 competent** computent **312 s.d.** [at l. 311 in F] **397 s.d. Exeunt** Exit

4.2. 6 in in in **38 clerestories** cleere stores **71 sport to** sport

4.3. 1 s.p. Sebastian [not in F] **35 s.d.** [F adds "Finis Actus Quartus"]

5.1. 190 s.d. [at l. 187 in F] **200 pavane** panyn **205 help? An** helpe an **389 tiny** tine **406 With hey** hey

Shakespeare's Sources

John Manningham's description of a performance of *Twelfth Night* on February 2, 1602, at the Middle Temple (one of the Inns of Court, where young men studied law in London), compares the play to Plautus' *The Menaechmi* and to an Italian play called *Inganni*. The comment offers a helpful hint on sources. *The Menaechmi* had been the chief source for Shakespeare's earlier play *The Comedy of Errors*, and that farce of mistaken identity clearly resembles *Twelfth Night* in the hilarious mixups resulting from the confusion of two look-alike twins. Shakespeare clearly profited from his earlier experimenting with this sort of comedy. *Twelfth Night* is not necessarily directly indebted to *The Menaechmi*, however, for Renaissance Italian comedy offered many imitations of Plautus from which Shakespeare could have taken his *Twelfth Night* plot. These include *Gl'Inganni* (1562) by Nicolò Secchi, another *Gl'Inganni* (1592) by Curzio Gonzaga, and most important an anonymous *Gl'Ingannati* (published 1537). This last play was translated into French by Charles Estienne as *Les Abusés* (1543) and adapted into Spanish by Lope de Rueda in *Los Engaños* (1567). A Latin version, *Laelia*, based on the French, was performed at Cambridge in the 1590s but never printed. Obviously, *Gl'Ingannati* was widely known, and Manningham was probably referring to it in his diary. To trace Shakespeare's own reading in this matter is difficult, owing to the large number of versions available to him, but we can note the suggestive points of comparison in each.

Both *Inganni* plays feature a brother and a sister mistaken for one another. In the later play (by Gonzaga), the sister uses the disguise name of "Cesare." In Secchi's *Inganni* the disguised sister is in love with her master, who is told that a woman the exact age of his supposed page is secretly in love with him. Another play by Secchi, *L'Interesse* (1581), has a comic duel involving a disguised heroine. Of the Italian plays considered here, however, *Gl'Ingannati* is closest to Shakespeare's play. A short prefatory entertainment included with it in most editions features the name Malevolti. In the play itself, the heroine, Lelia, disguises herself as a page in the service of Flaminio, whom she secretly loves, and is sent on embassies to Flaminio's disdainful mistress Isabella. This lady falls in love with "Fabio," as Lelia calls herself. Lelia's father, Virginio, learning of her disguise and resolving to marry her to old Gherardo (Isabella's father), seeks out Lelia but instead mistakenly arrests her long-lost twin brother, Fabrizio, who has just arrived in Modena. Fabrizio is locked up as a mad person in Isabella's room, whereupon Isabella takes the opportunity to betroth herself to the person she mistakes for "Fabio." A recognition scene clears up everything and leads to the marriages of Fabrizio to Isabella and Flaminio to Lelia. This story lacks the subplot of Malvolio, Sir Toby, et al. Nor is there a shipwreck.

Matteo Bandello based one of the stories in his *Novelle* (1554) on *Gl'Ingannati*, and this prose version was then translated into French by François de Belleforest in his *Histoires Tragiques* (1579 edition). Shakespeare may well have read both, for he consulted these collections of stories in writing *Much Ado about Nothing*. His most direct source, however, seems to have been the story of "Apollonius and Silla," by Barnabe Riche (an English soldier and fiction writer), in *Riche His Farewell to Military Profession* (1581), which was derived from Belleforest. A full modernized text of Riche's story appears in the following pages. Riche involves his characters in more serious moral predicaments than Shakespeare allows in his festive comedy. The plot situation is much the same: Silla (the equivalent of Shakespeare's Viola) is washed ashore near Constantinople, where, disguised as "Silvio," she takes service with a duke, Apollonius (Shakespeare's Orsino), and goes on embassies to the wealthy widow Julina (Shakespeare's Olivia), who proceeds at once to fall in love with "Silvio." When Silla's twin brother, the real Silvio, arrives, he is mistaken by Julina for his twin and is invited to a rendezvous, like Shakespeare's Sebastian. The differences at this point are marked, however, for Silvio becomes Julina's lover and leaves her pregnant when he departs the next day on his quest for Silla. Apollonius is understandably furious to learn of "Silvio's" apparent success with Julina and throws his page into prison. Julina is no less distressed when she learns that the supposed father of her child is in actuality a woman. Only Silla's revelation of her identity and Silvio's eventual return to marry Julina resolves these complications. Shakespeare eschews the pregnancy, the desertion, the imprisonment, and all of Riche's stern moralizings about the bestiality of lust that accompany this lurid tale. Moreover he adds the plot of Malvolio, for which Riche provides little suggestion. Shakespeare changes the location to Illyria, with its hint of delirium and illusion, and provides an English flavor in the comic scenes that intensifies the festive character of the play.

Shakespeare's reading may also have included the anonymous play *Sir Clyomon and Sir Clamydes* (c. 1570–1583), Sir Philip Sidney's *Arcadia* (1590), and Emmanuel Forde's prose romance *Parismus* (1598) in which one "Violetta" borrows the disguise of a page. Scholars have suggested that the Malvolio plot may reflect an incident at Queen Elizabeth's court in which the Comptroller of the Household, Sir William Knollys, interrupted a noisy late-night party dressed in only his nightshirt and a pair of spectacles, with a copy of the Italian pornographic writer Aretino's work in his hand. A similar confrontation between revelry and sobriety occurred in 1598: Ambrose Willoughby quieted a disturbance after the Queen had gone to bed, and was afterward thanked by her for doing his duty. Such incidents were no doubt common, however, and there is no compelling reason to suppose Shakespeare was sketching from current court gossip.

Riche His Farewell to Military Profession
Barnabe Riche
APOLLONIUS AND SILLA

Any departures from the original text are noted with an asterisk and appear at the bottom of the page in boldface; original readings are in roman.

Apollonius, Duke, having spent a year's service in the wars against the Turk, returning homeward with his company by sea, was driven by force of weather to the isle of Cyprus, where he was well received by Pontus, governor of the same isle; with whom Silla, daughter to Pontus, fell so strangely in love that after Apollonius was departed to Constantinople, Silla, with one man, followed. And coming to Constantinople she served Apollonius in the habit of a man; and after many pretty accidents falling out she was known to Apollonius, who, in requital of her love, married her.

There is no child that is born into this wretched world but, before it doth suck the mother's milk, it taketh first a sip* of the cup of error, which maketh us, when we come to riper years, not only to enter into actions of injury but many times to stray from that[1] is right and reason. But in[2] all other things wherein we show ourselves to be most drunken with this poisoned cup, it is in our actions of love. For the lover is so estranged from that[3] is right and wandereth so wide from the bounds of reason that he is not able to deem[4] white from black, good from bad, virtue from vice; but, only led[5] by the appetite of his own affections, and grounding them on the foolishness of his own fancies, will so settle his liking on such a one as either by desert or unworthiness will merit rather to be loathed than loved.

If a question might be asked, what is the ground indeed of reasonable love whereby the knot is knit of true and perfect friendship, I think those that be wise would answer: desert.[6] That is, where the party beloved doth requite us with the like. For otherwise, if the bare show of beauty or the comeliness of personage might be sufficient to confirm us in our love, those that be accustomed to go to fairs and

---

*sip soope

1 that that which **2 But in** i.e., but more than in **3 that** that which
4 deem distinguish **5 only led** led only **6 desert** deserving of recompense, offering something in return

markets might sometimes fall into love with twenty in a day. Desert must then be, of force,[7] the ground of reasonable love; for to love them that hate us, to follow them that fly from us, to fawn on them that frown on us, to curry favor with them that disdain us, to be glad to please them that care not how they offend us—who will not confess this to be an erroneous love, neither grounded upon wit nor reason? Wherefore, right courteous gentlewomen, if it please you with patience to peruse this history following, you shall see Dame Error so play her part with a leash[8] of lovers, a male and two females, as shall work a wonder to your wise judgment in noting the effect of their amorous devices and conclusions of their actions: the first neglecting the love of a noble dame, young, beautiful, and fair, who only for his good will[9] played the part of a servingman, contented to abide any manner of pain only to behold him. He again setting his love of[10] a dame that, despising him, being a noble duke, gave herself to a servingman, as she had thought. But it otherwise fell out, as the substance of this tale shall better describe. And because I have been something[11] tedious in my first discourse, offending your patient ears with the hearing of a circumstance[12] overlong, from henceforth that which I mind[13] to write shall be done with such celerity as the matter that I pretend to pen[14] may in any wise permit me. And thus followeth the history.

During the time that the famous city of Constantinople remained in the hands of the Christians, amongst many other noblemen that kept their abiding in that flourishing city there was one whose name was Apollonius, a worthy duke, who, being but a very young man and even then new come to his possessions, which were very great, levied a mighty band of men at his own proper charges,[15] with whom he served against the Turk during the space of one whole year; in which time, although it were very short, this young duke so behaved himself, as well by prowess and valiance showed with his own hands as otherwise by his wisdom and liberality used towards his soldiers, that all the

---

7 of force of necessity   **8 leash** set of three. (Said of hounds, hawks, etc.)
9 for his good will to obtain his affection   **10 setting his love of** fixing his love on   **11 something** somewhat   **12 a circumstance** an incident
13 mind intend   **14 pretend to pen** set forth, profess to write   **15 his own proper charges** his own expense

world was filled with the fame of this noble duke. When he had thus spent one year's service, he caused his trumpet to sound a retreat, and gathering his company together and embarking themselves, he set sail, holding his course towards Constantinople. But being upon the sea, by the extremity of a tempest which suddenly fell, his fleet was dissevered, some one way and some another; but he himself recovered[16] the isle of Cyprus, where he was worthily received by Pontus, duke and governor of the same isle, with whom he lodged while his ships were new repairing.

This Pontus, that was lord and governor of this famous isle, was an ancient[17] duke, and had two children, a son and a daughter. His son was named Silvio, of whom hereafter we shall have further occasion to speak; but at this instant he was in the parts of Africa, serving in the wars.

The daughter her[18] name was Silla, whose beauty was so peerless that she had the sovereignty amongst all other dames as well for her beauty as for the nobleness of her birth. This Silla, having heard of the worthiness of Apollonius, this young duke, who besides his beauty and good graces had a certain natural allurement, that, being now in his company in her father's court, she was so strangely attached with the love of Apollonius that there was nothing might content her but his presence and sweet sight. And although she saw no manner of hope to attain to that she most desired—knowing Apollonius to be but a guest and ready to take the benefit of the next wind and to depart into a strange country, whereby she was bereaved of all possibility ever to see him again, and therefore strived with herself to leave her fondness,[19] but all in vain—it would not be, but like the fowl which is once limed,[20] the more she striveth the faster she tieth herself. So Silla was now constrained, perforce[21] her will, to yield to love. Wherefore from time to time she used so great familiarity with him as her honor might well permit, and fed him with such amorous baits as the modesty of a maid could reasonably afford; which when she perceived did take but small effect, feeling herself so much outraged[22] with the extremity of her passion, by the

16 **recovered** reached   17 **ancient** of ancient family   18 **daughter her** daughter's   19 **fondness** doting   20 **limed** caught with sticky lime placed on a branch   21 **perforce** contrary to   22 **so much outraged** driven to such an intemperate passion

only countenance that she bestowed upon Apollonius it might have been well perceived that the very eyes pleaded unto him for pity and remorse. But Apollonius, coming but lately from out the field from the chasing of his enemies, and his fury not yet thoroughly dissolved nor purged from his stomach, gave no regard to those amorous enticements which, by reason of his youth, he had not been acquainted withal.[23] But his mind ran more to hear his pilots bring news of a merry[24] wind to serve his turn to Constantinople, which in the end came very prosperously; and giving Duke Pontus hearty thanks for his great entertainment, taking his leave of himself and the lady Silla, his daughter, departed with his company, and with a happy[25] gale arrived at his desired port.

Gentlewomen, according to my promise, I will here, for brevity's sake, omit to make repetition of the long and dolorous discourse recorded by Silla for this sudden departure of her Apollonius, knowing you to be as tenderly hearted as Silla herself, whereby you may the better conjecture the fury of her fever. But Silla, the further that she saw herself bereaved of all hope ever any more to see her beloved Apollonius, so much the more contagious were her passions, and made the greater speed to execute that[26] she had premeditated in her mind, which was this. Amongst many servants that did attend upon her, there was one whose name was Pedro, who had a long time waited upon her in her chamber, whereby she was well assured of his fidelity and trust; to that Pedro therefore she bewrayed[27] first the fervency of her love borne to Apollonius, conjuring him in the name of the Goddess of Love herself and binding him by the duty that a servant ought to have that tendereth[28] his mistress's safety and good liking, and desiring him, with tears trickling down her cheeks, that he would give his consent to aid and assist her in that[29] she had determined, which was for that[30] she was fully resolved to go to Constantinople, where she might again take the view of her beloved Apollonius; that he,[31] according to the trust she had reposed in him, would not refuse to give his consent secretly to con-

---

23 withal with   **24 merry** pleasant, favorable   **25 happy** prosperous
26 that what   **27 bewrayed** revealed   **28 tendereth** has a tender regard
for, holds dearly   **29 that** what   **30 for that** that   **31 he** i.e., Pedro

vey her from out her father's court according as she should give him direction; and also to make himself partaker of her journey and to wait upon her till she had seen the end of her determination.

Pedro, perceiving with what vehemency his lady and mistress had made request unto him, albeit he saw many perils and doubts depending in her pretense,[32] notwithstanding gave his consent to be at her disposition, promising her to further her with his best advice and to be ready to obey whatsoever she would please to command him. The match being thus agreed upon and all things prepared in a readiness for their departure, it happened there was a galley of Constantinople ready to depart, which Pedro, understanding, came to the captain, desiring him to have passage for himself and for a poor maid that was his sister which were bound to Constantinople upon certain urgent affairs. To which request the captain granted, willing him to prepare[33] aboard with all speed because the wind served him presently[34] to depart.

Pedro now coming to his mistress and telling her how he had handled the matter with the captain, she, liking very well of the device, disguising herself into very simple attire, stole away from out her father's court and came with Pedro—whom now she calleth brother—aboard the galley, where, all things being in readiness and the wind serving very well, they launched forth with their oars and set sail. When they were at the sea, the captain of the galley, taking the view of Silla, perceiving her singular beauty, he was better pleased in beholding of her face than in taking the height either of the sun or stars;* and thinking her by the homeliness of her apparel to be but some simple maiden, calling her into his cabin, he began to break[35] with her, after the sea fashion, desiring her to use his own cabin for her better ease, and during the time that she remained at the sea she should not want a bed; and then, whispering softly in her ear, he said that for want of a bedfellow he himself would supply that room. Silla, not being acquainted with any such talk, blushed for shame but made him no answer at all. My captain, feeling such a bickering within himself

*stars Starre
32 depending in her pretense arising from her profession of purpose
33 prepare i.e., get ready, come   **34 presently** immediately   **35 break**
converse, declare his intention

the like whereof he had never endured upon the sea, was like[36] to be taken prisoner aboard his own ship and forced to yield himself a captive without any cannon shot; wherefore, to salve all sores and thinking it the readiest way to speed,[37] he began to break with Silla in the way of marriage, telling her how happy a voyage she had made to fall into the liking of such a one as himself was, who was able to keep and maintain her like a gentlewoman, and for her sake would likewise take her brother into his fellowship, whom he would by some means prefer[38] in such sort that both of them should have good cause to think themselves thrice happy—she to light of[39] such a husband, and he to light of such a brother. But Silla, nothing pleased with these preferments, desired him to cease his talk for that she did think herself indeed to be too unworthy such a one as he was; neither was she minded yet to marry, and therefore desired him to fix his fancy upon some that were better worthy than herself was and that could better like of his courtesy than she could do. The captain, seeing himself thus refused, being in a great chafe he said as followeth:

"Then, seeing you make so little account of my courtesy, proffered to one that is so far unworthy of it, from henceforth I will use the office of my authority. You shall know that I am the captain of this ship and have power to command and dispose of things at my pleasure; and seeing you have so scornfully rejected me to be your loyal husband, I will now take you by force and use you at my will, and so long as it shall please me will keep you for mine own store. There shall be no man able to defend you nor yet to persuade me from that[40] I have determined."

Silla, with these words being struck into a great fear, did think it now too late to rue her rash attempt, determined[41] rather to die with her own hands than to suffer herself to be abused in such sort. Therefore she most humbly desired the captain so much as he could to save her credit,[42] and saying that she must needs be at his will and disposition, that for that present he would depart and suffer[43] her till night, when in the dark he might take his pleasure without any

---

36 was like was about   **37 speed** succeed   **38 prefer** give advancement to   **39 light of** happen upon   **40 that** what   **41 determined** i.e., and determined   **42 credit** reputation   **43 suffer** excuse, indulge

manner of suspicion to the residue of his company. The captain, thinking now the goal to be more than half won, was contented so far to satisfy her request and departed out, leaving her alone in his cabin.

Silla, being alone by herself, drew out her knife, ready to strike herself to the heart, and, falling upon her knees, desired God to receive her soul as an acceptable sacrifice for her follies which she had so willfully committed, craving pardon for her sins and so forth, continuing a long and pitiful reconciliation to God, in the midst whereof there suddenly fell a wonderful storm, the terror whereof was such that there was no man but did think the seas would presently have swallowed them. The billows so suddenly arose with the rage of the wind that they were all glad to fall to[44] heaving out of water, for otherwise their feeble galley had never been able to have brooked[45] the seas. This storm continued all that day and the next night; and they, being driven to put room[46]* before the wind to keep the galley ahead the billow, were driven upon the main shore, where the galley brake all to pieces. There was every man providing to save his own life. Some gat upon hatches, boards, and casks, and were driven with the waves to and fro; but the greatest number were drowned, amongst the which Pedro was one. But Silla herself being in the cabin, as you have heard, took hold of a chest that was the captain's, the which, by the only providence of God, brought her safe to the shore. The which when she had recovered,[47] not knowing what was become of Pedro her man, she deemed that both he and all the rest had been drowned, for that she saw nobody upon the shore but herself. Wherefore, when she had awhile made great lamentations, complaining her mishaps, she began in the end to comfort herself with the hope that she had to see her Apollonius, and found such means that she brake open the chest that brought her to land, wherein she found good store of coin and sundry suits of apparel that were the captain's. And now, to prevent a number of injuries that might be proffered to a woman that was left in her case, she determined to leave her own apparel and to sort herself into some of those suits, that, being taken for a man, she might pass

*room romer

44 fall to turn to   **45 brooked** endured   **46 room** sea room (? The original text reads "romer.")   **47 recovered** reached

through the country in the better safety. And as she changed her apparel she thought it likewise convenient to change her name, wherefore, not readily happening of any other, she called herself Silvio, by the name of her own brother, whom you have heard spoken of before.

In this manner she traveled to Constantinople, where she inquired out the palace of the Duke Apollonius; and thinking herself now to be both fit and able to play the serving-man, she presented herself to the Duke, craving his service. The Duke, very willing to give succor unto strangers, perceiving him to be a proper smug[48] young man, gave him entertainment. Silla thought herself now more than satisfied for all the casualties that had happened unto her in her journey that she might at her pleasure take but the view of the Duke Apollonius, and above the rest of his servants was very diligent and attendant upon him, the which the Duke perceiving began likewise to grow into good liking with the diligence of his man, and therefore made him one of his chamber. Who but Silvio then was most near about him in helping of him to make him ready in a morning, in the setting of his ruffs, in the keeping of his chamber? Silvio pleased his master so well that above all the rest of his servants about him he had the greatest credit, and the Duke put him most in trust.

At this very instant there was remaining in the city a noble dame, a widow whose husband was but lately deceased, one of the noblest men that were in the parts of Grecia, who left his lady and wife large possessions and great livings. This lady's name was called Julina, who, besides the abundance of her wealth and the greatness of her revenues, had likewise the sovereignty of all the dames of Constantinople for her beauty. To this Lady Julina, Apollonius became an earnest suitor; and, according to the manner of wooers, besides fair words, sorrowful sighs, and piteous countenances, there must be sending of loving letters, chains, bracelets, brooches, rings, tablets, gems, jewels, and presents—I know not what. So my Duke, who in the time that he remained in the isle of Cyprus had no skill at all in the art of love although it were more than half proffered unto him, was now become a scholar in love's school and had already

48 smug spruce, trim

learned his first lesson: that is, to speak pitifully, to look ruthfully, to promise largely, to serve diligently, and to please carefully. Now he was learning his second lesson: that is, to reward liberally, to give bountifully, to present willingly, and to write lovingly. Thus Apollonius was so busied in his new study that I warrant you there was no man that could challenge him for playing the truant, he followed his profession with so good a will. And who must be the messenger to carry the tokens and love letters to the Lady Julina but Silvio, his man. In him the Duke reposed his only confidence to go between him and his lady.

Now, gentlewomen, do you think there could have been a greater torment devised wherewith to afflict the heart of Silla than herself to be made the instrument to work her own mishap, and to play the attorney in a cause that made so much against herself? But Silla, altogether desirous to please her master, cared nothing at all to offend herself, followed[49] his business with so good a will as if it had been in her own preferment.

Julina, now having many times taken the gaze of this young youth, Silvio, perceiving him to be of such excellent perfect grace, was so entangled with the often sight of this sweet temptation that she fell into as great a liking with the man as the master was with herself. And on a time Silvio being sent from his master with a message to the Lady Julina, as he began very earnestly to solicit in his master's behalf, Julina, interrupting him in his tale, said, "Silvio, it is enough that you have said for your master. From henceforth either speak for yourself or say nothing at all." Silla, abashed to hear these words, began in her mind to accuse the blindness of love, that Julina, neglecting the good will of so noble a duke, would prefer her love unto such a one as nature itself had denied to recompense her liking.

And now, for a time leaving matters depending[50] as you have heard, it fell out that the right Silvio indeed—whom you have heard spoken of before, the brother of Silla—was come to his father's court into the isle of Cyprus; where, understanding that his sister was departed in manner as you have heard, conjectured that the very occasion did pro-

49 followed i.e., and followed   **50 depending** pending, awaiting outcome

ceed of some liking had between Pedro her man that was missing with her and herself. But Silvio, who loved his sister as dearly as his own life, and the rather for that—as she was his natural sister, both by father and mother—so the one of them was so like the other in countenance and favor that there was no man able to discern the one from the other by their faces saving by their apparel, the one being a man, the other a woman.

Silvio therefore vowed to his father not only to seek out his sister Silla but also to revenge the villainy which he conceived in Pedro for the carrying away of his sister. And thus departing, having traveled through many cities and towns without hearing any manner of news of those he went to seek for, at the last he arrived at Constantinople, where, as he was walking in an evening for his own recreation on a pleasant green yard without[51] the walls of the city, he fortuned to meet with the Lady Julina, who likewise had been abroad to take the air. And as she suddenly cast her eyes upon Silvio, thinking him to be her old acquaintance—by reason they were so like one another, as you have heard before—said[52] unto him, "Sir Silvio, if your haste be not the greater, I pray you, let me have a little talk with you, seeing I have so luckily met you in this place."

Silvio, wondering to hear himself so rightly named, being but a stranger not of above two days' continuance in the city, very courteously came towards her, desirous to hear what she would say.

Julina, commanding her train something[53] to stand back, said as followeth: "Seeing my good will and friendly love hath been the only cause to make me so prodigal to offer that[54] I see is so lightly rejected, it maketh me to think that men be of this condition rather to desire those things which they cannot come by than to esteem or value of that which both largely and liberally is offered unto them. But if the liberality of my proffer hath made to seem less the value of the thing that I meant to present, it is but in your own conceit,[55] considering how many noble men there hath been here before, and be yet at this present, which hath both served, sued, and most humbly entreated to attain to that

---

51 without outside of   **52 said** i.e., she said   **53 something** somewhat
54 that what   **55 conceit** conception

which to you of myself I have freely offered and, I perceive, is despised or at the least very lightly regarded."

Silvio, wondering at these words but more amazed that she could so rightly call him by his name, could not tell what to make of her speeches, assuring himself that she was deceived and did mistake him, did[56] think notwithstanding it had been a point of great simplicity[57] if he should forsake that which fortune had so favorably proffered unto him, perceiving by her train that she was some lady of great honor; and, viewing the perfection of her beauty and the excellency of her grace and countenance, did think it unpossible that she should be despised, and therefore answered thus:

"Madam, if before this time I have seemed to forget myself in neglecting your courtesy which so liberally you have meant[58] unto me, please it you to pardon what is past, and from this day forwards Silvio remaineth ready prest[59] to make such reasonable amends as his ability may any ways permit or as it shall please you to command."

Julina, the gladdest woman that might be to hear these joyful news, said, "Then, my Silvio, see you fail not tomorrow at night to sup with me at my own house, where I will discourse farther with you what amends you shall make me." To which request Silvio gave his glad consent, and thus they departed, very well pleased. And as Julina did think the time very long till she had reaped the fruit of her desire, so Silvio he[60] wished for harvest before corn could grow, thinking the time as long till he saw how matters would fall out. But, not knowing what lady she might be, he presently, before Julina was out of sight, demanded of one that was walking by what she was and how she was called, who satisfied Silvio in every point, and also in what part of the town her house did stand, whereby he might inquire it out.

Silvio, thus departing to his lodging, passed the night with very unquiet sleeps, and the next morning his mind ran so much of[61] his supper that he never cared neither for his breakfast nor dinner; and the day, to his seeming,

---

56 did i.e., he did   **57 simplicity** simplemindedness   **58 meant** intended to convey   **59 ready prest** ready and willing   **60 Silvio he** Silvio   **61 of** on

passed away so slowly that he had thought the stately steeds had been tired that draw the chariot of the sun, or else some other Joshua[62] had commanded them again to stand, and wished that Phaëthon[63] had been there with a whip.

Julina, on the other side, she had thought the clock setter had played the knave, the day came no faster forwards. But six o'clock being once strucken recovered comfort to both parties; and Silvio, hastening himself to the palace of Julina, where by her he was friendly welcomed and a sumptuous supper being made ready furnished with sundry sorts of delicate dishes, they sat them down, passing the suppertime with amorous looks, loving countenances, and secret glances conveyed from the one to the other, which did better satisfy them than the feeding of their dainty dishes.

Suppertime being thus spent, Julina did think it very unfitly[64] if she should turn Silvio to go seek his lodging in an evening, desired him therefore that he would take a bed in her house for that night; and, bringing him up into a fair chamber that was very richly furnished, she found such means that when all the rest of her household servants were abed and quiet, she came herself to bear Silvio company, where, concluding upon conditions that were in question between them, they passed the night with such joy and contentation[65] as might in that convenient time be wished for. But only[66] that Julina, feeding too much of some one dish above the rest, received a surfeit whereof she could not be cured in forty weeks after—a natural inclination in all women which are subject to longing and want[67] the reason to use a moderation in their diet. But, the morning approaching, Julina took her leave and conveyed herself into her own chamber; and when it was fair daylight, Silvio,* making himself ready, departed likewise about his affairs in the town, debating with himself how things had happened, being well assured that Julina had mistaken him; and therefore, for fear of further evils, determined to come no more there, but took his journey towards other places in

*__Silvio__ Silvano

62 Joshua (For Joshua's commanding the sun to stand still, see Joshua 10:12–13.) **63 Phaëthon** son of the sun-god, destroyed by Jupiter in his rash attempt to steer the sun-god's chariot **64 unfitly** unsuitable, inappropriate **65 contentation** contentment **66 But only** except **67 want** lack

the parts of Grecia to see if he could learn any tidings of his sister Silla.

The Duke Apollonius, having made a long suit and never a whit the nearer of his purpose, came to Julina to crave her direct answer, either to accept of him and such conditions as he proffered unto her or else to give him his last farewell.

Julina, as you have heard, had taken an earnest-penny[68] of another, whom she* had thought had been Silvio, the Duke's man, was[69] at a controversy in herself what she might do. One while[70] she thought, seeing her occasion served so fit, to crave the Duke's good will for the marrying of his man; then again, she could not tell what displeasure the Duke would conceive, in that she should seem to prefer his man before himself, did[71] think it therefore best to conceal the matter till she might speak with Silvio, to use his opinion how these matters should be handled; and hereupon resolving herself, desiring the Duke to pardon her speeches, said as followeth:

"Sir Duke, for that from this time forwards I am no longer of myself, having given my full power and authority over to another whose wife I now remain by faithful vow and promise, and albeit I know the world will wonder when they shall understand the fondness[72] of my choice, yet I trust you yourself will nothing dislike with me, sith[73] I have meant no other thing than the satisfying of mine own contentation and liking."

The Duke, hearing these words, answered: "Madam, I must then content myself, although against my will, having the law in your own hands to like of whom you list and to make choice where it pleaseth you."

Julina, giving the Duke great thanks that would content himself with such patience, desired him likewise to give his free consent and good will to the party whom she had chosen to be her husband.

"Nay, surely, madam," quoth the Duke, "I will never give my consent that any other man shall enjoy you than myself. I have made too great account of you than so lightly to pass you away with my good will. But seeing it lieth not in me to

*she he
68 earnest-penny small sum paid in earnest to secure a bargain   69 was i.e., and she was   70 One while on the one hand   71 did i.e., and did
72 fondness foolishness   73 nothing dislike with me, sith take no dislike to me, since

let[74] you, having, as you say, made your own choice, so from henceforwards I leave you to your own liking, always willing you well, and thus will take my leave."

The Duke departed towards his own house, very sorrowful that Julina had thus served him. But in the mean space[75] that the Duke had remained in the house of Julina, some of his servants fell into talk and conference with the servants of Julina, where, debating between them of the likelihood of the marriage between the Duke and the lady, one of the servants of Julina said that he never saw his lady and mistress use so good countenance to the Duke himself as she had done to Silvio his man, and began to report with what familiarity and courtesy she had received him, feasted him, and lodged him, and that in his opinion Silvio was like to speed[76] before the Duke or any other that were suitors.

This tale was quickly brought to the Duke himself, who, making better inquiry in the matter, found it to be true that was reported; and, better considering of the words which Julina had used towards himself, was very well assured that it could be no other than his own man that had thrust his nose so far out of joint. Wherefore, without any further respect,[77] caused[78] him to be thrust into a dungeon, where he was kept prisoner in a very pitiful plight.

Poor Silvio, having got intelligence by some of his fellows what was the cause that the Duke his master did bear such displeasure unto him, devised all the means he could, as well by mediation* by his fellows as otherwise by petitions and supplications to the Duke, that he would suspend his judgment till perfect proof were had in the matter, and then, if any manner of thing did fall out against him whereby the Duke had cause to take any grief, he would confess himself worthy not only of imprisonment but also of most vile and shameful death. With these petitions he daily plied the Duke, but all in vain, for the Duke thought he had made so good proof that he was thoroughly confirmed in his opinion against his man.

But the Lady Julina, wondering what made Silvio that he was so slack in his visitation and why he absented himself so long from her presence, began to think that all was not

---

*__mediation__ meditation

__74 let__ hinder   __75 space__ time   __76 like to speed__ likely to succeed
__77 respect__ consideration   __78 caused__ i.e., he caused

well. But in the end, perceiving no decoction[79] of her former surfeit—received as you have heard—and finding in herself an unwonted swelling in her belly, assuring herself to be with child, fearing to become quite bankrupt of her honor, did think it more than time to seek out a father, and made such secret search and diligent inquiry that she learned the truth how Silvio was kept in prison by the Duke his master. And minding[80] to find a present remedy, as well for the love she bare[81] to Silvio as for the maintenance of her credit and estimation, she speedily hasted to the palace of the Duke, to whom she said as followeth:

"Sir Duke, it may be that you will think my coming to your house in this sort doth something[82] pass the limits of modesty, the which, I protest before God, proceedeth of this desire that the world should know how justly I seek means to maintain my honor. But to the end I seem not tedious with prolixity of words, nor to use other than direct circumstances, know, sir, that the love I bear to my only beloved Silvio, whom I do esteem more than all the jewels in the world, whose personage I regard more than my own life, is the only cause of my attempted journey, beseeching you that all the whole displeasure which I understand you have conceived against him may be imputed unto my charge, and that it would please you lovingly to deal with him whom of myself I have chosen rather for the satisfaction of mine honest liking than for the vain preeminences or honorable dignities looked after[83] by ambitious minds."

The Duke, having heard this discourse, caused Silvio presently[84] to be sent for and to be brought before him, to whom he said: "Had it not been sufficient for thee, when I had reposed[85] myself in thy fidelity and the trustiness of thy service, that thou shouldst so traitorously deal with me, but since that time hast not spared still to abuse me with so many forgeries and perjured protestations, not only hateful unto me, whose simplicity thou thinkest to be such that by the plot of thy pleasant tongue thou wouldst make me believe a manifest untruth, but most abominable be thy doings in the presence and sight of God, that hast[86] not spared to blaspheme his holy name by calling him to be a witness

79 decoction diminishing   **80 minding** intending   **81 bare** bore
82 something somewhat   **83 looked after** sought after   **84 presently** immediately   **85 reposed** entrusted   **86 that hast** (you) who have

to maintain thy leasings,[87] and so detestably wouldst forswear thyself in a matter that is so openly known."

Poor Silvio, whose innocency was such that he might lawfully swear, seeing Julina to be there in place, answered thus:

"Most noble Duke, well understanding your conceived grief, most humbly I beseech you patiently to hear my excuse, not minding[88] thereby to aggravate or heap up your wrath and displeasure, protesting before God that there is nothing in the world which I regard so much or do esteem so dear as your good grace and favor, but desirous that Your Grace should know my innocency, and to clear myself of such impositions[89] wherewith I know I am wrongfully accused; which, as I understand, should be in the practicing[90] of the Lady Julina, who standeth here in place, whose acquittance for my better discharge[91] now I most humbly crave, protesting before the almighty God that neither in thought, word, nor deed I have not otherwise used myself than according to the bond and duty of a servant that is both willing and desirous to further his master's suits; which if I have otherwise said than that is true, you, Madam Julina, who can very well decide the depths of all this doubt, I most humbly beseech you to certify a truth if I have in anything missaid or have otherwise spoken than is right and just."

Julina, having heard this discourse which Silvio had made, perceiving that he stood in great awe of the Duke's displeasure, answered thus: "Think not, my Silvio, that my coming hither is to accuse you of any misdemeanor towards your master, so I do not deny but[92] in all such embassages wherein towards me you have been employed you have used the office of a faithful and trusty messenger. Neither am I ashamed to confess that the first day that mine eyes did behold the singular behavior, the notable courtesy, and other innummerable gifts wherewith my Silvio is endowed, but that beyond all measure my heart was so inflamed that impossible it was for me to quench the fervent love or extinguish the least part of my conceived torment before I had bewrayed[93] the same unto him and of my own motion craved

87 **leasings** lies   88 **minding** intending   89 **impositions** accusations
90 **practicing** devising   91 **discharge** clearing of blame   92 **so . . . but** and so I do not deny but that   93 **bewrayed** revealed

his promised faith and loyalty of marriage. And now is the time to manifest the same unto the world which hath been done before God and between ourselves, knowing that it is not needful to keep secret that which is neither evil done nor hurtful to any person. Therefore, as I said before, Silvio is my husband by plighted faith, whom I hope to obtain without offense or displeasure of anyone, trusting that there is no man that will so far forget himself as to restrain that which God hath left at liberty for every wight,[94] or that will seek by cruelty to force ladies to marry otherwise than according to their own liking. Fear not then, my Silvio, to keep your faith and promise which you have made unto me; and as for the rest, I doubt not things will so fall out as you shall have no manner of cause to complain."

Silvio, amazed to hear these words, for that Julina by her speech seemed to confirm that which he most of all desired to be quit of,[95] said: "Who would have thought that a lady of so great honor and reputation would herself be the ambassador of a thing so prejudicial and uncomely for her estate! What plighted promises be these which be spoken of? Altogether ignorant unto me, which, if it be otherwise than I have said, you, sacred goddess, consume me straight with flashing flames of fire! But what words might I use to give credit to the truth and innocency of my cause? Ah, Madam Julina! I desire no other testimony than your own honesty and virtue, thinking that you will not so much blemish the brightness of your honor, knowing that a woman is or should be the image of courtesy, continency, and shamefastness—from the which, so soon as she stoopeth and leaveth the office of her duty and modesty, besides the degradation of her honor, she thrusteth herself into the pit of perpetual infamy. And as I cannot think you would so far forget yourself by the refusal of a noble duke to dim the light of your renown and glory, which hitherto you have maintained amongst the best and noblest ladies, by such a one as I know myself to be, too far unworthy your degree and calling, so most humbly I beseech you to confess a truth whereto tendeth those vows and promises you speak of—which speeches be so obscure unto me as I know not for my life how I might understand them."

94 wight person **95 quit of** acquitted of

Julina, something nipped with[96] these speeches, said: "And what is the matter, that now you make so little account of your Julina? That, being my husband indeed, have the face to deny me to whom thou art contracted by so many solemn oaths? What? Art thou ashamed to have me to thy wife? How much oughtst thou rather to be ashamed to break thy promised faith and to have[97] despised the holy and dreadful name of God? But that time[98] constraineth me to lay open[99] that which shame rather willeth I should dissemble and keep secret. Behold me then here, Silvio, whom thou has gotten with child; who, if thou be of such honesty as I trust for all this[100] I shall find, then the thing is done without prejudice or any hurt to my conscience, considering that by the professed faith[101] thou didst account me for thy wife and I received thee for my spouse and loyal husband, swearing by the almighty God that no other than you have made the conquest and triumph of my chastity, whereof I crave no other witness than yourself and mine own conscience."

I pray you, gentlewomen, was not this a foul oversight of Julina, that would so precisely swear so great an oath that she was gotten with child by one that was altogether unfurnished with implements for such a turn? For God's love take heed, and let this be an example to you when you be with child how you swear who is the father before you have had good proof and knowledge of the party; for men be so subtle and full of sleight that, God knoweth, a woman may quickly be deceived.

But now to return to our Silvio, who, hearing an oath sworn so divinely that he had gotten a woman with child, was like to believe[102] that it had been true in very deed; but, remembering his own impediment, thought it impossible that he should commit such an act and therefore, half in a chafe,[103] he said:

"What law is able to restrain the foolish indiscretion of a woman that yieldeth herself to her own desires? What shame is able to bridle or withdraw her from her mind and

96 something nipped with somewhat taken aback by   **97 have** cause to be   **98 that time** i.e., the time of my pregnancy   **99 lay open** reveal **100 for all this** despite all this (denial)   **101 the professed faith** the faith we all profess   **102 like to believe** near to believing   **103 in a chafe** angry

madness, or with what snaffle is it possible to hold her back from the execution of her filthiness? But what abomination is this, that a lady of such a house should so forget the greatness of her estate, the alliance whereof she is descended, the nobility of her deceased husband, and maketh no conscience to shame and slander herself with such a one as I am, being so far unfit and unseemly for her degree! But how horrible is it to hear the name of God so defaced that we make no more account, but for the maintenance of our mischiefs we fear no whit at all to forswear his holy name, as though he were not in all his dealings most righteous, true, and just, and will not only lay open our leasings[104] to the world but will likewise punish the same with most sharp and bitter scourges."

Julina, not able to endure him to proceed any farther in his sermon, was already surprised with a vehement grief, began bitterly to cry out, uttering these speeches following:

"Alas! Is it possible that the sovereign justice of God can abide a mischief so great and cursed? Why may I not now suffer death rather than the infamy which I see to wander before mine eyes? Oh, happy, and more than right happy, had I been if inconstant Fortune had not devised this treason wherein I am surprised and caught! Am I thus become to be entangled with snares and in the hands of him who, enjoying the spoils of my honor, will openly deprive me of my fame by making me a common fable to all posterity in time to come? Ah, traitor and discourteous wretch! Is this the recompense of the honest and firm amity which I have borne thee? Wherein have I deserved this discourtesy? By loving thee more than thou art able to deserve? Is it I, arrant thief, is it I upon whom thou thinkest to work thy mischiefs? Dost thou think me no better worth but that thou mayst prodigally waste my honor at thy pleasure? Didst thou dare to adventure upon me, having my conscience wounded with so deadly a treason? Ah, unhappy and above all other most unhappy, that have so charily[105] preserved mine honor and now am made a prey to satisfy a young man's lust that hath coveted nothing but the spoil of my chastity and good name!"

104 leasings lies   **105 charily** carefully, frugally

Herewithal her tears so gushed down her cheeks that she was not able to open her mouth to use any farther speech.

The Duke, who stood by all this while and heard this whole discourse, was wonderfully moved with compassion towards Julina, knowing that from her infancy she had ever so honorably used herself that there was no man able to detect her of[106] any misdemeanor otherwise than beseemed a lady of her estate. Wherefore, being fully resolved that Silvio, his man, had committed this villainy against her, in a great fury, drawing his rapier, he said unto Silvio:

"How canst thou, arrant thief, show thyself so cruel and careless to such as do thee honor? Hast thou so little regard of such a noble lady as humbleth herself to such a villain as thou art, who, without any respect either of her renown or noble estate, canst be content to seek the wrack and utter ruin of her honor? But frame[107] thyself to make such satisfaction as she requireth—although I know, unworthy wretch, that thou art not able to make her the least part of amends—or I swear by God that thou shalt not escape the death which I will minister to thee with my own hands. And therefore advise thee well what thou dost."

Silvio, having heard this sharp sentence, fell down on his knees before the Duke, craving for mercy, desiring that he might be suffered to speak with the Lady Julina apart, promising to satisfy her according to her own contentation.[108]

"Well," quoth the Duke, "I take thy word; and therewithal I advise thee that thou perform thy promise, or otherwise I protest, before God, I will make thee such an example to the world that all traitors shall tremble for fear how they do seek the dishonoring of ladies."

But now Julina had conceived so great grief against Silvio that there was much ado to persuade her to talk with him. But remembering her own case, desirous to hear what excuse he could make, in the end she agreed, and, being brought into a place severally[109] by themselves, Silvio began with a piteous voice to say as followeth:

"I know not, madam, of whom I might make complaint, whether of you or of myself, or rather of Fortune, which

106 of in   **107 frame** prepare   **108 to her own contentation** to her heart's content   **109 severally** separately

hath conducted and brought us both into so great adversity. I see that you receive great wrong, and I am condemned against all right; you in peril to abide the bruit[110] of spiteful tongues, and I in danger to lose the thing that I most desire. And although I could allege many reasons to prove my sayings true, yet I refer myself to the experience and bounty of your mind." And herewithal loosing his garments down to his stomach, and showed Julina his breasts and pretty teats surmounting far the whiteness of snow itself, saying: "Lo, madam! Behold here the party whom you have challenged to be the father of your child. See, I am a woman, the daughter of a noble duke, who, only for the love of him whom you so lightly have shaken off, have forsaken my father, abandoned my country, and, in manner as you see, am become a servingman, satisfying myself but with the only[111] sight of my Apollonius. And now, madam, if my passion were not vehement and my torments without comparison, I would wish that my feigned griefs might be laughed to scorn and my dissembled pains to be rewarded with flouts. But my love being pure, my travail[112] continual, and my griefs endless, I trust, madam, you will not only excuse me of crime but also pity my distress, the which, I protest, I would still have kept secret if my fortune would so have permitted."

Julina did now think herself to be in a worse case than ever she was before, for now she knew not whom to challenge to be the father of her child; wherefore, when she had told the Duke the very certainty of the discourse which Silvio had made unto her, she departed to her own house with such grief and sorrow that she purposed never to come out of her own doors again alive to be a wonder and mocking stock to the world.

But the Duke, more amazed to hear this strange discourse of Silvio, came unto him, whom, when he had viewed with better consideration, perceived indeed that it was Silla, the daughter of Duke Pontus, and embracing her in his arms he said:

"Oh, the branch of all virtue and the flower of courtesy itself! Pardon me, I beseech you, of all such discourtesies as I have ignorantly committed towards you, desiring you that

---

110 bruit clamor   **111 but with the only** only with the   **112 travail** hardship

without farther memory of ancient griefs you will accept of me, who is more joyful and better contented with your presence than if the whole world were at my commandment. Where hath there ever been found such liberality in a lover which, having been trained up and nourished amongst the delicacies and banquets of the court, accompanied with trains of many fair and noble ladies, living in pleasure and in the midst of delights, would so prodigally adventure yourself, neither fearing mishaps nor misliking to take such pains as I know you have not been accustomed unto? O liberality never heard of before! O fact that can never be sufficiently rewarded! O true love most pure and unfeigned!" Herewithal sending for the most artificial workmen,[113] he provided for her sundry suits of sumptuous apparel, and the marriage day appointed, which was celebrated with great triumph through the whole city of Constantinople, everyone praising the nobleness of the Duke. But so many as did behold the excellent beauty of Silla gave her the praise above all the rest of the ladies in the troop.

The matter seemed so wonderful and strange that the bruit[114] was spread throughout all the parts of Grecia, insomuch that it came to the hearing of Silvio, who, as you have heard, remained in those parts to inquire of his sister. He, being the gladdest man in the world, hasted to Constantinople where, coming to his sister, he was joyfully received and most lovingly welcomed and entertained of the Duke his brother-in-law. After he had remained there two or three days, the Duke revealed unto Silvio the whole discourse how it happened between his sister and the Lady Julina, and how his sister was challenged for getting a woman with child. Silvio, blushing with these words, was stricken with great remorse to make Julina amends, understanding her to be a noble lady and was left defamed to the world through his default.[115] He therefore bewrayed[116] the whole circumstance to the Duke, whereof the Duke, being very joyful, immediately repaired[117] with Silvio to the house of Julina, whom they found in her chamber in great lamentation and mourning. To whom the Duke said: "Take courage, madam,

---

113 **artificial workmen** craftsmen skilled in their art   114 **bruit** rumor
115 **default** fault   116 **bewrayed** revealed   117 **repaired** went

for behold here a gentleman that will not stick[118] both to father your child and to take you for his wife; no inferior person, but the son and heir of a noble duke, worthy of your estate and dignity."

Julina, seeing Silvio in place, did know very well that he was the father of her child and was so ravished with joy that she knew not whether she were awake or in some dream. Silvio, embracing her in his arms, craving forgiveness of all that was past, concluded[119] with her the marriage day, which was presently accomplished with great joy and contentation to all parties. And thus, Silvio having attained a noble wife, and Silla, his sister, her desired husband, they passed the residue of their days with such delight as those that have accomplished the perfection of their felicities.

The text is based on Barnabe Riche, *Riche His Farewell to Military Profession*, London, 1581.

118 stick hesitate   **119 concluded** settled

Further Reading

Auden, W. H. "Music in Shakespeare." *"The Dyer's Hand" and Other Essays*. New York: Random House, 1948. Auden finds dark tones disturbing the comedy of *Twelfth Night*. Viola and Antonio are characters whose desires are too strong to be contained by the play's comic conventions. The songs, Auden argues, express the play's complex comic feeling: by themselves they are beautiful, but located within the psychological matrix of the play they are cruel, selfish, and self-indulgent.

Barber, C. L. "Testing Courtesy and Humanity in *Twelfth Night*." *Shakespeare's Festive Comedy*. Princeton, N.J.: Princeton Univ. Press, 1959. Focusing on the relation of the dramatic form to the social forms of Elizabethan holidays, Barber examines the Saturnalian patterns in Shakespearean comedy. In *Twelfth Night*, the reversal of sexual and social roles permits both characters and audiences to move, in Barber's phrase, "through release to clarification," as characters (with the telling exception of the puritanical Malvolio), caught up in delusions and misapprehensions, ultimately discover freedom, love, and self-knowledge through the festive action.

Barton, Anne. "*As You Like It* and *Twelfth Night*: Shakespeare's Sense of an Ending." In *Shakespearian Comedy*, ed. Malcolm Bradbury and D. J. Palmer. Stratford-upon-Avon Studies 14. London: Edward Arnold, 1972. Except for Malvolio, Barton argues, all characters and the audience participate in the play's festivity, but she finds the play's harmonies to be elusive and fragile: the improbable romantic world of escape, disguise, and irrational love is announced as a triumph of art, and Feste's final song gently leads us out of the golden world of fiction back to our imperfect world of fact.

Brown, John Russell. "Directions for *Twelfth Night*, or What You Will." *Tulane Drama Review* 5, no. 4 (1961): 77–88. Rpt. in *Shakespeare's Plays in Performance*. New York: St. Martin's Press, 1967. Brown surveys *Twelfth Night* on the stage in the 1950s to reveal the multiplicity of dramatic interpretations that it permits and to suggest the possibility of a production fully responsive to the play's range and complexity. He offers his own solution to the visual problems that *Twelfth Night* poses as an example of one way in which a director might use available theatrical resources to respond to the demands made by the unity and the imaginative power of the text.

Hartwig, Joan. "*Twelfth Night* and Parodic Subplot." *Shakespeare's Analogical Scene*. Lincoln, Neb.: Univ. of Nebraska Press, 1983. Finding the play to be concerned with the conflict between individual will and a design beyond human control, Hartwig considers the relation of the play's two plots. Only Malvolio's fate is determined by acts of human will, and the lack of forgiveness at his exit points to the central difference between the plots: the subplot is motivated by revenge, a human act that fragments and destroys; the main plot is directed by love, the concern of some benevolent higher agency, which creates and directs the play's harmonies.

Hollander, John. "*Twelfth Night* and the Morality of Indulgence." *Sewanee Review* 67 (1959): 220–238. Rpt. in *Discussions of Shakespeare's Romantic Comedy*, ed. Herbert Weil, Jr. Boston: D. C. Heath, 1966; and in *Essays in Shakespearean Criticism*, ed. James L. Calderwood and Harold E. Toliver. Englewood Cliffs, N.J.: Prentice-Hall, 1970. Arguing that in its use of a fully dramatized metaphor (of feasting and satiety) the play rejects the comic model provided by Ben Jonson (the characteristically static comedy of humors), Hollander sees *Twelfth Night* as a comedy of emotional and moral purgation in which excessive appetite is corrected through its indulgence. Except in the case of Malvolio, indulgence succeeds in releasing the fully human self from the limitations of comic stereotype.

Howard, Jean E. "The Orchestration of *Twelfth Night:* The Rhythm of Restraint and Release." *Shakespeare's Art of Orchestration: Stage Technique and Audience Response*. Urbana and Chicago: Univ. of Illinois Press, 1984. Howard considers how Shakespeare orchestrates an audience's experience of the play. The inadequacy of the characters' emotional postures is revealed through their inhibiting effects on the play's action and language. The audience's desire for the generosity and joy that has been frustrated is finally satisfied by the recognitions of the ending.

Jenkins, Harold. "Shakespeare's *Twelfth Night*." *Rice Institute Pamphlets* 45 (1959): 19–42. Rpt. in *Shakespeare, the Comedies: A Collection of Critical Essays*, ed. Kenneth Muir. Englewood Cliffs, N.J.: Prentice-Hall, 1965. Identifying *Twelfth Night*'s most important source as Shakespeare's own *The Comedy of Errors* and *The Two Gentlemen of Verona*, Jenkins examines the play's deepening of the emotional patterns of the earlier plays. The genuineness of Viola's feeling serves not only to measure the emotions of others but also to release both Orsino and Olivia from their self-indulgence, a movement that finds an ironic echo in the subplot as Malvolio remains locked in his self-love.

Kermode, Frank. "The Mature Comedies." In *Early Shakespeare*, ed. John Russell Brown and Bernard Harris. Stratford-upon-Avon Studies 3. London: Edward Arnold, 1961. In an essay seeking to characterize the achievement of the mature comedies, Kermode considers *Twelfth Night* in relation to two aspects of the Twelfth Night celebrations: its licensing of misrule and the confounding of identity and authority. The play's comic confusions and misapprehensions reflect the festive pattern, moving from a superficial comedy of errors to a complex and sophisticated comedy of identity.

King, Walter N., ed. *Twentieth Century Interpretations of "Twelfth Night."* Englewood Cliffs, N.J.: Prentice-Hall, 1968. King's introductory essay to this collection of criticism considers the collision of perspectives in *Twelfth Night*, and his selection of essays is designed to demonstrate the variety of critical approaches that it permits. King includes studies by Sylvan Barnet, H. B. Charlton, Alan Downer, and Leslie Hotson, as well as essays, considered here, by Barber, Hollander, Leech, Salingar, and Summers.

Leech, Clifford. "*Twelfth Night*, or What Delights You." *"Twelfth Night" and Shakespearian Comedy*. Toronto: Univ. of Toronto Press, 1965. *Twelfth Night*, according to Leech, tempers its harmonies with the awareness of the contrivance needed to produce them. The play is never harsh, Leech finds, but the precariousness of the comic triumph is evident—in our discomfort at Malvolio's humiliation, in the poignancy of Antonio's relationship with Sebastian, in the complicated sexual awareness produced by boy actors playing women disguised as men, and in the refusal of the ending fully to credit the imminent marriages.

Leggatt, Alexander. *"Twelfth Night." Shakespeare's Comedy of Love*. London: Methuen, 1974. Leggatt examines *Twelfth Night*'s emphasis upon individuals isolated by nature or circumstance. The play dramatizes the difficulties of forming relationships, and significantly, Leggatt finds, it ends not with a dance or procession of lovers but with the solitary figure of Feste. The love plot is resolved happily, but its resolution depends upon formal organization rather than upon psychological growth, revealing the tension between conventional and realistic art.

Lewalski, Barbara K. "Thematic Patterns in *Twelfth Night*." *Shakespeare Studies* 1 (1965): 168–181. Lewalski considers the religious dimension of *Twelfth Night*, exploring the significance of the play's title (Twelfth Night celebrates the journey of the Magi to Bethlehem and is observed on the twelfth and final day of the Christmas season, January 6). The play, Lewalski argues, is not an allegory of Christ's action in the world but a secular analogue of it: Sebastian and Viola bring peace and love to a disordered world, though Feste's final song reminds us that the real world is less easily perfected than the comic universe of the play.

Nevo, Ruth. "Nature's Bias." *Comic Transformations in Shakespeare*. London and New York: Methuen, 1980. Nevo regards *Twelfth Night* as Shakespeare's most brilliant realization of the possibilities of a dramatic form that is at once comic and corrective. The play enacts and exorcises characters' fantasies and obsessions. Nevo explores the gentle masculinity of Sebastian in this process, whose presence permits the joyful recognitions and remedies of the end.

Palmer, D. J. *Shakespeare, "Twelfth Night": A Casebook*. London: Macmillan, 1972. Palmer's introduction to this collection of critical commentary discusses the subtle play of lyrical and dissonant notes in *Twelfth Night* and usefully surveys the play's occasion, date, and sources as well as the history of criticism that it has provoked. The selections that he offers partially trace this history, from seventeenth-century comments on the play to the work of twentieth-century critics such as Barber, Bradley, Charlton, and Hotson.

Salingar, Leo G. "The Design of *Twelfth Night.*" *Shakespeare Quarterly* 9 (1958): 117–139. Rpt. in *Discussions of Shakespeare's Romantic Comedy*, ed. Herbert Weil, Jr. Boston: D. C. Heath, 1966. Salingar examines Shakespeare's transformation of classical and Renaissance romance materials into a comedy of misrule exploring the psychology of love. The narrative and emotional improbabilities of the sources are used to reveal love's folly as well as its life-affirming power. *Twelfth Night* presents and interrogates this paradoxical conception of love, as self-deception gives way to mistaken identities sorted out by the action of a fate responsive to human desire.

Summers, Joseph H. "The Masks of *Twelfth Night.*" *University Review of Kansas City* 22 (1955): 25–32. Rpt. in *Discussions of Shakespeare's Romantic Comedy*, ed. Herbert Weil, Jr. Boston: D. C. Heath, 1966; and in *Shakespeare: Modern Essays in Criticism*, ed. Leonard F. Dean. Rev. ed., London, Oxford, and New York: Oxford Univ. Press, 1967. *Twelfth Night*, according to Summers, in its elaborate dance of maskers enacts their pursuit of self-knowledge and happiness. Everyone wears a mask, and, in general, we laugh *with* those who are aware of and in control of the roles they play, and we laugh *at* those who are not. The clown, Feste—the one professional in the business of masking—is able to unmask the pretensions of others, even revealing the mask of the play itself to be only a fiction of an idealized world.

Welsford, Enid. *The Fool: His Social and Literary History.* Esp. pp. 251–252. London: Faber and Faber, 1935. In her study of the literary and social history of the Fool, Welsford considers Feste as a lord of misrule presiding over the festivities of *Twelfth Night*. His wit gives unity to the play's action, focusing its values. Appropriately he is given the play's final word, dissolving the fiction into a song that points to harsher realities than the comedy would admit.

Troilus and Cressida, with Tom Aldredge (l.) as Nestor and Roscoe Lee Browne as Ulysses, directed by Joseph Papp in 1965 at the Delacorte Theater in Central Park.

TROILUS
— AND —
CRESSIDA

TROILUS
AND CRESSIDA

Introductory Material
Foreword by Joseph Papp
Introduction
Troilus and Cressida in
Performance

THE PLAY

Supplementary Material
Date and Text
Textual Notes
Shakespeare's Sources
Further Reading

Foreword

If *Troilus and Cressida* is a problem play, as it is often called, then Troilus is definitely the problem—and Cressida the victim. When I directed this play, I found myself disliking the actor who played Troilus, because I was so much on Cressida's side. Troilus talks a lot, but he never does anything when it comes down to it. Instead of standing *up* for Cressida, he stands idly by watching the exchange of prisoners that sends her over to the Greek camp and effectively ends their relationship. What does he expect her to do, a lone woman against the whole Greek army? Of course she'll find herself someone else; she'll need a protector.

The Greeks themselves are something of a problem too, with their long, drawn-out scenes and speeches. Though there are some fine passages here and there—such as Ulysses' famous speech on honor, which begins, "The heavens themselves, the planets, and this center / Observe degree, priority, and place,"—the play can get bogged down in a lot of talk and stagnate.

Indeed, there is more *talk* about honor here than in any other play of Shakespeare's—but there's little honorable behavior. It is a play full of corruption and dishonor; people are selling out while putting up an "honorable" front. All of this ugliness is clothed in silk and powdered over with elegant makeup—which just makes the spread of moral infection and disease all the more disgusting. Look what the Greeks and the Trojans are fighting over—Helen, a woman who's portrayed in the play as nothing more than a whore. *Troilus and Cressida* is a stark, cynical portrayal of the internal rottenness and ugliness in people, and one you won't easily forget.

Joseph Papp

Joseph Papp gratefully acknowledges the help of Elizabeth Kirkland in preparing this Foreword.

Introduction

Troilus and Cressida has long proved a puzzling play. Its early printing history contains a number of obscurities. On February 7, 1603, the printer James Roberts entered his name on the Register of the Company of Stationers (booksellers and printers) to print, "when he hath gotten sufficient authority for it, the book of Troilus and Cressida as it is acted by my Lord Chamberlain's men." Evidently the authority was not forthcoming, for in 1609 the play was re-registered to R. Bonian and H. Walley and published by them that year in quarto as "*The History of Troilus and Cressida.* As it was acted by the King's Majesty's servants at the Globe. Written by William Shakespeare." Immediately afterward, and well before this first printing had sold out, a new title page was substituted as follows: "*The Famous History of Troilus and Cresseid.* Excellently expressing the beginning of their loves, with the conceited wooing of Pandarus, Prince of Lycia. Written by William Shakespeare." This second version had, moreover, a preface to the reader (something found in no other Shakespearean quarto) declaring *Troilus and Cressida* to be "a new play, never staled with the stage, never clapper-clawed with the palms of the vulgar," nor "sullied with the smoky breath of the multitude." The preface goes on to imply that the play's "grand possessors" (i.e., Shakespeare's acting company) had not wished to see the play released at all. What this substituted title page and added preface may suggest is that Bonian and Walley felt constrained to present their text as a new one, a literary rather than a theatrical text, and hence different from the version entered in the Stationers' Register "as it is acted by my Lord Chamberlain's men." Because that version had been legally registered in the name of James Roberts, the new publishers made their case for legal possession by offering a "new" play.

Later, the editors of the First Folio in 1623 seem to have had difficulty in obtaining permission to print *Troilus and Cressida*. Three pages of the play were actually printed to follow *Romeo and Juliet*, among the tragedies, but were then withdrawn to be replaced by *Timon of Athens*. Ultimately the play appeared in the Folio almost without pagination, unlisted in the table of contents, and placed with fitting ambiguity between the histories and tragedies.

This unusual printing history offers conflicting information about original stage performance. Against the evidence of the second version of the 1609 quarto with its preface proclaiming a play "never staled with the stage," we have the evidence of the first title page mentioning the King's Majesty's servants at the Globe and of the Stationers' Register entry in 1603 referring to the play "as it is acted." Since the 1609 preface may be part of a legal maneuver designed to represent the play as new, the case in favor of actual performance has some weight. We cannot be sure, however, that performance was successful, or that it reached a very large audience. Some scholars have hypothesized that Shakespeare's company mounted a special production of the play for a private audience at the Inns of Court (where young men studied law) or a similar place, even though an arrangement of this sort would have been most unusual if not unique; Shakespeare's company often took its regular plays to court or other special audiences, but no instance is positively known in which Shakespeare wrote on commission for a private showing. More likely, *Troilus and Cressida* was performed publicly without great success. A sequel, promised in the closing lines of the play by Pandarus to be presented some "two months hence," evidently did not materialize, perhaps because public demand was insufficient. The 1609 quarto, with its revised title page and added preface, may have attempted to capitalize on the play's public failure by touting it as sophisticated fare to be appreciated only by discerning readers. Possibly Shakespeare and his company took another look at *Troilus and Cressida* in 1608, after they had acquired the right to perform in their indoor theater at Blackfriars, where audiences tended to be more select, only to discover anew that the play did not draw. Its subsequent stage history, in any case, is largely a blank until the twentieth century, except for a much-changed Restoration adaptation by John Dryden (1679), in which Cressida remains true to Troilus and slays herself when accused of infidelity.

Shakespeare must have had some relative failures in the theater as well as enormous successes. Even if *Troilus and*

Cressida was a practical failure in its time, however, it enjoys high critical esteem today and has shown itself to be theatrically powerful. What we perceive is that its mordant wit, its satirical depiction of war, and its dispiriting portrayal of sexual infidelity call for a response very different from the one required for an appreciation of Shakespeare's romantic comedies and history plays of the 1590s. Were some of Shakespeare's audience put off at first by this difference? Certainly *Troilus and Cressida* is in a sense less "popular" than *As You Like It* or *A Midsummer Night's Dream*. *Troilus and Cressida*, written probably in 1601–1602 shortly before the Stationers' Register entry of 1603, is attuned to a new and darker mood emerging during this period in Shakespeare's work and in the work of his contemporaries.

In the early 1600s, dramatic satire enjoyed a sudden and highly visible notoriety. Catering in large part to select and courtly audiences, and given new impetus with the reopening of the boys' acting companies at the indoor theaters in 1599, satirical drama quickly employed the talents of Ben Jonson, John Marston, and George Chapman as well as other sophisticated dramatists. Jonson launched a series of plays he called comical satires, in which he rebuked the London citizenry and presumed to teach manners to the court as well. The so-called War of the Theaters among Jonson, Marston, and Thomas Dekker, although partly a personality clash of no consequence, was also a serious debate between public and more courtly or select stages on the proper uses of satire. Public dramatists complained about the libelous boldness of the new satire and were galled by the preference of some audiences for this new theatrical phenomenon; even Shakespeare fretted in *Hamlet* (2.2.339–362) about the rivalry. Yet as an artist in search of new forms, he also responded with positive interest. He experimented with a Jonsonian type of satirical plot in the exposure of Malvolio, in *Twelfth Night* (1600–1602). *Troilus and Cressida* seems to have been another and more ambitious experiment embracing a different kind of satire, not of witty exposure but of disillusionment.

This satiric genre is hard to classify according to the conventional definitions of tragedy, comedy, or history, but does have its own clearly defined rationale that makes special sense in terms of our modern theater. The play is nominally tragic in that it presents the fall of great Hector and adumbrates the fall of Troy, yet its love story merely dwindles into frustrated estrangement without the death of either lover. The play is comic only insofar as it is black comedy or comedy of the absurd. Its leering sexual titillation and its mood of spiritual paralysis link *Troilus and Cressida* to the problem comedies *All's Well That Ends Well* (c. 1601–1604) and *Measure for Measure* (1603–1604). The play is called a "history" on both its early title pages and assuredly deals with the great events of history's most famous war, but history has become essentially ironic. In this, *Troilus and Cressida* represents a culmination of Shakespeare's ironic exploration of history as begun in the impasses of *Richard II* or *Henry IV* and portrayed more fully in the sustained ambiguities of *Julius Caesar* (1599). However much Shakespeare may have been influenced by the contemporary vogue of satire in the boys' theater, his own satire of disillusion is integral to his development as an artist. *Troilus and Cressida* is a fitting companion and contemporary for *Hamlet* (c. 1599–1601). Like that play it evokes a universal disorder that may well reflect the Jacobean loss of an assured sense of philosophical reliance on the medieval hierarchies of the old Ptolemaic earth-centered cosmos.

Troilus and Cressida achieves its disillusioning effect through repeated ironic juxtaposition of heroic ideals and tarnished realities. Although it deals with the greatest war in history and a renowned love affair, we as audience know that Troy and the lovers will be overthrown by cunning and infidelity. Shakespeare partly inherited from his sources this duality of epic grandness and dispiriting conclusion. To learn of the war itself, he must have known George Chapman's translation of the *Iliad* (of which seven books were published in 1598), and of course Virgil's account of the destruction of Troy, but he relied more particularly on medieval romances: Raoul Lefevre's *Recueil des Histoires de Troyes* as translated and published by William Caxton, and perhaps John Lydgate's *Troy Book*, derived in part from Guido delle Colonne's *Historia Trojana*. These romances were Trojan in point of view and hence concerned with the fall of that city. For the bitter love story, Shakespeare went to Geoffrey Chaucer's *Troilus and Criseyde* (c. 1385–1386), which had been derived from the twelfth-century medieval romance of Benoît de Sainte-Maure, *Le Roman de Troie*, as amplified and retold in Boccaccio's *Il Filostrato*. Chaucer's Criseyde is an admirably self-possessed young woman, and her love for Troilus captures the spirit of the courtly love tradition upon which the story was based. After the late fourteenth century, however, Chaucer's heroine suffered a drastic decline in esteem. In Robert Henryson's *Testament of Cresseid*, for example, Cressida becomes a leper and beggar, the "lazar kite of Cressid's kind" to whom Pistol alludes in *Henry V*. Her name has become synonymous with womanly infidelity, as Shakespeare wryly points out in *Troilus and Cressida:* "Let all constant men be Troiluses, all false women Cressids, and all brokers-between Pandars" (3.2.201–203). Shakespeare is fascinated by this phenomenon of declining reputations. Just as the illustrious warrior Achilles must learn that envious time detracts from our best achievements and stigmatizes us for our worst failings, Troilus, Cressida, and Pandarus all anticipate the lasting consequences to their reputations of a failed love relationship. The passion to which they commit themselves eternally becomes not only an emblem of lost hopes and promises but a caricature to later generations of enervating and frustrated desire, promiscuity, and pandering. Thus Shakespeare finds in his materials both chivalric splendor and a deflation of it.

Stylistically, Shakespeare exploits this juxtaposition. He employs epic conventions more than is his custom. The narrative commences, as the chorus informs us, in medias res, "Beginning in the middle." Epic similes adorn the formal speeches of Ulysses, Agamemnon, and Nestor. The rhetoric of persuasion plays an important role, as in *Julius Caesar* and other Roman plays. The great names of antiquity are paraded past us in a roll call of heroes. Hector above all is an epic hero, although in the fashion of medieval romance he is also the prince of chivalry. He longs to resolve the war by a challenge to single combat, in tournament, with the breaking of lances and with each warrior defending the honor of his lady fair (1.3.264–283). The Greeks respond for a time to this stirring call to arms. Yet, in the broader context of the war itself, with its unworthy causes, its frustrating irresolution, and its debilitating effect on the morale of both sides, Hector's idealism cannot prevail. On the Greek side, Ulysses' ennobling vision of "degree, priority, and place" (1.3.86), by which the heavens show man the value of harmonious order, serves more to criticize and mock the present disorder of the Greek army than to offer guidance toward a restoration of that order. Epic convention becomes hollow travesty, as man's chivalric aspirations repeatedly dissolve into the sordid insinuations of Thersites or Pandarus. Despite the play's epic machinery, the gods are nowhere to be found.

A prevailing metaphor is that of disease (as also in *Hamlet*). Insubordinate conduct "infects" (1.3.187) the body politic. The Greek commanders hope to "physic" (1.3.377) Achilles lest his virtues, "like fair fruit in an unwholesome dish," rot untasted (2.3.119). Hector deplores the way his fellow Trojans "infectiously" enslave themselves to willful appetite (2.2.59). Elsewhere, love is described as an open ulcer and as an itch that must be scratched; Helen is "contaminated carrion" (4.1.73). Thersites most of all invites us to regard both love and war as disease-ridden, afflicted by boils, plagues, scabs, the "Neapolitan bone-ache" (syphilis), "lethargies, cold palsies, raw eyes, dirt-rotten livers, wheezing lungs, bladders full of impostume [abscesses], sciaticas," and still more (2.3.18 and 5.1.19–21). Pandarus ends the play on a similarly tawdry note by jesting about prostitutes (Winchester geese, he calls them) and the "sweating" or venereal diseases.

The war is both glorious and absurd. It calls forth brave deeds and heroic sacrifices. Yet it is correctly labeled by the Prologue a "quarrel," begun over an "old aunt" whom the Greeks have held captive and Helen, whom the Trojans abducted in reprisal. No one believes the original cause to justify the bloodletting that has ensued. Menelaus' cuckoldry is the subject of obscene mirth in the Greek camp. Among the Trojans, Troilus can argue only that one doesn't return soiled goods; since all Troy consented to Helen's abduction, Troy must continue the war to maintain its honor. The war thus assumes a grim momentum of its own. The combatants repeatedly discover that they are trapped in the ironies of a situation they helped make but can no longer unmake. Hector's challenge to single combat falls upon Ajax, his "father's sister's son." Achilles too has allegiances in the enemy's camp, since he is enamored of Priam's daughter Polyxena. In the parleys between the two sides, the warriors greet one another as long-lost brothers, though they vow to slaughter one another on the morrow. With fitting oxymoron, Paris comments on the paradox of this "most despiteful gentle greeting," this "noblest hateful love" (4.1.34–35). Only a barbarian could be free of regret for a peace that seems so near and is yet so far. The war offers insidious temptations to potentially worthy men, perverting Achilles' once-honorable quest for fame into maniacal ambition and an irresistible impulse to murder Hector. History and tradition, we know, will mock Achilles for this craven deed. It will put him down as a bully rather than a brave soldier, just as Troilus, Cressida, and Pandarus will come to be regarded in time as stereotypes of the cheated man, the whore, and the procurer. Even before the murder of Hector, Achilles sees his reputation for bravery tarnished by his inaction while Ajax is hoisted into prominence by the machinations of Ulysses and the other generals.

Hector's tragedy is in its own way no less ironic. Even though he emerges as the most thoughtful and courageous man on either side and advises his fellow Trojans to let Helen go in response to the "moral laws / Of nature and of nations," he nonetheless ends the Trojan council of war by resolving to fight on with them (2.2.184–185). This conclusion may represent in part a realization that the others will fight on in any case, and that he must therefore be loyal to them, but the choice also reflects hubris. Hector is not unlike Julius Caesar in his proud repudiation of his wife Andromache's ominous dreams, his sister Cassandra's mad but oracular prophecies, and his own conviction that Troy's pursuit of honor stems from a sickened appetite. He goes to his death because "The gods have heard me swear" (5.3.15). His character is his fate. Even his humane compunctions, like Brutus', are held against him; he spares the life of Achilles and is murdered in reward. War is no place for men of scruple, as Troilus reminds his older brother. Yet Hector is at least the better man for refusing to be corrupted by the savagery of war; we honor his memory even if we also view him as senselessly victimized by a meaningless conflict.

The lovers as well are caught in war's trap, not only Troilus and Cressida but Paris and Helen, Achilles and Polyxena. Achilles vows to Polyxena not to fight and thereby misses his cherished opportunity for fame; ironically he is aroused to vengeful action only by the death of a male friend, Patroclus, who is whispered to be his "male varlet" or "masculine whore" (5.1.15–17). Paris is obliged to ask his brother Troilus to return Cressida to the Greeks, so that Paris may continue to enjoy Helen. What else can Paris do? "There is no help," he complains. "The bitter disposition of the time / Will have it so" (4.1.50–51). Troilus prepares his own undoing when he argues in the Trojan council of war that Helen must be kept at all cost; the cost, it turns out, is his own Cressida. He sees this irony at once: "How my achievements mock me!" (4.2.71). That is, he has no sooner achieved her sexually than he must give her up so that the war may go on with Trojan honor intact and Helen still in Paris' bed. The love of Troilus and Cressida is dwarfed by the war, which has no regard for their private concerns. Troilus wins Cressida after many months of wooing, only to lose her the next day. Yet how could Cressida's father Calchas know of her personal situation? He wishes only to have his daughter back. And although the Trojan leaders do know of Troilus' affair, they must pay heed first to such matters of state as the exchange of prisoners.

So too must Troilus. Perhaps the greatest irony is that he must himself choose to send Cressida to the Greeks, placing duty above personal longing. He appears to have no real choice, but the result is surrounded by absurdities, and it is something that Cressida cannot comprehend. She has determined to stay no matter what the world may think; passionate love is more important to her. Although Cressida was first introduced to us as a sardonic and worldly young woman, urbane, mocking, self-possessed, witty, unsentimental, even scheming and opportunistic, above all wary of emotional commitment, her brief involvement with Troilus does touch deep emotion. For a moment she catches a glimpse of something precious to which she would cling, something genuine in her unstable world. Yet Troilus, caught between love and duty, consents to her departure to the Greek camp. There she reverts to her former disillusioned self, behaving as is expected of her. Who has deserted whom? Cressida gives up, hating herself for doing so. She knows she cannot be true because, like too many women in her experience, she is led by "The error of our eye" and is thus a prey to male importunity (5.2.113). Sometimes she seems, to Ulysses at least, one of those "sluttish spoils of opportunity / And daughters of the game" (4.5.63–64). Still, this surrender to will and appetite in her is not unsympathetic, and does not happen without inner struggle. Her weakness is emblematic of a universal disorder, and is partly caused by it. In the grim interplay of war and love, both men and women are powerless to assert their true selves. As the malcontent Thersites concludes, "Lechery, lechery, still wars and lechery; nothing else holds fashion."

The following is a complete text of the preface to the reader from the 1609 quarto:

A Never Writer, to an Ever Reader. News

Eternal reader, you have here a new play, never staled with the stage, never clapper-clawed with the palms of the vulgar, and yet passing full of the palm comical; for it is a birth of your brain that never undertook anything comical vainly. And were but the vain names of comedies changed for the titles of commodities, or of plays for pleas, you should see all those grand censors, that now style them such vanities, flock to them for the main grace of their gravities, especially this author's comedies, that are so framed to the life that they serve for the most common commentaries of all the actions of our lives, showing such a dexterity and power of wit that the most displeased with plays are pleased with his comedies. And all such dull and heavy-witted worldlings as were never capable of the wit of a comedy, coming by report of them to his representations, have found that wit there that they never found in themselves and have parted better witted than they came, feeling an edge of wit set upon them more than ever they dreamed they had brain to grind it on. So much and such savored salt of wit is in his comedies that they seem, for their height of pleasure, to be born in that sea that brought forth Venus. Amongst all there is none more witty than this; and had I time I would comment upon it, though I know it needs not, for so much as will make you think your testern well bestowed, but for so much worth as even poor I know to be stuffed in it. It deserves such a labor as well as the best comedy in Terence or Plautus. And believe this, that when he is gone and his comedies out of sale, you will scramble for them and set up a new English Inquisition. Take this for a warning, and at the peril of your pleasure's loss, and judgment's, refuse not, nor like this the less for not being sullied with the smoky breath of the multitude; but thank fortune for the scape it hath made amongst you, since by the grand possessors' wills I believe you should have prayed for them rather than been prayed. And so I leave all such to be prayed for, for the states of their wits' healths, that will not praise it. *Vale*.

Troilus and Cressida
in Performance

The stage history of *Troilus and Cressida* confirms our critical impression that Shakespeare never attempted a more puzzling, difficult, and uncompromisingly experimental play. With its mordant view of war and sexuality, it had to wait for the twentieth century to find its true audience. The play seems not to have prospered in Shakespeare's day (see the Introduction to the play, pp. 285–294); if performed publicly at all at the Globe Theatre, as the original quarto title page asserts, it evidently enjoyed so brief a run that the preface to a subsequent quarto printing could claim that the play had never been "staled with the stage" or "clapper-clawed with the palms of the vulgar."

This patrician sentiment of hostility toward popular taste and performance is the publisher's, not Shakespeare's; nonetheless, it raises questions about the play's intent. Did Shakespeare deliberately write a play that only sophisticated spectators or readers could appreciate? This elitist hypothesis has some appeal. Scholars have argued that *Troilus and Cressida* was performed at the Inns of Court (where lawyers were trained) for a select audience, and that it is full of topical references: to Ben Jonson's *Poetaster* (1601), to the vogue for satirical writing, and above all to the Earl of Essex. Since Shakespeare had already complimented Essex in his fifth Chorus of *Henry V* (1599), and since Essex was a favorite of the actors as well as a close associate of Shakespeare's first patron, the Earl of Southampton, Shakespeare may have had reason to be concerned about the political fortunes of this talented but mercurial aristocrat in the waning months of Queen Elizabeth's reign. George Chapman, in his translation of Homer's *Iliad*, had already extolled Essex as "the most honored now living instance of the Achilleian virtues," so that politically savvy audiences or readers might well have been expected to dwell on a possible analogy between the sulking Achilles of Shakespeare's play and England's unpredictable military hero of 1601. The analogy is an uncertain one; if Shakespeare had any such intention at all, he wisely did not make clear any object lesson. His portrait of Achilles is both admiring and critical, but mostly critical. Still, the play's experimental form and its satirical vein may have been prompted by a mood of disillusionment and anxiety in 1601–1602 at the end of Elizabeth's reign.

Whatever the immediate reason, *Troilus and Cressida* proved to be a play far ahead of its time. Until the twentieth century, the response to it was generally one of aversion, apathy, or bewilderment. It was either left unperformed or infrequently revived in a severely rewritten form. In fact, no performance of *Troilus and Cressida* is recorded after 1601–1602 (other than one of uncertain date but prior to the 1670s at Smock Alley, Dublin) until 1679, when, at the theater in Dorset Garden, London, John Dryden's *Troilus and Cressida, or Truth Found Too Late* undertook to remedy the play's presumed defects and make it palatable for Restoration audiences. Dryden not only brings dramatic structure into line with the classical "rules," as he had done in his more famous adaptation of Shakespeare's *Antony and Cleopatra* called *All for Love* (1678), but sentimentalizes Cressida into a heroine worthy of tragedy (as was his Cleopatra). Cressida remains faithful to Troilus and reluctantly accepts the attentions of Diomedes only as a ruse to make possible an escape back to Troy. The wooing scene witnessed by Troilus is thus only an illusion, and Cressida the victim of an ironic misunderstanding; betrayed by Diomedes' treachery and no longer trusted by Troilus, she commits suicide. Troilus, learning the truth too late, kills Diomedes and is at last slain in battle by the Greeks. The death of Hector is reported, not directly shown. Throughout, in fact, Dryden cuts back the gritty war material of Shakespeare's play, shortening the long council speeches and devising instead a quarrel between Hector and Troilus about the exchange of Cressida for Antenor—a conflict that relates to the love plot, not the war.

Dryden's adaptation enjoyed some success. Thomas Betterton played Troilus and also spoke the Prologue, "representing the ghost of Shakespeare." When the play was revived, at the Theatre Royal, Drury Lane, in 1709, Betterton took the part of Thersites. Performances took place in five other seasons in the early eighteenth century, the last at the Theatre Royal, Covent Garden, in 1734. From that date on, however, *Troilus and Cressida* remained wholly unknown for nearly two centuries.

Significantly, if unexpectedly, the play belatedly surfaced in Europe rather than in England. As literary critic and editor Kenneth Muir has shown, Shakespeare's play was performed at Munich in 1898 as a travesty of Homer with an all-male cast (*Proceedings of the Leeds Philosophical and Literary Society*, 8 [1958], 233–238). Several other productions followed in Germany in the succeeding decades, evidently devised as commentaries on current political crises in that country. The play was produced in Hungary in 1900, Vienna in 1902, and Prague in 1921. *Troilus and Cressida* had at last found a world in which human experience could match the desolation of Shakespeare's script.

Revivals in England, beginning in 1907 with a production by Charles Fry at London's Great Queen Street Theatre, and one by William Poel and the Elizabethan Stage Society at the King's Hall, Covent Garden, in 1912, explored the play's experimental and theatrical dimensions as well as its anguish and disillusionment. Working on a bare stage, Poel attempted to reproduce the theatrical conventions and conditions of the Elizabethan theater. An as yet unknown actress, Edith Evans, played Cressida, Poel played Pandarus, and Hermione Gingold was Cassandra. In 1922 a Marlowe Society production (with the women's parts played by men) at Cambridge caught the mood of war-weariness in the aftermath of World War I. In 1923, celebrating the three-hundredth anniversary of the publication of the First Folio, the Old Vic completed a ten-year project of staging the entire canon with a production of *Troilus and Cressida*. Ion Swinley played Troilus in Robert Atkins's production. Nugent Monck, who had served as William Poel's stage manager, produced the play in 1928 at the intimate Maddermarket Theatre in Norwich. Iden Payne, at Stratford-upon-Avon in 1936, provided a respectful version of Shakespeare's play in Elizabethan dress. Michael MacOwan, directing a production at London's Westminster Theatre in 1938, employed modern dress and contemporary weapons and battle effects to underscore the play's relevance to Neville Chamberlain's appeasement of the Nazis at Munich (September 1938), and a Marlowe Society revival in 1940, produced by George Rylands, similarly found pertinent material in the anxious months leading up to and following Dunkirk (May 1940).

By mid-twentieth century *Troilus and Cressida* had become a visible part of the Shakespearean repertory. Its timely bitterness seemed to invite a wide range of interpretations in the medium of modern theater, often in modern dress. In 1946 Robert Atkins again produced the play, this time in Regent's Park at the Open Air Theatre. Struggling against the difficulties of both the text and the weather, Atkins produced a thoughtful version whose evenhandedness is revealed in the program note identifying Thersites merely as "an independent-minded Grecian." Two years later, at Stratford-upon-Avon, Anthony Quayle directed Paul Scofield (as Troilus) in a production that emphasized the shabbiness of the Greek forces and the splendor of the Trojans. Quayle's production ended with Troilus' speech announcing Hector's death. In 1954 the play again was performed at Stratford-upon-Avon. Directed by Glen Byam Shaw, with Laurence Harvey as Troilus, the production eschewed any theatrical gimmickry to trace the emotional patterns of the play. Tyrone Guthrie's controversial production at the Old Vic in 1956 set the action in Edwardian England. With Pandarus in a gray top hat, Achilles in a chic dressing gown, Thersites as a war correspondent with sketchbook and camera, and Helen playing waltzes on a grand piano, Guthrie deftly exposed the affectation and folly that motivates the military action.

Troilus and Cressida's peculiarly modern fascination has perhaps been most eloquently realized by director John Barton in a series of collaborations. The production by Barton and Peter Hall (Stratford-upon-Avon, 1960) played up the cynicism of Thersites (Peter O'Toole) as well as the alluring sensuality of Cressida (Dorothy Tutin) at a time of growing unease with the sexual revolution and a deteriorating international climate. Barton's Stratford-upon-Avon productions in 1968 and 1976 exploited even further a mood of nihilism in the wake of a bitter European response to the war in Vietnam and to Europe's own social and political tensions. All nobility disappeared in these versions of the play, both of which were dominated by Thersites' sneering cynicism. In the 1968 production Achilles (Alan Howard) was a prancing homosexual with blond hair and shaved legs, Cressida (Helen Mirrin) a coarse tease, and Troilus (Michael Williams) weak and confused. In 1976 Barton (with co-director Barry Kyle) saw the play as an unnecessary and ignoble conflict between aging, purposeless Greeks, dressed in gray wool and brown leather, and young, sensual Trojans in pastel silks and gold jewelry. Today it is virtually impossible not to view the play as a bitter and timely commentary on war's dislocating effects. The performance history of *Troilus and Cressida* is an arresting instance of life imitating art.

In Shakespeare's original staging conception, assuming that the play was staged at all, tents and eavesdropping dominate the dramatic action in the Greek camp, while courtly debate and indolent amorous encounters characterize the scene at Troy. We cannot be sure how many actual tents are intended to be visible onstage, but their presence is continually invoked in the dialogue: Agamemnon encounters Aeneas " 'fore our tent" (1.3.215), Troilus overhears Cressida's disloyal courtship with Diomedes outside of Calchas' tent (5.2), and Achilles is repeatedly seen "at the opening of his tent" (2.3.83). This last tent must be functional to the extent of providing entries and exits. The eavesdroppings are at times elaborately choreographed, as in 5.2: Troilus and his guide Ulysses form one party to witness th wooing of Cressida by Diomedes, while the entire scene i witnessed in turn by Thersites as a gloating and obscene omniscient presence. In Troy, the ardent wooing of Cressida by Troilus is deflated by an implicit comparison with the amorous dalliance of Paris and Helen (3.1). Pandarus officiates in both courtships, and we are made continually aware of the irony that Troilus will have to give up Cressida in order that Paris may continue to enjoy Helen. Juxtaposition is an essential technique throughout: a council of war in the Greek camp (1.3) is echoed by one in Troy (2.2), long, eloquent speech answering long, eloquent speech as though to emphasize that rhetoric can prove anything. The juxtapositions of public oratory and eavesdropping, war and love, Greek camp and Trojan citadel, reputation and individual worth, public morality and private cynicism, all demand onstage an evocation of contrasting worlds irreconcilably at odds.

TROILUS
—AND—
CRESSIDA

[*Dramatis Personae*

PROLOGUE

PRIAM, *King of Troy*
HECTOR,
TROILUS,
PARIS,
DEIPHOBUS, } *his sons*
HELENUS, *a priest,*
MARGARELON, *a bastard,*
AENEAS   } *Trojan commanders*
ANTENOR
CALCHAS, *a Trojan priest, Cressida's father, and defector to the
    Greeks*
PANDARUS, *Cressida's uncle*
SERVANT *to Troilus*
SERVANT *to Paris*

CASSANDRA, *Priam's daughter, a prophetess*
ANDROMACHE, *Hector's wife*
HELEN, *former wife of Menelaus, now Paris' mistress*
CRESSIDA, *Calchas' daughter, loved by Troilus*
ALEXANDER, *Cressida's servant*

AGAMEMNON, *the Greek General*
MENELAUS, *brother of Agamemnon*
ACHILLES,
AJAX,
ULYSSES,   } *Greek commanders*
NESTOR,
DIOMEDES,
PATROCLUS, *Achilles' friend*
THERSITES, *a scurrilous fool*
SERVANT *to Diomedes*

Trojan and Greek Soldiers, and Attendants

SCENE: *Troy, and the Greek camp before it*]

Prologue

[*Enter the Prologue, in armor.*]

PROLOGUE

In Troy, there lies the scene. From isles of Greece
The princes orgulous, their high blood chafed,   2
Have to the port of Athens sent their ships,
Fraught with the ministers and instruments   4
Of cruel war. Sixty and nine, that wore
Their crownets regal, from th' Athenian bay   6
Put forth toward Phrygia, and their vow is made   7
To ransack Troy, within whose strong immures   8
The ravished Helen, Menelaus' queen,
With wanton Paris sleeps; and that's the quarrel.
To Tenedos they come,   11
And the deep-drawing barks do there disgorge   12
Their warlike freightage. Now on Dardan plains   13
The fresh and yet unbruisèd Greeks do pitch
Their brave pavilions. Priam's six-gated city—   15
Dardan, and Timbria, Helias, Chetas, Troien,   16
And Antenorides—with massy staples   17
And corresponsive and fulfilling bolts,   18
Spar up the sons of Troy.   19
Now expectation, tickling skittish spirits   20
On one and other side, Trojan and Greek,
Sets all on hazard. And hither am I come,   22
A prologue armed, but not in confidence   23
Of author's pen or actor's voice, but suited   24
In like conditions as our argument,   25

Prologue
2 orgulous proud. **chafed** heated, angered **4 Fraught** loaded. **ministers** agents, i.e., soldiers **6 crownets** coronets, crowns worn by nobles **7 Phrygia** district in western Asia Minor, identified as Troy by the Roman poets, and hence in Renaissance poetry **8 immures** walls **11 Tenedos** small island in the Aegean Sea off the coast of Asia Minor **12 deep-drawing barks** ships lying low in the water (with their heavy cargo) **13 Dardan** Trojan. (From *Dardanus,* son of Zeus and Electra, daughter of Atlas. According to legend, Dardanus was the ancestor of the Trojan race.) **15 brave pavilions** splendid tents **16–17 Dardan . . . Antenorides** (The names of Troy's six gates.) **17–18 massy . . . bolts** i.e., massive posts fitted with sockets to receive matching and well-fitted bolts **19 Spar** close **20 skittish** lively **22 Sets . . . hazard** puts all at risk **23 armed** in armor **23–24 not . . . voice** i.e., not to display arrogance on the part of author or actor **24–25 suited . . . argument** i.e., dressed in armor to match the character of the military plot. *Argument* means "plot of the story."

To tell you, fair beholders, that our play
Leaps o'er the vaunt and firstlings of those broils,   27
Beginning in the middle, starting thence away   28
To what may be digested in a play.
Like or find fault, do as your pleasures are;
Now good or bad, 'tis but the chance of war.

[Exit.]

❖

27 vaunt van, beginning.   **firstlings** firstfruits, beginning   **28 Beginning in the middle** (Alluding to the tradition of beginning epic poetry *in medias res.*)

1.1 *Enter Pandarus and Troilus.*

TROILUS
    Call here my varlet; I'll unarm again.   1
    Why should I war without the walls of Troy
    That find such cruel battle here within?
    Each Trojan that is master of his heart,
    Let him to field; Troilus, alas, hath none.   5
PANDARUS Will this gear ne'er be mended?   6
TROILUS
    The Greeks are strong, and skillful to their strength, 7
    Fierce to their skill, and to their fierceness valiant; 8
    But I am weaker than a woman's tear,
    Tamer than sleep, fonder than ignorance,   10
    Less valiant than the virgin in the night,
    And skilless as unpracticed infancy.
PANDARUS Well, I have told you enough of this. For my
    part, I'll not meddle nor make no farther. He that will 14
    have a cake out of the wheat must needs tarry the 15
    grinding.
TROILUS Have I not tarried?
PANDARUS Ay, the grinding, but you must tarry the
    bolting.   19
TROILUS Have I not tarried?
PANDARUS Ay, the bolting, but you must tarry the leav-
    ening.
TROILUS Still have I tarried.
PANDARUS Ay, to the leavening, but here's yet in the
    word "hereafter" the kneading, the making of the
    cake, the heating of the oven, and the baking; nay, you
    must stay the cooling too, or you may chance to burn
    your lips.
TROILUS
    Patience herself, what goddess e'er she be,   29

1.1. Location: Troy.
1 varlet page or servant of a knight **5 none** i.e., no heart to fight
6 gear business **7,8 to** in addition to, in proportion to **10 fonder** more
foolish **14 make** act, be involved **15 tarry** wait for **19 bolting** sifting **29 what goddess e'er** however much a goddess; or, if she is a
goddess

Doth lesser blench at sufferance than I do.   30
At Priam's royal table do I sit,
And when fair Cressid comes into my thoughts—
So, traitor! When she comes? When she is thence?   33
PANDARUS   Well, she looked yesternight fairer than ever
I saw her look, or any woman else.

TROILUS
I was about to tell thee—when my heart,
As wedgèd with a sigh, would rive in twain,   37
Lest Hector or my father should perceive me,
I have, as when the sun doth light a-scorn,   39
Buried this sigh in wrinkle of a smile;
But sorrow that is couched in seeming gladness   41
Is like that mirth fate turns to sudden sadness.

PANDARUS   An her hair were not somewhat darker than   43
Helen's—well, go to—there were no more compari-   44
son between the women. But, for my part, she is my   45
kinswoman; I would not, as they term it, praise her.
But I would somebody had heard her talk yesterday,
as I did. I will not dispraise your sister Cassandra's
wit, but—

TROILUS
O Pandarus! I tell thee, Pandarus—
When I do tell thee there my hopes lie drowned,
Reply not in how many fathoms deep
They lie indrenched. I tell thee I am mad
In Cressid's love. Thou answer'st she is fair;
Pour'st in the open ulcer of my heart
Her eyes, her hair, her cheek, her gait, her voice;
Handlest in thy discourse—O!—that her hand,   57
In whose comparison all whites are ink   58
Writing their own reproach, to whose soft seizure   59

---

30 Doth . . . sufferance flinches under suffering with less fortitude
33 So . . . thence (Troilus rebukes himself as a traitor to Love for implying that Cressida is ever out of his thoughts, as she would have to be
before she could come into them.)   **37 As wedgèd** as if cleft by a
wedge.   **rive** split   **39 a-scorn** scorningly, mockingly (?) (Troilus compares his face to that of the sun, putting on a false look of joviality.)
41 couched hidden   **43 An** if   **44 go to** i.e., never mind   **44–45 there . . .
comparison** i.e., there is no comparison   **57 Handlest** you handle.   **that
her hand** that hand of hers   **58 In whose comparison** in comparison
with which   **59 to** in comparison with.   **seizure** clasp

The cygnet's down is harsh, and spirit of sense   60
Hard as the palm of plowman. This thou tell'st me,
As true thou tell'st me, when I say I love her;
But saying thus, instead of oil and balm   63
Thou lay'st in every gash that love hath given me
The knife that made it.
PANDARUS   I speak no more than truth.
TROILUS   Thou dost not speak so much.   67
PANDARUS   Faith, I'll not meddle in it. Let her be as she
is. If she be fair, 'tis the better for her; an she be not,
she has the mends in her own hands.   70
TROILUS   Good Pandarus, how now, Pandarus?
PANDARUS   I have had my labor for my travail; ill   72
thought on of her and ill thought on of you; gone be-   73
tween and between, but small thanks for my labor.
TROILUS   What, art thou angry, Pandarus? What, with
me?
PANDARUS   Because she's kin to me, therefore she's not
so fair as Helen. An she were not kin to me, she would
be as fair o' Friday as Helen is on Sunday. But what   79
care I? I care not an she were a blackamoor; 'tis all one 80
to me.
TROILUS   Say I she is not fair?
PANDARUS   I do not care whether you do or no. She's a
fool to stay behind her father. Let her to the Greeks, 84
and so I'll tell her the next time I see her. For my part,
I'll meddle nor make no more i' the matter.
TROILUS   Pandarus—
PANDARUS   Not I.
TROILUS   Sweet Pandarus—
PANDARUS   Pray you, speak no more to me. I will leave
all as I found it, and there an end.   *Exit.*   91
                                        Sound alarum.

---

60 **cygnet's** young swan's.   **spirit of sense** i.e., the most delicate of all
material substances. (According to Renaissance physiology, spirits were
the invisible vapors that transmitted sense impressions to the soul.)
63 **oil and balm** ointments, salves   67 **so much** i.e., the whole truth about
Cressida (since she is indescribable)   70 **has . . . hands** i.e., can apply
remedy, such as cosmetics   72 **had** i.e., had only   73 **of** by   79 **as fair . . .
Sunday** i.e., as attractive in her plainest attire as Helen in her Sunday
best   80 **blackamoor** dark-skinned African   84 **her father** i.e., Calchas, a
Trojan priest, who, advised by the oracle of Apollo that Troy would fall,
fled to the Greeks   91 **s.d. alarum** trumpet signal to arms

TROILUS

Peace, you ungracious clamors! Peace, rude sounds!
Fools on both sides! Helen must needs be fair,
When with your blood you daily paint her thus.
I cannot fight upon this argument;   95
It is too starved a subject for my sword.   96
But Pandarus—O gods, how do you plague me!
I cannot come to Cressid but by Pandar,
And he's as tetchy to be wooed to woo   99
As she is stubborn-chaste against all suit.
Tell me, Apollo, for thy Daphne's love,   101
What Cressid is, what Pandar, and what we?   102
Her bed is India, there she lies, a pearl;
Between our Ilium and where she resides,   104
Let it be called the wild and wandering flood,
Ourself the merchant, and this sailing Pandar
Our doubtful hope, our convoy, and our bark.

   Alarum. Enter Aeneas.

AENEAS

How now, Prince Troilus, wherefore not afield?

TROILUS

Because not there. This woman's answer sorts,   109
For womanish it is to be from thence.
What news, Aeneas, from the field today?

AENEAS

That Paris is returnèd home and hurt.

TROILUS

By whom, Aeneas?

AENEAS   Troilus, by Menelaus.

TROILUS

Let Paris bleed. 'Tis but a scar to scorn;   114
Paris is gored with Menelaus' horn.   *Alarum.* 115

AENEAS

Hark, what good sport is out of town today!   116

---

95 upon this argument for this cause, theme   **96 starved** empty, trivial   **99 tetchy to be** irritable at being   **101 Apollo** (i.e., in his role of god
of music and poetry; the nymph Daphne was changed into a bay tree to
elude his pursuit)   **102 we** i.e., I   **104 Ilium** i.e., Troy generally, but here
Priam's palace   **109 sorts** is appropriate   **114 a scar to scorn** (1) a
wound not sufficiently serious to be regarded (2) a scar in return for
Paris' scorn of Menelaus   **115 horn** i.e., cuckold's horn, since Paris had
stolen Helen from Menelaus   **116 out of town** outside the walls

TROILUS
Better at home, if "would I might" were "may."　117
But to the sport abroad. Are you bound thither?
AENEAS
In all swift haste.
TROILUS　　　　　　Come, go we then together.　*Exeunt.*

❧

1.2　*Enter Cressida and her man [Alexander].*

CRESSIDA
Who were those went by?
ALEXANDER　　　　　Queen Hecuba and Helen.
CRESSIDA
And whither go they?
ALEXANDER　　　　Up to the eastern tower,
Whose height commands as subject all the vale,
To see the battle. Hector, whose patience
Is as a virtue fixed, today was moved.　5
He chid Andromache and struck his armorer,　6
And, like as there were husbandry in war,　7
Before the sun rose he was harnessed light,　8
And to the field goes he, where every flower
Did as a prophet weep what it foresaw
In Hector's wrath.
CRESSIDA　　　　　What was his cause of anger?
ALEXANDER
The noise goes, this: there is among the Greeks　12
A lord of Trojan blood, nephew to Hector;
They call him Ajax.
CRESSIDA　　　　Good; and what of him?
ALEXANDER
They say he is a very man per se　15
And stands alone.

---

117 Better . . . may i.e., if I had my wish, I'd have better entertainment
at home with Cressida
1.2. Location: Troy.
5 fixed steadfast.　**moved** angry (with wordplay on the antithesis between *fixed* and *moved*)　**6 chid** chided　**7 husbandry** thrift, good
management　**8 harnessed** dressed in armor　**12 noise** rumor　**15 per
se** i.e., unique, in the absolute sense

CRESSIDA So do all men, unless they are drunk, sick, or
have no legs.

ALEXANDER This man, lady, hath robbed many beasts
of their particular additions. He is as valiant as the 20
lion, churlish as the bear, slow as the elephant; a man
into whom nature hath so crowded humors that his 22
valor is crushed into folly, his folly sauced with discretion. There is no man hath a virtue that he hath not a
glimpse of, nor any man an attaint but he carries some 25
stain of it. He is melancholy without cause and merry
against the hair. He hath the joints of everything, but 27
everything so out of joint that he is a gouty Briareus, 28
many hands and no use, or purblind Argus, all eyes 29
and no sight.

CRESSIDA But how should this man, that makes me
smile, make Hector angry?

ALEXANDER They say he yesterday coped Hector in the 33
battle and struck him down, the disdain and shame
whereof hath ever since kept Hector fasting and
waking.

[*Enter Pandarus.*]

CRESSIDA Who comes here?

ALEXANDER Madam, your uncle Pandarus.

CRESSIDA Hector's a gallant man.

ALEXANDER As may be in the world, lady.

PANDARUS What's that? What's that?

CRESSIDA Good morrow, uncle Pandarus.

PANDARUS Good morrow, cousin Cressid. What do you 43
talk of? Good morrow, Alexander. How do you, cousin? When were you at Ilium? 45

CRESSIDA This morning, uncle.

PANDARUS What were you talking of when I came? Was
Hector armed and gone ere ye came to Ilium? Helen
was not up, was she?

---

20 additions qualities bestowing special distinction   **22 humors** temper-
amental characteristics   **25 glimpse** trace.   **attaint** defect, stain
27 against the hair contrary to natural tendency   **28 Briareus** Greek
mythological monster with fifty heads and one hundred hands; here, all
those hands are gouty   **29 Argus** a monster with one hundred eyes;
here, all are blind   **33 coped** encountered, came to blows with
43 cousin kinswoman, i.e., niece   **45 Ilium** the palace

CRESSIDA   Hector was gone, but Helen was not up.
PANDARUS   E'en so; Hector was stirring early.
CRESSIDA   That were we talking of, and of his anger.
PANDARUS   Was he angry?
CRESSIDA   So he says here.
PANDARUS   True, he was so. I know the cause too. He'll
lay about him today, I can tell them that; and there's 56
Troilus will not come far behind him. Let them take
heed of Troilus, I can tell them that too.
CRESSIDA   What, is he angry too?
PANDARUS   Who, Troilus? Troilus is the better man of
the two.
CRESSIDA   O Jupiter! There's no comparison.
PANDARUS   What, not between Troilus and Hector? Do
you know a man if you see him?
CRESSIDA   Ay, if I ever saw him before and knew him.
PANDARUS   Well, I say Troilus is Troilus.
CRESSIDA   Then you say as I say, for I am sure he is not
Hector.
PANDARUS   No, nor Hector is not Troilus in some de- 69
grees.
CRESSIDA   'Tis just to each of them; he is himself.   71
PANDARUS   Himself? Alas, poor Troilus! I would he
were.
CRESSIDA   So he is.
PANDARUS   Condition, I had gone barefoot to India.   75
CRESSIDA   He is not Hector.
PANDARUS   Himself? No, he's not himself. Would 'a 77
were himself! Well, the gods are above; time must
friend or end. Well, Troilus, well, I would my heart
were in her body. No, Hector is not a better man than
Troilus.
CRESSIDA   Excuse me.
PANDARUS   He is elder.
CRESSIDA   Pardon me, pardon me.
PANDARUS   Th' other's not come to 't. You shall tell me 85

---

56 lay about him fight fiercely   **69 in some** by several   **71 he** each
75 Condition . . . India i.e., Troilus is about as likely to be himself again
as I am to have walked barefoot on pilgrimage to India, which of course
I haven't   **77 'a** he   **85 to 't** i.e., to Hector's age

another tale when th' other's come to 't. Hector shall
not have his wit this year.   87

CRESSIDA   He shall not need it, if he have his own.

PANDARUS   Nor his qualities.

CRESSIDA   No matter.

PANDARUS   Nor his beauty.

CRESSIDA   'Twould not become him; his own's better.

PANDARUS   You have no judgment, niece. Helen herself
swore th' other day that Troilus, for a brown favor—   94
for so 'tis, I must confess—not brown neither—

CRESSIDA   No, but brown.   96

PANDARUS   Faith, to say truth, brown and not brown.

CRESSIDA   To say the truth, true and not true.

PANDARUS   She praised his complexion above Paris'.

CRESSIDA   Why, Paris hath color enough.

PANDARUS   So he has.

CRESSIDA   Then Troilus should have too much. If she
praised him above, his complexion is higher than his.   103
He having color enough, and the other higher, is too
flaming a praise for a good complexion. I had as lief   105
Helen's golden tongue had commended Troilus for a
copper nose.   107

PANDARUS   I swear to you, I think Helen loves him better than Paris.

CRESSIDA   Then she's a merry Greek indeed.   110

PANDARUS   Nay, I am sure she does. She came to him
th' other day into the compassed window—and, you   112
know, he has not past three or four hairs on his chin—

CRESSIDA   Indeed, a tapster's arithmetic may soon bring   114
his particulars therein to a total.

PANDARUS   Why, he is very young; and yet will he,
within three pound, lift as much as his brother Hector.

CRESSIDA   Is he so young a man and so old a lifter?   118

PANDARUS   But to prove to you that Helen loves him: she
came and puts me her white hand to his cloven chin—   120

---

87 his wit i.e., Troilus' intelligence   **94 for a brown favor** considering he
has a dark complexion   **96 but** merely   **103 higher than his** i.e., rud-
dier than Paris'   **105 lief** willingly   **107 copper** red   **110 merry Greek**
(Slang for a frivolous person, loose in morals.)   **112 compassed** bay
114 tapster barkeep. (Proverbially slow at simple addition.)   **118 lifter**
(with a quibble on the meaning "thief")   **120 puts me** i.e., puts. (*Me* is
merely an emphatic marker implying "listen to this.")

CRESSIDA Juno have mercy! How came it cloven?

PANDARUS Why, you know, 'tis dimpled. I think his smiling becomes him better than any man in all Phrygia.

CRESSIDA O, he smiles valiantly.

PANDARUS Does he not?

CRESSIDA O, yes, an 'twere a cloud in autumn.   127

PANDARUS Why, go to, then. But to prove to you that Helen loves Troilus—

CRESSIDA Troilus will stand to the proof, if you'll prove 130
it so.

PANDARUS Troilus! Why, he esteems her no more than I esteem an addle egg.   133

CRESSIDA If you love an addle egg as well as you love an idle head, you would eat chickens i' the shell.

PANDARUS I cannot choose but laugh to think how she tickled his chin. Indeed, she has a marvelous white 137
hand, I must needs confess—

CRESSIDA Without the rack.   139

PANDARUS And she takes upon her to spy a white hair on his chin.

CRESSIDA Alas, poor chin! Many a wart is richer.

PANDARUS But there was such laughing! Queen Hecuba laughed that her eyes ran o'er.

CRESSIDA With millstones.   145

PANDARUS And Cassandra laughed.

CRESSIDA But there was a more temperate fire under the pot of her eyes. Did her eyes run o'er too?

PANDARUS And Hector laughed.

CRESSIDA At what was all this laughing?

PANDARUS Marry, at the white hair that Helen spied on Troilus' chin.

CRESSIDA An 't had been a green hair, I should have 153
laughed too.

PANDARUS They laughed not so much at the hair as at his pretty answer.

---

127 an as if. **an . . . autumn** i.e., his smile is like a dark and threatening rain cloud in autumn. (Cressida is teasing her uncle by dispraising Troilus.) **130 stand . . . proof** i.e., not shrink from the test (with bawdy pun on *stand*, be erect) **133 addle** spoiled **137 marvelous** marvelously **139 rack** i.e., torture device **145 With millstones** i.e., mirthlessly, since nothing has been said funny enough to make the eyes weep tears of laughter **153 An** if

CRESSIDA What was his answer?

PANDARUS Quoth she, "Here's but two-and-fifty hairs   158
on your chin, and one of them is white."

CRESSIDA This is her question.

PANDARUS That's true, make no question of that. "Two-
and-fifty hairs," quoth he, "and one white. That white
hair is my father, and all the rest are his sons." "Jupiter!" quoth she, "which of these hairs is Paris my husband?" "The forked one," quoth he, "pluck 't out and   165
give it him." But there was such laughing! And Helen
so blushed, and Paris so chafed, and all the rest so   167
laughed, that it passed.   168

CRESSIDA So let it now, for it has been a great while   169
going by.

PANDARUS Well, cousin, I told you a thing yesterday;
think on 't.

CRESSIDA So I do.

PANDARUS I'll be sworn 'tis true; he will weep you an   174
'twere a man born in April.   175

CRESSIDA And I'll spring up in his tears an 'twere a   176
nettle against May.   *Sound a retreat.* 177

PANDARUS Hark, they are coming from the field. Shall
we stand up here and see them as they pass toward
Ilium? Good niece, do, sweet niece Cressida.

CRESSIDA At your pleasure.

PANDARUS Here, here, here's an excellent place; here
we may see most bravely. I'll tell you them all by their   183
names as they pass by, but mark Troilus above the
rest.

CRESSIDA Speak not so loud.

Enter Aeneas [and passes across the stage].

158 two-and-fifty (Priam had fifty sons. Some commentators assume
that the bastard Margarelon is to be included.) hairs (With a pun on
"heirs"; the Quarto spelling is "heires.") 165 forked (1) bifurcated
(2) bearing a cuckold's horns. (The suggestion is that Helen will cheat
Paris in love as she has done Menelaus.) 167 so chafed was so angry
168 it passed it exceeded all description. (But Cressida puns on the
sense of "passed by.") 169 it i.e., Pandarus' story 174–175 an 'twere
as if he were 175 April i.e., the season of showers 176–177 an 'twere
. . . May as if I were a nettle in anticipation of May 177 s.d. retreat
trumpet signal for withdrawal 183 bravely excellently

PANDARUS   That's Aeneas. Is not that a brave man? He's 187
one of the flowers of Troy, I can tell you. But mark
Troilus; you shall see anon.

Enter Antenor [and passes across the stage].

CRESSIDA   Who's that?
PANDARUS   That's Antenor. He has a shrewd wit, I can
tell you, and he's a man good enough. He's one o' the
soundest judgments in Troy whosoever, and a proper 193
man of person. When comes Troilus? I'll show you
Troilus anon. If he see me, you shall see him nod
at me.
CRESSIDA   Will he give you the nod?   197
PANDARUS   You shall see.
CRESSIDA   If he do, the rich shall have more.   199

Enter Hector [and passes across the stage].

PANDARUS   That's Hector, that, that, look you, that;
there's a fellow! Go thy way, Hector! There's a brave
man, niece. O brave Hector! Look how he looks!
There's a countenance! Is 't not a brave man?
CRESSIDA   O, a brave man!
PANDARUS   Is 'a not? It does a man's heart good. Look
you what hacks are on his helmet! Look you yonder, 206
do you see? Look you there. There's no jesting; there's
laying on, take 't off who will, as they say. There be 208
hacks!
CRESSIDA   Be those with swords?
PANDARUS   Swords, anything, he cares not; an the 211
devil come to him, it's all one. By God's lid, it does 212
one's heart good. Yonder comes Paris, yonder comes
Paris.

Enter Paris [and passes across the stage].

187 **brave** excellent   193 **proper** handsome   197 **nod** (with a pun on
noddy, fool, simpleton)   199 **the rich . . . more** i.e., the fool will become
more foolish (since foolish Pandarus will receive a nod or *noddy*)
206 **hacks** dents, gashes   208 **laying on** i.e., evidence of blows exchanged.   **take 't off who will** whatever anyone may say to the contrary
(with a pun on *taking off* as contrasted with *laying on*)   211 **an** if
212 **By God's lid** by God's eyelid. (An oath.)

Look ye yonder, niece; is 't not a gallant man too, is 't
not? Why, this is brave now. Who said he came hurt
home today? He's not hurt. Why, this will do Helen's
heart good now, ha! Would I could see Troilus now!
You shall see Troilus anon.

CRESSIDA Who's that?

Enter Helenus [and passes across the stage].

PANDARUS That's Helenus. I marvel where Troilus is.
That's Helenus. I think he went not forth today. That's   222
Helenus.

CRESSIDA Can Helenus fight, uncle?

PANDARUS Helenus? No. Yes, he'll fight indifferent   225
well. I marvel where Troilus is. Hark, do you not hear   226
the people cry "Troilus"? Helenus is a priest.

CRESSIDA What sneaking fellow comes yonder?

Enter Troilus [and passes across the stage].

PANDARUS Where? Yonder? That's Deiphobus. 'Tis
Troilus! There's a man, niece! Hem! Brave Troilus! The
prince of chivalry!

CRESSIDA Peace, for shame, peace!

PANDARUS Mark him, note him. O brave Troilus! Look
well upon him, niece. Look you how his sword is
bloodied, and his helm more hacked than Hector's,   235
and how he looks, and how he goes! O admirable   236
youth! He ne'er saw three-and-twenty. Go thy way,
Troilus, go thy way! Had I a sister were a grace, or a   238
daughter a goddess, he should take his choice. O
admirable man! Paris? Paris is dirt to him; and I warrant Helen, to change, would give an eye to boot.

CRESSIDA Here comes more.

[Common soldiers pass across the stage.]

PANDARUS Asses, fools, dolts! Chaff and bran, chaff
and bran! Porridge after meat! I could live and die in   244
the eyes of Troilus. Ne'er look, ne'er look. The eagles

---

222 **he** i.e., Troilus   225 **indifferent** moderately   226 **marvel** wonder
235 **helm** helmet   236 **goes** walks   238 **a grace** one of the three Graces,
handmaidens of Venus   244 **Porridge** soup (usually eaten before the
meat course; after, it would be an anticlimax)

are gone; crows and daws, crows and daws! I had 246
rather be such a man as Troilus than Agamemnon and
all Greece.

CRESSIDA   There is amongst the Greeks Achilles, a better
man than Troilus.

PANDARUS   Achilles? A drayman, a porter, a very camel. 251

CRESSIDA   Well, well.

PANDARUS   "Well, well"! Why, have you any discretion?
Have you any eyes? Do you know what a man is? Is
not birth, beauty, good shape, discourse, manhood,
learning, gentleness, virtue, youth, liberality, and such-
like the spice and salt that season a man?

CRESSIDA   Ay, a minced man; and then to be baked with 258
no date in the pie, for then the man's date is out. 259

PANDARUS   You are such a woman; a man knows not at 260
what ward you lie. 261

CRESSIDA   Upon my back to defend my belly, upon my
wit to defend my wiles, upon my secrecy to defend
mine honesty, my mask to defend my beauty, and 264
you to defend all these, and at all these wards I lie, at 265
a thousand watches. 266

PANDARUS   Say one of your watches.

CRESSIDA   Nay, I'll watch you for that; and that's one of
the chiefest of them too. If I cannot ward what I would
not have hit, I can watch you for telling how I took the
blow—unless it swell past hiding, and then it's past 271
watching. 272

PANDARUS   You are such another!

Enter [Troilus'] Boy.

BOY   Sir, my lord would instantly speak with you.

PANDARUS   Where?

---

246 daws jackdaws (glossy, black crowlike birds)   **251 drayman** one
who draws a cart   **258 minced** (1) made up of many diced ingredients
(2) affected   **259 the man's date is out** (1) the man is like a pie without
any dates, a common ingredient used for flavoring (2) the man is out of
fashion   **260–261 at what . . . lie** i.e., what defensive postures you
adopt. (*Ward* and *lie* are technical terms from fencing.)   **264 honesty**
i.e., reputation for chastity   **265–266 at a thousand watches** i.e., guarding myself in a thousand ways. (Subsequently, in the wordplay, *watch*
means "night watch," l. 267, "keep under observation," l. 268, and
"watch out lest you tell," l. 270.)   **271 swell** i.e., in pregnancy
271–272 past watching too late to be concerned about

BOY   At your own house; there he unarms him.
PANDARUS   Good boy, tell him I come.   [*Exit Boy.*]
     I doubt he be hurt. Fare ye well, good niece.   278
CRESSIDA   Adieu, uncle.
PANDARUS   I will be with you, niece, by and by.
CRESSIDA   To bring, uncle?   281
PANDARUS   Ay, a token from Troilus.
CRESSIDA   By the same token, you are a bawd.
                                   [*Exit Pandarus.*]
   Words, vows, gifts, tears, and love's full sacrifice
   He offers in another's enterprise;
   But more in Troilus thousandfold I see
   Than in the glass of Pandar's praise may be.
   Yet hold I off. Women are angels, wooing;   288
   Things won are done, joy's soul lies in the doing.
   That she beloved knows naught that knows not this: 290
   Men prize the thing ungained more than it is.   291
   That she was never yet that ever knew
   Love got so sweet as when desire did sue.   293
   Therefore this maxim out of love I teach: 294
   Achievement is command; ungained, beseech.   295
   Then though my heart's content firm love doth bear,   296
   Nothing of that shall from mine eyes appear.
                         Exit [*with Alexander*].

                         ❖

1.3   [*Sennet.*] *Enter Agamemnon, Nestor, Ulysses,*
           Diomedes, Menelaus, with others.

AGAMEMNON   Princes,
   What grief hath set the jaundice on your cheeks?

---

278 doubt fear   **281 To bring** i.e., are you bringing something? (But
Cressida's phrase also completes a colloquial expression, "be with you
to bring," meaning roughly, "I'll get even with you.")   **288 wooing** i.e.,
being wooed   **290 That she** that woman. (Also in l. 292.)   **291 than it is**
i.e., than it is worth in essence, in objective reality   **293 got** obtained
(by the man)   **294 out of** derived from   **295 Achievement . . . beseech**
i.e., to achieve (to win a woman) is to command her; unwon, she must be
besought   **296 content** i.e., essence, body.   **bear** bear the impress (of
love; or, the line may mean, "though I carry firm love as the content of
my heart")

1.3. Location: The Greek camp. Before Agamemnon's tent.
s.d. Sennet trumpet call signaling a processional entrance or exit

The ample proposition that hope makes   3
In all designs begun on earth below
Fails in the promised largeness. Checks and disasters 5
Grow in the veins of actions highest reared,   6
As knots, by the conflux of meeting sap,   7
Infects the sound pine and diverts his grain   8
Tortive and errant from his course of growth.   9
Nor, princes, is it matter new to us
That we come short of our suppose so far   11
That after seven years' siege yet Troy walls stand,   12
Sith every action that hath gone before,   13
Whereof we have record, trial did draw   14
Bias and thwart, not answering the aim   15
And that unbodied figure of the thought   16
That gave 't surmisèd shape. Why then, you princes,   17
Do you with cheeks abashed behold our works
And call them shames, which are indeed naught else
But the protractive trials of great Jove   20
To find persistive constancy in men?   21
The fineness of which metal is not found
In Fortune's love; for then the bold and coward,   23
The wise and fool, the artist and unread,   24
The hard and soft, seem all affined and kin.   25
But in the wind and tempest of her frown,   26
Distinction, with a broad and powerful fan,   27
Puffing at all, winnows the light away,   28
And what hath mass or matter by itself
Lies rich in virtue and unminglèd.   30
NESTOR
With due observance of thy godlike seat,   31

---

3 proposition offer **5–6 Checks . . . reared** i.e., hindrances and disaster
attend great enterprises **7 conflux** flowing together **8,9 his** its **9 Tortive
and errant** distorted and wandering **11 suppose** expectation **12 yet** still
13–17 Sith . . . shape i.e., since an attempt at performance (*trial*) has drawn
awry and crosswise every previous action of which we have record, so that
it has not corresponded to the aim of its originator nor to the impalpable
shape which it assumed in thought **20 protractive** delaying, drawing out
21 persistive enduring **23 In Fortune's love** i.e., when Fortune smiles
24 artist scholar **25 affined** related **26 her** i.e., Fortune's **27 Distinction**
the making of distinctions (between those who persevere and those who do
not) **28 winnows** sifts (in order to separate the wheat from the chaff).
the light i.e., the chaff, the inconstant **30 unminglèd** unalloyed, uncon-
taminated **31 observance** respect. **seat** throne, i.e., position as ruler

Great Agamemnon, Nestor shall apply   32
Thy latest words. In the reproof of chance   33
Lies the true proof of men. The sea being smooth,
How many shallow bauble boats dare sail   35
Upon her patient breast, making their way
With those of nobler bulk!
But let the ruffian Boreas once enrage   38
The gentle Thetis, and anon behold   39
The strong-ribbed bark through liquid mountains cut,
Bounding between the two moist elements   41
Like Perseus' horse. Where's then the saucy boat   42
Whose weak untimbered sides but even now   43
Corrivaled greatness? Either to harbor fled
Or made a toast for Neptune. Even so   45
Doth valor's show and valor's worth divide   46
In storms of Fortune. For in her ray and brightness   47
The herd hath more annoyance by the breese   48
Than by the tiger; but when the splitting wind
Makes flexible the knees of knotted oaks,
And flies fled under shade, why, then the thing of
    courage,   51
As roused with rage, with rage doth sympathize,
And with an accent tuned in selfsame key
Retorts to chiding Fortune.
ULYSSES   Agamemnon,
Thou great commander, nerves and bone of Greece,   55
Heart of our numbers, soul and only spirit,   56
In whom the tempers and the minds of all
Should be shut up, hear what Ulysses speaks.   58

32 apply i.e., extend the implications of, moralize   **33 reproof** rebuke,
defiance   **35 bauble** toy   **38 Boreas** north wind   **39 Thetis** a sea deity,
mother of Achilles; here used for the sea itself. (Probably confused with
Tethys, the wife of Oceanus.)   **41 moist elements** air and water   **42 Perseus' horse** Pegasus, a winged horse that sprang from the blood of
Medusa when Perseus cut off her head. (The horse was given to Bel-
lerophon by the gods. It is associated, however, with Perseus, probably
because Ovid relates that the latter hero was mounted on Pegasus when
he rescued Andromeda from the sea monster.)   **43 but even now** until
that moment   **45 toast** rich morsel to be swallowed, like toasted bread
floating in liquor   **46 show** mere appearance   **47 storms of Fortune**
trials and tests visited by misfortune.   **her** i.e., Fortune's   **48 breese**
gadfly   **51 fled** are fled.   **the thing of courage** any brave heart
55 nerves sinews   **56 numbers** armies   **58 shut up** gathered in,
embodied

Besides th' applause and approbation   59
The which, [*To Agamemnon*] most mighty for thy place
   and sway,
[*To Nestor*] And thou, most reverend for thy stretched-
   out life,
I give to both your speeches, which were such
As Agamemnon and the hand of Greece
Should hold up high in brass, and such again
As venerable Nestor, hatched in silver,   65
Should with a bond of air, strong as the axletree   66
On which heaven rides, knit all the Greekish ears   67
To his experienced tongue, yet let it please both,
Thou great, and wise, to hear Ulysses speak.

AGAMEMNON
Speak, Prince of Ithaca, and be 't of less expect   70
That matter needless, of importless burden,   71
Divide thy lips than we are confident,   72
When rank Thersites opes his mastic jaws,   73
We shall hear music, wit, and oracle.   74

ULYSSES
Troy, yet upon his basis, had been down,   75
And the great Hector's sword had lacked a master,
But for these instances.
The specialty of rule hath been neglected;   78
And look how many Grecian tents do stand   79
Hollow upon this plain, so many hollow factions.   80
When that the general is not like the hive   81
To whom the foragers shall all repair,   82
What honey is expected? Degree being vizarded,   83

---

59 approbation approval   **65 hatched in silver** (1) adorned with silver
hair, a sign of age and wisdom (2) born wise   **66 bond of air** i.e., his
breath or words as speech, powerful oration   **66–67 axletree . . . rides**
axis on which the heavens, in the Ptolemaic cosmology, revolve around
the earth   **70–74 be 't . . . oracle** i.e., we should expect unimportant
matter from you even less than we should expect music, wit, and truth
from Thersites   **70 expect** expectation   **73 mastic** abusive, scouring
75 yet . . . basis still standing on its foundations   **78 specialty of rule**
particular rights and responsibilities of supreme authority   **79 look
how many** however many, just as many   **80 Hollow** (1) empty, because
of the present assembly (2) symbolizing faction   **81 like the hive** i.e.,
serving as the focus of activity, the command center   **82 repair** return
83 Degree being vizarded when the hierarchical function of authority
is masked

Th' unworthiest shows as fairly in the mask.   84
The heavens themselves, the planets, and this center   85
Observe degree, priority, and place,
Insisture, course, proportion, season, form,   87
Office, and custom, in all line of order.
And therefore is the glorious planet Sol   89
In noble eminence enthroned and sphered   90
Amidst the other, whose med'cinable eye   91
Corrects the ill aspects of planets evil   92
And posts, like the commandment of a king,   93
Sans check, to good and bad. But when the planets   94
In evil mixture to disorder wander,   95
What plagues and what portents, what mutiny,
What raging of the sea, shaking of earth,
Commotion in the winds, frights, changes, horrors,
Divert and crack, rend and deracinate   99
The unity and married calm of states
Quite from their fixure! O, when degree is shaked,   101
Which is the ladder of all high designs,
The enterprise is sick. How could communities,
Degrees in schools, and brotherhoods in cities,   104
Peaceful commerce from dividable shores,   105
The primogeniture and due of birth,   106
Prerogative of age, crowns, scepters, laurels,
But by degree stand in authentic place?
Take but degree away, untune that string,
And hark what discord follows. Each thing meets
In mere oppugnancy. The bounded waters   111
Should lift their bosoms higher than the shores
And make a sop of all this solid globe;   113
Strength should be lord of imbecility,   114

84 **shows as fairly** appears as attractive (as the most noble)   **85 this
center** the earth, center of the Ptolemaic universe   **87 Insisture** steady
continuance in their path   **89 Sol** sun   **90 sphered** placed in its sphere
91 other others.   **med'cinable** healing   **92 aspects** relative positions of
the heavenly bodies as they appear to an observer on the earth's surface
at a given time, and the influence attributed thereto   **93 posts** speeds
94 Sans without   **95 mixture** conjunction   **99 deracinate** uproot
101 fixure stability   **104 Degrees in schools** academic rank.   **brotherhoods** corporations, guilds   **105 dividable** separated, which divide
106 primogeniture right of the eldest son to succeed to his father's
estate   **111 mere oppugnancy** total strife   **113 sop** piece of bread or
cake floating in liquor; pulp   **114 imbecility** weakness

And the rude son should strike his father dead;
Force should be right; or rather, right and wrong,
Between whose endless jar justice resides,   117
Should lose their names, and so should justice too.
Then everything includes itself in power,   119
Power into will, will into appetite;
And appetite, an universal wolf,
So doubly seconded with will and power,
Must make perforce an universal prey   123
And last eat up himself. Great Agamemnon,
This chaos, when degree is suffocate,   125
Follows the choking.   126
And this neglection of degree it is   127
That by a pace goes backward with a purpose   128
It hath to climb. The general's disdained   129
By him one step below, he by the next,
That next by him beneath; so every step,
Exampled by the first pace that is sick   132
Of his superior, grows to an envious fever
Of pale and bloodless emulation.
And 'tis this fever that keeps Troy on foot,
Not her own sinews. To end a tale of length,
Troy in our weakness stands, not in her strength.

NESTOR
Most wisely hath Ulysses here discovered   138
The fever whereof all our power is sick.   139

AGAMEMNON
The nature of the sickness found, Ulysses,
What is the remedy?

ULYSSES
The great Achilles, whom opinion crowns
The sinew and the forehand of our host,   143
Having his ear full of his airy fame,   144

117 **Between . . . resides** i.e., justice is arrived at only through an un-
ceasing conflict between right and wrong. (*Jar* means "collision.")
119 **includes** subsumes   123 **perforce** necessarily.   **prey** i.e., the act of
preying or devouring   125 **suffocate** suffocated   126 **choking** act of
suffocation   127 **neglection** neglect   128 **by a pace** step by step
128–129 **with . . . climb** when it intends to climb   132 **Exampled** shown
a precedent.   **first pace** i.e., he who is in second place, just below the
general.   **sick** envious   138 **discovered** revealed   139 **power** army
143 **forehand** first in might.   **host** army   144 **airy** unsubstantial, spoken by rumor

Grows dainty of his worth and in his tent   145
Lies mocking our designs. With him Patroclus
Upon a lazy bed the livelong day
Breaks scurril jests,
And with ridiculous and awkward action,
Which, slanderer, he imitation calls,
He pageants us. Sometimes, great Agamemnon,   151
Thy topless deputation he puts on,   152
And like a strutting player, whose conceit   153
Lies in his hamstring, and doth think it rich   154
To hear the wooden dialogue and sound   155
Twixt his stretched footing and the scaffoldage,   156
Such to-be-pitied and o'erwrested seeming   157
He acts thy greatness in; and when he speaks,
'Tis like a chime a-mending, with terms unsquared,   159
Which, from the tongue of roaring Typhon dropped,   160
Would seem hyperboles. At this fusty stuff   161
The large Achilles, on his pressed bed lolling,   162
From his deep chest laughs out a loud applause,
Cries, "Excellent! 'Tis Agamemnon just.   164
Now play me Nestor; hem, and stroke thy beard,
As he being dressed to some oration."   166
That's done, as near as the extremest ends
Of parallels, as like as Vulcan and his wife,   168
Yet god Achilles still cries, "Excellent!
'Tis Nestor right. Now play him me, Patroclus,
Arming to answer in a night alarm."   171
And then, forsooth, the faint defects of age   172
Must be the scene of mirth; to cough and spit,

145 **Grows dainty of** i.e., overvalues   151 **pageants** dramatizes, mimics
152 **topless deputation** supreme power   153 **conceit** understanding,
intelligence   154 **hamstring** tendon behind the knee.   **rich** admirable
155–156 **To hear . . . scaffoldage** i.e., to hear the echoing sound of his
marching to and fro on the stage or scaffolding   157 **to-be-pitied . . .
seeming** pitiful and exaggerated acting   159 **a-mending** being repaired
or retuned.   **terms unsquared** expressions unadapted to their subject,
ill-fitted (like unsquared stones in architecture)   160 **from** even if from.
Typhon Greek mythological monster with a hundred heads that
breathed fire; he made war against the gods and was destroyed by
one of Zeus' thunderbolts   161 **fusty** stale (and suggesting *fustian*, i.e.,
bombastic)   162 **pressed** weighed down (by its occupant)   164 **just**
exactly   166 **dressed to** ready for   168 **Vulcan . . . wife** i.e., the ugliest
god, and Venus, the most beautiful goddess   171 **answer in** respond
to   172 **faint** weak

And with a palsy, fumbling on his gorget,   174
Shake in and out the rivet. And at this sport
Sir Valor dies; cries, "O, enough, Patroclus,
Or give me ribs of steel! I shall split all
In pleasure of my spleen." And in this fashion,   178
All our abilities, gifts, natures, shapes,
Severals and generals of grace exact,   180
Achievements, plots, orders, preventions,
Excitements to the field, or speech for truce,   182
Success or loss, what is or is not, serves
As stuff for these two to make paradoxes.   184

NESTOR
And in the imitation of these twain—
Who, as Ulysses says, opinion crowns   186
With an imperial voice—many are infect.   187
Ajax is grown self-willed and bears his head
In such a rein, in full as proud a place   189
As broad Achilles; keeps his tent like him;   190
Makes factious feasts; rails on our state of war,   191
Bold as an oracle; and sets Thersites,
A slave whose gall coins slanders like a mint,   193
To match us in comparisons with dirt,
To weaken and discredit our exposure,   195
How rank soever rounded in with danger.   196

ULYSSES
They tax our policy and call it cowardice,   197
Count wisdom as no member of the war,
Forestall prescience, and esteem no act   199
But that of hand. The still and mental parts   200
That do contrive how many hands shall strike

---

174 palsy i.e., tremor. gorget piece of armor for the throat   178 spleen
(Regarded as the seat of laughter.)   180 Severals . . . exact well-ordered
gifts, individual and general   182 Excitements exhortations   184 paradoxes absurdities   186–187 crowns . . . voice i.e., regards most highly,
adulates   189 In . . . rein i.e., so haughtily   190 keeps keeps to
191 factious i.e., for his faction. state council   193 slave contemptible
person. gall the seat of bile and rancor   195 our exposure the danger
to which we are exposed   196 rank thickly. rounded in with surrounded by   197 tax our policy censure our prudent management
199 Forestall prescience condemn beforehand any attempts at foresight
200 that of hand i.e., an act involving physical combat

When fitness calls them on and know by measure   202
Of their observant toil the enemies' weight—   203
Why, this hath not a finger's dignity.   204
They call this bed work, mappery, closet war;   205
So that the ram that batters down the wall,
For the great swinge and rudeness of his poise,   207
They place before his hand that made the engine,   208
Or those that with the fineness of their souls   209
By reason guide his execution.   210

NESTOR
Let this be granted, and Achilles' horse   211
Makes many Thetis' sons.   [*A tucket.*]   212

AGAMEMNON   What trumpet? Look, Menelaus.

MENELAUS   From Troy.

[*Enter Aeneas, with a trumpeter.*]

AGAMEMNON   What would you 'fore our tent?

AENEAS
Is this great Agamemnon's tent, I pray you?

AGAMEMNON   Even this.

AENEAS
May one that is a herald and a prince
Do a fair message to his kingly ears?

AGAMEMNON
With surety stronger than Achilles' arm   220
'Fore all the Greekish host, which with one voice   221
Call Agamemnon head and general.

AENEAS
Fair leave and large security. How may   223
A stranger to those most imperial looks
Know them from eyes of other mortals?

AGAMEMNON   How?

202 **fitness** suitability of occasion   202–203 **by measure . . . weight** the enemy's strength by the reckoning up of laborious observation on the part of our mental faculties   204 **hath . . . dignity** is not worth a snap of the fingers   205 **bed work** i.e., armchair strategy.   **mappery** mere making of maps.   **closet** the study   207 **swinge** impetus of motion.   **rudeness** roughness.   **his poise** its weight   208 **place before** give precedence to   209 **fineness . . . souls** i.e., subtle skill of their intelligence   210 **his execution** i.e., the use of the battering ram   211–212 **Let . . . sons** i.e., if this is granted, then Achilles' horse in its brute strength outvalues many an Achilles (the son of Thetis)   212 **s.d. tucket** signal given on a trumpet   220 **surety** security   221 **'Fore** i.e., leading into battle   223 **Fair leave** courteous permission

AENEAS　Ay.
　I ask, that I might waken reverence,
　And bid the cheek be ready with a blush
　Modest as morning when she coldly eyes　　　　229
　The youthful Phoebus.　　　　　　　　　　　　230
　Which is that god in office, guiding men?
　Which is the high and mighty Agamemnon?
AGAMEMNON
　This Trojan scorns us, or the men of Troy
　Are ceremonious courtiers.
AENEAS
　Courtiers as free, as debonair, unarmed,　　　235
　As bending angels; that's their fame in peace.　　236
　But when they would seem soldiers, they have galls,　237
　Good arms, strong joints, true swords, and—Jove's
　　accord—　　　　　　　　　　　　　　　238
　Nothing so full of heart. But peace, Aeneas,　　239
　Peace, Trojan; lay thy finger on thy lips!
　The worthiness of praise distains his worth,　　241
　If that the praised himself bring the praise forth.
　But what the repining enemy commends,　　　243
　That breath fame blows; that praise, sole pure, tran-
　　scends.　　　　　　　　　　　　　　　244
AGAMEMNON
　Sir, you of Troy, call you yourself Aeneas?
AENEAS　Ay, Greek, that is my name.
AGAMEMNON　What's your affair, I pray you?
AENEAS
　Sir, pardon; 'tis for Agamemnon's ears.
AGAMEMNON
　He hears naught privately that comes from Troy.
AENEAS
　Nor I from Troy come not to whisper him.
　I bring a trumpet to awake his ear,　　　　251
　To set his sense on the attentive bent,　　　252

---

229 **she** i.e., Aurora, the dawn goddess　230 **Phoebus** Apollo, here
referred to as the sun-god　235 **free** generous.　**debonair** gentle, meek
236 **bending** bowing　237 **galls** i.e., spirit to resent injury. (See l. 193.)
238 **Jove's accord** Jove being in full accord　239 **Nothing . . . heart**
nothing is so full of heart (courage) as they　241 **distains his** sullies its
243 **repining** begrudging　244 **That . . . blows** fame proclaims abroad
that speech.　**sole** completely　251 **trumpet** trumpeter　252 **set . . .**
bent i.e., bend his sense of hearing attentively toward me

And then to speak.
AGAMEMNON   Speak frankly as the wind;
It is not Agamemnon's sleeping hour.
That thou shalt know, Trojan, he is awake,
He tells thee so himself.
AENEAS   Trumpet, blow loud;
Send thy brass voice through all these lazy tents,
And every Greek of mettle, let him know
What Troy means fairly shall be spoke aloud.
                              Sound trumpet.
We have, great Agamemnon, here in Troy
A prince called Hector—Priam is his father—
Who in this dull and long-continued truce
Is resty grown. He bade me take a trumpet   263
And to this purpose speak: Kings, princes, lords!
If there be one among the fair'st of Greece
That holds his honor higher than his ease,
That seeks his praise more than he fears his peril,
That knows his valor and knows not his fear,
That loves his mistress more than in confession   269
With truant vows to her own lips he loves,   270
And dare avow her beauty and her worth
In other arms than hers—to him this challenge.   272
Hector, in view of Trojans and of Greeks,
Shall make it good, or do his best to do it,
He hath a lady, wiser, fairer, truer,
Than ever Greek did compass in his arms,   276
And will tomorrow with his trumpet call
Midway between your tents and walls of Troy,
To rouse a Grecian that is true in love.
If any come, Hector shall honor him;
If none, he'll say in Troy when he retires,
The Grecian dames are sunburnt and not worth   282
The splinter of a lance. Even so much.   283
AGAMEMNON
This shall be told our lovers, Lord Aeneas.

263 resty sluggish, inactive, restive   **269–270 more . . . loves** more than
in protestation made with false vows to the lips of her whom he loves
272 In . . . hers i.e., in the arms of warfare rather than those of his
mistress   **276 compass** encompass, embrace   **282 sunburnt** i.e., unat-
tractive, according to Elizabethan tastes in beauty   **283 Even so much**
(A formulaic conclusion to a delivered message, meaning, "that is the
totality of what I am bid to say.")

If none of them have soul in such a kind,   285
We left them all at home. But we are soldiers;
And may that soldier a mere recreant prove   287
That means not, hath not, or is not in love!   288
If then one is, or hath, or means to be,
That one meets Hector; if none else, I am he.

NESTOR
Tell him of Nestor, one that was a man
When Hector's grandsire sucked. He is old now,
But if there be not in our Grecian host
One noble man that hath one spark of fire
To answer for his love, tell him from me
I'll hide my silver beard in a gold beaver,   296
And in my vambrace put this withered brawn,   297
And meeting him will tell him that my lady
Was fairer than his grandam and as chaste
As may be in the world. His youth in flood,   300
I'll prove this truth with my three drops of blood.

AENEAS
Now heavens forfend such scarcity of youth!   302
ULYSSES Amen.
AGAMEMNON
Fair Lord Aeneas, let me touch your hand;
To our pavilion shall I lead you first.
Achilles shall have word of this intent;
So shall each lord of Greece, from tent to tent.
Yourself shall feast with us before you go,
And find the welcome of a noble foe.
                    [*Exeunt all but Ulysses and Nestor.*]
ULYSSES Nestor!
NESTOR What says Ulysses?
ULYSSES
I have a young conception in my brain;
Be you my time to bring it to some shape.   313
NESTOR What is 't?

---

285 **such a kind** such a spirit   287 **mere recreant** utter coward
288 **means not** intends not to be   296 **beaver** face guard of a helmet
297 **vambrace** armor for the front part of the arm.   **brawn** i.e., arm
300 **His . . . flood** i.e., though his manhood and vigor be at their height
302 **forfend** forbid   313 **Be . . . time** i.e., act as midwife to my newly
conceived plan

ULYSSES This 'tis:
　　Blunt wedges rive hard knots; the seeded pride   316
　　That hath to this maturity blown up
　　In rank Achilles must or now be cropped   318
　　Or, shedding, breed a nursery of like evil   319
　　To overbulk us all.
NESTOR　　　　　　　Well, and how?   320
ULYSSES
　　This challenge that the gallant Hector sends,
　　However it is spread in general name,
　　Relates in purpose only to Achilles.
NESTOR
　　True, the purpose is perspicuous as substance,   324
　　Whose grossness little characters sum up,   325
　　And in the publication make no strain   326
　　But that Achilles, were his brain as barren
　　As banks of Libya—though, Apollo knows,   328
　　'Tis dry enough—will, with great speed of judgment,   329
　　Ay, with celerity, find Hector's purpose   330
　　Pointing on him.
ULYSSES　　And wake him to the answer, think you?
NESTOR
　　Yes, 'tis most meet. Who may you else oppose   333
　　That can from Hector bring his honor off
　　If not Achilles? Though 't be a sportful combat,
　　Yet in this trial much opinion dwells,   336
　　For here the Trojans taste our dear'st repute   337
　　With their fin'st palate. And trust to me, Ulysses,   338
　　Our imputation shall be oddly poised   339
　　In this vile action. For the success,   340
　　Although particular, shall give a scantling   341

316 **rive** split, break apart.　**seeded pride** pride that has gone to seed,
overblown　**318 rank** overripe, swollen.　**or** either　**319 shedding** i.e., if
it scatters its seeds　**320 overbulk** overwhelm　**324–325 perspicuous . . .
up** as perceivable as great wealth, the size of which can be rendered in
little figures　**326 in . . . strain** when it is publicly announced, have no
doubt　**328 banks** sandbanks　**329 dry** i.e., dull　**330 celerity** quickness
333 meet fitting.　**else** otherwise　**336 opinion** reputation　**337 taste
our dear'st repute** i.e., put to the test Achilles, our warrior of greatest
reputation　**338 their fin'st palate** i.e., Hector　**339 imputation** reputation.　**oddly poised** unequally balanced　**340 vile** trivial, paltry.　**success** outcome　**341 particular** relating to (two) particular men.　**scantling** specimen, sample

Of good or bad unto the general;   342
And in such indexes, although small pricks   343
To their subsequent volumes, there is seen   344
The baby figure of the giant mass
Of things to come at large. It is supposed
He that meets Hector issues from our choice;
And choice, being mutual act of all our souls,
Makes merit her election and doth boil,   349
As 'twere from forth us all, a man distilled
Out of our virtues; who miscarrying,   351
What heart from hence receives the conquering part,   352
To steel a strong opinion to themselves?   353
Which entertained, limbs are his instruments,   354
In no less working than are swords and bows   355
Directive by the limbs.   356

ULYSSES
Give pardon to my speech: therefore 'tis meet   357
Achilles meet not Hector. Let us like merchants
First show foul wares and think perchance they'll sell;
If not, the luster of the better shall exceed
By showing the worse first. Do not consent
That ever Hector and Achilles meet;
For both our honor and our shame in this
Are dogged with two strange followers.

NESTOR
I see them not with my old eyes. What are they?

ULYSSES
What glory our Achilles shares from Hector,   366
Were he not proud, we all should share with him.
But he already is too insolent,
And we were better parch in Afric sun   369
Than in the pride and salt scorn of his eyes,

342 **general** army at large   343 **indexes** indications, table of contents
343–344 **small . . . volumes** small indicators in comparison with the
volumes that follow   349 **election** basis of choice   351 **miscarrying** i.e.,
if he should fail   352 **What . . . part** what cheer will the conquering party, i.e., the Trojans, receive from this   353 **steel** strengthen
354–356 **Which . . . limbs** i.e., if one does entertain a strong opinion of
oneself, one's limbs become the instruments of that strong opinion, no
less efficacious and responsive to it than swords and bows are subject
to the direction of the limbs   357 **meet** fitting   366 **shares from** gains
at the expense of   369 **parch** to parch, to shrivel

Should he scape Hector fair. If he were foiled,   371
Why then we did our main opinion crush   372
In taint of our best man. No, make a lottery,   373
And, by device, let blockish Ajax draw
The sort to fight with Hector. Among ourselves   375
Give him allowance as the worthier man;   376
For that will physic the great Myrmidon,   377
Who broils in loud applause, and make him fall   378
His crest that prouder than blue Iris bends.   379
If the dull brainless Ajax come safe off,
We'll dress him up in voices; if he fail,   381
Yet go we under our opinion still
That we have better men. But, hit or miss,
Our project's life this shape of sense assumes: 384
Ajax employed plucks down Achilles' plumes.

NESTOR
Now, Ulysses, I begin to relish thy advice;
And I will give a taste thereof forthwith
To Agamemnon. Go we to him straight.
Two curs shall tame each other; pride alone
Must tar the mastiffs on, as 'twere their bone. *Exeunt.*   390

371 **scape Hector fair** escape from Hector victoriously   **372 main
opinion crush** destroy our general reputation   **373 In taint** in the
dishonor   **375 sort** lot   **376 allowance as** acknowledgment as   **377 physic**
purge medically.   **Myrmidon** i.e., Achilles. (So called here because
accompanied by a band of Myrmidon warriors, from a tribe living in
Thessaly.)   **378 broils in** basks in.   **fall** let fall, bow   **379 crest** plumes
on helmet.   **Iris** the messenger of Juno, i.e., the rainbow, and the blue
flower.   **bends** arches   **381 voices** applause   **384 life** success   **390 tar**
provoke, incite

2.1   *Enter Ajax and Thersites.*

AJAX   Thersites!

THERSITES   Agamemnon—how if he had boils, full, all over, generally?

AJAX   Thersites!

THERSITES   And those boils did run? Say so. Did not the General run then? Were not that a botchy core?   6

AJAX   Dog!

THERSITES   Then would come some matter from him; I   8 see none now.

AJAX   Thou bitch-wolf's son, canst thou not hear? [*Beating him.*] Feel, then.

THERSITES   The plague of Greece upon thee, thou mon-   12 grel beef-witted lord!   13

AJAX   Speak then, thou vinewed'st leaven, speak. I will   14 beat thee into handsomeness.

THERSITES   I shall sooner rail thee into wit and holiness; but I think thy horse will sooner con an oration than   17 thou learn a prayer without book. Thou canst strike,   18 canst thou? A red murrain o' thy jade's tricks!   19

AJAX   Toadstool, learn me the proclamation.   20

THERSITES   Dost thou think I have no sense, thou strik-   21 est me thus?

AJAX   The proclamation!

THERSITES   Thou art proclaimed fool, I think.

AJAX   Do not, porpentine, do not. My fingers itch.   25

THERSITES   I would thou didst itch from head to foot and I had the scratching of thee; I would make thee the loathsomest scab in Greece. When thou art forth in the incursions, thou strikest as slow as another.   29

AJAX   I say, the proclamation!

2.1. Location: The Greek camp.
6 botchy core central hard mass of a boil or tumor   **8 matter** (1) sense
(2) pus   **12–13 mongrel** (Ajax's mother was a Trojan, the sister of Priam;
cf. 2.2.77, note, 4.5.84, and 4.5.121.)   **13 beef-witted** i.e., slow-witted.
(Perhaps this refers to the belief that eating beef made one dull, or
Thersites may merely be calling Ajax a "stupid ox.")   **14 vinewed'st**
most moldy.   **leaven** dough   **17 con** memorize   **18 without book** by
heart   **19 murrain** plague.   **jade's tricks** i.e., ill-tempered kicking and
rearing, as of a worthless horse   **20 learn me** find out for me   **21 sense**
feeling   **25 porpentine** porcupine   **29 incursions** i.e., attacks upon the
Trojan forces

THERSITES Thou grumblest and railest every hour on
Achilles, and thou art as full of envy at his greatness as
Cerberus is at Proserpina's beauty, ay, that thou 33
bark'st at him.

AJAX Mistress Thersites!

THERSITES Thou shouldst strike him—   36

AJAX Cobloaf!   37

THERSITES He would pun thee into shivers with his fist, 38
as a sailor breaks a biscuit.

AJAX [*Beating him*] You whoreson cur!

THERSITES Do, do.

AJAX Thou stool for a witch!   42

THERSITES Ay, do, do, thou sodden-witted lord! Thou 43
hast no more brain than I have in mine elbows; an
asinego may tutor thee. Thou scurvy-valiant ass! Thou 45
art here but to thrash Trojans, and thou art bought 46
and sold among those of any wit, like a barbarian 47
slave. If thou use to beat me, I will begin at thy heel 48
and tell what thou art by inches, thou thing of no bow- 49
els, thou!   50

AJAX You dog!

THERSITES You scurvy lord!

AJAX [*Beating him*] You cur!

THERSITES Mars his idiot! Do, rudeness, do, camel, 54
do, do.

[*Enter Achilles and Patroclus.*]

ACHILLES Why, how now, Ajax, wherefore do ye thus? 56
How now, Thersites, what's the matter, man?

THERSITES You see him there, do you?

ACHILLES Ay; what's the matter?

THERSITES Nay, look upon him.

ACHILLES So I do. What's the matter?

THERSITES Nay, but regard him well.

ACHILLES Well, why, so I do.

33 Cerberus three-headed dog that guarded the entrance to Hades.
Proserpina Queen of Hades   **36 Thou** i.e., if thou   **37 Cobloaf** small
round loaf; a bun   **38 pun** pound   **42 stool** privy   **43 sodden-witted**
boiled-brained   **45 asinego** little ass   **46–47 bought and sold** i.e.,
treated like merchandise   **48 use** continue   **49 by inches** methodically,
inch by inch   **49–50 bowels** sensitivity, human feeling   **54 Mars his**
Mars'   **56 wherefore** why

THERSITES But yet you look not well upon him; for, whosoever you take him to be, he is Ajax.   65
ACHILLES I know that, fool.
THERSITES Ay, but that fool knows not himself.   67
AJAX Therefore I beat thee.
THERSITES Lo, lo, lo, lo, what modicums of wit he ut- 69 ters! His evasions have ears thus long. I have bobbed 70 his brain more than he has beat my bones. I will buy nine sparrows for a penny, and his pia mater is not 72 worth the ninth part of a sparrow. This lord, Achilles— Ajax, who wears his wit in his belly and his guts in his head--I'll tell you what I say of him.
ACHILLES What?
THERSITES I say, this Ajax—   [*Ajax threatens him.*]
ACHILLES Nay, good Ajax.
THERSITES Has not so much wit—
ACHILLES Nay, I must hold you.
THERSITES As will stop the eye of Helen's needle, for whom he comes to fight.
ACHILLES Peace, fool!
THERSITES I would have peace and quietness, but the fool will not—he there, that he. Look you there.
AJAX O thou damned cur! I shall—
ACHILLES Will you set your wit to a fool's?   87
THERSITES No, I warrant you, for a fool's will shame it.
PATROCLUS Good words, Thersites.   89
ACHILLES What's the quarrel?
AJAX I bade the vile owl go learn me the tenor of the proclamation, and he rails upon me.
THERSITES I serve thee not.
AJAX Well, go to, go to.
THERSITES I serve here voluntary.   95
ACHILLES Your last service was sufferance, 'twas not 96 voluntary; no man is beaten voluntary. Ajax was here the voluntary, and you as under an impress.   98

65 Ajax (with probable pun on *jakes*, a latrine) **67 that fool . . . himself** (Thersites answers as though Achilles had said, "I know that fool.")
69 modicums small amounts **70 have . . . long** i.e., are those of an ass, are asinine. **bobbed** thumped **72 pia mater** (Literally, membrane cover of the brain; used here for the brain.) **87 set your wit to** match wits with **89 Good words** i.e., speak gently **95 voluntary** voluntarily
96 sufferance something imposed **98 impress** (1) impressment, military draft (2) imprint (of blows)

THERSITES   E'en so; a great deal of your wit, too, lies in   99
your sinews, or else there be liars. Hector shall have a
great catch an 'a knock out either of your brains; 'a   101
were as good crack a fusty nut with no kernel.   102
ACHILLES   What, with me too, Thersites?
THERSITES   There's Ulysses and old Nestor, whose wit
was moldy ere your grandsires had nails on their toes,
yoke you like draft-oxen and make you plow up
the wars.
ACHILLES   What, what?
THERSITES   Yes, good sooth. To, Achilles! To, Ajax! To!   109
AJAX   I shall cut out your tongue.
THERSITES   'Tis no matter; I shall speak as much wit as
thou afterwards.   112
PATROCLUS   No more words, Thersites. Peace!
THERSITES   I will hold my peace when Achilles' brach   114
bids me, shall I?
ACHILLES   There's for you, Patroclus.
THERSITES   I will see you hanged like clodpolls ere I   117
come any more to your tents. I will keep where there
is wit stirring and leave the faction of fools.   *Exit.*
PATROCLUS   A good riddance.
ACHILLES
Marry, this, sir, is proclaimed through all our host:
That Hector, by the fifth hour of the sun,   122
Will with a trumpet 'twixt our tents and Troy
Tomorrow morning call some knight to arms
That hath a stomach, and such a one that dare   125
Maintain—I know not what, 'tis trash. Farewell.
AJAX   Farewell. Who shall answer him?
ACHILLES
I know not. 'Tis put to lottery. Otherwise
He knew his man.   [*Exit with Patroclus.*]   129
AJAX   O, meaning you? I will go learn more of it.
                                              [*Exit.*]

❖

99 E'en so exactly   101 an 'a if he   101–102 'a ... good he might as
well   102 fusty moldy   109 To ... To (Thersites impersonates Nestor and
Ulysses as drivers of a team, urging Achilles and Ajax to plow.)   112 afterwards i.e., even after my tongue is cut out   114 brach bitch hound. (The
quarto reading, *brooch,* could mean "bauble, plaything," referring to
Patroclus.)   117 clodpolls blockheads   122 fifth hour i.e., eleven o'clock
125 stomach appetite (for fighting)   129 knew would know

2.2   *Enter Priam, Hector, Troilus, Paris, and Helenus.*

PRIAM
  After so many hours, lives, speeches spent,
  Thus once again says Nestor from the Greeks:
  "Deliver Helen, and all damage else—
  As honor, loss of time, travail, expense,   4
  Wounds, friends, and what else dear that is consumed
  In hot digestion of this cormorant war—   6
  Shall be struck off." Hector, what say you to 't?   7
HECTOR
  Though no man lesser fears the Greeks than I
  As far as toucheth my particular,   9
  Yet, dread Priam,
  There is no lady of more softer bowels,   11
  More spongy to suck in the sense of fear,
  More ready to cry out, "Who knows what follows?"
  Than Hector is. The wound of peace is surety,   14
  Surety secure; but modest doubt is called   15
  The beacon of the wise, the tent that searches   16
  To th' bottom of the worst. Let Helen go.
  Since the first sword was drawn about this question,
  Every tithe soul, 'mongst many thousand dismes,   19
  Hath been as dear as Helen; I mean, of ours.
  If we have lost so many tenths of ours
  To guard a thing not ours—nor worth to us,
  Had it our name, the value of one ten—   23
  What merit's in that reason which denies
  The yielding of her up?
TROILUS   Fie, fie, my brother!
  Weigh you the worth and honor of a king
  So great as our dread father's in a scale

2.2. Location: Troy. The palace.
4 travail strenuous effort **6 cormorant** gluttonous (like the seabird)
7 struck off canceled **9 my particular** me personally **11 bowels**
mercy, pity **14 The . . . surety** i.e., the danger of peace is in the sense
of security it breeds **15 secure** overconfident. **modest doubt** a reasonable estimate of danger **16 beacon** warning signal. **tent** probe
19 Every tithe soul every soul exacted by the war as a tithe. **dismes**
tenths (of men sacrificed) **23 Had . . . name** i.e., even if Helen were a
Trojan. **one ten** i.e., one tithe exacted by the war, one Trojan life

Of common ounces? Will you with counters sum   28
The past-proportion of his infinite,   29
And buckle in a waist most fathomless
With spans and inches so diminutive   31
As fears and reasons? Fie, for godly shame!
HELENUS [*To Troilus*]
No marvel, though you bite so sharp at reasons,   33
You are so empty of them. Should not our father   34
Bear the great sway of his affairs with reason,
Because your speech hath none that tell him so?
TROILUS
You are for dreams and slumbers, brother priest;
You fur your gloves with reason. Here are your reasons: 38
You know an enemy intends you harm;
You know a sword employed is perilous,
And reason flies the object of all harm.
Who marvels then, when Helenus beholds
A Grecian and his sword, if he do set
The very wings of reason to his heels
And fly like chidden Mercury from Jove   45
Or like a star disorbed? Nay, if we talk of reason,   46
Let's shut our gates and sleep. Manhood and honor
Should have hare hearts, would they but fat their
          thoughts   48
With this crammed reason. Reason and respect   49
Make livers pale and lustihood deject.   50
HECTOR
Brother, she is not worth what she doth cost
The keeping.
TROILUS   What's aught but as 'tis valued?

28 counters pieces of coin-shaped metal used in calculation.   **sum** total
up   **29 The past-proportion . . . infinite** his infinitude past all comparison   **31 spans** measures of nine inches spanning the hand from thumb
to little finger   **33 reasons** (Pronounced like *raisins*, with pun.)   **34 not
our father** our father not   **38 fur** line with soft fur. (Troilus accuses
Helenus of using reason as a justification for personal comfort, explaining cowardly flight as prudence.)   **45 chidden Mercury** (Mercury as
Jove's errand boy was subject to his chiding or impatient bidding.)
46 disorbed removed from its sphere (like a shooting star)
48–49 thoughts . . . reason i.e., thoughts fattened or crammed with this
reason   **49 respect** caution   **50 livers pale** (A bloodless liver was
thought to be a sign of cowardice.)   **lustihood** bodily vigor

HECTOR

But value dwells not in particular will;	53
It holds his estimate and dignity	54
As well wherein 'tis precious of itself	55
As in the prizer. 'Tis mad idolatry	56
To make the service greater than the god;	
And the will dotes that is attributive	58
To what infectiously itself affects,	59
Without some image of th' affected merit.	60

TROILUS

I take today a wife, and my election	61
Is led on in the conduct of my will—	
My will enkindled by mine eyes and ears,	
Two traded pilots twixt the dangerous shores	64
Of will and judgment. How may I avoid,	65
Although my will distaste what it elected,	66
The wife I choose? There can be no evasion	
To blench from this and to stand firm by honor.	68
We turn not back the silks upon the merchant	
When we have soiled them, nor the remainder viands	70
We do not throw in unrespective sieve	71
Because we now are full. It was thought meet	
Paris should do some vengeance on the Greeks.	73
Your breath with full consent bellied his sails;	74
The seas and winds, old wranglers, took a truce	75
And did him service. He touched the ports desired,	
And for an old aunt whom the Greeks held captive	77

53 particular will i.e., one person's preference merely   **54 his** its. **dignity** worth   **55 of itself** intrinsically   **56 the prizer** i.e., the opinion of him who prizes it   **58–60 the will . . . merit** i.e., that will is mad which subserviently pays tribute to what the will itself prefers in a diseased way, without some appearance in the desired object of intrinsic merit   **61 I take today a wife** (Troilus, in setting up a hypothetical case that applies to Paris, is also stating his own credo about love.) **election** choice   **64 traded** skillful in their trade; trafficking back and forth   **65 avoid** rid myself of   **66 distaste** dislike (in time)   **68 blench** shrink.   **and** and simultaneously   **70 remainder viands** leftover food **71 unrespective sieve** worthless receptacle, i.e., garbage can   **73 vengeance** i.e., in return for Hesione's abduction; see l. 77 and note   **74 bellied** i.e., swelled   **75 old wranglers** traditional enemies   **77 an old aunt** i.e., Hesione, Priam's sister, rescued from the wrath of Poseidon by Hercules and bestowed by him on the Greek, Telamon, father of Ajax; we learn in 4.5.84 and 121 that she was Ajax' mother

He brought a Grecian queen, whose youth and freshness
Wrinkles Apollo's and makes stale the morning.   79
Why keep we her? The Grecians keep our aunt.
Is she worth keeping? Why, she is a pearl
Whose price hath launched above a thousand ships   82
And turned crowned kings to merchants.   83
If you'll avouch 'twas wisdom Paris went—
As you must needs, for you all cried, "Go, go"—
If you'll confess he brought home worthy prize—
As you must needs, for you all clapped your hands
And cried, "Inestimable!"—why do you now
The issue of your proper wisdoms rate   89
And do a deed that never Fortune did,
Beggar the estimation which you prized   91
Richer than sea and land? O, theft most base,
That we have stolen what we do fear to keep!
But thieves unworthy of a thing so stolen,   94
That in their country did them that disgrace   95
We fear to warrant in our native place!   96

CASSANDRA [*Within*]
      Cry, Trojans, cry!
PRIAM   What noise? What shriek is this?
TROILUS
'Tis our mad sister; I do know her voice.
CASSANDRA [*Within*]   Cry, Trojans!
HECTOR   It is Cassandra.

> *Enter Cassandra, raving, [with her hair about her ears].*

CASSANDRA
      Cry, Trojans, cry! Lend me ten thousand eyes,
      And I will fill them with prophetic tears.

79 Wrinkles Apollo's i.e., makes Apollo's youthful countenance look old and ugly by comparison   **82 Whose . . . ships** (Perhaps echoes the famous line from Marlowe's *Doctor Faustus:* "Was this the face that launched a thousand ships?")   **83 turned . . . merchants** i.e., made kings like merchants seeking a rare pearl. (Cf. Matthew 13:45.)   **89 The issue . . . rate** condemn the results of your own wise deliberation **91 Beggar . . . which** consider valueless the once-esteemed object which   **94 But** i.e., we are but   **95–96 That . . . place** i.e., who in Greece itself visited a disgrace upon the Greeks (by abducting Helen) which we are now afraid to justify through defending her right here in our own native land

HECTOR Peace, sister, peace!

CASSANDRA

Virgins and boys, mid-age and wrinkled eld,   104
Soft infancy, that nothing canst but cry,   105
Add to my clamors! Let us pay betimes   106
A moiety of that mass of moan to come.   107
Cry, Trojans, cry! Practice your eyes with tears!
Troy must not be, nor goodly Ilium stand;
Our firebrand brother, Paris, burns us all.   110
Cry, Trojans, cry! A Helen and a woe!
Cry, cry! Troy burns, or else let Helen go.   *Exit.*

HECTOR

Now, youthful Troilus, do not these high strains
Of divination in our sister work
Some touches of remorse? Or is your blood
So madly hot that no discourse of reason,
Nor fear of bad success in a bad cause,
Can qualify the same?

TROILUS   Why, brother Hector,
We may not think the justness of each act
Such and no other than th' event doth form it,   120
Nor once deject the courage of our minds   121
Because Cassandra's mad. Her brainsick raptures
Cannot distaste the goodness of a quarrel   123
Which hath our several honors all engaged
To make it gracious. For my private part,   125
I am no more touched than all Priam's sons,   126
And Jove forbid there should be done amongst us
Such things as might offend the weakest spleen   128
To fight for and maintain!

PARIS

Else might the world convince of levity   .   130
As well my undertakings as your counsels.
But I attest the gods, your full consent   132
Gave wings to my propension and cut off   133

---

104 eld old age   **105 nothing canst** can do nothing   **106 betimes** in advance   **107 moiety** part   **110 firebrand** (Paris' mother, Hecuba, dreamed when pregnant with Paris that she would be delivered of a firebrand destined to burn down Troy.)   **120 event** outcome   **121 once deject** ever abate   **123 distaste** render distasteful   **125 gracious** righteous, dignified (because our honorable selves "grace" the enterprise)   **126 touched** affected   **128 spleen** i.e., temper   **130 convince** convict   **132 attest** call to witness   **133 propension** propensity, inclination

All fears attending on so dire a project.
For what, alas, can these my single arms?　　135
What propugnation is in one man's valor　　136
To stand the push and enmity of those
This quarrel would excite? Yet, I protest,
Were I alone to pass the difficulties,　　139
And had as ample power as I have will,
Paris should ne'er retract what he hath done,
Nor faint in the pursuit.

PRIAM　　　　　　　　　　Paris, you speak
Like one besotted on your sweet delights.　　143
You have the honey still, but these the gall;
So to be valiant is no praise at all.　　145

PARIS
Sir, I propose not merely to myself
The pleasures such a beauty brings with it,
But I would have the soil of her fair rape　　148
Wiped off in honorable keeping her.
What treason were it to the ransacked queen,　　150
Disgrace to your great worths, and shame to me,
Now to deliver her possession up
On terms of base compulsion! Can it be
That so degenerate a strain as this
Should once set footing in your generous bosoms?　　155
There's not the meanest spirit on our party　　156
Without a heart to dare or sword to draw
When Helen is defended, nor none so noble
Whose life were ill bestowed or death unfamed　　159
Where Helen is the subject. Then I say,
Well may we fight for her whom we know well
The world's large spaces cannot parallel.

HECTOR
Paris and Troilus, you have both said well,
And on the cause and question now in hand
Have glozed—but superficially, not much　　165
Unlike young men, whom Aristotle thought

---

135 can . . . arms can my arms alone accomplish　136 propugnation
defense, might　139 pass experience, undergo　143 besotted drunk
145 So thus, under these circumstances　148 rape abduction
150 ransacked carried off　155 generous noble　156 party part, side
159 bestowed employed　165 glozed commented on

Unfit to hear moral philosophy. 167
The reasons you allege do more conduce 168
To the hot passion of distempered blood
Than to make up a free determination 170
Twixt right and wrong, for pleasure and revenge
Have ears more deaf than adders to the voice 172
Of any true decision. Nature craves 173
All dues be rendered to their owners. Now,
What nearer debt in all humanity
Than wife is to the husband? If this law
Of nature be corrupted through affection, 177
And that great minds, of partial indulgence 178
To their benumbèd wills, resist the same,
There is a law in each well-ordered nation
To curb those raging appetites that are
Most disobedient and refractory. 182
If Helen then be wife to Sparta's king,
As it is known she is, these moral laws
Of nature and of nations speak aloud
To have her back returned. Thus to persist
In doing wrong extenuates not wrong
But makes it much more heavy. Hector's opinion
Is this in way of truth; yet ne'ertheless,
My sprightly brethren, I propend to you 190
In resolution to keep Helen still,
For 'tis a cause that hath no mean dependence 192
Upon our joint and several dignities. 193
TROILUS
Why, there you touched the life of our design!
Were it not glory that we more affected 195
Than the performance of our heaving spleens, 196
I would not wish a drop of Trojan blood
Spent more in her defense. But, worthy Hector,

---

167 moral philosophy (Aristotle says this of political philosophy in the
Nichomachean Ethics.) **168 conduce** lead, tend **170 free** unbiased
172 adders (Cf. Psalms 58:4–5.) **173 craves** demands **177 affection**
passion **178 that** i.e., if that, if. **of partial** out of self-interested
182 refractory obstinate **190 sprightly** full of spirit. **propend** incline **192–193 'tis . . . dignities** i.e., it is a cause upon which depend to
no small degree our collective and individual honors **195 affected**
desired **196 heaving spleens** aroused anger

She is a theme of honor and renown,
A spur to valiant and magnanimous deeds,
Whose present courage may beat down our foes,   201
And fame in time to come canonize us;   202
For I presume brave Hector would not lose
So rich advantage of a promised glory
As smiles upon the forehead of this action
For the wide world's revenue.

HECTOR   I am yours,
You valiant offspring of great Priamus.
I have a roisting challenge sent amongst   208
The dull and factious nobles of the Greeks
Will strike amazement to their drowsy spirits.   210
I was advertised their great general slept,   211
Whilst emulation in the army crept.   212
This, I presume, will wake him.   *Exeunt.*

2.3   *Enter Thersites, solus.*

THERSITES   How now, Thersites? What, lost in the lab-
yrinth of thy fury? Shall the elephant Ajax carry it 2
thus? He beats me, and I rail at him. O, worthy satisfaction! Would it were otherwise, that I could beat
him whilst he railed at me. 'Sfoot, I'll learn to conjure 5
and raise devils but I'll see some issue of my spiteful 6
execrations. Then there's Achilles, a rare enginer! If 7
Troy be not taken till these two undermine it, the walls
will stand till they fall of themselves. O thou great
thunder-darter of Olympus, forget that thou art Jove,
the king of gods, and, Mercury, lose all the serpentine 11
craft of thy caduceus, if ye take not that little little less 12

201 Whose of which   **202 canonize** enroll among famous persons
208 roisting roistering, clamorous   **210 Will** that will   **211 advertised**
informed.   **their great general** i.e., Achilles; or possibly Agamemnon
212 emulation ambitious or jealous rivalry

2.3. Location: The Greek camp. Before Achilles' tent.
2 carry it carry off the honors   **5 'Sfoot** by His (God's) foot   **6 but I'll
see** unless I see   **7 execrations** curses.   **enginer** one who digs counter-
mines or tunnels underneath the enemy's battlements   **11–12 serpentine . . . caduceus** (Alludes to Mercury's wand, having two serpents
twined round it.)

than little wit from them that they have, which short- 13
armed ignorance itself knows is so abundant scarce it 14
will not in circumvention deliver a fly from a spider 15
without drawing their massy irons and cutting the 16
web! After this, the vengeance on the whole camp! Or
rather, the Neapolitan bone-ache! For that, methinks, 18
is the curse depending on those that war for a placket. 19
I have said my prayers, and devil Envy say "Amen."
What ho! My lord Achilles!

[*Enter Patroclus.*]

PATROCLUS Who's there? Thersites? Good Thersites,
come in and rail.

THERSITES If I could ha' remembered a gilt counterfeit, 24
thou wouldst not have slipped out of my contemplation. But it is no matter; thyself upon thyself! The com- 26
mon curse of mankind, folly and ignorance, be thine
in great revenue! Heaven bless thee from a tutor, and 28
discipline come not near thee! Let thy blood be thy 29
direction till thy death; then if she that lays thee out
says thou art a fair corpse, I'll be sworn and sworn
upon 't she never shrouded any but lazars. Amen. 32
Where's Achilles?

PATROCLUS What, art thou devout? Wast thou in prayer?
THERSITES Ay; the heavens hear me!
PATROCLUS Amen.

Enter Achilles.

ACHILLES Who's there?
PATROCLUS Thersites, my lord.

13–14 short-armed inadequate in its reach, finding everything beyond
its grasp   **15 circumvention** craft, stratagem   **16 massy irons** massive
swords (used with overkill on a mere spider's web)   **18 Neapolitan
bone-ache** i.e., venereal disease   **19 depending on** hanging over.
placket slit in a petticoat; hence (indecently) a woman   **24 ha'** have.
gilt counterfeit counterfeit coin (often called a "slip"; hence the quibble
in l. 25)   **26 thyself upon thyself** (Thersites, after alleging that he would
have cursed Patroclus along with Ajax and Achilles if he were not
counterfeit and hence so easily overlooked, now undertakes to curse
Patroclus with the most dire curse imaginable: may Patroclus simply be
himself, be plagued by himself.)   **28 great revenue** generous amounts.
bless thee from bless you by protecting you from (so as to preserve your
native ignorance)   **29 blood** violent passion   **32 lazars** lepers

ACHILLES Where, where? O, where? Art thou come?
Why, my cheese, my digestion, why hast thou not 40
served thyself in to my table so many meals? Come,
what's Agamemnon?

THERSITES Thy commander, Achilles. Then tell me, Patroclus, what's Achilles?

PATROCLUS Thy lord, Thersites. Then tell me, I pray
thee, what's thyself?

THERSITES Thy knower, Patroclus. Then tell me, Patroclus, what art thou?

PATROCLUS Thou mayst tell that knowest.

ACHILLES O, tell, tell.

THERSITES I'll decline the whole question. Agamemnon 51
commands Achilles, Achilles is my lord, I am Patroclus' knower, and Patroclus is a fool.

PATROCLUS You rascal!

THERSITES Peace, fool! I have not done.

ACHILLES He is a privileged man. Proceed, Thersites.   56

THERSITES Agamemnon is a fool, Achilles is a fool,
Thersites is a fool, and, as aforesaid, Patroclus is a
fool.

ACHILLES Derive this; come.   60

THERSITES Agamemnon is a fool to offer to command
Achilles, Achilles is a fool to be commanded of Agamemnon, Thersites is a fool to serve such a fool, and
this Patroclus is a fool positive.   64

PATROCLUS Why am I a fool?

THERSITES Make that demand of thy creator. It suffices
me thou art. Look you, who comes here?

*Enter [at a distance] Agamemnon, Ulysses, Nestor,
Diomedes, Ajax, and Calchas.*

ACHILLES Patroclus, I'll speak with nobody. Come in
with me, Thersites.   [*Exit.*]

THERSITES Here is such patchery, such juggling, and 70

---

40 cheese (Supposed, proverbially, to aid digestion.) **51 decline** go
through in order from beginning to end (as when declining a noun)
56 privileged man (Fools were permitted to speak without restraint.)
60 Derive give the origin of. (The grammatical metaphor is continued here and also in l. 64.) **64 positive** i.e., absolute **70 patchery**
knavery

such knavery! All the argument is a whore and a cuck- 71
old, a good quarrel to draw emulous factions and 72
bleed to death upon. Now, the dry serpigo on the 73
subject, and war and lechery confound all!   [*Exit.*]

AGAMEMNON   Where is Achilles?

PATROCLUS
Within his tent, but ill disposed, my lord.

AGAMEMNON
Let it be known to him that we are here.
He shent our messengers, and we lay by   78
Our appertainings, visiting of him.   79
Let him be told so, lest perchance he think
We dare not move the question of our place,   81
Or know not what we are.

PATROCLUS   I shall say so to him. [*Exit.*]

ULYSSES   We saw him at the opening of his tent. He is
not sick.

AJAX   Yes, lion-sick, sick of proud heart. You may call it 85
melancholy if you will favor the man, but, by my
head, 'tis pride. But why, why? Let him show us the
cause. A word, my lord. [*He takes Agamemnon aside.*]

NESTOR   What moves Ajax thus to bay at him?

ULYSSES   Achilles hath inveigled his fool from him.

NESTOR   Who, Thersites?

ULYSSES   He.

NESTOR   Then will Ajax lack matter, if he have lost his 93
argument.   94

ULYSSES   No, you see, he is his argument that has his 95
argument—Achilles.   96

NESTOR   All the better; their fraction is more our wish 97
than their faction. But it was a strong composure a fool 98
could disunite.

ULYSSES   The amity that wisdom knits not, folly may

---

71 **All the argument** i.e., the issue of the war   72 **draw** (1) attract (2) draw
blood; see l. 73.   **emulous** envious   73 **serpigo** skin eruption   78 **shent**
sent back insultingly   79 **appertainings** rights, prerogatives   81 **move the
question** insist upon the prerogatives   85 **lion-sick** i.e., sick with pride
93 **matter** subject matter (to rail upon)   93–94 **his argument** i.e., the
subject of his railing, Thersites   95–96 **he . . . Achilles** i.e., Achilles, who
now has Ajax' former subject of railing, Thersites, has himself become
Ajax' new target of raillery   97 **fraction** discord   98 **faction** i.e., union,
alliance.   **composure** union. (Said contemptuously.)

easily untie.

[*Enter Patroclus.*]

Here comes Patroclus.

NESTOR   No Achilles with him.

ULYSSES   The elephant hath joints, but none for cour-   104
tesy. His legs are legs for necessity, not for flexure.

PATROCLUS
Achilles bids me say he is much sorry
If anything more than your sport and pleasure
Did move your greatness and this noble state   108
To call upon him. He hopes it is no other
But for your health and your digestion's sake,
An after-dinner's breath.

AGAMEMNON   Hear you, Patroclus:
We are too well acquainted with these answers;
But his evasion, winged thus swift with scorn,
Cannot outfly our apprehensions.   114
Much attribute he hath, and much the reason   115
Why we ascribe it to him; yet all his virtues,
Not virtuously on his own part beheld,   117
Do in our eyes begin to lose their gloss,
Yea, like fair fruit in an unwholesome dish,
Are like to rot untasted. Go and tell him   120
We come to speak with him. And you shall not sin
If you do say we think him overproud
And underhonest, in self-assumption greater
Than in the note of judgment; and worthier than himself   124
Here tend the savage strangeness he puts on,   125
Disguise the holy strength of their command,
And underwrite in an observing kind   127
His humorous predominance—yea, watch   128
His pettish lunes, his ebbs, his flows, as if   129

---

104 elephant hath joints (Refers to a common belief that elephants' joints
did not enable them to lie down.)   **108 this noble state** i.e., the distinguished men accompanying Agamemnon   **114 apprehensions** understanding   **115 attribute** credit, reputation   **117 Not . . . beheld** not modestly
borne   **120 like** likely   **124 Than . . . judgment** than men of true judgment
know him to be; or, than in qualities of wise judgment   **125 tend** wait
upon.   **savage strangeness** uncivil aloofness   **127 underwrite** i.e., submit
to (as observers), subscribe to.   **in . . . kind** deferentially   **128 humorous
predominance** the currently dominant humor in him, i.e., blood, leading to
pride   **129 pettish lunes** ill-humored lunacies

The passage and whole carriage of this action
Rode on his tide. Go tell him this, and add
That if he overhold his price so much,   132
We'll none of him, but let him, like an engine   133
Not portable, lie under this report: 134
"Bring action hither, this cannot go to war."
A stirring dwarf we do allowance give   136
Before a sleeping giant. Tell him so.

PATROCLUS
I shall, and bring his answer presently.   [*Exit.*]

AGAMEMNON
In second voice we'll not be satisfied.
We come to speak with him. Ulysses, enter you.
                              [*Ulysses enters the tent.*]

AJAX   What is he more than another?

AGAMEMNON   No more than what he thinks he is.

AJAX   Is he so much? Do you not think he thinks himself a better man than I am?

AGAMEMNON   No question.

AJAX   Will you subscribe his thought and say he is?   146

AGAMEMNON   No, noble Ajax, you are as strong, as valiant, as wise, no less noble, much more gentle, and
altogether more tractable.

AJAX   Why should a man be proud? How doth pride
grow? I know not what pride is.

AGAMEMNON   Your mind is the clearer, Ajax, and your
virtues the fairer. He that is proud eats up himself.
Pride is his own glass, his own trumpet, his own   154
chronicle; and whatever praises itself but in the deed 155
devours the deed in the praise.

        Enter Ulysses.

AJAX   I do hate a proud man as I do hate the engendering of toads.

NESTOR [*Aside*]   And yet he loves himself. Is 't not
strange?

ULYSSES
Achilles will not to the field tomorrow.

---

132 overhold overvalue   **133 engine** military machine   **134 lie under**
suffer under   **136 allowance** approbation, praise   **146 subscribe** concur
in   **154 glass** mirror   **155 but in the deed** in any way other than doing
(praiseworthy) deeds

AGAMEMNON
  What's his excuse?
ULYSSES   He doth rely on none,
  But carries on the stream of his dispose   163
  Without observance or respect of any,
  In will peculiar and in self-admission.   165
AGAMEMNON
  Why will he not upon our fair request
  Untent his person and share th' air with us?
ULYSSES
  Things small as nothing, for request's sake only,   168
  He makes important. Possessed he is with greatness,
  And speaks not to himself but with a pride
  That quarrels at self-breath. Imagined worth   171
  Holds in his blood such swoll'n and hot discourse
  That twixt his mental and his active parts
  Kingdomed Achilles in commotion rages   174
  And batters down himself. What should I say?
  He is so plaguey proud that the death tokens of it   176
  Cry "No recovery."
AGAMEMNON   Let Ajax go to him.
  Dear lord, go you and greet him in his tent.
  'Tis said he holds you well and will be led,   179
  At your request, a little from himself.   180
ULYSSES
  O Agamemnon, let it not be so!
  We'll consecrate the steps that Ajax makes
  When they go from Achilles. Shall the proud lord
  That bastes his arrogance with his own seam   184
  And never suffers matter of the world   185
  Enter his thoughts, save such as doth revolve   186
  And ruminate himself, shall he be worshiped   187
  Of that we hold an idol more than he?   188

163 **dispose** bent of mind   **165 will peculiar** i.e., his own independent
will.   **self-admission** self-approbation   **168 for . . . only** only because
they are requested   **171 quarrels at self-breath** i.e., finds inadequate
even the praise he speaks of himself   **174 Kingdomed** i.e., like a microcosm of a state   **176 death tokens** symptoms of impending death
179 holds regards   **180 from himself** i.e., from his usual arrogant
behavior   **184 seam** fat, grease (i.e., Achilles feeds his own pride)
185 suffers allows   **186–187 doth . . . himself** i.e., serves for endless
self-contemplation   **188 Of that** by one whom (i.e., Ajax).   **idol** thing
worthy of worship

No, this thrice worthy and right valiant lord
Must not so stale his palm, nobly acquired,   190
Nor, by my will, assubjugate his merit,   191
As amply titled as Achilles' is,   192
By going to Achilles.
That were to enlard his fat-already pride
And add more coals to Cancer when he burns   195
With entertaining great Hyperion.   196
This lord go to him? Jupiter forbid,
And say in thunder, "Achilles go to him."
NESTOR [*Aside to Diomedes*]
O, this is well. He rubs the vein of him.   199
DIOMEDES [*Aside to Nestor*]
And how his silence drinks up this applause!
AJAX
If I go to him, with my armèd fist
I'll pash him o'er the face.   202
AGAMEMNON   O, no, you shall not go.
AJAX
An 'a be proud with me, I'll feeze his pride.   204
Let me go to him.
ULYSSES
Not for the worth that hangs upon our quarrel.   206
AJAX   A paltry, insolent fellow!
NESTOR [*Aside*]   How he describes himself!
AJAX   Can he not be sociable?
ULYSSES [*Aside*]   The raven chides blackness.
AJAX   I'll let his humor's blood.   211
AGAMEMNON   [*Aside*]   He will be the physician that should
    be the patient.
AJAX   An all men were o' my mind—
ULYSSES [*Aside*]   Wit would be out of fashion.
AJAX   'A should not bear it so, 'a should eat swords first. 216
    Shall pride carry it?

190 stale . . . acquired sully his nobly won honor   **191 assubjugate**
debase, reduce to subjection   **192 As . . . is** having as great a name as
Achilles'   **195–196 add . . . Hyperion** i.e., add a fire to the heat of
summer. (Cancer is the sign of the zodiac into which the sun [Hyperion]
enters at the beginning of summer.)   **199 vein** humor, disposition
202 pash smash   **204 feeze** settle the business of   **206 our quarrel** i.e.,
with the Trojans   **211 let . . . blood** bleed him (as a physician) to cure
his excessive humors   **216 eat swords** i.e., be beaten in fight

NESTOR [*Aside*]   An 'twould, you'd carry half.   218
ULYSSES [*Aside*]   'A would have ten shares.   219
AJAX   I will knead him; I'll make him supple.
NESTOR [*Aside*]   He's not yet through warm. Force him   221
    with praises. Pour in, pour in; his ambition is dry.
ULYSSES [*To Agamemnon*]
    My lord, you feed too much on this dislike.   223
NESTOR
    Our noble General, do not do so.
DIOMEDES
    You must prepare to fight without Achilles.
ULYSSES
    Why, 'tis this naming of him does him harm.   226
    Here is a man—but 'tis before his face;
    I will be silent.
NESTOR   Wherefore should you so?
    He is not emulous, as Achilles is.   229
ULYSSES
    Know the whole world, he is as valiant.
AJAX   A whoreson dog, that shall palter with us thus!   231
    Would he were a Trojan!
NESTOR   What a vice were it in Ajax now—
ULYSSES   If he were proud—
DIOMEDES   Or covetous of praise—
ULYSSES   Ay, or surly borne—
DIOMEDES   Or strange, or self-affected!   237
ULYSSES
    Thank the heavens, lord, thou art of sweet composure.   238
    Praise him that got thee, she that gave thee suck;   239
    Famed be thy tutor, and thy parts of nature   240
    Thrice famed, beyond, beyond all erudition;   241
    But he that disciplined thine arms to fight,   242
    Let Mars divide eternity in twain
    And give him half; and, for thy vigor,

---

218 An if   **219 ten shares** i.e., the whole without sharing   **221 through**
thoroughly   **223 this dislike** i.e., Achilles' truculence   **226 this . . . harm**
this continual citing of him as our chief hero that creates the difficulty   **229 emulous** envious, eager for glory   **231 palter** trifle, dodge
237 strange distant.   **self-affected** in love with himself   **238 composure**
temperament, constitution   **239 got** begot   **240–241 thy parts . . .**
erudition i.e., your natural gifts thrice exceeding what erudition can add
thereto (with an ironic double meaning, suggesting that erudition can
add little)   **242 But he** but as for him

Bull-bearing Milo his addition yield   245
To sinewy Ajax. I will not praise thy wisdom,   246
Which, like a bourn, a pale, a shore, confines   247
Thy spacious and dilated parts. Here's Nestor,   248
Instructed by the antiquary times;   249
He must, he is, he cannot but be wise.
But pardon, father Nestor, were your days
As green as Ajax' and your brain so tempered,
You should not have the eminence of him,
But be as Ajax.
AJAX   Shall I call you father?
NESTOR
Ay, my good son.
DIOMEDES   Be ruled by him, Lord Ajax.
ULYSSES
There is no tarrying here; the hart Achilles
Keeps thicket. Please it our great General   257
To call together all his state of war.   258
Fresh kings are come to Troy; tomorrow
We must with all our main of power stand fast.   260
And here's a lord—come knights from east to west,
And cull their flower, Ajax shall cope the best.   262
AGAMEMNON
Go we to council. Let Achilles sleep.
Light boats sail swift, though greater hulks draw deep.
                                       Exeunt.

❖

---

245 Bull-bearing . . . yield let bull-bearing Milo yield up his title. (Milo, a celebrated athlete of phenomenal strength, was able to carry a bull on his shoulders.) *Addition* means "title." **246 I will not** (1) I will forbear to (2) I won't **247 bourn** boundary. **pale** fence **248 dilated parts** extensive qualities **249 antiquary** ancient **257 Keeps thicket** i.e., stays hidden. (A *thicket* is a dense growth of shrubs or trees.) **258 state** council **260 main** full force **262 cull their flower** choose their flower of chivalry. **cope** prove a match for

3.1 [*Music within*]. *Enter* [*a Servant and*]
Pandarus.

PANDARUS Friend, you, pray you, a word. Do you not
follow the young Lord Paris?   2

SERVANT Ay, sir, when he goes before me.   3

PANDARUS You depend upon him, I mean?

SERVANT Sir, I do depend upon the lord.   5

PANDARUS You depend upon a noble gentleman; I
must needs praise him.   7

SERVANT The Lord be praised!

PANDARUS You know me, do you not?

SERVANT Faith, sir, superficially.   10

PANDARUS Friend, know me better. I am the Lord Pandarus.

SERVANT I hope I shall know your honor better.   13

PANDARUS I do desire it.

SERVANT You are in the state of grace.   15

PANDARUS Grace? Not so, friend. "Honor" and "lordship"
are my titles. What music is this?

SERVANT I do but partly know, sir. It is music in parts.

PANDARUS Know you the musicians?

SERVANT Wholly, sir.

PANDARUS Who play they to?

SERVANT To the hearers, sir.

PANDARUS At whose pleasure, friend?

SERVANT At mine, sir, and theirs that love music.

PANDARUS Command, I mean.

SERVANT Who shall I command, sir?

PANDARUS Friend, we understand not one another; I
am too courtly and thou too cunning. At whose request do these men play?

SERVANT That's to 't indeed, sir. Marry, sir, at the re-   30

3.1. Location: Troy. The palace.
2 follow serve. (But the servant takes it in the sense of "follow after.")
3 goes walks **5 lord** (quibbling on *lord*, referring to Paris, and "Lord" as
"God") **7 needs** necessarily **10 superficially** (1) by sight (2) not in
depth **13 know . . . better** (1) become better acquainted with you (2) see
you become a better man. (*Your honor* is a polite form of address to one of
social consequence.) **15 in . . . grace** i.e., in the way of salvation because
of desiring to be better. (Pandarus answers as though *grace* referred to the
courtly title applicable to a duke or prince.) **30 to 't** to the point

quest of Paris my lord, who is there in person; with
him, the mortal Venus, the heart-blood of beauty,
love's invisible soul—   33
PANDARUS Who, my cousin Cressida?
SERVANT No, sir, Helen. Could not you find out that by
her attributes?
PANDARUS It should seem, fellow, thou hast not seen
the Lady Cressid. I come to speak with Paris from the
Prince Troilus. I will make a complimental assault 39
upon him, for my business seethes.   40
SERVANT Sodden business! There's a stewed phrase in- 41
deed!

Enter Paris and Helen [attended].

PANDARUS Fair be to you, my lord, and to all this fair
company! Fair desires, in all fair measure, fairly guide
them! Especially to you, fair queen, fair thoughts be
your fair pillow!
HELEN Dear lord, you are full of fair words.
PANDARUS You speak your fair pleasure, sweet queen.
Fair prince, here is good broken music.   49
PARIS You have broke it, cousin, and, by my life, you 50
shall make it whole again; you shall piece it out with 51
a piece of your performance.—Nell, he is full of har-
mony.
PANDARUS Truly, lady, no.
HELEN O, sir—
PANDARUS Rude, in sooth; in good sooth, very rude.   56
PARIS Well said, my lord. Well, you say so in fits.   57
PANDARUS I have business to my lord, dear queen. My
lord, will you vouchsafe me a word?   59
HELEN Nay, this shall not hedge us out. We'll hear you 60
sing, certainly.
PANDARUS Well, sweet queen, you are pleasant with 62

---

33 love's invisible soul the very essence or spirit of love, personified in
Helen   **39 complimental** courteous   **40 seethes** boils, requires haste
41 Sodden, stewed (A play on *seethes* and with quibbling reference to
stews or brothels and to the sweating treatment for venereal disease.)
49 broken music music arranged for various instruments   **50 broke**
interrupted   **51 piece it out** mend it   **56 Rude** unpolished   **57 in fits**
(1) by fits and starts (2) in divisions of a song, in stanzas   **59 vouchsafe**
permit   **60 hedge** shut   **62 pleasant** jocular

me.—But, marry, thus, my lord: my dear lord and most
esteemed friend, your brother Troilus—

HELEN My lord Pandarus, honey-sweet lord—

PANDARUS Go to, sweet queen, go to—commends him- 66
self most affectionately to you—

HELEN You shall not bob us out of our melody. If you 68
do, our melancholy upon your head!

PANDARUS Sweet queen, sweet queen, that's a sweet
queen, i' faith.

HELEN And to make a sweet lady sad is a sour offense.

PANDARUS Nay, that shall not serve your turn, that shall
it not, in truth, la. Nay, I care not for such words, no, 74
no. And, my lord, he desires you that if the King call
for him at supper you will make his excuse.

HELEN My lord Pandarus—

PANDARUS What says my sweet queen, my very very
sweet queen?

PARIS What exploit's in hand? Where sups he tonight?

HELEN Nay, but, my lord—

PANDARUS What says my sweet queen? My cousin will 82
fall out with you.   83

HELEN [To Paris] You must not know where he sups.   84

PARIS I'll lay my life, with my disposer Cressida.   85

PANDARUS No, no, no such matter; you are wide.   86
Come, your disposer is sick.

PARIS Well, I'll make 's excuse.   88

PANDARUS Ay, good my lord. Why should you say
Cressida? No, your poor disposer's sick.

PARIS I spy.   91

PANDARUS You spy? What do you spy?—Come, give
me an instrument. [He is handed a musical instrument.]
Now, sweet queen.

HELEN Why, this is kindly done.

PANDARUS My niece is horribly in love with a thing you
have, sweet queen.

---

66 Go to (An expression of mild protest.) **68 bob** cheat **74 la** (An
exclamation accompanying a conventional phrase or address.)
82–83 My . . . you i.e., Paris (called *cousin* as a social equal) will be
angry with you for interrupting so **84 You must not** i.e., Pandarus does
not want you to. (Addressed to Paris.) **he** i.e., Troilus **85 lay** wager.
my disposer i.e., one who may dispose of me or order me as she
wishes (?) **86 wide** wide of the mark **88 make 's excuse** make his
(Troilus') excuse (to Priam) **91 I spy** i.e., I get it

HELEN She shall have it, my lord, if it be not my lord
Paris.

PANDARUS He? No, she'll none of him. They two are
twain.   101

HELEN Falling in, after falling out, may make them 102
three.   103

PANDARUS Come, come, I'll hear no more of this; I'll
sing you a song now.

HELEN Ay, ay, prithee now. By my troth, sweet lord,
thou hast a fine forehead.

PANDARUS Ay, you may, you may.   108

HELEN Let thy song be love. This love will undo us all.
O Cupid, Cupid, Cupid!

PANDARUS Love? Ay, that it shall, i' faith.

PARIS Ay, good now, love, love, nothing but love.

PANDARUS In good troth, it begins so: [*Sings.*]
"Love, love, nothing but love, still love, still more!
       For, O, love's bow
       Shoots buck and doe.   116
       The shaft confounds   117
       Not that it wounds,   118
But tickles still the sore.   119
These lovers cry O ho, they die!   120
       Yet that which seems the wound to kill,
Doth turn O ho! to ha, ha, he!
       So dying love lives still.   123
O ho! awhile, but ha, ha, ha!
O ho! groans out for ha! ha! ha!
Heigh-ho!"

HELEN In love, i' faith, to the very tip of the nose.

PARIS He eats nothing but doves, love, and that breeds
hot blood, and hot blood begets hot thoughts, and hot
thoughts beget hot deeds, and hot deeds is love.

PANDARUS Is this the generation of love? Hot blood, hot 131
thoughts, and hot deeds? Why, they are vipers. Is love

---

101 twain not in accord   **102–103 Falling . . . three** (Helen bawdily jokes
that Cressida's game will result in the birth of a child, a third person.)
108 you may i.e., go on, have your joke   **116 buck and doe** i.e., male and
female   **117 confounds** overwhelms   **118 Not that** either (1) not that
which, or (2) not so much that. (The erotic suggestion is that love does
its harm by penetrating and tickling.)   **119 sore** (1) wound (2) buck in its
fourth year   **120,123 die, dying** (quibbling on the idea of experiencing
orgasm)   **131 generation** genealogy

a generation of vipers? Sweet lord, who's afield 133
today?

PARIS Hector, Deiphobus, Helenus, Antenor, and all
the gallantry of Troy. I would fain have armed today,
but my Nell would not have it so. How chance my
brother Troilus went not?

HELEN He hangs the lip at something. You know all, 139
Lord Pandarus.

PANDARUS Not I, honey-sweet queen. I long to hear
how they sped today. You'll remember your brother's 142
excuse?

PARIS To a hair.   144

PANDARUS Farewell, sweet queen.

HELEN Commend me to your niece.

PANDARUS I will, sweet queen.   [*Exit.*]
                                      Sound a retreat.

PARIS
They're come from the field. Let us to Priam's hall,
To greet the warriors. Sweet Helen, I must woo you
To help unarm our Hector. His stubborn buckles,
With these your white enchanting fingers touched,
Shall more obey than to the edge of steel
Or force of Greekish sinews. You shall do more
Than all the island kings—disarm great Hector.   154
HELEN
'Twill make us proud to be his servant, Paris.
Yea, what he shall receive of us in duty
Gives us more palm in beauty than we have,   157
Yea, overshines ourself.
PARIS Sweet, above thought I love thee.   *Exeunt.*

❖

3.2 *Enter Pandarus [and] Troilus' Man, [meeting].*

PANDARUS How now, where's thy master? At my cousin Cressida's?

133 generation of vipers (See Matthew 3:7, 12:34, and 23:33.) **139 hangs the
lip** pouts, sulks **142 sped** succeeded **144 To a hair** to the last detail
154 island kings i.e., Greek chieftains **157 more palm** i.e., more honor

**3.2. Location: Troy. The garden of Cressida's house (where she lives with
her father Calchas).**
s.d. Man servant. (Probably the *varlet* referred to in 1.1.1.)

MAN   No, sir, he stays for you to conduct him thither.

[*Enter Troilus.*]

PANDARUS   O, here he comes.—How now, how now?

TROILUS   Sirrah, walk off.   [*Exit Man.*]

PANDARUS   Have you seen my cousin?

TROILUS

No, Pandarus. I stalk about her door

Like a strange soul upon the Stygian banks   8

Staying for waftage. O, be thou my Charon,   9

And give me swift transportance to those fields   10

Where I may wallow in the lily beds

Proposed for the deserver! O gentle Pandar,   12

From Cupid's shoulder pluck his painted wings,

And fly with me to Cressid!

PANDARUS   Walk here i' th' orchard; I'll bring her 15
straight.   [*Exit.*]

TROILUS

I am giddy; expectation whirls me round.

Th' imaginary relish is so sweet

That it enchants my sense. What will it be

When that the watery palate tastes indeed   20

Love's thrice repurèd nectar? Death, I fear me,   21

Swooning destruction, or some joy too fine,

Too subtle-potent, tuned too sharp in sweetness

For the capacity of my ruder powers.

I fear it much; and I do fear besides

That I shall lose distinction in my joys,   26

As doth a battle, when they charge on heaps   27

The enemy flying.

[*Enter Pandarus.*]

PANDARUS   She's making her ready; she'll come straight.
You must be witty now. She does so blush, and 30

8–9 a strange . . . Charon (Refers to the Greek mythological conception
of the fate of departed souls who had to wait on the banks of the Styx
or Acheron until the boatman Charon ferried them across to the infernal region.) **10 fields** i.e., the Elysian fields **12 Proposed for** promised
to **15 orchard** garden **20 watery palate** i.e., sense of taste watering
with anticipation **21 repurèd** refined, repurified **26 lose . . . joys** be
unable to distinguish one delight from another **27 battle** army
30 witty alert, resourceful in easy conversation

fetches her wind so short, as if she were frayed with 31
a spirit. I'll fetch her. It is the prettiest villain! She 32
fetches her breath as short as a new-ta'en sparrow.

[*Exit.*]

TROILUS
Even such a passion doth embrace my bosom.
My heart beats thicker than a feverous pulse,   35
And all my powers do their bestowing lose,   36
Like vassalage at unawares encountering   37
The eye of majesty.

Enter Pandarus and Cressida, [veiled].

PANDARUS Come, come, what need you blush?
Shame's a baby. Here she is now. Swear the oaths
now to her that you have sworn to me. [*Cressida draws
back.*] What, are you gone again? You must be watched 42
ere you be made tame, must you? Come your ways,
come your ways; an you draw backward, we'll put you
i' the thills.—Why do you not speak to her?—Come, 45
draw this curtain, and let's see your picture. [*He draws 46
back her veil.*] Alas the day, how loath you are to offend
daylight! An 'twere dark, you'd close sooner. So, so, 48
rub on, and kiss the mistress. [*They kiss.*] How now, 49
a kiss in fee-farm? Build there, carpenter, the air is 50
sweet. Nay, you shall fight your hearts out ere I part
you—the falcon as the tercel, for all the ducks i' the 52
river. Go to, go to.
TROILUS You have bereft me of all words, lady.
PANDARUS Words pay no debts; give her deeds. But
she'll bereave you o' the deeds too, if she call your ac- 56

---

31 fetches . . . short is short of breath   **31–32 frayed . . . spirit** frightened by a ghost   **32 villain** (Used endearingly.)   **35 thicker** faster
36 bestowing proper use   **37 vassalage** vassals.   **at unawares** unexpectedly   **42 watched** kept awake (like a hawk that is being tamed through
sleeplessness)   **45 thills** shafts of a cart or wagon   **46 curtain** veil.
(Curtains were hung in front of pictures.)   **48 close** (1) encounter
(2) come to terms   **49 kiss the mistress** (In bowls, to touch the central
target; to *rub* is to maneuver obstacles as the ball rolls; *mistress* is
analogous to "master," short for "master bowl," a small bowl placed as
a mark for players to aim at.)   **50 fee-farm** grant of lands in fee, that is,
forever; i.e., a kiss of endless duration   **52 the falcon . . . tercel** the
female hawk as well as the male   **56–57 bereave . . . question** i.e., wear
you down in lovemaking

tivity in question. What, billing again? Here's "In wit- 57
ness whereof the parties interchangeably—"Come in, 58
come in. I'll go get a fire.   [*Exit.*]

CRESSIDA Will you walk in, my lord?

TROILUS O Cressid, how often have I wished me thus!

CRESSIDA Wished, my lord! The gods grant—O my
lord!

TROILUS What should they grant? What makes this
pretty abruption? What too curious dreg espies my 65
sweet lady in the fountain of our love?

CRESSIDA More dregs than water, if my fears have eyes.

TROILUS Fears make devils of cherubins; they never see
truly.

CRESSIDA Blind fear, that seeing reason leads, finds safer 70
footing than blind reason stumbling without fear. To
fear the worst oft cures the worse.

TROILUS O, let my lady apprehend no fear. In all
Cupid's pageant there is presented no monster.

CRESSIDA Nor nothing monstrous neither?

TROILUS Nothing but our undertakings, when we vow 76
to weep seas, live in fire, eat rocks, tame tigers, thinking it harder for our mistress to devise imposition 78
enough than for us to undergo any difficulty imposed.
This is the monstrosity in love, lady, that the will is
infinite and the execution confined, that the desire is
boundless and the act a slave to limit.

CRESSIDA They say all lovers swear more performance
than they are able, and yet reserve an ability that they
never perform, vowing more than the perfection of ten 85
and discharging less than the tenth part of one. They
that have the voice of lions and the act of hares, are
they not monsters?

TROILUS Are there such? Such are not we. Praise us as
we are tasted, allow us as we prove; our head shall go 90
bare till merit crown it. No perfection in reversion 91

---

57 billing kissing   **57–58 In . . . interchangeably** (A legal formula used
for contracts, ending "have set their hand and seals.")   **65 abruption**
breaking off.   **curious** causing anxiety.   **dreg** impurity   **70 seeing**
clear-sighted   **76 undertakings** vows   **78 to devise imposition** to think
up tasks to impose   **85 perfection of ten** performance of ten perfect
lovers   **90 tasted** tried, proved.   **allow** acknowledge, approve
91 No . . . reversion no promise of perfection to come

shall have a praise in present; we will not name desert
before his birth, and, being born, his addition shall be 93
humble. Few words to fair faith. Troilus shall be such 94
to Cressid as what envy can say worst shall be a mock 95
for his truth, and what truth can speak truest not truer 96
than Troilus.

CRESSIDA Will you walk in, my lord?

[*Enter Pandarus.*]

PANDARUS What, blushing still? Have you not done
talking yet?

CRESSIDA Well, uncle, what folly I commit, I dedicate 101
to you.

PANDARUS I thank you for that. If my lord get a boy of
you, you'll give him me. Be true to my lord; if he
flinch, chide me for it.

TROILUS You know now your hostages: your uncle's
word and my firm faith.

PANDARUS Nay, I'll give my word for her too. Our
kindred, though they be long ere they be wooed, they
are constant being won. They are burrs, I can tell you;
they'll stick where they are thrown.   111

CRESSIDA
Boldness comes to me now and brings me heart.
Prince Troilus, I have loved you night and day
For many weary months.

TROILUS
Why was my Cressid then so hard to win?

CRESSIDA
Hard to seem won; but I was won, my lord,
With the first glance that ever—pardon me;
If I confess much, you will play the tyrant.
I love you now, but till now not so much
But I might master it. In faith, I lie;
My thoughts were like unbridled children, grown   121

---

93 addition title   **94 Few . . . faith** (Compare the proverb: "Where many
words are, the truth goes by.")   **95–96 as what . . . truth** that the worst
envy can do is to mock Troilus' loyalty   **101 folly** foolishness (though
Pandarus understands it to mean "lechery")   **111 thrown** tossed
(though Pandarus puns on a sexual meaning, to "throw down" a
woman, as at 3.3.209)   **121 unbridled** unrestrained

Too headstrong for their mother. See, we fools!
Why have I blabbed? Who shall be true to us
When we are so unsecret to ourselves?
But, though I loved you well, I wooed you not;
And yet, good faith, I wished myself a man,
Or that we women had men's privilege
Of speaking first. Sweet, bid me hold my tongue,
For in this rapture I shall surely speak
The thing I shall repent. See, see, your silence,
Cunning in dumbness, from my weakness draws
My very soul of counsel! Stop my mouth.   132

TROILUS
And shall, albeit sweet music issues thence.
                                    [*He kisses her.*]

PANDARUS   Pretty, i' faith.

CRESSIDA
My lord, I do beseech you, pardon me;
'Twas not my purpose thus to beg a kiss.
I am ashamed. O heavens, what have I done?
For this time will I take my leave, my lord.

TROILUS   Your leave, sweet Cressid?

PANDARUS   Leave! An you take leave till tomorrow   140
morning—

CRESSIDA   Pray you, content you.   142

TROILUS   What offends you, lady?

CRESSIDA   Sir, mine own company.

TROILUS   You cannot shun yourself.

CRESSIDA   Let me go and try.
I have a kind of self resides with you,
But an unkind self that itself will leave   148
To be another's fool. Where is my wit?   149
I would be gone. I speak I know not what.

TROILUS
Well know they what they speak that speak so wisely.

CRESSIDA
Perchance, my lord, I show more craft than love,
And fell so roundly to a large confession   153

---

132 My . . . counsel my inmost thoughts   **140 An** if   **142 content you**
i.e., be quiet   **148–149 that . . . fool** i.e., that will desert its true nature
to be your dupe or plaything   **153 roundly** outspokenly

To angle for your thoughts. But you are wise,
Or else you love not, for to be wise and love   155
Exceeds man's might; that dwells with gods above.

CRESSIDA

O, that I thought it could be in a woman—
As, if it can, I will presume in you—   158
To feed for aye her lamp and flames of love,
To keep her constancy in plight and youth,   160
Outliving beauty's outward, with a mind   161
That doth renew swifter than blood decays!   162
Or that persuasion could but thus convince me
That my integrity and truth to you
Might be affronted with the match and weight   165
Of such a winnowed purity in love;   166
How were I then uplifted! But, alas,
I am as true as truth's simplicity,
And simpler than the infancy of truth.

CRESSIDA

In that I'll war with you.

TROILUS   O virtuous fight,
When right with right wars who shall be most right!
True swains in love shall in the world to come
Approve their truth by Troilus. When their rhymes,   173
Full of protest, of oath and big compare,   174
Wants similes, truth tired with iteration,   175
As true as steel, as plantage to the moon,   176
As sun to day, as turtle to her mate,   177
As iron to adamant, as earth to the center,   178
Yet, after all comparisons of truth,
As truth's authentic author to be cited,
"As true as Troilus" shall crown up the verse
And sanctify the numbers.   182

155 **else** rather   158 **presume** presume that it is   160 **To . . . youth** to
keep her pledged constancy fresh   161 **outward** appearance   162 **blood
decays** passions wane   165 **affronted** equaled, matched.   **match and
weight** equal amount   166 **winnowed** i.e., absolute. (Literally, freed of
imperfections by sifting.)   173 **Approve** attest.   **by Troilus** i.e., using
Troilus as an ideal comparison   174 **protest** protestation (of love).
big compare extravagant comparisons   175 **Wants** are without
176 **plantage** vegetation (waxing in growth by the moon's influence)
177 **turtle** turtledove   178 **adamant** lodestone (magnetic)   182 **numbers** verses

CRESSIDA   Prophet may you be!
  If I be false or swerve a hair from truth,
  When time is old and hath forgot itself,
  When waterdrops have worn the stones of Troy,
  And blind oblivion swallowed cities up,
  And mighty states characterless are grated   187
  To dusty nothing, yet let memory,
  From false to false, among false maids in love,
  Upbraid my falsehood! When they've said "as false
  As air, as water, wind, or sandy earth,
  As fox to lamb, or wolf to heifer's calf,
  Pard to the hind, or stepdame to her son,"   193
  Yea, let them say, to stick the heart of falsehood, 194
  "As false as Cressid."
PANDARUS   Go to, a bargain made. Seal it, seal it; I'll be
  the witness. Here I hold your hand, here my cousin's.
  If ever you prove false one to another, since I have
  taken such pains to bring you together, let all pitiful
  goers-between be called to the world's end after my
  name; call them all Pandars. Let all constant men be
  Troiluses, all false women Cressids, and all brokers-
  between Pandars! Say "Amen."
TROILUS   Amen.
CRESSIDA   Amen.
PANDARUS   Amen. Whereupon I will show you a chamber, which bed, because it shall not speak of your   207
  pretty encounters, press it to death. Away!   208
                    Exeunt [Troilus and Cressida].
  And Cupid grant all tongue-tied maidens here   209
  Bed, chamber, pander to provide this gear!   *Exit.* 210

❖

187 **characterless** unrecorded, without a mark left   193 **Pard** leopard
or panther.   **hind** doe   194 **stick** pierce   207 **which bed** (The implied
antecedent is "a chamber with a bed.")   208 **press . . . death** (Alludes to
the usual punishment by weights for accused persons refusing to plead
or "speak.")   209 **here** i.e., in the audience   210 **gear** equipment

3.3   [*Flourish.*] *Enter Ulysses, Diomedes, Nestor,*
          Agamemnon, [Ajax, Menelaus, and] Calchas.

CALCHAS
     Now, princes, for the service I have done you,
     Th' advantage of the time prompts me aloud   2
     To call for recompense. Appear it to your mind   3
     That, through the sight I bear in things to come,   4
     I have abandoned Troy, left my possession,
     Incurred a traitor's name, exposed myself
     From certain and possessed conveniences   7
     To doubtful fortunes, sequestering from me all   8
     That time, acquaintance, custom, and condition
     Made tame and most familiar to my nature;   10
     And here, to do you service, am become   11
     As new into the world, strange, unacquainted.
     I do beseech you, as in way of taste,   13
     To give me now a little benefit
     Out of those many registered in promise,
     Which, you say, live to come in my behalf.
AGAMEMNON
     What wouldst thou of us, Trojan? Make demand.
CALCHAS
     You have a Trojan prisoner called Antenor
     Yesterday took; Troy holds him very dear.
     Oft have you—often have you thanks therefor—
     Desired my Cressid in right great exchange,   21
     Whom Troy hath still denied; but this Antenor,
     I know, is such a wrest in their affairs   23
     That their negotiations all must slack,
     Wanting his manage, and they will almost   25
     Give us a prince of blood, a son of Priam,
     In change of him. Let him be sent, great princes,   27

3.3. **Location: The Greek camp. Before Achilles' tent.**
2 advantage of favorable opportunity offered by   **3 Appear it** let it appear   **4 in** of   **7 From** turning from   **8 sequestering** separating, removing   **10 tame** familiar, domestic   **11 am** have   **13 taste** foretaste
21 right great exchange i.e., exchange for distinguished captives
23 wrest tuning key, i.e., one producing harmony and order   **25 Wanting** lacking.   **manage** management   **27 change of** exchange for

And he shall buy my daughter; and her presence
Shall quite strike off all service I have done
In most accepted pain.

AGAMEMNON   Let Diomedes bear him   30
And bring us Cressid hither. Calchas shall have
What he requests of us. Good Diomed,
Furnish you fairly for this interchange.
Withal bring word if Hector will tomorrow   34
Be answered in his challenge. Ajax is ready.   35

DIOMEDES
This shall I undertake, and 'tis a burden
Which I am proud to bear.   *Exit [with Calchas].* 37

Achilles and Patroclus stand in their tent.

ULYSSES
Achilles stands i' th' entrance of his tent.
Please it our General pass strangely by him,   39
As if he were forgot; and, princes all,
Lay negligent and loose regard upon him.
I will come last. 'Tis like he'll question me
Why such unplausive eyes are bent, why turned, on him. 43
If so, I have derision medicinable   44
To use between your strangeness and his pride,   45
Which his own will shall have desire to drink.
It may do good. Pride hath no other glass
To show itself but pride, for supple knees   48
Feed arrogance and are the proud man's fees.   49

AGAMEMNON
We'll execute your purpose and put on
A form of strangeness as we pass along.
So do each lord, and either greet him not
Or else disdainfully, which shall shake him more

---

30 In ... pain in pains (troubles, hardships) which I have endured most
willingly   **34 Withal** in addition   **35 Be answered in** meet the answerer
of   **37 s.d. stand in** i.e., enter and stand in the entrance of   **39 strangely**
i.e., as one who pretends to be a stranger   **43 unplausive** disapprov-
ing   **44 derision medicinable** scorn that can be used medicinally
45 strangeness aloofness   **48 To show ... pride** i.e., in which to see its
image except the pride of others   **48–49 for supple ... fees** i.e., obsequi-
ousness merely encourages arrogance by rewarding pride with the
adulation it expects

Than if not looked on. I will lead the way.
          [*They move in procession past Achilles' tent.*]
ACHILLES
What, comes the General to speak with me?
You know my mind. I'll fight no more 'gainst Troy.
AGAMEMNON
What says Achilles? Would he aught with us?   57
NESTOR
Would you, my lord, aught with the General?
ACHILLES   No.
NESTOR   Nothing, my lord.
AGAMEMNON   The better.   61
          [*Exeunt Agamemnon and Nestor.*]
ACHILLES [*To Menelaus*]   Good day, good day.
MENELAUS   How do you? How do you?   [*Exit.*]
ACHILLES   What, does the cuckold scorn me?
AJAX   How now, Patroclus?
ACHILLES   Good morrow, Ajax.
AJAX   Ha?
ACHILLES   Good morrow.
AJAX   Ay, and good next day too.
          Exit. [*Ulysses remains behind, reading.*]
ACHILLES
What mean these fellows? Know they not Achilles?
PATROCLUS
They pass by strangely. They were used to bend,   71
To send their smiles before them to Achilles,
To come as humbly as they used to creep
To holy altars.
ACHILLES   What, am I poor of late?
'Tis certain, greatness, once fall'n out with fortune,
Must fall out with men too. What the declined is
He shall as soon read in the eyes of others
As feel in his own fall; for men, like butterflies,
Show not their mealy wings but to the summer,   79
And not a man, for being simply man,
Hath any honor but honor for those honors
That are without him—as place, riches, and favor,   82

---

57 Would he aught does he want something **61 The better** so much the
better **71 used** accustomed **79 mealy** powdery **82 without** external to

Prizes of accident as oft as merit;
Which, when they fall, as being slippery standers,   84
The love that leaned on them, as slippery too,
Doth one pluck down another and together
Die in the fall. But 'tis not so with me;
Fortune and I are friends. I do enjoy
At ample point all that I did possess   89
Save these men's looks, who do, methinks, find out
Something not worth in me such rich beholding   91
As they have often given. Here is Ulysses;
I'll interrupt his reading.—How now, Ulysses?
ULYSSES   Now, great Thetis' son!
ACHILLES   What are you reading?
ULYSSES   A strange fellow here
Writes me that man, how dearly ever parted,   97
How much in having, or without or in,   98
Cannot make boast to have that which he hath,
Nor feels not what he owes, but by reflection;   100
As when his virtues, shining upon others,
Heat them, and they retort that heat again   102
To the first giver.
ACHILLES   This is not strange, Ulysses.
The beauty that is borne here in the face
The bearer knows not, but commends itself   105
To others' eyes; nor doth the eye itself,
That most pure spirit of sense, behold itself,   107
Not going from itself, but eye to eye opposed   108
Salutes each other with each other's form.
For speculation turns not to itself   110
Till it hath traveled and is mirrored there
Where it may see itself. This is not strange at all.

---

84 being . . . standers i.e., standing on uncertain foundation   **89 At ample point** to the full   **91 Something . . . beholding** something in me not worthy of such high respect   **97 Writes me** writes. (*Me* is merely an emphatic marker implying, "listen to me about this.")   **how . . . parted** however richly endowed with natural good qualities   **98 having** possession.   **or . . . in** whether with external or internal qualities   **100 owes** owns.   **by reflection** i.e., as reflected in others' opinions   **102 retort** reflect   **105 but** unless it   **107 most . . . sense** most exquisite of the five senses. (Cf. 1.1.60.)   **108 Not . . . itself** unless it could go out from itself.   **eye to eye opposed** i.e., two men's eyes gazing on one another   **110 speculation** power of sight

ULYSSES

I do not strain at the position—   113
It is familiar—but at the author's drift,   114
Who, in his circumstance, expressly proves   115
That no man is the lord of anything,
Though in and of him there be much consisting,   117
Till he communicate his parts to others;
Nor doth he of himself know them for aught   119
Till he behold them formed in the applause
Where they're extended; who, like an arch, reverb'rate   121
The voice again, or, like a gate of steel
Fronting the sun, receives and renders back   123
His figure and his heat. I was much rapt in this   124
And apprehended here immediately
Th' unknown Ajax. Heavens, what a man is there!   126
A very horse, that has he knows not what.
Nature, what things there are
Most abject in regard and dear in use!   129
What things again most dear in the esteem   130
And poor in worth! Now shall we see tomorrow—
An act that very chance doth throw upon him—
Ajax renowned. O heavens, what some men do,
While some men leave to do!   134
How some men creep in skittish Fortune's hall,   135
Whiles others play the idiots in her eyes!   136
How one man eats into another's pride,   137
While pride is fasting in his wantonness!   138
To see these Grecian lords—why, even already
They clap the lubber Ajax on the shoulder   140
As if his foot were on brave Hector's breast

---

113 strain at find difficulty in.   **position** i.e., general stance of the writer   **114 drift** i.e., particular application   **115 circumstance** detailed argument   **117 Though . . . consisting** although in him there are qualities from which much may be expected   **119 aught** anything   **121 Where they're extended** of those persons on whom they are bestowed   **123 Fronting** facing   **124 His** its, the sun's   **126 unknown Ajax** i.e., the Ajax whose true worth is not yet generally known   **129 abject . . . use** lowly esteemed and yet valuable, of practical value   **130 again** on the other hand   **134 to do** undone   **135 creep** i.e., are inobtrusive, draw no attention to themselves.   **skittish** fickle   **136 Whiles . . . eyes** while others attract the attention of the goddess Fortune by making fools of themselves   **137–138 How . . . wantonness** i.e., how one man, like Ajax, encroaches on another's glory, while that other man, like Achilles, starves his own glory through self-indulgence or caprice   **140 lubber** clumsy

And great Troy shrieking.

ACHILLES   I do believe it,
For they passed by me as misers do by beggars,
Neither gave to me good word nor look.
What, are my deeds forgot?

ULYSSES
Time hath, my lord, a wallet at his back,
Wherein he puts alms for oblivion,   147
A great-sized monster of ingratitudes.
Those scraps are good deeds past, which are devoured
As fast as they are made, forgot as soon
As done. Perseverance, dear my lord,
Keeps honor bright; to have done is to hang
Quite out of fashion, like a rusty mail   153
In monumental mock'ry. Take the instant way,   154
For honor travels in a strait so narrow
Where one but goes abreast. Keep then the path,
For emulation hath a thousand sons   157
That one by one pursue. If you give way,   158
Or hedge aside from the direct forthright,   159
Like to an entered tide they all rush by
And leave you hindmost;
Or, like a gallant horse fall'n in first rank,
Lie there for pavement to the abject rear,   163
O'errun and trampled on. Then what they do in present,
Though less than yours in past, must o'ertop yours;
For Time is like a fashionable host
That slightly shakes his parting guest by the hand,   167
And with his arms outstretched, as he would fly,
Grasps in the comer. The welcome ever smiles,   169
And farewell goes out sighing. Let not virtue seek
Remuneration for the thing it was;
For beauty, wit,
High birth, vigor of bone, desert in service,
Love, friendship, charity, are subjects all

---

147 alms for oblivion i.e., noble deeds to be forgotten   **153 mail** suit of
armor   **154 In . . . mock'ry** i.e., serving as a mocking trophy of forgotten noble deeds.   **instant way** way that lies immediately before you
now   **157 emulation** envious rivalry   **158 one by one pursue** follow one
another in single file   **159 forthright** straight path   **163 abject rear**
inferior specimens in the rear   **167 slightly** carelessly   **169 Grasps in**
welcomes, embraces

To envious and calumniating Time.   175
One touch of nature makes the whole world kin,   176
That all with one consent praise newborn gauds,
Though they are made and molded of things past,
And give to dust that is a little gilt   179
More laud than gilt o'erdusted.   180
The present eye praises the present object.
Then marvel not, thou great and complete man,
That all the Greeks begin to worship Ajax,
Since things in motion sooner catch the eye
Than what not stirs. The cry went once on thee,   185
And still it might, and yet it may again,
If thou wouldst not entomb thyself alive
And case thy reputation in thy tent,   188
Whose glorious deeds but in these fields of late   189
Made emulous missions 'mongst the gods themselves   190
And drave great Mars to faction.
ACHILLES   Of this my privacy   191
I have strong reasons.
ULYSSES   But 'gainst your privacy
The reasons are more potent and heroical.
'Tis known, Achilles, that you are in love
With one of Priam's daughters.
ACHILLES   Ha! Known?   195
ULYSSES   Is that a wonder?
The providence that's in a watchful state   197
Knows almost every grain of Pluto's gold,   198
Finds bottom in th' uncomprehensive deeps,   199
Keeps place with thought and almost, like the gods,   200
Do thoughts unveil in their dumb cradles.   201

175 calumniating slandering   **176 nature** i.e., natural human weakness;
here, the propensity of men to praise frivolous novelty (*newborn
gauds*)   **179 dust** i.e., trivial things.   **a little gilt** slightly gilded over
180 More . . . o'erdusted more praise than they give to gold, i.e., objects
worthy of praise, that are covered by dust (of oblivion)   **185 cry** acclaim   **188 case** box up, enclose   **189 but . . . late** only recently on the
battlefield   **190–191 Made . . . faction** i.e., caused the gods themselves
to join in the fighting on opposing sides, emulously, and even drove the
god of war to be partisan   **195 one . . . daughters** i.e., Polyxena
197 providence foresight   **198 Pluto's** (Pluto, god of the underworld,
was often confused with Plutus, god of riches.)   **199 uncomprehensive**
unfathomable   **200 Keeps . . . thought** keeps up with what is being
thought   **201 Do . . . cradles** discovers thought before it is conceived (in
the mind)

There is a mystery—with whom relation 202
Durst never meddle—in the soul of state, 203
Which hath an operation more divine
Than breath or pen can give expressure to. 205
All the commerce that you have had with Troy 206
As perfectly is ours as yours, my lord; 207
And better would it fit Achilles much
To throw down Hector than Polyxena.
But it must grieve young Pyrrhus now at home, 210
When Fame shall in our islands sound her trump, 211
And all the Greekish girls shall tripping sing,
"Great Hector's sister did Achilles win,
But our great Ajax bravely beat down him."
Farewell, my lord. I as your lover speak; 215
The fool slides o'er the ice that you should break. 216

                                    [*Exit.*]

PATROCLUS
To this effect, Achilles, have I moved you.
A woman impudent and mannish grown 218
Is not more loathed than an effeminate man
In time of action. I stand condemned for this;
They think my little stomach to the war 221
And your great love to me restrains you thus.
Sweet, rouse yourself, and the weak wanton Cupid
Shall from your neck unloose his amorous fold 224
And, like a dewdrop from the lion's mane,
Be shook to air.

ACHILLES   Shall Ajax fight with Hector?

PATROCLUS
Ay, and perhaps receive much honor by him.

ACHILLES
I see my reputation is at stake;
My fame is shrewdly gored.

PATROCLUS   O, then, beware! 229
Those wounds heal ill that men do give themselves.

202–203 with . . . meddle that can never be talked about **205 expressure** expression **206 commerce** dealings (i.e., with Polyxena) **207 is ours** i.e., is known to us of the Greek council **210 Pyrrhus** Achilles' son, also called Neoptolemus **211 trump** trumpet **215 lover** friend **216 The fool . . . break** i.e., the fool easily escapes dangers that to a man of your dignity would be fatal **218 impudent** shameless **221 little stomach to** lack of enthusiasm for **224 fold** embrace **229 shrewdly gored** severely wounded

Omission to do what is necessary
Seals a commission to a blank of danger;   232
And danger, like an ague, subtly taints   233
Even then when we sit idly in the sun.

ACHILLES
Go call Thersites hither, sweet Patroclus.
I'll send the fool to Ajax and desire him
T' invite the Trojan lords after the combat
To see us here unarmed. I have a woman's longing,
An appetite that I am sick withal,   239
To see great Hector in his weeds of peace,   240
To talk with him and to behold his visage,
Even to my full of view.

        Enter Thersites.

                                A labor saved!   242

THERSITES   A wonder!
ACHILLES   What?
THERSITES   Ajax goes up and down the field, asking for
himself.   246
ACHILLES   How so?
THERSITES   He must fight singly tomorrow with Hector
and is so prophetically proud of an heroical cudgeling
that he raves in saying nothing.
ACHILLES   How can that be?
THERSITES   Why, 'a stalks up and down like a peacock—
a stride and a stand; ruminates like an hostess that   253
hath no arithmetic but her brain to set down her reck-   254
oning; bites his lip with a politic regard, as who   255
should say, "There were wit in this head, an 'twould
out"—and so there is, but it lies as coldly in him as
fire in a flint, which will not show without knocking.
The man's undone forever, for if Hector break not his
neck i' the combat, he'll break 't himself in vainglory.
He knows not me. I said, "Good morrow, Ajax," and

232 Seals . . . danger i.e., gives danger unlimited license, a blank check.
(Literally, a warrant with blank spaces.)   233 ague fever.   taints infects   239 withal with   240 weeds garments   242 to . . . view to the
fullest satisfaction of my eyes   246 himself i.e., "Ajax" (with a quibble
on "a jakes" or latrine)   253–254 hostess . . . arithmetic (Tavern keepers
were proverbially poor at addition; cf. 1.2.114.)   255 politic regard
assumption of a knowing manner

he replies, "Thanks, Agamemnon." What think you of
this man, that takes me for the General? He's grown a
very land-fish, languageless, a monster. A plague of 264
opinion! A man may wear it on both sides, like a 265
leather jerkin. 266

ACHILLES   Thou must be my ambassador to him, Thersites.

THERSITES   Who, I? Why, he'll answer nobody; he pro- 269
fesses not answering. Speaking is for beggars; he 270
wears his tongue in 's arms. I will put on his presence. 271
Let Patroclus make his demands to me; you shall see
the pageant of Ajax.

ACHILLES   To him, Patroclus. Tell him I humbly desire
the valiant Ajax to invite the most valorous Hector to
come unarmed to my tent, and to procure safe-conduct
for his person of the magnanimous and most illustrious six-or-seven-times-honored Captain-General of
the Grecian army, Agamemnon, et cetera. Do this.

PATROCLUS   Jove bless great Ajax!

THERSITES   Hum!

PATROCLUS   I come from the worthy Achilles—

THERSITES   Ha?

PATROCLUS   Who most humbly desires you to invite
Hector to his tent—

THERSITES   Hum!

PATROCLUS   And to procure safe-conduct from Agamemnon.

THERSITES   Agamemnon?

PATROCLUS   Ay, my lord.

THERSITES   Ha!

PATROCLUS   What say you to 't?

THERSITES   God b' wi' you, with all my heart.

PATROCLUS   Your answer, sir.

THERSITES   If tomorrow be a fair day, by eleven of the
clock it will go one way or other. Howsoever, he shall 296
pay for me ere he has me.

PATROCLUS   Your answer, sir.

THERSITES   Fare you well, with all my heart.

---

264 land-fish i.e., monstrous creature   **265 opinion** reputation   **266 jerkin** close-fitting jacket   **269–270 professes** i.e., makes a point of   **271 put
. . . presence** assume his demeanor   **296 Howsoever** in either case

ACHILLES   Why, but he is not in this tune, is he?   300

THERSITES   No, but he's out o' tune thus. What music will be in him when Hector has knocked out his brains, I know not; but, I am sure, none, unless the fiddler Apollo get his sinews to make catlings on.   303 304

ACHILLES
Come, thou shalt bear a letter to him straight.

THERSITES   Let me carry another to his horse, for that's the more capable creature.   307

ACHILLES
My mind is troubled, like a fountain stirred,
And I myself see not the bottom of it.
                    [*Exeunt Achilles and Patroclus.*]

THERSITES   Would the fountain of your mind were clear again, that I might water an ass at it! I had rather be a tick in a sheep than such a valiant ignorance.   [*Exit.*]   312

❖

---

300 tune i.e., mood, disposition   **303–304 the fiddler Apollo** i.e., Apollo as god of music   **304 catlings** catgut, of which strings for instruments were made   **307 capable** intelligent   **312 ignorance** ignoramus, fool

4.1   *Enter, at one door, Aeneas, [and Servant with a torch;] at another, Paris, Deiphobus, Antenor, Diomedes the Grecian [and others], with torches.*

PARIS   See, ho! Who is that there?

DEIPHOBUS   It is the Lord Aeneas.

AENEAS   Is the Prince there in person?
Had I so good occasion to lie long
As you, Prince Paris, nothing but heavenly business
Should rob my bedmate of my company.

DIOMEDES
That's my mind too. Good morrow, Lord Aeneas.

PARIS
A valiant Greek, Aeneas; take his hand.
Witness the process of your speech, wherein   9
You told how Diomed, a whole week by days,   10
Did haunt you in the field.

AENEAS   Health to you, valiant sir,
During all question of the gentle truce;   13
But when I meet you armed, as black defiance   14
As heart can think or courage execute.

DIOMEDES
The one and other Diomed embraces.   16
Our bloods are now in calm; and so long, health!   17
But when contention and occasion meet,   18
By Jove, I'll play the hunter for thy life
With all my force, pursuit, and policy.   20

AENEAS
And thou shalt hunt a lion that will fly
With his face backward. In human gentleness,   22
Welcome to Troy! Now, by Anchises' life,   23
Welcome, indeed! By Venus' hand I swear,   24

4.1. Location: Troy. A street.
9 process drift   **10 a whole . . . days** every day for a week   **13 question**
discussion, parley (allowed by the truce)   **14 as black defiance** i.e.,
defiance as black   **16 The one and other** i.e., Aeneas' promises of *health*
and *defiance*   **17 so long** i.e., for as long as this truce lasts   **18 when
. . . meet** i.e., when the battle gives us opportunity   **20 policy** cunning
22 face backward i.e., bravely facing the enemy   **23, 24 Anchises, Venus**
(Aeneas' parents)

No man alive can love in such a sort   25
The thing he means to kill more excellently.

DIOMEDES
We sympathize. Jove, let Aeneas live,   27
If to my sword his fate be not the glory,
A thousand complete courses of the sun!
But, in mine emulous honor, let him die   30
With every joint a wound, and that tomorrow!

AENEAS   We know each other well.

DIOMEDES
We do, and long to know each other worse.

PARIS
This is the most despiteful gentle greeting,   34
The noblest hateful love, that e'er I heard of.
What business, lord, so early?

AENEAS
I was sent for to the King, but why, I know not.

PARIS
His purpose meets you. 'Twas to bring this Greek   38
To Calchas' house, and there to render him,   39
For the enfreed Antenor, the fair Cressid.
Let's have your company, or, if you please,
Haste there before us. [Aside to Aeneas.] I constantly
    do think—   42
Or rather, call my thought a certain knowledge—
My brother Troilus lodges there tonight.
Rouse him and give him note of our approach,   45
With the whole quality whereof. I fear   46
We shall be much unwelcome.

AENEAS   That I assure you.
Troilus had rather Troy were borne to Greece
Than Cressid borne from Troy.

PARIS   There is no help.
The bitter disposition of the time   50
Will have it so. On, lord; we'll follow you.

AENEAS   Good morrow, all.   [Exit with Servant.]

25 in . . . sort to such a degree   27 sympathize share your feeling
30 emulous ambitious   34 despiteful contemptuous   38 meets you i.e.,
I can tell you   39 render give   42 constantly confirmedly   45 note
news, notice   46 the . . . whereof all the causes thereof, reasons why
50 disposition (1) temperament (2) arrangement, ordering

PARIS

And tell me, noble Diomed, faith, tell me true,
Even in the soul of sound good-fellowship,　　　54
Who, in your thoughts, merits fair Helen most,
Myself or Menelaus?

DIOMEDES　　　　　　Both alike.

He merits well to have her that doth seek her,
Not making any scruple of her soilure,　　　58
With such a hell of pain and world of charge;　　　59
And you as well to keep her, that defend her,
Not palating the taste of her dishonor,　　　61
With such a costly loss of wealth and friends.
He, like a puling cuckold, would drink up　　　63
The lees and dregs of a flat 'tamèd piece;　　　64
You, like a lecher, out of whorish loins
Are pleased to breed out your inheritors.　　　66
Both merits poised, each weighs nor less nor more;　　　67
But he as he, the heavier for a whore.　　　68

PARIS

You are too bitter to your countrywoman.

DIOMEDES

She's bitter to her country. Hear me, Paris:
For every false drop in her bawdy veins
A Grecian's life hath sunk; for every scruple　　　72
Of her contaminated carrion weight　　　73
A Trojan hath been slain. Since she could speak,
She hath not given so many good words breath
As for her Greeks and Trojans suffered death.

PARIS

Fair Diomed, you do as chapmen do,　　　77
Dispraise the thing that they desire to buy.
But we in silence hold this virtue well:
We'll not commend what we intend to sell.
Here lies our way.　　　　　　　　*Exeunt.*

❖

54 soul spirit　**58 Not . . . scruple** not worrying about.　**soilure** dishonor, stain　**59 charge** cost　**61 Not palating** not tasting, being insensible of　**63 puling** complaining　**64 flat 'tamèd piece** wine cask so long opened that the wine is flat; hence, a used woman　**66 breed out** exhaust the breed, degenerate.　**inheritors** descendants　**67 poised** weighed.　**nor less** neither less　**68 he as he** i.e., the one like the other　**72 scruple** little bit (literally, one twenty-fourth of an ounce)　**73 carrion** putrified and rotten, like a carcass　**77 chapmen** traders, merchants

4.2   *Enter Troilus and Cressida.*

TROILUS
  Dear, trouble not yourself. The morn is cold.
CRESSIDA
  Then, sweet my lord, I'll call mine uncle down;
  He shall unbolt the gates.
TROILUS   Trouble him not;
  To bed, to bed. Sleep kill those pretty eyes,   4
  And give as soft attachment to thy senses   5
  As infants' empty of all thought!   6
CRESSIDA
  Good morrow, then.
TROILUS   I prithee now, to bed.
CRESSIDA   Are you aweary of me?
TROILUS
  O Cressida! But that the busy day,
  Waked by the lark, hath roused the ribald crows,   10
  And dreaming night will hide our joys no longer,
  I would not from thee.
CRESSIDA   Night hath been too brief.
TROILUS
  Beshrew the witch! With venomous wights she stays   13
  As tediously as hell, but flies the grasps of love
  With wings more momentary-swift than thought.
  You will catch cold, and curse me.
CRESSIDA
  Prithee, tarry. You men will never tarry.
  O foolish Cressid! I might have still held off,
  And then you would have tarried. Hark, there's one up.
PANDARUS [*Within*]   What's all the doors open here?   20
TROILUS   It is your uncle.

      [*Enter Pandarus.*]

CRESSIDA
  A pestilence on him! Now will he be mocking.
  I shall have such a life!

4.2. Location: Troy. The courtyard of Cressida's house.
4 **Sleep** let sleep. **kill** i.e., put to rest 5 **attachment** arrest, confinement 6 **infants'** i.e., infants' eyes 10 **ribald** offensively noisy, irrever-
ent 13 **Beshrew** curse. **the witch** i.e., the night. **venomous wights**
malignant beings 20 **What's** why are

PANDARUS   How now, how now, how go maidenheads?
Here, you maid! Where's my cousin Cressid?   25
CRESSIDA
   Go hang yourself, you naughty mocking uncle!
   You bring me to do—and then you flout me too.
PANDARUS   To do what, to do what? Let her say what.
What have I brought you to do?
CRESSIDA
   Come, come, beshrew your heart! You'll ne'er be good,
   Nor suffer others.   31
PANDARUS   Ha, ha! Alas, poor wretch! Ah, poor *capoc-* 32
chia! Has 't not slept tonight? Would he not, a naughty 33
man, let it sleep? A bugbear take him!   34
CRESSIDA
   Did not I tell you? Would he were knocked i' the head!
                           One knocks.
   Who's that at door? Good uncle, go and see.—
   My lord, come you again into my chamber.
   You smile and mock me, as if I meant naughtily.
TROILUS   Ha, ha!
CRESSIDA
   Come, you are deceived; I think of no such thing.
                              Knock.
   How earnestly they knock! Pray you, come in.
   I would not for half Troy have you seen here.
                Exeunt [Troilus and Cressida].
PANDARUS   Who's there? What's the matter? Will you
beat down the door? [*He opens the door.*] How now,
what's the matter?

    [*Enter Aeneas.*]

AENEAS   Good morrow, lord, good morrow.
PANDARUS   Who's there? My lord Aeneas! By my troth,
I knew you not. What news with you so early?
AENEAS   Is not Prince Troilus here?
PANDARUS   Here? What should he do here?   50

---

25 Where's . . . Cressid (Pandarus pretends not to recognize Cressida
now that she is no longer a virgin.)   **31 suffer others** allow others (to be
good)   **32–33 capocchia** dolt, simpleton. (Italian.)   **34 bugbear** hobgob-
lin   **50 should he do** would he be doing

AENEAS
  Come, he is here, my lord. Do not deny him.
  It doth import him much to speak with me.   52
PANDARUS Is he here, say you? It's more than I know,
  I'll be sworn. For my own part, I came in late. What 54
  should he do here?
AENEAS Hoo!—Nay, then. Come, come, you'll do him
  wrong ere you are ware. You'll be so true to him, to be 57
  false to him. Do not you know of him, but yet go fetch 58
  him hither; go.

    [*Enter Troilus.*]

TROILUS How now, what's the matter?
AENEAS
  My lord, I scarce have leisure to salute you,
  My matter is so rash. There is at hand   62
  Paris your brother, and Deiphobus,
  The Grecian Diomed, and our Antenor
  Delivered to us; and for him forthwith,
  Ere the first sacrifice, within this hour,   66
  We must give up to Diomedes' hand
  The Lady Cressida.
TROILUS   Is it so concluded?
AENEAS
  By Priam and the general state of Troy.   69
  They are at hand and ready to effect it.
TROILUS How my achievements mock me!
  I will go meet them. And, my lord Aeneas,
  We met by chance; you did not find me here.
AENEAS
  Good, good, my lord, the secrets of nature
  Have not more gift in taciturnity.
                    Exeunt [*Troilus and Aeneas*].
PANDARUS Is 't possible? No sooner got but lost? The
  devil take Antenor! The young prince will go mad. A
  plague upon Antenor! I would they had broke 's neck!

    Enter Cressida.

52 import concern **54 late** recently **57–58 You'll . . . of him** i.e., in
seeking to guard Troilus' secret, you'll protect him from knowing of a
matter that concerns him. Go ahead and pretend you don't know he is
here. **62 rash** urgent, pressing **66 Ere . . . sacrifice** i.e., before the first
religious ceremony of the day **69 state** council

CRESSIDA

How now? What's the matter? Who was here?

PANDARUS   Ah, ah!

CRESSIDA

Why sigh you so profoundly? Where's my lord?
Gone? Tell me, sweet uncle, what's the matter?

PANDARUS   Would I were as deep under the earth as I
am above!

CRESSIDA   O the gods! What's the matter?

PANDARUS   Pray thee, get thee in. Would thou hadst
ne'er been born! I knew thou wouldst be his death. O,
poor gentleman! A plague upon Antenor!

CRESSIDA   Good uncle, I beseech you, on my knees I
beseech you, what's the matter?

PANDARUS   Thou must be gone, wench, thou must be
gone; thou art changed for Antenor. Thou must to thy   92
father and be gone from Troilus. 'Twill be his death,
'twill be his bane; he cannot bear it.   94

CRESSIDA

O you immortal gods! I will not go.

PANDARUS   Thou must.

CRESSIDA

I will not, uncle. I have forgot my father.
I know no touch of consanguinity;   98
No kin, no love, no blood, no soul so near me
As the sweet Troilus. O you gods divine!
Make Cressid's name the very crown of falsehood
If ever she leave Troilus! Time, force, and death,
Do to this body what extremes you can;
But the strong base and building of my love
Is as the very center of the earth,
Drawing all things to it. I'll go in and weep—

PANDARUS   Do, do.

CRESSIDA

Tear my bright hair and scratch my praisèd cheeks,
Crack my clear voice with sobs, and break my heart
With sounding "Troilus." I will not go from Troy.   110

[*Exeunt.*]

✣

92 changed exchanged   **94 bane** death   **98 touch of consanguinity**
sense of kinship   **110 sounding** uttering

4.3 *Enter Paris, Troilus, Aeneas, Deiphobus,*
       Antenor, [and] Diomedes.

PARIS
   It is great morning, and the hour prefixed   1
   For her delivery to this valiant Greek
   Comes fast upon. Good my brother Troilus,
   Tell you the lady what she is to do,
   And haste her to the purpose.
                              Walk into her house.
TROILUS
   I'll bring her to the Grecian presently.   6
   And to his hand when I deliver her,
   Think it an altar, and thy brother Troilus
   A priest there offering to it his own heart.   *[Exit.]*
PARIS   I know what 'tis to love;
   And would, as I shall pity, I could help!   11
   Please you walk in, my lords.   *Exeunt.*

❖

4.4 *Enter Pandarus and Cressida.*

PANDARUS   Be moderate, be moderate.
CRESSIDA
   Why tell you me of moderation?
   The grief is fine, full, perfect, that I taste,   3
   And violenteth in a sense as strong   4
   As that which causeth it. How can I moderate it?
   If I could temporize with my affection,   6
   Or brew it to a weak and colder palate,   7
   The like allayment could I give my grief.   8
   My love admits no qualifying dross;   9
   No more my grief, in such a precious loss.

       Enter Troilus.

4.3. Location: Troy. Before Cressida's house.
1 great morning broad day.   **prefixed** earlier agreed upon   **6 presently**
immediately   **11 as** as much as

4.4. Location: Troy. Cressida's house.
3 fine refined, pure   **4 violenteth** is violent   **6 temporize** compromise,
come to terms with   **7 palate** taste   **8 allayment** relief, mitigation
9 dross impurity

PANDARUS   Here, here, here he comes. Ah, sweet
    ducks!

CRESSIDA   O Troilus! Troilus!   [Embracing him.]

PANDARUS   What a pair of spectacles is here! Let me em-   14
    brace too. "O heart," as the goodly saying is,
        "——O heart, heavy heart,
        Why sigh'st thou without breaking?"
    where he answers again,
        "Because thou canst not ease thy smart
        By friendship nor by speaking."
    There was never a truer rhyme. Let us cast away noth-
    ing, for we may live to have need of such a verse. We
    see it, we see it. How now, lambs?

TROILUS
    Cressid, I love thee in so strained a purity   24
    That the blest gods, as angry with my fancy,   25
    More bright in zeal than the devotion which
    Cold lips blow to their deities, take thee from me.

CRESSIDA   Have the gods envy?

PANDARUS   Ay, ay, ay, ay; 'tis too plain a case.

CRESSIDA
    And is it true that I must go from Troy?

TROILUS
    A hateful truth.

CRESSIDA   What, and from Troilus too?

TROILUS
    From Troy and Troilus.

CRESSIDA   Is 't possible?

TROILUS
    And suddenly, where injury of chance   33
    Puts back leave-taking, jostles roughly by   34
    All time of pause, rudely beguiles our lips
    Of all rejoindure, forcibly prevents   36
    Our locked embrasures, strangles our dear vows   37
    Even in the birth of our own laboring breath.
    We two, that with so many thousand sighs
    Did buy each other, must poorly sell ourselves

---

14 spectacles sights (with suggestion of "eyeglasses")   **24 strained**
purified as by filtering   **25 as** as if.   **fancy** love   **33 injury of chance**
injurious Fortune   **34 Puts back** forestalls, prevents   **36 rejoindure**
reunion (in a farewell kiss)   **37 embrasures** embraces

With the rude brevity and discharge of one.
Injurious Time now with a robber's haste
Crams his rich thievery up, he knows not how.   43
As many farewells as be stars in heaven,
With distinct breath and consigned kisses to them,   45
He fumbles up into a loose adieu   46
And scants us with a single famished kiss,   47
Distasted with the salt of broken tears.   48

AENEAS (*Within*)   My lord, is the lady ready?

TROILUS
Hark! You are called. Some say the genius so   50
Cries "Come!" to him that instantly must die.—
Bid them have patience; she shall come anon.

PANDARUS   Where are my tears? Rain, to lay this wind,   53
or my heart will be blown up by the root.   [*Exit.*]   54

CRESSIDA
I must then to the Grecians?

TROILUS   No remedy.

CRESSIDA
A woeful Cressid 'mongst the merry Greeks!
When shall we see again?

TROILUS
Hear me, my love. Be thou but true of heart—

CRESSIDA
I true? How now? What wicked deem is this?   59

TROILUS
Nay, we must use expostulation kindly,   60
For it is parting from us.
I speak not "be thou true" as fearing thee,   62
For I will throw my glove to Death himself   63
That there is no maculation in thy heart;   64
But "be thou true," say I, to fashion in   65

43 thievery stolen property.   **he . . . how** every which way, distractedly   **45 With . . . them** with the words of farewell and the kisses with
which those words are ratified   **46 fumbles** clumsily wraps   **47 scants**
inadequately supplies   **48 Distasted** rendered distasteful   **50 genius**
attendant spirit supposed to be assigned to a person at birth   **53 Rain
. . . wind** i.e., tears, to allay my sighs   **54 by the root** i.e., as though the
heart were a tree in a storm of sighs. (Sighs were thought to deprive the
heart of its blood.)   **59 deem** thought   **60 expostulation** opportunity for
discourse   **62 as fearing thee** i.e., as if not trusting your constancy
63 throw . . . to i.e., challenge   **64 maculation** stain of impurity
65 fashion in serve as introduction for

My sequent protestation: be thou true,
And I will see thee.

CRESSIDA

O, you shall be exposed, my lord, to dangers
As infinite as imminent! But I'll be true.

TROILUS

And I'll grow friend with danger. Wear this sleeve.

[*They exchange favors.*]

CRESSIDA

And you this glove. When shall I see you?

TROILUS

I will corrupt the Grecian sentinels,
To give thee nightly visitation.
But yet be true.

CRESSIDA   O heavens, "be true" again!

TROILUS   Hear why I speak it, love.
The Grecian youths are full of quality;   76
Their loving well composed with gifts of nature,   77
And flowing o'er with arts and exercise.   78
How novelty may move, and parts with person—   79
Alas, a kind of godly jealousy,
Which, I beseech you, call a virtuous sin—
Makes me afeard.

CRESSIDA   O heavens! You love me not.

TROILUS   Die I a villain, then!
In this I do not call your faith in question
So mainly as my merit. I cannot sing,   85
Nor heel the high lavolt, nor sweeten talk,   86
Nor play at subtle games—fair virtues all,
To which the Grecians are most prompt and pregnant—   88
But I can tell that in each grace of these
There lurks a still and dumb-discoursive devil   90
That tempts most cunningly. But be not tempted.

CRESSIDA   Do you think I will?

TROILUS   No.
But something may be done that we will not;   94
And sometimes we are devils to ourselves,

---

76 quality good qualities   **77 Their . . . composed** i.e., their skill in love-making is well endowed   **78 arts and exercise** skills sharpened by practice   **79 parts with person** accomplishments with personal charm
85 mainly strongly   **86 lavolt** lavolta, a lively dance for two   **88 pregnant** ready   **90 dumb-discoursive** eloquently silent   **94 will not** do not desire

When we will tempt the frailty of our powers,   96
Presuming on their changeful potency.   97
AENEAS (*Within*)
  Nay, good my lord—
TROILUS   Come, kiss, and let us part.
PARIS (*Within*)
  Brother Troilus!
TROILUS   Good brother, come you hither,
And bring Aeneas and the Grecian with you.
CRESSIDA   My lord, will you be true?
TROILUS
  Who, I? Alas, it is my vice, my fault.
Whiles others fish with craft for great opinion,   103
I with great truth catch mere simplicity;   104
Whilst some with cunning gild their copper crowns,
With truth and plainness I do wear mine bare.
Fear not my truth. The moral of my wit   107
Is "plain and true"; there's all the reach of it.   108

> [*Enter Aeneas, Paris, Antenor, Deiphobus, and
> Diomedes.*]

Welcome, Sir Diomed. Here is the lady
Which for Antenor we deliver you.
At the port, lord, I'll give her to thy hand,   111
And by the way possess thee what she is.   112
Entreat her fair, and by my soul, fair Greek,   113
If e'er thou stand at mercy of my sword,
Name Cressid, and thy life shall be as safe
As Priam is in Ilium.
DIOMEDES   Fair Lady Cressid,
So please you, save the thanks this prince expects.   117
The luster in your eye, heaven in your cheek,
Pleads your fair usage; and to Diomed
You shall be mistress, and command him wholly.

---

96 will tempt deliberately tempt   **97 changeful potency** power that may
change to failure   **103 craft** cunning.   **opinion** reputation (for wisdom)   **104 I . . . simplicity** I, in my use of simple truth, earn a reputation for being simple and plain   **107 moral** maxim   **108 all the reach**
full extent   **111 port** gate of the city   **112 possess** inform   **113 Entreat**
treat   **117 So please** if it please

TROILUS
Grecian, thou dost not use me courteously,
To shame the seal of my petition to thee   122
In praising her. I tell thee, lord of Greece,   123
She is as far high-soaring o'er thy praises
As thou unworthy to be called her servant.
I charge thee use her well, even for my charge;   126
For, by the dreadful Pluto, if thou dost not,
Though the great bulk Achilles be thy guard,
I'll cut thy throat.
DIOMEDES   O, be not moved, Prince Troilus.   129
Let me be privileged by my place and message
To be a speaker free. When I am hence,
I'll answer to my lust. And know you, lord,   132
I'll nothing do on charge. To her own worth   133
She shall be prized; but that you say "be 't so,"
I'll speak it in my spirit and honor, "no."
TROILUS
Come, to the port. I'll tell thee, Diomed,
This brave shall oft make thee to hide thy head.   137
Lady, give me your hand, and, as we walk,
To our own selves bend we our needful talk.
                  [*Exeunt Troilus, Cressida, and Diomedes.*
                                  Trumpet within.]
PARIS
Hark! Hector's trumpet.
AENEAS   How have we spent this morning!   140
The Prince must think me tardy and remiss,
That swore to ride before him to the field.
PARIS
'Tis Troilus' fault. Come, come, to field with him.
DEIPHOBUS   Let us make ready straight.
AENEAS
Yea, with a bridegroom's fresh alacrity,
Let us address to tend on Hector's heels.   146

122–123 **To . . . her** i.e., to praise her as though you were her lover and
thus scornfully refuse to consent to my petition that you treat her
courteously   126 **even . . . charge** simply because I demand that you do
so   129 **moved** angry   132 **my lust** my pleasures, desires   133 **on
charge** i.e., because you command it   137 **brave** boast, defiance
140 **spent** consumed by using   146 **address** get ready.   **tend** attend

The glory of our Troy doth this day lie
On his fair worth and single chivalry.   *Exeunt.* 148

❖

4.5   *Enter Ajax, armed, Achilles, Patroclus,
Agamemnon, Menelaus, Ulysses, Nestor, etc.*

AGAMEMNON
    Here art thou in appointment fresh and fair,   1
    Anticipating time with starting courage.   2
    Give with thy trumpet a loud note to Troy,
    Thou dreadful Ajax, that the appallèd air   4
    May pierce the head of the great combatant
    And hale him hither.
AJAX   Thou, trumpet, there's my purse. 6
                    [*He throws money to his trumpeter.*]
    Now crack thy lungs and split thy brazen pipe.
    Blow, villain, till thy spherèd bias cheek   8
    Outswell the colic of puffed Aquilon.   9
    Come, stretch thy chest, and let thy eyes spout blood;
    Thou blowest for Hector.   [*Trumpet sounds.*]
ULYSSES   No trumpet answers.
ACHILLES   'Tis but early days.   13

        [*Enter Diomedes, with Cressida.*]

AGAMEMNON
    Is not yond Diomed, with Calchas' daughter?
ULYSSES
    'Tis he. I ken the manner of his gait;   15
    He rises on the toe. That spirit of his
    In aspiration lifts him from the earth.

148 single chivalry individual prowess

4.5. Location: Near the Greek camp. Lists set out as an arena for combat.
1 appointment equipment, accoutrement   **2 starting courage** bold,
active defiance   **4 dreadful** inspiring dread   **6 trumpet** trumpeter
8 bias puffed out (and shaped like a weighted bowling ball used in
bowls)   **9 colic** i.e., swelling (like that caused by colic).   **Aquilon** the
north wind (here personified as distended by colic)   **13 days** in the
day   **15 ken** recognize

AGAMEMNON
  Is this the Lady Cressid?
DIOMEDES   Even she.
AGAMEMNON
  Most dearly welcome to the Greeks, sweet lady.
                                    [*He kisses her.*]
NESTOR
  Our general doth salute you with a kiss.
ULYSSES
  Yet is the kindness but particular;   21
  'Twere better she were kissed in general.   22
NESTOR
  And very courtly counsel. I'll begin.   [*He kisses her.*]
  So much for Nestor.
ACHILLES
  I'll take that winter from your lips, fair lady.   25
  Achilles bids you welcome.   [*He kisses her.*]
MENELAUS
  I had good argument for kissing once.   .   27
PATROCLUS
  But that's no argument for kissing now;
  For thus popped Paris in his hardiment,   29
  And parted thus you and your argument.
                                    [*He kisses her.*]
ULYSSES
  O deadly gall and theme of all our scorns,
  For which we lose our heads to gild his horns!
PATROCLUS
  The first was Menelaus' kiss; this, mine;
  Patroclus kisses you.   [*He kisses her again.*]
MENELAUS   O, this is trim!   34
PATROCLUS
  Paris and I kiss evermore for him.
MENELAUS
  I'll have my kiss, sir. Lady, by your leave.
CRESSIDA
  In kissing, do you render or receive?

---

21 particular single, limited to one   **22 in general** by everyone (with a
play on "by the general")   **25 that winter** (Alludes to Nestor's old age.)
27 argument i.e., Helen   **29 hardiment** bold exploits, boldness (with
bawdy double meaning of "hardness")   **34 trim** fine. (Said ironically.)

MENELAUS
  Both take and give.

CRESSIDA   I'll make my match to live,   38
  The kiss you take is better than you give;
  Therefore no kiss.

MENELAUS
  I'll give you boot; I'll give you three for one.   41

CRESSIDA
  You are an odd man; give even, or give none.   42

MENELAUS
  An odd man, lady? Every man is odd.

CRESSIDA
  No, Paris is not, for you know 'tis true
  That you are odd, and he is even with you.

MENELAUS
  You fillip me o' the head.

CRESSIDA   No, I'll be sworn.   46

ULYSSES
  It were no match, your nail against his horn.   47
  May I, sweet lady, beg a kiss of you?

CRESSIDA
  You may.

ULYSSES   I do desire it.

CRESSIDA   Why, beg then, too.

ULYSSES
  Why then for Venus' sake, give me a kiss
  When Helen is a maid again, and his.   51

CRESSIDA
  I am your debtor; claim it when 'tis due.

ULYSSES
  Never's my day, and then a kiss of you.   53

DIOMEDES
  Lady, a word. I'll bring you to your father.
                      [Exit with Cressida.]

NESTOR
  A woman of quick sense.   55

38 I'll . . . to live I'll wager my life **41 boot** odds, something in addition **42 odd** (1) strange (2) single, no longer having a wife **46 fillip . . . head** tap me on the head. (Suggesting the presence of cuckold's horns.) **47 It . . . horn** i.e., it would be an uneven contest between the fingernail with which you tap his head and Menelaus' cuckold's horn **51 his** i.e., Menelaus' wife **53 and . . . you** i.e., I'll never claim that kiss **55 quick sense** lively wit

ULYSSES   Fie, fie upon her!
There's language in her eye, her cheek, her lip,
Nay, her foot speaks; her wanton spirits look out
At every joint and motive of her body.   58
O, these encounterers, so glib of tongue,
That give accosting welcome ere it comes,   60
And wide unclasp the tables of their thoughts   61
To every tickling reader! Set them down   62
For sluttish spoils of opportunity   63
And daughters of the game.   64

> *Flourish. Enter all of Troy [Hector, Paris, Aeneas,*
> *Helenus, Troilus, and attendants].*

ALL
The Trojans' trumpet.
AGAMEMNON   Yonder comes the troop.
AENEAS
Hail, all you state of Greece! What shall be done   66
To him that victory commands? Or do you purpose   67
A victor shall be known? Will you the knights   68
Shall to the edge of all extremity   69
Pursue each other, or shall they be divided   70
By any voice or order of the field?
Hector bade ask.
AGAMEMNON   Which way would Hector have it?
AENEAS
He cares not; he'll obey conditions.
AGAMEMNON
'Tis done like Hector.
ACHILLES   But securely done,   74
A little proudly, and great deal misprizing   75
The knight opposed.
AENEAS   If not Achilles, sir,
What is your name?

58 motive moving limb or organ   **60 accosting** approaching, sidling up
to   **61 tables** tablets   **62 tickling** wanton   **63 sluttish ... opportunity**
"corrupt wenches, of whose chastity every opportunity may make a
prey" (Johnson)   **64 daughters of the game** i.e., prostitutes   **66 state**
noble lords.   **What ... done** i.e., what honors shall be afforded   **67 that
... commands** that wins the victory   **68 Will you** do you desire
69 edge ... extremity absolute limit   **70 divided** separated   **74 securely**
overconfidently   **75 misprizing** disdaining, underrating

ACHILLES   If not Achilles, nothing.

AENEAS
Therefore Achilles. But, whate'er, know this:
In the extremity of great and little,   79
Valor and pride excel themselves in Hector,   80
The one almost as infinite as all,
The other blank as nothing. Weigh him well,
And that which looks like pride is courtesy.
This Ajax is half made of Hector's blood,   84
In love whereof half Hector stays at home;
Half heart, half hand, half Hector comes to seek
This blended knight, half Trojan and half Greek.

ACHILLES
A maiden battle, then? O, I perceive you.   88

          [*Enter Diomedes.*]

AGAMEMNON
Here is Sir Diomed. Go, gentle knight,
Stand by our Ajax. As you and Lord Aeneas
Consent upon the order of their fight,   91
So be it, either to the uttermost,
Or else a breath. The combatants being kin   93
Half stints their strife before their strokes begin.
                    [*Ajax and Hector enter the lists.*]
ULYSSES   They are opposed already.
AGAMEMNON [*To Ulysses*]
What Trojan is that same that looks so heavy?   96
ULYSSES
The youngest son of Priam, a true knight,
Not yet mature, yet matchless, firm of word,
Speaking in deeds and deedless in his tongue,   99
Not soon provoked, nor being provoked soon calmed;
His heart and hand both open and both free,   101
For what he has he gives, what thinks he shows,
Yet gives he not till judgment guide his bounty,
Nor dignifies an impare thought with breath;   104

79–80 In . . . Hector i.e., Hector's valor excels in the extreme of greatness,
his pride in the extreme of littleness   84 Ajax . . . blood (Cf. 2.2.77, note,
and 4.5.120.)   88 maiden battle one without bloodshed   91 Consent
agree.   order procedure, rules   93 a breath mere exercise   96 heavy
sad   99 deedless in his tongue i.e., never boastful   101 free open, generous   104 impare unconsidered. (Or perhaps *impair*, unsuitable.)

Manly as Hector, but more dangerous,
For Hector in his blaze of wrath subscribes   106
To tender objects, but he in heat of action   107
Is more vindicative than jealous love.   108
They call him Troilus, and on him erect
A second hope, as fairly built as Hector.
Thus says Aeneas, one that knows the youth
Even to his inches, and with private soul   112
Did in great Ilium thus translate him to me.   113
                    Alarum. [*Hector and Ajax fight.*]
AGAMEMNON They are in action.
NESTOR Now, Ajax, hold thine own!
TROILUS Hector, thou sleep'st. Awake thee!
AGAMEMNON
His blows are well disposed. There, Ajax!   116
                              Trumpets cease.
DIOMEDES
You must no more.
AENEAS   Princes, enough, so please you.
AJAX
I am not warm yet; let us fight again.
DIOMEDES
As Hector pleases.
HECTOR   Why, then will I no more.
Thou art, great lord, my father's sister's son,
A cousin-german to great Priam's seed;   122
The obligation of our blood forbids
A gory emulation twixt us twain.   124
Were thy commixtion Greek and Trojan so   125
That thou couldst say, "This hand is Grecian all,
And this is Trojan; the sinews of this leg
All Greek, and this all Troy; my mother's blood
Runs on the dexter cheek, and this sinister   129
Bounds in my father's," by Jove multipotent,
Thou shouldst not bear from me a Greekish member
Wherein my sword had not impressure made   132

106–107 subscribes . . . objects i.e., yields mercy to those who awaken
his pity   **108 vindicative** vindictive   **112 Even . . . inches** i.e., every inch
of him.   **with private soul** in private confidence   **113 translate** interpret   **116 disposed** placed   **122 cousin-german** first cousin   **124 gory
emulation** bloody rivalry   **125 commixtion** mixture   **129 dexter** right.
sinister left   **132 impressure** impression

Of our rank feud. But the just gods gainsay   133
That any drop thou borrow'dst from thy mother,
My sacred aunt, should by my mortal sword
Be drained! Let me embrace thee, Ajax.
By him that thunders, thou hast lusty arms!   137
Hector would have them fall upon him thus.
Cousin, all honor to thee!   [*They embrace.*]

AJAX   I thank thee, Hector.
Thou art too gentle and too free a man.
I came to kill thee, cousin, and bear hence
A great addition earnèd in thy death.   142

HECTOR
Not Neoptolemus so mirable,   143
On whose bright crest Fame with her loud'st "Oyez"   144
Cries, "This is he," could promise to himself
A thought of added honor torn from Hector.

AENEAS
There is expectance here from both the sides   147
What further you will do.

HECTOR   We'll answer it;
The issue is embracement. Ajax, farewell.   149
          [*They embrace.*]

AJAX
If I might in entreaties find success—
As seld I have the chance—I would desire   151
My famous cousin to our Grecian tents.

DIOMEDES
'Tis Agamemnon's wish, and great Achilles
Doth long to see unarmed the valiant Hector.

HECTOR
Aeneas, call my brother Troilus to me,
And signify this loving interview   156
To the expecters of our Trojan part;   157
Desire them home. Give me thy hand, my cousin.   158

---

133 rank hot, intemperate. **gainsay** forbid   **137 By . . . thunders** i.e., by
Jove   **142 addition** honorable title   **143 Neoptolemus** (Evidently intended for Achilles; this is the name of Achilles' son.)   **mirable** to be
marveled at   **144 Oyez** hear ye (call of the public crier)   **147 expectance**
expectation   **149 issue** outcome   **151 seld** seldom   **156 signify** announce   **157 the expecters . . . part** i.e., those waiting the outcome on
our Trojan side   **158 home** to go home

I will go eat with thee and see your knights.
[*Agamemnon and the rest approach them.*]

AJAX
Great Agamemnon comes to meet us here.

HECTOR
The worthiest of them tell me name by name;
But for Achilles, my own searching eyes
Shall find him by his large and portly size.   163

AGAMEMNON
Worthy all arms! As welcome as to one   164
That would be of such an enemy—
But that's no welcome. Understand more clear:
What's past and what's to come is strewed with husks
And formless ruin of oblivion;
But in this extant moment, faith and troth,
Strained purely from all hollow bias-drawing,   170
Bids thee, with most divine integrity,
From heart of very heart, great Hector, welcome.

HECTOR
I thank thee, most imperious Agamemnon.   173

AGAMEMNON [*To Troilus*]
My well-famed lord of Troy, no less to you.

MENELAUS
Let me confirm my princely brother's greeting.
You brace of warlike brothers, welcome hither.

HECTOR
Who must we answer?

AENEAS   The noble Menelaus.

HECTOR
O, you, my lord? By Mars his gauntlet, thanks!
Mock not that I affect th' untraded oath;   179
Your quondam wife swears still by Venus' glove.   180
She's well, but bade me not commend her to you.

MENELAUS
Name her not now, sir; she's a deadly theme.

---

163 **portly** stately, dignified   164 **as to one** as it is possible to one
170 **Strained** refined, purged.   **hollow bias-drawing** i.e., insincerities,
obliquities, such as the bias gives the bowling ball in the game of
bowls   173 **imperious** imperial   179 **untraded** unhackneyed. (Hector
insists that his use of a new oath, "by Mars' gauntlet," is not an affectation.)   180 **quondam** former

HECTOR O, pardon! I offend.

NESTOR
I have, thou gallant Trojan, seen thee oft,
Laboring for destiny, make cruel way   185
Through ranks of Greekish youth, and I have seen thee,
As hot as Perseus, spur thy Phrygian steed,   187
Despising many forfeits and subduements,   188
When thou hast hung thy advancèd sword i' th' air,   189
Not letting it decline on the declined,
That I have said to some my standers-by,   191
"Lo, Jupiter is yonder, dealing life!"
And I have seen thee pause and take thy breath,
When that a ring of Greeks have hemmed thee in,   194
Like an Olympian wrestling. This have I seen;   195
But this thy countenance, still locked in steel,   196
I never saw till now. I knew thy grandsire   197
And once fought with him. He was a soldier good,
But, by great Mars, the captain of us all,
Never like thee. Let an old man embrace thee;
And, worthy warrior, welcome to our tents.
                                   [*They embrace.*]

AENEAS 'Tis the old Nestor.

HECTOR
Let me embrace thee, good old chronicle,   203
That hast so long walked hand in hand with Time.
Most reverend Nestor, I am glad to clasp thee.

NESTOR
I would my arms could match thee in contention
As they contend with thee in courtesy.

HECTOR I would they could.

NESTOR Ha!
By this white beard, I'd fight with thee tomorrow.
Well, welcome, welcome! I have seen the time.   211

---

185 Laboring for destiny employed in the service of fate, putting people to
death   **187 Perseus** (See 1.3.42, note.)   **188 Despising . . . subduements** i.e.,
ignoring those already vanquished, whose lives were forfeit; refusing easy
prey   **189 advancèd** raised aloft   **191 some** some of   **194 When that**
when   **195 Olympian** i.e., Olympian god   **196 still** always   **197 grandsire**
i.e., Laomedon, builder of the walls of Troy and defender of the city
against an earlier Greek army under Hercules   **203 chronicle** i.e., store-
house of memories   **211 I . . . time** i.e., there was such a time

ULYSSES
  I wonder now how yonder city stands
  When we have here her base and pillar by us.

HECTOR
  I know your favor, Lord Ulysses, well.   214
  Ah, sir, there's many a Greek and Trojan dead
  Since first I saw yourself and Diomed
  In Ilium, on your Greekish embassy.

ULYSSES
  Sir, I foretold you then what would ensue.
  My prophecy is but half his journey yet,
  For yonder walls, that pertly front your town,   220
  Yon towers, whose wanton tops do buss the clouds,   221
  Must kiss their own feet.

HECTOR   I must not believe you.
  There they stand yet, and modestly I think   223
  The fall of every Phrygian stone will cost
  A drop of Grecian blood. The end crowns all,
  And that old common arbitrator, Time,
  Will one day end it.

ULYSSES   So to him we leave it.
  Most gentle and most valiant Hector, welcome!
  After the General, I beseech you next
  To feast with me and see me at my tent.

ACHILLES
  I shall forestall thee, Lord Ulysses, thou!   231
  Now, Hector, I have fed mine eyes on thee;
  I have with exact view perused thee, Hector,
  And quoted joint by joint.

HECTOR   Is this Achilles?   234

ACHILLES   I am Achilles.

HECTOR
  Stand fair, I pray thee. Let me look on thee.   236

ACHILLES
  Behold thy fill.

HECTOR   Nay, I have done already.

ACHILLES
  Thou art too brief. I will the second time,
  As I would buy thee, view thee limb by limb.

---

214 favor face   **220 pertly front** boldly stand before   **221 buss** kiss
223 modestly without exaggeration   **231 forestall** prevent   **234 quoted**
noted, marked   **236 fair** i.e., still

HECTOR

O, like a book of sport thou'lt read me o'er;
But there's more in me than thou understand'st.
Why dost thou so oppress me with thine eye?

ACHILLES

Tell me, you heavens, in which part of his body
Shall I destroy him? Whether there, or there, or there?
That I may give the local wound a name
And make distinct the very breach whereout
Hector's great spirit flew. Answer me, heavens!

HECTOR

It would discredit the blest gods, proud man,
To answer such a question. Stand again.
Think'st thou to catch my life so pleasantly   250
As to prenominate in nice conjecture   251
Where thou wilt hit me dead?

ACHILLES   I tell thee, yea.

HECTOR

Wert thou an oracle to tell me so,
I'd not believe thee. Henceforth guard thee well;
For I'll not kill thee there, nor there, nor there,
But, by the forge that stithied Mars his helm,   256
I'll kill thee everywhere, yea, o'er and o'er.
You wisest Grecians, pardon me this brag;
His insolence draws folly from my lips.
But I'll endeavor deeds to match these words,
Or may I never—

AJAX   Do not chafe thee, cousin.   261
And you, Achilles, let these threats alone,
Till accident or purpose bring you to 't.
You may have every day enough of Hector,
If you have stomach. The general state, I fear,   265
Can scarce entreat you to be odd with him.   266

HECTOR

I pray you, let us see you in the field.
We have had pelting wars since you refused   268
The Grecians' cause.

ACHILLES   Dost thou entreat me, Hector?

250 pleasantly easily   **251 prenominate** name beforehand.   **nice** precise
256 stithied forged.   **helm** helmet   **261 chafe thee** anger yourself
265 stomach appetite (for fighting).   **general state** i.e., Greek commanders
in council   **266 be odd** be at odds, undertake to fight   **268 pelting** paltry

Tomorrow do I meet thee, fell as death;   270
Tonight all friends.

HECTOR   Thy hand upon that match.

[*They grasp hands.*]

AGAMEMNON
First, all you peers of Greece, go to my tent;
There in the full convive we. Afterwards,   273
As Hector's leisure and your bounties shall
Concur together, severally entreat him.   275
Beat loud the taborins, let the trumpets blow,   276
That this great soldier may his welcome know.

[*Flourish.*] *Exeunt* [*all except Troilus and Ulysses*].

TROILUS
My lord Ulysses, tell me, I beseech you,
In what place of the field doth Calchas keep?   279

ULYSSES
At Menelaus' tent, most princely Troilus.
There Diomed doth feast with him tonight,
Who neither looks on heaven nor on earth
But gives all gaze and bent of amorous view
On the fair Cressid.

TROILUS
Shall I, sweet lord, be bound to you so much,
After we part from Agamemnon's tent,
To bring me thither?

ULYSSES   You shall command me, sir.
As gentle tell me, of what honor was   288
This Cressida in Troy? Had she no lover there
That wails her absence?

TROILUS
O, sir, to such as boasting show their scars   291
A mock is due. Will you walk on, my lord?
She was beloved, she loved; she is, and doth.
But still sweet love is food for fortune's tooth. *Exeunt.* 294

♣

---

270 fell fierce   **273 convive** feast together   **275 severally** individually.
entreat invite   **276 taborins** drums   **279 keep** dwell   **288 As gentle** be
so courteous as to   **291 such as** those who   **294 still** always

5.1   *Enter Achilles and Patroclus.*

ACHILLES
I'll heat his blood with Greekish wine tonight,
Which with my scimitar I'll cool tomorrow.   2
Patroclus, let us feast him to the height.
PATROCLUS
Here comes Thersites.

Enter Thersites.

ACHILLES   How now, thou core of envy!   4
Thou crusty batch of nature, what's the news?   5
THERSITES   Why, thou picture of what thou seemest   6
and idol of idiot-worshipers, here's a letter for thee.
ACHILLES   From whence, fragment?   8
THERSITES   Why, thou full dish of fool, from Troy.
          [*He gives a letter. Achilles reads it.*]
PATROCLUS   Who keeps the tent now?   10
THERSITES   The surgeon's box, or the patient's wound.   11
PATROCLUS   Well said, adversity! And what need these
tricks?
THERSITES   Prithee, be silent, boy; I profit not by thy
talk. Thou art thought to be Achilles' male varlet.
PATROCLUS   Male varlet, you rogue? What's that?
THERSITES   Why, his masculine whore. Now, the rotten
diseases of the south, the guts-griping, ruptures, catarrhs, loads o' gravel i' the back, lethargies, cold pal-   19
sies, raw eyes, dirt-rotten livers, wheezing lungs,
bladders full of impostume, sciaticas, limekilns i' the   21

5.1. **Location: The Greek camp. Before Achilles' tent.**
2 scimitar sword. (Literally, a short, curved, single-bladed sword.)
4 core central hard mass of a boil or tumor   **5 crusty . . . nature** i.e.,
scabbed like a batch of overbaked bread. (*Batch* is sometimes emended
to *botch*, ulcer, boil.)   **6 picture** i.e., mere image   **8 fragment** i.e., crust
of bread   **10 Who . . . now** (Patroclus may be pointing out that Achilles
no longer keeps to his tent, thus depriving Thersites of an object of
satirical humor.)   **11 surgeon's box** (Thersites puns on *tent* in the
previous line, i.e., a probe for cleaning a wound.)   **19 gravel** i.e.,
stones.   **back** kidney   **21 impostume** abscesses.   **limekilns** burning
sensations

palm, incurable bone-ache, and the riveled fee-simple 22
of the tetter, take and take again such preposterous 23
discoveries! 24

PATROCLUS Why, thou damnable box of envy, thou,
what means thou to curse thus?

THERSITES Do I curse thee?

PATROCLUS Why, no, you ruinous butt, you whoreson 28
indistinguishable cur, no. 29

THERSITES No? Why art thou then exasperate, thou idle 30
immaterial skein of sleave silk, thou green sarcenet 31
flap for a sore eye, thou tassel of a prodigal's purse,
thou? Ah, how the poor world is pestered with such
waterflies, diminutives of nature!

PATROCLUS Out, gall!

THERSITES Finch egg! 36

ACHILLES
My sweet Patroclus, I am thwarted quite
From my great purpose in tomorrow's battle.
Here is a letter from Queen Hecuba,
A token from her daughter, my fair love,
Both taxing me and gaging me to keep 41
An oath that I have sworn. I will not break it.
Fall Greeks, fail fame, honor or go or stay; 43
My major vow lies here, this I'll obey.
Come, come, Thersites, help to trim my tent. 45
This night in banqueting must all be spent.
Away, Patroclus!   [*Exeunt Achilles and Patroclus.*]

THERSITES With too much blood and too little brain,
these two may run mad; but if with too much brain
and too little blood they do, I'll be a curer of madmen. 50
Here's Agamemnon, an honest fellow enough and
one that loves quails, but he has not so much brain as 52

---

22 riveled wrinkled. **fee-simple** absolute possession, i.e., incurable
disease **23 tetter** skin disease. **take** afflict with disease **23–24 pre-**
posterous discoveries i.e., the revelation of such relationships as exist
between Patroclus and Achilles **28 ruinous butt** dilapidated cask
29 indistinguishable shapeless **30 exasperate** exasperated, angry
31 skein coil. **sleave silk** floss silk, i.e., unwoven and hence worthless
(*immaterial*). **sarcenet** fine, soft silk **36 Finch egg** (The finch is a
small bird.) **41 taxing . . . gaging** i.e., urging . . . binding, pledging
43 or go either go **45 trim** prepare **50 I'll . . . madmen** i.e., a most
unlikely circumstance **52 quails** i.e., prostitutes. (Cant term.)

earwax; and the goodly transformation of Jupiter 53
there, his brother, the bull—the primitive statue and 54
oblique memorial of cuckolds, a thrifty shoeing-horn 55
in a chain, hanging at his brother's leg—to what form 56
but that he is should wit larded with malice and malice faced with wit turn him to? To an ass were noth- 58
ing, he is both ass and ox; to an ox were nothing, he's
both ox and ass. To be a dog, a mule, a cat, a fitch- 60
ew, a toad, a lizard, an owl, a puttock, or a herring 61
without a roe, I would not care; but to be Menelaus! I 62
would conspire against destiny. Ask me not what I
would be, if I were not Thersites, for I care not to be 64
the louse of a lazar, so I were not Menelaus. Heyday! 65
Sprites and fires! 66

Enter [Hector, Troilus, Ajax,] Agamemnon,
Ulysses, Nestor, [Menelaus,] and Diomedes, with
lights.

AGAMEMNON
We go wrong, we go wrong.
AJAX   No, yonder 'tis,
There, where we see the lights.
HECTOR   I trouble you.
AJAX
No, not a whit.
ULYSSES   Here comes himself to guide you.

   [Enter Achilles.]

ACHILLES
Welcome, brave Hector; welcome, princes all.

53–54 transformation . . . bull (Alludes ironically to the myth of Jupiter's rape of Europa, whom he encountered in a meadow after changing
himself into a bull. Thersites has in mind the bull's horns, which are
like Menelaus' cuckold's horns.)   54–55 primitive . . . cuckolds i.e., the
prototype and indirect reminder of cuckolds in having horns
55–56 thrifty . . . leg i.e., a convenient tool, always available to do
Agamemnon's will (the shoeing-horn having been suggested in Thersites' mind by the cuckold's horn)   58 faced covered, trimmed, adorned
60–61 fitchew polecat   61 puttock bird of prey of the kite kind
61–62 herring . . . roe i.e., least valuable kind of herring   64 I care not
to be I wouldn't mind being   65 lazar leper   66 Sprites and fires
(Thersites sees those who are entering with lights, reminding him of
will-o'-the-wisps and other spirits.)

AGAMEMNON
So now, fair Prince of Troy, I bid good night.
Ajax commands the guard to tend on you.
HECTOR
Thanks and good night to the Greeks' general.
MENELAUS   Good night, my lord.
HECTOR   Good night, sweet Lord Menelaus.
THERSITES   Sweet draft. "Sweet," quoth 'a! Sweet   76
sink, sweet sewer.   77
ACHILLES
Good night and welcome, both at once, to those
That go or tarry.
AGAMEMNON   Good night.
                          Exeunt Agamemnon [and] Menelaus.
ACHILLES
Old Nestor tarries; and you too, Diomed,
Keep Hector company an hour or two.
DIOMEDES
I cannot, lord. I have important business,
The tide whereof is now. Good night, great Hector.   84
HECTOR   Give me your hand.
ULYSSES [*Aside to Troilus*]
Follow his torch; he goes to Calchas' tent.
I'll keep you company.
TROILUS   Sweet sir, you honor me.
HECTOR
And so, good night.
        [*Exit Diomedes; Ulysses and Troilus following.*]
ACHILLES   Come, come, enter my tent.
        Exeunt [Achilles, Hector, Ajax, and Nestor].
THERSITES   That same Diomed's a false-hearted rogue, a
most unjust knave. I will no more trust him when he
leers than I will a serpent when he hisses. He will
spend his mouth and promise, like Brabbler the   92
hound, but when he performs, astronomers foretell it;   93
it is prodigious, there will come some change. The sun   94
borrows of the moon when Diomed keeps his word.   95

---

76 draft privy.   **'a** he   **77 sink** cesspool   **84 tide** time   **92 spend his
mouth** bay without scenting the game   **93–94 astronomers . . . change**
i.e., it is a rare and wondrous event   **95 borrows of** i.e., borrows reflected light from (reversing the natural superiority of the sun)

I will rather leave to see Hector than not to dog him. 96
They say he keeps a Trojan drab and uses the traitor 97
Calchas' tent. I'll after. Nothing but lechery! All incon-
tinent varlets!   [*Exit.*]

❖

5.2   *Enter Diomedes.*

DIOMEDES   What, are you up here, ho? Speak.
CALCHAS [*Within*]   Who calls?
DIOMEDES
Diomed. Calchas, I think. Where's your daughter?
CALCHAS [*Within*]   She comes to you.

> [*Enter Troilus and Ulysses, at a distance; after
> them, Thersites.*]

ULYSSES [*To Troilus*]
Stand where the torch may not discover us.   5
> [*He and Troilus conceal themselves in one place,
>   Thersites in another.*]

> *Enter Cressida.*

TROILUS
Cressid comes forth to him.
DIOMEDES   How now, my charge?
CRESSIDA
Now, my sweet guardian! Hark, a word with you.
                                    [*She whispers.*]
TROILUS   Yea, so familiar?
ULYSSES   She will sing any man at first sight.   9
THERSITES [*Aside*]   And any man may sing her, if he can
take her clef; she's noted.   11
DIOMEDES   Will you remember?
CRESSIDA   Remember? Yes.
DIOMEDES   Nay, but do, then,
And let your mind be coupled with your words.

96 leave to see cease looking upon.   **him** i.e., Diomedes   **97 drab** whore

5.2. Location: The Greek camp. Before Calchas' tent.
5 discover reveal   **9 sing** i.e., make music with, play upon   **11 clef** key
(with obscene pun on *cleft*).   **noted** set to music (with quibble on the
meaning "known," i.e., notorious)

TROILUS   What should she remember?
ULYSSES   List.
CRESSIDA
   Sweet honey Greek, tempt me no more to folly.
THERSITES [*Aside*]   Roguery!
DIOMEDES   Nay, then—
CRESSIDA   I'll tell you what—
DIOMEDES
   Foh, foh! Come, tell a pin. You are forsworn.   22
CRESSIDA
   In faith, I cannot. What would you have me do?
THERSITES [*Aside*]   A juggling trick—to be secretly   24
   open.   25
DIOMEDES
   What did you swear you would bestow on me?
CRESSIDA
   I prithee, do not hold me to mine oath;
   Bid me do anything but that, sweet Greek.
DIOMEDES   Good night.   [*He starts to go.*]
TROILUS   Hold, patience!
ULYSSES   How now, Trojan!
CRESSIDA   Diomed—
DIOMEDES
   No, no, good night. I'll be your fool no more.
TROILUS   Thy better must.
CRESSIDA   Hark, a word in your ear.
TROILUS   O plague and madness!
ULYSSES
   You are moved, Prince; let us depart, I pray,
   Lest your displeasure should enlarge itself
   To wrathful terms. This place is dangerous,   39
   The time right deadly. I beseech you, go.
                         [*He tries to lead Troilus away.*]
TROILUS
   Behold, I pray you!
ULYSSES   Nay, good my lord, go off.
   You flow to great distraction. Come, my lord.
TROILUS
   I prithee, stay.

22 tell a pin i.e., tell me no trifles   **24 juggling trick** magic trick (since
to be *secretly open* is an apparent contradiction in terms)   **25 open**
(1) frank (2) sexually available   **39 wrathful terms** i.e., a fight

ULYSSES   You have not patience; come.

TROILUS

I pray you, stay. By hell and all hell's torments,
I will not speak a word!

DIOMEDES

And so, good night.

CRESSIDA   Nay, but you part in anger.

TROILUS

Doth that grieve thee? O witherèd truth!

ULYSSES

How now, my lord!

TROILUS   By Jove, I will be patient.

CRESSIDA

Guardian!—Why, Greek!

DIOMEDES   Foh, foh! Adieu, you palter.   49

CRESSIDA

In faith, I do not. Come hither once again.

ULYSSES

You shake, my lord, at something. Will you go?
You will break out.

TROILUS   She strokes his cheek!

ULYSSES   Come, come.

TROILUS

Nay, stay. By Jove, I will not speak a word.
There is between my will and all offenses   54
A guard of patience. Stay a little while.

THERSITES [*Aside*] How the devil Luxury, with his fat   56
rump and potato finger, tickles these together! Fry,   57
lechery, fry!

DIOMEDES   But will you, then?

CRESSIDA

In faith, I will, la; never trust me else.

DIOMEDES

Give me some token for the surety of it.

CRESSIDA   I'll fetch you one.   *Exit.*

ULYSSES

You have sworn patience.

---

49 palter use trickery   **54 will** i.e., desire to speak and act   **56 Luxury**
lechery   **57 potato finger** (Potatoes were accounted stimulants to lechery.) **Fry** burn (with passion)

TROILUS   Fear me not, sweet lord.
I will not be myself, nor have cognition
Of what I feel. I am all patience.

Enter Cressida, [with Troilus' sleeve].

THERSITES [*Aside*]   Now the pledge; now, now, now!
CRESSIDA   Here, Diomed, keep this sleeve.
                              [*She gives it to him.*]
TROILUS
O beauty! Where is thy faith?
ULYSSES   My lord—
TROILUS
I will be patient; outwardly I will.
CRESSIDA
You look upon that sleeve; behold it well.
He loved me—O false wench!—Give 't me again.
                              [*She takes it back again.*]
DIOMEDES   Whose was 't?
CRESSIDA
It is no matter, now I ha 't again.
I will not meet with you tomorrow night.
I prithee, Diomed, visit me no more.
THERSITES [*Aside*]   Now she sharpens. Well said, whet- 76
stone!
DIOMEDES
I shall have it.
CRESSIDA   What, this?
DIOMEDES   Ay, that.
CRESSIDA
O all you gods! O pretty, pretty pledge!
Thy master now lies thinking in his bed
Of thee and me, and sighs, and takes my glove,
And gives memorial dainty kisses to it,
As I kiss thee. Nay, do not snatch it from me;
He that takes that doth take my heart withal.   84
DIOMEDES
I had your heart before; this follows it.
TROILUS   I did swear patience.

76 sharpens i.e., whets his appetite   **84 withal** with it

CRESSIDA
    You shall not have it, Diomed, faith, you shall not.
    I'll give you something else.
DIOMEDES   I will have this. Whose was it?
                            [*Getting the sleeve from her.*]
CRESSIDA   It is no matter.
DIOMEDES   Come, tell me whose it was.
CRESSIDA
    'Twas one's that loved me better than you will.
    But, now you have it, take it.
DIOMEDES   Whose was it?
CRESSIDA
    By all Diana's waiting-women yond,   94
    And by herself, I will not tell you whose.
DIOMEDES
    Tomorrow will I wear it on my helm
    And grieve his spirit that dares not challenge it.   97
TROILUS
    Wert thou the devil, and wor'st it on thy horn,   98
    It should be challenged.
CRESSIDA
    Well, well, 'tis done, 'tis past. And yet it is not;
    I will not keep my word.
DIOMEDES
    Thou never shalt mock Diomed again.
                            [*He starts to go.*]
CRESSIDA
    You shall not go. One cannot speak a word
    But it straight starts you.
DIOMEDES   I do not like this fooling.   104
THERSITES [*Aside*]   Nor I, by Pluto; but that that likes not 105
    you pleases me best.
DIOMEDES   What, shall I come? The hour?
CRESSIDA
    Ay, come—O Jove!—do come—I shall be plagued.
DIOMEDES
    Farewell till then.

94 **Diana's . . . yond** i.e., yonder stars. (Diana is the moon goddess and,
ironically, the goddess of chastity.)   97 **grieve** afflict   98 **wor'st** wore
104 **straight starts you** immediately starts you off on some abrupt
action   105 **likes** pleases

CRESSIDA   Good night. I prithee, come.
                                    [*Exit Diomedes.*]
    Troilus, farewell! One eye yet looks on thee,
    But with my heart the other eye doth see.
    Ah, poor our sex! This fault in us I find:
    The error of our eye directs our mind.
    What error leads must err; O, then conclude,
    Minds swayed by eyes are full of turpitude.   *Exit.* 115
THERSITES [*Aside*]
    A proof of strength she could not publish more,   116
    Unless she said, "My mind is now turned whore."
ULYSSES
    All's done, my lord.
TROILUS   It is.
ULYSSES   Why stay we, then?
TROILUS
    To make a recordation to my soul   119
    Of every syllable that here was spoke.
    But if I tell how these two did coact,
    Shall I not lie in publishing a truth?
    Sith yet there is a credence in my heart,
    An esperance so obstinately strong   124
    That doth invert th' attest of eyes and ears,   125
    As if those organs had deceptious functions,   126
    Created only to calumniate.   127
    Was Cressid here?
ULYSSES   I cannot conjure, Trojan.
TROILUS
    She was not, sure.
ULYSSES   Most sure she was.
TROILUS
    Why, my negation hath no taste of madness.
ULYSSES
    Nor mine, my lord. Cressid was here but now.
TROILUS
    Let it not be believed for womanhood!   132
    Think, we had mothers. Do not give advantage

---

115 **turpitude** wickedness   116 **A proof . . . more** she could not state
a stronger proof   119 **recordation** record   124 **esperance** hope
125 **attest** witness   126 **deceptious** deceiving   127 **calumniate** slander,
defame   132 **for** for the sake of

To stubborn critics, apt, without a theme   134
For depravation, to square the general sex   135
By Cressid's rule. Rather think this not Cressid.   136
ULYSSES
What hath she done, Prince, that can soil our mothers?
TROILUS
Nothing at all, unless that this were she.
THERSITES [*Aside*]   Will 'a swagger himself out on 's own   139
eyes?   140
TROILUS
This she? No, this is Diomed's Cressida.
If beauty have a soul, this is not she;
If souls guide vows, if vows be sanctimonies,   143
If sanctimony be the gods' delight,
If there be rule in unity itself,   145
This is not she. O, madness of discourse,   146
That cause sets up with and against itself!   147
Bifold authority, where reason can revolt   148
Without perdition, and loss assume all reason   149
Without revolt! This is and is not Cressid.   150
Within my soul there doth conduce a fight   151
Of this strange nature, that a thing inseparate   152
Divides more wider than the sky and earth,
And yet the spacious breadth of this division
Admits no orifex for a point as subtle   155
As Ariachne's broken woof to enter.   156
Instance, O, instance, strong as Pluto's gates,   157

134–136 apt . . . rule apt enough, even when they lack grounds for negative comment, to make Cressida the standard by which all womankind is measured. (To *square* is to use a carpenter's square or measuring tool.)
139–140 Will . . . eyes i.e., will he succeed in deceiving his own eyes
143 sanctimonies sacred things   **145 If . . . itself** i.e., if an entity (like Cressida) can only be itself and not two entities   **146 discourse** reason
147 That . . . up that sets up a debate or argument   **148 Bifold** divided in two   **148–150 where . . . Without revolt** where reason can revolt against itself (by denying the testimony of the senses that this is indeed Cressida) without becoming madness, and where loss of reason can put on the appearance of reason without actually revolting against it   **151 conduce** take place   **152 a thing inseparate** i.e., Cressida, an indivisible entity
155 orifex orifice   **156 Ariachne's broken woof** i.e., a thread of a spider's web. (Arachne [the correct spelling] challenged Minerva to a weaving contest; the goddess became angered, tore up Arachne's work, and turned her into a spider.)   **157 Instance** proof, evidence

Cressid is mine, tied with the bonds of heaven;
Instance, O, instance, strong as heaven itself,
The bonds of heaven are slipped, dissolved, and loosed,
And with another knot, five-finger-tied,   161
The fractions of her faith, orts of her love,   162
The fragments, scraps, the bits and greasy relics
Of her o'ereaten faith, are bound to Diomed.   164

ULYSSES
May worthy Troilus be half attached   165
With that which here his passion doth express?

TROILUS
Ay, Greek; and that shall be divulgèd well
In characters as red as Mars his heart
Inflamed with Venus. Never did young man fancy   169
With so eternal and so fixed a soul.
Hark, Greek: as much as I do Cressid love,
So much by weight hate I her Diomed.   172
That sleeve is mine that he'll bear on his helm.
Were it a casque composed by Vulcan's skill,   174
My sword should bite it. Not the dreadful spout   175
Which shipmen do the hurricano call,
Constringed in mass by the almighty sun,   177
Shall dizzy with more clamor Neptune's ear
In his descent than shall my prompted sword
Falling on Diomed.

THERSITES [Aside]   He'll tickle it for his concupy.   181

TROILUS
O Cressid! O false Cressid! False, false, false!
Let all untruths stand by thy stainèd name,
And they'll seem glorious.

ULYSSES   O, contain yourself;
Your passion draws ears hither.

        Enter Aeneas.

AENEAS
I have been seeking you this hour, my lord.

---

161 five-finger-tied i.e., tied by giving her hand to Diomedes   **162 orts**
leftovers, fragments   **164 o'ereaten** i.e., surfeiting through overfeeding
165 half attached half as much affected (as it appears)   **169 fancy**
love   **172 So . . . weight** to the same extent   **174 casque** headpiece,
helmet   **175 spout** waterspout   **177 Constringed** compressed
181 concupy (1) concupiscence, lust; or (2) concubine, i.e., Cressida

Hector, by this, is arming him in Troy;
Ajax, your guard, stays to conduct you home.

TROILUS
Have with you, Prince. My courteous lord, adieu.   189
Farewell, revolted fair! And, Diomed,
Stand fast, and wear a castle on thy head!   191

ULYSSES   I'll bring you to the gates.

TROILUS   Accept distracted thanks.

Exeunt Troilus, Aeneas, and Ulysses.

THERSITES   Would I could meet that rogue Diomed! I
would croak like a raven; I would bode, I would bode.   195
Patroclus will give me anything for the intelligence of   196
this whore. The parrot will not do more for an almond
than he for a commodious drab. Lechery, lechery, still   198
wars and lechery; nothing else holds fashion. A burn-   199
ing devil take them!   *Exit.*   200

❖

5.3   *Enter Hector, [armed,] and Andromache.*

ANDROMACHE
When was my lord so much ungently tempered
To stop his ears against admonishment?
Unarm, unarm, and do not fight today.

HECTOR
You train me to offend you. Get you in.   4
By all the everlasting gods, I'll go!

ANDROMACHE
My dreams will, sure, prove ominous to the day.   6

HECTOR
No more, I say.

Enter Cassandra.

CASSANDRA   Where is my brother Hector?

ANDROMACHE
Here, sister, armed, and bloody in intent.

---

189 **Have with you** let us go together   191 **castle** fortress, i.e., strong
helmet   195 **bode** warn, prognosticate   196 **intelligence** news   198 **commodious** accommodating   199–200 **A burning devil** i.e., venereal disease

5.3. **Location:** Troy. The palace.
4 **train** tempt, induce   6 **ominous to** prophetic of

Consort with me in loud and dear petition;   9
Pursue we him on knees. For I have dreamt
Of bloody turbulence, and this whole night
Hath nothing been but shapes and forms of slaughter.

CASSANDRA
O, 'tis true.

HECTOR   Ho! Bid my trumpet sound.

CASSANDRA
No notes of sally, for the heavens, sweet brother.   14

HECTOR
Begone, I say. The gods have heard me swear.

CASSANDRA
The gods are deaf to hot and peevish vows.
They are polluted offerings, more abhorred
Than spotted livers in the sacrifice.

ANDROMACHE
O, be persuaded! Do not count it holy
To hurt by being just. It is as lawful,
For we would give much, to use violent thefts,   21
And rob in the behalf of charity.

CASSANDRA
It is the purpose that makes strong the vow,
But vows to every purpose must not hold.   24
Unarm, sweet Hector.

HECTOR   Hold you still, I say.
Mine honor keeps the weather of my fate.   26
Life every man holds dear, but the dear man   27
Holds honor far more precious-dear than life.

     Enter Troilus.

How now, young man, mean'st thou to fight today?

ANDROMACHE
Cassandra, call my father to persuade.

                 Exit Cassandra.

HECTOR
No, faith, young Troilus, doff thy harness, youth;   31
I am today i' the vein of chivalry.

---

9 dear ardent   **14 sally** sallying, going forth to battle   **21 For** because.   **would give** want to give   **24 vows . . . hold** not every vow must be held sacred   **26 keeps the weather of** keeps to the windward side of, takes precedence over   **27 dear man** worthy man, man of nobility
31 harness armor

Let grow thy sinews till their knots be strong,
And tempt not yet the brushes of the war.   34
Unarm thee, go, and doubt thou not, brave boy,
I'll stand today for thee and me and Troy.

TROILUS
Brother, you have a vice of mercy in you,
Which better fits a lion than a man.   38

HECTOR
What vice is that? Good Troilus, chide me for it.

TROILUS
When many times the captive Grecian falls,   40
Even in the fan and wind of your fair sword,
You bid them rise and live.

HECTOR
O, 'tis fair play.

TROILUS   Fool's play, by heaven, Hector.

HECTOR
How now, how now?

TROILUS   For th' love of all the gods,
Let's leave the hermit Pity with our mothers,
And when we have our armors buckled on,
The venomed vengeance ride upon our swords,
Spur them to ruthful work, rein them from ruth.   48

HECTOR
Fie, savage, fie!

TROILUS   Hector, then 'tis wars.   49

HECTOR
Troilus, I would not have you fight today.

TROILUS   Who should withhold me?
Not fate, obedience, nor the hand of Mars
Beck'ning with fiery truncheon my retire,   53
Not Priamus and Hecuba on knees,
Their eyes o'ergallèd with recourse of tears,   55
Nor you, my brother, with your true sword drawn,
Opposed to hinder me, should stop my way,
But by my ruin.

---

34 brushes hostile encounters   **38 better fits a lion** (Lions were thought
to be merciful to submissive prey.)   **40 captive** overpowered in battle
48 ruthful lamentable, i.e., causing lamentation.   **ruth** pity, mercy
49 then 'tis wars i.e., war is like that **53 truncheon** staff of office.   **retire**
withdrawal **55 o'ergallèd** inflamed.   **recourse** flowing down repeatedly

Enter Priam and Cassandra.

CASSANDRA
Lay hold upon him, Priam, hold him fast;
He is thy crutch. Now if thou lose thy stay,   60
Thou on him leaning, and all Troy on thee,
Fall all together.

PRIAM   Come, Hector, come, go back.
Thy wife hath dreamt, thy mother hath had visions,
Cassandra doth foresee, and I myself
Am like a prophet suddenly enrapt   65
To tell thee that this day is ominous.
Therefore, come back.

HECTOR   Aeneas is afield,
And I do stand engaged to many Greeks,
Even in the faith of valor, to appear   69
This morning to them.

PRIAM   Ay, but thou shalt not go.

HECTOR   I must not break my faith.
You know me dutiful; therefore, dear sir,
Let me not shame respect, but give me leave   73
To take that course by your consent and voice
Which you do here forbid me, royal Priam.

CASSANDRA
O Priam, yield not to him!

ANDROMACHE   Do not, dear Father.

HECTOR
Andromache, I am offended with you.
Upon the love you bear me, get you in.

                                        Exit Andromache.

TROILUS
This foolish, dreaming, superstitious girl
Makes all these bodements.

CASSANDRA   O, farewell, dear Hector!   80
Look how thou diest! Look how thy eye turns pale!
Look how thy wounds do bleed at many vents!
Hark, how Troy roars, how Hecuba cries out,
How poor Andromache shrills her dolors forth!   84
Behold, distraction, frenzy, and amazement,

---

60 stay prop   **65 enrapt** carried away, inspired   **69 faith of valor** word of
honor   **73 shame respect** i.e., violate my filial duty   **80 Makes** causes.
bodements omens of ill fortune   **84 shrills her dolors** wails her grief

Like witless antics, one another meet,   86
And all cry, "Hector! Hector's dead! O Hector!"

TROILUS   Away! away!

CASSANDRA
Farewell. Yet soft! Hector, I take my leave.
Thou dost thyself and all our Troy deceive.   [*Exit.*]

HECTOR
You are amazed, my liege, at her exclaim.   91
Go in and cheer the town. We'll forth and fight,
Do deeds worth praise, and tell you them at night.

PRIAM
Farewell. The gods with safety stand about thee!
          [*Exeunt separately Priam and Hector.*] *Alarum.*

TROILUS
They are at it, hark! Proud Diomed, believe
I come to lose my arm or win my sleeve.

          Enter Pandarus.

PANDARUS   Do you hear, my lord? Do you hear?

TROILUS   What now?

PANDARUS   Here's a letter come from yond poor girl.
                                        [*He gives a letter.*]

TROILUS   Let me read.

PANDARUS   A whoreson tisick, a whoreson rascally tis-   101
ick so troubles me, and the foolish fortune of this girl,   102
and what one thing, what another, that I shall leave
you one o' th's days; and I have a rheum in mine eyes   104
too, and such an ache in my bones that, unless a man
were cursed, I cannot tell what to think on 't.—What
says she there?

TROILUS
Words, words, mere words, no matter from the heart;
Th' effect doth operate another way.   109
          [*He tears the letter and tosses it away.*]
Go, wind, to wind! There turn and change together.   110
My love with words and errors still she feeds,
But edifies another with her deeds.   *Exeunt.* 112

❖

86 antics fools   **91 amazed** dumbstruck.   **exclaim** outcry   **101–102 tisick**
phthisic, consumptive cough   **104 rheum** watery discharge   **109 Th' effect**
. . . way i.e., her actions belie her words   **110 Go, wind, to wind** go, empty
words, to the air   **112 s.d. Exeunt** (In the Folio version, Pandarus is angrily
dismissed at this point, in the lines printed by the Quarto at 5.10.32–34.)

5.4   [*Alarum.*] *Enter Thersites. Excursions.*

THERSITES   Now they are clapper-clawing one another; 1
I'll go look on. That dissembling abominable varlet,
Diomed, has got that same scurvy doting foolish
young knave's sleeve of Troy there in his helm. I
would fain see them meet, that that same young
Trojan ass, that loves the whore there, might send
that Greekish whoremasterly villain with the sleeve
back to the dissembling luxurious drab, of a sleeveless 8
errand. O' th' other side, the policy of those crafty
swearing rascals, that stale old mouse-eaten dry
cheese, Nestor, and that same dog-fox, Ulysses, is not
proved worth a blackberry. They set me up, in policy, 12
that mongrel cur, Ajax, against that dog of as bad a
kind, Achilles. And now is the cur Ajax prouder than
the cur Achilles, and will not arm today, whereupon
the Grecians begin to proclaim barbarism, and policy 16
grows into an ill opinion.

[*Enter Diomedes, Troilus following.*]

Soft! Here comes Sleeve, and t'other.

TROILUS
Fly not, for shouldst thou take the River Styx,
I would swim after.

DIOMEDES   Thou dost miscall retire.   20
I do not fly, but advantageous care   21
Withdrew me from the odds of multitude.   22
Have at thee!   [*They fight.*]

THERSITES   Hold thy whore, Grecian!—Now for thy
whore, Trojan!—Now the sleeve, now the sleeve!

[*Exeunt Troilus and Diomedes, fighting.*]

Enter Hector.

**5.4. Location: Between Troy and the Greek camp. The battlefield is the
setting for the rest of the play.**
s.d. Excursions sorties or issuings forth of soldiers   **1 clapper-clawing**
mauling, thrashing   **8 luxurious** lecherous.   **sleeveless** futile   **12 set
me** set. (*Me* is used colloquially.)   **16 proclaim barbarism** i.e., declare
they will be governed by *policy* or established government no longer
20 miscall retire call my retirement by the wrong name of retreat
21–22 advantageous . . . multitude care for my own advantage prompted
me to withdraw from facing heavy odds

HECTOR
What art thou, Greek? Art thou for Hector's match?
Art thou of blood and honor?   27
THERSITES   No, no, I am a rascal, a scurvy railing knave,
a very filthy rogue.
HECTOR   I do believe thee. Live.   [*Exit.*]
THERSITES   God-a-mercy, that thou wilt believe me; but
a plague break thy neck for frighting me! What's become of the wenching rogues? I think they have swallowed one another. I would laugh at that miracle—yet,
in a sort, lechery eats itself. I'll seek them.   *Exit.* 35

5.5   *Enter Diomedes and Servant.*

DIOMEDES
Go, go, my servant, take thou Troilus' horse;
Present the fair steed to my lady Cressid.
Fellow, commend my service to her beauty;
Tell her I have chastised the amorous Trojan
And am her knight by proof.
SERVANT   I go, my lord.   [*Exit.*]

        Enter Agamemnon.

AGAMEMNON
Renew, renew! The fierce Polydamas   6
Hath beat down Menon; bastard Margarelon
Hath Doreus prisoner,
And stands colossus-wise, waving his beam,   9
Upon the pashèd corpses of the kings   10
Epistrophus and Cedius; Polyxenes is slain,
Amphimachus and Thoas deadly hurt,
Patroclus ta'en or slain, and Palamedes
Sore hurt and bruised. The dreadful Sagittary   14

---

27 **blood** noble blood   35 **in a sort** in a way

5.5. Location: As before; the battle continues.
6 **Renew** i.e., get ready to attack again   9 **colossus-wise** like the Colossus (the great bronze statue of Apollo at Rhodes, one of the seven
wonders of the ancient world).   **beam** lance   10 **pashèd** battered
14 **Sagittary** (Literally, the archer; a centaur, i.e., a monster half man,
half horse, who according to medieval legends fought in the Trojan War
against the Greeks.)

Appals our numbers. Haste we, Diomed,   15
To reinforcement, or we perish all.

    Enter Nestor [and soldiers].

NESTOR
  Go, bear Patroclus' body to Achilles,
  And bid the snail-paced Ajax arm for shame.
                            [Exeunt some.]
  There is a thousand Hectors in the field.
  Now here he fights on Galathe his horse,
  And there lacks work; anon he's there afoot,
  And there they fly or die, like scalèd schools   22
  Before the belching whale; then is he yonder,
  And there the strawy Greeks, ripe for his edge,   24
  Fall down before him, like the mower's swath.
  Here, there, and everywhere he leaves and takes,   26
  Dexterity so obeying appetite
  That what he will he does, and does so much
  That proof is called impossibility.   29

    Enter Ulysses.

ULYSSES
  O, courage, courage, princes! Great Achilles
  Is arming, weeping, cursing, vowing vengeance.
  Patroclus' wounds have roused his drowsy blood,
  Together with his mangled Myrmidons,   33
  That noseless, handless, hacked and chipped, come to
    him,
  Crying on Hector. Ajax hath lost a friend   35
  And foams at mouth, and he is armed and at it,
  Roaring for Troilus, who hath done today
  Mad and fantastic execution,   38
  Engaging and redeeming of himself   39
  With such a careless force and forceless care   40

---

15 Appals our numbers dismays our troops   **22 scalèd schools** scattering
schools of fish   **24 strawy** like straw ready for mowing   **26 leaves and
takes** i.e., leaves one dead and takes on another (?)   **29 proof** fact, accomplished deed   **33 Myrmidons** soldiers of Thessaly (whom Achilles led to
Troy)   **35 Crying on** complaining of, exclaiming against   **38 execution**
deeds   **39 Engaging** committing to battle   **40 forceless care** easy dexterity

As if that luck, in very spite of cunning,
Bade him win all.

Enter Ajax.

AJAX
Troilus! Thou coward Troilus!   *Exit.*
DIOMEDES   Ay, there, there.
NESTOR
So, so, we draw together.   ·   *Exit.*

Enter Achilles.

ACHILLES   Where is this Hector?
Come, come, thou boy-queller, show thy face!   45
Know what it is to meet Achilles angry.
Hector! Where's Hector? I will none but Hector.
                          Exit [with others].

5.6   *Enter Ajax.*

AJAX
Troilus, thou coward Troilus, show thy head!

Enter Diomedes.

DIOMEDES
Troilus, I say! Where's Troilus?
AJAX   What wouldst thou?
DIOMEDES   I would correct him.
AJAX
Were I the general, thou shouldst have my office
Ere that correction. Troilus, I say! What, Troilus!   5

Enter Troilus.

TROILUS
O traitor Diomed! Turn thy false face, thou traitor,
And pay thy life thou owest me for my horse!
DIOMEDES   Ha, art thou there?

---

45 boy-queller boy killer; i.e., slayer of Patroclus
5.6. Location: As before; the battle continues.
5 Ere that correction i.e., sooner than take from me the privilege of
chastising Troilus

AJAX
  I'll fight with him alone. Stand, Diomed.   9
DIOMEDES
  He is my prize. I will not look upon.   10
TROILUS
  Come, both you cogging Greeks, have at you both!   11
                            [*Exeunt, fighting.*]

          [*Enter Hector.*]

HECTOR
  Yea, Troilus? O, well fought, my youngest brother!

      Enter Achilles.

ACHILLES
  Now do I see thee, ha! Have at thee, Hector!
                       [*They fight; Achilles tires.*]
HECTOR   Pause, if thou wilt.
ACHILLES
  I do disdain thy courtesy, proud Trojan.
  Be happy that my arms are out of use.
  My rest and negligence befriends thee now,
  But thou anon shalt hear of me again;
  Till when, go seek thy fortune.   *Exit.*
HECTOR   Fare thee well.
  I would have been much more a fresher man,
  Had I expected thee.

      Enter Troilus.

                    How now, my brother!
TROILUS
  Ajax hath ta'en Aeneas! Shall it be?
  No, by the flame of yonder glorious heaven,
  He shall not carry him. I'll be ta'en too,   24
  Or bring him off. Fate, hear me what I say!   25
  I reck not though thou end my life today.   *Exit.* 26

      Enter one in armor.

HECTOR
  Stand, stand, thou Greek; thou art a goodly mark.

---

9 Stand i.e., stand aside   **10 look upon** remain an onlooker   **11 cogging**
deceitful   **24 carry him** i.e., into captivity   **25 bring him off** rescue
him   **26 reck** care

No? Wilt thou not? I like thy armor well;
I'll frush it and unlock the rivets all,   29
But I'll be master of it. [*Exit one in armor.*] Wilt thou not,
   beast, abide?
Why, then fly on, I'll hunt thee for thy hide.   31

                           Exit [*in pursuit*].

5.7 *Enter Achilles, with Myrmidons.*

ACHILLES
Come here about me, you my Myrmidons;
Mark what I say. Attend me where I wheel.
Strike not a stroke, but keep yourselves in breath,   3
And when I have the bloody Hector found,
Empale him with your weapons round about;   5
In fellest manner execute your arms.   6
Follow me, sirs, and my proceedings eye.
It is decreed Hector the great must die.   *Exeunt.*

   Enter Thersites; Menelaus [*and*] *Paris* [*fighting*].

THERSITES The cuckold and the cuckold maker are at it.
Now, bull! Now, dog! 'Loo, Paris, 'loo! Now my dou-   10
ble-horned Spartan! 'Loo, Paris, 'loo! The bull has the   11
game. Ware horns, ho!   12

             Exeunt Paris and Menelaus.

   Enter Bastard [*Margarelon*].

MARGARELON Turn, slave, and fight.
THERSITES What art thou?
MARGARELON A bastard son of Priam's.
THERSITES I am a bastard too; I love bastards. I am bastard begot, bastard instructed, bastard in mind, bastard in valor, in everything illegitimate. One bear will
not bite another, and wherefore should one bastard?

---

29 frush bruise **31 hide** i.e., armor

5.7. Location: As before; the battle continues.
3 in breath in readiness **5 Empale** fence **6 fellest** fiercest. **execute**
your arms bring your weapons into operation **10 bull** i.e., Menelaus, a
cuckold, a horned creature. **'Loo** (A cry to incite a dog against the bull
in the sport of bullbaiting in Shakespeare's England.) **11–12 has the**
game wins **12 Ware** beware

Take heed, the quarrel's most ominous to us. If the
son of a whore fight for a whore, he tempts judgment.
Farewell, bastard.   [*Exit.*]
MARGARELON   The devil take thee, coward!   *Exit.*

5.8   *Enter Hector, [bearing the armor he has taken].*

HECTOR
  Most putrefièd core, so fair without,   1
  Thy goodly armor thus hath cost thy life.
  Now is my day's work done; I'll take good breath.
  Rest, sword; thou hast thy fill of blood and death.
                                        [*He disarms.*]

  Enter Achilles and Myrmidons.

ACHILLES
  Look, Hector, how the sun begins to set,
  How ugly night comes breathing at his heels.
  Even with the vail and darkening of the sun,   7
  To close the day up, Hector's life is done.
HECTOR
  I am unarmed. Forgo this vantage, Greek.
ACHILLES
  Strike, fellows, strike! This is the man I seek.
                                        [*Hector falls.*]
  So, Ilium, fall thou next! Come, Troy, sink down!
  Here lies thy heart, thy sinews, and thy bone.
  On, Myrmidons, and cry you all amain,
  "Achilles hath the mighty Hector slain."
                                        Retreat [*sounded*].
  Hark! A retire upon our Grecian part.   15
MYRMIDON
  The Trojan trumpets sound the like, my lord.
ACHILLES
  The dragon wing of night o'erspreads the earth,
  And, stickler-like, the armies separates.   18
  My half-supped sword, that frankly would have fed,   19

5.8. Location: As before; the battle continues.
1 core i.e., the body of the Greek from whom Hector has taken the
armor   **7 vail** going down   **15 retire** call to retreat   **18 stickler-like** like
a referee   **19 frankly** freely

Pleased with this dainty bait, thus goes to bed.   20
                    [*He sheathes his sword.*]
Come, tie his body to my horse's tail;
Along the field I will the Trojan trail.
                    Exeunt [*with Hector's body*].

5.9   *Enter Agamemnon, Ajax, Menelaus, Nestor,*
          Diomedes, and the rest, marching. [*Shouts*
          within.]

AGAMEMNON   Hark! Hark! What shout is that?
NESTOR   Peace, drums!
SOLDIERS (*Within*)
    Achilles! Achilles! Hector's slain! Achilles!
DIOMEDES
    The bruit is, Hector's slain, and by Achilles.   4
AJAX
    If it be so, yet bragless let it be;   5
    Great Hector was as good a man as he.
AGAMEMNON
    March patiently along. Let one be sent
    To pray Achilles see us at our tent.
    If in his death the gods have us befriended,
    Great Troy is ours, and our sharp wars are ended.
                    Exeunt.

5.10   *Enter Aeneas, Paris, Antenor,* [*and*]
          Deiphobus.

AENEAS
    Stand, ho! Yet are we masters of the field.   1

          Enter Troilus.

TROILUS
    Never go home; here starve we out the night.   2
    Hector is slain.

20 **dainty bait** tasty snack

5.9. Location: The battlefield; the battle has concluded.
4 **bruit** rumor, noise   5 **bragless** without boasting

5.10. Location: The battlefield after the battle.
1 **Yet** still   2 **starve we out** i.e., let us endure, outlast

ALL   Hector! The gods forbid!
TROILUS
He's dead, and at the murderer's horse's tail,
In beastly sort, dragged through the shameful field.
Frown on, you heavens, effect your rage with speed!
Sit, gods, upon your thrones and smile at Troy!   7
I say, at once let your brief plagues be mercy,   8
And linger not our sure destructions on!   9
AENEAS
My lord, you do discomfort all the host.   10
TROILUS
You understand me not that tell me so.
I do not speak of flight, of fear, of death,   12
But dare all imminence that gods and men   13
Address their dangers in. Hector is gone.   14
Who shall tell Priam so, or Hecuba?
Let him that will a screech owl aye be called
Go in to Troy, and say there, "Hector's dead."
There is a word will Priam turn to stone,
Make wells and Niobes of the maids and wives,   19
Cold statues of the youth, and, in a word,
Scare Troy out of itself. But march away.
Hector is dead. There is no more to say.
Stay yet. You vile abominable tents,
Thus proudly pitched upon our Phrygian plains,
Let Titan rise as early as he dare,   25
I'll through and through you! And, thou great-sized
    coward,   26
No space of earth shall sunder our two hates.
I'll haunt thee like a wicked conscience still,
That moldeth goblins swift as frenzy's thoughts.

7 smile i.e., mockingly   8 let . . . mercy i.e., let your afflictions end us
quickly, be mercifully brief   9 linger draw out, protract   10 discomfort
discourage.   host army   12 of flight i.e., merely of disordered retreat
13 imminence impending evils, threats of imminent disaster
14 Address . . . in level their threats with   19 Niobes (Niobe boasted
that her six sons and six daughters made her superior to Latona,
mother of Apollo and Diana, for which she was punished by seeing
them put to death by the arrows of these two deities. While weeping she
was changed into a stone, but her tears continued to flow from the
rock.)   25 Titan i.e., Helios, the sun-god, one of the Titans   26 coward
i.e., Achilles, craven slayer of Hector

Strike a free march to Troy! With comfort go.
Hope of revenge shall hide our inward woe.
                              [*Exeunt Aeneas and soldiers.*]
          Enter Pandarus.
PANDARUS   But hear you, hear you!
TROILUS
Hence, broker-lackey! Ignomy and shame
Pursue thy life, and live aye with thy name!
                              Exeunt all but Pandarus.
PANDARUS   A goodly medicine for my aching bones! O
world, world, world! Thus is the poor agent despised.
O traders and bawds, how earnestly are you set   37
a-work, and how ill requited! Why should our en-
deavor be so desired and the performance so loathed?
What verse for it? What instance for it? Let me see:

Full merrily the humble-bee doth sing,   41
Till he hath lost his honey and his sting;
And being once subdued in armèd tail,
Sweet honey and sweet notes together fail.

Good traders in the flesh, set this in your painted   45
cloths: 46
As many as be here of Pandar's hall,   47
Your eyes, half out, weep out at Pandar's fall;   48
Or if you cannot weep, yet give some groans,
Though not for me, yet for your aching bones.   50
Brethren and sisters of the hold-door trade,   51
Some two months hence my will shall here be made.
It should be now, but that my fear is this:
Some gallèd goose of Winchester would hiss.   54
Till then I'll sweat and seek about for eases,   55
And at that time bequeath you my diseases.   [*Exit.*]

---

37 **traders** i.e., traders in sex   41 **humble-bee** bumblebee
45–46 **painted cloths** cheap wall hangings worked or painted with
scenes and mottoes   47 **hall** fraternity   48 **half out** i.e., already half
eaten away by venereal disease   50 **aching bones** (A symptom of venereal disease.)   51 **hold-door trade** i.e., brothel keeping   54 **gallèd ...
Winchester** i.e., a prostitute having venereal disease; so called because
the brothels of Southwark were under the jurisdiction of the Bishop of
Winchester   55 **sweat** (A common treatment for venereal disease.)

Date and Text

The textual history of *Troilus and Cressida* is complicated. On February 7, 1603, James Roberts entered on the Stationers' Register, the official record book of the London Company of Stationers (booksellers and printers), "when he hath gotten sufficient aucthority for yt, The booke of Troilus and Cresseda as yt is acted by my lord Chamberlens Men." On January 28, 1609, however, a new entry appeared on the Register as though the first had never been made: "Richard Bonion Henry Walleys. Entred for their Copy vnder thandes of Master Segar deputy to Sir George Bucke and master warden Lownes a booke called the history of Troylus and Cressida." Later that year appeared the first quarto with the following title:

> THE Historie of Troylus and Cresseida. *As it was acted by the Kings Maiesties* seruants at the Globe.
> *Written by* William Shakespeare. LONDON Imprinted by *G. Eld* for *R Bonian* and *H. Walley,* and are to be sold at the spred Eagle in Paules Church-yeard, ouer against the great North doore. 1609.

Before the first printing had sold out, still in 1609, the original title leaf was replaced by two new leaves containing a new title and an epistle. The title reads:

> THE Famous Historie of Troylus *and* Cresseid. *Excellently expressing the beginning* of their loues, with the conceited wooing of *Pandarus* Prince of *Licia. Written by* William Shakespeare.

The epistle is addressed "A neuer writer, to an euer reader. Newes," and begins, "Eternall reader, you haue heere a new play, neuer stal'd with the Stage, neuer clapper-clawd with the palmes of the vulger, and yet passing full of the palme comicall."

The First Folio editors originally intended *Troilus and Cressida* to follow *Romeo and Juliet*. After three pages had been set up in this position, however, the play was removed (perhaps owing to copyright difficulties) and *Timon of Athens* inserted instead. Later, *Troilus* was placed between the Histories and the Tragedies, almost entirely without pagination. See the Introduction for some possible explanations of the unusual publishing history.

The quarto text was evidently set from a transcript of Shakespeare's foul papers (i.e., his working draft), made either by Shakespeare or by a scribe, or else from the foul papers themselves. The first three pages of the Folio text, those originally intended to follow *Romeo and Juliet*, were set from this first quarto. The remaining pages of the First Folio, however, seem to have been based on the quarto collated with a manuscript source, either Shakespeare's draft or more probably the promptbook, which may itself have been a transcript of Shakespeare's fair ("clean") copy of his foul papers. As a result, both the quarto and Folio texts have independent textual authority. Recent editorial study has paid increasing attention to the Folio text on the theory that its readings, when not manifestly corrupt, may represent either Shakespeare's second thoughts as he fair copied or at least what the Folio collator found in Shakespeare's draft. Hence this edition, though using the first quarto as its control text, introduces more Folio readings than are usually found in some previous editions; the Folio readings have been rejected only when there is some textual evidence against them.

The possibility that the play may not have been publicly performed and the failure of Shakespeare's company to provide the sequel promised at the end of *Troilus* suggest that the play was written not long before the first Stationers' Register entry of February 1603. Certainly the play was not an old favorite in the company's repertoire. Failure as a stage play might have led to an attempt at quick publication, aimed at sophisticated readers. The current fad for satire would also have provided a motive for prompt publication. Stylistically, *Troilus* belongs to the period of *Hamlet* (c. 1599–1601). A seeming allusion in the Prologue of *Troilus* to the "armed" Prologue of Ben Jonson's *Poetaster* (1601) helps set a probable early limit for date of composition. George Chapman's *Seven Books of the Iliads of Homer,* a source of information about the Trojan War, had appeared in 1598.

Textual Notes

These textual notes are not a historical collation, either of the early quarto and the early folios or of more recent editions; they are simply a record of departures in this edition from the copy text. The reading adopted in this edition appears in boldface, followed by the rejected reading from the copy text, i.e., the quarto of 1609. Only major alterations in punctuation are noted. Changes in lineation are not indicated, nor are some minor and obvious typographical errors.

Abbreviations used:
F the First Folio
Q the quarto of 1609
s.d. stage direction
s.p. speech prefix

Copy text: the quarto of 1609, which may represent Shakespeare's revision of the play, although the First Folio text represents an independent and valuable textual authority. All adopted readings are from [F] unless otherwise indicated; [eds.] means that the reading is that of some editor since the First Folio.

Prologue [F; not in Q]   **8 immures** emures [F]   **12 barks** [eds.] Barke [F]   **17 Antenorides** Antenonidus [F]   **19 Spar** [eds.] Stirre [F]

1.1. 15 must needs must   **26 of the** the   **27 you** yea   **to burn** burne   **33 When** [eds.] then   **73 on of you** of you   **78 not kin** kin   **80 care I** I   **85 her. For** her for   **99 woo** [eds.] woe   **100 stubborn-chaste** stubborn, chast   **104 resides** reides

1.2. 1 s.p. [and throughout] Alexander Man   **17 they** the   **34 struck** stroke   **48 ye** [eds.] yea   **85 come** eome   **87 wit** [eds.] will   **117 lift** liste   **125 valiantly** valianty   **130 the** [eds.] thee   **177 s.d.** [at l. 175 in Q]   **180 Ilium** Ilion   **186 s.d.** [at l. 185 in Q]   **205 man's** man   **214 s.d.** [at l. 210 in Q]   **269 too** two

1.3. 2 the jaundice on these Iaundies ore   **13 every** euer   **31 thy** the   **36 patient** ancient   **48 breese** Bryze   **54 Retorts** [eds.] Retires   **61 thy** the   **70–74** [F; not in Q]   **75 basis** bases   **92 ill . . . evil** influence of euill Planets   **106 primogeniture** primogenitie   **110 meets** melts   **119 includes** include   **143 sinew** sinnow   **149 awkward** sillie   **159 unsquared** vnsquare   **164 just** right   **188 willed** wild   **195 and** our   **209 fineness** finesse   **219 ears** eyes   **221 host** [eds.] heads   **236 fame** same   **238 Jove's** great Ioues   **247 affair** affaires   **250 him** with him   **252 sense** seat   **the** that   **256 loud** alowd   **262 this** his   **267 That seeks** And feeds   **276 compass** couple   **289 or means** a meanes   **294 One . . . one** A . . . no   **297 this withered brawn** my withered braunes   **298 will tell** tell   **302 youth** men   **304 s.p. Agamemnon** [F; not in Q]   **305 first** sir   **315 This 'tis** [F; not in Q]   **327 were** weare   **333 Yes** Why   **334 his honor** those honours   **336 this** the   **352 from hence receives the** receiues from hence a   **354–356** [F; not in Q]   **354 his** [eds.] in his [F]   **369 we** it   **372 did** do   **390 tar** arre   **their** a

2.1. 14 vinewed'st [eds.] vnsalted [Q] whinid'st [F]   **17 oration** oration without booke   **18 learn a** learne   **19 o'** ath   **27 thee** the   **38, 40, 41 s.p. Thersi-**

tes, Ajax, Thersites [F; not in Q]   45 Thou scurvy you scuruy   71 I will It
will   75 I'll I   88 for a the   101 an 'a and [Q] if he [F]   out at   105 your
[eds.] their   nails on their toes nailes   111 wit as as   114 brach [eds.]
brooch   122 fifth first

2.2. 3 damage domage   14, 15 surety surely   33 at of   47 Let's Sets
64 shores shore   71 sieve siue   79 stale pale   82 launched lansh't   86 he
be   100 s.d. [at l. 96 in Q]   104 eld old [F] elders [Q]   120 th' event [eds.]
euent   149 off of   210 strike shrike

2.3. 1 s.p. Thersites [not in Q]   24 ha' a   25 wouldst couldst   31 art art
not   46 thyself Thersites   49 mayst must   54–59 [F; not in Q]
62–63 commanded of Agamemnon commanded   66 of thy creator of the
Prouer   68 Patroclus Come Patroclus   73–74 Now . . . all [F; not in Q]
73 serpigo [eds.] Suppeago [F]   78 shent [eds.] sent [F] sate [Q]   87 the a
88 A word, my lord [F; not in Q]   111 Hear Heere   129 pettish lunes course,
and time [Q] pettish lines [F]   his flows and flowes   as and   130 carriage
of this action streame of his commencement   140 enter you entertaine
152 clearer, Ajax cleerer   190 Must Shall   192 titled liked   200 this his
202 pash push   204 'a he   211 let tell   humors humorous   214 o' of
218 'twould two'od   219 'A . . . shares [assigned in Q to Ajax]   221 He's . . .
warm [assigned in Q to Ajax]   222 praises praiers   in; his his   225 You
Yon   241 beyond all all thy   247 bourn boord   248 Thy This   262 cull call

3.1. 3. s.p. [and elsewhere] Servant Man   6 noble notable   41 There's
theirs   76 supper you super. You   90 poor disposer's disposer is   106 lord
lad   107 hast haste   113 [F; not in Q]   117 shaft confounds shafts confound   148 They're Their   149 woo woe   151 these this   159 thee her

3.2. 3 he stays stays   8 a to a   10 those these   20 palate tastes pallats
taste   23 subtle-potent subtill, potent   37 unawares vnwares   38 s.d. Pandarus and Cressida pandar and Cressid   45 thills filles   67 fears [eds.]
teares   80 This is This   91 crown it. No perfection louer part no affection
121 grown grone   131 Cunning Comming   149–150 Where . . . what I would
be gone: / Where is my wit? I know not what I speake   159 aye age
179 Yet, after After   184 and or   199 pains paine

3.3. s.d. Calchas Chalcas   3 to your to   4 come [eds.] loue   29 off of
43 unplausive vnpaulsiue   69 s.d. Exit Exeunt   101 shining ayming
103 giver giuers   111 mirrored [eds.] married   129 abject obiect   141 on
one   142 shrieking [eds.] shriking [Q] shrinking [F]   153 mail male
156 one on   159 hedge turn   161 hindmost him, most   162–164 Or . . . on
[F; not in Q]   163 rear [eds.] neere [F]   165 past passe   179 give [eds.] goe
185 Than That   not stirs stirs not   198 grain . . . gold thing   199 deeps
depth   225 like a like   234 we they   242 s.d. Enter Thersites [after
"saud'd" in Q]   267 ambassador to him Ambassador   272 make his his
275 the most the   279 Grecian [not in Q]   et cetera. Do Do   299 you yee
301 but he's but   o' of   306 carry beare

4.1. s.d. [and elsewhere] Diomedes Diomed   5 you your   18 But Lul'd
42 do think beleeue   46 whereof wherefore   54 the soul soule   55 merits
deserues   most best   58 soilure soyle

4.2. 18 off of   32–33 capocchia [eds.] chipochia   35 s.d. One knocks [after
l. 36 in Q]   56 Hoo! [eds.] Who   65 us; and for him him, and   74 nature
neighbor Pandar   79 s.p. Cressida [not in Q]   89–90 knees I beseech knees

4.4. 6 affection affections **50 genius so** Genius **51 "Come"** so **54 the root**
my throate **58 my love** loue **70 Wear** were **77** [F; not in Q] **gifts** guift [F]
78 flowing swelling **79 person** portion **106 wear** were **135 I'll speak** I
speake **144–148** [F; not in Q] **144 s.p. Deiphobus** [eds.] Dio [F]

4.5. s.d. Nestor Nester, Calcas **2 time . . . courage.** time. With starting courage **16 toe** too **38 s.p. Menelaus** [eds.] Patr **44 not** nor **49 then, too** then
60 accosting a coasting **62 tickling** ticklish **66 you** the **74 s.p. Achilles** [not in Q] **95** [F; not in Q] **96 s.p. Agamemnon** Vlises **99 in deeds**
deeds **133 Of our rank feud** [F; not in Q] **134 drop** day **166–171** [F; not
in Q] **179 that I** thy **oath** earth **189 thy** th' **194 hemmed** shrupd
200 Let O let **207** [F; not in Q] **256 stithied** stichied **276 Beat . . . taborins**
To taste your bounties **282 on heaven nor on** vpon the heauen nor **288 As**
But **293 she loved** my Lord

5.1. 4 core curre **12 need these** needs this **14 boy** box **15 thought** said
18–19 catarrhs [F; not in Q] **20 wheezing** whissing **31 sarcenet** sacenet
32 tassel toslell **51 Here's** her's **54 brother** be **56 hanging . . . leg** at his
bare legge **59 he's** her's **60 dog** day **mule** Moyle **60–61 fitchew**
Fichooke **63 me not** me **71 good** God **77 sewer** [eds.] sure **78 both at
once** both

5.2. 5 s.d. Enter Cressida [after "to him" in l. 6 in Q] **11 clef** Cliff **13 s.p.
Cressida** [eds.] Cal **16 should** shall **41 Nay** Now **42 distraction** distruction **49 Adieu, you** you **57 tickles these** tickles **59 But will** will **60 la**
[eds.] lo **63 sweet** my **69** [F; not in Q] **70 s.p. Cressida** Troy. **80 in** on
83 Nay . . . me [assigned in Q, F to Diomedes] **87 s.p. Cressida** [F; not in
Q] **92 one's** [eds.] on's [Q] one [F] **94 By** And by **121 coact** Court
126 had were **deceptious** deceptions **137 soil** spoile **146 is** was **161 five**
finde **164 bound** giuen **171 as I** [eds.] I

5.3. 14 s.p. Cassandra Cres **20–22** [F; not in Q] **21 give** [eds.] count giue [F]
use [eds.] as [F] **23 s.p. Cassandra** [F; not in Q] **45 mothers** Mother **58** [F;
not in Q] **85 distraction** distruction

5.4. 4 young knave's knaues **16 begin** [eds.] began **26 art thou** art

5.5. 5 s.p. Servant Man **11 Cedius** [eds.] Cedus **12 Thoas** [eds.] Thous
22 scaled scaling **25 the** a **41 luck** lust **43 s.p. Ajax** [F; not in Q]

5.6. 1 s.p. Ajax [F; not in Q] **2 s.p. Diomedes** [F; not in Q] **13 s.p. Achilles**
[F; not in Q] **21 s.d. Enter Troilus** [after "brother" in l. 21 in Q] **26 reck**
[eds.] wreake **thou end** I end

5.7. 1 s.p. Achilles [F; not in Q] **8 s.d. Exeunt** [eds.] Exit **10 'Loo** [eds.]
lowe **10–11 double-horned Spartan** [eds.] double hen'd spartan [Q] double-
henned sparrow [F] **12 s.d. Exeunt** [eds.] Exit **13 s.p. [and throughout
scene] Margarelon** Bast

5.8. 3 good my **15 part** prat **16 s.p. Myrmidon** One **Trojan trumpets**
Troyans trumpet

5.9. 1 shout is that is this

5.10. 17 there their **21 Scare** Scarre **21–22 But . . . dead** [F; not in Q]
23 vile proud **33 Ignomy and** ignomyny **36 world, world, world** world,
world **37 traders** traitors **39 desired** lou'd **50 your** my **51 hold-door**
hold-ore

Shakespeare's Sources

Shakespeare had access to Homer for information about the Trojan War, since George Chapman's translation of *Seven Books of the Iliads of Homer* had appeared in 1598, and earlier English translations of the entire *Iliad* were also available. Shakespeare ends his play with the death of Hector, as do Homer and some post-Homeric historians of the war, and portrays Achilles as a figure in tragic conflict with his sense of pride, as does Homer. Thersites and Nestor are based ultimately on the *Iliad*, as can be seen in the excerpt from Chapman's translation that follows. Ajax' ludicrous boastfulness may owe something to Homer's Ajax Telamon, as well as to Ovid's account of the quarrel between Ulysses and Ajax over Achilles' armor (*Metamorphoses*, 12–13). Yet for Shakespeare, and for most Englishmen of his time, the chief sources of information about the Trojan War were medieval romances. These were all pro-Trojan in their bias, since Englishmen traced their own mythic history to the lineage of Aeneas and tended to look on Homer as suspiciously pro-Greek. Medieval European culture generally was far more oriented to Roman than to Greek civilization; Greek texts went almost unread. In these circumstances, a pro-Trojan account of the war emerged and grew to considerable proportions, in which non-Homeric material became increasingly important.

The central work dealing with this expanded account of the war was Benoît de Sainte-Maure's *Roman de Troie* (c. 1160), a romance freely based on earlier accounts of two supposed eyewitnesses named Dictys the Cretan and Dares the Phrygian. Benoît not only narrates the war from Troy's point of view but introduces the love story of Troilus, "Breseida," and Diomedes. Benoît found a hint for this story in the *Iliad*, where two Trojan maidens named Chryseis and Briseis are captured and given to Agamemnon and Achilles respectively. When Chryseis' father calls down a plague on the Greeks for refusing to return Chryseis, Agamemnon reluctantly gives her up but then seizes Briseis from Achilles, thereby precipitating Achilles' angry retirement to his tent and all that disastrously follows. Benoît freely transforms this situation into the rivalry of Troilus and Diomed, who appear in Homer but in entirely different roles.

Benoît's *Roman de Troie* became the inspiration for subsequent medieval accounts of the Trojan War. Guido delle Colonne translated Benoît in his *Historia Troiana* (completed 1287). Giovanni Boccaccio based his *Il Filostrato* (c. 1338) on Guido and Benoît but made significant alterations: the love story became the focus of attention, and Pandarus assumed the important role of go-between. (In Homer, Pandarus is a fierce warrior.) Geoffrey Chaucer based his *Troilus and Criseyde* (c. 1385–1386) on Boccaccio, giving still greater attention to the states of mind of the two lovers and endowing Pandarus with a humorous disposition, as is illustrated in the selection that follows. Shakespeare certainly knew Chaucer's masterpiece. He also consulted, however, at least two other medieval accounts of the war: John Lydgate's *The History, Siege, and Destruction of Troy* (first printed 1513), based on Guido and Chaucer and known also as the *Troy Book*, and William Caxton's *The Recuyell of the Histories of Troy* (printed 1474, the first book printed in English), a translation from the French of Raoul Lefevre who had followed Guido rather closely. In Caxton, for example, Shakespeare found materials for the Trojan debate in Act 2, scene 2 (see the selection from Caxton that follows) and for Hector's visit to the Greek camp (Act 4, scene 5). In addition, Shakespeare was certainly familiar with the degeneration of Cressida's character since the time of Chaucer, as reflected for example in Robert Henryson's *The Testament of Cresseid* (published 1532), in which Cressida is punished for her faithlessness by leprosy and poverty.

Shakespeare pays a good deal more attention to the war than does Chaucer and portrays the lovers as caught in a conflict beyond their control. Shakespeare's Cressida is more sardonic and experienced in the ways of the world than is Chaucer's heroine, even though Chaucer's Criseyde is a widow and Shakespeare's Cressida is unmarried. The subtle and elaborate code of courtly love evoked by Chaucer has almost completely disappeared in Shakespeare's work, leaving in its wake a more dispiriting and cynical impression. Shakespeare's Troilus is still a faithful and earnest lover, as in Chaucer, but betrayed by his own chauvinistic ideals about honor and patriotism in a way that Chaucer's Troilus is not. Pandarus is more leering, giddy, vapid, and coarse than his Chaucerian counterpart. Diomedes is also changed for the worse, being more hard and cynical.

Among the non-Chaucerian characters, Achilles is made to appear more guilty and brutal than in Shakespeare's sources: Achilles orders his Myrmidons (i.e., his soldiers) to murder the unarmed Hector, even though Hector had previously spared Achilles in battle. Lydgate and Caxton report that Achilles' Myrmidons kill Troilus, not Hector (in Caxton, Achilles cuts off Troilus' head and then drags Troilus' body behind his horse), whereas in Homer Achilles kills Hector in battle and only then do his Myrmidons desecrate the body. Shakespeare refuses to glamorize the war just as he refuses to glamorize the love story. He also compresses time, as he did with so many of his sources. The play begins only a short time before Cressida surrenders to Troilus; she is transferred to the Greeks immediately after she and Troilus become lovers; her surrender to Diomedes follows quickly after her transfer. This telescoping provides not only dramatic unity but a sense of sudden and violent change.

Other plays on Troilus and Cressida are known to have existed in Shakespeare's time, such as a "new" play acted by the Admiral's men, an acting company, in 1596 and another by Thomas Dekker and Henry Chettle in 1599. Shakespeare may have known and even written in response to such productions by rival theatrical companies, but today nothing is known about these lost plays.

Seven Books of the Iliads of Homer
Translated by George Chapman
BOOK 2

[Morale is so low among the Greeks, after years of being in Troy with no victory yet in sight, that, when Agamemnon tests his army by inviting them to leave Troy, a mutiny nearly occurs. In the council meeting that ensues to discuss matters, the most disaffected and insubordinate trouble-maker is Thersites.]

All sat and silent used their seats, Thersites sole
    except—   1
A man of tongue, whose ravenlike voice a tuneless
    jarring kept,   2
Who in his rank mind copy had of unregarded words   3
That rashly and beyond all rule used to oppugn the
    lords.   4
But whatsoever came from him was laughed at
    mightily—
The filthiest Greek that came to Troy. He had a
    goggle eye;   6
Stark lame he was of either foot; his shoulders were
    contract   7
Into his breast and crook'd withal; his head was
    sharp compact,   8
And here and there it had a hair. To mighty Thetides 9
And wise Ulysses he retained much anger and
    disease,   10
For still he chid them eagerly, and then against the
    state   11
Of Agamemnon he would rail. The Greeks in
    vehement hate
And high disdain conceited him, yet he with violent
    throat   13
Would needs upbraid the General, and thus himself
    forgot: 14
    "Atrides, why complain'st thou now? What dost
    thou covet more?   15

1 Thersites sole except except only Thersites **2 kept** kept up **3 rank**
haughty, rebellious; gross. **unregarded** un-looked-after, disordered
4 oppugn assail, controvert **6 goggle** protuberant; squinting **7 Stark**
severely. **either foot** both feet. **contract** contracted, shrunken
8 withal in addition. **his . . . compact** i.e., his skull went up to a point
9–10 To . . . disease i.e., Thersites provoked much anger and annoyance
in mighty Achilles and Ulysses. **Thetides** Achilles, son of Thetis
10 disease annoyance, grievance **11 still** continually. **eagerly** keenly,
violently. **state** dignity, office **13 conceited** regarded **14 Would needs**
felt compelled to. **himself forgot** i.e., forgot his manners **15 Atrides**
Agamemnon, son of Atreus

Thy thrifty tents are full of coin, and thou hast
    women store,   16
Fair and well-favored, which we Greeks at every town
    we take   17
Resign to thee. Think'st thou, thou want'st some
    treasure thou might make   18
To be deduced thee out of Troy by one that comes to
    seek   19
His son for ransom, who myself or any other Greek   20
Should bring thee captive? Or a wench, filled with
    her sweets of youth,   21
Which thou mayst love and private keep for thy
    insatiate tooth?
But it becomes not kings to tempt by wicked
    precedent
Their subjects to dishonesty. O minds most impotent,
Not Argives but Achaean girls, come fall aboard and
    home!   25
Let him concoct his prey alone, alone Troy overcome, 26
To make him know if our free ears his proud
    commands would hear   27
In anything, or not disdain his longer yoke to bear 28
Who hath with contumely wronged a better man than
    he—   29
Achilles, from whose arms, in spite that all the world
    might see,
He took a prize won with his sword. But now it plain
    appears   31
Achilles hath no spleen in him, but most remissly
    bears   32

16 store in great abundance   **17 well-favored** attractive
18–21 Think'st . . . captive i.e., are you hankering after some huge sum
you might get from a Trojan father as ransom for his son whom I or
another Greek would capture and turn over to you. **deduced thee**
brought (from Troy) to you **25 Argives** i.e., Greeks, from Argos.
Achaean i.e., Greek, from Achaea. **come fall aboard and home** go
aboard ship and head home **26 Let him concoct** let Agamemnon digest
or mull over **27 free** i.e., free to hear what we wish **28 or . . . bear** or
rather disdain to bear his yoke any longer **29 contumely** insult, insolence **31 prize** i.e., Briseis, whom Agamemnon has taken away from
Achilles when Agamemnon's prize, Chryseis (compare Criseyde or
Cressida), had to be returned to the Trojans. **his** i.e., Achilles'
32 spleen indignation; resolution

A female stomach; else, be sure, the robbery of his
   meed,   33
O Agamemnon, would have proved thy last injurious
   deed."
   Thus did Thersites chide the king to whom all
     Greece did bow;
When wise Ulysses straight stood up, and, with
   contracted brow,   36
Beholding him, used this rebuke: "Prating Thersites,
   cease,
Though thou canst rail so cunningly, nor dare to
   tempt the peace   38
Of sacred kings; for well thou knowest I know well
   what thou art.   39
A baser wretch came not to Troy to take the Grecians'
   part.   40
Profane not kings, then, with thy lips. Examine our
   retreat,   41
Whereof ourselves are ignorant, nor are our states so
   great   42
That we dare urge upon the King what he will only
   know.   43
Sit then and cease thy barbarous taunts to him whom
   all we owe
So much observance, though from thee these insolent
   poisons flow.   45
But I protest, and will perform if I shall deprehend   46
Such frenzy in thy pride again as now doth all offend:
Then let Ulysses lose his head, and cease inglorious   48
To be the native father called of young Telemachus,   49
If from thee to thy nakedness thy garments be not
   stripped   50
And from the council to the fleet thou be not soundly
   whipped."   51

---

33 female stomach i.e., feminine lack of courage. **meed** reward, i.e., the
prize Briseis **36 straight** straightway, at once **38–39 tempt . . . kings**
flout the general peace provided by the authority of kings **40 take . . .
part** fight on the Grecian side **41 retreat** i.e., military option of retreating
42 states statures, ranks **43 what . . . know** what only he can know
45 observance deference **46 protest** insist. **deprehend** detect
48–51 Then let . . . whipped i.e., may I lose my very life and claims of
paternity if I do not whip you and send you packing back to the ships if I
catch you doing this again. **inglorious** having lost all fame and glory

This said, his back and shoulder blades he with his
    scepter smit;
Who then shrunk round, and down his cheeks the
    servile tears did flit.
The golden scepter in his flesh a bloody print did
    raise,
With which he, trembling, took his seat and, looking
    twenty ways,   55
Ill-favoredly he wiped the tears from his self-pitying
    eyes.
    And then, though all the host were sad, they
        laughed to hear his cries.   57
When thus flew speeches intermixed: "O gods, what
    endless good
Ulysses still bestows on us, that to the field of blood   59
Instructs us, and in council doth for chief director
    serve!
Yet never action passed his hands that did more
    praise deserve   61
Than to disgrace this railing fool in all the army's
    sight,
Whose rudeness henceforth will take heed how he
    doth princes bite."

[Ulysses then speaks, casting more scorn on those discontents and cowards who would go home, and reminding them of Calchas' prophecy that the Greeks will win at the end of ten years.]

Ulysses having spoken thus, his words so likèd were
That of his praise the ships, the tents, the shore did
    witness bear,
Resounding with the people's noise, who gave his
    speech the prize.
Th' applause once ceased, from seat to speak old
    Nestor doth arise.
    "Fie, Greeks, what infamy is this? Ye play at
        children's game,

55 looking twenty ways i.e., his eyes shifting **57 sad** serious **59 still** always. **field of blood** battlefield **61 Yet . . . hands** never yet did he do anything

Your warlike actions thus far brought, now to neglect
their fame.   69
O, whither from our lips profane shall oaths and
compacts fly?
The councils and the cares of men now in the fire
shall die   71
With those our sacred offerings made by pure
unmixèd wine
And our right hands with which our faiths we freely
did combine.   73
The cause is, since amongst ourselves we use
discursive words,   74
And go not manlike to the field to manage it with
swords,   75
Nor with the fineness of our wits by stratagems
devise
In all this while against a world to work our
enterprise.   77
But, great Atrides, as at first, thy counsel being
sound,
Command to field! And be not led corruptly from the
ground   79
Of our endeavors by the moods of one or two that
use   80
Councils apart. They shall not go to Greece till Jove
refuse   81
To ratify his promise made, or we may surely know
If those ostents were true or false that he from
heaven did show. . . .   83
But if some be so mutinous, whom nothing may
restrain,
Let him but touch his black-armed bark that he may
first be slain.   85

69 Your . . . fame now to neglect to pursue the glory of the warlike
action you have brought thus far   **71 in . . . die** i.e., will not fly up to
the gods and be heard. (The sacrificial fire will not be efficacious.)
73 And i.e., and by.   **faiths** pledges.   **combine** i.e., make mutually
74 since i.e., that.   **discursive** unfocused, indecisive   **75 manage it**
control the fighting successfully   **77 against a world** against great odds
79 ground arena   **80–81 use Councils apart** i.e., conspire separately and
seek to divide authority   **83 ostents** portents   **85 him** i.e., that traitorous person.   **black-armed bark** ship outfitted and armed in black

Then, great Atrides, be advised, and others reasons
   see:
It shall not prove an abject speech that I will utter
   thee.
In tribes and nations let thy men be presently
   arrayed,   88
That still the tribes may second tribes, and nations
   nations aid.   89
Of every chief and soldier thus the proof shall rest in
   sight,
For both will thirst their country's fame and press
   for single fight.
What soldier, when he is allowed his countryman for
   guide,
Will not more closely stick to him than to a
   stranger's side?
Thus shalt thou know if gods detain thy hand from
   Ilion's harms   94
Or else the faintness of thy men and ignorance in
   arms."

[Agamemnon thanks Nestor for his inspiring address, says
he wishes he had ten such counselors, and urges an end to
the strife that has divided Greek against Greek, so that they
may turn their energies to leveling the Trojan citadel.]

George Chapman's translation of *Seven Books of the Iliads of Homer* was
published in London in 1598. This modernized text is based on that edition.

88 tribes and nations political divisions.   **presently** at once   **89 still**
always.   **second** support, assist   **94 from Ilion's harms** from inflicting
harm on Troy

The Recuyell of the Histories of Troy
By William Caxton
BOOK 3

[King Priant (Priam) assembles a council of Trojans to consider what should be done about the fact that the Greeks hold captive his sister, Exione (Hesione). The debate resembles that in Act 2, scene 2, of Shakespeare's play, where the capture of Hesione is talked about (ll. 77 ff.), except that the present debate takes place years earlier, before the Trojans seize Helen in retaliation and thereby provide the immediate provocation for the Trojan War. Priant speaks first.]

My sons, ye have well in your memory the death of your grandfather[1] [and] the servitude of your Aunt Exione, that men holdeth by your living[2] in manner of a common woman. And ye be so puissant, meseemeth,[3] that reason should ensign you for to employ you[4] to avenge this great injury and shame. And if this move you not thereto, yet ye ought to do it to satisfy my will and pleasure, for I die for sorrow and anguish, to which[5] ye ought and been bound for to remedy to your power,[6] that have do you so well be[7] nourished and brought forth.

"And thou, Hector, my right dear son, that art the oldest of thy brethren, the most wise and the most strong: I pray thee first that thou emprise[8] to put in execution this my will,

---

Title: **Recuyell** receuil, literary compilation
1 death of your grandfather (Laomedon, King of Troy, earned the wrath of Poseidon by refusing to pay him and Apollo for building the walls of Troy. When Poseidon sent a sea monster against Troy, Laomedon was told he could avert the danger only by sacrificing his daughter Hesione to it. Though assisted by Heracles in getting rid of the monster, Laomedon likewise defrauded Heracles of the famous horses he had promised as a reward. Heracles raised an army and captured Troy, slaying Laomedon and giving Hesione to Telamon.)   **2 by your living** during your lifetime (?), from your possession (?)   **3 puissant, meseemeth** powerful, it seems to me   **4 ensign you for to employ you** instruct you to employ yourselves   **5 to which** to whom   **6 to your power** to the extent of your power   **7 that have . . . be** I who have caused you to be so well **8 emprise** undertake

and that thou be duke and prince of thy brethren in this work, and all the other[9] shall obey gladly unto thee. And in like wise shall do all they[10] of this realm, for[11] the great prowess that they know in thee. And know that from this day forth I despoil me[12] of all this work and put it upon thee that art the most strong and asper[13] to maintain the battles. And I am ancient and old and may not forth on help[14] myself so well as I was wont to do,'' etc.

To these words answered Hector right soberly and sweetly, saying,

"My Father and my right dear and sovereign lord, there is none of all your sons but that it seemeth to him thing human[15] to desire vengeance of these injuries. And also to us that been of high noblesse[16] a little injury ought to be great.[17] As it is so that the quality of the person groweth and minisheth,[18] so ought the quality of the injury. And if we desire and have appetite to take vengeance of[19] our injuries, we forsake not ne[20] leave the nature human, for in like wise do and usen[21] the dumb beasts in the same manner, and nature ensigneth and giveth hem[22] thereto. My right dear lord and Father, there is none of all your sons that ought more to desire the vengeance of the injury and death of our aiel[23] or grandfather than I, that am the oldest.

"But I will,[24] if it please you, that ye consider in this emprise[25] not only the beginning but also the middle and the end to what thing we may come hereafter, for otherwhile little profiten[26] some things well begun that come unto an evil end. Then methinketh[27] that it is much more allowable to a man to abstain him for to begin things whereof the ends been dangerous and whereof may come more evil than good, for the thing is not said eurous[28] or happy unto[29] the time that it come unto a good end.

---

9 other others **10 all they** all those **11 for** on account of **12 despoil me** disrobe, divest myself **13 asper** hardy, warlike **14 on help** in way of assistance **15 thing human** a human trait **16 noblesse** nobility **17 a little . . . great** even a little insult ought to be regarded as a great one **18 As . . . minisheth** i.e., and just as the rank of the person to whom the injury has been done is greater or lesser **19 of** for **20 ne** nor **21 usen** practice, behave **22 ensigneth and giveth hem** instructs and inclines them **23 aiel** grandfather **24 will** wish **25 emprise** enterprise, undertaking **26 little profiten** of little profit are **27 methinketh** it seems to me **28 eurous** lucky, prosperous **29 unto** until

"I say not these things for any evil or cowardice, but only to the end that ye begin not a thing—and specially that thing that ye have on[30] your heart—to put it lightly in ure,[31] but that ye first be well counseled. . . . Exione is not of so high price that it behooveth all us to put us in peril and doubt[32] of death for her. She hath been now long time there where she is yet. It were better that she perform forth her time, that,[33] I trow, hath but little time to live, than we should put us all in such perils.

"And meekly I beseech you not to suppose in no manner that I say these things for cowardice, but I doubt[34] the turns of Fortune and that under the shadow of this thing she[35] not beat ne[36] destroy your great seigniory, and that we ne begin thing[37] that we ought to leave for to eschew[38] more great mischief," etc.

When Hector had made an end of his answer, Paris was nothing well content therewith. He stood up on his feet and said in this wise:

"My right dear lord, I beseech you to hear me say to what end ye may come if ye begin the war against the Greeks. How be not we garnished of[39] so many and noble chivalry as they been? Certes that be we which[40] in all the world is none that may discomfit.[41] And therefore begin ye hardily[42] that emprise[43] that ye have thought, and send of your ships and of your people to run[44] in Greece and to take the people and damage the country. And if it please you to send me, I shall do it with a good will and heart, for I am certain that, if ye send me, that I shall do great damage unto the Greeks. And I shall take some noble lady[45] of Greece and bring her with me to this realm. And by the commutation[46] of her ye may recover your sister Exione. And if ye will understand and know how I am certain of this thing, I shall say it to you how the gods have promised it to me.

---

30 on in   **31 ure** use, practice   **32 doubt** fear, danger   **33 perform . . . time, that** live out her life, who   **34 doubt** fear   **35 she** i.e., Fortune   **36 ne** nor   **37 ne begin thing** do not begin something   **38 leave for to eschew** avoid in order to escape   **39 How . . . garnished of** in what way are we not provided with   **40 Certes . . . which** certainly we are the ones who   **41 discomfit** defeat   **42 hardily** boldly   **43 emprise** enterprise   **44 run** move about freely and quickly   **45 some noble lady** (This lady of course turns out to be Helen.)   **46 commutation** exchanging

[Paris expounds to his father and the other Trojans a vision he has had, and the promise made to him by the goddess Venus. He is followed and seconded by Deiphoebus.]

After this spake Helenus, the fourth son of King Priant, that said thus:

"Ha, ha, right puissant King and right sovereign dominator upon[47] us your humble subjects and obedient sons! Beware that coveteise of[48] vengeance put not you in such danger as lieth herein. Ye know well how I know and can the science[49] to know the things future and to come, as ye have proved[50] many times without finding fault. The gods forbid that it never come that Paris be sent into Greece! For know ye for certain that, if he go to make any assault, ye shall see this noble and worshipful city destroyed by the Greeks, the Trojans slain and we all that been your children. . . ."

When the King heard Helenus thus speak he was all abashed, and began to counterpoise[51] and think, and held his peace and spake not of[52] a great while. And so did all the other.[53]

Then arose upon his feet Troilus, the youngest son of King Priant, and began to speak in this manner:

"O noble men and hardy, how be ye abashed for the words of this coward priest here? Is it not the custom of priests for to dread the battles by[54] pusillanimity, and for to love the delices[55] and to fat and increase hem[56] and fill their bellies with good wines and with good meats? Who is he that believeth that any man may know the things to come but if[57] the gods show it hem by revelation? It is but folly for to tarry upon this or to believe such things. If Helenus be afeard, let him go into the temple and sing the divine service. And let the other[58] take vengeance of their injuries by force of arms. O right dear Father and lord, wherefore art thou so troubled for these words? Send thy ships into Greece, and thy knights wise and hardy, that may render to the Greeks their injuries that they have done to us."

47 **dominator upon** lord over   48 **coveteise of** covetousness of, desire for   49 **can the science** am master of the knowledge   50 **proved** discovered   51 **counterpoise** weigh one possibility against another   52 **of** for   53 **other** others   54 **by** by reason of   55 **delices** sensual pleasures   56 **hem** themselves   57 **but if** unless   58 **other** others

All they that heard Troilus thus speak, they allowed[59] him, saying that he had well spoken. And thus they finished their parliament and went to dinner.

William Caxton translated *The Recuyell* from the French version by Raoul Lefevre in about 1474 and printed it in that same year. This modernized text is based on the 1474 edition.

Troilus and Criseyde
By Geoffrey Chaucer

BOOK 3

[With much ado, Criseyde's uncle Pandarus has managed to persuade her to take pity on the suffering of Troilus by allowing him to visit her at night in her chambers. An assignation is not mentioned; the pretense is that nothing short of seeing her immediately can save Troilus' life.]

"Then, em," quod she, "doth hereof as you list.	939
But ere he come, I will up first arise,	940
And, for the love of God, syn all my trist	941
Is on you two, and ye been bothe wise,	942
So werketh now in so discreet a wise	943
That I honor may have, and he pleasaunce;	944
For I am here all in your governaunce."	945
"That is well said," quod he, "my nece deere.	946
There good thrift on that wise gentle herte!	947
But liggeth still, and taketh him right here;	948
It needeth not no ferther for him sterte.	949
And each of you ease otheres sorwes smerte,	950

59 allowed praised

939 em uncle.   **quod** quoth, said.   **doth . . . list** do in this as you please
940 ere before   **941 syn** since.   **trist** trust   **942 on** in.   **been** be
943 werketh work, arrange matters   **944 pleasaunce** pleasure   **945 all**
entirely   **946 nece deere** dear niece   **947 There good thrift on** may good
success come to   **948 liggeth** lie.   **taketh** take, receive   **949 It . . . sterte**
there's no need to go anywhere else as far as he is concerned
950 sorwes smerte painful sorrows

For love of God; and Venus, I thee herye; 951
For soon hope I we shull been alle merrye." 952

This Troilus full soon on knees him sette 953
Full soberly, right by her beddes head, 954
And in his beste wise his lady grette. 955
But, Lord, so she wex sodeynliche red! 956
Ne though men sholde smitten off her head 957
She couthe not a word aright out bringe 958
So sodeynly, for his sodeyn cominge. 959

But Pandarus, that so well coulde feele 960
In everything, to play anon began, 961
And saide, "Nece, see how this lord can kneele!
Now, for your trouthe, see this gentle man!" 963
And with that word he for a quysshen ran, 964
And saide, "Kneeleth now, while that you leste, 965
There God your hertes bringe soon at reste!" 966

Can I not seyn, for she bade him not rise, 967
If sorwe it put out of her remembraunce, 968
Or elles that she took it in the wise 969
Of dewete, as for his observaunce; 970
But well find I she did him this pleasaunce, 971
That she him kissed, although she siked sore, 972
And bade him sit adown withouten more. 973

Quod Pandarus: "Now wol ye well beginne. 974
Now doth him sitte, goode nece deere, 975
Upon your beddes side all there withinne, 976

951 Venus, I thee herye Venus, I praise you **952 shull** shall **953 him sette** set himself **954 soberly** gravely, demurely. **by her beddes head** by the head of her bed **955 grette** greeted **956 wex sodeynliche** waxed suddenly **957 Ne . . . head** even if men were to smite off her head **958 couthe** could **959 for** on account of **960 so . . . feele** was so perceptive **961 play** jest **963 for your trouthe** i.e., by your troth. (A mild oath.) **964 quysshen** cushion **965 Kneeleth** kneel. **while . . . leste** while you please **966 There . . . bringe** may God bring your hearts **967 Can . . . rise** I can't say, since she didn't bid him rise **968 it put** put it **969 that** if. **wise** manner, way **970 dewete** duty. **as for his observaunce** as a part of his duty to her (in his capacity as her servant in the courtly love relationship) **971 find I she did** I find (as I look into the history of this love story) that she did **972 siked sore** sighed sorely **973 more** more ado **974 Now . . . beginne** i.e., now you can begin **975 doth him sitte** have him sit **976 there withinne** i.e., within the bed curtains

That each of you the bet may other heere." 977
And with that word he drow him to the feere, 978
And took a light, and fond his contenaunce 979
As for to look upon an old romaunce. 980

Criseyde, that was Troilus' lady right, 981
And clear stood on a ground of sikernesse, 982
All thoughte she her servant and her knight 983
Ne should of right none untruth in her guesse, 984
Yet natheless, considered his distresse, 985
And that love is in cause of swich follye, 986
Thus to him spake she of his jealousy:

"Lo, herte mine, as would the excellence 988
Of love, ageyns the which that no man may 989
Ne ought eke goodly make resistance; 990
And eke because I felte well and say 991
Youre grete truth and service every day, 992
And that your herte all mine was, soth to sayn, 993
This drof me for to rew upon your pain. 994

"And your goodness have I founden alway yit, 995
Of which, my deere herte and all my knight, 996
I thank it you, as fer as I have wit, 997
All can I not as much as it were right; 998
And I, emforth my cunning and my might, 999
Have and ay shall, how sore that me smerte, 1000
Been to you trew and whole with all mine herte; 1001

977 **the bet . . . heere** may hear the other better   978 **drow him to** drew himself to, approached.   **feere** i.e., fireplace   979 **fond his contenaunce** set his expression, made a show   980 **As . . . upon** as though he were reading   981 **right** completely   982 **clear . . . sikernesse** stood on a secure foundation   983 **All thoughte she her** was entirely of the opinion that her   984 **Ne . . . guesse** by rights should not suspect any lack of fidelity in her   985 **natheless, considered** nevertheless, having considered   986 **in cause** the cause.   **swich** such   988–989 **as . . . love** i.e., as love in all its excellence wishes me to do   989 **ageyns the which that** against which   990 **Ne . . . resistance** nor ought indeed to make strong resistance   991 **eke** also.   **felte well and say** was well aware of and saw   992 **truth** troth, fidelity   993 **soth to sayn** to say the truth   994 **drof** drove, induced.   **for to rew** to take pity   995 **yit** yet   996 **all** entirely   997 **fer** far   998 **All . . . right** albeit I can't thank you as much as I ought   999 **emforth** to the extent of   1000 **ay** always.   **how . . . smerte** how grievously soever it may cause me pain   1001 **whole** perfect, loyal

And dredeless, that shall be found at preve. 1002
But, herte mine, what all this is to sayne 1003
Shall well be told, so that ye nought you greve, 1004
Though I to you right on yourself complaine. 1005
For therewith mean I finally the paine 1006
That halt your herte and mine in heaviness 1007
Fully to slain, and every wrong redress. 1008

My goode mine, noot I forwhy ne how 1009
That jealousy, alas, that wicked wyvere, 1010
Thus causeless is croppen into you, 1011
The harm of which I woulde fain delivere. 1012
Alas, that he, all whole, or of him slivere, 1013
Should han his refut in so digne a place. 1014
There Jove him soon out of your herte arace! 1015

"But O, thou Jove, O auctour of nature, 1016
Is this an honor to thy deity
That folk unguiltif sufferen hire injure, 1018
And who that guiltif is, all quit goth he? 1019
O, were it leful for to plain on thee, 1020
That undeserved sufferest jealousy, 1021
Of that I would upon thee plain and cry! 1022

"Eke all my woe is this, that folk now usen 1023
To sayn right thus: "Yea, jealousy is love!" 1024
And would a bushel venom all excusen, 1025

1002 dredeless without doubt. **at preve** at proof, when tested **1003 to sayne** to say **1004 nought you greve** do not grieve yourself at all **1005 right . . . complaine** complain in downright fashion of your behavior **1006–1008 therewith . . . slain** by that means I intend finally to slay fully the pain that holds your heart and mine in sorrow. **halt** holds **1009 My goode mine** i.e., my dear love **1009–1010 noot . . . That** I do not know why or how **1010 wyvere** viper **1011 Thus . . . you** has crept thus without cause into you **1012 woulde fain delivere** would gladly do away with **1013 of him slivere** even a sliver of him (Jealousy) **1014 han** have. **refut** refuge. **digne** worthy **1015 There . . . arace** may Jove soon root him out of your heart **1016 auctour** author, creator **1018 folk . . . injure** innocent folk suffer unjust wrongs inflicted on them. **hire** their **1019 who that** he who. **quit** acquitted **1020 leful** allowable. **plain on thee** complain against you (Jove) **1021 That . . . jealousy** who permit undeserved jealousy **1022 upon thee plain** complain against you **1023 Eke** also. **usen** make it a practice **1024 sayn right thus** say exactly as follows **1025 would . . . excusen** would excuse a bushel of venom

For that o grain of love is on it shove. 1026
But that wot heighe God that sit above, 1027
If it be liker love, or hate, or grame; 1028
And after that it oughte bear his name. 1029

"But certain is, some manner jealousy 1030
Is excusable more than some, iwis; 1031
As when cause is, and some swich fantasy 1032
With piety so well repressed is 1033
That it unnethe doth or saith amiss, 1034
But goodly drinketh up all his distresse; 1035
And that excuse I, for the gentilesse. 1036

"And some so full of fury is and despite
That it surmounteth his repressioun. 1038
But, herte mine, ye be not in that plight,
That thank I God; for which your passioun 1040
I woll nought call it but illusioun,
Of habundaunce of love and busy cure, 1042
That doth your herte this disease endure. 1043

"Of which I am right sorry, but nought wroth; 1044
But, for my devoir and your hertes reste, 1045
Whereso you list, by ordeal or by oath, 1046
By sort, or in what wise so you leste, 1047
For love of God, lat preve it for the beste; 1048

1026 For that o because one single. **shove** placed, contained. (People would save a whole bushel of jealousy for the one grain of love in it.) **1027 But . . . above** but God who sits above on high knows **1028 If it be liker** whether it (jealousy) is more like. **grame** anger **1029 after . . . name** it ought to bear the name of what it most resembles, i.e., wrath **1030 some manner** some kinds of **1031 iwis** to be sure **1032 As . . . is** as when there is genuine cause (for jealousy) **1032–1035 and some . . . distresse** or when some jealousy based in fantasy is so well and dutifully repressed that the sufferer scarcely does or says anything to offend others, but instead drinks the cup of his own private sorrow **swich** such. **unnethe** scarcely **1036 for the gentilesse** for its courteous behavior **1038 surmounteth his repressioun** surmounts any attempt at repression **1040 for which** because of which **1042 Of habundaunce** generated by an oversupply. **busy cure** attentive and anxious caring **1043 doth** causes. **this disease endure** to endure this grief **1044 nought wroth** not at all angry **1045 for my devoir** i.e., to satisfy the duty I owe **1046 Whereso you list** wherever you wish. **ordeal** trial by ordeal **1047 sort** trial by drawing of lots. **leste** list, wish **1048 lat preve it** let it be proven, tested

And if that I be guiltif, do me deye! 1049
Alas, what might I more done or saye?" 1050

With that a fewe brighte teris newe 1051
Out of her eyen fell, and thus she saide: 1052
"Now God, thou wost, in thought ne deed untrewe 1053
To Troilus was never yet Criseyde." 1054
With that her head down in the bed she laide,
And with the sheet it wreigh, and sighte sore, 1056
And held her peace; not o word spake she more. 1057

But now help God to quenchen all this sorwe!
So hope I that he shall, for he best may.
For I have seen, of a full misty morwe 1060
Followen full oft a merry summer's day;
And after winter followeth greene May.
Men seen all day, and readen eke in stories, 1063
That after sharpe showers been victories. 1064

This Troilus, when he her wordes herde, 1065
Have ye no care, him liste not to sleepe; 1066
For it thought him no strokes of a yerde 1067
To hear or seen Criseyde, his lady, weepe; 1068
But well he felt about his herte creepe, 1069
For every tear which that Criseyde asterte, 1070
The cramp of death to strain him by the herte. 1071

And in his mind he gan the time accurse
That he come there, and that he was born; 1073
For now is wikke turned into worse, 1074
And all that labor he hath done biforn 1075
He weened it lost; he thought he nas but lorn. 1076

1049 do me deye have me put to death **1050 done** do **1051 teris** tears
1052 eyen eyes **1053 thou wost** thou knowest **1053–1054 in
thought . . . Criseyde** Criseyde was never yet untrue in thought or deed
to Troilus **1056 it wreigh** covered it. **sighte sore** sighed sorrowfully
1057 o one **1060 of** i.e., after. **morwe** morning **1063 seen** see
1064 showers attacks **1065 herde** heard **1066 Have ye no care** i.e.,
don't you worry, you can be sure. **him . . . sleepe** he had no desire to
sleep **1067 it . . . yerde** i.e., it seemed to him no mere blow of a rod
in comparison **1068 seen** see **1069 well** very much **1070 tear . . .
asterte** tear that Criseyde allowed to escape **1071 strain** constrain
1073 come came **1074 wikke** wicked, evil **1075 biforn** before, earlier
1076 weened thought. **nas but lorn** was utterly lost, as good as lost

"O Pandarus," thought he, "alas, thy wile   1077
Serveth of nought, so welaway the while!"   1078

And therewithal he heng adown the head,   1079
And fell on knees, and sorwfully he sighte.   1080
What might he sayn? He felt he nas but dead,   1081
For wroth was she that should his sorwes lighte.   1082
But natheless, when that he speken mighte,   1083
Then said he thus: "God wot that of this game,   1084
When all is wist, then am I not to blame."   1085

Therewith the sorwe so his herte shette   1086
That from his eyen fell there not a tere,   1087
And every spirit his vigor in knette,   1088
So they astoned or oppressed were.   1089
The feeling of his sorwe, or of his fere,   1090
Or of aught elles, fled was out of town,
And down he fell all sodeynly a-swoon.

This was no little sorwe for to see;
But all was hushed, and Pandar up as faste.   1094
"O, nece, peace, or we be lost!" quod he,   1095
"Beth naught aghast!" But certain, at the laste,   1096
For this or that, he into bed him caste,   1097
And said, "O thief, is this a mannes herte?"   1098
And off he rent all to his bare sherte;   1099

And saide, "Nece, but ye help us now,   1100
Alas, your owen Troilus is lorn!"   1101

1077 wile guile   **1078 Serveth of nought** serves for nothing. **welaway** alas   **1079 heng adown** hung down   **1080 sighte** sighed   **1081 might he sayn** could he say. **nas but dead** was utterly dead   **1082 For . . . lighte** since she who should lighten his sorrows was angry   **1083 natheless . . . mighte** nevertheless, when he could speak   **1084–1085 God . . . blame** God knows that, when all the truth of this business is known, I will be found blameless   **1086 shette** shut down   **1087 eyen . . . tere** eyes not a tear fell   **1088–1089 And . . . were** and every spirit contracted its vigor, so stunned and oppressed were they. (The three spirits that controlled bodily function were associated with the heart, liver, and brain; when they shut down, as here, the result was a swoon.)   **1090 fere** fear   **1094 up as faste** was on his feet as fast as possible   **1095 nece** niece. **peace** be calm   **1096 Beth** be   **1097 For this or that** for one reason or another. **into . . . caste** threw him into the bed   **1098 thief** i.e., villain, scoundrel. (Here a term of affectionate abuse.)   **1099 off he rent** off he tore (Troilus' clothes)   **1100 but** unless   **1101 owen** own. **lorn** lost

"Iwis, so would I, an I wiste how,   1102
Full fain," quod she. "Alas, that I was born!"   1103
"Yea, nece, woll ye pullen out the thorn
That sticketh in his herte," quod Pandare,
"Say 'all foryeve,' and stint is all this fare."   1106

"Yea, that to me," quod she, "full levere were   1107
Than all the good the sun aboute goth."   1108
And therewithal she sware him in his ere,   1109
"Iwis, my deere herte, I am not wroth,
Have here my truth!" and many another oath;   1111
"Now speak to me, for it am I, Criseyde!"
But all for naught; yet might he not abreyde.   1113

Therewith his pous and palmes of his hondes   1114
They gan to frote, and eke his temples twain;   1115
And to deliveren him from bitter bondes,
She oft him kissed; and shortly for to sayn,   1117
Him to revoken she did all her pain.   1118
And at the last he gan his breath to drawe,
And of his swough soon after that adawe,   1120

And gan bet mind and reason to him take,   1121
But wonder sore he was abayst, iwis.   1122
And with a sik, when he gan bet awake,   1123
He said, "O mercy, God, what thing is this?"
"Why do ye with yourselven thus amiss?"   1125
Quod tho Criseyde, "Is this a mannes game?   1126
What, Troilus, wol ye do thus for shame?"

And therewithal her arm over him she laide,
And all foryaf, and ofte time him keste.   1129
He thanked her, and to her spake, and saide

1102–1103 Iwis . . . fain certainly I would if I knew how, most gladly
1106 all foryeve all is forgiven. **stint** stinted, ceased. **fare** ado
1107 full levere were would be far more desirable **1108 Than . . . goth**
than all the worldly wealth that the sun goes around **1109 him** i.e.,
Troilus. **ere** ear **1111 truth** troth, vow **1113 abreyde** awake
1114 pous pulse **1115 frote** chafe. **eke** also **1117 shortly . . . sayn**
to put it briefly **1118 revoken** recall (from his swoon) **1120 swough**
swoon. **adawe** awaken. (Literally, dawn.) **1121 gan . . . take** began to
gather his mind and reason to him better **1122 wonder** wondrously.
abayst abashed **1123 sik** sigh. **bet** better **1125 Why . . . amiss** why
do you wrong yourself so, behave so wrongly **1126 Quod tho** said then
1129 all foryaf forgave all. **keste** kissed

As fell to purpose for his hertes reste;
And she to that answerde him as her leste,   1132
And with her goodly wordes him disporte   1133
She gan, and oft his sorwes to comforte.

Chaucer wrote *Troilus and Criseyde* in about 1385–1387. Some sixteen manuscripts are extant, and we appear to have two Chaucerian readings in some lines. This selection, based on Corpus Christi College, Cambridge, ms. 61, has been lightly modernized in such a way as not to interfere unduly with Chaucerian pronunciation and scansion: *him* for *hym, yea* for *ye, thee* for *the, her* for *hire*, etc.

In the following, the departure from the original text appears in boldface; the original reading is in roman.

940 up first first up   **941 for the** for   **942 been** beth   **944 honor may have** may haue honour   **950 ease** eseth   **977 may other** may   **980 an** and   **1024–1025** [partially defective in ms. 61]   **1073 that** that that [the reading can be defended]   **1091 was** were **1106 stint is** stynte   **1115 eke** wete   **1131 hertes** herte

1132 as her leste as seemed pleasing to her   **1133 him disporte** to cheer him up

Further Reading

Adelman, Janet. " 'This Is and Is Not Cressid': The Characterization of Cressida." In *The (M)other Tongue: Essays in Feminist Psychoanalytic Interpretation,* ed. Shirley Nelson Garner, Claire Kahane, and Madelon Sprengnether. Ithaca, N.Y., and London: Cornell Univ. Press, 1985. Finding Cressida's inconstancy paralleled by an inconsistency in characterization, Adelman contends that the play traps an audience in Troilus' psychological need to split Cressida into a betrayer and an idealized, unthreatening lover. The split Troilus requires becomes part of our experience of the play as Cressida's character, initially psychologically complete and available to us, becomes opaque in Act 4, scene 4. Thus, our relationship with Cressida breaks down at the same point that Troilus' does, and the play itself enacts Troilus' fantasy.

Bayley, John. "Time and the Trojans." *Essays in Criticism* 25 (1975): 55–73. Rpt. in *Shakespeare, "Troilus and Cressida": A Casebook,* ed. Priscilla Martin. London: Macmillan, 1976. For Bayley, *Troilus and Cressida* strives for dramatic and intellectual effects different from those Shakespeare successfully achieves elsewhere; the play eschews the density of time and character that normally marks Shakespeare's art in favor of a disturbing insistence on present time detached from past and future. The play, according to Bayley, parodies traditional notions of representation and action as it presents a world in which all assurances of selfhood are dissolved.

Berry, Ralph. *"Troilus and Cressida." Changing Styles in Shakespeare.* London: George Allen and Unwin, 1981. In his study of how productions of Shakespearean plays have changed on the modern stage, Berry examines the post–World War II stage history of *Troilus and Cressida* as it reflects theatrical and intellectual movements of the last forty years. Until Peter Hall's 1960 production, Ulysses was usually taken as the moral center of the play; beginning with Hall, however, Ulysses has been seen as an example of the collapse of values, and his speech on "degree" as a self-serving strategy rather than a cultural norm.

Campbell, Oscar James. *Comicall Satyre and Shakespeare's "Troilus and Cressida."* Los Angeles: Huntington Library, 1938. Seeing *Troilus and Cressida* as Shakespeare's single experiment with the genre of "comical satire" invented by Ben Jonson and John Marston, Campbell first traces the development of the new literary form and then focuses on Shakespeare's adaptation of its themes and techniques. Once seen in its proper dramatic context, Campbell claims, *Troilus and Cressida* reveals its ethical dimension, emerging as a satire on the irrational and impassioned codes of love and war that threatened to disrupt the social order of the last years of Elizabeth's reign.

Coghill, Neville. *Shakespeare's Professional Skills*, pp. 78–127. Cambridge: Cambridge Univ. Press, 1964. Coghill devotes two chapters of his book to *Troilus and Cressida*: chapter four considers its early performances and texts as they cast light on its nature and meaning, and chapter five offers an analysis of the play's structure. For Coghill, the play is a tragedy of the fall of a great tradition of honor and faith before a new world of force and fraud, and it organizes the conflict between materialism and idealism so that our sympathies rest with the values and fate of Troy.

Foakes, R. A. "Shakespeare and Satirical Comedy." *Shakespeare, the Dark Comedies to the Last Plays: From Satire to Celebration.* Charlottesville, Va.: Univ. Press of Virginia, 1971. Attending to the dramatic context and shape of *Troilus and Cressida*, Foakes argues that the play reflects Shakespeare's use of satiric techniques learned from Ben Jonson and John Marston to explore and expand the satiric mode. The play, he finds, is the most balanced of the problem plays, exposing the inadequacies of the heroic and romantic action but preserving the ideals that are betrayed in the play.

Frye, Northrop. "The Reverse Side of Reality." *The Myth of Deliverance: Reflections on Shakespeare's Problem Comedies.* Toronto: Univ. of Toronto Press, 1983. In his study of the problem comedies as enactments of the "myth of deliverance" in which redemptive forces are released by forgiveness and reunification, Frye treats *Troilus and Cressida* as a play in which the ironic emphasis is too powerful to be redeemed by the comic drive. It is a play, Frye contends, that reveals, in its presentation of a disillusioning world of egotism and brutality, not the triumph of deliverance but the need for it.

Kermode, Frank. " 'Opinion' in *Troilus and Cressida.*" In *Teaching the Text*, ed. Susanne Kappeler and Norman Bryson. London: Routledge and Kegan Paul, 1983. Arguing that the play explores the gap between opinion and truth, Kermode first traces the development and semantic range of the word "opinion" and then examines how the term emerges as a preoccupation of the play. *Troilus and Cressida*, Kermode finds, organizes the tensions between opinion and truth into a complex structure that neither yields a simple ethical sense nor fits a particular genre.

Kernan, Alvin B. *The Cankered Muse: Satire of the English Renaissance*, pp. 194–198. New Haven, Conn.: Yale Univ. Press, 1959. Excerpt rpt. in *Shakespeare, "Troilus and Cressida": A Casebook*, ed. Priscilla Martin. London: Macmillan, 1976. In Kernan's seminal study of Renaissance satire, *Troilus and Cressida* appears as a play that explores and criticizes the satiric vision itself. Thersites' perspective represents an extreme, if typical, satiric view of a turbulent world, one that is discovered to be inadequate in the face of the play's dark power. Hector, Troilus, and Ulysses are no better able than Thersites to reform the world of the play, but their efforts, Kernan finds, are at least serious engagements with the world rather than projections of a diseased mind.

Kimbrough, Robert. *Shakespeare's "Troilus and Cressida" and Its Setting*. Cambridge, Mass.: Harvard Univ. Press, 1964. Kimbrough locates *Troilus and Cressida* in its theatrical and literary contexts and finds that the play embraces often contradictory conventions and concerns of both Shakespeare's own public theater and the private stage. The result is not always successful as drama, but the play's formal experimentation, Kimbrough finds, permitted Shakespeare to develop techniques necessary for the great tragedies and final romances, and produced a play that, by requiring its audience to view it in a detached, intellectual manner, seems peculiarly and powerfully modern.

Knight, G. Wilson. "The Philosophy of *Troilus and Cressida.*" *The Wheel of Fire: Interpretations of Shakespeare's Tragedy*, 1930. Rev. and enl., New York: Meridian, 1957. Finding in *Troilus and Cressida* a powerful conceptual unity, Knight argues that the play dramatizes the opposition of intellect and intuition. The Greeks and the Trojans represent opposing modes of human consciousness: the Greeks, rational, tending toward cynicism, and the Trojans, emotional, relying on romantic faith. Between these two modes, Knight finds, Troilus is caught, unable to choose between or reconcile them.

Knights, L. C. "The Theme of Appearance and Reality in *Troilus and Cressida.*" *Some Shakespearean Themes.* London: Chatto and Windus, 1959. Insisting that Shakespeare's exploration of the idea of appearance and reality is dramatic rather than discursive, Knights examines the play's deliberate presentation of the theme. For Knights, Greek "reason" and Trojan "idealism" are not opposed but complementary modes of apprehension, each subjected in the play to radical criticism for committing their adherents to the world of appearance and time.

Long, Michael. "The Comedy of Troilus and Cressida." *The Unnatural Scene: A Study in Shakespearean Tragedy.* London: Methuen, 1976. Provocatively assessing the tone of the play, Long maintains that *Troilus and Cressida* joins the tragic and the absurd, not as a "problem" play, but as a play demanding a derisive laughter that is itself a human value. The play, according to Long, forces an audience to laugh at the images of heroic and romantic pretension even when it is clear that real suffering will be the price of the human ineptness that has been revealed.

Ornstein, Robert. *The Moral Vision of Jacobean Tragedy*, pp. 240–249. Madison and Milwaukee: Univ. of Wisconsin Press, 1960. Ornstein treats the play not as comical satire but as a serious if disillusioned study of heroic and romantic aspiration. The play presents ironically and analytically the traditional concerns of tragedy, probing the conflict between the human desire for ideal values and the ego's willingness to accept decadent substitutes.

Presson, Robert K. *Shakespeare's "Troilus and Cressida" and the Legends of Troy*. Madison: Univ. of Wisconsin Press, 1953. Presson's account of Shakespeare's use of his sources in *Troilus and Cressida* centers mainly on his debts to Homer, William Caxton, and Thomas Heywood. Presson argues that Chapman's 1598 translation of seven books of the *Iliad* (and a portion of an eighth) was of central importance in shaping the theme, structure, and characterization of Shakespeare's play, and that study of the sources reveals the play's relationship to the concerns and dramaturgy of Shakespeare's tragedies.

Rabkin, Norman. "*Troilus and Cressida:* The Uses of the Double Plot." *Shakespeare Studies* 1 (1965): 265–282. Rpt. and rev. in *Shakespeare and the Common Understanding*. New York: The Free Press, 1967. Rpt. also in *Essays in Shakespearean Criticism,* ed. James L. Calderwood and Harold E. Toliver. Englewood Cliffs, N.J.: Prentice-Hall, 1970. Focusing on Shakespeare's use of the convention of the double plot in *Troilus and Cressida* to organize the play's complex theme, Rabkin examines the presentation of the love story and the military action as independent but parallel explorations of the subjectivity of value. The two plots are juxtaposed to reveal that value is not what is willed but what is winnowed by the flux of time.

Rossiter, A. P. "*Troilus and Cressida.*" In *Angel with Horns and Other Shakespearean Lectures,* ed. Graham Storey. London: Longmans, Green, 1961. Rpt. as "*Troilus* as 'Inquisition'*"* in *Shakespeare, "Troilus and Cressida": A Casebook,* ed. Priscilla Martin. London: Macmillan, 1976. Rossiter locates the play in the skeptical, Jacobean intellectual environment, engaged by the contradictions rather than the achievements of Renaissance individualism. We see the play as a subtle comedy of deflation; values are debased, as in each of the play's three actions characters consistently act without faith or honor, blinded to their own motives by egotism and impassioned will.

Shaw, George Bernard. "*Troilus and Cressida.*" *Shaw on Shakespeare,* ed. Edwin Wilson. New York: E. P. Dutton, 1961. In a paper presented in 1884 Shaw holds that

Shakespeare treats the play's Homeric material "as an iconoclast treats an idol," undermining the claims of heroic virtue that Shakespeare had endorsed in *Henry V* ("It was to expose and avenge his mistake and failure in writing *Henry V* that he wrote *Troilus and Cressida*"). Elsewhere, Shaw notes the modernity of Shakespeare's play: "We find him ready and willing to start at the twentieth century if the seventeenth would only let him."

Taylor, Gary. "*Troilus and Cressida*: Bibliography, Performance, and Interpretation." *Shakespeare Studies* 15 (1982): 99–136. Taylor's analysis of the two substantive texts of *Troilus and Cressida* (the 1609 quarto and the First Folio of 1623) reveals that the Folio version represents a more authoritative version, based on a promptbook of the original productions. Our interpretation of the play's tone and meaning, Taylor argues, is affected by the choice of text: the quarto's epilogue and placement of Troilus' rejection of Pandarus at the end produces a play more alienating and distanced than the Folio's experimental but clearly tragic drama.

All's Well that Ends Well, with (l. to r.) Marian Hailey as Diana, Barbara Barrie as Helena, and Jane Rose as Widow Capilet, directed by Joseph Papp in 1966 at the Delacorte Theater in Central Park.

ALL'S WELL
—THAT—
ENDS WELL

ALL'S WELL
THAT ENDS WELL

Introductory Material
Foreword by Joseph Papp
Introduction
All's Well That Ends Well
in Performance

THE PLAY

Supplementary Material
Date and Text
Textual Notes
Shakespeare's Sources
Further Reading

Foreword

All's Well That Ends Well is usually thought of as a difficult play. The "hero" of the play, Bertram, isn't someone
the audience exactly warms to—in fact, he's easy to dislike.
There are questions about Helena, the heroine, too; she is
dogged in her pursuit of him, but why she wants a cad like
Bertram is a mystery to us all. The Widow Capilet and Diana, who help Helena trick Bertram into her bed, aren't
particularly likable either. The whole play seems to have an
air of unpleasant realism about it, unlike some of the
lighter comedies such as *As You Like It* or *A Midsummer
Night's Dream*.

And yet for all of its drawbacks, *All's Well* is playable. Audiences like the bed trick, for everyone wants the snobbish
young Bertram to get his richly deserved comeuppance at
the end, especially after he tries to worm out of what he's
done. Parolles, that blustering braggart, that second-rate
Falstaffian poltroon, who barks loudly but bites not at all,
is entertaining. There is a funny scene where Bertram's soldiers kidnap and blindfold Parolles and talk gibberish to
him, a scene that works well on the stage and even engen-
ders some sympathy for him.

And in the end, though it's not easy, we just have to accept
Helena at face value: she wants Bertram, rogue though he
is, and that's that. It's as if Shakespeare is giving Bertram a
second chance here, just as he gives another chance to the
hypocrite Angelo at the end of *Measure for Measure*, to the
treacherous Oliver in *As You Like It*, and to the unforgivable
Proteus in *The Two Gentlemen of Verona*.

This belief that people can and will change really works
only in the comedies. Shakespeare can't apply this generosity to the histories, where unyielding historical fact determines who's executed, who's banished, and who's allowed
to survive. No, such humanizing forgiveness flourishes
only in comedy, where no factual restraints apply, and
where no character is so bad that he cannot undergo a process of reformation.

Joseph Papp

Joseph Papp gratefully acknowledges the help of Elizabeth Kirkland in preparing this Foreword.

Introduction

All's Well That Ends Well belongs to that period of Shakespeare's creative life when he concentrated on his great tragedies and wrote little comedy. The few apparent exceptions do not fit readily into conventional dramatic genres. *Measure for Measure* (1603–1604), usually called a problem play, is darkly preoccupied with human carnality and injustice. *Troilus and Cressida* (c. 1601–1602), printed between the histories and the tragedies in the Folio of 1623, is a disillusioning satire of love and war somewhat akin to the black comedy of our modern theater. *All's Well* shares to an extent the satiric and brooding spirit of these two plays. Its "bed trick," in which one woman is substituted for another in an assignation with the protagonist, Bertram, poses ethical problems for the audience (as does a similar trick in *Measure for Measure*). Helena, in arranging the substitution, may seem too much of a schemer. The relations between the sexes are problematic in this play, written as it seemingly was at a time when Shakespeare was preoccupied with tragedies that are haunted by images of destructive femaleness and of debasing sexuality. The action of *All's Well* is to a large extent controlled by an admirable and attractive woman, and yet the play dwells more than any previous comedy on the potential hazards of sexuality. For these and other reasons, *All's Well* is often grouped with the problem plays.

At the same time, the play also looks forward to Shakespeare's late romances, *Pericles*, *Cymbeline*, *The Winter's Tale*, and *The Tempest*. Here the mode of comedy turns toward the miraculous and tragicomic, with journeys of separation ending in tearful reunion, and sinful error ending in spiritual rebirth. This mode was not unknown in Shakespeare's comedies of the late 1590s: *As You Like It* ends with the sudden and implausible conversion of its villains, and *Much Ado about Nothing* offers forgiveness to the undeserving Claudio while restoring his traduced fiancée, Hero, to a new life. *Measure for Measure* follows a similar pattern of redemptive pardon for the corrupted Angelo and providential deliverance for Isabella. Both *All's Well* and

Measure for Measure contain features of this comedy of forgiveness, even if admittedly the ironies surrounding the gesture of forgiving are far less controlled than in the late romances.

Certainly, in any case, *All's Well* occupies a central position in the line of development from the early comedies to the late romances. Helena points back to earlier comic women in her role as engineer of the love plot, and forward to women of the late romances in her role as daughter, victim, and savior (though early comedy and late romance are, to be sure, not as neatly distinguishable as this antithesis suggests). Bertram, who is virtually without precedent in earlier comedies, anticipates to a degree Posthumus in *Cymbeline*, Florizel in *The Winter's Tale*, and Ferdinand in *The Tempest* in that he takes part in a marriage sanctioned and defined largely by paternal intervention. *All's Well*, like the romances and unlike the earlier comedies, affords a remarkably prominent role to the older generation.

The probable date of *All's Well* is consistent with such a transitional function. Its dates are hard to fix by external evidence, for it was neither registered nor printed until 1623, and allusions to it are scarce. Some scholars think that it is the *Love's Labor's Won* intriguingly mentioned by Francis Meres in *Palladis Tamia* in 1598, which Shakespeare might then have revised some time around 1601–1604. Portions of the play do feature the rhymed couplets, letters in sonnet form, and witty conceits that we normally associate with Shakespeare's early style. These old-fashioned effects may have been deliberate on Shakespeare's part, however, not unlike the anachronisms he later introduces in *Pericles* and *Cymbeline*. Certainly a major portion of the play dates stylistically from 1601–1604 or even later. Here the language is elliptical and compact, the images complexly interwoven, the verse rhythms free.

In any event, with its two contrasting styles poised between romance and satire, *All's Well* plaintively seeks comic reassurance amid the pessimistic ironies of Shakespeare's tragic period. It lacks many of the felicities we associate with the festive comedies of the 1590s: the love songs, the innocently hedonistic joy, the well-mated young lovers escaping from stern parents or an envious court. *All's Well* has too often been judged negatively for its failure to achieve a festive mood that Shakespeare probably did not intend it to have. The hero, Bertram, is undeniably a cad, and Helena is perhaps wrong to force Bertram to marry her against his will. As the undeserving hero forgiven in spite of his waywardness, however, Bertram plays an essential role in the play's problematic resolution—or failure to achieve complete resolution. He is, in the common Renaissance view of all mankind, unworthy of the forgiveness he receives, whereas Helena's generosity in forgiving him (however flawed by her aggressiveness) suggests at least a capability in mankind for decency and compassion. We are left, as in *Measure for Measure*, with a sense of the perennially unbridgeable gap between human ideals and their achievement, and yet we view this dilemma in a comic context where second chances and hope are bestowed even on those who appear to deserve them least.

The satiric mode in *All's Well* is conveyed chiefly through Lavatch the clown and through Parolles, the boastful cowardly knave who accompanies Bertram to the wars. Lavatch, with the bitter and riddling wit of the professional fool, gives expression to many of the satirical themes that are also illustrated by the exposure of Parolles. Lavatch jests about cuckoldry and the other marital difficulties that cause men to flee from women; he pokes fun at court manners, and apes the prodigal disobedience of his master Bertram. He is, like Parolles, called a "foulmouthed and calumnious knave" (1.3.56–57), although the inversion of appearance and reality is evident here as with all Shakespearean fools: Parolles is truly more fool and knave than his mocking counterpart. Parolles is all pretense. Full of sound, but hollow like the drum to which he is compared, he is a swaggerer and a fashionmonger whose clothes conceal his lack of inner substance. He is a recognizable satiric type that goes back to the Latin dramatists Plautus and Terence: the braggart soldier. He is, to be sure, endearing in his outrageousness; Shakespeare endows him with that vitality we find also in those earlier braggart soldiers, Falstaff and Pistol. Yet because Parolles lacks the self-awareness of Falstaff, we merely laugh at him rather than with him. To the impressionable young Bertram, hungry for fame, Parolles represents smartness and military style. Bertram rejects the true worth of Helena because she lacks family position and, ironically, embraces the false worth of a parvenu. Parolles and Helena are foils from their first encounter, when the braggart sardonically derides virginity as unnatural and out of fashion. Parolles stands opposite also to Lafew, the Countess, and the King, those dignified embodiments of a traditional chivalrous order, whose generous teachings Bertram rejects for the company of Parolles and of attractive young women. By disguising his slick insolence in the guise of fashionable manliness, Parolles is able to win Bertram's friendship for a time. Parolles is not really a tempter, for we never see him bending Bertram from his true inclination; rather, Bertram is himself too much in love with sham reputation, too rebellious against the civilized decencies of his elders. He is the Prodigal Son, or Youth in the old morality play, perversely eager to prove his own worst enemy.

Yet Bertram is not without a redeeming nobleness—he bears himself bravely in the Florentine wars—and cannot be fooled indefinitely by his roguish companion. The exposure of Parolles is one of satiric humiliation, like that of Malvolio in *Twelfth Night* or one of Ben Jonson's humorous gulls. The engineers of Parolles's exposure use the language of Jonsonian satire in their devices to outwit him: their game is a "sport" done "for the love of laughter," employing a snare whereby the "fox" or the "woodcock" will entrap himself (3.6.34–102 and 4.1.92). The device of public humiliation is particularly appropriate because Parolles is himself a railing slanderer, like Lucio in *Measure for Measure,* caustically brilliant in his invective but nonetheless a slayer of men's reputations. The punishment of ridicule fits his particular crime. His callous disregard for the good name of various French military commanders is parallel to Bertram's indifference to the public shame he has heaped upon his virtuous wife. Once Parolles's bluff has been called, Bertram is in part disabused of his folly; but other more wondrous and spiritual means are needed to convince him of the wrong he has done to Helena. Indeed, Bertram's very coldness in turning away from Parolles shows a lack of that humility, which he must learn by being tricked, exposed, and humiliated himself.

The fabulous romancelike aspect of *All's Well* is conveyed chiefly through its folktale plot and through the character of Helena. The story is derived from the third "day" of Giovanni Boccaccio's *Decameron,* a day devoted to tales of lovers obliged to overcome seemingly impossible obstacles in order to achieve love's happiness. The story was translated into English by William Painter in *The Palace of Pleasure* (1566). To win the nobly born Beltramo, Giletta of Narbonne must cure the French king with her physician-father's secret remedy and then must perform the riddling tasks assigned her by Beltramo as his means of being rid of her. Both these motifs have ancient antecedents in folklore, and, as in his late romances, Shakespeare puts great stress on the wondrous and improbable nature of these events.

All common sense warns against the likelihood of Helena's success. She is vastly below Bertram in social station or in "blood," even though she excels in "virtue." (This low station is unique among Shakespeare's comic heroines, and it contributes to what is so unusual about this play.) Her only hope is a desperate gamble: to cure the ailing King and so win Bertram as her reward. No one supposes at first she will even be admitted to the King, who has given up all hope of living; his "congregated college" of learned doctors "have concluded / That laboring art can never ransom nature / From her inaidible estate" (2.1.119–121). Helena transcends these rational doubts through resourcefulness and above all through a faith in help from above. She is willing to "hazard" all for love. She senses that her father's legacy will "be sanctified / By th' luckiest stars in heaven" (1.3.243–244), and she manages to convince not only the Countess and Lafew (persons who do not appear in Boccaccio) but also the King himself. Believing, like George Bernard Shaw's Saint Joan, that God will perform his greatest works through the humblest of his creatures, Helena inspires her listeners with faith in the impossible. Lafew is so moved by her simple eloquence that he proclaims to the King, "I have seen a medicine / That's able to breathe life into a stone" (2.1.73–74). Soon the King too is persuaded that in Helena "some blessèd spirit doth speak / His powerful sound within an organ weak" (ll. 177–178). Once the King's cure has been effected, even Parolles and Bertram must agree with Lafew that the age of miracles, long thought to have passed, is with them again. The King's cure by the "Very hand of heaven," through the agency of a "weak— / And debile minister," is matter for a pious ballad or an old tale (2.3.31–34). At the same time, Helena is very determined and is willing to use whatever means are necessary to get what she wants.

The impossible tasks Helena must perform are stated as riddles, as is usual in a folktale, and must be solved by riddling or paradoxical means. Bertram writes that she must "get the ring upon my finger, which never shall come off, and show me a child begotten of thy body that I am father to" (3.2.57–59). Such a challenge invites ingenuity, as in Boccaccio, but in Shakespeare the solution also requires providential aid. Helena's first sad response is to set Bertram free and renounce her audacious pretentions. Her pilgrimage of grief takes her to Florence, where Bertram happens to be serving in the wars. Is this mere coincidence, or conscious scheming on her part? Throughout, her motives are at once virtuous and deceitful, lawful and sinful, just as her very sexuality, so unlike that of earlier Shakespearean heroines, is wholesome and yet is seen by us in a context of debased human nature. Her acts are prompted at once by providence and by shrewd calculation. Even if providence must be credited with introducing her to Diana, the very lady whom Bertram is importuning in love, Helena makes the most of such opportunities afforded her, never doubting that "heaven" has "fated" her both to help Diana and simultaneously to serve her own turn (4.4.18–20). The bed trick is a "plot," but a virtuous one, a "deceit" that is "lawful," a deed that is "not sin, and yet a sinful fact" (3.7.38–47). Diana repeatedly plays upon these same riddles in accusing Bertram before the King: he is "guilty, and he is not guilty" (5.3.290).

The conundrums, although playful and entertaining in Shakespeare's highly complicated denouement (not found in Boccaccio), also hint at paradoxes in the nature of humanity. Bertram's typically human waywardness justifies a cunning response. "I think 't no sin," argues Diana, "To cozen him that would unjustly win" (4.2.75–76). Justice on earth, as in *Measure for Measure*, must take forms only roughly approximating those of heavenly justice, for human depravity sometimes requires a harsh remedy in kind. Yet by a providential paradox, humanity's thwarted and evil nature, seemingly so fatal, leads instead to regeneration: by being humbled, humanity is enabled to rise. "The web of our life is of a mingled yarn, good and ill together," says a sympathetic observer of Bertram. "Our virtues would be proud if our faults whipped them not, and our crimes would despair if they were not cherished by our virtues" (4.3.70–73). Human perversity accentuates the need for divine grace.

Helena is a romantic heroine, only metaphorically the "angel" who must "Bless this unworthy husband," reprieving him by her "prayers" from "the wrath / Of greatest justice" (3.4.25–29). Indeed, she is capable of being quite threatening to Bertram. If Bertram typifies the "Natural rebellion" of all youth, and Helena the "herb of grace" whom he has willfully rejected (5.3.6 and 4.5.17), Helena is also an aggressive woman whose clever plans to win Bertram against his will produce an understandable reluctance in the young man. Still, the spiritual overtones are not extraneous to this bittersweet comedy. However much we may sympathize with his desire to choose in love for himself, Bertram's revolt is incomprehensible to every witness except Parolles. Bertram himself confesses, too late it seems, that he has recognized Helena's precious worth. This note of "love that comes too late," wherein the penitent sinner confesses "That's good that's gone," hovers over the play with its tragicomic mood (5.3.58–61). Helena is a "jewel" thrown away and seemingly forever lost (5.3.1). The semblance of her death is in fact only another one of her inventive schemes, along with the bewildering contretemps of the final scene. Yet when she reappears, setting all to rights, she comes as "one that's dead" but is now "quick," alive again, merely a "shadow" of her former self (5.3.304–308). Bertram has not actually committed the evil he intended; by a providential sophistry he is innocent, like Claudio in *Much Ado* or Angelo in *Measure for Measure*, and so is reconciled to the goodness he has failed to merit. Even Parolles is given a second chance by the magnanimous Lafew. As the play's title implies, all might have miscarried through man's "rash faults" that "Make trivial price of serious things we have" (5.3.61–62), were it not for a forgiving power that can make humanity's worst failings an instrument of penitence and recovery. This resolution fleetingly comforts us in the final scene, even though it must do battle with such manifest imbalances as the prolonged shaming of Bertram and the scant attention paid to his reunion with Helena. The web of human life remains a mingled yarn.

All's Well That Ends Well
in Performance

No record exists of any performance of *All's Well That Ends Well* during Shakespeare's lifetime. The first of which we know, in fact, took place in 1741 at a theater in Goodman's Fields, London. The following year, the play was added to the repertory at the Theatre Royal, Drury Lane, with Theophilus Cibber as Parolles (to the great displeasure of Charles Macklin, who had to settle for the role of Lavatch). The fact that they fought over the role of Parolles and not Bertram suggests that eighteenth-century audiences, when they saw the play at all, saw a cut and revised version that concentrated on the play's satirical comedy. Playgoers and producers of that era evidently concurred in the judgment of Charles I, who had written "Monsieur Parolles" next to the play's title in his copy of the Second Folio. The actor and producer David Garrick continued this emphasis on the satiric and comic in his revival at Drury Lane in 1756, even assigning the epilogue to Parolles. John Bell's acting edition of 1775 made substantial cuts in order to focus on the bawdy of Parolles and Lavatch, the quarrel of Lafew and Parolles, and most of all the unmasking of the braggart soldier. Frederick Pilon's production at the Haymarket Theatre in 1785 so reshaped the play to accommodate the comic skills of John Bannister in the role of Parolles that the first three acts of Shakespeare's play were virtually eliminated. It was not until 1794 (at Drury Lane) that John Philip Kemble became the first leading actor to play Bertram, and even then his effort to refocus the play as the sentimental story of thwarted love was not a success.

In the nineteenth century, audiences generally found the morality of the play distasteful. Even an operatic version by Frederic Reynolds (the Theatre Royal, Covent Garden, 1832), with generous borrowings from other Shakespeare plays, such as a masque of Oberon and Robin Goodfellow (adapted out of *A Midsummer Night's Dream*) and various arias, including "Love is a smoke made with the fume of sighs" (*Romeo and Juliet*), "Sometimes lurk I in a gossip's bowl" and "Trip away, make no stay" (*A Midsummer Night's Dream*), and "If she be made of white and red" (*Love's Labor's Lost*), failed to overcome Victorian aversion for a tale of bed tricks and faithless husbands. Actor-manager Samuel Phelps, at the Sadler's Wells Theatre in 1852, took out the bed trick and other offensive material, but to no avail; the verdict seems to have been that the play was morally irredeemable. Theater managers knew when they were beaten and gave up entirely for over forty years. George Bernard Shaw reviewed the next production negatively (at the Irving Dramatic Club in 1895) and later concluded that the best parts of the play were simply too good and too modern for public taste.

The coming of the women's emancipation movement in the early twentieth century provided an opportunity to consider the play in modern terms as Shaw proposed. Directors Frank Benson, at Stratford-upon-Avon in 1916, and William Poel, in 1920, took up the challenge of viewing Bertram as a callow young man in need of redemption by a woman's means. It was Benson who first restored Shakespeare's text to the stage.

Tyrone Guthrie deserves credit for what may have been the play's first genuine theatrical success, in 1953 at Stratford, Canada, and then in 1959 at Stratford-upon-Avon. Guthrie set the play in Edwardian England, with the scenes of military action located in the North African desert. Helena (Irene Worth in Canada, Zoe Caldwell in England) was serious and purposeful, austerely dressed in black and with her hair set in a tight bun. Parolles's inquisitors were guerrilla soldiers with automatic weapons, while the officers sported jodhpurs and riding whips. In the Canadian production Alec Guinness played the French King in a wheelchair. Lavatch's role disappeared; Diana was a cockney tart who worked in a wartime factory and flirted with the soldiers. To a disillusioned postwar world, the perfidies of Bertram no longer seemed inexplicable and shocking, as they had to many Victorians.

Other directors have found ways in which *All's Well* can speak to modern audiences. Michael Benthall, in the Old Vic company's production in 1953, produced a farcical fairy tale, with a beautiful Claire Bloom as Helena (by way of Cinderella) and John Neville's Bertram as a callow

Prince Charming misled by Michael Hordern's Parolles (who dominated the performance not as a hapless boaster but, in the words of one reviewer, as a sort of "amateurish Mephistopheles"). Whereas this production used comic business to alleviate the play's bitterness, Noel Willman (Stratford-upon-Avon, 1955) chose to exploit it. In his version Lavatch was a hunchbacked dwarf; Helena, pertinacious and even aggressive, pursued Bertram with a thoroughness that gave new insight into the anxieties generated in this play about male unwillingness to cope with dominant women. In 1959, at Stratford, Connecticut, John Houseman directed the play as a moving tragicomedy, emphasizing the characters' unawareness of the implications of their willful behavior. John Barton's 1967 production for the Royal Shakespeare Company responded to the mood of the 1960s by accentuating the generational gap between youth and age and by taking an ironic view of war as a gentleman's game. The exposure of Parolles (Clive Swift) was remorseless, even cruel, that of Bertram (Ian Richardson) more understanding and comic. Trevor Nunn (Royal Shakespeare Company, 1981) explored the pre–World War era of Edwardian England from a later and disenchanted point of view; the military scenes suggested the Crimean War, while elder figures such as the Countess and Lafew were Victorian gentlefolk confronting an uncertain future of shifting social values. Bertram's ambivalent view of women was not sympathetically presented, and he was denied any final opportunity to redeem himself. David Jones's successful staging at Stratford, Canada, in 1977, with William Hutt (the French King), Margaret Tyzack (the Countess), Nicholas Pennell (Bertram), and Martha Henry (Helena), was movingly autumnal, opening with Lavatch sweeping dead leaves from the base of a sundial.

Symptomatic of this play's peculiar modernism, perhaps, is its success on television. No other production in the BBC Shakespeare series has succeeded better than *All's Well* under Elijah Moshinsky's direction. The intimacy of the camera does much to reveal the play's emotional energies and allows a kind of frankness that seems especially appropriate for a problem play about sexual anxiety.

On its original stage the play made little effort to exploit the spatial resources of the theater; there are few large scenes, a minimum of ceremony, no battle sequences (even the military action in this play is drama of comic intrigue), no demand for the gallery or discovery space or trapdoor. What Shakespeare's audiences thought of *All's Well* we do not know. Shakespeare seems to have written an understated, disturbing play, far ahead of its time and only now gaining the critical and theatrical recognition it deserves.

ALL'S WELL
—— THAT ——
ENDS WELL

[*Dramatis Personae*

COUNTESS OF ROSSILLION, *Bertram's mother and Helena's guardian*
BERTRAM, *Count of Rossillion*
HELENA (*or* HELEN), *orphaned daughter of the Countess's physician*
PAROLLES, *a follower of Bertram*
RINALDO, *a steward,*
LAVATCH, *a clown or fool,* } *servants of the Countess of Rossillion*
PAGE,

KING OF FRANCE
LAFEW, *an old lord*
Two FRENCH LORDS, *the brothers Dumain, later captains in the Florentine army*
Other LORDS
Two FRENCH SOLDIERS
A GENTLEMAN
A MESSENGER

DUKE OF FLORENCE
WIDOW CAPILET *of Florence*
DIANA, *her daughter*
MARIANA, *neighbor and friend of the Widow*

Lords, Attendants, Soldiers, Citizens

SCENE: *Rossillion; Paris; Florence; Marseilles*]

1.1   *Enter young Bertram, Count of Rossillion, his*
mother [the Countess], and Helena, [with] Lord
Lafew, all in black.

COUNTESS   In delivering my son from me, I bury a sec- 1
ond husband.

BERTRAM   And I in going, madam, weep o'er my father's death anew. But I must attend His Majesty's 4
command, to whom I am now in ward, evermore in 5
subjection.

LAFEW   You shall find of the King a husband, madam; 7
you, sir, a father. He that so generally is at all times 8
good must of necessity hold his virtue to you, whose 9
worthiness would stir it up where it wanted rather 10
than lack it where there is such abundance.

COUNTESS   What hope is there of His Majesty's amend- 12
ment? 13

LAFEW   He hath abandoned his physicians, madam, under whose practices he hath persecuted time with 15
hope, and finds no other advantage in the process but 16
only the losing of hope by time.

COUNTESS   This young gentlewoman had a father—O,
that "had," how sad a passage 'tis!—whose skill was 19
almost as great as his honesty; had it stretched so far, 20
would have made nature immortal, and death should
have play for lack of work. Would for the King's sake 22
he were living! I think it would be the death of the
King's disease.

LAFEW   How called you the man you speak of, madam?

1.1. **Location: Rossillion, i.e., Roussillon, in southern France, on the**
Spanish border near the Mediterranean. The Count's residence.
1 delivering sending (with play on "giving birth to" and "freeing")
4 attend obey   **5 in ward** (According to a feudal custom, the King
became the guardian of orphaned heirs to estates, who remained "in
ward" so long as they were minors. The King's jurisdiction extended
even so far as the bestowal of his ward in marriage, but only to someone of equal rank.)   **7 of** in the person of   **8 generally** to all people
9 hold continue to devote   **10 wanted** is lacking   **12–13 amendment**
recovery   **15–16 hath . . . hope** i.e., spends his days in painful treatment
in hope of cure   **19 passage** (1) phrase, expression (2) passing away
20 honesty integrity of character   **22 Would** if only

COUNTESS He was famous, sir, in his profession, and it
was his great right to be so: Gerard de Narbonne.   27

LAFEW He was excellent indeed, madam. The King
very lately spoke of him admiringly and mourningly.
He was skillful enough to have lived still, if knowledge 30
could be set up against mortality.

BERTRAM What is it, my good lord, the King languishes of?

LAFEW A fistula, my lord.   34

BERTRAM I heard not of it before.

LAFEW I would it were not notorious. Was this gentlewoman the daughter of Gerard de Narbonne?

COUNTESS His sole child, my lord, and bequeathed to
my overlooking. I have those hopes of her good that 39
her education promises her dispositions she inherits,
which makes fair gifts fairer; for where an unclean 41
mind carries virtuous qualities, there commendations
go with pity—they are virtues and traitors too. In her 43
they are the better for their simpleness; she derives her 44
honesty and achieves her goodness.   45

LAFEW Your commendations, madam, get from her
tears.

COUNTESS 'Tis the best brine a maiden can season her 48
praise in. The remembrance of her father never approaches her heart but the tyranny of her sorrows
takes all livelihood from her cheek.—No more of this, 51
Helena. Go to, no more, lest it be rather thought you 52
affect a sorrow than to have—   53

HELENA I do affect a sorrow indeed, but I have it too. 54

LAFEW Moderate lamentation is the right of the dead, 55
excessive grief the enemy to the living.

---

27 his great right i.e., his right in proportion to his greatness   **30 still**
(1) now as before (2) forever   **34 fistula** ulcerous sore   **39 overlooking**
supervision   **39–41 that . . . fairer** that her upbringing adds to her
inherited qualities, which will make her natural qualities even more
attractive   **41–43 where . . . pity** i.e., when an innately evil disposition is
given the accomplishments of a good education, in that instance praises
are mingled with regrets   **43 virtues and traitors too** i.e., accomplishments that serve evil purposes. **In her** i.e., in Helena   **44 simpleness**
purity, being unmixed with vice.   **derives** inherits   **45 achieves** i.e., by
her own efforts in response to her upbringing   **48 season** preserve (as
with salt)   **51 livelihood** animation   **52 Go to** i.e., come, come
53 affect enjoy, appreciate   **54 affect** feign   **55 right** rightful due

COUNTESS   If the living be enemy to the grief, the excess   57
makes it soon mortal.   58

BERTRAM   Madam, I desire your holy wishes.

LAFEW   How understand we that?   60

COUNTESS
Be thou blest, Bertram, and succeed thy father
In manners as in shape! Thy blood and virtue   62
Contend for empire in thee, and thy goodness
Share with thy birthright! Love all, trust a few,   64
Do wrong to none. Be able for thine enemy   65
Rather in power than use, and keep thy friend   66
Under thy own life's key. Be checked for silence   67
But never taxed for speech. What heaven more will,   68
That thee may furnish and my prayers pluck down,   69
Fall on thy head! Farewell.—My lord,
'Tis an unseasoned courtier; good my lord,   71
Advise him.

LAFEW   He cannot want the best   72
That shall attend his love.   73

COUNTESS   Heaven bless him! Farewell, Bertram.
                                                    [*Exit.*]

BERTRAM   The best wishes that can be forged in your   75
thoughts be servants to you! [*To Helena.*] Be comfort-   76
able to my mother, your mistress, and make much of   77
her.

LAFEW   Farewell, pretty lady. You must hold the credit   79
of your father.   [*Exeunt Bertram and Lafew.*]

HELENA
O, were that all! I think not on my father,
And these great tears grace his remembrance more   82

57–58 If . . . mortal if those who live resist excessive grief, the excess
will soon extinguish itself   60 How . . . that i.e., what holy wishes do
you desire (?)   62 Thy may thy (also in l. 63).   blood noble birth, inherited qualities; also passion   64 birthright inherited qualities   65–66 Be
able . . . use i.e., be powerful enough to keep your enemies in awe
without having to use that power   66–67 keep . . . key protect your
friend's life as you protect your own   67 checked reproved   68 taxed
for speech rebuked for idle talk.   will may bestow   69 pluck draw
71 unseasoned inexperienced   72 want the best lack the best advice
73 attend his love accompany my love for him   75 forged devised
76–77 comfortable comforting, serviceable   77 make much of be
devoted to   79 hold uphold.   credit reputation   82 his i.e.,
Bertram's (?)

Than those I shed for him. What was he like?   83
I have forgot him. My imagination
Carries no favor in 't but Bertram's.   85
I am undone; there is no living, none,
If Bertram be away. 'Twere all one
That I should love a bright particular star
And think to wed it, he is so above me.
In his bright radiance and collateral light   90
Must I be comforted, not in his sphere.
Th' ambition in my love thus plagues itself;
The hind that would be mated by the lion   93
Must die for love. 'Twas pretty, though a plague,   94
To see him every hour, to sit and draw
His archèd brows, his hawking eye, his curls,   96
In our heart's table—heart too capable   97
Of every line and trick of his sweet favor.
But now he's gone, and my idolatrous fancy   99
Must sanctify his relics. Who comes here?   100

　　　Enter Parolles.

[*Aside.*] One that goes with him. I love him for his sake;   101
And yet I know him a notorious liar,
Think him a great way fool, solely a coward.   103
Yet these fixed evils sit so fit in him   104
That they take place when virtue's steely bones   105
Looks bleak i' th' cold wind. Withal, full oft we see   106
Cold wisdom waiting on superfluous folly.   107
PAROLLES   Save you, fair queen!   108
HELENA   And you, monarch!

---

83 for him i.e., for my father when he died   **85 favor** (1) face (2) love
token   **90 collateral** distant, shed from a different sphere. (The different
Ptolemaic spheres were said to move collaterally, the implication here
being that the distance cannot be closed.)   **93 hind** female deer
94 pretty pleasing   **96 hawking** keen   **97 table** drawing board.   **capable** susceptible   **99 fancy** love   **100 sanctify** revere, worship   **101 his**
i.e., Bertram's   **103 a great way** in large measure a.   **solely** completely   **104 fixed** ineradicable, firmly established.   **sit so fit** are so
natural and plausible (in him)   **105–106 take . . . wind** find acceptance,
while virtue, in its uncompromising severity, is left out in the cold
106 Withal consequently   **107 Cold . . . folly** naked and unprovided
wisdom being forced to defer to overdressed folly   **108 Save** i.e., God
save.   **queen** (A hyperbolical compliment, which Helena answers in
kind, whereupon they both deny their titles.)

PAROLLES   No.

HELENA   And no.

PAROLLES   Are you meditating on virginity?

HELENA   Ay. You have some stain of soldier in you; let   113
me ask you a question. Man is enemy to virginity;
how may we barricado it against him?   115

PAROLLES   Keep him out.

HELENA   But he assails, and our virginity, though valiant, in the defense yet is weak. Unfold to us some   118
warlike resistance.

PAROLLES   There is none. Man setting down before   120
you will undermine you and blow you up.   121

HELENA   Bless our poor virginity from underminers and
blowers-up! Is there no military policy how virgins   123
might blow up men?

PAROLLES   Virginity being blown down, man will
quicklier be blown up. Marry, in blowing him down   126
again, with the breach yourselves made you lose your
city. It is not politic in the commonwealth of nature to   128
preserve virginity. Loss of virginity is rational in-   129
crease, and there was never virgin got till virginity was   130
first lost. That you were made of is metal to make vir-   131
gins. Virginity by being once lost may be ten times   132
found; by being ever kept, it is ever lost. 'Tis too cold   133
a companion. Away with 't!

HELENA   I will stand for 't a little, though therefore I die   135
a virgin.

PAROLLES   There's little can be said in 't; 'tis against the   137
rule of nature. To speak on the part of virginity is to   138

---

113 **stain** tinge   115 **barricado** barricade   118 **Unfold** reveal
120–121 **setting . . . you** laying siege (as though to a town, but with
bawdy quibbling that is elaborated in the following lines. To *blow up* is
to "explode with mines" and "impregnate.")   123 **policy** stratagem
126 **blown up** i.e., reinflated, given an erection.   **Marry** (A mild oath
derived from "by the Virgin Mary.")   126–128 **in blowing . . . city** i.e., in
satisfying his desire by making a breach in your virginity, you will be
forced to surrender entirely, paying the loss of your virginity for the
subsiding of his erection   128 **politic** expedient   129 **rational** (1) reasonable (2) of rational beings   130 **got** begotten   131 **That** that which.
metal substance (with idea also of *mettle*, spirit, temperament)
132–133 **may . . . found** i.e., may reproduce itself tenfold   135 **stand**
fight, stand up.   **die** (with probable quibble on "experience orgasm")
137 **in 't** in its behalf   138 **on the part of** in behalf of

accuse your mothers, which is most infallible disobe- 139
dience. He that hangs himself is a virgin; virginity 140
murders itself, and should be buried in highways out 141
of all sanctified limit, as a desperate offendress against 142
nature. Virginity breeds mites, much like a cheese,
consumes itself to the very paring, and so dies with 144
feeding his own stomach. Besides, virginity is pee- 145
vish, proud, idle, made of self-love, which is the most
inhibited sin in the canon. Keep it not; you cannot 147
choose but lose by 't. Out with 't! Within th' one year it 148
will make itself two, which is a goodly increase, and
the principal itself not much the worse. Away with 't! 150
HELENA   How might one do, sir, to lose it to her own 151
liking?
PAROLLES   Let me see. Marry, ill, to like him that ne'er 153
it likes. 'Tis a commodity will lose the gloss with lying; 154
the longer kept, the less worth. Off with 't while 'tis
vendible; answer the time of request. Virginity, like 156
an old courtier, wears her cap out of fashion, richly
suited, but unsuitable, just like the brooch and the 158
toothpick, which wear not now. Your date is better in 159
your pie and your porridge than in your cheek; and 160
your virginity, your old virginity, is like one of our
French withered pears—it looks ill, it eats drily. Marry, 162
'tis a withered pear; it was formerly better; marry, yet
'tis a withered pear. Will you anything with it?

139 infallible certain   **140 is a virgin** i.e., is like a virgin, since virginity
is a kind of suicide   **141–142 buried . . . limit** (Suicides were customarily buried at crossroads of highways, not in consecrated ground.)
144 paring covering rind   **145 his** its.   **stomach** (1) maw (2) pride
147 inhibited prohibited.   **canon** catalogue of sins. (Pride is the first of
the Deadly Sins.)   **Keep** hoard   **148 Out with 't** put it out at interest
150 principal original investment, i.e., the former virgin   **151 How**
what   **153–154 ill . . . likes** i.e., one must do ill, by liking a man that
dislikes virginity   **154 will** that will.   **gloss** gloss of newness.   **with
lying** with being unused (with quibble on "lying down")   **156 vendible**
marketable.   **the time of request** when there is demand   **158 unsuitable** unfashionable   **159 wear not** are not in fashion (i.e., brooches in
hats and the affectation of using toothpicks, once fashionable, are no
longer so)   **159–160 Your . . . cheek** i.e., the date does better as an
ingredient in cooking than as an emblem of withering in your cheek
162 withered pears i.e., objects of (sexual) appetite that have become
unappetizing through age and atrophy.   **eats drily** tastes dry

HELENA
　Not my virginity, yet . . .   165
　There shall your master have a thousand loves,   166
　A mother, and a mistress, and a friend,   167
　A phoenix, captain, and an enemy,
　A guide, a goddess, and a sovereign,
　A counselor, a traitress, and a dear;
　His humble ambition, proud humility,
　His jarring concord, and his discord dulcet,
　His faith, his sweet disaster; with a world   173
　Of pretty, fond, adoptious christendoms   174
　That blinking Cupid gossips. Now shall he—   175
　I know not what he shall. God send him well!
　The court's a learning place, and he is one—
PAROLLES What one, i' faith?
HELENA That I wish well. 'Tis pity—
PAROLLES What's pity?
HELENA
　That wishing well had not a body in 't   181
　Which might be felt, that we, the poorer born,   182
　Whose baser stars do shut us up in wishes,   183
　Might with effects of them follow our friends   184
　And show what we alone must think, which never 185
　Returns us thanks.   186

　　　　Enter Page.

PAGE Monsieur Parolles, my lord calls for you.   [*Exit.*]
PAROLLES Little Helen, farewell. If I can remember thee,
　I will think of thee at court.
HELENA Monsieur Parolles, you were born under a
　charitable star.

165 Not . . . yet the moment for surrendering my virginity has not yet
arrived (?). (There may be a textual omission here.)   **166 There** i.e., at
court   **167–173 A mother . . . disaster** (Helena here provides a catalogue of
various emotional relationships and paradoxical emotional attitudes.)
174 adoptious christendoms pet names   **175 blinking . . . gossips** blind
Cupid is godfather to, sponsors   **181–182 That . . . felt** i.e., that good
wishing does not have a tangible body which could be perceived by the
object (Bertram) of this wishing   **183 Whose . . . wishes** whose lower
births confine us to mere wishing   **184 Might . . . them** i.e., might with the
assistance of our fulfilled wishes   **185–186 show . . . thanks** achieve what
we can in fact only think, and for which we receive no thanks

PAROLLES   Under Mars, I.

HELENA   I especially think under Mars.

PAROLLES   Why under Mars?

HELENA   The wars hath so kept you under that you   195
must needs be born under Mars.

PAROLLES   When he was predominant.   197

HELENA   When he was retrograde, I think rather.   198

PAROLLES   Why think you so?

HELENA   You go so much backward when you fight.

PAROLLES   That's for advantage.

HELENA   So is running away, when fear proposes the
safety. But the composition that your valor and fear   203
makes in you is a virtue of a good wing, and I like the   204
wear well.   205

PAROLLES   I am so full of businesses I cannot answer
thee acutely. I will return perfect courtier, in the which   207
my instruction shall serve to naturalize thee, so thou   208
wilt be capable of a courtier's counsel and understand   209
what advice shall thrust upon thee; else thou diest in
thine unthankfulness, and thine ignorance makes thee   211
away. Farewell. When thou hast leisure, say thy pray-   212
ers; when thou hast none, remember thy friends. Get
thee a good husband, and use him as he uses thee. So,
farewell.   [*Exit.*]

HELENA

Our remedies oft in ourselves do lie,

Which we ascribe to heaven. The fated sky   217

Gives us free scope, only doth backward pull

Our slow designs when we ourselves are dull.   219

What power is it which mounts my love so high,   220

---

195 under down   **197 predominant** in the ascendant, ruling   **198 retrograde** moving backward (i.e., in a direction from east to west relative to
the fixed positions of the signs of the zodiac)   **203 composition** mixture   **204 of a good wing** strong in flight (and hence useful in rapid
retreat; with a quibble on a sartorial sense of *wing*, meaning "an ornamental shoulder flap")   **205 wear** fashion   **207 perfect** complete.   **in
the which** i.e., in which courtly behavior   **208 naturalize** familiarize;
also, deflower.   **so** provided that   **209 capable** receptive (with bawdy
double meaning, continued in *understand, thrust,* and *diest*)
211–212 makes thee away destroys, puts an end to you   **217 fated**
invested with the power of destiny   **219 dull** slow, sluggish   **220 so
high** to so exalted an object, i.e., Bertram

That makes me see, and cannot feed mine eye?   221
The mightiest space in fortune nature brings   222
To join like likes and kiss like native things.   223
Impossible be strange attempts to those   224
That weigh their pains in sense and do suppose
What hath been cannot be. Who ever strove   226
To show her merit, that did miss her love?   227
The King's disease—my project may deceive me,
But my intents are fixed and will not leave me.   *Exit.*

❖

1.2   *Flourish cornets. Enter the King of France,*
       with letters, and divers attendants.

KING
   The Florentines and Senoys are by th' ears,   1
   Have fought with equal fortune and continue
   A braving war.
FIRST LORD   So 'tis reported, sir.   3
KING
   Nay, 'tis most credible. We here receive it
   A certainty, vouched from our cousin Austria,   5
   With caution that the Florentine will move us   6
   For speedy aid, wherein our dearest friend   7
   Prejudicates the business, and would seem   8
   To have us make denial.
FIRST LORD   His love and wisdom,

221 That . . . eye i.e., that puts a desirable object in my mind but will
not let me feed my longings in his presence   **222–223 The . . . things**
i.e., natural affection causes those separated by the widest diversity in
social status to come together   **224–226 Impossible . . . be** extraordinary attempts (at surmounting social barriers) seem impossible to those
who too carefully calculate the extent and cost of their difficulties and
suppose something to be impossible which in fact has been done before (?)   •
227 miss fail to achieve

1.2. Location: Paris. The royal court.
1 Senoys natives of Siena.   **by th' ears** at variance, quarreling
3 braving war war of mutual defiance   **5 our cousin** my fellow sovereign of   **6 move** petition   **7 friend** i.e., the Duke of Austria   **8 Prejudicates** prejudges

Approved so to Your Majesty, may plead   10
For amplest credence.
KING   He hath armed our answer,   11
And Florence is denied before he comes.
Yet, for our gentlemen that mean to see   13
The Tuscan service, freely have they leave
To stand on either part.
SECOND LORD   It well may serve   15
A nursery to our gentry, who are sick   16
For breathing and exploit.
KING   What's he comes here?   17

Enter Bertram, Lafew, and Parolles.

FIRST LORD
It is the Count Rossillion, my good lord,
Young Bertram.
KING   Youth, thou bear'st thy father's face.
Frank nature, rather curious than in haste,   20
Hath well composed thee. Thy father's moral parts   21
Mayst thou inherit too! Welcome to Paris.

BERTRAM
My thanks and duty are Your Majesty's.

KING
I would I had that corporal soundness now   24
As when thy father and myself in friendship
First tried our soldiership! He did look far   26
Into the service of the time, and was   27
Discipled of the bravest. He lasted long,   28
But on us both did haggish age steal on,   29
And wore us out of act. It much repairs me   30
To talk of your good father. In his youth
He had the wit which I can well observe
Today in our young lords; but they may jest

---

10 Approved demonstrated, proved   **11 credence** belief.   **armed** fortified (against denial)   **13 for** as for.   **see** i.e., participate in   **15 stand**
serve, fight.   **part** side.   **serve** serve as   **16 nursery** training school.
sick longing   **17 For breathing** for want of vigorous exercise   **20 Frank**
generous, bountiful.   **curious** careful, skillful   **21 parts** qualities
24 corporal soundness physical health   **26 tried** tested   **26–27 did look
far Into** understood deeply, from experience   **27 service** military affairs   **28 Discipled of** followed by   **29 haggish** like a hag, malevolent
30 wore . . . act deprived us of ability to be active.   **repairs** restores

Till their own scorn return to them unnoted   34
Ere they can hide their levity in honor.   35
So like a courtier, contempt nor bitterness   36
Were in his pride or sharpness; if they were,   37
His equal had awaked them, and his honor,   38
Clock to itself, knew the true minute when   39
Exception bid him speak, and at this time   40
His tongue obeyed his hand. Who were below him   41
He used as creatures of another place   42
And bowed his eminent top to their low ranks,   43
Making them proud of his humility
In their poor praise he humbled. Such a man   45
Might be a copy to these younger times,   46
Which, followed well, would demonstrate them now   47
But goers backward.
BERTRAM   His good remembrance, sir,   48
Lies richer in your thoughts than on his tomb.
So in approof lives not his epitaph   50
As in your royal speech.
KING
Would I were with him! He would always say—
Methinks I hear him now; his plausive words   53
He scattered not in ears, but grafted them   54
To grow there and to bear—"Let me not live"—
This his good melancholy oft began
On the catastrophe and heel of pastime,   57
When it was out—"Let me not live," quoth he,   58

34 **unnoted** unnoticed   35 **hide . . . honor** i.e., cover their frivolous
jesting of youth with truly honorable action   36–37 **So . . . sharpness**
i.e., so like a true courtier as he was, he showed no contemptuousness
in his proper self-esteem nor bitterness of tongue in his sharpness of
wit   37 **if they were** i.e., if he ever spoke sharply   38 **equal** i.e., social
equal, not an inferior   39 **Clock to itself** i.e., self-governing.   **true**
exact   40 **Exception** disapproval   41 **obeyed his hand** i.e., said no more
than the hand of his clock of honor indicated, or than his own hand was
ready to maintain.   **Who** those who   42 **creatures . . . place** people of a
different (i.e., more elevated) station   43 **top** head   45 **In . . . humbled**
i.e., he humbling himself in the praise of them, poor though they were
46 **copy** model   47–48 **demonstrate . . . backward** i.e., show today's
young men to be inferior to him   50 **So . . . epitaph** i.e., the epitaph on
his tomb is nowhere so amply confirmed   53 **plausive** praiseworthy
54 **scattered not** did not strew haphazardly   57 **On . . . pastime** i.e., at
the drawing to a close of some sport (such as hunting)   58 **it was out**
i.e., the sport was over

"After my flame lacks oil, to be the snuff   59
Of younger spirits, whose apprehensive senses   60
All but new things disdain; whose judgments are   61
Mere fathers of their garments; whose constancies   62
Expire before their fashions." This he wished.
I, after him, do after him wish too,   64
Since I nor wax nor honey can bring home,   65
I quickly were dissolvèd from my hive   66
To give some laborers room.
SECOND LORD   You're loved, sir.
They that least lend it you shall lack you first.   68
KING
I fill a place, I know 't. How long is 't, Count,
Since the physician at your father's died?
He was much famed.
BERTRAM   Some six months since, my lord.
KING
If he were living, I would try him yet.—
Lend me an arm.—The rest have worn me out   73
With several applications. Nature and sickness   74
Debate it at their leisure. Welcome, Count;   75
My son's no dearer.
BERTRAM   Thank Your Majesty.
                              Exeunt. Flourish.

❖

1.3   *Enter Countess, Steward [Rinaldo], and Clown
          [Lavatch].*

COUNTESS I will now hear. What say you of this gentle-
    woman?

---

59 snuff burned wick that interferes with proper burning of the candle,
hence, hindrance **60 apprehensive** quick to perceive, keen but impatient **61–62 whose . . . garments** i.e., whose wisdom produces nothing
but new fashions **62 constancies** loyalties **64 I . . . too** I, surviving
him, wish as he did **65 nor . . . nor** neither . . . nor **66 dissolvèd**
separated **68 lend it you** give love (or perhaps *room* of l. 67) to you.
lack miss **73 The rest** i.e., my physicians **74 several applications**
various medical treatments **75 Debate . . . leisure** i.e., contend over my
condition at length

1.3. Location: Rossillion.

and all flesh and blood are, and indeed I do marry
that I may repent.   37

COUNTESS Thy marriage, sooner than thy wickedness.   38

LAVATCH I am out o' friends, madam; and I hope to have
friends for my wife's sake.

COUNTESS Such friends are thine enemies, knave.

LAVATCH You're shallow, madam, in great friends, for the 42
knaves come to do that for me which I am aweary of.
He that ears my land spares my team and gives me 44
leave to in the crop; if I be his cuckold, he's my 45
drudge. He that comforts my wife is the cherisher of 46
my flesh and blood; he that cherishes my flesh and
blood loves my flesh and blood; he that loves my flesh
and blood is my friend. Ergo, he that kisses my wife
is my friend. If men could be contented to be what 50
they are, there were no fear in marriage; for young 51
Charbon the Puritan and old Poysam the Papist, how- 52
soe'er their hearts are severed in religion, their heads
are both one—they may jowl horns together, like any 54
deer i' the herd.

COUNTESS Wilt thou ever be a foulmouthed and calum- 56
nious knave?   57

LAVATCH A prophet I, madam, and I speak the truth the
next way: 59

For I the ballad will repeat
Which men full true shall find:
Your marriage comes by destiny,
Your cuckoo sings by kind.   63

---

37 repent i.e., (1) atone for my carnal ways by making them legitimate
(2) regret marrying   **38 Thy marriage** i.e., you'll repent your marriage
(since proverbially hasty marriage leads to regret)   **42 shallow . . . in** a
superficial judge of   **44–45 He . . . crop** i.e., he that plows (*ears*) my wife
sexually takes the load off my *team*, my sexual organs, and provides me
with a *crop* of children   **45 in** bring in, harvest.   **cuckold** a man whose
wife is unfaithful   **46 drudge** menial laborer   **50–51 what they are** i.e.,
cuckolds   **52 Charbon, Poysam** (Corruptions of *chairbonne*, good meat,
and *poisson*, fish, the fast-day diets of Puritans and Catholics respectively.)   **54 both one** alike (in having cuckolds' horns).   **jowl** dash,
knock   **56 ever** always   **56–57 calumnious** slandering   **59 next** nearest, most direct   **63 kind** nature (i.e., cuckoldry is natural)

RINALDO   Madam, the care I have had to even your con- 3
tent I wish might be found in the calendar of my past 4
endeavors; for then we wound our modesty, and
make foul the clearness of our deservings, when of
ourselves we publish them. 7

COUNTESS   What does this knave here? Get you gone,
sirrah. The complaints I have heard of you I do not all 9
believe. 'Tis my slowness that I do not, for I know you
lack not folly to commit them and have ability enough
to make such knaveries yours.

LAVATCH   'Tis not unknown to you, madam, I am a poor
fellow.

COUNTESS   Well, sir.

LAVATCH   No, madam, 'tis not so well that I am poor,
though many of the rich are damned; but if I may
have your ladyship's good will to go to the world, Isbel 18
the woman and I will do as we may.

COUNTESS   Wilt thou needs be a beggar?

LAVATCH   I do beg your good will in this case.

COUNTESS   In what case?

LAVATCH   In Isbel's case and mine own. Service is no her- 23
itage, and I think I shall never have the blessing of 24
God till I have issue o' my body; for they say bairns 25
are blessings.

COUNTESS   Tell me thy reason why thou wilt marry.

LAVATCH   My poor body, madam, requires it. I am driven
on by the flesh, and he must needs go that the devil 29
drives.

COUNTESS   Is this all your worship's reason?

LAVATCH   Faith, madam, I have other holy reasons, such
as they are.

COUNTESS   May the world know them?

LAVATCH   I have been, madam, a wicked creature, as you

3–4 to . . . content to meet your expectations   4 calendar record
7 publish make known   9 sirrah (Form of address to a social inferior.)   18 go . . . world i.e., marry   23 case (with a bawdy pun on
"female pudenda")   23–24 Service is no heritage i.e., being a servant
gives me little to bequeath to my heirs   25 bairns children   29 needs
necessarily

COUNTESS Get you gone, sir. I'll talk with you more
anon.

RINALDO May it please you, madam, that he bid Helen
come to you. Of her I am to speak.

COUNTESS Sirrah, tell my gentlewoman I would speak
with her—Helen, I mean.

LAVATCH [*Sings*]
    "Was this fair face the cause," quoth she,   70
      "Why the Grecians sackèd Troy?
    Fond done, done fond,   72
      Was this King Priam's joy?"   73
    With that she sighèd as she stood,
    With that she sighèd as she stood,
      And gave this sentence then: 76
    "Among nine bad if one be good,
    Among nine bad if one be good,
      There's yet one good in ten."

COUNTESS What, one good in ten? You corrupt the   80
song, sirrah.   81

LAVATCH One good woman in ten, madam, which is a
purifying o' the song. Would God would serve the   83
world so all the year! We'd find no fault with the tithe-   84
woman if I were the parson. One in ten, quoth 'a? An   85
we might have a good woman born but or every blaz-   86
ing star or at an earthquake, 'twould mend the lottery   87
well; a man may draw his heart out ere 'a pluck one.   88

COUNTESS You'll be gone, sir knave, and do as I command you?

LAVATCH That man should be at woman's command,

---

70 fair face i.e., of Helen of Troy   **72 Fond** foolishly   **73 Priam's joy** i.e.,
Paris, son of King Priam of Troy   **76 sentence** maxim   **80–81 You . . .
song** (The song must have had one *bad* in ten, referring probably to
Paris as Priam's one bad son; but the clown indicates he is singing of
women, for whom one *good* in ten is a *purifying* or improvement.)
83 Would if only   **84–85 tithe-woman** (An allusion to the practice of
paying tithes, or a tenth part of one's farm produce, in kind rather than
in money. The parson ought to be satisfied with one good woman in
ten.)   **85 quoth 'a** said he, i.e., forsooth.   **An** if   **86–87 but . . . star** i.e.,
only as commonly as a comet appears   **87 mend the lottery** improve
the current odds   **88 pluck one** i.e., draw one good woman

and yet no hurt done! Though honesty be no Puritan, 92
yet it will do no hurt; it will wear the surplice of humility over the black gown of a big heart. I am going, 94
forsooth. The business is for Helen to come hither.

Exit.

COUNTESS Well, now.

RINALDO I know, madam, you love your gentlewoman
entirely.

COUNTESS Faith, I do. Her father bequeathed her to me,
and she herself, without other advantage, may lawfully make title to as much love as she finds. There is 101
more owing her than is paid, and more shall be paid
her than she'll demand.

RINALDO Madam, I was very late more near her than I 104
think she wished me. Alone she was, and did communicate to herself her own words to her own ears;
she thought, I dare vow for her, they touched not any 107
stranger sense. Her matter was, she loved your son. 108
Fortune, she said, was no goddess, that had put such
difference betwixt their two estates; Love no god, that
would not extend his might only where qualities were 111
level; Dian no queen of virgins, that would suffer her 112
poor knight surprised without rescue in the first as- 113
sault or ransom afterward. This she delivered in the 114
most bitter touch of sorrow that e'er I heard virgin ex- 115
claim in, which I held my duty speedily to acquaint
you withal, sithence, in the loss that may happen, it 117
concerns you something to know it. 118

92–94 Though . . . heart i.e., though my hearty good nature (my *honesty*)
is manly and impulsive (*no Puritan*), it will not offend authority; it will,
like the Puritan, hide its proud spirit (*big heart*) beneath the guise of
humble obedience. (The metaphor concerns those Puritans who de-
murred at obedience to some of the rubrics and canons pertaining to
public worship; some of them, to *do no hurt*, conformed in some respect
by wearing the surplice; nevertheless they wore it over the black Gene-
van gown customarily worn by Calvinistic Protestants on the Continent.)
101 make title lay claim **104 late** recently **107–108 any stranger sense**
any other person's sense of hearing **108 matter** theme **111 extend his
might only** exercise his (Love's) power except **111–112 qualities were
level** social rank was equal **112 Dian** Diana, goddess of chastity
112–113 suffer . . . surprised allow her hapless devotee to be captured
114 delivered spoke **115 touch** note **117 withal** with. **sithence** since
118 something somewhat

COUNTESS   You have discharged this honestly; keep it to   119
yourself. Many likelihoods informed me of this before,   120
which hung so tottering in the balance that I could neither believe nor misdoubt. Pray you, leave me. Stall   122
this in your bosom, and I thank you for your honest
care. I will speak with you further anon.

                                            Exit Steward [Rinaldo].

    Enter Helena.

Even so it was with me when I was young.
  If ever we are nature's, these are ours. This thorn   126
Doth to our rose of youth rightly belong;
  Our blood to us, this to our blood is born.   128
It is the show and seal of nature's truth,   129
Where love's strong passion is impressed in youth.
By our remembrances of days forgone,
Such were our faults, or then we thought them none.   132
Her eye is sick on 't; I observe her now.   133
HELENA   What is your pleasure, madam?
COUNTESS
You know, Helen, I am a mother to you.
HELENA
Mine honorable mistress.
COUNTESS   Nay, a mother.
Why not a mother? When I said "a mother,"
Methought you saw a serpent. What's in "mother"
That you start at it? I say I am your mother,
And put you in the catalogue of those
That were enwombèd mine. 'Tis often seen
Adoption strives with nature, and choice breeds   142
A native slip to us from foreign seeds.   143
You ne'er oppressed me with a mother's groan,   144

---

119 discharged performed   **120 likelihoods** indications   **122 misdoubt**
doubt.   **Stall** lodge   **126 these** i.e., these pangs of love (signs of which
the Countess sees manifested in Helena)   **128 blood** natural feeling,
especially *love's strong passion,* l. 130, and linked to the sexual suggestion of *thorn* and *rose* in ll. 126–127   **129 show and seal** sign and
guarantee   **132 or . . . none** i.e., though at the time we didn't consider
them faults   **133 on 't** with it   **142 strives** vies (in strength of attachment)   **142–143 choice . . . seeds** choice of a grafting or scion grown
from an unrelated stock makes wholly ours what was originally foreign   **144 with a mother's groan** i.e., in childbirth

Yet I express to you a mother's care.
God's mercy, maiden, does it curd thy blood
To say I am thy mother? What's the matter,
That this distempered messenger of wet,   148
The many-colored Iris, rounds thine eye?   149
Why? That you are my daughter?
HELENA   That I am not.   150
COUNTESS
    I say I am your mother.
HELENA   Pardon, madam;
    The Count Rossillion cannot be my brother.
    I am from humble, he from honored name;
    No note upon my parents, his all noble.   154
    My master, my dear lord he is, and I
    His servant live and will his vassal die.
    He must not be my brother.
COUNTESS   Nor I your mother?
HELENA
    You are my mother, madam; would you were—
    So that my lord your son were not my brother—
    Indeed my mother! Or were you both our mothers,   160
    I care no more for than I do for heaven,
    So I were not his sister. Can 't no other   162
    But, I your daughter, he must be my brother?   163
COUNTESS
    Yes, Helen, you might be my daughter-in-law.
    God shield you mean it not! "Daughter" and "mother"   165
    So strive upon your pulse. What, pale again?
    My fear hath catched your fondness. Now I see   167
    The mystery of your loneliness and find
    Your salt tears' head. Now to all sense 'tis gross: 169
    You love my son. Invention is ashamed,   170

148 distempered . . . wet immoderate tear   149 Iris Juno's messenger;
also the rainbow (which appears refracted in Helena's tears). rounds
encircles   150 not i.e., not daughter-in-law   154 note mark of distinction. parents ancestors   160 both our mothers mother of us both
162 So so long as   162–163 Can 't . . . daughter must it be that if I'm
your daughter   165 shield forbid. (But the construction with not is
ambiguous.)   167 catched caught. fondness love (of Bertram); or
foolishness. (The Countess speaks ambiguously while she tests Helena.)   169 head source. sense perception. gross palpable, apparent
170 Invention i.e., of excuses

Against the proclamation of thy passion,   171
To say thou dost not. Therefore tell me true,
But tell me then 'tis so, for look, thy cheeks
Confess it th' one to th' other, and thine eyes
See it so grossly shown in thy behaviors
That in their kind they speak it. Only sin   176
And hellish obstinacy tie thy tongue,
That truth should be suspected. Speak, is 't so?   178
If it be so, you have wound a goodly clew;   179
If it be not, forswear 't. Howe'er, I charge thee,   180
As heaven shall work in me for thine avail,   181
To tell me truly.

HELENA   Good madam, pardon me!

COUNTESS
Do you love my son?

HELENA   Your pardon, noble mistress!

COUNTESS
Love you my son?

HELENA   Do not you love him, madam?

COUNTESS
Go not about; my love hath in 't a bond   185
Whereof the world takes note. Come, come, disclose   186
The state of your affection, for your passions
Have to the full appeached.

HELENA [*Kneeling*]   Then I confess   188
Here on my knee, before high heaven and you,
That before you, and next unto high heaven,   190
I love your son.
My friends were poor but honest; so's my love.   192
Be not offended, for it hurts not him
That he is loved of me. I follow him not
By any token of presumptuous suit,   195
Nor would I have him till I do deserve him,

171 **Against** in the face of   176 **in their kind** in their natural way, i.e., by
weeping   178 **suspected** surmised (by me) rather than openly declared;
or, rendered suspect   179 **wound . . . clew** wound up a fine ball of thread,
i.e., snarled things up beautifully   180 **forswear 't** deny it under oath.
Howe'er in any case   181 **avail** benefit   185 **Go not about** don't evade
me.   **bond** i.e., maternal bond   186 **Whereof . . . note** which society
acknowledges   188 **appeached** informed against (you)   190 **before you**
more than (I love) you   192 **friends** kinfolk   195 **By . . . suit** with any
indication of my presumptuous love

Yet never know how that desert should be.
I know I love in vain, strive against hope;
Yet in this captious and intenible sieve   199
I still pour in the waters of my love
And lack not to lose still. Thus, Indian-like,   201
Religious in mine error, I adore
The sun, that looks upon his worshiper
But knows of him no more. My dearest madam,   204
Let not your hate encounter with my love   205
For loving where you do; but if yourself,
Whose agèd honor cites a virtuous youth,   207
Did ever in so true a flame of liking   208
Wish chastely and love dearly, that your Dian   209
Was both herself and Love, O, then, give pity   210
To her whose state is such that cannot choose
But lend and give where she is sure to lose;
That seeks not to find that her search implies,   213
But riddle-like lives sweetly where she dies.   214

COUNTESS
Had you not lately an intent—speak truly—
To go to Paris?

HELENA   Madam, I had.

COUNTESS   Wherefore?   216
Tell true.

HELENA
I will tell truth, by grace itself I swear.
You know my father left me some prescriptions
Of rare and proved effects, such as his reading
And manifest experience had collected   221
For general sovereignty; and that he willed me   222
In heedfull'st reservation to bestow them,   223

199 **captious** deceptive; also, capacious. **intenible** incapable of holding
201 **lack . . . still** still have enough to keep pouring without diminishing my
supply; also, continually lose. **Indian-like** idolatrously, like the savage
(who worships the sun) 204 **no more** nothing else 205 **encounter with**
oppose 207 **agèd honor cites** honorable old age bespeaks, gives evidence
of 208 **liking** love 209 **that** so that 210 **both . . . Love** i.e., both Diana
and Venus, chaste and passionate 213 **that . . . implies** i.e., what her
search is for 214 **riddle-like** paradoxically, with an unguessed mystery
216 **Wherefore** why 221 **manifest experience** i.e., the practice, in antithesis to the theory (reading) 222 **general sovereignty** general efficacy and
use 223 **In . . . them** to employ them only with the greatest care

As notes whose faculties inclusive were   224
More than they were in note. Amongst the rest   225
There is a remedy, approved, set down,   226
To cure the desperate languishings whereof
The King is rendered lost.   228

COUNTESS
This was your motive for Paris, was it? Speak.

HELENA
My lord your son made me to think of this,
Else Paris and the medicine and the King
Had from the conversation of my thoughts   232
Happily been absent then.

COUNTESS   But think you, Helen,   233
If you should tender your supposèd aid,   234
He would receive it? He and his physicians
Are of a mind: he, that they cannot help him,
They, that they cannot help. How shall they credit   237
A poor unlearnèd virgin, when the schools,
Emboweled of their doctrine, have left off   239
The danger to itself?

HELENA   There's something in 't
More than my father's skill, which was the great'st
Of his profession, that his good receipt   242
Shall for my legacy be sanctified
By th' luckiest stars in heaven; and would your honor 244
But give me leave to try success, I'd venture   245
The well-lost life of mine on His Grace's cure   246
By such a day and hour.   247

COUNTESS   Dost thou believe 't?

HELENA   Ay, madam, knowingly.   249

COUNTESS
Why, Helen, thou shalt have my leave and love,

224–225 As . . . note i.e., as prescriptions whose power was greater than
recognized   226 approved tested   228 rendered lost reckoned to be
incurable   232 conversation movement, train   233 Happily haply,
perhaps   234 tender offer   237 credit trust   239 Emboweled emp-
tied.   left off abandoned   242 that whereby.   receipt prescription
244 luckiest i.e., most able to confer luck   245 try success test the
outcome.   venture risk, wager   246 well-lost i.e., well lost in such a
cause, worthless otherwise   247 such a i.e., a specific   249 knowingly
knowing what I'm doing

Means and attendants, and my loving greetings
To those of mine in court. I'll stay at home
And pray God's blessing into thy attempt.   253
Begone tomorrow, and be sure of this:
What I can help thee to thou shalt not miss.   *Exeunt.* 255

253 into upon   **255 miss** be lacking

2.1 *Enter the King [in his chair] with divers young*
Lords taking leave for the Florentine war:
[Bertram] Count Rossillion, and Parolles.
Flourish cornets.

KING
Farewell, young lords. These warlike principles   1
Do not throw from you. And you, my lords, farewell.   2
Share the advice betwixt you; if both gain all,   3
The gift doth stretch itself as 'tis received   4
And is enough for both.
FIRST LORD   'Tis our hope, sir,
After well-entered soldiers, to return   6
And find Your Grace in health.
KING
No, no, it cannot be; and yet my heart
Will not confess he owes the malady   9
That doth my life besiege. Farewell, young lords.
Whether I live or die, be you the sons
Of worthy Frenchmen. Let higher Italy—   12
Those bated that inherit but the fall   13
Of the last monarchy—see that you come   14
Not to woo honor, but to wed it. When   15
The bravest questant shrinks, find what you seek,   16
That fame may cry you loud. I say, farewell.   17
SECOND LORD
Health at your bidding serve Your Majesty!
KING
Those girls of Italy, take heed of them.
They say our French lack language to deny

2.1. Location: Paris. The royal court.
1 **These warlike principles** this military advice   2 **Do . . . you** i.e.,
remember   3 **if . . . all** i.e., if both groups (one going to the aid of
Florence, one of Siena) wish to follow all of my advice   4 **as 'tis re-**
ceived i.e., to accommodate the demand   6 **After . . . soldiers** after
having become seasoned soldiers; or, in the manner of experienced
soldiers   9 **owes** owns   12 **higher Italy** (1) the knightly class of Italy,
corresponding to *worthy Frenchmen,* or (2) Tuscany, of which Florence
and Siena are cities   13–14 **Those . . . monarchy** i.e., except those who
have merely profited as upstarts by recent engagements involving the
fall of a monarchy (?)   15 **woo** flirt with.   **wed** possess as your own
16 **questant** seeker   17 **cry you loud** proclaim you loudly

If they demand. Beware of being captives   21
Before you serve.

BOTH   Our hearts receive your warnings.

KING
Farewell.—Come hither to me. [*The King converses
privately with various lords; Bertram and his companions move apart.*]

FIRST LORD
O my sweet lord, that you will stay behind us!

PAROLLES
'Tis not his fault, the spark.

SECOND LORD   O, 'tis brave wars!   25

PAROLLES   Most admirable. I have seen those wars.

BERTRAM   I am commanded here and kept a coil with   27
"Too young," and "The next year," and "'Tis too early."

PAROLLES   An thy mind stand to 't, boy, steal away   29
bravely.   30

BERTRAM
I shall stay here the forehorse to a smock,   31
Creaking my shoes on the plain masonry,   32
Till honor be bought up and no sword worn   33
But one to dance with. By heaven, I'll steal away!   34

FIRST LORD
There's honor in the theft.

PAROLLES   Commit it, Count.

SECOND LORD
I am your accessory; and so, farewell.

BERTRAM   I grow to you, and our parting is a tortured   37
body.   38

FIRST LORD   Farewell, Captain.

SECOND LORD   Sweet Monsieur Parolles!

PAROLLES   Noble heroes, my sword and yours are kin.

21 captives i.e., to love   **25 spark** elegant young man.   **brave** splendid
27 here i.e., to remain here.   **kept a coil** pestered, fussed over   **29 An**
if   **30 bravely** (1) worthily (2) valiantly   **31 forehorse . . . smock** the lead
horse of a team driven by a woman   **32 plain masonry** smooth masonry
floor (instead of a battlefield)   **33 Till . . . up** till opportunity for winning honor in the wars is past, all consumed   **34 one . . . with** i.e., a
light ornamental weapon   **37 grow to** grow deeply attached to, become
as one with   **37–38 a tortured body** i.e., as painful as a body being torn
apart by torture

Good sparks and lustrous, a word, good metals: you   42
shall find in the regiment of the Spinii one Captain
Spurio, with his cicatrice, an emblem of war, here on   44
his sinister cheek; it was this very sword entrenched it.   45
Say to him I live, and observe his reports for me.   46

FIRST LORD   We shall, noble Captain.

PAROLLES   Mars dote on you for his novices!   48

　　　　　　　　　　　　　　　　　　 [*Exeunt Lords.*]

[*To Bertram.*]   What will ye do?

BERTRAM   Stay the King.   50

PAROLLES [*To Bertram*]   Use a more spacious ceremony   51
to the noble lords; you have restrained yourself within
the list of too cold an adieu. Be more expressive to   53
them, for they wear themselves in the cap of the time;   54
there do muster true gait, eat, speak, and move under   55
the influence of the most received star; and, though the   56
devil lead the measure, such are to be followed. After   57
them, and take a more dilated farewell.   58

BERTRAM   And I will do so.

PAROLLES   Worthy fellows, and like to prove most sin-   60
ewy swordmen.　　　 *Exeunt* [*Bertram and Parolles*].   61

　　　Enter Lafew [*and approaches the King*].

LAFEW [*Kneeling*]
Pardon, my lord, for me and for my tidings.   62

KING   I'll fee thee to stand up.   63

LAFEW [*Rising*]
Then here's a man stands that has brought his pardon.   64
I would you had kneeled, my lord, to ask me mercy,
And that at my bidding you could so stand up.

---

42 metals i.e., "blades"; spirits of mettle   **44 Spurio** (This name suggests "spurious," "counterfeit.")   **cicatrice** scar   **45 sinister** left
46 reports reply   **48 Mars** may Mars.   **novices** devotees   **50 Stay the
King** support or wait on the King. (But also interpreted, with different
punctuation, as "Stay; the King wills it" or "Stay; the King approaches.")   **51 spacious ceremony** effusive courtesy   **53 list** boundary   **54 wear . . . time** stand out as ornaments of the fashionable
world   **55 muster true gait** set the right pace   **56 received** fashionable   **57 measure** dance   **58 dilated** protracted; expansive   **60 like**
likely   **60–61 sinewy** energetic, forceful   **62 tidings** news, information   **63 I'll . . . up** i.e., I bid you rise; or, I will rather reward you for
rising   **64 pardon** i.e., something to win the King's indulgence

KING

    I would I had, so I had broke thy pate   67

    And asked thee mercy for 't.

LAFEW   Good faith, across!   68

    But, my good lord, 'tis thus: will you be cured

    Of your infirmity?

KING   No.

LAFEW   O, will you eat   70

    No grapes, my royal fox? Yes, but you will   71

    My noble grapes, an if my royal fox   72

    Could reach them. I have seen a medicine   73

    That's able to breathe life into a stone,

    Quicken a rock, and make you dance canary   75

    With sprightly fire and motion, whose simple touch

    Is powerful to araise King Pepin, nay,   77

    To give great Charlemagne a pen in 's hand

    And write to her a love line.

KING   What "her" is this?   79

LAFEW

    Why, Doctor She! My lord, there's one arrived,

    If you will see her. Now by my faith and honor,

    If seriously I may convey my thoughts

    In this my light deliverance, I have spoke   83

    With one that in her sex, her years, profession,   84

    Wisdom, and constancy hath amazed me more   85

    Than I dare blame my weakness. Will you see her,   86

    For that is her demand, and know her business?

    That done, laugh well at me.

KING   Now, good Lafew,

67–68 so . . . for 't i.e., that would be like wounding you on the head and begging your pardon for it   **68 across** i.e., a weak jest. (A metaphor derived from tilting, where to break a lance *across* an opponent was to strike awkwardly and ineffectively instead of directly with the point.) **70–71 will . . . fox** i.e., will you be like the fox in Aesop's fable and call the grapes sour because they are beyond your reach   **72 an if** if **73 medicine** i.e., physician   **75 Quicken** bring to life.   **canary** a lively Spanish dance   **77 araise** raise from the dead.   **King Pepin** French king of the eighth century, father of Charlemagne   **79 love line** (Some of Lafew's terms, such as *stone, quicken, fire and motion, touch, araise,* and *pen in 's hand,* have possible erotic undertones that link recovery to restored potency.)   **83 light deliverance** frivolous utterance   **84 profession** what she professes to be able to do   **85–86 more . . . weakness** more than I can attribute to my feebleness or susceptibility as an old man

Bring in the admiration, that we with thee   89
May spend our wonder too, or take off thine   90
By wondering how thou took'st it.
LAFEW   Nay, I'll fit you,   91
And not be all day neither.   [*He goes to the door.*]
KING
Thus he his special nothing ever prologues.   93
LAFEW   Nay, come your ways.   94

    Enter Helena.

KING   This haste hath wings indeed.
LAFEW   Nay, come your ways.
This is His Majesty; say your mind to him.
A traitor you do look like, but such traitors
His Majesty seldom fears. I am Cressid's uncle,   99
That dare leave two together. Fare you well.   *Exit.*
KING
Now, fair one, does your business follow us?   101
HELENA   Ay, my good lord.
Gerard de Narbonne was my father;
In what he did profess, well found.
KING   I knew him.   104
HELENA
The rather will I spare my praises towards him;
Knowing him is enough. On 's bed of death
Many receipts he gave me; chiefly one,   107
Which, as the dearest issue of his practice,   108
And of his old experience th' only darling,
He bade me store up as a triple eye,   110
Safer than mine own two, more dear. I have so;   111
And, hearing Your High Majesty is touched
With that malignant cause wherein the honor   113
Of my dear father's gift stands chief in power,   114

---

89 admiration wonder   **90 spend** expend.   **take off** dispel   **91 took'st**
conceived (with a play on *take* in the previous line).   **fit** satisfy
93 special nothing particular trifles.   **prologues** introduces   **94 come
your ways** come along   **99 Cressid's uncle** Pandarus, go-between for the
lovers Troilus and Cressida   **101 follow** concern   **104 well found** i.e., to
be good   **107 receipts** remedies   **108 issue** product   **110 triple** third
111 Safer more safely   **113–114 cause . . . power** disease for which my
father's remedy is most particularly effective

I come to tender it and my appliance   115
With all bound humbleness.

KING   We thank you, maiden,   116
But may not be so credulous of cure   117
When our most learnèd doctors leave us and
The congregated college have concluded   119
That laboring art can never ransom nature   120
From her inaidible estate. I say we must not
So stain our judgment, or corrupt our hope,   122
To prostitute our past-cure malady   123
To empirics, or to dissever so   124
Our great self and our credit, to esteem   125
A senseless help when help past sense we deem.   126

HELENA
My duty then shall pay me for my pains.   127
I will no more enforce mine office on you,   128
Humbly entreating from your royal thoughts
A modest one to bear me back again.   130

KING
I cannot give thee less, to be called grateful.
Thou thought'st to help me, and such thanks I give
As one near death to those that wish him live.
But what at full I know, thou know'st no part,   134
I knowing all my peril, thou no art.

HELENA
What I can do can do no hurt to try,
Since you set up your rest 'gainst remedy.   137
He that of greatest works is finisher
Oft does them by the weakest minister.
So holy writ in babes hath judgment shown,

115 **tender** offer. **appliance** treatment   **116 bound** dutiful
117 credulous of ready to believe in   **119 congregated college** college of
physicians   **120 art** skill, i.e., medicine   **122 stain** pervert   **123 prostitute** submit, subject   **124 empirics** quack doctors   **124–125 dissever . . .
credit** divorce thus my kingly self from my reputation, or from my
faith   **125 esteem** value, put faith in   **126 A senseless help** unreasona-
ble treatment.   **past sense** beyond reason   **127 My duty** i.e., having
tried to do my duty   **128 office** dutiful service   **130 A modest one** i.e.,
a favorable regard commensurate with my humble station, and with my
maidenly modesty.   **bear me back** bear back with me   **134 no part** not
at all   **137 set . . . rest** stake your all. (A figure from gambling.)

When judges have been babes; great floods have flown   141
From simple sources, and great seas have dried   142
When miracles have by the great'st been denied.
Oft expectation fails, and most oft there
Where most it promises, and oft it hits   145
Where hope is coldest and despair most fits.

KING
I must not hear thee. Fare thee well, kind maid.
Thy pains, not used, must by thyself be paid;   148
Proffers not took reap thanks for their reward.   149

HELENA
Inspirèd merit so by breath is barred.   150
It is not so with Him that all things knows
As 'tis with us that square our guess by shows;   152
But most it is presumption in us when
The help of heaven we count the act of men.   154
Dear sir, to my endeavors give consent!
Of heaven, not me, make an experiment.   156
I am not an impostor that proclaim   157
Myself against the level of mine aim;   158
But know I think, and think I know most sure,
My art is not past power, nor you past cure.   160

KING
Art thou so confident? Within what space   161
Hop'st thou my cure?

HELENA   The great'st grace lending grace,   162
Ere twice the horses of the sun shall bring
Their fiery torcher his diurnal ring,   164
Ere twice in murk and occidental damp   165

---

141 babes i.e., babyish, foolish. (The inversion of babes and wise men appears several times in the New Testament.)   **142 simple** small, insignificant   **145 hits** succeeds, is confirmed   **148 by . . . paid** i.e., be their own reward   **149 thanks** i.e., nothing but thanks   **150 Inspirèd . . . barred** divinely inspired virtue is thus denied by mere spoken words   **152 square . . . shows** support our conjectures on the basis of appearances   **154 count** account   **156 experiment** trial   **157–158 proclaim . . . aim** claim something other than what I aim to accomplish   **160 My . . . power** my professed skill (as a doctor) is not beyond my range of ability   **161 space** period of time   **162 Hop'st thou** do you hope for.
great'st grace divine grace (i.e., with God's help)   **164 torcher** torchbearer.   **diurnal ring** daily round   **165 occidental** western, sunset

Moist Hesperus hath quenched her sleepy lamp,   166
Or four-and-twenty times the pilot's glass   167
Hath told the thievish minutes how they pass,
What is infirm from your sound parts shall fly,
Health shall live free, and sickness freely die.

KING
Upon thy certainty and confidence
What dar'st thou venture?   Tax of impudence,   172
HELENA
A strumpet's boldness, a divulgèd shame
Traduced by odious ballads; my maiden's name   174
Seared otherwise; nay, worse of worst, extended   175
With vilest torture let my life be ended.

KING
Methinks in thee some blessèd spirit doth speak
His powerful sound within an organ weak;
And what impossibility would slay   179
In common sense, sense saves another way.   180
Thy life is dear, for all that life can rate   181
Worth name of life in thee hath estimate: 182
Youth, beauty, wisdom, courage, all
That happiness and prime can happy call.   184
Thou this to hazard needs must intimate   185
Skill infinite, or monstrous desperate.   186
Sweet practicer, thy physic I will try,   187
That ministers thine own death if I die.   188

HELENA
If I break time or flinch in property   189
Of what I spoke, unpitied let me die,
And well deserved. Not helping, death's my fee;   191
But, if I help, what do you promise me?

166 **Hesperus** evening star (actually Venus)   167 **glass** hourglass
172 **venture** risk, wager.   **Tax** accusation   174 **Traduced** slandered
175 **Seared** branded.   **otherwise** in other ways as well.   **extended**
stretched out on the rack; or, drawn out in time   179–180 **what . . . way**
what common sense would regard as impossible, a higher sense (faith)
can regard as possible   181 **rate** value, consider   182 **hath estimate**
must be reckoned present   184 **happiness** good fortune.   **prime**
youth   185 **Thou . . . intimate** that you are prepared to hazard all this
argues   186 **monstrous desperate** (that you are) extremely reckless
187 **physic** medicine   188 **ministers** administers   189 **break** infringe,
fail to keep.   **flinch in property** fall short in any detail   191 **Not helping** i.e., if I do not help

KING
  Make thy demand.
HELENA   But will you make it even?   193
KING
  Ay, by my scepter and my hopes of heaven.
HELENA
  Then shalt thou give me with thy kingly hand
  What husband in thy power I will command.
  Exempted be from me the arrogance
  To choose from forth the royal blood of France,
  My low and humble name to propagate
  With any branch or image of thy state;
  But such a one, thy vassal, whom I know
  Is free for me to ask, thee to bestow.
KING
  Here is my hand. The premises observed,
  Thy will by my performance shall be served.
  So make the choice of thy own time, for I,
  Thy resolved patient, on thee still rely.   206
  More should I question thee, and more I must—
  Though more to know could not be more to trust—
  From whence thou cam'st, how tended on; but rest   209
  Unquestioned welcome and undoubted blest.—   210
  Give me some help here, ho!—If thou proceed
  As high as word, my deed shall match thy meed.   212
              Flourish. Exeunt, [the King carried in].

                          ❖

2.2   *Enter Countess and Clown [Lavatch].*

COUNTESS   Come on, sir; I shall now put you to the   1
  height of your breeding.   2
LAVATCH   I will show myself highly fed and lowly taught. 3
  I know my business is but to the court.

---

193 make it even carry it out   **206 still** continually   **209 tended on**
attended   **210 Unquestioned** (1) without being questioned (2) unquestionably   **212 high as word** fully as you have promised.   **meed** merit

2.2. Location: Rossillion.
1–2 put . . . breeding test your good manners   **3 highly . . . taught**
overfed and underdisciplined. ("Better fed than taught" was proverbial
for a spoiled child.)

COUNTESS To the court? Why, what place make you 5
special, when you put off that with such contempt? 6
But to the court!

LAVATCH Truly, madam, if God have lent a man any
manners, he may easily put it off at court. He that can- 9
not make a leg, put off 's cap, kiss his hand, and say 10
nothing has neither leg, hands, lip, nor cap; and indeed such a fellow, to say precisely, were not for the
court. But for me, I have an answer will serve all men.

COUNTESS Marry, that's a bountiful answer that fits all
questions.

LAVATCH It is like a barber's chair that fits all buttocks:
the pin-buttock, the quatch-buttock, the brawn-buttock, 17
or any buttock.

COUNTESS Will your answer serve fit to all questions?

LAVATCH As fit as ten groats is for the hand of an attor- 20
ney, as your French crown for your taffety punk, as 21
Tib's rush for Tom's forefinger, as a pancake for 22
Shrove Tuesday, a morris for May Day, as the nail to 23
his hole, the cuckold to his horn, as a scolding quean 24
to a wrangling knave, as the nun's lip to the friar's
mouth, nay, as the pudding to his skin. 26

COUNTESS Have you, I say, an answer of such fitness
for all questions?

LAVATCH From below your duke to beneath your constable, it will fit any question.

COUNTESS It must be an answer of most monstrous size
that must fit all demands.

LAVATCH But a trifle neither, in good faith, if the learned 33
should speak truth of it. Here it is, and all that belongs
to 't. Ask me if I am a courtier; it shall do you no harm
to learn.

5–6 make you special do you consider special   **6 put off** dismiss   **9 put
it off** carry it off   **10 leg** respectful bow   **17 pin** narrow, pointed.
quatch fat, wide.   **brawn** hefty, fleshy   **20 ten groats** forty pence
21 French crown (1) coin (2) *corona veneris*, a scab on the head symptomatic of syphilis, the "French disease."   **taffety punk** prostitute finely
dressed   **22 Tib's rush** (Refers to a folk custom of exchanging rings
made of rushes in a marriage without benefit of clergy.)   **pancake**
(Traditionally eaten as a last feast on the final day before Lent, Shrove
Tuesday.)   **23 morris** morris dance, country dance common at May Day
celebrations   **24 his** its.   **quean** wench   **26 pudding** sausage   **33 But
. . . neither** on the contrary, it's only a trifle

COUNTESS To be young again, if we could! I will be a
fool in question, hoping to be the wiser by your answer. I pray you, sir, are you a courtier?

LAVATCH O, Lord, sir!—There's a simple putting off. 40
More, more, a hundred of them.

COUNTESS Sir, I am a poor friend of yours, that loves
you.

LAVATCH O, Lord, sir!—Thick, thick, spare not me.   44

COUNTESS I think, sir, you can eat none of this homely 45
meat.   46

LAVATCH O Lord, sir!—Nay, put me to 't, I warrant you.

COUNTESS You were lately whipped, sir, as I think.

LAVATCH O Lord, sir!—Spare not me.

COUNTESS Do you cry, "O Lord, sir!" at your whipping,
and "spare not me"? Indeed your "O Lord, sir!" is 51
very sequent to your whipping; you would answer 52
very well to a whipping, if you were but bound to 't. 53

LAVATCH I ne'er had worse luck in my life in my "O
Lord, sir!" I see things may serve long, but not serve
ever.

COUNTESS
I play the noble huswife with the time,
To entertain it so merrily with a fool.

LAVATCH O Lord, sir!—Why, there 't serves well again.

COUNTESS
An end, sir! To your business. Give Helen this,
                              [*Giving a letter*]
And urge her to a present answer back.   61
Commend me to my kinsmen and my son.
This is not much.

LAVATCH Not much commendation to them?

COUNTESS Not much employment for you. You understand me?

LAVATCH Most fruitfully. I am there before my legs.

COUNTESS Haste you again.   *Exeunt* [*separately*]. 68

❧

40 **O, Lord, sir** (A foppish phrase currently in vogue at court.) **putting
off** evasion **44 Thick** quickly **45–46 homely meat** plain fare **51–52 is
very sequent to** is a pertinent response to (because it would be a plea
for mercy) **52–53 answer . . . to** (1) reply cleverly to (2) repay, serve as a
suitable subject for **53 bound to 't** (1) obliged to reply (2) tied up for
it **61 present** immediate **68 again** back again

2.3   *Enter Count [Bertram], Lafew, and Parolles.*

LAFEW   They say miracles are past, and we have our
philosophical persons to make modern and familiar 2
things supernatural and causeless. Hence is it that we 3
make trifles of terrors, ensconcing ourselves into seem- 4
ing knowledge when we should submit ourselves to
an unknown fear.   6
PAROLLES   Why, 'tis the rarest argument of wonder that 7
hath shot out in our latter times.   8
BERTRAM   And so 'tis.
LAFEW   To be relinquished of the artists—   10
PAROLLES   So I say, both of Galen and Paracelsus.   11
LAFEW   Of all the learned and authentic fellows—   12
PAROLLES   Right, so I say.
LAFEW   That gave him out incurable—   14
PAROLLES   Why, there 'tis; so say I too.
LAFEW   Not to be helped.
PAROLLES   Right! As 'twere a man assured of a—
LAFEW   Uncertain life and sure death.
PAROLLES   Just, you say well; so would I have said.   19
LAFEW   I may truly say it is a novelty to the world.
PAROLLES   It is, indeed. If you will have it in showing, 21
you shall read it in—what-do-ye-call there?
                    [*He points to a ballad in Lafew's hand.*]
LAFEW [*Reading*]   "A showing of a heavenly effect in an
earthly actor."
PAROLLES   That's it. I would have said the very same.
LAFEW   Why, your dolphin is not lustier. 'Fore me, I 26
speak in respect—   27

2.3. Location: Paris. The royal court.
2 modern commonplace   **3 causeless** inexplicable by any natural
cause   **4 ensconcing** taking refuge, fortifying   **6 unknown fear** awe of
the unknown   **7 argument** theme, proof   **8 shot out** suddenly appeared.   **latter** recent   **10 relinquished of** abandoned by.   **artists** i.e.,
physicians   **11 Galen** Greek physician of the second century; the traditional authority.   **Paracelsus** Swiss physician of the sixteenth century;
the new and more radical authority   **12 authentic fellows** those properly licensed to practice   **14 gave him out** proclaimed him   **19 Just**
exactly   **21 showing** i.e., print   **26 dolphin** (A sportive and vigorous sea
animal; with a pun perhaps on *dauphin*, French crown prince.)   **'Fore
me** i.e., on my soul   **27 in respect** i.e., intending no disrespect

PAROLLES   Nay, 'tis strange, 'tis very strange, that is the   28
  brief and the tedious of it; and he's of a most facinor-   29
  ous spirit that will not acknowledge it to be the—   30
LAFEW   Very hand of heaven.
PAROLLES   Ay, so I say.
LAFEW   In a most weak—
PAROLLES   And debile minister; great power, great tran-   34
  scendence, which should indeed give us a further use
  to be made than alone the recovery of the King, as to
  be—
LAFEW   Generally thankful.   38

    Enter King, Helena, and attendants. [The King
    sits.]

PAROLLES   I would have said it; you say well. Here
  comes the King.
LAFEW   Lustick, as the Dutchman says. I'll like a maid   41
  the better whilst I have a tooth in my head. Why, he's   42
  able to lead her a coranto.   43
PAROLLES   *Mort du vinaigre!* Is not this Helen?   44
LAFEW   'Fore God, I think so.
KING
  Go, call before me all the lords in court.
                       [Exit an Attendant.]
  Sit, my preserver, by thy patient's side,   *[She sits.]*
  And with this healthful hand, whose banished sense   48
  Thou hast repealed, a second time receive   49
  The confirmation of my promised gift,
  Which but attends thy naming.   51

    Enter four Lords.

  Fair maid, send forth thine eye. This youthful parcel   52
  Of noble bachelors stand at my bestowing,   53

28–29 the brief . . . it i.e., the short and the long of it   **29–30 facinorous**
infamous, wicked   **34 debile minister** weak agent   **38 Generally** universally   **41 Lustick** lusty.   **Dutchman** i.e., from any Germanic country
42 have a tooth (with a play on the meaning "have a taste still for
girls")   **43 coranto** lively dance   **44 Mort du vinaigre** (Possibly an oath
by the vinegar in Christ's wounds; literally, "death of vinegar.")
48 banished sense loss of feeling   **49 repealed** recalled (from the banishment of illness)   **51 attends** waits upon   **52 parcel** group   **53 stand . . .
bestowing** i.e., are my wards, whom I may give in marriage

O'er whom both sovereign power and father's voice
I have to use. Thy frank election make;   55
Thou hast power to choose, and they none to forsake. 56

HELENA
To each of you one fair and virtuous mistress
Fall, when Love please! Marry, to each but one.

LAFEW [*Aside*]
I'd give bay Curtal and his furniture   59
My mouth no more were broken than these boys',   60
And writ as little beard.

KING   Peruse them well.   61
Not one of those but had a noble father.

HELENA   Gentlemen,
Heaven hath through me restored the King to health.

ALL THE LORDS
We understand it, and thank heaven for you.

HELENA
I am a simple maid, and therein wealthiest
That I protest I simply am a maid.—
Please it Your Majesty, I have done already.
The blushes in my cheeks thus whisper me,
"We blush that thou shouldst choose; but, be refused, 70
Let the white death sit on thy cheek forever,   71
We'll ne'er come there again."

KING   Make choice and see.
Who shuns thy love shuns all his love in me.   73

HELENA
Now, Dian, from thy altar do I fly,   74
And to imperial Love, that god most high,   75
Do my sighs stream. (*She addresses her to a Lord.*) Sir,
will you hear my suit?

FIRST LORD
And grant it.

HELENA   Thanks, sir; all the rest is mute.   77

---

55 frank election uninhibited choice   **56 forsake** refuse   **59 bay . . .
furniture** i.e., my dock-tailed horse and his trappings   **60 My . . . than**
i.e., I had lost no more teeth than   **61 writ** i.e., and that I laid claim to.
(Lafew wishes he were young enough to be a suitor of Helena.)   **70 be
refused** i.e., if you are refused   **71 the white death** i.e., death in its
pallor   **73 Who** he who   **74 Dian** Diana, the goddess of chastity
75 imperial Love i.e., the god of love, Cupid   **77 all . . . mute** I have
nothing more to say to you

LAFEW [*Aside*]   I had rather be in this choice than throw
ambs-ace for my life.   79
HELENA [*To Second Lord*]
The honor, sir, that flames in your fair eyes
Before I speak too threateningly replies.
Love make your fortunes twenty times above
Her that so wishes, and her humble love!   83
SECOND LORD
No better, if you please.
HELENA   My wish receive,   84
Which great Love grant! And so I take my leave.
LAFEW [*Aside*]   Do all they deny her? An they were sons 86
of mine, I'd have them whipped, or I would send them
to the Turk, to make eunuchs of.
HELENA [*To Third Lord*]
Be not afraid that I your hand should take;
I'll never do you wrong for your own sake.
Blessing upon your vows, and in your bed
Find fairer fortune if you ever wed!
LAFEW [*Aside*]   These boys are boys of ice; they'll none
have her. Sure they are bastards to the English; the 94
French ne'er got 'em.   95
HELENA [*To Fourth Lord*]
You are too young, too happy, and too good
To make yourself a son out of my blood.
FOURTH LORD   Fair one, I think not so.
LAFEW [*Aside*]   There's one grape yet; I am sure thy fa- 99
ther drunk wine. But if thou be'st not an ass, I am a 100
youth of fourteen; I have known thee already.   101
HELENA [*To Bertram*]
I dare not say I take you, but I give
Me and my service, ever whilst I live,
Into your guiding power.—This is the man.

---

79 ambs-ace two aces, the lowest possible throw in dice. (To throw ambs-
ace with one's life at stake is to risk all on a throw.)   **83 Her . . . wishes**
her that speaks this wish, i.e., Helena herself   **84 No better** i.e., I wish
for no one better than yourself.   **My wish receive** i.e., take my wish for
your fortunate marriage   **86 Do . . . her** (Lafew, unable to hear, misin-
terprets her passing from one to another.)   **An** if   **94 Sure** certainly.
bastards to illegitimate children of   **95 got** begot   **99 grape** i.e., scion of
a good family.   **thy** i.e., Bertram's   **100 drunk wine** i.e., was red-blooded.
thou i.e., the fourth lord   **101 known** i.e., seen through

KING
  Why, then, young Bertram, take her; she's thy wife.
BERTRAM
  My wife, my liege? I shall beseech Your Highness,
  In such a business give me leave to use
  The help of mine own eyes.
KING   Know'st thou not, Bertram,
  What she has done for me?
BERTRAM   Yes, my good lord,
  But never hope to know why I should marry her.
KING
  Thou know'st she has raised me from my sickly bed.
BERTRAM
  But follows it, my lord, to bring me down   112
  Must answer for your raising? I know her well;
  She had her breeding at my father's charge.
  A poor physician's daughter my wife? Disdain   115
  Rather corrupt me ever!   116
KING
  'Tis only title thou disdain'st in her, the which   117
  I can build up. Strange is it that our bloods,
  Of color, weight, and heat, poured all together,
  Would quite confound distinction, yet stands off   120
  In differences so mighty. If she be   121
  All that is virtuous—save what thou dislik'st,
  A poor physician's daughter—thou dislik'st
  Of virtue for the name. But do not so.   124
  From lowest place when virtuous things proceed,   125
  The place is dignified by th' doer's deed.
  Where great additions swell 's, and virtue none,   127
  It is a dropsied honor. Good alone   128
  Is good without a name; vileness is so;   129
  The property by what it is should go,   130
  Not by the title. She is young, wise, fair;

112 **bring me down** i.e., to a socially inferior wife, to the (marriage)
bed **115–116 Disdain . . . ever** i.e., rather let my disdain for her ruin
me forever in your favor **117 title** i.e., her lack of title **120 Would . . .
distinction** could not be distinguished at all. **stands off** stand separated **121 differences** i.e., social differences **124 name** i.e., lack of a
name (title) **125 proceed** emanate **127 great . . . swell 's** pompous
titles puff us up **128 dropsied** unhealthily swollen **128–129 Good . . .
name** i.e., what is in itself good is so without a title **129 so** the same
130 property quality. **go** i.e., be judged, be valued

In these to nature she's immediate heir,   132
And these breed honor. That is honor's scorn   133
Which challenges itself as honor's born
And is not like the sire. Honors thrive   135
When rather from our acts we them derive
Than our forgoers. The mere word's a slave
Debauched on every tomb, on every grave   138
A lying trophy, and as oft is dumb   139
Where dust and damned oblivion is the tomb
Of honored bones indeed. What should be said?   141
If thou canst like this creature as a maid,
I can create the rest. Virtue and she   143
Is her own dower; honor and wealth from me.   144

BERTRAM
I cannot love her nor will strive to do 't.

KING
Thou wrong'st thyself if thou shouldst strive to choose.   146

HELENA
That you are well restored, my lord, I'm glad.
Let the rest go.

KING
My honor's at the stake, which to defeat   149
I must produce my power. Here, take her hand,
Proud scornful boy, unworthy this good gift,
That dost in vile misprision shackle up   152
My love and her desert; that canst not dream,   153
We, poising us in her defective scale,   154
Shall weigh thee to the beam; that wilt not know   155
It is in us to plant thine honor where   156

132 In . . . heir in these qualities she inherits directly from nature
133–135 That . . . sire true honor is scornful of any claim to honor
based only on the fact of noble birth rather than the imitation of the
noble behavior of one's forebears   138 Debauched debased   139 trophy
memorial.   dumb silent   141 honored bones indeed i.e., the remains of
those who were genuinely honorable   143–144 Virtue . . . dower i.e., her
marriage gift to you will be her virtue and herself   146 strive to choose
try to assert your own choice   149 which i.e., which threat to my honor
152 misprision contempt and poor judgment (with a play on "undeserved imprisonment").   shackle up confine, limit   153–155 that . . .
beam you who cannot imagine that I, weighing my royal self on her
underweight (defective) side of the scales, will outweigh yours and pull
it up to the cross-beam   156 in us within my royal power

We please to have it grow. Check thy contempt;   157
Obey our will, which travails in thy good;   158
Believe not thy disdain, but presently   159
Do thine own fortunes that obedient right   160
Which both thy duty owes and our power claims,
Or I will throw thee from my care forever
Into the staggers and the careless lapse   163
Of youth and ignorance, both my revenge and hate
Loosing upon thee in the name of justice   165
Without all terms of pity. Speak; thine answer.   166

BERTRAM
Pardon, my gracious lord; for I submit
My fancy to your eyes. When I consider   168
What great creation and what dole of honor   169
Flies where you bid it, I find that she, which late   170
Was in my nobler thoughts most base, is now
The praisèd of the King, who, so ennobled,
Is as 'twere born so.

KING   Take her by the hand
And tell her she is thine, to whom I promise
A counterpoise, if not to thy estate,   175
A balance more replete.

BERTRAM   I take her hand.   176

KING
Good fortune and the favor of the King
Smile upon this contract, whose ceremony   178
Shall seem expedient on the now-born brief   179
And be performed tonight. The solemn feast   180
Shall more attend upon the coming space,   181
Expecting absent friends. As thou lov'st her,   182

---

157 Check curb, restrain   **158 travails in** labors for   **159 Believe not** do not place faith in or obey.   **presently** at once   **160 obedient right** right of obedience   **163 staggers** giddy decline.   **careless lapse** irresponsible fall   **165 Loosing** giving vent to, letting loose   **166 all ... pity** pity in any form   **168 fancy** affection   **169 great creation** creating of greatness.   **dole** share, doling out   **170 which late** who lately   **175–176 A counterpoise ... replete** i.e., an equal weight of money as dowry, if not an amount even exceeding your estate   **178–179 whose ... brief** i.e., the consecration of which will serve as a fitting or rapid conclusion to the agreement just made (?)   **180 solemn** solemnizing   **181–182 more ... friends** be delayed for a time until absent friends and relatives can arrive. (There is to be a wedding tonight, and a celebratory feast later on when all can gather.)

Thy love's to me religious; else, does err.   183
> *Exeunt. Parolles and Lafew stay behind,*
> *commenting of this wedding.*

LAFEW   Do you hear, monsieur? A word with you.

PAROLLES   Your pleasure, sir?

LAFEW   Your lord and master did well to make his recantation.

PAROLLES   Recantation? My lord? My master?

LAFEW   Ay. Is it not a language I speak?

PAROLLES   A most harsh one, and not to be understood
without bloody succeeding. My master?   191

LAFEW   Are you companion to the Count Rossillion?

PAROLLES   To any count, to all counts, to what is man.   193

LAFEW   To what is count's man. Count's master is of   194
another style.

PAROLLES   You are too old, sir; let it satisfy you, you are   196
too old.

LAFEW   I must tell thee, sirrah, I write man, to which   198
title age cannot bring thee.

PAROLLES   What I dare too well do, I dare not do.   200

LAFEW   I did think thee, for two ordinaries, to be a   201
pretty wise fellow; thou didst make tolerable vent of   202
thy travel; it might pass. Yet the scarves and the ban-   203
nerets about thee did manifoldly dissuade me from   204
believing thee a vessel of too great a burden. I have   205
now found thee. When I lose thee again, I care not; yet   206
art thou good for nothing but taking up, and that   207
thou'rt scarce worth.

PAROLLES   Hadst thou not the privilege of antiquity
upon thee—

LAFEW   Do not plunge thyself too far in anger, lest thou

---

183 to me religious holy and faithful to me (i.e., you will take her if you
love me). **else** otherwise   **183 s.d. of** on   **191 succeeding** consequences;
i.e., a fight   **193 what is man** i.e., any true man; or, what is manly
194 count's man i.e., servant. (Said belittlingly.)   **196 too old** i.e., for me
to duel with.   **let . . . you** i.e., take that as a satisfaction instead of a
duel   **198 write man** i.e., account myself a man, lay claim to that title
200 What . . . not do i.e., what I could too easily accomplish—beat you—I
must not do because of your age   **201 for two ordinaries** during the
space of two meals   **202 didst . . . of** discoursed tolerably upon
203–204 scarves, bannerets i.e., soldier's scarves, reminding Lafew of a
ship's pennants   **205 burden** cargo   **206 found** found out   **207 taking
up** contradicting; arresting; picking up (as opposed to *losing*)

hasten thy trial; which if—Lord have mercy on thee 212
for a hen! So, my good window of lattice, fare thee 213
well. Thy casement I need not open, for I look through 214
thee. Give me thy hand.

PAROLLES My lord, you give me most egregious indig- 216
nity.

LAFEW Ay, with all my heart, and thou art worthy of it.

PAROLLES I have not, my lord, deserved it.

LAFEW Yes, good faith, every dram of it, and I will not 220
bate thee a scruple.   221

PAROLLES Well, I shall be wiser.   222

LAFEW Even as soon as thou canst, for thou hast to pull 223
at a smack o' the contrary. If ever thou be'st bound in 224
thy scarf and beaten, thou shall find what it is to be
proud of thy bondage. I have a desire to hold my ac- 226
quaintance with thee, or rather my knowledge, that I
may say in the default, "He is a man I know."   228

PAROLLES My lord, you do me most insupportable vexation.

LAFEW I would it were hell-pains for thy sake, and my 231
poor doing eternal; for doing I am past, as I will by 232
thee, in what motion age will give me leave.   *Exit.* 233

PAROLLES Well, thou hast a son shall take this disgrace 234
off me—scurvy, old, filthy, scurvy lord! Well, I must 235
be patient; there is no fettering of authority. I'll beat 236
him, by my life, if I can meet him with any convenience, an he were double and double a lord. I'll have 238

---

212 thy trial i.e., the testing of your supposed valor   **213 hen** i.e.,
cackling, cowardly female.   **window of lattice** wooden frame with cross-
hatched slats (instead of glass), often painted red and used as the sign of
an alehouse   **214 casement** window sash   **216 egregious** outrageous,
flagrant   **220 dram** bit (literally, an eighth of an ounce)   **221 bate** abate,
remit.   **scruple** smallest bit (literally, a third of a dram)   **222 wiser** i.e.,
wiser than to deal with such dotards in the future   **223–224 for . . .
contrary** i.e., because you have to taste your own folly   **226 bondage**
i.e., the scarf, in which you would be bound and of which you are now
vainly proud.   **hold** continue   **228 in the default** when you default, i.e.,
show your emptiness on being brought to trial   **231–232 my poor doing**
i.e., my inadequate power to teach you a lesson   **232 for doing** for
energetic activity (with a sexual suggestion)   **232–233 will by thee** i.e.,
will pass by you (punning on *past*—passed)   **233 in . . . leave** with
whatever speed age will allow me   **234–235 shall . . . me** i.e., on whom I
will vindicate myself for these insults   **236 fettering** restraining
238 an even if

no more pity of his age than I would have of—I'll beat
him, an if I could but meet him again.   240

    Enter Lafew.

LAFEW Sirrah, your lord and master's married; there's
news for you. You have a new mistress.

PAROLLES I most unfeignedly beseech your lordship to
make some reservation of your wrongs. He is my good   244
lord; whom I serve above is my master.   245

LAFEW Who? God?

PAROLLES Ay, sir.

LAFEW The devil it is that's thy master. Why dost thou 248
garter up thy arms i' this fashion? Dost make hose of
thy sleeves? Do other servants so? Thou wert best set 250
thy lower part where thy nose stands. By mine honor,
if I were but two hours younger, I'd beat thee. Methink'st thou art a general offense, and every man
should beat thee. I think thou wast created for men to
breathe themselves upon thee.   255

PAROLLES This is hard and undeserved measure, my
lord.

LAFEW Go to, sir. You were beaten in Italy for picking 258
a kernel out of a pomegranate. You are a vagabond   259
and no true traveler. You are more saucy with lords
and honorable personages than the commission of   261
your birth and virtue gives you heraldry. You are not 262
worth another word, else I'd call you knave. I leave
you.   *Exit.*

PAROLLES Good, very good! It is so then. Good, very
good. Let it be concealed awhile.

    Enter [Bertram] Count Rossillion.

BERTRAM Undone, and forfeited to cares forever!

PAROLLES What's the matter, sweetheart?

---

240 an if if   **244 make . . . wrongs** put some restraint upon your insults   **244 make . . . wrongs** qualify the insults you've given me
244–245 good lord i.e., patron (not master, as Lafew has insultingly
said)   **245 whom** i.e., he whom (God)   **248–250 Why . . . sleeves**
(Parolles apparently has decorative scarves tied around the sleeves of
his outfit.)   **255 breathe** exercise   **258–259 for . . . pomegranate** i.e., for
some petty offense, or on a slight pretext   **261 commission** warrant
262 gives you heraldry entitles you to be

BERTRAM Although before the solemn priest I have sworn, I will not bed her.

PAROLLES What, what, sweetheart?

BERTRAM

O my Parolles, they have married me!
I'll to the Tuscan wars, and never bed her.

PAROLLES France is a dog-hole, and it no more merits the tread of a man's foot. To th' wars!

BERTRAM There's letters from my mother. What th' import is I know not yet. 276

PAROLLES Ay, that would be known. To th' wars, my boy, to th' wars!
He wears his honor in a box unseen
That hugs his kicky-wicky here at home, 281
Spending his manly marrow in her arms, 282
Which should sustain the bound and high curvet 283
Of Mars's fiery steed. To other regions!
France is a stable, we that dwell in 't jades. 285
Therefore, to th' war!

BERTRAM

It shall be so. I'll send her to my house,
Acquaint my mother with my hate to her
And wherefore I am fled; write to the King
That which I durst not speak. His present gift
Shall furnish me to those Italian fields 291
Where noble fellows strike. War is no strife
To the dark house and the detested wife. 293

PAROLLES

Will this capriccio hold in thee? Art sure? 294

BERTRAM

Go with me to my chamber and advise me.
I'll send her straight away. Tomorrow 296
I'll to the wars, she to her single sorrow.

---

276 letters i.e., a letter   **281 kicky-wicky** woman (with sexual suggestion, as also in *box* in the previous line and *Spending* and *marrow* in the following line)   **282 manly marrow** masculine essence   **283 curvet** leap   **285 jades** worn-out horses   **291 furnish me** (Knights customarily provided themselves with trappings and armed retainers when enlisting in warlike enterprises.)   **293 To . . . house** i.e., compared to the madhouse (of marriage)   **294 capriccio** caprice   **296 straight** at once

PAROLLES

   Why, these balls bound; there's noise in it. 'Tis hard!   298
A young man married is a man that's marred.
Therefore away, and leave her bravely; go.
The King has done you wrong, but hush, 'tis so.

                                          Exeunt.

                     ❖

2.4   *Enter Helena [with a letter], and Clown
[Lavatch].*

HELENA

   My mother greets me kindly. Is she well?

LAVATCH She is not well, but yet she has her health. She's 2
very merry, but yet she is not well. But thanks be
given, she's very well and wants nothing i' the world;
but yet she is not well.

HELENA If she be very well, what does she ail that she's
not very well?

LAVATCH Truly, she's very well indeed but for two
things.

HELENA What two things?

LAVATCH One, that she's not in heaven, whither God
send her quickly! The other, that she's in earth, from
whence God send her quickly!

     Enter Parolles.

PAROLLES Bless you, my fortunate lady!

HELENA I hope, sir, I have your good will to have mine
own good fortunes.

PAROLLES You had my prayers to lead them on, and to
keep them on have them still.—O my knave, how does
my old lady?

LAVATCH So that you had her wrinkles and I her money,
I would she did as you say.

PAROLLES Why, I say nothing.

298 Why . . . hard i.e., now you're talking; that's the way to behave.
(*Balls* here are tennis balls.)

2.4. Location: Paris. The royal court.
2 not well (Referring to the Elizabethan euphemism by which the dead
were spoken of as "well.")

LAVATCH Marry, you are the wiser man; for many a
man's tongue shakes out his master's undoing. To say 24
nothing, to do nothing, to know nothing, and to have
nothing is to be a great part of your title, which is 26
within a very little of nothing.

PAROLLES Away! Thou'rt a knave.

LAVATCH You should have said, sir, "Before a knave 29
thou'rt a knave"; that's, "Before me thou'rt a knave." 30
This had been truth, sir.

PAROLLES Go to, thou art a witty fool; I have found 32
thee.   33

LAVATCH Did you find me in yourself, sir? Or were you 34
taught to find me? The search, sir, was profitable; and
much fool may you find in you, even to the world's
pleasure and the increase of laughter.

PAROLLES
A good knave, i' faith, and well fed.   38
Madam, my lord will go away tonight;
A very serious business calls on him.
The great prerogative and rite of love
Which, as your due, time claims, he does acknowledge, 42
But puts it off to a compelled restraint;   43
Whose want and whose delay is strewed with sweets, 44
Which they distill now in the curbèd time   45
To make the coming hour o'erflow with joy
And pleasure drown the brim.

HELENA   What's his will else?   47

PAROLLES
That you will take your instant leave o' the King
And make this haste as your own good proceeding,   49

---

24 man's servant's. **shakes out** i.e., brings about by talking too freely
26 title worth   **29 Before** in presence of   **30 Before me** i.e., upon my
soul. (But by substituting *me* for *knave* Lavatch suggests that Parolles
call himself a knave.)   **32–33 found thee** found you to be a fool   **34 in
yourself** (1) by your own efforts (2) in your reflection   **38 well fed**
(Referring to the proverb "better fed than taught," as at 2.2.3.)   **42 time**
i.e., the present time   **43 to** owing to   **44 Whose want** the lack of which
(rite of love). The postponing of love's rites makes them sweeter, like
perfume made sweeter by distillation.   **sweets** sweet-smelling flowers
45 they i.e., the lack and delay.   **curbèd time** period of restraint (and
also of distillation, as in the making of perfume from *curbing* flowers or
sweets, l. 44, in a still)   **47 else** besides   **49 make** represent.   **proceeding** course of action

Strengthened with what apology you think
May make it probable need.
HELENA   What more commands he? 51
PAROLLES
That, having this obtained, you presently
Attend his further pleasure.   53
HELENA
In everything I wait upon his will.
PAROLLES   I shall report it so.   *Exit Parolles.*
HELENA   I pray you.—Come, sirrah.

                          Exit [with Lavatch].

❖

2.5   *Enter Lafew and Bertram.*

LAFEW   But I hope your lordship thinks not him a sol-
dier.
BERTRAM   Yes, my lord, and of very valiant approof.   3
LAFEW   You have it from his own deliverance.   4
BERTRAM   And by other warranted testimony.
LAFEW   Then my dial goes not true. I took this lark for a 6
bunting.   7
BERTRAM   I do assure you, my lord, he is very great in
knowledge, and accordingly valiant.   9
LAFEW   I have then sinned against his experience and
transgressed against his valor; and my state that way is 11
dangerous, since I cannot yet find in my heart to re-   12
pent. Here he comes. I pray you, make us friends; I
will pursue the amity.

        Enter Parolles.

51 probable need plausibly appear to be necessary   **53 Attend** await.
pleasure command
2.5. Location: Paris. The royal court.
3 valiant approof proven valor   **4 deliverance** testimony, word   **6 dial**
clock, compass, i.e., judgment   **6–7 I . . . bunting** i.e., I underestimated
him. (The bunting resembles the lark but lacks the lark's beautiful
song.) Lafew ironically suggests that Parolles sings (i.e., talks) well
enough but is all show and no substance.   **9 accordingly** correspond-
ingly   **11 my state** i.e., the state of my soul. (Lafew uses ironically an
elaborate metaphor of religious penitence.)   **12 find in** find it in

PAROLLES [*To Bertram*]   These things shall be done, sir.

LAFEW   Pray you, sir, who's his tailor?   16

PAROLLES   Sir?

LAFEW   O, I know him well. Ay, sir, he, sir, 's a good   18
workman, a very good tailor.   19

BERTRAM [*Aside to Parolles*]   Is she gone to the King?

PAROLLES   She is.

BERTRAM   Will she away tonight?

PAROLLES   As you'll have her.

BERTRAM

I have writ my letters, casketed my treasure,
Given order for our horses; and tonight,
When I should take possession of the bride,
End ere I do begin.

LAFEW   A good traveler is something at the latter end of   28
a dinner; but one that lies three thirds, and uses a   29
known truth to pass a thousand nothings with, should
be once heard and thrice beaten. God save you, Captain.

BERTRAM [*To Parolles*]   Is there any unkindness be-   33
tween my lord and you, monsieur?

PAROLLES   I know not how I have deserved to run into
my lord's displeasure.

LAFEW   You have made shift to run into 't, boots and   37
spurs and all, like him that leapt into the custard; and   38
out of it you'll run again, rather than suffer question   39
for your residence.   40

BERTRAM   It may be you have mistaken him, my lord.   41

LAFEW   And shall do so ever, though I took him at 's
prayers. Fare you well, my lord, and believe this of

16 who's his tailor i.e., what tailor made this stuffed (bombast) figure.
(Lafew says this to Bertram, but is taunting Parolles, who replies indignantly.)   **18–19 O . . . tailor** (Lafew mockingly takes Parolles's *Sir* in
l. 17 as the name of his tailor.)   **28–29 A good . . . dinner** i.e., a person
with many traveling experiences is an asset as a storyteller after dinner   **29 three thirds** i.e., all the time   **33 unkindness** ill will   **37 made
shift** contrived (at our previous meeting)   **38 like . . . custard** i.e., like a
clown at an annual city entertainment jumping into a large, deep custard   **39 you'll run** you will want to run   **39–40 suffer . . . residence**
undergo questioning about your being there, i.e., explain how your
cowardice displeased me   **41 mistaken him** misjudged or misidentified
him. (But Lafew deliberately takes the phrase in the sense of "taken
exception to his behavior.")

me: there can be no kernel in this light nut. The soul
of this man is his clothes. Trust him not in matter of
heavy consequence. I have kept of them tame, and   46
know their natures.—Farewell, monsieur. I have spoken
better of you than you have or will to deserve at my   48
hand; but we must do good against evil.   [*Exit.*]

PAROLLES An idle lord, I swear.   50

BERTRAM I think so.

PAROLLES Why, do you not know him?

BERTRAM
Yes, I do know him well, and common speech
Gives him a worthy pass. Here comes my clog.   54

Enter Helena.

HELENA
I have, sir, as I was commanded from you,
Spoke with the King, and have procured his leave
For present parting; only he desires
Some private speech with you.

BERTRAM   I shall obey his will.
You must not marvel, Helen, at my course,
Which holds not color with the time, nor does   60
The ministration and requirèd office
On my particular. Prepared I was not   62
For such a business; therefore am I found
So much unsettled. This drives me to entreat you
That presently you take your way for home;
And rather muse than ask why I entreat you,   66
For my respects are better than they seem,   67
And my appointments have in them a need   68
Greater than shows itself at the first view
To you that know them not. This to my mother.
                              [*Giving a letter.*]

---

46 heavy serious.   **I . . . tame** I have kept tame creatures of this kind
(for the amusement they provide)   **48 have . . . deserve** have deserved or
are likely to deserve   **50 idle** foolish   **54 pass** reputation.   **clog** a heavy
weight attached to the leg or neck of a man or animal to prevent free-
dom of movement   **60–62 Which . . . particular** which does not appear
to suit with the occasion (of our marriage), nor does it fulfill what is
incumbent upon me as a husband   **66 muse** wonder   **67 respects**
motives   **68 appointments** purposes

'Twill be two days ere I shall see you, so
I leave you to your wisdom.
HELENA   Sir, I can nothing say
But that I am your most obedient servant.
BERTRAM
Come, come, no more of that.
HELENA   And ever shall
With true observance seek to eke out that   75
Wherein toward me my homely stars have failed   76
To equal my great fortune.
BERTRAM   Let that go.
My haste is very great. Farewell; hie home.   78
                              [*He starts to go.*]
HELENA
Pray, sir, your pardon.
BERTRAM   Well, what would you say?
HELENA
I am not worthy of the wealth I owe,   80
Nor dare I say 'tis mine, and yet it is;
But, like a timorous thief, most fain would steal   82
What law does vouch mine own.
BERTRAM   What would you have? 83
HELENA
Something, and scarce so much; nothing, indeed.
I would not tell you what I would, my lord. Faith, yes—
Strangers and foes do sunder, and not kiss.   86
BERTRAM
I pray you, stay not, but in haste to horse.   87
HELENA
I shall not break your bidding, good my lord.
BERTRAM
Where are my other men, monsieur?—Farewell.
                              Exit [*Helena*].
Go thou toward home, where I will never come
Whilst I can shake my sword or hear the drum.
Away, and for our flight.
PAROLLES   Bravely, *coraggio*!   [*Exeunt.*] 92

❖

75 **observance** service. **eke out** add to   76 **homely stars** i.e., lowly
origin   78 **hie** hasten   80 **owe** own   82 **fain** gladly   83 **vouch** affirm to
be   86 **sunder** separate   87 **stay** delay   92 **coraggio** courage, bravo

3.1 *Flourish. Enter the Duke of Florence*
[attended]; the two Frenchmen, with a
troop of soldiers.

DUKE
So that from point to point now have you heard
The fundamental reasons of this war,
Whose great decision hath much blood let forth   3
And more thirsts after.

FIRST LORD   Holy seems the quarrel
Upon Your Grace's part, black and fearful
On the opposer.   6

DUKE
Therefore we marvel much our cousin France   7
Would in so just a business shut his bosom
Against our borrowing prayers.

SECOND LORD   Good my lord,   9
The reasons of our state I cannot yield   10
But like a common and an outward man   11
That the great figure of a council frames   12
By self-unable motion, therefore dare not   13
Say what I think of it, since I have found
Myself in my incertain grounds to fail
As often as I guessed.

DUKE   Be it his pleasure.   16

FIRST LORD
But I am sure the younger of our nature,   17
That surfeit on their ease, will day by day   18
Come here for physic.

DUKE   Welcome shall they be,   19
And all the honors that can fly from us   20
Shall on them settle. You know your places well;

3.1. Location: Florence.
3 decision combat to decide an issue   **6 the opposer** i.e., the opposer's
part   **7 cousin** i.e., fellow sovereign   **9 borrowing prayers** prayers for
assistance   **10 yield** communicate, produce   **11 But** except.   **outward**
not having intimate knowledge of things   **12 figure** scheme.   **frames**
constructs   **13 self-unable motion** i.e., his own imperfect guess   **16 Be**
. . . pleasure i.e., be it as the King of France wishes   **17 nature** outlook,
disposition   **18 surfeit** grow sick   **19 physic** i.e., cure of their surfeit
(through bloodletting)   **20 can fly from us** i.e., we can grant

When better fall, for your avails they fell.   22
Tomorrow to the field.   *Flourish*. [*Exeunt*.]

❖

3.2   *Enter Countess and Clown* [*Lavatch*].

COUNTESS   It hath happened all as I would have had it,
save that he comes not along with her.
LAVATCH   By my troth, I take my young lord to be a very 3
melancholy man.
COUNTESS   By what observance, I pray you?   5
LAVATCH   Why, he will look upon his boot and sing,
mend the ruff and sing, ask questions and sing, pick 7
his teeth and sing. I know a man that had this trick of 8
melancholy sold a goodly manor for a song.
COUNTESS   Let me see what he writes and when he
means to come.   [*Opening a letter*.]
LAVATCH   I have no mind to Isbel since I was at court.
Our old ling and our Isbels o' the country are nothing 13
like your old ling and your Isbels o' the court. The
brains of my Cupid's knocked out, and I begin to love
as an old man loves money, with no stomach.   16
COUNTESS   What have we here?
LAVATCH   E'en that you have there.   *Exit*.
COUNTESS (*Reads a letter*) "I have sent you a daughter-
in-law. She hath recovered the King and undone me. 20
I have wedded her, not bedded her, and sworn to
make the 'not' eternal. You shall hear I am run away; 22
know it before the report come. If there be breadth
enough in the world, I will hold a long distance. My 24
duty to you.
                    Your unfortunate son,
                         Bertram."

22 better fall i.e., better places fall vacant.   **fell** will have fallen

3.2. Location: Rossillion.
3 troth faith   **5 observance** observation   **7 mend the ruff** adjust the
loose turned-over flap at the top of his boot   **7–8 pick his teeth** (An
affected mannerism, as at 1.1.159.)   **8 trick** habit   **13 old ling** i.e., men.
(Literally, salted cod, but with a bawdy meaning referring to the penis.)   **16 stomach** appetite   **20 recovered** cured   **22 not** (with a pun on
knot)   **24 hold a long distance** stay far away

This is not well, rash and unbridled boy,
To fly the favors of so good a king,
To pluck his indignation on thy head   30
By the misprizing of a maid too virtuous   31
For the contempt of empire.   32

    Enter Clown [Lavatch].

LAVATCH O madam, yonder is heavy news within be- 33
tween two soldiers and my young lady!
COUNTESS What is the matter?
LAVATCH Nay, there is some comfort in the news, some
comfort. Your son will not be killed so soon as I
thought he would.
COUNTESS Why should he be killed?
LAVATCH So say I, madam, if he run away, as I hear he
does. The danger is in standing to 't; that's the loss of 41
men, though it be the getting of children. Here they 42
come will tell you more. For my part, I only hear your
son was run away.   [*Exit.*] 44

    Enter Helena and [the] two [French] Gentlemen
    [or Lords].

SECOND LORD Save you, good madam.
HELENA
  Madam, my lord is gone, forever gone!
FIRST LORD Do not say so.
COUNTESS
  Think upon patience. Pray you, gentlemen,
  I have felt so many quirks of joy and grief   49
  That the first face of neither, on the start,   50
  Can woman me unto 't. Where is my son, I pray you?   51
FIRST LORD
  Madam, he's gone to serve the Duke of Florence.
  We met him thitherward; for thence we came,   53

30 pluck bring down **31 misprizing** scorning, failing to appreciate
32 of empire of even an emperor **33 heavy** sad **41 standing to 't**
standing one's ground (with sexual pun) **42 getting** begetting **44 was**
has **49 quirks** sudden shifts **50 face** appearance. **on the start** appearing suddenly **51 woman me unto 't** i.e., make me respond emotionally, weep **53 thitherward** on his way there

And, after some dispatch in hand at court,   54
Thither we bend again.

HELENA
Look on his letter, madam; here's my passport.   56
[*Reads*.] "When thou canst get the ring upon my finger, which never shall come off, and show me a child
begotten of thy body that I am father to, then call me
husband; but in such a 'then' I write a 'never.' "
This is a dreadful sentence.

COUNTESS
Brought you this letter, gentlemen?

FIRST LORD   Ay, madam,
And for the contents' sake are sorry for our pains.

COUNTESS
I prithee, lady, have a better cheer.
If thou engrossest all the griefs are thine,   65
Thou robb'st me of a moi'ty. He was my son,   66
But I do wash his name out of my blood,
And thou art all my child.—Towards Florence is he?   68

FIRST LORD
Ay, madam.

COUNTESS   And to be a soldier?

FIRST LORD
Such is his noble purpose; and, believe 't,
The Duke will lay upon him all the honor
That good convenience claims.

COUNTESS   Return you thither?   72

SECOND LORD
Ay, madam, with the swiftest wing of speed.

HELENA [*Reads*]
"Till I have no wife, I have nothing in France."
'Tis bitter.

COUNTESS   Find you that there?

HELENA   Ay, madam.

SECOND LORD
'Tis but the boldness of his hand, haply,   76
Which his heart was not consenting to.

---

54 dispatch in hand business to be taken care of   **56 passport** license to
wander as a beggar   **65 thou engrossest** you monopolize.   **are** that are
66 moi'ty half   **68 all my** my only   **72 convenience** propriety   **76 haply**
perhaps

COUNTESS
Nothing in France, until he have no wife!
There's nothing here that is too good for him
But only she, and she deserves a lord
That twenty such rude boys might tend upon
And call her hourly mistress. Who was with him?

SECOND LORD
A servant only, and a gentleman
Which I have sometime known.

COUNTESS Parolles, was it not?

SECOND LORD Ay, my good lady, he.

COUNTESS
A very tainted fellow, and full of wickedness.
My son corrupts a well-derivèd nature
With his inducement.

SECOND LORD   Indeed, good lady,   89
The fellow has a deal of that too much   90
Which holds him much to have.   91

COUNTESS You're welcome, gentlemen.
I will entreat you, when you see my son,
To tell him that his sword can never win
The honor that he loses. More I'll entreat you
Written to bear along.

FIRST LORD   We serve you, madam,   96
In that and all your worthiest affairs.

COUNTESS
Not so, but as we change our courtesies.   98
Will you draw near?   *Exit [with Gentlemen].*   99

HELENA
"Till I have no wife, I have nothing in France."
Nothing in France, until he has no wife!
Thou shalt have none, Rossillion, none in France;   102
Then hast thou all again. Poor lord, is 't I
That chase thee from thy country and expose
Those tender limbs of thine to the event   105
Of the none-sparing war? And is it I

---

89 With his inducement i.e., by Parolles's corrupt influence **90–91 has
. . . have** i.e., has considerably too much of that ingratiating and persuasive quality which he uses to his advantage **96 Written** in writing
98 but . . . courtesies i.e., only if I can repay your courtesy with my
own **(change:** exchange.) **99 draw near** come with me **102 Rossillion**
i.e., Bertram (whom Helena refers to by his title) **105 event** hazard

That drive thee from the sportive court, where thou   107
Wast shot at with fair eyes, to be the mark   108
Of smoky muskets? O you leaden messengers,   109
That ride upon the violent speed of fire,
Fly with false aim; move the still-piecing air,   111
That sings with piercing; do not touch my lord!   112
Whoever shoots at him, I set him there;
Whoever charges on his forward breast,
I am the caitiff that do hold him to 't;   115
And, though I kill him not, I am the cause
His death was so effected. Better 'twere
I met the ravin lion when he roared   118
With sharp constraint of hunger; better 'twere
That all the miseries which nature owes   120
Were mine at once. No, come thou home, Rossillion,
Whence honor but of danger wins a scar,   122
As oft it loses all. I will be gone.   123
My being here it is that holds thee hence.
Shall I stay here to do 't? No, no, although
The air of paradise did fan the house
And angels officed all. I will be gone,   127
That pitiful rumor may report my flight   128
To consolate thine ear. Come, night; end, day!   129
For with the dark, poor thief, I'll steal away.   *Exit.*

❖

3.3   *Flourish. Enter the Duke of Florence, [Bertram, Count] Rossillion, drum and trumpets, soldiers, Parolles.*

DUKE
The General of our Horse thou art, and we,

107 **sportive** amorous   108 **mark** target   109 **leaden messengers** i.e., bullets   111 **still-piecing** always closing or repairing itself again. (The Folio reading, *still-peering,* is possible in the sense of "always observing.")   112 **sings with piercing** i.e., whistles when a bullet passes through it   115 **caitiff** base wretch   118 **ravin** ravenous   120 **nature owes** human nature possesses, suffers   122–123 **Whence . . . all** i.e., from war, in which honor is at best rewarded for danger with a scar, and often loses life itself   127 **officed all** performed all domestic duties   128 **pitiful** compassionate   129 **consolate** console

3.3. Location: Florence.

Great in our hope, lay our best love and credence   2
Upon thy promising fortune.

BERTRAM   Sir, it is
A charge too heavy for my strength, but yet
We'll strive to bear it for your worthy sake
To th' extreme edge of hazard.

DUKE   Then go thou forth,   6
And fortune play upon thy prosperous helm   7
As thy auspicious mistress!

BERTRAM   This very day,
Great Mars, I put myself into thy file.   9
Make me but like my thoughts, and I shall prove   10
A lover of thy drum, hater of love.   *Exeunt omnes.*

❖

3.4   *Enter Countess and Steward [Rinaldo].*

COUNTESS
Alas! And would you take the letter of her?
Might you not know she would do as she has done,
By sending me a letter? Read it again.

RINALDO (*Reads the letter*)
"I am Saint Jaques' pilgrim, thither gone.   4
     Ambitious love hath so in me offended
That barefoot plod I the cold ground upon,
     With sainted vow my faults to have amended.   7
Write, write, that from the bloody course of war
     My dearest master, your dear son, may hie.   9
Bless him at home in peace, whilst I from far
     His name with zealous fervor sanctify.
His taken labors bid him me forgive;   12
     I, his despiteful Juno, sent him forth   13

---

2 Great pregnant, expectant. **lay** wager. **credence** trust **6 edge of
hazard** limit of peril **7 helm** helmet **9 file** battle line; ranks, catalogue **10 like my thoughts** i.e., as valiant as I aspire to be

3.4. Location: Rossillion.
4 Saint Jaques' pilgrim i.e., a pilgrim to the shrine of Saint James,
presumably the famous shrine of Santiago de Compostela in Spain
7 sainted holy **9 hie** hasten **12 His taken labors** the labors he has
undertaken **13 despiteful** spiteful. **Juno** goddess who persecuted
Hercules by assigning him the twelve labors

From courtly friends, with camping foes to live   14
    Where death and danger dogs the heels of worth.
He is too good and fair for death and me;
Whom I myself embrace, to set him free.''   17
COUNTESS
Ah, what sharp stings are in her mildest words!
Rinaldo, you did never lack advice so much   19
As letting her pass so. Had I spoke with her,
I could have well diverted her intents,
Which thus she hath prevented.
RINALDO   Pardon me, madam.   22
If I had given you this at overnight,   23
She might have been o'erta'en; and yet she writes
Pursuit would be but vain.
COUNTESS   What angel shall
Bless this unworthy husband? He cannot thrive,
Unless her prayers, whom heaven delights to hear   27
And loves to grant, reprieve him from the wrath
Of greatest justice. Write, write, Rinaldo,
To this unworthy husband of his wife.   30
Let every word weigh heavy of her worth   31
That he does weigh too light. My greatest grief,
Though little he do feel it, set down sharply.
Dispatch the most convenient messenger.   34
When haply he shall hear that she is gone,   35
He will return; and hope I may that she,
Hearing so much, will speed her foot again,
Led hither by pure love. Which of them both
Is dearest to me, I have no skill in sense   39
To make distinction. Provide this messenger.
My heart is heavy and mine age is weak;
Grief would have tears, and sorrow bids me speak.
                           Exeunt.

❖

14 **camping** fighting, contending   17 **Whom** i.e., death   19 **advice** judgment   22 **prevented** forestalled   23 **at overnight** last night   27 **her** i.e.,
Helena's. (Helena is likened to the Virgin Mary and other saints who
can intercede with heaven on behalf of a sinner.)   30 **unworthy . . . wife**
husband unworthy of his wife   31 **weigh heavy of** emphasize   34 **convenient** appropriate   35 **haply** perhaps   39 **in sense** in what I feel

3.5   *A tucket afar off. Enter old Widow of Florence,*
her daughter [Diana], and Mariana, with other
citizens.

WIDOW   Nay, come, for if they do approach the city we
shall lose all the sight.   2

DIANA   They say the French count has done most honorable service.

WIDOW   It is reported that he has taken their great'st   5
commander, and that with his own hand he slew the
Duke's brother. [*Tucket.*] We have lost our labor; they
are gone a contrary way. Hark! You may know by
their trumpets.

MARIANA   Come, let's return again and suffice our-   10
selves with the report of it. Well, Diana, take heed of
this French earl. The honor of a maid is her name, and   12
no legacy is so rich as honesty.   13

WIDOW   I have told my neighbor how you have been   14
solicited by a gentleman his companion.

MARIANA   I know that knave, hang him! One Parolles,
a filthy officer he is in those suggestions for the young   17
earl. Beware of them, Diana; their promises, enticements, oaths, tokens, and all these engines of lust are   19
not the things they go under. Many a maid hath been   20
seduced by them; and the misery is, example, that so   21
terrible shows in the wrack of maidenhood, cannot for
all that dissuade succession, but that they are limed   23
with the twigs that threatens them. I hope I need not   24
to advise you further, but I hope your own grace will   25
keep you where you are, though there were no further   26
danger known but the modesty which is so lost.   27

3.5. Location: Florence. Outside the walls.
s.d. tucket a trumpet fanfare   **2 lose . . . sight** miss seeing them
5 their i.e., the Sienese's   **10 suffice** content   **12 earl** i.e., Count
Bertram.   **her name** her reputation (for chastity)   **13 honesty** chastity
14 my neighbor i.e., Mariana   **17 officer** agent.   **suggestions for** solicit-
ings on behalf of   **19 engines** artifices, devices   **20 go under** pretend to
be   **21–23 example . . . succession** the dreadful example of what happens with the loss of virginity nonetheless cannot dissuade another
from a similar course   **23–24 they . . . twigs** i.e., other maidens are
caught in the traps. (Birdlime was smeared on twigs to ensnare birds.)
25 grace virtue   **26–27 further danger** i.e., pregnancy

DIANA You shall not need to fear me.   28

Enter Helena [disguised like a pilgrim].

WIDOW I hope so.—Look, here comes a pilgrim. I
know she will lie at my house; thither they send one 30
another. I'll question her.—God save you, pilgrim!
Whither are bound?   32

HELENA To Saint Jaques le Grand.
Where do the palmers lodge, I do beseech you?   34

WIDOW
At the Saint Francis here beside the port.   35

HELENA Is this the way?   *(A march afar.)*

WIDOW
Ay, marry, is 't. Hark you, they come this way.
If you will tarry, holy pilgrim,
But till the troops come by,
I will conduct you where you shall be lodged;
The rather, for I think I know your hostess
As ample as myself.   42

HELENA Is it yourself?

WIDOW If you shall please so, pilgrim.

HELENA
I thank you, and will stay upon your leisure.   45

WIDOW
You came, I think, from France?

HELENA   I did so.

WIDOW
Here you shall see a countryman of yours
That has done worthy service.

HELENA   His name, I pray you?

DIANA
The Count Rossillion. Know you such a one?

HELENA
But by the ear, that hears most nobly of him.
His face I know not.

DIANA   Whatsoe'er he is,
He's bravely taken here. He stole from France,   52

28 fear worry about **30 lie** lodge **32 are** are you **34 palmers** pilgrims
35 port city gate **42 ample** fully, completely **45 stay . . . leisure** await
your convenience **52 bravely taken** highly regarded

As 'tis reported, for the King had married him   53
Against his liking. Think you it is so?
HELENA
Ay, surely, mere the truth. I know his lady.   55
DIANA
There is a gentleman that serves the Count
Reports but coarsely of her.
HELENA   What's his name?
DIANA
Monsieur Parolles.
HELENA   O, I believe with him.   58
In argument of praise, or to the worth   59
Of the great Count himself, she is too mean
To have her name repeated. All her deserving   61
Is a reservèd honesty, and that   62
I have not heard examined.
DIANA   Alas, poor lady!   63
'Tis a hard bondage to become the wife
Of a detesting lord.
WIDOW
I warrant, good creature, wheresoe'er she is,
Her heart weighs sadly. This young maid might do her
A shrewd turn, if she pleased.
HELENA   How do you mean?   68
Maybe the amorous Count solicits her
In the unlawful purpose?
WIDOW   He does indeed,
And brokes with all that can in such a suit   71
Corrupt the tender honor of a maid.
But she is armed for him and keeps her guard
In honestest defense.   74

> *Drum and colors. Enter [Bertram] Count*
> *Rossillion, Parolies, and the whole army.*

MARIANA The gods forbid else!   75
WIDOW So, now they come.

---

53 **for** because 55 **mere** absolutely 58 **believe** agree 59 **In argument
of** as a subject for. **to** compared to 61–62 **All . . . honesty** her only
merit is a well-preserved chastity 63 **examined** doubted, questioned
68 **shrewd** malicious, hurtful 71 **brokes** bargains 74 **honestest** most
chaste 75 **else** that it should be otherwise

That is Antonio, the Duke's eldest son;
That, Escalus.
HELENA   Which is the Frenchman?
DIANA   He,
That with the plume. 'Tis a most gallant fellow.
I would he loved his wife. If he were honester   80
He were much goodlier. Is 't not a handsome gentle-
man?
HELENA   I like him well.
DIANA
'Tis pity he is not honest. Yond's that same knave
That leads him to these places. Were I his lady
I would poison that vile rascal.
HELENA   Which is he?
DIANA
That jackanapes with scarves. Why is he melancholy?   86
HELENA   Perchance he's hurt i' the battle.
PAROLLES   Lose our drum? Well.
MARIANA   He's shrewdly vexed at something. Look, he   89
has spied us.
WIDOW   Marry, hang you!
MARIANA   And your courtesy, for a ring-carrier!   92
              Exeunt [Bertram, Parolles, and army].
WIDOW
The troop is past. Come, pilgrim, I will bring you
Where you shall host. Of enjoined penitents   94
There's four or five, to great Saint Jaques bound,
Already at my house.
HELENA   I humbly thank you.
Please it this matron and this gentle maid   97
To eat with us tonight, the charge and thanking   98
Shall be for me; and, to requite you further,   99
I will bestow some precepts of this virgin   100
Worthy the note.
BOTH   We'll take your offer kindly.   101
                                        Exeunt.

❖

80 honester more honorable   **86 jackanapes** monkey   **89 shrewdly**
sorely   **92 courtesy** ceremonious bow.   **ring-carrier** go-between
94 host lodge.   **enjoined penitents** those bound by oath to undertake
a pilgrimage as penance for sin   **97 Please it** if it please   **98–99 the
charge . . . me** i.e., I will bear the expense and be grateful at the same
time   **99 for me** mine   **100 of** on   **101 kindly** gratefully

3.6   *Enter [Bertram] Count Rossillion and the [two] Frenchmen, as at first.*

FIRST LORD   Nay, good my lord, put him to 't; let him 1
have his way.

SECOND LORD   If your lordship find him not a hilding, 3
hold me no more in your respect.

FIRST LORD   On my life, my lord, a bubble.

BERTRAM   Do you think I am so far deceived in him?

FIRST LORD   Believe it, my lord, in mine own direct
knowledge, without any malice, but to speak of him
as my kinsman, he's a most notable coward, an infi- 9
nite and endless liar, an hourly promise-breaker, the
owner of no one good quality worthy your lordship's
entertainment.   12

SECOND LORD   It were fit you knew him, lest, reposing 13
too far in his virtue, which he hath not, he might at
some great and trusty business in a main danger fail 15
you.

BERTRAM   I would I knew in what particular action to
try him.   18

SECOND LORD   None better than to let him fetch off his 19
drum, which you hear him so confidently undertake
to do.

FIRST LORD   I, with a troop of Florentines, will suddenly
surprise him; such I will have whom I am sure 23
he knows not from the enemy. We will bind and
hoodwink him so, that he shall suppose no other but 25
that he is carried into the leaguer of the adversaries, 26
when we bring him to our own tents. Be but your
lordship present at his examination. If he do not, for
the promise of his life and in the highest compulsion
of base fear, offer to betray you and deliver all the in- 30
telligence in his power against you, and that with the 31
divine forfeit of his soul upon oath, never trust my
judgment in anything.

3.6. Location: The Florentine camp.
1 to 't i.e., to the test   **3 hilding** good-for-nothing   **9 as** as if he were
12 entertainment patronage   **13 reposing** trusting   **15 trusty** demanding trustworthiness   **18 try** test   **19 fetch off** recapture   **23 surprise**
capture   **25 hoodwink** blindfold   **26 leaguer** camp   **30–31 intelligence
in his power** information at his command

SECOND LORD   O, for the love of laughter, let him fetch
his drum; he says he has a stratagem for 't. When your
lordship sees the bottom of his success in 't, and to 36
what metal this counterfeit lump of ore will be melted,
if you give him not John Drum's entertainment, your 38
inclining cannot be removed. Here he comes.   39

   Enter Parolles.

FIRST LORD [*Aside to Bertram*] O, for the love of
laughter, hinder not the honor of his design. Let him
fetch off his drum in any hand.   42

BERTRAM   How now, monsieur? This drum sticks sorely 43
in your disposition.   44

SECOND LORD   A pox on 't, let it go; 'tis but a drum.

PAROLLES   But a drum! Is 't but a drum? A drum so lost!
There was excellent command—to charge in with our
horse upon our own wings, and to rend our own sol-   48
diers!

SECOND LORD   That was not to be blamed in the com- 50
mand of the service; it was a disaster of war that Cae- 51
sar himself could not have prevented, if he had been
there to command.

BERTRAM   Well, we cannot greatly condemn our suc-   54
cess. Some dishonor we had in the loss of that drum, 55
but it is not to be recovered.

PAROLLES   It might have been recovered.

BERTRAM   It might, but it is not now.

PAROLLES   It is to be recovered. But that the merit of ser- 59
vice is seldom attributed to the true and exact per-
former, I would have that drum or another, or *hic* 61
jacet.   62

BERTRAM   Why, if you have a stomach, to 't, monsieur!
If you think your mystery in stratagem can bring this 64

---

36 bottom extent   **38 John Drum's entertainment** (Slang phrase for a
thorough beating and unceremonious dismissal.)   **39 inclining** partiality
(for Parolles)   **42 in any hand** in any case   **43–44 sticks . . . disposition**
i.e., greatly troubles you   **48 wings** flanks.   **rend** cut up, attack
50–51 in . . . service i.e., upon the generalship   **51 disaster** accident
54–55 we . . . success i.e., we were successful enough   **59 But that** were
it not that   **61–62 hic jacet** Latin for *here lies*, the beginning phrase of
tomb inscriptions. Hence, Parolles means "I would die in the attempt."
64 mystery skill

instrument of honor again into his native quarter, be 65
magnanimous in the enterprise and go on; I will grace 66
the attempt for a worthy exploit. If you speed well in 67
it, the Duke shall both speak of it and extend to you
what further becomes his greatness, even to the ut- 69
most syllable of your worthiness.

PAROLLES   By the hand of a soldier, I will undertake it.

BERTRAM   But you must not now slumber in it.

PAROLLES   I'll about it this evening, and I will presently 73
pen down my dilemmas, encourage myself in my cer- 74
tainty, put myself into my mortal preparation; and by 75
midnight look to hear further from me.

BERTRAM   May I be bold to acquaint His Grace you are
gone about it?

PAROLLES   I know not what the success will be, my lord,
but the attempt I vow.

BERTRAM   I know thou'rt valiant, and to the possibility 81
of thy soldiership will subscribe for thee. Farewell.   82

PAROLLES   I love not many words.   *Exit.*

FIRST LORD   No more than a fish loves water. Is not this
a strange fellow, my lord, that so confidently seems to
undertake this business, which he knows is not to be
done, damns himself to do, and dares better be 87
damned than to do 't?

SECOND LORD   You do not know him, my lord, as we
do. Certain it is that he will steal himself into a man's
favor and for a week escape a great deal of discover- 91
ies; but when you find him out, you have him ever 92
after.

BERTRAM   Why, do you think he will make no deed at 94
all of this that so seriously he does address himself
unto?

FIRST LORD   None in the world, but return with an in- 97
vention, and clap upon you two or three probable lies. 98

---

65 again . . . quarter back home again   **66 grace** honor   **67 speed**
succeed   **69 becomes** suits, is worthy of   **73 presently** immediately
74 pen . . . dilemmas contain my uncertainties   **75 mortal preparation**
extreme unction; or, death-dealing readiness   **81 possibility** capacity
82 subscribe vouch   **87 damns** condemns.   **better** rather   **91–92 es-**
cape . . . discoveries i.e., almost get away with it   **92 have him** have a
true knowledge of him   **94 deed** attempt   **97–98 invention** fabrication
98 probable plausible

But we have almost embossed him. You shall see his 99
fall tonight; for indeed he is not for your lordship's
respect.

SECOND LORD   We'll make you some sport with the fox
ere we case him. He was first smoked by the old lord 103
Lafew. When his disguise and he is parted, tell me 104
what a sprat you shall find him, which you shall see 105
this very night.

FIRST LORD
I must go look my twigs. He shall be caught.   107

BERTRAM
Your brother he shall go along with me.   108

FIRST LORD
As 't please your lordship. I'll leave you.   [*Exit.*]

BERTRAM
Now will I lead you to the house and show you
The lass I spoke of.

SECOND LORD   But you say she's honest.   111

BERTRAM
That's all the fault. I spoke with her but once
And found her wondrous cold; but I sent to her,
By this same coxcomb that we have i' the wind,   114
Tokens and letters which she did re-send,   115
And this is all I have done. She's a fair creature.
Will you go see her?

SECOND LORD   With all my heart, my lord.
                                        Exeunt.

❖

3.7   *Enter Helena and Widow.*

HELENA
If you misdoubt me that I am not she,   1

---

99 embossed driven to exhaustion, cornered. (A hunting term.)
103 case skin, strip, unmask.   **smoked** smelled out; smoked out into the
open   **104 is parted** are separated   **105 sprat** a small fish; a contemptible creature   **107 look my twigs** i.e., see to my trap (as in catching
birds with birdlime on twigs)   **108 Your brother** i.e., the Second Lord
111 honest chaste   **114 coxcomb** fool.   **have i' the wind** have to our
downwind side, whom we are tracking   **115 re-send** send back

3.7. Location: Florence. The Widow's house.
1 misdoubt doubt

I know not how I shall assure you further
But I shall lose the grounds I work upon.   3

WIDOW
Though my estate be fall'n, I was well born,   4
Nothing acquainted with these businesses,
And would not put my reputation now   6
In any staining act.

HELENA   Nor would I wish you.
First give me trust the Count he is my husband,   8
And what to your sworn counsel I have spoken   9
Is so from word to word; and then you cannot,   10
By the good aid that I of you shall borrow,   11
Err in bestowing it.

WIDOW   I should believe you,
For you have showed me that which well approves   13
You're great in fortune.

HELENA [*Giving money*]   Take this purse of gold,
And let me buy your friendly help thus far,
Which I will overpay and pay again
When I have found it. The Count he woos your daughter, 17
Lays down his wanton siege before her beauty,
Resolved to carry her. Let her in fine consent,   19
As we'll direct her how 'tis best to bear it.   20
Now his important blood will naught deny   21
That she'll demand. A ring the County wears,   22
That downward hath succeeded in his house
From son to son some four or five descents
Since the first father wore it. This ring he holds
In most rich choice, yet, in his idle fire,   26
To buy his will it would not seem too dear,   27
Howe'er repented after.

WIDOW
Now I see the bottom of your purpose.   29

---

3 But . . . upon i.e., unless I give up my basic plan (of concealing my
identity from Bertram) **4 estate** worldly condition **6 put** risk **8 give
me trust** believe me **9 counsel** secrecy **10 so . . . word** true in every
word **11 By** with regard to **13 approves** proves **17 found it** i.e.,
received your help with success **19 carry** win. **in fine** finally, in the
end (as also in l. 33) **20 bear** manage **21 important** importunate,
urgent. **blood** passion **22 County** Count **26 choice** estimation,
regard. **idle fire** reckless passion **27 will** desire **29 bottom** i.e.,
extent

HELENA
You see it lawful, then. It is no more
But that your daughter, ere she seems as won,
Desires this ring; appoints him an encounter;   32
In fine, delivers me to fill the time,
Herself most chastely absent. After,
To marry her, I'll add three thousand crowns   35
To what is passed already.
WIDOW   I have yielded.
Instruct my daughter how she shall persever,
That time and place with this deceit so lawful
May prove coherent. Every night he comes   39
With musics of all sorts and songs composed   40
To her unworthiness. It nothing steads us   41
To chide him from our eaves, for he persists   42
As if his life lay on 't.
HELENA   Why then tonight   43
Let us assay our plot, which, if it speed,   44
Is wicked meaning in a lawful deed,   45
And lawful meaning in a lawful act,
Where both not sin, and yet a sinful fact.   47
But let's about it.   [*Exeunt.*]

❖

32 **appoints him an encounter** arranges a meeting   35 **To marry her** i.e.,
to give her a dowry   39 **coherent** suitable   40 **musics** musicians   41 **To
her unworthiness** to her, his social inferior; or, to the end of persuading
her to do an unworthy deed.   **nothing steads** profits not at all   42 **chide**
drive   43 **lay** depended   44 **assay** try.   **speed** succeed   45 **meaning**
intention (on Bertram's part)   47 **fact** deed (which is sinful because of
Bertram's intention)

4.1 *Enter one of the Frenchmen [the First Lord]*
with five or six other Soldiers, in ambush.

FIRST LORD   He can come no other way but by this
hedge corner. When you sally upon him, speak what 2
terrible language you will. Though you understand it 3
not yourselves, no matter; for we must not seem to
understand him, unless someone among us whom 5
we must produce for an interpreter.

FIRST SOLDIER   Good Captain, let me be th' interpreter.

FIRST LORD   Art not acquainted with him? Knows he not
thy voice?

FIRST SOLDIER   No, sir, I warrant you.

FIRST LORD   But what linsey-woolsey hast thou to speak 11
to us again?

FIRST SOLDIER   E'en such as you speak to me.

FIRST LORD   He must think us some band of strangers 14
i' th' adversary's entertainment. Now he hath a smack 15
of all neighboring languages. Therefore we must every
one be a man of his own fancy, not to know what we
speak one to another; so we seem to know is to know 18
straight our purpose: choughs' language, gabble 19
enough and good enough. As for you, interpreter,
you must seem very politic. But couch, ho! Here he 21
comes, to beguile two hours in a sleep, and then to 22
return and swear the lies he forges.   [*They hide.*]

Enter Parolles.

PAROLLES   Ten o'clock. Within these three hours 'twill
be time enough to go home. What shall I say I have
done? It must be a very plausive invention that carries 26
it. They begin to smoke me, and disgraces have of late 27
knocked too often at my door. I find my tongue is too

4.1. Location: Outside the Florentine camp.
2 sally rush out   **3 terrible** terrifying   **5 unless** except for   **11 linsey-woolsey** a fabric woven from wool and flax; figuratively, a hodgepodge
14 strangers foreigners   **15 entertainment** service.   **smack** smattering
18 so provided that   **19 choughs' language** the chattering of a small
species of the crow family, the jackdaw   **21 politic** shrewd, cunning.
couch take concealment   **22 beguile** while away.   **sleep** nap   **26 plausive**
plausible   **26–27 carries it** carries it off   **27 smoke** detect

foolhardy; but my heart hath the fear of Mars before
it, and of his creatures, not daring the reports of my   30
tongue.   31

FIRST LORD [*Aside*] This is the first truth that e'er thine
own tongue was guilty of.

PAROLLES What the devil should move me to undertake
the recovery of this drum, being not ignorant of the
impossibility and knowing I had no such purpose? I
must give myself some hurts and say I got them in
exploit. Yet slight ones will not carry it—they will say,
"Came you off with so little?"—and great ones I dare
not give. Wherefore? What's the instance? Tongue, I   40
must put you into a butter-woman's mouth and buy   41
myself another of Bajazeth's mule, if you prattle me   42
into these perils.

FIRST LORD [*Aside*] Is it possible he should know
what he is, and be that he is?

PAROLLES I would the cutting of my garments would
serve the turn, or the breaking of my Spanish sword.   47

FIRST LORD [*Aside*] We cannot afford you so.   48

PAROLLES Or the baring of my beard, and to say it was 49
in stratagem.

FIRST LORD [*Aside*] 'Twould not do.

PAROLLES Or to drown my clothes, and say I was
stripped.

FIRST LORD [*Aside*] Hardly serve.

PAROLLES Though I swore I leapt from the window of
the citadel—

FIRST LORD [*Aside*] How deep?

PAROLLES Thirty fathom.   58

FIRST LORD [*Aside*] Three great oaths would scarce
make that be believed.

---

30 his creatures i.e., soldiers   **30–31 not . . . tongue** not daring to carry
out my boasts   **40 Wherefore** why.   **instance** motive, cause (i.e., why
did I ever open my mouth?)   **41 butter-woman** dairywoman, i.e., a
proverbial scold and garrulous talker   **42 of Bajazeth's mule** i.e., from
a Turkish mule, since mules are notoriously mute (?) (Many emenda-
tions have been proposed, including *mute* for *mule*.)   **47 serve the turn**
suffice   **48 afford you so** i.e., let you off for that   **49 baring** shaving
58 fathom (A fathom is a unit of measure equal to six feet.)

PAROLLES   I would I had any drum of the enemy's. I
would swear I recovered it.

FIRST LORD [*Aside*]   You shall hear one anon.   63

PAROLLES   A drum now of the enemy's—

                                             Alarum within.

FIRST LORD [*Coming forward*]   *Throca movousus, cargo,*
cargo, cargo.

ALL   *Cargo, cargo, cargo, villianda par corbo, cargo.*

                        [*They seize and blindfold him.*]

PAROLLES

O, ransom, ransom! Do not hide mine eyes.

FIRST SOLDIER   *Boskos thromuldo boskos.*

PAROLLES

I know you are the Muskos' regiment,   70
And I shall lose my life for want of language.   71
If there be here German, or Dane, Low Dutch,
Italian, or French, let him speak to me;
I'll discover that which shall undo the Florentine.   74

FIRST SOLDIER   *Boskos vauvado.* I understand thee and
can speak thy tongue. *Kerelybonto.* Sir, betake thee to   76
thy faith, for seventeen poniards are at thy bosom.   77

PAROLLES   O!

FIRST SOLDIER   O, pray, pray, pray! *Manka revania*
dulche.

FIRST LORD   *Oscorbidulchos volivorco.*

FIRST SOLDIER

The General is content to spare thee yet,
And, hoodwinked as thou art, will lead thee on   83
To gather from thee. Haply thou mayst inform   84
Something to save thy life.

PAROLLES   O, let me live,
And all the secrets of our camp I'll show,
Their force, their purposes; nay, I'll speak that
Which you will wonder at.

FIRST SOLDIER   But wilt thou faithfully?

PAROLLES

If I do not, damn me.

---

63 anon immediately   **70 Muskos'** Muscovites'   **71 want** lack   **74 dis-**
cover reveal   **76–77 betake . . . faith** i.e., say your prayers   **83 hood-**
winked blindfolded   **on** onward, elsewhere   **84 gather** get information.   **Haply** perhaps

FIRST SOLDIER   *Acordo linta.*
  Come on; thou art granted space.   90
                              Exit [with Parolles guarded].
                              A short alarum within.
FIRST LORD
  Go tell the Count Rossillion and my brother
  We have caught the woodcock and will keep him muffled 92
  Till we do hear from them.
SECOND SOLDIER   Captain, I will.
FIRST LORD
  'A will betray us all unto ourselves;
  Inform on that.   95
SECOND SOLDIER   So I will, sir.
FIRST LORD
  Till then I'll keep him dark and safely locked. *Exeunt.*

❖

4.2   *Enter Bertram and the maid called Diana.*

BERTRAM
  They told me that your name was Fontibell.
DIANA
  No, my good lord, Diana.
BERTRAM   Titled goddess,   2
  And worth it, with addition! But, fair soul,   3
  In your fine frame hath love no quality?   4
  If the quick fire of youth light not your mind,   5
  You are no maiden, but a monument.   6
  When you are dead, you should be such a one
  As you are now; for you are cold and stern,
  And now you should be as your mother was
  When your sweet self was got.   10
DIANA
  She then was honest.   11

---

90 space time   **92 woodcock** (A proverbially stupid bird.)   **muffled**
blindfolded   **95 Inform on** report

4.2. Location: Florence. The Widow's house.
2–3 Titled . . . addition you who have the name of a goddess, and who
deserve that and more   **4 quality** position   **5 quick** lively   **6 monument**
statue, lifeless effigy   **10 got** begotten   **11 honest** chaste, true to marriage vows. (But Bertram uses it to mean "frank.")

BERTRAM   So should you be.

DIANA   No.

My mother did but duty—such, my lord,
As you owe to your wife.

BERTRAM   No more o' that.

I prithee, do not strive against my vows.   14
I was compelled to her, but I love thee
By love's own sweet constraint and will forever
Do thee all rights of service.

DIANA   Ay, so you serve us

Till we serve you; but when you have our roses,   18
You barely leave our thorns to prick ourselves   19
And mock us with our bareness.

BERTRAM   How have I sworn!   20

DIANA

'Tis not the many oaths that makes the truth,
But the plain single vow that is vowed true.
What is not holy, that we swear not by,
But take the High'st to witness. Then pray you, tell me,
If I should swear by Jove's great attributes
I loved you dearly, would you believe my oaths
When I did love you ill? This has no holding,   27
To swear by Him whom I protest to love,   28
That I will work against Him. Therefore your oaths   29
Are words and poor conditions but unsealed,   30
At least in my opinion.

BERTRAM   Change it, change it!

Be not so holy-cruel. Love is holy,   32
And my integrity ne'er knew the crafts   33
That you do charge men with. Stand no more off,
But give thyself unto my sick desires,   35
Who then recovers. Say thou art mine, and ever   36
My love, as it begins, shall so persever.

---

14 vows i.e., vows to live apart from Helena   **18 serve you** i.e., sexually.
(The sexual suggestion is continued in *roses* and in *prick*, l. 19.)   **19 barely**
bare   **20 our bareness** i.e., the loss of our rose of virginity   **27 ill** wick-
edly, and hence contrary to the purport of an oath sworn to God. **hold-**
ing power to bind; consistency   **28 protest** profess   **29 work against**
Him i.e., defy God's injunction against carnal and illicit sex   **30 words . . .**
unsealed mere words and invalid provisos, unratified and hence lacking
in legally binding force   **32 holy-cruel** i.e., cruel to me in your holiness   **33 crafts** deceits   **35 sick** i.e., unfulfilled   **36 Who** which.
recovers recover

DIANA

I see that men may rope 's in such a snare   38
That we'll forsake ourselves. Give me that ring.

BERTRAM

I'll lend it thee, my dear, but have no power
To give it from me.

DIANA   Will you not, my lord?

BERTRAM

It is an honor 'longing to our house,
Bequeathèd down from many ancestors,
Which were the greatest obloquy i' the world   44
In me to lose.

DIANA   Mine honor's such a ring.
My chastity's the jewel of our house,
Bequeathèd down from many ancestors,
Which were the greatest obloquy i' the world
In me to lose. Thus your own proper wisdom   49
Brings in the champion Honor on my part   50
Against your vain assault.

BERTRAM   Here, take my ring!
My house, mine honor, yea, my life, be thine,
And I'll be bid by thee.   [*He gives the ring.*] 53

DIANA

When midnight comes, knock at my chamber window.
I'll order take my mother shall not hear.   55
Now will I charge you in the bond of truth,
When you have conquered my yet maiden bed,
Remain there but an hour, nor speak to me.
My reasons are most strong, and you shall know them
When back again this ring shall be delivered.
And on your finger in the night I'll put
Another ring, that what in time proceeds   62
May token to the future our past deeds.   63
Adieu till then; then, fail not. You have won
A wife of me, though there my hope be done.   65

---

38 rope 's rope us, entrap us. (F reads *make rope's in such a scarre*.)
44 obloquy disgrace (as also in l. 48)   **49 proper** pertaining to yourself
50 part side   **53 bid** commanded   **55 order take** make provision
62 that . . . proceeds which, whatever may happen   **63 token** betoken,
indicate   **65 though . . . done** although all hope (of marriage) is thereby
destroyed for me

BERTRAM
  A heaven on earth I have won by wooing thee.

                                              [Exit.]

DIANA
  For which live long to thank both heaven and me!
  You may so in the end.
  My mother told me just how he would woo,
  As if she sat in 's heart; she says all men
  Have the like oaths. He had sworn to marry me   71
  When his wife's dead; therefore I'll lie with him
  When I am buried. Since Frenchmen are so braid,   73
  Marry that will, I live and die a maid.   74
  Only in this disguise I think 't no sin
  To cozen him that would unjustly win.   *Exit.* 76

❖

4.3   *Enter the two French Captains and some two*
        or three Soldiers.

FIRST LORD   You have not given him his mother's letter?
SECOND LORD   I have delivered it an hour since. There is 2
  something in 't that stings his nature, for on the reading it he changed almost into another man.
FIRST LORD   He has much worthy blame laid upon him 5
  for shaking off so good a wife and so sweet a lady.
SECOND LORD   Especially he hath incurred the everlasting displeasure of the King, who had even tuned his 8
  bounty to sing happiness to him. I will tell you a 9
  thing, but you shall let it dwell darkly with you. 10
FIRST LORD   When you have spoken it, 'tis dead, and I
  am the grave of it.
SECOND LORD   He hath perverted a young gentlewoman
  here in Florence, of a most chaste renown, and this

---

71 had has (?) would have (?)   **73 braid** i.e., deceitful. (A *braid* is a trick.)
74 Marry let those marry   **76 cozen** cheat

4.3. Location: The Florentine camp.
2 since ago   **5 worthy** deserved   **8 even** accurately   **9 bounty** generosity
10 darkly secretly

night he fleshes his will in the spoil of her honor. He 15
hath given her his monumental ring and thinks him- 16
self made in the unchaste composition.   17

FIRST LORD   Now, God delay our rebellion! As we are 18
ourselves, what things are we!   19

SECOND LORD   Merely our own traitors. And as in the 20
common course of all treasons we still see them reveal 21
themselves till they attain to their abhorred ends, so 22
he that in this action contrives against his own nobility 23
in his proper stream o'erflows himself.   24

FIRST LORD   Is it not meant damnable in us to be trum- 25
peters of our unlawful intents? We shall not then have
his company tonight?

SECOND LORD   Not till after midnight, for he is dieted to 28
his hour.

FIRST LORD   That approaches apace. I would gladly have
him see his company anatomized, that he might take 31
a measure of his own judgments wherein so curiously 32
he had set this counterfeit.   33

SECOND LORD   We will not meddle with him till he 34
come, for his presence must be the whip of the other. 35

FIRST LORD   In the meantime, what hear you of these
wars?

SECOND LORD   I hear there is an overture of peace.

FIRST LORD   Nay, I assure you, a peace concluded.

SECOND LORD   What will Count Rossillion do then? Will
he travel higher or return again into France?   41

---

15 fleshes his will gratifies his lust (like a hunter giving some meat to his
hounds from the hunted animal, the quarry or *spoil*)   **16 monumental**
i.e., serving as a token of his identity   **17 made** a made man. **composition** bargain   **18 delay our rebellion** assuage our lustful appetites
18–19 are ourselves i.e., unaided by God   **20 Merely** absolutely, entirely
21–22 still . . . themselves always see traitors reveal themselves for what
they are   **22 attain . . . ends** achieve their abhorrent desires and the
inevitable consequences of them   **23–24 he . . . himself** i.e., Bertram,
who thus seduces a woman, subverts his own nobility by abusing the
qualities that should channel and perpetuate it. (Like all traitors, indeed
like all people, Bertram is most of all a traitor to himself, betraying by
his actions his own wickedness.)   **25 meant damnable** a revelation or
confirmation of wickedness (?)   **28 dieted** restricted   **31 company**
companion. **anatomized** dissected, exposed   **32 curiously** carefully,
elaborately   **33 counterfeit** false jewel, i.e., Parolles   **34 him . . . he** i.e.,
Parolles . . . Bertram   **35 his . . . the other** i.e., Bertram's . . . Parolles
41 higher farther

FIRST LORD   I perceive, by this demand, you are not al- ⁴²
together of his council. ⁴³

SECOND LORD   Let it be forbid, sir! So should I be a great
deal of his act. ⁴⁵

FIRST LORD   Sir, his wife some two months since fled
from his house. Her pretense is a pilgrimage to Saint ⁴⁷
Jaques le Grand, which holy undertaking with most
austere sanctimony she accomplished. And, there re- ⁴⁹
siding, the tenderness of her nature became as a prey
to her grief; in fine, made a groan of her last breath, ⁵¹
and now she sings in heaven.

SECOND LORD   How is this justified? ⁵³

FIRST LORD   The stronger part of it by her own letters,
which makes her story true even to the point of her ⁵⁵
death. Her death itself, which could not be her office
to say is come, was faithfully confirmed by the rector
of the place.

SECOND LORD   Hath the Count all this intelligence?

FIRST LORD   Ay, and the particular confirmations, point
from point, to the full arming of the verity. ⁶¹

SECOND LORD   I am heartily sorry that he'll be glad of
this.

FIRST LORD   How mightily sometimes we make us com- ⁶⁴
forts of our losses! ⁶⁵

SECOND LORD   And how mightily some other times we
drown our gain in tears! The great dignity that his
valor hath here acquired for him shall at home be encountered with a shame as ample.

FIRST LORD   The web of our life is of a mingled yarn,
good and ill together. Our virtues would be proud if
our faults whipped them not, and our crimes would ⁷²
despair if they were not cherished by our virtues. ⁷³

Enter a [Servant as] messenger.

How now? Where's your master?

---

42 demand question   **43 of his council** in his confidence   **45 of his act**
i.e., an accessory to his misdeeds   **47 pretense** intent   **49 sanctimony**
holiness   **51 in fine** at last   **53 justified** made certain   **55 point** time,
moment   **61 arming** corroboration, strengthening. **verity** truth
64–65 make . . . losses i.e., take as apparent benefits what actually are
great deprivations   **72 whipped** chastened. **crimes** i.e., sins   **73 cherished** i.e., improved, compensated for

SERVANT He met the Duke in the street, sir, of whom
he hath taken a solemn leave. His lordship will next 76
morning for France. The Duke hath offered him letters
of commendations to the King.
SECOND LORD They shall be no more than needful there, 79
if they were more than they can commend. 80

Enter [Bertram] Count Rossillion.

FIRST LORD They cannot be too sweet for the King's tart-
ness. Here's his lordship now.—How now, my lord,
is 't not after midnight?
BERTRAM I have tonight dispatched sixteen businesses,
a month's length apiece, by an abstract of success: I 85
have congeed with the Duke, done my adieu with his 86
nearest, buried a wife, mourned for her, writ to my 87
lady mother I am returning, entertained my convoy, 88
and between these main parcels of dispatch effected 89
many nicer needs. The last was the greatest, but that I 90
have not ended yet.
SECOND LORD If the business be of any difficulty, and
this morning your departure hence, it requires haste
of your lordship.
BERTRAM I mean, the business is not ended, as fearing
to hear of it hereafter. But shall we have this dialogue
between the fool and the soldier? Come, bring forth
this counterfeit module; he's deceived me like a dou- 98
ble-meaning prophesier. 99
SECOND LORD Bring him forth. [*Exeunt Soldiers.*] He's
sat i' the stocks all night, poor gallant knave.
BERTRAM No matter; his heels have deserved it, in
usurping his spurs so long. How does he carry himself?
SECOND LORD I have told your lordship already, the
stocks carry him. But to answer you as you would be

76 **will** i.e., will depart   79 **no . . . needful** i.e., urgently needed   80 **if . . .
commend** even if they were stronger than any recommendation could
be   85 **by . . . success** i.e., by successfully condensing my affairs; or, by a
series of successful moves, as follows   86 **congeed with** taken leave of
86–87 **his nearest** those persons nearest him   88 **entertained my convoy**
arranged my transportation   89 **main . . . dispatch** major items of
business   90 **nicer** more delicate.   **The last** i.e., the affair with Diana
98 **module** mere image   98–99 **double-meaning** ambiguous, equivocating

understood, he weeps like a wench that had shed her 107
milk. He hath confessed himself to Morgan, whom he
supposes to be a friar, from the time of his remem- 109
brance to this very instant disaster of his setting i' the 110
stocks. And what think you he hath confessed?

BERTRAM Nothing of me, has 'a?

SECOND LORD His confession is taken, and it shall be
read to his face. If your lordship be in 't, as I believe
you are, you must have the patience to hear it.

    Enter Parolles [guarded] with [First Soldier as]
    his interpreter.

BERTRAM A plague upon him! Muffled! He can say 116
nothing of me.

FIRST LORD Hush, hush! Hoodman comes!—*Portotar-* 118
tarosa.

FIRST SOLDIER He calls for the tortures. What will you
say without 'em?

PAROLLES I will confess what I know without constraint. If ye pinch me like a pasty, I can say no more. 123

FIRST SOLDIER *Bosko chimurcho.*

FIRST LORD *Boblibindo chicurmurco.*

FIRST SOLDIER You are a merciful general.—Our general
bids you answer to what I shall ask you out of a note. 127

PAROLLES And truly, as I hope to live.

FIRST SOLDIER [*Reads*] "First demand of him how many
horse the Duke is strong." What say you to that? 130

PAROLLES Five or six thousand, but very weak and un-
serviceable. The troops are all scattered and the commanders very poor rogues, upon my reputation and
credit and as I hope to live.

FIRST SOLDIER Shall I set down your answer so?

                                  [He writes.]

PAROLLES Do. I'll take the Sacrament on 't, how and
which way you will.

BERTRAM [*Aside to the Lords*] All's one to him. What a
past-saving slave is this!

---

107 shed spilled **109–110 the time . . . remembrance** as far back as he
can recall **110 instant** present **116 Muffled** blindfolded **118 Hoodman
comes** (Customary call in the game of blindman's buff.) **123 pasty** meat
pie **127 note** memorandum or list **130 horse** horsemen, cavalry troops

FIRST LORD [*Aside to Bertram*]   You're deceived, my lord.
This is Monsieur Parolles, the "gallant militarist"—that 141
was his own phrase—that had the whole theoric of 142
war in the knot of his scarf and the practice in the
chape of his dagger.   144

SECOND LORD [*Aside*]   I will never trust a man again for
keeping his sword clean, nor believe he can have 146
everything in him by wearing his apparel neatly.

FIRST SOLDIER   Well, that's set down.

PAROLLES   "Five or six thousand horse," I said—I will
say true—"or thereabouts," set down, for I'll speak
truth.

FIRST LORD [*Aside*]   He's very near the truth in this.

BERTRAM [*Aside*]   But I con him no thanks for 't, in the 153
nature he delivers it.   154

PAROLLES   "Poor rogues," I pray you, say.

FIRST SOLDIER   Well, that's set down.

PAROLLES   I humbly thank you, sir. A truth's a truth. The
rogues are marvelous poor.

FIRST SOLDIER [*Reads*]   "Demand of him of what
strength they are afoot." What say you to that?

PAROLLES   By my troth, sir, if I were to live this present 161
hour, I will tell true. Let me see: Spurio, a hundred and
fifty; Sebastian, so many; Corambus, so many; Jaques, 163
so many; Guiltian, Cosmo, Lodowick, and Gratii, two
hundred fifty each; mine own company, Chitopher,
Vaumond, Bentii, two hundred fifty each; so that the
muster-file, rotten and sound, upon my life, amounts 167
not to fifteen thousand poll, half of the which dare not 168
shake the snow from off their cassocks lest they shake 169
themselves to pieces.

BERTRAM [*Aside to the Lords*]   What shall be done to
him?

FIRST LORD [*Aside*]   Nothing, but let him have thanks.—
Demand of him my condition and what credit I have
with the Duke.

FIRST SOLDIER   Well, that's set down. [*Reads.*] "You shall
demand of him whether one Captain Dumain be i'

---

141 militarist military expert   **142 theoric** theory   **144 chape** scabbard
tip   **146 clean** i.e., polished   **153 con** offer. (Literally, "know.")
154 nature manner   **161 live** i.e., live only   **163 so** as, equally   **167 file**
roll   **168 poll** heads   **169 cassocks** cloaks

the camp, a Frenchman; what his reputation is with
the Duke; what his valor, honesty, and expertness in
wars; or whether he thinks it were not possible, with
well-weighing sums of gold, to corrupt him to a 181
revolt." What say you to this? What do you know
of it?

PAROLLES I beseech you, let me answer to the particular
of the inter'gatories. Demand them singly.   185

FIRST SOLDIER Do you know this Captain Dumain?

PAROLLES I know him. 'A was a botcher's prentice in 187
Paris, from whence he was whipped for getting the
sheriff's fool with child—a dumb innocent, that 189
could not say him nay.

BERTRAM [Aside to First Lord, who makes as if to strike
Parolles] Nay, by your leave, hold your hands—
though I know his brains are forfeit to the next tile 193
that falls.   194

FIRST SOLDIER Well, is this captain in the Duke of Florence's camp?

PAROLLES Upon my knowledge, he is, and lousy.   197

FIRST LORD [Aside to Bertram] Nay, look not so upon
me; we shall hear of your lordship anon.

FIRST SOLDIER What is his reputation with the Duke?

PAROLLES The Duke knows him for no other but a poor
officer of mine, and writ to me this other day to turn
him out o' the band. I think I have his letter in my
pocket.

FIRST SOLDIER Marry, we'll search.
                              [They search his pockets.]

PAROLLES In good sadness, I do not know; either it is 206
there, or it is upon a file with the Duke's other letters
in my tent.

FIRST SOLDIER Here 'tis, here's a paper. Shall I read it to
you?

PAROLLES I do not know if it be it or no.

BERTRAM [Aside] Our interpreter does it well.

FIRST LORD [Aside] Excellently.

---

181 **well-weighing** heavy and persuasive   185 **inter'gatories** questions
187 **botcher's** mender's, especially a tailor or cobbler who makes repairs
189 **sheriff's fool** feeble-minded girl in the sheriff's custody   **193–194 his
. . . falls** i.e., such a liar is headed straight for sudden and violent death
197 **lousy** (1) contemptible (2) infested with lice   **206 sadness** seriousness

FIRST SOLDIER [*Reads*]
  "Dian, the Count's a fool, and full of gold—"
PAROLLES That is not the Duke's letter, sir; that is an
  advertisement to a proper maid in Florence, one   216
  Diana, to take heed of the allurement of one Count
  Rossillion, a foolish idle boy, but for all that very rut-   218
  tish. I pray you, sir, put it up again.   219
FIRST SOLDIER Nay, I'll read it first, by your favor.
PAROLLES My meaning in 't, I protest, was very honest
  in the behalf of the maid; for I knew the young Count
  to be a dangerous and lascivious boy, who is a whale
  to virginity and devours up all the fry it finds.   224
BERTRAM [*Aside*] Damnable both-sides rogue!
FIRST SOLDIER (*Reads the letter*)
  "When he swears oaths, bid him drop gold, and take it;
    After he scores, he never pays the score.   227
  Half won is match well made; match, and well make it;   228
    He ne'er pays after-debts, take it before.   229
  And say a soldier, Dian, told thee this:
    Men are to mell with, boys are not to kiss.   231
  For count of this, the Count's a fool, I know it,   232
    Who pays before, but not when he does owe it.   233
          Thine, as he vowed to thee in thine ear,
                                        Parolles."
BERTRAM [*Aside*] He shall be whipped through the
  army with this rhyme in 's forehead.
SECOND LORD [*Aside*] This is your devoted friend, sir,
  the manifold linguist and the armipotent soldier.   239
BERTRAM [*Aside*] I could endure anything before but a
  cat, and now he's a cat to me.   241
FIRST SOLDIER I perceive, sir, by our general's looks, we
  shall be fain to hang you.   243
PAROLLES My life, sir, in any case! Not that I am afraid

---

216 advertisement warning. **proper** respectable   **218–219 ruttish** lecherous   **224 fry** small fish   **227 scores** (1) buys on credit (2) hits the mark,
scores sexually.   **score** bill   **228 Half . . . made** one is halfway to success
if the *match* or bargain is well started with clearly defined agreements
229 after-debts debts payable after the goods are received. **it** i.e., payment   **231 mell** meddle (sexually)   **232 count of** take note of   **233 before**
in advance (when he is required to do so). **owe it** (1) owe payment for
something already received (2) possess it, i.e., her maidenhood   **239 manifold linguist** speaker of many languages. **armipotent** powerful in arms
241 cat (A term of contempt.)   **243 fain** obliged

to die, but that, my offenses being many, I would repent out the remainder of nature. Let me live, sir, in a   246
dungeon, i' the stocks, or anywhere, so I may live.

FIRST SOLDIER   We'll see what may be done, so you confess freely. Therefore, once more to this Captain Dumain. You have answered to his reputation with the
Duke, and to his valor. What is his honesty?

PAROLLES   He will steal, sir, an egg out of a cloister. For
rapes and ravishments he parallels Nessus. He pro-   253
fesses not keeping of oaths; in breaking 'em he is   254
stronger than Hercules. He will lie, sir, with such vol-   255
ubility that you would think truth were a fool. Drunk-   256
enness is his best virtue, for he will be swine-drunk,
and in his sleep he does little harm save to his bed-
clothes about him; but they know his conditions, and   259
lay him in straw. I have but little more to say, sir, of
his honesty. He has everything that an honest man
should not have; what an honest man should have, he
has nothing.

FIRST LORD [Aside]   I begin to love him for this.

BERTRAM [Aside]   For this description of thine honesty?
A pox upon him for me, he's more and more a cat.

FIRST SOLDIER   What say you to his expertness in war?

PAROLLES   Faith, sir, he's led the drum before the En-   268
glish tragedians. To belie him I will not, and more of   269
his soldiership I know not, except in that country he
had the honor to be the officer at a place there called
Mile End, to instruct for the doubling of files. I would   272
do the man what honor I can, but of this I am not
certain.

FIRST LORD [Aside]   He hath out-villained villainy so far
that the rarity redeems him.   276

BERTRAM [Aside]   A pox on him, he's a cat still.

---

246 remainder of nature i.e., what is left of my natural life   **253 Nessus**
a centaur who attempted to rape the wife of Hercules   **253–254 professes** makes a practice of   **255–256 volubility** fluency, facility
256 truth were a fool i.e., truth here seems so easily put down
259 they i.e., his servants   **268–269 led . . . tragedians** (It was a custom
of actors to parade the street before the
performance of a play.)   **272 Mile End** place near London where citizen
militiamen were regularly exercised.   **doubling of files** (Simple drill
maneuvers.)   **276 rarity** excellence

FIRST SOLDIER   His qualities being at this poor price, I
need not to ask you if gold will corrupt him to revolt.

PAROLLES   Sir, for a cardecu he will sell the fee simple   280
of his salvation, the inheritance of it, and cut th' entail   281
from all remainders, and a perpetual succession for it
perpetually.   283

FIRST SOLDIER   What's his brother, the other Captain
Dumain?

SECOND LORD [*Aside*]   Why does he ask him of me?

FIRST SOLDIER   What's he?

PAROLLES   E'en a crow o' the same nest; not altogether
so great as the first in goodness, but greater a great
deal in evil. He excels his brother for a coward, yet his
brother is reputed one of the best that is. In a retreat
he outruns any lackey; marry, in coming on he has the   292
cramp.

FIRST SOLDIER   If your life be saved, will you undertake to
betray the Florentine?

PAROLLES   Ay, and the Captain of his Horse, Count Ros-   296
sillion.

FIRST SOLDIER   I'll whisper with the General and know
his pleasure.

PAROLLES [*To himself*]   I'll no more drumming; a plague
of all drums! Only to seem to deserve well, and to beguile the supposition of that lascivious young boy the   302
Count, have I run into this danger. Yet who would
have suspected an ambush where I was taken?

FIRST SOLDIER   There is no remedy, sir, but you must
die. The General says, you that have so traitorously
discovered the secrets of your army and made such   307
pestiferous reports of men very nobly held can serve   308
the world for no honest use; therefore you must die.
Come, headsman, off with his head.

PAROLLES   O Lord, sir, let me live, or let me see my
death!

---

280 cardecu quart d'écu, quarter of a French crown.   **fee simple** total
and perpetual ownership   **281–283 cut . . . perpetually** prevent it from
being passed on successively to subsequent heirs   **292 lackey** running
footman.   **coming on** moving forward   **296 Captain of his Horse** cavalry commander   **302 supposition** judgment   **307 discovered** revealed
308 pestiferous malicious, pernicious.   **held** regarded

FIRST SOLDIER   That shall you, and take your leave of all
    your friends. [*Unblinding him.*] So, look about you.
    Know you any here?
BERTRAM   Good morrow, noble Captain.
SECOND LORD   God bless you, Captain Parolles.
FIRST LORD   God save you, noble Captain.
SECOND LORD   Captain, what greeting will you to my   319
    Lord Lafew? I am for France.   320
FIRST LORD   Good Captain, will you give me a copy of
    the sonnet you writ to Diana in behalf of the Count
    Rossillion? An I were not a very coward, I'd compel it   323
    of you; but fare you well. *Exeunt [Bertram and Lords]*.
FIRST SOLDIER   You are undone, Captain, all but your
    scarf; that has a knot on 't yet.
PAROLLES   Who cannot be crushed with a plot?
FIRST SOLDIER   If you could find out a country where but
    women were that had received so much shame, you
    might begin an impudent nation. Fare ye well, sir; I   330
    am for France too. We shall speak of you there.
                                        Exit [with Soldiers].
PAROLLES
    Yet am I thankful. If my heart were great,
    'Twould burst at this. Captain I'll be no more,
    But I will eat and drink, and sleep as soft
    As captain shall. Simply the thing I am
    Shall make me live. Who knows himself a braggart,   336
    Let him fear this, for it will come to pass
    That every braggart shall be found an ass.
    Rust, sword! Cool, blushes! And, Parolles, live
    Safest in shame! Being fooled, by foolery thrive!   340
    There's place and means for every man alive.
    I'll after them.   *Exit*.

❖

319 **will you** i.e., do you wish to send   320 **for** bound for, off to   323 **An**
if   330 **impudent** shameless   336 **Who** he who   340 **Being . . . thrive**
i.e., since they have made a fool of me, I will now thrive by playing the
fool

4.4   *Enter Helena, Widow, and Diana.*

HELENA
That you may well perceive I have not wronged you,
One of the greatest in the Christian world
Shall be my surety; 'fore whose throne 'tis needful,   3
Ere I can perfect mine intents, to kneel.
Time was, I did him a desirèd office,
Dear almost as his life, which gratitude   6
Through flinty Tartar's bosom would peep forth
And answer thanks. I duly am informed
His Grace is at Marseilles, to which place
We have convenient convoy. You must know   10
I am supposèd dead. The army breaking,   11
My husband hies him home, where, heaven aiding,   12
And by the leave of my good lord the King,
We'll be before our welcome.
WIDOW   Gentle madam,   14
You never had a servant to whose trust
Your business was more welcome.
HELENA   Nor you, mistress,
Ever a friend whose thoughts more truly labor
To recompense your love. Doubt not but heaven
Hath brought me up to be your daughter's dower,
As it hath fated her to be my motive   20
And helper to a husband. But O, strange men!
That can such sweet use make of what they hate,
When saucy trusting of the cozened thoughts   23
Defiles the pitchy night; so lust doth play   24
With what it loathes for that which is away.   25
But more of this hereafter. You, Diana,
Under my poor instructions yet must suffer   27
Something in my behalf.

4.4. Location: Florence. The Widow's house.
3 **surety** guarantee   6 **which gratitude** gratitude for which   10 **convenient convoy** suitable transport   11 **breaking** disbanding   12 **hies him** hastens   14 **be . . . welcome** i.e., arrive before we are expected
20 **motive** means   23–24 **When . . . night** when lascivious yielding to the deceptions of lust makes blacker the already black night   25 **for** i.e., believing it to be.   **away** absent. (Helena describes how Bertram has lustfully enjoyed Helena, making *sweet use* of what he hates, believing her to be the absent Diana.)   27 **yet** for a time yet. (Also at l. 30.)

DIANA   Let death and honesty   28
Go with your impositions, I am yours   29
Upon your will to suffer.
HELENA   Yet, I pray you;   30
But with the word the time will bring on summer,   31
When briers shall have leaves as well as thorns,   32
And be as sweet as sharp. We must away;
Our wagon is prepared, and time revives us.   34
All's well that ends well. Still the fine's the crown; 35
Whate'er the course, the end is the renown.   *Exeunt.* 36

❖

4.5   *Enter Clown [Lavatch], Old Lady [Countess],
          and Lafew.*

LAFEW   No, no, no, your son was misled with a snipped- 1
taffeta fellow there, whose villainous saffron would   2
have made all the unbaked and doughy youth of a na-   3
tion in his color. Your daughter-in-law had been alive
at this hour, and your son here at home, more
advanced by the King than by that red-tailed humble-   6
bee I speak of.   7
COUNTESS   I would I had not known him! It was the
death of the most virtuous gentlewoman that ever nature had praise for creating. If she had partaken of my

---

28 Let death and honesty i.e., even if death (provided my honor be
maintained)   **29 your impositions** what you impose or command
30 Upon . . . suffer to suffer as you wish.   **Yet** i.e., let us go on   **31 with
. . . summer** i.e., if we go on, time will bring on a happier state of
affairs, with rewards to compensate for our suffering   **32 briers . . .
leaves** (Helena refers to the sweetbrier or eglantine, a species of small
rose, which has prickly stems and highly aromatic leaves.)   **34 revives**
will revive   **35 the fine's the crown** the end is the crown of all   **36 is
the renown** will determine what is thought of us and make our story
famous

4.5. Location: Rossillion.
1 with by   **1–2 snipped-taffeta** wearing taffeta silk garments with
slashes to allow the under material to be visible   **2 saffron** bright
yellow spice used in making pastry and also in dyeing starched ruffs
and collars   **3 unbaked and doughy** raw and unformed   **6–7 humble-
bee** bumblebee

flesh and cost me the dearest groans of a mother, I [11]
could not have owed her a more rooted love. [12]

LAFEW 'Twas a good lady, 'twas a good lady. We may
pick a thousand salads ere we light on such another
herb.

LAVATCH Indeed, sir, she was the sweet marjoram of the
salad, or rather the herb of grace. [17]

LAFEW They are not herbs, you knave, they are nose- [18]
herbs. [19]

LAVATCH I am no great Nebuchadnezzar, sir. I have not [20]
much skill in grass. [21]

LAFEW Whether dost thou profess thyself, a knave or a [22]
fool?

LAVATCH A fool, sir, at a woman's service, and a knave
at a man's.

LAFEW Your distinction?

LAVATCH I would cozen the man of his wife and do his [27]
service. [28]

LAFEW So you were a knave at his service, indeed.

LAVATCH And I would give his wife my bauble, sir, to do [30]
her service.

LAFEW I will subscribe for thee, thou art both knave [32]
and fool.

LAVATCH At your service.

LAFEW No, no, no! [35]

LAVATCH Why, sir, if I cannot serve you, I can serve as
great a prince as you are.

LAFEW Who's that, a Frenchman?

LAVATCH Faith, sir, 'a has an English name, but his phys- [39]
nomy is more hotter in France than there. [40]

---

11 groans of a mother i.e., pains of childbirth   **12 rooted** firm   **17 herb
of grace** rue   **18 not herbs** i.e., not edible salad herbs or greens
18–19 nose-herbs fragrant herbs used for bouquets, not salads
20–21 Nebuchadnezzar . . . grass (In Daniel 4:28–37, King Nebuchadnezzar is reported to have gone mad and eaten grass like an ox.)   **21 grass**
(with a pun on *grace;* the word in the Folio is *grace*)   **22 Whether** which
of the two   **27 cozen** cheat   **27–28 do his service** i.e., usurp his sexual
role   **30 bauble** stick carried by a court fool (with bawdy suggestion)
32 subscribe vouch   **35 No, no, no** i.e., not under the terms of service
you have described   **39 English name** i.e., the Black Prince, a widely
known name for the eldest son of Edward III who defeated the French
39–40 physnomy physiognomy

LAFEW   What prince is that?

LAVATCH   The black prince, sir, alias the prince of darkness, alias the devil.

LAFEW   Hold thee, there's my purse. [*He gives money.*] I
give thee not this to suggest thee from thy master thou 45
talk'st of; serve him still.

LAVATCH   I am a woodland fellow, sir, that always loved a 47
great fire, and the master I speak of ever keeps a good
fire. But sure he is the prince of the world; let his
nobility remain in 's court. I am for the house with the
narrow gate, which I take to be too little for pomp to 51
enter. Some that humble themselves may, but the
many will be too chill and tender, and they'll be for 53
the flowery way that leads to the broad gate and the 54
great fire.

LAFEW   Go thy ways. I begin to be aweary of thee; and 56
I tell thee so before, because I would not fall out with 57
thee. Go thy ways. Let my horses be well looked to,
without any tricks.

LAVATCH   If I put any tricks upon 'em, sir, they shall be
jades' tricks, which are their own right by the law of 61
nature.   *Exit.*

LAFEW   A shrewd knave and an unhappy.   63

COUNTESS   So 'a is. My lord that's gone made himself
much sport out of him. By his authority he remains
here, which he thinks is a patent for his sauciness; and
indeed he has no pace, but runs where he will.   67

LAFEW   I like him well; 'tis not amiss. And I was about
to tell you, since I heard of the good lady's death, and
that my lord your son was upon his return home, I
moved the King my master to speak in the behalf of
my daughter, which, in the minority of them both, His

---

45 suggest tempt   **47 woodland** rustic   **51 narrow gate** (Compare
Matthew 7:14: "Strait is the gate, and narrow is the way, which leadeth
unto life.")   **53 many** multitude.   **chill and tender** sensitive to cold (and
hence preferring the hotter place)   **54 broad gate** (Compare Matthew
7:13: "Wide is the gate, and broad is the way, that leadeth to destruction.")   **56 Go thy ways** get along with you   **57 before** i.e., before I
grow thoroughly weary   **61 jades' tricks** (1) malicious tricks played on
jades, or broken-down horses (2) the ill-tempered behavior of a jade
63 shrewd sharp-tongued and witty.   **unhappy** discontented   **67 has no
pace** observes no restraint

Majesty, out of a self-gracious remembrance, did first 73
propose. His Highness hath promised me to do it, and
to stop up the displeasure he hath conceived against
your son, there is no fitter matter. How does your
ladyship like it?

COUNTESS With very much content, my lord, and I wish
it happily effected.

LAFEW His Highness comes post from Marseilles, of as 80
able body as when he numbered thirty. 'A will be here 81
tomorrow, or I am deceived by him that in such intel- 82
ligence hath seldom failed.

COUNTESS It rejoices me that I hope I shall see him ere 84
I die. I have letters that my son will be here tonight. I
shall beseech your lordship to remain with me till they
meet together.

LAFEW Madam, I was thinking with what manners I
might safely be admitted.   89

COUNTESS You need but plead your honorable privi- 90
lege.   91

LAFEW Lady, of that I have made a bold charter, but I 92
thank my God it holds yet.

Enter Clown [Lavatch].

LAVATCH O madam, yonder's my lord your son with a
patch of velvet on 's face. Whether there be a scar under 't or no, the velvet knows, but 'tis a goodly patch
of velvet. His left cheek is a cheek of two pile and a 97
half, but his right cheek is worn bare.   98

LAFEW A scar nobly got, or a noble scar, is a good livery 99
of honor; so belike is that.   100

LAVATCH But it is your carbonadoed face.   101

---

73 self-gracious remembrance thoughtful recollection that came to him
without prompting **80 post** posthaste **81 numbered thirty** was thirty
years old **82 him** i.e., a messenger **84 that . . . shall** that I can hope
to **89 admitted** i.e., allowed to stay on for that meeting **90–91 honorable privilege** privilege due your honor **92 made . . . charter** asserted
my claim as far as I dare **97–98 two . . . half** i.e., a thick velvet
98 worn bare i.e., without a velvet patch **99 livery** uniform **100 belike**
probably **101 carbonadoed** slashed or scored across with gashes, as to
broil meat (here suggesting a cut made to drain a venereal ulcer and
covered with a velvet patch)

LAFEW   Let us go see your son, I pray you. I long to talk
   with the young noble soldier.
LAVATCH   Faith, there's a dozen of 'em, with delicate fine
   hats, and most courteous feathers, which bow the
   head and nod at every man.   *Exeunt.*

❖

5.1 *Enter Helena, Widow, and Diana, with two attendants.*

HELENA
But this exceeding posting day and night   1
Must wear your spirits low; we cannot help it.
But since you have made the days and nights as one
To wear your gentle limbs in my affairs,   4
Be bold you do so grow in my requital   5
As nothing can unroot you.

　　　　　Enter a Gentleman.

　　　　　　　　　　　　　In happy time!   6
This man may help me to His Majesty's ear,
If he would spend his power.—God save you, sir.   8
GENTLEMAN　And you.
HELENA
Sir, I have seen you in the court of France.
GENTLEMAN　I have been sometimes there.
HELENA
I do presume, sir, that you are not fallen
From the report that goes upon your goodness;
And therefore, goaded with most sharp occasions   14
Which lay nice manners by, I put you to   15
The use of your own virtues, for the which
I shall continue thankful.
GENTLEMAN　　　　　　　　What's your will?
HELENA　That it will please you
To give this poor petition to the King
　　　　　　　　　[*Showing a petition*]
And aid me with that store of power you have
To come into his presence.
GENTLEMAN
The King's not here.
HELENA　　　　　　Not here, sir?
GENTLEMAN　　　　　　　　　　Not indeed.

5.1. Location: Marseilles. A street.
1 posting riding in haste　**4 wear** wear out　**5 bold** confident.　**requital**
i.e., debt, thankfulness　**6 happy** opportune　**8 spend** expend　**14 sharp**
occasions urgent circumstances　**15 nice** scrupulous.　**put** urge

He hence removed last night, and with more haste   23
Than is his use.
WIDOW   Lord, how we lose our pains!   24
HELENA   All's well that ends well yet,
Though time seem so adverse and means unfit.
I do beseech you, whither is he gone?
GENTLEMAN
Marry, as I take it, to Rossillion,
Whither I am going.
HELENA   I do beseech you, sir,
Since you are like to see the King before me,
Commend the paper to his gracious hand,   31
                              [*Giving the petition*]
Which I presume shall render you no blame
But rather make you thank your pains for it.
I will come after you with what good speed
Our means will make us means.
GENTLEMAN   This I'll do for you.   35
HELENA
And you shall find yourself to be well thanked,
Whate'er falls more. We must to horse again.   37
Go, go, provide.   [*Exeunt separately.*]

❖

5.2   *Enter Clown* [*Lavatch*], *and Parolles.*

PAROLLES   Good Monsieur Lavatch, give my Lord Lafew this letter. [*He offers a letter.*] I have ere now, sir,
been better known to you, when I have held familiarity
with fresher clothes; but I am now, sir, muddied in
Fortune's mood, and smell somewhat strong of her
strong displeasure.
LAVATCH   Truly, Fortune's displeasure is but sluttish if it
smell so strongly as thou speak'st of. I will henceforth
eat no fish of Fortune's buttering. Prithee, allow the   9
wind.   10

23 **removed** departed   24 **use** usual practice   31 **Commend** deliver
35 **Our . . . means** our resources will allow   37 **falls more** else may happen
5.2. Location: Rossillion.
9 **of Fortune's buttering** i.e., prepared and served by Fortune
9–10 **allow the wind** let me have the windward side of you (since you
have been befouled by evil-smelling Fortune)

PAROLLES Nay, you need not to stop your nose, sir; I spake but by a metaphor.

LAVATCH Indeed, sir, if your metaphor stink I will stop my nose, or against any man's metaphor. Prithee, get thee further.

PAROLLES Pray you, sir, deliver me this paper.

LAVATCH Foh! Prithee, stand away. A paper from Fortune's close-stool to give to a nobleman! Look, here he 18 comes himself.

Enter Lafew.

Here is a purr of Fortune's, sir, or of Fortune's cat—but 20 not a musk cat—that has fallen into the unclean fish- 21 pond of her displeasure, and, as he says, is muddied withal. Pray you, sir, use the carp as you may, for he 23 looks like a poor, decayed, ingenious, foolish, rascally 24 knave. I do pity his distress in my similes of comfort, 25 and leave him to your lordship.   [*Exit.*]

PAROLLES My lord, I am a man whom Fortune hath cruelly scratched.

LAFEW And what would you have me to do? 'Tis too late to pare her nails now. Wherein have you played the knave with Fortune that she should scratch you, who of herself is a good lady and would not have knaves thrive long under her? There's a cardecu for 33 you. [*He gives money.*] Let the justices make you and For- 34 tune friends; I am for other business.

[*He starts to leave.*]

PAROLLES I beseech your honor to hear me one single word.

LAFEW You beg a single penny more. Come, you shall ha 't; save your word.

PAROLLES My name, my good lord, is Parolles.

---

18 close-stool privy   **20 purr** (The multiple pun here may include "male child," "piece of dung," "the purr of a cat," and the name given to the jack or knave in the card game post and pair.)   **21 musk cat** musk deer, prized for its musk scent   **23 carp** (1) a fish often bred in sewage-rich fishponds or moats (2) a chatterer   **24 ingenious** stupid, lacking in genius or intellect (?)   **25 similes of comfort** comforting similes   **33 cardecu** quart d'écu, quarter of a French crown   **34 justices** i.e., Justices of the Peace, responsible in Elizabethan England for tending to the deserving poor

LAFEW You beg more than "word," then. Cox my pas- 41
sion! Give me your hand. How does your drum?   42

PAROLLES O my good lord, you were the first that
found me!   44

LAFEW Was I, in sooth? And I was the first that lost 45
thee.

PAROLLES It lies in you, my lord, to bring me in some
grace, for you did bring me out.   48

LAFEW Out upon thee, knave! Dost thou put upon me
at once both the office of God and the devil? One
brings thee in grace and the other brings thee out.
[*Trumpets sound.*] The King's coming; I know by his
trumpets. Sirrah, inquire further after me. I had talk of
you last night; though you are a fool and a knave, you
shall eat. Go to, follow.

PAROLLES I praise God for you.   [*Exeunt.*]

❖

5.3 *Flourish. Enter King, Old Lady [Countess],*
Lafew, the two French Lords, with attendants.

KING
We lost a jewel of her, and our esteem   1
Was made much poorer by it; but your son,
As mad in folly, lacked the sense to know   3
Her estimation home.

COUNTESS   'Tis past, my liege,   4
And I beseech Your Majesty to make it
Natural rebellion, done i' the blade of youth,   6
When oil and fire, too strong for reason's force,
O'erbears it and burns on.

KING   My honored lady,
I have forgiven and forgotten all,

---

41 more than "word" i.e., many words; *Parolles* suggests a plural of the
French *parole*, word   **41–42 Cox my passion** i.e., by God's (Christ's)
passion on the cross   **44 found me** found me out   **45 lost** abandoned
48 grace favor.   **out** out of favor

5.3. Location: Rossillion.
s.d. Lafew (Lafew may remain onstage from the end of the previous
scene.)   **1 of** in.   **our esteem** my own value   **3–4 know . . . home** appreciate her value fully   **6 Natural rebellion** rebellion by the passions.
blade greenness, freshness

Though my revenges were high bent upon him   10
And watched the time to shoot.
LAFEW   This I must say—   11
But first I beg my pardon—the young lord
Did to His Majesty, his mother, and his lady
Offense of mighty note; but to himself
The greatest wrong of all. He lost a wife
Whose beauty did astonish the survey   16
Of richest eyes, whose words all ears took captive,   17
Whose dear perfection hearts that scorned to serve
Humbly called mistress.
KING   Praising what is lost
Makes the remembrance dear. Well, call him hither;
We are reconciled, and the first view shall kill
All repetition. Let him not ask our pardon;   22
The nature of his great offense is dead,
And deeper than oblivion we do bury
Th' incensing relics of it. Let him approach,   25
A stranger, no offender; and inform him   26
So 'tis our will he should.
GENTLEMAN   I shall, my liege.   [*Exit.*] 27
KING
What says he to your daughter? Have you spoke?
LAFEW
All that he is hath reference to Your Highness.   29
KING
Then shall we have a match. I have letters sent me
That sets him high in fame.

          Enter Count Bertram.

LAFEW   He looks well on 't.
KING   I am not a day of season,   33
For thou mayst see a sunshine and a hail
In me at once. But to the brightest beams

---

10 high bent i.e., as with a fully drawn bow   **11 watched** waited for
16 astonish the survey dazzle the sight   **17 richest** i.e., richest in experience   **22 repetition** rehearsing what is past   **25 incensing relics** re-
minders that kindle anger   **26 A stranger** i.e., as one whose story is
unknown   **27 s.p. Gentleman** (This could be one of the two French
lords, or some other person in attendance.)   **29 hath reference to** defers
to   **33 of season** i.e., of one consistent kind of weather

Distracted clouds give way; so stand thou forth.   36
The time is fair again.
BERTRAM   My high-repented blames,
Dear sovereign, pardon to me.
KING   All is whole.
Not one word more of the consumèd time.
Let's take the instant by the forward top;   40
For we are old, and on our quick'st decrees
Th' inaudible and noiseless foot of Time
Steals ere we can effect them. You remember
The daughter of this lord?
BERTRAM   Admiringly, my liege. At first
I stuck my choice upon her, ere my heart   46
Durst make too bold a herald of my tongue;
Where the impression of mine eye infixing,   48
Contempt his scornful perspective did lend me,   49
Which warped the line of every other favor,   50
Scorned a fair color, or expressed it stolen,   51
Extended or contracted all proportions   52
To a most hideous object. Thence it came   53
That she whom all men praised, and whom myself,   54
Since I have lost, have loved, was in mine eye
The dust that did offend it.
KING   Well excused.   56
That thou didst love her strikes some scores away
From the great compt. But love that comes too late,   58
Like a remorseful pardon slowly carried,   59
To the great sender turns a sour offense,   60
Crying, "That's good that's gone." Our rash faults

---

36 Distracted . . . way clouds disperse and give way   **40 forward top** forelock   **46 stuck** made, fixed   **48 Where** i.e., in my heart.   **the impression . . .
infixing** i.e., the image of her entering first at my eye and then fixing itself in
my heart. (Bertram seems to say that he loved Lafew's daughter some time
ago but dared not speak of his love, and on her account came to despise all
women—especially Helena, who was like an offending speck in his eye,
though since then he has learned to love the memory of the wife he lost.)
49 perspective an optical glass for producing distorted images   **50 favor**
face   **51 expressed it stolen** declared it to be painted cosmetically
52–53 Extended . . . object elongated or compressed all other forms until
they made a hideous sight   **54 she** i.e., Helena   **56 offend it** (1) give it
offense (2) blur its vision   **58 compt** account, reckoning   **59 slowly carried**
i.e., arriving too late   **60 turns . . . offense** i.e., turns sour on him

Make trivial price of serious things we have,   62
Not knowing them until we know their grave.   63
Oft our displeasures, to ourselves unjust,   64
Destroy our friends, and after weep their dust;   65
Our own love waking cries to see what's done,
While shameful hate sleeps out the afternoon.   67
Be this sweet Helen's knell, and now forget her.
Send forth your amorous token for fair Maudlin.   69
The main consents are had, and here we'll stay
To see our widower's second marriage day.

COUNTESS
Which better than the first, O dear heaven, bless!
Or, ere they meet, in me, O nature, cesse!   73

LAFEW
Come on, my son, in whom my house's name
Must be digested, give a favor from you   75
To sparkle in the spirits of my daughter,
That she may quickly come. [*Bertram gives a ring.*] By
  my old beard,
And every hair that's on 't, Helen that's dead
Was a sweet creature; such a ring as this,
The last that e'er I took her leave at court,   80
I saw upon her finger.
BERTRAM   Hers it was not.

KING
Now, pray you, let me see it; for mine eye,
While I was speaking, oft was fastened to 't.
                    [*The ring is given to the King.*]
This ring was mine, and when I gave it Helen
I bade her, if her fortunes ever stood
Necessitied to help, that by this token   86
I would relieve her. Had you that craft to reave her   87
Of what should stead her most?   88

---

62 Make trivial price of greatly undervalue   **63 knowing** i.e., appreciating.   **know their grave** i.e., are aware of their irrevocable loss   **64 displeasures** offenses   **65 weep their dust** mourn over their remains
67 sleeps . . . afternoon i.e., sleeps at ease having done its work
69 Maudlin i.e., Magdalen, the daughter of Lafew   **73 ere they meet** i.e., before the two marriages come to resemble one another in unhappiness.
cesse cease   **75 digested** assimilated.   **favor** token   **80 took her leave** took leave of her   **86 Necessitied to** in need of   **87 reave** deprive, rob   **88 stead** help

BERTRAM   My gracious sovereign,   88
  Howe'er it pleases you to take it so,
  The ring was never hers.
COUNTESS   Son, on my life,
  I have seen her wear it, and she reckoned it
  At her life's rate.
LAFEW   I am sure I saw her wear it.   92
BERTRAM
  You are deceived, my lord; she never saw it.
  In Florence was it from a casement thrown me,
  Wrapped in a paper, which contained the name
  Of her that threw it. Noble she was, and thought
  I stood engaged; but when I had subscribed   97
  To mine own fortune, and informed her fully   98
  I could not answer in that course of honor   99
  As she had made the overture, she ceased   100
  In heavy satisfaction, and would never   101
  Receive the ring again.
KING   Plutus himself,   102
  That knows the tinct and multiplying med'cine,   103
  Hath not in nature's mystery more science   104
  Than I have in this ring. 'Twas mine, 'twas Helen's,
  Whoever gave it you. Then, if you know   106
  That you are well acquainted with yourself,   107
  Confess 'twas hers, and by what rough enforcement
  You got it from her. She called the saints to surety 109
  That she would never put it from her finger
  Unless she gave it to yourself in bed,
  Where you have never come, or sent it us
  Upon her great disaster.
BERTRAM   She never saw it.   113
KING
  Thou speak'st it falsely, as I love mine honor,

---

92 rate value   **97 engaged** i.e., pledged to her; or, possibly, not pledged
to another. (The F spelling, *ingag'd*, may suggest a negative prefix.)
97–98 subscribed . . . fortune i.e., explained my true situation (of my
marriage)   **99–100 answer . . . overture** respond honorably to the proposal (of marriage) that she honorably made   **101 heavy satisfaction**
doleful resignation   **102 Plutus** the god of wealth   **103 tinct . . . med'-
cine** the alchemical elixir for transmuting base metals into gold   **104 science** knowledge   **106–107 if . . . yourself** i.e., if you knew this to be a
fact as self-evident as your knowing your own self   **109 to surety** to
witness   **113 Upon . . . disaster** on the occasion of a disaster to her

And mak'st conjectural fears to come into me   115
Which I would fain shut out. If it should prove   116
That thou art so inhuman—'twill not prove so,
And yet I know not—thou didst hate her deadly,
And she is dead, which nothing but to close
Her eyes myself could win me to believe,
More than to see this ring. Take him away.
My forepast proofs, howe'er the matter fall,   122
Shall tax my fears of little vanity,   123
Having vainly feared too little. Away with him!   124
We'll sift this matter further.
BERTRAM   If you shall prove
  This ring was ever hers, you shall as easy
  Prove that I husbanded her bed in Florence,
  Where yet she never was.   [*Exit, guarded.*]

      Enter a Gentleman.

KING
  I am wrapped in dismal thinkings.
GENTLEMAN   Gracious sovereign,
  Whether I have been to blame or no, I know not.
  Here's a petition from a Florentine, [*Giving petition*]
  Who hath for four or five removes come short   132
  To tender it herself. I undertook it,   133
  Vanquished thereto by the fair grace and speech   134
  Of the poor suppliant, who by this I know   135
  Is here attending. Her business looks in her   136
  With an importing visage, and she told me,   137
  In a sweet verbal brief, it did concern   138
  Your Highness with herself.
KING (*Reads a letter*) "Upon his many protestations to
  marry me when his wife was dead, I blush to say it,
  he won me. Now is the Count Rossillion a widower,

115 **conjectural** suspicious   116 **fain** willingly   122 **My forepast proofs**
the evidence I already have.   **fall** turn out   123–124 **Shall . . . little** will
hardly censure my fears (concerning Helena) as inconsequential; indeed,
I have foolishly been too little apprehensive   132 **for . . . short** on
account of four or five shifts of residence of the court (as it moved from
Marseilles to Rossillion) come too late   133 **tender** offer   134 **Vanquished** won   135 **by this** by this time   136 **looks** manifests itself
137 **importing** urgent and full of import   138 **brief** summary

his vows are forfeited to me, and my honor's paid to   143
him. He stole from Florence, taking no leave, and I
follow him to his country for justice. Grant it me, O
King! In you it best lies; otherwise a seducer flourishes and a poor maid is undone.   Diana Capilet"

LAFEW   I will buy me a son-in-law in a fair, and toll for   148
this. I'll none of him.   149

KING
The heavens have thought well on thee, Lafew,
To bring forth this discovery. Seek these suitors.   151
Go speedily and bring again the Count.
                    [*Exeunt some attendants.*]
I am afeard the life of Helen, lady,
Was foully snatched.

COUNTESS   Now, justice on the doers!

    Enter Bertram [guarded].

KING
I wonder, sir, since wives are monsters to you,
And that you fly them as you swear them lordship,   156
Yet you desire to marry.

    Enter Widow [and] Diana.

                    What woman's that?   157

DIANA
I am, my lord, a wretched Florentine,
Derivèd from the ancient Capilet.   159
My suit, as I do understand, you know,
And therefore know how far I may be pitied.

WIDOW
I am her mother, sir, whose age and honor
Both suffer under this complaint we bring,
And both shall cease, without your remedy.

---

143 are . . . me i.e., are debts to which I am legally entitled   **148 in a fair**
i.e., where stolen and disreputable merchandise are common. (Lafew says
he can do better at such a place than with Bertram.)   **148–149 toll for
this** i.e., put Bertram up for sale. (Merchants wishing to sell at market
paid a toll or fee in order to enter their goods in a register.)   **151 suitors**
petitioners   **156 as** as soon as.   **swear them lordship** swear to be their
lord and husband   **157 Yet** still   **159 Derivèd** descended

KING
  Come hither, Count. Do you know these women?
BERTRAM
  My lord, I neither can nor will deny
  But that I know them. Do they charge me further?
DIANA
  Why do you look so strange upon your wife?
BERTRAM
  She's none of mine, my lord.
DIANA   If you shall marry,
  You give away this hand, and that is mine;   170
  You give away heaven's vows, and those are mine;
  You give away myself, which is known mine;
  For I by vow am so embodied yours
  That she which marries you must marry me,
  Either both or none.
LAFEW [*To Bertram*]   Your reputation comes too short for
  my daughter; you are no husband for her.
BERTRAM
  My lord, this is a fond and desperate creature,   178
  Whom sometime I have laughed with. Let Your High-
    ness
  Lay a more noble thought upon mine honor
  Than for to think that I would sink it here.
KING
  Sir, for my thoughts, you have them ill to friend   182
  Till your deeds gain them. Fairer prove your honor
  Than in my thought it lies!
DIANA   Good my lord,
  Ask him upon his oath if he does think
  He had not my virginity.
KING   What sayst thou to her?
BERTRAM   She's impudent, my lord,   188
  And was a common gamester to the camp.   189
DIANA
  He does me wrong, my lord; if I were so,
  He might have bought me at a common price.
  Do not believe him. O, behold this ring,
                                [*Showing a ring*]

170 **this hand** i.e., Bertram's hand   178 **fond** foolish   182 **you . . . friend**
they are not well disposed toward you   188 **impudent** shameless
189 **gamester** prostitute

Whose high respect and rich validity   193
Did lack a parallel; yet for all that
He gave it to a commoner o' the camp,
If I be one.
COUNTESS   He blushes, and 'tis hit.   196
Of six preceding ancestors, that gem,
Conferred by testament to th' sequent issue,   198
Hath it been owed and worn. This is his wife;   199
That ring's a thousand proofs.
KING   Methought you said
You saw one here in court could witness it.
DIANA
I did, my lord, but loath am to produce
So bad an instrument. His name's Parolles.
LAFEW
I saw the man today, if man he be.
KING
Find him, and bring him hither.   [*Exit an Attendant.*]
BERTRAM   What of him?
He's quoted for a most perfidious slave,   206
With all the spots o' the world taxed and debauched,   207
Whose nature sickens but to speak a truth.
Am I or that or this for what he'll utter,   209
That will speak anything?
KING   She hath that ring of yours.
BERTRAM
I think she has. Certain it is I liked her,
And boarded her i' the wanton way of youth.   212
She knew her distance and did angle for me,   213
Madding my eagerness with her restraint,   214
As all impediments in fancy's course   215
Are motives of more fancy; and, in fine,   216
Her infinite cunning, with her modern grace,   217
Subdued me to her rate. She got the ring,   218

---

193 **validity** value   196 **'tis hit** i.e., that point scored   198 **sequent issue**
next heir   199 **owed** owned   206 **quoted for** set down as   207 **With . . .**
debauched censured for being debauched with all the vices in the world
209 **Am I** am I to be considered.   **or . . . or** either . . . or.   **for** because of
212 **boarded** accosted (with sexual meaning)   213 **knew her distance** i.e.,
knew how to keep her distance, knew her value   214 **Madding** making
mad, exciting   215 **fancy's** love's   216 **motives** causes.   **fine** conclusion
217 **modern** commonplace   218 **her rate** her terms

And I had that which any inferior might
At market price have bought.

DIANA   I must be patient.
You that have turned off a first so noble wife
May justly diet me. I pray you yet—   222
Since you lack virtue, I will lose a husband—
Send for your ring, I will return it home,
And give me mine again.

BERTRAM   I have it not.

KING   What ring was yours, I pray you?

DIANA
Sir, much like the same upon your finger.

KING
Know you this ring? This ring was his of late.

DIANA
And this was it I gave him, being abed.

KING
The story then goes false you threw it him   231
Out of a casement?

DIANA   I have spoke the truth.

Enter Parolles [attended].

BERTRAM
My lord, I do confess the ring was hers.

KING
You boggle shrewdly; every feather starts you.—   234
Is this the man you speak of?

DIANA   Ay, my lord.

KING
Tell me, sirrah—but tell me true, I charge you,
Not fearing the displeasure of your master,
Which on your just proceeding I'll keep off—   238
By him and by this woman here what know you?   239

PAROLLES   So please Your Majesty, my master hath been
an honorable gentleman. Tricks he hath had in him,
which gentlemen have.

KING   Come, come, to the purpose. Did he love this
woman?

PAROLLES   Faith, sir, he did love her; but how?

222 **diet** restrain; provide for   231 **The story . . . false** the story then is
not true that   234 **boggle shrewdly** startle violently.   **starts** startles
238 **on . . . proceeding** if you speak honestly   239 **By** concerning

KING How, I pray you?

PAROLLES He did love her, sir, as a gentleman loves a
woman.   248

KING How is that?

PAROLLES He loved her, sir, and loved her not.   250

KING As thou art a knave, and no knave. What an
equivocal companion is this!   252

PAROLLES I am a poor man, and at Your Majesty's command.

LAFEW He's a good drum, my lord, but a naughty or-   255
ator.

DIANA Do you know he promised me marriage?

PAROLLES Faith, I know more than I'll speak.

KING But wilt thou not speak all thou know'st?

PAROLLES Yes, so please Your Majesty. I did go between
them, as I said; but more than that, he loved her, for
indeed he was mad for her, and talked of Satan and
of Limbo and of Furies and I know not what. Yet I was
in that credit with them at that time that I knew of   264
their going to bed, and of other motions, as promising 265
her marriage, and things which would derive me ill   266
will to speak of; therefore I will not speak what I know.

KING Thou hast spoken all already, unless thou canst
say they are married. But thou art too fine in thy evi- 269
dence; therefore stand aside.

This ring, you say, was yours?

DIANA   Ay, my good lord.

KING
Where did you buy it? Or who gave it you?

DIANA
It was not given me, nor I did not buy it.

KING
Who lent it you?

DIANA   It was not lent me neither.

KING
Where did you find it, then?

DIANA   I found it not.

---

248 woman i.e., not a gentlewoman **250 loved her not** i.e., desired her
only sexually **252 equivocal** equivocating. **companion** knave
255 drum drummer. **naughty** worthless **264 in . . . with them** so
much in their confidence **265 motions** proposals **266 derive** gain
269 fine subtle

KING
    If it were yours by none of all these ways,
    How could you give it him?
DIANA   I never gave it him.
LAFEW This woman's an easy glove, my lord; she goes
    off and on at pleasure.
KING
    This ring was mine; I gave it his first wife.
DIANA
    It might be yours or hers, for aught I know.
KING
    Take her away; I do not like her now.
    To prison with her. And away with him.
    Unless thou tell'st me where thou hadst this ring,
    Thou diest within this hour.
DIANA   I'll never tell you.
KING
    Take her away.
DIANA   I'll put in bail, my liege.   286
KING
    I think thee now some common customer.   287
DIANA
    By Jove, if ever I knew man, 'twas you.   288
KING
    Wherefore hast thou accused him all this while?   289
DIANA
    Because he's guilty, and he is not guilty.
    He knows I am no maid, and he'll swear to 't;
    I'll swear I am a maid, and he knows not.
    Great King, I am no strumpet, by my life;
    I am either maid or else this old man's wife.
                                        [Pointing to Lafew.]
KING
    She does abuse our ears. To prison with her!
DIANA
    Good Mother, fetch my bail. Stay, royal sir.
                                        [Exit Widow.]
    The jeweler that owes the ring is sent for,   297
    And he shall surety me. But for this lord,   298

286 put in bail make bail, i.e., produce evidence to assure my liberty
287 customer i.e., prostitute 288 knew i.e., sexually 289 Wherefore
why 297 owes owns 298 surety me be my security

Who hath abused me, as he knows himself,
Though yet he never harmed me, here I quit him.   300
He knows himself my bed he hath defiled,
And at that time he got his wife with child.
Dead though she be, she feels her young one kick.
So there's my riddle: one that's dead is quick—   304
And now behold the meaning.

    Enter Helena and Widow.

KING   Is there no exorcist   305
Beguiles the truer office of mine eyes?
Is 't real that I see?
HELENA   No, my good lord,
'Tis but the shadow of a wife you see,
The name and not the thing.
BERTRAM   Both, both. O, pardon!
HELENA
O my good lord, when I was like this maid   310
I found you wondrous kind. There is your ring,   311
And, look you, here's your letter. [*She produces a letter.*]
   This it says:
"When from my finger you can get this ring
And are by me with child," etc. This is done.
Will you be mine, now you are doubly won?
BERTRAM
If she, my liege, can make me know this clearly,
I'll love her dearly, ever, ever dearly.
HELENA
If it appear not plain and prove untrue,
Deadly divorce step between me and you!   319
O my dear mother, do I see you living?
LAFEW
Mine eyes smell onions; I shall weep anon.
[*To Parolles.*] Good Tom Drum, lend me a handkerchief.
So, I thank thee. Wait on me home; I'll make sport
with thee. Let thy curtsies alone; they are scurvy ones.
KING
Let us from point to point this story know,

300 quit (1) acquit (2) repay   **304 quick** alive (and pregnant)
305 exorcist one who conjures up spirits   **310 like this maid** i.e., disguised as Diana   **311 There** i.e., on Diana's finger (unless Diana has
returned the ring to Helena)   **319 Deadly divorce** divorcing death

To make the even truth in pleasure flow.   326
[*To Diana.*] If thou be'st yet a fresh uncroppèd flower,
Choose thou thy husband, and I'll pay thy dower;
For I can guess that by thy honest aid
Thou kept'st a wife herself, thyself a maid.
Of that and all the progress, more and less,
Resolvedly more leisure shall express.   332
All yet seems well, and if it end so meet,   333
The bitter past, more welcome is the sweet. *Flourish.*   334

[Epilogue]

[KING, *advancing*]
The king's a beggar, now the play is done.
All is well ended, if this suit be won,
That you express content; which we will pay,   3
With strife to please you, day exceeding day.   4
Ours be your patience then, and yours our parts;   5
Your gentle hands lend us, and take our hearts.   6
                                        Exeunt omnes.

326 **even** precise, plain   332 **Resolvedly** so that all doubts are removed
333 **meet** fittingly   334 **past** being past

Epilogue
3 **express content** i.e., applaud   4 **strife** effort   5 **Ours . . . parts** i.e., we
will patiently attend, like an audience, while you undertake the active
role by applauding   6 **hearts** i.e., gratitude

Date and Text

All's Well That Ends Well was first registered in the Stationers' Register, the official record book of the London Company of Stationers (booksellers and printers), in November of 1623 and published in the Folio of that same year. The text contains numerous inconsistencies and vague stage directions, indicating it was set from the author's working papers, but these errors are not as extensive as once thought and the text is basically sound. Shakespeare's manuscript may have been sporadically annotated by the bookkeeper. Its printing in the First Folio is unusually laden with errors. Information on the date of the play is sparse. Francis Meres does not mention it in 1598 in his *Palladis Tamia: Wit's Treasury* (a slender volume on contemporary literature and art; valuable because it lists most of the plays of Shakespeare that existed at that time), unless it is the intriguing *Loue labours wonne* on his list. Its themes and style are more suggestive of the period of *Hamlet* and the problem plays, *Measure for Measure* and *Troilus and Cressida*. The common assumption today is that the play was written some time around 1601–1604. The role of Lavatch is clearly designed for the actor Robert Armin, who did not join Shakespeare's acting company until 1599. Scholars once argued that *All's Well* is an early play later revised, but this means of explaining the inconsistencies in the text no longer seems necessary.

Textual Notes

These textual notes are not a historical collation, either of the early folios or of more recent editions; they are simply a record of departures in this edition from the copy text. The reading adopted in this edition appears in boldface, followed by the rejected reading from the copy text, i.e., the First Folio. Only major alterations in punctuation are noted. Changes in lineation are not indicated, nor are some minor and obvious typographical errors.

Abbreviations used:
F the First Folio
s.d. stage direction
s.p. speech prefix

Copy text: the First Folio.

1.1. 1 s.p. [and elsewhere] Countess Mother   **3 s.p. [and elsewhere] Bertram**
Ros   **130 got** goe   **148 th' one** ten   **159 wear** were

1.2. 3 s.p. [and elsewhere] First Lord 1. Lo. G   **15 s.p. [and elsewhere] Second Lord** 2. Lo. E   **18 Rossillion** Rosignoll   **52 him! He** him he   **76 s.d.
Exeunt** Exit

1.3. 3 s.p. [and elsewhere] Rinaldo Ste   **13 s.p. [and elsewhere] Lavatch**
Clo   **19 I** w   **75 With . . . stood** bis   **112 Dian no queen** Queene   **124 s.d.
[and elsewhere] Helena** Hellen   **125** [F has s.p. here, Old. Cou., used subsequently in other s.p.]   **127 rightly** righlie   **168 loneliness** louelinesse
174 th' one to th' other 'ton to oth to th' other   **199 intenible** intemible
247 and an

2.1. 5 s.p. First Lord Lord. G   **18 s.p. Second Lord** L.G   **25 s.p. Second Lord**
2 Lo. E   **44 with his cicatrice** his sicatrice, with   **63 fee** see   **146 fits**
shifts   **157 impostor** Impostrue   **175 nay** ne   **194 heaven** helpe   **212 meed**
deed   **s.d. Exeunt** Exit

2.2. 1 s.p. [and elsewhere in scene] Countess Lady   **60 An** And

2.3. 1 s.p. [and elsewhere] Lafew Ol. Laf   **44 Mort du vinaigre** Mor du
vinager   **51 s.d. four** 3 or 4   **65 s.p. All the lords** All   **76 s.d.** [at l. 62 in F]
94 her heere   **96 s.p. Helena** La   **99 s.p. Lafew** Ol. Lord   **125 when**
whence   **130 it is** is is   **213 lattice** Lettice   **266 s.d.** [at l. 264 in F]   **292 War**
Warres   **293 detested** detected   **301 s.d. Exeunt** Exit

2.4. 16 fortunes fortune

2.5. 27 End And   **29 one** on   **31 heard** hard   **89 s.p. Bertram** [at l. 90 in F]

3.1. 9 s.p. Second Lord French E   **17 s.p. First Lord** Fren. G   **23 to the** to 'th
the

3.2. 9 sold hold   **13 ling** Lings   **18 E'en** In   **19 s.p. Countess Reads** [not in
F]   **45 s.p. [and throughout scene] Second Lord** French E   **47 s.p. [and
throughout scene] First Lord** French G   **64 s.p. Countess** Old La   **111 still-
piercing** still-peering

3.4. 4 s.p. Rinaldo (reads the [not in F]   **18 s.p. Countess** [not in F]

3.5. s.d. daughter daughter, Violenta   **10 s.p. [and elsewhere]   Mariana**
Maria   **33 le** la   **66 warrant** write   **92 s.d. Exeunt** Exit

3.6. 1 s.p. [and throughout scene until l. 109] First Lord Cap. E   **3 s.p. [and
throughout scene until l. 109] Second Lord** Cap. G   **36 his** this   **37 ore**
ours   **109 s.p. First Lord** Cap. G   **111, 117 s.p. Second Lord** Cap. E

3.7. 19 Resolved Resolue   **41 steads** steeds

4.1. 1 s.p. [and throughout scene] First Lord 1. lord E   **69 s.p. [and throughout scene] First Soldier** Inter   **90 art** are   **93 s.p. Second soldier** Sol [and at
l. 96]   **97 s.d. Exeunt** Exit

4.2. 38 may make   **snare** scarre

4.3. 1 s.p. [and throughout scene] First Lord Cap. G   **2 s.p. [and throughout
scene] Second Lord** Cap. E   **81 s.p. First Lord** Ber   **89 effected** affected
118 Hush, hush [assigned in F to Bertram]   **125 s.p. First Lord** Cap

138 All's one to him [assigned in F to Parolles]   **199 lordship** Lord   **226 s.p. Reads the** [not in F]   **242 our** your   **316 s.p. Bertram** Count

4.4. 16 you your

4.5. 21 grass grace   **39 name** maine   **46 of** off

5.1. 6 s.d. a Gentleman a gentle Astringer

5.2. 25 similes smiles   **33 under her** vnder

5.3. 50 warped warpe   **72 s.p. Countess** [not in F]   **102 Plutus** Platus
115 conjectural connecturall   **123 tax** taze   **140 s.p. King Reads** [not in F]   **154 s.d.** [at l. 152 in F]   **155 since** sir   **157 s.d. Diana** Diana, and Parrolles   **208 sickens but** sickens; but   **217 infinite** insuite   **cunning** comming   **314 are** is

Epilogue 4 strife strift

Shakespeare's Sources

Shakespeare's only known source for *All's Well That Ends Well* is the tale of Giglietta of Nerbone from Boccaccio's *Decameron* (c. 1348–1358), as translated into English by William Painter in *The Palace of Pleasure* (1566, 1575). Painter may have based his translation on a French intermediary by Antoine le Maçon, and Shakespeare possibly knew the Italian and French versions although the English was the most available to him. All three are essentially the same except for the forms of the proper names. The Helena story is also widely dispersed in folk tales.

Painter's version appears in the following pages with modernized spelling. From it we see that, except for Helena, many of the characters' names in Shakespeare's play are derived from this source: Helena is Giletta in Painter, but her father is Gerardo of Narbona (compare Shakespeare's Gerard de Narbon or Narbonne), and the young man she vainly loves is Beltramo, Count of Rossiglione (i.e., Bertram, Count of Rossillion), who is left after his father's death "under the royal custody of the King" of France. Giletta is no ward and helpless dependent, however, as in Shakespeare; she is well-to-do, is cared for by her kinsfolk after her father's death, and refuses many favorable offers of marriage before journeying to Paris to cure the King of a fistula and claim her reward. Shakespeare's Helena on the other hand is not rich, and so can serve as an example of innate virtue or "gentleness" in contrast with Bertram's hereditary nobility. Shakespeare enhances the roles of the Countess and Lafew and makes the King more sympathetic than in Painter to Helena's (or Giletta's) cause: in Painter, the King is reluctant to give Giletta to Beltramo, whereas in Shakespeare the King becomes a spokesman for faith in the miraculous. Other courtiers in Shakespeare's play join the King in approving of Helena, so that, however much Bertram's resistance to an enforced marriage might seem understandable in most circumstances, his refusal of Helena is made to appear willful. Lavatch, the Countess's fool, quizzically expounds questions of moral consequence that are absent in Painter. Conversely, the added character

Parolles highlights the callowness and insensitivity of Bertram and serves as a scapegoat when Bertram belatedly gains a better understanding of himself. At the same time, Shakespeare eschews Painter's easy romantic ending for one that is highly problematic: he does not offer Bertram much opportunity to show a real change of heart toward Helena, as Painter does, and thus places a greater strain on credibility in this comedy of forgiveness. Helena, because she is so far below Bertram in wealth and position, is obliged to be more aggressive than her counterpart in Painter, an aggressiveness which raises troublesome issues of female assertiveness. She does not enjoy Giletta's prerogative of governing Rossiglione in her husband's absence and winning such love from her advisers and subjects that they all lament her public resolution to go on a pilgrimage; Helena is thrown more on her own resources and so is at once more self-reliant and self-asserting.

Shakespeare also gives his play a unity of construction and an economy of time not found in the sources. Characters such as the King and Diana are not discarded once their primary roles have been discharged but are brought importantly into the denouement. As in his use of other Italianate fictional sources, Shakespeare compresses time: for example, Helena vows to cure the King in two days rather than eight (as in Painter), and Helena sleeps with Bertram once rather than often. No convincing source has been found for the comic exposure of Parolles.

The Palace of Pleasure
By William Painter

THE THIRTY-EIGHTH NOVEL: GILETTA OF NARBONNE

Any departures from the original text are noted with an asterisk and appear at the bottom of the page in boldface; original readings are in roman.

Giletta, a physician's daughter of Narbonne, healed the French King of a fistula, for reward whereof she demanded Beltramo, Count of Rossiglione, to husband.[1] *The Count, being married against his will, for despite fled to Florence and loved another. Giletta, his wife, by policy found means to lie*

1 **to husband** as husband

*with her husband in place of his lover and was begotten
with child of two sons, which known to her husband, he received her again, and afterwards she lived in great honor
and felicity.*

In France there was a gentleman called Isnardo, the Count
of Rossiglione, who, because he was sickly and diseased,
kept always in his house a physician named Master Gerardo
of Narbonne. This Count had only one son, called Beltramo,
a very young child, pleasant and fair, with whom there was
nourished and brought up many other children of his age—
amongst whom[2] one of the daughters of the said physician,
named Giletta, who fervently fell in love with Beltramo,
more than was meet for a maiden of her age.

This Beltramo, when his father was dead, and left[3] under
the royal custody of the King, was sent to Paris, for whose
departure the maiden was very pensive. A little while after,
her father being likewise dead, she was desirous to go to
Paris, only to see the young Count, if for that purpose she
could get any good occasion.[4] But being diligently looked
unto[5] by her kinsfolk, because she was rich and fatherless,
she could see no convenient way for her intended journey.
And being now marriageable, the love she bare to the Count
was never out of her remembrance, and refused[6] many husbands with whom her kinsfolk would have placed her without making them privy to the occasion of her refusal.[7]

Now it chanced that she burned more in love with Beltramo than ever she did before, because she heard tell that
he was grown to the state of a goodly young gentleman. She
heard by report that the French King had a swelling upon
his breast which by reason of ill cure was grown to a fistula
and did put him to marvelous[8] pain and grief, and that there
was no physician to be found, although many were proved,[9]
that could heal it, but rather did impair[10] the grief and

---

2 amongst whom amongst whom was   **3 and left** i.e., and he, Beltramo,
being left   **4 get any good occasion** find any good excuse   **5 looked
unto** attended to. (Her relatives are attentive to the question of her
marriage because she is mistress of her own considerable inheritance;
they would not be happy to have her slip away unattended.)   **6 and
refused** and she refused   **7 without . . . refusal** without letting them in
on her secret reasons for refusing   **8 marvelous** excruciating   **9 proved**
tested   **10 impair** make worse

made it worse and worse. Wherefore the King, like one that was in despair, would take no more counsel or help. Whereof the young maiden was wonderful glad, and thought to have by this means not only a lawful occasion to go to Paris but, if the disease were such as she supposed, easily to bring to pass that she might have the Count Beltramo to her husband.

Whereupon, with such knowledge as she had learned at her father's hands beforetime, she made a powder of certain herbs which she thought meet for that disease and rode to Paris. And the first thing she went about when she came thither was to see the Count Beltramo. And then she repaired to[11] the King, praying His Grace to vouchsafe to show her his disease.

The King, perceiving her to be a fair young maiden and a comely, would not hide it but opened the same unto her. So soon as she saw it, she put him in comfort that she was able to heal him, saying:

"Sire, if it shall please Your Grace, I trust in God, without any pain or grief unto Your Highness, within eight days I will make you whole of this disease."

The King, hearing her say so, began to mock her, saying: "How is it possible for thee, being a young woman, to do that which the best-renowned physicians in the world cannot?" He thanked her for her good will and made her a direct answer that he was determined no more to follow the counsel of any physician. Whereunto the maiden answered: "Sire, you despise my knowledge because I am young and a woman. But I assure you that I do not minister physic[12] by profession but by the aid and help of God and with the cunning of Master Gerardo of Narbonne, who was my father and a physician of great fame so long as he lived."

The King, hearing those words, said to himself: "This woman, peradventure, is sent unto me of God, and therefore why should I disdain to prove her cunning, sithence[13] she promiseth to heal me within a little space,[14] without any offense or grief unto me?" And being determined to prove[15] her, he said: "Damosel, if thou dost not heal me, but make

11 **repaired to** went to   12 **physic** medicine   13 **sithence** seeing that
14 **space** space of time   15 **prove** test

me to break my determination,[16] what wilt thou shall follow thereof?"[17]

"Sire," said the maiden, "let me be kept in what guard and keeping you list. And if I do not heal you within these eight days, let me be burnt. But if I do heal Your Grace, what recompense shall I have then?"

To whom the King answered: "Because thou art a maiden and unmarried, if thou heal me according to thy promise I will bestow thee upon some gentleman that shall be of right good worship[18] and estimation."

To whom she answered: "Sire, I am very well content that you bestow me in marriage. But I will have such a husband as I myself shall demand, without presumption to any of your children or other of your blood." Which request the King incontinently[19] granted.

The young maiden began to minister her physic, and in short space, before her appointed time, she had thoroughly cured the King. And when the King perceived himself whole, he* said unto her: "Thou hast well deserved a husband, Giletta, even such a one as thyself shalt choose."

"I have, then, my lord," quod she, "deserved the County[20] Beltramo of Rossiglione, whom I have loved from my youth."

The King was very loath to grant him unto her. But because he had made a promise which he was loath to break, he caused him to be called forth and said unto him: "Sir Count, because you are a gentleman of great honor, our pleasure is that you return home to your own house to order your estate according to your degree,[21] and that you take with you a damosel which I have appointed to be your wife."

To whom the Count gave his humble thanks and demanded what[22] she was.

"It is she," quoth the King, "that with her medicines hath healed me."

The Count knew her well and had already seen her; although she was fair, yet, knowing her not to be of a stock

*he [not in 1566]
16 determination i.e., to follow no more the advice of any physician
17 what . . . thereof what do you wish to see happen as a consequence
18 worship rank, distinction   **19 incontinently** immediately   **20 quod . . .
County** quoth, said . . . Count   **21 degree** rank, social position
22 demanded what asked who

convenable to[23] his nobility, disdainfully said unto the King: "Will you then, sire, give me a physician to wife? It is not the pleasure of God that ever I should in that wise bestow myself."

To whom the King said: "Wilt thou, then, that we should break our faith which we to recover health have given to the damosel, who for a reward thereof asked thee to husband?"

"Sire," quoth Beltramo, "you may take from me all that I have and give my person to whom you please, because I am your subject. But I assure you I shall never be contented with that marriage."

"Well, you shall have her," said the King, "for the maiden is fair and wise and loveth you most entirely, thinking[24] verily you shall lead a more joyful life with her than with a lady of a greater house."[25]

The Count therewithal held his peace, and the King made great preparation for the marriage. And when the appointed day was come, the Count, in the presence of the King, although it were against his will, married the maiden, who loved him better than her own self. Which done, the Count, determining before what he would do, prayed license to return to his country to consummate the marriage. And when he was on horseback he went not thither but took his journey into Tuscany, where, understanding that the Florentines and Senois were at wars, he determined to take the Florentines' part and was willingly received and honorably entertained, and made Captain of a certain number of men, continuing in their service a long time.

The new-married gentlewoman, scarce contented with that and hoping by her well-doing to cause him to return into his country, went to Rossiglione, where she was received of all his subjects for their lady. And perceiving that through the Count's absence all things were spoiled and out of order, she, like a sage lady, with great diligence and care disposed all things in order again, whereof the subjects rejoiced very much, bearing to her their hearty love and affection, greatly blaming the Count because he could not content himself with her.

This notable gentlewoman, having restored all the coun-

---

23 convenable to consistent with   **24 thinking** i.e., I do this being of the opinion that   **25 house** family

try again, sent word thereof to the Count her husband by two knights of the country, which she sent to signify unto him that, if it were for her sake that he had abandoned his country, he should send her word thereof and she, to do him pleasure, would depart from thence. To whom he churlishly said: "Let her do what she list. For I do purpose to dwell with her when she shall have this ring"—meaning a ring which he wore—"upon her finger and a son in her arms begotten by me." He greatly loved that ring, and kept it very carefully and never took it off from his finger, for a certain virtue that he knew it had.

The knights, hearing the hard condition of two things impossible and seeing that by them he could not be removed from his determination, they returned again to the lady, telling her his answer, who, very sorrowful, after she had a good while bethought herself,[26] purposed to find means to attain to those two things, to the intent that thereby she might recover her husband. And having advised with herself what to do, she assembled the noblest and chiefest of her country, declaring unto them in lamentable wise what she had already done to win the love of the Count, showing them also what followed thereof. And in the end said unto them that she was loath the Count for her sake should dwell in perpetual exile; therefore she determined to spend the rest of her time in pilgrimages and devotion, for preservation of her soul, praying them to take the charge and government of the country, and that they would let the Count understand that she had forsaken his house and was removed far from thence with purpose never to return to Rossiglione again.

Many tears were shed by the people as she was speaking these words, and divers supplications were made unto him to alter his opinion, but all in vain. Wherefore, commending them all unto God, she took her way with her maid and one of her kinsmen, in the habit[27] of a pilgrim, well furnished with silver and precious jewels, telling no man whither she went, and never rested till she came to Florence; where, arriving by fortune at a poor widow's house, she contented herself with the state of a poor pilgrim, desirous to hear

26 **bethought herself** thought to herself about this 27 **habit** dress, garb

news of her lord, whom by fortune she saw the next day passing by the house where she lay, on horseback with his company. And although she knew him well enough, yet she demanded of the goodwife of the house what he was, who answered that he was a strange[28] gentleman called the Count Beltramo of Rossiglione, a courteous knight and well-beloved in the city, and that he was marvelously in love with a neighbor of hers that was a gentlewoman, very poor and of small substance, nevertheless of right honest life and report, and by reason of her poverty was yet unmarried and dwelt with her mother, that was a wise and honest lady.

The Countess, well noting these words, and by little and little debating every particular point thereof, comprehending the effect of those news, concluded what to do; and, when she had well understanded which was the house and the name of the lady and of her daughter that was beloved of the Count, upon a day repaired to the house secretly in the habit of a pilgrim; where, finding the mother and daughter in poor estate amongst their family, after she had saluted them, told the mother that she had to say[29] unto her. The gentlewoman, rising up, courteously entertained her, and being entered alone into a chamber, they sat down, and the Countess began to say unto her in this wise:

"Madam, methink that ye be one upon whom Fortune doth frown so well as[30] upon me. But, if you please, you may both comfort me and yourself."

The lady answered that there was nothing in the world whereof she was more desirous than of honest comfort. The Countess, proceeding in her talk, said unto her: "I have need now of your fidelity and trust, whereupon, if I do stay[31] and you deceive me, you shall both undo me and yourself."

"Tell me then what it is, hardly,"[32] said the gentlewoman, "if it be your pleasure, for you shall never be deceived of[33] me."

Then the Countess began to recite her whole estate[34] of love, telling her[35] what she was and what had chanced to that

---

28 strange foreign   **29 to say** something to say   **30 so well as** just as
31 stay stand firm, rely   **32 hardly** hardily, boldly   **33 of** by   **34 estate**
circumstance, condition   **35 what** who

present day in such perfect order that the gentlewoman, believing her words because she had partly heard report thereof before, began to have compassion upon her. And after that[36] the Countess had rehearsed all the whole circumstance, she continued her purpose,[37] saying: "Now you have heard, amongst other my troubles, what two things they be which behooveth me to have if I do[38] recover my husband, which I know none can help me to obtain but only you, if it be true that I hear: which is that the Count, my husband, is far in love with your daughter."

To whom the gentlewoman said: "Madam, if the Count love my daughter, I know not, albeit the likelihood is great. But what am I able to do in that which you desire?"

"Madam," answered the Countess, "I will tell you. But first I will declare what I mean to do for you if my determination be brought to effect. I see your fair daughter of good age, ready to marry, but, as I understand, the cause why she is unmarried is the lack of substance to bestow upon her. Wherefore I purpose, for recompense of the pleasure which you shall do for me, to give so much ready money to marry her honorably as you shall think sufficient."

The Countess's offer was very well liked of the lady, because she was but poor. Yet, having a noble heart, she said unto her:

"Madam, tell me wherein I may do you service, and if it be a thing honest I will gladly perform it; and, the same being brought to pass, do as it shall please you."

Then said the Countess: "I think it requisite that, by someone whom you trust, that you give knowledge to the Count my husband that your daughter is and shall be at his commandment. And to the intent she may be well assured that he loveth her indeed above any other, that she prayeth him to send her a ring that he weareth upon his finger, which ring, she heard tell, he loved very dearly. And when he sendeth the ring, you shall give it unto me, and afterwards send him word that your daughter is ready to accomplish his pleasure. And then you shall cause him secretly to come hither, and place me by him instead of your daughter. Per-

---

36 after that after **37 she continued her purpose** i.e., the Countess continued laying out her plan **38 do** am to

adventure[39] God will give me the grace that I may be with child. And so, having this ring on my finger and the child in mine arms begotten by him, I shall recover him and by your means continue with him as a wife ought to do with her husband."

This thing seemed difficult unto the gentlewoman, fearing that there would follow reproach unto her daughter. Notwithstanding, considering what an honest part it were to be a means that the good lady should recover her husband and that she should do it for a good purpose, having affiance in her honest affection,[40] not only promised the Countess to bring this to pass, but in few days, with great subtlety, following the order wherein she was instructed, she had gotten the ring—although it was with the Count's ill will—and took order that the Countess instead of her daughter did lie with him. And at the first meeting, so affectuously[41] desired by the Count, God so disposed the matter that the Countess was begotten with child of two goodly sons, and her delivery chanced[42] at the due time. Whereupon the gentlewoman not only contented the Countess at that time with the company of her husband, but at many other times, so secretly that it was never known—the Count not thinking that he had lien with his wife but with her whom he loved. To whom at his uprising in the morning he used many courteous and amiable words and gave divers fair and precious jewels, which the Countess kept most carefully.

And when she perceived herself with child, she determined no more to trouble the gentlewoman, but said unto her: "Madam, thanks be to God and you, I have the thing that I desire; and even so[43] it is time to recompense your desert, that afterwards I may depart."

The gentlewoman said unto her that if she had done any pleasure agreeable to her mind she was right glad thereof, which she did not for hope of reward but because it appertained to her by well-doing so to do.[44] Whereunto the Countess said: "Your saying pleaseth me well, and likewise for

---

39 Peradventure perhaps   **40 having . . . affection** i.e., the Countess thus able to have a marriage fulfilled in chaste affection   **41 affectuously** ardently   **42 chanced** occurred   **43 even so** accordingly   **44 appertained . . . to do** befitted her to do so in the name of virtue

my part I do not purpose to give unto you the thing you shall demand of me in reward, but for consideration of your well-doing, which duty forceth me so to do."[45]

The gentlewoman then, constrained with[46] necessity, demanded[47] of her with great bashfulness an hundred pounds to marry her daughter. The Countess, perceiving the shame-fastness[48] of the gentlewoman and hearing her courteous demand, gave her five hundred pounds and so many fair and costly jewels which almost amounted to like valor.[49] For which the gentlewoman, more than contented, gave most hearty thanks to the Countess, who departed from the gentlewoman and returned to her lodging. The gentlewoman, to take occasion from the Count of any farther repair[50] or sending to her house, took her daughter with her and went into the country to her friends. The Count Beltramo, within few days after, being revoked[51] home to his own house by his subjects, hearing that the Countess was departed from thence, returned.

The Countess, knowing that her husband was gone from Florence and returned into his country, was very glad and contented, and she continued in Florence till the time of her childbed was come and was brought abed of two sons, which were very like unto their father, and caused them carefully to be nursed and brought up. And when she saw time, she took her journey, unknown to any man, and arrived at Montpellier. And resting herself there for certain days, hearing news of the Count and where he was, and that upon the day of All Saints he purposed to make a great feast and assembly of ladies and knights, in her pilgrim's weed she went thither. And knowing that they were all assembled at the palace of the Count, ready to sit down at the table, she passed through the people without change of apparel with her two sons in her arms; and when she was come up into the hall, even to the place where the Count was, falling down prostrate at his feet, weeping, said unto him:

"My lord, I am thy poor infortunate wife who, to the intent thou mightest return and dwell in thine own house,

45 I do not . . . to do i.e., I do not intend to give you what you ask as a reward but prompted by my own sense of duty in consideration of your virtuous act **46 with** by **47 demanded** asked **48 shamefastness** modesty, decency **49 valor** worth **50 farther repair** additional visit **51 revoked** recalled

have been a great while begging about the world. Therefore I now beseech thee, for the honor of God, that thou wilt observe the conditions which the two knights that I sent unto thee did command me to do. For behold here in mine arms not only one son begotten by thee but twain, and likewise thy ring. It is now time, then, if thou keep promise, that I should be received as thy wife."

The Count, hearing this, was greatly astonied,[52] and knew the ring, and the children also, they were so like him.

"But tell me," quoth he, "how is this come to pass?"

The Countess, to the great admiration[53] of the Count and of all those that were in presence, rehearsed unto them in order all that which had been done and the whole discourse thereof. For which cause the Count, knowing the things she had spoken to be true and perceiving her constant mind and good wit and the two fair young boys, to keep his promise made, and to please his subjects and the ladies that made suit unto him to accept her from that time forth as his lawful wife and to honor her, abjected[54] his obstinate rigor, causing her to rise up, and embraced and kissed her, acknowledging her again for his lawful wife. And after he had appareled her according to her estate, to the great pleasure and contentation of those that were there and of all his other friends, not only that day but many others he kept great cheer, and from that time forth he loved and honored her as his dear spouse and wife.

Text based on *The Palace of Pleasure, Beautified, Adorned, and Well Furnished with Pleasant Histories and Excellent Novels, Selected out of Divers Good and Commendable Authors. By William Painter . . . 1566. Imprinted at London by Henry Denham for Richard Tottell and William Jones.*

52 astonied astonished   **53 admiration** astonishment   **54 abjected** cast off

Further Reading

Bradbrook, M. C. "Virtue is the True Nobility: A Study of the Structure of *All's Well That Ends Well*." *Review of English Studies*, n.s. 1 (1950): 289–301. Rpt. in *Shakespeare, the Comedies: A Collection of Critical Essays*, ed. Kenneth Muir. Englewood Cliffs, N.J.: Prentice-Hall, 1965; and in *Bradbrook on Shakespeare*. Totowa, N.J.: Barnes and Noble, 1984. Examining the structure of *All's Well* in the context of Renaissance ideas of virtue, Bradbrook argues that in the play the romantic logic of comic plotting is subordinated to the play's ethical concerns, as Helena's inherent virtue is contrasted with Bertram's merely inherited nobility.

Cole, Howard C. *The All's Well Story from Boccaccio to Shakespeare*. Urbana, Ill., Chicago, and London: Univ. of Illinois Press, 1981. Cole traces the development of the story of Giletta di Narbona, on which Shakespeare based his play, from Giovanni Boccaccio's *Decameron* to its appearance in fifteenth- and sixteenth-century redactions and translations. Considering this literary tradition and several relevant nonliterary contexts, Cole offers an ironic reading of the play in which Helena appears essentially self-seeking and self-deceived.

Donaldson, Ian. "*All's Well That Ends Well:* Shakespeare's Play of Endings." *Essays in Criticism* 27 (1977): 34–55. Donaldson discovers the complexity and coherence of *All's Well* in its insistence upon the difficulties of ending. The play's refusal to end well in either formal or human terms becomes for Donaldson evidence of its recognition that problems of ending are problems of life as well as art.

Foakes, R. A. "Shakespeare and Satirical Comedy." *Shakespeare, the Dark Comedies to the Last Plays: From Satire to Celebration*, esp. pp. 7–16. Charlottesville, Va.: Univ. Press of Virginia, 1971. Arguing that Parolles and Lavatch control the tone of the play, Foakes sees *All's Well* as a modified version of romantic comedy, one that achieves the fulfillment of the comic form but never the festive comic tone. The play is marked by an insistence upon the intractability of human nature (revealed both by Bertram's unattractiveness and by Helena's obsession with him) that resists the idealizations of the world of romance.

Frye, Northrop. "The Reversal of Energy." *The Myth of Deliverance: Reflections on Shakespeare's Problem Comedies.* Toronto: Univ. of Toronto Press, 1983. For Frye, *All's Well* reveals the fundamental rhythm of comedy found in the natural cycles of renewal. The play dramatizes the transformation of self-destructive energies such as Bertram's lust or Parolles's cowardice into creative social and emotional patterns that rejuvenate the family, the state, and perhaps even Bertram's nature.

Hunter, Robert Grams. *"All's Well That Ends Well." Shakespeare and the Comedy of Forgiveness.* New York: Columbia Univ. Press, 1965. Examining the play in the context of medieval dramatic forebears that celebrate God's forgiveness of erring sinners, Hunter sees *All's Well That Ends Well* as a secular "comedy of forgiveness": Helena achieves her romantic goal in marrying Bertram, but the comic conclusion of the play depends not (as in romantic comedy) upon the marriage but upon Bertram's moral regeneration, accomplished through the agency of Helena's redemptive love.

Johnson, Samuel. *"All's Well That Ends Well." Johnson on Shakespeare,* ed. Arthur Sherbo. *The Yale Edition of the Works of Samuel Johnson,* vol. 7. New Haven, Conn.: Yale Univ. Press, 1968. In a celebrated and influential criticism, Johnson faults the play's ending for its violation of moral decorum: "I cannot reconcile my heart to Bertram," he writes, finding him cowardly and ungenerous yet inexplicably "dismissed to happiness."

Kastan, David Scott. *"All's Well That Ends Well* and the Limits of Comedy." *ELH* 52 (1985): 575–589. Kastan argues that *All's Well* is Shakespeare's most insistent exploration of the formal and moral implications of comedy. Resisting the desires of both the characters and the audience for neat solutions, the play, unlike romantic comedy, refuses to shape itself into comforting patterns of wish-fulfillment.

Kirsch, Arthur. *"All's Well That Ends Well." Shakespeare and the Experience of Love.* Cambridge and New York:

Cambridge Univ. Press, 1981. Provocatively mingling Pauline theology and twentieth-century psychology, Kirsch examines the disjunctions of tone and action that distinguish the play. He discusses the tensions and contradictions that emerge from its profound exploration of the paradoxes of flesh and spirit inherent in human sexuality.

Knight, G. Wilson. "The Third Eye." *The Sovereign Flower*. London: Methuen, 1958. Rpt. in *Shakespeare, the Comedies: A Collection of Critical Essays*, ed. Kenneth Muir. Englewood Cliffs, N.J.: Prentice-Hall, 1965. In Knight's exuberant, idealistic response to *All's Well*, Helena emerges as the medium by which the transcendent, redemptive possibilities of love enter into the play's world. Knight finds that all of Helena's actions are designed to serve Bertram's better self, and he insists upon an analogy between Helena's love, which sees and creates Bertram as he potentially is, and the creative and purifying power of Shakespeare's own art.

Lawrence, W. W. *"All's Well That Ends Well." Shakespeare's Problem Comedies*, 1931. Rpt. Harmondsworth, Eng.: Penguin, 1960. Lawrence discusses Helena's healing of the King and satisfaction of Bertram's apparently impossible conditions in the context of their origin in folktales exalting clever and devoted wives. Helena is thus to be understood as honorable, courageous, and resolute, and Bertram's repentance as both an appropriate and a believable response to his wife's virtue.

Leech, Clifford. "The Theme of Ambition in *All's Well That Ends Well*." *ELH* 21 (1954): 17–29. Rpt. in *Discussions of Shakespeare's Problem Comedies*, ed. Robert Ornstein. Boston: D. C. Heath, 1961. In the face of efforts by his contemporaries to explain away the problems of this so-called problem comedy (see, for example, Lawrence above), Leech focuses on the problematic element of ambition in Helena's love. Helena is not the wholly virtuous heroine of folk tradition or of romantic comedy, but a woman whose love is often willful and self-absorbed.

Muir, Kenneth, and Stanley Wells, eds. *Aspects of Shakespeare's "Problem Plays": Articles Reprinted from "Shakespeare Survey."* Cambridge: Cambridge Univ. Press, 1982. Muir and Wells have edited a collection of criticism on the play published originally in *Shakespeare Survey*, including the essay by Roger Warren (see below) and an interview with Royal Shakespeare Company director John Barton about the problems of directing the "problem plays."

Price, Joseph G. *The Unfortunate Comedy: A Study of "All's Well That Ends Well" and Its Critics.* Toronto: Univ. of Toronto Press, 1968. Price's work, the first book-length study of *All's Well*, begins with valuable surveys of the play's stage and critical history and ends with his own interpretation of its unity and coherence. Price argues that the play dramatizes the maturation of Bertram's understanding of honor, a process that is completed only when he and Helena stand together at the end, dramatically reconciling the nobility of birth and of virtue.

Rossiter, A. P. *"All's Well That Ends Well." Angel With Horns and Other Shakespeare Lectures,* ed. Graham Storey. London: Longmans, Green, 1961. Rossiter examines Shakespeare's additions to and alterations of his source (Painter's translation of Boccaccio) in tracing the play's deliberate reversal of comic expectations. The play, for Rossiter, is a "tragi-comedy" marked by disquieting ambiguities raised by the conflict between its fairy-tale plot and the psychological exposure of its characters.

Styan, J. L. *All's Well That Ends Well.* Dover, N.H., and Manchester, Eng.: Manchester Univ. Press, 1984. Focusing on a number of influential productions of the play, Styan discusses the range of interpretations discovered in performance and permitted by the text. After identifying some of the central issues the play raises, he offers a scene-by-scene analysis demonstrating how productions have responded to and revealed the play's complex tone.

Warren, Roger. "Why Does It End Well? Helena, Bertram, and the Sonnets." *Shakespeare Survey* 22 (1969): 79–92. Warren clarifies the complex emotional concerns of the play by a comparison with Shakespeare's sonnets, where similarly a focus on intensity of love despite rejection is central. This parallel enables Warren to understand Bertram's cruelty and Helena's devotion in the context of Shakespeare's belief in the power of love to survive and overcome humiliation.

Wheeler, Richard P. "Imperial Love and the Dark House:

All's Well That Ends Well." Shakespeare's Development and the Problem Comedies. Berkeley, Los Angeles, and London: Univ. of California Press, 1981. Wheeler argues that the play brings to the foreground conflicts and contradictions latent in romantic comedy, where the claims of society yield comfortably to the claims of young love. In *All's Well* Wheeler finds this accommodation strained, and he exposes and explores the tensions provoked by the forced marriage between the play's comic design and its psychological content.

Measure for Measure, with Mariette Hartley as Isabella and Mark Lenard as the Duke of Vienna, directed by Alan Schneider in 1960 at the Belvedere Lake Theater in Central Park.

MEASURE
—FOR—
MEASURE

MEASURE
FOR MEASURE

Introductory Material
Foreword by Joseph Papp
Introduction
Measure for Measure in Performance

THE PLAY

Supplementary Material
Date and Text
Textual Notes
Shakespeare's Sources
Further Reading

Foreword

Measure for Measure surprised me; I didn't really understand the play until I directed it, which just goes to show that Shakespeare can always teach us something new. The play is often called a dark comedy, or a problem play—mostly, I think, because the character of the Duke has puzzled many directors and critics.

When I started work on the play in preparation for directing it a few years ago, I began under the influence of previous interpretations of the Duke, in which he was seen as Christ-like, or sinister and cruel, or almost psychotically manipulative. Whatever the approach, it invariably darkened the production and made it into a disjointed and strange drama about political corruption. But it was placed among the Comedies in the First Folio, and I had to take that seriously, so I began trying to figure out how the term was justified.

After a while I realized that *Measure for Measure* is a love story between the Duke and Isabella. He's falling in love with this rigidly chaste young woman during the events in the course of the play that draw them together. She is adamantly and religiously bound to preserving her chastity above all else, cutting herself off from life in the process, but throughout the play the Duke is gradually winning her over.

It's not so different in kind from what goes on between Petruchio and Kate in *The Taming of the Shrew,* but where Petruchio *breaks* his shrew, Kate, the Duke *softens* his nun, Isabella. Once I realized that the play was really a light comedy, it stopped being a problem play for me and I knew just how to cast the Duke—as a young romantic type who's a perfect match for Isabella, not some weird psychotic that she picks up at the end for lack of anything better.

One of my favorite characters in the play is Barnardine, the prisoner who indignantly refuses to die when he's called up to the gallows to suit the machinations of the plot. I cast him as an elegant but faded gentleman wearing once-sumptuous clothes now in tatters. He stumped out with a cane, furious with those who would have him die before he's ready to go, and exclaimed, "You rogue, I have been drinking all night. I am not fitted for 't.'' It's a small moment, but he almost stole the show.

Measure for Measure is full of interesting, "playable" characters—the Provost, who is put into a difficult position as a middleman; Elbow, another constable figure who could be Dogberry's (from *Much Ado about Nothing)* twin brother; and Escalus, who stands out because of his wisdom. Though it took me a long time to cast these characters, because it took awhile to understand the play in its new light, in the end it worked quite well. "Problem" or not, *Measure for Measure* is a terrific play.

Joseph Papp

Joseph Papp gratefully acknowledges the help of Elizabeth Kirkland in preparing this Foreword.

Introduction

"A play Caled Mesur for Mesur" by "Shaxberd" was performed at court, for the new King James I, by "his Maiesties plaiers" on December 26, 1604. Probably it had been composed that same year, or in late 1603. The play dates from the very height of Shakespeare's tragic period, three years or so after *Hamlet*, contemporary with *Othello*, shortly before *King Lear* and *Macbeth*. This period includes very little comedy of any sort, and what there is differs markedly from the festive comedy of the 1590s. *Troilus and Cressida* (c. 1601–1602), hovering between satire and tragedy, bleakly portrays a hopeless love affair caught in the toils of a pointless and stalemated war. *All's Well That Ends Well* (c. 1601–1604) resembles *Measure for Measure* in its portrayal of an undeserving protagonist who must be deceived into marriage by the ethically ambiguous trick of substituting one woman for another in the protagonist's bed. *Measure for Measure*, the last such comedy from the tragic period, illustrates most clearly of all what critics usually mean by "problem comedy" or "problem play."

Its chief concern is not with the triumphs of love, as in the happy comedies, but with moral and social problems: "filthy vices" arising from sexual desire, and the abuses of judicial authority. Images of disease abound in this play. We see corruption in Vienna "boil and bubble / Till it o'errun the stew" (5.1.326–327). The protagonist, Angelo, is for most of the play a deeply torn character, abhorring his own perverse sinfulness, compulsively driven to an attempted murder in order to cover up his lust for the heroine, Isabella. His soliloquies are introspective, tortured, focused on the psychological horror of an intelligent mind succumbing to criminal desire. The disguised Duke, witnessing this fall into depravity and despair, can offer Angelo's intended victims no better philosophical counsel than Christian renunciation of the world and all its vain hopes. Tragedy is averted only by providential intervention and by the harsh trickery of "Craft against vice" (3.2.270), in which the Duke becomes involved as chief manipulator and stage manager. Of the concluding marriages, two are foisted on the bridegrooms (Angelo and Lucio) against their wills, whereas that of the Duke and Isabella jars oddly with his stoical teachings and with her previous determination to be a nun. The ending thus seems arbitrary; both justice and romantic happiness are so perilously achieved in this play that they seem inconsistent with the injustice and lechery that have prevailed until the last.

Yet the very improbability of the ending, and the sense of tragedy narrowly averted, are perhaps intentional. These features are appropriate not only for problem comedy but for tragicomedy or comedy of forgiveness, overlapping genres toward which Shakespeare gravitated in his late romances. Angelo is, like Leontes in *The Winter's Tale* (or, earlier, like Bertram in *All's Well* or Claudio in *Much Ado about Nothing*), an erring protagonist forgiven in excess of his deserving, spared by a benign overseeing providence from destroying that which is most precious to him.

The play's title, *Measure for Measure*, introduces a paradox of human justice which this "problem" play cannot wholly resolve. How is fallible man to judge the sins of his fellow mortals and still obey Christ's injunction of the Sermon on the Mount, "Judge not that ye be not judged"? Three positions emerge from the debate: absolute justice at one extreme, mercy at the other, and equity as a middle ground. Isabella speaks for mercy, and her words ring with biblical authority. Since all men would be condemned to eternal darkness were God not merciful as well as just, should not men also be merciful? The difficulty, however, is that Vienna shows all too clearly the effects of leniency under the kindly Duke. Vice is rampant; stern measures are needed. Though he has not wished to crack the whip himself, the Duke firmly endorses "strict statutes and most biting laws, / The needful bits and curbs to headstrong steeds" (1.3.19–20). To carry out necessary reform, the Duke has chosen Lord Angelo, spokesman for absolute justice, to represent him. Angelo's position is cold but consistent. Only by a literal and impartial administering of the statutes, he maintains, can the law deter potential offenders. If the judge is found guilty, he must pay the penalty as well. One difficulty here, however, is that literal enforcement of the statute on fornication seems ironically to catch the wrong culprits. Claudio and Juliet, who are about to be married and are already joined by a "true contract" of betrothal, are sentenced to the severest limit of the law, whereas the pimps and whores of Vienna's suburbs manage at first to evade punishment entirely. Angelo's deputy, Escalus, can only shake his head in dismay at this unjust result of strict justice. Angelo has not remembered fully the terms of his commission from the Duke: he was enjoined to practice both "Mortality and mercy" in Vienna, to "enforce or qualify the laws / As to your soul seems good." The attributes of a ruler, like those of God, must include "terror" but also "love" (1.1.20–67).

Escalus's compassionate and pragmatic approach to law illustrates equity, or the flexible application of the law to particular cases. Because Claudio is only technically guilty (though still guilty), Escalus would pronounce for him a light sentence. Pompey and Mistress Overdone, on the other hand, require vigorous prosecution. The problem of policing vice is compounded by the law's inefficiency as well as by erring human nature, which will never be wholly tamed. Constable Elbow, like Dogberry in *Much Ado*, is a pompous user of malapropisms, less clever by far than the criminals he would arrest. His evidence against Pompey is so absurdly circumstantial that Escalus is first obliged to let off this engaging pimp with a stern warning. Yet Escalus patiently and tenaciously attends to such proceedings, unlike Angelo, whose interest in the law is too theoretical. Escalus deals with day-to-day problems effectively. He orders reforms of the system by which constables are selected, instructs Elbow in the rudiments of his office, and so proceeds ultimately to an effective arrest. Vice is not eliminated; as Pompey defiantly points out, unless someone plans to "geld and splay all the youth of the city," they "will to 't then" (2.1.229–233). Still, vice is held in check. Law can shape the outer man and hope for some inner reform. Even Pompey is taught a trade, albeit a grisly one, as an apprentice hangman. The law must use both "correction" and "instruction."

The solutions arrived at in the comic subplot do not fit the case of Angelo, for he is powerful enough to be above the Viennese law. Indeed, he tries finally to brazen it out, pitting his authority against that of the seemingly friendless Isabella, much like the biblical Elders when justly accused of immorality by the innocent Susannah. Society is on Angelo's side—even the well-meaning Escalus; only providence can rescue the defenseless. The Duke of Vienna, hovering in the background and seeing all that happens, intervenes just at those points when tragedy threatens to become irreversible. Moreover, the Duke is testing those he observes. As he says to Friar Thomas, explaining why he has delegated his power to Angelo: "Hence shall we see, / If power change purpose, what our seemers be" (1.3.53–54). The Duke obviously expects Angelo to fall. Indeed, he has known all along that Angelo had dishonorably repudiated his solemn contract to Mariana when her marriage dowry disappeared at sea (3.1.215–225). Like an all-seeing deity who keeps a reckoning of men's good and evil deeds, the Duke has found out Angelo's great weakness. As Angelo confesses, "I perceive Your Grace, like power divine, / Hath looked upon my passes" (5.1.377–378). Paradoxically, however, this seemingly tragic story of temptation and fall yields precious benefits of remorse and humility. Angelo is rescued from his self-made nightmare of seduction, murder, and tyranny. Knowing now that he is prone like other men to fleshly weakness, he knows also that he needs spiritual assistance and that as judge he ought to use mercy. Seen in restrospect, his panic, despair, and humiliation are curative.

The Duke is no less a problematic character than Angelo, Isabella, and the rest. Vienna's deep corruption is in part the result of his unwillingness to bear down on vice, and yet, rather than undertake to remedy the failure himself, this strange "Duke of dark corners" (4.3.157) elects to leave the business to one he suspects will make matters worse. The Duke has a great deal to learn about his own dislike of crowds, his complacent tolerance of human weakness, and his naive supposition that all his subjects speak well of him. He is a highly manipulative character, the one most responsible in the play for the ethically dubious solutions through which craft must be employed against vice. The comforting words of spiritual counsel he offers Claudio, Juliet, and the rest are spoken by a secular ruler fraudulently disguised as a friar. Certainly the Duke is no allegorized god-figure, for all his omniscience and final role as both punisher and forgiver. As deus ex machina of this problem comedy, the Duke is human, frail, and vulnerable—as indeed he ought to be in a play that explores with such rich complexity the ironic distance between divine and human justice.

Yet for all his manifest and even comic weaknesses, the Duke is finally the authority figure who must attempt to bring order to the imperfect world of Vienna. If his role is more that of artist than ruler or deity, his being so is appropriate to the artistically contrived and theatrical world that Shakespeare presents to us. Within the world of this play, the disguised Duke's chief function is to test the other characters and to mislead them intentionally into expecting the worst, in order to try their resolve. On a comic level, he exposes the amiable but loose-tongued Lucio as a slanderer against the Duke himself, and devises for Lucio a suitably satirical exposure and witty punishment. More seriously, as confessor to Juliet he assures her that her beloved Claudio must die on the morrow. As she ought, she penitentially accepts "shame with joy," and so is cleansed (2.3.37). Because the Duke is not really a friar, he does not have the spiritual authority to do this, and the ruse strikes us as theatrical, employing devices of illusion that actors and dramatists use. Even so, it provides real comfort for Juliet. The very theatricality of the illusion, by reminding us that we are in the theater, enables us to see the Duke as a kind of morally persuasive playwright who can change the lives of his characters for the better.

Similarly, the counsel of Christian renunciation offered to Claudio by the bogus friar (3.1) is at once illusory and comforting. The Duke's poignant reflection on the vanity of human striving is made ironic but not invalid by our awareness that we are viewing a deception with an ultimately benign purpose, that of persuading Claudio to see matters in their true perspective. The Duke characterizes life as a breath, a dreamlike "after-dinner's sleep," a fever of inconstancy in which timorous man longs fretfully for what he does not have and spurns those things he has. Claudio responds as he ought, resolving to "find life" by "seeking death" (3.1.5–43). He achieves this calm, however, in the face of certain execution; ironically, what he must then learn to overmaster is the desperate hope of living by means of his sister's dishonor. Claudio is broken by this test, and perversely begs for a few years of guilty life at the cost of eternal shame for himself and Isabella. From this harrowing experience he emerges at length with a better understanding of his own weakness and a greater compassion toward the weakness of others.

The searing encounter between Claudio and Isabella puts her to the test as well, and her response seems hysterical and no doubt prudish to modern audiences. She has much to learn about the complexities of human behavior. Although she is sincere in protesting that she would lay down her life for her brother and is correct, in the play's terms, to prefer virtue to mere existence, her tone is too strident. Like other major characters, she must be humbled before she can rise. She and Claudio must heed the Duke's essential admonition: "Do not satisfy your resolution with hopes that are fallible" (3.1.170–171). Only then, paradoxically, can Isabella and Claudio go on to achieve earthly happiness.

In her final testing, Isabella shows greatness of spirit. Here Shakespeare significantly alters his chief sources, George Whetstone's *Promos and Cassandra* (1578), Cinthio's *Hecatommithi*, and Whetstone's *Heptameron of Civil Discourses* (the last of which is reprinted on pages 124–133 of this volume). In all these versions, the character corresponding to Angelo does actually ravish the heroine, and in Cinthio he also murders her brother. Shakespeare, by withholding these irreversible acts, not only gives to Angelo a technical innocence, but allows the Duke as *deus ex machina* to practice virtuous deception on Isabella one more time. Can she forgive the supposed murderer of her brother? Her affirmative answer confutes the Old Testament ethic of "An Angelo for Claudio, death for death" whereby "Like doth quit like, and measure still for measure" (5.1.417–419). Although Angelo concedes that he deserves to die for what he intended, the forfeit need not be paid so long as humanity can reveal itself capable of Isabella's godlike mercy.

With its apparently unsuitable marriages and its improbable plotting, *Measure for Measure* does end by dealing directly with the problems of human nature confronted in the earlier scenes. The bed trick (switching Mariana for Isabella) may seem a legalistic and contrived way to bring Angelo to terms with his own carnality, but it is instructive, not only to him but to Isabella; she, like Angelo, must learn to accept the realities of the human condition. By helping Mariana to achieve her legitimate desire to couple and marry, Isabella sees into her own need. Her begging for Angelo's life is not merely an act of forgiveness to an enemy; it is a gift of continued marriage to Mariana. This realization helps to prepare Isabella herself for a marriage that, although dramatically surprising onstage (and even rejected by her in some modern productions), may be intended to demonstrate her having given up the cloistered life for all that marriage signifies. *Measure for Measure* is thus essentially comic (unlike *Troilus and Cressida*), despite its harrowing scenes of conflict and its awareness of vice everywhere in human nature. The play celebrates the *felix culpa* of human nature, the fall from grace that is an integral part of humanity's rise to happiness and self-knowledge. Throughout, in the play's finest scenes, poignancy is tempered by a wit and humor that are ultimately gracious. The formal and substantive emphasis on marriage stresses not just the benefits of remorse and humility but also the real possibility of psychic and spiritual growth: Isabella can acknowledge that she is a woman, Angelo can be genuinely freed from repression, and Claudio can value life more intensely because he has confronted death. All these recognitions affirm the acceptance and proper use of the physical and sexual side of human nature, and yet they are achieved only through charity and forgiveness. Humanity can learn, however slowly and painfully, that the talents entrusted to it by providence are to be used wisely.

Measure for Measure
in Performance

Measure for Measure has been a controversial and sometimes neglected play through much of its stage history.
With an ethically dubious bed trick, impersonations of religious authority, a whimsical presentation of civil authority,
and a detailed exploration of the world of vice in Vienna,
the play has had to wait for the twentieth century to find
audiences that could be amused and challenged by the
work as Shakespeare wrote it. As with the other problem
plays, *All's Well That Ends Well* and *Troilus and Cressida*,
Shakespeare seems to have written a play that was centuries ahead of its time.

A performance of "Mesur for Mesur" by "Shaxberd" and
acted by the King's men took place, according to the Revels
Accounts, at the palace at Whitehall on December 26, 1604.
No other performance is known to have occurred until the
Restoration, when, on February 18, 1662, diarist Samuel
Pepys saw the Duke's company at the theater in Lincoln's
Inn Fields, London, in *The Law against Lovers*. Pepys
thought it "a good play and well performed, especially the
little girl's (whom I never saw act before) dancing and singing." The remarkable innovations introduced by William
Davenant as he adapted Shakespeare's play suggest the extent to which *Measure for Measure* was thought to be in
need of "improvement." The "little girl" so much admired
by Pepys is Viola (from *Twelfth Night*), now a younger sister
of Beatrice, who, along with Benedick, is imported from
Much Ado about Nothing. Benedick is made a brother to
Angelo, while Beatrice is Angelo's ward. Benedick and Beatrice are soon involved in a plot to liberate Claudio (the
Claudio of *Measure for Measure*) and his lover Juliet from
jail. Juliet is Beatrice's cousin (Hero is nowhere to be seen),
in a much augmented role. It is she, not Claudio, who begs
Isabella to save Claudio's life at the expense of her chastity,
in reply to which Isabella proposes that Juliet instead take
her place in Angelo's bed. Juliet thus plays a part like that
of Mariana in Shakespeare's play. Angelo turns out not to

be the villain Shakespeare made him after all; he has long loved Isabella and tempts her only to test her virtue. Angelo is punished by the Duke for what he has done but is then permitted to marry Isabella. The low comedy is expunged, and even Lucio becomes nearly respectable. Pepys's little girl, Viola, sings a song, is then joined in a chorus ("Our Ruler has got the Vertigo of State") by Benedick, Beatrice, Escalus, and Lucio, and dances a saraband with castanets. The language of almost the whole play, said one observer, was "borrowed from Shakespeare, yet, where the language is rough or obsolete, our author has taken care to polish it."

Charles Gildon was the next to "improve" the play in his *Measure for Measure, or Beauty the Best Advocate,* acted at Lincoln's Inn Fields in 1699–1700 by Thomas Betterton (Angelo) and Anne Bracegirdle (Isabella) some five years after they and some other actors had seceded from the Theatre Royal in Drury Lane. Gildon did away with the additions from *Much Ado,* but otherwise his production shows again the preference of the age for avoiding moral blemishes and unpleasantness. The lowlife characters—Froth, Pompey, Mistress Overdone, Abhorson, Barnardine—all disappear, and Lucio is limited to the first scene. Because Angelo and Mariana have married in secret, the bed trick poses no problem of morality. Claudio too is clandestinely married to Juliet, and his speech to his sister on the horrors of death (a speech that also offended Davenant) is excused on the grounds that he is really asking that Juliet be looked after when he is dead. The characters are all redeemable, even noble, and marital propriety is never offended. The Duke does not marry Isabella. Gildon also flatters the taste of the age by adding to the music that Davenant had included. In fact the piece becomes nearly operatic. Escalus undertakes to honor Angelo's birthday with a four-part masque. Musical episodes unfold as the play proceeds, providing a grand entry at the end of each act based on the fable of Dido and Aeneas and employing elaborate machinery to create the effects of storms, ships, witches, dancing furies, Phoebus and Venus in their chariots, Nereides and Tritons rising out of the sea, nymphs, morris dancers, and still more.

James Quin produced the play in 1720 at Lincoln's Inn Fields, with Quin as the Duke and Anna Seymour as Isabella, in a version that made some effort to restore Shakespeare's text to the stage. Quin revived the play the following year, and he chose it for his benefit performance in 1737 at Drury Lane in which Susannah Cibber appeared as Isabella. She then chose the play for her benefit the following year. Quin and Cibber acted the play at the Theatre Royal, Covent Garden, in the 1742–1743 season and again in 1746–1747. After Quin retired, Cibber regularly played Isabella opposite Henry Mossop.

The play was popular throughout the eighteenth century, having had the support of strong actors: in addition to Quin and Mossop as the Duke, William Smith successfully acted the role; Lacy Ryan acted Claudio; Charles Macklin, Lucio; and a succession of fine actresses, in addition to Susannah Cibber, played Isabella, including Peg Woffington, Hannah Pritchard, George Anne Bellamy, Mary Ann Yates, and above all Sarah Siddons (in 1779 and the following years). David Garrick staged the play at Drury Lane but never took a part himself. Sarah Siddons's brother, John Philip Kemble, had success with the play around the turn of the century, first taking the part of the Duke in 1794 at Drury Lane. Even in this era of relative success, however, the play was egregiously bowdlerized. John Bell's acting edition of 1773 suggests what audiences did and did not see. Mistress Overdone almost entirely disappears, along with the bawdy talk among Lucio and the gentlemen in scene 2. The trial of Pompey and Froth before Escalus is retained but with the excision of some seven pages of "absolute ribaldry." Pompey is kept mainly for his clowning in the prison scenes.

The nineteenth century evidently found even this remainder of a play too much, and it was seldom performed. Kemble revived the play in 1803 at Covent Garden, and in 1811, in her last year onstage, Sarah Siddons performed the play eight times, despite the fact that she was now so weak with age that she needed the Duke's aid to rise after kneeling before him in the final scene. Eliza O'Neill successfully played Isabella at Covent Garden, in 1816, with Harriet Faucit (Helen Faucit's mother) as Mariana. William Charles Macready played the Duke for three performances at Drury Lane in 1824; and Samuel Phelps produced the play in 1846 at the Sadler's Wells Theatre. Adelaide Neilson was notable as Isabella at the Haymarket Theatre in 1876 and 1878, but the play did not appear again in London until 1893 when William Poel produced the play in the Royalty Theatre. Taking the role of Angelo, Poel converted the Royalty Theatre into a near replica of the Fortune playhouse (built in 1600) in order that he might present "an Elizabethan play under the conditions it was written to fulfill." In 1888 Helena Modjeska acted Isabella in the United States at the Hollis Street Theatre in New York. Oscar Asche revived the play in 1906 at London's Adelphi Theatre, playing Angelo, with Lily Brayton as Isabella.

Still, *Measure for Measure* did not seem an appropriate vehicle for the prosperous actor-managers such as Henry Irving and Herbert Beerbohm Tree. The play as Shakespeare wrote it seemed unnecessarily unpleasant and disreputable. When Richard Wagner wrote an operatic version called *Das Liebesverbot* (first performed in 1842), he converted Angelo into a romantic hero who has long been in love with Isabella, much as William Davenant had done in 1662. In 1906, when Shakespeare's play was put on by the Oxford University Dramatic Society, residents complained of its obscenity. Even the theater historian George Odell, writing in 1920, declared the play to be "exceedingly offensive" onstage and wondered if it should ever be acted.

In spite of a successful production at the Old Vic in 1933, directed by Tyrone Guthrie and starring Charles Laughton, the play continued to outrage public decency. In 1936 *The Scotsman* protested a production of the play in Edinburgh, and in the following year the inclusion of a production by Tyrone Guthrie in the Buxton Theatre Festival led Canon Charles Scott-Moncrieff to attack the festival organizers for allowing a play so obviously "disfigured" by its sexual preoccupations. This prudery seems no doubt quaint to modern audiences familiar with women's liberation and the sexual revolution. By 1950, Peter Brook could successfully direct John Gielgud (as Angelo) at Stratford-upon-Avon in an austere production in which the sordid and the sacred uncomfortably coexisted.

Today, the play perhaps demands an even tougher sensibility, and it is not uncommon to see Isabella refuse the surprising offer of marriage made by the Duke in Act 5. Estelle Kohler, in John Barton's production in 1970 at Stratford-upon-Avon, was obviously shocked by the Duke's proposal and was left alone onstage as the Duke went off bewildered by her reaction. In a fine production at Stratford, Canada, in 1975, Martha Henry, directed by Robin Phillips, expressed the resentment and pent-up fury of a woman thoroughly wronged by men and sharing with Mariana a sense of victimization. On the male side, the play's painful candor about sexuality has prompted searing performances of the roles of Angelo and Claudio. At Stratford-upon-Avon in 1962, Marius Goring played Angelo as a sado-masochistic Puritan whose public arrogance was countered by his private indulgence in flagellation. Jonathan Pryce, in Barry Kyle's 1978 production at Stratford-upon-Avon, appeared "trapped between duty and desire," repelled by his own actions but unable to resist Isabella. On the modern stage the Duke has also become a complex character, no longer a benign agent of an active Providence but an enigmatic meddler in the lives of others. Directors have not always taken kindly to him as an authority figure, and his management of affairs is apt to suggest a capricious universe in which all authority is lacking or flawed by self-indulgence. Perhaps the most extreme example of this tendency was Barrie Ingham's Duke in Keith Hack's 1974 production at Stratford-upon-Avon. Ingham's Duke was deeply implicated in the corruption of Vienna. His manipulations were transparently hypocritical, and he was obviously resented by those whose lives he undertook to manage. In the final act, he descended from the flies (the space over the stage where equipment and scenery are hung), literalizing his chosen role as a deus ex machina. In modern productions, Lucio has also come into his own as an ingratiating rake, no doubt overly licentious and loose-tongued but endearing and vivacious, as in Lenny Baker's performance in John Pasquin's 1976 production for the New York Shakespeare Festival at the Delacorte Theatre (starring Meryl Streep as Isabella and Sam Waterston as the Duke).

The comic figures thrive as well. Michael Bogdanov's *Measure for Measure* at Stratford, Canada, in 1985 shows how far performances of this play have come from the sheltered days of Victorian England. Bogdanov's company positively reveled in decadence. For thirty minutes or so before show time the theater became a cabaret with bar and barstools, actors who chatted with theatergoers in the lobby or lounged about talking inaudibly among themselves, a sleazy master of ceremonies announcing that gentlemen might not remove their trousers but that ladies could remove anything they wished, transvestite dancers, headline items about nightclub raids and drug charges, and the like. In the play itself Bogdanov added to rather than subtracted from the bawdy exchanges of Pompey and Lucio by some invented dialogue and some borrowings from the bordello scene in *Pericles*. Added business in Mistress Overdone's club provided at various times an entourage of soldiers and other customers, quantities of black leather, strobe lighting, the wail of sirens, and a raid in which policemen checked the aisles. For her scene at the Moated Grange, Mariana wore a "Walkman" radio and listened to rock music. Isabella (Barbara March) was a modern nun in black skirt and sweater, Angelo (Nicholas Pennell) an administrator in a business suit, the Provost an official in a blazer. The Duke (Alan Scarfe) made his reappearance in Act 5 carrying his car keys, while offstage were heard the sounds of traffic, a helicopter, and television coverage. Not everyone was happy with the relentlessly modern tempo of this production, but it did provide an interpretation of *Measure for Measure* that earlier generations would have found inconceivable. A troubling play has found a troubled world in which it can make its case.

MEASURE
—FOR—
MEASURE

The Names of All the Actors

VINCENTIO, *the Duke*
ANGELO, *the deputy*
ESCALUS, *an ancient lord*
CLAUDIO, *a young gentleman*
LUCIO, *a fantastic*
Two other like GENTLEMEN
PROVOST
THOMAS, } *two friars*
PETER,
[A JUSTICE]
[VARRIUS, *a friend of the Duke*]

ELBOW, *a simple constable*
FROTH, *a foolish gentleman*
CLOWN [POMPEY, *a servant to Mistress Overdone*]
ABHORSON, *an executioner*
BARNARDINE, *a dissolute prisoner*

ISABELLA, *sister to Claudio*
MARIANA, *betrothed to Angelo*
JULIET, *beloved of Claudio*
FRANCISCA, *a nun*
MISTRESS OVERDONE, *a bawd*

[A SERVANT *of Angelo*
BOY *singer*
A MESSENGER *from Angelo*

Lords, Officers, Citizens, Servants, and other Attendants]

SCENE: *Vienna*

Names of All the Actors. **fantastic** one given to dandified dress (?)

1.1   *Enter Duke, Escalus, lords, [and attendants].*

DUKE Escalus.
ESCALUS   My lord.
DUKE

Of government the properties to unfold   3
Would seem in me t' affect speech and discourse,   4
Since I am put to know that your own science   5
Exceeds, in that, the lists of all advice   6
My strength can give you. Then no more remains   7
But that to your sufficiency   . . .   8
. . . . as your worth is able,   9
And let them work. The nature of our people,
Our city's institutions, and the terms   11
For common justice, you're as pregnant in
As art and practice hath enrichèd any   13
That we remember. There is our commission,
                                    [*Giving a paper*]
From which we would not have you warp. Call hither,   15
I say, bid come before us Angelo. [*Exit an Attendant.*]
What figure of us think you he will bear?   17
For you must know, we have with special soul   18
Elected him our absence to supply,   19
Lent him our terror, dressed him with our love,   20
And given his deputation all the organs   21
Of our own power. What think you of it?
ESCALUS

If any in Vienna be of worth
To undergo such ample grace and honor,   24

1.1. Location: Vienna. The court of Duke Vincentio.
3 Of . . . unfold to explain the qualities needed in governing well   **4 seem
. . . discourse** i.e., make me seem enamored of the sound of my own
voice   **5 put to know** obliged to admit.   **science** knowledge   **6 that** i.e.,
properties of government (l. 3).   **lists** limits   **7 strength** power of mind
8–9 But . . . able (The passage appears in the Folio as a single line.
Several attempts at emendation have been made, but the most plausible
explanation is that something has been deleted or inadvertently omitted.)   **11 terms** terms of court; or, methods of procedure   **13 art** learning, theory   **15 warp** deviate   **17 What . . . bear** i.e., how do you think he
will do as my substitute   **18 special soul** all the powers of the mind;
whole heart   **19 supply** fill, make up for   **20 terror** power to inspire awe
and fear   **21 his deputation** him as deputy.   **organs** instruments
24 undergo bear the weight of

It is Lord Angelo.

Enter Angelo.

DUKE   Look where he comes.
ANGELO
  Always obedient to Your Grace's will,
  I come to know your pleasure.
DUKE   Angelo,
  There is a kind of character in thy life   28
  That to th' observer doth thy history
  Fully unfold. Thyself and thy belongings   30
  Are not thine own so proper as to waste   31
  Thyself upon thy virtues, they on thee.
  Heaven doth with us as we with torches do,
  Not light them for themselves; for if our virtues
  Did not go forth of us, 'twere all alike   35
  As if we had them not. Spirits are not finely touched   36
  But to fine issues, nor Nature never lends   37
  The smallest scruple of her excellence   38
  But, like a thrifty goddess, she determines   39
  Herself the glory of a creditor,   40
  Both thanks and use. But I do bend my speech   41
  To one that can my part in him advertise.   42
  Hold, therefore, Angelo:
  In our remove be thou at full ourself.   44
  Mortality and mercy in Vienna   45
  Live in thy tongue and heart. Old Escalus,
  Though first in question, is thy secondary.   47
  Take thy commission.   [*He gives a paper.*]
ANGELO   Now, good my lord,

---

28 character writing   **30 belongings** attributes, endowments   **31 proper**
exclusively.   **waste** expend   **35 Did . . . us** i.e., were not active in the
world.   **all alike** exactly the same   **36 Spirits** souls.   **finely touched**
excellently endowed   **37 fine issues** noble purposes   **38 scruple** bit.
(Literally, a small weight.)   **39 determines** assumes   **40 Herself** for herself.   **glory** privileges   **41 use** interest.   **bend** direct   **42 my . . . advertise** instruct that part of me now vested in him, i.e., knows more already
than I know   **44 remove** absence.   **at full** in every respect.   **ourself** i.e.,
myself. (The royal plural.)   **45 Mortality** the full rigor of the law, the
death sentence   **47 first in question** senior and first appointed

Let there be some more test made of my mettle   49
Before so noble and so great a figure
Be stamped upon it.
DUKE   No more evasion.
We have with a leavenèd and preparèd choice   52
Proceeded to you; therefore take your honors.
Our haste from hence is of so quick condition   54
That it prefers itself and leaves unquestioned   55
Matters of needful value. We shall write to you,   56
As time and our concernings shall importune,   57
How it goes with us, and do look to know   58
What doth befall you here. So, fare you well.
To th' hopeful execution do I leave you   60
Of your commissions.
ANGELO   Yet give leave, my lord,   61
That we may bring you something on the way.   62
DUKE   My haste may not admit it;
Nor need you, on mine honor, have to do   64
With any scruple. Your scope is as mine own,   65
So to enforce or qualify the laws
As to your soul seems good. Give me your hand.
I'll privily away. I love the people
But do not like to stage me to their eyes;   69
Though it do well, I do not relish well
Their loud applause and "aves" vehement,   71
Nor do I think the man of safe discretion   72
That does affect it. Once more, fare you well.   73
ANGELO
The heavens give safety to your purposes!

---

49 mettle substance, quality (with play on *metal,* a common variant spelling, continued in the coining imagery of ll. 50–51)   **52 leavened** i.e., carefully considered (just as yeast leavens dough)   **54–55 Our . . . itself** the cause for my hasty departure is so urgent (*quick*) that it takes precedence over all other matters   **55 unquestioned** not yet considered   **56 needful** indispensable   **57 concernings** affairs.   **importune** urge   **58 look to know** expect to be informed   **60 To . . . you** i.e., full of hope am I, leaving you to the execution. (*Hopeful* modifies *I leave you.*)   **61 leave** permission   **62 bring you something** accompany you for a short distance   **64 have to do** have concern   **65 scruple** misgiving   **69 stage me** make a show of myself   **71 aves** hails of acclamation   **72 safe** sound   **73 affect** desire, court

ESCALUS
Lead forth and bring you back in happiness!
DUKE   I thank you. Fare you well.   *Exit.*
ESCALUS
I shall desire you, sir, to give me leave
To have free speech with you; and it concerns me
To look into the bottom of my place.   79
A power I have, but of what strength and nature
I am not yet instructed.
ANGELO
'Tis so with me. Let us withdraw together,
And we may soon our satisfaction have
Touching that point.
ESCALUS   I'll wait upon your honor.
                                        Exeunt.

❖

1.2   *Enter Lucio and two other Gentlemen.*

LUCIO   If the Duke with the other dukes come not to
composition with the King of Hungary, why then all   2
the dukes fall upon the King.   3
FIRST GENTLEMAN   Heaven grant us its peace, but not
the King of Hungary's!
SECOND GENTLEMAN   Amen.
LUCIO   Thou conclud'st like the sanctimonious pirate
that went to sea with the Ten Commandments but
scraped one out of the table.   9
SECOND GENTLEMAN   "Thou shalt not steal"?
LUCIO   Ay, that he razed.   11
FIRST GENTLEMAN   Why, 'twas a commandment to command the captain and all the rest from their functions;
they put forth to steal. There's not a soldier of us all
that, in the thanksgiving before meat, do relish the 15
petition well that prays for peace.
SECOND GENTLEMAN   I never heard any soldier dislike it.

79 the bottom of my place the extent of my commission and authority

1.2. Location: A public place.
2 composition agreement   **3 fall upon** attack   **9 table** tablet   **11 razed**
scraped out. (The word may also suggest *rased*, "erased.")   **15 thanksgiving** prayer of thanksgiving, grace.   **meat** the meal

LUCIO   I believe thee, for I think thou never wast where
grace was said.

SECOND GENTLEMAN   No? A dozen times at least.

FIRST GENTLEMAN   What, in meter?

LUCIO   In any proportion or in any language.   22

FIRST GENTLEMAN   I think, or in any religion.

LUCIO   Ay, why not? Grace is grace, despite of all con- 24
troversy; as, for example, thou thyself art a wicked villain, despite of all grace.

FIRST GENTLEMAN   Well, there went but a pair of shears 27
between us.   28

LUCIO   I grant; as there may between the lists and the 29
velvet. Thou art the list.   30

FIRST GENTLEMAN   And thou the velvet. Thou art good
velvet; thou'rt a three-piled piece, I warrant thee. I had 32
as lief be a list of an English kersey as be piled, as thou 33
art piled, for a French velvet. Do I speak feelingly now? 34

LUCIO   I think thou dost, and indeed with most painful
feeling of thy speech. I will, out of thine own confession, learn to begin thy health but, whilst I live, forget 37
to drink after thee.   38

FIRST GENTLEMAN   I think I have done myself wrong, 39
have I not?

22 **proportion** form   24 **Grace is grace** (Refers to the Catholic–Protes-
tant *controversy*, ll. 24–25, as to whether man can be saved by works or
by grace alone; with punning on *grace* as "thanks for a meal," l. 19, and
"gracefulness" or "becomingness," l. 26.)   **27–28 there . . . between us**
i.e., we're cut from the same cloth   **29–30 as . . . list** (Lucio jokes that
the shears might also cut between, i.e., distinguish between, the mere
lists or selvages, edges of a woven fabric, and the *velvet* betokening a
true gentlemen. Lucio wittily asserts himself to be a true gentleman, the
other not.)   **32 three-piled** having a threefold pile or nap (the best grade of
velvet)   **33 as lief** as soon, rather.   **kersey** a coarse woolen fabric. (The
First Gentleman turns the joke on Lucio by saying he would rather be a
plain, homespun Englishman than a Frenchified velvet gentleman in decay
and threadbare. *Velvet* suggests prostitutes and disease, as in the following
notes.)   **be piled** (1) have a cloth nap (2) suffer from hemorrhoids (3) be
pilled or peeled, i.e., hairless, bald, as a result of mercury treatment for
venereal disease (known as the French disease; see *French velvet* in the
next line and *French crown*, l. 50)   **34 feelingly** to the purpose. (But Lucio's reply quibbles on "painfully," meaning the Gentleman's mouth is
affected by the French disease; hence Lucio will not drink from the same
cup after him.)   **37 begin thy health** begin drinking to your health
37–38 forget . . . thee take care not to drink from your cup   **39 done
myself wrong** i.e., asked for that

SECOND GENTLEMAN   Yes, that thou hast, whether thou
art tainted or free.   42

Enter Bawd [Mistress Overdone].

LUCIO   Behold, behold, where Madam Mitigation   43
comes! I have purchased as many diseases under her
roof as come to—
SECOND GENTLEMAN   To what, I pray?
LUCIO   Judge.   47
SECOND GENTLEMAN   To three thousand dolors a year.   48
FIRST GENTLEMAN   Ay, and more.
LUCIO   A French crown more.   50
FIRST GENTLEMAN   Thou art always figuring diseases in   51
me, but thou art full of error. I am sound.
LUCIO   Nay, not, as one would say, healthy, but so
sound as things that are hollow. Thy bones are hollow;   54
impiety has made a feast of thee.
FIRST GENTLEMAN   [*To Mistress Overdone*] How now,
which of your hips has the most profound sciatica?   57
MISTRESS OVERDONE   Well, well; there's one yonder ar-
rested and carried to prison was worth five thousand
of you all.
SECOND GENTLEMAN   Who's that, I pray thee?
MISTRESS OVERDONE   Marry, sir, that's Claudio, Signor
Claudio.
FIRST GENTLEMAN   Claudio to prison? 'Tis not so.
MISTRESS OVERDONE   Nay, but I know 'tis so. I saw him
arrested, saw him carried away; and, which is more,   66
within these three days his head to be chopped off.
LUCIO   But, after all this fooling, I would not have it so.   68
Art thou sure of this?
MISTRESS OVERDONE   I am too sure of it; and it is for
getting Madam Julietta with child.
LUCIO   Believe me, this may be. He promised to meet me

---

42 tainted infected   **43 Mitigation** (So called because her function is to
relieve desire.)   **47 Judge** guess   **48 dolors** (quibbling on *dollars;* spelled
Dollours in the Folio)   **50 French crown** (1) gold coin (2) bald head
incurred through syphilis, the "French disease"   **51 figuring** (1) imagining (2) reckoning (recalling the monetary puns of ll. 48 and 50)
54 sound resounding (with hollow bones caused by syphilis)   **57 sciatica**
a disease affecting the sciatic nerve in the hip and thigh, thought to be a
symptom of syphilis   **66 which** what   **68 after** notwithstanding

two hours since, and he was ever precise in promise- 73
keeping.

SECOND GENTLEMAN Besides, you know, it draws 75
something near to the speech we had to such a pur- 76
pose. 77

FIRST GENTLEMAN But most of all agreeing with the
proclamation.

LUCIO Away! Let's go learn the truth of it.

Exit [Lucio with the Gentlemen].

MISTRESS OVERDONE Thus, what with the war, what
with the sweat, what with the gallows, and what with 82
poverty, I am custom-shrunk. 83

Enter Clown [Pompey].

How now, what's the news with you?

POMPEY Yonder man is carried to prison.

MISTRESS OVERDONE Well, what has he done? 86

POMPEY A woman.

MISTRESS OVERDONE But what's his offense?

POMPEY Groping for trouts in a peculiar river. 89

MISTRESS OVERDONE What? Is there a maid with child
by him?

POMPEY No, but there's a woman with maid by him. 92
You have not heard of the proclamation, have you?

MISTRESS OVERDONE What proclamation, man?

POMPEY All houses in the suburbs of Vienna must be 95
plucked down.

MISTRESS OVERDONE And what shall become of those in
the city?

POMPEY They shall stand for seed. They had gone 99
down too, but that a wise burgher put in for them. 100

---

73 ever always   **75–76 it . . . near to** i.e., it sounds somewhat like
76–77 to . . . purpose on that topic   **82 sweat** sweating sickness; a form
of the plague   **83 custom-shrunk** having fewer customers   **86 done**
(Pompey quibbles in l. 87 on a sexual sense of the word, present also in
Mistress Overdone's name.)   **89 peculiar** privately owned (with bawdy
suggestion)   **92 woman with maid** (Pompey playfully corrects Mistress
Overdone's use of the word "maid," joking that a pregnant woman
cannot be a virgin [*maid*] though the child she carries is one.)
95 houses i.e., brothels.   **suburbs** (Location of the brothels in Shakespeare's London.)   **99 for seed** to preserve the species (with ribald
pun)   **100 burgher** citizen.   **put . . . them** interceded on their behalf

MISTRESS OVERDONE   But shall all our houses of resort in
the suburbs be pulled down?

POMPEY   To the ground, mistress.

MISTRESS OVERDONE   Why, here's a change indeed in
the commonwealth! What shall become of me?

POMPEY   Come, fear not you. Good counselors lack no
clients. Though you change your place, you need not
change your trade; I'll be your tapster still. Courage! 108
There will be pity taken on you. You that have worn 109
your eyes almost out in the service, you will be con- 110
sidered.

MISTRESS OVERDONE   What's to do here, Thomas Tapster? Let's withdraw.

POMPEY   Here comes Signor Claudio, led by the Pro- 114
vost to prison; and there's Madam Juliet.   *Exeunt.* 115

   Enter Provost, Claudio, Juliet, officers; Lucio and
   two Gentlemen [follow].

CLAUDIO

Fellow, why dost thou show me thus to the world?
Bear me to prison, where I am committed.

PROVOST

I do it not in evil disposition,
But from Lord Angelo by special charge.

CLAUDIO

Thus can the demigod Authority
Make us pay down for our offense by weight   121
The words of heaven. On whom it will, it will;   122
On whom it will not, so; yet still 'tis just.   123

LUCIO

Why how now, Claudio? Whence comes this restraint?

CLAUDIO

From too much liberty, my Lucio, liberty.
As surfeit is the father of much fast,   126
So every scope by the immoderate use   127

108 **tapster** one who draws beer in an alehouse   **109–110 worn . . . out**
i.e., worked so hard (perhaps with an ironic reference to the traditional
image of the blind Cupid)   **114–115 Provost** officer charged with apprehension, custody, and punishment of offenders   **121–123 pay . . . so** pay
the exact amount due for our offense, thus confirming the biblical
observation (Romans 9:18): "Therefore hath he [God] mercy on whom he
will have mercy, and whom he will he hardeneth"   **126 surfeit** excess.
fast abstinence   **127 scope** freedom

Turns to restraint. Our natures do pursue,
Like rats that ravin down their proper bane,   129
A thirsty evil, and when we drink we die.

LUCIO If I could speak so wisely under an arrest, I
would send for certain of my creditors. And yet, to say   132
the truth, I had as lief have the foppery of freedom as   133
the morality of imprisonment. What's thy offense,
Claudio?

CLAUDIO
What but to speak of would offend again.

LUCIO What, is 't murder?

CLAUDIO   No.

LUCIO   Lechery?

CLAUDIO
  Call it so.

PROVOST   Away, sir, you must go.

CLAUDIO
One word, good friend.—Lucio, a word with you.

LUCIO
A hundred, if they'll do you any good.
Is lechery so looked after?   141

CLAUDIO
Thus stands it with me: upon a true contract   142
I got possession of Julietta's bed.
You know the lady; she is fast my wife,   144
Save that we do the denunciation lack   145
Of outward order. This we came not to   146
Only for propagation of a dower   147
Remaining in the coffer of her friends,   148
From whom we thought it meet to hide our love
Till time had made them for us. But it chances   150
The stealth of our most mutual entertainment
With character too gross is writ on Juliet.   152

---

129 ravin . . . bane greedily devour what is poisonous to them
132 creditors (who would arrest me for debt)   **133 lief** willingly.
foppery foolishness   **141 so looked after** taken so seriously   **142 true
contract** i.e., in the presence of witnesses, though without a religious
ceremony. (The Church recognized the validity of such a marriage but
demanded a Church service before it could be consummated.)   **144 fast
my wife** i.e., firmly bound by precontract   **145 denunciation** formal
declaration   **146 outward order** public ceremony   **147 propagation**
increase, begetting   **148 friends** relatives   **150 made . . . us** disposed
them in our favor   **152 character too gross** letters too large

LUCIO
  With child, perhaps?
CLAUDIO   Unhappily, even so.
  And the new deputy now for the Duke—
  Whether it be the fault and glimpse of newness,   155
  Or whether that the body public be
  A horse whereon the governor doth ride,
  Who, newly in the seat, that it may know
  He can command, lets it straight feel the spur;   159
  Whether the tyranny be in his place,   160
  Or in his eminence that fills it up,   161
  I stagger in—but this new governor   162
  Awakes me all the enrollèd penalties   163
  Which have, like unscoured armor, hung by the wall
  So long that nineteen zodiacs have gone round   165
  And none of them been worn; and for a name   166
  Now puts the drowsy and neglected act
  Freshly on me. 'Tis surely for a name.
LUCIO   I warrant it is, and thy head stands so tickle on 169
  thy shoulders that a milkmaid, if she be in love, may
  sigh it off. Send after the Duke and appeal to him.
CLAUDIO
  I have done so, but he's not to be found.
  I prithee, Lucio, do me this kind service:
  This day my sister should the cloister enter   174
  And there receive her approbation.   175
  Acquaint her with the danger of my state;
  Implore her, in my voice, that she make friends
  To the strict deputy; bid herself assay him.   178
  I have great hope in that, for in her youth
  There is a prone and speechless dialect   180
  Such as move men; besides, she hath prosperous art   181
  When she will play with reason and discourse,   182
  And well she can persuade.

155 the fault . . . newness the faulty flashiness of novelty   159 straight
at once   160 in his place inherent in the office   161 his eminence the
eminence of him   162 I stagger in I am uncertain   163 Awakes
me i.e., awakes. (Me is used colloquially.)   165 zodiacs i.e., years
166 for a name for reputation's sake   169 tickle uncertain, unstable
174 cloister i.e., convent   175 approbation novitiate, period of probation   178 To with.   assay test   180 prone eager.   dialect language
181 prosperous art skill or ability to gain favorable results   182 play
with use

LUCIO   I pray she may, as well for the encouragement of
the like, which else would stand under grievous im- 185
position, as for the enjoying of thy life, who I would 186
be sorry should be thus foolishly lost at a game of tick- 187
tack. I'll to her.   188
CLAUDIO   I thank you, good friend Lucio.
LUCIO   Within two hours.
CLAUDIO   Come, officer, away!   *Exeunt.*

❖

1.3   *Enter Duke and Friar Thomas.*

DUKE
No, holy Father, throw away that thought;
Believe not that the dribbling dart of love   2
Can pierce a complete bosom. Why I desire thee   3
To give me secret harbor hath a purpose   4
More grave and wrinkled than the aims and ends   5
Of burning youth.
FRIAR THOMAS   May Your Grace speak of it?
DUKE
My holy sir, none better knows than you
How I have ever loved the life removed
And held in idle price to haunt assemblies   9
Where youth and cost witless bravery keeps.   10
I have delivered to Lord Angelo,
A man of stricture and firm abstinence,   12
My absolute power and place here in Vienna,
And he supposes me traveled to Poland;
For so I have strewed it in the common ear,
And so it is received. Now, pious sir,
You will demand of me why I do this.
FRIAR THOMAS   Gladly, my lord.

185 the like i.e., similar offenders.   **else** otherwise   **185–186 imposition**
accusation   **187–188 tick-tack** a form of backgammon in which pegs
were fitted into holes (here applied bawdily)

1.3. Location: A friary.
2 dribbling falling short or wide of the mark   **3 complete** perfect,
whole, strong   **4 harbor** shelter   **5 wrinkled** i.e., mature   **9 held ...**
price i.e., thought it foolish. *Idle* means "unprofitable."   **10 cost** costly
expenditure.   **witless ... keeps** maintain a foolish display   **12 stricture**
strictness

DUKE
We have strict statutes and most biting laws,
The needful bits and curbs to headstrong steeds,   20
Which for this fourteen years we have let slip,   21
Even like an o'ergrown lion in a cave
That goes not out to prey. Now, as fond fathers,   23
Having bound up the threatening twigs of birch
Only to stick it in their children's sight
For terror, not to use, in time the rod
Becomes more mocked than feared, so our decrees,
Dead to infliction, to themselves are dead,   28
And liberty plucks justice by the nose;   29
The baby beats the nurse, and quite athwart   30
Goes all decorum.
FRIAR THOMAS   It rested in Your Grace
To unloose this tied-up justice when you pleased;
And it in you more dreadful would have seemed
Than in Lord Angelo.
DUKE   I do fear, too dreadful.
Sith 'twas my fault to give the people scope,   35
'Twould be my tyranny to strike and gall them
For what I bid them do; for we bid this be done   37
When evil deeds have their permissive pass   38
And not the punishment. Therefore indeed, my father,
I have on Angelo imposed the office,   40
Who may, in th' ambush of my name, strike home,   41
And yet my nature never in the fight   42
To do in slander. And to behold his sway   43
I will, as 'twere a brother of your order,
Visit both prince and people. Therefore, I prithee,
Supply me with the habit, and instruct me
How I may formally in person bear   47
Like a true friar. More reasons for this action

---

20 steeds (The Folio reading, *weeds,* is possible in the sense of "lawless and uncontrolled impulses.")   **21 fourteen** (Claudio mentions nineteen years at 1.2.169; possibly the compositor confused *xiv* and *xix.*)
23 fond doting   **28 Dead to infliction** dead in that they are not executed   **29 liberty** license   **30 athwart** wrongly, awry   **35 Sith** since
37 we . . . done i.e., we virtually order a crime to be committed   **38 pass** sanction   **40 office** duty   **41 in th' ambush** under cover.   **name** i.e., ducal authority   **42 nature** i.e., personal identity (as distinguished from my official capacity)   **43 do in slander** be put in disrepute   **47 bear** i.e., bear myself

At our more leisure shall I render you.   49
Only this one: Lord Angelo is precise,   50
Stands at a guard with envy, scarce confesses   51
That his blood flows or that his appetite   52
Is more to bread than stone. Hence shall we see,   53
If power change purpose, what our seemers be.

                     Exeunt.

❖

1.4   *Enter Isabella and Francisca, a nun.*

ISABELLA
And have you nuns no farther privileges?
FRANCISCA   Are not these large enough?
ISABELLA
Yes, truly. I speak not as desiring more,
But rather wishing a more strict restraint
Upon the sisterhood, the votarists of Saint Clare.   5
LUCIO (*Within*)
Ho! Peace be in this place!
ISABELLA   Who's that which calls?
FRANCISCA
It is a man's voice. Gentle Isabella,
Turn you the key, and know his business of him.
You may, I may not; you are yet unsworn.   9
When you have vowed, you must not speak with men
But in the presence of the prioress;
Then if you speak you must not show your face,
Or if you show your face you must not speak.
He calls again. I pray you, answer him.   [*Exit.*]
ISABELLA
Peace and prosperity! Who is 't that calls?

   [*She opens the door. Enter Lucio.*]

---

49 more greater   **50 precise** strict, puritanical   **51 at . . . envy** in a
defensive posture against malice   **52–53 his appetite . . . stone** i.e., he
has any normal human appetites

1.4. Location: A convent.
5 votarists of Saint Clare an order founded in 1212 by Saint Francis of
Assisi and Saint Clare; its members were enjoined to a life of poverty,
service, and contemplation   **9 you . . . unsworn** i.e., you have not yet
taken your formal vows to enter the convent

LUCIO

Hail, virgin, if you be, as those cheek roses   16
Proclaim you are no less. Can you so stead me   17
As bring me to the sight of Isabella,   18
A novice of this place, and the fair sister
To her unhappy brother Claudio?

ISABELLA

Why "her unhappy brother"? Let me ask,
The rather for I now must make you know
I am that Isabella, and his sister.

LUCIO

Gentle and fair, your brother kindly greets you.
Not to be weary with you, he's in prison.   25

ISABELLA   Woe me! For what?

LUCIO

For that which, if myself might be his judge,
He should receive his punishment in thanks:
He hath got his friend with child.

ISABELLA

Sir, make me not your story.

LUCIO   'Tis true.   30
I would not—though 'tis my familiar sin
With maids to seem the lapwing, and to jest,   32
Tongue far from heart—play with all virgins so.
I hold you as a thing enskied and sainted   34
By your renouncement, an immortal spirit,
And to be talked with in sincerity,
As with a saint.

ISABELLA

You do blaspheme the good in mocking me.

LUCIO

Do not believe it. Fewness and truth, 'tis thus: 39
Your brother and his lover have embraced.
As those that feed grow full, as blossoming time
That from the seedness the bare fallow brings   42
To teeming foison, even so her plenteous womb   43

16 cheek roses i.e., blushes   **17–18 Can . . . As** can you be so helpful as
to. (*Stead* means "help.")   **25 weary** wearisome   **30 story** subject for
mirth   **32 lapwing** peewit or plover (with reference to its habit of
running away from its nest in order to draw away enemies from its
young)   **34 enskied** placed in heaven   **39 Fewness and truth** in few
words and truly   **42 seedness** sowing.   **fallow** untilled land   **43 teeming foison** abundant harvest

Expresseth his full tilth and husbandry.   44

ISABELLA
Someone with child by him? My cousin Juliet?

LUCIO   Is she your cousin?

ISABELLA
Adoptedly, as schoolmaids change their names   47
By vain though apt affection.

LUCIO   She it is.   48

ISABELLA
O, let him marry her.

LUCIO   This is the point.
The Duke is very strangely gone from hence;
Bore many gentlemen, myself being one,   51
In hand and hope of action; but we do learn,   52
By those that know the very nerves of state,
His givings-out were of an infinite distance   54
From his true-meant design. Upon his place,
And with full line of his authority,
Governs Lord Angelo, a man whose blood
Is very snow broth; one who never feels   58
The wanton stings and motions of the sense,   59
But doth rebate and blunt his natural edge   60
With profits of the mind, study, and fast.
He—to give fear to use and liberty,   62
Which have for long run by the hideous law,
As mice by lions—hath picked out an act,
Under whose heavy sense your brother's life   65
Falls into forfeit. He arrests him on it
And follows close the rigor of the statute
To make him an example. All hope is gone,
Unless you have the grace by your fair prayer
To soften Angelo. And that's my pith of business   70
Twixt you and your poor brother.

ISABELLA   Doth he so
Seek his life?

44 tilth tillage. **husbandry** (1) tillage (2) duties of a husband
47 change exchange   **48 vain though apt** foolish though natural
51–52 Bore . . . action i.e., misleadingly kept us in expectation of some
military action   **54 givings-out** public statements   **58 snow broth**
melted snow (i.e., icewater)   **59 motions** promptings   **60 rebate** dull,
abate.   **his** its.   **edge** sharpness of desire   **62 use and liberty** habitual
licentiousness   **65 heavy sense** severe interpretation   **70 my pith of
business** the essence of my business

LUCIO   He's censured him already,   72
  And, as I hear, the Provost hath a warrant
  For 's execution.
ISABELLA   Alas, what poor
  Ability's in me to do him good?
LUCIO Assay the power you have.   76
ISABELLA
  My power? Alas, I doubt.
LUCIO   Our doubts are traitors,
  And makes us lose the good we oft might win,   78
  By fearing to attempt. Go to Lord Angelo,
  And let him learn to know, when maidens sue
  Men give like gods; but when they weep and kneel,
  All their petitions are as freely theirs   82
  As they themselves would owe them.   83
ISABELLA I'll see what I can do.
LUCIO But speedily.
ISABELLA I will about it straight,
  No longer staying but to give the Mother   87
  Notice of my affair. I humbly thank you.
  Commend me to my brother. Soon at night   89
  I'll send him certain word of my success.   90
LUCIO
  I take my leave of you.
ISABELLA   Good sir, adieu.
                              Exeunt [separately].

❖

72 **He's censured** he has passed sentence on   76 **Assay** test   78 **makes**
i.e., make   82 **their petitions** i.e., the things the maidens ask for   83 **As**
as if.   **they** i.e., the maidens.   **owe** possess   87 **Mother** Mother Superior, prioress   89 **Soon at night** early tonight   90 **my success** how I
have succeeded

2.1 *Enter Angelo, Escalus, and servants, [a] Justice.*

ANGELO
  We must not make a scarecrow of the law,
  Setting it up to fear the birds of prey,   2
  And let it keep one shape till custom make it
  Their perch and not their terror.
ESCALUS   Ay, but yet
  Let us be keen and rather cut a little   5
  Than fall and bruise to death. Alas, this gentleman   6
  Whom I would save had a most noble father!
  Let but your honor know,   8
  Whom I believe to be most strait in virtue,
  That, in the working of your own affections,   10
  Had time cohered with place, or place with wishing,
  Or that the resolute acting of your blood   12
  Could have attained th' effect of your own purpose,
  Whether you had not sometime in your life   14
  Erred in this point which now you censure him,
  And pulled the law upon you.
ANGELO
  'Tis one thing to be tempted, Escalus,
  Another thing to fall. I not deny
  The jury passing on the prisoner's life
  May in the sworn twelve have a thief or two
  Guiltier than him they try. What's open made to justice,
  That justice seizes. What knows the laws   22
  That thieves do pass on thieves? 'Tis very pregnant,   23
  The jewel that we find, we stoop and take 't
  Because we see it; but what we do not see
  We tread upon, and never think of it.
  You may not so extenuate his offense
  For I have had such faults; but rather tell me,   28
  When I that censure him do so offend,

2.1. Location: A court of justice.
2 fear frighten   **5 keen** sharp   **6 fall** let fall heavily.   **bruise** i.e.,
crush   **8 know** consider   **10 affections** desires   **12 blood** passion
14 had would have.   **sometime** on some occasion   **22–23 What . . . on
thieves** i.e., what cognizance can the laws take of the possibility that
thieves may pass sentence upon thieves   **23 pregnant** clear   **28 For**
because

Let mine own judgment pattern out my death   30
And nothing come in partial. Sir, he must die.   31

    Enter Provost.

ESCALUS
Be it as your wisdom will.
ANGELO   Where is the Provost?
PROVOST
Here, if it like your honor.
ANGELO   See that Claudio   33
Be executed by nine tomorrow morning.
Bring him his confessor; let him be prepared.
For that's the utmost of his pilgrimage.   36

                            [*Exit Provost.*]
ESCALUS
Well, heaven forgive him and forgive us all!
Some rise by sin and some by virtue fall;
Some run from breaks of ice and answer none,   39
And some condemnèd for a fault alone.

    Enter Elbow, Froth, Clown [Pompey], officers.

ELBOW   Come, bring them away. If these be good peo-   41
ple in a commonweal that do nothing but use their   42
abuses in common houses, I know no law. Bring them   43
away.
ANGELO   How now, sir, what's your name? And what's
the matter?
ELBOW   If it please your honor, I am the poor Duke's   47
constable, and my name is Elbow. I do lean upon jus-   48
tice, sir, and do bring in here before your good honor
two notorious benefactors.
ANGELO   Benefactors? Well, what benefactors are they?
Are they not malefactors?
ELBOW   If it please your honor, I know not well what

---

30 judgment pattern out sentence (imposed in this and similar cases)
serve as a model for   **31 nothing . . . partial** let there be no mitigation
33 like please   **36 utmost** furthest point.   **pilgrimage** i.e., life   **39 Some
. . . none** i.e., some commit sin (grossly violate chastity) and escape the
consequences (?). (A famous crux; the Folio reads *brakes of ice*.)   **41 away**
onward   **42–43 use . . . houses** practice their vices in bawdy houses
47 poor Duke's i.e., Duke's poor   **48 lean upon** rely on, appeal to (with
an unintended comic reference to the idea of leaning on one's elbow)

they are; but precise villains they are, that I am sure 54
of, and void of all profanation in the world that good 55
Christians ought to have.

ESCALUS [*To Angelo*] This comes off well. Here's a wise
officer.

ANGELO Go to. What quality are they of? Elbow is your 59
name? Why dost thou not speak, Elbow?

POMPEY He cannot, sir; he's out at elbow.   61

ANGELO What are you, sir?

ELBOW He, sir? A tapster, sir, parcel-bawd, one that 63
serves a bad woman, whose house, sir, was, as they
say, plucked down in the suburbs; and now she pro- 65
fesses a hothouse, which, I think, is a very ill house 66
too.

ESCALUS How know you that?

ELBOW My wife, sir, whom I detest before heaven and 69
your honor—

ESCALUS How? Thy wife?

ELBOW Ay, sir; whom I thank heaven is an honest
woman—

ESCALUS Dost thou detest her therefore?

ELBOW I say, sir, I will detest myself also, as well as she,
that this house, if it be not a bawd's house, it is pity 76
of her life, for it is a naughty house.   77

ESCALUS How dost thou know that, Constable?

ELBOW Marry, sir, by my wife, who, if she had been a
woman cardinally given, might have been accused in 80
fornication, adultery, and all uncleanliness there.

ESCALUS By the woman's means?

ELBOW Ay, sir, by Mistress Overdone's means; but as
she spit in his face, so she defied him.   84

---

54 precise complete (or perhaps a blunder unintentionally recalling the
description of Angelo as *precise*, i.e., strict or puritanical, at 1.3.50)
55 profanation (A blunder for *profession*? Elbow already has used
several seeming malapropisms, including *lean upon*, *benefactors*, and
precise.) **59 quality** occupation **61 out at elbow** (1) impoverished,
threadbare, hence without any ideas (2) missing his cue, i.e., silent (or
out) after being called by his name **63 parcel-bawd** part-time bawd
(and part-time tapster) **65–66 professes a hothouse** professes to run a
bathhouse **69 detest** (For *protest*.) **76–77 pity of her life** i.e., a sad
state of affairs for her **77 naughty** wicked **80 cardinally** (For *carnally*.) **given** inclined **84 his** i.e., Pompey's, who was carrying out
Mistress Overdone's wishes and was therefore her *means*

POMPEY   Sir, if it please your honor, this is not so.

ELBOW   Prove it before these varlets here, thou honor- 86
able man, prove it. 87

ESCALUS [*To Angelo*]   Do you hear how he misplaces?

POMPEY   Sir, she came in great with child, and longing,
saving your honor's reverence, for stewed prunes. Sir, 90
we had but two in the house, which at that very dis- 91
tant time stood, as it were, in a fruit dish, a dish of 92
some   threepence—your   honors   have   seen   such
dishes; they are not China dishes, but very good
dishes—

ESCALUS   Go to, go to. No matter for the dish, sir.

POMPEY   No indeed, sir, not of a pin; you are therein 97
in the right. But to the point. As I say, this Mistress
Elbow, being, as I say, with child, and being great-
bellied, and longing, as I said, for prunes; and having
but two in the dish, as I said, Master Froth here, this
very man, having eaten the rest, as I said, and, as I
say, paying for them very honestly—for, as you
know, Master Froth, I could not give you threepence
again. 105

FROTH   No indeed.

POMPEY   Very   well;   you   being   then,   if   you   be
remembered, cracking the stones of the foresaid 108
prunes—

FROTH   Ay, so I did indeed.

POMPEY   Why, very well; I telling you then, if you be
remembered, that such a one and such a one were past
cure of the thing you wot of, unless they kept very 113
good diet, as I told you—

FROTH   All this is true.

POMPEY   Why, very well, then—

ESCALUS   Come, you are a tedious fool. To the purpose.

86–87 varlets . . . honorable (Elbow reverses or *misplaces* these epithets.)   **90 saving . . . reverence** i.e., begging your pardon for what I'm
about to say.   **stewed prunes** (Commonly served in houses of prostitu-
tion, or *stews*, and therefore suggesting prostitutes. The pronunciation
is suggested by the Folio spelling *prewyns*.)   **91–92 distant** (Blunder
for *instant?*)   **97 a pin** i.e., an insignificant trifle   **105 again** back
108 stones pits   **113 the thing . . . of** you know what I mean (i.e., venereal disease)

What was done to Elbow's wife, that he hath cause to
complain of? Come me to what was done to her.   119
POMPEY   Sir, your honor cannot come to that yet.
ESCALUS   No, sir, nor I mean it not.
POMPEY   Sir, but you shall come to it, by your honor's
leave. And, I beseech you, look into Master Froth here,
sir, a man of fourscore pound a year, whose father   124
died at Hallowmas.—Was 't not at Hallowmas, Master 125
Froth?
FROTH   All-hallond eve.   127
POMPEY   Why, very well. I hope here be truths. He, sir,
sitting, as I say, in a lower chair, sir—'twas in the 129
Bunch of Grapes, where indeed you have a delight to 130
sit, have you not?
FROTH   I have so, because it is an open room and good 132
for winter.
POMPEY   Why, very well, then. I hope here be truths.
ANGELO
This will last out a night in Russia,
When nights are longest there. I'll take my leave
And leave you to the hearing of the cause,
Hoping you'll find good cause to whip them all.
ESCALUS
I think no less. Good morrow to your lordship.
                              Exit [*Angelo*].
Now, sir, come on. What was done to Elbow's wife,   140
once more?
POMPEY   Once, sir? There was nothing done to her
once.
ELBOW   I beseech you, sir, ask him what this man did
to my wife.
POMPEY   I beseech your honor, ask me.
ESCALUS   Well, sir, what did this gentleman to her?
POMPEY   I beseech you, sir, look in this gentleman's

---

119 Come me i.e., come. (*Me* is used colloquially. Pompey makes a
vulgar joke on the word *come*.)   **124 of . . . year** i.e., well off   **125 Hallowmas** All Saints' Day, November 1   **127 All-hallond eve** Halloween,
October 31   **129 a lower chair** i.e., a chair of special dignity, or an easy
chair for the infirm (?)   **130 Bunch of Grapes** (It was not uncommon to
designate particular rooms in inns by such names.)   **132 open** public
140 done (Pompey, in his answer, uses *done* in a sexual sense.)

face. Good Master Froth, look upon his honor; 'tis for
a good purpose. Doth your honor mark his face?   150

ESCALUS   Ay, sir, very well.

POMPEY   Nay, I beseech you, mark it well.

ESCALUS   Well, I do so.

POMPEY   Doth your honor see any harm in his face?

ESCALUS   Why, no.

POMPEY   I'll be supposed upon a book, his face is the   156
worst thing about him. Good, then; if his face be the
worst thing about him, how could Master Froth do the
constable's wife any harm? I would know that of your
honor.

ESCALUS   He's in the right, Constable. What say you
to it?

ELBOW   First, an it like you, the house is a respected   163
house; next, this is a respected fellow; and his mistress
is a respected woman.

POMPEY   By this hand, sir, his wife is a more respected
person than any of us all.

ELBOW   Varlet, thou liest! Thou liest, wicked varlet! The
time is yet to come that she was ever respected with
man, woman, or child.

POMPEY   Sir, she was respected with him before he married with her.

ESCALUS   Which is the wiser here, Justice or Iniquity? Is   173
this true?

ELBOW   O thou caitiff! O thou varlet! O thou wicked   175
Hannibal! I respected with her before I was married to   176
her? If ever I was respected with her, or she with me,
let not your worship think me the poor Duke's officer.
Prove this, thou wicked Hannibal, or I'll have mine
action of battery on thee.   180

ESCALUS   If he took you a box o' th' ear, you might have   181
your action of slander too.

ELBOW   Marry, I thank your good worship for it. What

---

150 mark observe   **156 supposed** (A malapropism for *deposed*, i.e.,
sworn.)   **book** i.e., Bible   **163 an it like** if it please.   **respected** (For
suspected.)   **173 Justice or Iniquity** (Personified characters in a morality
play.)   **175 caitiff** knave, villain   **176 Hannibal** (A blunder for *cannibal*,
perhaps also suggested by the fact that Hannibal and Pompey were both
famous generals in the classical world.)   **180 battery** (An error for
slander, as Escalus amusedly points out.)   **181 took** gave

is 't your worship's pleasure I shall do with this
wicked caitiff?

ESCALUS   Truly, officer, because he hath some offenses
in him that thou wouldst discover if thou couldst, let   187
him continue in his courses till thou know'st what   188
they are.

ELBOW   Marry, I thank your worship for it. Thou seest,
thou wicked varlet, now, what's come upon thee: thou
art to continue now, thou varlet, thou art to continue.

ESCALUS [*To Froth*]   Where were you born, friend?

FROTH   Here in Vienna, sir.

ESCALUS   Are you of fourscore pounds a year?   195

FROTH   Yes, an 't please you, sir.

ESCALUS   So. [*To Pompey.*] What trade are you of, sir?

POMPEY   A tapster, a poor widow's tapster.

ESCALUS   Your mistress' name?

POMPEY   Mistress Overdone.

ESCALUS   Hath she had any more than one husband?

POMPEY   Nine, sir. Overdone by the last.   202

ESCALUS   Nine?—Come hither to me, Master Froth. Master Froth, I would not have you acquainted with tap-
sters. They will draw you, Master Froth, and you will   205
hang them. Get you gone, and let me hear no more of   206
you.

FROTH   I thank your worship. For mine own part, I
never come into any room in a taphouse but I am
drawn in.

ESCALUS   Well, no more of it, Master Froth. Farewell.
[*Exit Froth.*] Come you hither to me, Master Tapster.
What's your name, Master Tapster?

POMPEY   Pompey.

ESCALUS   What else?

POMPEY   Bum, sir.

ESCALUS   Troth, and your bum is the greatest thing
about you, so that in the beastliest sense you are Pom-

---

187 **discover** reveal   188 **courses** courses of action   195 **of** possessed
of   202 **Overdone . . . last** (1) her name, Overdone, was given her by her
last husband (2) she has been worn out (*overdone*) by the last one
205 **draw** (1) cheat, take in (2) empty, deplete (with a pun on the tapster's trade of drawing liquor from a barrel, and on Froth's name)
(3) disembowel, or drag to execution   205–206 **will hang them** will be
the cause of their hanging

pey the Great. Pompey, you are partly a bawd, Pompey, howsoever you color it in being a tapster, are you 220
not? Come, tell me true. It shall be the better for you.

POMPEY   Truly, sir, I am a poor fellow that would live.   222

ESCALUS   How would you live, Pompey? By being a
bawd? What do you think of the trade, Pompey? Is it
a lawful trade?

POMPEY   If the law would allow it, sir.

ESCALUS   But the law will not allow it, Pompey; nor it
shall not be allowed in Vienna.

POMPEY   Does your worship mean to geld and splay all 229
the youth of the city?

ESCALUS   No, Pompey.

POMPEY   Truly, sir, in my poor opinion, they will to 't
then. If your worship will take order for the drabs and 233
the knaves, you need not to fear the bawds.

ESCALUS   There is pretty orders beginning, I can tell
you. It is but heading and hanging.   236

POMPEY   If you head and hang all that offend that way
but for ten year together, you'll be glad to give out a
commission for more heads. If this law hold in Vienna 239
ten year, I'll rent the fairest house in it after threepence 240
a bay. If you live to see this come to pass, say Pompey 241
told you so.

ESCALUS   Thank you, good Pompey. And, in requital of 243
your prophecy, hark you: I advise you let me not find
you before me again upon any complaint whatsoever;
no, not for dwelling where you do. If I do, Pompey, I
shall beat you to your tent and prove a shrewd Caesar 247
to you; in plain dealing, Pompey, I shall have you
whipped. So for this time, Pompey, fare you well.

POMPEY   I thank your worship for your good counsel.
[Aside.] But I shall follow it as the flesh and fortune
shall better determine.

Whip me? No, no, let carman whip his jade.   253

---

220 color disguise   **222 live** make a living   **229 splay** spay   **233 take
order for** attend to.   **drabs** prostitutes   **236 heading** beheading
239 commission order.   **hold** remain in force   **240 after** at the rate of
241 bay division of a house included under one gable   **243 requital of**
return for   **247 shrewd** harsh, severe.   **Caesar** (Escalus refers to Julius
Caesar's defeat of Pompey at Pharsalus in 48 B.C.)   **253 carman** one
who drives a cart.   **jade** broken-down horse

The valiant heart's not whipped out of his trade.

Exit.

ESCALUS   Come hither to me, Master Elbow; come
hither, Master Constable. How long have you been in
this place of constable?

ELBOW   Seven year and a half, sir.

ESCALUS   I thought, by your readiness in the office, you   259
had continued in it some time. You say, seven years
together?

ELBOW   And a half, sir.

ESCALUS   Alas, it hath been great pains to you. They do
you wrong to put you so oft upon 't. Are there not
men in your ward sufficient to serve it?   265

ELBOW   Faith, sir, few of any wit in such matters. As
they are chosen, they are glad to choose me for them.   267
I do it for some piece of money and go through with   268
all.   269

ESCALUS   Look you bring me in the names of some six
or seven, the most sufficient of your parish.

ELBOW   To your worship's house, sir?

ESCALUS   To my house. Fare you well.   [*Exit Elbow.*]
What's o'clock, think you?

JUSTICE   Eleven, sir.

ESCALUS   I pray you home to dinner with me.   276

JUSTICE   I humbly thank you.

ESCALUS
It grieves me for the death of Claudio;
But there's no remedy.

JUSTICE
Lord Angelo is severe.

ESCALUS   It is but needful.
Mercy is not itself, that oft looks so;   281
Pardon is still the nurse of second woe.   282
But yet—poor Claudio! There is no remedy.
Come, sir.   *Exeunt.*

---

259 readiness proficiency, alacrity   **265 sufficient** able   **267 for them** i.e.,
to take their place   **268–269 go . . . all** i.e., perform my duties thoroughly   **276 dinner** (Dinner was customarily eaten just before midday.)
281 Mercy . . . so i.e., what seems merciful may not really be so (since it
may encourage crime and hence lead to more punishment)   **282 still** always

2.2   *Enter Provost [and a] Servant.*

SERVANT
  He's hearing of a cause; he will come straight.   1
  I'll tell him of you.
PROVOST   Pray you, do. [*Exit Servant.*] I'll know
  His pleasure; maybe he will relent. Alas,
  He hath but as offended in a dream!   4
  All sects, all ages smack of this vice—and he   5
  To die for 't!

      Exit Angelo.

ANGELO   Now, what's the matter, Provost?
PROVOST
  Is it your will Claudio shall die tomorrow?
ANGELO
  Did not I tell thee yea? Hadst thou not order?
  Why dost thou ask again?
PROVOST   Lest I might be too rash.
  Under your good correction, I have seen   11
  When, after execution, judgment hath
  Repented o'er his doom.   13
ANGELO   Go to; let that be mine.   14
  Do you your office, or give up your place,
  And you shall well be spared.   16
PROVOST   I crave your honor's pardon.
  What shall be done, sir, with the groaning Juliet?   18
  She's very near her hour.
ANGELO   Dispose of her   19
  To some more fitter place, and that with speed.

      [*Enter a Servant.*]

SERVANT
  Here is the sister of the man condemned
  Desires access to you.   22

2.2. Location: Adjacent to the court of justice, perhaps at Angelo's
official residence.
1 hearing . . . cause listening to a case   **4 He** i.e., Claudio   **5 sects**
classes of people, ranks.   **smack** partake of   **11 Under . . . correction**
i.e., allow me to say   **13 doom** sentence   **14 mine** my business   **16 well
be spared** easily be done without   **18 groaning** (with labor pains)
19 hour time of delivery   **22 Desires** who desires

ANGELO   Hath he a sister?
PROVOST
  Ay, my good lord, a very virtuous maid,
  And to be shortly of a sisterhood,   24
  If not already.
ANGELO   Well, let her be admitted.

                                    [*Exit Servant.*]
  See you the fornicatress be removed.
  Let her have needful, but not lavish, means;
  There shall be order for 't.

        Enter Lucio and Isabella.

PROVOST   Save your honor!   28
ANGELO [*To Provost*]
  Stay a little while. [*To Isabella.*] You're welcome. What's
    your will?
ISABELLA
  I am a woeful suitor to your honor,
  Please but your honor hear me.
ANGELO   Well, what's your suit?
ISABELLA
  There is a vice that most I do abhor
  And most desire should meet the blow of justice,
  For which I would not plead, but that I must;
  For which I must not plead, but that I am
  At war twixt will and will not.
ANGELO   Well, the matter?
ISABELLA
  I have a brother is condemned to die.
  I do beseech you, let it be his fault,   38
  And not my brother.
PROVOST [*Aside*]   Heaven give thee moving graces!
ANGELO
  Condemn the fault and not the actor of it?
  Why, every fault's condemned ere it be done.
  Mine were the very cipher of a function,
  To fine the faults whose fine stands in record   43
  And let go by the actor.
ISABELLA   O just but severe law!

---

24 sisterhood i.e., convent   **28 Save** may God save   **38 let . . . fault** i.e.,
let the fault die   **43 fine . . . fine** punish . . . penalty.   **in record** in the
statutes

I had a brother, then. Heaven keep your honor!

LUCIO [*Aside to Isabella*]
Give 't not o'er so. To him again, entreat him!   47
Kneel down before him; hang upon his gown.
You are too cold. If you should need a pin,   49
You could not with more tame a tongue desire it.
To him, I say!

ISABELLA [*To Angelo*]
Must he needs die?

ANGELO   Maiden, no remedy.

ISABELLA
Yes, I do think that you might pardon him,
And neither heaven nor man grieve at the mercy.

ANGELO
I will not do 't.

ISABELLA   But can you, if you would?

ANGELO
Look what I will not, that I cannot do.   56

ISABELLA
But might you do 't, and do the world no wrong,
If so your heart were touched with that remorse   58
As mine is to him?

ANGELO   He's sentenced; 'tis too late.

LUCIO [*Aside to Isabella*]   You are too cold.

ISABELLA
Too late? Why, no; I that do speak a word
May call it back again. Well, believe this:
No ceremony that to great ones longs,   64
Not the king's crown, nor the deputed sword,   65
The marshal's truncheon, nor the judge's robe,   66
Become them with one half so good a grace
As mercy does.
If he had been as you, and you as he,
You would have slipped like him; but he, like you,
Would not have been so stern.

ANGELO   Pray you, begone.

---

47 Give 't . . . so don't give up so soon   **49 need a pin** i.e., ask for the
smallest trifle   **56 Look what** whatever   **58 remorse** pity   **64 longs** is
fitting, belongs   **65 deputed sword** sword of justice entrusted by God to
his deputy   **66 truncheon** staff borne by military officers

ISABELLA
  I would to heaven I had your potency,
  And you were Isabel! Should it then be thus?
  No, I would tell what 'twere to be a judge
  And what a prisoner.
LUCIO [*Aside to Isabella*] Ay, touch him; there's the vein.   75
ANGELO
  Your brother is a forfeit of the law,   76
  And you but waste your words.
ISABELLA   Alas, alas!
  Why, all the souls that were were forfeit once,   78
  And He that might the vantage best have took   79
  Found out the remedy. How would you be,   80
  If He, which is the top of judgment, should   81
  But judge you as you are? O, think on that,
  And mercy then will breathe within your lips,
  Like man new-made.
ANGELO   Be you content, fair maid.   84
  It is the law, not I, condemn your brother.
  Were he my kinsman, brother, or my son,
  It should be thus with him. He must die tomorrow.
ISABELLA
  Tomorrow! O, that's sudden. Spare him, spare him!
  He's not prepared for death. Even for our kitchens
  We kill the fowl of season. Shall we serve heaven   90
  With less respect than we do minister
  To our gross selves? Good, good my lord, bethink you:
  Who is it that hath died for this offense?
  There's many have committed it.
LUCIO [*Aside to Isabella*]   Ay, well said.
ANGELO
  The law hath not been dead, though it hath slept.
  Those many had not dared to do that evil
  If the first that did th' edict infringe

---

75 there's the vein i.e., that's the right approach. (*Vein* means "lode to
be profitably mined.")   **76 a forfeit** one who must incur the penalty
78–80 Why . . . remedy (A reference to God's Redemption of sinful
humanity when He would have been justified in destroying humankind.)   **81 top of judgment** supreme judge   **84 new-made** i.e., new-
created by salvation, born again   **90 of season** that is in season and
properly mature

Had answered for his deed. Now 'tis awake,
Takes note of what is done, and like a prophet
Looks in a glass that shows what future evils,   100
Either now, or by remissness new-conceived,   101
And so in progress to be hatched and born,   102
Are now to have no successive degrees,   103
But, ere they live, to end.
ISABELLA   Yet show some pity.   104
ANGELO
I show it most of all when I show justice;
For then I pity those I do not know,
Which a dismissed offense would after gall,   107
And do him right that, answering one foul wrong,   108
Lives not to act another. Be satisfied;
Your brother dies tomorrow. Be content.
ISABELLA
So you must be the first that gives this sentence,
And he, that suffers. O, it is excellent
To have a giant's strength, but it is tyrannous
To use it like a giant.
LUCIO [*Aside to Isabella*]   That's well said.
ISABELLA   Could great men thunder
As Jove himself does, Jove would never be quiet,   116
For every pelting, petty officer   117
Would use his heaven for thunder,
Nothing but thunder! Merciful Heaven,
Thou rather with thy sharp and sulfurous bolt   120
Splits the unwedgeable and gnarlèd oak   121
Than the soft myrtle; but man, proud man,
Dressed in a little brief authority,
Most ignorant of what he's most assured,   124
His glassy essence, like an angry ape,   125

---

100 glass magic crystal   **101 Either . . . new-conceived** i.e., both evils
already hatched and those that would be encouraged by continued
laxity of enforcement   **102 in progress** in the course of time   **103 successive degrees** successors   **104 ere they live** i.e., before they can be
committed   **107 dismissed** forgiven.   **gall** irritate, injure   **108 right**
justice   **116 be quiet** have any quiet   **117 pelting** paltry   **120 bolt**
thunderbolt   **121 unwedgeable** unable to be split   **124 of what . . .
assured** i.e., of his own spiritual essence, his natural infirmity and need
for God's grace, something his faith should make him certain of
125 glassy essence i.e., his soul, which is reflected from God; *glassy*
refers to a mirror.   **angry ape** i.e., ludicrous buffoon

Plays such fantastic tricks before high heaven
As makes the angels weep; who, with our spleens,   127
Would all themselves laugh mortal.   128

LUCIO [*Aside to Isabella*]
O, to him, to him, wench! He will relent.
He's coming, I perceive 't.

PROVOST [*Aside*]   Pray heaven she win him!   130

ISABELLA
We cannot weigh our brother with ourself.   131
Great men may jest with saints; 'tis wit in them,
But in the less foul profanation.   133

LUCIO [*Aside to Isabella*]
Thou'rt i' the right, girl; more o' that.

ISABELLA
That in the captain's but a choleric word   135
Which in the soldier is flat blasphemy.   136

LUCIO [*Aside to Isabella*]   Art advised o' that? More on 't.   137

ANGELO
Why do you put these sayings upon me?   138

ISABELLA
Because authority, though it err like others,
Hath yet a kind of medicine in itself
That skins the vice o' the top. Go to your bosom;   141
Knock there, and ask your heart what it doth know
That's like my brother's fault. If it confess
A natural guiltiness such as is his,
Let it not sound a thought upon your tongue
Against my brother's life.

ANGELO [*Aside*]   She speaks, and 'tis such sense   147
That my sense breeds with it.—Fare you well.   148

                    [*He starts to go.*]

---

127 with our spleens i.e., if they laughed at folly as we do. (The spleen
was thought to be the seat of laughter.)   **128 themselves laugh mortal**
laugh themselves out of heaven and into our mortal condition (because
of the lack of charity the laughter demonstrates)   **130 coming** coming
around   **131 cannot . . . ourself** cannot judge our fellow men by the
same standards we use in judging ourselves (because we are so blinded
to justice)   **133 in the less** in men of lesser stature (it is)   **135 That . . .**
word i.e., we treat the abusive language a commanding officer uses in anger
merely as an outburst; we are indulgent toward the failings of *great men*
136 blasphemy defamation   **137 advised** informed, aware   **138 put . . .**
me apply these sayings to me   **141 skins . . . top** covers over the sore
with skin, leaving it unhealed. (The *medicine* of l. 140 is thus only a
palliative.)   **147–148 sense . . . sense** import . . . sensuality

ISABELLA   Gentle my lord, turn back.   149

ANGELO
  I will bethink me. Come again tomorrow.

ISABELLA
  Hark how I'll bribe you. Good my lord, turn back.

ANGELO   How? Bribe me?

ISABELLA
  Ay, with such gifts that heaven shall share with you.   153

LUCIO [*Aside to Isabella*]   You had marred all else.   154

ISABELLA
  Not with fond sicles of the tested gold,   155
  Or stones whose rate are either rich or poor   156
  As fancy values them, but with true prayers
  That shall be up at heaven and enter there
  Ere sunrise—prayers from preservèd souls,   159
  From fasting maids whose minds are dedicate   160
  To nothing temporal.

ANGELO   Well, come to me tomorrow.

LUCIO [*Aside to Isabella*]   Go to, 'tis well. Away!

ISABELLA
  Heaven keep your honor safe!

ANGELO [*Aside*]   Amen!
  For I am that way going to temptation,
  Where prayers cross.

ISABELLA   At what hour tomorrow   165
  Shall I attend your lordship?

ANGELO   At any time 'fore noon.

ISABELLA   Save your honor!   168
                    [*Exeunt Isabella, Lucio, and Provost.*]

ANGELO   From thee, even from thy virtue!
  What's this, what's this? Is this her fault or mine?
  The tempter or the tempted, who sins most, ha?
  Not she, nor doth she tempt; but it is I
  That, lying by the violet in the sun,
  Do as the carrion does, not as the flower,   174

---

149 **Gentle my lord** my noble lord   153 **that** as   154 **else** otherwise
155 **fond** i.e., foolishly valued.   **sicles** shekels (Hebrew coins).   **tested**
purest, tested by the touchstone   156 **rate** values   159 **preservèd** protected (from the world)   160 **dedicate** dedicated   165 **cross** are at cross
purposes   168 **Save** may God save   174 **carrion** decaying flesh

Corrupt with virtuous season. Can it be   175
That modesty may more betray our sense   176
Than woman's lightness? Having waste ground enough,   177
Shall we desire to raze the sanctuary
And pitch our evils there? O, fie, fie, fie!   179
What dost thou, or what art thou, Angelo?
Dost thou desire her foully for those things
That make her good? O, let her brother live!
Thieves for their robbery have authority
When judges steal themselves. What, do I love her,
That I desire to hear her speak again
And feast upon her eyes? What is 't I dream on?
O cunning enemy that, to catch a saint,
With saints dost bait thy hook! Most dangerous
Is that temptation that doth goad us on
To sin in loving virtue. Never could the strumpet,
With all her double vigor, art, and nature,   191
Once stir my temper; but this virtuous maid   192
Subdues me quite. Ever till now,
When men were fond, I smiled and wondered how.   194

Exit.

❖

2.3   *Enter, [meeting,] Duke [disguised as a friar]
            and Provost.*

DUKE
Hail to you, Provost—so I think you are.
PROVOST
I am the Provost. What's your will, good Friar?
DUKE
Bound by my charity and my blest order,
I come to visit the afflicted spirits

---

175 Corrupt . . . season i.e., putrefy while all else flourishes. (The warmth
of flowering time causes the violet, Isabella, to blossom, but causes the
carrion lying beside it, Angelo, to rot.)   **176 modesty** virtue, chastity.
sense sensual nature   **177 lightness** immodesty, lust   **179 pitch our evils
there** i.e., erect a privy not on *waste ground* (l. 177) but on sanctified
ground   **191 vigor** power.   **art** artifice.   **nature** sensual nature   **192 temper** mental balance, temperament   **194 fond** foolishly in love

2.3. Location: A prison.

Here in the prison. Do me the common right   5
To let me see them and to make me know
The nature of their crimes, that I may minister
To them accordingly.

PROVOST
I would do more than that, if more were needful.

Enter Juliet.

Look, here comes one: a gentlewoman of mine,
Who, falling in the flaws of her own youth,   11
Hath blistered her report. She is with child,   12
And he that got it, sentenced—a young man   13
More fit to do another such offense
Than die for this.

DUKE
When must he die?

PROVOST   As I do think, tomorrow.
[*To Juliet.*] I have provided for you. Stay awhile,   17
And you shall be conducted.   18

DUKE
Repent you, fair one, of the sin you carry?

JULIET
I do, and bear the shame most patiently.

DUKE
I'll teach you how you shall arraign your conscience,   21
And try your penitence, if it be sound   22
Or hollowly put on.   23

JULIET   I'll gladly learn.

DUKE   Love you the man that wronged you?

JULIET
Yes, as I love the woman that wronged him.

DUKE
So then it seems your most offenseful act
Was mutually committed?

JULIET   Mutually.

DUKE
Then was your sin of heavier kind than his.

---

5 common right i.e., right of all clerics   **11 flaws** sudden gusts (of passion)   **12 blistered her report** marred her reputation   **13 got** begot   **17 provided** provided a place to stay   **18 conducted** taken there   **21 arraign** accuse   **22 try** test   **23 hollowly** falsely

JULIET
　I do confess it, and repent it, Father.
DUKE
　'Tis meet so, daughter. But lest you do repent　　　31
　As that the sin hath brought you to this shame,　　32
　Which sorrow is always toward ourselves, not heaven,　33
　Showing we would not spare heaven as we love it,　　34
　But as we stand in fear—
JULIET
　I do repent me as it is an evil,
　And take the shame with joy.
DUKE　　　　　　　　　　　There rest.　　　37
　Your partner, as I hear, must die tomorrow,
　And I am going with instruction to him.
　Grace go with you. *Benedicite!*　　　　　　*Exit.* 40
JULIET
　Must die tomorrow? O injurious love,
　That respites me a life, whose very comfort　　　42
　Is still a dying horror!
PROVOST　　　　　　　'Tis pity of him.　　　*Exeunt.* 43

❖

2.4　*Enter Angelo.*

ANGELO
　When I would pray and think, I think and pray
　To several subjects. Heaven hath my empty words,　　2
　Whilst my invention, hearing not my tongue,　　3
　Anchors on Isabel; Heaven in my mouth,
　As if I did but only chew His name,　　　5
　And in my heart the strong and swelling evil

31 **'Tis meet so** it is fitting that you do so　32 **As that** because
33 **toward ourselves** i.e., narrowly self-concerned rather than loving
virtue for its own sake　34 **spare heaven** i.e., spare heaven the sorrow
felt there for unconfessed sins.　**as** because (also in ll. 35 and 36)
37 **There rest** hold fast to that truth　40 **Benedicite** blessings on you
42 **respites** prolongs, does not forfeit. (Her life is spared, unlike
Claudio's.)　**42–43 whose . . . horror** i.e., whose greatest comfort will
always be a deadly horror　43 **pity of** a pity about

2.4. Location: Angelo's official residence.
2 **several** separate　3 **invention** imagination　5 **His** i.e., Heaven's, God's

Of my conception. The state, whereon I studied,   7
Is like a good thing, being often read,
Grown sere and tedious; yea, my gravity,   9
Wherein—let no man hear me—I take pride,
Could I with boot change for an idle plume,   11
Which the air beats for vain. O place, O form,   12
How often dost thou with thy case, thy habit,   13
Wrench awe from fools and tie the wiser souls
To thy false seeming! Blood, thou art blood.   15
Let's write "good angel" on the devil's horn,   16
'Tis not the devil's crest.

    Enter Servant.

                     How now? Who's there?   17

SERVANT
One Isabel, a sister, desires access to you.
ANGELO   Teach her the way. [*Exit Servant.*] O heavens!   19
Why does my blood thus muster to my heart,   20
Making both it unable for itself   21
And dispossessing all my other parts
Of necessary fitness?
So play the foolish throngs with one that swoons,
Come all to help him, and so stop the air
By which he should revive; and even so
The general subject to a well-wished king   27
Quit their own part and in obsequious fondness   28
Crowd to his presence, where their untaught love   29
Must needs appear offense.   30

    Enter Isabella.

---

7 conception thought.   **The state** statecraft   **9 sere** withered, old
11 Could . . . boot I could advantageously   **12 the air beats** beats the
air.   **vain** vanity.   **place** official position, rank.   **form** dignity of office   **13 case** outward appearance.   **habit** garb   **15 Blood . . . blood** i.e.,
passions are inherent in human nature, under all these outward appearances   **16 Let's write** i.e., if we were to write.   **good angel** (with a play
on Angelo's name)   **17 'Tis . . . crest** that still would not make it a true
sign of the devil's identity (i.e., it would not make the devil an angel
merely to write "good angel" on his horn). The *crest* is an identifying emblem worn on the helmet or coat of arms.   **19 Teach** show   **20 muster to**
assemble in   **21 unable** ineffectual   **27 general subject** i.e., commoners,
subjects   **28 Quit . . . part** abandon their proper function and (politely distant) place   **29 untaught** ignorant, unsophisticated   **30 Must needs** will
necessarily

How now, fair maid?

ISABELLA   I am come to know your pleasure.

ANGELO
That you might know it would much better please me   32
Than to demand what 'tis. Your brother cannot live.

ISABELLA   Even so. Heaven keep your honor!   34

[She turns to leave.]

ANGELO
Yet may he live awhile; and, it may be,
As long as you or I. Yet he must die.

ISABELLA   Under your sentence?

ANGELO   Yea.

ISABELLA
When, I beseech you? That in his reprieve,
Longer or shorter, he may be so fitted   40
That his soul sicken not.

ANGELO
Ha? Fie, these filthy vices! It were as good
To pardon him that hath from nature stolen   43
A man already made, as to remit   44
Their saucy sweetness that do coin heaven's image   45
In stamps that are forbid. 'Tis all as easy   46
Falsely to take away a life true made
As to put metal in restrainèd means   48
To make a false one.

ISABELLA
'Tis set down so in heaven, but not in earth.   50

ANGELO
Say you so? Then I shall pose you quickly: 51
Which had you rather, that the most just law
Now took your brother's life, or, to redeem him,

---

32 know it i.e., know my pleasure, my desire. (Angelo is thinking of
his desire for Isabella.)   **34 Even so** i.e., so be it   **40 fitted** prepared
43–44 To . . . made i.e., to pardon a murderer   **44 remit** pardon
45 Their . . . sweetness the wanton pleasures of those persons
45–46 coin . . . forbid i.e., produce illegitimate offspring, like counterfeit coiners   **48 metal** (with a play on *mettle*, a variant spelling,
and as it is spelled in the Folio; i.e., substance).   **restrainèd** prohibited, illicit   **50 'Tis . . . earth** i.e., equating murder and bastardiz-
ing accords with divine law but not with human law, to which murder
is more heinous   **51 pose** put a question to

Give up your body to such sweet uncleanness
As she that he hath stained?
ISABELLA   Sir, believe this,
I had rather give my body than my soul.
ANGELO
I talk not of your soul. Our compelled sins   57
Stand more for number than for account.
ISABELLA   How say you?   58
ANGELO
Nay, I'll not warrant that, for I can speak   59
Against the thing I say. Answer to this:
I, now the voice of the recorded law,
Pronounce a sentence on your brother's life;
Might there not be a charity in sin
To save this brother's life?
ISABELLA   Please you to do 't,   64
I'll take it as a peril to my soul;   65
It is no sin at all, but charity.
ANGELO
Pleased you to do 't at peril of your soul   67
Were equal poise of sin and charity.   68
ISABELLA
That I do beg his life, if it be sin,
Heaven let me bear it! You granting of my suit,
If that be sin, I'll make it my morn prayer
To have it added to the faults of mine,
And nothing of your answer.
ANGELO   Nay, but hear me.   73
Your sense pursues not mine. Either you are ignorant
Or seem so craftily; and that's not good.
ISABELLA
Let me be ignorant, and in nothing good
But graciously to know I am no better.   77
ANGELO
Thus wisdom wishes to appear most bright

57–58 compelled . . . account sins committed under compulsion are
recorded but not charged to our spiritual account   **59 I'll . . . that** i.e.,
I'm not necessarily endorsing the view I just expressed   **64 Please you**
if you please   **65 take** accept   **67 Pleased** if it pleased   **68 Were equal
poise** there would be equal balance   **73 of your answer** to which you
will have to answer   **77 graciously** through divine grace

When it doth tax itself, as these black masks   79
Proclaim an enshield beauty ten times louder   80
Than beauty could, displayed. But mark me.
To be receivèd plain, I'll speak more gross: 82
Your brother is to die.

ISABELLA So.

ANGELO
And his offense is so, as it appears,
Accountant to the law upon that pain.   86

ISABELLA True.

ANGELO
Admit no other way to save his life—   88
As I subscribe not that, nor any other,   89
But in the loss of question—that you, his sister,   90
Finding yourself desired of such a person
Whose credit with the judge, or own great place,
Could fetch your brother from the manacles
Of the all-binding law; and that there were
No earthly means to save him, but that either
You must lay down the treasures of your body
To this supposed, or else to let him suffer.   97
What would you do?

ISABELLA
As much for my poor brother as myself:
That is, were I under the terms of death,   100
Th' impression of keen whips I'd wear as rubies,
And strip myself to death as to a bed
That longing have been sick for, ere I'd yield   103
My body up to shame.

ANGELO Then must your brother die.

ISABELLA And 'twere the cheaper way.
Better it were a brother died at once   107

---

79 **tax itself** accuse itself (of ignorance). **these** (Generically referring to
any.) **80 enshield** enshielded, protected from view behind the black
masks **82 receivèd plain** plainly understood. **gross** openly **86 Accountant** accountable. **pain** penalty **88 Admit** suppose **89 subscribe**
assent to **90 But . . . question** i.e., provided nothing more can be said
to defend Claudio's case. (*Loss* means "default.") **97 supposed** hypothetical person. **him** i.e., Claudio **100 terms** i.e., sentence **103 longing . . . for** i.e., that I have been sick with longing for **107 died at once**
i.e., should experience physical death (as contrasted to the death of the
soul through sin, to *die forever,* l. 109)

Than that a sister, by redeeming him,
Should die forever.

ANGELO
Were not you then as cruel as the sentence
That you have slandered so?

ISABELLA
Ignomy in ransom and free pardon   112
Are of two houses. Lawful mercy   113
Is nothing kin to foul redemption.   114

ANGELO
You seemed of late to make the law a tyrant,
And rather proved the sliding of your brother   116
A merriment than a vice.

ISABELLA
O, pardon me, my lord. It oft falls out,
To have what we would have, we speak not what we
    mean.
I something do excuse the thing I hate   120
For his advantage that I dearly love.

ANGELO
We are all frail.

ISABELLA   Else let my brother die,
If not a fedary but only he   123
Owe and succeed thy weakness.   124

ANGELO   Nay, women are frail too.

ISABELLA
Ay, as the glasses where they view themselves,   126
Which are as easy broke as they make forms.   127
Women? Help, Heaven! Men their creation mar   128
In profiting by them. Nay, call us ten times frail,
For we are soft as our complexions are,   130

---

112 Ignomy ignominy **113 of two houses** i.e., utterly different, of
different kinds **114 nothing** not at all **116 proved** argued, condoned
120 something to some extent **123 fedary** associate, i.e., one of the
whole group of mankind **124 Owe . . . weakness** possess and own
through succession or inheritance the weakness you speak of, or the
weakness to which all men as a class are prone. (Isabella argues
that Claudio should die only if he is the only man who is frail.)
126 glasses mirrors **127 forms** (1) images (2) copies of themselves, i.e.,
children **128 their . . . mar** debase their nature **130 complexions**
constitutions

And credulous to false prints.

ANGELO   I think it well.   131
And from this testimony of your own sex—
Since I suppose we are made to be no stronger
Than faults may shake our frames—let me be bold.   134
I do arrest your words. Be that you are,   135
That is, a woman; if you be more, you're none.   136
If you be one, as you are well expressed   137
By all external warrants, show it now
By putting on the destined livery.   139

ISABELLA
I have no tongue but one. Gentle my lord,   140
Let me entreat you speak the former language.   141

ANGELO   Plainly conceive, I love you.

ISABELLA   My brother did love Juliet,
And you tell me that he shall die for 't.

ANGELO
He shall not, Isabel, if you give me love.

ISABELLA
I know your virtue hath a license in 't,   146
Which seems a little fouler than it is   147
To pluck on others.

ANGELO   Believe me, on mine honor,   148
My words express my purpose.

ISABELLA
Ha! Little honor to be much believed,
And most pernicious purpose! Seeming, seeming!
I will proclaim thee, Angelo, look for 't!
Sign me a present pardon for my brother,   153
Or with an outstretched throat I'll tell the world aloud
What man thou art.

ANGELO   Who will believe thee, Isabel?
My unsoiled name, th' austereness of my life,

---

131 credulous . . . prints susceptible to false impressions. (The metaphor is from the stamping of metal.)   **134 Than** than that   **135 arrest your words** take what you have said and hold you to it.   **that** what   **136 if . . . none** i.e., if you strive for the perfection of chastity, you are no longer a woman as we have defined that term   **137 expressed** shown to be   **139 putting . . . livery** i.e., assuming the characteristic frailty that all women possess   **140 tongue** language   **141 former** i.e., customary   **146–148 your . . . others** i.e., you, although virtuous, are pretending foul purposes in order to mislead (*pluck on*) me   **153 present** immediate

My vouch against you, and my place i' the state   157
Will so your accusation overweigh
That you shall stifle in your own report
And smell of calumny. I have begun,   160
And now I give my sensual race the rein.   161
Fit thy consent to my sharp appetite;
Lay by all nicety and prolixious blushes   163
That banish what they sue for. Redeem thy brother   164
By yielding up thy body to my will,
Or else he must not only die the death,
But thy unkindness shall his death draw out
To lingering sufferance. Answer me tomorrow,   168
Or, by the affection that now guides me most,   169
I'll prove a tyrant to him. As for you,
Say what you can, my false o'erweighs your true.
                                                    Exit.

ISABELLA
To whom should I complain? Did I tell this,   172
Who would believe me? O perilous mouths,
That bear in them one and the selfsame tongue,
Either of condemnation or approof,   175
Bidding the law make curtsy to their will,
Hooking both right and wrong to th' appetite,   177
To follow as it draws! I'll to my brother.   178
Though he hath fall'n by prompture of the blood,   179
Yet hath he in him such a mind of honor
That, had he twenty heads to tender down   181
On twenty bloody blocks, he'd yield them up
Before his sister should her body stoop
To such abhorred pollution.
Then, Isabel, live chaste, and, brother, die;
More than our brother is our chastity.
I'll tell him yet of Angelo's request,
And fit his mind to death, for his soul's rest.   *Exit.*

157 **vouch** testimony   160 **calumny** slander   161 **race** natural or inherited disposition (with a probable quibble on "horse race")   163 **by** aside.   **nicety** modesty, reserve.   **prolixious** tedious   164 **banish** i.e., seem to thrust away   168 **sufferance** torture   169 **affection** passion   172 **Did I tell** if I told   175 **approof** approval, sanction   177 **Hooking** attaching   178 **as it draws** wherever it drags   179 **prompture** prompting, suggestion   181 **tender down** lay down in payment

3.1 *Enter Duke [disguised as before], Claudio, and Provost.*

DUKE

So then you hope of pardon from Lord Angelo?

CLAUDIO

The miserable have no other medicine
But only hope.
I have hope to live and am prepared to die.

DUKE

Be absolute for death. Either death or life
Shall thereby be the sweeter. Reason thus with life:
If I do lose thee, I do lose a thing
That none but fools would keep. A breath thou art,
Servile to all the skyey influences   9
That dost this habitation where thou keep'st   10
Hourly afflict. Merely, thou art death's fool,   11
For him thou labor'st by thy flight to shun,
And yet runn'st toward him still. Thou art not noble,
For all th' accommodations that thou bear'st   14
Are nursed by baseness. Thou'rt by no means valiant,   15
For thou dost fear the soft and tender fork   16
Of a poor worm. Thy best of rest is sleep,   17
And that thou oft provok'st, yet grossly fear'st   18
Thy death, which is no more. Thou art not thyself,
For thou exists on many a thousand grains
That issue out of dust. Happy thou art not,
For what thou hast not, still thou striv'st to get,
And what thou hast, forget'st. Thou art not certain,   23
For thy complexion shifts to strange effects,   24
After the moon. If thou art rich, thou'rt poor,   25
For, like an ass whose back with ingots bows,
Thou bear'st thy heavy riches but a journey,
And death unloads thee. Friend hast thou none,

3.1. Location: The prison.
9 skyey influences influence of the stars   **10 this habitation** i.e., the earth (and possibly "the body" as well).   **keep'st** dwell   **11 Merely** utterly, only   **14 accommodations** conveniences, civilized comforts   **15 nursed by baseness** nurtured by ignoble means   **16 fork** forked tongue   **17 worm** snake   **18 thou oft provok'st** you often invoke, summon   **23 certain** steadfast   **24 complexion** constitution.   **effects** appearances, manifestations **25 After** in obedience to, under the influence of

For thine own bowels which do call thee sire,   29
The mere effusion of thy proper loins,   30
Do curse the gout, serpigo, and the rheum   31
For ending thee no sooner. Thou hast nor youth nor age,   32
But as it were an after-dinner's sleep   33
Dreaming on both, for all thy blessèd youth
Becomes as agèd and doth beg the alms   35
Of palsied eld; and, when thou art old and rich,   36
Thou hast neither heat, affection, limb, nor beauty   37
To make thy riches pleasant. What's yet in this
That bears the name of life? Yet in this life
Lie hid more thousand deaths; yet death we fear,
That makes these odds all even.

CLAUDIO   I humbly thank you.   41
To sue to live, I find I seek to die,   42
And, seeking death, find life. Let it come on.

Enter Isabella.

ISABELLA
What, ho! Peace here; grace and good company!

PROVOST
Who's there? Come in. The wish deserves a welcome.
          [*He goes to greet her.*]

DUKE [*To Claudio*]
Dear sir, ere long I'll visit you again.

CLAUDIO   Most holy sir, I thank you.

ISABELLA
My business is a word or two with Claudio.

PROVOST
And very welcome. Look, signor, here's your sister.

DUKE [*Aside to Provost*]   Provost, a word with you.

PROVOST   As many as you please.

DUKE
Bring me to hear them speak, where I may be
Concealed.   [*The Duke and the Provost withdraw.*]

CLAUDIO   Now, sister, what's the comfort?

---

29 **bowels** i.e., offspring   30 **mere** very.   **proper** own   31 **serpigo** a skin
eruption.   **rheum** catarrh   32 **nor youth** neither youth   33 **after-dinner's**
i.e., afternoon's   35 **as agèd** like old age, having to depend on it. (Youth is
penniless and dependent on the aged, whereas the old lack the physical
capacity of youth.)   36 **eld** old age   37 **heat** vigor.   **affection** passion
41 **makes . . . even** i.e., resolves all these difficulties   42 **To sue** suing

ISABELLA   **Why,**
  As all comforts are: most good, most good indeed.
  Lord Angelo, having affairs to heaven,
  Intends you for his swift ambassador,
  Where you shall be an everlasting leiger.   57
  Therefore your best appointment make with speed;   58
  Tomorrow you set on.
CLAUDIO   **Is there no remedy?**   59
ISABELLA
  None but such remedy as, to save a head,
  To cleave a heart in twain.
CLAUDIO But is there any?
ISABELLA Yes, brother, you may live.
  There is a devilish mercy in the judge,
  If you'll implore it, that will free your life
  But fetter you till death.
CLAUDIO   **Perpetual durance?**   66
ISABELLA
  Ay, just; perpetual durance, a restraint,   67
  Though all the world's vastidity you had,   68
  To a determined scope.
CLAUDIO   **But in what nature?**   69
ISABELLA
  In such a one as, you consenting to 't,
  Would bark your honor from that trunk you bear   71
  And leave you naked.
CLAUDIO   **Let me know the point.**
ISABELLA
  O, I do fear thee, Claudio, and I quake   73
  Lest thou a feverous life shouldst entertain,   74
  And six or seven winters more respect   75
  Than a perpetual honor. Dar'st thou die?
  The sense of death is most in apprehension,   77
  And the poor beetle that we tread upon

---

57 leiger resident ambassador **58 appointment** preparation **59 set on**
set out **66 durance** imprisonment **67 just** just so **67–69 restraint . . .**
scope a confinement to fixed limits or bounds (i.e., to certain damnation
and perpetual remorse for the sinful bargain you had struck), even if
you had the entire vastness of the world to wander in **71 bark** strip off
(as one strips bark from a tree *trunk*) **73 fear** fear for **74 feverous**
feverish. **entertain** maintain, desire **75 respect** value **77 apprehen-**
sion anticipation

In corporal sufferance finds a pang as great
As when a giant dies.
CLAUDIO   Why give you me this shame?
Think you I can a resolution fetch   82
From flowery tenderness? If I must die,   83
I will encounter darkness as a bride
And hug it in mine arms.

ISABELLA
There spake my brother! There my father's grave
Did utter forth a voice. Yes, thou must die.
Thou art too noble to conserve a life
In base appliances. This outward-sainted deputy,   89
Whose settled visage and deliberate word   90
Nips youth i' the head, and follies doth enew   91
As falcon doth the fowl, is yet a devil;
His filth within being cast, he would appear   93
A pond as deep as hell.
CLAUDIO   The prenzie Angelo?   94

ISABELLA
O, 'tis the cunning livery of hell,
The damned'st body to invest and cover   96
In prenzie guards! Dost thou think, Claudio,   97
If I would yield him my virginity,
Thou mightst be freed!
CLAUDIO   O heavens, it cannot be.

ISABELLA
Yes, he would give 't thee, from this rank offense,   100
So to offend him still. This night's the time   101
That I should do what I abhor to name,
Or else thou diest tomorrow.
CLAUDIO   Thou shalt not do 't.
ISABELLA   O, were it but my life,

---

82 resolution fixity of purpose. **fetch** derive **83 flowery tenderness**
i.e., comforting figures of speech **89 In base appliances** by means of
ignoble devices, remedies. **outward-sainted** outwardly holy **90 settled
visage** composed features **91 Nips . . . head** i.e., strikes at the head,
like a falcon swooping upon its prey. **enew** drive prey down into the
water or into covert **93 cast** vomited; cleared out; reckoned up (?)
94, 97 prenzie (A word unknown elsewhere, perhaps meaning "princely"
or "precise.") **96 invest** clothe **97 guards** trimmings. **Dost thou think**
i.e., would you believe **100 give 't thee** i.e., grant you license. **from** in
return for **101 So . . . still** i.e., to continue with your fornication

I'd throw it down for your deliverance
As frankly as a pin.

CLAUDIO   Thanks, dear Isabel.   107

ISABELLA
Be ready, Claudio, for your death tomorrow.

CLAUDIO   Yes. Has he affections in him   109
That thus can make him bite the law by the nose   110
When he would force it? Sure, it is no sin,   111
Or of the deadly seven it is the least.

ISABELLA   Which is the least?

CLAUDIO
If it were damnable, he being so wise,
Why would he for the momentary trick   115
Be perdurably fined? O Isabel!   116

ISABELLA
What says my brother?

CLAUDIO   Death is a fearful thing.

ISABELLA   And shamèd life a hateful.

CLAUDIO
Ay, but to die, and go we know not where,
To lie in cold obstruction and to rot,   120
This sensible warm motion to become   121
A kneaded clod; and the delighted spirit   122
To bathe in fiery floods, or to reside
In thrilling region of thick-ribbèd ice,   124
To be imprisoned in the viewless winds   125
And blown with restless violence round about
The pendent world; or to be worse than worst   127
Of those that lawless and incertain thought   128
Imagine howling—'tis too horrible!
The weariest and most loathèd worldly life
That age, ache, penury, and imprisonment   131

---

107 frankly freely   **109 affections** passions   **110 bite . . . nose** i.e., flout
the law   **111 force** enforce. (Claudio wonders that lust can drive
Angelo to make a mockery of the law even while seeking to enforce it.)
115 trick trifle   **116 perdurably fined** everlastingly punished
120 obstruction cessation of vital functions   **121 sensible** endowed with
feeling.   **motion** organism   **122 kneaded clod** shapeless lump of
earth.   **delighted spirit** spirit attended with delight; or, beloved spirit
124 thrilling piercingly cold   **125 viewless** invisible   **127 pendent**
hanging in space. (A Ptolemaic concept.)   **128 lawless . . . thought** i.e.,
wild conjecture   **131 penury** extreme poverty

Can lay on nature is a paradise
To what we fear of death.

ISABELLA Alas, alas!

CLAUDIO Sweet sister, let me live.
What sin you do to save a brother's life,
Nature dispenses with the deed so far   137
That it becomes a virtue.

ISABELLA   O you beast!
O faithless coward! O dishonest wretch!
Wilt thou be made a man out of my vice?
Is 't not a kind of incest, to take life
From thine own sister's shame? What should I think?
Heaven shield my mother played my father fair!   143
For such a warpèd slip of wilderness   144
Ne'er issued from his blood. Take my defiance,
Die, perish! Might but my bending down   146
Reprieve thee from thy fate, it should proceed.
I'll pray a thousand prayers for thy death,
No word to save thee.

CLAUDIO
Nay, hear me, Isabel.

ISABELLA   O, fie, fie, fie!
Thy sin's not accidental, but a trade.   151
Mercy to thee would prove itself a bawd;   152
'Tis best that thou diest quickly.

CLAUDIO O, hear me, Isabella!

[*The Duke comes forward.*]

DUKE
Vouchsafe a word, young sister, but one word.   155

ISABELLA What is your will?

DUKE Might you dispense with your leisure, I would
by and by have some speech with you. The satisfac-
tion I would require is likewise your own benefit.   159

ISABELLA I have no superfluous leisure—my stay must

---

137 **dispenses with** grants a dispensation for, excuses   143 **shield** defend
144 **warpèd . . . wilderness** perverse scion of a wild stock   146 **but**
merely   151 **trade** established habit   152 **prove . . . bawd** provide opportunity for sexual license   155 **Vouchsafe** allow   159 **require** ask

be stolen out of other affairs—but I will attend you   161
awhile.   [*She walks apart.*]
DUKE   Son, I have overheard what hath passed between
you and your sister. Angelo had never the purpose to
corrupt her; only he hath made an assay of her virtue   165
to practice his judgment with the disposition of na-   166
tures. She, having the truth of honor in her, hath made   167
him that gracious denial which he is most glad to receive. I am confessor to Angelo, and I know this to be
true; therefore prepare yourself to death. Do not satisfy
your resolution with hopes that are fallible. Tomorrow
you must die. Go to your knees and make ready.
CLAUDIO   Let me ask my sister pardon. I am so out of
love with life that I will sue to be rid of it.
DUKE   Hold you there. Farewell. [*Claudio retires.*] Pro-   175
vost, a word with you.

          [*The Provost comes forward.*]

PROVOST   What's your will, Father?
DUKE   That now you are come, you will be gone. Leave
me awhile with the maid. My mind promises with my   179
habit no loss shall touch her by my company.   180
PROVOST   In good time.   *Exit* [*Provost with Claudio*].   181

          [*Isabella comes forward.*]

DUKE   The hand that hath made you fair hath made you
good. The goodness that is cheap in beauty makes   183
beauty brief in goodness; but grace, being the soul of   184
your complexion, shall keep the body of it ever fair.   185
The assault that Angelo hath made to you, fortune
hath conveyed to my understanding; and, but that   187
frailty hath examples for his falling, I should wonder   188
at Angelo. How will you do to content this substitute   189
and to save your brother?

---

161 attend await   **165 assay** test   **166–167 to practice . . . natures** to
test his ability to judge people's characters   **175 Hold you there** hold
fast to that resolution   **179–180 with my habit** as well as my priestly
garb (that)   **181 In good time** i.e., very well   **183–184 The goodness . . .
in goodness** i.e., the physical graces that come easily with beauty make
beauty soon cease to be morally good   **185 complexion** character and
appearance   **187 but that** were it not that   **188 examples** precedents
189 this substitute i.e., the deputy, Angelo

ISABELLA   I am now going to resolve him. I had rather 191
my brother die by the law than my son should be unlawfully born. But, O, how much is the good Duke
deceived in Angelo! If ever he return and I can speak
to him, I will open my lips in vain, or discover his 195
government.   196

DUKE   That shall not be much amiss. Yet, as the matter
now stands, he will avoid your accusation; he made 198
trial of you only. Therefore fasten your ear on my ad-
visings. To the love I have in doing good a remedy presents itself. I do make myself believe that you may
most uprighteously do a poor wronged lady a merited
benefit, redeem your brother from the angry law, do
no stain to your own gracious person, and much
please the absent Duke, if peradventure he shall ever
return to have hearing of this business.

ISABELLA   Let me hear you speak farther. I have spirit to
do anything that appears not foul in the truth of my
spirit.

DUKE   Virtue is bold, and goodness never fearful. Have 210
you not heard speak of Mariana, the sister of Frederick,
the great soldier who miscarried at sea?

ISABELLA   I have heard of the lady, and good words
went with her name.

DUKE   She should this Angelo have married, was affi- 215
anced to her by oath, and the nuptial appointed; between which time of the contract and limit of the so- 217
lemnity, her brother Frederick was wrecked at sea, 218
having in that perished vessel the dowry of his sister.
But mark how heavily this befell to the poor gentlewoman. There she lost a noble and renowned brother,
in his love toward her ever most kind and natural;
with him, the portion and sinew of her fortune, her 223
marriage dowry; with both, her combinate husband, 224
this well-seeming Angelo.

---

191 resolve answer   **195–196 discover his government** i.e., expose
Angelo's misconduct   **198 avoid** repudiate   **210 fearful** afraid   **215 She
. . . was** i.e., Angelo was supposed to have married her, was
217–218 limit . . . solemnity date set for the ceremony   **223 sinew** i.e.,
mainstay   **224 combinate husband** i.e., betrothed

ISABELLA   Can this be so? Did Angelo so leave her?

DUKE   Left her in her tears, and dried not one of them
with his comfort; swallowed his vows whole, pretend-   228
ing in her discoveries of dishonor; in few, bestowed   229
her on her own lamentation, which she yet wears for   230
his sake; and he, a marble to her tears, is washed with   231
them but relents not.

ISABELLA   What a merit were it in death to take this poor
maid from the world! What corruption in this life, that
it will let this man live! But how out of this can she
avail?   236

DUKE   It is a rupture that you may easily heal, and the
cure of it not only saves your brother but keeps you
from dishonor in doing it.

ISABELLA   Show me how, good Father.

DUKE   This forenamed maid hath yet in her the continuance of her first affection; his unjust unkindness, that
in all reason should have quenched her love, hath, like
an impediment in the current, made it more violent
and unruly. Go you to Angelo; answer his requiring
with a plausible obedience; agree with his demands to   246
the point. Only refer yourself to this advantage, first,   247
that your stay with him may not be long, that the time
may have all shadow and silence in it, and the place   249
answer to convenience. This being granted in
course—and now follows all—we shall advise this
wronged maid to stead up your appointment, go in   252
your place. If the encounter acknowledge itself here-   253
after, it may compel him to her recompense. And here,   254
by this, is your brother saved, your honor untainted,
the poor Mariana advantaged, and the corrupt deputy
scaled. The maid will I frame and make fit for his at-   257

228–229 **pretending** alleging   229 **in her** i.e., to have found in her.   **in
few** in short   229–230 **bestowed . . . lamentation** left her to her grief
(with quibble on *bestowed* meaning "gave in marriage")   231 **a marble
to** i.e., unmoved by   236 **avail** benefit   246–247 **to the point** precisely
247 **refer . . . advantage** i.e., obtain as a proviso the following favorable
condition   249 **shadow** darkness, secrecy   252 **stead . . . appointment**
go in your stead   253–254 **If the . . . hereafter** i.e., if she should become pregnant   257 **scaled** weighed (and found wanting).   **frame**
prepare

tempt. If you think well to carry this as you may, the doubleness of the benefit defends the deceit from reproof. What think you of it?

ISABELLA   The image of it gives me content already, and I trust it will grow to a most prosperous perfection.

DUKE   It lies much in your holding up. Haste you speed- 263
ily to Angelo. If for this night he entreat you to his bed, give him promise of satisfaction. I will presently to Saint Luke's; there, at the moated grange, resides 266
this dejected Mariana. At that place call upon me, and dispatch with Angelo, that it may be quickly.   268

ISABELLA   I thank you for this comfort. Fare you well, good Father.   *Exit. [The Duke remains.]*

3.2   *Enter [to the Duke] Elbow, Clown [Pompey, and] officers.*

ELBOW   Nay, if there be no remedy for it but that you will needs buy and sell men and women like beasts, we shall have all the world drink brown and white bastard.   4

DUKE   O heavens, what stuff is here?

POMPEY   'Twas never merry world since, of two usu- 6
ries, the merriest was put down, and the worser al- 7
lowed by order of law a furred gown to keep him 8
warm, and furred with fox on lambskins too, to sig- nify that craft, being richer than innocency, stands 10
for the facing.   11

ELBOW   Come your way, sir.—Bless you, good Father Friar.

DUKE   And you, good Brother Father. What offense hath 14
this man made you, sir?

---

263 holding up ability to carry it off   **266 moated grange** country house surrounded by a ditch   **268 dispatch** settle, conclude (business)

3.2. Location: Scene continues. The Duke remains onstage.
4 bastard sweet Spanish wine (used quibblingly)   **6–7 two usuries** i.e., moneylending (the *worser*) and procuring for fornication (the *merriest*), both of which yield increase   **8 furred gown** (Characteristic attire of usurers.)   **10–11 stands . . . facing** represents the outer covering. (Fox symbolizes *craft* or craftiness, lambskin *innocency*.)   **14 Brother Father** (The Duke's retort to Elbow's *Father Friar*, i.e., Father Brother.)

ELBOW   Marry, sir, he hath offended the law; and, sir,
we take him to be a thief too, sir, for we have found
upon him, sir, a strange picklock, which we have sent   18
to the deputy.

DUKE
Fie, sirrah, a bawd, a wicked bawd!
The evil that thou causest to be done,
That is thy means to live. Do thou but think
What 'tis to cram a maw or clothe a back   23
From such a filthy vice; say to thyself,
From their abominable and beastly touches
I drink, I eat, array myself, and live.
Canst thou believe thy living is a life,
So stinkingly depending? Go mend, go mend.

POMPEY   Indeed, it does stink in some sort, sir; but yet,
sir, I would prove—   30

DUKE
Nay, if the devil have given thee proofs for sin,   31
Thou wilt prove his. Take him to prison, officer.   32
Correction and instruction must both work
Ere this rude beast will profit.

ELBOW   He must before the deputy, sir; he has given   35
him warning. The deputy cannot abide a whoremas-
ter. If he be a whoremonger, and comes before him,
he were as good go a mile on his errand.   38

DUKE
That we were all, as some would seem to be,   39
From our faults, as faults from seeming, free!   40

Enter Lucio.

ELBOW   His neck will come to your waist—a cord, sir.   41
POMPEY   I spy comfort; I cry bail. Here's a gentleman
and a friend of mine.

---

18 strange picklock (referring to a chastity belt)   **23 cram a maw** fill a
stomach   **30 prove** i.e., argue   **31 proofs for** arguments in defense of
32 prove turn out to be   **35 must** must go.   **deputy** i.e., Angelo, though
Escalus gave Pompey the warning   **38 he . . . errand** i.e., he will have a
hard road to travel   **39 That** would that   **40 From . . . free** i.e., free
from faults, and our faults free from dissembling   **41 His . . . cord** i.e.,
he is likely to hang by a cord like that around your waist. (The Duke is
habited like a friar.)

LUCIO   How now, noble Pompey? What, at the wheels
of Caesar? Art thou led in triumph? What, is there 45
none of Pygmalion's images, newly made woman, to 46
be had now, for putting the hand in the pocket and
extracting it clutched? What reply, ha? What sayst thou 48
to this tune, matter, and method? Is 't not drowned i' 49
the last rain, ha? What sayst thou, trot? Is the world 50
as it was, man? Which is the way? Is it sad, and few 51
words? Or how? The trick of it? 52

DUKE   Still thus, and thus; still worse!

LUCIO   How doth my dear morsel, thy mistress? Pro-
cures she still, ha?

POMPEY   Troth, sir, she hath eaten up all her beef, and 56
she is herself in the tub. 57

LUCIO   Why, 'tis good. It is the right of it; it must be so.
Ever your fresh whore and your powdered bawd; an 59
unshunned consequence, it must be so. Art going to 60
prison, Pompey?

POMPEY   Yes, faith, sir.

LUCIO   Why, 'tis not amiss, Pompey. Farewell. Go, say I
sent thee thither. For debt, Pompey? Or how?

ELBOW   For being a bawd, for being a bawd.

LUCIO   Well, then, imprison him. If imprisonment be
the due of a bawd, why, 'tis his right. Bawd is he
doubtless, and of antiquity too; bawd-born. Farewell, 68
good Pompey. Commend me to the prison, Pompey.
You will turn good husband now, Pompey; you will 70
keep the house. 71

---

45 Caesar (who defeated Pompey at Pharsalia, and led his sons in
triumph) **46 Pygmalion's images** i.e., prostitutes, so called because
they "painted" with cosmetics like a painted statue. (Pygmalion was a
sculptor, according to legend, whose female statue came to life.)
48 clutched i.e., with money in it   **49–50 drowned . . . rain** i.e., out of
fashion (?)   **50 trot** old bawd   **51 Which . . . way** i.e., how goes the
world   **52 trick** custom, fashion   **56 eaten . . . beef** i.e., run through all
her prostitutes   **57 in the tub** (1) being pickled, as in preserving beef
(2) being treated for venereal disease by the sweating-tub treatment
59 Ever . . . bawd i.e., it always happens that young whores turn into
old bawds, preserved as in salt pickling brine and caked with cosmetics   **60 unshunned** unshunnable, unavoidable   **68 antiquity** long continuance   **70 good husband** thrifty manager   **71 keep the house** stay
indoors (with pun on the pimp's function as doorkeeper)

POMPEY   I hope, sir, your good worship will be my bail.

LUCIO   No indeed will I not, Pompey; it is not the wear. I will pray, Pompey, to increase your bondage. 74 If you take it not patiently, why, your mettle is the 75 more. Adieu, trusty Pompey.—Bless you, Friar.

DUKE   And you.

LUCIO   Does Bridget paint still, Pompey, ha?   78

ELBOW   Come your ways, sir, come.   79

POMPEY   You will not bail me, then, sir?

LUCIO   Then, Pompey, nor now.—What news abroad, 81 Friar? What news?

ELBOW   Come your ways, sir, come.

LUCIO   Go to kennel, Pompey, go. [*Exeunt Elbow, Pompey, and officers.*] What news, Friar, of the Duke?

DUKE   I know none. Can you tell me of any?

LUCIO   Some say he is with the Emperor of Russia; other some, he is in Rome. But where is he, think you?

DUKE   I know not where; but wheresoever, I wish him well.

LUCIO   It was a mad fantastical trick of him to steal from 91 the state and usurp the beggary he was never born to. 92 Lord Angelo dukes it well in his absence; he puts 93 transgression to 't.   94

DUKE   He does well in 't.

LUCIO   A little more lenity to lechery would do no harm in him. Something too crabbed that way, Friar.   97

DUKE   It is too general a vice, and severity must cure it.

LUCIO   Yes, in good sooth, the vice is of a great kindred; 99 it is well allied. But it is impossible to extirp it quite, 100 Friar, till eating and drinking be put down. They say this Angelo was not made by man and woman after this downright way of creation. Is it true, think you? 103

DUKE   How should he be made, then?

---

74 **wear** fashion   **75 mettle** spirit (with quibble on *metal*, i.e., the irons with which he will be shackled)   **78 paint** use cosmetics   **79 your ways** i.e., along   **81 Then** neither then   **91 steal** steal away   **92 beggary** i.e., status of a wanderer or traveler (with unconscious ironic appropriateness; Lucio clearly does not see through the Duke's disguise.)
93–94 puts . . . to 't puts lawbreaking under severe restraint   **97 Something** somewhat.   **crabbed** harsh   **99 kindred** i.e., family   **100 extirp** eradicate   **103 downright** ordinary, usual

LUCIO Some report a sea maid spawned him; some, 105
that he was begot between two stockfishes. But it is 106
certain that when he makes water his urine is con-
gealed ice, that I know to be true. And he is a motion 108
generative, that's infallible. 109

DUKE You are pleasant, sir, and speak apace. 110

LUCIO Why, what a ruthless thing is this in him, for the
rebellion of a codpiece to take away the life of a man! 112
Would the Duke that is absent have done this? Ere he
would have hanged a man for the getting a hundred
bastards, he would have paid for the nursing a thousand. He had some feeling of the sport; he knew the
service, and that instructed him to mercy.

DUKE I never heard the absent Duke much detected for 118
women. He was not inclined that way.

LUCIO O, sir, you are deceived.

DUKE 'Tis not possible.

LUCIO Who, not the Duke? Yes, your beggar of fifty;
and his use was to put a ducat in her clack-dish. The 123
Duke had crotchets in him. He would be drunk too, 124
that let me inform you.

DUKE You do him wrong, surely.

LUCIO Sir, I was an inward of his. A shy fellow was 127
the Duke, and I believe I know the cause of his
withdrawing.

DUKE What, I prithee, might be the cause?

LUCIO No, pardon. 'Tis a secret must be locked within
the teeth and the lips. But this I can let you understand: the greater file of the subject held the Duke to 133
be wise.

DUKE Wise? Why, no question but he was.

LUCIO A very superficial, ignorant, unweighing fellow. 136

---

105 sea maid mermaid   **106 stockfishes** dried codfish   **108–109 motion generative** masculine puppet, without power of generation
110 pleasant jocose   **112 codpiece** an appendage to the front of close-fitting hose or breeches worn by men, often ornamented and indelicately conspicuous; hence, slang for "penis"   **118 detected** accused
123 clack-dish beggar's wooden dish with a lid, which was "clacked" to attract attention; probably used metaphorically here for the female pudenda   **124 crotchets** whims   **127 inward** intimate acquaintance
133 the greater . . . subject the majority of his subjects   **136 unweighing** not considering carefully

DUKE   Either this is envy in you, folly, or mistaking. The 137
very stream of his life and the business he hath helmed 138
must, upon a warranted need, give him a better proc- 139
lamation. Let him be but testimonied in his own 140
bringings-forth, and he shall appear to the envious a 141
scholar, a statesman, and a soldier. Therefore you
speak unskillfully; or, if your knowledge be more, it is 143
much darkened in your malice.

LUCIO   Sir, I know him, and I love him.

DUKE   Love talks with better knowledge, and knowledge with dearer love.

LUCIO   Come, sir, I know what I know.

DUKE   I can hardly believe that, since you know not
what you speak. But if ever the Duke return, as our
prayers are he may, let me desire you to make your
answer before him. If it be honest you have spoke,
you have courage to maintain it. I am bound to call
upon you; and, I pray you, your name?

LUCIO   Sir, my name is Lucio, well known to the Duke.

DUKE   He shall know you better, sir, if I may live to report you.

LUCIO   I fear you not.

DUKE   O, you hope the Duke will return no more, or
you imagine me too unhurtful an opposite. But indeed 160
I can do you little harm; you'll forswear this again. 161

LUCIO   I'll be hanged first. Thou art deceived in me, Friar.
But no more of this. Canst thou tell if Claudio die tomorrow or no?

DUKE   Why should he die, sir?

LUCIO   Why? For filling a bottle with a tundish. I would 166
the Duke we talk of were returned again. This ungen- 167
itured agent will unpeople the province with conti- 168
nency. Sparrows must not build in his house eaves, 169
because they are lecherous. The Duke yet would have

---

137 envy malice   **138 helmed** steered   **139 upon . . . need** if a warrant
were needed   **139–140 give . . . proclamation** proclaim him better (than
you assert)   **140–141 in . . . bringings-forth** by his own public actions
141 to the envious even to the malicious   **143 unskillfully** in ignorance   **160 too . . . opposite** too harmless an adversary   **161 forswear
this** deny under oath what you've said   **166 tundish** funnel (here representing the penis)   **167–168 ungenitured agent** sexless deputy
169 Sparrows (Proverbially lecherous birds.)

dark deeds darkly answered; he would never bring 171
them to light. Would he were returned! Marry, this
Claudio is condemned for untrussing. Farewell, good 173
Friar. I prithee, pray for me. The Duke, I say to thee
again, would eat mutton on Fridays. He's not past it 175
yet, and I say to thee he would mouth with a beggar, 176
though she smelt brown bread and garlic. Say that I 177
said so. Farewell.   *Exit.*

DUKE
No might nor greatness in mortality   179
Can censure scape; back-wounding calumny   180
The whitest virtue strikes. What king so strong
Can tie the gall up in the slanderous tongue?
But who comes here?

Enter Escalus, Provost, and [officers with] Bawd
[Mistress Overdone].

ESCALUS Go, away with her to prison.
MISTRESS OVERDONE Good my lord, be good to me.
Your honor is accounted a merciful man. Good my
lord.
ESCALUS Double and treble admonition, and still forfeit 188
in the same kind! This would make mercy swear and 189
play the tyrant.
PROVOST A bawd of eleven years' continuance, may it
please your honor.
MISTRESS OVERDONE My lord, this is one Lucio's infor- 193
mation against me. Mistress Kate Keepdown was with 194
child by him in the Duke's time; he promised her marriage. His child is a year and a quarter old, come Philip 196
and Jacob. I have kept it myself; and see how he goes 197
about to abuse me!

171 **darkly answered** not made public   173 **untrussing** undressing. (Specifically, untying the points used to fasten hose to doublet.)   175 **mutton** i.e.,
prostitute. (To *eat mutton on Fridays* is to violate religious observance by
eating meat on fast days, i.e., to frequent prostitutes.)   **past it** i.e., past his
prime, impotent   176 **mouth** kiss   177 **smelt brown bread** smelled of
coarse bran bread   179 **mortality** humankind   180 **scape** escape.   **back-
wounding calumny** backbiting slander   188–189 **forfeit . . . kind** guilty of
the same offense   189 **mercy** i.e., even mercy   193–194 **information**
accusation   196–197 **Philip and Jacob** the Feast of Saint Philip and Saint
James (*Jacobus* in Latin), May 1

ESCALUS   That fellow is a fellow of much license. Let
him be called before us. Away with her to prison!
Go to, no more words. [*Exeunt officers with Mistress
Overdone.*] Provost, my brother Angelo will not be al-   202
tered; Claudio must die tomorrow. Let him be furnished with divines and have all charitable prep-   204
aration. If my brother wrought by my pity, it should   205
not be so with him.

PROVOST   So please you, this friar hath been with him,
and advised him for th' entertainment of death.   208

ESCALUS   Good even, good Father.

DUKE   Bliss and goodness on you!

ESCALUS   Of whence are you?

DUKE
Not of this country, though my chance is now
To use it for my time. I am a brother   213
Of gracious order, late come from the See   214
In special business from His Holiness.

ESCALUS   What news abroad i' the world?

DUKE   None but that there is so great a fever on goodness that the dissolution of it must cure it. Novelty is   218
only in request, and, as it is, as dangerous to be aged   219
in any kind of course as it is virtuous to be constant   220
in any undertaking. There is scarce truth enough alive   221
to make societies secure, but security enough to make   222
fellowships accursed. Much upon this riddle runs the   223
wisdom of the world. This news is old enough, yet it
is every day's news. I pray you, sir, of what disposition was the Duke?

---

202 brother i.e., fellow officer of state   **204 divines** clergymen
205 wrought . . . pity acted in accord with my impulses of pity   **208 entertainment** reception, acceptance   **213 use** dwell in   **214 the See**
Rome   **218 the dissolution . . . cure it** i.e., only by dying can goodness be
rid of the disease   **218–219 is only in request** is the only thing people
desire   **219–221 as it . . . undertaking** as things currently stand, (it is) as
dangerous to be constant in any undertaking as it is virtuous to be thus
constant   **221–223 There . . . accursed** i.e., there is hardly enough integrity and trust extant to bind men in sincere affection, but binding con-
tractual obligations enough to make ordinary transactions intolerable.
(The Duke thus puns on *security* [1] a sense of trust [2] financial pledge
required to borrow money, and on *fellowship* [1] friendship [2] corporations formed for tracking ventures.)   **223 upon this riddle** in this riddling fashion

ESCALUS One that, above all other strifes, contended es- 227
pecially to know himself.

DUKE What pleasure was he given to?

ESCALUS Rather rejoicing to see another merry than
merry at anything which professed to make him rejoice—a gentleman of all temperance. But leave we him
to his events, with a prayer they may prove prosper- 233
ous, and let me desire to know how you find Claudio
prepared. I am made to understand that you have lent 235
him visitation. 236

DUKE He professes to have received no sinister measure 237
from his judge but most willingly humbles himself to
the determination of justice; yet had he framed to him- 239
self, by the instruction of his frailty, many deceiving 240
promises of life, which I, by my good leisure, have
discredited to him, and now is he resolved to die.

ESCALUS You have paid the heavens your function, and
the prisoner the very debt of your calling. I have la- 244
bored for the poor gentleman to the extremest shore of 245
my modesty, but my brother justice have I found so 246
severe that he hath forced me to tell him he is indeed
Justice.

DUKE If his own life answer the straitness of his pro- 249
ceeding, it shall become him well; wherein if he
chance to fail, he hath sentenced himself.

ESCALUS I am going to visit the prisoner. Fare you well.

DUKE Peace be with you!

                    [*Exeunt Escalus and Provost.*]
He who the sword of heaven will bear
Should be as holy as severe;
Pattern in himself to know, 256
Grace to stand, and virtue go; 257

---

227 strifes endeavors   **233 his events** the outcome of his affairs
235–236 lent him visitation paid him a visit   **237 sinister** unfair, unjust   **239–240 framed to himself** formulated in his mind   **240 by . . .
frailty** at the prompting of his natural human weakness   **244 the prisoner . . . calling** what your calling as a friar obliges you to give the
prisoner, i.e., the comforts of spiritual counsel   **245–246 shore . . .
modesty** limit of propriety   **249 straitness** strictness   **256 Pattern . . .
know** to find an example or *pattern* in himself by which to conduct
himself or judge others   **257 Grace . . . go** (to find in himself) grace to
keep himself upright and virtue to guide himself forward

More nor less to others paying   258
Than by self-offenses weighing.   259
Shame to him whose cruel striking
Kills for faults of his own liking!
Twice treble shame on Angelo,
To weed my vice and let his grow!   263
O, what may man within him hide,
Though angel on the outward side!
How may likeness made in crimes,   266
Making practice on the times,   267
To draw with idle spiders' strings
Most ponderous and substantial things!   269
Craft against vice I must apply.
With Angelo tonight shall lie
His old betrothèd but despisèd;
So disguise shall, by the disguisèd,
Pay with falsehood false exacting   274
And perform an old contracting.   *Exit.* 275

❖

258–259 **More . . . weighing** inflicting no more and no less punishment
on others than he would inflict upon himself for his own offenses
263 **my vice** i.e., another's sin   266–269 **How . . . things** (Seemingly a
corrupt passage, perhaps missing two lines.)   267 **Making . . . times**
practicing deception on the world   274 **falsehood** illusion, i.e.,
Mariana's disguise.   **false exacting** extortion, bribery (by Angelo)
275 **perform . . . contracting** fulfill an old contract

4.1 *Enter Mariana, and Boy singing.*

Song.

BOY
> Take, O, take those lips away,
>   That so sweetly were forsworn,
> And those eyes, the break of day,
>   Lights that do mislead the morn;   4
> But my kisses bring again, bring again,
> Seals of love, but sealed in vain, sealed in vain.   6

Enter Duke [disguised as before].

MARIANA
Break off thy song, and haste thee quick away.
Here comes a man of comfort, whose advice
Hath often stilled my brawling discontent. [*Exit Boy.*]   9
I cry you mercy, sir, and well could wish   10
You had not found me here so musical.
Let me excuse me, and believe me so,
My mirth it much displeased, but pleased my woe.   13

DUKE
'Tis good; though music oft hath such a charm
To make bad good, and good provoke to harm.   15
I pray you, tell me, hath anybody inquired for me here
today? Much upon this time have I promised here to   17
meet.

MARIANA You have not been inquired after. I have sat
here all day.

Enter Isabella.

DUKE I do constantly believe you. The time is come   21
even now. I shall crave your forbearance a little. May-   22

4.1. Location: The moated grange at Saint Luke's.
4 mislead the morn i.e., into thinking the sun has risen **6 Seals** confirmations, pledges **9 brawling** clamorous **10 cry you mercy** beg your
pardon **13 My . . . woe** i.e., it suited not a merry but a melancholy
mood **15 bad good** i.e., bad seem good, attractive. (The Duke, echoing
Renaissance conceptions of the psychological effects of music, warns
that music may soothe melancholy at times but may also produce
distressing effects on the mind.) **17 upon** about **21 constantly** confidently **22 crave . . . little** i.e., ask you to withdraw briefly

be I will call upon you anon, for some advantage to 23
yourself.

MARIANA   I am always bound to you.   *Exit.*

DUKE   Very well met, and welcome.
What is the news from this good deputy?

ISABELLA

He hath a garden circummured with brick,   28
Whose western side is with a vineyard backed;
And to that vineyard is a planchèd gate,   30
That makes his opening with this bigger key.   31
                     [*She shows keys.*]
This other doth command a little door
Which from the vineyard to the garden leads;
There have I made my promise, upon the
Heavy middle of the night, to call upon him.

DUKE

But shall you on your knowledge find this way?

ISABELLA

I have ta'en a due and wary note upon 't.
With whispering and most guilty diligence,
In action all of precept, he did show me   39
The way twice o'er.

DUKE   Are there no other tokens
Between you 'greed concerning her observance?   41

ISABELLA

No, none, but only a repair i' the dark,   42
And that I have possessed him my most stay   43
Can be but brief; for I have made him know
I have a servant comes with me along,
That stays upon me, whose persuasion is   46
I come about my brother.

DUKE   'Tis well borne up.   47
I have not yet made known to Mariana
A word of this.—What, ho, within! Come forth!

Enter Mariana.

---

23 anon presently   **28 circummured** walled about   **30 planchèd** made
of boards, planks   **31 his** its   **39 In action . . . precept** i.e., teaching
by demonstration   **41 her observance** what she is supposed to do
42 repair act of going or coming to a place   **43 possessed** informed.
my most stay my stay at the longest   **46 stays upon** waits for   **47 borne
up** sustained, carried out

I pray you, be acquainted with this maid;
She comes to do you good.

ISABELLA   I do desire the like.

DUKE

Do you persuade yourself that I respect you?   52

MARIANA

Good Friar, I know you do, and have found it.   53

DUKE

Take, then, this your companion by the hand,
Who hath a story ready for your ear.
I shall attend your leisure. But make haste;
The vaporous night approaches.

MARIANA Will 't please you walk aside?

Exit [with Isabella].

DUKE

O place and greatness! Millions of false eyes
Are stuck upon thee. Volumes of report   60
Run with these false and most contrarious quests 61
Upon thy doings; thousand escapes of wit   62
Make thee the father of their idle dream   63
And rack thee in their fancies.

Enter Mariana and Isabella.

Welcome. How agreed? 64

ISABELLA

She'll take the enterprise upon her, Father,
If you advise it.

DUKE   It is not my consent,   66
But my entreaty too.

ISABELLA   Little have you to say   67
When you depart from him but, soft and low,
"Remember now my brother."

MARIANA   Fear me not.   69

DUKE

Nor, gentle daughter, fear you not at all.

52 respect you are concerned for your welfare **53 found it** i.e., found it
to be true **60 stuck** fastened. **report** rumor **61 contrarious quests**
perverse or conflicting inquiries **62 escapes** sallies **63 Make . . .
dream** credit you with being the source of their fantasies **64 rack**
stretch as on the rack, distort **66 not** not only **67 Little . . . say** say
little **69 Fear me not** i.e., don't worry about my carrying out my part

He is your husband on a precontract;   71
To bring you thus together, 'tis no sin,
Sith that the justice of your title to him   73
Doth flourish the deceit. Come, let us go.   74
Our corn's to reap, for yet our tithe's to sow. *Exeunt.*   75

❖

4.2   *Enter Provost and Clown [Pompey].*

PROVOST   Come hither, sirrah. Can you cut off a man's
head?

POMPEY   If the man be a bachelor, sir, I can; but if he be
a married man, he's his wife's head, and I can never   4
cut off a woman's head.   5

PROVOST   Come, sir, leave me your snatches and yield   6
me a direct answer. Tomorrow morning are to die
Claudio and Barnardine. Here is in our prison a com-   8
mon executioner, who in his office lacks a helper. If   9
you will take it on you to assist him, it shall redeem
you from your gyves; if not, you shall have your full   11
time of imprisonment and your deliverance with an
unpitied whipping, for you have been a notorious
bawd.

POMPEY   Sir, I have been an unlawful bawd time out of
mind, but yet I will be content to be a lawful hangman. I would be glad to receive some instruction from
my fellow partner.

PROVOST   What, ho, Abhorson! Where's Abhorson,
there?

Enter Abhorson.

71 precontract legally binding agreement entered into before any church
ceremony. (Compare Claudio's and Juliet's *true contract* at 1.2.142.)
73 Sith since   **74 flourish** embellish, make fair   **75 Our corn's . . . sow**
we must first sow grain before we can expect to reap a harvest; i.e., we
must get started.   **tithe** grain sown for tithe dues

4.2. Location: The prison.
4 wife's head (Compare Ephesians 5:23: "The husband is the head of
the wife.")   **5 head** i.e., maidenhead   **6 leave . . . snatches** leave off your
quips   **8–9 common** public   **11 gyves** fetters, shackles

ABHORSON Do you call, sir?

PROVOST Sirrah, here's a fellow will help you tomorrow in your execution. If you think it meet, compound 23 with him by the year, and let him abide here with you; if not, use him for the present and dismiss him. He cannot plead his estimation with you; he hath 26 been a bawd..

ABHORSON A bawd, sir? Fie upon him! He will discredit our mystery.   29

PROVOST Go to, sir, you weigh equally; a feather will turn the scale.   *Exit*.

POMPEY Pray, sir, by your good favor—for surely, sir, 32 a good favor you have, but that you have a hanging 33 look—do you call, sir, your occupation a mystery? 34

ABHORSON Ay, sir, a mystery.

POMPEY Painting, sir, I have heard say, is a mystery, 36 and your whores, sir, being members of my occupation, using painting, do prove my occupation a mystery. But what mystery there should be in hanging, if I should be hanged, I cannot imagine.

ABHORSON Sir, it is a mystery.

POMPEY Proof?

ABHORSON Every true man's apparel fits your thief. If it 43 be too little for your thief, your true man thinks it big 44 enough; if it be too big for your thief, your thief thinks 45 it little enough. So every true man's apparel fits your 46 thief.

Enter Provost.

PROVOST Are you agreed?

POMPEY Sir, I will serve him, for I do find your hang-

---

23 compound make an agreement **26 plead his estimation** claim any respect on account of his reputation **29 mystery** craft, occupation **32–33 favor . . . favor** leave . . . face **33–34 hanging look** (1) downcast look (2) look of a hangman **36 Painting** (1) painting of pictures (2) applying cosmetics **43–46 Every . . . enough** (Just as Pompey argues that whores belong to a skilled craft because they are like painters, Abhorson implies that hangmen are skilled craftsmen because they are like thieves, who in turn are like tailors; both thieves and tailors "fit" honest men's apparel, by stealing or adjusting it. Hangmen in turn are like thieves because they receive the garments of the men they execute.) **44–45 big enough** i.e., enough of a loss **46 little enough** little enough for his efforts (since, because it is *too big*, it can't be worn)

man is a more penitent trade than your bawd: he doth 50
oftener ask forgiveness.   51

PROVOST   You, sirrah, provide your block and your ax
tomorrow four o'clock.

ABHORSON   Come on, bawd. I will instruct thee in my
trade. Follow!

POMPEY   I do desire to learn, sir; and I hope, if you have
occasion to use me for your own turn, you shall find 57
me yare. For truly, sir, for your kindness I owe you a 58
good turn.

PROVOST
Call hither Barnardine and Claudio.
                              Exit [Pompey, with Abhorson].
Th' one has my pity; not a jot the other,
Being a murderer, though he were my brother.

            Enter Claudio.

Look, here's the warrant, Claudio, for thy death.
'Tis now dead midnight, and by eight tomorrow
Thou must be made immortal. Where's Barnardine?   65
CLAUDIO
As fast locked up in sleep as guiltless labor   66
When it lies starkly in the traveler's bones.   67
He will not wake.
PROVOST   Who can do good on him?
Well, go, prepare yourself. [*Knocking within.*] But hark,
what noise?
Heaven give your spirits comfort! [*Exit Claudio.*] By and
by.—
I hope it is some pardon or reprieve
For the most gentle Claudio.

        Enter Duke [disguised as before].

                    Welcome, Father.

50–51 he doth . . . forgiveness (The executioner perfunctorily asked
forgiveness of those whose lives he was about to take.)   **57 for . . . turn**
(1) as a pimp to provide for your sexual needs (2) as your hangman
when it is your turn to be hanged   **58 yare** ready, alacritous   **65 made
immortal** i.e., executed   **66 fast** firmly, soundly.   **guiltless labor** (A
personification of the well-earned weariness that tires the innocent
laborer.)   **67 starkly** stiffly.   **traveler's** laborer's, or one who travails

DUKE
  The best and wholesom'st spirits of the night
  Envelop you, good Provost! Who called here of late?
PROVOST   None since the curfew rung.
DUKE
  Not Isabel?
PROVOST   No.
DUKE   They will, then, ere 't be long.
PROVOST   What comfort is for Claudio?
DUKE
  There's some in hope.
PROVOST   It is a bitter deputy.
DUKE
  Not so, not so. His life is paralleled   79
  Even with the stroke and line of his great justice.   80
  He doth with holy abstinence subdue
  That in himself which he spurs on his power   82
  To qualify in others. Were he mealed with that 83
  Which he corrects, then were he tyrannous;
  But this being so, he's just. [*Knocking within.*] Now are
    they come.

                    [*The Provost goes to the door.*]

  This is a gentle provost; seldom when   86
  The steelèd jailer is the friend of men.   87

                              [*Knocking within.*]

  How now? What noise? That spirit's possessed with
    haste
  That wounds th' unsisting postern with these strokes. 89
PROVOST [*Speaking at the door*]
  There he must stay until the officer
  Arise to let him in; he is called up.

                        [*He returns to the Duke.*]

DUKE
  Have you no countermand for Claudio yet,
  But he must die tomorrow?
PROVOST   None, sir, none.

79–80 is paralleled . . . with runs parallel and in exact conformity
with   **80 stroke and line** rigorous and exact course   **82 spurs on** encourages, urges   **83 qualify** mitigate.   **mealed** spotted, stained   **86 seldom when** i.e., it is seldom that   **87 steelèd** hardened   **89 unsisting**
unassisting, or unresisting (?).   **postern** small door

DUKE
  As near the dawning, Provost, as it is,
  You shall hear more ere morning.
PROVOST   Happily   95
  You something know, yet I believe there comes
  No countermand; no such example have we.   97
  Besides, upon the very siege of justice   98
  Lord Angelo hath to the public ear
  Professed the contrary.

          Enter a Messenger.

                          This is his lordship's man.
DUKE   And here comes Claudio's pardon.
MESSENGER [*Giving a paper*]   My lord hath sent you this
  note, and by me this further charge, that you swerve
  not from the smallest article of it, neither in time, mat-
  ter, or other circumstance. Good morrow; for, as I take
  it, it is almost day.
PROVOST   I shall obey him.   [*Exit Messenger.*]
DUKE [*Aside*]
  This is his pardon, purchased by such sin
  For which the pardoner himself is in.   109
  Hence hath offense his quick celerity,   110
  When it is borne in high authority.   111
  When vice makes mercy, mercy's so extended
  That for the fault's love is th' offender friended.— 113
  Now, sir, what news?
PROVOST   I told you. Lord Angelo, belike thinking me 115
  remiss in mine office, awakens me with this un- 116
  wonted putting-on—methinks strangely, for he hath 117
  not used it before.
DUKE   Pray you, let's hear.
PROVOST   (*Reads the letter*)   "Whatsoever you may
  hear to the contrary, let Claudio be executed by four of
  the clock, and in the afternoon Barnardine. For my
  better satisfaction, let me have Claudio's head 123

95 **Happily** haply, perhaps   97 **example** precedent   98 **siege** seat
109 **in** engaged   110–111 **Hence . . . authority** i.e., any offense of which
the person in authority is himself guilty will be quickly pardoned. (*His*
means "its own.")   113 **the fault's love** love of the fault.   **friended**
befriended   115 **belike** perchance   116–117 **unwonted** unaccustomed
117 **putting-on** urging   123 **better satisfaction** greater assurance

sent me by five. Let this be duly performed, with a thought that more depends on it than we must yet deliver. Thus fail not to do your office, as you will 126 answer it at your peril."
What say you to this, sir?

DUKE   What is that Barnardine who is to be executed in th' afternoon?

PROVOST   A Bohemian born, but here nursed up and 131 bred; one that is a prisoner nine years old. 132

DUKE   How came it that the absent Duke had not either delivered him to his liberty or executed him? I have heard it was ever his manner to do so.

PROVOST   His friends still wrought reprieves for him; and indeed his fact, till now in the government of Lord 137 Angelo, came not to an undoubtful proof.

DUKE   It is now apparent?

PROVOST   Most manifest, and not denied by himself.

DUKE   Hath he borne himself penitently in prison? How seems he to be touched? 142

PROVOST   A man that apprehends death no more dread- 143 fully but as a drunken sleep—careless, reckless, and 144 fearless of what's past, present, or to come; insensible 145 of mortality, and desperately mortal. 146

DUKE   He wants advice. 147

PROVOST   He will hear none. He hath evermore had the 148 liberty of the prison; give him leave to escape hence, he would not. Drunk many times a day, if not many days entirely drunk. We have very oft awaked him as if to carry him to execution, and showed him a seeming warrant for it; it hath not moved him at all.

DUKE   More of him anon. There is written in your brow, Provost, honesty and constancy; if I read it not truly, my ancient skill beguiles me, but, in the boldness of 156 my cunning, I will lay myself in hazard. Claudio, 157 whom here you have warrant to execute, is no greater

126 deliver make known   131 here i.e., in Vienna   132 a prisoner . . . old nine years a prisoner   137 fact crime   142 touched affected 143–144 no more dreadfully with no more dread   145–146 insensible . . . mortal incapable of comprehending the meaning of death, and without hope of immortality or of escaping execution   147 wants needs   148 evermore constantly   156–157 in the . . . hazard confident in my knowledge (of human character), I will risk my life

forfeit to the law than Angelo who hath sentenced him.
To make you understand this in a manifested effect, I   160
crave but four days' respite, for the which you are to
do me both a present and a dangerous courtesy.   162
PROVOST   Pray, sir, in what?
DUKE   In the delaying death.
PROVOST   Alack, how may I do it, having the hour lim-   165
ited and an express command, under penalty, to de-   166
liver his head in the view of Angelo? I may make my
case as Claudio's, to cross this in the smallest.
DUKE   By the vow of mine order I warrant you, if my
instructions may be your guide. Let this Barnardine
be this morning executed, and his head borne to Angelo.
PROVOST   Angelo hath seen them both and will dis-   173
cover the favor.   174
DUKE   O, death's a great disguiser, and you may add to
it. Shave the head and tie the beard, and say it was   176
the desire of the penitent to be so bared before his
death. You know the course is common. If anything
fall to you upon this more than thanks and good for-   179
tune, by the saint whom I profess, I will plead against
it with my life.
PROVOST   Pardon me, good Father, it is against my oath.
DUKE   Were you sworn to the Duke or to the deputy?
PROVOST   To him and to his substitutes.
DUKE   You will think you have made no offense if the
Duke avouch the justice of your dealing?   186
PROVOST   But what likelihood is in that?
DUKE   Not a resemblance, but a certainty. Yet since I see
you fearful, that neither my coat, integrity, nor persua-
sion can with ease attempt you, I will go further than   190
I meant, to pluck all fears out of you. Look you, sir,
here is the hand and seal of the Duke. [*He shows a
letter.*] You know the character, I doubt not, and the   193
signet is not strange to you.
PROVOST   I know them both.
DUKE   The contents of this is the return of the Duke.

160 in . . . effect by means of concrete proof   162 present immediate
165–166 limited fixed, set   173–174 discover the favor recognize the
face   176 tie trim, dress (?)   179 fall to befall   186 avouch confirm
190 attempt win, influence   193 character handwriting

You shall anon overread it at your pleasure, where
you shall find within these two days he will be here.
This is a thing that Angelo knows not, for he this very
day receives letters of strange tenor, perchance of the
Duke's death, perchance entering into some monas-
tery, but by chance nothing of what is writ. Look, th' 202
unfolding star calls up the shepherd. Put not yourself 203
into amazement how these things should be; all difficulties are but easy when they are known. Call your
executioner, and off with Barnardine's head. I will give
him a present shrift and advise him for a better place. 207
Yet you are amazed, but this shall absolutely resolve 208
you. Come away; it is almost clear dawn. 209

        Exit [*with Provost*].

❖

4.3 *Enter Clown* [*Pompey*].

POMPEY I am as well acquainted here as I was in our 1
house of profession. One would think it were Mistress
Overdone's own house, for here be many of her old
customers. First, here's young Master Rash; he's in for 4
a commodity of brown paper and old ginger, nine- 5
score and seventeen pounds, of which he made five
marks, ready money. Marry, then ginger was not
much in request, for the old women were all dead. 8
Then is there here one Master Caper, at the suit of 9

---

202 writ i.e., written here (?) **203 unfolding star** i.e., morning star,
Venus, which bids the shepherd lead his sheep from the fold
207 present shrift immediate absolution for sins (after confession)
208 Yet still **208–209 resolve you** dispel your uncertainties

4.3. Location: The prison.
1 well widely **4 Rash** (All the names mentioned by Pompey apparently
glance at contemporary social affectations and defects. *Rash* means, of
course, reckless.) **5 a commodity . . . ginger** (To circumvent the laws
against excessive rates of interest, moneylenders often advanced cheap
commodities such as brown paper to gullible borrowers in lieu of cash
at a high rate of interest. Master Rash, having agreed to a valuation of
197 pounds for such merchandise, has been able to resell it for five
marks, each mark worth about two thirds of a pound, and has been
thrown into prison for debt.) **8 old women** (Proverbially fond of ginger.) **9 Caper** (To *caper* was to dance or leap gracefully.)

Master Three-pile the mercer, for some four suits of 10
peach-colored satin, which now peaches him a beggar. 11
Then have we here young Dizzy, and young Master 12
Deep-vow, and Master Copper-spur, and Master 13
Starve-lackey the rapier and dagger man, and young 14
Drop-heir that killed lusty Pudding, and Master Forth- 15
light the tilter, and brave Master Shoe-tie the great 16
traveler, and wild Half-can that stabbed Pots, and I 17
think forty more, all great doers in our trade, and are
now "for the Lord's sake."   19

    Enter Abhorson.

ABHORSON   Sirrah, bring Barnardine hither.
POMPEY   Master Barnardine! You must rise and be
   hanged, Master Barnardine!
ABHORSON   What, ho, Barnardine!
BARNARDINE   (*Within*) A pox o' your throats! Who
   makes that noise there? What are you?
POMPEY   Your friends, sir, the hangman. You must be
   so good, sir, to rise and be put to death.
BARNARDINE   [*Within*] Away, you rogue, away! I am
   sleepy.
ABHORSON   Tell him he must awake, and that quickly
   too.
POMPEY   Pray, Master Barnardine, awake till you are ex-
   ecuted, and sleep afterwards.
ABHORSON   Go in to him and fetch him out.
POMPEY   He is coming, sir, he is coming. I hear his
   straw rustle.

---

10 Three-pile (*Three-pile* defines the thickest nap and most expensive
grade of velvet.)   **mercer** cloth merchant   **11 peaches him** denounces
him as   **12 Dizzy** (i.e., giddy, foolish?)   **13 Deep-vow** (One who swears
earnestly and often.)   **Copper-spur** (Copper was often used fraudulently
to simulate gold.)   **14 Starve-lackey** (Spendthrift gallants often virtually
starved their pages.)   **15 Drop-heir** (Perhaps referring to those who
disinherited or preyed on unsuspecting heirs.)   **lusty** vigorous.   **Pudding** (i.e., sausage)   **15–16 Forthlight** (Unexplained. Perhaps an error for
Forthright, referring to a style of tilting.)   **16 tilter** jouster.   **brave**
showy, splendidly dressed.   **Shoe-tie** (Evidently a nickname for travelers
and others who affected the foreign fashion of elaborate rosettes on the
tie of the shoe.)   **17 Half-can** (i.e., a small drinking tankard).   **Pots** (i.e.,
ale pots)   **19 for . . . sake** (The cry of prisoners from jail windows to
passers-by to give them food or alms.)

Enter Barnardine.

ABHORSON Is the ax upon the block, sirrah?

POMPEY Very ready, sir.

BARNARDINE How now, Abhorson? What's the news
with you?

ABHORSON Truly, sir, I would desire you to clap into 41
your prayers; for, look you, the warrant's come.

BARNARDINE You rogue, I have been drinking all night.
I am not fitted for 't.

POMPEY O, the better, sir, for he that drinks all night
and is hanged betimes in the morning may sleep the 46
sounder all the next day.

Enter Duke [disguised as before].

ABHORSON Look you, sir, here comes your ghostly fa- 48
ther. Do we jest now, think you?

DUKE Sir, induced by my charity, and hearing how hast-
ily you are to depart, I am come to advise you, comfort you, and pray with you.

BARNARDINE Friar, not I. I have been drinking hard all
night, and I will have more time to prepare me, or
they shall beat out my brains with billets. I will not 55
consent to die this day, that's certain.

DUKE
O, sir, you must, and therefore I beseech you
Look forward on the journey you shall go.

BARNARDINE I swear I will not die today for any man's
persuasion.

DUKE But hear you—

BARNARDINE Not a word. If you have anything to say
to me, come to my ward, for thence will not I today. 63

                                              Exit.

Enter Provost.

DUKE
Unfit to live or die. O gravel heart!   64
After him, fellows. Bring him to the block.

                    [*Exeunt Abhorson and Pompey.*]

---

41 clap into quickly begin **46 betimes** early **48 ghostly** spiritual
55 billets cudgels, blocks of wood **63 ward** cell **64 gravel** stony

PROVOST
Now, sir, how do you find the prisoner?

DUKE
A creature unprepared, unmeet for death;   67
And to transport him in the mind he is   68
Were damnable.

PROVOST   Here in the prison, Father,
There died this morning of a cruel fever
One Ragozine, a most notorious pirate,
A man of Claudio's years, his beard and head
Just of his color. What if we do omit   73
This reprobate till he were well inclined,
And satisfy the deputy with the visage
Of Ragozine, more like to Claudio?

DUKE
O, 'tis an accident that heaven provides!
Dispatch it presently; the hour draws on   78
Prefixed by Angelo. See this be done,   79
And sent according to command, whiles I
Persuade this rude wretch willingly to die.

PROVOST
This shall be done, good Father, presently.
But Barnardine must die this afternoon.
And how shall we continue Claudio,   84
To save me from the danger that might come
If he were known alive?

DUKE   Let this be done:
Put them in secret holds, both Barnardine and Claudio.   87
Ere twice the sun hath made his journal greeting   88
To yond generation, you shall find   89
Your safety manifested.

PROVOST   I am your free dependent.   91

DUKE
Quick, dispatch, and send the head to Angelo.
                                        Exit [*Provost*].

---

67 unmeet unready, unfit **68 transport him** i.e., send him to his doom
73 omit ignore, overlook **78 presently** immediately (as also in l. 82)
79 Prefixed appointed beforehand, stipulated **84 continue** preserve
87 holds cells, dungeons **88 journal** daily **89 yond** i.e., beyond these
walls, outside the perpetually dark prison (?). Sometimes emended to *th'*
under, the people of the Antipodes, on the opposite side of the earth, or,
people under the sun, the human race. **91 free dependent** willing servant

Now will I write letters to Varrius—   93
The Provost, he shall bear them—whose contents
Shall witness to him I am near at home,
And that, by great injunctions, I am bound   96
To enter publicly. Him I'll desire
To meet me at the consecrated fount   98
A league below the city; and from thence,   99
By cold gradation and well-balanced form,   100
We shall proceed with Angelo.

    Enter Provost [with Ragozine's head].

PROVOST
  Here is the head. I'll carry it myself.
DUKE
  Convenient is it. Make a swift return,   103
  For I would commune with you of such things   104
  That want no ear but yours.
PROVOST   I'll make all speed. *Exit.* 105
ISABELLA (*Within*) Peace, ho, be here!
DUKE
  The tongue of Isabel. She's come to know
  If yet her brother's pardon be come hither.
  But I will keep her ignorant of her good,
  To make her heavenly comforts of despair
  When it is least expected.

    Enter Isabella.

ISABELLA   Ho, by your leave!
DUKE
  Good morning to you, fair and gracious daughter.
ISABELLA
  The better, given me by so holy a man.
  Hath yet the deputy sent my brother's pardon?

93 to Varrius (The Folio reads *to Angelo*, but see l. 99 below and
4.5.12–14; evidently the Duke's plan is to meet Varrius "a league below
the city" and then proceed to the rendezvous with Angelo.) **96 by great
injunctions** by powerful precedent, or for compelling reasons **98 fount**
spring **99 league** (a measure of varying length but usually about three
miles) **100 cold . . . form** i.e., moving deliberately and with proper
observance of all formalities **103 Convenient** timely, fitting **104 commune** converse **105 want** require

DUKE
　He hath released him, Isabel, from the world.
　His head is off and sent to Angelo.
ISABELLA
　Nay, but it is not so!
DUKE　　　　　　　　It is no other.
　Show your wisdom, daughter, in your close patience.　118
ISABELLA
　O, I will to him and pluck out his eyes!
DUKE
　You shall not be admitted to his sight.
ISABELLA
　Unhappy Claudio! Wretched Isabel!
　Injurious world! Most damnèd Angelo!
DUKE
　This nor hurts him nor profits you a jot.　　　　123
　Forbear it therefore; give your cause to heaven.
　Mark what I say, which you shall find
　By every syllable a faithful verity:
　The Duke comes home tomorrow. Nay, dry your eyes;
　One of our convent, and his confessor,
　Gives me this instance. Already he hath carried　129
　Notice to Escalus and Angelo,
　Who do prepare to meet him at the gates,
　There to give up their pow'r. If you can, pace your wis-
　　dom　　　　　　　　　　　　　　　　　　132
　In that good path that I would wish it go,
　And you shall have your bosom on this wretch,　134
　Grace of the Duke, revenges to your heart,　　135
　And general honor.
ISABELLA　　　　　　　I am directed by you.
DUKE
　This letter, then, to Friar Peter give.
　　　　　　　　　[He gives her a letter.]
　'Tis that he sent me of the Duke's return.
　Say, by this token, I desire his company
　At Mariana's house tonight. Her cause and yours

118 close patience silent enduring　123 nor hurts neither hurts　129 instance proof　132 pace teach to move in response to your will, as with a
horse　134 bosom desire　135 Grace of manifestation of favor from.
to in accord with

I'll perfect him withal, and he shall bring you   141
Before the Duke, and to the head of Angelo   142
Accuse him home and home. For my poor self,   143
I am combinèd by a sacred vow,   144
And shall be absent. Wend you with this letter.   145
Command these fretting waters from your eyes   146
With a light heart; trust not my holy order
If I pervert your course. Who's here?

    Enter Lucio.

LUCIO   Good even. Friar, where's the Provost?
DUKE   Not within, sir.
LUCIO   O pretty Isabella, I am pale at mine heart to see   151
thine eyes so red. Thou must be patient. I am fain to   152
dine and sup with water and bran; I dare not for my   153
head fill my belly; one fruitful meal would set me   154
to 't. But they say the Duke will be here tomorrow.   155
By my troth, Isabel, I loved thy brother. If the old fan-
tastical Duke of dark corners had been at home, he
had lived.   *[Exit Isabella.]*
DUKE   Sir, the Duke is marvelous little beholding to   159
your reports; but the best is, he lives not in them.   160
LUCIO   Friar, thou knowest not the Duke so well as I do.
He's a better woodman than thou tak'st him for.   162
DUKE   Well, you'll answer this one day. Fare ye well.
                        [He starts to go.]
LUCIO   Nay, tarry, I'll go along with thee. I can tell thee
pretty tales of the Duke.
DUKE   You have told me too many of him already, sir, if
they be true; if not true, none were enough.
LUCIO   I was once before him for getting a wench with
child.
DUKE   Did you such a thing?

---

141 perfect acquaint completely   **142 head** i.e., face   **143 home and
home** thoroughly   **144 combinèd** bound   **145 Wend** go   **146 fretting**
corroding   **151 I am . . . heart** i.e., from sighing, since sighs cost the
heart loss of blood   **152 fain** compelled (as also in l. 171)   **153–154 for
my head** i.e., on my life   **154 fruitful** abundant   **154–155 set me to 't**
i.e., awaken my lust and thus place me in danger of Angelo's edict
159 beholding beholden   **160 he . . . them** i.e., he is not accurately
described by them   **162 woodman** i.e., hunter (of women)

LUCIO   Yes, marry, did I, but I was fain to forswear it.
They would else have married me to the rotten medlar.   172
DUKE   Sir, your company is fairer than honest. Rest you
well.
LUCIO   By my troth, I'll go with thee to the lane's end. If
bawdy talk offend you, we'll have very little of it. Nay,
Friar, I am a kind of burr; I shall stick.   *Exeunt.*

❖

4.4   *Enter Angelo and Escalus, [reading letters].*

ESCALUS   Every letter he hath writ hath disvouched   1
other.
ANGELO   In most uneven and distracted manner. His actions show much like to madness. Pray heaven his
wisdom be not tainted! And why meet him at the
gates and redeliver our authorities there?
ESCALUS   I guess not.   7
ANGELO   And why should we proclaim it in an hour be-   8
fore his entering, that if any crave redress of injustice,
they should exhibit their petitions in the street?
ESCALUS   He shows his reason for that: to have a dispatch of complaints, and to deliver us from devices   12
hereafter, which shall then have no power to stand
against us.
ANGELO   Well, I beseech you, let it be proclaimed. Be-   15
times i' the morn I'll call you at your house. Give no-   16
tice to such men of sort and suit as are to meet him.   17
ESCALUS   I shall, sir. Fare you well.
ANGELO   Good night.   *Exit [Escalus].*
This deed unshapes me quite, makes me unpregnant   20
And dull to all proceedings. A deflowered maid,
And by an eminent body that enforced   22
The law against it! But that her tender shame   23
Will not proclaim against her maiden loss,

172 **medlar** a fruit that was eaten after it had begun to rot; here, signifying a prostitute

4.4. Location: In Vienna.
1 **disvouched** contradicted   **7 guess not** cannot guess   **8 in an hour** i.e.,
a full hour   **12 devices** contrived complaints   **15–16 Betimes** early
17 sort rank.   **suit** such as owe attendance   **20 unpregnant** unapt
22 body person   **23 But that** were it not that

How might she tongue me! Yet reason dares her no,   25
For my authority bears of a credent bulk   26
That no particular scandal once can touch
But it confounds the breather. He should have lived,   28
Save that his riotous youth, with dangerous sense,   29
Might in the times to come have ta'en revenge,
By so receiving a dishonored life   31
With ransom of such shame. Would yet he had lived!
Alack, when once our grace we have forgot,
Nothing goes right; we would, and we would not.

Exit.

4.5   *Enter Duke [in his own habit] and Friar Peter.*

DUKE
These letters at fit time deliver me.   [*Giving letters.*] 1
The Provost knows our purpose and our plot.
The matter being afoot, keep your instruction,   3
And hold you ever to our special drift,   4
Though sometimes you do blench from this to that   5
As cause doth minister. Go call at Flavius' house,   6
And tell him where I stay. Give the like notice
To Valencius, Rowland, and to Crassus,
And bid them bring the trumpets to the gate;   9
But send me Flavius first.
FRIAR PETER   It shall be speeded well.   [*Exit.*] 11

     Enter Varrius.

DUKE
I thank thee, Varrius, thou hast made good haste.
Come, we will walk. There's other of our friends
Will greet us here anon. My gentle Varrius!   *Exeunt.*

✤

25 tongue i.e., reproach, accuse.   **dares her no** i.e., frightens her to do
nothing   **26 bears ... bulk** bears a huge credibility   **28 But ... breather**
without confounding the person who speaks   **29 sense** passion (?)   **31 By** for

4.5. Location: Outside the city.
1 me for me   **3 keep** keep to   **4 drift** plot   **5 blench** deviate   **6 minister**
provide occasion   **9 trumpets** trumpeters   **11 speeded** accomplished

4.6   *Enter Isabella and Mariana.*

ISABELLA
  To speak so indirectly I am loath.
  I would say the truth, but to accuse him so,
  That is your part. Yet I am advised to do it,
  He says, to veil full purpose.
MARIANA   Be ruled by him.
ISABELLA
  Besides, he tells me that, if peradventure   5
  He speak against me on the adverse side,
  I should not think it strange, for 'tis a physic   7
  That's bitter to sweet end.

          Enter [Friar] Peter.

MARIANA
  I would Friar Peter—
ISABELLA   O, peace, the Friar is come.
FRIAR PETER
  Come, I have found you out a stand most fit,   10
  Where you may have such vantage on the Duke
  He shall not pass you. Twice have the trumpets sounded.
  The generous and gravest citizens   13
  Have hent the gates, and very near upon   14
  The Duke is entering. Therefore hence, away!
                              Exeunt.

❖

4.6. Location: Near the city gate.
5 peradventure perhaps   **7 physic** remedy   **10 stand** place to stand
13 generous highborn   **14 hent** reached, occupied.   **very near upon**
almost immediately now

5.1   *Enter Duke, Varrius, lords, Angelo, Escalus,*
Lucio, [Provost, officers, and] citizens at several
doors.

DUKE
My very worthy cousin, fairly met!   1
Our old and faithful friend, we are glad to see you.

ANGELO, ESCALUS
Happy return be to Your Royal Grace!

DUKE
Many and hearty thankings to you both.
We have made inquiry of you, and we hear
Such goodness of your justice that our soul
Cannot but yield you forth to public thanks,   7
Forerunning more requital.   8

ANGELO   You make my bonds still greater.   9

DUKE
O, your desert speaks loud, and I should wrong it
To lock it in the wards of covert bosom,   11
When it deserves with characters of brass   12
A forted residence 'gainst the tooth of time   13
And rasure of oblivion. Give me your hand,   14
And let the subject see, to make them know   15
That outward courtesies would fain proclaim   16
Favors that keep within. Come, Escalus,   17
You must walk by us on our other hand,
And good supporters are you.

   Enter [Friar] Peter and Isabella.

FRIAR PETER
Now is your time. Speak loud, and kneel before him.

ISABELLA [*Kneeling*]
Justice, O royal Duke! Vail your regard   21
Upon a wronged—I would fain have said a maid!

5.1. Location: The city gate.
s.d. several separate   **1 cousin** fellow nobleman. (Addressed to
Angelo.)   **7 yield . . . to** i.e., present you with   **8 more requital** further
reward   **9 bonds** obligations   **11 To lock . . . bosom** i.e., to keep it
locked up in my heart   **12 characters** writing, letters   **13 forted** fortified   **14 rasure** effacement   **15 the subject** those who are subjects
16 fain happily (as also in l. 22)   **17 keep** reside.   **within** i.e., in the
heart   **21 Vail your regard** look down

O worthy Prince, dishonor not your eye
By throwing it on any other object
Till you have heard me in my true complaint
And given me justice, justice, justice, justice!

DUKE
Relate your wrongs. In what? By whom? Be brief.
Here is Lord Angelo shall give you justice.   28
Reveal yourself to him.

ISABELLA   O worthy Duke,
You bid me seek redemption of the devil.
Hear me yourself; for that which I must speak
Must either punish me, not being believed,   32
Or wring redress from you.
Hear me, O, hear me, hear!

ANGELO
My lord, her wits, I fear me, are not firm.
She hath been a suitor to me for her brother
Cut off by course of justice—

ISABELLA   By course of justice!

ANGELO
And she will speak most bitterly and strange.

ISABELLA
Most strange, but yet most truly, will I speak.
That Angelo's forsworn, is it not strange?
That Angelo's a murderer, is 't not strange?
That Angelo is an adulterous thief,
An hypocrite, a virgin-violator,
Is it not strange, and strange?

DUKE   Nay, it is ten times strange.

ISABELLA
It is not truer he is Angelo
Than this is all as true as it is strange.
Nay, it is ten times true, for truth is truth
To th' end of reck'ning.

DUKE   Away with her! Poor soul,
She speaks this in th' infirmity of sense.   50

ISABELLA
O Prince, I conjure thee, as thou believ'st
There is another comfort than this world,

---

28 shall who shall   **32 not being** if it is not   **50 in . . . sense** out of a
sick mind, out of the weakness of passion

That thou neglect me not with that opinion
That I am touched with madness! Make not impossible   54
That which but seems unlike. 'Tis not impossible   55
But one the wicked'st caitiff on the ground   56
May seem as shy, as grave, as just, as absolute   57
As Angelo; even so may Angelo,
In all his dressings, characts, titles, forms,   59
Be an archvillain. Believe it, royal Prince,
If he be less, he's nothing; but he's more,   61
Had I more name for badness.

DUKE   By mine honesty,
If she be mad—as I believe no other—
Her madness hath the oddest frame of sense,   64
Such a dependency of thing on thing,   65
As e'er I heard in madness.

ISABELLA   O gracious Duke,
Harp not on that, nor do not banish reason   67
For inequality, but let your reason serve   68
To make the truth appear where it seems hid,
And hide the false seems true.   70

DUKE   Many that are not mad
Have, sure, more lack of reason. What would you say?

ISABELLA
I am the sister of one Claudio,
Condemned upon the act of fornication
To lose his head, condemned by Angelo.
I, in probation of a sisterhood,   76
Was sent to by my brother; one Lucio
As then the messenger—

LUCIO   That's I, an 't like Your Grace.
I came to her from Claudio and desired her
To try her gracious fortune with Lord Angelo
For her poor brother's pardon.

ISABELLA   That's he indeed.

---

54 Make consider   **55 unlike** unlikely   **56 But one the wicked'st caitiff**
but that the most wicked villain   **57 absolute** flawless   **59 dressings**
ceremonial robes.   **characts** insignia, symbols of office   **61 If . . . nothing**
i.e., even if he were less than an archvillain he would be worthless
64 frame of sense form of reason   **65 dependency . . . on thing** coherence   **67–68 do . . . inequality** i.e., do not assume lack of reason on my
part because of the inconsistency between my story and Angelo's refuta-
tion, or because of the inequality in our reputations   **70 hide** remove
from consideration.   **seems** that seems   **76 in probation** i.e., a novice

DUKE
  You were not bid to speak.
LUCIO   No, my good lord,
  Nor wished to hold my peace.
DUKE   I wish you now, then.
  Pray you, take note of it. And when you have
  A business for yourself, pray heaven you then
  Be perfect.   86
LUCIO   I warrant your honor.   87
DUKE
  The warrant's for yourself; take heed to 't.
ISABELLA
  This gentleman told somewhat of my tale—
LUCIO   Right.
DUKE
  It may be right, but you are i' the wrong
  To speak before your time.—Proceed.
ISABELLA   I went
  To this pernicious caitiff deputy—
DUKE
  That's somewhat madly spoken.
ISABELLA   Pardon it;
  The phrase is to the matter.   95
DUKE   Mended again. The matter; proceed.   96
ISABELLA
  In brief, to set the needless process by,   97
  How I persuaded, how I prayed, and kneeled,
  How he refelled me, and how I replied—   99
  For this was of much length—the vile conclusion
  I now begin with grief and shame to utter.
  He would not, but by gift of my chaste body
  To his concupiscible intemperate lust,   103
  Release my brother; and after much debatement   104
  My sisterly remorse confutes mine honor,   105
  And I did yield to him. But the next morn betimes,   106

---

86 perfect prepared   **87 warrant** assure. (The Duke, however, quibbles
in l. 88 on the meaning "judicial writ.")   **95 to the matter** to the purpose   **96 Mended again** i.e., again you have explained seemingly mad
speech. **The matter** i.e., proceed to the main point   **97 to set . . . by**
not to dwell on unnecessary details in the story   **99 refelled** refuted
103 concupiscible lustful   **104 debatement** argument, debate
105 remorse pity.   **confutes** confounds, silences   **106 betimes** early

His purpose surfeiting, he sends a warrant   107
For my poor brother's head.

DUKE   This is most likely!

ISABELLA
O, that it were as like as it is true!

DUKE
By heaven, fond wretch, thou know'st not what thou
   speak'st,   110
Or else thou art suborned against his honor   111
In hateful practice. First, his integrity   112
Stands without blemish. Next, it imports no reason   113
That with such vehemency he should pursue
Faults proper to himself. If he had so offended,   115
He would have weighed thy brother by himself   116
And not have cut him off. Someone hath set you on.
Confess the truth, and say by whose advice
Thou cam'st here to complain.

ISABELLA   And is this all?
Then, O you blessèd ministers above,
Keep me in patience, and with ripened time
Unfold the evil which is here wrapped up   122
In countenance! Heaven shield Your Grace from woe,   123
As I thus wrongèd hence unbelievèd go!

                          [*She starts to leave.*]

DUKE
I know you'd fain be gone. An officer!
To prison with her. Shall we thus permit
A blasting and a scandalous breath to fall   127
On him so near us? This needs must be a practice.
Who knew of your intent and coming hither?

ISABELLA
One that I would were here, Friar Lodowick.

DUKE
A ghostly father, belike. Who knows that Lodowick?

LUCIO
My lord, I know him; 'tis a meddling friar.

---

107 surfeiting becoming satiated   **110 fond** foolish   **111 suborned**
induced to give false testimony   **112 practice** machination, conspiracy   **113 imports no reason** i.e., makes no sense   **115 proper to himself**
of which he himself is guilty   **116 weighed** judged   **122 Unfold** disclose   **122–123 wrapped ... countenance** concealed by means of authority   **127 blasting** blighting

I do not like the man. Had he been lay, my lord,   133
For certain words he spake against Your Grace
In your retirement, I had swinged him soundly.   135

DUKE
Words against me? This' a good friar, belike!   136
And to set on this wretched woman here
Against our substitute! Let this friar be found.

LUCIO
But yesternight, my lord, she and that friar,
I saw them at the prison. A saucy friar,
A very scurvy fellow.

FRIAR PETER   Blessed be Your Royal Grace!
I have stood by, my lord, and I have heard
Your royal ear abused. First, hath this woman
Most wrongfully accused your substitute,
Who is as free from touch or soil with her
As she from one ungot.   147

DUKE   We did believe no less.
Know you that Friar Lodowick that she speaks of?

FRIAR PETER
I know him for a man divine and holy,
Not scurvy, nor a temporary meddler,   151
As he's reported by this gentleman;
And, on my trust, a man that never yet
Did, as he vouches, misreport Your Grace.

LUCIO
My lord, most villainously, believe it.

FRIAR PETER
Well, he in time may come to clear himself;
But at this instant he is sick, my lord,
Of a strange fever. Upon his mere request,   158
Being come to knowledge that there was complaint   159
Intended 'gainst Lord Angelo, came I hither,
To speak, as from his mouth, what he doth know
Is true and false, and what he with his oath
And all probation will make up full clear,   163
Whensoever he's convented. First, for this woman,   164
To justify this worthy nobleman,

133 **lay** not a cleric   135 **swinged** beaten   136 **This'** this is   147 **ungot**
unbegotten   151 **temporary meddler** meddler in temporal affairs
158 **Upon . . . request** solely at his request   159 **Being . . . knowledge** he
having learned   163 **probation** proof   164 **convented** summoned

So vulgarly and personally accused,   166
Her shall you hear disprovèd to her eyes,
Till she herself confess it.
DUKE   Good Friar, let's hear it.
                    [*Isabella is led off, guarded.*]
Do you not smile at this, Lord Angelo?
O heaven, the vanity of wretched fools!   170
Give us some seats. [*They sit.*] Come, cousin Angelo,
In this I'll be impartial. Be you judge
Of your own cause.

        Enter Mariana, [*veiled*].

                    Is this the witness, Friar?
First, let her show her face, and after speak.
MARIANA
Pardon, my lord, I will not show my face
Until my husband bid me.
DUKE   What, are you married?
MARIANA   No, my lord.
DUKE   Are you a maid?
MARIANA   No, my lord.
DUKE   A widow, then?
MARIANA   Neither, my lord.
DUKE   Why, you are nothing then, neither maid,
widow, nor wife?
LUCIO   My lord, she may be a punk, for many of them   185
are neither maid, widow, nor wife.
DUKE
Silence that fellow. I would he had some cause
To prattle for himself.   188
LUCIO   Well, my lord.
MARIANA
My lord, I do confess I ne'er was married,
And I confess besides I am no maid.
I have known my husband, yet my husband   192
Knows not that ever he knew me.
LUCIO   He was drunk then, my lord; it can be no better.
DUKE   For the benefit of silence, would thou wert so too!

166 vulgarly publicly   **170 vanity** folly   **185 punk** harlot   **188 To . . .**
himself to speak in his own defense. (The Duke hints that there might well
be charges pending against Lucio.)   **192 known** had intercourse with

LUCIO Well, my lord.

DUKE

This is no witness for Lord Angelo.

MARIANA Now I come to 't, my lord:
She that accuses him of fornication
In selfsame manner doth accuse my husband,
And charges him, my lord, with such a time   201
When, I'll depose, I had him in mine arms   202
With all th' effect of love.   203

ANGELO Charges she more than me?   204

MARIANA Not that I know.

DUKE No? You say your husband?

MARIANA

Why, just, my lord, and that is Angelo,
Who thinks he knows that he ne'er knew my body,
But knows, he thinks, that he knows Isabel's.

ANGELO

This is a strange abuse. Let's see thy face.   210

MARIANA

My husband bids me. Now I will unmask.

                              [*She unveils.*]

This is that face, thou cruel Angelo,
Which once thou swor'st was worth the looking on;
This is the hand which, with a vowed contract,
Was fast belocked in thine; this is the body   215
That took away the match from Isabel,   216
And did supply thee at thy garden house
In her imagined person.

DUKE Know you this woman?

LUCIO Carnally, she says.

DUKE Sirrah, no more!

LUCIO Enough, my lord.

ANGELO

My lord, I must confess I know this woman,
And five years since there was some speech of marriage
Betwixt myself and her, which was broke off,
Partly for that her promisèd proportions   226

201 with . . . time with doing the deed at just the same time 202 depose testify under oath 203 effect manifestations 204 Charges . . . me
does she (Isabella) bring charges against persons besides myself
210 abuse deception 215 fast belocked firmly locked 216 match
meeting 226 proportions dowry

Came short of composition, but in chief   227
For that her reputation was disvalued   228
In levity. Since which time of five years   229
I never spake with her, saw her, nor heard from her,
Upon my faith and honor.
MARIANA   Noble Prince,
As there comes light from heaven and words from
    breath,
As there is sense in truth and truth in virtue,
I am affianced this man's wife as strongly
As words could make up vows; and, my good lord,
But Tuesday night last gone in 's garden house
He knew me as a wife. As this is true,
Let me in safety raise me from my knees,
Or else forever be confixèd here,   239
A marble monument!
ANGELO   I did but smile till now.
Now, good my lord, give me the scope of justice;   242
My patience here is touched. I do perceive   243
These poor informal women are no more   244
But instruments of some more mightier member   245
That sets them on. Let me have way, my lord,
To find this practice out.
DUKE   Ay, with my heart,
And punish them to your height of pleasure.
Thou foolish friar, and thou pernicious woman,
Compact with her that's gone, think'st thou thy oaths,   250
Though they would swear down each particular saint,   251
Were testimonies against his worth and credit
That's sealed in approbation?—You, Lord Escalus,   253
Sit with my cousin; lend him your kind pains
To find out this abuse, whence 'tis derived.
There is another friar that set them on;
Let him be sent for.
                    [*The Duke rises; Escalus takes his chair.*]
FRIAR PETER
Would he were here, my lord! For he indeed

227 **composition** agreement   228–229 **disvalued In levity** discredited for
lightness   239 **confixèd** firmly fixed   242 **scope** full authority
243 **touched** injured, affected   244 **informal** rash, distracted   245 **But**
than   250 **Compact** in collusion   251 **swear . . . saint** call down to
witness every single saint   253 **sealed in approbation** ratified by proof

Hath set the women on to this complaint.
Your Provost knows the place where he abides,
And he may fetch him.

DUKE   Go do it instantly. [*Exit Provost.*]
And you, my noble and well-warranted cousin,
Whom it concerns to hear this matter forth,   263
Do with your injuries as seems you best,   264
In any chastisement. I for a while
Will leave you; but stir not you till you have
Well determined upon these slanderers.   267

ESCALUS My lord, we'll do it throughly. *Exit* [*Duke*]. 268
Signor Lucio, did not you say you knew that Friar
Lodowick to be a dishonest person?

LUCIO *Cucullus non facit monachum;* honest in noth- 271
ing but in his clothes, and one that hath spoke most
villainous speeches of the Duke.

ESCALUS We shall entreat you to abide here till he come
and enforce them against him. We shall find this friar 275
a notable fellow.   276

LUCIO As any in Vienna, on my word.

ESCALUS Call that same Isabel here once again. I would
speak with her. [*Exit an Attendant.*] Pray you, my lord,
give me leave to question. You shall see how I'll handle
her.

LUCIO Not better than he, by her own report.

ESCALUS Say you?

LUCIO Marry, sir, I think, if you handled her privately,
she would sooner confess; perchance publicly she'll be
ashamed.

ESCALUS I will go darkly to work with her.   287

LUCIO That's the way, for women are light at midnight. 288

    Enter Duke [*disguised as a friar*], *Provost,*
    Isabella, [*and officers*].

ESCALUS Come on, mistress. Here's a gentlewoman
denies all that you have said.

263 forth through   **264 Do with your injuries** respond to the wrongs done
to you.   **seems you** seems to you   **267 determined** reached judgment
268 throughly thoroughly   **271 Cucullus . . . monachum** a cowl doesn't
make a monk   **275 enforce them** forcefully charge them   **276 notable**
notorious   **287 darkly** subtly, slyly   **288 light** wanton, unchaste

LUCIO My lord, here comes the rascal I spoke of, here
with the Provost.

ESCALUS In very good time. Speak not you to him till
we call upon you.

LUCIO Mum.

ESCALUS Come, sir, did you set these women on to
slander Lord Angelo? They have confessed you did.

DUKE 'Tis false.

ESCALUS How? Know you where you are?

DUKE
Respect to your great place! And let the devil   300
Be sometimes honored for his burning throne!   301
Where is the Duke? 'Tis he should hear me speak.

ESCALUS
The Duke's in us, and we will hear you speak.
Look you speak justly.

DUKE
Boldly, at least. But O, poor souls,
Come you to seek the lamb here of the fox?
Good night to your redress! Is the Duke gone?
Then is your cause gone too. The Duke's unjust,
Thus to retort your manifest appeal,   309
And put your trial in the villain's mouth
Which here you come to accuse.

LUCIO This is the rascal. This is he I spoke of.

ESCALUS
Why, thou unreverend and unhallowed friar,
Is 't not enough thou hast suborned these women
To accuse this worthy man, but, in foul mouth
And in the witness of his proper ear,   316
To call him villain? And then to glance from him
To th' Duke himself, to tax him with injustice?   318
Take him hence. To th' rack with him! We'll touse you   319
Joint by joint, but we will know his purpose.
What, "unjust"?

DUKE   Be not so hot. The Duke
Dare no more stretch this finger of mine than he
Dare rack his own. His subject am I not,

300–301 let . . . throne i.e., may all authority be respected, even the
devil's. (Said sardonically.)   **309 retort** turn back.   **manifest** obviously
just   **316 in . . . ear** within his own hearing   **318 tax him with** accuse
him of   **319 touse** tear

Nor here provincial. My business in this state   324
Made me a looker-on here in Vienna,
Where I have seen corruption boil and bubble
Till it o'errun the stew; laws for all faults,   327
But faults so countenanced that the strong statutes   328
Stand like the forfeits in a barber's shop,   329
As much in mock as mark.
ESCALUS   Slander to th' state!   330
Away with him to prison.
ANGELO
What can you vouch against him, Signor Lucio?
Is this the man that you did tell us of?
LUCIO 'Tis he, my lord. Come hither, Goodman Bald-   334
pate. Do you know me?   335
DUKE I remember you, sir, by the sound of your voice.
I met you at the prison, in the absence of the Duke.
LUCIO O, did you so? And do you remember what you
said of the Duke?
DUKE Most notedly, sir.   340
LUCIO Do you so, sir? And was the Duke a flesh-
monger, a fool, and a coward, as you then re-
ported him to be?
DUKE You must, sir, change persons with me ere you
make that my report. You indeed spoke so of him, and
much more, much worse.
LUCIO O thou damnable fellow! Did not I pluck thee by
the nose for thy speeches?
DUKE I protest I love the Duke as I love myself.
ANGELO Hark how the villain would close now, after his   350
treasonable abuses!
ESCALUS Such a fellow is not to be talked withal. Away
with him to prison! Where is the Provost? Away with
him to prison! Lay bolts enough upon him. Let him   354
speak no more. Away with those giglots too, and with   355

---

324 provincial subject to the religious authority of this province or
state   **327 stew** (1) stewpot (2) brothel   **328 countenanced** allowed
329 forfeits i.e., lists of rules and minor fines (which barbers apparently
hung in their shops as guides to appropriate behavior)   **330 As . . .
mark** i.e., as often flouted as observed   **334–335 Goodman Baldpate**
(Lucio refers to the tonsure he assumes this "friar" must have.)
340 notedly particularly   **350 close** come to terms, compromise
354 bolts iron fetters   **355 giglots** wanton women

the other confederate companion!   356
        [*The Provost lays hands on the Duke.*]

DUKE [*To Provost*]   Stay, sir, stay awhile.

ANGELO   What, resists he? Help him, Lucio.

LUCIO   Come, sir, come, sir, come, sir; foh, sir! Why,
you bald-pated, lying rascal, you must be hooded,
must you? Show your knave's visage, with a pox to
you! Show your sheep-biting face, and be hanged an   362
hour! Will 't not off?   363
        [*He pulls off the friar's hood, and discovers*
                the Duke. Escalus rises.]

DUKE

Thou art the first knave that e'er mad'st a duke.

First, Provost, let me bail these gentle three.   365

[*To Lucio.*] Sneak not away, sir, for the Friar and you

Must have a word anon.—Lay hold on him.

LUCIO   This may prove worse than hanging.

DUKE [*To Escalus*]

What you have spoke I pardon. Sit you down.

We'll borrow place of him. [*To Angelo.*] Sir, by your leave.
        [*He takes Angelo's seat. Escalus also sits.*]

Hast thou or word, or wit, or impudence,

That yet can do thee office? If thou hast,

Rely upon it till my tale be heard,

And hold no longer out.

ANGELO [*Kneeling*]   O my dread lord,

I should be guiltier than my guiltiness

To think I can be undiscernible,

When I perceive Your Grace, like power divine,

Hath looked upon my passes. Then, good prince,   378

No longer session hold upon my shame,

But let my trial be mine own confession.

Immediate sentence then and sequent death   381

Is all the grace I beg.

DUKE   Come hither, Mariana.

Say, wast thou e'er contracted to this woman?

ANGELO   I was, my lord.

---

356 confederate companion i.e., Friar Peter   **362 sheep-biting** knavish
(from the action of wolves or dogs that prey on sheep)   **362–363 hanged
an hour** (a sardonic way of saying "hanged")   **365 gentle three** i.e.,
Mariana, Isabella, and Friar Peter   **378 passes** trespasses   **381 sequent**
subsequent

DUKE
Go take her hence and marry her instantly.
Do you the office, Friar, which consummate,   386
Return him here again. Go with him, Provost.
          *Exit [Angelo, with Mariana, Friar Peter, and
                                        Provost].*

ESCALUS
My lord, I am more amazed at his dishonor
Than at the strangeness of it.

DUKE   Come hither, Isabel.
Your friar is now your prince. As I was then
Advertising and holy to your business,   391
Not changing heart with habit, I am still
Attorneyed at your service.

ISABELLA   O, give me pardon,   393
That I, your vassal, have employed and pained   394
Your unknown sovereignty!

DUKE   You are pardoned, Isabel.
And now, dear maid, be you as free to us.   396
Your brother's death, I know, sits at your heart;
And you may marvel why I obscured myself,
Laboring to save his life, and would not rather
Make rash remonstrance of my hidden power   400
Than let him so be lost. O most kind maid,
It was the swift celerity of his death,
Which I did think with slower foot came on,
That brained my purpose. But peace be with him!   404
That life is better life past fearing death
Than that which lives to fear. Make it your comfort,
So happy is your brother.

          *Enter Angelo, Mariana, [Friar] Peter, [and]
          Provost.*

ISABELLA   I do, my lord.   407
DUKE
For this new-married man approaching here,
Whose salt imagination yet hath wronged   409

386 **Do . . . office** you perform the service. **consummate** being completed 391 **Advertising** attentive 393 **Attorneyed at** serving as agent in 394 **pained** put to trouble 396 **free to us** i.e., generous in pardoning me 400 **rash remonstrance** sudden manifestation 404 **brained** dashed, defeated 407 **So** thus 409 **salt** lecherous

Your well-defended honor, you must pardon
For Mariana's sake. But as he adjudged your brother—
Being criminal, in double violation
Of sacred chastity and of promise-breach   413
Thereon dependent, for your brother's life—   414
The very mercy of the law cries out   415
Most audible, even from his proper tongue,   416
"An Angelo for Claudio, death for death!"
Haste still pays haste, and leisure answers leisure;   418
Like doth quit like, and measure still for measure.   419
Then, Angelo, thy fault's thus manifested,
Which, though thou wouldst deny, denies thee vantage.   421
We do condemn thee to the very block
Where Claudio stooped to death, and with like haste.
Away with him!
MARIANA   O my most gracious lord,
I hope you will not mock me with a husband!
DUKE
It is your husband mocked you with a husband.
Consenting to the safeguard of your honor,
I thought your marriage fit; else imputation,   428
For that he knew you, might reproach your life   429
And choke your good to come. For his possessions,   430
Although by confiscation they are ours,
We do instate and widow you withal   432
To buy you a better husband.
MARIANA   O my dear lord,
I crave no other, nor no better man.
DUKE
Never crave him; we are definitive.   435
MARIANA [*Kneeling*]
Gentle my liege—
DUKE   You do but lose your labor.
Away with him to death! [*To Lucio.*] Now, sir, to you.

413–414 promise-breach . . . dependent i.e., breaking his promise made
in return for the yielding up of chastity   **415 The very . . . law** i.e., even
mercy itself   **416 his proper** its own   **418 still** always   **419 quit** requite   **421 though** even if.   **vantage** i.e., any advantage. (Angelo must
suffer the same penalty as Claudio.)   **428 fit** appropriate.   **imputation**
accusation, slander   **429 For that** because.   **knew** had sexual relations
with   **430 For** as for   **432 instate and widow** grant to you the estate
appropriate to a widow   **435 definitive** firmly resolved

MARIANA

O my good lord! Sweet Isabel, take my part!
Lend me your knees, and all my life to come
I'll lend you all my life to do you service.

DUKE

Against all sense you do importune her.
Should she kneel down in mercy of this fact,   442
Her brother's ghost his pavèd bed would break   443
And take her hence in horror.

MARIANA   Isabel,
Sweet Isabel, do yet but kneel by me!
Hold up your hands, say nothing; I'll speak all.
They say best men are molded out of faults,   447
And, for the most, become much more the better   448
For being a little bad. So may my husband.
O Isabel, will you not lend a knee?

DUKE

He dies for Claudio's death.

ISABELLA [*Kneeling*]   Most bounteous sir,
Look, if it please you, on this man condemned
As if my brother lived. I partly think
A due sincerity governed his deeds,
Till he did look on me. Since it is so,
Let him not die. My brother had but justice,
In that he did the thing for which he died.
For Angelo,
His act did not o'ertake his bad intent,
And must be buried but as an intent   460
That perished by the way. Thoughts are no subjects,   461
Intents but merely thoughts.

MARIANA   Merely, my lord.

DUKE

Your suit's unprofitable; stand up, I say.   463

                                        [*They stand.*]

I have bethought me of another fault.
Provost, how came it Claudio was beheaded
At an unusual hour?

PROVOST   It was commanded so.

442 in . . . fact pleading mercy for this crime   **443 pavèd bed** grave
covered with a stone slab   **447 best men** even the best of men
448 most most part   **460 buried** i.e., forgotten   **461 no subjects** i.e., not
subject to the state's authority   **463 unprofitable** worthless

DUKE
  Had you a special warrant for the deed?
PROVOST
  No, my good lord, it was by private message.
DUKE
  For which I do discharge you of your office.
  Give up your keys.
PROVOST   Pardon me, noble lord.
  I thought it was a fault, but knew it not,   472
  Yet did repent me after more advice;   473
  For testimony whereof, one in the prison,
  That should by private order else have died,
  I have reserved alive.
DUKE   What's he?
PROVOST   His name is Barnardine.
DUKE
  I would thou hadst done so by Claudio.
  Go fetch him hither. Let me look upon him.
                                        [*Exit Provost.*]
ESCALUS
  I am sorry one so learnèd and so wise
  As you, Lord Angelo, have still appeared,   482
  Should slip so grossly, both in the heat of blood
  And lack of tempered judgment afterward.
ANGELO
  I am sorry that such sorrow I procure,
  And so deep sticks it in my penitent heart
  That I crave death more willingly than mercy.
  'Tis my deserving, and I do entreat it.   488

    Enter Barnardine and Provost, Claudio [*muffled*],
    [*and*] *Juliet.*

DUKE
  Which is that Barnardine?
PROVOST   This, my lord.
DUKE
  There was a friar told me of this man.
  Sirrah, thou art said to have a stubborn soul
  That apprehends no further than this world,

472 knew it not was not sure   **473 advice** consideration   **482 still**
always   **488 s.d. muffled** wrapped up so as to conceal identity (as also
in l. 497)

And squar'st thy life according. Thou'rt condemned;   493
But, for those earthly faults, I quit them all,   494
And pray thee take this mercy to provide
For better times to come. Friar, advise him;
I leave him to your hand. What muffled fellow's that?

PROVOST
This is another prisoner that I saved,
Who should have died when Claudio lost his head,
As like almost to Claudio as himself.

                    [*He unmuffles Claudio.*]

DUKE [*To Isabella*]
If he be like your brother, for his sake
Is he pardoned, and for your lovely sake,
Give me your hand and say you will be mine;
He is my brother too. But fitter time for that.
By this Lord Angelo perceives he's safe;
Methinks I see a quickening in his eye.
Well, Angelo, your evil quits you well.   507
Look that you love your wife, her worth worth yours.
I find an apt remission in myself;   509
And yet here's one in place I cannot pardon.
[*To Lucio.*] You, sirrah, that knew me for a fool, a coward,
One all of luxury, an ass, a madman—   512
Wherein have I so deserved of you
That you extol me thus?

LUCIO   Faith, my lord, I spoke it but according to the
trick. If you will hang me for it, you may; but I had   516
rather it would please you I might be whipped.

DUKE
Whipped first, sir, and hanged after.
Proclaim it, Provost, round about the city,
If any woman wronged by this lewd fellow—
As I have heard him swear himself there's one
Whom he begot with child—let her appear,
And he shall marry her. The nuptial finished,
Let him be whipped and hanged.

LUCIO   I beseech Your Highness, do not marry me to a
whore. Your Highness said even now I made you a   526

---

493 squar'st regulates   **494 for** as for.   **quit** pardon   **507 quits** rewards, requites   **509 remission** readiness to show mercy   **512 luxury** lechery   **516 trick** fashion   **526 even** just

duke; good my lord, do not recompense me in making
me a cuckold.

DUKE
  Upon mine honor, thou shalt marry her.
  Thy slanders I forgive and therewithal   530
  Remit thy other forfeits. Take him to prison,   531
  And see our pleasure herein executed.   532
LUCIO Marrying a punk, my lord, is pressing to death,   533
  whipping, and hanging.
DUKE Slandering a prince deserves it.
                          [*Exeunt officers with Lucio.*]
  She, Claudio, that you wronged, look you restore.
  Joy to you, Mariana! Love her, Angelo.
  I have confessed her, and I know her virtue.
  Thanks, good friend Escalus, for thy much goodness;
  There's more behind that is more gratulate.   540
  Thanks, Provost, for thy care and secrecy;
  We shall employ thee in a worthier place.
  Forgive him, Angelo, that brought you home
  The head of Ragozine for Claudio's;
  Th' offense pardons itself. Dear Isabel,
  I have a motion much imports your good,   546
  Whereto if you'll a willing ear incline,
  What's mine is yours and what is yours is mine.
  So, bring us to our palace, where we'll show   549
  What's yet behind that's meet you all should know.   550
                                           [*Exeunt.*]

---

530 **therewithal** consequently 531 **Remit . . . forfeits** i.e., cancel the
sentences of whipping and hanging 532 **see . . . executed** i.e., see that
my order be carried out that Lucio marry Kate Keepdown (see
3.2. 194–196) 533 **pressing to death** i.e., by having heavy weights placed
on the chest. (A standard form of executing those who refused to plead
to a felony charge.) Lucio wryly complains that marrying a whore is as
bad as death by torture. 540 **behind** in store, to come. **gratulate**
gratifying 546 **motion** proposal (which) 549 **bring** escort 550 **What's
yet behind** what is still to be told

Date and Text

Measure for Measure first appeared in the First Folio of 1623. The text was evidently set from scrivener Ralph Crane's copy of Shakespeare's own draft; the usual inconsistencies of composition have not yet been smoothed away by use in the theater. A more recent and controversial hypothesis is that Crane transcribed a promptbook in use after Shakespeare's death, one that incorporates some theatrical adaptation by Thomas Middleton and some other reviser. The first recorded performance was on December 26, 1604, St. Stephen's Night, when "a play Caled Mesur for Mesur" by "Shaxberd" was acted in the banqueting hall at Whitehall "by his Maiesties plaiers." Shakespeare's acting company, previously the Lord Chamberlain's men, had become the King's men after the accession to the throne of James I in 1603.

Several allusions in the play seem to point to the summer of 1604, when the theaters, having been closed for a year because of the plague, were reopened. A reference to the King of Hungary (1.2.1–5) may reflect anxieties in England over James's negotiations for a settlement with Spain; censorship would forbid a direct mentioning of Spain. Mistress Overdone's complaint about the war, the "sweat" (plague), the "gallows" (public executions), and poverty (1.2.81–83) are all suggestive of events in 1603–1604, when war with Spain and the plague were still very much in evidence. Duke Vincentio's reticent habits have been seen as a flattering reference to James's well-known dislike of crowds. Stylistically the play is clearly later than *Twelfth Night* (1600–1602), so that a date close to the first recorded performance in 1604 is a necessity even if we cannot be positive about all the supposed allusions to King James.

Textual Notes

These textual notes are not a historical collation, either of the early folios or of more recent editions; they are simply a record of departures in this edition from the copy text. The reading adopted in this edition appears in boldface, followed by the rejected reading from the copy text, i.e., the First Folio. Only major alterations in punctuation are noted. Changes in lineation are not indicated, nor are some minor and obvious typographical errors.

Abbreviations used:
F the First Folio
s.d. stage direction
s.p. speech prefix

Copy text: the First Folio.

1.1. 76 s.d. [at l. 75 in F]

1.2. 58 s.p. [and elsewhere] Mistress Overdone Bawd   **83 s.d.** [at l. 84 in F] **85 s.p. [and elsewhere] Pompey** Clo   **115** [F begins "Scena Tertia" here] **134 morality** mortality

1.3. [F labels as "Scena Quarta"]   **20 steeds** weedes   **27 Becomes more** More   **54 s.d. Exeunt** Exit

1.4. [F labels as "Scena Quinta"]   **s.d. [and elsewhere] Isabella** Isabell **2 s.p. [and throughout] Francisca** Nun   **17 stead** steed   **54 givings-out** giuing-out

2.1. 12 your our   **39 breaks** brakes   **139 s.d.** [at l. 138 in F]

2.2. 63 back again againe   **104 ere** here

2.4. 9 sere feard   **17 s.d. Enter Servant** [after l. 17 in F]   **30 s.d. Enter Isabella** [after l. 30 in F]   **53 or** and   **75 craftily** crafty   **76 me be** be   **94 all-binding** all-building

3.1. 29 sire fire   **52 me to hear them** them to heare me   **68 Though** Through   **91 enew** emmew   **96 damned'st** damnest   **131 penury** periury **216 by oath** oath

3.2. 26 array away   **48 it clutched** clutched   **74–75 bondage . . . why** bondage if . . . patiently: Why   **147 dearer** deare   **214 See** Sea

4.1. 1 s.p. Boy [not in F]   **20 s.d. Isabella** Isabell   **49 s.d.** [at l. 48 in F] **61 quests** Quest   **64 s.d. Enter . . . Isabella** [after l. 64 in F]

4.2. 43–47 If . . . thief [assigned in F to Clown]   **58 yare** y'are   **60 s.d.** [at l. 59 in F]   **72 s.d. Enter Duke** [after l. 72 in F]   **100 This . . . man** [assigned in F to Duke]   **lordship's** Lords   **101 s.p. Duke** Pro   **120 s.p. Provost (Reads** [not in F]

4.3. 92 s.d. [at l. 91 in F]   **93 Varrius** Angelo   **100 well** weale

4.4. 6 redeliver reliuer   **15–16 proclaimed. Betimes** proclaim'd betimes

4.5. 6 Flavius' Flauia's

5.1. 14 me we   **34 hear!** heere   **173 s.d. Enter Mariana** [after l. 173 in F] **174 her face** your face   **268 s.d.** [at l. 267 in F]   **288 s.d.** [at l. 286 in F] **407 s.d. Mariana** Maria   **431 confiscation** confutation   **488 s.d. Juliet** Iulietta   **550 that's** that

Shakespeare's Sources

Stories about corrupt magistrates are ancient and universal, but Shakespeare's particular story in *Measure for Measure* seems to go back to an actual incident in the sixteenth-century Italian court of Don Ferdinando de Gonzaga. A Hungarian student named Joseph Macarius, writing from Vienna, tells about an Italian citizen accused of murder whose wife submitted to the embraces of the magistrate in hopes of saving her husband. When the magistrate executed her husband despite her having fulfilled her bargain, she appealed to the Duke who ordered the magistrate to give her a dowry and marry her. Thereafter the Duke ordered the magistrate to be executed. This incident seems to have inspired a Senecan drama by Claude Rouillet called *Philanira* (1556), a French translation of this play (1563), a novella in the *Hecatommithi* of G. B. Giraldi Cinthio (1565), and a play by Cinthio called *Epitia* (posthumously published in 1583). Shakespeare may have known both the prose and the dramatic versions by Cinthio.

In Cinthio's story, the wise Emperor Maximian appoints his friend Juriste to govern Innsbruck, warning him to rule justly or expect no mercy from the Emperor. Juriste rules long and well, to the satisfaction of his master and the people of Innsbruck. When a young man named Vico is brought before him for ravishing a virgin, Juriste assigns the mandatory sentence of death. Vico's sister, Epitia, an extraordinarily beautiful virgin of eighteen, pleads for Vico's life, urging that his deed was one of passion and that he stands ready to marry the girl he forced. The judge, secretly inflamed with lust for Epitia, promises to consider the matter carefully. She reports this seemingly encouraging news to Vico, who urges her to persevere. When, however, the judge proposes to take her chastity in return for her brother's life, Epitia is mortified and refuses unless Juriste will marry her. During another interim in these negotiations, Vico begs his sister to save his life at any cost. She then submits to Juriste on the condition that he will both marry her and spare Vico. Next morning, however, the jailer brings her the body of her decapitated brother. She lays her complaint before the Emperor, who confronts Juriste with his guilt. Conscience-stricken, Juriste confesses and begs for mercy. At first Epitia demands strict justice, but when the Emperor compels Juriste to marry her and then be beheaded, she reveals "her natural kindness" and begs successfully for the life of her wronger. There are several important differences between this account and Shakespeare's play: Vico is actually killed, unlike Claudio, and Epitia sleeps with Juriste and then is married to him. No equivalent to Mariana appears, or to Lucio, Pompey, Mistress Overdone, Elbow, and other characters in the comic scenes of Shakespeare's play. No duke oversees the career of Juriste and ensures that no fatal wrong will occur.

Shakespeare may also have consulted Cinthio's play *Epitia,* but his chief sources were George Whetstone's two-part play *Promos and Cassandra* (1578) and a novella on the same subject. In the English play, the corrupt judge is Promos, administrator of the city of Julio under the King of Hungary. The law forbidding adultery has lain in abeyance for some years when a young gentleman named Andrugio is arrested and condemned for "incontinency." His sister Cassandra, like Epitia in Cinthio, lays down her precious chastity to Promos in response to her brother's piteous entreaties. Promos gives his assurance that he will marry her and save Andrugio's life. When Promos instead treacherously orders the execution of Andrugio, the jailer secretly substitutes the head of a felon, newly executed and so mutilated as to be unrecognizable even by Cassandra. (This rescue is seen as an intervention "by the providence of God.") The King sentences Promos just as the Emperor sentences Juriste in Cinthio, but in Whetstone's play the King refuses Cassandra's pleas for the life of her new husband until Andrugio reveals himself to be still alive and offers to die for Promos. The King forgives Andrugio on condition that he marry Polina, whom he wronged. The play also features a courtesan named Lamia and her man, Rosko, who ingratiate themselves with the corrupt officer (Phallax) in charge of investigating their case. Phallax is ultimately caught and dismissed from office while Lamia is publicly humiliated.

Whetstone wrote a prose novella of this same story in the *Heptameron of Civil Discourses* (1582). Shakespeare appears to have consulted it as well as the play, for the prose version mentions the names of Isabella (as the narrator of the story) and Crassus (compare *Measure for Measure*, 4.5.8), and the King's awarding of measure for measure in his sentencing of Promos—"You shall be measured with the grace you bestowed on Andrugio"—may have given Shakespeare an idea for the title of his play. The prose version is given in the following pages, since the two-part play is far too long for inclusion and since the novella gives much of what Shakespeare used, other than the important dramatic structure of *Promos and Cassandra*. Shakespeare was also indebted for a few details to a version in Thomas Lupton's *Too Good to Be True* (1581).

Even though Shakespeare's play is closely related to Whetstone's play and novella, Shakespeare has changed much. He adds the motif of the Duke's mysterious disguise. (A not very compelling analogue to this motif occurs in Sir Thomas Elyot's *The Image of Governance*, 1541.) Shakespeare introduces the use of the bed trick, found also in his presumably earlier play *All's Well that Ends Well*. Most important, Shakespeare stresses the moral and legal complexity of his story. Isabella is about to renounce the world by entering a convent. By contrast, Lucio, a Shakespearean addition, is an engaging cynic, hedonist, and slanderer. Claudio, although guilty of fornication, is only technically in violation of the laws against sexual license. Isabella does not surrender her chastity. Her breakdown in the scene with Claudio intensifies her emotional crisis and renders all the more triumphant her final ability to forgive Angelo. Angelo himself is made puritanical in temperament, and is spared the actual consequences of his worst intentions so that he can be worthy of being forgiven. Isabella need not marry Angelo, since he has not actually seduced her; she is thus free to marry the Duke. No felon need be executed in Claudio's stead, for providence provides a natural death in the prison. In the subplot, going well beyond the merest hints in Whetstone, Pompey is a brilliantly original innovation, Elbow a characteristically Shakespearean clown modeled on the earlier Dogberry of *Much Ado about Nothing*, and Escalus a significant spokesman for a moderate and practical course of equity in the law.

An Heptameron[1] of Civil Discourses
By George Whetstone

THE RARE HISTORY OF PROMOS AND CASSANDRA

[*The story is narrated by a lady called Isabella at the court of Queen Aurelia.*]

At what time[2] Corvinus, the scourge of the Turks, reigned as King of Bohemia, for to[3] well govern the free cities of his realm he sent divers worthy magistrates. Among the rest he gave the Lord Promos the lieutenantship of Julio, who in the beginning of his government purged the city of many ancient vices and severely punished new offenders.

In this city there was an old custom, by the suffering[4] of some magistrates grown out of use,[5] that what man soever committed adultery should lose his head, and the woman offender should ever after be infamously noted by the wearing of some disguised apparel.[6] For the man was held to be the greatest offender and therefore had the severest punishment. Lord Promos, with a rough execution, revived this statute, and in the highest degree of injury brake it himself, as shall appear by the sequel of Andrugio's adventures.

This Andrugio, by the yielding favor[7] of fair Polina, trespassed against this ordinance, who through envy[8] was accused, and by Lord Promos condemned to suffer execution.

The woeful Cassandra, Andrugio's sister, prostrates herself at Lord Promos's feet, and with more tears than words thus pleaded for her brother's life:

"Most noble lord and worthy judge, vouchsafe me the favor to speak, whose case is so desperate as,[9] unless you behold me with the eyes of mercy, the frail trespass of condemned Andrugio, my brother, will be the death of sorrowful Cassandra, his innocent sister. I will not presume to

---

1 **An Heptameron** a collection of stories, represented (on the pattern of Boccaccio's *Decameron*) as having been told on seven successive days
2 **At what time** when   3 **for to** in order to   4 **suffering** allowance
5 **grown out of use** fallen into disuse   6 **disguised apparel** i.e., distinctive costume appropriate to her shame   7 **by the yielding favor** through the compliant and unresisting indulgence   8 **envy** malice   9 **as** that

excuse his offense or reproach the law of rigor.[10] For in the general construction[11] he hath done most evil, and the law hath judged but what is right. But, reverend judge, pardon that necessity maketh me here tell that[12] your wisdom already knoweth. The most sovereign Justice is crowned with laurel,[13] although she be girt with a sword; and this privilege she giveth unto her administrators, that they shall mitigate the severity of the law according to the quality of the offense. Then, that justice be not robbed of her gracious pity, listen, good Lord Promos, to the nature of my brother's offense and his able means to repair the injury. He hath defiled no nuptial bed, the stain whereof dishonoreth the guiltless husband. He hath committed no violent rape, in which act the injured maid can have no amends. But with yielding consent of his mistress Andrugio hath only sinned through love, and never meant but with marriage to make amends. I humbly beseech you to accept his satisfaction, and by this example you shall be as much beloved for your clemency as feared for your severity. Andrugio shall be well warned, and he, with his sister, woeful Cassandra, shall ever remain your lordship's true servants."

Promos's ears were not so attentive to hear Cassandra's ruthful[14] tale as his eyes were settled to regard her excellent beauty. And love, that was the appointed headsman[15] of Andrugio, became now the sovereign of his judge's thought. But because he would seem to bridle his passions, he answered:

"Fair damsel, have patience. You importune me with an impossibility. He is condemned by law. Then, without injury to law, he cannot be saved."

"Princes' and their deputies' prerogatives," quoth she, "are above the law. Besides, law, truly construed, is but the amends of[16] injury, and where the fault may be valued and amends had,[17] the breach of law is sufficiently repaired."

Quoth Lord Promos:

"Your passions moveth more than your proofs. And for

---

10 reproach . . . rigor accuse the law of being too rigorous   **11 general construction** interpretation of people generally   **12 that** that which   **13 laurel** (Here symbolic of mercy, balanced against the sword of rigor.)   **14 ruthful** pitiful   **15 headsman** executioner (with a play on *sovereign*)   **16 amends of** compensation for   **17 where . . . had** where a price tag may be put on the offense and paid accordingly

your sake I will reprieve Andrugio and study how to do you ease without apparent breach of law."

Cassandra, recomforted,[18] with humble thanks received his favor, and in great haste goeth to participate[19] this hope with her dying brother. But, O, that authority should have power to make the virtuous to do amiss, as well as through correction to enforce the vicious to fall unto goodness! Promos is a witness of this privilege,[20] who, not able to subdue his incontinent[21] love, and withal resolved[22] that Cassandra would never be overcome with fair words, large promises, or rich rewards, demanded the spoil of her virginity for ransom of her brother's liberty.

Cassandra imagined at the first that Lord Promos used this speech but to try her behavior; answered[23] him so wisely as, if he had not been the rival[24] of virtue, he could not but have suppressed his lewd affection and have subscribed to her just petition. But to leave circumstances,[25] Promos was fired with a vicious desire which must be quenched with Cassandra's yielding love, or Andrugio must die.

Cassandra, moved with a chaste disdain, departed with the resolution rather to die herself than to stain her honor, and with this heavy news greeted her condemned brother. Poor man, alas! What should he do? Life was sweet. But to be redeemed with his sister's infamy could not but be always unsavory. To persuade her to consent was unnatural; to yield to death was more grievous. To choose the least of these evils was difficult; to study long was dangerous. Fain[26] would he live, but shame closed his mouth when he attempted to persuade his sister. But necessity, that mastereth both shame and fear, brake a passage[27] for his imprisoned intent.

"Sweet Cassandra," quoth he, "that men love is usual, but to subdue affection is impossible, and so thorny are the motions of incontinent desire as, to find ease, the tongue is only occupied to persuade, the purse is ever open to entice, and, where neither words nor gifts can corrupt—with the mighty—force shall constrain or despite[28] avenge. That Pro-

---

18 recomforted relieved   **19 participate** share   **20 privilege** i.e., abuse of authority   **21 incontinent** lacking in self-restraint   **22 withal resolved** in addition persuaded   **23 answered** i.e., and answered   **24 rival** opponent   **25 to leave circumstances** to make a long story short
26 Fain gladly, eagerly   **27 brake a passage** broke a way out of prison
28 despite malice

mos do love is but just; thy beauty commands him. That Promos be refused is more just, because consent is thy shame. Thou mayst refuse and live. But he being rejected, I die. For wanting his will[29] in thee, he will wreak his teen[30] on me. This is my hard estate: my life lieth in thy infamy, and thy honor in my death. Which of these evils be least I leave for thee to judge."

The woeful Cassandra answered that death was the least, whose dart we cannot shun, when[31] honor, in death's despite, outliveth time.

"It is true," quoth Andrugio, "but thy trespass will be in the least degree of blame. For, in forced faults, justice saith there is no intent of evil."

"O Andrugio," quoth she, "intent is nowadays little considered. Thou art not condemned by the intent but by the strict word of the law. So shall my crime be reproached and the forced cause pass unexcused.[32] And, such is the venom of envy, one evil deed shall disgrace ten good turns; and in this yielding, so shall I be valued. Envy, disdain, spite, malice, slander, and many more furies will endeavor to shame me, and the meanest[33] virtue will blush to help to support my honor; so that I see no liberty for thee but death nor no ease for me but to hasten my end."

"O, yes," quoth Andrugio, "for if this offense be known, thy fame will be enlarged, because it will likewise be known that thou receivedst dishonor to give thy brother life. If it be secret, thy conscience will be without scruple of guiltiness. Thus, known or unknown, thou shalt be deflowered but not dishonested;[34] and for amends[35] we both shall live. This further hope remaineth: that, as the gillyflower both pleaseth the eye and feedeth the sense, even so the virtue of thy chaste behavior may so grace thy beauty as Promos's filthy lust may be turned into faithful love and so move him to salve thy honor in making thee his wife, or for conscience forbear to do so heinous an injury."

---

29 **wanting his will** failing to achieve his desire   30 **wreak his teen** exercise his wrath   31 **when** whereas   32 **and . . . unexcused** i.e., and the fact that I was compelled to commit my crime of unchastity will not excuse it   33 **meanest** least   34 **dishonested** proclaimed as unchaste 35 **for amends** by way of compensation

Sovereign madam, and you fair gentlewomen (quoth Isabella),[36] I entreat you in Cassandra's behalf, these reasons well weighed, to judge her yielding a constraint and no consent, who, weary of her own life and tender over her brother's, with the tears of her lovely eyes bathed his cheeks with this comfortable sentence:

"Live, Andrugio, and make much of this kiss, which breatheth my honor into thy bowels and draweth the infamy of thy first trespass into my bosom."

The sharp encounters between life and death so occupied Andrugio's senses that his tongue had not the virtue[37] to bid her farewell. To grieve you with the hearing of Cassandra's secret plaints were an injury, virtuous ladies, for they concluded with their good fortune and everlasting fame.[38] But for that[39] her offense grew neither of frailty, free will, or any motion of a woman, but by the mere[40] enforcement of a man, because she would not stain the modest weeds of her kind[41] she attired herself in the habit of a page, and with the bashful grace of a pure virgin she presented wicked Promos Andrugio's precious ransom.

This devil in human shape, more vicious than Heliogabalus of Rome[42] and withal as cruel as Denis of Sicily,[43] received this jewel with a thousand protestations of favor.[44] But what should I say? In the beginning of his love Promos was metamorphosed into Priapus.[45] And of a fiend what may we expect but vengeance heaped upon villainy? And therefore let it not seem strange that, after this hellhound had dishonored Cassandra, he sent his warrant to the jailer privily[46] to execute Andrugio, and, with his head, crowned with these two briefs, in Promos's name to present Cassandra:[47]

> Fair Cassandra, as Promos promised thee,
> From prison, lo, he sends thy brother free.

36 Isabella (The narrator of this story at the court of Queen Aurelia.) **37 virtue** strength **38 with . . . fame** i.e., with prayers for good fortune and an everlasting reputation for virtue **39 for that** because **40 by the mere** utterly by the **41 weeds of her kind** i.e., feminine dress **42 Heliogabalus of Rome** Elagabalus, notoriously licentious Roman emperor from 218 to 222 **43 Denis of Sicily** i.e., Dionysius, tyrant of Syracuse, who died in 367 B.C. **44 protestations of favor** promises of showing favor **45 Priapus** god of lechery **46 privily** secretly **47 with . . . Cassandra** i.e., and to present to Cassandra in Promos's name the head of Andrugio crowned with the following short lines

This was his charge,[48] whose cursed will had been executed had not God, by an especial providence, at the hour of his death possessed Andrugio with the virtues of the two brave Romans, Marcus Crassus and Marius,[49] one of which by the force of his tongue and the other by the motions of his eyes caused the ax to fall out of the headsman's hand and mollified his cruel mind. With like compassion the jailer, in hearing Andrugio's hard adventure, left his resolution, and upon a solemn oath to live unknown, yea, to his dear sister,[50] he gave him life, and in the dead of the night betook[51] him to God and to good fortune. Which done, this good jailer took the head of a young man new executed who somewhat resembled Andrugio, and according to lewd Promos's commandment made a present thereof to Cassandra.

How unwelcome this present was, the testimony of her former sorrows somewhat discover. But to give her present passion a true grace were the task of Prometheus,[52] or such a one as hath had experience of the anguishes of hell.

"O," quoth she, "sweet Andrugio, whether shall I first[53] lament thy death, exclaim of[54] Promos's injury, or bemoan my own estate, deprived of honor, and, which is worse, cannot die but by the violence of my own hands? Alas, the least of these griefs are too heavy a burden for a man! Then all, joined in one poor woman's heart, cannot be eased but by death, and to be avenged of injurious Fortune I will forthwith cut my fillet[55] of life. But so[56] shall Promos's lewdness escape unpunished. What remedy? I am not of power to revenge. To complain, I express my own infamy, but withal proclaim his villainy; and to hear his lewdness reproved would take away the bitterness of my death. I will go unto the King, who is just and merciful. He shall hear the ruthful events of Promos's tyranny, and to give him example of vengeance I will seal my complaints with my dearest blood."

---

48 his charge his orders   **49 Marcus Crassus** (d. 53 B.C.) one of the first triumvirate   **Marius** (157–87 B.C.) Roman general and statesman
50 to live . . . sister i.e., that Andrugio would conceal himself and live unknown even to his sister   **51 betook** committed   **52 Prometheus** Greek hero who stole fire from heaven, in punishment for which he was chained to a rock where an eagle fed daily on his liver   **53 whether shall I first** which of these shall I do first   **54 of** on   **55 fillet** thread **56 so** accordingly

Continuing this determination, Cassandra buried her imagined brother's head, and with speed journeyed unto King Corvinus's court, before whose presence when she arrived, her mourning attire, but especially her modest countenance, moved him to behold her with an especial regard. Cassandra, upon the grant of audience, with her eyes overcharged with tears, reported the already discoursed accidents[57] with such an appearance of grief as the King and his attendants were astonied to hear her; and sure, had she not been happily[58] prevented, she had concluded her determination with chaste Lucretia's[59] destiny. The King comforted her with many gracious words and promised to take such order that, although he[60] could not be revived, her brother's death should fully be revenged and her crazed[61] honor repaired without blemish of her former reputation.

Cassandra, upon these comfortable words, a little succored her afflicted heart and with patience attended the justice of the King, who with a chosen company made a progress to Julio and entered the town with a semblance of great favor towards Promos, by that color to learn what other corrupt magistrates ruled in the city. For well he knew that birds of a feather would fly together, and wicked men would join in affection to bolster each other's evil.

After this gracious king had by heedful intelligence understood the factions of the people, unlooked-for of the magistrates he caused a proclamation to be published in which was a clause that, if any person could charge any magistrate or officer with any notable or heinous offense, treason, murder, rape, sedition, or with any such notorious crime, where they were the judges of the multitude he would himself be the judge of them, and do justice unto the meanest.[62] Upon this proclamation it was a hell to hear the exclamations of the poor, and the festered consciences of the rich appeared as loathsome as the River of Styx.[63]

Among many that complained and received judgment of comfort, Cassandra's process[64] was presented, who, led be-

---

57 **accidents** happenings   58 **astonied . . . happily** astonished . . . luckily
59 **Lucretia** Roman matron who committed suicide rather than outlive the shame of having been raped by Tarquin   60 **he** i.e., Andrugio
61 **crazed** shattered   62 **meanest** least (citizen)   63 **Styx** river of the underworld   64 **process** story

tween sorrow and shame, accused Promos to his face. The evidence was so plain as[65] the horror of a guilty conscience reaved[66] Promos of all motions of excuse; so that, holding up his hand among the worst degree of thieves, the little hope that was left moved him to confess the crime and with repentance to sue for mercy.

"O," quoth the King, "such especial mercy were tyranny to a commonwealth. No, Promos, no. *Hoc facias alteri, quod tibi vis fieri.*[67] You shall be measured with the grace you bestowed on Andrugio. O God," quoth he, "if men durst bark as dogs, many a judge in the world would be bewrayed for[68] a thief. It behooveth a prince to know to whom he committeth authority, lest the sword of justice, appointed to chasten the lewd, wound the good, and where good subjects are wronged, evil officers receive the benefit and their sovereigns beareth the blame. Well, wicked Promos, to scourge thy impious offenses, I here give sentence that thou forthwith marry Cassandra, to repair her honor by thee violated, and that the next day thou lose thy head, to make satisfaction for her brother's death."

This just judgment of the good King in the first point was forthwith executed. But sacred is the authority[69] that the virtues of the good are a shield unto the lewd. So sweet Cassandra, who simply by virtue overcame the spite of Fortune, in this marriage was charged with a new assault of sorrow, and preferring the duty of a wife before the natural zeal of a sister, where she before prosecuted the revenge of her brother's death she now was an humble suitor to the King for her husband's life.

The gracious King sought to appease her with good words, but he could not do her this private favor without injury unto the public weal. "For though," quoth he, "your suit be just and the bounden[70] duty of a wife, yet I in fulfilling the same should do unjustly and generally injure my subjects. And therefore, good gentlewoman, have patience, and no doubt virtue in the end will give you power over all your afflictions."

---

65 as that   **66 reaved** bereaved   **67 Hoc . . . fieri** (The King freely translates in his next sentence.)   **68 bewrayed for** revealed as
69 sacred is the authority i.e., we have scriptural authority for it
70 bounden bound, required

There was no remedy; Cassandra must depart out of hope to obtain her suit. But, as the experience is in daily use,[71] the doings of princes post through the world on Pegasus' back,[72] and as their actions are good or bad so is their fame. With the like speed the King's justice and Promos's execution was spread abroad, and by the tongue of a clown[73] was blown into Andrugio's ears, who till then lived like an outlaw in the desert woods. But upon these news, covertly in the habit[74] of an hermit, by the divine motion of the soul who directs us in things that be good and the flesh in actions of evil, Andrugio goes to see the death of his capital enemy. But on the other part,[75] regarding the sorrow of his sister, he wished him life as a friend.

To conclude, as well to give terror to the lewd as comfort to his good subjects, the King personally came to see the execution of Promos; who, guarded with officers and strengthened with the comfortable persuasions of his ghostly fathers[76] (among whom Andrugio was), meekly offered his life as a satisfaction for his offenses—which were many more than the law took knowledge of. And yet, to say the truth, such was his repentance as the multitude did both forgive and pity him. Yea, the King wondered that his life was governed with no more virtue, considering the grace he showed at his death.

Andrugio, beholding this ruthful spectacle, was so overcome with love towards his sister as, to give her comfort, he frankly consented anew to imperil his own life. And following this resolution, in his hermit's weed upon his knees he humbly desired the King to give him leave to speak. The King graciously granted him audience. Whereupon quoth he: "Regarded[77] sovereign, if law may possibly be satisfied, Promos's true repentance meriteth pardon."

"Good father," quoth the King, "he cannot live and the law satisfied, unless by miracle Andrugio be revived."

"Then," quoth the hermit, "if Andrugio live, the law is satisfied and Promos discharged."

---

71 as . . . daily use as we see every day **72 post . . . back** i.e., travel quickly far and near. (Pegasus is a winged horse of Greek mythology.) **73 clown** rustic **74 habit** garb, dress **75 part** hand **76 ghostly fathers** spiritual fathers, priests or monks **77 Regarded** highly respected

"Ay," quoth the King, "if your prayer can revive the one, my mercy shall acquit the other."

"I humbly thank Your Majesty," quoth Andrugio, and discovering himself showed the providence of God and the means of his escape; and tendering his sister's comfort above his own safety, he prostrated himself at His Majesty's feet, humbly to obey the sentence of his pleasure.

The King, upon the report of this strange adventure, after good deliberation pardoned Promos, to keep his word and withal[78] holding an opinion that it was more beneficial for the citizens to be ruled by their old evil governor, new reformed, than to adventure upon a new whose behaviors were unknown. And to perfect Cassandra's joy, he pardoned her brother Andrugio, with condition that he should marry Polina. Thus, from between the teeth of danger every party was preserved and in the end established in their hearts' desire.

George Whetstone's *An Heptameron of Civil Discourses, Containing the Christmas Exercise of Sundry Well-Courted Gentlemen and Gentlewomen* was published in London in 1582. The present text is based on the original edition.

78 withal in addition

Further Reading

Bennett, Josephine Waters. *"Measure for Measure" as Royal Entertainment.* New York: Columbia Univ. Press, 1966. Bennett argues that Shakespeare carefully designed the play for its performance at court in December of 1604. Accordingly, she sees the play as a comedy enacting the spirit of the Christmas season and reflecting and reinforcing the political views the King had expressed in his recently reissued *Basilicon Doron.* Bennett even suggests that Shakespeare may have played the role of the Duke himself as part of his effort to recommend himself and his company to King James.

Berry, Ralph. *"Measure for Measure." Changing Styles in Shakespeare.* London: George Allen and Unwin, 1981. Berry examines recent productions of the play in relation to changing social and sexual attitudes. In 1950 Peter Brook's production presented a dignified and benevolent Duke successfully united with Isabella. Contrastingly, in the 1960s the emerging feminism and distrust of authority figures required a shift to productions that portrayed the Duke as manipulative and Isabella as ambivalent (and sometimes horrified) at the prospect of marrying him. Since the late 1970s, however, productions seem to be moving toward a greater dramatic and political balance, responding fully to the ambiguities of the play text.

Chambers, R. W. "The Jacobean Shakespeare and *Measure for Measure." Proceedings of the British Academy* 23 (1938 for 1937): 135–192. Rpt. in *Shakespeare, the Comedies: A Collection of Critical Essays,* ed. Kenneth Muir. Englewood Cliffs, N.J.: Prentice-Hall, 1965. Chambers defends *Measure for Measure* against critics who find Isabella uncharitable and the play bitter or cynical. When viewed in the historical context of Renaissance Christian thought, he argues, the play's characters and action are coherent and comprehensible. The play affirms the central values of Christianity: repentance, forgiveness, mercy, and the paradoxical rewards of adversity.

Coleridge, Samuel Taylor. *"Measure for Measure." Coleridge's Writings on Shakespeare,* ed. Terence Hawkes. New York: G. P. Putnam's Sons, 1959. Anticipating the modern emphasis upon the disturbing qualities of the comic action, Coleridge finds *Measure for Measure* "the most painful—say rather, the only painful" work of Shakespeare. He is troubled by the conjunction of its comic and tragic aspects, and he finds Angelo's pardon and marriage not merely baffling to "the strong indignant claim of justice" but "likewise degrading to the character of woman."

Dollimore, Jonathan. "Transgression and Surveillance in *Measure for Measure.*" In *Political Shakespeare: New Essays in Cultural Materialism,* ed. Jonathan Dollimore and Alan Sinfield. Ithaca, N.Y., and London: Cornell Univ. Press, 1985. Dollimore argues that the play's concern with sexual transgression reflects political rather than ethical considerations. The effort to control sexual license is revealed to be part of a deeper cultural anxiety about control of the lower classes. The crisis in Vienna is attributed to unregulated desire, but the play discloses that this desire, rather than undermining government control, in fact permits the legitimation of its authority.

Frye, Northrop. "The Reversal of Action." *The Myth of Deliverance: Reflections on Shakespeare's Problem Comedies.* Toronto: Univ. of Toronto Press, 1983. In a stimulating analysis of dramatic form and its relation to social experience in the so-called problem comedies, Frye focuses on the remarkable shift midway through *Measure for Measure* from a tragic to a comic action. In containing (instead of avoiding) tragic aspects of experience through this reversal, the comedy satisfies our desire for a "myth of deliverance"—a triumph of love over law, and the release of energies that permit reconciliation and renewal.

Gless, Darryl J. *"Measure for Measure," the Law, and the Convent.* Princeton, N.J.: Princeton Univ. Press, 1979. Gless explores the intellectual contexts invoked by the play's language and action. In his analysis of the play's legal and theological concerns, Isabella and Claudio, no less than Angelo, appear as examples of the necessary spiritual depravity of fallen humanity who are, however, finally redeemed by the working of a benign Providence through the agency of the Duke.

Hawkins, Harriett. " 'They That Have Power to Hurt and Will Do None': Tragic Facts and Comic Fictions in *Mea-*

sure for Measure." *Likenesses of Truth in Elizabethan and Restoration Drama.* Oxford: Oxford Univ. Press, 1972. The play for Hawkins is a failure, though a magnificent one. The conclusion never satisfies the tragic expectations aroused by the powerful and emotionally gripping first half of the play. When Shakespeare, through the omniscient Duke, initiates an artificial comic resolution, the audience, Hawkins argues, feels cheated and is left with the conviction that the yoking of tragic and comic action results in irreconcilable contradictions.

Hazlitt, William. *"Measure for Measure." Characters of Shakespear's Plays.* London, 1817. Hazlitt finds the play to be "as full of genius as it is of wisdom," but admits that it does not allow an audience to admire its characters: "our sympathies are repulsed and defeated in all directions." Even the Duke, Hazlitt finds (anticipating much recent criticism), is "more absorbed in his own plots and gravity than anxious for the welfare of the state."

Hunter, Robert Grams. *"Measure for Measure." Shakespeare and the Comedy of Forgiveness.* New York: Columbia Univ. Press, 1965. *Measure for Measure,* Hunter finds, offers a secular version of the pattern of moral regeneration in the medieval drama. Three times in the play someone stands caught between the conflicting claims of Mercy and Justice, and the comic action of the play, like that of its sacred prototypes, insists upon the rejection of self-righteousness in favor of a generous recognition of human weakness. In *Measure for Measure* only charity permits a solution to the complex problems of sexual morality explored in the play.

Kirsch, Arthur. *"Measure for Measure." Shakespeare and the Experience of Love.* Cambridge: Cambridge Univ. Press, 1981. Emphasizing the psychological and theological assumptions that Elizabethans would have brought to the theater, Kirsch argues that *Measure for Measure* explores the paradoxical conditions of Christian experience. Though the play emphasizes the sinfulness of fallen humanity, the grace offered at the play's conclusion appropriately completes the pattern of the fortunate fall that the play enacts; and for Kirsch, what the Duke's "play" becomes for the characters onstage—a process leading to self-knowledge and a recognition of what it means to be mortal—is mirrored in the audience's own experience of Shakespeare's tragicomic play.

Knight, G. Wilson. *"Measure for Measure and the Gospels."* *The Wheel of Fire: Interpretations of Shakespeare's Tragedy*, 1930. 4th rev. ed. London: Methuen, 1949. Knight invites us to read *Measure for Measure* as a Christian parable, an allegorical and symbolic representation of the Gospel's injunction that man, as sinner, is unfit to stand in judgment of other men. The Duke, for Knight, is a figure of Christ's merciful authority, embodying the Christian ethic at the center of the play.

Leavis, F. R. "The Greatness of *Measure for Measure.*" *The Common Pursuit*. London: Chatto and Windus, 1952. Leavis challenges the critical view that the play is problematic and morbidly pessimistic. He proposes instead that in balancing the need for social order against the New Testament injunction "Judge not, that ye be not judged," Shakespeare achieves a delicate complexity of attitudes toward justice and sexuality that is the measure of the play's coherence, and not an indication, as many critics have maintained, of Shakespeare's own moral uncertainty.

Miles, Rosalind. *The Problem of "Measure for Measure."* New York: Barnes and Noble, 1976. In the first half of her book Miles provides a valuable overview of the play's fate at the hands of critics, actors, illustrators, and imitators; its critical history suggests how susceptible has been the interpretation of the play to shifts in taste and morality. Miles then locates Shakespeare's achievement within the context of the drama of his age, by focusing on the play's use of dramatic conventions, especially its use of disguisings, stock character types, and the bed trick. She concludes that Shakespeare never fully assimilates and transcends his models and that the result, though always intellectually provocative, is something less than a total dramatic success.

Schanzer, Ernest. *"Measure for Measure."* *The Problem Plays of Shakespeare: A Study of "Julius Caesar," "Measure for Measure," and "Antony and Cleopatra."* New York: Schocken, 1963. Like Shakespeare's other problem plays, *Measure for Measure* deals with moral issues (here, justice and mercy) that the dramatist presents in such a way as to make us unsure of our moral bearings. Schanzer's analysis focuses on how these ethical conflicts—both personal and political—are embodied in Shakespeare's complex characters, and how Shakespeare shapes our moral response to character and action in the play.

Stead, C. K., ed. Shakespeare, "Measure for Measure": A Casebook. London: Macmillan, 1971. Stead divides his collection of essays into three sections. The first contains selections from early critics of the play (including Coleridge and Hazlitt; see above). The second provides discussions of the play's editorial and stage history. The third offers a selection of modern critical essays (including those by Knight and Schanzer; see above).

Stevenson, David L. The Achievement of Shakespeare's "Measure for Measure." Ithaca, N.Y.: Cornell Univ. Press, 1966. Stevenson's book offers a careful reading of the play, concluding that Measure for Measure is Shakespeare's greatest and most ingeniously constructed comedy. Its ironies, reversals, and resolution lead Stevenson to liken its structure to that of a poem by John Donne. This surface structure, he argues, serves to "unlock" deeper levels of awareness of the human condition and of the inevitability of moral paradox. Stevenson includes in an appendix a revision of an earlier historical study of the impact on the play of King James I and his political doctrine.

Wheeler, Richard P. "Vincentio and the Sins of Others: The Expense of Spirit in Measure for Measure." Shakespeare's Development and the Problem Comedies. Berkeley, Los Angeles, and London: Univ. of California Press, 1981. For Wheeler, Measure for Measure possesses a disturbing power derived from the psychological complexity of the experience of its protagonists, something we are more accustomed to discovering in Shakespeare's tragedies. The providential and comic ending does not clarify or resolve the inner conflicts of the characters. The tension between sexuality and moral order remains unresolved, and the unsatisfying marriage of the Duke and Isabella "is the appropriate barren conclusion" to a problematic play that exposes the artificiality of the comic form.

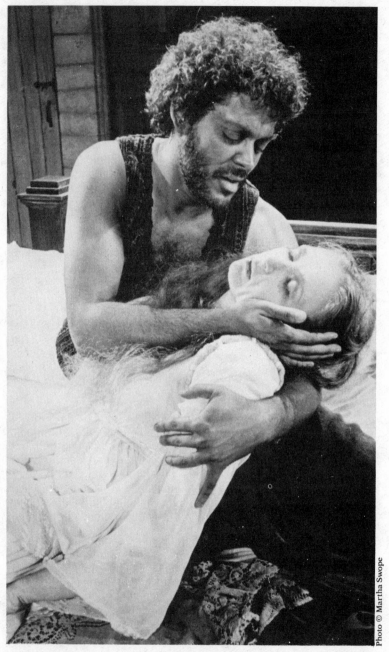

From the 1979 New York Shakespeare Festival production of *Othello*, with Raul Julia as Othello and Frances Conroy as Desdemona, directed by Wilford Leach at the Delacorte Theater in Central Park.

—OTHELLO—

OTHELLO

Foreword

Othello is filled with extraordinary characters and speeches. There's Othello himself, with his blind and fatal trust in the wrong people. There's the remarkably strong Desdemona, whose defiance of her father to marry Othello would have been exceptional for that time. Lieutenant Cassio plays a vital role as the instrument employed by Iago to feed Othello's jealousy by winning Desdemona's sympathy.

And of course, Iago is Shakespeare's ultimate villain, that fiendishly smooth serpent of a man. I see him as a graceful, slender, elegant type, sophisticated, and, like Richard III, totally devoid of any moral sense. Possessed of that fine-tuned awareness of other people's weaknesses that psychopathic people often have, Iago knows precisely where to prick Othello. Slowly and surely, he moves in for the kill; we marvel at his finesse and subtlety as we watch.

How he does it—and not why—is what makes the play interesting. Iago himself gives several reasons for his hatred of the Moor—Iago wasn't promoted, he suspects Othello of sleeping with his wife, he loves Othello's wife Desdemona—but in the end none of these really account for what he does. He has the capacity to create the right circumstances, and then he makes them work for his purposes.

To all of these characters Shakespeare brings his amazing powers of perception as he examines a variety of human natures. We recognize Othello, or Desdemona, or Cassio, because we've seen them recreated countless times in ourselves and in other people—people who are jealous, or unfairly accused, or unwitting victims of someone else's cruelty. There's nothing in Shakespeare that isn't within the realm of human possibility. His characters aren't false, soap opera versions of real people; they *are* real people.

As in all of his plays, Shakespeare wrote some extraordinary speeches for *Othello*. Cassio's heartbroken outcry in Act 2, scene 3, about his reputation—in contrast to Falstaff's disdaining of "honor" as a mere word—is one example. Othello's explanation to the Venetian senators of how he and Desdemona fell in love, as he told her the story of his life, is gorgeously eloquent:

> She thanked me,
> And bade me, if I had a friend that loved her,
> I should but teach him how to tell my story
> And that would woo her. Upon this hint I spake.
> She loved me for the dangers I had passed,
> And I loved her that she did pity them.

The frank, surprisingly contemporary discussion Desdemona and Emilia have about marriage and infidelity, in Act 4, scene 3, has always been a favorite of mine.

DESDEMONA
　　Dost thou in conscience think—tell me, Emilia—
　　That there be women do abuse their husbands
　　In such gross kind?
EMILIA　　　　　　　There be some such, no question.
DESDEMONA
　　Wouldst thou do such a deed for all the world?
EMILIA
　　Why, would not you?
DESDEMONA　　　　　　No, by this heavenly light!
EMILIA
　　Nor I neither by this heavenly light;
　　I might do 't as well i' the dark.
DESDEMONA
　　Wouldst thou do such a deed for all the world?
EMILIA
　　The world's a huge thing. It is a great price
　　For a small vice.
DESDEMONA
　　Good troth, I think thou wouldst not.

Throughout this scene, Emilia's worldliness is contrasted to Desdemona's utter innocence and faith, which Shakespeare deliberately emphasizes shortly before Othello comes in to murder her. It's an ingenious dramatic prelude to the crime.

Othello's murder of Desdemona is one of Shakespeare's great scenes, though it can cause a slight problem for the director, who has to figure out how Desdemona can speak after she's been throttled. If not handled gingerly, this can easily lead to laughter, which will obviously destroy the delicate pathos of the scene. Nineteenth-century producers often solved the problem by having Othello stab Desdemona with a dagger instead of smothering her, but I consider that a coward's way out.

In a moving conclusion to the tragedy, before he takes his own life, Othello utters the poignant speech that begins, "Soft you; a word or two before you go":

> I pray you, in your letters,
> When you shall these unlucky deeds relate,
> Speak of me as I am; nothing extenuate,
> Nor set down aught in malice. Then must you speak
> Of one that loved not wisely but too well.

Othello is such a rich play, with its characters drawn straight from life and its array of gorgeous speeches, that it deserves to be read and performed over and over—as does all of Shakespeare.

Joseph Papp

Joseph Papp gratefully acknowledges the help of Elizabeth Kirkland in preparing this Foreword.

Introduction

Othello differs in several respects from the other three major Shakespearean tragedies with which it is usually ranked. Written seemingly about the time of its performance at court by the King's men (Shakespeare's acting company) on November 1, 1604, after *Hamlet* (c. 1599–1601) and before *King Lear* (c. 1605) and *Macbeth* (c. 1606–1607), *Othello* shares with these other plays a fascination with evil in its most virulent and universal aspect. These plays study the devastating effects of ambitious pride, ingratitude, wrath, jealousy, and vengeful hate—the deadly sins of the spirit—with only a passing interest in the political strife to which Shakespeare's Roman or classical tragedies are generally devoted. Of the four, *Othello* is the most concentrated upon one particular evil. The action concerns sexual jealousy, and although human sinfulness is such that jealousy ceaselessly touches on other forms of depravity, the center of interest always returns in *Othello* to the destruction of a love through jealousy. *Othello* is a tragic portrait of a marriage. The protagonist is not a king or prince, as in the tragedies already mentioned, but a general recently married. There are no supernatural visitations as in *Hamlet* and *Macbeth*. Ideas of divine justice, while essential to *Othello*'s portrayal of a battle between good and evil for the allegiance of the protagonist, do not encompass the wide sweep of *King Lear;* nor do we find here the same broad indictment of humanity. Social order is not seriously shaken by Othello's tragedy. The fair-minded Duke of Venice remains firmly in control, and his deputy Lodovico oversees a just conclusion on Cyprus.

By the same token, *Othello* does not offer the remorseless questioning about man's relationship to the cosmos that we find in *King Lear, Hamlet,* and *Macbeth*. The battle of good and evil is of course cosmic, but in *Othello* that battle is realized through a taut narrative of jealousy and murder. Its poetic images are accordingly focused to a large extent on the natural world. One cluster of images is domestic and animal, having to do with goats, monkeys, wolves, baboons, guinea hens, wildcats, spiders, flies, asses, dogs, copulating horses and sheep, serpents, and toads; other images, more wide-ranging in scope, include green-eyed monsters, devils, blackness, poisons, money purses, tarnished jewels, music untuned, and light extinguished. The story is immediate and direct, retaining the sensational atmosphere of its Italian prose source by Giovanni Baptista Giraldi Cinthio, in his *Hecatommithi* of 1565 (translated into French in 1584). Events move even more swiftly than in Cinthio, for Shakespeare has compressed the story into two or three nights and days (albeit with an intervening sea journey and with an elastic use of stage time to allow for the maturing of long-term plans, as when we learn that Iago has begged Emilia "a hundred times" to steal Desdemona's handkerchief, or that Iago has accused Cassio of making love to Desdemona "a thousand times"). *Othello* does not have a fully developed double plot as in *King Lear* or a comparatively large group of characters serving as foils to the protagonist as in *Hamlet*. *Othello*'s cast is small and the plot is concentrated to an unusual degree on Othello, Desdemona, and Iago. What *Othello* may lose in breadth it gains in dramatic intensity.

Daringly, Shakespeare opens this tragedy of love not with a direct and sympathetic portrayal of the lovers themselves, but with a scene of vicious insinuation about their marriage. The images employed by Iago to describe the coupling of Othello and Desdemona are revoltingly animalistic, sodomistic. "Even now, now, very now, an old black ram / Is tupping your white ewe," he taunts Desdemona's father Brabantio. ("Tupping" is a word used specifically for the copulating of sheep.) "You'll have your daughter covered with a Barbary horse; you'll have your nephews neigh to you"; "your daughter and the Moor are now making the beast with two backs"; "the devil will make a grandsire of you" (1.1.90–93, 113–120). This degraded view reduces the marriage to one of utter carnality, with repeated emphasis on the word "gross": Desdemona has yielded "to the gross clasps of a lascivious Moor," and has made "a gross revolt" against her family and society (ll. 129, 137). Iago's second theme, one that is habitual with him, is money. "What ho, Brabantio! Thieves, thieves, thieves! / Look to your house, your daughter, and your bags!" (ll. 81–82). The implication is of a sinister bond between thievery in sex and thievery in gold. Sex and money are both commodities to be protected by watchful fathers against libidinous and opportunistic children.

We as audience make plentiful allowance for Iago's bias in all this, since he has admitted to Roderigo his knavery and resentment of Othello. Even so, the carnal vision of love we confront is calculatedly disturbing, because it seems so equated with a pejorative image of blackness. Othello is unquestionably a black man, referred to disparagingly by his detractors as the "thick-lips," with a "sooty bosom" (1.1.68; 1.2.71); Elizabethan usage applied the term "Moor" to Africans without attempting to distinguish between Arabian and Negroid peoples. From the ugly start of the play, Othello and Desdemona have to prove the worth of their love in the face of preset attitudes against miscegenation. Brabantio takes refuge in the thought that Othello must have bewitched Desdemona. His basic assumption—one to be echoed later by Iago and by Othello himself—is that miscegenation is unnatural by definition. In confronting and accusing Othello he repeatedly appeals "to all things of sense" (that is, to common sense) and asks if it is not "gross in sense" (self-evident) that Othello has practiced magic on her, since nothing else could prompt human nature so to leave its natural path. "For nature so preposterously to err, / Being not deficient, blind, or lame of sense, / Sans witchcraft could not" (1.2.65, 73; 1.3.64–66). We as audience do not endorse Brabantio's view and recognize in him the type of imperious father who conventionally opposes romantic love. It is sadly ironic that he should now prefer Roderigo as a son-in-law, evidently concluding that any white Venetian would be preferable to the prince of blacks. Still, Brabantio has been hospitable to the Moor and trusting of his daughter. He is a sorrowful rather than ridiculous figure, and the charge he levels at the married pair, however much based on a priori assumptions of what is "natural" in human behavior, remains to be answered.

After all, we find ourselves wondering, what did attract Othello and Desdemona to each other? Even though he certainly did not use witchcraft, may Othello not have employed a subtler kind of enchantment in the exotic character of his travels among "the Cannibals that each other eat, / The Anthropophagi, and men whose heads / Do grow beneath their shoulders" (1.3.145–147)? These "passing strange" events fascinate Desdemona as they do everyone including the Duke of Venice ("I think this tale would win my daughter too"). Othello has not practiced unfairly on her—"This only is the witchcraft I have used" (ll. 162, 173, 171). Yet may he not represent for Desdemona a radical novelty, being a man at once less devious and more mysterious than the dissolute Venetian swaggerers such as Roderigo and the "wealthy curlèd darlings of our nation" (1.2.69) who follow her about? Was her deceiving of her father by means of the elopement a protest, an escape from conventionality? Why has she been attracted to a man so much older than herself? For his part, Othello gives the impression of being inexperienced with women, at least of Desdemona's rank and complexion, and is both intrigued and flattered by her attentions. "She loved me for the dangers I had passed, / And I loved her that she did pity them" (1.3.169–170). Desdemona fulfills a place in Othello's view of himself. Does she also represent status for him in Venetian society, where he has been employed as a military commander but treated nonetheless as something of an alien?

These subtle but impertinent ways of doubting the motivations of Othello and Desdemona are thrust upon us by the play's opening and are later crucial to Iago's strategy of breeding mistrust. Just as important, however, these insinuations are refuted by Othello and especially by Desdemona. Whatever others may think, she never gives the slightest indication of regarding her husband as different or exotic because he is black and old. In fact the images of blackness and age are significantly reversed during the play's early scenes. Othello's blackness, like that of the natives dwelling in heathen lands, could betoken to Elizabethan audiences an innocent proneness to accept Christianity, and Othello is one who has already embraced the Christian faith. His first appearance onstage, when he confronts a party of torch-bearing men coming to arrest him and bids his followers sheathe their swords, is sufficiently reminiscent of Christ's arrest in the Garden of Gethsemane to convey a fleeting comparison between Othello and the Christian God whose charity and forbearance he seeks to emulate. Othello's blackness may be used in part as an emblem of fallen man, but so are we all fallen. His age similarly strengthens our impression of his wisdom, restraint, leadership. Any suggestions of comic sexual infidelity in the marriage of an old man and an attractive young bride are confuted by what we see in Desdemona's chaste yet sensual regard for the good man she has chosen.

Desdemona is utterly fond of Othello, admiring, and faithful. We believe her when she says that she does not even know what it means to be unfaithful; the word "whore" is not in her vocabulary. She is defenseless against the charges brought against her because she does not even comprehend them, cannot believe that anyone would imagine such things. Her love, both erotic and chaste, is of that transcendent wholesomeness common to several late Shakespearean heroines such as Cordelia in *King Lear* and Hermione in *The Winter's Tale*. Her "preferring" Othello to her father, like Cordelia's placing her duty to a husband before that to a father, is not ungrateful but natural and proper. And Othello, however much he may regard Desdemona as an extension of himself (he calls her "my fair warrior"), does cherish Desdemona as she deserves. "I cannot speak enough of this content," he exclaims when he rejoins her on Cyprus. "It stops me here; it is too much of joy" (2.1.181, 196–197). The passionate intensity of his love prepares the way for his tragedy, for he knows only too well that "when I love thee not, / Chaos is come again" (3.3.99–100). Iago speaks truly when he observes that Othello "Is of a constant, loving, noble nature" (2.1.290). Othello's tragedy is not that he is easily duped, but that his strong faith can be destroyed at such terrible cost. Othello never forgets how much he is losing. The threat to his love is not an initial lack of wholesomeness, but rather the insidious assumption that Desdemona cannot love him because such a love is unnatural. The fear of being unlovable exists in Othello's mind, but the human instrument of this vicious gospel is Iago.

Iago belongs to a select group of villains in Shakespeare who, while plausibly motivated in human terms, also take delight in evil for its own sake: Aaron the Moor in *Titus Andronicus*, Richard III, Don John in *Much Ado*, Iago, Edmund in *King Lear*. They are not, like Macbeth or like Claudius in *Hamlet*, men driven by ambition to commit crimes they clearly recognize to be wrong. Although Edmund does belatedly try to make amends, these villains are essentially conscienceless, sinister, and amused at their own cunning. They are related to one another by a stage metaphor of personified evil derived from the Vice of the morality play, whose typical role is to win the Mankind figure away from virtue and to corrupt him with worldly enticements. Like that engaging tempter, Shakespeare's villains in these plays take the audience into their confidence, boast in soliloquy of their cleverness, exult in the triumph of evil, and improvise plans with daring and resourcefulness. They are all superb actors, deceiving virtually every character onstage until late in the action with their protean and hypocritical display. They take pleasure in this "sport" and amaze us by their virtuosity. The role is paradoxically comic in its use of ingenious and resourceful deception, although it is the grim and ironic comedy of vice. We know that we are to condemn morally even while we applaud the skill.

The tradition of vice comedy may best explain a puzzling feature of Iago, noted long ago and memorably phrased by Samuel Taylor Coleridge as "the motive-hunting of motiveless malignity." Iago does offer plausible motives for what he does. Despite his resemblance to the morality Vice, he is no allegorized abstraction but an ensign in the army, a junior field officer who hates being outranked by a theoretician or staff officer. As an old-school professional he also resents that he has not been promoted on the basis of seniority, the "old gradation" (1.1.38). Even his efforts at using influence with Othello have come to naught, and Iago can scarcely be blamed for supposing that Cassio's friendship with Othello has won him special favor. Thus Iago has reason to plot against Cassio as well as Othello. Nevertheless a further dimension is needed to explain the gloating, the utter lack of moral reflection, the concentration on destroying Desdemona (who has not wronged Iago), the absorption in ingenious methods of plotting, the finesse and the style. Hatred precedes any plausible motive in Iago, and ultimately does not depend on psychological causality. Probably the tradition of the stage Machiavel (another type of gloating villain based on stereotyped attitudes toward the heretical political ideas of Niccolò Machiavelli), as in

Marlowe's *Jew of Malta,* adds an ingredient; this tradition was readily assimilated with that of the Vice.

Iago's machinations yield him both "sport" and "profit" (1.3.387); that is, he enjoys his evildoing, although he is also driven by a motive. This Vice-like behavior in human garb creates a restless sense of a dark metaphysical reality lying behind his visible exterior. Even his stated motives do not always make sense. When in an outburst of hatred he soliloquizes that "I hate the Moor; / And it is thought abroad that twixt my sheets / He's done my office," Iago goes on to concede the unlikelihood of this charge. "I know not if 't be true; / But I, for mere suspicion in that kind, / Will do as if for surety" (ll. 387–391). The charge is so absurd, in fact, that we have to look into Iago himself for the origin of this jealous paranoia. The answer may be partly emblematic: as the embodiment and genius of sexual jealousy, Iago suffers with ironic appropriateness from the evil he preaches, and without external cause. Emilia understands that jealousy is not a rational affliction but a self-induced disease of the mind. Jealous persons, she tells Desdemona, "are not ever jealous for the cause, / But jealous for they're jealous. It is a monster / Begot upon itself, born on itself" (3.4.161–163). Iago's own testimonial bears this out, for his jealousy is at once wholly irrational and agonizingly self-destructive. "I do suspect the lusty Moor / Hath leaped into my seat, the thought whereof / Doth, like a poisonous mineral, gnaw my innards" (2.1.296–298). In light of this nightmare, we can see that even his seemingly plausible resentment of Cassio's promotion is jealous envy. The "daily beauty" in Cassio's life makes Iago feel "ugly" by comparison (5.1.19–20), engendering in Iago a profound sense of lack of worth from which he can temporarily find relief only by reducing Othello and others to his own miserable condition. He is adept at provoking self-hatred in others because he suffers from it himself.

Othello comes at last to regard Iago as a "demi-devil" who has tempted Othello to damn himself "beneath all depth in hell"; Lodovico speaks of Iago in the closing lines of the play as a "hellish villain" (5.2.309, 142, 379); and Iago himself boasts that "When devils will the blackest sins put on, / They do suggest at first with heavenly shows, / As I do now" (2.3.345–347). Iago thus bears some affinity to both Vice and devil, suggesting his relationship both to Othello's inner temptation and to a preexistent evil force in the universe itself. Conversely, Desdemona is in Emilia's words an "angel," purely chaste, "So come my soul to bliss as I speak true" (5.2.134, 259). When Desdemona lands on Cyprus, she is greeted in words that echo the *Ave Maria:* "Hail to thee, lady! And the grace of heaven . . . Enwheel thee round!" (2.1.87–89). These images introduce metaphorically a conflict of good and evil in which Othello, typical of fallen man, has chosen evil and destroyed the good at the prompting of a diabolical counselor. Again we see the heritage of the morality play, especially of the later morality in which the Mankind figure was sometimes damned rather than saved. Even so, to allegorize *Othello* is to obscure and misread its clash of human passion. In fact, we see that the impulse to reduce human complexity to simplistic moral absolutes is a fatal weakness in Othello; by insisting on viewing Desdemona as a type or abstraction, he loses sight of her wonderful humanity. The theological issue of salvation or damnation is not relevant in dramatic terms; the play is not a homily on the dangers of jealousy. The metaphysical dimensions of a homiletic tradition are transmuted into human drama. Acknowledging these limitations, we can notwithstanding see a spiritual analogy in Iago's devil-like method of undoing his victims.

His trick resembles that of the similarly mischief-making Don John in *Much Ado about Nothing:* an optical illusion by which the blameless heroine is impugned as an adulteress. The concealed Othello must watch Cassio boasting of sexual triumphs and believe he is talking about Desdemona. Like the devil, Iago is given power over men's frail senses, especially the eyes. He can create illusions to induce Othello to see what Iago wants him to see, as Don John does with Claudio, but Othello's acceptance of the lie must be his own responsibility, a failure of his corrupted will. Iago practices on Othello with an a priori logic used before on Brabantio and Roderigo, urging the proneness of all mortals to sin and the unnaturalness of a black-white marriage. All women have appetites; Desdemona is a woman; hence Desdemona has appetites. "The wine she drinks is made of grapes," he scoffs to Roderigo. "If she had been blessed, she would never have loved the Moor" (2.1.253–255). She is a Venetian, and "In Venice they do let God see the pranks / They dare not show their husbands" (3.3.216–217). Therefore she too is a hypocrite; "She did deceive her father" (l. 220). Most of all, it stands to reason that she must long for a man of her own race. As Iago succeeds in getting Othello to ponder: "And yet, how nature erring from itself—" (l. 243). This proposition that Nature teaches all persons, including Desdemona, to seek a harmonious matching of "clime, complexion, and degree" strikes a responsive chord in Othello, since he knows that he is black and alien. "Haply, for I am black / And have not those soft parts of conversation / That chamberers have." Then, too, he is sensitive that he is considerably older than she, "declined / Into the vale of years" (ll. 246, 279–282), "the young affects / In me defunct" (1.3.266–267). And so, if one must conclude from the preceding that Desdemona will seek a lover, the only question is who. "This granted—as it is a most pregnant and unforced position—who stands so eminent in the degree of this fortune as Cassio does?" (2.1.237–239). Once Othello has accepted this syllogistic sequence of proofs, specious not through any lapse in logic but because the axiomatic assumptions about human nature are degraded and do not apply to Desdemona, Othello has arrived at an unshakable conclusion to which all subsequent evidence must be forced as "a foregone conclusion." "Villain, be sure thou prove my love a whore," he commissions Iago (3.3.443, 375). Desdemona's innocent pleading for Cassio only makes things look worse. Cassio's reputed muttering while asleep, like the handkerchief seen in his possession or his giddy talk about his mistress Bianca, "speaks against her [Desdemona] with the other proofs" (l. 456).

How has Othello fallen so far in so short a time? His bliss with Desdemona as they are reunited on Cyprus knows no limit. These two persons represent married love at its very best, erotic and spiritual, she enhancing his manliness, he cherishing her beauty and virtue. His blackness and age are positive images in him, despite earlier insinuations to the contrary. He is a man of public worthiness, of command, of self-assurance. Desdemona is the most domestic of Shakespeare's tragic heroines, even while she is also representative of so much that is transcendent. Husband and wife are bound happily in one of Shakespeare's few detailed portraits of serious commitment in marriage. What then gives way? We look at Iago for one important insight, but ultimately the cause must be in Othello himself. Arthur Kirsch has argued persuasively (in *Shakespeare and the Experience of Love*, 1981) that Othello's most grave failing is an insufficient regard for himself. It is in part an inability to counter the effects on him of a culture that regards him as an outsider; he is at last persuaded to see himself with the eyes of Venice, not just of Iago but of Brabantio (who gladly entertains Othello until he has the presumption to elope with Brabantio's white daughter) and others. The resulting destruction of self-regard is devastating. Othello's jealousy stems from a profound suspicion that others cannot love him because he does not deem himself lovable.

Othello has loved Desdemona as an extension of himself, and in his moments of greatest contentedness his marriage is sustained by an idealized vision of Desdemona serving as the object of his exalted romantic passion. When he destroys Desdemona, as he realizes with a terrible clarity, Othello destroys himself; the act is a prelude to his actual suicide. Iago's mode of temptation, then, is to persuade Othello to regard himself with the eyes of Venice, to accept the view that Othello is himself alien and that any woman who loves him does so perversely. In Othello's tainted state of mind, Desdemona's very sexuality becomes an unbearable threat to him, her warmth and devotion a "proof" of disloyalty. Othello's most tortured speeches (3.4.57–77, 4.2.49–66) reveal the extent to which he equates the seemingly betraying woman he has so depended on for happiness with his own mother, who gave Othello's father a handkerchief and threatened him with loss of her love if he should lose it. Othello has briefly learned and then forgotten the precious art of harmonizing erotic passion and spiritual love, and as these two great aims of love are driven apart in him, he comes to loathe and fear the sexuality that puts him so much in mind of his physical frailty and dependence on woman. The horror and pity of *Othello* rests above all in the spectacle of a love that was once so whole and noble made filthy by self-hatred.

The increasing surrender of Othello's judgment to passion can be measured in three successive trial scenes in the play: the entirely fair trial of Othello himself by the Venetian senate concerning the elopement, Othello's trial of Cassio for drinking and rioting (when, ominously, Othello's "blood begins my safer guides to rule"; 2.3.199), and finally the prejudged sentencing of Desdemona without any opportunity for her to defend herself. In a corollary decline, Othello falls from the Christian compassion of the opening scenes (he customarily confesses to heaven "the vices of my blood," 1.3.125) to the pagan savagery of his vengeful and ritualistic execution of his wife. "My heart is turned to stone" (4.1.182–183), he vows, and at the play's end he grievingly characterizes himself as a "base Indian" who "threw a pearl away / Richer than all his tribe" (5.2.357–358). (The First Folio reading of "Iudean" or "Judean" refers perhaps to Judas Iscariot or to Herod; most editors prefer the quarto reading of "Indian.") Iago knows that he must persuade Othello to sentence and execute Desdemona himself, for only by active commitment to evil will Othello damn himself. In nothing does Iago so resemble the devil as in his wish to see Othello destroy the innocence and goodness on which his happiness depends.

The fate of some of the lesser characters echoes that of Othello, for Iago's evil intent is to "enmesh them all" (2.3.356). Cassio in particular is, like Othello, an attractive man with a single but fatally vulnerable weakness, in his case a fleshly appetite for wine and women. For him, alternately idolizing and depreciating women as he does, the gap between spiritual and sensual love remains vast, but he is essentially good-natured and trustworthy. His seemingly genial flaws lead to disaster because they put him at the mercy of a remorseless enemy. Iago is, with fitting irony, the apostle of absolute self-control: "Our bodies are our gardens, to the which our wills are gardeners" (1.3.323–324). Thus, Cassio's tragedy is anything but a straightforward homily on the virtues of temperance. Similarly, Bianca is undone not through any simple cause-and-effect punishment of her sexual conduct—she is, after all, fond of Cassio and loyal to him, even if he will not marry her—but because Iago is able to turn appearances against her. With his usual appeal to a priori logic, he builds a case that she and Cassio are in cahoots: "I do suspect this trash / To be a party in this injury. . . . This is the fruits of whoring" (5.1.86–87, 118). Roderigo is another of Iago's victims, a contemptible one, led by the nose because he too has surrendered reason to passion. Emilia cannot escape Iago's evil influence and gives the handkerchief to him despite knowing its value for Desdemona. Flaws are magnified into disasters by a remorseless evil intelligence. Men must be ceaselessly circumspect; a good reputation is sooner lost than recovered. Emilia is a conventionally decent enough woman—she would be faithless in marriage, she tells Desdemona, only for a very high price—and yet her one small compromise with her conscience contributes to the murder of her mistress. Like Othello she offers atonement too late, by denouncing her husband. Desdemona is the only person in the play too good to be struck down through some inner flaw, which may explain why Iago is committed above all else to seeing that she be destroyed.

As a tragic hero, Othello obtains self-knowledge at a terrible price. He knows finally that what he has destroyed was ineffably good. The discovery is too late for him to make amends, and he dies by his own hand as atonement. The deaths of Othello and Desdemona are, in their separate ways, equally devastating: he is in part the victim of racism, though he nobly refuses to deny his own culpability, and she is the victim of sexism, lapsing sadly into the stereotypical role of passive and silent sufferer that has been demanded of her. Despite the loss, however, Othello's reaffirmation of faith in Desdemona's goodness undoes what the devil-like Iago had most hoped to achieve: the separation of Othello from a belief in goodness. In this important sense, Othello's self-knowledge is cathartic and a compensation for the terrible price he has paid. The very existence of a person as good as Desdemona gives the lie to Iago's creed that everyone has his or her price. She is the sacrificial victim who must die for Othello's loss of faith and, by dying, rekindle that faith. ("My life upon her faith!" Othello prophetically affirms, in response to her father's warning that she may deceive him [1.3.297].) She cannot restore him to himself, for self-hatred has done its ugly work, but she is the means by which he understands at last the chimerical and wantonly destructive nature of his jealousy. His greatness appears in his acknowledgment of this truth, and in the heroic struggle with which he has confronted an inner darkness we all share.

Othello
in Performance

To a remarkable extent, the history of *Othello* in performance is the history of lead actors in the roles of Othello and Iago. Desdemona occasionally captures attention, sometimes even Cassio, but the rest of the play is largely forgotten. Scenic effects are not essential. Props are at a minimum. Indeed, there are only thirteen speaking parts. The play onstage depends almost entirely on the personal magnetism of the leading player and one or two others. Small wonder that Othello's role has been coveted by most of the famous actors in every age.

Richard Burbage played Othello in Shakespeare's company, regularly at the Globe Theatre, and at court in 1604 and again in 1613. An elegy written upon Burbage's death in 1619 remembers his "grieved Moor" among his great roles. Thomas Killigrew, who obtained the rights to *Othello* after the Restoration, performed the play with his King's men at the Cockpit. Samuel Pepys saw this production on October 11, 1660, remarking in his diary: "a pretty lady that sat by me called out to see Desdemona smothered." Thomas Betterton played Othello with great intensity from 1683 to 1709, primarily after 1703 at the theater in Lincoln's Inn Fields, London. One contemporary witness testified that "his aspect was serious, venerable, and majestic." Barton Booth, James Quin, and Spranger Barry were the great Othellos after Betterton on the Restoration and eighteenth-century stage. Oddly, David Garrick was not successful in the role: he acted Othello in two seasons only, abandoning the part for Iago in 1746. Garrick's small, wiry body and his nervous emotional intensity did not match the age's preference for a heroic protagonist. John Philip Kemble first played Othello in 1785 and struggled through various productions until 1805, but had no better luck. Kemble failed because of what his biographer James Boaden has called the "philosophy in his bearing and reason in his rage." Audiences seemed to demand from Othello either the towering violent jealousy projected by Betterton or the grandeur and presence of Quin. Spranger Barry, combining something of both, was the most successful Othello of the century, fierce in his rage but so poignant in his grief that, as a reviewer noted, "the audience seemed to lose the energies of their hands, and could only thank him with their tears." Iago, played by Lacy Ryan, Colley Cibber, and Charles Macklin, among others, required melodramatic villainy, though Macklin also provided some real depth of characterization, naturalizing his performance so that (in Macklin's words) Iago's "seeming openness and concealed revenge" became a plausible, if terrifying, human response to the goodness surrounding him. Anne Bracegirdle and Susannah Cibber were the outstanding Desdemonas of the age, energetically asserting their innocence. The play was enormously popular throughout the period, no doubt because of the persuasive acting of its principals. It was staged in all but seven years of the entire eighteenth century.

The play was cut to center attention on its main figures and to enhance the tragic nobility of the protagonist. Bell's acting version of 1773 is representative of the tradition. It omits Othello's mention of anthropophagi, cannibals, and "antres vast," does away with the storm scene for the landing in Cyprus in Act 2, cuts the Clown scene (3.1) in the interests of classical unity and decorum, banishes Bianca for reasons of moral decency, takes away the scene in which Othello's jealousy is confirmed by seeing the handkerchief in Cassio's hand, and deprives Desdemona of her conversation with Emilia before her death. The death itself is accomplished by stabbing. What remains in the text is chiefly a series of lofty tragic scenes for Othello and Iago.

Othello in the nineteenth century belonged for the most part to Edmund Kean, Edwin Booth, and Tommaso Salvini; Samuel Phelps also succeeded in the role. Kean's Othello was the most celebrated, described by critic William Hazlitt as "the finest piece of acting in the world." Kean's appalling fury and final desolation moved audiences to tears. Booth describes his father as believing that "no mortal man could equal Kean in the rendering of Othello's despair and rage." Booth himself was a more noble and humane Othello, as in his production at Booth's Theatre in New York in 1869, but was perhaps more arresting in his portrayal of a gloating and demonic Iago, as at the Winter Garden Theatre in 1866. In 1881, Booth and Henry Irving appeared at London's Lyceum Theatre, alternating the roles of Othello and Iago, with Ellen Terry as Desdemona. The production was a great success, artistically and financially. Irving had played Othello only once before, in 1876, to little acclaim, and he had never played Iago. Still, he was the greatest English actor of his generation, and people flocked to see the collision of titans from England and America. As Othello, Irving could not match the power of Booth's brooding Moor. Irving's Iago, on the other hand, was more than a match for his rival, believably genial in public and savagely sardonic when alone. Yet Irving's success with Iago was not enough to compensate him for being overpowered in the role of Othello. Although the English critics applauded Irving, the measure of Booth's triumph is that Irving never again acted either part. The Italian actor Tommaso Salvini first appeared as Othello in New York at the Academy of Music in 1873 and two years later in London at the Theatre Royal, Drury Lane. His was a fiery, sensual Moor, powerful and dangerous. The theater critic William Winter, disgusted by Salvini's barbaric Othello, claimed that "only because of the excitement that it diffused throughout the nervous systems of the multitude, it possesses a worldwide renown." What Winter intended as a slight seems high praise indeed today.

Though William Charles Macready acted the part often in his career, first in 1814, he felt that he never achieved "the real pathos and terrible fury which belong to the character." Still, his Othello was powerful and dignified, and, in keeping with the attention to realistic detail for which Macready was famous, always correctly attired as a sixteenth-century Venetian officer. When, in 1816, Macready and Charles Mayne Young alternated in the two leading parts, Macready achieved greater success as Iago. Hazlitt remembered Young's Othello as "a great humming-top, and Macready, in Iago, like a mischievous boy whipping him." Samuel Phelps and Charles Fechter also acted Othello with something like Macready's dignity and restraint. Phelps alternated with Macready in the parts of Iago and Othello in 1839 at the Haymarket Theatre, with Helen Faucit as Desdemona. Once again, Macready achieved success with his

Iago, but Phelps's unfussy, gentle Othello, much to Macready's discomfort, carried the day. The *Weekly Dispatch* delightedly remarked: "He was of all things that which we have never witnessed since the death of Kean—natural." The *Sunbeam* proclaimed, even more enthusiastically, "we are now convinced that the Othello of Mr. Phelps is the Othello of Shakespeare." His productions at the Sadler's Wells Theatre, in fifteen of his eighteen years as manager, were great successes, and he continued alternating in the two male leads in seasons when he had another actor capable of performing both. Charles Fechter's Othello was more sentimental than Phelps's, intelligent and affectionate, perhaps better suited, as the *Morning Advertiser* put it, to be the hero of a "French melodrama" than of Shakespeare's agonizing tragedy.

In some remarkable way, the emotional intensity demanded in the playing of *Othello* seemed to encourage actors to carry their theatrical roles over into their private lives. Kean was correspondent in a notorious divorce trial in 1825. In 1833 Kean collapsed into the arms of his son Charles during a performance of *Othello* and died shortly thereafter. The American actor Edwin Forrest brought to his performance of Othello the experience of divorcing his wife for adultery only to be found guilty himself and ordered to pay alimony. Court appeals dragged on for years, leaving Forrest embittered and alienated. The nineteenth-century American black actor Ira Aldridge, who successfully played Othello and other tragic parts in Europe for four decades before his death in 1867, was married to a white woman. Stories such as these, at any rate, fed a popular conception of *Othello* as a shocking and sensational affair, one well suited to the savage fury and sensuality of Salvini's performance. The scene of Desdemona's murder in Salvini's rendition was especially violent, and the production took London by storm. The famous actresses of the age—Sarah Siddons, Anna Mowatt, most of all Ellen Terry—captured the sympathies of audiences by playing to the full the melodramatic role of womanly innocence traduced and overwhelmed.

Sensationalism of this kind is made for opera, and it is no coincidence that the *Othello* of the nineteenth-century stage gave rise to immortal operatic rendition. Gioachino

Rossini's *Otello* (1816) departs too widely from Shakespeare's text to allow meaningful comparison (he relied on Cinthio's story), but Giuseppe Verdi's great *Otello* (1887), the libretto by Arrigo Boito, is integrally a part of the stage history of Shakespeare's play. The omission of the first act in Venice, the concentration on the roles of Otello, Iago, and Desdemona, the ending with Otello's last kiss of his dead wife—all are comparable to those means used by actor-managers to focus the play on the intensely emotional confrontations of the tragic protagonists. Verdi eloquently interpreted the play as it was understood by his generation, and did so with such power that his operatic version remains a central formative influence in today's theater.

The twentieth century has not brought with it a major revision in the staging of *Othello*, in part perhaps because the play does not lend itself to topical appropriation as with the antiwar satire often applied to Shakespeare's histories or the disillusioning view of sex and politics often seen in productions of *Troilus and Cressida* or *Hamlet*. *Othello* does not easily adapt itself to Edwardian decor or the American frontier West, as in some productions of *All's Well That Ends Well* or *Much Ado about Nothing*. In most twentieth-century productions the text is more nearly restored to the original than in those of the previous century, and the balance of parts gives new visibility to Roderigo, Brabantio, Emilia, and Bianca, but the text was never as rearranged as it was for many other plays. Because *Othello* is a play written around a few major roles, the nineteenth century did not have to change a great deal to get what it wanted from this play.

Changes in perception of *Othello* in the twentieth century have accordingly focused on a few delicate and critical issues, most notably that of the relations of the races. For Paul Robeson, a black American actor, the central issue was not sexual jealousy but the granting of human dignity to blacks. Starring in a production with Peggy Ashcroft as Desdemona, Sybil Thorndike as Emilia, and Ralph Richardson as Roderigo at London's Savoy Theatre in 1930, Robeson brought together his personal convictions and professional ambitions in a way very different from that of Kean or Forrest. Earlier actors of Othello, excepting Ira Aldridge, had been whites who could choose to portray a black Othello or a more Arabian and Moorish Othello to suit their own acting styles. Robeson was black, a large man, sonorous of voice, commanding, magisterial. He was also a believer in a cause, and, although limited theatrically to this one role in which he must show violence and loss of emotional control (prejudices of the time did not permit him to play Iago as Booth, Kean, and Phelps had done), the very fact of his sharing the spotlight with Peggy Ashcroft (and later in 1943 with Jose Ferrer and Uta Hagen in Margaret Webster's production at the Shubert Theatre in New York) was in itself significant. He was a man of memorable dignity and presence, and his work opened the way for other blacks, especially Earle Hyman (New York, Jan Hus Auditorium, 1953, and Stratford, Connecticut, 1957), Moses Gunn (Stratford, Connecticut, 1970), and James Earl Jones (New York Shakespeare Festival, 1964, and Stratford, Connecticut, 1981), to succeed in the part. Robeson became a controversial figure and something of an outcast, whereas, when Jones played opposite Christopher Plummer in 1981 at Stratford, Connecticut (a production that in February of 1982 opened at New York's Winter Garden Theatre), his race no longer occasioned comment; Jones had by then already won considerable praise for his portrayal of King Lear.

Today, the role of Othello is available to any leading player, and has been acted by Ralph Richardson in Tyrone Guthrie's production at the Old Vic in 1938, with Laurence Olivier as Iago; by Richard Burton, again at the Old Vic, in 1956, alternating with John Neville in the parts of Othello and Iago; by Emrys James at Stratford-upon-Avon in 1971; by Raul Julia, as a passionate, tortured Othello in Wilford Leach's production for the New York Shakespeare Festival in 1979; by Anthony Hopkins, opposite Bob Hoskins's Iago, in Jonathan Miller's BBC television version in 1981; and by Ben Kingsley, who powerfully revealed the violence at the center of Othello's achieved calm, at Stratford-upon-Avon in 1985. Laurence Olivier played Othello with great success at the Old Vic for the newly established National Theatre in 1964, although he was less convincing in his film version of the production the next year, perhaps because the close-ups made too much of Oliver's West Indian mannerisms and appearance. With his virtuoso performance of an Othello both proud and self-dramatizing, Olivier demonstrated at least that the play remains what it always has been, the vehicle for an astonishing display of acting ability by one of the great actors of the age.

When we locate *Othello* on the Elizabethan stage, we see that the absence of scenery accentuates the focus on character; indeed, scenic effects have seldom played a big part in productions of this play. The Elizabethan actor needs to build the scene around him by his commanding presence and the magic of his words. Costuming and spatial arrangement are also important: in Act 1, scene 1, we know in the Elizabethan theater that we are before Brabantio's house when Desdemona's father appears in the gallery above, at his window, and then reemerges below in his nightgown *"with servants and torches."* Torches are repeatedly necessary in *Othello*, not to illuminate the stage but to signal nighttime. Theatrical signs of darkness are often intensified by violent action, as in the drinking on watch (2.3) or the killing of Roderigo and the wounding of Cassio (5.1). The latter scene, particularly, reveals how actors on the bare Elizabethan stage, in full daylight, convey a sense of darkness and dread: they grope about, look apprehensive, call for lights, and gradually come to understand what the audience, in its omniscience, has known all along.

Illusion-making of this sort is central to a play that is so concerned with deceptive appearances and overhearing. Iago is the master of illusion, and his dominance as a baleful kind of dramatist indicates how hard it is not to be deceived by show. We watch Roderigo, Othello, and indeed virtually everyone fall under the influence of his image-making ability. What are we as audience to believe? We are left in Act 5 with a stage image that focuses our attention on this problem of truth and reputation: Desdemona's bed. Thrust onstage or set in the discovery space at the rear of the stage for the play's final scene, it is a central stage property that tests the very nature of theatrical illusion. Desdemona lies slain within its bed curtains, while Emilia and others struggle to discover what has occurred. Othello, who has begun the scene believing he could snuff out the life of Desdemona as simply as snuffing out a candle, learns too late that Desdemona is not what he, in his diseased imagination, has pictured her to be. The final "tragic loading of this bed" leaves us with an unforgettable picture of Othello's failure, but also of the innocence that his doubt and Iago's slander cannot finally unsay.

—OTHELLO—

The Names of the Actors

OTHELLO, *the Moor*
BRABANTIO, [*a senator,*] *father to Desdemona*
CASSIO, *an honorable lieutenant* [*to Othello*]
IAGO, [*Othello's ancient,*] *a villain*
RODERIGO, *a gulled gentleman*
DUKE OF VENICE
SENATORS [*of Venice*]
MONTANO, *Governor of Cyprus*
GENTLEMEN *of Cyprus*
LODOVICO *and* GRATIANO, [*kinsmen to Brabantio,*] *two noble
    Venetians*
SAILORS
CLOWN

DESDEMONA, [*daughter to Brabantio and*] *wife to Othello*
EMILIA, *wife to Iago*
BIANCA, *a courtesan* [*and mistress to Cassio*]

[A MESSENGER
A HERALD
A MUSICIAN

Servants, Attendants, Officers, Senators, Musicians, Gentlemen

SCENE: *Venice; a seaport in Cyprus*]

1.1 *Enter Roderigo and Iago.*

RODERIGO
Tush, never tell me! I take it much unkindly   1
That thou, Iago, who hast had my purse
As if the strings were thine, shouldst know of this.   3
IAGO   'Sblood, but you'll not hear me.   4
If ever I did dream of such a matter,
Abhor me.
RODERIGO
Thou toldst me thou didst hold him in thy hate.
IAGO   Despise me
If I do not. Three great ones of the city,
In personal suit to make me his lieutenant,
Off-capped to him; and by the faith of man,   11
I know my price, I am worth no worse a place.
But he, as loving his own pride and purposes,
Evades them with a bombast circumstance   14
Horribly stuffed with epithets of war,   15
And, in conclusion,
Nonsuits my mediators. For, "Certes," says he,   17
"I have already chose my officer."
And what was he?
Forsooth, a great arithmetician,   20
One Michael Cassio, a Florentine,
A fellow almost damned in a fair wife,   22
That never set a squadron in the field
Nor the division of a battle knows   24
More than a spinster—unless the bookish theoric,   25
Wherein the togaed consuls can propose   26
As masterly as he. Mere prattle without practice

1.1. Location: Venice. A street.
1 never tell me don't talk to me   **3 this** i.e., Desdemona's elopement
4 'Sblood by His (Christ's) blood   **11 him** i.e., Othello   **14 bombast
circumstance** wordy evasion. (*Bombast* is cotton padding.)   **15 epithets
of war** military expressions   **17 Nonsuits** rejects the petition of.   **Certes**
certainly   **20 arithmetician** i.e., a man whose military knowledge is
merely theoretical, based on books of tactics   **22 A . . . wife** (Cassio
does not seem to be married, but his counterpart in Shakespeare's
source does have a woman in his house. See also 4.1.131.)   **24 division
of a battle** disposition of a military unit   **25 a spinster** i.e., a housewife,
one whose regular occupation is spinning.   **theoric** theory   **26 togaed**
wearing the toga.   **consuls** counselors, senators.   **propose** discuss

Is all his soldiership. But he, sir, had th' election;
And I, of whom his eyes had seen the proof   29
At Rhodes, at Cyprus, and on other grounds
Christened and heathen, must be beleed and calmed   31
By debitor and creditor. This countercaster,   32
He, in good time, must his lieutenant be,   33
And I—God bless the mark!—his Moorship's ancient.   34

RODERIGO
By heaven, I rather would have been his hangman.   35

IAGO
Why, there's no remedy. 'Tis the curse of service;
Preferment goes by letter and affection,   37
And not by old gradation, where each second   38
Stood heir to the first. Now, sir, be judge yourself
Whether I in any just term am affined   40
To love the Moor.

RODERIGO   I would not follow him, then.

IAGO   O sir, content you.   43
I follow him to serve my turn upon him.
We cannot all be masters, nor all masters
Cannot be truly followed. You shall mark   46
Many a duteous and knee-crooking knave
That, doting on his own obsequious bondage,
Wears out his time, much like his master's ass,
For naught but provender, and when he's old, cashiered. 50
Whip me such honest knaves. Others there are   51
Who, trimmed in forms and visages of duty,   52
Keep yet their hearts attending on themselves,
And, throwing but shows of service on their lords,

29 his i.e., Othello's   31 Christened i.e., Christian. beleed and calmed
left to leeward without wind, becalmed. (A sailing metaphor.)
32 debitor and creditor (A name for a system of bookkeeping, here used
as a contemptuous nickname for Cassio.)   countercaster i.e., bookkeeper, one who tallies with *counters* or metal disks. (Said contemptuously.)   33 in good time i.e., forsooth   34 God bless the mark (Perhaps
originally a formula to ward off evil; here an expression of impatience.)   ancient standard-bearer, ensign   35 his hangman the executioner of him   37 Preferment promotion.   letter and affection personal
influence and favoritism   38 old gradation step-by-step seniority, the
traditional way   40 term respect.   affined bound   43 content you don't
you worry about that   46 truly faithfully   50 cashiered dismissed from
service   51 Whip me whip, as far as I'm concerned   52 trimmed . . .
duty dressed up in the mere form and show of dutifulness

Do well thrive by them, and when they have lined their
   coats,   55
Do themselves homage. These fellows have some soul,   56
And such a one do I profess myself. For, sir,
It is as sure as you are Roderigo,
Were I the Moor I would not be Iago.   59
In following him, I follow but myself—
Heaven is my judge, not I for love and duty,
But seeming so for my peculiar end.   62
For when my outward action doth demonstrate
The native act and figure of my heart   64
In compliment extern, 'tis not long after   65
But I will wear my heart upon my sleeve
For daws to peck at. I am not what I am.   67

RODERIGO
What a full fortune does the thick-lips owe   68
If he can carry 't thus!

IAGO   Call up her father.   69
Rouse him, make after him, poison his delight,
Proclaim him in the streets; incense her kinsmen,
And, though he in a fertile climate dwell,   72
Plague him with flies. Though that his joy be joy,   73
Yet throw such changes of vexation on 't   74
As it may lose some color.   75

RODERIGO
Here is her father's house. I'll call aloud.

IAGO
Do, with like timorous accent and dire yell   77

---

55 lined their coats i.e., stuffed their purses   **56 Do themselves homage**
i.e., attend to self-interest solely   **59 Were . . . Iago** i.e., if I were able to
assume command I certainly would not choose to remain a subordi-
nate   **62 peculiar** particular, personal   **64 native** innate. **figure** shape,
intent   **65 compliment extern** outward show (conforming in this case to
the inner workings and intention of the heart)   **67 I am not what I am**
i.e., I am not one who wears his heart on his sleeve   **68 full** swelling.
thick-lips (Elizabethans often applied the term "Moor" to Negroes.)
owe own   **69 carry 't thus** carry this off   **72–73 though . . . flies** i.e.,
though he seems prosperous and happy now, vex him with misery
73 Though . . . be joy i.e., although he seems fortunate and happy.
(Repeats the idea of l. 72.)   **74 changes of vexation** vexing changes
75 As it may that may cause it to. **some color** i.e., some of its fresh
gloss   **77 timorous** frightening

As when, by night and negligence, the fire   78
Is spied in populous cities.

RODERIGO
What ho, Brabantio! Signor Brabantio, ho!

IAGO
Awake! What ho, Brabantio! Thieves, thieves, thieves!
Look to your house, your daughter, and your bags!
Thieves, thieves!   83

Brabantio [enters] above [at a window].

BRABANTIO
What is the reason of this terrible summons?
What is the matter there?   85

RODERIGO
Signor, is all your family within?

IAGO
Are your doors locked?

BRABANTIO   Why, wherefore ask you this?

IAGO
Zounds, sir, you're robbed. For shame, put on your
    gown!   88
Your heart is burst; you have lost half your soul.
Even now, now, very now, an old black ram
Is tupping your white ewe. Arise, arise!   91
Awake the snorting citizens with the bell,   92
Or else the devil will make a grandsire of you.   93
Arise, I say!

BRABANTIO   What, have you lost your wits?

RODERIGO
Most reverend signor, do you know my voice?

BRABANTIO   Not I. What are you?

RODERIGO   My name is Roderigo.

BRABANTIO   The worser welcome.
I have charged thee not to haunt about my doors.
In honest plainness thou hast heard me say
My daughter is not for thee; and now, in madness,

---

78 and negligence i.e., caused by negligence   **83 s.d. at a window** (This
stage direction, from the quarto, probably calls for an appearance on
the gallery above and rearstage.)   **85 the matter** your business
88 Zounds by His (Christ's) wounds   **91 tupping** covering, copulating
with. (Said of sheep.)   **92 snorting** snoring   **93 the devil** (The devil was
conventionally pictured as black.)

Being full of supper and distempering drafts,   102
Upon malicious bravery dost thou come   103
To start my quiet.   104

RODERIGO
Sir, sir, sir—

BRABANTIO   But thou must needs be sure
My spirits and my place have in their power   106
To make this bitter to thee.

RODERIGO   Patience, good sir.

BRABANTIO
What tell'st thou me of robbing? This is Venice;
My house is not a grange.

RODERIGO   Most grave Brabantio,   109
In simple and pure soul I come to you.   110

IAGO   Zounds, sir, you are one of those that will not
serve God if the devil bid you. Because we come to do
you service and you think we are ruffians, you'll have
your daughter covered with a Barbary horse; you'll
have your nephews neigh to you; you'll have coursers   115
for cousins and jennets for germans.   116

BRABANTIO   What profane wretch art thou?

IAGO   I am one, sir, that comes to tell you your daughter
and the Moor are now making the beast with two
backs.

BRABANTIO
Thou art a villain.

IAGO   You are—a senator.

BRABANTIO
This thou shalt answer. I know thee, Roderigo.   122

RODERIGO
Sir, I will answer anything. But, I beseech you,
If 't be your pleasure and most wise consent—
As partly I find it is—that your fair daughter,
At this odd-even and dull watch o' the night,   126

102 **distempering** intoxicating   103 **Upon malicious bravery** with hostile intent to defy me   104 **start** startle, disrupt   106 **My spirits and my place** my temperament and my authority of office.   **have in** have it in   109 **grange** isolated farmhouse   110 **simple** sincere   115 **nephews** i.e., grandsons.   **coursers** powerful horses   116 **cousins** kinsmen.   **jennets** small Spanish horses.   **germans** near relatives   122 **answer** be held accountable for   126 **odd-even** between one day and the next, i.e., about midnight

Transported with no worse nor better guard   127
But with a knave of common hire, a gondolier,   128
To the gross clasps of a lascivious Moor—
If this be known to you and your allowance   130
We then have done you bold and saucy wrongs.   131
But if you know not this, my manners tell me
We have your wrong rebuke. Do not believe
That, from the sense of all civility,   134
I thus would play and trifle with your reverence.   135
Your daughter, if you have not given her leave,
I say again, hath made a gross revolt,
Tying her duty, beauty, wit, and fortunes   138
In an extravagant and wheeling stranger   139
Of here and everywhere. Straight satisfy yourself.   140
If she be in her chamber or your house,
Let loose on me the justice of the state
For thus deluding you.
BRABANTIO   Strike on the tinder, ho!   144
Give me a taper! Call up all my people!
This accident is not unlike my dream.   146
Belief of it oppresses me already.
Light, I say, light!   *Exit [above].*
IAGO   Farewell, for I must leave you.
It seems not meet nor wholesome to my place
To be produced—as, if I stay, I shall—   150
Against the Moor. For I do know the state,
However this may gall him with some check,   152
Cannot with safety cast him, for he's embarked   153
With such loud reason to the Cyprus wars,   154
Which even now stands in act, that, for their souls,   155
Another of his fathom they have none   156

127 **with** by   128 **But with a knave** than by a low fellow, a servant
130 **allowance** permission   131 **saucy** insolent   134 **from** contrary to.
civility good manners, decency   135 **your reverence** the respect due to
you   138 **wit** intelligence   139 **extravagant** expatriate, wandering far
from home.   **wheeling** roving about, vagabond.   **stranger** foreigner
140 **Straight** straightway   144 **tinder** charred linen ignited by a spark
from flint and steel, used to light torches or *tapers* (ll. 145, 170)
146 **accident** occurrence, event   150 **producted** produced (as a witness)   152 **gall** rub; oppress.   **check** rebuke   153 **cast** dismiss.   **embarked** engaged   154 **loud** i.e., self-evident, boldly proclaimed
155 **stands in act** are going on   156 **fathom** i.e., ability, depth of
experience

To lead their business; in which regard,   157
Though I do hate him as I do hell pains,
Yet for necessity of present life   159
I must show out a flag and sign of love,
Which is indeed but sign. That you shall surely find him,
Lead to the Sagittary the raisèd search,   162
And there will I be with him. So farewell.   *Exit.*   163

> *Enter [below] Brabantio [in his nightgown] with*
> *servants and torches.*

BRABANTIO
It is too true an evil. Gone she is;
And what's to come of my despisèd time   165
Is naught but bitterness. Now, Roderigo,
Where didst thou see her?—O unhappy girl!—
With the Moor, sayst thou?—Who would be a father!—
How didst thou know 'twas she?—O, she deceives me
Past thought!—What said she to you?—Get more tapers.
Raise all my kindred.—Are they married, think you?
RODERIGO   Truly, I think they are.
BRABANTIO
O heaven! How got she out? O treason of the blood!
Fathers, from hence trust not your daughters' minds
By what you see them act. Is there not charms   175
By which the property of youth and maidhood   176
May be abused? Have you not read, Roderigo,   177
Of some such thing?
RODERIGO   Yes, sir, I have indeed.
BRABANTIO
Call up my brother.—O, would you had had her!—
Some one way, some another.—Do you know
Where we may apprehend her and the Moor?
RODERIGO
I think I can discover him, if you please   182
To get good guard and go along with me.

---

157 in which regard out of regard for which   **159 life** livelihood
162 Sagittary (An inn where Othello and Desdemona are staying.)
raisèd search search party roused out of sleep   **163 s.d. nightgown**
dressing gown. (This costuming is specified in the quarto text.)   **165 time**
i.e., remainder of life   **175 charms** spells   **176 property** special quality,
nature   **177 abused** deceived   **182 discover** reveal, uncover

BRABANTIO
  Pray you, lead on. At every house I'll call;
  I may command at most.—Get weapons, ho!   185
  And raise some special officers of night.—
  On, good Roderigo. I will deserve your pains.   187

                                      Exeunt.

❖

1.2   *Enter Othello, Iago, attendants with torches.*

IAGO
  Though in the trade of war I have slain men,
  Yet do I hold it very stuff o' the conscience   2
  To do no contrived murder. I lack iniquity   3
  Sometimes to do me service. Nine or ten times
  I had thought t' have yerked him here under the ribs. 5
OTHELLO
  'Tis better as it is.
IAGO   Nay, but he prated,
  And spoke such scurvy and provoking terms
  Against your honor
  That, with the little godliness I have,
  I did full hard forbear him. But, I pray you, sir,   10
  Are you fast married? Be assured of this,
  That the magnifico is much beloved,   12
  And hath in his effect a voice potential   13
  As double as the Duke's. He will divorce you,   14
  Or put upon you what restraint and grievance
  The law, with all his might to enforce it on,
  Will give him cable.
OTHELLO   Let him do his spite.   17
  My services which I have done the seigniory   18

---

185 command demand assistance   **187 deserve** show gratitude for

1.2. Location: Venice. Another street, before Othello's lodgings.
2 very stuff essence, basic material (continuing the metaphor of *trade*
from l. 1)   **3 contrived** premeditated   **5 yerked** stabbed. **him** i.e.,
Roderigo   **10 I . . . him** I restrained myself with great difficulty from
assaulting him   **12 magnifico** Venetian grandee, i.e., Brabantio   **13 in
his effect** at his command. **potential** powerful   **14 double** doubly
powerful (in comparison with other senators)   **17 cable** i.e., scope
18 seigniory Venetian government

Shall out-tongue his complaints. 'Tis yet to know—   19
Which, when I know that boasting is an honor,
I shall promulgate—I fetch my life and being
From men of royal siege, and my demerits   22
May speak unbonneted to as proud a fortune   23
As this that I have reached. For know, Iago,
But that I love the gentle Desdemona,
I would not my unhousèd free condition   26
Put into circumscription and confine   27
For the sea's worth. But look, what lights come yond? 28

Enter Cassio [and certain Officers] with torches.

IAGO
Those are the raisèd father and his friends.
You were best go in.
OTHELLO   Not I. I must be found.
My parts, my title, and my perfect soul   31
Shall manifest me rightly. Is it they?
IAGO   By Janus, I think no.   33
OTHELLO
The servants of the Duke? And my lieutenant?
The goodness of the night upon you, friends!
What is the news?
CASSIO   The Duke does greet you, General,
And he requires your haste-post-haste appearance
Even on the instant.
OTHELLO   What is the matter, think you? 38
CASSIO
Something from Cyprus, as I may divine.   39
It is a business of some heat. The galleys   40
Have sent a dozen sequent messengers   41
This very night at one another's heels,

19 yet to know not yet widely known   **22 siege** i.e., rank. (Literally, a
seat used by a person of distinction.)   **demerits** deserts   **23 unbonneted**
without removing the hat, i.e., on equal terms (? Or "with hat off," "in
all due modesty.")   **26 unhousèd** unconfined, undomesticated   **27 circumscription and confine** restriction and confinement   **28 the sea's
worth** all the riches at the bottom of the sea   **s.d. Officers** (The quarto
text calls for "Cassio with lights, officers with torches.")   **31 My . . .
soul** my natural gifts, my position or reputation, and my unflawed
conscience   **33 Janus** Roman two-faced god of beginnings   **38 matter**
business   **39 divine** guess   **40 heat** urgency   **41 sequent** successive

And many of the consuls, raised and met,   43
Are at the Duke's already. You have been hotly called for;
When, being not at your lodging to be found,
The Senate hath sent about three several quests   46
To search you out.
OTHELLO   'Tis well I am found by you.
I will but spend a word here in the house
And go with you.   [*Exit.*]
CASSIO   Ancient, what makes he here?   49
IAGO
Faith, he tonight hath boarded a land carrack.   50
If it prove lawful prize, he's made forever.   51
CASSIO
I do not understand.
IAGO   He's married.
CASSIO   To who?

                    [*Enter Othello.*]

IAGO
Marry, to—Come, Captain, will you go?   53
OTHELLO   Have with you.   54
CASSIO
Here comes another troop to seek for you.   55

                    *Enter Brabantio, Roderigo, with officers and
                    torches.*

IAGO
It is Brabantio. General, be advised.   56
He comes to bad intent.
OTHELLO   Holla! Stand there!
RODERIGO
Signor, it is the Moor.
BRABANTIO   Down with him, thief!
                                        [*They draw on both sides.*]
IAGO
You, Roderigo! Come, sir, I am for you.

43 consuls senators   **46 several** separate   **49 makes** does   **50 boarded**
gone aboard and seized as an act of piracy (with sexual suggestion).
carrack large merchant ship   **51 prize** booty   **53 Marry** (An oath,
originally "by the Virgin Mary.")   **54 Have with you** i.e., let's go
55 s.d. officers and torches (The quarto text calls for "others with lights
and weapons.")   **56 be advised** be on your guard

OTHELLO
Keep up your bright swords, for the dew will rust them. 60
Good signor, you shall more command with years
Than with your weapons.

BRABANTIO
O thou foul thief, where hast thou stowed my daughter?
Damned as thou art, thou hast enchanted her!
For I'll refer me to all things of sense, 65
If she in chains of magic were not bound
Whether a maid so tender, fair, and happy,
So opposite to marriage that she shunned
The wealthy curlèd darlings of our nation,
Would ever have, t' incur a general mock,
Run from her guardage to the sooty bosom 71
Of such a thing as thou—to fear, not to delight.
Judge me the world if 'tis not gross in sense 73
That thou hast practiced on her with foul charms,
Abused her delicate youth with drugs or minerals 75
That weakens motion. I'll have 't disputed on; 76
'Tis probable, and palpable to thinking.
I therefore apprehend and do attach thee 78
For an abuser of the world, a practicer
Of arts inhibited and out of warrant.— 80
Lay hold upon him! If he do resist,
Subdue him at his peril.

OTHELLO   Hold your hands,
Both you of my inclining and the rest. 83
Were it my cue to fight, I should have known it
Without a prompter.—Whither will you that I go
To answer this your charge?

BRABANTIO   To prison, till fit time
Of law and course of direct session 88
Call thee to answer.

OTHELLO   What if I do obey?

---

60 Keep up i.e., sheathe   **65 refer me** submit my case.   **things of sense**
commonsense understandings, or, creatures possessing common
sense   **71 guardage** guardianship   **73 gross in sense** obvious   **75 minerals** i.e., poisons   **76 weakens motion** impair the vital faculties.
disputed on argued in court by professional counsel, discussed by
experts   **78 attach** arrest   **80 inhibited** prohibited.   **out of warrant**
illegal   **83 inclining** following, party   **88 course of direct session**
regular or specially convened legal proceedings

How may the Duke be therewith satisfied,
Whose messengers are here about my side
Upon some present business of the state
To bring me to him?

OFFICER   'Tis true, most worthy signor.
The Duke's in council, and your noble self,
I am sure, is sent for.

BRABANTIO   How? The Duke in council?
In this time of the night? Bring him away.   96
Mine's not an idle cause. The Duke himself,   97
Or any of my brothers of the state,
Cannot but feel this wrong as 'twere their own;
For if such actions may have passage free,
Bondslaves and pagans shall our statesmen be.

                                        Exeunt.

                    ❖

1.3   *Enter Duke [and] Senators [and sit at a table,
            with lights], and Officers. [The Duke and
            Senators are reading dispatches.]*

DUKE
There is no composition in these news   1
That gives them credit.

FIRST SENATOR   Indeed, they are disproportioned.   3
My letters say a hundred and seven galleys.

DUKE
And mine, a hundred forty.

SECOND SENATOR   And mine, two hundred.
But though they jump not on a just account—   6
As in these cases, where the aim reports   7
'Tis oft with difference—yet do they all confirm
A Turkish fleet, and bearing up to Cyprus.

DUKE
Nay, it is possible enough to judgment.

---

96 away right along   **97 idle** trifling

1.3. Location: Venice. A council chamber.
s.d. Enter . . . Officers (The quarto text calls for the Duke and Senators
to "sit at a table with lights and attendants.")   **1 composition** consistency   **3 disproportioned** inconsistent   **6 jump** agree.   **just** exact
7 the aim conjecture

I do not so secure me in the error   11
But the main article I do approve   12
In fearful sense.
SAILOR (*Within*)   What ho, what ho, what ho!

    Enter Sailor.

OFFICER   A messenger from the galleys.
DUKE   Now, what's the business?
SAILOR
The Turkish preparation makes for Rhodes.   16
So was I bid report here to the state
By Signor Angelo.
DUKE
How say you by this change?
FIRST SENATOR   This cannot be   19
By no assay of reason. 'Tis a pageant   20
To keep us in false gaze. When we consider   21
Th' importancy of Cyprus to the Turk,
And let ourselves again but understand
That, as it more concerns the Turk than Rhodes,
So may he with more facile question bear it,   25
For that it stands not in such warlike brace,   26
But altogether lacks th' abilities   27
That Rhodes is dressed in—if we make thought of this, 28
We must not think the Turk is so unskillful   29
To leave that latest which concerns him first,   30
Neglecting an attempt of ease and gain
To wake and wage a danger profitless.   32
DUKE
Nay, in all confidence, he's not for Rhodes.
OFFICER   Here is more news.

    Enter a Messenger.

11–12 I do not . . . approve I do not take such (false) comfort in the
discrepancies that I fail to perceive the main point, i.e., that the Turkish
fleet is threatening   **16 preparation** fleet prepared for battle   **19 by**
about   **20 assay** test.   **pageant** mere show   **21 in false gaze** looking the
wrong way   **25 may . . . it** he (the Turk) can more easily capture it
(Cyprus)   **26 For that** since.   **brace** state of defense   **27 abilities** means
of self-defense   **28 dressed in** equipped with   **29 unskillful** deficient in
judgment   **30 latest** last   **32 wake** stir up.   **wage** risk

MESSENGER
  The Ottomites, reverend and gracious,
  Steering with due course toward the isle of Rhodes,
  Have there injointed them with an after fleet.   37
FIRST SENATOR
  Ay, so I thought. How many, as you guess?
MESSENGER
  Of thirty sail; and now they do restem   39
  Their backward course, bearing with frank appearance   40
  Their purposes toward Cyprus. Signor Montano,
  Your trusty and most valiant servitor,   42
  With his free duty recommends you thus,   43
  And prays you to believe him.
DUKE   'Tis certain then for Cyprus.
  Marcus Luccicos, is not he in town?
FIRST SENATOR   He's now in Florence.
DUKE
  Write from us to him, post-post-haste. Dispatch.
FIRST SENATOR
  Here comes Brabantio and the valiant Moor.

  Enter Brabantio, Othello, Cassio, Iago, Roderigo,
  and officers.

DUKE
  Valiant Othello, we must straight employ you   50
  Against the general enemy Ottoman.   51
  [*To Brabantio.*] I did not see you; welcome, gentle signor.   52
  We lacked your counsel and your help tonight.
BRABANTIO
  So did I yours. Good Your Grace, pardon me;
  Neither my place nor aught I heard of business   55
  Hath raised me from my bed, nor doth the general care
  Take hold on me, for my particular grief   57
  Is of so floodgate and o'erbearing nature   58

---

37 injointed them joined themselves.   **after** second   **39–40 restem . . .
course** retrace their original course   **40 frank appearance** i.e., undis-
guised intent   **42 servitor** officer under your command   **43 free duty**
freely given and loyal service.   **recommends** commends himself and
reports to   **50 straight** straightway   **51 general** universal, i.e., against
all Christendom   **52 gentle** noble   **55 place** official position
57 particular personal   **58 floodgate** i.e., overwhelming (as when flood-
gates are opened)

That it engluts and swallows other sorrows   59
And it is still itself.
DUKE   Why, what's the matter?   60
BRABANTIO
My daughter! O, my daughter!
DUKE AND SENATORS   Dead?
BRABANTIO   Ay, to me.
She is abused, stol'n from me, and corrupted   62
By spells and medicines bought of mountebanks;
For nature so preposterously to err,
Being not deficient, blind, or lame of sense,   65
Sans witchcraft could not.   66
DUKE
Whoe'er he be that in this foul proceeding
Hath thus beguiled your daughter of herself,
And you of her, the bloody book of law
You shall yourself read in the bitter letter
After your own sense—yea, though our proper son   71
Stood in your action.
BRABANTIO   Humbly I thank Your Grace.   72
Here is the man, this Moor, whom now it seems
Your special mandate for the state affairs
Hath hither brought.
ALL   We are very sorry for 't.
DUKE [*To Othello*]
What, in your own part, can you say to this?
BRABANTIO   Nothing, but this is so.
OTHELLO
Most potent, grave, and reverend signors,
My very noble and approved good masters: 79
That I have ta'en away this old man's daughter,
It is most true; true, I have married her.
The very head and front of my offending   82
Hath this extent, no more. Rude am I in my speech,   83
And little blessed with the soft phrase of peace;
For since these arms of mine had seven years' pith,   85

59 engluts engulfs   **60 is still itself** remains undiminished   **62 abused**
deceived   **65 deficient** defective   **66 Sans** without   **71 After . . . sense**
according to your own interpretation.   **our proper** my own   **72 Stood
. . . action** were under your accusation   **79 approved** proved, esteemed   **82 head and front** height and breadth, entire extent   **83 Rude**
unpolished   **85 pith** strength, vigor (i.e., since I was seven)

Till now some nine moons wasted, they have used   86
Their dearest action in the tented field;   87
And little of this great world can I speak
More than pertains to feats of broils and battle,
And therefore little shall I grace my cause
In speaking for myself. Yet, by your gracious patience,
I will a round unvarnished tale deliver   92
Of my whole course of love—what drugs, what charms,
What conjuration, and what mighty magic,
For such proceeding I am charged withal,   95
I won his daughter.
BRABANTIO   A maiden never bold;
Of spirit so still and quiet that her motion   97
Blushed at herself; and she, in spite of nature,   98
Of years, of country, credit, everything,   99
To fall in love with what she feared to look on!
It is a judgment maimed and most imperfect
That will confess perfection so could err   102
Against all rules of nature, and must be driven
To find out practices of cunning hell   104
Why this should be. I therefore vouch again   105
That with some mixtures powerful o'er the blood,   106
Or with some dram conjured to this effect,   107
He wrought upon her.
DUKE   To vouch this is no proof,
Without more wider and more overt test   109
Than these thin habits and poor likelihoods   110
Of modern seeming do prefer against him.   111
FIRST SENATOR   But, Othello, speak.
Did you by indirect and forcèd courses
Subdue and poison this young maid's affections?
Or came it by request and such fair question   115
As soul to soul affordeth?

86 Till . . . wasted until some nine months ago (since when Othello
has evidently not been on active duty, but in Venice)   87 dearest most
valuable   92 round plain   95 withal with   97–98 her . . . herself her
very emotions prompted her to blush at discovering such feelings in
herself   99 years i.e., difference in age.   credit virtuous reputation
102 confess concede (that)   104 practices plots   105 vouch assert
106 blood passions   107 conjured to this effect made by magical spells
to have this effect   109 more wider fuller   110 habits garments, i.e.,
appearances   111 modern seeming commonplace assumption.   prefer
bring forth   115 question conversation

OTHELLO   I do beseech you,
  Send for the lady to the Sagittary
  And let her speak of me before her father.
  If you do find me foul in her report,
  The trust, the office I do hold of you
  Not only take away, but let your sentence
  Even fall upon my life.
DUKE   Fetch Desdemona hither.
OTHELLO
  Ancient, conduct them. You best know the place.
                 [*Exeunt Iago and attendants.*]
  And, till she come, as truly as to heaven
  I do confess the vices of my blood,   125
  So justly to your grave ears I'll present   126
  How I did thrive in this fair lady's love,
  And she in mine.
DUKE   Say it, Othello.
OTHELLO
  Her father loved me, oft invited me,
  Still questioned me the story of my life   131
  From year to year—the battles, sieges, fortunes,
  That I have passed.
  I ran it through, even from my boyish days
  To th' very moment that he bade me tell it,
  Wherein I spoke of most disastrous chances,
  Of moving accidents by flood and field,   137
  Of hairbreadth scapes i' th' imminent deadly breach,   138
  Of being taken by the insolent foe
  And sold to slavery, of my redemption thence,
  And portance in my travels' history,   141
  Wherein of antres vast and deserts idle,   142
  Rough quarries, rocks, and hills whose heads touch
    heaven,   143
  It was my hint to speak—such was my process—   144
  And of the Cannibals that each other eat,
  The Anthropophagi, and men whose heads   146

125 **blood** passions, human nature   126 **justly** truthfully, accurately
131 **Still** continually   137 **accidents** happenings   138 **imminent . . .**
breach death-threatening gaps made in a fortification   141 **portance**
conduct   142 **antres** caverns.   **idle** barren, desolate   143 **Rough**
quarries rugged rock formations   144 **hint** occasion, opportunity
146 **Anthropophagi** man-eaters. (A term from Pliny's *Natural History*.)

Do grow beneath their shoulders. These things to hear
Would Desdemona seriously incline;
But still the house affairs would draw her thence,
Which ever as she could with haste dispatch
She'd come again, and with a greedy ear
Devour up my discourse. Which I, observing,
Took once a pliant hour, and found good means   153
To draw from her a prayer of earnest heart
That I would all my pilgrimage dilate,   155
Whereof by parcels she had something heard,   156
But not intentively. I did consent,   157
And often did beguile her of her tears,
When I did speak of some distressful stroke
That my youth suffered. My story being done,
She gave me for my pains a world of sighs.
She swore, in faith, 'twas strange, 'twas passing strange,   162
'Twas pitiful, 'twas wondrous pitiful.
She wished she had not heard it, yet she wished
That heaven had made her such a man. She thanked me,
And bade me, if I had a friend that loved her,
I should but teach him how to tell my story,
And that would woo her. Upon this hint I spake.   168
She loved me for the dangers I had passed,
And I loved her that she did pity them.
This only is the witchcraft I have used.
Here comes the lady. Let her witness it.

Enter Desdemona, Iago, [and] attendants.

DUKE
    I think this tale would win my daughter too.
    Good Brabantio,
    Take up this mangled matter at the best.   175
    Men do their broken weapons rather use
    Than their bare hands.
BRABANTIO   I pray you, hear her speak.
    If she confess that she was half the wooer,
    Destruction on my head if my bad blame

---

153 **pliant** well-suiting   155 **dilate** relate in detail   156 **by parcels**
piecemeal   157 **intentively** with full attention   162 **passing** exceedingly   168 **hint** opportunity   175 **Take . . . best** make the best of a bad
bargain

Light on the man!—Come hither, gentle mistress.
Do you perceive in all this noble company
Where most you owe obedience?

DESDEMONA   My noble Father,
I do perceive here a divided duty.
To you I am bound for life and education;   184
My life and education both do learn me   185
How to respect you. You are the lord of duty;
I am hitherto your daughter. But here's my husband,
And so much duty as my mother showed
To you, preferring you before her father,
So much I challenge that I may profess   190
Due to the Moor my lord.

BRABANTIO   God be with you! I have done.
Please it Your Grace, on to the state affairs.
I had rather to adopt a child than get it.   194
Come hither, Moor.   [*He joins the hands of Othello
and Desdemona.*]
I here do give thee that with all my heart   196
Which, but thou hast already, with all my heart   197
I would keep from thee.—For your sake, jewel,   198
I am glad at soul I have no other child,
For thy escape would teach me tyranny,   200
To hang clogs on them.—I have done, my lord.   201

DUKE
Let me speak like yourself, and lay a sentence   202
Which, as a grece or step, may help these lovers   203
Into your favor.
When remedies are past, the griefs are ended   205
By seeing the worst, which late on hopes depended.   206
To mourn a mischief that is past and gone   207
Is the next way to draw new mischief on.   208

---

184 education upbringing   **185 learn** teach   **190 challenge** claim
194 get beget   **196 with all my heart** wherein my whole affection has
been engaged   **197 with all my heart** willingly, gladly   **198 For your
sake** on your account   **200 escape** elopement   **201 clogs** (Literally,
blocks of wood fastened to the legs of criminals or convicts to inhibit
escape.)   **202 like yourself** i.e., as you would, in your proper temper.
sentence maxim (also at l. 219)   **203 grece** step   **205 remedies** hopes of
remedy   **206 which** i.e., the griefs.   **late . . . depended** were sustained
until recently by hopeful anticipation   **207 mischief** misfortune, injury   **208 next** nearest

What cannot be preserved when fortune takes,   209
Patience her injury a mockery makes.   210
The robbed that smiles steals something from the thief;
He robs himself that spends a bootless grief.   212

BRABANTIO
So let the Turk of Cyprus us beguile,
We lose it not, so long as we can smile.
He bears the sentence well that nothing bears   215
But the free comfort which from thence he hears,   216
But he bears both the sentence and the sorrow   217
That, to pay grief, must of poor patience borrow.   218
These sentences, to sugar or to gall,   219
Being strong on both sides, are equivocal.   220
But words are words. I never yet did hear
That the bruised heart was piercèd through the ear.   222
I humbly beseech you, proceed to th' affairs of state.

DUKE   The Turk with a most mighty preparation makes
for Cyprus. Othello, the fortitude of the place is best 225
known to you; and though we have there a substitute   226
of most allowed sufficiency, yet opinion, a sovereign 227
mistress of effects, throws a more safer voice on you. 228
You must therefore be content to slubber the gloss of 229
your new fortunes with this more stubborn and   230
boisterous expedition.

OTHELLO
The tyrant custom, most grave senators,
Hath made the flinty and steel couch of war
My thrice-driven bed of down. I do agnize   234

---

209 What whatever   **210 Patience . . . makes** patience laughs at the
injury inflicted by fortune (and thus eases the pain)   **212 spends a
bootless grief** indulges in unavailing grief   **215–218 He bears . . .
borrow** i.e., a person well bears out your maxim who takes with him
only the philosophic consolation it teaches him, a comfort free from
sorrow; but anyone whose grief bankrupts his poor patience is left with
your saying and his sorrow too. (*Bears the sentence* also plays on the
meaning, "receives judicial sentence.")   **219–220 These . . . equivocal**
i.e., these fine maxims are equivocal, either sweet or bitter in their
application   **222 piercèd . . . ear** i.e., surgically lanced and cured by
mere words of advice   **225 fortitude** strength   **226 substitute** deputy
227 allowed acknowledged   **227–228 opinion . . . on you** general opinion, an important determiner of affairs, chooses you as the best man
229 slubber soil, sully   **230 stubborn** harsh, rough   **234 thrice-driven**
thrice sifted, winnowed.   **agnize** know in myself, acknowledge

A natural and prompt alacrity
I find in hardness, and do undertake   236
These present wars against the Ottomites.
Most humbly therefore bending to your state,   238
I crave fit disposition for my wife,
Due reference of place and exhibition,   240
With such accommodation and besort   241
As levels with her breeding.   242

DUKE
Why, at her father's.

BRABANTIO   I will not have it so.

OTHELLO
Nor I.

DESDEMONA   Nor I. I would not there reside,
To put my father in impatient thoughts
By being in his eye. Most gracious Duke,
To my unfolding lend your prosperous ear,   247
And let me find a charter in your voice   248
T' assist my simpleness.

DUKE   What would you, Desdemona?

DESDEMONA
That I did love the Moor to live with him,
My downright violence and storm of fortunes   252
May trumpet to the world. My heart's subdued   253
Even to the very quality of my lord.   254
I saw Othello's visage in his mind,
And to his honors and his valiant parts   256
Did I my soul and fortunes consecrate.
So that, dear lords, if I be left behind
A moth of peace, and he go to the war,   259
The rites for why I love him are bereft me,   260
And I a heavy interim shall support

236 hardness hardship   **238 bending . . . state** bowing or kneeling to
your authority   **240 reference . . . exhibition** provision of place to live
and allowance of money   **241 accommodation** suitable provision.
besort attendance   **242 levels** equals, suits   **247 unfolding** explanation,
proposal.   **prosperous** propitious   **248 charter** privilege, authorization   **252 My . . . fortunes** my plain and total breach of social custom,
taking my future by storm and disrupting my whole life   **253–254 My
heart's . . . lord** my heart is brought wholly into accord with Othello's
virtues; I love him for his virtues   **256 parts** qualities   **259 moth** i.e.,
one who consumes merely   **260 rites** rites of love (with a suggestion too
of *rights*, sharing)

By his dear absence. Let me go with him.   262
OTHELLO   Let her have your voice.   263
   Vouch with me, heaven, I therefor beg it not
   To please the palate of my appetite,
   Nor to comply with heat—the young affects   266
   In me defunct—and proper satisfaction,   267
   But to be free and bounteous to her mind.   268
   And heaven defend your good souls that you think   269
   I will your serious and great business scant
   When she is with me. No, when light-winged toys
   Of feathered Cupid seel with wanton dullness   272
   My speculative and officed instruments,   273
   That my disports corrupt and taint my business,   274
   Let huswives make a skillet of my helm,
   And all indign and base adversities   276
   Make head against my estimation!   277
DUKE
   Be it as you shall privately determine,
   Either for her stay or going. Th' affair cries haste,
   And speed must answer it.
A SENATOR   You must away tonight.
DESDEMONA
   Tonight, my lord?
DUKE   This night.
OTHELLO   With all my heart.
DUKE
   At nine i' the morning here we'll meet again.
   Othello, leave some officer behind,
   And he shall our commission bring to you,
   With such things else of quality and respect   285
   As doth import you.
OTHELLO   So please Your Grace, my ancient;   286
   A man he is of honesty and trust.

---

262 dear (1) heartfelt (2) costly   **263 voice** consent   **266 heat** sexual
passion.   **young affects** passions of youth, desires   **267 proper** personal   **268 free** generous   **269 defend** forbid.   **think** should think
272 seel i.e., make blind (as in falconry, by sewing up the eyes of the
hawk during training)   **273 speculative ... instruments** i.e., perceptive
faculties used in the performance of duty   **274 That** so that.   **disports**
sexual pastimes.   **taint** impair   **276 indign** unworthy, shameful
277 Make head raise an army.   **estimation** reputation   **285 of quality
and respect** of importance and relevance   **286 import** concern

To his conveyance I assign my wife,
With what else needful Your Good Grace shall think
To be sent after me.
DUKE   Let it be so.
  Good night to everyone. [*To Brabantio.*] And, noble
    signor,
  If virtue no delighted beauty lack,   292
  Your son-in-law is far more fair than black.
FIRST SENATOR
  Adieu, brave Moor. Use Desdemona well.
BRABANTIO
  Look to her, Moor, if thou hast eyes to see.
  She has deceived her father, and may thee.
                    Exeunt [Duke, Brabantio, Cassio, Senators,
                                        and Officers].
OTHELLO
  My life upon her faith! Honest Iago,
  My Desdemona must I leave to thee.
  I prithee, let thy wife attend on her,
  And bring them after in the best advantage.   300
  Come, Desdemona. I have but an hour
  Of love, of worldly matters and direction,   302
  To spend with thee. We must obey the time.
                              Exit [with Desdemona].
RODERIGO Iago—
IAGO What sayst thou, noble heart?
RODERIGO What will I do, think'st thou?
IAGO Why, go to bed and sleep.
RODERIGO I will incontinently drown myself.   308
IAGO If thou dost, I shall never love thee after. Why,
  thou silly gentleman?
RODERIGO It is silliness to live when to live is torment;
  and then have we a prescription to die when death is 312
  our physician.
IAGO O villainous! I have looked upon the world for 314
  four times seven years, and, since I could distinguish
  betwixt a benefit and an injury, I never found man

292 delighted capable of delighting   **300 in . . . advantage** at the most
favorable opportunity   **302 direction** instructions   **308 incontinently**
immediately   **312 prescription** (1) right based on long-established
custom (2) doctor's prescription   **314 villainous** i.e., what perfect
nonsense

that knew how to love himself. Ere I would say I
would drown myself for the love of a guinea hen, I   318
would change my humanity with a baboon.

RODERIGO   What should I do? I confess it is my shame
to be so fond, but it is not in my virtue to amend it.   321

IAGO   Virtue? A fig! 'Tis in ourselves that we are thus or   322
thus. Our bodies are our gardens, to the which our
wills are gardeners; so that if we will plant nettles or
sow lettuce, set hyssop and weed up thyme, supply it   325
with one gender of herbs or distract it with many, ei-   326
ther to have it sterile with idleness or manured with   327
industry—why, the power and corrigible authority of   328
this lies in our wills. If the beam of our lives had not   329
one scale of reason to poise another of sensuality, the   330
blood and baseness of our natures would conduct us   331
to most preposterous conclusions. But we have reason
to cool our raging motions, our carnal stings, our un-   333
bitted lusts, whereof I take this that you call love to be   334
a sect or scion.   335

RODERIGO   It cannot be.

IAGO   It is merely a lust of the blood and a permission
of the will. Come, be a man. Drown thyself? Drown
cats and blind puppies. I have professed me thy friend,
and I confess me knit to thy deserving with cables of
perdurable toughness. I could never better stead thee   341
than now. Put money in thy purse. Follow thou the
wars; defeat thy favor with an usurped beard. I say,   343
put money in thy purse. It cannot be long that Desdemona should continue her love to the Moor—put
money in thy purse—nor he his to her. It was a vio-

---

318 guinea hen (A slang term for a prostitute.)   **321 fond** infatuated.
virtue strength, nature   **322 fig** (To give a fig is to thrust the thumb
between the first and second fingers in a vulgar and insulting gesture.)   **325 hyssop** a herb of the mint family   **326 gender** kind.
distract it with divide it among   **327 idleness** want of cultivation
328 corrigible authority power to correct   **329 beam** balance
330 poise counterbalance   **331 blood** natural passions   **333 motions**
appetites   **333–334 unbitted** unbridled, uncontrolled   **335 sect or scion**
cutting or offshoot   **341 perdurable** very durable.   **stead** assist
343 defeat thy favor disguise your face.   **usurped** (The suggestion is
that Roderigo is not man enough to have a beard of his own.)

lent commencement in her, and thou shalt see an an- 347
swerable sequestration—put but money in thy purse. 348
These Moors are changeable in their wills—fill thy 349
purse with money. The food that to him now is as
luscious as locusts shall be to him shortly as bitter as 351
coloquintida. She must change for youth; when she is 352
sated with his body, she will find the error of her
choice. She must have change, she must. Therefore
put money in thy purse. If thou wilt needs damn thyself, do it a more delicate way than drowning. Make 356
all the money thou canst. If sanctimony and a frail vow 357
betwixt an erring barbarian and a supersubtle Vene- 358
tian be not too hard for my wits and all the tribe of
hell, thou shalt enjoy her. Therefore make money. A
pox of drowning thyself! It is clean out of the way.
Seek thou rather to be hanged in compassing thy joy 362
than to be drowned and go without her.

RODERIGO Wilt thou be fast to my hopes if I depend on 364
the issue?

IAGO Thou art sure of me. Go, make money. I have
told thee often, and I retell thee again and again, I hate
the Moor. My cause is hearted; thine hath no less rea- 368
son. Let us be conjunctive in our revenge against him. 369
If thou canst cuckold him, thou dost thyself a pleasure,
me a sport. There are many events in the womb of
time which will be delivered. Traverse, go, provide thy 372
money. We will have more of this tomorrow. Adieu.

RODERIGO Where shall we meet i' the morning?

IAGO At my lodging.

RODERIGO I'll be with thee betimes. [*He starts to leave.*] 376

IAGO Go to, farewell.—Do you hear, Roderigo?

RODERIGO What say you?

IAGO No more of drowning, do you hear?

347–348 an answerable sequestration a corresponding separation or
estrangement **349 wills** carnal appetites **351 locusts** fruit of the carob
tree (see Matthew 3:4), or perhaps honeysuckle **352 coloquintida**
colocynth or bitter apple, a purgative **356 Make** raise, collect
357 sanctimony sacred ceremony **358 erring** wandering, vagabond,
unsteady **362 compassing** encompassing, embracing **364 fast** true
368 hearted fixed in the heart, heartfelt **369 conjunctive** united
372 Traverse (A military marching term.) **376 betimes** early

RODERIGO I am changed.

IAGO Go to, farewell. Put money enough in your purse.

RODERIGO I'll sell all my land.   *Exit.*

IAGO

Thus do I ever make my fool my purse;
For I mine own gained knowledge should profane
If I would time expend with such a snipe   386
But for my sport and profit. I hate the Moor;
And it is thought abroad that twixt my sheets   388
He's done my office. I know not if 't be true;   389
But I, for mere suspicion in that kind,
Will do as if for surety. He holds me well;   391
The better shall my purpose work on him.
Cassio's a proper man. Let me see now: 393
To get his place and to plume up my will   394
In double knavery—How, how?—Let's see:
After some time, to abuse Othello's ear   396
That he is too familiar with his wife.   397
He hath a person and a smooth dispose   398
To be suspected, framed to make women false.
The Moor is of a free and open nature,   400
That thinks men honest that but seem to be so,
And will as tenderly be led by the nose   402
As asses are.
I have 't. It is engendered. Hell and night
Must bring this monstrous birth to the world's light.

                                        [*Exit.*]

❖

386 snipe woodcock, i.e., fool   388 it is thought abroad i.e., it is rumored   389 my office i.e., my sexual function as husband   391 do . . .
surety act as if on certain knowledge.   holds me well regards me
favorably   393 proper handsome   394 plume up glorify, gratify
396 abuse deceive   397 he i.e., Cassio   398 dispose manner, bearing
400 free frank, generous.   open unsuspicious   402 tenderly readily

2.1 *Enter Montano and two Gentlemen.*

MONTANO
  What from the cape can you discern at sea?
FIRST GENTLEMAN
  Nothing at all. It is a high-wrought flood.   2
  I cannot, twixt the heaven and the main,   3
  Descry a sail.
MONTANO
  Methinks the wind hath spoke aloud at land;
  A fuller blast ne'er shook our battlements.
  If it hath ruffianed so upon the sea,   7
  What ribs of oak, when mountains melt on them,   8
  Can hold the mortise? What shall we hear of this?   9
SECOND GENTLEMAN
  A segregation of the Turkish fleet.   10
  For do but stand upon the foaming shore,
  The chidden billow seems to pelt the clouds;   12
  The wind-shaked surge, with high and monstrous mane,   13
  Seems to cast water on the burning Bear   14
  And quench the guards of th' ever-fixèd pole.
  I never did like molestation view   16
  On the enchafèd flood.   17
MONTANO   If that the Turkish fleet   18
  Be not ensheltered and embayed, they are drowned;   19
  It is impossible to bear it out.   20

  Enter a [Third] Gentleman.

THIRD GENTLEMAN   News, lads! Our wars are done.

2.1. **Location: A seaport in Cyprus. An open place near the quay.**
2 high-wrought flood very agitated sea   **3 main** ocean (also at l. 41)
7 ruffianed raged   **8 mountains** i.e., of water   **9 hold the mortise** hold
their joints together. (A *mortise* is the socket hollowed out in fitting
timbers.)   **10 segregation** dispersion   **12 chidden** i.e., rebuked, repelled
(by the shore), and thus shot into the air   **13 monstrous mane** (The surf
is like the mane of a wild beast.)   **14 the burning Bear** i.e., the constellation Ursa Minor or the Little Bear, which includes the polestar (and
hence regarded as the *guards of th' ever-fixèd pole* in the next line;
sometimes the term *guards* is applied to the two "pointers" of the Big
Bear or Dipper, which may be intended here.)   **16 like molestation**
comparable uproar   **17 enchafèd** angry   **18 If that** if   **19 embayed**
sheltered by a bay   **20 bear it out** survive, weather the storm

The desperate tempest hath so banged the Turks
That their designment halts. A noble ship of Venice   23
Hath seen a grievous wreck and sufferance   24
On most part of their fleet.
MONTANO   How? Is this true?
THIRD GENTLEMAN   The ship is here put in,
A Veronesa; Michael Cassio,   28
Lieutenant to the warlike Moor Othello,
Is come on shore; the Moor himself at sea,
And is in full commission here for Cyprus.
MONTANO
I am glad on 't. 'Tis a worthy governor.
THIRD GENTLEMAN
But this same Cassio, though he speak of comfort
Touching the Turkish loss, yet he looks sadly   34
And prays the Moor be safe, for they were parted
With foul and violent tempest.
MONTANO   Pray heaven he be,
For I have served him, and the man commands
Like a full soldier. Let's to the seaside, ho!   38
As well to see the vessel that's come in
As to throw out our eyes for brave Othello,
Even till we make the main and th' aerial blue   41
An indistinct regard.
THIRD GENTLEMAN   Come, let's do so,   42
For every minute is expectancy   43
Of more arrivance.   44

    Enter Cassio.

CASSIO
Thanks, you the valiant of this warlike isle,
That so approve the Moor! O, let the heavens   46
Give him defense against the elements,
For I have lost him on a dangerous sea.
MONTANO   Is he well shipped?

---

23 designment enterprise. **halts** is lame **24 wreck** shipwreck.
sufferance disaster **28 Veronesa** i.e., fitted out in Verona for Venetian
service, or possibly *Verennessa* (the Folio spelling), a cutter (from *ver-
rinare*, to cut through) **34 sadly** gravely **38 full** perfect **41 the main
. . . blue** the sea and the sky **42 An indistinct regard** indistinguishable
in our view **43 is expectancy** gives expectation **44 arrivance** arrival
46 approve admire, honor

CASSIO
  His bark is stoutly timbered, and his pilot
  Of very expert and approved allowance;   51
  Therefore my hopes, not surfeited to death,   52
  Stand in bold cure.
                [A cry] within: "A sail, a sail, a sail!"   53
CASSIO   What noise?
A GENTLEMAN
  The town is empty. On the brow o' the sea
  Stand ranks of people, and they cry "A sail!"
CASSIO
  My hopes do shape him for the governor.
                                  [A shot within.]

SECOND GENTLEMAN
  They do discharge their shot of courtesy;   58
  Our friends at least.
CASSIO   I pray you, sir, go forth,
  And give us truth who 'tis that is arrived.
SECOND GENTLEMAN   I shall.   *Exit.*
MONTANO
  But, good Lieutenant, is your general wived?
CASSIO
  Most fortunately. He hath achieved a maid
  That paragons description and wild fame,   64
  One that excels the quirks of blazoning pens,   65
  And in th' essential vesture of creation   66
  Does tire the enginer.

     Enter [Second] Gentleman.

                  How now? Who has put in?   67
SECOND GENTLEMAN
  'Tis one Iago, ancient to the General.

---

51 approved allowance tested reputation   **52 surfeited to death** i.e.,
overextended, worn thin through repeated application or delayed fulfillment   **53 in bold cure** in strong hopes of fulfillment   **58 discharge . . .**
courtesy fire a salute in token of respect and courtesy   **64 paragons**
surpasses.   **wild fame** extravagant report   **65 quirks** witty conceits.
blazoning setting forth as though in heraldic language   **66–67 in . . .**
enginer in her real beauty (she) defeats any attempt to praise her.
enginer engineer, i.e., poet, one who devises   **s.d. Second Gentleman**
(So identified in the quarto text here and in ll. 58, 61, 68, and 96; the
Folio calls him a gentleman.)   **put in** i.e., to harbor

CASSIO
  He's had most favorable and happy speed.
  Tempests themselves, high seas, and howling winds,
  The guttered rocks and congregated sands—   71
  Traitors ensteeped to clog the guiltless keel—   72
  As having sense of beauty, do omit   73
  Their mortal natures, letting go safely by   74
  The divine Desdemona.
MONTANO   What is she?
CASSIO
  She that I spake of, our great captain's captain,
  Left in the conduct of the bold Iago,
  Whose footing here anticipates our thoughts   78
  A sennight's speed. Great Jove, Othello guard,   79
  And swell his sail with thine own powerful breath,
  That he may bless this bay with his tall ship,   81
  Make love's quick pants in Desdemona's arms,
  Give renewed fire to our extinct spirits,
  And bring all Cyprus comfort!

      Enter Desdemona, Iago, Roderigo, and Emilia.

                              O, behold,
  The riches of the ship is come on shore! [*He kneels.*]
  You men of Cyprus, let her have your knees.
  Hail to thee, lady! And the grace of heaven
  Before, behind thee, and on every hand
  Enwheel thee round!   [*He rises.*]
DESDEMONA   I thank you, valiant Cassio.
  What tidings can you tell me of my lord?
CASSIO
  He is not yet arrived, nor know I aught
  But that he's well and will be shortly here.
DESDEMONA
  O, but I fear—How lost you company?
CASSIO
  The great contention of the sea and skies
  Parted our fellowship.
                         (*Within*) "A sail, a sail!" [*A shot.*]
                         But hark. A sail!

71 **guttered** jagged, trenched 72 **ensteeped** lying under water 73 **As** as
if. **omit** forbear to exercise 74 **mortal** deadly 78 **footing** landing
79 **sennight's** week's 81 **tall** splendid, gallant

SECOND GENTLEMAN
    They give their greeting to the citadel.
    This likewise is a friend.
CASSIO   See for the news.
                    [*Exit Second Gentleman.*]
    Good Ancient, you are welcome. [*Kissing Emilia.*]
        Welcome, mistress.
    Let it not gall your patience, good Iago,
    That I extend my manners. 'Tis my breeding   100
    That gives me this bold show of courtesy.
IAGO
    Sir, would she give you so much of her lips
    As of her tongue she oft bestows on me,
    You would have enough.
DESDEMONA   Alas, she has no speech!
IAGO   In faith, too much.
    I find it still, when I have list to sleep.   107
    Marry, before your ladyship, I grant,
    She puts her tongue a little in her heart
    And chides with thinking.
EMILIA   You have little cause to say so. 110
IAGO
    Come on, come on. You are pictures out of doors,   111
    Bells in your parlors, wildcats in your kitchens,   112
    Saints in your injuries, devils being offended,   113
    Players in your huswifery, and huswives in your beds. 114
DESDEMONA   O, fie upon thee, slanderer!
IAGO
    Nay, it is true, or else I am a Turk.
    You rise to play, and go to bed to work.
EMILIA
    You shall not write my praise.
IAGO   No, let me not.
DESDEMONA
    What wouldst write of me, if thou shouldst praise me?

---

100 extend show   107 still always. list desire   110 with thinking i.e.,
in her thoughts only   111 pictures out of doors i.e., silent and well-
behaved in public   112 Bells i.e., jangling, noisy, and brazen. in your
kitchens i.e., in domestic affairs. (Ladies would not do the cooking.)
113 Saints martyrs   114 Players idlers, triflers, or deceivers. huswif-
ery housekeeping. huswives hussies (i.e., women are "busy" in bed, or
thrifty in dispensing sexual favors)

IAGO
    O gentle lady, do not put me to 't,
    For I am nothing if not critical.   121
DESDEMONA
    Come on, assay.—There's one gone to the harbor?   122
IAGO Ay, madam.
DESDEMONA
    I am not merry, but I do beguile
    The thing I am by seeming otherwise.   125
    Come, how wouldst thou praise me?
IAGO
    I am about it, but indeed my invention
    Comes from my pate as birdlime does from frieze—   128
    It plucks out brains and all. But my Muse labors,   129
    And thus she is delivered:
    If she be fair and wise, fairness and wit,
    The one's for use, the other useth it.   132
DESDEMONA
    Well praised! How if she be black and witty?   133
IAGO
    If she be black, and thereto have a wit,
    She'll find a white that shall her blackness fit.   135
DESDEMONA
    Worse and worse.
EMILIA   How if fair and foolish?
IAGO
    She never yet was foolish that was fair,
    For even her folly helped her to an heir.   138
DESDEMONA   These are old fond paradoxes to make fools   139
    laugh i' th' alehouse. What miserable praise hast thou
    for her that's foul and foolish?   141
IAGO
    There's none so foul and foolish thereunto,
    But does foul pranks which fair and wise ones do.   143

---

121 critical censorious   **122 assay** try   **125 The thing I am** i.e., my
anxious self   **128 birdlime** sticky substance used to catch small birds.
frieze coarse woolen cloth   **129 labors** (1) exerts herself (2) prepares to
deliver a child (with a following pun on *delivered* in l. 130)   **132 The
one's . . . it** i.e., her cleverness will make use of her beauty   **133 black**
dark complexioned, brunette   **135 white** a fair person (with wordplay
on *wight,* a person).   **fit** (with sexual suggestion of mating)   **138 folly**
(with added meaning of "lechery, wantonness").   **to an heir** i.e., to bear
a child   **139 fond** foolish   **141 foul** ugly   **143 foul** sluttish

DESDEMONA   O heavy ignorance! Thou praisest the worst
best. But what praise couldst thou bestow on a deserving woman indeed, one that, in the authority of her
merit, did justly put on the vouch of very malice itself?   147

IAGO
She that was ever fair, and never proud,
Had tongue at will, and yet was never loud,
Never lacked gold and yet went never gay,   150
Fled from her wish, and yet said, "Now I may,"   151
She that being angered, her revenge being nigh,
Bade her wrong stay and her displeasure fly,   153
She that in wisdom never was so frail
To change the cod's head for the salmon's tail,   155
She that could think and ne'er disclose her mind,
See suitors following and not look behind,
She was a wight, if ever such wight were—

DESDEMONA   To do what?

IAGO
To suckle fools and chronicle small beer.   160

DESDEMONA   O most lame and impotent conclusion! Do
not learn of him, Emilia, though he be thy husband.
How say you, Cassio? Is he not a most profane and   163
liberal counselor?   164

CASSIO   He speaks home, madam. You may relish him   165
more in the soldier than in the scholar.   166

              [Cassio and Desdemona stand together,
                        conversing intimately.]

IAGO [Aside]   He takes her by the palm. Ay, well said,   167
whisper. With as little a web as this will I ensnare as
great a fly as Cassio. Ay, smile upon her, do; I will
gyve thee in thine own courtship. You say true; 'tis so,   170
indeed. If such tricks as these strip you out of your

---

147 put . . . vouch compel the approval   150 gay extravagantly
clothed   151 Fled . . . may avoided temptation where the choice was
hers   153 Bade . . . stay i.e., resolved to put up with her injury patiently   155 To . . . tail i.e., to exchange a lackluster husband for a
sexy lover (?) (Cod's head is slang for penis, and tail for pudendum.)
160 suckle fools breastfeed babies.   chronicle small beer i.e., keep petty
household accounts, keep track of trivial matters   163 profane irrever-
ent, ribald   164 liberal licentious, free-spoken   165 home i.e., without
reserve.   relish appreciate   166 in in the character of   167 well said
well done   170 gyve fetter, shackle.   courtship courtesy, show of
courtly manners

lieutenantry, it had been better you had not kissed your three fingers so oft, which now again you are most apt to play the sir in. Very good; well kissed! An 174 excellent courtesy! 'Tis so, indeed. Yet again your fingers to your lips? Would they were clyster pipes for your 176 sake! [*Trumpet within.*] The Moor! I know his trumpet.

CASSIO 'Tis truly so.

DESDEMONA Let's meet him and receive him.

CASSIO Lo, where he comes!

Enter Othello and attendants.

OTHELLO
O my fair warrior!

DESDEMONA   My dear Othello!

OTHELLO
It gives me wonder great as my content
To see you here before me. O my soul's joy!
If after every tempest come such calms,
May the winds blow till they have wakened death!
And let the laboring bark climb hills of seas
Olympus-high, and duck again as low
As hell's from heaven! If it were now to die,
'Twere now to be most happy, for I fear
My soul hath her content so absolute
That not another comfort like to this
Succeeds in unknown fate.

DESDEMONA   The heavens forbid   192
But that our loves and comforts should increase
Even as our days do grow!

OTHELLO Amen to that, sweet powers!
I cannot speak enough of this content.
It stops me here; it is too much of joy.
And this, and this, the greatest discords be   198

                                        [*They kiss*]

That e'er our hearts shall make!

IAGO [*Aside*] O, you are well tuned now!

---

174 the sir i.e., the fine gentleman   **176 clyster pipes** tubes used for enemas and douches   **192 Succeeds . . . fate** i.e., can follow in the unknown future   **198 s.d. They kiss** (The direction is from the quarto.)

But I'll set down the pegs that make this music,   201
As honest as I am.

OTHELLO Come, let us to the castle.

News, friends! Our wars are done, the Turks are
    drowned.

How does my old acquaintance of this isle?—

Honey, you shall be well desired in Cyprus;   206

I have found great love amongst them. O my sweet,

I prattle out of fashion, and I dote   208

In mine own comforts.—I prithee, good Iago,

Go to the bay and disembark my coffers.   210

Bring thou the master to the citadel;   211

He is a good one, and his worthiness

Does challenge much respect.—Come, Desdemona.—   213

Once more, well met at Cyprus!

                    Exeunt Othello and Desdemona [and all
                                but Iago and Roderigo].

IAGO [*To an attendant*] Do thou meet me presently at
the harbor. [*To Roderigo.*] Come hither. If thou be'st
valiant—as, they say, base men being in love have   217
then a nobility in their natures more than is native to
them—list me. The Lieutenant tonight watches on the   219
court of guard. First, I must tell thee this: Desdemona   220
is directly in love with him.

RODERIGO With him? Why, 'tis not possible.

IAGO Lay thy finger thus, and let thy soul be instructed.   223
Mark me with what violence she first loved the Moor,
but for bragging and telling her fantastical lies.   225
To love him still for prating? Let not thy discreet
heart think it. Her eye must be fed; and what delight
shall she have to look on the devil? When the blood is
made dull with the act of sport, there should be, again
to inflame it and to give satiety a fresh appetite, love-
liness in favor, sympathy in years, manners, and   231

---

201 set down loosen (and hence untune the instrument)   **206 desired**
welcomed   **208 out of fashion** irrelevantly (?)   **210 coffers** chests,
baggage   **211 master** ship's captain   **213 challenge** lay claim to, deserve   **217 base men** even lowly born men   **219 list** listen to   **220 court
of guard** guardhouse. (Cassio is in charge of the watch.)   **223 thus** i.e.,
on your lips   **225 but** only   **231 favor** appearance.   **sympathy** corre-
spondence, similarity

beauties—all which the Moor is defective in. Now, for
want of these required conveniences, her delicate ten- 233
derness will find itself abused, begin to heave the 234
gorge, disrelish and abhor the Moor. Very nature will 235
instruct her in it and compel her to some second
choice. Now, sir, this granted—as it is a most preg- 237
nant and unforced position—who stands so eminent 238
in the degree of this fortune as Cassio does? A knave
very voluble, no further conscionable than in putting 240
on the mere form of civil and humane seeming for the 241
better compassing of his salt and most hidden loose 242
affection. Why, none, why, none. A slipper and subtle 243
knave, a finder out of occasions, that has an eye can 244
stamp and counterfeit advantages, though true advantage 245
never present itself; a devilish knave. Besides, the
knave is handsome, young, and hath all those requi-
sites in him that folly and green minds look after. A 248
pestilent complete knave, and the woman hath found 249
him already. 250

RODERIGO　I cannot believe that in her. She's full of most
blessed condition. 252

IAGO　Blessed fig's end! The wine she drinks is made of 253
grapes. If she had been blessed, she would never have
loved the Moor. Blessed pudding! Didst thou not see 255
her paddle with the palm of his hand? Didst not mark
that?

RODERIGO　Yes, that I did; but that was but courtesy.

IAGO　Lechery, by this hand. An index and obscure pro- 259
logue to the history of lust and foul thoughts. They
met so near with their lips that their breaths embraced
together. Villainous thoughts, Roderigo! When these
mutualities so marshal the way, hard at hand comes 263

233 conveniences compatibilities　**234–235 heave the gorge** experience
nausea　**237–238 pregnant** evident, cogent　**240 conscionable** conscien-
tious, conscience-bound　**241 humane** polite, courteous　**242 salt**
licentious　**243 affection** passion.　**slipper** slippery　**244–245 an eye
can stamp** an eye that can coin, create　**245 advantages** favorable
opportunities　**248 folly** wantonness.　**green** immature　**249–250 found
him** sized him up　**252 condition** disposition　**253 fig's end** (See 1.3.322
for the vulgar gesture of the fig.)　**255 pudding** sausage　**259 index**
table of contents.　**obscure** (i.e., the *lust and foul thoughts*, l. 260, are
secret, hidden from view)　**263 mutualities** exchanges, intimacies.
hard at hand closely following

the master and main exercise, th' incorporate conclu- 264
sion. Pish! But, sir, be you ruled by me. I have brought
you from Venice. Watch you tonight; for the com- 266
mand, I'll lay 't upon you. Cassio knows you not. I'll 267
not be far from you. Do you find some occasion to
anger Cassio, either by speaking too loud, or tainting 269
his discipline, or from what other course you please,
which the time shall more favorably minister.   271
RODERIGO Well.
IAGO Sir, he's rash and very sudden in choler, and hap- 273
ly may strike at you. Provoke him that he may, for 274
even out of that will I cause these of Cyprus to mutiny, 275
whose qualification shall come into no true taste again 276
but by the displanting of Cassio. So shall you have a
shorter journey to your desires by the means I shall
then have to prefer them, and the impediment most 279
profitably removed, without the which there were no
expectation of our prosperity.
RODERIGO I will do this, if you can bring it to any
opportunity.
IAGO I warrant thee. Meet me by and by at the citadel. 284
I must fetch his necessaries ashore. Farewell.
RODERIGO Adieu.   *Exit.*
IAGO
That Cassio loves her, I do well believe 't;
That she loves him, 'tis apt and of great credit.   288
The Moor, howbeit that I endure him not,
Is of a constant, loving, noble nature,
And I dare think he'll prove to Desdemona
A most dear husband. Now, I do love her too,
Not out of absolute lust—though peradventure
I stand accountant for as great a sin—   294
But partly led to diet my revenge   295
For that I do suspect the lusty Moor
Hath leaped into my seat, the thought whereof

---

264 **incorporate** carnal   266 **Watch you** stand watch   266–267 **for the command . . . you** I'll arrange for you to be appointed, given orders   269 **tainting** disparaging   271 **minister** provide   273 **choler** wrath   273–274 **haply** perhaps   275 **mutiny** riot   276 **qualification** appeasement.   **true taste** acceptable state   279 **prefer** advance   284 **warrant** assure.   **by and by** immediately   288 **apt** probable.   **credit** credibility   294 **accountant** accountable   295 **diet** feed

Doth, like a poisonous mineral, gnaw my innards;
And nothing can or shall content my soul
Till I am evened with him, wife for wife,
Or failing so, yet that I put the Moor
At least into a jealousy so strong
That judgment cannot cure. Which thing to do,
If this poor trash of Venice, whom I trace   304
For his quick hunting, stand the putting on,   305
I'll have our Michael Cassio on the hip,   306
Abuse him to the Moor in the rank garb—   307
For I fear Cassio with my nightcap too—   308
Make the Moor thank me, love me, and reward me
For making him egregiously an ass
And practicing upon his peace and quiet   311
Even to madness. 'Tis here, but yet confused.
Knavery's plain face is never seen till used.   *Exit.*

2.2   *Enter Othello's Herald with a proclamation.*

HERALD   It is Othello's pleasure, our noble and valiant
general, that, upon certain tidings now arrived, importing the mere perdition of the Turkish fleet, every 3
man put himself into triumph: some to dance, some
to make bonfires, each man to what sport and revels
his addiction leads him. For, besides these beneficial 6
news, it is the celebration of his nuptial. So much was
his pleasure should be proclaimed. All offices are open, 8
and there is full liberty of feasting from this present
hour of five till the bell have told eleven. Heaven bless
the isle of Cyprus and our noble general Othello!
                                                    Exit.

❖

304 **trace** i.e., train, or follow (?), or perhaps *trash*, a hunting term,
meaning to put weights on a hunting dog in order to slow him down
305 **For** to make more eager.   **stand . . . on** respond properly when I
incite him to quarrel   306 **on the hip** at my mercy, where I can throw
him. (A wrestling term.)   307 **Abuse** slander.   **rank garb** coarse manner,
gross fashion   308 **with my nightcap** i.e., as a rival in my bed, as one
who gives me cuckold's horns   311 **practicing upon** plotting against

2.2. Location: Cyprus. A street.
3 **mere perdition** complete destruction   6 **addiction** inclination
8 **offices** rooms where food and drink are kept

2.3   *Enter Othello, Desdemona, Cassio, and*
           attendants.

OTHELLO
  Good Michael, look you to the guard tonight.
  Let's teach ourselves that honorable stop   2
  Not to outsport discretion.   3
CASSIO
  Iago hath direction what to do,
  But notwithstanding, with my personal eye
  Will I look to 't.
OTHELLO   Iago is most honest.
  Michael, good night. Tomorrow with your earliest   7
  Let me have speech with you. [*To Desdemona.*] Come,
    my dear love,
  The purchase made, the fruits are to ensue;   9
  That profit's yet to come 'tween me and you.—   10
  Good night.
           Exit [Othello, with Desdemona and attendants].

           Enter Iago.

CASSIO Welcome, Iago. We must to the watch.
IAGO Not this hour, Lieutenant; 'tis not yet ten o' the   13
  clock. Our general cast us thus early for the love of his   14
  Desdemona; who let us not therefore blame. He hath   15
  not yet made wanton the night with her, and she is
  sport for Jove.
CASSIO She's a most exquisite lady.
IAGO And, I'll warrant her, full of game.
CASSIO Indeed, she's a most fresh and delicate creature.
IAGO What an eye she has! Methinks it sounds a parley   21
  to provocation.
CASSIO An inviting eye, and yet methinks right modest.
IAGO And when she speaks, is it not an alarum to love?   24

2.3. Location: Cyprus. The citadel.
2 stop restraint   **3 outsport** celebrate beyond the bounds of   **7 with
your earliest** at your earliest convenience   **9–10 The purchase . . . you**
i.e., though married, we haven't yet consummated our love   **13 Not this
hour** not for an hour yet   **14 cast** dismissed   **15 who** i.e., Othello
21 sounds a parley calls for a conference, issues an invitation
24 alarum signal calling men to arms (continuing the military metaphor
of *parley*, l. 21)

CASSIO She is indeed perfection.

IAGO Well, happiness to their sheets! Come, Lieutenant,
I have a stoup of wine, and here without are a brace 27
of Cyprus gallants that would fain have a measure to 28
the health of black Othello.

CASSIO Not tonight, good Iago. I have very poor and
unhappy brains for drinking. I could well wish courtesy would invent some other custom of entertainment.

IAGO O, they are our friends. But one cup! I'll drink
for you.   35

CASSIO I have drunk but one cup tonight, and that was
craftily qualified too, and behold what innovation it 37
makes here. I am unfortunate in the infirmity and 38
dare not task my weakness with any more.

IAGO What, man? 'Tis a night of revels. The gallants
desire it.

CASSIO Where are they?

IAGO Here at the door. I pray you, call them in.

CASSIO I'll do 't, but it dislikes me.   *Exit.* 44

IAGO
If I can fasten but one cup upon him,
With that which he hath drunk tonight already,
He'll be as full of quarrel and offense
As my young mistress' dog. Now, my sick fool Roderigo,
Whom love hath turned almost the wrong side out,
To Desdemona hath tonight caroused   50
Potations pottle-deep; and he's to watch.   51
Three lads of Cyprus—noble swelling spirits,   52
That hold their honors in a wary distance,   53
The very elements of this warlike isle—   54
Have I tonight flustered with flowing cups,
And they watch too. Now, 'mongst this flock of
  drunkards   56

---

27 stoup measure of liquor, two quarts. **without** outside. **brace** pair
28 have a measure drink a toast **35 for you** in your place. (Iago will do
the steady drinking to keep the gallants company while Cassio has only
one cup.) **37 qualified** diluted. **innovation** disturbance, insurrection
38 here i.e., in my head **44 dislikes** displeases **50 caroused** drunk
off **51 pottle-deep** to the bottom of the tankard **52 swelling** proud
53 hold . . . distance i.e., are extremely sensitive of their honor **54 very
elements** true representatives **56 watch** are members of the guard

Am I to put our Cassio in some action
That may offend the isle.—But here they come.

> *Enter Cassio, Montano, and gentlemen; [servants
> following with wine].*

If consequence do but approve my dream,   59
My boat sails freely both with wind and stream.   60
CASSIO 'Fore God, they have given me a rouse already.   61
MONTANO Good faith, a little one; not past a pint, as I
am a soldier.
IAGO Some wine, ho!

> [*Sings.*] "And let me the cannikin clink, clink,   65
> And let me the cannikin clink.
> A soldier's a man,
> O, man's life's but a span;   68
> Why, then, let a soldier drink."

Some wine, boys!
CASSIO 'Fore God, an excellent song.
IAGO I learned it in England, where indeed they are
most potent in potting. Your Dane, your German, and   73
your swag-bellied Hollander—drink, ho!—are noth-
ing to your English.
CASSIO Is your Englishman so exquisite in his drinking?
IAGO Why, he drinks you, with facility, your Dane   77
dead drunk; he sweats not to overthrow your Almain;   78
he gives your Hollander a vomit ere the next pottle can
be filled.
CASSIO To the health of our general!
MONTANO I am for it, Lieutenant, and I'll do you justice.   82
IAGO O sweet England! [*Sings.*]

> "King Stephen was and-a worthy peer,
> His breeches cost him but a crown;
> He held them sixpence all too dear;
> With that he called the tailor lown.   87

59 If . . . dream if subsequent events will only substantiate my
scheme **60 stream** current **61 rouse** full draft of liquor **65 cannikin**
small drinking vessel **68 span** i.e., brief span of time. (Compare Psalm
39:5 as rendered in the Book of Common Prayer: "Thou hast made my
days as it were a span long.") **73 potting** drinking **77 drinks you**
drinks. **your Dane** your typical Dane **78 Almain** German **82 I'll . . .
justice** i.e., I'll drink as much as you **87 lown** lout, rascal

He was a wight of high renown,
    And thou art but of low degree.
'Tis pride that pulls the country down;   90
    Then take thy auld cloak about thee."   91

Some wine, ho!

CASSIO 'Fore God, this is a more exquisite song than the other.

IAGO Will you hear 't again?

CASSIO No, for I hold him to be unworthy of his place that does those things. Well, God's above all; and there be souls must be saved, and there be souls must not be saved.

IAGO It's true, good Lieutenant.

CASSIO For mine own part—no offense to the General, nor any man of quality—I hope to be saved.   102

IAGO And so do I too, Lieutenant.

CASSIO Ay, but, by your leave, not before me. The lieutenant is to be saved before the ancient. Let's have no more of this. Let's to our affairs. God forgive us our sins! Gentlemen, let's look to our business. Do not think, gentlemen, I am drunk. This is my ancient; this is my right hand, and this is my left. I am not drunk now. I can stand well enough, and speak well enough.

GENTLEMEN Excellent well.

CASSIO Why, very well then. You must not think then that I am drunk.   *Exit.*

MONTANO

To th' platform, masters. Come, let's set the watch.   114

                    [Exeunt Gentlemen.]

IAGO

You see this fellow that is gone before.
He's a soldier fit to stand by Caesar
And give direction; and do but see his vice.
'Tis to his virtue a just equinox,   118
The one as long as th' other. 'Tis pity of him.
I fear the trust Othello puts him in,
On some odd time of his infirmity,
Will shake this island.

90 pride i.e., extravagance in dress **91 auld** old **102 quality** rank
114 set the watch mount the guard **118 just equinox** exact counterpart.
(*Equinox* is an equal length of days and nights.)

MONTANO   But is he often thus?

IAGO
'Tis evermore the prologue to his sleep.
He'll watch the horologe a double set,   124
If drink rock not his cradle.

MONTANO   It were well
The General were put in mind of it.
Perhaps he sees it not, or his good nature
Prizes the virtue that appears in Cassio
And looks not on his evils. Is not this true?

        Enter Roderigo.

IAGO [*Aside to him*]   How now, Roderigo?
I pray you, after the Lieutenant; go.   [*Exit Roderigo.*]

MONTANO
And 'tis great pity that the noble Moor
Should hazard such a place as his own second   133
With one of an engraffed infirmity.   134
It were an honest action to say so
To the Moor.

IAGO   Not I, for this fair island.
I do love Cassio well and would do much
To cure him of this evil.   [*Cry within:* "Help! Help!"]
                              But hark! What noise?   138

        Enter Cassio, pursuing Roderigo.

CASSIO   Zounds, you rogue! You rascal!

MONTANO   What's the matter, Lieutenant?

CASSIO   A knave teach me my duty? I'll beat the knave
into a twiggen bottle.   142

RODERIGO   Beat me?

CASSIO   Dost thou prate, rogue?   [*He strikes Roderigo.*]

MONTANO   Nay, good Lieutenant. [*Staying him.*] I pray
you, sir, hold your hand.

CASSIO   Let me go, sir, or I'll knock you o'er the maz-   147
ard.   148

---

124 watch . . . set stay awake twice around the clock or *horologe*
133–134 hazard . . . With risk giving such an important position as his
second in command to   **134 engraffed** engrafted, inveterate   **138 s.d.**
pursuing (The quarto text reads, "driving in.")   **142 twiggen** wicker-
covered. (Cassio vows to assail Roderigo until his skin resembles
wickerwork, or until he has driven Roderigo through the holes in a
wickerwork.)   **147–148 mazard** i.e., head. (Literally, a drinking vessel.)

MONTANO   Come, come, you're drunk.

CASSIO   Drunk?   [*They fight.*]

IAGO [*Aside to Roderigo*]

Away, I say. Go out and cry a mutiny. [*Exit Roderigo.*] 151
Nay, good Lieutenant—God's will, gentlemen—
Help, ho!—Lieutenant—sir—Montano—sir—
Help, masters!—Here's a goodly watch indeed!   154
                                    [*A bell rings.*]
Who's that which rings the bell?—Diablo, ho!   155
The town will rise. God's will, Lieutenant, hold!   156
You'll be ashamed forever.

   Enter Othello and attendants [*with weapons*].

OTHELLO
What is the matter here?

MONTANO   Zounds, I bleed still.
I am hurt to th' death. He dies! [*He thrusts at Cassio.*]

OTHELLO   Hold, for your lives!

IAGO
Hold, ho! Lieutenant—sir—Montano—gentlemen—
Have you forgot all sense of place and duty?
Hold! The General speaks to you. Hold, for shame!

OTHELLO
Why, how now, ho! From whence ariseth this?
Are we turned Turks, and to ourselves do that
Which heaven hath forbid the Ottomites?   165
For Christian shame, put by this barbarous brawl!
He that stirs next to carve for his own rage   167
Holds his soul light; he dies upon his motion.   168
Silence that dreadful bell. It frights the isle
From her propriety. What is the matter, masters?   170
Honest Iago, that looks dead with grieving,
Speak. Who began this? On thy love, I charge thee.

IAGO
I do not know. Friends all but now, even now,

---

151 mutiny riot   **154 masters** sirs   **s.d. A bell rings** (This direction is
from the quarto, as are *Exit Roderigo* at l. 131, *They fight* at l. 150, and
with weapons at l. 157.)   **155 Diablo** the devil   **156 rise** grow riotous
165 forbid i.e., prevented, by destroying their fleet, so that the Venetians
need not fight them   **167 carve for** i.e., indulge, satisfy   **168 Holds . . .
light** i.e., places little value on his life.   **upon his motion** if he moves
170 propriety proper state or condition

In quarter and in terms like bride and groom   174
Devesting them for bed; and then, but now—   175
As if some planet had unwitted men—
Swords out, and tilting one at other's breast
In opposition bloody. I cannot speak   178
Any beginning to this peevish odds;   179
And would in action glorious I had lost
Those legs that brought me to a part of it!

OTHELLO
How comes it, Michael, you are thus forgot?   182

CASSIO
I pray you, pardon me. I cannot speak.

OTHELLO
Worthy Montano, you were wont be civil;   184
The gravity and stillness of your youth   185
The world hath noted, and your name is great
In mouths of wisest censure. What's the matter   187
That you unlace your reputation thus   188
And spend your rich opinion for the name   189
Of a night-brawler? Give me answer to it.

MONTANO
Worthy Othello, I am hurt to danger.
Your officer, Iago, can inform you—
While I spare speech, which something now offends
  me—   193
Of all that I do know; nor know I aught
By me that's said or done amiss this night,
Unless self-charity be sometimes a vice,
And to defend ourselves it be a sin
When violence assails us.

OTHELLO   Now, by heaven,
My blood begins my safer guides to rule,   199
And passion, having my best judgment collied,   200

---

174 In quarter in friendly conduct, within bounds. **in terms** on good
terms   **175 Devesting them** undressing themselves   **178 speak** explain   **179 peevish odds** childish quarrel   **182 are thus forgot** have
forgotten yourself thus   **184 wont be** accustomed to be   **185 stillness**
sobriety   **187 censure** judgment   **188 unlace** undo, lay open (as one
might loose the strings of a purse containing reputation)   **189 opinion**
reputation   **193 something** somewhat. **offends** pains   **199 blood**
passion (of anger). **guides** i.e., reason   **200 collied** darkened

Assays to lead the way. Zounds, if I stir,   201
Or do but lift this arm, the best of you
Shall sink in my rebuke. Give me to know
How this foul rout began, who set it on;   204
And he that is approved in this offense,   205
Though he had twinned with me, both at a birth,
Shall lose me. What? In a town of war
Yet wild, the people's hearts brim full of fear,
To manage private and domestic quarrel?   209
In night, and on the court and guard of safety?   210
'Tis monstrous. Iago, who began 't?

MONTANO [*To Iago*]
If partially affined, or leagued in office,   212
Thou dost deliver more or less than truth,
Thou art no soldier.

IAGO   Touch me not so near.
I had rather have this tongue cut from my mouth
Than it should do offense to Michael Cassio;
Yet, I persuade myself, to speak the truth
Shall nothing wrong him. Thus it is, General.
Montano and myself being in speech,
There comes a fellow crying out for help,
And Cassio following him with determined sword
To execute upon him. Sir, this gentleman   222
                        [*Indicating Montano*]
Steps in to Cassio and entreats his pause.
Myself the crying fellow did pursue,
Lest by his clamor—as it so fell out—
The town might fall in fright. He, swift of foot,
Outran my purpose, and I returned, the rather   227
For that I heard the clink and fall of swords
And Cassio high in oath, which till tonight
I ne'er might say before. When I came back—
For this was brief—I found them close together
At blow and thrust, even as again they were

---

201 Assays undertakes   **204 rout** riot   **205 approved in** found guilty of
209 manage undertake   **210 on . . . safety** at the main guardhouse or head-
quarters and on watch   **212 partially affined** made partial by some personal
relationship.   **leagued in office** in league as fellow officers   **222 execute**
give effect to (his anger)   **227 rather** sooner

When you yourself did part them.
More of this matter cannot I report.
But men are men; the best sometimes forget.   235
Though Cassio did some little wrong to him,
As men in rage strike those that wish them best,   237
Yet surely Cassio, I believe, received
From him that fled some strange indignity,
Which patience could not pass.
OTHELLO   I know, Iago,   240
Thy honesty and love doth mince this matter,
Making it light to Cassio. Cassio, I love thee,
But nevermore be officer of mine.

    Enter Desdemona, attended.

Look if my gentle love be not raised up.
I'll make thee an example.
DESDEMONA
What is the matter, dear?
OTHELLO   All's well now, sweeting;
Come away to bed. [*To Montano.*] Sir, for your hurts,
Myself will be your surgeon.—Lead him off.   248
                    [*Montano is led off.*]
Iago, look with care about the town
And silence those whom this vile brawl distracted.
Come, Desdemona. 'Tis the soldiers' life
To have their balmy slumbers waked with strife.
           Exit [*with all but Iago and Cassio*].
IAGO What, are you hurt, Lieutenant?
CASSIO Ay, past all surgery.
IAGO Marry, God forbid!
CASSIO Reputation, reputation, reputation! O, I have
lost my reputation! I have lost the immortal part of
myself, and what remains is bestial. My reputation,
Iago, my reputation!
IAGO As I am an honest man, I thought you had re-
ceived some bodily wound; there is more sense in that
than in reputation. Reputation is an idle and most

---

235 forget forget themselves **237 those . . . best** i.e., even those who are
well disposed **240 pass** pass over, overlook **248 be your surgeon** i.e.,
make sure you receive medical attention

false imposition, oft got without merit and lost with- 263
out deserving. You have lost no reputation at all, unless you repute yourself such a loser. What, man, there
are ways to recover the General again. You are but now 266
cast in his mood—a punishment more in policy than in 267
malice, even so as one would beat his offenseless dog 268
to affright an imperious lion. Sue to him again and 269
he's yours.

CASSIO   I will rather sue to be despised than to deceive
so good a commander with so slight, so drunken, and 272
so indiscreet an officer. Drunk? And speak parrot? 273
And squabble? Swagger? Swear? And discourse fustian with one's own shadow? O thou invisible spirit
of wine, if thou hast no name to be known by, let us
call thee devil!

IAGO   What was he that you followed with your sword?
What had he done to you?

CASSIO   I know not.

IAGO   Is 't possible?

CASSIO   I remember a mass of things, but nothing distinctly; a quarrel, but nothing wherefore. O God, that 283
men should put an enemy in their mouths to steal
away their brains! That we should, with joy, pleas-
ance, revel, and applause transform ourselves into
beasts!

IAGO   Why, but you are now well enough. How came
you thus recovered?

CASSIO   It hath pleased the devil drunkenness to give
place to the devil wrath. One unperfectness shows me
another, to make me frankly despise myself.

IAGO   Come, you are too severe a moraler. As the time, 293
the place, and the condition of this country stands, I
could heartily wish this had not befallen; but since it is

---

263 **imposition** thing artificially imposed and of no real value   266 **recover** regain favor with   267 **cast in his mood** dismissed in a moment
of anger.   **in policy** done for expediency's sake and as a public gesture
268–269 **would . . . lion** i.e., would make an example of a minor offender
in order to deter more important and dangerous offenders   269 **Sue** petition   272 **slight** worthless   273 **speak parrot** talk nonsense, rant. (*Discourse
fustian*, ll. 274–275, has much the same meaning.)   283 **wherefore** why
293 **moraler** moralizer

as it is, mend it for your own good.

CASSIO   I will ask him for my place again; he shall tell
me I am a drunkard! Had I as many mouths as Hydra, 298
such an answer would stop them all. To be now a sensible man, by and by a fool, and presently a beast! O,
strange! Every inordinate cup is unblessed, and the ingredient is a devil.

IAGO   Come, come, good wine is a good familiar creature, if it be well used. Exclaim no more against it.
And, good Lieutenant, I think you think I love you.

CASSIO   I have well approved it, sir. I drunk!   306

IAGO   You or any man living may be drunk at a time,   307
man. I'll tell you what you shall do. Our general's wife
is now the general—I may say so in this respect, for   309
that he hath devoted and given up himself to the con-   310
templation, mark, and denotement of her parts and   311
graces. Confess yourself freely to her; importune her
help to put you in your place again. She is of so free,   313
so kind, so apt, so blessed a disposition, she holds it a
vice in her goodness not to do more than she is requested. This broken joint between you and her husband entreat her to splinter; and, my fortunes against 317
any lay worth naming, this crack of your love shall   318
grow stronger than it was before.

CASSIO   You advise me well.

IAGO   I protest, in the sincerity of love and honest kind- 321
ness.

CASSIO   I think it freely; and betimes in the morning I   323
will beseech the virtuous Desdemona to undertake for
me. I am desperate of my fortunes if they check me   325
here.

IAGO   You are in the right. Good night, Lieutenant. I
must to the watch.

---

298 **Hydra** the Lernaean Hydra, a monster with many heads and the
ability to grow two heads when one was cut off; slain by Hercules as
the second of his twelve labors   306 **approved** proved   307 **at a time** at
one time or another   309–310 **in . . . that** in view of this fact, that
311 **mark, and denotement** (Both words mean "observation.")   **parts**
qualities   313 **free** generous   317 **splinter** bind with splints   318 **lay**
stake, wager   321 **protest** insist, declare   323 **freely** unreservedly
325 **check** repulse

CASSIO   Good night, honest Iago.   *Exit Cassio.*

IAGO
 And what's he then that says I play the villain,
 When this advice is free I give and honest,   331
 Probal to thinking, and indeed the course   332
 To win the Moor again? For 'tis most easy
 Th' inclining Desdemona to subdue   334
 In any honest suit; she's framed as fruitful 335
 As the free elements. And then for her   336
 To win the Moor—were 't to renounce his baptism,
 All seals and symbols of redeemèd sin—
 His soul is so enfettered to her love
 That she may make, unmake, do what she list,
 Even as her appetite shall play the god
 With his weak function. How am I then a villain, 342
 To counsel Cassio to this parallel course 343
 Directly to his good? Divinity of hell!   344
 When devils will the blackest sins put on, 345
 They do suggest at first with heavenly shows, 346
 As I do now. For whiles this honest fool
 Plies Desdemona to repair his fortune,
 And she for him pleads strongly to the Moor,
 I'll pour this pestilence into his ear,
 That she repeals him for her body's lust; 351
 And by how much she strives to do him good,
 She shall undo her credit with the Moor.
 So will I turn her virtue into pitch,
 And out of her own goodness make the net
 That shall enmesh them all.

  Enter Roderigo.

        How now, Roderigo?
RODERIGO   I do follow here in the chase, not like a

---

331 free (1) free from guile (2) freely given **332 Probal** probable, reasonable **334 inclining** favorably disposed. **subdue** persuade **335 fruitful**
generous **336 free elements** i.e., earth, air, fire, and water, which
sustain life (?) **342 function** exercise of faculties (weakened by his
fondness for her) **343 parallel** corresponding to these facts and to his
best interests **344 Divinity of hell** inverted theology of hell (which
seduces the soul to its damnation) **345 put on** further, instigate
346 suggest tempt **351 repeals him** i.e., attempts to get him restored

hound that hunts, but one that fills up the cry. My 358
money is almost spent; I have been tonight exceedingly well cudgeled; and I think the issue will be I
shall have so much experience for my pains, and so, 361
with no money at all and a little more wit, return again
to Venice.

IAGO
How poor are they that have not patience!
What wound did ever heal but by degrees?
Thou know'st we work by wit, and not by witchcraft,
And wit depends on dilatory time.
Does 't not go well? Cassio hath beaten thee,
And thou, by that small hurt, hast cashiered Cassio.   369
Though other things grow fair against the sun,   370
Yet fruits that blossom first will first be ripe.   371
Content thyself awhile. By the Mass, 'tis morning!
Pleasure and action make the hours seem short.
Retire thee; go where thou art billeted.
Away, I say! Thou shalt know more hereafter.
Nay, get thee gone.   *Exit Roderigo.*
               Two things are to be done.
My wife must move for Cassio to her mistress;   377
I'll set her on;
Myself the while to draw the Moor apart
And bring him jump when he may Cassio find   380
Soliciting his wife. Ay, that's the way.
Dull not device by coldness and delay.   *Exit.* 382

358 fills up the cry merely takes part as one of the pack   **361 so
much** just so much and no more   **369 cashiered** dismissed from service
370–371 Though . . . ripe i.e., the first part of our plan has already ripened
to fruition, and other parts are maturing in their own good time   **377 move**
plead   **380 jump** precisely   **382 device** plot.   **coldness** lack of zeal

3.1   *Enter Cassio [and] Musicians.*

CASSIO
    Masters, play here—I will content your pains—   1
    Something that's brief, and bid "Good morrow,
      General."   [*They play.*]

    [*Enter*] *Clown.*

CLOWN Why, masters, have your instruments been in
Naples, that they speak i' the nose thus?   4
A MUSICIAN How, sir, how?
CLOWN Are these, I pray you, wind instruments?
A MUSICIAN Ay, marry, are they, sir.
CLOWN O, thereby hangs a tail.
A MUSICIAN Whereby hangs a tale, sir?
CLOWN Marry, sir, by many a wind instrument that I   10
know. But, masters, here's money for you. [*He gives
money.*] And the General so likes your music that he
desires you, for love's sake, to make no more noise   13
with it.
A MUSICIAN Well, sir, we will not.
CLOWN If you have any music that may not be heard,   16
to 't again; but, as they say, to hear music the General
does not greatly care.
A MUSICIAN We have none such, sir.
CLOWN Then put up your pipes in your bag, for I'll   20
away. Go, vanish into air, away!   *Exeunt Musicians.*   21
CASSIO Dost thou hear, mine honest friend?
CLOWN No, I hear not your honest friend; I hear you.
CASSIO Prithee, keep up thy quillets. There's a poor   24
piece of gold for thee. [*He gives money.*] If the gentlewoman that attends the General's wife be stirring, tell

---

3.1. Location: Before the chamber of Othello and Desdemona.
1 content reward. **pains** efforts **4 speak i' the nose** (1) sound nasal
(2) sound like one whose nose has been attacked by syphilis. (Naples
was popularly supposed to have a high incidence of venereal disease.)
10 wind instrument (With a joke on flatulence. The *tail*, l. 8, that hangs
nearby the *wind instrument* suggests the penis.) **13 for love's sake**
(1) out of friendship and affection (2) for the sake of lovemaking in
Othello's marriage **16 may not** cannot **20–21 I'll away** (Possibly a
misprint, or a snatch of song?) **24 keep up** do not bring out, do not
use. **quillets** quibbles, puns

her there's one Cassio entreats her a little favor of   27
speech. Wilt thou do this?   28
CLOWN   She is stirring, sir. If she will stir hither, I shall
seem to notify unto her.   30
CASSIO
Do, good my friend.   *Exit Clown.*

  Enter Iago.

                    In happy time, Iago.   31
IAGO You have not been abed, then?
CASSIO Why, no. The day had broke
Before we parted. I have made bold, Iago,
To send in to your wife. My suit to her
Is that she will to virtuous Desdemona
Procure me some access.
IAGO I'll send her to you presently;
And I'll devise a means to draw the Moor
Out of the way, that your converse and business
May be more free.
CASSIO
I humbly thank you for 't.   *Exit [Iago].*
                    I never knew
A Florentine more kind and honest.   43

  Enter Emilia.

EMILIA
Good morrow, good Lieutenant. I am sorry
For your displeasure; but all will sure be well.   45
The General and his wife are talking of it,
And she speaks for you stoutly. The Moor replies
That he you hurt is of great fame in Cyprus
And great affinity, and that in wholesome wisdom   49
He might not but refuse you; but he protests he loves you
And needs no other suitor but his likings
To take the safest occasion by the front   52
To bring you in again.
CASSIO   Yet I beseech you,

27–28 a little . . . speech the favor of a brief talk 30 seem deem it
good, think fit 31 In happy time i.e., well met 43 Florentine i.e.,
even a fellow Florentine. (Iago is a Venetian, Cassio a Florentine.)
45 displeasure fall from favor 49 affinity kindred, family connection
52 occasion . . . front opportunity by the forelock

If you think fit, or that it may be done,
Give me advantage of some brief discourse
With Desdemon alone.
EMILIA   Pray you, come in.
I will bestow you where you shall have time
To speak your bosom freely.   58
CASSIO   I am much bound to you.   [*Exeunt.*]

3.2   *Enter Othello, Iago, and Gentlemen.*

OTHELLO [*Giving letters*]
These letters give, Iago, to the pilot,
And by him do my duties to the Senate.   2
That done, I will be walking on the works;   3
Repair there to me.
IAGO   Well, my good lord, I'll do 't.   4
OTHELLO
This fortification, gentlemen, shall we see 't?
GENTLEMEN   We'll wait upon your lordship.   *Exeunt.* 6

3.3   *Enter Desdemona, Cassio, and Emilia.*

DESDEMONA
Be thou assured, good Cassio, I will do
All my abilities in thy behalf.
EMILIA
Good madam, do. I warrant it grieves my husband
As if the cause were his.
DESDEMONA
O, that's an honest fellow. Do not doubt, Cassio,
But I will have my lord and you again
As friendly as you were.

---

58 bosom inmost thoughts

3.2. Location: The citadel.
2 do my duties convey my respects   **3 works** breastworks, fortifications   **4 Repair** return, come   **6 wait upon** attend

3.3. Location: The garden of the citadel.

CASSIO   Bounteous madam,
  Whatever shall become of Michael Cassio,
  He's never anything but your true servant.
DESDEMONA
  I know 't. I thank you. You do love my lord;
  You have known him long, and be you well assured
  He shall in strangeness stand no farther off   12
  Than in a politic distance.
CASSIO   Ay, but, lady,   13
  That policy may either last so long,
  Or feed upon such nice and waterish diet,   15
  Or breed itself so out of circumstance,   16
  That, I being absent and my place supplied,   17
  My general will forget my love and service.
DESDEMONA
  Do not doubt that. Before Emilia here   19
  I give thee warrant of thy place. Assure thee,
  If I do vow a friendship I'll perform it
  To the last article. My lord shall never rest.
  I'll watch him tame and talk him out of patience;   23
  His bed shall seem a school, his board a shrift;   24
  I'll intermingle everything he does
  With Cassio's suit. Therefore be merry, Cassio,
  For thy solicitor shall rather die   27
  Than give thy cause away.   28

          Enter Othello and Iago [at a distance].

EMILIA   Madam, here comes my lord.
CASSIO   Madam, I'll take my leave.
DESDEMONA   Why, stay, and hear me speak.
CASSIO
  Madam, not now. I am very ill at ease,
  Unfit for mine own purposes.
DESDEMONA   Well, do your discretion.   *Exit Cassio.* 34

---

12 strangeness aloofness   **13 politic** required by wise policy   **15 Or . . .
diet** or sustain itself at length upon such a trivial and meager means of
support   **16 breed . . . circumstance** continually renew itself so out of
chance events, or yield so few chances for my being pardoned
17 supplied filled by another person   **19 doubt** fear   **23 watch him
tame** tame him by keeping him from sleeping. (A term from falconry.)
out of patience past his endurance   **24 shrift** confessional   **27 solicitor**
advocate   **28 away** up   **34 do your discretion** act according to your own
discretion

IAGO   Ha? I like not that.

OTHELLO   What dost thou say?

IAGO
Nothing, my lord; or if—I know not what.

OTHELLO
Was not that Cassio parted from my wife?

IAGO
Cassio, my lord? No, sure, I cannot think it,
That he would steal away so guiltylike,
Seeing you coming.

OTHELLO   I do believe 'twas he.

DESDEMONA   How now, my lord?
I have been talking with a suitor here,
A man that languishes in your displeasure.

OTHELLO   Who is 't you mean?

DESDEMONA
Why, your lieutenant, Cassio. Good my lord,
If I have any grace or power to move you,
His present reconciliation take;   49
For if he be not one that truly loves you,
That errs in ignorance and not in cunning,   51
I have no judgment in an honest face.
I prithee, call him back.

OTHELLO   Went he hence now?

DESDEMONA   Yes, faith, so humbled
That he hath left part of his grief with me
To suffer with him. Good love, call him back.

OTHELLO
Not now, sweet Desdemon. Some other time.

DESDEMONA   But shall 't be shortly?

OTHELLO   The sooner, sweet, for you.

DESDEMONA   Shall 't be tonight at supper?

OTHELLO   No, not tonight.

DESDEMONA   Tomorrow dinner, then?   63

OTHELLO   I shall not dine at home.
I meet the captains at the citadel.

DESDEMONA
Why, then, tomorrow night, or Tuesday morn,
On Tuesday noon, or night, on Wednesday morn.

49 present immediate   **51 in cunning** wittingly   **63 dinner** (The noon-
time meal.)

I prithee, name the time, but let it not
Exceed three days. In faith, he's penitent;
And yet his trespass, in our common reason—   70
Save that, they say, the wars must make example   71
Out of her best—is not almost a fault   72
T' incur a private check. When shall he come?   73
Tell me, Othello. I wonder in my soul
What you would ask me that I should deny,
Or stand so mammering on. What? Michael Cassio,   76
That came a-wooing with you, and so many a time,
When I have spoke of you dispraisingly,
Hath ta'en your part—to have so much to do
To bring him in! By 'r Lady, I could do much—   80

OTHELLO
Prithee, no more. Let him come when he will;
I will deny thee nothing.

DESDEMONA   Why, this is not a boon.
'Tis as I should entreat you wear your gloves,
Or feed on nourishing dishes, or keep you warm,
Or sue to you to do a peculiar profit   86
To your own person. Nay, when I have a suit
Wherein I mean to touch your love indeed,
It shall be full of poise and difficult weight,   89
And fearful to be granted.

OTHELLO   I will deny thee nothing.
Whereon, I do beseech thee, grant me this,   92
To leave me but a little to myself.

DESDEMONA
Shall I deny you? No. Farewell, my lord.

OTHELLO
Farewell, my Desdemona. I'll come to thee straight.   95

DESDEMONA
Emilia, come.—Be as your fancies teach you;   96
Whate'er you be, I am obedient.   *Exit [with Emilia].*

---

70 **common reason** everyday judgments   71–72 **Save . . . best** were it
not that, as the saying goes, military discipline requires making an
example of the very best men. (*Her* refers to *wars* as a singular concept.)   72 **not almost** scarcely   73 **a private check** even a private repri-
mand   76 **mammering on** wavering about   80 **bring him in** restore him
to favor   86 **peculiar** particular, personal   89 **poise** weight, heaviness;
or equipoise, delicate balance involving hard choice   92 **Whereon** in
return for which   95 **straight** straightway   96 **fancies** inclinations

OTHELLO
  Excellent wretch! Perdition catch my soul   98
  But I do love thee! And when I love thee not,   99
  Chaos is come again.
IAGO   My noble lord—
OTHELLO   What dost thou say, Iago?
IAGO
  Did Michael Cassio, when you wooed my lady,
  Know of your love?
OTHELLO
  He did, from first to last. Why dost thou ask?
IAGO
  But for a satisfaction of my thought;
  No further harm.
OTHELLO   Why of thy thought, Iago?
IAGO
  I did not think he had been acquainted with her.
OTHELLO
  O, yes, and went between us very oft.
IAGO   Indeed?
OTHELLO
  Indeed? Ay, indeed. Discern'st thou aught in that?
  Is he not honest?
IAGO   Honest, my lord?
OTHELLO   Honest. Ay, honest.
IAGO   My lord, for aught I know.
OTHELLO   What dost thou think?
IAGO   Think, my lord?
OTHELLO
  "Think, my lord?" By heaven, thou echo'st me,
  As if there were some monster in thy thought
  Too hideous to be shown. Thou dost mean something.
  I heard thee say even now, thou lik'st not that,
  When Cassio left my wife. What didst not like?
  And when I told thee he was of my counsel   123
  In my whole course of wooing, thou criedst "Indeed?"
  And didst contract and purse thy brow together   125

---

98 wretch (A term of affectionate endearment.)   **99 But I do** if I do
not   **123 of my counsel** in my confidence   **125 purse** knit

As if thou then hadst shut up in thy brain
Some horrible conceit. If thou dost love me,   127
Show me thy thought.

IAGO   My lord, you know I love you.

OTHELLO   I think thou dost;
And, for I know thou'rt full of love and honesty,
And weigh'st thy words before thou giv'st them breath,
Therefore these stops of thine fright me the more;   133
For such things in a false disloyal knave
Are tricks of custom, but in a man that's just   135
They're close dilations, working from the heart   136
That passion cannot rule.

IAGO   For Michael Cassio,   137
I dare be sworn I think that he is honest.

OTHELLO
I think so too.

IAGO   Men should be what they seem;
Or those that be not, would they might seem none!   140

OTHELLO
Certain, men should be what they seem.

IAGO
Why, then, I think Cassio's an honest man.

OTHELLO   Nay, yet there's more in this.
I prithee, speak to me as to thy thinkings,
As thou dost ruminate, and give thy worst of thoughts
The worst of words.

IAGO   Good my lord, pardon me.
Though I am bound to every act of duty,
I am not bound to that all slaves are free to.   148
Utter my thoughts? Why, say they are vile and false,
As where's that palace whereinto foul things
Sometimes intrude not? Who has that breast so pure
But some uncleanly apprehensions

---

127 **conceit** fancy   **133 stops** pauses   **135 of custom** customary
136 close dilations secret or involuntary expressions or delays
137 That passion cannot rule i.e., that are too passionately strong to
be restrained (referring to the workings), or, that cannot rule its own
passions (referring to the heart)   **140 none** i.e., not to be men,
or not seem to be honest   **148 that** that which.   **free to** i.e.,
free with respect to

Keep leets and law days, and in sessions sit 153
With meditations lawful? 154

OTHELLO
Thou dost conspire against thy friend, Iago, 155
If thou but think'st him wronged and mak'st his ear
A stranger to thy thoughts.

IAGO   I do beseech you,
Though I perchance am vicious in my guess— 158
As I confess it is my nature's plague
To spy into abuses, and oft my jealousy 160
Shapes faults that are not—that your wisdom then, 161
From one that so imperfectly conceits, 162
Would take no notice, nor build yourself a trouble
Out of his scattering and unsure observance. 164
It were not for your quiet nor your good,
Nor for my manhood, honesty, and wisdom,
To let you know my thoughts.

OTHELLO   What dost thou mean?

IAGO
Good name in man and woman, dear my lord,
Is the immediate jewel of their souls. 169
Who steals my purse steals trash; 'tis something,
   nothing;
'Twas mine, 'tis his, and has been slave to thousands;
But he that filches from me my good name
Robs me of that which not enriches him
And makes me poor indeed.

OTHELLO   By heaven, I'll know thy thoughts.

IAGO
You cannot, if my heart were in your hand, 176
Nor shall not, whilst 'tis in my custody.

OTHELLO
Ha?

IAGO   O, beware, my lord, of jealousy!

---

153 Keep leets and law days i.e., hold court, set up their authority in
one's heart. (*Leets* are a kind of manor court; *law days* are the days
courts sit in session, or those sessions.) **154 With** along with. **lawful**
innocent **155 thy friend** i.e., Othello **158 vicious** wrong **160 jealousy**
suspicion of evil **161 then** on that account **162 one** i.e., myself,
Iago. **conceits** judges, conjectures **164 scattering** random
169 immediate essential, most precious **176 if** even if

It is the green-eyed monster which doth mock   179
The meat it feeds on. That cuckold lives in bliss   180
Who, certain of his fate, loves not his wronger;   181
But O, what damnèd minutes tells he o'er   182
Who dotes, yet doubts, suspects, yet fondly loves!
OTHELLO   O misery!
IAGO
Poor and content is rich, and rich enough,   185
But riches fineless is as poor as winter   186
To him that ever fears he shall be poor.
Good God, the souls of all my tribe defend
From jealousy!
OTHELLO   Why, why is this?
Think'st thou I'd make a life of jealousy,
To follow still the changes of the moon   192
With fresh suspicions? No! To be once in doubt   193
Is once to be resolved. Exchange me for a goat   194
When I shall turn the business of my soul
To such exsufflicate and blown surmises   196
Matching thy inference. 'Tis not to make me jealous   197
To say my wife is fair, feeds well, loves company,
Is free of speech, sings, plays, and dances well;
Where virtue is, these are more virtuous.
Nor from mine own weak merits will I draw
The smallest fear or doubt of her revolt,   202
For she had eyes, and chose me. No, Iago,
I'll see before I doubt; when I doubt, prove;
And on the proof, there is no more but this—
Away at once with love or jealousy.

179–180 doth mock . . . on mocks and torments the heart of its victim, the man who suffers jealousy   **181 his wronger** i.e., his faithless wife. (The unsuspecting cuckold is spared the misery of loving his wife only to discover she is cheating on him.)   **182 tells** counts   **185 Poor . . . enough** to be content with what little one has is the greatest wealth of all. (Proverbial.)   **186 fineless** boundless   **192–193 To follow . . . suspicions** to be constantly imagining new causes for suspicion, changing incessantly like the moon   **194 once** once and for all.   **resolved** free of doubt, having settled the matter   **196 exsufflicate and blown** inflated and blown up, rumored about; or, spat out and flyblown, hence, loathsome, disgusting   **197 inference** description or allegation   **202 doubt . . . revolt** fear of her unfaithfulness

IAGO

I am glad of this, for now I shall have reason
To show the love and duty that I bear you
With franker spirit. Therefore, as I am bound,
Receive it from me. I speak not yet of proof.
Look to your wife; observe her well with Cassio.
Wear your eyes thus, not jealous nor secure.   212
I would not have your free and noble nature,
Out of self-bounty, be abused. Look to 't.   214
I know our country disposition well;
In Venice they do let God see the pranks
They dare not show their husbands; their best
   conscience
Is not to leave 't undone, but keep 't unknown.

OTHELLO   Dost thou say so?

IAGO

She did deceive her father, marrying you;
And when she seemed to shake and fear your looks,
She loved them most.

OTHELLO   And so she did.

IAGO   Why, go to, then!   222
She that, so young, could give out such a seeming,   223
To seel her father's eyes up close as oak,   224
He thought 'twas witchcraft! But I am much to blame.
I humbly do beseech you of your pardon
For too much loving you.

OTHELLO   I am bound to thee forever.   228

IAGO

I see this hath a little dashed your spirits.

OTHELLO

Not a jot, not a jot.

IAGO   I' faith, I fear it has.
I hope you will consider what is spoke
Comes from my love. But I do see you're moved.
I am to pray you not to strain my speech

---

212 **not** neither. **secure** free from uncertainty 214 **self-bounty** inherent or natural goodness and generosity. **abused** deceived 222 **go to** (An expression of impatience.) 223 **seeming** false appearance 224 **seel** blind. (A term from falconry.) **oak** (A close-grained wood.) 228 **bound** indebted (but perhaps with ironic sense of "tied")

To grosser issues nor to larger reach   234
Than to suspicion.
OTHELLO   I will not.
IAGO   Should you do so, my lord,
My speech should fall into such vile success   238
Which my thoughts aimed not. Cassio's my worthy
    friend.
My lord, I see you're moved.
OTHELLO   No, not much moved.
I do not think but Desdemona's honest.   241
IAGO
Long live she so! And long live you to think so!
OTHELLO
And yet, how nature erring from itself—
IAGO
Ay, there's the point! As—to be bold with you—
Not to affect many proposèd matches   245
Of her own clime, complexion, and degree,
Whereto we see in all things nature tends—
Foh! One may smell in such a will most rank,   248
Foul disproportion, thoughts unnatural.   249
But pardon me. I do not in position   250
Distinctly speak of her, though I may fear
Her will, recoiling to her better judgment,   252
May fall to match you with her country forms   253
And happily repent.
OTHELLO   Farewell, farewell!   254
If more thou dost perceive, let me know more.
Set on thy wife to observe. Leave me, Iago.
IAGO [*Going*]   My lord, I take my leave.
OTHELLO
Why did I marry? This honest creature doubtless
Sees and knows more, much more, than he unfolds.

---

234 issues significances. **reach** meaning, scope **238 success** effect,
result **241 honest** chaste **245 affect** prefer, desire **248 will** sensuality, appetite **249 disproportion** abnormality **250 position** argument,
proposition **252 recoiling** reverting. **better** i.e., more natural and
reconsidered **253 fall . . . forms** undertake to compare you with Venetian norms of handsomeness **254 happily repent** haply repent her
marriage

IAGO [*Returning*]
　My Lord, I would I might entreat your honor
　To scan this thing no farther. Leave it to time.
　Although 'tis fit that Cassio have his place—
　For, sure, he fills it up with great ability—
　Yet, if you please to hold him off awhile,
　You shall by that perceive him and his means.
　Note if your lady strain his entertainment   266
　With any strong or vehement importunity;
　Much will be seen in that. In the meantime,
　Let me be thought too busy in my fears—
　As worthy cause I have to fear I am—
　And hold her free, I do beseech your honor.   271
OTHELLO　Fear not my government.   272
IAGO　I once more take my leave.   *Exit.*
OTHELLO
　This fellow's of exceeding honesty,
　And knows all qualities, with a learnèd spirit,   275
　Of human dealings. If I do prove her haggard,   276
　Though that her jesses were my dear heartstrings,   277
　I'd whistle her off and let her down the wind   278
　To prey at fortune. Haply, for I am black   279
　And have not those soft parts of conversation   280
　That chamberers have, or for I am declined   281
　Into the vale of years—yet that's not much—
　She's gone. I am abused, and my relief   283
　Must be to loathe her. O curse of marriage,
　That we can call these delicate creatures ours
　And not their appetites! I had rather be a toad
　And live upon the vapor of a dungeon
　Than keep a corner in the thing I love
　For others' uses. Yet, 'tis the plague of great ones;
　Prerogatived are they less than the base.   290

266 strain his entertainment urge his reinstatement　**271 hold her free**
regard her as innocent　**272 government** self-control, conduct
275 qualities natures, types　**276 haggard** wild (like a wild female
hawk)　**277 jesses** straps fastened around the legs of a trained hawk
278 I'd . . . wind i.e., I'd let her go forever. (To release a hawk downwind
was to invite it not to return.)　**279 prey at fortune** fend for herself in
the wild.　**Haply, for** perhaps because　**280 soft . . . conversation**
pleasing graces of social behavior　**281 chamberers** gallants
283 abused deceived　**290 Prerogatived** privileged (to have honest
wives).　**the base** ordinary citizens

'Tis destiny unshunnable, like death.
Even then this forkèd plague is fated to us   292
When we do quicken. Look where she comes.   293

    Enter Desdemona and Emilia.

If she be false, O, then heaven mocks itself!
I'll not believe 't.
DESDEMONA   How now, my dear Othello?
Your dinner, and the generous islanders   296
By you invited, do attend your presence.   297
OTHELLO
I am to blame.
DESDEMONA   Why do you speak so faintly?
Are you not well?
OTHELLO
I have a pain upon my forehead here.
DESDEMONA
Faith, that's with watching. 'Twill away again.   301
           [*She offers her handkerchief.*]
Let me but bind it hard, within this hour
It will be well.
OTHELLO   Your napkin is too little.   303
Let it alone. Come, I'll go in with you.   304
        [*He puts the handkerchief from him,*
                and it drops.]

DESDEMONA
I am very sorry that you are not well.
             Exit [*with Othello*].
EMILIA [*Picking up the handkerchief*]
I am glad I have found this napkin.
This was her first remembrance from the Moor.
My wayward husband hath a hundred times   308
Wooed me to steal it, but she so loves the token—
For he conjured her she should ever keep it—
That she reserves it evermore about her

---

292 forkèd (An allusion to the horns of the cuckold.)   **293 quicken**
receive life. (*Quicken* may also mean to swarm with maggots as the
body festers, as in 4.2.69, in which case ll. 292–293 suggest that *even
then*, in death, we are cuckolded by *forkèd* worms.)   **296 generous**
noble   **297 attend** await   **301 watching** too little sleep   **303 napkin**
handkerchief   **304 Let it alone** i.e., never mind   **308 wayward**
capricious

To kiss and talk to. I'll have the work ta'en out,   312
And give 't Iago. What he will do with it
Heaven knows, not I;
I nothing but to please his fantasy.   315

     Enter Iago.

IAGO
How now? What do you here alone?
EMILIA
Do not you chide. I have a thing for you.
IAGO
You have a thing for me? It is a common thing—   318
EMILIA Ha?
IAGO To have a foolish wife.
EMILIA
O, is that all? What will you give me now
For that same handkerchief?
IAGO What handkerchief?
EMILIA What handkerchief?
Why, that the Moor first gave to Desdemona;
That which so often you did bid me steal.
IAGO Hast stolen it from her?
EMILIA
No, faith. She let it drop by negligence,
And to th' advantage I, being here, took 't up.   329
Look, here 'tis.
IAGO   A good wench! Give it me.
EMILIA
What will you do with 't, that you have been so earnest
To have me filch it?
IAGO [*Snatching it*]   Why, what is that to you?
EMILIA
If it be not for some purpose of import,
Give 't me again. Poor lady, she'll run mad
When she shall lack it.
IAGO   Be not acknown on 't.   335
I have use for it. Go, leave me.   *Exit Emilia.*

---

312 work ta'en out design of the embroidery copied   **315 fantasy**
whim   **318 common thing** (with bawdy suggestion; *common* suggests
coarseness and availability to all comers, and *thing* is a slang term for
the pudendum)   **329 to th' advantage** taking the opportunity   **335 Be
. . . on 't** do not confess knowledge of it

I will in Cassio's lodging lose this napkin   337
And let him find it. Trifles light as air
Are to the jealous confirmations strong
As proofs of Holy Writ. This may do something.
The Moor already changes with my poison.
Dangerous conceits are in their natures poisons,   342
Which at the first are scarce found to distaste,   343
But with a little act upon the blood   344
Burn like the mines of sulfur.

    Enter Othello.

                          I did say so.
Look where he comes! Not poppy nor mandragora   346
Nor all the drowsy syrups of the world
Shall ever medicine thee to that sweet sleep
Which thou owedst yesterday.

OTHELLO   Ha, ha, false to me?   349

IAGO
Why, how now, General? No more of that.

OTHELLO
Avaunt! Begone! Thou hast set me on the rack.
I swear 'tis better to be much abused
Than but to know 't a little.

IAGO   How now, my lord?

OTHELLO
What sense had I of her stolen hours of lust?
I saw 't not, thought it not, it harmed not me.
I slept the next night well, fed well, was free and merry; 356
I found not Cassio's kisses on her lips.
He that is robbed, not wanting what is stolen,   358
Let him not know 't and he's not robbed at all.

IAGO I am sorry to hear this.

OTHELLO
I had been happy if the general camp,
Pioners and all, had tasted her sweet body,   362
So I had nothing known. O, now, forever   363

---

337 lose (The Folio spelling, *loose*, is a normal spelling for "lose," but it
may also contain the idea of "let go," "release.") **342 conceits** fancies,
ideas **343 distaste** be distasteful **344 act** action, working **346 mandragora** an opiate made of the mandrake root **349 thou owedst** you did own
356 free carefree **358 wanting** missing **362 Pioneers** diggers of mines,
the lowest grade of soldiers **363 So** provided

Farewell the tranquil mind! Farewell content!
Farewell the plumèd troops and the big wars   365
That makes ambition virtue! O, farewell!
Farewell the neighing steed and the shrill trump,
The spirit-stirring drum, th' ear-piercing fife,
The royal banner, and all quality,   369
Pride, pomp, and circumstance of glorious war!   370
And O, you mortal engines, whose rude throats   371
Th' immortal Jove's dread clamors counterfeit,   372
Farewell! Othello's occupation's gone.

IAGO Is 't possible, my lord?

OTHELLO
Villain, be sure thou prove my love a whore!
Be sure of it. Give me the ocular proof,
Or, by the worth of mine eternal soul,
Thou hadst been better have been born a dog
Than answer my waked wrath!

IAGO   Is 't come to this?

OTHELLO
Make me to see 't, or at the least so prove it
That the probation bear no hinge nor loop   381
To hang a doubt on, or woe upon thy life!

IAGO My noble lord—

OTHELLO
If thou dost slander her and torture me,
Never pray more; abandon all remorse;   385
On horror's head horrors accumulate;   386
Do deeds to make heaven weep, all earth amazed;   387
For nothing canst thou to damnation add
Greater than that.

IAGO   O grace! O heaven forgive me!
Are you a man? Have you a soul or sense?
God b' wi' you; take mine office. O wretched fool,   391
That lov'st to make thine honesty a vice!   392
O monstrous world! Take note, take note, O world,

---

365 big stately   **369 quality** character, essential nature   **370 Pride** rich
display.   **circumstance** pageantry   **371 mortal engines** i.e., cannon.
(*Mortal* means "deadly.")   **372 Jove's dread clamors** i.e., thunder
381 probation proof   **385 remorse** pity   **386 horrors accumulate** add
still more horrors   **387 amazed** confounded with horror   **391 O
wretched fool** (Iago addresses himself as a fool for having carried
honesty too far.)   **392 vice** failing, something overdone

To be direct and honest is not safe.
I thank you for this profit, and from hence   395
I'll love no friend, sith love breeds such offense.   396
OTHELLO   Nay, stay. Thou shouldst be honest.   397
IAGO
I should be wise, for honesty's a fool
And loses that it works for.
OTHELLO   By the world,   399
I think my wife be honest and think she is not;
I think that thou art just and think thou art not.
I'll have some proof. My name, that was as fresh
As Dian's visage, is now begrimed and black   403
As mine own face. If there be cords, or knives,
Poison, or fire, or suffocating streams,
I'll not endure it. Would I were satisfied!
IAGO
I see, sir, you are eaten up with passion.
I do repent me that I put it to you.
You would be satisfied?
OTHELLO   Would? Nay, and I will.
IAGO
And may; but how? How satisfied, my lord?
Would you, the supervisor, grossly gape on?   411
Behold her topped?
OTHELLO   Death and damnation! O!
IAGO
It were a tedious difficulty, I think,
To bring them to that prospect. Damn them then,   414
If ever mortal eyes do see them bolster   415
More than their own. What then? How then?   416
What shall I say? Where's satisfaction?
It is impossible you should see this,
Were they as prime as goats, as hot as monkeys,   419
As salt as wolves in pride, and fools as gross   420

395 profit profitable instruction. hence henceforth 396 sith since.
offense i.e., harm to the one who offers help and friendship 397 Thou
shouldst be it appears that you are. (But Iago replies in the sense of
"ought to be.") 399 that what 403 Dian Diana, goddess of the moon
and of chastity 411 supervisor onlooker 414 Damn them then i.e.,
they would have to be really incorrigible 415 bolster go to bed together, share a bolster 416 More other 419 prime lustful 420 salt
wanton, sensual. pride heat

As ignorance made drunk. But yet, I say,
If imputation and strong circumstances
Which lead directly to the door of truth
Will give you satisfaction, you might have 't.

OTHELLO
Give me a living reason she's disloyal.

IAGO   I do not like the office.
But sith I am entered in this cause so far,   427
Pricked to 't by foolish honesty and love,   428
I will go on. I lay with Cassio lately,
And being troubled with a raging tooth
I could not sleep. There are a kind of men
So loose of soul that in their sleeps will mutter
Their affairs. One of this kind is Cassio.
In sleep I heard him say, "Sweet Desdemona,
Let us be wary, let us hide our loves!"
And then, sir, would he grip and wring my hand,
Cry "O sweet creature!" then kiss me hard,
As if he plucked up kisses by the roots
That grew upon my lips; then laid his leg
Over my thigh, and sighed, and kissed, and then
Cried, "Cursèd fate that gave thee to the Moor!"

OTHELLO
O monstrous! Monstrous!

IAGO   Nay, this was but his dream.

OTHELLO
But this denoted a foregone conclusion.   443
'Tis a shrewd doubt, though it be but a dream.   444

IAGO
And this may help to thicken other proofs
That do demonstrate thinly.

OTHELLO   I'll tear her all to pieces.

IAGO
Nay, yet be wise. Yet we see nothing done;
She may be honest yet. Tell me but this:
Have you not sometimes seen a handkerchief
Spotted with strawberries in your wife's hand?   450

---

427 **sith** since   428 **Pricked** spurred   443 **foregone conclusion** concluded experience or action   444 **shrewd doubt** suspicious circumstance   450 **Spotted with strawberries** embroidered with a strawberry
pattern

OTHELLO
I gave her such a one. 'Twas my first gift.
IAGO
I know not that; but such a handkerchief—
I am sure it was your wife's—did I today
See Cassio wipe his beard with.
OTHELLO   If it be that—
IAGO
If it be that, or any that was hers,
It speaks against her with the other proofs.
OTHELLO
O, that the slave had forty thousand lives!   457
One is too poor, too weak for my revenge.
Now do I see 'tis true. Look here, Iago,
All my fond love thus do I blow to heaven.   460
'Tis gone.
Arise, black vengeance, from the hollow hell!
Yield up, O love, thy crown and hearted throne   463
To tyrannous hate! Swell, bosom, with thy freight,   464
For 'tis of aspics' tongues!   465
IAGO   Yet be content.   466
OTHELLO   O, blood, blood, blood!
IAGO
Patience, I say. Your mind perhaps may change.
OTHELLO
Never, Iago. Like to the Pontic Sea,   469
Whose icy current and compulsive course
Ne'er feels retiring ebb, but keeps due on
To the Propontic and the Hellespont,   472
Even so my bloody thoughts with violent pace
Shall ne'er look back, ne'er ebb to humble love,
Till that a capable and wide revenge   475
Swallow them up. Now, by yond marble heaven,   476
[Kneeling] In the due reverence of a sacred vow
I here engage my words.

---

457 the slave i.e., Cassio   460 fond foolish   463 hearted fixed in
the heart / 464 freight burden   465 aspics' venomous serpents'
466 content calm   469 Pontic Sea Black Sea   472 Propontic body of
water between the Bosporus and Hellespont   475 capable comprehen-
sive   476 marble i.e., gleaming like marble

IAGO   Do not rise yet.
[*He kneels*.] Witness, you ever-burning lights above,   479
You elements that clip us round about,   480
Witness that here Iago doth give up
The execution of his wit, hands, heart,   482
To wronged Othello's service! Let him command,
And to obey shall be in me remorse,   484
What bloody business ever.   [*They rise*.]
OTHELLO   I greet thy love,   485
Not with vain thanks, but with acceptance bounteous,
And will upon the instant put thee to 't.
Within these three days let me hear thee say
That Cassio's not alive.
IAGO   My friend is dead;
'Tis done at your request. But let her live.
OTHELLO
Damn her, lewd minx! O, damn her, damn her!   491
Come, go with me apart. I will withdraw
To furnish me with some swift means of death
For the fair devil. Now art thou my lieutenant.
IAGO   I am your own forever.   *Exeunt*.

❧

3.4   *Enter Desdemona, Emilia, and Clown.*

DESDEMONA   Do you know, sirrah, where Lieutenant 1
Cassio lies?   2
CLOWN   I dare not say he lies anywhere.
DESDEMONA   Why, man?
CLOWN   He's a soldier, and for me to say a soldier lies,
'tis stabbing.
DESDEMONA   Go to. Where lodges he?
CLOWN   To tell you where he lodges is to tell you where
I lie.

479 s.d. He kneels (In the quarto text, Iago kneels here after Othello has
knelt at l. 477.)   **480 clip** encompass   **482 execution** exercise, action.
wit mind   **484 remorse** pity (for Othello's wrongs)   **485 ever** soever
491 minx wanton

3.4. Location: Before the citadel.
1 sirrah (A form of address to an inferior.)   **2 lies** lodges. (But the Clown
makes the obvious pun.)

DESDEMONA   Can anything be made of this?

CLOWN   I know not where he lodges, and for me to devise a lodging and say he lies here, or he lies there,
were to lie in mine own throat.   13

DESDEMONA   Can you inquire him out, and be edified
by report?

CLOWN   I will catechize the world for him; that is, make
questions, and by them answer.

DESDEMONA   Seek him, bid him come hither. Tell him I
have moved my lord on his behalf and hope all will be   19
well.

CLOWN   To do this is within the compass of man's wit,
and therefore I will attempt the doing it.   *Exit Clown.*

DESDEMONA
Where should I lose that handkerchief, Emilia?

EMILIA   I know not, madam.

DESDEMONA
Believe me, I had rather have lost my purse
Full of crusadoes; and but my noble Moor   26
Is true of mind and made of no such baseness
As jealous creatures are, it were enough
To put him to ill thinking.

EMILIA   Is he not jealous?

DESDEMONA
Who, he? I think the sun where he was born
Drew all such humors from him.

EMILIA   Look where he comes. 31

     Enter Othello.

DESDEMONA
I will not leave him now till Cassio
Be called to him.—How is 't with you, my lord?

OTHELLO
Well, my good lady. [*Aside.*] O, hardness to dissemble!—
How do you, Desdemona?

DESDEMONA   Well, my good lord.

OTHELLO
Give me your hand. [*She gives her hand.*] This hand is
moist, my lady.

---

13 lie . . . throat lie egregiously and deliberately   **19 moved** petitioned
26 crusadoes Portuguese gold coins   **31 humors** (Refers to the four
bodily fluids thought to determine temperament.)

DESDEMONA
   It yet hath felt no age nor known no sorrow.
OTHELLO
   This argues fruitfulness and liberal heart.   38
   Hot, hot, and moist. This hand of yours requires
   A sequester from liberty, fasting and prayer,   40
   Much castigation, exercise devout;   41
   For here's a young and sweating devil here
   That commonly rebels. 'Tis a good hand,
   A frank one.
DESDEMONA   You may indeed say so,   44
   For 'twas that hand that gave away my heart.
OTHELLO
   A liberal hand! The hearts of old gave hands,   46
   But our new heraldry is hands, not hearts.   47
DESDEMONA
   I cannot speak of this. Come now, your promise.
OTHELLO   What promise, chuck?   49
DESDEMONA
   I have sent to bid Cassio come speak with you.
OTHELLO
   I have a salt and sorry rheum offends me;   51
   Lend me thy handkerchief.
DESDEMONA   Here, my lord. [*She offers a handkerchief.*]
OTHELLO
   That which I gave you.
DESDEMONA   I have it not about me.
OTHELLO   Not?
DESDEMONA   No, faith, my lord.
OTHELLO   That's a fault. That handkerchief
   Did an Egyptian to my mother give.
   She was a charmer, and could almost read   59
   The thoughts of people. She told her, while she kept it,

38 argues gives evidence of. **fruitfulness** generosity, amorousness, and
fecundity. **liberal** generous and sexually free   **40 sequester** separation,
sequestration   **41 castigation** corrective discipline   **44 frank** generous,
open (with sexual suggestion)   **46 The hearts . . . hands** i.e., in former
times people would give their hearts when they gave their hands to
something   **47 But . . . hearts** i.e., in our decadent times the joining of
hands is no longer a badge to signify the giving of hearts   **49 chuck** (A
term of endearment.)   **51 salt . . . rheum** distressful head cold or watering of the eyes   **59 charmer** sorceress

'Twould make her amiable and subdue my father   61
Entirely to her love, but if she lost it
Or made a gift of it, my father's eye
Should hold her loathèd and his spirits should hunt
After new fancies. She, dying, gave it me,   65
And bid me, when my fate would have me wived,
To give it her. I did so; and take heed on 't;   67
Make it a darling like your precious eye.
To lose 't or give 't away were such perdition   69
As nothing else could match.
DESDEMONA   Is 't possible?
OTHELLO
'Tis true. There's magic in the web of it.   71
A sibyl, that had numbered in the world
The sun to course two hundred compasses,   73
In her prophetic fury sewed the work;   74
The worms were hallowed that did breed the silk,
And it was dyed in mummy which the skillful   76
Conserved of maidens' hearts.
DESDEMONA   I' faith! Is 't true?   77
OTHELLO
Most veritable. Therefore look to 't well.
DESDEMONA
Then would to God that I had never seen 't!
OTHELLO   Ha? Wherefore?
DESDEMONA
Why do you speak so startingly and rash?   81
OTHELLO
Is 't lost? Is 't gone? Speak, is 't out o' the way?   82
DESDEMONA   Heaven bless us!
OTHELLO   Say you?
DESDEMONA
It is not lost; but what an if it were?   85
OTHELLO   How?

---

61 amiable desirable   **65 fancies** loves   **67 her** i.e., to my wife
69 perdition loss   **71 web** fabric, weaving   **73 compasses** annual cir-
clings. (The *sibyl*, or prophetess, was 200 years old.)   **74 prophetic fury**
frenzy of prophetic inspiration   **76 mummy** medicinal or magical
preparation drained from mummified bodies   **77 Conserved of** prepared or preserved out of   **81 startingly and rash** disjointedly and
impetuously, excitedly   **82 out o' the way** lost, misplaced   **85 an if** if

DESDEMONA
I say it is not lost.

OTHELLO   Fetch 't. Let me see 't.

DESDEMONA
Why, so I can, sir, but I will not now.
This is a trick to put me from my suit.
Pray you, let Cassio be received again.

OTHELLO
Fetch me the handkerchief! My mind misgives.

DESDEMONA   Come, come,
You'll never meet a more sufficient man.   93

OTHELLO
The handkerchief!

DESDEMONA   I pray, talk me of Cassio.   94

OTHELLO
The handkerchief!

DESDEMONA   A man that all his time   95
Hath founded his good fortunes on your love,
Shared dangers with you—

OTHELLO   The handkerchief!

DESDEMONA   I' faith, you are to blame.

OTHELLO   Zounds!   *Exit Othello.*

EMILIA   Is not this man jealous?

DESDEMONA   I ne'er saw this before.
Sure, there's some wonder in this handkerchief.
I am most unhappy in the loss of it.

EMILIA
'Tis not a year or two shows us a man.   105
They are all but stomachs, and we all but food;   106
They eat us hungerly, and when they are full   107
They belch us.

          Enter Iago and Cassio.

                    Look you, Cassio and my husband.

IAGO
There is no other way; 'tis she must do 't.
And, lo, the happiness! Go and importune her.   110

---

93 sufficient able, complete   **94 talk** talk to   **95 all his time** throughout
his career   **105 'Tis . . . man** i.e., you can't really know a man even
in a year or two of experience (?) or, real men come along seldom (?)
106 but nothing but   **107 hungerly** hungrily   **110 the happiness** in
happy time, fortunately met

DESDEMONA
How now, good Cassio? What's the news with you?

CASSIO
Madam, my former suit. I do beseech you
That by your virtuous means I may again   113
Exist, and be a member of his love
Whom I with all the office of my heart   115
Entirely honor. I would not be delayed.
If my offense be of such mortal kind   117
That nor my service past nor present sorrows,   118
Nor purposed merit in futurity,
Can ransom me into his love again,
But to know so must be my benefit;   121
So shall I clothe me in a forced content,
And shut myself up in some other course,
To fortune's alms.

DESDEMONA   Alas, thrice-gentle Cassio,   124
My advocation is not now in tune.   125
My lord is not my lord; nor should I know him,
Were he in favor as in humor altered.   127
So help me every spirit sanctified
As I have spoken for you all my best
And stood within the blank of his displeasure   130
For my free speech! You must awhile be patient.
What I can do I will, and more I will
Than for myself I dare. Let that suffice you.

IAGO
Is my lord angry?

EMILIA   He went hence but now,
And certainly in strange unquietness.

IAGO
Can he be angry? I have seen the cannon
When it hath blown his ranks into the air,
And like the devil from his very arm
Puffed his own brother—and is he angry?

---

113 virtuous efficacious   **115 office** loyal service   **117 mortal** fatal
118 nor . . . nor neither . . . nor   **121 But . . . benefit** merely to know
that my case is hopeless must be all I can expect   **124 To fortune's
alms** throwing myself on the mercy of fortune   **125 advocation** advo-
cacy   **127 favor** appearance   **130 within the blank** within point-blank
range. (The *blank* is the center of the target.)

Something of moment then. I will go meet him.   140
There's matter in 't indeed, if he be angry.

DESDEMONA
I prithee, do so.   *Exit [Iago].*

                Something, sure, of state,   142
Either from Venice, or some unhatched practice   143
Made demonstrable here in Cyprus to him,
Hath puddled his clear spirit; and in such cases   145
Men's natures wrangle with inferior things,
Though great ones are their object. 'Tis even so;
For let our finger ache, and it indues   148
Our other healthful members even to a sense
Of pain. Nay, we must think men are not gods,
Nor of them look for such observancy   151
As fits the bridal. Beshrew me much, Emilia,   152
I was, unhandsome warrior as I am,   153
Arraigning his unkindness with my soul;   154
But now I find I had suborned the witness,   155
And he's indicted falsely.

EMILIA   Pray heaven it be
State matters, as you think, and no conception
Nor no jealous toy concerning you.   158

DESDEMONA
Alas the day! I never gave him cause.

EMILIA
But jealous souls will not be answered so;
They are not ever jealous for the cause,
But jealous for they're jealous. It is a monster   162
Begot upon itself, born on itself.   163

DESDEMONA
Heaven keep that monster from Othello's mind!

EMILIA   Lady, amen.

DESDEMONA
I will go seek him. Cassio, walk hereabout.

---

140 of moment of immediate importance, momentous   **142 of state**
concerning state affairs   **143 unhatched practice** as yet unexecuted or
undiscovered plot   **145 puddled** muddied   **148 indues** brings to the
same condition   **151 observancy** attentiveness   **152 bridal** wedding
(when a bridegroom is newly attentive to his bride).   **Beshrew me** (A
mild oath.)   **153 unhandsome** insufficient, unskillful   **154 with** before
the bar of   **155 suborned the witness** induced the witness to give false
testimony   **158 toy** fancy   **162 for** because   **163 Begot upon itself**
generated solely from itself

If I do find him fit, I'll move your suit
And seek to effect it to my uttermost.

CASSIO   I humbly thank your ladyship.

> *Exit [Desdemona with Emilia].*

> *Enter Bianca.*

BIANCA
Save you, friend Cassio!

CASSIO   What make you from home?   170
How is 't with you, my most fair Bianca?
I' faith, sweet love, I was coming to your house.

BIANCA
And I was going to your lodging, Cassio.
What, keep a week away? Seven days and nights?
Eightscore-eight hours? And lovers' absent hours
More tedious than the dial eightscore times?   176
O weary reckoning!

CASSIO   Pardon me, Bianca.
I have this while with leaden thoughts been pressed;
But I shall, in a more continuate time,   179
Strike off this score of absence. Sweet Bianca,   180

> *[Giving her Desdemona's handkerchief]*

Take me this work out.

BIANCA   O Cassio, whence came this?   181
This is some token from a newer friend.   182
To the felt absence now I feel a cause.
Is 't come to this? Well, well.

CASSIO   Go to, woman!
Throw your vile guesses in the devil's teeth,
From whence you have them. You are jealous now
That this is from some mistress, some remembrance.
No, by my faith, Bianca.

BIANCA   Why, whose is it?

CASSIO
I know not, neither. I found it in my chamber.
I like the work well. Ere it be demanded—   190
As like enough it will—I would have it copied.   191
Take it and do 't, and leave me for this time.

---

170 Save God save.   **make** do   **176 the dial** a complete revolution of the
clock   **179 continuate** uninterrupted   **180 Strike . . . score** settle this
account   **181 Take . . . out** copy this embroidery for me   **182 friend**
mistress   **190 demanded** inquired for   **191 like** likely

BIANCA　Leave you? Wherefore?

CASSIO

　I do attend here on the General,

　And think it no addition, nor my wish,　　　　195

　To have him see me womaned.

BIANCA　Why, I pray you?

CASSIO　Not that I love you not.

BIANCA　But that you do not love me.

　I pray you, bring me on the way a little,　　　200

　And say if I shall see you soon at night.

CASSIO

　'Tis but a little way that I can bring you,

　For I attend here; but I'll see you soon.

BIANCA

　'Tis very good. I must be circumstanced.　　　204

Exeunt omnes.

❖

195 addition i.e., addition to my reputation　**200 bring** accompany
204 be circumstanced be governed by circumstance, yield to your
conditions

4.1 *Enter Othello and Iago.*

IAGO
  Will you think so?
OTHELLO   Think so, Iago?
IAGO   What,
  To kiss in private?
OTHELLO   An unauthorized kiss!
IAGO
  Or to be naked with her friend in bed
  An hour or more, not meaning any harm?
OTHELLO
  Naked in bed, Iago, and not mean harm?
  It is hypocrisy against the devil.
  They that mean virtuously, and yet do so,
  The devil their virtue tempts, and they tempt heaven.
IAGO
  If they do nothing, 'tis a venial slip.   9
  But if I give my wife a handkerchief—
OTHELLO   What then?
IAGO
  Why then, 'tis hers, my lord, and being hers,
  She may, I think, bestow 't on any man.
OTHELLO
  She is protectress of her honor too.
  May she give that?
IAGO
  Her honor is an essence that's not seen;
  They have it very oft that have it not.   17
  But, for the handkerchief—
OTHELLO
  By heaven, I would most gladly have forgot it.
  Thou saidst—O, it comes o'er my memory
  As doth the raven o'er the infectious house,   21
  Boding to all—he had my handkerchief.
IAGO
  Ay, what of that?

4.1. Location: Before the citadel.
9 venial pardonable   **17 They have it** i.e., they enjoy a reputation for
it   **21 raven . . . house** (Allusion to the belief that the raven hovered over
a house of sickness or infection, such as one visited by the plague.)

OTHELLO   That's not so good now.

IAGO   What

If I had said I had seen him do you wrong?

Or heard him say—as knaves be such abroad,   25

Who having, by their own importunate suit,

Or voluntary dotage of some mistress,   27

Convincèd or supplied them, cannot choose   28

But they must blab—

OTHELLO   Hath he said anything?

IAGO

He hath, my lord; but, be you well assured,

No more than he'll unswear.

OTHELLO   What hath he said?

IAGO

Faith, that he did—I know not what he did.

OTHELLO   What? What?

IAGO

Lie—

OTHELLO   With her?

IAGO   With her, on her; what you will.

OTHELLO   Lie with her? Lie on her? We say "lie on her"

when they belie her. Lie with her? Zounds, that's ful- 36

some.—Handkerchief—confessions—handkerchief! 37

—To confess and be hanged for his labor—first to be 38

hanged and then to confess.—I tremble at it. Nature 39

would not invest herself in such shadowing passion 40

without some instruction. It is not words that shakes 41

me thus. Pish! Noses, ears, and lips.—Is 't possible?—

Confess—handkerchief!—O devil!

Falls in a trance.

IAGO   Work on,

My medicine, work! Thus credulous fools are caught,

And many worthy and chaste dames even thus,

---

25 abroad around about   **27 voluntary dotage** willing infatuation
28 Convincèd or supplied seduced or gratified   **36 belie** slander
36–37 fulsome foul   **38–39 first . . . to confess** (Othello reverses the
proverbial *confess and be hanged;* Cassio is to be given no time to
confess before he dies.)   **39–41 Nature . . . instruction** i.e., without some
foundation in fact, nature would not have dressed herself in such an
overwhelming passion that comes over me now and fills my mind with
images, or in such a lifelike fantasy as Cassio had in his dream of lying
with Desdemona   **41 words** mere words

All guiltless, meet reproach.—What ho! My lord!
My lord, I say! Othello!

Enter Cassio.

                       How now, Cassio?

CASSIO What's the matter?

IAGO
My lord is fall'n into an epilepsy.
This is his second fit. He had one yesterday.

CASSIO
Rub him about the temples.

IAGO   No, forbear.
The lethargy must have his quiet course.   53
If not, he foams at mouth, and by and by
Breaks out to savage madness. Look, he stirs.
Do you withdraw yourself a little while.
He will recover straight. When he is gone,
I would on great occasion speak with you.   58
                          [*Exit Cassio.*]
How is it, General? Have you not hurt your head?

OTHELLO
Dost thou mock me?

IAGO   I mock you not, by heaven.   60
Would you would bear your fortune like a man!

OTHELLO
A hornèd man's a monster and a beast.

IAGO
There's many a beast then in a populous city,
And many a civil monster.   64

OTHELLO Did he confess it?

IAGO Good sir, be a man.
Think every bearded fellow that's but yoked   67
May draw with you. There's millions now alive   68
That nightly lie in those unproper beds   69

---

53 lethargy coma. **his** its   **58 on great occasion** on a matter of great
importance   **60 mock** (Othello takes Iago's question about hurting his
head to be a mocking reference to the cuckold's horns.)   **64 civil** i.e.,
dwelling in a city   **67 yoked** (1) married (2) put into the yoke of infamy
and cuckoldry   **68 draw with you** pull as you do like oxen who are
yoked, i.e., share your fate as cuckold   **69 unproper** not exclusively
their own

Which they dare swear peculiar. Your case is better.   70
O, 'tis the spite of hell, the fiend's arch-mock,
To lip a wanton in a secure couch   72
And to suppose her chaste! No, let me know,
And knowing what I am, I know what she shall be.   74
OTHELLO O, thou art wise. 'Tis certain.
IAGO Stand you awhile apart;
Confine yourself but in a patient list.   77
Whilst you were here o'erwhelmèd with your grief—
A passion most unsuiting such a man—
Cassio came hither. I shifted him away,   80
And laid good 'scuses upon your ecstasy,   81
Bade him anon return and here speak with me,
The which he promised. Do but encave yourself   83
And mark the fleers, the gibes, and notable scorns   84
That dwell in every region of his face;
For I will make him tell the tale anew,
Where, how, how oft, how long ago, and when
He hath and is again to cope your wife.   88
I say, but mark his gesture. Marry, patience!
Or I shall say you're all-in-all in spleen,   90
And nothing of a man.
OTHELLO   Dost thou hear, Iago?
I will be found most cunning in my patience;
But—dost thou hear?—most bloody.
IAGO   That's not amiss;
But yet keep time in all. Will you withdraw?   94
                    [*Othello stands apart.*]
Now will I question Cassio of Bianca,
A huswife that by selling her desires   96
Buys herself bread and clothes. It is a creature
That dotes on Cassio—as 'tis the strumpet's plague
To beguile many and be beguiled by one.

---

70 peculiar private, their own. **better** i.e., because you know the truth **72 lip** kiss. **secure** free from suspicion **74 what I am** i.e., a cuckold. **she shall be** i.e., an adulteress who must die **77 in . . . list** within the bounds of patience **80 shifted him away** used a dodge to get rid of him **81 ecstasy** trance **83 encave** conceal **84 fleers** sneers. **notable** obvious **88 cope** encounter with, have sex with **90 all-in-all in spleen** utterly governed by passionate impulses **94 keep time** keep yourself steady (as in music) **96 huswife** hussy

He, when he hears of her, cannot restrain   100
From the excess of laughter. Here he comes.

    Enter Cassio.

As he shall smile, Othello shall go mad;
And his unbookish jealousy must conster   103
Poor Cassio's smiles, gestures, and light behaviors
Quite in the wrong.—How do you now, Lieutenant?

CASSIO
The worser that you give me the addition   106
Whose want even kills me.

IAGO
Ply Desdemona well and you are sure on 't.
[*Speaking lower.*] Now, if this suit lay in Bianca's power,
How quickly should you speed!

CASSIO [*Laughing*]   Alas, poor caitiff!   111

OTHELLO   Look how he laughs already!

IAGO
I never knew a woman love man so.

CASSIO
Alas, poor rogue! I think, i' faith, she loves me.

OTHELLO
Now he denies it faintly, and laughs it out.

IAGO
Do you hear, Cassio?

OTHELLO   Now he importunes him
To tell it o'er. Go to! Well said, well said.   117

IAGO
She gives it out that you shall marry her.
Do you intend it?

CASSIO   Ha, ha, ha!

OTHELLO
Do you triumph, Roman? Do you triumph?   121

CASSIO   I marry her? What? A customer? Prithee, bear   122
some charity to my wit; do not think it so unwhole-   123
some. Ha, ha, ha!

100 restrain refrain   **103 unbookish** uninstructed.   **conster** construe
106 addition title   **111 caitiff** wretch   **117 Well said** well done
121 Roman (The Romans were noted for their *triumphs* or triumphal
processions.)   **122 customer** i.e., prostitute   **122–123 bear . . . wit** be
more charitable to my judgment

OTHELLO So, so, so, so! They laugh that win.   125

IAGO Faith, the cry goes that you shall marry her.   126

CASSIO Prithee, say true.

IAGO I am a very villain else.

OTHELLO Have you scored me? Well.   129

CASSIO This is the monkey's own giving out. She is persuaded I will marry her, out of her own love and flattery, not out of my promise.   132

OTHELLO Iago beckons me. Now he begins the story.   133

CASSIO She was here even now; she haunts me in every place. I was the other day talking on the seabank with certain Venetians, and thither comes the bauble, and, 136 by this hand, she falls me thus about my neck—

                    [*He embraces Iago.*]

OTHELLO Crying, "O dear Cassio!" as it were; his gesture imports it.

CASSIO So hangs and lolls and weeps upon me, so shakes and pulls me. Ha, ha, ha!

OTHELLO Now he tells how she plucked him to my chamber. O, I see that nose of yours, but not that dog I shall throw it to.

CASSIO Well, I must leave her company.

IAGO Before me, look where she comes.   146

        Enter Bianca [with Othello's handkerchief].

CASSIO 'Tis such another fitchew! Marry, a perfumed 147 one.—What do you mean by this haunting of me?

BIANCA Let the devil and his dam haunt you! What did 149 you mean by that same handkerchief you gave me even now? I was a fine fool to take it. I must take out the work? A likely piece of work, that you should find 152 it in your chamber and know not who left it there! This is some minx's token, and I must take out the

---

125 They . . . win i.e., they that laugh last laugh best **126 cry** rumor
129 scored me scored off me, beaten me, made up my reckoning,
branded me **132 flattery** self-flattery, self-deception **133 beckons**
signals **136 bauble** plaything **146 Before me** i.e., on my soul **147 'Tis
. . . fitchew** what a polecat she is! Just like all the others. **fitchew**
(Polecats were often compared with prostitutes because of their rank
smell and presumed lechery.) **149 dam** mother **152 A likely . . . work**
a fine story

work? There; give it your hobbyhorse. [*She gives him* 155
the handkerchief.] Wheresoever you had it, I'll take out
no work on 't.

CASSIO   How now, my sweet Bianca? How now? How now?

OTHELLO   By heaven, that should be my handkerchief!   159

BIANCA   If you'll come to supper tonight, you may; if
you will not, come when you are next prepared for.   161
                                                    Exit.

IAGO   After her, after her.

CASSIO   Faith, I must. She'll rail in the streets else.

IAGO   Will you sup there?

CASSIO   Faith, I intend so.

IAGO   Well, I may chance to see you, for I would very
fain speak with you.

CASSIO   Prithee, come. Will you?

IAGO   Go to. Say no more.   [*Exit Cassio.*]   169

OTHELLO [*Advancing*]   How shall I murder him, Iago?

IAGO   Did you perceive how he laughed at his vice?

OTHELLO   O, Iago!

IAGO   And did you see the handkerchief?

OTHELLO   Was that mine?

IAGO   Yours, by this hand. And to see how he prizes
the foolish woman your wife! She gave it him, and he
hath given it his whore.

OTHELLO   I would have him nine years a-killing. A fine
woman! A fair woman! A sweet woman!

IAGO   Nay, you must forget that.

OTHELLO   Ay, let her rot, and perish, and be damned
tonight, for she shall not live. No, my heart is turned
to stone; I strike it, and it hurts my hand. O, the world
hath not a sweeter creature! She might lie by an emperor's side and command him tasks.

IAGO   Nay, that's not your way.   186

OTHELLO   Hang her! I do but say what she is. So delicate
with her needle! An admirable musician! O, she will
sing the savageness out of a bear. Of so high and plenteous wit and invention!   190

---

155 hobbyhorse harlot   **159 should be** must be   **161 when . . . for** when
I'm ready for you (i.e., never)   **169 Go to** (An expression of remonstrance.)   **186 your way** i.e., the way you should think of her
190 invention imagination

IAGO   She's the worse for all this.

OTHELLO   O, a thousand, a thousand times! And then,
of so gentle a condition!   193

IAGO   Ay, too gentle.   194

OTHELLO   Nay, that's certain. But yet the pity of it, Iago!
O, Iago, the pity of it, Iago!

IAGO   If you are so fond over her iniquity, give her patent   197
to offend, for if it touch not you it comes near nobody.

OTHELLO   I will chop her into messes. Cuckold me?   199

IAGO   O, 'tis foul in her.

OTHELLO   With mine officer?

IAGO   That's fouler.

OTHELLO   Get me some poison, Iago, this night. I'll not
expostulate with her, lest her body and beauty un-   204
provide my mind again. This night, Iago.   205

IAGO   Do it not with poison. Strangle her in her bed,
even the bed she hath contaminated.

OTHELLO   Good, good! The justice of it pleases. Very good.

IAGO   And for Cassio, let me be his undertaker. You   209
shall hear more by midnight.

OTHELLO
Excellent good. [*A trumpet within.*] What trumpet is
that same?

IAGO   I warrant, something from Venice.

Enter Lodovico, Desdemona, and attendants.

'Tis Lodovico. This comes from the Duke.
See, your wife's with him.

LODOVICO
God save you, worthy General!

OTHELLO   With all my heart, sir.   215

LODOVICO [*Giving him a letter*]
The Duke and the senators of Venice greet you.

OTHELLO
I kiss the instrument of their pleasures.
                         [*He opens the letter, and reads.*]

---

193 gentle a condition wellborn and wellbred   **194 gentle** generous,
yielding (to other men)   **197 fond** foolish.   **patent** license   **199 messes**
portions of meat, i.e., bits   **204–205 unprovide** weaken, render unfit
209 be his undertaker undertake to dispatch him   **215 With all my
heart** i.e., I thank you most heartily

DESDEMONA
  And what's the news, good cousin Lodovico?
IAGO
  I am very glad to see you, signor.
  Welcome to Cyprus.
LODOVICO
  I thank you. How does Lieutenant Cassio?
IAGO Lives, sir.
DESDEMONA
  Cousin, there's fall'n between him and my lord
  An unkind breach; but you shall make all well.   224
OTHELLO Are you sure of that?
DESDEMONA My lord?
OTHELLO [*Reads*] "This fail you not to do, as you will—"
LODOVICO
  He did not call; he's busy in the paper.
  Is there division twixt my lord and Cassio?
DESDEMONA
  A most unhappy one. I would do much
  T' atone them, for the love I bear to Cassio.   231
OTHELLO Fire and brimstone!
DESDEMONA My lord?
OTHELLO Are you wise?
DESDEMONA
  What, is he angry?
LODOVICO   Maybe the letter moved him;
  For, as I think, they do command him home,
  Deputing Cassio in his government.   237
DESDEMONA By my troth, I am glad on 't.   238
OTHELLO Indeed?
DESDEMONA My lord?
OTHELLO I am glad to see you mad.   241
DESDEMONA Why, sweet Othello—
OTHELLO [*Striking her*] Devil!
DESDEMONA I have not deserved this.
LODOVICO
  My lord, this would not be believed in Venice,

---

224 unkind unnatural, contrary to their natures; hurtful **231 atone**
reconcile **237 government** office **238 on 't** of it **241 I am . . . mad**
i.e., I am glad to see that you are insane enough to rejoice in Cassio's
promotion (? Othello bitterly plays on Desdemona's *I am glad*.)

Though I should swear I saw 't. 'Tis very much.   246
Make her amends; she weeps.

OTHELLO   O devil, devil!
If that the earth could teem with woman's tears,   248
Each drop she falls would prove a crocodile.   249
Out of my sight!

DESDEMONA   I will not stay to offend you. [*Going.*]

LODOVICO   Truly, an obedient lady.
I do beseech your lordship, call her back.

OTHELLO   Mistress!

DESDEMONA [*Returning*]   My lord?

OTHELLO   What would you with her, sir?   255

LODOVICO   Who, I, my lord?

OTHELLO
Ay, you did wish that I would make her turn.
Sir, she can turn, and turn, and yet go on
And turn again; and she can weep, sir, weep;
And she's obedient, as you say, obedient,   260
Very obedient.—Proceed you in your tears.—
Concerning this, sir—O well-painted passion!—   262
I am commanded home.—Get you away;
I'll send for you anon.—Sir, I obey the mandate
And will return to Venice.—Hence, avaunt!
                              [*Exit Desdemona.*]
Cassio shall have my place. And, sir, tonight
I do entreat that we may sup together.
You are welcome, sir, to Cyprus.—Goats and monkeys! 268
                              Exit.

LODOVICO
Is this the noble Moor whom our full Senate
Call all in all sufficient? Is this the nature
Whom passion could not shake? Whose solid virtue
The shot of accident nor dart of chance
Could neither graze nor pierce?

IAGO   He is much changed.

246 very much too much, outrageous   **248 teem** breed, be impreg-
nated   **249 falls** lets fall.   **crocodile** (Crocodiles were supposed to weep
hypocritical tears for their victims.)   **255 What . . . sir** (Othello implies
that Desdemona is pliant and will do a *turn*, ll. 257–259, for any man.)
260 obedient (with much the same sexual connotation as *turn* in
ll. 257–259)   **262 passion** i.e., grief   **268 Goats and monkeys** (See
3.3.419.)

LODOVICO
　Are his wits safe? Is he not light of brain?
IAGO
　He's that he is. I may not breathe my censure　　275
　What he might be. If what he might he is not,　　276
　I would to heaven he were!
LODOVICO　　　　　　　　What, strike his wife?　　277
IAGO
　Faith, that was not so well; yet would I knew
　That stroke would prove the worst!
LODOVICO　　　　　　　　　Is it his use?　　279
　Or did the letters work upon his blood　　280
　And new-create his fault?
IAGO　　　　　　　　　Alas, alas!
　It is not honesty in me to speak
　What I have seen and known. You shall observe him,
　And his own courses will denote him so
　That I may save my speech. Do but go after,
　And mark how he continues.
LODOVICO
　I am sorry that I am deceived in him.　　　　*Exeunt.*

4.2　　*Enter Othello and Emilia.*

OTHELLO　You have seen nothing then?
EMILIA
　Nor ever heard, nor ever did suspect.
OTHELLO
　Yes, you have seen Cassio and she together.
EMILIA
　But then I saw no harm, and then I heard
　Each syllable that breath made up between them.
OTHELLO　What, did they never whisper?
EMILIA　Never, my lord.
OTHELLO　Nor send you out o' the way?

275–277 I may . . . were i.e., I dare not venture an opinion as to whether
he's of unsound mind, as you suggest; but if he isn't, then it might be
better to wish he were in fact insane, since only that could excuse his
wild behavior　**279 use** custom　**280 blood** passions
4.2. Location: The citadel.

EMILIA   Never.

OTHELLO

To fetch her fan, her gloves, her mask, nor nothing?

EMILIA   Never, my lord.

OTHELLO   That's strange.

EMILIA

I durst, my lord, to wager she is honest,
Lay down my soul at stake. If you think other,   14
Remove your thought; it doth abuse your bosom.
If any wretch have put this in your head,
Let heaven requite it with the serpent's curse!   17
For if she be not honest, chaste, and true,   .
There's no man happy; the purest of their wives
Is foul as slander.

OTHELLO   Bid her come hither. Go.

                                             Exit Emilia.

She says enough; yet she's a simple bawd   21
That cannot say as much. This is a subtle whore,   22
A closet lock and key of villainous secrets.   23
And yet she'll kneel and pray; I have seen her do 't.

                Enter Desdemona and Emilia.

DESDEMONA   My lord, what is your will?

OTHELLO   Pray you, chuck, come hither.

DESDEMONA

What is your pleasure?

OTHELLO   Let me see your eyes.
Look in my face.

DESDEMONA   What horrible fancy's this?

OTHELLO [*To Emilia*]   Some of your function, mistress.   29
Leave procreants alone and shut the door;   30
Cough or cry "hem" if anybody come.
Your mystery, your mystery! Nay, dispatch.   32

                                             Exit Emilia.

14 at stake as the wager   **17 the serpent's curse** the curse pronounced
by God on the serpent for deceiving Eve, just as some man has done to
Othello and Desdemona. (See Genesis 3:14.)   **21–22 she's . . . much** i.e.,
any procuress or go-between who couldn't make up as convincing a
story as Emilia's would have to be pretty stupid   **22 This** i.e., Desdemona   **23 closet lock and key** i.e., concealer   **29 Some . . . function** i.e.,
practice your chosen profession, that of bawd (by guarding the door)
30 procreants mating couples   **32 mystery** trade, occupation

DESDEMONA [*Kneeling*]
  Upon my knees, what doth your speech import?
  I understand a fury in your words,
  But not the words.
OTHELLO
  Why, what art thou?
DESDEMONA   Your wife, my lord, your true
  And loyal wife.
OTHELLO   Come, swear it, damn thyself,
  Lest, being like one of heaven, the devils themselves   38
  Should fear to seize thee. Therefore be double damned:
  Swear thou art honest.
DESDEMONA   Heaven doth truly know it.
OTHELLO
  Heaven truly knows that thou art false as hell.
DESDEMONA
  To whom, my lord? With whom? How am I false?
OTHELLO [*Weeping*]
  Ah, Desdemon! Away, away, away!
DESDEMONA
  Alas the heavy day! Why do you weep?
  Am I the motive of these tears, my lord?   45
  If haply you my father do suspect
  An instrument of this your calling back,
  Lay not your blame on me. If you have lost him,
  I have lost him too.
OTHELLO   Had it pleased heaven
  To try me with affliction, had they rained   50
  All kinds of sores and shames on my bare head,
  Steeped me in poverty to the very lips,
  Given to captivity me and my utmost hopes,
  I should have found in some place of my soul
  A drop of patience. But, alas, to make me
  A fixèd figure for the time of scorn   56
  To point his slow and moving finger at!   57
  Yet could I bear that too, well, very well.

---

38 being . . . heaven looking like an angel **45 motive** cause **50 they**
i.e., heavenly powers **56 time of scorn** i.e., scornful world **57 his** its.
slow and moving finger i.e., hour hand of the clock, moving so slowly it
seems hardly to move at all. (Othello envisages himself as being eternally pointed at by the scornful world as the numbers on a clock are
pointed at by the hour hand.)

But there where I have garnered up my heart,   59
Where either I must live or bear no life,
The fountain from the which my current runs   61
Or else dries up—to be discarded thence!
Or keep it as a cistern for foul toads   63
To knot and gender in! Turn thy complexion there,   64
Patience, thou young and rose-lipped cherubin—   65
Ay, there look grim as hell!   66

DESDEMONA
I hope my noble lord esteems me honest.   67

OTHELLO
O, ay, as summer flies are in the shambles,   68
That quicken even with blowing. O thou weed,   69
Who art so lovely fair and smell'st so sweet
That the sense aches at thee, would thou hadst ne'er
   been born!

DESDEMONA
Alas, what ignorant sin have I committed?   72

OTHELLO
Was this fair paper, this most goodly book,
Made to write "whore" upon? What committed?
Committed? O thou public commoner!   75
I should make very forges of my cheeks,
That would to cinders burn up modesty,
Did I but speak thy deeds. What committed?
Heaven stops the nose at it and the moon winks;   79
The bawdy wind, that kisses all it meets,   80
Is hushed within the hollow mine of earth   81
And will not hear 't. What committed?
Impudent strumpet!

DESDEMONA   By heaven, you do me wrong.

OTHELLO   Are not you a strumpet?

DESDEMONA   No, as I am a Christian.

---

59 garnered stored **61 fountain** spring **63 cistern** cesspool **64 knot**
i.e., couple. **gender** engender. **Turn . . . there** change your color, grow
pale, at such a sight **65–66 Patience . . . hell** (Even Patience, that rose-
lipped cherub, will look grim and pale at this spectacle.) **67 honest**
chaste **68 shambles** slaughterhouse **69 quicken** come to life. **with
blowing** i.e., with the puffing up of something rotten in which maggots
are breeding **72 ignorant sin** sin in ignorance **75 commoner** prostitute **79 winks** closes her eyes. (The moon symbolizes chastity.)
80 bawdy kissing one and all **81 mine** cave (where the winds were
thought to dwell)

If to preserve this vessel for my lord   86
From any other foul unlawful touch
Be not to be a strumpet, I am none.
OTHELLO What, not a whore?
DESDEMONA No, as I shall be saved.
OTHELLO Is 't possible?
DESDEMONA
O, heaven forgive us!
OTHELLO   I cry you mercy, then.   92
I took you for that cunning whore of Venice
That married with Othello. [*Calling out.*] You, mistress,
That have the office opposite to Saint Peter
And keep the gate of hell!

    Enter Emilia.

                  You, you, ay, you!
We have done our course. There's money for your
    pains.   [*He gives money.*] 97
I pray you, turn the key and keep our counsel. *Exit.*
EMILIA
Alas, what does this gentleman conceive?   99
How do you, madam? How do you, my good lady?
DESDEMONA Faith, half asleep.   101
EMILIA
Good madam, what's the matter with my lord?
DESDEMONA With who?
EMILIA Why, with my lord, madam.
DESDEMONA
Who is thy lord?
EMILIA   He that is yours, sweet lady.
DESDEMONA
I have none. Do not talk to me, Emilia.
I cannot weep, nor answers have I none
But what should go by water. Prithee, tonight   108
Lay on my bed my wedding sheets, remember;
And call thy husband hither.
EMILIA Here's a change indeed!   *Exit.*

---

86 vessel i.e., body **92 cry you mercy** beg your pardon **97 course**
business (with an indecent suggestion of "trick," turn at sex)
99 conceive suppose, think **101 half asleep** i.e., dazed **108 go by
water** be expressed by tears

DESDEMONA

'Tis meet I should be used so, very meet.   112

How have I been behaved, that he might stick   113

The small'st opinion on my least misuse?   114

Enter Iago and Emilia.

IAGO

What is your pleasure, madam? How is 't with you?

DESDEMONA

I cannot tell. Those that do teach young babes

Do it with gentle means and easy tasks.

He might have chid me so, for, in good faith,

I am a child to chiding.

IAGO   What is the matter, lady?

EMILIA

Alas, Iago, my lord hath so bewhored her,

Thrown such despite and heavy terms upon her,

That true hearts cannot bear it.

DESDEMONA   Am I that name, Iago?

IAGO   What name, fair lady?

DESDEMONA

Such as she said my lord did say I was.

EMILIA

He called her whore. A beggar in his drink

Could not have laid such terms upon his callet.   128

IAGO   Why did he so?

DESDEMONA [*Weeping*]

I do not know. I am sure I am none such.

IAGO   Do not weep, do not weep. Alas the day!

EMILIA

Hath she forsook so many noble matches,

Her father and her country and her friends,

To be called whore? Would it not make one weep?

DESDEMONA

It is my wretched fortune.

IAGO   Beshrew him for 't!   135

How comes this trick upon him?

DESDEMONA   Nay, heaven doth know.   136

---

112 meet fitting   **113 stick** attach   **114 opinion** censure.   **least misuse**
slightest misconduct   **128 callet** whore   **135 Beshrew** curse   **136 trick**
strange behavior, delusion

EMILIA
   I will be hanged if some eternal villain,   137
   Some busy and insinuating rogue,   138
   Some cogging, cozening slave, to get some office,   139
   Have not devised this slander. I will be hanged else.

IAGO
   Fie, there is no such man. It is impossible.

DESDEMONA
   If any such there be, heaven pardon him!

EMILIA
   A halter pardon him! And hell gnaw his bones!   143
   Why should he call her whore? Who keeps her
      company?
   What place? What time? What form? What likelihood? 145
   The Moor's abused by some most villainous knave,
   Some base notorious knave, some scurvy fellow.
   O heavens, that such companions thou'dst unfold,   148
   And put in every honest hand a whip
   To lash the rascals naked through the world
   Even from the east to th' west!

IAGO   Speak within door.   151

EMILIA
   O, fie upon them! Some such squire he was   152
   That turned your wit the seamy side without   153
   And made you to suspect me with the Moor.

IAGO
   You are a fool. Go to.

DESDEMONA   Alas, Iago,   155
   What shall I do to win my lord again?
   Good friend, go to him; for, by this light of heaven,
   I know not how I lost him. Here I kneel. [*She kneels.*]
   If e'er my will did trespass 'gainst his love,
   Either in discourse of thought or actual deed,   160
   Or that mine eyes, mine ears, or any sense   161
   Delighted them in any other form;   162

---

137 **eternal** inveterate   138 **insinuating** ingratiating, fawning, whee-
dling   139 **cogging** cheating. **cozening** defrauding   143 **halter** hangman's noose   145 **form** appearance, circumstance   148 **companions**
fellows. **unfold** expose   151 **within door** i.e., not so loud   152 **squire**
fellow   153 **seamy side without** wrong side out   155 **Go to** i.e., that's
enough   160 **discourse of thought** process of thinking   161 **that** if (also
in l. 163)   162 **Delighted them** took delight

Or that I do not yet, and ever did,   163
And ever will—though he do shake me off
To beggarly divorcement—love him dearly,
Comfort forswear me! Unkindness may do much,   166
And his unkindness may defeat my life,   167
But never taint my love. I cannot say "whore."
It does abhor me now I speak the word;   169
To do the act that might the addition earn   170
Not the world's mass of vanity could make me.   171

IAGO
I pray you, be content. 'Tis but his humor.   172
The business of the state does him offense,
And he does chide with you.

DESDEMONA   If 'twere no other—

IAGO   It is but so, I warrant.   [*Trumpets within.*]
Hark, how these instruments summon you to supper!
The messengers of Venice stays the meat.   178
Go in, and weep not. All things shall be well.
                    Exeunt Desdemona and Emilia.

    Enter Roderigo.

How now, Roderigo?

RODERIGO   I do not find that thou deal'st justly with me.

IAGO   What in the contrary?

RODERIGO   Every day thou daff'st me with some device, 183
    Iago, and rather, as it seems to me now, keep'st from
    me all conveniency than suppliest me with the least 185
    advantage of hope. I will indeed no longer endure it, 186
    nor am I yet persuaded to put up in peace what al-   187
    ready I have foolishly suffered.

IAGO   Will you hear me, Roderigo?

RODERIGO   Faith, I have heard too much, for your words
    and performances are no kin together.

IAGO   You charge me most unjustly.

RODERIGO   With naught but truth. I have wasted myself
    out of my means. The jewels you have had from me to

---

163 **yet** still   166 **Comfort forswear** may heavenly comfort forsake
167 **defeat** destroy   169 **abhor** (1) fill me with abhorrence (2) make me
whorelike   170 **addition** title   171 **vanity** showy splendor   172 **humor**
mood   178 **stays the meat** are waiting to dine   183 **thou daff'st me** you
put me off.   **device** excuse, trick   185 **conveniency** advantage, opportunity   186 **advantage** increase   187 **put up** submit to, tolerate

deliver Desdemona would half have corrupted a vo- 195
tarist. You have told me she hath received them and 196
returned me expectations and comforts of sudden re- 197
spect and acquaintance, but I find none. 198

IAGO Well, go to, very well.

RODERIGO "Very well"! "Go to"! I cannot go to, man, nor 200
'tis not very well. By this hand, I think it is scurvy, and
begin to find myself fopped in it. 202

IAGO Very well.

RODERIGO I tell you 'tis not very well. I will make myself 204
known to Desdemona. If she will return me my jewels,
I will give over my suit and repent my unlawful solic-
itation; if not, assure yourself I will seek satisfaction 207
of you.

IAGO You have said now? 209

RODERIGO Ay, and said nothing but what I protest in- 210
tendment of doing. 211

IAGO Why, now I see there's mettle in thee, and even
from this instant do build on thee a better opinion
than ever before. Give me thy hand, Roderigo. Thou
hast taken against me a most just exception; but yet I
protest I have dealt most directly in thy affair.

RODERIGO It hath not appeared.

IAGO I grant indeed it hath not appeared, and your suspicion is not without wit and judgment. But, Roderigo, if thou hast that in thee indeed which I have
greater reason to believe now than ever—I mean purpose, courage, and valor—this night show it. If thou
the next night following enjoy not Desdemona, take
me from this world with treachery and devise engines 224
for my life. 225

RODERIGO Well, what is it? Is it within reason and compass?

---

195 deliver deliver to   **195–196 votarist** nun   **197–198 sudden respect**
immediate consideration   **200 I cannot go to** (Roderigo changes Iago's
go to, an expression urging patience, to *I cannot go to*, "I have no
opportunity for sex.")   **202 fopped** fooled, duped   **204 not very well**
(Roderigo changes Iago's *very well*, "all right, then," to *not very well*,
"not at all good.")   **207 satisfaction** repayment. (The term normally
means the settling of accounts in a duel.)   **209 You . . . now** have you
finished   **210–211 intendment** intention   **224–225 engines for** plots
against

IAGO   Sir, there is especial commission come from Venice to depute Cassio in Othello's place.

RODERIGO   Is that true? Why, then Othello and Desdemona return again to Venice.

IAGO   O, no; he goes into Mauritania and takes away
with him the fair Desdemona, unless his abode be
lingered here by some accident; wherein none can be
so determinate as the removing of Cassio.   235

RODERIGO   How do you mean, removing of him?

IAGO   Why, by making him uncapable of Othello's
place—knocking out his brains.

RODERIGO   And that you would have me to do?

IAGO   Ay, if you dare do yourself a profit and a right.
He sups tonight with a harlotry, and thither will I go   241
to him. He knows not yet of his honorable fortune. If
you will watch his going thence, which I will fashion
to fall out between twelve and one, you may take him   244
at your pleasure. I will be near to second your attempt,
and he shall fall between us. Come, stand not amazed
at it, but go along with me. I will show you such a
necessity in his death that you shall think yourself
bound to put it on him. It is now high suppertime,   249
and the night grows to waste. About it.   250

RODERIGO   I will hear further reason for this.

IAGO   And you shall be satisfied.   *Exeunt.*

❖

4.3   *Enter Othello, Lodovico, Desdemona, Emilia,
and attendants.*

LODOVICO
I do beseech you, sir, trouble yourself no further.

OTHELLO
O, pardon me; 'twill do me good to walk.

LODOVICO
Madam, good night. I humbly thank your ladyship.

---

235 determinate effective   **241 harlotry** slut   **244 fall out** occur
249 high fully   **250 grows to waste** wastes away

4.3. Location: The citadel.

DESDEMONA
  Your honor is most welcome.
OTHELLO   Will you walk, sir?
  O, Desdemona!
DESDEMONA   My lord?
OTHELLO   Get you to bed on th' instant. I will be re-
  turned forthwith. Dismiss your attendant there. Look 't
  be done.
DESDEMONA   I will, my lord.
              Exit [Othello, with Lodovico and attendants].
EMILIA   How goes it now? He looks gentler than he did.
DESDEMONA
  He says he will return incontinent,   12
  And hath commanded me to go to bed,
  And bid me to dismiss you.
EMILIA   Dismiss me?
DESDEMONA
  It was his bidding. Therefore, good Emilia,
  Give me my nightly wearing, and adieu.
  We must not now displease him.
EMILIA   I would you had never seen him!
DESDEMONA
  So would not I. My love doth so approve him
  That even his stubbornness, his checks, his frowns—   21
  Prithee, unpin me—have grace and favor in them.
              [Emilia prepares Desdemona for bed.]
EMILIA   I have laid those sheets you bade me on the
  bed.
DESDEMONA
  All's one. Good faith, how foolish are our minds!   25
  If I do die before thee, prithee shroud me
  In one of these same sheets.
EMILIA   Come, come, you talk.   27
DESDEMONA
  My mother had a maid called Barbary.
  She was in love, and he she loved proved mad   29
  And did forsake her. She had a song of "Willow."
  An old thing 'twas, but it expressed her fortune,

12 incontinent immediately   **21 stubbornness** roughness.   **checks**
rebukes   **25 All's one** all right. It doesn't really matter   **27 talk** i.e.,
prattle   **29 mad** wild, i.e., faithless

And she died singing it. That song tonight
Will not go from my mind; I have much to do   33
But to go hang my head all at one side   34
And sing it like poor Barbary. Prithee, dispatch.
EMILIA   Shall I go fetch your nightgown?   36
DESDEMONA   No, unpin me here.
This Lodovico is a proper man.   38
EMILIA   A very handsome man.
DESDEMONA   He speaks well.
EMILIA   I know a lady in Venice would have walked
barefoot to Palestine for a touch of his nether lip.
DESDEMONA [*Singing*]
   "The poor soul sat sighing by a sycamore tree,
     Sing all a green willow;   44
   Her hand on her bosom, her head on her knee,
     Sing willow, willow, willow.
   The fresh streams ran by her and murmured her
     moans;
     Sing willow, willow, willow;
   Her salt tears fell from her, and softened the
     stones—"
Lay by these.
[*Singing*.] "Sing willow, willow, willow—"
Prithee, hie thee. He'll come anon.   52
[*Singing*.] "Sing all a green willow must be my garland.
   Let nobody blame him; his scorn I approve—"
Nay, that's not next.—Hark! Who is 't that knocks?
EMILIA   It's the wind.
DESDEMONA [*Singing*]
   "I called my love false love; but what said he then?
     Sing willow, willow, willow;
   If I court more women, you'll couch with more
     men."
So, get thee gone. Good night. Mine eyes do itch;
Doth that bode weeping?
EMILIA   'Tis neither here nor there.

33–34 I . . . hang I can scarcely keep myself from hanging
36 nightgown dressing gown   **38 proper** handsome   **44 willow** (A
conventional emblem of disappointed love.)   **52 hie thee** hurry.   **anon**
right away

DESDEMONA
  I have heard it said so. O, these men, these men!
  Dost thou in conscience think—tell me, Emilia—
  That there be women do abuse their husbands   64
  In such gross kind?
EMILIA   There be some such, no question.
DESDEMONA
  Wouldst thou do such a deed for all the world?
EMILIA
  Why, would not you?
DESDEMONA   No, by this heavenly light!
EMILIA
  Nor I neither by this heavenly light;
  I might do 't as well i' the dark.
DESDEMONA
  Wouldst thou do such a deed for all the world?
EMILIA
  The world's a huge thing. It is a great price
  For a small vice.
DESDEMONA
  Good troth, I think thou wouldst not.
EMILIA By my troth, I think I should, and undo 't when
  I had done. Marry, I would not do such a thing for a
  joint ring, nor for measures of lawn, nor for gowns,   76
  petticoats, nor caps, nor any petty exhibition. But for   77
  all the whole world! Uds pity, who would not make   78
  her husband a cuckold to make him a monarch? I
  should venture purgatory for 't.
DESDEMONA
  Beshrew me if I would do such a wrong
  For the whole world.
EMILIA Why, the wrong is but a wrong i' the world, and
  having the world for your labor, 'tis a wrong in your
  own world, and you might quickly make it right.
DESDEMONA
  I do not think there is any such woman.
EMILIA Yes, a dozen, and as many

---

64 abuse deceive **76 joint ring** a ring made in separate halves. **lawn**
fine linen **77 exhibition** gift **78 Uds** i.e., God's

To th' vantage as would store the world they played for. 88
But I do think it is their husbands' faults
If wives do fall. Say that they slack their duties 90
And pour our treasures into foreign laps, 91
Or else break out in peevish jealousies,
Throwing restraint upon us? Or say they strike us, 93
Or scant our former having in despite? 94
Why, we have galls, and though we have some grace, 95
Yet have we some revenge. Let husbands know
Their wives have sense like them. They see, and smell, 97
And have their palates both for sweet and sour,
As husbands have. What is it that they do
When they change us for others? Is it sport? 100
I think it is. And doth affection breed it? 101
I think it doth. Is 't frailty that thus errs?
It is so too. And have not we affections,
Desires for sport, and frailty, as men have?
Then let them use us well; else let them know,
The ills we do, their ills instruct us so.

DESDEMONA
Good night, good night. God me such uses send 107
Not to pick bad from bad, but by bad mend! 108

Exeunt.

❧

88 To th' vantage in addition, to boot.   **store** populate.   **played**
(1) gambled (2) sported sexually   **90 duties** marital duties   **91 pour . . .
laps** i.e., are unfaithful, give what is rightfully ours (semen) to other
women   **93 Throwing . . . us** i.e., jealously restricting our freedom to
see other men   **94 scant . . . despite** reduce our allowance to spite us
95 have galls i.e., are capable of resenting injury and insult   **97 sense**
physical sense   **100 sport** sexual pastime   **101 affection** passion
107 uses habit, practice   **108 Not . . . mend** i.e., not to learn bad conduct from others' badness (as Emilia has suggested women learn from
men), but to mend my ways by perceiving what badness is, making
spiritual benefit out of evil and adversity

5.1   *Enter Iago and Roderigo.*

IAGO
  Here stand behind this bulk. Straight will he come.   1
  Wear thy good rapier bare, and put it home.   2
  Quick, quick! Fear nothing. I'll be at thy elbow.
  It makes us or it mars us. Think on that,
  And fix most firm thy resolution.
RODERIGO
  Be near at hand. I may miscarry in 't.
IAGO
  Here, at thy hand. Be bold, and take thy stand.
        [*Iago stands aside. Roderigo conceals himself.*]
RODERIGO
  I have no great devotion to the deed;
  And yet he hath given me satisfying reasons.
  'Tis but a man gone. Forth, my sword! He dies.
                              [*He draws.*]
IAGO
  I have rubbed this young quat almost to the sense,   11
  And he grows angry. Now, whether he kill Cassio
  Or Cassio him, or each do kill the other,
  Every way makes my gain. Live Roderigo,   14
  He calls me to a restitution large
  Of gold and jewels that I bobbed from him   16
  As gifts to Desdemona.
  It must not be. If Cassio do remain,
  He hath a daily beauty in his life
  That makes me ugly; and besides, the Moor
  May unfold me to him; there stand I in much peril.   21
  No, he must die. Be 't so. I hear him coming.

        Enter Cassio.

RODERIGO [*Coming forth*]
  I know his gait, 'tis he.—Villain, thou diest!
                    [*He makes a pass at Cassio.*]
CASSIO
  That thrust had been mine enemy indeed,

5.1. Location: A street in Cyprus.
1 bulk framework projecting from the front of a shop **2 bare** un-
sheathed **11 quat** pimple, pustule. **to the sense** to the quick **14 Live
Roderigo** if Roderigo live **16 bobbed** swindled **21 unfold** expose

But that my coat is better than thou know'st.   25
I will make proof of thine.
                    [*He draws, and wounds Roderigo.*]
RODERIGO   O, I am slain!   [*He falls.*] 26
                    [*Iago from behind wounds Cassio
                         in the leg, and exit.*]
CASSIO
I am maimed forever. Help, ho! Murder! Murder!

Enter Othello.

OTHELLO
The voice of Cassio! Iago keeps his word.
RODERIGO   O, villain that I am!
OTHELLO   It is even so.
CASSIO   O, help, ho! Light! A surgeon!
OTHELLO
'Tis he. O brave Iago, honest and just,
That hast such noble sense of thy friend's wrong!
Thou teachest me. Minion, your dear lies dead,   34
And your unblest fate hies. Strumpet, I come.   35
Forth of my heart those charms, thine eyes, are blotted; 36
Thy bed, lust-stained, shall with lust's blood be spotted.
                              Exit Othello.

Enter Lodovico and Gratiano.

CASSIO
What ho! No watch? No passage? Murder! Murder!   38
GRATIANO
'Tis some mischance. The voice is very direful.
CASSIO   O, help!
LODOVICO   Hark!
RODERIGO   O wretched villain!
LODOVICO
Two or three groan. 'Tis heavy night;   43
These may be counterfeits. Let's think 't unsafe
To come in to the cry without more help.   45
                    [*They remain near the entrance.*]

25 coat (Possibly a garment of mail under the outer clothing, or simply
a tougher coat than Roderigo expected.)   **26 proof** a test   **34 Minion**
hussy (i.e., Desdemona)   **35 hies** hastens on   **36 Forth of** from out
38 passage people passing by   **43 heavy** thick, dark   **45 come in to**
approach

RODERIGO
Nobody come? Then shall I bleed to death.

Enter Iago [in his shirtsleeves, with a light].

LODOVICO   Hark!

GRATIANO
Here's one comes in his shirt, with light and weapons.

IAGO
Who's there? Whose noise is this that cries on murder?   49

LODOVICO
We do not know.

IAGO   Did not you hear a cry?

CASSIO
Here, here! For heaven's sake, help me!

IAGO   What's the matter?
                              [He moves toward Cassio.]

GRATIANO *[To Lodovico]*
This is Othello's ancient, as I take it.

LODOVICO *[To Gratiano]*
The same indeed, a very valiant fellow.

IAGO *[To Cassio]*
What are you here that cry so grievously?   54

CASSIO
Iago? O, I am spoiled, undone by villains!   55
Give me some help.

IAGO
O me, Lieutenant! What villains have done this?

CASSIO
I think that one of them is hereabout,
And cannot make away.

IAGO   O treacherous villains!   59
[To Lodovico and Gratiano.] What are you there? Come
    in, and give some help.   *[They advance.]*

RODERIGO   O, help me there!

CASSIO
That's one of them.

IAGO   O murderous slave! O villain!
                              [He stabs Roderigo.]

RODERIGO
O damned Iago! O inhuman dog!

49 cries on cries out   **54 What** who (also at ll. 60 and 66)   **55 spoiled**
ruined, done for   **59 make** get

IAGO
    Kill men i' the dark?—Where be these bloody thieves?—
    How silent is this town!—Ho! Murder, murder!—
    [*To Lodovico and Gratiano.*] What may you be? Are you
      of good or evil?
LODOVICO   As you shall prove us, praise us.   67
IAGO   Signor Lodovico?
LODOVICO   He, sir.
IAGO
    I cry you mercy. Here's Cassio hurt by villains.   70
GRATIANO   Cassio?
IAGO   How is 't, brother?
CASSIO   My leg is cut in two.
IAGO   Marry, heaven forbid!
    Light, gentlemen! I'll bind it with my shirt.
                  [*He hands them the light, and tends*
                              to Cassio's wound.]

    Enter Bianca.

BIANCA
    What is the matter, ho? Who is 't that cried?
IAGO   Who is 't that cried?
BIANCA   O my dear Cassio!
    My sweet Cassio! O Cassio, Cassio, Cassio!
IAGO
    O notable strumpet! Cassio, may you suspect
    Who they should be that have thus mangled you?
CASSIO   No.
GRATIANO
    I am sorry to find you thus. I have been to seek you.
IAGO
    Lend me a garter. [*He applies a tourniquet.*] So.—O,
      for a chair,   83
    To bear him easily hence!
BIANCA
    Alas, he faints! O Cassio, Cassio, Cassio!
IAGO
    Gentlemen all, I do suspect this trash
    To be a party in this injury.—
    Patience awhile, good Cassio.—Come, come;

67 praise appraise   **70 I cry you mercy** I beg your pardon   **83 chair**
litter

Lend me a light. [*He shines the light on Roderigo.*] Know
  we this face or no?
Alas, my friend and my dear countryman
Roderigo! No.—Yes, sure.—O heaven! Roderigo!
GRATIANO What, of Venice?
IAGO Even he, sir. Did you know him?
GRATIANO Know him? Ay.
IAGO
Signor Gratiano? I cry your gentle pardon.   95
These bloody accidents must excuse my manners   96
That so neglected you.
GRATIANO   I am glad to see you.
IAGO
How do you, Cassio? O, a chair, a chair!
GRATIANO Roderigo!
IAGO
He, he, 'tis he. [*A litter is brought in.*] O, that's well said;
  the chair.   100
Some good man bear him carefully from hence;
I'll fetch the General's surgeon. [*To Bianca.*] For you,
  mistress,
Save you your labor.—He that lies slain here, Cassio, 103
Was my dear friend. What malice was between you? 104
CASSIO
None in the world, nor do I know the man.
IAGO [*To Bianca*]
What, look you pale?—O, bear him out o' th' air. 106
              [*Cassio and Roderigo are borne off.*]
Stay you, good gentlemen.—Look you pale, mistress?— 107
Do you perceive the gastness of her eye?— 108
Nay, if you stare, we shall hear more anon.— 109
Behold her well; I pray you, look upon her.
Do you see, gentlemen? Nay, guiltiness
Will speak, though tongues were out of use.

    [*Enter Emilia.*]

---

95 **gentle** noble   96 **accidents** sudden events   100 **well said** well done
103 **Save . . . labor** i.e., never you mind tending Cassio   104 **malice**
enmity   106 **bear . . . air** (Fresh air was thought to be dangerous for a
wound.)   107 **Stay you** (Lodovico and Gratiano are evidently about to
leave.)   108 **gastness** terror   109 **stare** (Iago pretends to interpret
Bianca's wild looks as an involuntary confession of guilt.)

EMILIA
  'Las, what's the matter? What's the matter, husband?
IAGO
  Cassio hath here been set on in the dark
  By Roderigo and fellows that are scaped.
  He's almost slain, and Roderigo dead.
EMILIA
  Alas, good gentleman! Alas, good Cassio!
IAGO
  This is the fruits of whoring. Prithee, Emilia,
  Go know of Cassio where he supped tonight.   119
  [*To Bianca.*] What, do you shake at that?
BIANCA
  He supped at my house, but I therefore shake not.
IAGO
  O, did he so? I charge you go with me.
EMILIA   O, fie upon thee, strumpet!
BIANCA
  I am no strumpet, but of life as honest   124
  As you that thus abuse me.
EMILIA   As I? Faugh! Fie upon thee!
IAGO
  Kind gentlemen, let's go see poor Cassio dressed.—   127
  Come, mistress, you must tell 's another tale.
  Emilia, run you to the citadel
  And tell my lord and lady what hath happed.—
  Will you go on afore? [*Aside.*] This is the night
  That either makes me or fordoes me quite.   *Exeunt.* 132

❖

5.2   *Enter Othello [with a light], and Desdemona in her bed.*

OTHELLO
  It is the cause, it is the cause, my soul.   1
  Let me not name it to you, you chaste stars!
  It is the cause. Yet I'll not shed her blood,

119 know learn   **124 honest** chaste   **127 Cassio dressed** Cassio's wounds dressed   **132 fordoes** undoes, ruins

5.2. Location: A bedchamber in the citadel.
s.d. in her bed (The bed is presumably "thrust out" onstage as the scene begins.)   **1 cause** i.e., cause of justice, the offense itself, which Othello must correct as an agent of justice

Nor scar that whiter skin of hers than snow,
And smooth as monumental alabaster.   5
Yet she must die, else she'll betray more men.
Put out the light, and then put out the light.   7
If I quench thee, thou flaming minister,   8
I can again thy former light restore,
Should I repent me; but once put out thy light,   10
Thou cunning'st pattern of excelling nature,   11
I know not where is that Promethean heat   12
That can thy light relume. When I have plucked thy rose, 13
I cannot give it vital growth again;
It needs must wither. I'll smell thee on the tree.
                            [*He kisses her.*]
O balmy breath, that dost almost persuade
Justice to break her sword! One more, one more.
Be thus when thou art dead, and I will kill thee,
And love thee after. One more, and that's the last.
                            [*He kisses her.*]
So sweet was ne'er so fatal. I must weep,
But they are cruel tears. This sorrow's heavenly;   21
It strikes where it doth love. She wakes.   22
DESDEMONA Who's there? Othello?
OTHELLO Ay, Desdemona.
DESDEMONA Will you come to bed, my lord?
OTHELLO Have you prayed tonight, Desdemon?
DESDEMONA Ay, my lord.
OTHELLO
If you bethink yourself of any crime   28
Unreconciled as yet to heaven and grace,
Solicit for it straight.   30
DESDEMONA
Alack, my lord, what may you mean by that?
OTHELLO
Well, do it, and be brief. I will walk by.

---

5 monumental i.e., used in making tombs and funeral monuments
7 the light . . . light the torch or lamp . . . Desdemona's life   **8 flaming
minister** torch or lamp that serves me   **10 repent me** change my
mind   **11 Thou . . . pattern** you skillfully wrought perfect example
12 Promethean heat divine fire. (Alluding to the theft of fire from
heaven by Prometheus.)   **13 relume** rekindle   **21 cruel** unrelenting
22 It . . . love (Compare Hebrews 12:6: "For whom the Lord loveth he
chasteneth.")   **28 crime** sin   **30 Solicit** petition, pray.   **straight**
immediately

I would not kill thy unp#repar#èd spirit.
No, heaven forfend! I would not kill thy soul.   34
DESDEMONA
Talk you of killing?
OTHELLO   Ay, I do.
DESDEMONA   Then heaven
Have mercy on me!
OTHELLO   Amen, with all my heart!
DESDEMONA
If you say so, I hope you will not kill me.
OTHELLO   Humh!
DESDEMONA
And yet I fear you; for you're fatal then
When your eyes roll so. Why I should fear I know not,
Since guiltiness I know not; but yet I feel I fear.
OTHELLO
Think on thy sins.
DESDEMONA   They are loves I bear to you.   42
OTHELLO   Ay, and for that thou diest.
DESDEMONA
That death's unnatural that kills for loving.
Alas, why gnaw you so your nether lip?
Some bloody passion shakes your very frame.
These are portents; but yet I hope, I hope,
They do not point on me.   48
OTHELLO   Peace, and be still!
DESDEMONA   I will so. What's the matter?
OTHELLO
That handkerchief which I so loved and gave thee
Thou gav'st to Cassio.
DESDEMONA   No, by my life and soul!
Send for the man and ask him.
OTHELLO
Sweet soul, take heed, take heed of perjury.
Thou art on thy deathbed.
DESDEMONA
Ay, but not yet to die.
OTHELLO   Yes, presently.   56

34 forfend forbid   **42 They are . . . you** i.e., if I sinned, it was in loving
you more than my father, or more than God   **48 point on** point at,
predict what is to happen to   **56 presently** immediately

Therefore confess thee freely of thy sin;
For to deny each article with oath
Cannot remove nor choke the strong conception   59
That I do groan withal. Thou art to die.   60

DESDEMONA
Then Lord have mercy on me!

OTHELLO   I say, amen.

DESDEMONA
And have you mercy too! I never did
Offend you in my life; never loved Cassio   63
But with such general warranty of heaven   64
As I might love. I never gave him token.

OTHELLO
By heaven, I saw my handkerchief in 's hand.
O perjured woman! Thou dost stone my heart,   67
And makes me call what I intend to do
A murder, which I thought a sacrifice.
I saw the handkerchief.

DESDEMONA   He found it, then.
I never gave it him. Send for him hither;
Let him confess a truth.

OTHELLO   He hath confessed.

DESDEMONA   What, my lord?

OTHELLO
That he hath used thee.

DESDEMONA   How? Unlawfully?

OTHELLO   Ay.

DESDEMONA
He will not say so.

OTHELLO   No, his mouth is stopped;
Honest Iago hath ta'en order for 't.   76

DESDEMONA
O, my fear interprets. What, is he dead?

OTHELLO
Had all his hairs been lives, my great revenge
Had stomach for them all.

DESDEMONA
Alas, he is betrayed and I undone!   [*She weeps.*]

---

59 conception (1) belief in your guilt (2) plan in my mind   **60 groan
withal** (1) groan at in sorrow (2) groan as in giving birth   **63 Offend**
wrong   **64 warranty** sanction   **67 stone** turn to stone, harden   **76 ta'en
order** taken measures

OTHELLO
  Out, strumpet! Weep'st thou for him to my face?
DESDEMONA
  O, banish me, my lord, but kill me not!
OTHELLO   Down, strumpet!
DESDEMONA
  Kill me tomorrow; let me live tonight!
OTHELLO   Nay, if you strive—
DESDEMONA
  But half an hour!
OTHELLO   Being done, there is no pause.   86
DESDEMONA
  But while I say one prayer!
OTHELLO   It is too late.
                                        Smothers her.

EMILIA (*At the door*)
  My lord, my lord! What ho! My lord, my lord!
OTHELLO
  What noise is this? Not dead? Not yet quite dead?
  I that am cruel am yet merciful;
  I would not have thee linger in thy pain.
                              [*He dispatches her.*]
  So, so.
EMILIA (*Within*)   What ho! My lord, my lord!
OTHELLO   Who's there?
EMILIA [*Within*]
  O, good my lord, I would speak a word with you!
OTHELLO
  Yes, 'tis Emilia.—By and by.—She's dead.
  'Tis like she comes to speak of Cassio's death.—   95
  The noise was here. Ha! No more moving?   96
  Still as the grave. Shall she come in? Were 't good?—
  I think she stirs again. No. What's best to do?
  If she come in, she'll sure speak to my wife.
  My wife! My wife! What wife? I have no wife.
  O, insupportable! O heavy hour!
  Methinks it should be now a huge eclipse

86 Being done i.e., since justice has begun its relentless course   **95 like**
likely that   **96 here** (The Folio's *high* is possible, suggesting that the
commotion of the attack on Cassio was loud.)

Of sun and moon, and that th' affrighted globe
Should yawn at alteration.
EMILIA [*Within*]   I do beseech you   104
That I may speak with you, O, good my lord!
OTHELLO
I had forgot thee. O, come in, Emilia.—
Soft, by and by. Let me the curtains draw.—   107
                    [*He closes the bed-curtains and
                        opens the door.*]
Where art thou?

          Enter Emilia.

              What's the matter with thee now?
EMILIA
O, my good lord, yonder's foul murders done!
OTHELLO   What, now?
EMILIA   But now, my lord.
OTHELLO
It is the very error of the moon;   112
She comes more nearer earth than she was wont,
And makes men mad.
EMILIA
Cassio, my lord, hath killed a young Venetian
Called Roderigo.
OTHELLO   Roderigo killed?
And Cassio killed?
EMILIA   No, Cassio is not killed.
OTHELLO
Not Cassio killed? Then murder's out of tune,
And sweet revenge grows harsh.
DESDEMONA   O, falsely, falsely murdered!
EMILIA   O Lord, what cry is that?
OTHELLO   That? What?
EMILIA
Out and alas, that was my lady's voice.   123
                    [*She opens the bed-curtains.*]

---

104 yawn gape in amazement, i.e., move in an earthquake. (According to
Pliny, earthquakes often happen during eclipses.)   **at alteration** at these
cataclysmic events in nature, well suited to express the horror of Desdemona's death   **107 Soft** wait a minute   **112 error** aberration, irregular-
ity   **123 Out** (A cry of dismay, intensifying *alas*.)

Help, help, ho, help! O lady, speak again!
Sweet Desdemona! O sweet mistress, speak!
DESDEMONA   A guiltless death I die.
EMILIA   O, who hath done this deed?
DESDEMONA   Nobody; I myself. Farewell.
Commend me to my kind lord. O, farewell! [*She dies.*]
OTHELLO
Why, how should she be murdered?
EMILIA   Alas, who knows?
OTHELLO
You heard her say herself it was not I.
EMILIA
She said so. I must needs report the truth.
OTHELLO
She's like a liar gone to burning hell!
'Twas I that killed her.
EMILIA   O, the more angel she,
And you the blacker devil!
OTHELLO
She turned to folly, and she was a whore.   136
EMILIA
Thou dost belie her, and thou art a devil.   137
OTHELLO   She was false as water.
EMILIA   Thou art rash as fire to say
That she was false. O, she was heavenly true!
OTHELLO
Cassio did top her. Ask thy husband else.   141
O, I were damned beneath all depth in hell
But that I did proceed upon just grounds
To this extremity. Thy husband knew it all.
EMILIA   My husband?
OTHELLO   Thy husband.
EMILIA   That she was false to wedlock?
OTHELLO
Ay, with Cassio. Nay, had she been true,
If heaven would make me such another world
Of one entire and perfect chrysolite,   150
I'd not have sold her for it.
EMILIA   My husband?

136 folly i.e., wantonness, fleshly sin   **137 belie** slander   **141 else** i.e., if you don't believe me   **150 chrysolite** precious topaz

OTHELLO
  Ay, 'twas he that told me on her first.
  An honest man he is, and hates the slime
  That sticks on filthy deeds.
EMILIA   My husband?
OTHELLO
  What needs this iterance, woman? I say thy husband.   157
EMILIA
  O mistress, villainy hath made mocks with love!   158
  My husband say she was false?
OTHELLO   He, woman;
  I say thy husband. Dost understand the word?
  My friend, thy husband, honest, honest Iago.
EMILIA
  If he say so, may his pernicious soul
  Rot half a grain a day! He lies to th' heart.
  She was too fond of her most filthy bargain.
OTHELLO   Ha?   [*He draws.*]
EMILIA   Do thy worst!
  This deed of thine is no more worthy heaven
  Than thou wast worthy her.
OTHELLO   Peace, you were best.   168
EMILIA
  Thou hast not half that power to do me harm
  As I have to be hurt. O gull! O dolt!   170
  As ignorant as dirt! Thou hast done a deed—
  I care not for thy sword; I'll make thee known,
  Though I lost twenty lives.—Help! Help, ho, help!
  The Moor hath killed my mistress! Murder, murder!

      Enter Montano, Gratiano, and Iago.

MONTANO
  What is the matter? How now, General?
EMILIA
  O, are you come, Iago? You have done well,
  That men must lay their murders on your neck.
GRATIANO   What is the matter?
EMILIA [*To Iago*]
  Disprove this villain, if thou be'st a man.

___

157 iterance iteration, repetition   **158 made mocks with** derided, made
sport of   **168 you were best** it would be best for you   **170 to be hurt**
i.e., to endure hurt.   **gull** dupe

He says thou toldst him that his wife was false.
I know thou didst not; thou'rt not such a villain.
Speak, for my heart is full.

IAGO
I told him what I thought, and told no more
Than what he found himself was apt and true.   184

EMILIA
But did you ever tell him she was false?

IAGO   I did.

EMILIA
You told a lie, an odious, damnèd lie!
Upon my soul, a lie, a wicked lie.
She false with Cassio? Did you say with Cassio?

IAGO
With Cassio, mistress. Go to, charm your tongue.   190

EMILIA
I will not charm my tongue; I am bound to speak.
My mistress here lies murdered in her bed—

ALL   O heavens forfend!

EMILIA
And your reports have set the murder on.

OTHELLO
Nay, stare not, masters. It is true indeed.

GRATIANO   'Tis a strange truth.

MONTANO
O monstrous act!

EMILIA   Villainy, villainy, villainy!
I think upon 't—I think I smell 't! O villainy!
I thought so then—I'll kill myself for grief—   199
O villainy, villainy!

IAGO
What, are you mad? I charge you, get you home.

EMILIA
Good gentlemen, let me have leave to speak.
'Tis proper I obey him, but not now.
Perchance, Iago, I will ne'er go home.

184 apt plausible   **190 charm** keep silent (as though by a magic spell)
199 then (Perhaps at 3.3.331–332 and 4.2.137–154.)

OTHELLO

   O! O! O!   [*Othello falls on the bed.*]

EMILIA   Nay, lay thee down and roar,   205

   For thou hast killed the sweetest innocent

   That e'er did lift up eye.

OTHELLO [*Rising*]   O, she was foul!   207

   I scarce did know you, uncle. There lies your niece,

   Whose breath indeed these hands have newly stopped.

   I know this act shows horrible and grim.   210

GRATIANO

   Poor Desdemon! I am glad thy father's dead.

   Thy match was mortal to him, and pure grief

   Shore his old thread in twain. Did he live now,   213

   This sight would make him do a desperate turn,   214

   Yea, curse his better angel from his side,

   And fall to reprobance.   216

OTHELLO

   'Tis pitiful. But yet Iago knows

   That she with Cassio hath the act of shame

   A thousand times committed. Cassio confessed it;

   And she did gratify his amorous works   220

   With that recognizance and pledge of love   221

   Which I first gave her. I saw it in his hand;

   It was a handkerchief, an antique token

   My father gave my mother.

EMILIA   O God! O heavenly God!

IAGO

   Zounds, hold your peace.

EMILIA   'Twill out, 'twill out! I peace?

   No, I will speak as liberal as the north.   227

   Let heaven and men and devils, let them all,

   All, all, cry shame against me, yet I'll speak.

IAGO

   Be wise, and get you home.

---

205 s.d. Othello . . . bed (This direction is from the quarto, as also *He kisses her* at l. 19 and *She dies* at l. 129.)   **207 lift up eye** i.e., lift her eyes to heaven   **210 shows** looks   **213 Shore** sheared, cut   **214 turn** deed   **216 reprobance** damnation, i.e., suicide   **220 gratify** reward   **221 recognizance** token   **227 liberal as the north** freely as the north wind (blows)

EMILIA   I will not.
                               [*Iago threatens Emilia.*]
GRATIANO   Fie,
Your sword upon a woman?
EMILIA
O thou dull Moor! That handkerchief thou speak'st of
I found by fortune and did give my husband;
For often, with a solemn earnestness,
More than indeed belonged to such a trifle,   235
He begged of me to steal 't.
IAGO   Villainous whore!
EMILIA
She give it Cassio? No, alas! I found it,
And I did give 't my husband.
IAGO   Filth, thou liest!
EMILIA
By heaven, I do not, I do not, gentlemen.
O murderous coxcomb! What should such a fool   240
Do with so good a wife?
OTHELLO   Are there no stones in heaven   242
But what serves for the thunder?—Precious villain!   243
          [*He runs at Iago; Montano disarms Othello.*
           Iago, from behind, stabs Emilia.]
GRATIANO
The woman falls! Sure he hath killed his wife.
EMILIA
Ay, ay. O, lay me by my mistress' side.
                               [*Exit Iago.*]
GRATIANO   He's gone, but his wife's killed.
MONTANO
'Tis a notorious villain. Take you this weapon,
Which I have here recovered from the Moor.
Come, guard the door without. Let him not pass,
But kill him rather. I'll after that same villain,
For 'tis a damnèd slave.
               Exit [*with all but Othello and Emilia,*
               who has been laid by Desdemona's side].

235 **belonged** was appropriate 240 **coxcomb** fool. (Addressed to
Othello.) 242 **stones** bolts, such as those used for thunderbolts
243 **Precious** i.e., arrant, utter **s.d. He . . . Emilia** (The quarto text
reads, "The Moor runs at Iago. Iago kills his wife." The quarto also
specifies the exit of Iago at l. 245 and the death of Emilia at l. 260.)

OTHELLO   I am not valiant neither,
But every puny whipster gets my sword.   253
But why should honor outlive honesty?   254
Let it go all.
EMILIA   What did thy song bode, lady?
Hark, canst thou hear me? I will play the swan,
And die in music. [*She sings.*] "Willow, willow, willow."
Moor, she was chaste. She loved thee, cruel Moor.
So come my soul to bliss as I speak true.
So speaking as I think, alas, I die.   [*She dies.*]
OTHELLO
I have another weapon in this chamber;
It was a sword of Spain, the ice-brook's temper—   262
O, here it is. [*He finds a sword.*] Uncle, I must come forth.
GRATIANO [*Within*]
If thou attempt it, it will cost thee dear.
Thou hast no weapon, and perforce must suffer.
OTHELLO
Look in upon me then and speak with me,
Or, naked as I am, I will assault thee.   267

        [*Enter Gratiano.*]

GRATIANO
What is the matter?
OTHELLO   Behold, I have a weapon;
A better never did itself sustain
Upon a soldier's thigh. I have seen the day
That, with this little arm and this good sword,
I have made my way through more impediments
Than twenty times your stop. But O, vain boast!   273
Who can control his fate? 'Tis not so now.
Be not afraid, though you do see me weaponed;
Here is my journey's end, here is my butt   276
And very seamark of my utmost sail.   277
                            [*Gratiano steps back.*]
Do you go back dismayed? 'Tis a lost fear;   278

---

253 whipster contemptible fellow   **254 honor** i.e., the bravery for which
one enjoys a soldier's reputation.   **honesty** true integrity   **262 the ice-
brook's temper** tempered in ice-cold water   **267 naked** unarmed
273 stop power (to stop)   **276 butt** goal, limit. (An archery term.)
277 seamark beacon (marking his destination or limit)   **278 lost** wasted,
unneeded

Man but a rush against Othello's breast   279
And he retires. Where should Othello go?
                    [*He turns to Desdemona.*]
Now, how dost thou look now? O ill-starred wench!
Pale as thy smock! When we shall meet at compt,   282
This look of thine will hurl my soul from heaven,
And fiends will snatch at it. Cold, cold, my girl?
Even like thy chastity. O cursèd, cursèd slave!   285
Whip me, ye devils,
From the possession of this heavenly sight!
Blow me about in winds! Roast me in sulfur!
Wash me in steep-down gulfs of liquid fire!
O Desdemon! Dead, Desdemon! Dead! O! O!   290

> *Enter Lodovico, Cassio [carried in a litter],*
> *Montano, and Iago [prisoner], with officers.*

LODOVICO
Where is this rash and most unfortunate man?
OTHELLO
That's he that was Othello. Here I am.
LODOVICO
Where is that viper? Bring the villain forth.
                    [*Iago is led forward.*]
OTHELLO
I look down towards his feet; but that's a fable.   294
If that thou be'st a devil, I cannot kill thee.
                    [*He wounds Iago.*]
LODOVICO
Wrench his sword from him.   [*Othello is disarmed.*]
IAGO   I bleed, sir, but not killed.
OTHELLO
I am not sorry neither. I'd have thee live,
For in my sense 'tis happiness to die.   298
LODOVICO
O thou Othello, that was once so good,
Fall'n in the practice of a cursèd slave,   300
What shall be said to thee?

279 Man . . . rush wield no more than a reed   **282 compt** account,
judgment day   **285 slave** i.e., Othello himself   **290 s.d. in a litter** (The
quarto specifies that Cassio is "in a chair.")   **294 towards his feet** i.e.,
to see if they are cloven like the devil's   **298 in my sense** to one who
feel as I do   **300 in the practice** through the plotting.   **slave** villain

OTHELLO   Why, anything.
  An honorable murderer, if you will,
  For naught I did in hate, but all in honor.
LODOVICO
  This wretch hath part confessed his villainy.
  Did you and he consent in Cassio's death?   305
OTHELLO   Ay.
CASSIO
  Dear General, I never gave you cause.
OTHELLO
  I do believe it, and I ask your pardon.
  Will you, I pray, demand that demi-devil
  Why he hath thus ensnared my soul and body?
IAGO
  Demand me nothing. What you know, you know.
  From this time forth I never will speak word.
LODOVICO   What, not to pray?
GRATIANO   Torments will ope your lips.   314
OTHELLO   Well, thou dost best.
LODOVICO
  Sir, you shall understand what hath befall'n,
  Which, as I think, you know not. Here is a letter
  Found in the pocket of the slain Roderigo;
  And here another. [*He produces letters.*] The one of them
    imports
  The death of Cassio, to be undertook
  By Roderigo.
OTHELLO
  O villain!
CASSIO   Most heathenish and most gross!   322
LODOVICO [*Showing another paper*]
  Now here's another discontented paper   323
  Found in his pocket too. And this, it seems,
  Roderigo meant t' have sent this damnèd villain;
  But that belike Iago in the interim   326
  Came in and satisfied him.   327
OTHELLO   O thou pernicious caitiff!—
  How came you, Cassio, by that handkerchief
  That was my wife's?

305 consent agree   **314 Torments** torture   **322 gross** monstrous   **323 discontented** full of discontent   **326 belike** most likely   **327 Came in**
interposed

CASSIO   I found it in my chamber;
And he himself confessed it but even now
That there he dropped it for a special purpose
Which wrought to his desire.
OTHELLO   O fool, fool, fool!   333
CASSIO
There is besides in Roderigo's letter
How he upbraids Iago, that he made him
Brave me upon the watch, whereon it came   336
That I was cast; and even but now he spake,   337
After long seeming dead, Iago hurt him,
Iago set him on.
LODOVICO [*To Othello*]
You must forsake this room and go with us.
Your power and your command is taken off,   341
And Cassio rules in Cyprus. For this slave,
If there be any cunning cruelty
That can torment him much and hold him long,   344
It shall be his. You shall close prisoner rest   345
Till that the nature of your fault be known
To the Venetian state.—Come, bring away.
OTHELLO
Soft you; a word or two before you go.   348
I have done the state some service, and they know 't.
No more of that. I pray you, in your letters,
When you shall these unlucky deeds relate,   351
Speak of me as I am; nothing extenuate,
Nor set down aught in malice. Then must you speak
Of one that loved not wisely but too well;
Of one not easily jealous but, being wrought,   355
Perplexed in the extreme; of one whose hand,   356
Like the base Indian, threw a pearl away   357

---

333 wrought . . . desire worked out as he wished, fitted in with his
plan   **336 Brave** defy   **337 cast** dismissed   **341 taken off** taken away
344 hold him long keep him alive a long time (during his torture)
345 rest remain   **348 Soft you** one moment   **351 unlucky** unfortunate
355 wrought worked upon   **356 Perplexed** distraught   **357 Indian** (This
reading from the quarto pictures an ignorant savage who cannot recognize the value of a precious jewel. The Folio reading, *Iudean* or *Judean*,
i.e., infidel or disbeliever, may refer to Herod, who slew Miriamne in a
fit of jealousy, or to Judas Iscariot, the betrayer of Christ.)

Richer than all his tribe; of one whose subdued eyes,   358
Albeit unusèd to the melting mood,
Drops tears as fast as the Arabian trees
Their medicinable gum. Set you down this;   361
And say besides that in Aleppo once,
Where a malignant and a turbaned Turk
Beat a Venetian and traduced the state,
I took by th' throat the circumcisèd dog
And smote him, thus.   [*He stabs himself.*] 366
LODOVICO   O bloody period!   367
GRATIANO   All that is spoke is marred.
OTHELLO
I kissed thee ere I killed thee. No way but this,
Killing myself, to die upon a kiss.
                    [*He kisses Desdemona and*] *dies.*
CASSIO
This did I fear, but thought he had no weapon;
For he was great of heart.
LODOVICO [*To Iago*]   O Spartan dog,   372
More fell than anguish, hunger, or the sea!   373
Look on the tragic loading of this bed.
This is thy work. The object poisons sight;
Let it be hid. Gratiano, keep the house,   376
                    [*The bed-curtains are drawn*]
And seize upon the fortunes of the Moor,   377
For they succeed on you. [*To Cassio.*] To you, Lord
   Governor,   378
Remains the censure of this hellish villain,   379
The time, the place, the torture. O, enforce it!
Myself will straight aboard, and to the state
This heavy act with heavy heart relate.   *Exeunt.*

---

358 subdued i.e., overcome by grief   **361 gum** i.e., myrrh   **366 s.d. He stabs himself** (This direction is in the quarto text.)   **367 period** termination, conclusion   **372 Spartan dog** (Spartan dogs were noted for their savagery and silence.)   **373 fell** cruel   **376 Let it be hid** i.e., draw the bed-curtains. (No stage direction specifies that the dead are to be carried offstage at the end of the play.)   **keep** remain in   **377 seize upon** take legal possession of   **378 succeed on** pass as though by inheritance to   **379 censure** sentencing

Date and Text

On October 6, 1621, Thomas Walkley entered in the Stationers' Register, the official record book of the London Company of Stationers (booksellers and printers), "The Tragedie of Othello, the moore of Venice," and published the play in the following year:

THE Tragoedy of Othello, The Moore of Venice. *As it hath beene diuerse times acted at the* Globe, and at the Black-Friers, by *his Maiesties Seruants. Written by* VVilliam Shakespeare. LONDON, Printed by *N. O.* [Nicholas Okes] for *Thomas Walkley,* and are to be sold at his shop, at the Eagle and Child, in Brittans Bursse. 1622.

The text of this quarto is a good one, based probably on a transcript of Shakespeare's foul papers (working manuscript), although it is some 160 lines shorter than the Folio text of 1623 and may have been cut in the printing house to meet the constraints of space when the printer's copy was allocated to a fixed number of pages. The Folio text may have been derived (via an intermediate transcript) from a copy of the original foul papers, one in which Shakespeare himself copied over his work and made a large number of synonymous or nearly synonymous changes as he did so. These papers, edited by someone else to remove profanity as required by law and introducing other stylistic changes in the process, seemingly became the basis of the prompt-book and also of the Folio text.

The textual situation is thus complex. The Folio text appears to contain a significant number of authorial changes, but it was also worked on by one or more sophisticating scribes and by compositors whose changes are sometimes hard to distinguish from those of Shakespeare. The quarto text was printed by a printing establishment not known for careful work, but does stand close in some ways to a Shakespearean original. Editorially, then, the Folio's readings are to be preferred when the quarto is not clearly right and especially when the Folio gives us genuinely new words; but the quarto's readings demand careful consideration when the Folio text may be suspected of mechanical error (e.g., the shortening of words in full lines) or compositorial substitution of alternative forms, normalizations, and easy adjustments of meter. There are times when the Folio's compositor may have been misled by nearby words or letters in his copy. And because the Folio's stage directions are probably scribal, attention should be paid to those in the quarto.

The earliest mention of the play is on "Hallamas Day, being the first of Nouembar," 1604, when "the Kings Maiesties plaiers" performed "A Play in the Banketinge house att Whit Hall Called The Moor of Venis." The play is attributed to "Shaxberd." The authenticity of this Revels account, first printed by Peter Cunningham in 1842, was once challenged, but it is now accepted as genuine. On stylistic grounds the play is usually dated in 1603 or 1604, although arguments are sometimes presented for a date as early as 1601 or 1602.

Textual Notes

These textual notes are not a historical collation, either of the early quartos and folios or of more recent editions; they are simply a record of departures in this edition from the copy text. The reading adopted in this edition appears in boldface, followed by the rejected reading from the copy text, i.e., the First Folio. Only major alterations in punctuation are noted. Changes in lineation are not indicated, nor are some minor and obvious typographical errors.

Abbreviations used:
F the First Folio
Q1 the quarto of 1622
s.d. stage direction
s.p. speech prefix

Copy text: the First Folio. The adopted readings are from the quarto of 1622 [Q1], unless otherwise indicated; [eds.] means that the adopted reading was first proposed by some editor subsequent to the First Folio.

1.1. 1 Tush, never Neuer **4 'Sblood, but** but **16 And, in conclusion** [Q1; not in F] **26 togaed** Tongued **30 other** others **34 God bless** blesse **68 full fall** **thick-lips** Thick-lips **74 changes** chances **75 [and elsewhere] lose** [eds.] loose **81 Thieves, thieves, thieves** Theeues, Theeues **83 s.d. Brabantio above** [in F, printed as a speech prefix to l. 84] **88 Zounds, sir** Sir [also at l. 111] **103 bravery** knauerie **119 are now** are **158 pains** apines **161 sign. That** [eds.] signe) that **186 night** might

1.2. 15 and or **34 Duke** Dukes **50 carrack** Carract **64 her!** [eds.] her **69 darlings** Deareling **89 I do** do

1.3. 1 There is There's **these** this **61 s.p. Duke and Senators** [All Q1] Sen **101 maimed** main'd **108 s.p. Duke** [Q1; not in F] **109 overt** ouer **112 s.p. [and elsewhere] First Senator** Sen **124 till** tell **132 battles** Battaile **fortunes** Fortune **141 travels'** Trauellours **143 rocks, and** Rocks **heads** head **145 other** others **147 Do grow** Grew **149 thence** hence **157 intentively** instinctiuely **161 sighs** kisses **204 Into your favor** [Q1; not in F] **222 ear** eares **227 sovereign** more soueraigne **233 couch** [eds.] Coach [F] Cooch [Q1] **237 These** [eds.] This **244 Nor I. I would not** Nor would I **251 did love** loue **267 me** [eds.] my **273 instruments** Instrument **281 Desdemona. Tonight, my lord? Duke. This night** [Q1; not in F] **285 With** And **294 s.p. First Senator** Sen **296 s.d. Exeunt** Exit **302 matters** matter **303 the** the the **329 beam** [eds.] braine [F] ballance [Q1] **333–334 our unbitted** or vnbitted **335 scion** [eds.] Seyen [F] syen [Q1] **353 error** errors **354 She . . . she must** [Q1; not in F] **358 a supersubtle** super-subtle **378–382 Roderigo. What . . . purse** [Q1; not in F] **386 a snipe** Snpe **389 He's** [Ha's Q1] She ha's **396 ear** eares

2.1. 35 prays praye **36 heaven** Heauens **42 s.p. Third Gentleman** Gent **44 arrivance** Arriuancie **45 this** the **58 s.p. Second Gentleman** Gent [also at ll. 61, 68, and 95] **72 clog** enclogge **84 And . . . comfort** [Q1; not in F] **90 tell me** tell **94 the sea** Sea **96 their** this **107 list** leaue **111 doors**

doore   **156 [and elsewhere] ne'er** neu'r   **158 such wight** such wightes
170 gyve [eds.] giue   **174 An** and   **175 courtesy** Curtsie   **176 clyster pipes**
Cluster-pipes   **214 s.d. Exeunt** [eds.] Exit   **216 hither** thither   **229 again** a
game   **239 fortune** Forune   **242 compassing** compasse   **244 finder out**
finder   **occasions** occasion   **has** he's   **263 mutualities** mutabilities
300 for wife for wift   **307 rank** right   **308 nightcap** Night-Cape

2.2. 6 addiction [eds.] addition   **10 Heaven bless** Blesse

2.3. 27 stoup [eds.] stope   **38 unfortunate** infortunate   **52 lads** else   **57 to
put** put to   **61, 71 God** heauen   **76 Englishman** Englishmen   **91 Then . . .
auld** [Then . . . owd *Q1*] And take thy awl'd   **93 'Fore God** Why   **97 God's**
heau'ns   **106 God forgive** Forgiue   **110 speak** I speake   **123 the** his
138 s.d. Cry within: Help! Help [from Q1: "Helpe, helpe, within"]
139 Zounds, you You   **152 God's will** Alàs   **153 Montano—sir** Montano
156 God's will, Lieutenant, hold Fie, fie Lieutenant   **158 Zounds, I** I
161 sense of place [eds.] place of sense   **177 breast** breastes   **184 wont be**
wont to be   **201 Zounds, if I** If I once   **212 leagued** [eds.] league   **218 Thus**
This   **227 the** then   **246 well now** well   **250 vile** vil'd   **255 God** Heauen
260 thought had thought   **266 ways** more wayes   **283 O God** Oh   **308 I'll**
I   **311 denotement** [eds.] deuotement   **325–326 me here** me   **337 were 't**
were   **369 hast** hath   **372 By the Mass** Introth   **378 on;** [on, *Q1*] on   **379 the**
[eds.] a

3.1. s.d. Musicians [eds.] Musicians, and Clowne   **21 s.d. Exeunt** [eds.]
Exit   **22 hear** heare me   **26 General's wife** Generall   **31 Cassio. Do, good
my friend** [Q1; not in F]   **42 s.d. Exit** [at l. 41 in F]   **52 To . . . front** [Q1; not
in F]

3.3. 16 circumstance Circumstances   **41 you** your   **55 Yes, faith** I sooth
66 or on   **80 By'r Lady** Trust me   **103 you** he   **118 By heaven** Alas   **124 In
Of**   **148 that all** that: All   **free to free**   **152 But some** Wherein   **160 oft** of
161 wisdom then wisdome   **175 By heaven, I'll** Ile   **183 fondly** [eds.]
soundly [F] strongly [Q1]   **188 God** Heauen   **194 Is once** Is   **196 blown**
blow'd   **199 dances well** Dances   **216 God** Heauen   **218 keep 't** [eds.] keepe
[Q1] kept [F]   **230 I' faith** Trust me   **232 my** your   **249 disproportion**
disproportions   **264 to hold** to   **275 qualities** Quantities   **289 of** to   **294 O,
then heaven mocks** Heauen mock'd   **301 Faith** Why   **305 s.d. Exit** [at l. 304
in F]   **328 faith** but   **345 s.d. Enter Othello** [after "I did say so" in F]
354 of her in her   **385 remorse;** [remorce. *Q1*] remorce. *Q1*] remorse   **407 see, sir** see
411 supervisor super-vision   **439 then laid** laid   **440 Over** ore   **sighed**
sigh   **kissed** kisse   **441 Cried** cry   **455 any that was** [eds.] any, it was
468 mind perhaps minde   **471 Ne'er feels** [eds.] Neu'r keepes

3.4. 23 that the   **37 It yet** It   **56 faith** indeed   **77 I' faith** Indeed   **79 God**
Heauen   **83 Heaven bless** Blesse   **88 can, sir** can   **94–95 Desdemona. I pray
. . . Cassio. Othello. The handkerchief!** [Q1; not in F]   **99 I' faith** Insooth
100 Zounds Away   **164 that** the   **172 I' faith** Indeed   **182 friend.** [eds.]
friend,   **183 absence** [eds.] absence, [Q1] Absence: [F]   **188 by my faith** in
good troth

4.1. 32 Faith Why   **36 Zounds, that's** that's   **45 work** workes   **52 No,
forbear** [Q1; not in F]   **72 couch** [Coach *Q1*] Cowch;   **79 unsuiting** [Q1
corrected] vnfitting [Q1 uncorrected] resulting [F]   **97 clothes** Cloath
103 conster conserue   **105 you now** you   **109 power** dowre   **114 i' faith**

indeed   121 **Do you** Do ye   122 **marry her** marry   125 **win** [eds.] winnes
126 **Faith** Why   **shall marry** marry   133 **beckons** becomes   137 **by this
hand, she** [Q1; not in F]   163 **Faith, I** I   165 **Faith** Yes   212 **s.d.** [at. l. 210 in
F]   215 **God save** Saue   238 **By my troth** Trust me   251 **Truly, an** Truely
284 **denote** deonte [F uncorrected] deuote [F corrected]

4.2. 32 Nay May   33 **knees** knee   35 **But not the words** [Q1; not in F]
51 **kinds** kind   56 **A** The   66 **Ay, there** [eds.] I heere   71 **ne'er** neuer
83 **Impudent strumpet** [Q1; not in F]   96 **keep** [eds.] keepes   **s.d. Enter
Emilia** [at l. 94 in F]   162 **them in** [eds.] them: or   174 **And . . . you** [Q1; not
in F]   177 **you to** to   190 **Faith, I** I   **for** and   201 **By this hand** Nay
232 **takes** taketh   236 **of** [Q1; not in F]

4.3. 10 s.d. Exit [at l. 9 in F]   22 **favor in them** fauour   25 **faith** Father
26 **before thee** before   43 **sighing** [eds.] singing [F corrected] sining [F
uncorrected]   73 **Good troth** Introth   74 **By my troth** Introth   78 **Uds pity**
why   107 **God** Heauen

5.1. 1 bulk Barke   22 **Be 't** But   **hear** heard   36 **Forth** For   50 **Did** Do
91 **O heaven** Yes, 'tis   106 **out o'** o'   113 **'Las, what's . . .** What's Alas, what
is . . . What is   116 **dead** quite dead   126 **Faugh!** Fie Fie

5.2. 34 heaven Heauens   37 **say so** say   56 **Yes, presently** Presently
61 **Then Lord** O Heauen   96 **here** high   104 **Should** Did   121 **O Lord** Alas
131 **heard** heare   148 **Nay, had** had   225 **O God! O heavenly God** Oh
Heauen! oh heauenly Powres   226 **Zounds** Come   248 **have here** haue
317 **not. Here** [not: here *Q1*] not) heere   357 **Indian** Iudean

Shakespeare's Sources

Shakespeare's main source for *Othello* was the seventh story from the third decade of G. B. Giraldi Cinthio's *Hecatommithi* (1565). Cinthio was available in French but not in English translation during Shakespeare's lifetime. The verbal echoes in Shakespeare's play are usually closer to the Italian original than to Gabriel Chappuys's French version of 1584. Cinthio's account may have been based on an actual incident occurring in Venice around 1508.

Shakespeare is considerably indebted to Cinthio's story for the essentials of the narrative, as can be seen in the following new translation: the marriage of a Moorish captain to a Venetian lady, Disdemona, whose relatives wish her to marry someone else, the mutual attraction to noble qualities of mind in both husband and wife, their happiness together at first, the dispatching of the Moor to Cyprus to take charge of the garrison there, Disdemona's insistence on accompanying her husband through whatever dangers may occur (though the sea voyage, as it turns out, is a very calm one), the ensign's treachery and resolve to destroy the Moor's happiness with Disdemona, her begging her husband to reinstate the squadron leader whom the Moor has demoted for fighting on guard duty (although no mention is made of drunkenness or of the ensign's role in starting the trouble), the ensign's insinuations to the Moor that his wife is cuckolding him because she is becoming weary of her marriage with a black man, the ensign's difficulty in providing ocular proof, his planting of Disdemona's handkerchief in the squadron leader's quarters and his showing the Moor that the handkerchief is now in the squadron leader's possession, his arranging for the Moor to witness at a distance a conversation between the ensign and squadron leader that is in fact not about Disdemona, Disdemona's confusion when she is asked to produce the handkerchief, the attack on the squadron leader in the dark, the murder of Disdemona in her bed, the Moor's deep regret at the loss of his wife, the eventual punishment of both the Moor and the ensign, and the telling of the story publicly by the ensign's wife, who has heretofore kept silent because of her fear of her husband.

Although these correspondences in the story are many, Shakespeare has changed a great deal. He provides Desdemona with a caring and saddened father, Brabantio, out of Cinthio's brief suggestion of family opposition to her marriage, and adds the entire opening scene in which Iago arouses the prejudices of Brabantio. Roderigo is a brilliantly invented character used to reveal Iago's skill in manipulation. Cinthio's ensign, though thoroughly wicked, never expresses a resentment for the squadron leader's promotion and favored treatment by the Moor; instead, the ensign lusts for Disdemona and turns against her and the Moor only when his passion is unrequited. In his complex portrayal of a consuming and irrational jealousy in Iago, Shakespeare goes far beyond his source, making use as well of the inventive villainy of the Vice in the English late medieval morality play. In Cinthio's account the ensign filches the handkerchief from Disdemona while she is hugging the ensign's three-year-old daughter; the ensign's wife is uninvolved in this mischief, though she does unwillingly learn of her husband's villainy (since he has an idea of using her in his plot) and later feels constrained to hold her tongue when Disdemona asks her if she knows why the Moor is behaving so strangely. (As is usual in prose narrative, the passage of time is much more extended than in Shakespeare's play.)

In the later portions of the story, the changes are more marked. Cinthio relates an episode in which the squadron leader, finding the handkerchief in his room, takes it back to Disdemona while the Moor is out but is interrupted by the Moor's unexpected return home; Shakespeare instead has Cassio approach Desdemona (earlier in the story) to beg her assistance in persuading Othello to reinstate him. Cinthio tells of a woman in the squadron leader's household who copies the embroidery of the handkerchief before it is returned and is seen with it at a window by the Moor; here Shakespeare finds a suggestion for Bianca, but her role is considerably augmented, partly with the help of a passing remark in Cinthio that the squadron leader is attacked and wounded as he leaves the house of a courtesan with whom he occasionally takes his pleasure. In the absence of any character corresponding to Roderigo, the Cinthio narrative assigns to the ensign himself the role of wounding the squadron leader. The manner in which Disdemona is murdered is strikingly different. Cinthio has nothing equivalent to the tender scene between Desdemona and Emilia as Desdemona prepares to go to bed. Cinthio's Moor hides the ensign in a dressing room next to his bedroom and commissions the ensign to bludgeon her to death with a sand-filled stocking, after which the two murderers cause the ceiling of the room to collapse on her and create the impression that a rafter has smashed her skull.

Cinthio also treats the aftermath of the murder in a very different way. The Moor, distracted with grief, turns on the ensign and demotes him, whereupon the ensign persuades the squadron commander to take vengeance on the Moor as his attacker (according to the lying ensign) and killer of Disdemona. When the squadron commander accuses the Moor before the Seigniory, the Moor keeps silent but is banished and eventually killed by Disdemona's relatives. The ensign, returning to his own country, gets in trouble by making a false accusation and dies as the result of torture. Cinthio sees this as God's retribution. The ensign's wife lives to tell her story, unlike Shakespeare's Emilia.

The changed ending is essential to Shakespeare's play. Emilia becomes a more complex figure than the ensign's wife: Shakespeare implicates her in the taking of the handkerchief but also accentuates her love for Desdemona and her brave denunciation of her husband when at last she knows the full truth. Othello's ritual slaying of Desdemona avoids the appalling butchery of the source story. Shakespeare's ending is more unified, and brings both Othello and Iago to account for the deeds they have committed in this play. Most important, Shakespeare transforms a sensational murder story into a moving tragedy of love.

Hecatommithi (A Hundred Tales)
By Giovanni Battista Giraldi Cinthio
Translated by David Bevington and Kate Bevington

THIRD DECADE, SEVENTH NOVELLA

A Moorish captain takes as his wife a woman who is a citizen of Venice. An ensign in his company accuses her to her husband of adultery. The husband undertakes to have the ensign kill the supposed adulterer. The captain kills his wife. Having been publicly accused by the ensign, the Moor does not confess but is banished nonetheless on clear evidence of guilt. The villainous ensign, thinking to harm still other persons, brings on himself a wretched death.

There once lived in Venice a Moor, a very brave man, who, by virtue of his personal qualities and by having given proof in war of great prudence and energetic ability, was highly regarded by those signors who, in rewarding honorable actions, ever advance the interests of the republic. Now it happened that a virtuous lady of marvelous beauty, called Disdemona, drawn not by a woman's appetite but the innate qualities of the Moor himself, fell in love with him. And he, vanquished by her beauty and nobleness of mind, similarly burned with love for the lady. Their love was so well-disposed and mutual that, although the lady's relatives did what they could to get her to choose some other husband, the two were united in matrimony. And they lived together in such peace and harmony, while they were in Venice, that nothing but affectionate words ever passed between them.

Now it happened that the signors of Venice made a change in the garrison they maintained on Cyprus, and they chose the Moor to command the troops they dispatched there. He, although greatly pleased by the honor thus offered him—since such a distinguished rank is conferred only on men who are noble, mighty, and loyal, and who have shown themselves to be unusually brave—was not so happy when he considered the length and dangers of the voyage, thinking that Disdemona would be distressed by it. But the lady, who had no other happiness on earth than the Moor and was greatly pleased with the testimonial to his merits that her husband had received from so powerful and noble a republic, eagerly awaited the hour when her husband, with his men, should set forth on his way, and she accompanying him to such an honorable post.

It grieved her to see the Moor troubled. And so, not knowing what the reason could be, she said to him one day as they sat at dinner: "Why is it, my Moor, that you, who have been promoted to such a distinguished rank by the Seigniory, are nevertheless so depressed?"

The Moor said to Disdemona: "The love I have for you troubles my contentedness with the honor I have received, because I see that one of two things must necessarily happen: either I must take you with me over the perils of the sea, or I must leave you in Venice to avoid this hardship. The first of these cannot help but weigh heavily on me, since every fatigue you endured and every danger we encountered would make me extremely anxious. The second of these, having to leave you behind, would be hateful to me, since in parting from you I should be parting from my very life."

Disdemona, hearing this, said: "Alas, my husband, what thoughts are these that are going through your head? Why do you give in to such vexing ideas? I want to come with you wherever you go, even if I should have to walk through fire in my chemise rather than going by sea in a perfectly safe and handsomely furnished ship. If there are going to be dangers and fatigues, I want to share them with you. I would think you didn't love me very much if you thought of leaving me in Venice rather than taking me to sea with you, or persuaded yourself that I would prefer to stay here in safety rather than be with you in such danger. I want you to get ready for the voyage with all the cheerfulness your seniority of rank deserves."

The Moor threw his arms joyfully around his wife's neck and said with an affectionate kiss: "May God keep us long in such love, my dear wife!"

Soon after that, putting on his armor and making everything ready for the expedition, he went on board the galley with his lady and all their followers, hoisted sail, and got under way, and, favored with a perfectly tranquil sea, they made their journey to Cyprus.

Among the officers of the Moor's company was an ensign, a man of handsome appearance but of the most depraved nature in the world. He was much in favor with the Moor, who didn't have the slightest idea of his wickedness. For although his mind was utterly vile, he concealed that villainy in his heart with such high-sounding and noble speech and such pleasing demeanor that he made himself out to be a veritable Hector or Achilles. This rascal had also taken his wife, a beautiful and virtuous young woman, to Cyprus, and being of Italian birth, she was much loved by the Moor's wife, who spent the greater part of the day with her.

In the same company there was also a squadron leader of whom the Moor was very fond. He went often to the Moor's house and frequently dined with him and his wife. And so the lady, knowing how much he meant to her husband, gave him proofs of the greatest kindness. This greatly pleased the Moor.

The villainous ensign, not heeding at all the vows he had made to his wife or the friendship, loyalty, and duty he owed the Moor, fell head over heels in love with Disdemona and bent all his thoughts to see if he could enjoy her, but he didn't dare show his passion openly for fear that, if the Moor should notice, he would quickly be a dead man. And so he sought various ways, as guilefully as he could, to let the lady know that he loved her. But she, who was so entirely taken up with the Moor, never gave a thought to the ensign or anyone else. Everything he did to kindle passion in her toward him had no more effect than as if he hadn't even tried.

Then he took it into his head that this neglect was the result of her being in love with the squadron leader, and he began to wonder how he might remove this person from her sight. Not only did his mind turn to this, but the love he had for the lady changed into the bitterest hatred, and he gave himself entirely to the study of how he might bring it about that, once the squadron leader had been killed, if he himself could not enjoy the lady, the Moor would not be able to enjoy her either.

Turning over in his mind various ideas, all of them villainous and evil, the ensign finally decided to accuse her of adultery to her husband and to make him believe that the adulterer was none other than the squadron leader. But, knowing the single-hearted love the Moor had for Disdemona, and the friendship he had for the squadron leader, the ensign recognized clearly that, unless he could dupe the Moor with some clever fraud, it would be impossible to get him to listen to either accusation. For which reason he set himself to wait until time and place should open up a way for him to begin his villainous project.

Not long afterward, it happened that the Moor, because the squadron leader drew his sword on a soldier while on guard duty and wounded him, demoted him in rank. This distressed Disdemona greatly. Many times she tried to bring about a reconciliation between her husband and him. At this the Moor said to the villainous ensign that his wife was putting up such a fuss on behalf of the squadron leader that he feared he would be constrained at last to reinstate the officer. The villain took this opportunity to set in motion the deception he had planned, and said: "Perhaps Disdemona has good reason to look so kindly on him."

"And why would that be?" said the Moor.

"I have no desire," answered the ensign, "to come between husband and wife, but if you keep your eyes open, you'll see for yourself."

Nothing the Moor did could persuade the ensign to go beyond what he had said. Nevertheless, his words left such a sharp, stinging thorn in the Moor's mind that he gave himself up to thinking intently what these words could mean, and he fell into a deep melancholy.

One day, when his wife was trying to soften his anger toward the squadron leader, beseeching him not to consign to oblivion the service and friendship of so many years for a mere peccadillo, especially since matters had been patched up between the squadron leader and the soldier he wounded, the Moor burst into a rage and said to her: "There must be some extraordinary reason, Disdemona, that you should take so much trouble over this man. He isn't your brother, after all, or even a kinsman, to be so near your heart."

The lady said, courteously and humbly: "Please don't be angry with me. Nothing prompts me to do this except that it saddens me to see you deprived of such a dear friend as I know, by your own testimony, the squadron leader has been to you. He hasn't done anything to deserve so much hatred from you. But you Moors are so naturally hot-tempered that every little thing provokes you to anger and revenge."

The Moor, made still angrier by these words, answered: "Anyone who doesn't believe this can easily find proof that it's true! I will be revenged for the wrongs done to me! I will be satisfied!"

The lady was frightened at these words, and, seeing her husband to be inflamed with anger against her, quite beyond his usual self, she said humbly: "I have only the best of motives in speaking to you about this. But, not to give you any cause to be angry with me, I won't say another word about it from now on."

Seeing the earnestness with which his wife had pleaded anew on behalf of the squadron leader, the Moor guessed that the words which the ensign had spoken to him signified that Disdemona was in love with the squadron leader. And so, deeply depressed, he went to the villainous ensign and tried to get him to speak more frankly. The ensign, bent on doing injury to the unfortunate lady, after pretending not to want to say anything that might displease the Moor, gave the appearance of being brought around by the Moor's urging and said: "I can't deny that it pains me terribly to have to say anything to you that must disturb you extremely. But since you insist I tell you, and since the concern I ought to have for your honor as my commanding officer also spurs me on to tell you, I will not now refuse to obey your request and my own sense of duty. You must realize, then, that your lady's only reason for being unhappy to see the squadron leader out of favor with you is that she takes her pleasure with him whenever he comes to your house. That's how she consoles herself for the disgust she feels about your blackness."

These words penetrated to the very core of the Moor's heart. But, in order to know more (though he now believed what the ensign had told him to be true, through the suspicion that had already been born in his mind), he said, with a fierce expression: "I don't know what keeps me from cutting out that audacious tongue of yours, which has had the effrontery to offer such an insult to my lady."

Then the ensign said: "I didn't expect, Captain, any other reward for my friendly service. But, since the duty I owe you and the care I have for your honor have brought me thus far, let me repeat to you that matters stand just as you've heard. And if your lady, with her show of affection for you, has blinded your eyes to such an extent that you are unable to see what is right in front of you, that doesn't at all mean that I haven't been telling the truth. Believe me, this same squadron leader, being one of those people who don't think their happiness complete until they have made someone else acquainted with it, has told me everything." And he added: "If I hadn't feared your anger, I should, when he told me this, have given him the recompense he justly deserved by killing him. But since, by letting you know what concerns you more than any other person, I have earned for myself such an unbefitting reward, I wish I had kept silent and thus avoided falling into your disfavor."

Then the Moor, in torment, said: "If you do not make me see with my own eyes what you've told me, rest assured that I will give you reason to think you would have been better off to have been born without a tongue."

"It would have been easy enough," answered the scoundrel, "when he used to come to your house. But now that you have driven him away—and, I must say, not for any compelling need but for the most trivial of reasons—it's bound to be difficult for me, for, even though I feel sure that he enjoys Disdemona whenever you give him the chance, he must do so much more cautiously than before, now that he sees he has fallen into your disfavor. Still, I do not lose hope of being able to make you see what you are so unwilling to believe." And with these words they went their own ways.

The wretched Moor, as if struck by the most piercing of arrows, went home to await the day when the ensign would make him see that which would make him forever unhappy. But the ensign meanwhile was no less troubled by the chaste behavior with which he knew the lady to govern herself, since it seemed to him impossible to discover a way of making the Moor believe what he had falsely told him. And so, turning this over in his mind in every possible direction, the scoundrel hit at last on a new piece of cunning.

As I have told you, the Moor's wife often went to the house

of the ensign's wife and spent the better part of the day with her. Whereupon the ensign, seeing that she sometimes carried with her a handkerchief which, he knew, the Moor had given her, and which had been embroidered with an intricate Moorish design, and which was especially dear to the lady and no less so to the Moor, he devised a scheme to take it from her by stealth and thereby prepare her final ruin. He had a young daughter, three years old, and much beloved of Disdemona. One day, when the poor lady had gone to pass the time of day at the villain's house, he took up the little girl in his arms and presented her to the lady, who took the child and hugged her to her breast. The traitor, who was very quick in sleight of hand, lifted the handkerchief from her sash so adroitly that she took no notice. And so, glad at heart, he took his leave of her.

Disdemona, unaware of what had happened, went home and, busy with other considerations, never gave a thought to the handkerchief. But a few days afterward, when she went to look for it and couldn't find it, she was terribly afraid that the Moor would ask her for it as he often did.

Meantime the villainous ensign, taking a suitable occasion, visited the squadron leader in his room and, with crafty malice, left the handkerchief at the head of the bed in such a way that the squadron leader took no notice until the following morning when, as he got out of bed, and the handkerchief by this time having fallen to the floor, he put his foot on it. Not being able to imagine how it had gotten into his house, knowing it to be Disdemona's, he determined to give it back to her. And so, waiting until the Moor had gone out, he went to the back door and knocked.

Fortune seemed to have conspired with the ensign to bring about the death of the poor woman, for at that very moment the Moor came back home. Hearing a knock at the door, he went to a window and very angrily shouted: "Who is knocking?" The squadron leader, hearing the Moor's voice and fearing that he would come downstairs and do him some harm, without answering a word took to his heels. The Moor ran downstairs and, opening the door, went out into the street and looked around but found no one. Then, going back inside, filled with spite, he demanded of his wife who it was that had knocked at the downstairs door. The lady answered truthfully that she didn't know. But the Moor said: "To me it looked like the squadron leader." "I don't know," she said, "whether it was he or someone else." The Moor held in his fury, though he burned with wrath.

He didn't want to do anything before he had spoken with the ensign, and so he went to him immediately and told him what had happened, and begged him to find out from the squadron leader what he could about the business. He, delighted with the way things were going, readily agreed to do so.

And so one day he spoke with the squadron leader while the Moor was standing in a place where he could see the two of them in conversation. As they talked of all sorts of things having nothing to do with the lady, the ensign laughed with huge gusto and made as if to show great surprise, gesturing a lot with his head and hands as if he heard some incredible tale. The Moor went to the ensign as soon as he saw the two separate, in order to know what the other had told him. The ensign, after making the Moor beg for a long time, finally said to him: "He hasn't hidden a thing from me. He says that he has enjoyed your wife every time that you've given him opportunity by being away. And, he says, on the last such time he was with her, she gave him the handkerchief which you gave her as a gift when you married her." The Moor thanked the ensign, and it seemed to him obvious that if the lady no longer had the handkerchief in her possession, all must be as the ensign had said.

And so one day, after they had dined, as he discussed various things with his lady, the Moor asked for the handkerchief. The poor woman, who had been so afraid of this question, turned all red in the face, and, in order to hide her blushes, which the Moor had already taken good notice of, she ran to her chest and pretended to look for it. After she had searched a good deal, she said: "I don't know why I can't find it now. Do you have it, by any chance?" "If I had it," he said, "why would I be asking you for it? But you will look for it more easily and comfortably some other time."

And, leaving her, the Moor began to think how he might kill his lady and the squadron leader at the same time in such a way that the guilt for her death would not be laid at his door. Thinking of this day and night, he couldn't prevent his lady from noticing that he was not the same toward her as before. She said to him several times: "What thing is bothering you? What is troubling you? You, who used to be the merriest person on earth, are now the most melancholy person alive." The Moor found various excuses in replying to his lady, but she was not at all easy in her mind.

Even though she knew that no misconduct on her part could have troubled the Moor so greatly, she feared nonetheless that through the excessive amount of lovemaking he engaged in with her, he had become bored. Sometimes she would say to the ensign's wife: "I don't know what to make of the Moor. He used to be so loving to me, and now, in I don't know how short a time, he's become quite another person. I'm greatly worried that I shall prove a warning to young women not to marry against their parents' wishes, and that Italian ladies will learn by my example not to be linked in marriage with the kind of man who is separated from us by nature, Heaven itself, and an entire way of life. But because I know he is on good terms with your husband and shares with him his most private affairs, I beg of you that, if you've learned anything from him that you can tell me about, you won't fail to help me." And as she said all this she wept uncontrollably.

The ensign's wife, who knew everything (since her husband wished to use her as a means to the death of the lady, though she had never willingly consented), did not dare, for the fear she had of her husband, to say a word of this thing to Disdemona. She said only: "Take care not to give your husband the least suspicion, and strive as hard as you can to make him realize your love and loyalty to him." "Why, so I do," Disdemona said, "but nothing helps."

The Moor, meanwhile, sought every way of confirming more certainly the very thing he did not want to discover. He begged the ensign to arrange matters in such a way that he could see the handkerchief in the squadron leader's possession, and, although this request put the scoundrel rather on the spot, he promised the Moor nonetheless to make every effort to give him the proof he desired.

The squadron leader had a woman in the house who made the most marvelous embroidery on fine linen. She, seeing the handkerchief and hearing that it belonged to the Moor's wife and that it was to be given back to her, undertook to make a copy of it before it was returned. While she was doing this, it struck the ensign that she had placed herself next to a window from which she could be seen by whoever passed by in the street. He made sure that the Moor saw this, who accordingly held it for certain that his utterly chaste lady was in fact an adulteress.

The Moor came to an agreement with the ensign to kill her and the squadron leader, and as the two of them discussed between them how it was to be done, the Moor implored the ensign that he would agree to be the one to kill the squadron leader, promising to remain eternally obliged to him for doing so. Although the ensign at first refused to undertake such a difficult and exceedingly dangerous thing, since the squadron leader was no less skillful than valorous, after having been begged repeatedly and bribed with a sufficient quantity of money, he was at length induced to say that he would undertake to tempt fortune.

One evening after these matters had been settled, as the squadron leader was leaving the house of a courtesan with whom he liked to solace himself, the night being dark, the ensign accosted him with sword in hand and directed a blow at his legs to cause him to fall, and in so doing cut the right thigh entirely through so that the poor man did indeed fall to the ground. The ensign was instantly upon him to finish him off. But the squadron leader, who was brave and accustomed to blood and death, drew his own sword and, wounded though he was, put himself on guard to defend his life and shouted in a loud voice: "Help! Murder!"

At this the ensign, hearing people running toward him, and among them some soldiers who were billeted in the neighborhood, took to his heels so as not to be taken there, and then, doubling back on his tracks, made it appear that he also was running toward the noise. Blending in among the others, and seeing the leg that had been lopped off, he judged that the squadron leader, if not virtually dead already, would die in any case of such a wound. And, although he rejoiced to himself at this, he nevertheless offered condolences to the squadron leader as if he had been his brother.

Next morning the news was all over the city, and came too

to the ears of Disdemona. She, loving as always, and not thinking that she might suffer harm from it, showed the greatest sorrow for what had happened. The Moor put the worst possible construction on her behavior. He went to find the ensign and said to him: "Do you know that my fool of a wife is in such a state about what has happened to the squadron leader that she is very nearly out of her mind?"

"What else could you expect," said the ensign, "since he is her very heart and soul?"

"Heart and soul, you say?" answered the Moor. "I'll tear her heart and soul right out of her body! I couldn't think myself a man if I didn't rid the world of such a depraved creature."

As they went on discussing alternatives, whether the lady should die by poison or the knife, and not coming to an agreement between them on one or the other, the ensign said: "A way has come into my head that should satisfy you and lead to no suspicion. Here it is. The house you occupy is very old, and the ceiling in your room is full of cracks. My idea is that we pummel Disdemona with a stocking filled with sand until she dies, since this way there will appear on her body no sign of a beating. Once she is dead we can cause part of the ceiling to cave in, and we can break the lady's head in such a way as to make it appear that a falling rafter smashed her skull and killed her. This way no one will suspect you, supposing instead that her death came about by accident."

This cruel advice pleased the Moor, and he waited only for a convenient opportunity, some night when he would share his bed with Disdemona. First he concealed the ensign in a dressing room that opened off their bedroom. Then the ensign, according to the plan they had made between them, made some sort of noise in the dressing room. Hearing this, the Moor said very suddenly to his wife: "Did you hear that noise?"

"Yes, I did," she said.

"Get up and see what it is," the Moor rejoined.

Poor Disdemona got up. As soon as she had come close to the dressing room, the ensign rushed out and, being strong and muscular, gave her a terrible blow in the small of her back with the stocking he had ready, so that the lady fell immediately, hardly able to draw her breath. With the little voice she had left she called on the Moor to help her. But he, leaping out of bed, said to her: "You most wicked of women! This is the reward for your unchastity. This is what they get who, pretending to love their husbands, put horns on their heads instead."

The poor lady, hearing this and sensing that her end was near—since the ensign had landed another blow—said that she called on divine justice to attest to her fidelity, since earthly justice failed to come to her aid. And as she called on God to help her, she was struck by a third blow and lay dead, slain by the impious ensign.

Then, putting her on the bed and smashing her skull, he and the Moor caused the ceiling of the room to cave in as they had planned between them, whereupon the Moor began to cry for help, that the house was falling down. At which cry the neighbors came running, and discovered the bed, and found the lady dead under the rafters. All were amazed and grieved at this, because her life had been so good.

On the following day Disdemona was buried with deep grieving on everybody's part. But God, the just examiner of all human souls, did not wish that such monstrous evil should go without suitable punishment. He decreed that the Moor, who had loved the lady more than his own life, seeing himself deprived of her, should begin to have such an intense longing for her that he went about like one who was out of his mind, searching for her in every imaginable place in the house. And coming to the conclusion that it was the ensign who had caused him to lose, along with the lady, every joy of his life and indeed his very being, he came to loathe the villain so intensely that he couldn't even bear to look at him. If he had not been afraid of the inviolable justice of the Venetian Seigniory, the Moor would have killed him right out in the open. But since he couldn't do so safely, he instead demoted the ensign and refused to let him serve any longer in his company, whereupon was born such a bitter enmity between them that it would be impossible to imagine one more immense or deadly.

On this score the ensign, that worst of all villains, turned all his thoughts to doing harm to the Moor. Seeking out the squadron leader, who had recovered by now and who got about on a wooden leg in place of the one that had been cut off, the ensign said to him: "The time has come for you to be revenged for your cut-off leg. If you'll come with me to Venice, I will tell you who the malefactor was. I don't dare talk about it here for many reasons. And I will testify for you in court."

The squadron leader, knowing himself to have been deeply wronged but not understanding the real truth of the matter, thanked the ensign and accompanied him to Venice. When they had arrived, the ensign told him that the Moor was the one who had cut off his leg because of an idea he had gotten into his head that he, the squadron leader, had lain with Disdemona, and that for this same reason the Moor had killed her and afterward spread the report of her having been killed by the falling ceiling.

The squadron leader, hearing this, accused the Moor before the Seigniory of having cut off his leg and of having killed the lady, and he called as his witness the ensign, who said that both things were true, which he knew because the Moor had told him everything and had tried to induce him to commit both crimes; and that, having then killed his wife, impelled by the bestial jealousy that had come into his head, the Moor had told to the ensign the manner in which he had done her in.

The Venetian Seigniory, upon learning of this cruel deed perpetrated by a barbarian foreigner on a Venetian citizen, issued orders for the Moor to be arrested in Cyprus and brought back to Venice, where through numerous tortures they tried to find out the truth. But he was able to endure all the tortures with his mightiness of spirit and denied everything so steadfastly that they could not get anything out of him. And although by his steadfastness he escaped death, he was, after being confined many days in prison, condemned to perpetual exile. There he was finally put to death by Disdemona's relatives, as he deserved.

The ensign went back to his own country, and, not being inclined to change his ways, accused a companion of his of having tried to get him, the ensign, to kill one of this fellow's enemies, a person of good birth. On the basis of this accusation the fellow was taken and put to the torture.

When he denied the truth of what his accuser had said, the ensign too was put to the torture in order that their stories might be compared. There he was so badly tortured that his internal organs ruptured. Afterward he was released from prison and taken home, where he died a miserable death. Thus did God avenge the innocence of Disdemona. And now that he was dead, the ensign's wife, who knew the whole story, told what had happened just as I have told you.

Gli Hecatommithi by Giovanni Battista Giraldi Cinthio was first published in Italy in 1565. This new translation is based on the edition of 1566.

Further Reading

Adamson, Jane. *"Othello" as Tragedy: Some Problems of Judgment and Feeling*. Cambridge and New York: Cambridge Univ. Press, 1980. Adamson finds the unity of *Othello* in the similarities between the problems of judgment and feeling that characters confront and those experienced by an audience of the play. We are made uncomfortable with our own desire for certainty as we see characters who, in theirs, urgently construe and misconstrue actions and personalities.

Bayley, John. "Love and Identity." *The Characters of Love: A Study in the Literature of Personality*. London: Constable, 1960. Examining the psychological and philosophical implications of Shakespeare's revision of G. B. Giraldi Cinthio's novella, Bayley sees the play as an intensely personal tragedy rooted in the difficulties of truly knowing another being. Both Desdemona and Othello reveal powerful conceptions of love but are tragically incapable of understanding any other kind of love or of being separated from their own sense of identity.

Boose, Lynda E. "Othello's Handkerchief: 'The Recognizance and Pledge of Love.'" *English Literary Renaissance* 5 (1975): 360–374. Boose discovers in the "strawberry spotted handkerchief" the motive forces of the play itself: the concerns with fidelity and justice. Examining Shakespeare's transformation of his source material and exploring Renaissance marriage customs, Boose finds that the handkerchief functions as an emblem of marital consummation, and that Othello's chosen role as judicial executioner derives from marriage laws and rituals that prescribe the death of a wife whose wedding sheets fail to provide proof of her bridal virginity.

Bradley, A. C. *"Othello." Shakespearean Tragedy*, 1904. Rpt., New York: St. Martin's Press, 1985. Bradley's deservedly influential study focuses on character: Othello is heroic, noble, not innately jealous but unreflective; Desdemona is passive, armed with nothing to oppose evil except endurance and forgiveness; and Iago is a liar, supremely evil, motivated by an unconscious longing for power and superiority.

Cavell, Stanley. "Literature as the Knowledge of the Outsider." *The Claim of Reason: Wittgenstein, Scepticism, Morality, and Tragedy.* New York: Oxford Univ. Press, 1979. Rpt. as "On *Othello*," in *Shakespeare, the Tragedies: New Perspectives,* ed. Robert B. Heilman. Englewood Cliffs, N.J.: Prentice-Hall, 1984. Cavell sees the play enacting the tragic implications of the individual's need for the existence of—and acknowledgment by—another. Othello needs Desdemona to confirm his image of himself but simultaneously has to reject Desdemona for exposing his need. Othello's tragedy is then not the tragedy of a man who lacks certainty but of one who knows too much— about himself as dependent and imperfect—and is unable to confront that knowledge.

Coleridge, Samuel Taylor. "*Othello*." *Coleridge's Writings on Shakespeare,* ed. Terence Hawkes. New York: G. P. Putnam's Sons, 1959. Coleridge regards Othello as a noble and majestic figure, not jealous by nature but aroused by offended honor, moral indignation, and regret at his discovery that Desdemona's virtue is apparently impure and worthless. Coleridge views Iago as a "passionless character, all *will* and intellect," and, in a famous phrase, characterizes Iago's rationalizations of his hatred for Othello as "the motive-hunting of motiveless malignity."

Doran, Madeleine. "Iago's 'If': An Essay on the Syntax of *Othello*." In *The Drama of the Renaissance: Essays for Leicester Bradner,* ed. Elmer M. Blistein. Providence, R.I.: Brown Univ. Press, 1970. Rpt. and rev. as "Iago's 'If—': Conditional and Subjunctive in *Othello*." *Shakespeare's Dramatic Language.* Madison: Univ. of Wisconsin Press, 1976. Analyzing Shakespeare's use of syntax to inform the dramatic structure of *Othello,* Doran discovers two dominant syntactic patterns counterpointed in the play: conditional and declarative sentences. The conditionals (which initiate every significant phase of the tragic action) disrupt and finally destroy the world of Othello's assurance. His absolutism and ultimately his whole being fall victim to the terrifying ambiguities released by Iago's "if."

Empson, William. " 'Honest' in *Othello.*" *The Structure of Complex Words.* New York: New Directions, 1951. Empson argues that Shakespeare's complex handling of the words "honest" and "honesty" (which appear over fifty times in the play) is central to an understanding of Iago's character and motivation. Shakespeare exploits the words' various possibilities of meaning, and a Renaissance audience, alert to the ironies and ambiguities of the words, would necessarily see Iago as less purely evil and more complexly human than most twentieth-century critics have allowed.

Gardner, Helen. "The Noble Moor." In *Proceedings of the British Academy* 41 (1956 for 1955): 189–205. Rpt. in *Shakespeare Criticism, 1935–60,* ed. Anne Ridler. London and New York: Oxford Univ. Press, 1963. As her title suggests, Gardner sees Othello as a noble and heroic figure in a play of poetic, intellectual, and moral beauty. The play's subject is not pride, egoism, or self-deception, but is, rather, loss of faith stemming from sexual jealousy. In *Othello* we are presented with the fall of a noble man from a great happiness to ruin, but a fall that affirms the value of the life and love that have been lost.

Garner, S. N. "Shakespeare's Desdemona." *Shakespeare Studies* 9 (1976): 233–252. Finding *Othello* to be among the "bleakest" of the tragedies, Garner traces Desdemona's tragic trajectory from her initial courage and confidence to her "appalling innocence" and passivity of the last two acts. Exactly like Othello, she never fully knows herself or her spouse, and both fail to "understand the way the world fosters their misperceptions."

Greenblatt, Stephen. "The Improvisation of Power." *Renaissance Self-Fashioning.* Chicago: Univ. of Chicago Press, 1980. In Greenblatt's suggestive cultural anthropology, *Othello* emerges as a play expressing the central social and psychic realities of the Renaissance. Iago's understanding that the self is something "fashioned" permits him the improvisational freedom to enter into the psychic structure of another and turn it to his advantage. Playing upon the ambivalence of Othello's relationship to Venetian society, Iago activates Othello's terrifying sexual anxieties and mistrust.

Heilman, Robert B. *Magic in the Web: Action and Language in "Othello."* Lexington, Ky.: Univ. of Kentucky Press, 1956. *Othello,* Heilman argues in his account of the play's imagery and dramatic action, is a "dramatic poem" about love. Othello's tragedy stems from his failure to recognize the transformative power of Desdemona's love. His histrionic bent, his self-pity, and his self-love allow him to be seduced by Iago's wit and reason, and he dies never knowing the true value of what he has lost.

Johnson, Samuel. *"Othello." Johnson on Shakespeare,* ed. Arthur Sherbo. *The Yale Edition of the Works of Samuel Johnson,* vol. 8. New Haven and London: Yale Univ. Press, 1969. Johnson praises the play for its moral qualities, its dramatic construction, and its vivid characterization. Othello is "boundless in his confidence, ardent in his affection, inflexible in his resolution, and obdurate in his revenge." Johnson also admires Desdemona's "soft simplicity" and finds her murder unbearable: "I am glad that I have ended my revisal of this dreadful scene. It is not to be endured."

Jones, Eldred. *Othello's Countrymen: The African in English Renaissance Drama.* London: Oxford Univ. Press, 1965. Jones surveys the Elizabethan knowledge of Africans and their representation on the stage and finds that *Othello* marks a significant departure from the traditional dramatic treatment of Moors: Shakespeare endows Othello with noble, human qualities, though the play invokes—in order to reject—racial stereotypes in the prejudice of Iago and Brabantio.

Kirsch, Arthur. "The Polarization of Erotic Love in *Othello." Modern Language Review* 73 (1978): 721–740. Rpt. as *"Othello." Shakespeare and the Experience of Love.* Cambridge and New York: Cambridge Univ. Press, 1981. According to Kirsch, Shakespeare in the play, and most deeply in Othello's character, explores the powerful and often paradoxical forces of erotic love. Drawing on both Christian and Freudian theories of desire, Kirsch understands *Othello* not as a tragedy of moral or psychological failure but as an enactment of the tragic potential of a human love born necessarily in vulnerability and need.

Knight, G. Wilson. "The *Othello* Music." *The Wheel of Fire: Interpretation of Shakespeare's Tragedy,* 1930. Rev. and enl., New York: Meridian, 1957. Iago's corrosive cynicism represents for Knight a "spirit of negation" that would destroy "the domesticity, the romance, the idealized humanity of the *Othello* world." But, while Iago succeeds in destroying the love and beauty of that world, his triumph is not complete. At the end Othello recovers his former dignity, rising above the chaos into which he has sunk and denying Iago an absolute victory.

Leavis, F. R. "Diabolic Intellect and the Noble Hero: A Note on *Othello." Scrutiny* 6 (1937): 259–283. Rpt. in *The Common Pursuit.* London: Chatto and Windus, 1952; New York: New York Univ. Press, 1964. Leavis attacks what he calls the "Sentimentalists' Othello," promulgated by Coleridge, Johnson, and Bradley (see above). In place of their heroic and noble figure seduced by a supremely evil villain, he argues for an Othello driven by pride, sentimentality, and a lack of self-knowledge that makes him succumb "with an extraordinary promptness to suggestion."

Neely, Carol Thomas. "Women and Men in *Othello:* 'What Should Such a Fool / Do With So Good a Woman?'" *Shakespeare Studies* 10 (1977): 133–158. Rpt. in *The Woman's Part: Feminist Criticism of Shakespeare,* ed. Carolyn Ruth Swift Lenz, Gayle Greene, and Carol Thomas Neely. Urbana, Chicago, and London: Univ. of Illinois Press, 1980. Neely proposes that the play's central conflict is not between good and evil but between men and women. Unlike Shakespeare's comedies, where witty heroines are able to dispel male folly, *Othello* defines a world where male fantasies remain tragically unaffected by female wit and energy. Here the conflicts are never resolved, and at the end we do not celebrate the pairing of lovers but can only look at the dead bodies of Emilia, Desdemona, and Othello.

Orkin, Martin. "Othello and the 'Plain Face' of Racism." *Shakespeare Quarterly* 38 (1987): 166–188. Orkin traces attitudes toward race and color in Renaissance England and ways in which a "racist mythology inscribes critical responses to the play." In a final section, Orkin examines the specific case of the play as it is treated in the academic criticism of South Africa.

Rosenberg, Marvin. *The Masks of "Othello": The Search for the Identity of Othello, Iago, and Desdemona by Three Centuries of Actors and Critics.* Berkeley and Los Angeles: Univ. of California Press, 1961. Rosenberg's subtitle indicates the contents of his book. He examines the play on the stage from the eighteenth through the twentieth centuries, provides an overview of critical approaches, and attends to the ways in which the text has been reshaped for performance. In the two concluding chapters he argues against either symbolic or skeptical approaches to *Othello,* maintaining that *Othello*'s deep and complex humanity is most powerfully realized in the theater.

Synder, Susan. "Beyond Comedy: *Romeo and Juliet* and *Othello." The Comic Matrix of Shakespeare's Tragedies,* esp. pp. 70–90. Princeton, N.J.: Princeton Univ. Press, 1979. Responding to the play's movement from an initial comic design to a fully developed tragic action, Snyder maintains that the power of *Othello* derives from Shakespeare's radical questioning of the fundamental assumption of romantic comedy: that self-definition and fulfillment can be achieved through union with another. The play enacts and explores the tragic implications of emotional ties that necessarily reveal the dependency and vulnerability that Iago exploits.

Spivack, Bernard. "Iago Revisited." *Shakespeare and the Allegory of Evil.* New York: Columbia Univ. Press, 1958. Finding no plausible motivation within the play for Iago's exuberant evil, Spivack discovers an explanation for his behavior not in Iago's psychology but in his literary ancestry in the medieval drama. Iago's logic and energy derive from the allegorical Vice of the morality plays, and Spivack explores the implications of this legacy for the moral dynamics of the play.

Stoll, E. E. *"Othello": An Historical and Comparative Study,* 1915. Rpt., New York: Haskell House, 1964. Stoll responds sharply to the psychological critics (notably Bradley, see above) who discuss the play's characters as if they were real people. Instead, Stoll argues for the primacy of plot, language, and stage conventions, and invites us to reconsider the play in light of the expectations and values of an Elizabethan audience.

WILLIAM SHAKESPEARE was born in Stratford-upon-Avon in April, 1564, and his birth is traditionally celebrated on April 23. The facts of his life, known from surviving documents, are sparse. He was one of eight children born to John Shakespeare, a merchant of some standing in his community. William probably went to the King's New School in Stratford, but he had no university education. In November 1582, at the age of eighteen, he married Anne Hathaway, eight years his senior, who was pregnant with their first child, Susanna. She was born on May 26, 1583. Twins, a boy, Hamnet (who would die at age eleven), and a girl, Judith, were born in 1585. By 1592 Shakespeare had gone to London, working as an actor and already known as a playwright. A rival dramatist, Robert Greene, referred to him as "an upstart crow, beautified with our feathers." Shakespeare became a principal shareholder and playwright of the successful acting troupe the Lord Chamberlain's men (later, under James I, called the King's men). In 1599 the Lord Chamberlain's men built and occupied the Globe Theatre in Southwark near the Thames River. Here many of Shakespeare's plays were performed by the most famous actors of his time, including Richard Burbage, Will Kempe, and Robert Armin. In addition to his 37 plays, Shakespeare had a hand in others, including *Sir Thomas More* and *The Two Noble Kinsmen*, and he wrote poems, including *Venus and Adonis* and *The Rape of Lucrece*. His 154 sonnets were published, probably without his authorization, in 1609. In 1611 or 1612 he gave up his lodgings in London and devoted more and more of his time to retirement in Stratford, though he continued writing such plays as *The Tempest* and *Henry VIII* until about 1613. He died on April 23, 1616, and was buried in Holy Trinity Church, Stratford. No collected edition of his plays was published during his lifetime, but in 1623 two members of his acting company, John Heminges and Henry Condell, published the great collection now called the First Folio.